# THE YALE EDITION

OF

# HORACE WALPOLE'S

# CORRESPONDENCE

EDITED BY W. S. LEWIS

(1895–1979)

*VOLUME FORTY-FOUR*

# HORACE WALPOLE'S CORRESPONDENCE

## COMPLETE INDEX

*COMPILED BY*
WARREN HUNTING SMITH
*WITH THE ASSISTANCE OF*
EDWINE M. MARTZ, RUTH K. McCLURE,
*AND* WILLIAM T. LA MOY

I

A. A. *TO* CONSTANT

NEW HAVEN
*YALE UNIVERSITY PRESS*
OXFORD · OXFORD UNIVERSITY PRESS

1983

# TABLE OF CONTENTS

## *VOLUME I*

# PREFACE TO THE INDEX

This is an index to the eighteenth century as reflected in Horace Walpole's correspondence and in the supporting materials affixed to it.

'This edition, through its index, hopes to lead the scholar, whether the subject of his research is Dr Johnson or ballooning, to whatever Walpole's correspondence may have to say about it'—so wrote W. S. Lewis in his preface to our first volume, in 1937. He envisioned this final index as 'the index to end all indexes.'

We index not only Walpole's correspondence but his own footnotes to that correspondence, and also such unpublished MSS, and extracts from periodicals, as we have printed in appendices or quoted in our own footnotes.

Besides hundreds of individuals, this index includes events, objects, publications, and the whole fabric of political, social, financial, artistic, military, and literary history so far as it is portrayed in our volumes. There are special group-headings for topics such as Costume, Food, Landscape effects, Law, Medicine, Music, Opera, Painting, Religion, Theatre, War, etc.

From beginning to end, our volumes are consecutively numbered in arabic numerals, while the multi-volume component correspondences are internally numbered in roman letters. Therefore the volume numbers in this final index are in bold-face arabic numerals, followed by page numbers in plain arabic numerals.

When an important biographical footnote identifies any individual whose index entries are numerous, its location is usually indicated by a page number in italic type. This is considered unnecessary for famous people who are to be found in all the reference books.

Footnote references are distinguished by 'n' after the page number.

Women are indexed under their maiden names and peers under their family names, with cross-reference from married name or title. In giving the peerage-number of English noblemen, we have followed Walpole's own practice of omitting from the numbering any female title-holders who might have held that peerage—for instance, Walpole considered it improper to call a man *second* Earl Temple when the *first* holder of the earldom had been a Countess. However, in certain baronies (such as Dacre), there were so many Baronesses that this would be confusing. Where we have

omitted female title-holders in the numbering, we add, in brackets, to that number the number which the peer properly held without that omission.

Walpole sometimes jotted names of people and objects on the backs of letters, to serve as memoranda. Such unexplained names or words we index as 'HW mentions.'

Walpole's 'Paris Journals' in our Vol. 7 are filled with lists of people he met at parties. These we indexed in Vol. 8 (the Du Deffand index) under the names of hosts and guests as 'social relations of, with—' The final index does not reprint all those entries, but merely refers the reader to the appropriate pages in Vol. 8.

We usually do not anglicize the names of foreign monarchs, but 'Leghorn,' 'Florence,' and a few other place-names are here in anglicized form. We use 'St Petersburg' rather than 'Petrograd' or 'Leningrad.'

In alphabetizing first names, we follow the hierarchy of the *Nouvelle biographie générale*: saints, popes, emperors, kings (divided according to the alphabetical order of the names of their countries), princes, dukes, and commoners.

We alphabetize all two- and three-word items as if they were spelt solid up to the first comma—*Middlemarch*; 'Middle of the Forest'; Middle Temple; Middlewood, etc.

In alphabetizing the subheads, HW (for Horace Walpole himself) precedes all other words beginning with H, but SH (for Strawberry Hill) is placed where it would be if spelled out.

Nouns are indexed in singular rather than plural form, and are alphabetized accordingly.

The following abbreviations and contractions are used in the index:

| | |
|---|---|
| Abp | Archbishop |
| Adm. | Admiral |
| b. | born |
| Bn | Baron |
| Bns | Baroness |
| Bp | Bishop |
| Bt | Baronet |
| c. | century |
| ca | circa |
| Col. | Colonel |
| cr. | created |
| Cts | Countess |
| d. | died |
| D. | Duke |

| | |
|---|---|
| dau. | daughter |
| D. D. | Doctor of Divinity |
| Dr | Doctor |
| Ds | Duchess |
| E. | Earl |
| edn | edition |
| fl. | flourished |
| F. R. S. | Fellow of the Royal Society |
| F. S. A. | Fellow of the Society of Artists |
| G. C. B. | Knight Grand Cross of the Order of the Bath |
| Gen. | General |
| gov. | governor |
| gov.-gen. | governor-general |
| Hon. | Honourable |
| HW | Horace Walpole |
| K. | King |
| K. B. | Knight of the Order of the Bath |
| K. G. | Knight of the Order of the Garter |
| Kt | Knight |
| K. T. | Knight of the Order of the Thistle |
| LL. D. | Doctor of Laws |
| Lt | Lieutenant |
| Lt-Col. | Lieutenant-Colonel |
| Lt-Gen. | Lieutenant-General |
| m. | married |
| M. | Marquess |
| Maj. | Major |
| Maj.-Gen. | Major-General |
| M. P. | Member of Parliament |
| n. | footnote |
| n. c. | of a new creation |
| P. | Prince |
| Ps | Princess |
| Q. | Queen |
| Rear-Adm. | Rear-Admiral |
| Rev. | Reverend |
| SH | Strawberry Hill |
| s. j. | *suo jure* |
| *temp.* | in the reign of |
| Vice-Adm. | Vice-Admiral |
| Vct | Viscount |
| Vcts | Viscountess |

The following abbreviations of the names of English counties are often used with the place-names in this index. They represent counties as they existed during most of the edition's progress, not the present counties as reconstituted and renamed.

| | |
|---|---|
| Beds | Bedfordshire |
| Berks | Berkshire |
| Bucks | Buckinghamshire |
| Cambs | Cambridgeshire |
| Glos | Gloucestershire |
| Hants | Hampshire |
| Herefs | Herefordshire |
| Herts | Hertfordshire |
| Hunts | Huntingdonshire |
| Lancs | Lancashire |
| Leics | Leicestershire |
| Lincs | Lincolnshire |
| Northants | Northamptonshire |
| Notts | Nottinghamshire |
| Oxon | Oxfordshire |
| Salop | Shropshire |
| Staffs | Staffordshire |
| Wilts | Wiltshire |
| Worcs | Worcestershire |
| Yorks | Yorkshire |

# ACKNOWLEDGMENTS

Our style for indexing was established at the Yale University Press by Mrs Nicholas Moseley for our first two volumes (the correspondence with William Cole) in 1937. This style was then slightly altered before Mrs Moseley collaborated with me and others for the index to the correspondence with Madame du Deffand which appeared in 1939; she also read the galley-proofs of the index to the correspondence with George Montagu (1941), an index compiled by Mrs Eunice B. Gettell and myself.

The indexes for Vols. 11–16 and 28–29 were mostly prepared by the late Charles H. Bennett with the help of Mrs Louis Martz. The massive index to the eleven-volume correspondence with Sir Horace Mann was compiled by me with aid from Charles H. Bennett and other members of our staff, the contributions of Laurence R. Veysey and Joseph Ambash as typists being especially noteworthy. The Ossory index was largely Mrs Martz's work; the indexes to Vols. 30 and 31 were prepared by Robert A. Smith.

The present final index coordinates the various printed indexes for Vols. 1–34 with manuscript indexes to Vols. 35–43, as well as the manuscript index to selected material in our annotation—all interwoven together into one alphabetical sequence, with some inevitable inconsistencies of style. Such a major undertaking could not have been accomplished without the help of the three people named on its title-pages, but there were many occasional assistants, especially Mrs Victoria Wolf and David Mandel, to whom our thanks are due. The staffs of the Yale University Press in New Haven, and of Heritage Printers in Charlotte, N.C., are to be commended for their cooperation and endurance in dealing with this large and highly complicated enterprise.

W. H. S.

# A

A. A., Mr:

Paris visited by, en route to Munich, **30**. 215

Aachen. *See* Aix-la-Chapelle

Aaron:

rod of, **39**. 254

Abano, baths of:

Mann, Horace II and Lady Lucy, to visit, **24**. 108

visitors to: Pitt, Anne, **24**. 9, 22, 105, 108, 233; Tylney, **24**. 22

'Abarasser.' *See* Balthazar

Abarca de Bolea, Don Pedro Pablo (1719–98), Conde de Aranda; Spanish ambassador to France; president of the council of Castile:

Almodóvar informs, of England's rejection of Spanish ultimatum, **24**. 463n

biographical information on, corrected, **43**. 95, 249

Brest visited by, to make Spanish admiral give precedence to Du Chaffault, **24**. 528

Brunoy's house taken by, **5**. 406

courier brings news to, of plot against George III, **6**. 230

French and Spanish fleets' departure to be observed by, **24**. 527n, 528n

French domination of, **25**. 33n

Fuentes' house too small for, **5**. 405–6

has seen no one, **5**. 405

Jesuits opposed by, **26**. 49, **41**. 203

member of Ordre du St-Esprit, **6**. 401

Minorca's surrender announced by, **25**. 255n

picture of, on watch, **41**. 203

Rochford tells St Paul to observe, **24**. 101n

said to be mortally wounded, **18**. 154

said to be president of Castile, **41**. 203

social relations of, with: Du Deffand, Mme, **6**. 303, **7**. 348, 351, 432, (?) 446; Maurepas, Comte and Comtesse de, **7**. 432; Necker, M. and Mme, **6**. 381

'Tonton' likes, **6**. 447

Treaty of Paris preliminaries signed by, **25**. 356n

Voltaire's verses to, **41**. 203

Abatisti, Academy of:

*giuoco della sibilla* performed in, **21**. 48

Abbaye, L', prison in Paris:

Echlin imprisoned at, **7**. 110

Fleury, Duchesse de, lived near, **34**. 165

La Trémoïlle, Duchesse de, imprisoned in, **12**. 3n

massacre at, **6**. 57n, **7**. 137n

priests butchered in, **34**. 165

prisoners transferred to, **6**. 256

'Abbé.' *See* Nicholls, Rev. Norton

'Abbé, le grand.' *See* Barthélemy, Jean-Jacques

Abbé, the, Mann's spy at Rome:

a poor spy, **18**. 485

at Rome, **18**. 466

(?) HW calls, Mann's 'little friend,' **17**. 3

Mann does not hear rumour from, **19**. 140

money given to, **17**. 114

Scottish visitors to Old Pretender revealed by, **17**. 145

Young Pretender's departure from Rome told by, **17**. 113

Abbé; abbés:

Clement XIII regulates dress and conduct of, **21**. 224, 230

costume of, **17**. 136, **19**. 49, **21**. 224, 230

Craon, Princesse de, entertains, French, **17**. 16

French and German, pervade Rome, **37**. 57

Genoese: Conway told by, how holy relics are esteemed there, **37**. 320; said to be Lady Mary Wortley Montagu's cicisbeo, **30**. 11

Gondi, Mme, attended by, **17**. 136, **18**. 289

HW wishes, in England, **9**. 268

Pannoni's influenced by false rumours from, **18**. 557

Pius VI's edicts regulate, **24**. 107

*See also* Vance, Abbé de

Abberley Lodge, Worcs:

Bromley of, **2**. 154n

Abbé-secretary, Richecourt's. *See* Niccoli, Abbé

Abbeville:

Écu de Brabant, l', inn at, **7**. 371, **37**. 40

HW writes from, **3**. 344, 350, 352, **7**. 386

La Barre beheaded at, **4**. 101n

suitable for over-night stay, **37**. 40

Tête de Bœuf inn at, **7**. 334, 371n

visitors to: Gray, **13**. 162n; Gunnings, **11**. 229n; HW, **3**. 2, 344, 350, 352, **6**. 221, **7**. 259, 314, 324, 333, 334, 353, 386, **13**. 162n

woolen factory at, **37**. 41

Abbey; abbeys:

at Pisa, **23**. 504

HW imparts gloomth of, to SH, **20**. 372

HW's love of, will not put him against Reformation, **35**. 146

Mantuan and Milanese, income of, **18**. 55n

More, Hannah, sees, in Wye valley, **31**. 320

ruined, farm turned into, at Wentworth Castle, **37**. 561

Sussex the 'holy land' of, **35**. 131

Valenti loses, **18**. 55

Abbondanza:

robbery of, **19**. 473, **20**. 220

Abbot, George (1562–1633), Abp of Canterbury, 1611:

Abbot's Hospital, Guildford, founded by, **16**. 197

James I flattered by, **2**. 95–6, 99

Abbot; abbots:

figure of, on gateway at Peterborough, **10**. 347

'purple,' at Netley Abbey, **35**. 251

tomb of, with crozier, at Bayham Abbey, **35**. 137

'Abbot of Strawberry':

HW calls himself, **10**. 127

Abbot's Hospital, Guildford:
Lort asks about chapel windows of, **16.** 197
Abbots Ripton, Hants:
Bonfoy of, **13.** 166n, **14.** 51n
Abbotstone, Hants, D. of Bolton's seat:
HW might visit, **9.** 216
Abbreviations:
HW's, unintelligible save to Kirgate, **34.** 127
Abbs Court. *See* Apps Court
*A, B, C, L'. See under* Voltaire
*Abcedario.* See *Abecedario*
Abd el Malek *or* Muley Moloch (d. 1578), K.
of Morocco:
bashaws and viceroys of, spread destruction,
**42.** 78
HW refers to Gulston as, **1.** 289
Abdolonimus:
Mason tells story of, in *English Garden,* **28.**
272
Abdul-Hamid I (1725–89), Sultan of Turkey
1774–89:
Austria and Russia may get concessions from,
**25.** 399n, 409n, 410n
interpreter needed for interview with, **32.** 339
Russian encroachments must be resented by,
**25.** *436*
Russia to get indemnity from, **24.** 40
subjects of, riotous, **25.** 360, 436
withdraws protection from Poland, **24.** 40
Abdurissak Effendi, Turkish delegate:
Bucharest congress left by, **23.** 469n
Abdy, Anne Hester (fl. 1770), m. Charles Nel-
son Cole:
marriage of, **1.** 283n, 284n
Abdy, Sir Anthony Thomas (ca 1690–1733), 3d
Bt:
daughter inherits Felix Hall from, **9.** 66n
Abdy, Sir Anthony Thomas (d. 1775), 5th Bt:
sister of, marries, **1.** 283n, 284n
Abdy, Charlotte, m. (1744) John Williams:
Felix Hall inherited by, from father, **9.** 66n
*Abecedario pittorico. See under* Orlandi, Pel-
legrino Antonio
Abel:
HW jokes about Cain and, **35.** 335
Abélard, Pierre (1079–1142), philosopher:
Du Deffand, Mme, dislikes, **3.** 8
letters of, *see under* Hughes, John
Nuneham church worthy of entombing, **35.**
460
Paraclete of, Haistwell's etching of, **42.** 53n
'Abelard and Eloisa' (print). *See under*
Bowles, Carrington
Abercairny:
Stirling of, **11.** 165n
Abercorn, Cts of. *See* Clifton, Katherine (ca
1592–1637); Plumer, Anne (1690–1776)
Abercorn, E. of. *See* Hamilton, George (ca 1636–
before 1683); Hamilton, James (ca 1661–
1734); Hamilton, James (1686–1744); Ham-
ilton, James (1712–89)
Abercorn, E. and M. of. *See* Hamilton, John
James (1756–1818)

Abercorn, Marchioness of. *See* Copley, Catharine (d. 1791)
Abercromby, James (? 1706–81), army officer:
Pitt sends Mann extract of letter of, **21.** 233n
Abercromby, Sir Ralph (1734–1801), K. B.,
1795:
returns from West Indies to England, **12.** 212
Aberdeen:
ball to be held at, **37.** 225
Boys, Commodore, pursues Thurot towards,
**21.** 346n, 352n
cathedral at: **15.** 149n; stripped of lead, **32.**
225n
colleges of, have Jamesone portraits, **40.** 267
elegy on Jamesone printed at, **40.** 262, 268
Fitzjames's horsemen arrive at, **19.** 209n
Jamesone born at, **40.** 263
King's College at, **43.** 196
magistrates of, offer low price for Jamesone's
full-length of Charles I, **40.** 267
Newton College at, has Jamesone's portrait
of Johnston, **40.** 269
Reid professor at, **40.** 320
St Nicholas's church at, festival hangings of,
**40.** 266
visitors to: Conway, **37.** 222–5, 226, 227–37;
Cornwallis, **37.** 235; Cumberland, D. of,
**19.** 228, 233
Aberdeen gloves:
Masters gives, to Cole, **2.** 197
Aberdour, Bn. *See* Douglas, George (1761–1827)
Abergavenny, Bn. *See* Nevill, George (1727–
85); Nevill, Henry (after 1527–87); Nevill,
William (d. 1744)
Abergavenny, Bns. *See* Fitzalan, Joan (d.
1435); Herbert, Lady Rebecca (d. 1758);
Pelham, Henrietta (1730–68); Tatton, Kath-
erine (d. 1729)
Abergavenny, E. of. *See* Nevill, George (1727–
85)
Abimelech:
Biblical misquotation about, **7.** 375, **32.** 268
Sarah and, **34.** 21
Abingdon, E. of. *See* Bertie, Willoughby (1740–
99)
Abingdon, Berks:
church spire at, **28.** 337
Harcourt's vale bounded by, **35.** 459
Southcote of, **9.** 116n
Abingdon St, Westminster:
Bentley's last residence, **33.** 372n
Abington, James (fl. 1759), royal trumpeter:
wife of, **7.** 142n, **29.** 44n
Abington, Mrs James. *See* Barton, Frances
Abington, Great *and* Little, Cambs:
Cole drives with Middleton towards, **15.** 313
Cole's birthplace, **1.** 2n
Gideon supposedly at, **2.** 118
Lagden dies at, **1.** 364n
Nichols vicar of, **2.** 371n
Western buried at, **1.** 364

Abington. *See also* Abingdon

Abington Buildings, London:
Cock, Dr, in, **2**. 172n

Abishag:
Fagnani, Maria, called, **33**. 142
HW's term for Louis XV's mistresses, **22**. 4, 23. 258
Van der Werff's picture of, **43**. 124

Ablaincourt. *See* Bruhier d'Ablaincourt

Ablancourt. *See* Perrot d'Ablancourt

Abo, Treaty of:
Russia and Sweden sign, **18**. 275n
Swedish succession proclaimed by, **18**. 203n, 275n

Abou-al-eb-Saba-bedin-lolo-ab-alnin:
HW jokes about, **20**. 197

Aboul-Cacem *or* Aboulcasem Basry:
(?) HW the heir of, **3**. 99
Pétis de la Croix's *Persian and Turkish Tales* tell of, **37**. 466

Aboulcaum. *See* Aboul-Cacem

Aboulensem. *See* Aboul-Cacem

Aboyne, Cts of. *See* Cope, Catherine Anne (1771–1832); Douglas, Lady Mary (1737–1816)

Aboyne, E. of. *See* Gordon, George (1761–1853)

Abraham:
bosom of, **33**. 181, **35**. 113
HW's correspondence as long-lived as, **25**. 417
stained glass depicts, **9**. 385n
wives of, **34**. 21

'Abraham and Hagar.' *See under* Barbieri, Giovanni Francesco

Abrahams, Moses:
jewels stolen by, **11**. 206n

Abrahams. *See also* Abrams

Abrams, Eliza, singer:
sings glees at Mrs Udny's, **11**. 109

Abrams, Harriet (1760–ca 1825), soprano:
sings at Cambridge, **2**. 331
sings glees at Mrs Udny's, **11**. 109

Abrams, Theodosia (ca 1758–ca 1822), m. Joseph Garrow; contralto:
biographical information on, corrected, **43**. 76, 144
sings at Cambridge, **2**. 331
sings glees at Mrs Udny's, **11**. *109*

*Abrégé chronologique de l'histoire de France.*
*See under* Hénault, Charles-Jean-François

Abreu y Bertodano, Felix de (d. ?1765), Spanish envoy to England 1754–60:
Alt's conversation with, on Munster's capture, **21**. 315–16
(?) death of, **7**. 397
Fox, Henry, suggests Gibraltar–Port Mahon exchange to, **20**. 574n
Garrick's dinner includes, **35**. 244
La Galissonnière's account sent to, **20**. *561*
Townshend's witticism to, **37**. 474

Abruzzo:
Austrians overrun, **18**. 460

Spaniards retire towards, **18**. 438
troops from, approach Foligno, **17**. 291

'Absalom.' *See* Frederick Louis, P. of Wales

*Absalom and Achitophel. See under* Dryden, John

Abscess; abscesses:
HW's on left leg, **34**. 227
in head, occurrences of, **38**. 361
occurrences of, **36**. 292, **42**. 436, 438
Rockingham believed he had, **25**. 288

Abs Court Farm. *See* Apps Court Farm

Absentee Tax. *See under* Tax

Absolution:
*in articulo mortis*, Louis XV hopes for, **23**. 518, **24**. 8
Johnson, Bp, might give, to Young Pretender, **22**. 324

Abuna of Abyssinia:
Yasous II unable to install, **39**. 476

*Abuse of Parliament. See* Ralph, James: *Detection of the Use and Abuse of Parliaments*

Abyssinia, Dowager Empress of. *See* Welleta Georgis

Abyssinia, K. of. *See* Socinios; Yasous I; Yasous II

Abyssinia:
Bruce lived at court of, **24**. 21
—— said to have sent camels to, **32**. 242
——'s stories of music of, **28**. 204, 249–50
——'s story of monarch of, ridiculed by HW, **28**. 248–9
HW's name for France, **11**. 139, 141
letters to, HW's compared to, **11**. 160
Páez said to build palaces and convents in, **39**. 476–7
travel to, still novel, **28**. 219
Wortley Montagu to visit, **22**. 113

Acacia; acacias:
Arabians worship, **10**. 156
HW's: at SH, **10**. 127, 156; covered with flowers, **31**. 36, **38**. 90; HW offers, to Cole, **1**. 183, 190; HW should not languish under, **31**. 25; HW to send, to Montagu, **9**. 177
wind harmful to, **9**. 177

*Academia nobilissimæ artis pictoriæ. See under* Sandrart, Joachim von

*Academiæ Cantabrigiensis luctus:*
Frederick, P. of Wales lamented in, **20**. 260

Académie de belles-lettres, at Florence:
Richecourt entertains, in honour of Margravine of Bayreuth, **20**. 476–7

Académie des inscriptions et belles-lettres, at Paris:
Chesterfield thanks, in letter, for electing him, **37**. 408
Duclos leaves vacancy in, **5**. 209
*Histoire* of, **7**. 357
Joseph II at, **6**. 443
(?) London not to be reformed by, **34**. 173
prize offered by, **35**. 336
Sainte-Palaye's publications at, **40**. 303

Académie des sciences:
  Alembert's pension from, **41.** 62
  Duclos secretary of, **22.** 531
  Leroy member of, **6.** 211, 442
  London not to be reformed by, **34.** 173
  Pringle defeated by Tronchin for, **7.** 12
  Tronchin elected to Haller's place in, **7.** 12
  visitors to: Brunswick, P. of, **3.** 49; Gustav III,
    **5.** 36, 39; Joseph II, **6.** 440, 443
Académie française:
  Alembert reads eulogies at public sessions of,
    **6.** 189, **7.** 68
  ———'s eulogies read at, *see* Alembert, Jean le
    Rond d': *Éloges lus . . .*
  ——— to be secretary of, **5.** 209, 211, 222
  Baretti's connection with, **28.** 97
  Batteux candidate for secretary of, **5.** 222
  Beauvau talks at, **5.** 354
  Boismont's funeral oration at, for Louis XV,
    **6.** 80
  Brunswick, D. of, dines with members of, **3.**
    41–2
  Catherine II admired by members of, **33.** 410
  Chamfort's prize from, **7.** 326n
  Court influence in elections of, **5.** 211
  Delille's election to, vetoed, **5.** 234
  dictionary of, **4.** 439
  Du Deffand, Mme, mentions session of, **7.** 170
  ———'s opinion of members of, **7.** 68
  ———'s opinion of works of members of, **5.** 222
  Franciscans' masses at deaths of members of,
    **7.** 48
  Frederick II the ape of, **34.** 34
  Gaillard director of, **6.** 208
  ———'s speech before, **5.** 46, 58
  Garrick should be included in, for moderniz-
    ing *Hamlet*, **28.** 58, 60
  HW fit for, **4.** 255
  HW imagines ships christened by, **34.** 76
  HW supposes D. of Manchester will be elected
    to, **33.** 399
  hall of, **5.** 209
  Lemierre candidate for, **7.** 240
  Louis XV vetoes election to, **5.** 234
  Louis XVI and, exchange compliments, **28.**
    221
  ——— receives deputation from, **6.** 60
  members of: Aix, Abp of, **6.** 260, 274; Alem-
    bert, **5.** 222, **7.** 48; Beauvau, **5.** 34–5, 458;
    Chabanon, **7.** 438; Chastellux, **6.** 116; Ches-
    terfield, **37.** 408; Colardeau, **6.** 274, 284,
    333; Ducis, **7.** 100, 104, 118; Duclos, **5.** 209,
    222; Dupré de St-Maur, **6.** 116; Gresset, **6.**
    497, **7.** 10; La Harpe, **6.** 324, 333; Millot,
    **6.** 497, **7.** 10; Saint-Aignan, **6.** 274, 284;
    Voisenon, **6.** 260, 274; Voltaire, **7.** 51, 85,
    100, 118
  Merry's ode dull enough to succeed with, **34.**
    117
  Necker's prize address at, **5.** 395, 400, 405
    (*see also* Necker, Jacques: *Éloge de M.
    Colbert*)

  Nivernais reads fables to, **28.** 84
  opening session of, **6.** 232
  postilion may get éloges from, **39.** 270
  Radonvilliers president of, **7.** 118
  speeches at: **6.** 278, 324, 341, 345, **7.** 10, 118;
    sent to HW, **5.** 46, 48, 57, **6.** 277, 281, 324,
    325, **7.** 118, 121
  Suard's election to, vetoed, **5.** 142n, 234
  Tressan candidate for, **7.** 240
  vacancies in, **4.** 489, **7.** 240
  value of secretaryship of, **5.** 209, 222
  visitors to: Brunswick, P. of, **3.** 41–2, 54; Gus-
    tav III, **5.** 36; Joseph II, **6.** 443; Luxem-
    bourg, Mme de, **6.** 333; Montagu, Mrs, **6.**
    354, 358; Richmond, **6.** 333
  Voltaire eulogized at, **7.** 172
  ——— receives deputation from, **7.** 18
  ———'s invective in, against Shakespeare, **24.**
    267
  ———'s place in: Ducis receives, **7.** 100; no
    claimants for, **7.** 51; verses on, **7.** 85
  ———'s plans for, **7.** 53
  ———'s successor in, not to be welcomed by
    Radonvilliers, **7.** 48
Académie royale de chirurgie, Paris:
  HW has not seen, **32.** 160
  (?) HW visits, **7.** 348
Académies de sciences et de belles lettres. *See*
  Académie des inscriptions et belles-lettres;
  Académie des sciences
Academy; academies:
  in Lorraine, **42.** 90
  literary, in Ansbach, of Bns Craven, **34.** 27n
  *See also* Abatisti, Academy of; Académie;
    Accademia
Academy, French. *See* Académie française
Academy of Arts and Sciences. *See* Society for
  the Encouragement of Arts, Manufacture,
  and Commerce
Acadia. *See* Nova Scotia
*Acadiade, L'. See under* Chevrier, François-
  Antoine
Acapulco, Mexico:
  galleon treasure from, paraded through Lon-
    don, **30.** 53–4
Acapulco, ship from. *See Nuestra Señora del
  Cabadongo*
Accademia, at Florence:
  attendants at: Chute, **18.** 187; Goldsworthy,
    Mrs, **35.** 23; Whithed, **18.** 187, **35.** 23
  balls at, **19.** 115
  (?) Dashwood's, **40.** 33
  Mann entertains, **18.** 12–13, 29
  Medici, Filippo, starts, **18.** 178
Accademia degli Armonici:
  concerts by, **23.** 458n
Accademia degli Immobili, Florence:
  founded in Palazzo Ughi, **17.** 56n
  masked ball given by, **25.** 50n
  Teatro della Pergola owned by, **18.** 439n,
    **19.** 355n
Accademia degli Intronati, Siena:
  Bibiena rebuilds, after fire, **20.** 391n

*Tito Manlio*, opera, at reopening of, **20.** 391n

Accademia dei Filomusi:
poetry readings by, **23.** 458n

Accademia dei Gelati, Bologna:
device of, **13.** 193
West wants his translation sent to, **13.** 198

Accademia dei nobili, Florence:
Leopold II to see celebration by, in great theatre, **22.** 367
masked ball given by, **25.** 51n

Accademia della Crusca, Florence:
Cork presents Dr Samuel Johnson's *Dictionary* to, **25.** 643n
dictionary (*Vocabolario*) of: **35.** 186; Chute more conversant with, **28.** 107; does not include English business terms, **21.** 549; (?) HW consults, **20.** 196; HW does not own, **20.** 196n; Kaunitz receives, from Ginori, **17.** 49
Florentines think Lady Charlotte Fermor brightest foreigner ever to honour, **30.** 15
Mason alludes to, **28.** 97
Merry, member of, **11.** 136n
Mozzi president of, **21.** 70n
poetry of English imitators of, lacking in sense, **34.** 91

Accademia del Teatro Nuovo:
masked ball given by, in Teatro della Palla a Corda, **25.** 50n

Accademici:
Medici, Filippo de', denied use of theatre by, for his opera, **18.** 439, 445

*Accesso*:
dignity conferred by Tuscan Court, **22.** 528

Acciaioli, Mme. *See* Acciaioli, Marianna (b. 1725); Serlupi-Crescenzi, Teresa (d. 1779)

Acciaioli, Anna (b. 1698), m. (1717) Cavaliere Pietro Frescobaldi:
Bologna visited by, **18.** 65
Mann entertains, **18.** 98
——'s neighbour, **18.** 145
Ricasoli, Baronessa, entertains, **17.** 136
Strozzi cicisbeo to, **18.** 145

Acciaioli, Antonfrancesco (1696–1760):
daughter of, **17.** 477n
Mann takes Mme Bichi to call on, **19.** 407–8
Rome left by, for Florence, **19.** 407–8
villa of, **20.** 160, 165–6, 191

Acciaioli, Clarice (b. 1727), m. (1747) Andrea Minerbetti:
Acciaioli, Cardinal, and Mme Bolognetti to be visited by, **21.** 462
daughter of, to marry, **23.** 295, 306
English wives presented by, to Grand Duke, **23.** 527n
Mann's cicisbea, **23.** 295, 306
(?) Mann's cicisbea at opera only, **22.** 180
Mann seeks fans for, **21.** 462, 483
——'s legacies to, **25.** 667n

Acciaioli, Faustina (d. 1776), m. (1720) Conte Giacomo Bolognetti:
Bologna visited by, **18.** 65

Minerbetti, Mme, seeks fans for visit to, **21.** 462
social relations of, with: Craon, **17.** 37; Craon, Mme de, **17.** *10*, 16, 37, **18.** 65; Mann, **18.** 65; Old Pretender and sons, **17.** 10, 16

Acciaioli, Filippo (1700–66), cardinal, 1759; nuncio to Lisbon 1754–60:
Archinto assures, that Clement XIII will not change Benedict XIV's Jesuit policy, **21.** 340n
*Dimostrazione* accuses, of conspiring, **21.** 476n
José Manoel's injury blamed by, on a fall, **21.** 264–5, 276
Lisbon earthquake described in letters by, **20.** *519*
Minerbetti, Mme, seeks fans for visit to, **21.** 462
Portugal expels, for not illuminating house for royal marriage, **21.** 422–3, 476
returns Clement XIII's letter by valet-de-chambre, **21.** 340–1
Roman Court publishes account of expulsion of, from Lisbon, **21.** 476
Torregiani and Palhava brothers said to join, in plot against José Manoel, **21.** 475, 476n

Acciaioli, Giacinto Emmanuele (1710–82), of Madeira:
Bocchineri, Mme, compromised by, in Mann's garden, **19.** 497, 502
'canary bird,' **18.** (?) 446, **19.** 497
Madeira origins of, **17.** 444, 477, **18.** 65
marriage of, **17.** *444*, 474, 477n, **18.** 65, (?) 446
wife dislikes, **20.** 116

Acciaioli, Marianna (b. 1725), m. (1742) Giacinto Emmanuele Acciaioli:
Boothby's departure leaves, in tears, **21.** 481–2
Corsi, Mme, invited by, to meet Ds of Grafton, **22.** 27–8
fans still liked by, **21.** 462
fortune of, **17.** 474
Grafton, Ds of, to be attended by, **22.** 27–8
health of: smallpox, **18.** 65
husband disliked by, **20.** 116
Langlois succeeded by Pucci as cicisbeo to, **20.** 284, **37.** 323–4
Mann entertains, **19.** 501
marriage of, **17.** *444*, 474, 477n, **18.** 65, (?) 446
'near the bloom of her wrinkles,' **21.** 482
Pelham's affair with, **20.** 115, 129, 172, 284, **37.** 323–4
Pisa baths visited by, **20.** 158
Pucci in love with, **37.** 323–4
ugly, **18.** 65, **37.** 323–4

Acciaioli, Nicola (1753–1834):
birth of, **20.** 116n

Acciaioli family:
descent of, from Dukes of Athens, **20.** 116
heir wanted by, **20.** 116
Pelham liked by, **20.** 172

6 INDEX

[Acciaioli family, *continued*]

——'s intrigue with Mme Acciaioli abetted by, **20**. 116

Accouchement:

toilets displayed at Lady Charlotte Finch's, **19**. 442–3

Accoucheur:

godparent might give money to, at baptism, **24**. 199

Leopold and Maria Louisa accompanied by, on travels, **23**. 220

Secker was, according to Ds of Bedford, **38**. 264

*Account of a Conference between his Grace George late Duke of Buckingham and Father Fitzgerald, An:*

HW tells story from, **18**. 306–7

*Account of Corsica. See under* Boswell, James

*Account of Divers Choice Remarks. See under* Veryard, Ellis

*Account of her Conduct. See under* Jennings, Sarah, Ds of Marlborough

*Account of Hogarth's Tour. See under* Gostling, William

*Account of my Conduct,* by HW:

HW justifies his sinecures in, **35**. 501n

HW's Customs place explained in, **26**. 52–4

*Account of Roman Antiquities Discovered at Woodchester, An. See under* Lysons, Samuel

*Account of Russia, An. See under* Whitworth, Charles

*Account of the Behaviour of the late Earl of Kilmarnock. See under* Foster, James

*Account of the Behaviour of William, late Earl of Kilmarnock and Arthur, late Lord Balmerino. See under* Ford, T.

*Account of the Birth, Life, and Negotiations of the Marechal Belisle, An:*

Belle-Isle compared to Trojan horse in, **18**. 564n

*Account of the Conduct of the Dowager Duchess of Marlborough. See under* Hooke, Nathaniel

*Account of the Earthquakes. See under* Hamilton, Sir William

*Account of the Earthquakes which Happened at Leghorn in Italy, An. See under* Horton, Rev. Thomas

*Account of the Exact Time when Miracles Ceased. See under* Whiston, William

*Account of the Expedition to Carthagena, An:*

Wentworth's actions assailed in, **18**. 143n

*Account of the Giants Lately Discovered, An,* by HW ('l'écrit des Patagons'):

Aiguillon, Mme d', reads, **3**. 172, 177

Cole gives reports on, **1**. 129–30

—— wants to see copy of, **1**. 126, 128, 129–30

Du Deffand, Mme, reads, **3**. 176, 187

HW not to repeat, **33**. 365

HW's copy of, **43**. 49

HW to have copy of translation of, **3**. 188, 190, 200, 212

HW wants reports on, **1**. 128

(?) HW writes, at Bath, **31**. 132

Hertford gives, to Mme d'Aiguillon, **3**. 187

*Journal encyclopédique* reviews, **4**. 62

out of print, **1**. 128

popularity of, **30**. 238

published, **13**. 42

Redmond translates, **3**. 188, 190, 212n

Selwyn reads, in French translation, **30**. 238

Williams, G. J., praises, and quotes it, **30**. 238

—— tells HW of French rage for, **30**. 238

—— to send, to Selwyn, **30**. 238

*Account of the Institution and Progress of the Society of Antiquaries of Scotland. See under* Smellie, William

*Account of the Life . . . of John Napier, An. See under* Erskine, David Steuart

*Account of the Pelew Islands. See under* Keate, George

*Account of the Remains of the Worship of Priapus. See under* Knight, Richard Payne

*Account of the Revolution at Bengal, An. See* Campbell, John (1708–75): *Memoir of the Revolution in Bengal*

*Account of the Voyages . . . in the Southern Hemisphere. See under* Hawkesworth, John

'Account of . . . Tibet.' *See under* Stewart, John

Aceuil; Aceville. *See* Lacueil

Achard des Joumards, Angélique-Gabrielle (1716–82), m. (1738) François-Alexandre, Comte de Galard de Béarn; 'la dame présentante':

daughter of, marries, **6**. 5

(?) Du Barry, Mme, accompanies, to salon, **4**. 233

joked about, **4**. 194, 203, **6**. 5

Achates:

Boswell compared to, **11**. 275

Aché, Comte d':

Pocock does not battle with, off Karikal, India, **21**. 283n

Acheron, river in Hades:

HW's verses mention, **31**. 120

Achesoun *or* Atkinson, John (fl. 1553–5):

coins struck by, **15**. 113n, **42**. 321n

*Achille in Sciro. See under* Metastasio, Pietro

Achilles:

story of Lady Mary Coke and Knyphausen like that of, **38**. 11

*Achilles,* French ship:

capture of, near Cadiz, **21**. 523

Achmet (*or* Ahmed) III (1673–1736), Sultan of Turkey 1703–30:

in Voltaire's *Candide* and in opera, **33**. 587

Achonry, Ireland:

Sherlock surrogate of, **29**. 104n

Achy, Marquise d'. *See* Jubert de Bouville, Marie-Catherine-Jeanne

Acland, Lady Christian. *See* Fox Strangways, Lady Christian Henrietta Caroline

Acland, John Dyke (1746–78), M.P.; army officer:

Callington's M.P. on Lord Orford's interest, **35**. 416n

death of, 33. 71, 41. 375
elected M.P., 32. 212
escapes in America, 33. 71
Fox debates with, 32. 278
wounded at Saratoga, 32. 402

Acon, Bp of. See Talbot, Thomas Joseph (1727–75)

Acorn; acorns:
HW jokes about eating, 31. 325

A'Court (after 1768 Ashe A'Court or A'Court Ashe), William (ca 1708–81), M.P.; army officer:
dismissed for anti-Court voting, 38. 295n
House of Commons entered by, 38. 320
Keppel, Bp, clashes with Rich over, 38. 295

Acquaviva, Pasquale (1719–88), cardinal, 1770:
vice-legate at Avignon, 19. 368

Acquaviva, Trajano (1695–1747), cardinal, 1732; Spanish ambassador at Rome:
Austrian party persecuted by, 19. 113–14
Belloni gets passports from, for Shuttleworth, 19. 77
Benedict XIV blesses, 19. 329–30
—— discusses Neapolitan invasion with, 17. 110
——'s conversation with, about Austrian defeat, 17. 465
——'s permission asked by, for Don Philip to have Parma and Placentia, 17. 201
Bernis alone lives as magnificently as, 23. 389
Caprarola, house of, 17. 389, 18. 377
Charles of Naples visited by, 18. 533
Chute hates, 19. 318, 339
death of, expected, 19. 329–30
English visitors refused passports for Naples by, 19. 15
faction of: Conclave activities of, 13. 220n, 21. 207; encouraged, 35. 59
Franchini exposed to insults because close to, 19. 114
Goddard's pardon not procured by, from Old Pretender, 18. 434
health of, 19. 136, 339
Lamberti assists, 21. 391
Louis XV wants French candidate elected by, 17. 20–1
Monreale archdiocese of, 19. 416
Montemar told by, to invade Tuscany, 17. 266
Naples not allowed by, to be shut off from Rome, 18. 270
Old Pretender aided by, 19. 339n
—— confers with, 19. 85
—— receives information from couriers of, 18. 426n
Pontano seized by order of, 18. 55–6
Protector of Spain, 19. 339n
Roman mob fired on by guard of, 19. 113–14, 136
Spanish army receives Roman recruits from, 18. 542
Trasteverini revolt would ruin, 18. 462
Valenti directed by, 19. 114, 158

votes controlled by, in Conclave, 17. 16n
Young Pretender aided by, 18. 376–8, 388–9

Acquittance, general:
Mozzi awaits, as it is needed for tax declaration, 25. 521

Acropolis. See under Athens

Acrostics:
knotting verses superior to, 33. 263

Act; acts. See Parliament: acts of

Actæon:
mentioned in HW's verses, 12. 258
picture with, 2. 49

Actæon, British frigate:
lost near Charleston, 24. 236, 32. 318

Acta sanctorum ordinis S. Benedicti. See under Mabillon, Jean

Acting:
HW's reflections on, 32. 39, 38. 524

Actions (investments):
Chute to talk about, with Sir Robert Brown, 35. 86

Active, British frigate:
Hermione captured by, 2. 368n, 22. 45
(?) Howe sends dispatches by, 32. 337n, 339n
Pike lieutenant on, 32. 318n

Acton, Commodore John (d. 1766), Tuscan naval official:
Algerines to be fought by, 20. 473, 480
death of, 22. 548
East India Co.'s former employee, 22. 548
Florence visited by, to see mistress, 20. 480
hydrophobia cure witnessed by, 20. 509
Niccolini accused of conniving at capture by, of prizes, 20. 2n
rear-admiral in Francis I's navy, 20. 98n
Toussaint accompanied by, to Florence, 20. 99n
—— confers with, at Florence, 20. 98
Tuscan grand dukes pension, for services in Indian scheme, 22. 548
Tuscan ships outfitted by, at Porto Ferrajo, 20. 472n

Acton, Sir John Francis Edward (1736–1811), Neapolitan prime minister:
Caramanico displaced by, 33. 242n
Hamilton hears from, about Spanish ultimatum, 24. 486n

Acton, Middlesex:
'Old Hat,' the, near, 10. 104

Acton Road:
Holland House has coach road into, 30. 114n

Actor; actors:
ambassador is nothing but an, 21. 335
at Calais, resent D. and Ds of Cumberland's paltry gratuities, 23. 519–20, 32. 150–1
Baskerville less prosperous than, 40. 275
buckram worn by, 25. 624
Conway would be indifferent as, 37. 86
Dublin's better than Bath's, 37. 412
fat, Townshend, Vcts, remarks on, 19. 119
footman fails as, 37. 14
footman preferable to, as son-in-law, 38. 367
French, in London: at Lady William Gor-

[Actor; actors, *continued*]
don's, **39.** 441; Cliveden visited by, **18.** 305; mob silences, **17.** 166; mobs violent about, **20.** 48; riots against, **20.** 100n; Trentham champions, **20.** 100n
HW's reflections on, **32.** 39
HW wishes he could send, to Cts of Ailesbury, **39.** 35
kings and emperors compared with, **25.** 552
new political play is old farce by new set of, **37.** 86
return by, after retirement, fatal, **25.** 308
Actress; actresses:
jewels borrowed from, **38.** 109
Acuña. *See* Sarmiento de Acuña
Acunha. *See* Cunha Manuel
Adage:
Italian, about correspondence, **40.** 299
Adair, ——, army agent, at Chidley Court, Pall Mall:
Suckling hears from, of vacant cornetcy, **42.** 47
Adair, Lady Caroline. *See* Keppel, Lady Caroline
Adair, Dr Robert (ca 1711–90); surgeon:
Duval's letter from, **24.** 325n, 326n
George III receives bi-weekly letters from, **23.** 369
—— sends, to Italy, to attend D. of Gloucester, **23.** *356*
Gloucester, Ds of, receives food from, **36.** 142
—— sends to England for, **24.** 314, 317
—— slightly encouraged by, about husband's health, **24.** 321, 322–3
Gloucester, D. of, attended by, **23.** 384n, **24.** (?) 76, 321, 322–3, 329, 369, **28.** 323n, **32.** 362, 373, 376, **34.** 247, **35.** 475, **36.** 127, 130, 139, 141, 142
—— may be enabled by, to finish his journey, **24.** 329
—— to be met by, **26.** 51
Gloucester, D. and Ds of, part with, in France, **36.** 149n
HW first meets, at Lady Shelburne's, **32.** *153–4*
letter from, about D. of Gloucester, **32.** 376–7
Mann told by, of Ps of Wales's illness, **23.** 358
Pius VI receives surgical instruments from, **24.** 129n
Stiell's letter from, about D. of Gloucester, **36.** 139
Trent visited by, **36.** 127
Venice to be visited by, **36.** 143, 149
Weymouth gets bulletins from, about D. of Gloucester, **36.** 130
Adam:
and Eve: clothes of, eaten by goat on the Ark, **39.** 294; married couples left alone in the country like, **38.** 14; resemble Cook's savages, **33.** 436; Teniers' painting of, **7.** 286
Arenberg traces descent from, **20.** 195
Arne calls, 'royal youth,' **28.** 55

'father of lies,' **12.** 45
figleaf of, **35.** 531, **39.** 294
George I almost coeval with, **12.** 12
HW jokes about, **35.** 335
Milton's, comparable to Apollo Belvedere, **16.** 270
Montagu, Lady Mary Wortley, jokes about, **20.** 282
Norfolk, D. of, probably scorns, as a relation, **12.** 209
'own prime ancestor,' **33.** 469
Pineda thinks, understood all sciences but politics, **37.** 293
Prior's *Alma* mentions, **11.** 185
Stanhopes trace descent from, **20.** 181, 195
Strawbridge, Mrs, would have outwitted, **34.** 263
Vertot should have written about, **31.** 329
'Adam.' *See* Beauvau, Charles-Just de
Adam, Antoine (b. 1705), priest:
Voltaire's Jesuit friend, **7.** 278
Adam, James (d. 1794), architect:
Bonomi invited by, to England, **42.** 101n
Boulton encouraged by, **23.** 212n
brother advised by, to write to Mann, **22.** 418n
lottery of brother and, **29.** 38
nephew of, **24.** 537
Parliament votes land to brother and, **28.** 108
Sandby joint architect with, of H. M. Office of Works, **1.** 208n
satirical account of, **16.** 186n
Adam, Robert (1728–92), architect:
Adelphi buildings of: HW disparages, **28.** 102; lottery for, **28.** 108, **29.** 38
'all gingerbread, filigraine, and fan-painting,' **24.** 93
Bonomi invited to England by, **42.** 101n
Boulton encouraged by, **23.** 212n
Breton ordered by, to do bas relief for Wolfe's tomb, **21.** 421–2, 436
bridge and gateway by, at Sion House, **35.** 331n
brother advises, to write to Mann, **22.** 418n
Carteret's house remodelled by, **33.** 548
Cornwall's dinner attended by, **33.** 588n
Derby's house 'filigreed' by, **32.** 371
designs by: for garden-cottage at SH, **4.** 147n; for Ds of Northumberland's monument, **41.** 411n; for Hertford's saloon, **38.** 16, 18, 26; for Roger Townshend's monument, **21.** 421n, **40.** 167n; for Wolfe's tomb, **21.** 428
'gingerbread and sippets of embroidery' in architecture of, **33.** 500
HW and Hertford to meet with, **38.** 16
HW's correspondence with, **41.** 39
HW sends books to, for designs for SH, **41.** 39
HW to call on, **41.** 39
'harlequinades' of, **29.** 184
Kedleston designed by, **10.** 230
Mason calls brother and, 'self-puffing Scotch coxcombs,' **28.** 107

Montagu, Mrs, offended by, **29.** 184n

nephew of, **24.** 537

Osterley Park decorated by, **10.** 103n, **28.** 413, **32.** 125n, *126*, **34.** 237–8

Parliament votes land to brother and, **28.** 108

satirical account of, **16.** 186n

Shelburne House begun by, for Bute, **33.** 125n

Sion House rebuilt by, **9.** 169n, **32.** 125n, **38.** 429

SH chimney-piece designed by, **2.** 370n, **35.** 407

tables designed by, brittle, **28.** 102

Theban harp of Bruce might have been designed by, **28.** 249

Townshend's monument by: **40.** 167n; uses Breton's bas-relief, **21.** 421n

Tuscan order should be used by, instead of filigraine, for ancient families' seats, **41.** 361

Villiers's house influenced by, **32.** 371

*Works in Architecture* of: bridge at Sion in, **28.** 108; first number of, published, **28.** *101–2*, 107

Adam, Thomas (fl. 1433–65), sea-captain:

(?) brought over Margaret of Anjou, **14.** 75

Adam, William (1751–1839), M.P.:

biographical information on, corrected, **43.** 287, 304, 352

Fitzpatrick replies to, **33.** 238

Fox, C. J., wounded by, in duel, **24.** 537, **25.** 2, 37, **28.** *481–2*, **29.** 12, 87, **33.** *144*, 146–7, 267

Hardinge could not endure hearing, in Parliament, **35.** 620

Macdonald as absurd as, **28.** 486

Parliamentary speeches by, **24.** 537, **35.** 620

Powys called to order by, **35.** 620n

preferment desired by, **33.** 267

Adam. *See also* Adame; Adami; Adams

Adam, l'Isle. *See* Isle-Adam

Adame, Rev. Robert (fl. ca 1473):

Haslingfield vicar, **2.** 256

Adami, Andrea (1663–1742), of Bolsena:

*Osservazioni per ben regolare il coro della capella pontificizia*, **21.** 467, 477, 482, 492

'Adams, Miss':

Euston said to have married, **30.** 28

Adams, Charles:

France visited by, with father, **39.** 345n

Adams, John (1735–1826), 2d President of the United States:

American minister plenipotentiary to England, **33.** 127n

arrives in Paris, **28.** *382*

France visited by, **28.** 382, **39.** 344–5

Gage to be executed instead of, **28.** 219

Howe receives, **24.** 270

'independency' used by, **15.** 44n

peace preliminaries signed by, **25.** 347n

presidency of, corrected, **43.** 303

sons accompany, **39.** 344–5

Adams, John Quincy (1767–1848), 6th President of the United States:

France visited by, with father, **39.** 345n

Adams. *See also* Adam; Adame; Adami

Adamson, John, printer:

Bachaumont's *Mémoires secrets* printed by, **6.** 478, **28.** 324, **43.** 301

'Ad Bacchum.' *See under* West, Richard

Addenbrooke's Hospital, Cambridge:

benefit concert for, **1.** 267n, **2.** 95n

Hayles attends at, **1.** 371n

Hopkins attends at, **1.** 240n

sermon for, **2.** 331n

Adderbury, Oxon:

best route, by way of Islip, **10.** 261

Buccleuchs to return to, for Christmas, **10.** 284

fever prevalent in vicinity of, **10.** 287

HW jokes about climate at, **10.** 312

life at, simple, **10.** 281

Montagu's garden at, **10.** 257, 286

——'s health improves at, **10.** 266, 267

——'s house at: description of, by Montagu, **10.** 257–8; dry, **10.** 267; fire at, smokes, **10.** 281; gate at, **10.** 261; glass at, **10.** 258, 281; HW asks for address of, **10.** 260; HW's objections to, **10.** 258–9, 262, 267, 276; hay at, **10.** 261; Montagu criticized for improving, **10.** 281; Montagu prefers, to Greatworth, **10.** 267; Montagu's opinion of, **10.** 261; Montagu takes, **10.** 257; Montagu to spend Christmas at, **10.** 299; parlour in, **10.** 310; remodelling of, **10.** 266, 286–7; rent of, low, **10.** 258, 267

—— spends little time in, **10.** 287

mud of, **10.** 274

post from, **10.** 300

visitors to Montagu at: Boscawen, **10.** 295–6; Boston, **10.** 284; Burgoyne, **10.** 295–6; Chute, **10.** 264; Guilford, **10.** 308; HW, **10.** 258; 261–4, 310–13, **39.** 107; Osborn, Sir George, **10.** 288, 295–6; Osborn, John, **10.** 288, 295–6; Osborns' clergyman and squire, **10.** 295–6

Addington, Justice:

rioters examined by, at Bow St, **33.** 179n

Addington, Mr, of Teddington:

SH visited by, **12.** 241

Addington, Anne (d. 1806), m. (1770) William Goodenough, M.D.:

SH visited by, **12.** 243

Addington, Anthony (1713–90), M.D., 1744:

Bute-Chatham negotiation involves, **33.** 64n

Chute might call in, **35.** 95

formerly a 'mad doctor,' **22.** 505

Pitt (Chatham) attended by, **22.** 505, 552n, **24.** 371n

—— dissuaded by, from going to Parliament, **24.** 370

Addington, Henry (1757–1844), speaker of the House of Commons 1789–1801; cr. (1805) Vct Sidmouth; prime minister:

Dunkirk cannot be recaptured by, **39.** 504

[Addington, Henry, *continued*]
re-elected speaker, **11.** 147n
rumour concerning, **12.** 19n
sister of, **12.** 243
'Addington, Sir William':
Kelly's *School for Wives* produced under name of, **32.** 170n
Addington, Northants:
church at: Cole does not see, **10.** 343; HW tells Cole about, **10.** 343; Vere tombs said to be in, **10.** 343
visited by HW and Lady Catherine Beauclerk, **10.** 343
Addison, Joseph (1672–1719), writer:
'better Christian than antiquarian,' **15.** 22
*Campaign, The*: HW paraphrases, **9.** 180, **34.** 208; HW quotes, **35.** 173
*Cato*: Balmerinoch's words an echo of, **19.** 301n; Conway paraphrases, **37.** 7; Davies compares Johnson's *Irene* to, **29.** 34; Dennis's criticism of, reprinted by Johnson, **29.** 97; Garrick and Goldsmith act scene in, **33.** 171; HW calls, dull, **38.** 446; HW lays in scraps of, for his last words, **9.** 23; HW paraphrases, **31.** 114; HW quotes or alludes to, **12.** 38, 97, **17.** 434, **18.** 221, 315, 481, 562, **19.** 27, **21.** 518, **28.** 30, 162, **29.** 205, 370, **30.** 81, **33.** 129, 524, 536, **38.** 267, **39.** 108, 330; HW sees performance of, by Ps Elizabeth and her family, **21.** 327; Lovel paraphrases, **35.** 39; Mann quotes, **19.** 11; Mason paraphrases, **29.** 320; Swift describes rehearsal of, **10.** 219
Cole on, **1.** 40
*Drummer, The*: apostle spoons mentioned in, **1.** 313n; Hurstmonceaux chamber may give name to, **35.** 139; Rucellai translates, from Destouches' translation, **20.** 118, 151
English still prefer Shakespeare and Milton to, **40.** 379
epitaph quoted by, **1.** 40, 41
'Essay on the Georgics,' Virgil complimented in, **16.** 269
HW ascribes death of, to drinking, **9.** 236
HW compares, with Shakespeare, **9.** 356n
humour in, **35.** 648
Hurd's dialogues the 'offspring' of, **16.** 34
interest in, survives to next age, **28.** 280
*Letter from Italy, A*: HW paraphrases, **28.** 108; HW quotes, **18.** 255, **35.** 85, 337, **38.** 196
life of, in *Biographia Britannica*, **2.** 95, 98
master of grace, **16.** 269
Pope's attack on, despite 'Sir Roger de Coverley,' **35.** 563
professional jealousy of Pope and, **2.** 252
prologues and epilogues of, talk of Sophocles and Euripides, **33.** 553
*Remarks on Several Parts of Italy*: HW imitates, **13.** 85–90; HW refers to, **13.** 204; might have been written without leaving England, **16.** 52, **42.** 244; sarcophagus at Bolsena mentioned in, **15.** 22

*Rosamond* by: Chambers, Miss, acts in, **13.** 97n; Norfolk heiress sings song from, **18.** 317
rough drafts of, probably comparable to Cts Temple's, **40.** 294
Scotch wish to replace, by Ossian, **29.** 105
Shakespeare would have acquired elegance from age of, **41.** 153
Somers characterized by, **2.** 95, 98
*Spectator, The*: Boufflers, Comtesse de, imitates, **22.** 271; Cocchi imitates, **22.** 73n; could alone do justice to Cts Harcourt's verses, **35.** 491; HW paraphrases line in, **28.** 162; Pinkerton's revision of paper from, **16.** 265; portrait in, resembles HW, **31.** 256–7; ridicules fashions in patching, **16.** 258; 'Will Wimble' in, praised, **16.** 269–70
style of, **31.** 224
Tickell 'a poor short-winded imitator of,' **14.** 35
—— friend of, **28.** 384
travelled through poets, not Italy, **13.** 231
Van der Gucht's portrait of, **35.** 515–16
Walpole, Sir Robert, gives Bland's translation to, **42.** 18
West mentions poetical works of, **13.** 131
wife of, **1.** 183n
Young's *Conjectures* describes death of, **9.** 236
See also under *Spectator, The*
Addison, Leonard (ca 1699–1772), D.D.; Fellow of Pembroke College, Cambridge:
Brown's rival as successor to Dr Long, **14.** 89
'creature' of Horatio Walpole (1678–1757), **14.** 90
*Additional Lives to the First Edition of Anecdotes of Painting in England*, by HW:
printing of, **1.** 79n
reviewed in *The Critical Review*, **1.** 139n
Tuer's possible inclusion in, **1.** 78, **43.** 47
*Additional Militia Bill. See under* Parliament: acts of: militia bill
*Additions to the Works of Alexander Pope*:
Gay's 'Mr Pope's Welcome from Greece' printed in, **31.** 418
Addollo. *See* Agdollo
Address; addresses:
anti-American, from English trading towns, **24.** 132, **39.** 270n
approbation of German treaties implied by, **20.** 510
England expresses thanks in, to the Crown, **25.** 484
from Essex, among loyal ones, **23.** 98
Irish Volunteers send, **35.** 382
loyal, presented by Oxford and Cambridge, **30.** 98
of letters, *see under* Letter; letters: direction of
on George III's accession, **16.** 41
Parliamentary opposition moves amendment to, **24.** 534

Parliament may produce, on national disgraces, **24**. 133–4

venal, cannot efface England's stigmas, **35**. 363

*See also under* Parliament; Parliament, Irish

*Address to the Inhabitants . . . of Great Britain and Ireland. Relating to . . . Abolition of the Slave Trade*:

slavery vindicated in, **31**. 280n

*Address to the National Assembly of France, An*:

Burke attacked in, **11**. 169n

*Address to the Opposers of the Repeal of the Corporation and Test Acts. See under* Aikin, Anna Letitia (Mrs Barbauld)

*Address to the Public on the Late Dismission of a General Officer. See under* Guthrie, William

Addy, W.:

print of, **40**. 236

Adela (ca 1062–1137), dau. of William the Conqueror, m. (1080) Stephen, E. of Blois:

verses written by, **12**. 263–4

Adélaïde, Mme, dau. of Louis XV. *See* Marie-Adélaïde

*Adélaïde de Hongrie. See under* Dorat, Claude-Joseph

*Adélaïde du Guesclin. See under* Voltaire

Adeliza (Adela, Adelaide) (ca 1103–51) of Louvain, m. 1 (1121) Henry I of England; m. 2 (1138) William d'Aubigny, 1st E. of Arundel:

second marriage of, **12**. 205, **42**. 422

Adelphi, the, buildings in London:

fire at, **32**. 109

HW visits Hannah More at, **31**. 259, 392

HW visits Mrs Garrick at, **31**. 259, 351, 392

lottery for, **28**. 108, **29**. 38

More, Hannah, might sleep at, during London visit, **31**. 256

residents of: Beauclerk, **10**. 270n, **32**. 170n; Garrick, David, **31**. 211n; Garrick, Mrs, **11**. 249, **31**. 211n; Hardinge, **35**. 598, 599; Macdonald, Lady Louisa, **11**. 217n; More, Hannah, **11**. 249, **31**. 211, 256, 259, 291, 392, 393

Society of Arts in, **29**. 292n

'warehouses laced down the seams,' **28**. 102

Ademar; Adhémar, Comte d'. *See* Azémar de Montfalcon

*Adenochoiradelogia. See under* Brown, John

Ader, Augustin (d. 1783), lawyer:

(?) judgment on, in Goëzmann case, **6**. 23

Adhémar, Comte d'. *See* Azémar de Montfalcon, Jean-Balthazar d'

Adhémar, Comtesse d'. *See* Bouthillier, Gabrielle-Pauline

Adhémar de Monteil. *See* Castellane-Adhémar de Monteil

*Adieux d'Andromaque et d'Hector. See under* André, Pierre-Nicolas; Gruet, ——

Adige ('Adice'), Italian river:

overflowing of, **21**. 134

Adinolfi, Pasquale, Papal physician:

Clement XIV's autopsy by, **24**. 43

Adjutant-General:

Barré dismissed as, **38**. 255

Adlard, Henry:

engraving by, **11**. 134n

Adlestrop, Glos:

Leigh of, **12**. 128n

Administration; administrations, English:

change in, always predicted in summer, **42**. 499

*See also under names of prime ministers; see also* Ministers (cabinet)

Admiral; admirals:

Admiralty lords intimidate, **19**. 359–60

boroughs contested by, **21**. 484

Conway wishes HW had sent preventative against lying of, **37**. 469

Keppel's court martial opposed by, **33**. 82

*See also* Vice-Admiral

*Admiral Hosier's Ghost. See under* Glover, Richard

Admiralty, English:

Arbuthnot's arrangements for Channel Islands reported by, **39**. 320

Argyll names board of, **17**. 355, 363

Barnard may have post in, **17**. 333

Bedford, D. of, first lord of, **37**. 200

Bedford, Henry, employed at, **42**. 492

Boscawen does not write to, **20**. 511

bribes accepted in, for releases from impressment, **39**. 290

Byng leniently treated by, **21**. 55

—— quarrels with, **21**. 3

——'s execution warrant signed by, **21**. 63

Carteret appoints Hardy and Phillipson to, without the Pelhams' knowledge, **18**. 349

—— said to allow George II no power in, **18**. 81

changes in: **9**. 33, 39, 72, 115, 180–1, 204, **10**. 35, 45, 69, **17**. 333, 346, 355–6, 363, 366, 436n, 451, 487, **18**. 349, 550, **19**. 34, 211, 256, 419, 464, **20**. 12, 259, 517, **21**. 17, 25, 73, 103–4, 490, **22**. 42, 449, 472, **23**. 180, 262–3, **25**. 262, 391, 392, **34**. 9n, **38**. 370

Charles Emmanuel III scolds, for court-martialling Townshend, **19**. 332

Chetwynd may be lord of, **17**. 356

Cleveland first secretary to, **20**. 560n, **21**. 309n

—— ordered by, to send Byng extract of La Galissonnière's letter, **20**. 561n

Cotton may be lord of, **17**. 356, 363

court martial recommends Byng to mercy of, **21**. 51

court of, in Doctors Commons, **21**. 287n

Fowke and Byng send, minutes of Gibraltar council, by O'Hara, **20**. 560n

France threatens invasion to force Boscawen's recall by, **29**. 579n

frigates ordered by, to bring Bristol from Lisbon, **21**. 548n

George II chooses members of, **17**. 366, **20**. 17

—— coldly receives lords of, **37**. 481

—— insists on keeping Winchilsea in, **21**. 99

[Admiralty, English, *continued*]

George III may replace Sandwich by Howe in, **24**. 445n

Gower refuses, **22**. 449

Granard said to be in, **17**. 355

Grenville, George, retires to, **38**. 184

high court of, Brough marshal of, **21**. 66n

Howe and friends resign from, discontented by naval promotions, **39**. 462

Howe may succeed Keppel in, **25**. 311n

—— resigns as first lord of, **34**. 9n

—— said to have rejected leadership of, **24**. 439

inquiry into Navy docks ordered by, **20**. 8on

Jersey news from, **39**. 349

Keppel's court martial ordered by, **24**. 432, **33**. 75n

——'s letter to, **39**. 306

Kinnoull's home near, **21**. 364n

*Kouli Kan's* seizure to be adjudged by, **24**. 365n

Long wishes Mann were head of, **18**. 470

lords of: sympathetic towards Townshend, **19**. 325n; tell news to Hertford at Court, **33**. 101

Mathews's court martial conducted by, **19**. 328

members of: Anson, **18**. 550, **20**. 259, **21**. 17, 25, 103; Baltimore, **17**. 366, **18**. 565, **19**. 360n, **30**. 304n; Barrington, **17**. 436n; Bateman, **20**. 517, **21**. 25; Beauclerk, Lord Vere, **17**. 356, **18**. 550, 565, **20**. 80; Bedford, D. of, **18**. 550; Boscawen, **20**. 259, **21**. 25, 73; Brett, **22**. 472, **23**. 180; Campbell, **19**. 256; Carysfort, **21**. 73; Cavendish, **17**. 366; Cockburn, **17**. 355, 366, **18**. 550; Duncannon, **19**. 256, **20**. 157n, **21**. 25; Edgcumbe, **20**. 517; Egmont, **22**. 167, 449; Elliot, **21**. 25, 73; Ellis, **19**. 419, **20**. 517; Forbes, **21**. 25; Fox, C. J. **23**. 188, **34**. 253; Grenville, George, **18**. 550, **19**. 388, 419, **22**. 91; Halifax, **22**. 91; Hamilton, Lord Archibald, **17**. 366; Hamilton, William Gerard, **21**. 73; Hardy, **18**. 349, 550; Hawke, **22**. 472, **23**. 262–3; Hay, **21**. 25, 73; Hunter, **21**. 25, **22**. 9; Hyde, **21**. 25; Keppel, **25**. 262, 391; Lee, **17**. 242n, 333, 356, 366, 451, **18**. 550, **20**. 30; Legge, **19**. 34, 256, 457n, **21**. 92; Mostyn, **21**. 73; Palliser, **24**. 444; Palmerston, **24**. 135, 144; Phillipson, **18**. 349, 550; Pitt, John, **21**. 25; Rowley, **20**. 259, **21**. 25, 73; Sandwich, **18**. 550, **19**. 176, 388, 464, **23**. 263, **24**. 435n, 438n; Sandys, **21**. 73; Saunders, **22**. 449, 471, **41**. 86; Stanhope, John, **19**. 463, **20**. 12; Stanley, **22**. 292, 327, **43**. 280; Temple, **21**. 18, 25, 73; Townshend, Charles, **20**. 517, **22**. 130; Townshend, Hon. John, **25**. 392; Trentham, **20**. 100n; Trevor, **17**. 366; Villiers, **19**. 458n, **20**. 12, 17, **21**. 25; West, **20**. 583n, **21**. 25; Winchilsea, **17**. 355, **18**. 470, 550, **19**. 211, **21**. 73, 99, **22**. 310; Yonge, **23**. 180

Minorcan papers from, presented to House of Commons, **21**. 76n

Navy Bill supported by, with bribes, **20**. 33

Palliser resigns seat in, **24**. 444

——'s demand for trial not as eagerly received by, as Keppel's **24**. 444–5

Pelham and Pitt oppose, over Navy Bill, **20**. 38

Pitt (Chatham) asks, for transports for Belle-Île expedition, **21**. 438n

—— demands place in: for Legge, **21**. 92; for Temple, **21**. 12n

—— puts Jenkinson into, to please Bute, **22**. 472n

——'s board of, **21**. 104

promotions in, rumoured, **30**. 162

resignations from, **39**. 122

Richmond names Saunders for, **41**. 86

Rodney recalled by, **25**. 278

sailors stopped by, from leaving Portsmouth to join mob, **38**. 560

Sandwich best fitted to be head of, **23**. 263

secretary to, *see* Clevland, John; Gashry, Francis

Spencer may get post in, **22**. 569n

Stanley expects changes in, **22**. 327

Townshend, Charles, recommended for, **22**. 130

Wager refuses post in, **17**. 346

Walpole, Sir Robert, one of council to P. George in, **22**. 26

Warren a candidate for, **20**. 17

waterman to petition, for release from imprisonment, **39**. 290–1

Wilmington refers merchants to, **17**. 211

Young, Capt., ordered by, to sail for Byng's trial, **20**. 590n

Admiralty, Russian:

Catherine II tells, to take care of Ds of Kingston's yacht, **24**. 333

Admiralty Office:

express reaches, from Carolina, **38**. 169

Grasse and Keppel dine at, **33**. 351n

guards will especially protect, **24**. 438

Howe's capture of French ships reported to, **12**. 81

letters from Keppel received at, **28**. 414

messenger from Howe said to reach, **12**. 73, **39**. 506

Palliser escapes to, **24**. 442

Spanish left few islands for, **28**. 94

*Admiranda romanorum . . . vestigia. See under* Bartoli, Pietro Santo; Bellori, Giovanni Pietro

Adolf I, (fl. 1406), Duke of Cleves:

wife of, **14**. 77n

Adolf Fredrik (1710–71), Bp of Lübeck 1727–50; K. of Sweden 1751–71:

Alembert eulogizes, **5**. 39

death of, **5**. 36

France may aid, against Russia, **4**. 203

Frederick II tried to aid, **23**. 439

handsome, **18**. 278

matrimonial plans of, **18**. *203, 219,* 275, 278, 303–4, 305
peace overture by, **21**. 498n, 502n
Stanislas II's treaty with, over Polish dissidents, **22**. 574n
Swedes give succession to, under treaty of Abo, **18**. 203n, 219, 278
Adolf Friedrich IV (1738–94), D. of Mecklenburg-Strelitz:
Garter granted to, **22**. 227, **38**. *377*
George III and Charlotte give Chelsea china to, **22**. 121–2
George IV's godfather, **38**. *174*
Hurd will protect, **33**. 245
name of, corrected, **43**. 353
Adolphus, Gustavus. *See* Gustavus Adolphus
Adolphus Frederick (1774–1850), cr. (1801) D. of Cambridge, son of George III:
birth of, **23**. 557, **32**. 171n
Dundas visits, **12**. 25n
father requests provision for, **24**. 371
Göttingen university attended by, **11**. 145n
travels of, **34**. 213
York, Ds of, visits, at Windsor Castle, **12**. 9
Adolphus Frederick, D. of Mecklenburg. *See* Adolf Friedrich IV
Adonis:
gentlemen of three-score can look as sleek as, **32**. 348
Giberne does not resemble, **20**. 90
HW calls Massereene, **30**. 211
HW compares himself to grandfather of, **10**. 176
HW jokes about himself as, **32**. 13, 23, 220
Mount Stuart an, **32**. 19
Adonis wig. *See under* Wig
'Adoration of the Magi':
Van Eyck's painting of, **42**. 66
'Ad Pyrrham.' *See under* West, Richard
Adrian IV (d. 1159), pope:
fortress built by, **13**. 205n
Adrian (fl. 1291), Bp of the Tartars:
Edward I's deposition before, **1**. 317, 319, 322–4
Adrian. *See also* Hadrian
*Adriano in Siria. See under* Bach, Johann Christian; Metastasio, Pietro
Adrianople, Abp of. *See* Lercari, Giovanni (d. 1802)
Adrianople:
Montagu, Lady Mary Wortley, observes inoculations at, **42**. 183n
plague at, **11**. 302n
Adriatic Sea:
Charles of Naples sends barks to, **19**. 220
Del Monte said to have sailed on, **20**. 444
English ships for, **17**. 455, **18**. 396, **19**. 206n, 220, 231, 235
English ships said to be in, **21**. 135
German reinforcements to cross, **19**. 206
Lee, Capt., requests pilots for, **17**. 455n
Spaniards to receive artillery by way of, **19**. 30

Spanish barks may escape to, **18**. 288
Adrienne. *See* Andrienne
Adultery:
bishops try to stop, **24**. 455
Worsley, Lady, tried for, **25**. 245
Adultery Bill. *See under* Parliament: acts of
Advent:
York, D. of, should not come to Florence during gloom of, **22**. 179
*Adventurer, The*:
Wilton said to be mentioned in, **20**. 395n
*Adventures of Peregrine Pickle; Adventures of Roderick Random. See under* Smollett, Tobias George
Advertisement; advertisements:
for Shorter's will, **37**. 372n
for tabby fabric, **35**. 300
HW contributes, anonymously, to *Public Advertiser*, **42**. 455–6
HW never reads, **25**. 297
HW responds to appeals in, for needy persons, **40**. 270, 345, **41**. 384, **42**. 454, 455
HW's, prevents spurious edition of *Mysterious Mother*, **39**. 372, **42**. 155
Henley's, **30**. 56, **35**. 170–1
in Cambridge newspapers, of estate sale, **1**. 97
of Dublin plays, to be sent to HW, **37**. 412
of list of nobility and gentry who fled from London for fear of earthquake, **20**. 137
on C. H. Williams's 'Lord Bath to Ambition,' **30**. 319
Ossory, Cts of, sends, to HW, **33**. 569, **34**. 6
*Advice, The*:
copies of, **43**. 128–9
HW writes, to Frances Pelham, **10**. 54–5
(?) transcript of, sent to Lady Mary Coke, **43**. 330–1
Advocate, Lord. *See* Lord Advocate
Advocates' Library. *See under* Edinburgh
Advowson; advowsons:
for Norfolk parishes, sold by Orford, **36**. 95
perpetual, to be sold by (?) Catherine Daye, **36**. 53
Æacus:
Du Deffand, Mme, compares Choiseul to, **8**. 122
*Ædes Strawberrianæ. See Description of the Villa of Horace Walpole . . . at Strawberry Hill, A*
*Ædes Walpolianæ* ('Houghton catalogue') by HW:
Cocchi's and Mann's praises of, **20**. 79, 85
Cole's copy of, **2**. 159, 166, 167, **43**. 69
delayed at Marseille, **20**. 68
Domenichino painting mentioned in, **20**. 69
editions of, **13**. 17
Gough's *British Topography* mentions, **2**. 215
Guido's 'Simeon' mentioned in, **32**. 169
HW on Flemish and Dutch painters in preface to, **2**. 189, **34**. 243
HW regrets having printed, **20**. 261
HW sells, **28**. 23n

[*Ædes Walpolianæ*, continued]
HW sends: to Bibliothèque du Roi, **41**. 58n; to Frederick, P. of Wales, **9**. 88–9; to Mann and Cocchi, **19**. 496–7, 504, 505, 511, **20**. 55, 64, 68
HW's sermon on painting in, **13**. 13, **28**. 103n
Houghton pictures described in, **13**. 17
Livy quoted in, **9**. 89, 90n
presentation copy of, finely bound, **9**. 89
priced copy of, **2**. 157–9, 162, 165–8
Schaub has copy of, **9**. 88
Walpole, Sir Edward, made jealous by, **20**. 41–2, 55
——'s verses in, **1**. 52
Whaley hopes to see, **40**. 42
Ædie, Mrs George. *See* Jamesone, Mary (ca 1637–84)
Æetes, father of Medea:
Medea said to have chopped, into cutlets, **33**. 241
Ægean Islands. *See* Greek Islands
Ægean Sea:
HW dicourages Lady Craven from visiting, **42**. 507
Russian fleet to go to, **23**. 212, 306–7
Ægidius:
portrait of, **1**. 170
Ægyptian. *See* Egyptian
*Ælia Lælia*:
Chudleigh, Elizabeth, called, in light of old epitaph, **9**. 276, **24**. 196n
Ælius Cæsar (d. 137):
medal of, **26**. 7
Æneas:
Creusa lost by, **33**. 196
Dido and, **32**. 128, **33**. 223
HW compares himself with, **32**. 220
Horace quoted on, **42**. 272
messenger to Elysian Fields, **10**. 282
Romans not descended from, **41**. 177
voyages of, **11**. 20
*Æneid. See under* Virgil
Æolian harp:
reviewer's mistake about, **25**. 194
Æolipile; æolipiles:
Plot's *Staffordshire* depicts, **40**. 76–7
*Æolus*, English ship:
Elliot, John, capt. of, **21**. 376n
Russian naval news brought by, from Gibraltar, **23**. 148n
Thurot pursued by, **21**. 376
Æolus:
HW imagines himself as, **33**. 116
'let loose,' **33**. 454
'Æolus, little.' *See* Russell, John (1710–71), D. of Bedford
'Æquitas'; 'Æquus':
popular signatures for letters to newspapers, **42**. 500
Aeronaut, aeronauts. *See under* Balloon
Æschylus (525–456 B.C.):
Potter translates, **28**. 347–8, **29**. 308

*Prometheus*, HW disapproves of Io in, **28**. 348
Æsculapius:
mentioned in verses on HW, **12**. 96
Middleton's marble figure of, **15**. 16
Æson, father of Jason:
confused with Æetes, **33**. 241
'too old to try a new kettle,' **34**. 146
Æsop:
fable should be made by, of tiger and monkey elements in human makeup, **23**. 192
fables of, **16**. 79, **25**. 386, **32**. 205, **33**. 392, **34**. 107, **37**. 7
*Select Fables* of, printed by Baskerville, **31**. 58n
Æthiopia. *See* Abyssinia; Ethiopia
Ætna, Mt:
'burst in flames above,' **14**. 87
HW compares Frederick II and Joseph II to, **24**. 38
HW jokes about balloon arriving from, **39**. 425
Hamilton not to dive into caverns of, **35**. 415
*Affaires de l'Angleterre et de l'Amérique*:
(?) Du Deffand, Mme, prefers, among the journals, **6**. 396
Affectation:
HW's reflections on, **39**. 79
Affection; affections:
HW draws, carmine for contemporaries, and purple for newcomers, **39**. 296–7
'Afflem,' a monk:
Chatterton ascribes invention of painted glass to, **34**. 150
Affliction; afflictions:
Middleton's reflections on, **15**. 5–6
Affluent, the:
HW thinks that advantages of, are not appreciated especially in illness, **25**. 620
Affry, Louis-Auguste-Augustin (1713–93), Comte d'; Col. of Swiss Guards; diplomatist:
Barthélemy's pension negotiated by, **5**. 167–8, 168
Broglie sends account of victory to, **21**. 287n
Charles III's meeting with Charles Emmanuel III at Lyon believed by, **21**. 283n
France said by, to be ready to negotiate with England through Spain, **21**. 360n
French invasion plans and Old Pretender's leadership denied by, **21**. 298n
gout of, cured, **41**. 341
mission of, to change Dutch government and make it anti-British, **21**. 298n
pension of, **5**. 168
refused permission to visit Chanteloup, **5**. 76n
social relations of, with: Geoffrin, Mme, **7**. 307; Hénault, **7**. 317
States General told by, of plan to invade England, **21**. 298
Swiss Guards administered by, **5**. 168
Yorke gets false news from, at The Hague, **37**. 469

Afreet:
in Arabian Nights, 34. 102
Africa:
beef-steaks said to be eaten alive in, 33. 237
Bragança's acquaintance with, 7. 9
Bristol's trade with, 31. 248
Bruce makes, fashionable, 24. 21
——'s writings on, ridiculed, 33. 237, 34. 92–3
civilization never flowered in, save in Egypt and Carthage, 25. 47
cruelties worthy of, in Paris, 34. 56
emperors and empresses of, 31. 162
English trade with, 31. 248n
Europe as unknown as, to England, 25. 116
fate of, to be decided, 31. 296
giants from, in Heroic Epistle, 28. 45
HW's letters to Mann may have to go by way of, 21. 259
jerboa from, 9. 142
Kent compared with, 33. 222
molehills of, 39. 430, 42. 117
monarchs of, 11. 207
More, Hannah, hopes for redemption of, 31. 321
oppression of, 31. 284
Parliamentary bill on trade with, 20. 135n
Pitt the 'conqueror' of, 9. 395, 21. 541
'princes' from, 20. 40, 56
Selwyn's joke on Guinea coast in, 33. 181
Sessaracoa returns to, 20. 40n
slaves from, observe European crews destroyed by hurricane, 25. 109
slave trade in, 15. 282, 20. 126
weather worthy of, 39. 498
African Company:
Parliament debates over sale of slaves by, 20. 126
'Africani':
title acquired by Romans, 33. 421
African lamb. See Lamb, Astrakhan
African Trade the Great Pillar and Support of the British Trade in America, The:
HW owns, 20. 126n
Afrite:
in Arabian Nights, 34. 102
After-room:
HW suggests, as drawing-card for London churches, 11. 15
most popular part of London assemblies, 11. 15
Agamemnon, Greek leader:
Colman compared with, 33. 207
grief of, not shown in picture, 32. 172
Agamemnon. See under Thomson, James
Agamemnon, prose play:
acted at Florence, 18. 128
Agamemnon, English ship:
French and Spanish fleets seen by, 25. 182n
Aganippe, spring on Mt Helicon:
water from, 29. 5, 32. 88
Agar, Charles (1736–1809), Abp of Cashel, 1779, of Dublin 1801–9; cr. (1795) Bn and

(1800) Vct Somerton, and (1806) E. of Normanton:
arrives in Twickenham, 12. 157
Hardinge invites HW to dine with, 12. 166
(?) SH visited by, 12. 202, 43. 157
Agar, Mrs Charles. See Benson, Jane
Agar, Diana (d. 1814), sister of Charles Agar:
Mendip, Lord, visited by, 12. 158
SH visited by, 12. 158, 249
Agar, Ellis (ca 1708–89), m. 1 (1726) Theobald Bourke, 7th Vct Mayo; m. 2 (1745) Francis Bermingham, 14th Bn Athenry; cr. (1758) Cts of Brandon, s.j.:
Beauvau asks about family of, 41. 331
nosegay of, brilliant, 37. 442
supper given by, 37. 442
Agar, Emily Anne (d. 1821):
SH visited by, 15. 327
Agar (after 1804, Ellis) Henry Welbore (1761–1836), 2d Vct Clifden, 1789, 2d Bn Mendip, 1802:
fractional sum subscribed by, for French clergy, 34. 167
HW thinks, agreeable, 12. 156–7
Ireland, return from, of, 12. 156
Mendip, Lord, visited by, 12. 156
Ramsgate visited by, 12. 156
SH visited by, 12. (?) 202, 231, 15. 327
Agar, James (1734–89), cr. (1781) Vct Clifden:
SH visited by, 12. 231
Agar, Mrs James. See Martin, Lucia
Agar, Mary, m. (1742) James Smyth of Tenny Park:
Beauvau asks about family of, 41. 332
Agar, Welbore Ellis:
Calcraft succeeded by, as deputy commissary-gen. of musters, 38. 248n
Agar family:
Mendip, Lady, visited by, 12. 202
Mendip, Lord, patriarch of, 12. 157
Agate:
steel mirror of, 32. 323
Agathocle. See under Voltaire
Agathocles (ca 360–289 B.C.):
Carthage invaded by, 29. 82
Agay, Marie-François-Bruno (1722–1805), Comte d', intendant of Picardy:
Fenouilhet, Lady, gets request from, to give up house to Bienassise, 5. 399, 402, 405, 408
Agdalo. See Agdollo
Agdollo, Gregorio, Saxon minister to Tuscany:
Apamea, Abp of, corresponds with, 17. 114
Asiatic, 17. 168n
debts of, may cause his departure, 17. 148, 149
Eleonora, Ps, negotiates with, 17. 149
Franceschi's bankruptcy causes loss to, 17. 62
Frederick Augustus II employs, 17. 168n
leaves Florence for Dresden, 17. 148–50
prisoner at Leghorn, 17. 168n
Age, old:
absence of pain the pleasure of, 24. 327

[Age, old, *continued*]
    affectations in, are pretensions, **39.** 296
    apologia of, by Comtesse de Forcalquier,
        **3.** 10
    at 65, too late to look forwards, **33.** 345
    cannot adopt follies of recent generation,
        **32.** 348
    comfortable if one resigns one's self to it,
        **39.** 209
    consequences of, are not remediable acci-
        dents, **24.** 342–3
    Du Deffand, Mme, reflects upon, **3.** 156, 213,
        273, 295, **4.** 50, 59–60, 82, 200, 240, 348,
        491, **5.** 17, 50, 59–60, 184, 287, 325, **6.** 465
    ——'s verses on, **5.** 413
    egotism the food of, **35.** 649
    experience often taken by, for spectacles, **24.**
        359
    folly of trying to conceal, **25.** 535
    France makes one forget, **32.** 27, 29–30
    giving advice is a weakness of, **16.** 284
    golden age always regarded in, as period
        when one was young, **34.** 218
    gout adds dignity to, **32.** 27
    HW acquires indifference with, **24.** 351
    HW afraid of acting too young for his, **32.**
        320
    HW anticipates his healthiness in, **25.** 242
    HW can ameliorate his, better than most
        people, **39.** 317–18
    HW considers, to be like a dipping in the
        Styx, **25.** 510
    HW does not want to grow old, **32.** 27
    HW dreads seeming not apprised of his
        antiquity and decay, **33.** 311
    HW has 'fit' of, **37.** 255, 256
    HW in his youth saw follies of those who
        forgot, **25.** 502
    HW's: as agreeable as he desires it, **24.** 283;
        'by no means, an uncomfortable season,'
        **42.** 265; 'has its satisfactions,' **42.** 272;
        makes him 'less fit to be informing or enter-
        taining,' **35.** 362
    HW's horror for 'juvenile ancientry,' **33.** 271
    HW 'slides into decline very agreeably,' **33.**
        19
    HW's memory fails in, **25.** 298
    HW's philosophy in, forced and selfish, **24.**
        373
    HW's reflections on, **1.** 279, 330–1, 337, **2.**
        18, 46, 55–6, 155, 178, 194, 217, 269, 327,
        **12.** 108, 122, **16.** 255, 258, **22.** 372–3, **24.**
        277, 279, 283, 324–5, 327, 342–3, 351, 359,
        373, **25.** 48, 109, 164–5, 242, 296, 298, 502,
        539, **29.** 298, **30.** 280, **31.** 257, 305, **32.** 211,
        216, 316, 320–1, 348, 364, **33.** 128, 130, **35.**
        352, 353, 362–3, **39.** 148–9, 295–6, 317; *see
        also under* Old people; Youth and old age
    HW thinks that people are seldom converted
        in, **25.** 48
    HW will not hobble in, like Nestor to the
        siege of Troy, **25.** 296

    health care in, is merely a preparation for
        death, **35.** 414
    ideas a resource for, **11.** 62
    insensibility of, increases upon HW, **24.** 278
    London's late hours unsuitable for, **35.** 358–9
    loss of friends one of discomforts of, **25.**
        502–3, **33.** 230, 232
    marks of, **33.** 73
    memory in, produces 'genealogy of gossiping,'
        **34.** 219
    must do what is right, **33.** 2
    'one must not play the fool,' **33.** 227
    parade and ridicule both to be avoided in,
        **39.** 79
    peace more desirable to, than storm, **33.**
        160–1
    playthings help assuage disabilities of, **34.**
        217
    pleasures of, **28.** 280, 295
    senseless people enjoy, because they do not
        remember how they once ridiculed the
        elderly, **25.** 109
    tranquillity in, achieved by indifference to
        others, but endangered by love of money,
        **34.** 192
    unreserved intimacies lacking in, **39.** 148–9
    vanity of visions in, **33.** 450
    youth less censorious than, about differing
        customs, **35.** 370
    youth should not be bored with woes of,
        **32.** 44
    *See also* Aged, the; Old people; Youth and
        old age
Age, the present:
    HW cannot and will not try to please, **39.** 277
    prefers riding on streets to roads or turf,
        **25.** 317
Aged, the:
    treatment of, in England and France, **5.** 245
Agen, Bp of. *See* Usson de Bonac, Jean-Louis d'
Agencourt. *See* Agincourt
Ageno, Francesco Maria (1727–88), Genoese
    minister to England 1760–6:
    George III to be congratulated by, **21.** 509
    SH visited by, **12.** 222
Agenois, Duc d'. *See* Vignerot du Plessis-Riche-
    lieu, Armand-Désiré
Agent; agents (diplomatic):
    American, to France, *see* Deane, Silas
    colonial, in London, **39.** 231
    English, at Marseille, *see* Birback
    English, at Rome, *see* Jenkins, Thomas
        (1722–98)
    English, at Rotterdam, *see* Wolters, Richard
        (1713–71)
    English, Del Nero not to employ Stosch as,
        **18.** 308
    French, in London, *see* Gérard de Rayneval,
        Joseph-Matthias
    French, in Russia, *see* Rossignol d'Anneville
    Genoese, at Rome, *see* Casale, Scipione
        Giuseppe

Neapolitan, in Tuscany, *see* Vernaccini, Abate Francesco (fl. 1783–5); Viviani, Luigi (1709–80)
Prussian, at Rome. *See* Ciofani
Prussian, at Venice. *See* Cataneo, Giovanni
Spanish, at Florence. *See* Ascanio, Père Salvator Maria (ca 1655–1741); Vernaccini, Abate Ranieri (d. 1759)
Tuscan, at Paris. *See* Favi, Francesco (fl. 1780–92); Niccoli, Abbé Raimondo (d. 1780)
Tuscan, at Venice. *See* Bozzini, Michelangelo
Tuscan, in London. *See* Pucci, Vincenzo (ca 1675–1757)
Agent (estate). *See under* Servant
Agent (military):
 Conway's regimental, *see* Taylor, Henry
 *See also* Adair; Mann, Edward Louisa; Mann, Galfridus; Mann, James
'Age of Abortions':
 HW's term for his era, **20.** 453, 461, 469, 472, **21.** 109, **23.** 29, 346, **25.** 47
Aggas, Ralph (?1540–1621), map-maker:
 view of London by, **1.** 172
Agincourt, Chevalier d'. *See* Seroux d'Agincourt
Agincourt, battle of:
 Aumerle, E. of, killed at, **42.** 138
 English always expect to repeat, **18.** 224
 English victories to surpass, **19.** 327
 HW does not enjoy prospect of a second, **21.** 211
 HW puns on, **39.** 291
 HW's childhood fondness for stories of, **37.** 200, 203
 modern battles incongruous with, **37.** 200
 newspapers of the time would not have printed tittle-tattle of, **35.** 364
 Onslows not present at, **30.** 288
 Orléans, Duc d', captured at, **14.** 72n, **34.** 6
 Pepys's collection of ballads dates from, **15.** 63
 would make no impression now, **28.** 174
Aginussa, Gen. (of Algeria):
 Spaniards capture, **20.** 480
*Agis. See under* Home, John
Agneaux, Charles-Jean-Baptiste d' (1728–92), Dom Devienne:
 *Histoire de la ville de Bordeaux*, offered to HW by Mme d'Aiguillon, **5.** 200, 202, 210, 220
Agnew, —— (d. 1752), convict:
 Newgate turnkey murdered by, **20.** 312n
Agnew, Mrs. *See* Astley, Anne
Agostini, François, (?) Theodore of Corsica's secretary:
 (?) Mann hears from, about Theodore, **20.** 379
 Theodore chooses, to carry instructions to Tunis, **20.** 379n
Agoult, Marquis d'. *See* Vincens de St-Michel, Louis-Fouquet d'
Agra:

HW may be with Great Mogul at, **37.** 278
Agrarian laws:
 Roman, **3.** 108
Agrate, Marco Ferreri d' (fl. 1540–ca 1570), sculptor:
 statue of St Bartholomew by, in Milan Cathedral, **33.** 564
*Agreeable Surprise. See under* O'Keeffe, John
'Agréments':
 HW to bring, from Paris for new cottage, **10.** 168
*Agricola. See under* Tacitus
Agriculture:
 barley, beans, oats, peas, wheat, **1.** 276
 bean-planting, **1.** 106
 Coke, Lady Mary, discusses, **31.** 200
 Cole little concerned in, **1.** 276
 ——'s fondness for, **1.** 146
 ——'s hay and harvest, **1.** 339
 French, **30.** 203, **31.** 200, **39.** 270
 HW does not understand, **30.** 203
 HW receives letters about, **31.** 363
 innovations in, shunned at first by farmers, **31.** 325
'Agriculture and the Arts,' print. *See under* Hogarth, William
Agrigento, Sicily:
 Hamilton sees Gothic paintings at, **35.** 409
Agrippa, Biblical character:
 HW quotes, **34.** 166
Agrippa, Marcus Vipsanius (63–12 B.C.), Roman general:
 head of, cut on Rowley's seal, **19.** 9
 possessions of, in Sicily, **13.** 115n
Agrippina (d. A.D. 33), wife of Germanicus:
 Brundusium experiences of, might be paralleled by Ds of Gloucester's, **24.** 326
 Poussin's drawing of, **7.** 279
*Agrippina. See under* Gray, Thomas
'Agrippina.' *See under* Racine, Jean: *Britannicus*
Ague:
 cure of, 'melting away,' **38.** 138
 HW jokes about, **10.** 262
 indigenous to local areas, **22.** 456
 occurrences of, **1.** 35, **9.** 59, **10.** 245, **16.** 193, **17.** 164, **20.** 88, **21.** 222n, 300, **30.** 82, **33.** 436, **34.** 126, **38.** 138, 141, 478
 peace negotiations suffer from, **25.** 355
 tertian, **1.** 29
Aguesseau, Henri-Cardin-Jean-Baptiste (1746–1826), Comte d':
 avocat général of Paris parliament, **6.** 168n
Aguesseau, Henri-François d' (1668–1751), chancellor:
 exiled for refusal to sign bull *unigenitus*, **7.** 276
 Jonzac, Mme de, tells anecdote of, **7.** 276
Aguesseau, Henriette-Anne-Louise d' (1737–94), m. (1755) Jean-Louis-François-Paul de Noailles, Duc d'Ayen:
 La Fayette's departure distresses, **6.** 427

Aguiari *or* Agujari, Lucrezia (1743–83), called
La Bastardella *or* Bastardina:
HW to hear, at Lady Bingham's, **39**. 223–4
salary of, for singing at Pantheon, **39**. 224
Yates, Mrs, does not agree with, **39**. 223–4
Aguilar, ——, mayor of Perpignan:
Mirabeau takes refuge with, **39**. 474
Aguilar. *See also* Aquilar
Agujari. *See* Aguiari
*Ah! ma voisine, es-tu-fâchée?*:
verses to air of, **6**. 407
Ahmet Resni Effendi (1700–83), Turkish dip-
lomatist:
Kücük Kainardje treaty signed by, **24**. 40
Aholah and Aholibah, Biblical sisters:
prophets censure, **28**. 392
*Ah quel Conte! See under* Crébillon, Claude-
Prosper Jolyot de
Ahriman:
Ormuzd gets the better of, by turns, **23**. 192
Aickin (*or* Aikin), James (ca 1735–1803), actor:
birth date of, corrected, **43**. 297
plays rôle of Almada in *Braganza*, **41**. 287n
ridiculous in *Braganza*, **28**. 177
Aide-de-camp; aides-de-camp:
Arenberg's, **37**. 158
Bertie reprimands, **19**. 464
Clinton's, Pelham Clinton, Lord Thomas, to
be, **24**. 263n
Conway's, **30**. 198–9; *see also* Hamilton, Sir
William; Hotham, George; Hyde, West
Conway visited by, at Park Place, **38**. 13
Cornwallis's, *see* Ross, ——
Cumberland, D. of, has, at lodge at Windsor,
**37**. 258n
——'s: accompanies him to Hulst, **19**. 395;
Bury is, **19**. 177, 204; Conway is, **19**. 26,
177, 204; Keppel is, **20**. 459n; Townshend
is, **20**. 33
Eliott's, *see* Koehler, George Frederick
Erskine is, to Northumberland in Ireland,
**31**. 41n
Ferdinand of Brunswick's, **30**. 157, **38**. 93n;
*see also* Fitzroy, Charles, Bn Southampton;
Lennox, Charles, D. of Richmond
Frederick II's, *see* Grant, John; Lentulus,
Robert Scipio
George III's, Shelburne dismissed as, **38**. 255
Hanoverians named as, **37**. 459
Hastings's, *see* Cooper, Charles
Hertford's, **30**. 198–200
horse-racing bets placed by, **20**. 74
Howe's, *see* Cuyler, Cornelius
Irish Regency members have, **20**. 316
Leghorn governor sends, to ask about D. of
Gloucester, **23**. 335
Northumberland's, **30**. 198
Rutland's, in Ireland, **39**. 421
Sackville's, *see* Smith, John (d. 1804)
Sandwich is, to D. of Richmond, **19**. 176
Villars's, **20**. 159
'Aigle, Comte d'.' *See* Nay, Emmanuel-François-
Joseph-Ignace de

Aigle, Comtesse de l'. *See* Waës, Anne-Salomé-
Joséphine de
*Aigrette, L'*, French frigate:
Vilaine entrance defended by, **21**. 351
Aigueblanche, Marchese di. *See* Carron, Giu-
seppe Angelo Maria
Aiguillon, Duc d'. *See* Vignerot du Plessis-
Richelieu, Emmanuel-Armand
Aiguillon, Duchesse d'. *See* Bréhan-Plélo,
Louise-Félicité de (1726–96); Crussol de
Florensac, Anne-Charlotte de (1700–72)
Aiguillon:
Aiguillon, Duc d', sent to, **6**. 200
——'s release from exile at, **6**. 323n
Aiguillon, Duchy of:
stripped of rights and privileges of the peer-
age, **4**. 449n
Aiguillon, Hôtel d', at Paris:
Pontchartrain-Béarn marriage at, **6**. 5
Aiguilly. *See* Aiguillon
Aikin, Anna Letitia (1743–1825), m. (1774)
Rev. Rochemont Barbauld; poetess, editor:
*Address to the Opposers of the Repeal of the
Corporation and Test Acts*: **31**. 361n; shows
liberal tendencies of, **11**. 169n
anti-slavery sentiments of, factious, **31**. 362
Burke's Amazonian foe, **11**. *169*
*Castle of Otranto* imitated by, **29**. *382*, **41**.
410
Crown and Anchor invitation of, **11**. 320
*Epistle to William Wilberforce* by: HW not
to read, **31**. 361; More, Hannah, praises, **31**.
*357*–8
French Revolution approved by, **11**. 320, **31**.
361
HW calls, 'Deborah,' **11**. 320, **31**. 361
HW denounces, **31**. 361–2
just married, **32**. 197
name of, corrected, **43**. 343
politics of, might be forgiven for her poetry,
**31**. 358
SH visited by, **32**. 197
Aikin. *See also* Aickin; Aitkin
Aikman, William (1682–1731), painter:
Kent's portrait by, **15**. 143n
Ailesbury, Cts of. *See* Campbell, Caroline
(1721–1803); Grey, Diana (d. 1689); Hoare,
Susanna (1732–83); Rawdon, Anne (1753–
1813)
Ailesbury, E. of. *See* Bruce, Charles (1682–
1747); Bruce, Robert (ca 1626–85); Bruce,
Thomas (1656–1741); Bruce Brudenell,
Thomas Bruce (1729–1814)
Ailesbury, E. and M. of. *See* Brudenell Bruce,
Charles (1773–1856)
Ailesbury (Bucks). *See* Aylesbury
Aillecourt, Comte d'. *See* Choiseul-Beaupré,
Michel-Félix-Victor de
Aillecourt, Comtesse d'. *See* Rouillé du Cou-
dray, Marie-Eugénie
Ailred. *See* Ethelred
Ainslie, Lady Mary. *See* Mackenzie, Lady Mary

Air:
  change of, recommended, **33**. 254
  'fixed,' discussed, **33**. 128
  HW's pun on, **33**. 73
  London's, *see under* London
  travel by, *see under* Balloon
  *See also* Sea air
Air (dancing posture):
  HW uses, **43**. 354
Air; airs (musical):
  Mann sends copies of, to HW, **17**. 181, 212
  Venetian, Amorevoli and Salembeni sing, **17**. 101, 240
Air balloon. *See* Balloon
Aire, France:
  Ligonier, Vcts, misbehaves at, with Irish brigade, **30**. 255n
  visitors to: Conway, **39**. 536; HW, **7**. 315, 343; Scott, **39**. 536
Aire, river in Yorkshire:
  navigation on, **16**. 29n
'Airgonauts':
  HW's name for aeronauts, **33**. 458
Airlie, E. of. *See* Ogilvie, David (1725–1803)
Airmine (Armine), Lady. *See* Talbot, Mary
Air St, Piccadilly, London:
  Comyn, Mrs, in, **9**. 19
  Simco, bookseller in, **41**. 388n
Aislabie, William (?1699–1781), of Studley Royal, Yorks, M.P.:
  birth date of, corrected, **43**. 294
  HW may visit, **28**. 37
Aisne, department of, in France:
  members for: Condorcet, **12**. 66n; Rochemont, **12**. 1n
Aitken, James (1752–77), called 'John the Painter'; incendiary:
  fires started by, not an American plot, **28**. 283–4, **32**. 346n
  Temple entraps, **24**. 362
  —— says, was in pay of American agent, **28**. 286–7
  trial of, **28**. 288n
Aix, Abp of. *See* Boisgelin de Cucé, Jean-de-Dieu-Raymond de
Aix, ——:
  Hancarville's *Collection of . . . Antiquities* edited by, **23**. 448n
Aix, île d':
  Conway's bravery on, **21**. 155
  English capture of, **21**. 355n, **30**. 139, **35**. 285, **37**. 506, 510
  roads of, **6**. 403n
Aix, Parliament of. *See under* Aix-en-Provence
Aix, roadstead of:
  Conway in ship at, **37**. 506, 507
Aix-en-Provence:
  (?) gambling at, **23**. 530, 536
  Gardes Lorraines reassembled at, **19**. 54n
  HW's imitations of Horace written at, **17**. 174n
  parliament of: Parliament of Toulouse sup-

ported by, in protest, **38**. 301; reformed, **5**. 106
Pembroke's family detained at, by daughter's illness, **25**. 493
residents of: Rochechouart, Marquise de, **31**. 161; Vence, Mme de, **3**. 405n
Sturgis inquires about, **17**. 95
Vanloo born in, **2**. 57n
Villars's country house between Marseille and, **7**. 365, **22**. 553
visitors to: Almada, **21**. 340n; Brownlow, Lady Betty, **18**. 479; Carlisle, Cts of, **36**. 193; Coke, Lady Mary, **31**. 143–4, 161; Francis III, **19**. 314n; HW, **13**. 11, **17**. 109, 116, **18**. 479; Herbert family, **25**. 493; (?) Orford, Cts of, **23**. 155, 161, **35**. 410; Philip, Don, **17**. 361–2, **19**. 314n; Warner, **36**. 193, 195
Aix-la-Chapelle:
  Devonshire may take warm baths at, **38**. 429, 444
  French defeated at, **31**. 386n
  (?) gambling at, **23**. 530, 536
  George III may be crowned at, **21**. 515
  Niccolini to visit, **19**. 485
  Sandwich and Puisieux decide that Congress should be held at, **19**. 430n
  Sandwich's conduct at, makes breach with Newcastle, **20**. 120n
  statesmen to go to, **18**. 304–5
  treaty of: Amelia, Ps, gets no husband from, **9**. 57; anecdotes of time of, **34**. 65; Aranjuez treaty based on, **20**. 294n; Austrian-Modenese treaty resembles, **20**. 400; Austria persuades Louis XV to leave Don Philip at Parma in spite of, **21**. 323n; Charles of Naples opposes Neapolitan arrangements of, **21**. 264n; Charles of Naples's paper sets aside, **21**. 323; Charles Emmanuel III reluctantly consents to, **19**. 508, **21**. 264n; Congress to meet for, **19**. 448; Courts interested in, will protest against nomination of King of Two Sicilies, **21**. 330; debated in Parliament, **20**. 3; delayed, **19**. 503–4; Dunkirk to be demolished according to terms of, **19**. 481, **20**. 527; Frenchman's bon mot about, **20**. 400; Genoa to regain Finale by, **19**. 481; HW's fears before, **28**. 296; HW's poem on fireworks for, **13**. 22n; Holland obliged by, to aid England if Protestant succession is in peril, **21**. 298n; Kaunitz's reservations at, **19**. 488n; Keene repairs Sandwich's omissions at, **20**. 198; London indignant at, **9**. 55; Maria Theresa consents to, **19**. 488; Maria Theresa favoured by, **19**. 479n; Maria Theresa not to demand reversion of Parma to Austria under, **21**. 280n; Maria Theresa objects to, **19**. 479–80; Maria Theresa said to have halted negotiations at, **19**. 495–6; Mill misinformed about opposition to, **20**. 43; ministers at, should

[Aix-la-Chapelle, *continued*]

avert slaughter, **19**. 466; Modena returns to Francis III by, **19**. 481; negotiators of, **20**. 400n; Newcastle's instructions to Sandwich concerning, **19**. 448n, 479n; Old Pretender said to be promised pension by, **9**. 55; Old Pretender's renunciation stipulated by, **19**. 481–2; Parliament will probably approve of, **20**. 27; Philip, Don, would have received Naples crown from, **21**. 330; Placentia and Guastalla reversions under, **21**. 275n; plenipotentiaries to, get passports, **19**. 446n; preliminaries to, ratified, **9**. 55n, **19**. 479–83, 487, 488n, **37**. 284–5; proclaimed and celebrated, **20**. 46–51; Prussia and Sardinia get necessary cessions by, **19**. 479n; reported broken off, **9**. 58; Sandwich at, **19**. 422n; Sandwich concludes, **9**. 48n; Sandwich opposes Williams's hope of attending, **19**. 456n; Sardinian ambassador refuses to sign, **19**. 480; Sardinia's claims to Placentia and Guastalla under, **21**. 280n; separate article I of Treaty of Seville not renewed by, **20**. 198n; signed, **9**. 58, **19**. 511; signers of, do not oppose French conquest of Corsica, **23**. 54; signers of, may all object to France's Corsican policy, **23**. 38; Spain delays, **19**. 485, 511; Spain signs preliminaries of, **19**. 488n; Sussex hostage under, **10**. 339; West Indies' navigation limits established by, do not satisfy England, **20**. 171n; will let Conway come home, **37**. 290

visitors to: Aubeterre, Vicomtesse d', **4**. 259; Biron, Duchesse de, **11**. 291n; Bolingbroke, **18**. 304–5; Boufflers, **11**. 88n; Conway, **37**. 275, **39**. 537; Fénelon, **18**. 304n; Goodwin, Mrs, **20**. 103; Morice, **7**. 239; Scott, David, **39**. 537; Sinsheim, **18**. 304n; Sporke, Bn, **18**. 304n

waters of, William IV of Orange dies from drinking, **20**. 279

Aix-les-Bains:

HW visits, **13**. 181

(?) Orford, Cts of, at, **23**. 155, 161, **35**. 410

Ajaccio, Corsica:

Corsican rebels threaten, **19**. 163, 171, **22**. 536

France sends engineer to raise batteries at, **20**. 573n

Genoa reserves, **20**. 273n

Jesuits land at, **22**. 526n, 535n, 545n

*St Isidore* disabled at, **18**. 189

*Ajax*, English ship:

Rodney detaches, **25**. 24n

'Ajax Supporting the Dead Patroclus':

at end of Ponte Vecchio, Florence, **22**. 124n

Akenside, Mark (1721–70), poet and physician:

beneath even Voltaire's envy, **28**. 278

Charlotte, Q., has, as physician, **35**. 566n

compared to Virgil, **11**. 20

HW criticizes, **31**. 211

HW quotes ode by, **19**. 28

HW's and Pinkerton's opinions of, **33**. 492

Johnson admires, **29**. 97, 111

Mason's memoirs of Gray mention, **28**. 152

More, Hannah, likes, **31**. 211

*Pleasures of Imagination, The,* by, **11**. 20n, **29**. 97n, **37**. 262, 263

*Poems,* praised by Hardinge, **35**. 563–4, 566

political apostacy of, **35**. 566

politics of, 'illegible,' **35**. 648

popularity of, **9**. 215

wit lacked by, **35**. 647

Akinside. *See* Akenside

Akinsioff, Maj., Russian courier:

Florence visited by, on way to Orlov's forces, **23**. 444

Ala, Italy:

Gloucester, D. of, at, **26**. 50

'Alabaster.' *See* Balthazar

Alabaster:

columns of, at Kedleston, **10**. 230

cupids of, **24**. 312n

of Volterra, not big enough for large vases, **20**. 582, **21**. 133

statues of, **42**. 68

tomb of, at Horton, **10**. 333

vases or urns of, *see under* Vase

Alacoque, Marguerite-Marie (1647–90), St; nun:

Coke, Lady Mary, compared with, **24**. 179, **33**. 382

Aladdin:

lantern of, **35**. 515

*À la façon de Barbarie*:

verses to air of, **6**. 411

Alais, France:

Montmorency owns, **14**. 127n

Narbonne-Pelet at, **4**. 104n

Alam. *See* Shah Alam

À la main, à la mains:

Court, American news reported by, **24**. 216

from Paris: HW jokes about Cole's reading, **2**. 123; in newspaper, **37**. 103

Alamanni, Marchesa. *See* Del Nero, Maria Maddalena (d. 1742)

Alamanni, Marchese:

(?) death of, **18**. 127

*À la mémoire de Mme Geoffrin. See under* Thomas, Antoine-Léonard

Alamgir II (d. 1759), Mogul emperor:

grandmother of, **21**. 378

'Alans':

in Pope quotation, **33**. 362

Alanson. *See* Alençon

Alaric (ca 370–410), Vandal king:

HW's term for Joseph II, **25**. 613

remembered while his soldiers are not, **29**. 295

*Alarm*, English frigate:

Gloucester, D. of, comes in, **23**. 353

—— sends baggage by, **23**. 407n

Jervis commands, **23**. 353

Spanish ships taken by, **24**. 306–7

Alba; Alva, Duque d'. *See* Alvarez de Toledo,

Fernando (1508–82); Silva Alvarez de Toledo, Fernando de (1714–76)

Alban (d. ca 304), St:
apocryphal account of, 1. 186, 192

Albani, Principessa. See Casati, Teresa (fl. 1783–6); Cybo, Maria Anna Matilda (1726–97)

Albani, Alessandro (1692–1779), cardinal:
Anhalt's letter from, 22. 478
Austrian camp visited by, 18. 532
Austrian-sympathizing mob at Rome might be aroused by, 19. 114
Austro-Sardinian treaty revealed by, to Niccolini, 17. 342
ball given by, for D. of York, 22. 233–4
Benedict XIV gets complaint from, against Acquaviva's attack on mob, 19. 114
Brettingham brings, measurements of Northumberland's gallery, 20. 329n
cardinal-deacons headed by, 21. 207n
cardinals headed by, in remonstrance to Clement XIV, 23. 148n
Catherine II called 'heroine of the north' in circular letter by, 22. 76
Charles of Naples sends refusal to, to let paintings be 'veiled,' 20. 328n
Cheroffini, Contessa, mistress of, 21. 406
Chute and Whithed befriended by, 19. 59, 121–2, 149, 196, 197, 198
Clement XI's nephew, 18. 467n
Clement XIII tells, to promise Mann a Roman welcome for D. of York, 22. 171
Conclave of 1740's French and Imperial delegates want to switch to faction of, 37. 70
Conclave of 1774 involves party of, 24. 59n
couriers sent by: to Mann with letter about Young Pretender, 19. 86; to Vienna, 19. 114
dismissal of, for meddling with Maria Theresa's affairs at Rome, 19. 475
eagle's purchase for HW facilitated by, 19. 66, 121–2, 135, 149
English captains dine with, 19. 12
English cause warmly supported by, 22. 384
'extravagance' of, 13. 208
Falkirk news alarms, 19. 218
Fantoni recommended by, 22. 527
France said by, to permit Spanish invasion of Tuscany, 19. 30–1, 38
Francis I honours, 19. 475
Gages seizes letters of, 18. 359n
George III buys drawings and prints of, 22. 107, 115
Gloucester, D. and Ds of, occupy Albano villa of, 24. 214, 248
Gotti of faction of, 17. 22n
HW and Deskford call on, at Conclave door, 17. 9, 37. 57
HW's civilities from, 14. 240, 37. 57
HW's correspondence with, 40. 29–30
Hamerani strikes medal for, to celebrate Francis I's election, 19. 184
Hoare copies Antinous bas-relief of, 20. 86n
keys of Del Anima church held by, 23. 36

Kingston, Ds of, takes her treasure to villa of, 24. 70
Lobkowitz calls on, 18. 447
maestro delle strade under control of, 17. 29n
Mann asked by, to send Genoese edict to Rome, 21. 394n
—— assured by, of messenger's veracity, 19. 7
—— flattered by, in order to get ships, 18. 460–1
—— informed by, of Papal-Genoese clash, 21. 405n
—— receives messenger from, from Gages's army, 19. 2
—— recommends Astley to, 43. 270
—— recommends Conway and Stormont to, 20. 298
—— satisfies demand of, for English naval help, 18. 471
——'s correspondence with, 18. 453, 460–1, 467, 476–7, 486, 489–91, 504, 19. 30–1, 51–2, 113, 136, 311–12, 21. 405n, 22. 215, 368, 384, 386–7, 408, 527, 23. 397, 427n, 25. 526
—— sends translation to, of HW's inscription on Benedict XIV, 21. 127
—— sent by, a copy of Winckelmann's will, 23. 113
——'s friendship with, 19. 13
—— to recommend Pars to, 23. 135
—— to thank, for attentions to D. of York, 22. 179
—— would like cameos and medals from, for HW, 18. 477
Maria Carolina, Leopold, and Maria Louisa not to visit, 23. 2
Maria Josefa's birth reported by, 18. 478
—— to stay at villa of, 22. 556
Maria Theresa's minister at Rome, 18. 467n
Mathews's friendship to Austria doubted by, 18. 476
Moretti recommended by, to Mann, 20. 37, 46
Muzell dedicates Winckelmann's Description to, 21. 186n
nephew of, to marry, 19. 475
Old Pretender's motions reported by, 19. 94, 96–7
——'s negotiations with Benedict XIV known to, 19. 90
Orford, Cts of, corresponds with, 19. 51
Petroni does honours for, 37. 57
Pitture antiche di Ercolano might be procured by, for HW, 21. 262
Richecourt not trusted by, 19. 2
Rinuccini benefits by Electress's contract with, over rights to church lands, 18. 169
San Severino recommended by, to Mann, 20. 369
Stanley meets, 22. 327n
Stosch's medals sent by, 18. 478
Taylor to treat one eye of, 20. 458
Valenti induced by, to release statues for Leicester, 20. 104n
—— makes offer through, to Stosch, 21. 192

[Albani, Alessandro, *continued*]
Vienna refers letters of, to Lobkowitz, 18. 515
villa of: architect of, is Marchionni, 24. 344n; at Albano, 23. 214, 248; at Rome, surpasses all other Roman sights, 22. 229; York, D. of, to hear concert at, 22. 229
Winckelmann in service of, 22. 113
York, D. of, receives civilities from, 22. 155n, 229, 233–4
Young Pretender's marriage predicted by, 19. 335

Albani, Annibale (1682–1751), cardinal, 1711, camerlengo:
cardinals promise votes to, 17. 16
faction led by, in Conclave, 13. 212n, 220, 227

Albani, Carlo Francesco Saverio Giuseppe (b. 1749), Principe di Soriano:
SH visited by, 33. 530

Albani *or* Albano, Francesco (1578–1660), painter:
Beauclerk, Lady Diana, rivals, in drawing children, 28. *244*, 35. 426
Cipriani's paintings replace those of, at Houghton, 25. 316
Cupids of, all alike, 29. 104
Francis III sells paintings by, to K. of Poland, 19. 314n
HW buys painting by, of Holy Family, 26. 7
HW likes 'glut' of buildings in landscapes of, 9. 122
Mereworth reminiscent of landscapes of, 35. 143
Milton's Eden has colouring of, 16. 270
Nuneham Courtenay Church inspired by, 29. 85
Stowe reminds HW of paintings of, 9. 122, 10. 44, 315, 35. 75
'sweet neatness of,' 34. 243

Albani, Giovanni Francesco (1649–1721), *see* Clement XI

Albani, Giovanni Francesco (1720–1803), cardinal, 1747:
Clement XIII consults, about Young Pretender, 22. 389
—— receives communication from, 22. 369n
Lepri, Marchesa, defended by, 25. 385n
pro-Jesuit cardinals led by, 23. 89n
York, Cardinal, corresponds with, 22. 388n
—— intimate with, 22. 389
—— reveals letter of, to congregation of cardinals, 22. 389
—— to be taken on tour by, after Old Pretender's death, 21. 392n
Young Pretender asks Clement XIII through, to let him return to Rome, 22. 368

Albani, Orazio Francesco (1717–92), Principe di Soriano:
dates of, 43. 264
wife of, 17. 47n, 19. 475, 33. 530n

Albani, Palazzo, at Castel Gandolfo:
Albani builds, below Papal gardens near Savelli castle, 24. 214n

—— lends, to D. and Ds of Gloucester, 24. 214, 248

Albani, Villa:
Marchionni, architect of, 24. 344n

Albani faction:
Mosca's election as Pope sought by, despite Louis XV's request, 21. 207

Albania:
brigands of, called by Turks to slaughter Greeks, 23. 212n
possible revolt by, against Turks, 23. 146n

Albano, painter. *See* Albani, Francesco

Albano, Italy:
Altieri summoned from, 13. 216
Benedict XIV might have exiled Virgin to, along with Stuarts, 22. 227
Gloucester, D. and Ds of, to spend summer at Albani's villa at, 24. 214, 248
Lobkowitz approaches, 18. 447
Mann's spy visits father at, 19. 141
Old Pretender and family at, said to be stirring, 21. 252
Old Pretender does not visit, 20. 442
—— goes to, 19. 99n
——'s health reported from, 21. 217
——'s preparations for escaping from, 19. 135
——'s sojourn at, will be interrupted, 18. 447
——'s villa at, 19. 99n, 21. 404n, 22. 257n
—— with guards and Cardinal York retires to, 20. 590
Patriots used to think of, when dismissed from St James's, 22. 257
Strange may make pilgrimage to, 21. 404
visitors to: Cologne, Elector of, 20. 508n; HW, 17. 28; Inverness, Ds of, 17. 28; Mahony, Comtesse, 17. 28; Spinelli, 20. 590
Young Pretender believed to be ill at, 18. 377, 387–8
——'s valet goes to, 19. 312
*See also* Albani

Albans, St. *See* Saint Albans

Albany, Count *or* Earl of. *See* Charles Edward (Stuart)

Albany, Countess of. *See* Stolberg-Gedern, Luise-Maximiliane of (1752–1824)

Albany, Ds of. *See* Stuart, Charlotte (d. 1789)

Albany, D. of. *See* Stewart, Alexander (ca 1454–ca 1485); Stewart, John (d. 1536)

Albany, E. of. *See* Charles Edward (Stuart)

Albany, N.Y.:
Montcalm threatens, 21. 229n, 30. 138n

Albaret. *See* Ponte d'Albaret

Albemarle, Cts of. *See* Lennox, Lady Anne (1703–89); Miller, Anne (d. 1824)

Albemarle, Ds of. *See* Cavendish, Lady Elizabeth (1654–1734)

Albemarle, D. of. *See* Edward (Plantagenet) (ca 1373–1415); Monck, Christopher (1653–88); Monck, George (1608–70)

Albemarle, E. of. *See* Keppel, George (1724–72); Keppel, William Anne van (1702–54)

Albemarle, family of:
numerous fatalities in, 33. 316
*See also* Keppel family
Albemarle St, London:
HW's acquaintance in, 9. 133
Ladies Club in, *see* Ladies Club
name of, corrected, 43. 347
residents of: Bromley, 2. 154n; Davis, Sir
John, 25. 494; Livett, 36. 259n; Monson,
42. 219n; Nivernais, 38. 172; Pomfret, Cts
of, and Lady Juliana Fermor, 20. 97n;
Waldegrave, 10. 56–7, 32. 67n, 38. 294
Wildman's Club in, 32. 67n, 38. 294, 461n
Albenga:
Charles Emmanuel III's quarters at, 19. 312
Maillebois and Don Philip reach, 19. 58
Albergo d'Aquila, Florentine inn:
Modenese princess at, 17. 68n
Solis stays at, 24. 68n
Albergotti, (?) Albergotto, *or* Angiolo Tom-
maso, *or* Girolamo:
Mann asked by, to intercede in quarrel, 17.
111–12
Romana, the, arouses jealousy of, at burletta,
17. 162–3
Tesi, the, insulted by, 18. 368
Albermarle. *See* Albemarle
Alberoni, Julio (1664–1752), cardinal, 1717;
prime minister to Philip V of Spain:
Benedict XIV recalls, from Bologna, 18. 199n
Hervey, Bp, compared to, 25. 455
Montemar said to warn Elizabeth Farnese
against, 18. 7
Noailles does not discuss, 6. 434
Traun seizes property of, in Plaisanteri, 18.
199
Alberstroff, Cts of. *See* Walkinshaw, Clementina
Maria Sophia
Albert II (1397–1439), Holy Roman Emperor
1438–9:
Bavarian deed of, denied by Austrians when
Frederick II produces it, 24. 403
Bavaria's renunciation by, found by Joseph
II, 24. 400
'Albert, Duke.' *See* Albrecht Kasimir August
Albert (1738–1822), P., of Saxony:
Pressburg the residence of, as viceroy of Hun-
gary, 39. 538
Albert, Charles-Philippe d' (1695–1758), Duc
de Luynes:
*Mémoires* of, has *Copie d'une lettre du Roi
de Prusse* inserted, 21. 141n
widow of, 3. 379n, 8. 36–7
Albert, Joseph-François-Ildefonse-Raymond
(1721–90), lieutenant of police:
dismissed, 6. 331
made lieutenant of police, 6. 184
Sartine would not get on with, 6. 300
Turgot's protégé, 6. 184–5, 300
Albert, Louis-Joseph-Marie-Charles-Amable d'
(1748–1807), Duc de Luynes:
attends parliament of Paris, 8. 172
wife of, 4. 352n

Albert d'Ailly, Charles d' (1625–98), Duc de
Chaulnes:
Brittany more interesting under rule of, 31.
74
Albert d'Ailly, Marie-Joseph-Louis d' (1741–93),
Duc de Pecquigny; later Duc de Chaulnes:
attacks cabinet-maker, 4. 85
Bedford entertains, at Woburn, 38. 276, 295
Bedford, Ds of, offends, at whist match, 38.
295
Buckingham Gate assignation of, escaped by
Virrette, 38. 313
café au lait mistaken by, for snuff, 38. 215
Garlies almost duels with, at Milton's ball,
38. 295
Guerchy sends away, after arrest, 38. 322
HW mentions, 6. 20
Harrington, Cts of, alarmed by attendance of,
at her assembly, 38. 234
London revisited by, after duel, 38. 322
Stanhope, Lady Caroline, forbidden to speak
to, 38. 234
Virrette wins money from, and is challenged,
38. 306–7, 313, 322
witticism by, on Sandwich injuring him in
horse-play, 38. 295
Albert d'Ailly, Michel-Ferdinand d' (1714–
69), Duc de Chaulnes:
Albemarle settles cartel with, 21. 261n
chargé des chevau-légers, 7. 370
château of, at Picquigny, 7. 259
Hertford offered renewal by, of lease of Hôtel
de Grimbergh, 38. 304–5, 306, 313, 351
son of, 38. 306
Albert de Luynes, Marie-Charles-Louis d'
(1717–71), Duc de Chevreuse; gov. of Paris:
daughter of, has smallpox, 4. 321
ill, 3. 106
Louis's malapropism about, 10. 202
Albert de Luynes, Paul d' (1703–88), Bp of
Bayeux, 1729; Abp of Sens, 1753; cardinal,
1756:
Choiseul orders, to exclude Cavalchini, 21.
215n
clarity of, 3. 288
Conclave expects, 21. 207n, 215n, 23. 95n
Dauphiness's almoner, 20. 464n
Louis XV's exclusion of Cavalchini an-
nounced by, 21. 215–16
Old Pretender nominates, to college of cardi-
nals, 20. 464
Rome approached by, with great suite, 23.
104n
Albert de Luynes, Pauline-Sophie d' (b. 1756):
smallpox attacks, despite inoculation, 4. 321
Alberti. *See* Degli Alberti
Albertini, Prince. *See* San Severino Albertini,
Giovanni Battista
Albigensians:
Toulouse seat of, 31. 276n
Albion Mills, Southwark:
burning of, 11. 212–13
*Albion Queens, The. See under* Banks, John

Albizzi, Gaetano, printer:
Gualtieri's book printed by, 18. 88
Albizzi. *See also* Degli Albizzi
Albon, Comtesse d'. *See* Albon, Julie-Claude-Hilaire-Françoise d' (1695–1748); Castellane, Angélique-Charlotte d' (b. 1751)
Albon, Claude-Camille-François (1751–89), Comte d'; Prince d'Yvetot:
Du Deffand, Mme, annoyed by claim of relationship by, 6. 25–6
marriage of, 5. 225
verses by, on Mme du Deffand's blindness, 6. 9, 25
Albon, Julie-Claude-Hilaire-Françoise d' (1695–1748), m. (1711) Claude d'Albon, Comte de St-Marcel:
Lespinasse, Julie de, daughter of, 3. 290n
Albon de St-Marcel, Marie-Camille-Diane d' (1714–73), m. (1739) Gaspard-Nicolas de Vichy, Comte de Champrond:
Albon connected to Mme du Deffand through, 6. 26
nephew of, 5. 225, 6. 9n, 26
Albon family:
Lespinasse, Julie de, mentions, in will, 6. 328
Albrecht (1773–4) of Tuscany, Archduke:
death of: 25. 549; announced to foreign ministers, 24. 23
inoculation of, 24. 7
Albrecht Kasimir August (1738–1822), D. of Saxe-Teschen; Austrian general; 'Duke Albert':
Florence left by, for Rome, 24. 190n
HW wants sketches of architecture of, 39. 182
Lloyd, Rachel, discusses, 33. 291
Albreda. *See* Emma
Albret, Maréchale d'. *See* Guénégaud, Madeleine de
Albret, Henri d', K. of Navarre:
wife of, 15. 155n
Albury:
Hardinge writes from, 35. 594
Alby, Comte d'. *See* Sartine, Antoine-Raimond-Jean-Gualbert-Gabriel de
Alby, Comtesse d'. *See* Hardy du Plessis, Marie-Anne
Alcæus, Greek poet:
Horace impersonates, 35. 568
Alcántara Guzman Pacheco y Silva, Don Pedro (d. 1779), 14th D. of Medina Sidonia:
death of, said to have occurred on peace mission, 24. 440
*Alceste. See under* Lulli, Jean-Baptiste; Quinault, Philippe
Alcester, Warwickshire:
HW sees Greville tombs at, 9. 224
Ragley near, 9. 117n, 38. 53
*Alchemist; Alchymist. See under* Jonson, Ben
Alcibiades:
character in *Ballet de la Paix*, 18. 496
dog of, 3. 225

*Alcide*, French ship:
English capture, 35. 235n
Alcides:
Silva's, 19. 383
Alciphron (fl. 2d century), rhetorician:
Beloe translates, 15. 217n
*Alcmena*, British frigate:
escapes to Ireland, 25. 152
Alcock, John (1430–1500), Bp of Rochester, 1472, of Worcester, 1476, of Ely, 1486:
Clare made justice of peace for Ely by, 2. 256
Henry VII's comptroller of works and buildings, 1. 147–8
repair of chapel of, at Ely, 1. 278
Alcoforado, Marianna (1640–1723), nun:
*Lettres d'amour d'une religieuse portugaise . . .*: date of, 43. 81; Du Deffand, Mme, disparages, 3. 54, 55, 87, 143, 4. 152; HW taunts Mme du Deffand with imitating, 3. *44*, 54, 4. 152
Alcon, E. of Richmond:
priory given to abbey by, 2. 257–8
Alcorans:
ancient, could not foresee modern contingencies, 25. 21
Alcubierre, Roque Joaquin de (d. 1780):
Herculaneum excavated by, 13. 222n
Aldborough, Cts of. *See* Hamilton, Elizabeth (d. 1846); Herbert, Barbara (1742–85)
Aldborough, E. of. *See* Stratford, Edward Augustus
*Aldborough*, English ship:
Thurot pursued by, from Portsmouth, 21. 374n
Aldborough, Norfolk:
Cole rector of, 1. 283n
Aldborough House:
Herbert builds, 33. 376n
Aldborough. *See also* Aldeburgh
Aldeburgh, Suffolk:
corruption in borough of, 22. 585n
storm at, 10. 241
Sudbourne near, 6. 137n
Alderman; aldermen:
Blakiston is, 20. 261n
Bury altar tablets may depict, 16. 184
Carte's history to be inspected by, 18. 480
Gloucester pew worthy of queen of, 35. 154
HW does not wish to be, 32. 40
Marlborough's general retorts to remark by, at Lord Mayor's dinner, 21. 198, 24. 29, 414, 25. 340
members of Parliament probably bribe, 24. 132
might match his daughter with the King, 21. 518
military loved by, when danger threatens, 23. 34
nine die in one year, 11. 106
protest by, against London's remonstrance, 23. 196
Westminster chooses, for City of London, 35. 334

Wilkes may have become quiet as, **23**. 208
—— resolves to become, **23**. 206
—— triumphs over, in London, **32**. 52–3
*See also under* London: City of
Alderney:
Conway might combine, with Channel Islands into United Provinces, **39**. 299
cows of. *See under* Cow
*Alderney*, English ship:
*Sampson* chased by, **24**. 468n
Aldersbrook House, Essex:
Lethieullier of, **1**. 12n, **2**. 238n
Aldersgate St, London:
Gilding's house in, **34**. 98n
Thanet House in, **43**. 383
Alderson, ——:
ensigncy sought for, from Conway, **39**. 401–2, **42**. 54
Alderson, Rev. Christopher (ca 1737–1814), Mason's curate; rector of Aston 1797–1814:
antiquarianism disliked by, **28**. 63, 73, 165
at Lady Holdernesse's in Hertford St, **42**. 54
HW's correspondence with, **42**. 54–5
HW sends compliments to, **28**. 43
HW's MSS owned by, **36**. 314
HW's or Mason's letters and MSS carried or forwarded by, **28**. 73, 76, 81, 438, 440, 442, **29**. 50, 302–4
Holdernesse's corpse attended to Hornby by, **28**. 399
Hornby Castle visited by, **28**. 321
Mason's correspondence with, **28**. 23n, 150, 484
——'s tithes to be regulated by, **28**. 231
—— would dismiss, if insipid, **28**. 106
relative of, applies to Conway for ensigncy, **29**. 303, 307–8, **39**. 401–2, **42**. 54
Syon Hill visited by, **28**. 150
Alderson, William:
transcribes Gray's journal, **28**. 106n
Aldgate, London:
Parsons of, **1**. 379n
Tower of London and, **9**. 112n
Aldhelm (ca 639–709), Bp of Sherborne:
*De laudibus virginitatis*, Saxon drawing in, **40**. 248
Aldingham, Lancs:
Ashton rector of, **9**. 29n, **13**. 161n, **14**. 234
—— to resign living of, to brother, **43**. 189
living of, vacated by Tullie's death, sought by HW for Ashton, **13**. 249n, **40**. 37, 39
verses dated from, **14**. 235n
Aldobrandini, Maria Camilla (1718–83), m. (1737) Marchese Folco Rinuccini:
father-in-law's legacy to, **19**. 461
HW sees brocatelle in bedchamber of, **21**. 458
Madonna di Loreto to be visited by, to aid conception of son, **30**. 15
Mann thanked by, for HW's attentions to her husband, **19**. *349*
name of, corrected, **43**. 313
son born to, **17**. 473
Aldobrandini villa. *See under* Rome

Aldovrandi. *See* Aldrovandi
Aldreth, Cambs:
Cole's estate in, **1**. 167, 243n
Aldrich, Henry (1647–1710), dean of Christ Church, Oxford:
Millemet MS of, **1**. 148
preface to Clarendon's *History* attributed to, **16**. 8
Tyson's account of, **1**. 172
Aldridge. *See* Aldrich
Aldrovandi, ——, of Bologna:
York, D. of, greeted by, **22**. 232n
Aldrovandi, Pompeo (1668–1752), cardinal:
papal candidacy of, **13**. 227
Aldsworth. *See* Aldworth
Aldus Manutius. *See* Manutius, Aldus
Aldwarke, Yorks:
Foljambe of, **28**. 50n
Aldworth, Richard Neville. *See* Neville, Richard Neville Aldworth
Ale:
Anna, Czarina, kills herself with, **40**. 43
Burton-upon-Trent's chief product, **40**. 43
drunk in half-pint bumpers, at Crewe Hall, **10**. 96
Hardwicke, Cts of, forbids procurement of, **21**. 4
'nasty,' in Northampton, **10**. 256
Newton opposes brewing of, in college, **30**. 89
—— thinks, wholesome, **30**. 89
Norfolk squires over-indulge in, **35**. 42
Nottingham, **17**. 506
savages drink, from skull, **10**. 255
served at Ranelagh, **17**. 401
Aleatico wine. *See under* Wine
Alecto (fury):
East India Co. should be corrected by, **23**. 442
HW's name for: Campbell sisters, **33**. 458; Catherine II, **22**. 253, **31**. 373; Elizabeth of Russia, **21**. 498; Wollstonecraft, Mary, **31**. 397
HW's verses mention, **31**. 120
Alectus. *See* Allectus
Ale-house; ale-houses:
adulterated beer and porter sold at, **40**. 257
at Messing, Essex, **33**. 206, **34**. 22
at Ranelagh, **17**. 401
called 'mug-house' in Birmingham, **35**. 147
Cock Lane séances profitable to, **10**. 6
English, full of French revolutionary agents, **42**. 376
full of topers, **39**. 498
HW offers to take a pot with Phyllis at, **42**. 222
hedge, **10**. 239
in Sion Lane, **38**. 60
near Oxford, *see* 'Louse Hall'
'saints' from, rescue ferry-boat, **39**. 187
signs for: Queen Anne's head on, **35**. 58; Vernon's portrait on, **18**. 423
tables and benches back-to-back in, **38**. 335
tax on, **37**. 445

[Ale-house; ale-houses, *continued*]
violin from, 33. 283–4
*See also* Tavern
Alehouse Man:
English, sketched by Anne Seymour Conway, 38. 156
Alembert, Jean le Rond d' (1717–83), 'philosophe':
Académie française's éloges by, of: Bossuet, 6. 89; Crébillon, 7. 68; Fénelon, 7. 68; Gustav III, 5. 36, 39; La Motte, 7. 68; Millot, 7. 10; Rose, 7. 68; Sacy, 6. 324n; (?) Toulouse, 6. 189
Académie française to have, as secretary, 5. 209, 211, 222
adulation by, of philosophic sovereigns, 25. 39, 613–14
agreeable, and 'of irreproachable morals,' 41. 62
appendix and preface of *Exposé succinct* written by, 3. 158, 163, 171, 176, 180, 41. 49
Bossuet's eulogy by, at Académie, 6. 89
Brunswick, P. of, honours, 3. *49*
Caracciolo admires, 5. 211
Catherine II praised by, 25. 39, 613–14, 33. 36–7, 312
——'s and Frederick II's offers refused by, 41. 62
Catherine II's conduct edifies, 28. 475–6
——'s interest in, 4. 214
——'s request to educate her son refused by, 25. 39n, 31. 62, 32. 59n
(?) Châtillon, Duchesse de, and Mlle de Lespinasse, friendship of, attributed to, 6. 102
Christian VII hears speech by, 4. 168–9
Christina's memoirs abridged by, 15. 56, 29. 119–20
'Déclaration' by, to *Exposé succinct,* 43. 83
Duclos leaves diamond to, 5. 211
——'s relations with, 43. 93
Du Deffand, Mme, alludes to, 4. 217
—— fears, will hear of Voltaire's letters to her, 3. 388
—— inquired after by, 7. 54
—— ridicules conspiracy of Cellamare to, 7. 278
——'s account of speech of, before Gustav III, 5. 39–40
—— seldom mentions, 41. 55
——'s opinion of, 4. 246–7, 6. 382, 41. 55
——'s 'portrait' of, 8. 94–5
——'s quarrel with, 8. 64
——'s remark on *La Belle Poule* admired by, 7. 54
éloges and Tacitus scraps by, HW glad not to be credited with, 41. 53
*Éloges lus dans les séances publiques de l'Académie française,* 7. 103, 106, (?) 123
Frederick II praised by, 25. 39, 613–14
——'s correspondence with, 5. 300, 302–3, 6. 363, 382

——'s offers refused by, 41. 62
Geoffrin, Mme, leaves annuities to, 6. 484
——'s social relations with, 7. 312, 316
good at impersonation, 3. 302
Gustav III eulogized by, at Académies, 5. 36, 39, 25. 39, 613–14
HW as Mme du Deffand's friend may be resented by, 41. 49, 54, 61
HW owns works by, 41. 62n
HW's letter to Rousseau attributed by, to Mme du Deffand, 28. 420
HW's letter to Rousseau attributed to, 3. 97, 41. 53, 54
HW speaks of, 3. 174
HW's proposed epic about, 4. 214–15, 217
HW's style discussed by, 3. 158
HW unacquainted with, 30. 223
Hume informed by, of Paris opinion regarding Rousseau controversy, 41. 24, 43–4, 61
—— prefers, 41. 25n
——'s friendship for, 3. 112n
——'s letter to Holbach read by, 3. 89
*Influence et l'utilité réciproques de la philosophie envers les princes, L',* 4. 168–9
Joseph II emulates, 29. 151
La Ferté-Imbault, Mme, keeps, away from Mme Geoffrin, 6. 296n, 363
Lespinasse, Julie de, affair of, with, 5. 209, 6. 110, 363
—— names, as executor, 6. 328
*Lettre de M. d'Alembert à . . . Condorcet sur Mme Geoffrin,* 6. 498
Marmontel protégé of, 3. 229
——'s verses for portrait of, 7. 54
office to be given to, 6. 154–5
pensions of, 41. 62
Rousseau's delusions concerning, 3. 97, 30. 223, 41. 53, 56
Sévigné letters transmitted by, 5. 373
style and delivery of, 7. 68, 102–3
*Sur la destruction des Jésuites,* Hertford sends, to HW, 38. 537, 554
Tacitus translation of, less creditable than his algebra and geometry, 41. 62
Tencin, Mme de, mother of, 28. *291*
Voltaire's correspondence with, 5. 307, 338, 12. 9
Voltaire sends epistle to K. of Prussia to, 5. 338
——'s successor to be received into Académie by, 7. 48
—— wishes to show libel to, 7. 25
Alençon, Duc de. *See* Jean II
Alençon, Ducs de:
HW dreams of imprisoning, 21. 212
*À Léon Franco,* Spanish galleon:
in Spanish fleet, 17. 286
Aleppo, consul at. *See* Drummond, Alexander (d. 1769); Pollard, Arthur (d. 1754)
*Alert,* English ship:
*La Belle Poule* approached by, 24. 395n

Alessandri. *See* Degli Alessandri

Alessandria (in Italy):
Charles Emmanuel III brings Liechtenstein to save, **19.** 231
—— camps near, **19.** 82
French may besiege, **19.** 75
HW and Gray pass through, **13.** 192n
Lobkowitz ready to move to, **19.** 36–7, 40–1
Mann receives letter from, **19.** 84
Parma, D. of, used to write from, **22.** 213
Sardinian troops assemble near, **19.** 258
Spaniards endanger, **19.** 36, 75, 120, 136–7, 226, 227

*Alessandro. See under* Handel, George Frideric

'Alessandro Magno.' *See* Alexander the Great

*Alessandro nell' Indie. See under* Hasse, J. A.; Metastasio, Pietro

Alet, Bp of. *See* La Cropte de Chanterac, Charles de

Alet. *See also* Alais

'Alexander, Cardinal.' *See* Albani, Alessandro

Alexander VI (Roderigo Borgia) (1431–1503), pope 1492–1503:
cardinals murdered by, **22.** 254
Charles VIII's Neapolitan conquest contemporary with, **4.** 243
Maupeou would have served, **24.** 35
Voltaire questions poisonings by, **22.** 253n

Alexander VII (Fabio Chigi) (1599–1667), pope 1655–67:
Pantheon's modernization first proposed by, **21.** 37n

Alexander VIII (Pietro Ottoboni) (1610–91), pope 1689–91:
aged, **1.** 163, **2.** 253
great-nephew of, **13.** 214n
HW quotes remark by, **15.** 247

Alexander (356–323 B.C.) the Great; Emperor:
America could be subdued only by, **24.** 46
American war compared to campaign of, **32.** 388
cameo of, on snuff-box, **22.** 234n
Charlotte, Q., will feel she is marrying, **21.** 517
Clive compared with, **23.** 530
Cornwallis an, **34.** 147
Du Deffand, Mme, prefers Cæsar to, **3.** 321
England compared to, **21.** 338
English counterparts of, **35.** 258
fame of, **31.** 21
Fox, C. J., compared with, **34.** 354
Frederick II compared with, **21.** 171, **34.** 34, **39.** 273
George II does not emulate, despite Voltaire's epigram, **21.** 31
Germain can look as well as, **32.** 348
Gordian knot cut by, **34.** 111
Granby's soul worthy of, **40.** 241
Guadagni plays, **23.** 272
HW jokes about Thalestris and, **31.** 160
HW pardons, **3.** 318

HW prefers D. of Cumberland to, **37.** 258
histories of, do not fire Conway, **37.** 37
'incontinencies' of, depicted at Wanstead, **35.** 238
Indian expedition of, to be theme of opera, **18.** 353
Jupiter Ammon adopted, **30.** 217
Le Brun's paintings of battles of, **7.** 339, **35.** 344
North's losses greater than conquests of, **24.** 139
plumes usually worn by, in opera, **24.** 222
Porus's treatment from, **25.** 545, 642
question about, at giuoco della sibilla, **20.** 477
Rigby's health drunk by, **30.** 332
schoolboys' pleasures better than those of, **9.** 3
statue of, Mann advises Botta to put, in loggia, **22.** 124
transmigration should convert, into a beast, **35.** 356
Voltaire alludes to, **4.** 396
weeps at having no more to conquer, **13.** 135
Wilkes uses magnanimity of, **24.** 89
yellow fever would cause, to look wretched, **21.** 290

Alexander (208–35) Severus, Roman emperor 222–35:
Egyptian birds delight, **14.** 290
HW's *medaglioncino* of, **13.** 233, **15.** 13, **16.** 254n, **23.** 383
Lampridius's life of, **42.** 268

Alexander I (1777–1825), Czar of Russia 1801–25:
marriage of, **12.** 54
said to have travelled with Catherine II, **33.** 562

Alexander Leopold Joseph (1772–95), of Tuscany; Archduke:
Gloucester, D. and Ds of, see, at Poggio Imperiale, **24.** 297
(?) grandmother to meet, at Gorïzia, **24.** 191
living, **25.** 549

Alexander, Mr:
HW says, is Cts of Ailesbury's friend, **38.** 75

Alexander, Mr, of Teddington:
SH visited by, **12.** 233

Alexander, Alexandre (fl. 1727–51), banker at Paris:
book to be forwarded through, to Conway, **40.** 29
HW's correspondence forwarded by, **13.** 184, 239, **17.** 23n
(?) Montagu's Paris banker and forwarder of mail, **9.** 9

Alexander, Daniel:
conspiracy by, against Sir Edward Walpole, **43.** 365

Alexander, Elizabeth:
Sarah the dwarf's servant, **40.** 161

Alexander, John (fl. 1715–52), engraver; sometimes called Alexander Jamesone:
biographical information on, corrected, **43.**
195
Jamesone's paintings owned by, **40.** 266
print by, of Jamesone family picture, **15.** 75,
**40.** 261, **43.** 195
Alexander, Mrs John (Frances ——), of Teddington:
(?) SH visited by, **12.** 230
Alexander, Mrs John. *See* Jamesone, Marjory
Alexander, Thomas:
Criquitt replaced by, as servant to Hudson
the dwarf, **41.** 161
Alexander, Sir William (?1567–1640), cr. (1633)
E. of Stirling:
print of, **1.** 182
psalms translated by, **16.** 366n
Alexander, William (ca 1690–1761), M. P.;
lord provost of Edinburgh; banker:
(?) death of, **38.** 104
Alexander, William (1726–83), self-styled **E.**
of Stirling; American Brig.-Gen.:
court martial rumoured for, **24.** 406
Lee's court martial conducted by, **24.** 406n
Long Island defeat of, **24.** 249
one of Washington's generals, **28.** 434n
Alexander brothers, Paris bankers:
evade Hon. Thomas Walpole's claims on
property in Grenada, **7.** 180n
*See also* Alexander, Alexandre
*Alexander in Persia*, opera:
Amorevoli unable to sing in, **37.** 116
Galuppi adapts music for, **17.** 184n
performed in London, **17.** 183, 185, 186, 190–
1, 197, 208, 209, 211
Pescetti's music included in, **17.** 302n
Rolli and Vaneschi adapt lyrics for, **17.** 184n
*Alexander's Feast, See under* Dryden, John;
Handel, George Frideric
*Alexander the Great. See under* Lee, Nathaniel
Alexandre, Paris banker. *See* Alexander, Alex-
andre; Alexander brothers
Alexandre, João, Portuguese Jesuit:
Portugal does not release, **21.** 341
*Alexandreis. See under* Gaultier de Châtillon,
Philippe
Alexandria, Egypt:
library at, burned by Omar, **31.** 279
ships bound for, when captured, **21.** 274n
view of, **40.** 283
Alexandria, Italy. *See* Alessandria
Alexiano, Capt., Russian agent at Port Mahon:
Murray sends, to Leghorn for supplies, **24.**
380n
Alexis (1746–87) of Brunswick-Wolfenbüttel:
Catherine II releases, with his sisters, **34.** 3
death of, **34.** 3
*Alexis Comnène. See* Voltaire: *Irene*
Alfani, Mgr Onofrio, Papal official:
discovery of Gunpowder Plot papers an-
nounced by, **23.** 522

Jesuit archives delivered to, **23.** 517n
Alfieri, Vittorio (1749–1803), Count; poet:
Albany, Cts of, instructed by, **25.** *107*
—— lived alone with, **25.** 535
—— may marry, **25.** 397, **33.** 438–9
—— separated from husband through plot
by, **25.** 396–7, 535
—— wooed by, **25.** 106–7, 538n, **26.** 48
breakfasts with HW, **11.** *302, 303*
Francès told by, of disgust at Vcts Ligonier's
affair, **30.** 255–6
Leopold II, Pius VI, and Cardinal York de-
luded by, **25.** 396–7
Ligonier's duel with, **5.** 77n, **25.** 538n, **26.** 48
Ligonier, Vcts, has affair with, **35.** 453
Piedmontese, **25.** 538n, **26.** 48
Pius VI banishes, **25.** 397
SH visited by, **12.** 238
writer of tragedies, **25.** 396–7, 535
Alfonso V (1394–1458), K. of Aragon 1416–58,
of Naples 1442–58:
Van Eyck sends painting to, of Adoration
of Magi, **42.** 66
Alford, E. of. *See* Graeme, John
Alford, Rev. Samuel (ca 1705–?99), vicar of
Curry Rivel, Somerset:
(?) Pynsent's will drawn by, **22.** 276–7
Alfred (849–901), K. of the West Saxons:
print of, **1.** 172
will of, sent to HW by Astle, **42.** 223
Alfred, P. (1780–82), son of George III:
at point of death, **25.** 309
Cornwallis baptizes, **29.** 87
death of, **25.** 403, 413, **34.** 355
Hunter, Dr, might teach, **33.** 319
not inoculated, **25.** 413
'Prince Duodecimus,' **33.** 355
sisters bathe with, in sea, **25.** 413
*Alfred. See under* Home, John
*Alfred*, opera:
Arne puts on, in Dublin, **37.** 412n
*Alfred*, English ship:
captain of, killed, **25.** 278n
*Alfred*, American war ship:
Glasgow's battle with, **24.** 216
Algajola, Corsica:
Jesuits land at, **22.** 526n, 535n, 545n
Algarotti, Francesco (1712–64), Conte; author:
Frederick II summons, by letter, **37.** 63–4
—— visited by, on way to St Petersburg with
Baltimore, **37.** 64
genteel dialogue of, **28.** 161
Gray cites passage in Leghorn edn of works
of, **14.** 165
——'s correspondence with, **28.** 153
Hervey intimate with, in London, **37.** 64
Mann told by, of Peter III's generosity, **22.** 22
Montagu, Lady Mary Wortley, and, **43.** 190
writes military news from Bologna, **21.** 271
Algebra:
Alembert's work on, **41.** 62

English heraldry would be, to Florentine sculptor, **25**. 227

Algeria. *See* Algerians; Algiers

Algerians ('Algerines'; 'Algerins'):
English aided by, in Minorca, **25**. 205
Mann calls, 'pirates,' **25**. 270
Tuscan ships respected by all nations but, **25**. 270
Tuscany making peace with, **25**. 270

Algiers, Dey ('Bey') of:
painting of, at Hinchingbrooke, **40**. 283
*See also* Ali Bassa (d. 1766); Muhammed-Ben-Othman (ca 1710–91)

Algiers, Mufti of:
rewards promised by, to those who fight the Spaniards, **24**. 122

Algiers:
Acton to proceed against, **20**. 480
'Alī Pāsha usurps Tunisian throne with aid of, **20**. 318n
Charles III demolishes, **39**. 420
*corpo santo* on Spanish expedition to, **25**. 26
corsairs of, prey on Tuscan trade, **20**. 472
Dey of, expels Stendardi and declares war on Tuscany, **20**. 472n
English ships behave like pirates of, **20**. 494
France may aid Spain against, **24**. 179
French ship from, carries plague, **17**. 105
HW calls, metropolitan see of thieves, **39**. 420
Hardinge prefers, to London, **35**. 604
Johnston dies of wounds received at, **12**. 64–5n
La Condamine visits, **22**. 147n
Mann's captain reports from, **25**. 416
sea captain imprisoned at, keeps chickens, **22**. 586, **23**. 4
Spain's attack on, **32**. 239n
Spaniards attack, **28**. 217
Spaniards capture vessels and general from, **20**. 480
Spanish armada fails at, **24**. 119, 120, 122, **25**. 26, 415–16, **28**. 217
Tuscan consul ill-treated and dismissed by, **22**. 259
Tuscany cannot afford war with, **20**. 487
Tuscany's treaty with, **20**. 472
vessels of, said to have landed in Minorca to aid English, **25**. 205

Alhambra, the:
Moorish mosaics said to adorn, **42**. 53
prints of, **2**. 149, 150, 151–2

Ali I (d. 1796) Karamanliya; Dey of Tripoli 1755–93, 1795–6:
minister sent by, to Holland, **23**. 24

Alias; aliases:
in D. of Kingston's will, **23**. 520, **24**. 30
street walkers at Old Bailey indicted under, **23**. 520

Ali Bassa (d. 1766), Dey of Algiers:
letters may be intercepted by, **21**. 263
Tuscany receives apologies from, for ill-treating consul, **22**. 259n

'Alī ben Muhammed ben 'Alī (d. 1756), Bey of Tunis 1735–56:
son massacres wives of, and puts out his eyes, **20**. 319n
son's revolt against, **20**. 319
Tunisian throne usurped from Husain ben 'Alī by, with Algerian help, **20**. 318n

Alicante:
Court's fleet said to have reached, **18**. 415
Dutchman meets Rowley near, **18**. 525
French fleet at, **18**. 420
French ships may flee to, **21**. 188
Hervey to take E. of Bristol to, **21**. 225
*Postilion*, Spanish polacre from, captured, **19**. 82n

Alice Holt Forest:
house near, **37**. 305

Aligre, Étienne d' (d. 1635), chancellor:
tomb of, **7**. 277

Aligre, Étienne d' (1592–1677), chancellor:
tomb of, **7**. 277

Aligre, Étienne-François d' (1726–98), President of Parliament of Paris:
anecdote of new councillor and, **6**. 72
attends session of parliament of Paris, **8**. 171
harangue of, at lit de justice, **4**. 183–4
hunts, **4**. 179
marriage of, **3**. 395n
parliament of Paris sends, to Louis XV in Séguier affair, **4**. 493
social relations of, with Comtesse de Boufflers, **7**. 306

Aligre, Mme Étienne-François d'. *See* Talon, Françoise-Madeleine

Alincourt:
epitaph at, **41**. 308–9

'Alī Pāsha. *See* 'Alī ben Muhammed ben 'Alī (d. 1756)

Alipes (wing-footed horse):
HW to forsake Pegasus for, **32**. 131

Alison, Rev. Archibald (1757–1839):
HW never saw, **34**. 70
HW thanks, for *Essays on the Nature and Principles of Taste*, **42**. 264, 273
wife of, **6**. 357n

Alison, Mrs Archibald. *See* Gregory, Dorothea

*Alix et Alexis. See under* Poinsinet, Antoine-Alexandre-Henri

Alla. *See* Ala

Alladin. *See* Aladdin

Allahabad:
treaty of, **25**. 13n

Allan, David (1744–96):
illustrations to *Scotland's Skaith* drawn by, **42**. 432n

Allan, George (1736–1800), antiquary:
HW invited by, to see his collection, **41**. 351
HW receives prints from, **2**. 28n, **41**. 350
HW's correspondence with, **41**. 350–1
private press of, at Blackwell Grange, **41**. 351n
*Sketch of the Life and Character of . . .*

[Allan, George, *continued*]
*Richard Trevor* by, frontispiece to, **41.** 350n
Allanson. *See* Alison
Allard, Marie:
Vestris's son by, **25.** 134n
Allectus (d. 276), Roman usurper:
coins of, **17.** 378, **18.** 347n
Allegory:
HW dislikes, **32.** 182
Allegranti, Teresa Maddalena (b. ca 1754, living 1801), m. (ca 1798) —— Harrison; soprano:
HW hears, **25.** 242–3
HW to hear, **33.** 322
is applauded more than Vestris, **25.** 243
'nightingale-woman,' **29.** 174
Allegri, Antonio (1494–1534), called Correggio; painter:
angels by: have 'curled smiles,' **33.** 287; not as fresh-looking as Lady Sarah Lennox, **33.** 130
Berry, Mary, expresses opinion of, **11.** 150n
Cooper's print after, **15.** 100
Damer, Mrs, equals, **35.** 437
fame of, **30.** 325
faultless line of, **11.** 338
Félibien and Du Fresnoy praise, **30.** 325
Furoni a pupil of, **21.** 200
HW's opinion of, **11.** 149–50
Hamilton brings 'Venus, Cupid and Satyr' allegedly by, to England, **23.** 350, **26.** 46, **32.** 70, 71, **35.** 409
Julienne has boys' heads and sleeping woman by, **7.** 287
'La Notte' by, **18.** 323
Madonna and Child with St Jerome by, at Parma: Bragge says, is not original, **18.** 355; Carracci engraves, **17.** 167; Chute likes, **35.** 5; French kings make offers for, **18.** 338; Mann might procure, for Sir Robert Walpole, **17.** 167, 199, 268, **18.** 323, 337–8, 351, 370, 373, **35.** 5, 12; Parma, D. of, buys, **17.** 167n
Magdalen by, **9.** 335
Monaco, P. of, has 'sainte face' attributed to, **7.** 335
paintings by: at Marigny's, **39.** 15; Hamilton to bring, to England, **35.** 415; in Mariette's sale, **32.** 266; Louis XIV admires, **18.** 338n; Siries shows, to Mann, **20.** 314; Trevisani's copy of, bought by HW, **26.** 7
West asks for list of works of, in England, **40.** 312
Allegri, Gregorio (1582–1652), composer:
*Miserere* by: Haymarket Theatre to have performance of, **18.** 211; performed on Good Fridays at Rome, **18.** 211n
Allegrini, Francesco (b. 1729), artist:
heads of Medici by, **21.** 533, 561, **25.** 226, 434
*Allegro, L'. See under* Milton, John
'Allemand, Prince':
Ossory, Cts of, sends 'portrait' of, **34.** 48

Allemande (dance):
Christian VII's love affairs last as long as, **35.** 323
HW unable to dance, **31.** 140
Allemani. *See* Alamanni
Allen, Vcts. *See* Du Pass, Margaret (d. 1758)
Allen, ——, apothecary:
son of, **23.** 346
Allen, Capt.:
Bacon, Anthony, hears of Hatton from, **33.** 256n
Allen, Cardinal:
Baynes, secretary to, **42.** 64n
Allen, Lady, wife of Sir Timothy Allen:
Montagu Dunk, Ladies Elizabeth and Frances, to be entertained by, **9.** 415
Allen, Maj.:
Hervey Aston, Henry, dies after duel with, **25.** 566n
Allen, Bennet (b. ca 1737, d. 1782 or after), miscellaneous writer:
Dulany fatally wounded by, **32.** 181n
Granby's alleged collaborator, **32.** 181
Allen, Edward, English consul at Naples ca 1737–53:
called 'Spanish consul,' **18.** *453*
Charles of Naples might seize, as hostage, **19.** 57–8
Florence to be visited by, on way to England, **19.** 477
(?) Mann fails to get explanation from, **20.** 431
Martin sends, ashore at Naples, **18.** 42
Mathews to receive horse bought by, **18.** 453
Walpole, Bns, described by, **17.** 71n
Allen, Mrs Edward. *See* Shadwell, Catherine
Allen, Elizabeth (d. 1738), m. William Coventry, 5th E. of Coventry:
natural dau. of, **9.** 29n
Allen, Ethan (1738–89), American patriot:
Ticonderoga's capture by, **32.** 370n
Allen, Frances (d. 1801) m. (1758) William Mayne, cr. (1763) Bt, and (1776) Bn Newhaven:
HW mentions, **7.** 177
'Lilliputian,' **33.** 127
Tunbridge Wells visited by, **33.** 127
Vesey, Mrs, makes sarcastic remark to, **33.** 127
Allen, Mrs James. *See* Fitzroy, Louisa
Allen, Rev. John (1699–1778), Fellow of Trinity College, Cambridge:
Cole plans to visit, **1.** 34, 87n
——'s opinion of, **1.** 4n
—— visits, **1.** 4
death of, **2.** 137n
fellow of Trinity College, **1.** 4, **43.** 38
HW's *Account of the Giants* entertains, **1.** 129
has seen Cole's MSS, **2.** 42
(?) painting of Henry VII's court owned by, **14.** 78

Allen, John (1771–1843), M.D.; Lord Holland's librarian:
HW's letters transcribed by, 26. 36, 37, 38, 39, 43. 232
Allen, Joshua (1728–1816), 5th Vct Allen; army officer; M.P.:
opera attended by, drunk, insulting Rigby, 38. 247
Allen, Ralph (1694–1764), philanthropist:
HW compares, to Atticus, 9. 394
peace terms called 'adequate' by, 10. 108
Pitt's bequest from, 22. 277n
wife of, 10. 228n
Allen, Mrs Ralph. See Holder, Elizabeth
Allen, William (before 1726–86), gentleman usher to Q. Charlotte:
application of, to be Mann's proxy at Bath installation, 23. 326–7, 346, 356, 362, 364, 366, 371, 408
Allen, William (ca 1749–68):
guards shoot, 23. 20, 98
Allen, William, sr:
master of Horseshoe Inn and livery stables, Blackman St, Southwark, 23. 20n
Allen. See also Allan; Alleyn; Alleyne
Alleon, —— d':
departed from Florence, 20. 431
Mann was to have been told by, about Nicoll affair, 20. 431
Allerthorpe, Yorks:
Montagu of, 9. 258n
Allesandri. See Degli Alessandri
Allestree, Richard (1619–81):
Whole Duty of Man, The, attributed to, 16. 137n, 28. 154n
Allestrie, Catherine (d. 1811), m. Henry Lyell [Hendrik Leijel]:
Du Deffand, Mme, sends parcels by friends of, 5. 414, 416
——'s opinion of, 5. 414
Allet, Bryan or Brian:
Mann gets inquiry from, about Tortola lands, 24. 168–9, 200, 220
(?) offer made by, for Tortola lands, 24. 265
Alletz, Pons-Augustin (ca 1705–85), writer:
Esprit des femmes célèbres du siècle de Louis XIV et celui de Louis XV, L'. 4. 26, 33, 37
Magasin des adolescents, Le, 8. 33n
Alleurs. See Puchot des Alleurs
Allexandria. See Alessandria
Alleyn, Edward (1566–1626), actor:
founder of Dulwich College, 11. 288
Alleyne, Mary Anne (ca 1730–1819), m. (1761) Robert Molesworth, 5th Vct Molesworth, 1793:
in Yorkshire, 39. 109
All for Love. See under Dryden, John
'All Gamesters Day.' See Twelfth Night
All Hallows, Barking, London:
image of the Virgin at, 1. 322–3
picture possibly from, 16. 185n
Alliance, American ship:
Jones escapes in, 39. 347n

Alliance between Church and State. See under Warburton, William
'Allicholy':
Shakespeare's use of, 43. 110
Allier, France:
commissioners from department of, 12. 56n
Alligators:
infest ocean, 34. 155
Alligri, Abbate, Venetian musician:
social relations of, with: Holbach, 7. 263; Macdonald, 7. 265
Allingham, ——, undertaker of the Tower of London:
(?) carpenter to the Mint Office, 19. 300n
men of, receive Kilmarnock's head, 19. 300
Allington, Cordell, m. Sir John Stanhope:
HW's ancestress, 1. 375n
Allington, Lady Dorothy. See Cecil, Lady Dorothy
Allington, Sir Giles (1572–1638), Kt:
HW descended from, 12. 165n
marriage of, 1. 374
tomb of wife of, 1. 48, 49–50, 52
Allington, Susan (1605–81), m. Sir Robert Crane, 1st Bt:
marriage of, 1. 374
Allington family:
crest of, 1. 49
HW related to, 1. 150, 43. 63
pedigree of, 1. 50, 52, 374
'All in the Downs,' ballad. See under Gay, John
All in the Wrong. See under Murphy, Arthur
Alliot, François-Antoine (ca 1696–1779), intendant of Stanislas I's household:
(?) Stanislas I reassured by, about expenses, 22. 403
Allison. See Alison
Alliteration:
HW's remarks on, 7. 373–4
Allobroges:
Matta and Senantes talk about, in Gramont, 34. 17
Allodials:
of Guastalla, Francis III sells, to Don Philip, 22. 144
of the Farnese family, in Castro and Ronciglione, 17. 204n
Tuscan: Electress's death may strengthen Spanish pretensions to, 18. 176; Naples presents memorial to Tuscan Regency on, 18. 177; Spanish pretensions to, 17. 238
Allonville, Antoine-Charles-Augustin (1733 or 5–92), Chevalier d':
(?) Pecquigny steals away from, to fight duel, 38. 322
social relations of, with HW, 7. 268
Allott, Robert (fl. 1600):
Englands Parnassus by, 16. 367
Allowances, diplomatic:
Stanley's, for equipage as ambassador to Russia, 30. 233
'All Saints'; 'All the Saints.' See Toussaint

All Souls' College, Oxford:
Chichele's motives in founding, **35**. 387
Codrington's library at, **35**. 178
HW attributes new buildings at, to Gibbs, **35**. 155n:
All Souls Day:
Arundell and Booth do not travel on, **21**. 339
*Allure, mon cousin, L'*:
verses to air of, **5**. 70
*Alma. See under* Prior, Matthew
Almac. *See* Almack
Almack, William (d. 1781), ballroom-manager; caterer:
advertisements by, **29**. 109, **38**. 512
assembly-room of, to be opened, **10**. 138
HW's letter from, on Orford's debt, **33**. 23
Almack's (club), later Brooks's:
assembly-room of, opens, **10**. 138n, **38**. 511–12
Bellenden drinks hard at dinner at, for Drummond family, **38**. 84
Blake might order a live sheep for supper at, **24**. 21
Bryant's accidental account of, **28**. 140
'buttery-book' at, **30**. 258
Clarence, D. of, gives ball at, **39**. 465n
club for both sexes to be organized at rooms of, **10**. 305
cornfields, meadows, and villages gambled away at, **35**. 423
Cumberland, D. of, attends, **38**. 512
Damer's suicide provokes moralizing over, **32**. 314
debts contracted at, **28**. 104
dullness of, **31**. 94
'Female Coterie' meets at, **32**. 67n
festino in King St by, **39**. 322
foundresses of club at, **10**. 305
Fox, C. J., shines at, **23**. 188
Fox, Stephen, and Ossory would be good recruits for, **38**. 517
Fox brothers could spend entire inheritance in few nights at, **24**. 29
gambling at, **32**. 74
HW avoids, **41**. 277
HW does not belong to, **32**. 195
HW hopes, will be re-established, **32**. 67
HW to belong to club at, **10**. 305
HW would be in fashion if he went to, **32**. 191
Hare witty at, **33**. 6–7
macaronies loll out of windows at, **35**. 458
Northumberland, D. of, loses at, **33**. 6
Pactolus dry in, **32**. 184
Parliament resembles, **24**. 81
sangfroid of an 'Almackian,' **32**. 123
Selwyn and Lady Mary Fox know stories of, **32**. 103
Selwyn gambles at, **6**. 282n
—— sits up all night at, **30**. 191
Seymour-Conway, Hon. Henry, writes from, **39**. 75
subject of dinner conversation, **38**. 530

Waldegrave, Lady Elizabeth Laura, goes to, **36**. 325
White's eclipsed by, as gaming centre, **23**. 187
Almada de Mendonça, Francisco de (fl. 1756–70), Portuguese minister at Rome:
Bourbon ministers treat, with contempt, **23**. 221
Clement XIII advised by Cardinals not to negotiate when, is in Rome, **21**. 425
—— refuses audience to, **21**. 423
——'s brief against Parma to be opposed by, from Siena, **23**. 26
Corsini treats with, **21**. 423–4, 425
—— warns, of Clement XIII's change, **21**. 426
directed by Corsini and Passionei, **21**. *383*
Jesuits denounced by, to Benedict XIV, **21**. 217n
——' suppression again demanded by, **23**. 214, **26**. 49
Mann escorts, into Florence, **21**. 436
—— given *Sentença* by, **21**. 275n
paper by, attacks Torreggiani and announces Portuguese break with Rome, **21**. 423
Portuguese arms removed from door of, at Rome, **21**. 426
Regency councillors seen by, in Florence, **21**. 436
Rome left by, for Corsini's villa at San Casciano, **21**. 426
San Casciano left by, **21**. 436
second edict of, annuls breach with Rome, **21**. 423, 425
secretary of, *see* Rodriguez, P. F. Antonio Giuseppe
Torreggiani's brief to José I given to, at Aix, **21**. 340n
Turin to be winter residence of, to escape Jesuits, **21**. 436
Villa Corsini frequented by, with secretary, **21**. 430
Alma Mater:
HW's term for: Lennox, Lady George, **31**. 355; More, Hannah, **31**. 338
'Alma Mater and her nurslings' (? verses or drawings by Mason):
HW amused by, **28**. 38, 43
Almanac; almanacs:
Beaune sends, to Gibbon, **7**. 5, 8
country topics discussed according to, **23**. 122
farmers' adherence to, **35**. 173
French regulate lives by, **31**. 72
HW jokes about, copying Arabian, **31**. 305–6
ploughman reads, **10**. 184
Rider's, HW jokes about reading, **30**. 34
*See also Poor Robin's Almanac*
*Almanach de Liège*:
predictions of, **6**. 67
*Almanach des Muses*:
Chauvelin's song attributed by, to Mme du Deffand, **6**. 26
*Almanach royal*:
Du Deffand, Mme, offers to send, to HW, **5**. 320, 322

Gloucester and Cumberland, Duchesses of, not included in, 6. 320
Almanac-maker:
HW would not be good as, 38. 486
Almanza:
battle of, 30. 55n
'Almanzor.' See Ashton, Rev. Thomas; see also under Dryden, John: Conquest of Granada
Almanzor and Almahide. See under Dryden, John
Almodóvar, Countess:
jealous, 24. 413
Almodóvar, Marqués and Duque de. See Luján Silva y Góngora, Pedro Francisco
Almon, John (1737–1805), printer; publisher:
Debrett takes over business of, 29. 213n
Gray's verses on Lord Holland printed by, in New Foundling Hospital for Wit, 28. 209
HW approached by, about writing for Opposition weekly, 22. 263n
HW calls, a rogue, 28. 126
HW informed by, of disguised gentlemen leading weavers, 38. 559n
HW's Counter-Address printed by, 28. 126n, 29. 253
Inquiry into the Doctrine addressed to, 22. 274n
Keppel's court martial printed by, 24. 427n
Letter to Jenkinson by, praised by HW, 29. 172
Mason's Heroic Epistle printed by, 28. 82, 84
——'s Heroic Postscript printed by, 28. 126–7, 129, 137
Stockdale succeeds, 29. 157n
Temple's pamphlet exhibited in shop window of, 30. 237
——'s relations with, 30. 225–6
trial of, for libel, 35. 553n
Almond; almonds:
lady carries, in pocket, 37. 22
Almond tree; almond trees:
HW recommends, to Montagu, 9. 177
one bud of, opens, 38. 155
Alms:
charity often confused with, 25. 584
Alms-boxes:
prisons hang out pewter pots as, 21. 238
Alms-houses:
in Cambridge, 13. 80
Almsmen:
George II's funeral attended by, 9. 322
Alnwick Castle, Northumberland, D. of Northumberland's seat:
Northumberlands build at, 20. 341
—— may exclude D. and Ds of Gloucester from, 36. 323
Percy, Rev. Thomas, at, 43. 309
Selby of, 11. 17n
Somerset, D. of, leaves furniture of, to E. of Hertford, 20. 10n
visitors to: March, 9. 265; Dashkov, Ps, 33. 172n

Aloe; aloes:
in quack medicine, 7. 208
late blooming of, 38. 493
virtue compared to, 33. 18
Aloisiæ Sigeæ Toletanæ satyra sotadica de arcanis Amoris et Veneris. See under Chorier, Nicolas
Alonzo. See under Home, John
Alphabet:
HW would make, of colours for different ages, 39. 296–7
parody of, 33. 500
Trollope's verses on, 28. 174
'Alphonso.' See under Congreve, William, Mourning Bride
Alps, the:
Austria expects Charles Emmanuel III to defend, 19. 478
Bentley's taste for, 35. 268
Conway considers, impassable in winter, 37. 324
HW and Gray cross, 13. 9, 189
HW avoids, by sea voyage, 17. 107
HW dreads recrossing, 13. 238
HW's description of, makes West shudder, 13. 185, 196
HW's dog seized in crossing, 17. 257n, see also under 'Tory'
HW unequal to trip over, 22. 332, 340
Kingston, Ds of, fears to cross, 24. 87n
Mann's uncomfortable crossing of, in hot July, 17. 107
Old Pretender forced to live south of, 22. 393
Robin's Wood Hill as high as, 35. 152
useless in the North, 23. 465–6
vultures might write to birds in, 35. 367
Young Pretender disappears at foot of, 23. 324
—— on other side of, 18. 384
Alresford, Hants:
Grange, the, near, 9. 222n, 12. 188n
Alsace, Cardinal d'. See Alsace-Hénin-Liétard, Thomas-Philippe d'
Alsace:
Charles, P., may invade, 18. 290, 37. 160
clergy of, protest, 34. 71n
French army bound for, 25. 546
French army goes into winter quarters in, 18. 276n
French in, reported routed, 12. 89n
Jews in, appeal against persecution, 31. 331n
Khevenhüller tells hussars to take, 18. 293
military divisions of, 6. 322
Prussians fear Austrian domination of, 12. 67n
Seven Years War extends from Russia to, 35. 290
unrest in, 11. 215n, 34. 71
Alsace-Hénin-Liétard, Charles-Alexandre Marc-Marcellin d' (1744–94), Prince d'Hénin:
colonelcy of grenadiers given to, 4. 330
dances at Mirepoix ball, 3. 217
death of, in Paris, 12. 101

[Alsace-Hénin-Liétard, Charles, *continued*]
marriage of, 3. 123, 127, 136, 152, 4. 298n, 12. 14n
Mirepoix, Mme de, aunt of, 28. 290
—— lacks influence to help, 5. 30
social relations of, with: Du Deffand, Mme, 3. *123*, 205; Luxembourg, Mme de, 4. 361; Mirepoix, Mme de, 7. 336, 340, 351
to be captain of guards to Artois, 5. 220
Alsace-Hénin-Liétard, Gabrielle-Françoise-Charlotte d' (1729–1809), m. (1755) Jacques-François-Xavier-Régis-Ignace, Vicomte de Cambis, later Comte de Cambis-Orsan; 'oiseau de Steinkerque':
afraid of highwaymen on Hounslow Heath, 11. 329
Boufflers, Chevalier de, asked by, to write verses, 6. 462
—— letters of, shown by, to Mme du Deffand, 4. 289, 305
Boufflers, Comtesse de, attached to, 5. 226
Boufflers, Marquise de, at odds with, 4. 368, 381, 5. 270
brother-in-law of, weds, 7. 84
Bushey Park visited by, 11. 329
Caraman, Comte and Comtesse de, visited by, 5. 120, 6. 210, 212, 7. 73; *see also* Roissy: visitors to
Caraman, Comtesse de, sister to, 7. 213
Chaillot visited by, 6. 357
Chesterfield translated by, 6. 461, 462, 465
Cholmondeley, Mrs, compared with, 6. 280
—— cordially treated by, 4. 477
—— in danger from, 4. 326, 327
Churchill, Lady Mary, acquaintance of, 5. 23
Coke, Lady Mary, relations of, with, 6. 56
'comédie du magistrat' read by, 7. 441
comes to England, 34. 77
Conway and Cts of Ailesbury constantly with, in Paris, 39. 218
Conway's verses to, with porcelain *déjeuné*, 6. 138, 151, 39. 243n
Craufurd's friendship with, 5. 280, 285, 286, 288, 295, 374n, 6. 482, 488, 489
Damer, Mrs, friend of, 5. 267, 7. 88
—— gets letter from, 39. 260, 43. 108
—— to bring, to SH, 39. 403–4
Du Deffand, Mme, agrees with HW's cautions against, 4. 273–4, 324, 326, 327
—— asks HW to send message to, 6. 227
—— discusses Mme de Boisgelin's finances with, 4. 366, 368
—— has not seen or heard of, 4. 273, 277, 281–2, 5. 170
—— leaves furnishings to, 8. 9, 24–6, 44
—— mentions, 4. 310, 342
——'s correspondence with, 7. 428
——'s informant, 7. 34
——'s neighbour, 6. 356
——'s opinion of, 4. 286, 322, 381, 421, 461, 5. 122, 137–8, 152, 196, 206, 260, 436, 6. 219, 431, 496, 7. 65, 150, 213, 222
——'s relations with, 4. 322, 5. 137, 142, 148,

152, 154, 426, 434, 436, 6. 227, 241, 356, 431, 499, 7. 102, 150, 222
—— tells Martha Turk's story to, 5. 438
—— to see less of, 4. 295
—— wagers with, about Mme de Châtillon, 6. 223
—— wants fan for, 5. 157
Dunkirk visited by, 7. 332
Durfort, Chevalier de, important to, 5. 434–5, 436, 438, 474n
English studied by, 6. 430, 461
Englishwomen cultivated by, 6. 241
family of, 34. 77
friend of both d'Aiguillon and Choiseul camps, 5. 13
gambles, 4. 316, 317, 326, 328, 337, 367, 461
George IV seen by, 35. 532
Gibbon's relations with, 6. 490, 7. 222
Goodwood visited by, 39. 492
HW accompanies, to theatre, 7. 336, 351
HW admired by, 4. 287
HW claims Mme du Deffand is jealous of, 6. 499, 7. 65
HW escorts, through Bushey Park, 11. 329
HW exchanges compliments with, 5. 97, 6. 227, 234
HW recommends, to Conway, 39. 201
HW's dinner might be thought 'Gothic' by, 39. 404
HW sees, at Richmond, 39. 502
HW's *Gramont* given to, 5. 305
HW's illness distresses, 7. 100
HW's informant, 15. 219n, 39. 492
HW thanked by, for kindness to Sourches, 7. 224
HW visits, 34. 80
health of, 7. 449, 461
Isle-Adam visited by, 5. 98, 403
La Vallière, Mme, writes 'portrait' of, 6. 314–15, 318
Leinster, Ds of, sends tea to, 36. 168
Lenoncourt, Mme de, friend of, 4. 338
Le Val visited by, 7. 424, 461
Lorraine visited by, 5. 23
Luxembourg, Mme de, attached to, 5. 206, 226
—— visited by, 4. 319
Melbourne, Vcts, brought by, to SH, 35. 532
Monaco, P. of, friend of, 5. 86
Montmorency visited by, 4. 319, 5. 301, 6. 499
Mount Edgcumbe, Cts of, lends coach to, 12. 41
Nicolet attended by, 7. 336
Park Place visited by, 11. 357, 360
Port-à-l'Anglois, le, visited by, 5. 396
Raincy visited by, 6. 232
Richmond, D. of, hears news of Hon. Thomas Walpole's law suit from, 36. 204
—— receives Boufflers' *Œuvres* from, 36. 196
——'s correspondence with, 7. 42, 60, 96, 97, 234
——'s friendship with, 6. 331, 338, 356, 372,

430, 441, 444, 446, 458, 461, 474, 496, **7.**
16, 108, 222
——'s portrait sent by, to Mme du Deffand,
**7.** 127
—— told by, of Mme du Deffand's bequest to
HW, 36. 181
Richmond Green house taken by, 11. 22*r*
Roissy visited by, **5.** 120, **6.** 210, 212, 462,
474, 482, 484, 485, **7.** 65, 68, 75, 150, 176, 334
Sabran, Comtesse de, friend of, **5.** 269
Saint-Ouen visited by, **6.** 342
sings, **5.** 137, 206, **6.** 219, 338, **7.** 96, 97, 98,
**39.** 208, 218
social relations of, with: Beauvaus, **7.** 444;
Boufflers, Comtesse de, **6.** 225, 241, 265,
**7.** 136, 351; Caraman, **5.** 312, 320; Caraman, Mme de, **4.** 368, **5.** 312, 320, **7.** 334,
426, 427, Châtillon, Mme de, **6.** 221; Cholmondeley, Mrs, **4.** 283, 315, 316, 317, 367;
Du Deffand, Mme, **4.** 283 to **7.** 461, *passim*;
Durfort, Chevalier de, **7.** 341; Fitzgerald,
Lord Charles and (?) Lady Charlotte, **6.**
330; Fox, **4.** 316; Garrick, Mrs, **11.** 329;
HW, **5.** 83, 86, **7.** 341, **11.** 329, **12.** 5, 203,
235, **34.** 80, **35.** 532, **39.** 404; La Reynière,
Mme de, **7.** 435; Lauzuns, **4.** 328; La Vallière, Mme de, **6.** 221, **7.** 344, 349; Leinster,
Ds of, **6.** 330, **7.** 160; Luxembourg, Mme
de, **4.** 315, **7.** 352, 448; Melbourne, Vcts,
**35.** 532; Mirepoix, Mme de, **5.** 314, 396, **6.**
329, **7.** 330, 336, 340, 341, 347, 349, 351;
Monconseil, Marquise de, **7.** 332; Montagu,
Mrs, **6.** 357; Neckers, **6.** 329, 343, 381, **7.**
441; Ogilvie, **6.** 330; Richmond, D. of, **6.**
330, **39.** 492; Rochfords, **3.** *311*; Rondé,
Mme, **7.** 345; Viry, Contessa di, **6.** 310
Stanhope, Lady Harriet, friend of, **6.** 240, 241
SH visited by, **12.** 203, 235, **35.** 532
to leave Paris, **5.** 353
to remain in Paris, **6.** 462
to return to Paris, **6.** 499, **7.** 75
Valentinois, Mme de, former friend of, **6.** 71
—— leaves money to, **6.** 71
verses by, on Mme du Deffand's tonneau,
4. 289–90
Villers-Cotterêts visit of, **6.** 342, 462, 466
Walpole, Hon. Thomas, attentive to, **7.** 222
weeps with Cts of Ailesbury at Farmain de
Rozoi's *Henri IV*, **39.** 218
Alsace-Hénin-Liétard, Marie-Anne-Gabrielle-
Josèphe-Françoise-Xavière d' (1728–1810), m.
(1750) Victor-Maurice de Riquet, Comte de
Caraman:
Boisgelin, Mme de, visits, **6.** 86
Boufflers, Comtesse de, praised by, **3.** 18
—— visits, **6.** 86
Cambis, Vicomtesse de, sister of, **7.** 213
—— surpasses, **39.** 212
—— visits, **5.** 120, **6.** 210, 212, **7.** 73
child expected by, **39.** 16
children and servants of, to give show, **5.** 269
crystal baskets bought by, **3.** 219, 237, 246,
260, 271, 277, 283

daughters of, to marry, **6.** 189, 198, 413, 419
Du Deffand, Mme, defends, to Choiseul, **3.**
369
—— may visit, **6.** 56, 212
——'s correspondence with, **7.** 425
——'s neighbour, **7.** 213
——'s opinion of, **3.** 17, **5.** 233, 436, **6.** 431
—— talks with, about Marquise de Bussy,
**3.** 18
—— visits, **6.** 86, 210
—— wishes Selwyn to be kind to son-in-law
of, **7.** 213
—— writes letter of introduction for friends
of, **6.** 28, 29, 32, 34
family amity of, **6.** 86, 210, **7.** 73
family of, 34. 77
Greville, Mrs, friend of, **5.** 323
HW asked to buy woolen material for, **6.** 246
HW attends ball at house of, **32.** 260, **34.** 77
HW compliments, **3.** 26, **6.** 419
HW may visit, **6.** 212
HW's *Gramont* given to, **5.** 306
HW's kindness to son-in-law of, **7.** 213, 217–
18, 221, 223
husband of, to go to England, **38.** 520
La Salle visits, **6.** 86
La Vallière, Mme de, puts Mme du Deffand
in good graces of, **3.** 369
(?) Mirepoix, Mme de, on bad terms with,
**6.** 270
Mirepoix, Mme de, related to, **38.** 520
—— visits, **6.** 56, 81, 86
not entertaining at Roissy, **6.** 373
O'Kelly visits, **6.** 210
'Pompom' sent to call on, in monk's garb, **7.** 2
returns from country, **5.** 120, 122, 426, **6.**
237, 380, **7.** 436
Roissy country-seat of, **3.** 369
—— occupied by, **4.** 243, 256, **5.** 260, 269, 353,
370, 404, 413, **6.** 56, 72, 210, **7.** 44, 179, 334,
346, 426, 453, 454, 460
—— to be occupied by, **5.** 225, 231, 233, 350,
**6.** 33, 49, 272, 281
Shuvalov visits, **6.** 86
social relations of, in Paris, *see index entries
ante* 8. 225
son born to, **5.** 142
Vic, M. and Mme, friends of, **6.** 29, 32, 34
visitors to, at Roissy, *see* Roissy, visitors to
Alsace-Hénin-Liétard, Philippe-Gabriel-Maurice-Joseph d' (1736–1804), Prince de Chimay:
England visited by, **6.** 366
(?) Fitzjames thought to have been at odds
with, **6.** 366
HW not acquainted with, **11.** 269
social relations of, with Richmonds, **7.** 274
wife of, 4. 367n
Alsace-Hénin-Liétard, Thomas-Philippe d'
(1679–1759), Cardinal d'Alsace:
Conclave shunned by, **21.** 207n

Alscott Park, Glos:
  West MSS at, **40**. 312n
  West of, **15**. 122n
Alsop, Robert (d. 1785), sheriff of London; lord mayor of London, 1752:
  Newcastle's controversy with, about Lovat's head, **37**. 267
Alston, Anne, m. Stephen Soame:
  husband of, **38**. 463
Alston, Carlotta *or* Charlotte, m. (1743) Francis Hare Naylor:
  assemblies given by, on Sunday, **20**. 136
  bedchamber of, has two beds, **20**. 136
  Chudleigh, Elizabeth, strikes name of, from list for concert, **9**. 329
  HW entertained by, **20**. 136
  marriage of, **18**. 268, **43**. 120
  morals of, lax, **9**. *217*, 274, 329, **20**. 136
  sister of, **38**. 463
Alston, Mary (d. 1660), m. Sir James Langham:
  print of, **1**. *179*, 188
Alston, Mary Margaret (ca 1700–84), m. (1728) Francis Hare, Bp of Chichester:
  Walpole, Sir Robert, entertains, at Houghton, **18**. 63
Alston, Sarah (d. 1692), m. 1 George Grimston; m. 2 (ca 1656) John Seymour, 4th D. of Somerset; m. 3 (1682) Henry Hare, 2d Bn Coleraine:
  Rose gardener to, **2**. 200n, **29**. 45n
Alston, Thomas (ca 1724–74), 5th Bt; M.P.:
  Address debated by, **37**. 415
Alstone. *See* Alston
Alsworth. *See* Neville
Alt, Jost Heinrich (1698–1768), Hessian minister to England 1741–68:
  Abreu and Pitt talk with, about Munster capture and Russian defeat, **21**. 315–16
  biographical information about, corrected, **43**. 275
Alta, Italy:
  Gloucester, D. and Ds of, to go to, **34**. 247
Altar; altars:
  at: Hurstmonceaux, **35**. 138; Magdalen-House Chapel, **9**. 273; SH, **10**. 61; Versailles chapel, **10**. 292; Wachtendonck's bedside, **17**. 110; Westminster Abbey, **38**. 122
  busts at foot of, on Shakespeare's monument, **35**. 151
  candlesticks stolen from, **17**. 85, **34**. 98–9
  Conway's, smoke for Venus only, **37**. 76
  Diana's, in Chersonesus, **22**. 196
  HW will build, for Mme de Sévigné's portrait, **35**. 198
  high: at Gloucester, **35**. 154; at Mereworth, **35**. 144
  in George Townshend's caricature, **21**. 78, 90
  in Leghorn public square, **17**. 303
  Methodist, is a plain table, **35**. 119
  philosophers erect, to themselves, **35**. 117
  sepulchral, procured by Mann for HW's gar-

den, **20**. 325, 333, 352–3, 365, 368, 372, 388, 391; *see also* Pedestal
  Townshend, Vcts, kneels before, in Roman Catholic chapel, **10**. 216
  *See also* Pedestal
Altar-cloth:
  Fuller's, at Magdalen and Wadham Colleges, **42**. 380n
  purple and silver, for Vyne chapel, **35**. 640
Altar doors:
  from Bury St Edmunds abbey, **2**. 30–2, 35–6, 219–21, **43**. 65
  given to Cole by HW, **2**. 327–8, 329
Altar-piece:
  at Glamis Castle, **42**. 346–7
  given to Cole by HW, **2**. 327–8, 329
  HW designs, for Westminster Abbey, **28**. 214, 216
  Mann hopes to exchange, for Correggio picture, **17**. 199
  Mason paints, for Nuneham church, **35**. 527
  too large for private houses, **33**. 487
Altar rails:
  at: Easton Mauduit, **10**. 338; Horton, **10**. 333
Altar table:
  HW's, from Bury St Edmunds, portrays Duke Humphrey and others, **42**. 246–7
Altar tablets:
  HW buys, from Ives, **16**. 184
  Lort sees, at Bonus's, **16**. 186
Altar-tombs:
  dimensions of, probably constant, **21**. 471
  Wood's tomb might be copied from, **41**. 247
Altash, Ozoro:
  Bruce mentions, **39**. 476n
Altemps. *See* Attems
Altena:
  Albemarle, Cts of, visits, **18**. 341
Altenburg, D. of. *See* Ernst II
*Alter Alexius. See under* Faustinus Cranius, Father
Althan, Michael Anton Ignaz (1716–74), Graf von; army officer:
  horse of, lost, **18**. 164
  Lobkowitz sends, to Vienna with dispatches, **18**. *486*
Althorp, Vct. *See* Spencer, George John (1758–1834); Spencer, John (1734–83)
Althorp, Vcts. *See* Bingham, Hon. Lavinia (1762–1831)
Althorp Park, Northants, seat of E. Spencer:
  art gallery at, **9**. 299
  furniture of, goes to heir, **33**. 428n
  Garrick reads plays at, **28**. 347
  HW asks Montagu the location of, **9**. 290
  HW likes, **32**. 256
  housekeeper of, surprised at HW's knowledge of portraits, **35**. 305
  Montagu wants to see, **9**. 286
  portraits at, **9**. 119n, **10**. 1n, 79n, **16**. 324n
  Raphael tapestries at, **16**. 157n, 159n
  Spencer leaves reversion of, to Pitt, **9**. 34

Stanley's suicide at, **7.** 201n, **29.** 5, **33.** 161–2
Stanley writes from, **41.** 116–17, 127
visitors to: Craufurd, **32.** 174, **41.** 281–2; Garrick, **28.** 347; HW, **9.** 5–6, 285, 299, **32.** 356, **35.** 305; Howe, Mrs, **39.** 273; Lloyd, Rachel, **39.** 273; Stanley, **41.** 116–17, 127
Althorpe; Althrop. *See* Althorp
Altieri, Emilio. *See* Clement X
Altieri, Giambattista (1673–1740), cardinal: death of, **13.** 217
Altieri, Lorenzo (1671–1741), cardinal: at Conclave, **13.** 216–17
Altiero, Ferdinando:
Dizionario italiano ed inglese owned by HW, **20.** 196n
Alum:
cunts braced with, **30.** 309
Grosvernor, Anne, tells HW to use, for teeth, **10.** 276
HW's teeth fortified by, **10.** 276, **39.** 106
Alva *or* Alba, D. of. *See* Alvarez de Toledo, Fernando (1508–82); Silva Alvarez de Toledo, Fernando de (1714–76)
'Alva, D. of.' *See* Sackville, Lord George
Alva:
Erskine of, **28.** 242n
Alvanley, Bn. *See* Arden, Richard Pepper
Alvarez de Toledo, Fernando (1508–82), Duque d'Alba ('D. of Alva'):
Germain as cruel as, **39.** 239
Watson's *History of . . . Philip II* treats, **32.** 339–40
Alvarez Ferreira, Antonio (d. 1759): burnt alive, **21.** 267n
Alvensleben, Philipp Karl (1745–1802), Graf von; Prussian minister to England 1788–90: SH visited by, **12.** 233
Alwalton, Hunts:
Neve rector of, **15.** 309n
Alziary de Roquefort, Marie-Blanche (1752–1836), actress:
(?) Berrys see, at Lyon, **11.** 140n
(?) HW prefers another actress to, **11.** 140
Alziary de Roquefort, Marie-Pauline (1743–1830), called Mlle Saint-Val; actress:
(?) Berry, Mary, sees, at Lyon, **11.** 140n
(?) HW prefers another actress to, **11.** 140
*Alzire. See under* Voltaire
*Alzuma. See under* Murphy, Arthur
*Amabella. See under* Jerningham, Edward
*À Madame Lullin. See under* Voltaire
'Amadis, Admiral.' *See* Anson, George
*Amadis de Gaule:*
Ariosto a more agreeable version of, **29.** 256
Conway longs to read, **37.** 151
Crébillon, Mme de la Fayette, and Marivaux supersede, in HW's esteem, **37.** 203
Du Deffand, Mme, cites or mentions, **3.** 134, 270, **5.** 6
—— likes, **7.** 118, 133, 136–7
—— offers, to HW, **7.** 118, 122–3, 128
—— sends, to HW, **7.** 128, 133

HW knew, by heart, **37.** 189
HW's copy of, **43.** 104
HW severe on, **7.** 136
hero's son continues the adventures of, **25.** 487
Johnston's valour worthy of, **40.** 242
Levite preferable to, **25.** 424
Plough Monday at Cambridge reminds Gray of, **13.** 74
*Traduction libre* of, *see under* La Vergne, Louis-Élisabeth de
Amalasunta:
HW's term for Catherine II, **25.** 613
Amalekites:
HW compares Hertford's sons to those of, **38.** 215
Amalia, Empress. *See* Wilhelmine Amalie
Amalia (1699–1778), Ps of Modena:
baths taken by, **17.** 65
Bologna visited by, after family rupture, **22.** 144
Braitwitz and Mme Vitelli praise, **19.** 170
Braitwitz praises, **19.** 257
Charles Emmanuel III said to give pension to, **18.** 223
Chute and Whithed see, at Bologna, **19.** 257
Craon, Princesse de, has rift with, **17.** 60, 65, **19.** 476
dinner for, at Scarperia, **17.** 56
Electress cannot arrange ceremonial with, **17.** 65, 99
expenses of, **17.** 64–5
Fermor, Lady Sophia, informed by, about HW, **43.** 169
Florence visited by, **17.** 55–6, 60–1, 64–5, 68–9, 99
Grifoni, Signora, attends, **17.** 66, 70, 78
HW sends compliments to, **19.** 257, 272–3
house at Bologna rented by, **18.** 223
itinerary of, **17.** 99
Leghorn visit of, **17.** 66, 70, 78
Lucca to be visited by, **17.** 56
Mann complimented by, **19.** 170
—— discusses HW with, **17.** 61, 64
Modena, Ds of, must be bored by, **18.** 237
presents distributed by, **17.** 64–5, 70, 78
Pucci, Mme, enters service of, **17.** 39n
Suares, Mme, entertains, with play, **17.** 104, 121
—— to give comedy for, **17.** 65, 99, 100
Amalia (1780–98), archduchess: living, **25.** 549
Amalia. *See also* Amalie; Amelia
Amalie (1752–1828) of Pfalz-Zweibrücken, m. (1769) Frederick Augustus III, Elector, 1763, and K., 1806, of Saxony:
Conway presented to, **39.** 537
Amalie. *See also* Amalia; Amelia
Amalthæa:
cornucopia of, **37.** 22
*Amant bourru, L'. See under* Boutet de Monvel, Jacques-Marie

*Amant indécis, L'. See under* Vichy-Champrond, Marie de, Mme du Deffand
*Amants réunis, Les. See under* Noverre, ——
*Amant voleur, L':*
Ossory, Cts of, tells HW story of, **33.** 375
Amat y Junient Planella Aimeric y Saint-Pau, Manuel de; viceroy of Chile 1755–61, of Peru, 1761–76:
wealth of, disregarded, **22.** 89
*Amazon,* British frigate:
West Indian news brought by, **25.** 235n
Amazon; Amazons:
Coke, Lady Mary, compared with, **25.** 564, **31.** 160, 185
—— does not send, to HW, **31.** 164
costume of, **18.** 353, 361
English, **11.** 169, 274
French, **11.** 96–7
French fishwives called, **31.** 332
HW's term for ladies watching Parliament sessions, **38.** 327
of both political parties, **25.** 477
political activities of, **34.** 41
women of fashion should not 'go aboard,' **33.** 548
*Amazones, Les. See under* Le Page, Anne-Marie, Mme du Boccage
*Ambassade, L':*
Du Deffand, Mme, sings, **4.** 277
verses to air of, **4.** 289–91
*See also under* Boufflers, Stanislas-Jean
*Ambassadeur et ses fonctions, L'. See under* Wicquefort, Abraham van
Ambassador; ambassadors (*see also* Agent; Envoy; Minister; Resident):
actor and philosopher comprise functions of, **21.** 335
apt to be failures because they resemble their masters, **22.** 212
barbarian, to Rome, *see* Cineas
Botetourt to have appurtenances of, **23.** 44n
bullying the function of, **21.** 337
Chesterfield's anecdote about, questioned by HW, **12.** 93
England and Genoa may exchange, **18.** 346
English, HW compares himself to, **32.** 53
falseness of, **21.** 167
French, forbidden to receive émigrés, **11.** 259
French court uses ministers plenipotentiary in absence of, **22.** 356
from American colonies to Holland, *see* Laurens, Henry
from Austria to England, *see* Joachim Egon (1749–1828) of Furstenberg; Kageneck, Graf Friedrich (fl. 1778–94); Reviczky; Seilern, Christian August (1717–1801), Wasner, Johann Ignaz (ca 1688–1767), Freiherr von
from Austria to France, *see* Mercy-Argenteau, Florimond-Claude-Charles (1727–94), Comte de; Starhemberg, Georg Adam (1724–1807)
from Austria to Rome, *see* Turinetti, Ercole (1717–81)
from Austria to Russia, Peter III notifies, of pro-Prussian policy, **22.** 19n
from Austria to Venice, *see* Durazzo, Conte *or* Marchese Giacomo (1718–95); Turinetti, Giovanni Antonio (1687–1757)
from Denmark to England, *see* Söhlenthal, Baron Henrik Frederik
from Denmark to Naples, *see* Osten, Greve Adolph Siegfried von der
from England to Austria, *see* Murray, David (1727–96), Vct Stormont; Robinson, Sir Thomas (1695–1770), 1st Bn Grantham; Robinson, Thomas (1738–86), 2d Bn Grantham
from England to Denmark, *see* Howard, Charles (ca 1629–85), E. of Carlisle
from England to France: Choiseul wants HW to be, **4.** 344, 356, **23.** 183; not yet appointed after Albemarle's death, **35.** 203, 207, 212; *see also* Bentinck, William (ca 1645–1709), 1st E. of Portland; Berkeley, Charles (d. 1665), E. of Falmouth; Conway, Francis Seymour (1718–94), E. of Hertford; Dalrymple, John (1673–1747), E. of Stair; Harcourt, Simon (1714–77), E. Harcourt; Harris, James (1746–1820), 1st E. of Malmesbury; Keppel, William Anne van (1702–54), 2d E. of Albemarle; Lennox, Charles (1735–1806), 3d D. of Richmond; Montagu, George (1737–88), D. of Manchester; Murray, David (1727–96), 7th Vct Stormont; Nassau de Zuylestein, William Henry (1717–81), 4th E. of Rochford; Osborne, Francis Godolphin (1751–99), M. of Carmarthen; Russell, John (1710–71), 4th D. of Bedford; Sackville, John Frederick (1745–99), D. of Dorset; Villiers, George (1628–87), 2d D. of Buckingham; Waldegrave, James (1715–63), 2d E.; Walpole, Horatio (1678–1757), 1st Bn Walpole of Wolterton
from England to Holland, *see* Dalrymple, John (1673–1747), E. of Stair; Eden, William (1744–1814), Bn Auckland; Finch, William (d. 1766); Montagu, John (1718–92), 4th E. of Sandwich; Spencer, Lord Henry John (1770–95); Yorke, Sir Joseph (1724–92)
from England to Prussia: Cholmondeley named as, but resigns, **25.** 319–20,
from England to Russia, *see* Cathcart, Charles Schaw (1721–76); Finch, Hon. Edward (d. 1771); Harris, James (1746–1820), 1st E. of Malmesbury; Hobart, John (1723–93), 2d E. of Buckinghamshire; Howard, Charles (ca 1629–85), E. of Carlisle; Macartney, Sir George (1737–1806); Stanley, Hans (1721–80); Williams, Sir Charles Hanbury (1708–59)
from England to Sardinia, *see* Capell, Wil-

liam (1697–1743), E. of Essex; Nassau de Zuylestein, William Henry, 4th E. of Rochford

from England to Spain: Mount Stuart receives promise of, **25.** 345; *see also* Fanshawe, Sir Richard (1608–66); Gray, Sir James (ca 1708–73); Harris, Sir James (1746–1820); Hervey, George William (1721–75), 2d E. of Bristol; Keene, Sir Benjamin (1697–1757); Montagu, Edward (1625–72); Robinson, Sir Thomas (1695–1770), 1st Bn Grantham; Robinson, Thomas (1738–86), 2d Bn Grantham; Stanhope, Philip (1755–1815), E. of Chesterfield; Stuart, John (1744–1814), styled Vct Mount Stuart

from England to Sweden, *see* Finch, Hon. Edward; Howard, Charles (ca 1629–85), E. of Carlisle

from England to Turkey, *see* Fane, Charles (ca 1708–66); Fawkener, Sir Everard (1684–1758); Grenville, Hon. Henry (1717–84); Montagu, Edward Wortley (1678–1761); Murray, John (d. 1775); Porter, James (1710–86)

from England to Venice, *see* Compton, Charles (1737–63), E. of Northampton; Darcy, Robert (1718–78), E. of Holdernesse

from Epirus to ancient Rome, *see* Cineas

from France to Austria, *see* Durand de Distroff, François-Marie (1714–78); Durfort-Civrac, Émeric-Joseph de (1716–87); Le Tonnelier, Louis-Auguste (1730–1801), Baron de Breteuil; Noailles, Emmanuel-Marie-Louis (1743–1822), Marquis de; Rohan, Louis-René-Édouard (1734–1803)

from France to England, *see* Azémar de Montfalcon, Jean-Balthazar d' (1731–91), Comte d'Adhémar; Barillon d'Amoncourt, Paul (ca 1630–91), Marquis de Branges; Bonnières, Adrien-Louis de (1735–1806), Duc de Guines; Broglie, François-Marie de (1671–1745); Du Châtelet, Louis-Marie-Florent (1727–93), Comte; La Luzerne, Anne-César de (1741–91), Marquis de; Lévis de Lomagne, Gaston-Charles-Pierre de (1699–1757), Marquis and Duc de Mirepoix; Mancini-Mazarini, Louis-Jules-Barbon (1716–98), Duc de Nivernais; Noailles, Emmanuel-Marie-Louis (1743–1822), Marquis de; Regnier, Claude-Louis-François de (1715–67), Comte de Guerchy

from France to Holland, *see* Affry, Louis-Auguste-Augustin (1713–93), Comte d'; Noailles, Emmanuel-Marie-Louis (1743–1822), Marquis de; Usson, François-Armand d' (1716–78)

from France to Italian states, now conciliate English, **20.** 497

from France to Naples, *see* Choiseul, Renaud-César-Louis (1735–91), Vicomte de; Clermont, Jean-Baptiste-Charles-François

(1728–92), Chevalier de; Le Tonnelier, Louis-Charles-Auguste (1733–1807), Baron de Breteuil; L'Hôpital, Paul-François (1697–1776), Marquis de; Ossun, Pierre-Paul (1713–88), Marquis d'

from France to Poland, *see* Conflans d'Armentières, Louis-Gabriel (1735–89); Du Bec-Crespin, Renée (ca 1603–59), Maréchale de Guébriant

from France to Portugal, *see* Blosset, Paul (1728–after 1780), Marquis de; Clermont, Jean-Baptiste-Charles-François (1728–92), Chevalier de; Dunn, James

from France to Prussia, *see* Pons, Louis-Marie, Marquis de

from France to Rome (Holy See), *see* Beauvillier, Paul-Hippolyte de (1686–1776), Duc de St-Aignan; Bouchard d'Esparbez de Lussan, Henri-Joseph (1714–88), Marquis d'Aubeterre; Choiseul-Stainville, Étienne-François de (1719–85), Duc de Choiseul; La Rochefoucauld, Frédéric-Jérôme de Roye de (1701–57); Mancini-Mazarini, Louis-Jules-Barbon (1716–98), Duc de Nivernais; Pierre, François-Joachim de (1715–94), Cardinal de Bernis; Rochechouart, Jean-François-Joseph de (1708–77)

from France to Russia: Peter III notifies, of pro-Prussian policy, **22.** 19n; *see also* Durand de Distroff, François-Marie (1714–78); L'Hôpital, Paul-François (1697–1776), Marquis de; Trotti, Joachim-Jacques (1705–59), Marquis de la Chétardie

from France to Sardinia, *see* Chauvelin, François-Claude (1716–73)

from France to Scotland (Jacobite), *see* Boyer, Alexandre-Jean-Baptiste de (d. 1785)

from France to Spain, *see* Beauvillier, Paul-Hippolyte de (1684–1776), Duc de St-Aignan; Montmorin, Comte de; Ossun, Pierre-Paul (1713–88), Marquis d'

from France to Sweden, *see* Gravier de Vergennes, Charles (1719–87), Comte de Vergennes; Usson de Bonac, Pierre-Chrysostome (1724–82), Comte d'Usson

from France to Switzerland, *see* Barbérie, Jacques-Dominique de (ca 1697–1767), Marquis de Courteille

from France to Turkey, *see* Huguet de Sémonville, Charles-Louis (1759–1839), Comte and Marquis de Sémonville; Puchot, Roland (d. 1755), Comte des Alleurs

from France to Venice: **15.** 81; sent to Naples, **21.** 333n; *see also* Froullay, Charles-François

from Genoa to Austria, *see* Durazzo, Conte *or* Marchese Giacomo (1718–95)

from Genoa to England, *see* Ageno, Francesco Maria

from Hanover to Imperial Diet, *see* Münchhausen, Gerlach Adolph

[Ambassador; ambassadors, *continued*]
from Holland to Austria, *see* Wassenaer Obdam, Carel George (1733–1800)
from Holland to England, *see* Boreel, Jacob (1711–78)
from Holland to France, *see* Lestevenon de Berkenroode, Matthijs (1719–97); Van Hoey, Abraham (1684–1766)
from (?) Lucca to Naples and Tuscany, *see* Diodati, Lorenzo
from Lucca to the Empire, Modena, and Parma, *see* Bernardini, Francesco Paolino
from Malta to France, *see* Le Tonnelier, Jacques-Laure, Bailli de Breteuil
from Malta to Naples, *see* Rosset de Fleury, Pons-François de
from Malta to Rome, *see* Guérin de Tencin, Jean-Aloyse (fl. 1742–7), Comte and Bailli; Le Tonnelier, Jacques-Laure (1723–85), Bailli de Breteuil
from Modena to France, *see* Cioia de Forges, Bernardo
from Morocco to England, HW resembles, 35. 303
from Morocco to Tuscany, *see* Muhemed ben Milas
from Naples to England, *see* Aquino, Francesco d' (1736–95); Caracciolo, Domenico (1715–89); Ruffo, Fabrizio (1763–1832), Principe di Castelcicala
from Naples to France, *see* Baesa e Visentelo, Don Giuseppe (d. ?1770), Conte di Cantillana, (?) Marchese di Castromonte; Caracciolo, Domenico (1715–89)
from Naples to Portugal, *see* San Severino Albertini, Giovanni Battista
from Naples to Sardinia, *see* (?) Baesa e Visentelo, Don Giuseppe, Conte di Cantillana, (?) Marchese di Castromonte
from Naples to Spain, *see* Boncompagni, Gaetano
from Poland to England, *see* Bukaty, Franciszik; Dzialynski, Paul
from Portugal to France, *see* Souza Coutinho, Dom Vicente de
from Prussia to England, *see* Knyphausen, Dodo Heinrich, Baron von
from Russia to England, *see* Chernyshev, Count Ivan Grigor'evich (1726–97); Chernyshev, Petr Grigor'evich (1712–67); Musin Pushkin, Alexei Semenovich (1732–1817); Vorontsov, Alexander Romanovich (1741–1805); Vorontsov, Semen Romanovich
from Russia to France, *see* Golitsyn, Dimitrii Mikhailovich
from Russia to Holland, *see* Golovkin, Count
from Russia to Poland, nuncio said to be illtreated by, 22. 577n
from Sardinia to Aix treaty, *see* Borré de Chavannes, Joseph; Osorio-Alarcon, Cavaliere Giuseppe
from Sardinia to England, *see* Osorio-Alarcon,

Cavaliere Giuseppe; Viry, Francesco Giuseppe di (d. 1766)
from Sardinia to France, *see* Ferrero di Biella, Filippo Francesco Maria (1719–89), Conte della Marmora; Sallier de la Tour, Vittorio Amedeo (1726–1800), Marchese di Cordon; Solaro di Breglio, Roberto Ignazio (ca 1715–65); Viry, Francesco Maria Giuseppe Giustino (1736–1813), Conte di Viry
from Sardinia to Naples, Philip Anton's imbecility noticed by, 21. 322n
from Sardinia to Rome, *see* Balbis de Rivera, Simeone
from Sardinia to Spain, *see* Viry, Francesco Maria Giuseppe Giustino di (1736–1813), Conte di Viry
from Savoy to England, *see* Carron di San Tommaso, Giuseppe Gioacchino
from Siam to France, *see* Brah Visūtra Sundara (Kosā Pān); Hlvān Kalyāna Rājmaitri; Khun Shrīvisāla Vācā
from Spain to England, *see* Abreu, Chevalier d'; Cárdenas, Don Alonso; Del Campo, Bernardo (fl. ca 1783–95); Ferrero di Biella, Marino (1721–72), Conte di Laragna; Ferrero di Biella, Vittorio Filippo (1713–77), Principe di Masserano; Luján Silva y Góngora, Pedro Francisco (1727–94), Marqués de Almodóvar; Pignatelli de Aragón, Juan Joaquín Atanasio (1724–76), Conde de Fuentes; Ronquillo, Don Pedro (1630–91); Sarmiento de Acuña, Diego (1567–1626), Conde de Gondomar; Wall, Gen. Richard (1694–1778)
from Spain to France: Minorca's surrender announced by, 25. 255n; *see also* Abarca de Bolea, Pedro Pablo (1718–99), Conde de Aranda; Grimaldi Palavicini y Spinola, Pablo Geronimo (1720–86); Guzman, Don Jaime de, Marqués de la Mina; Pignatelli de Aragón, Juan Joaquín Atanasio, Conde de Fuentes
from Spain to Naples, *see* Boncompagni, Gaetano (1706–77), Principe di Piombino
from Spain to Parma, *see* Pignatelli, Gian Domenico
from Spain to Rome, *see* Moñino y Redondo, José (1728–1809), Conde di Floridablanca
from Spain to Venice, *see* Guzmann, José Joaquín, Duca di Montallegre; Mari, Marchese Stefano (d. 1748)
from Sweden to France, *see* Creutz, Gustaf Philip (1731–85), greve; Scheffer, Carl Fredrik (1715–86), greve; Staël-Holstein, Eric Magnus (d. 1802), Baron
from Sweden to Russia, Peter III notifies, of pro-Prussian policy, 22. 19n
from the Empire to Naples, *see* Eszterházy von Galántha, Paul Anton
from Tripoli to Austria, *see* Hasan Efendi
from Tripoli to England, *see* Hūsejn Bej
from Turkey to France, *see* Said Effendi

from Turkey to Russia, *see* Hāggī Mehmed Paša

from Venice to Austria, *see* Foscarini, Marco (1695–1763); Tron, Andrea (1712–85)

from Venice to England, *see* Capello, Pietro Andrea (1702–63); Grimani, Pietro (1677–1752); Morosini, Cavaliere Francesco (fl. 1744–85); Querini, Tommasso

from Venice to France, *see* Gradenigo, Bartolommeo Andrea; Mocenigo, Alvise

from Venice to Rome, *see* Capello, Pietro Andrea (1702–63); Corraro, Pietro (1707–68); Foscarini, Marco (1695–1763)

from Venice to Russia, *see* Grimani, Gian Pietro

from Venice to Sardinia, *see* Foscarini, Marco (1695–1763)

from Venice to Spain, *see* Correr, Geronimo; Michieli, Antonio

from Venice to Turkey, *see* Diedo

HW's reflections on, **33**. 488–9

leg of, used in proxy marriage, **9**. 99, **32**. 246, **39**. 256

Macartney's profession as, **30**. 274

'many fools' sent as, **33**. 488

Moroccan, HW looks like, **35**. 303

Neapolitan, sees his legs enlarged by his spectacles, **41**. 101

public days set for visitors to, **20**. 85

taciturnity demanded for profession of, **30**. 274

Trojan, answered by Tiberius, **36**. 280

Venetian, house of, at Lago di Garda may be taken for summer by D. and Ds of Gloucester, **24**. 290

women in capacity of, **31**. 102, **32**. 209

Wotton's definition of, **21**. 276

Amber; ambers:

at Elizabeth Chudleigh's, **9**. 277

box of, HW asks, from Thomas Walpole jr, **36**. 228

hartshorn jelly looks like, **37**. 442

Ambersley. *See* Ombersley

*Ambigu:*

informal supper, **28**. 215

'Ambiguous Lines':

cited about Conway, **32**. 309

HW quotes, **11**. 186

Ambition:

and content, HW's reflections on, **1**. 91

crime and, **3**. 300

exists by destruction of everybody else's visions, **24**. 521

HW considers, a natural appetite, **24**. 516

HW lacks, **10**. 317

HW never felt, **33**. 132

HW's aversion to, **24**. 100–1

HW's reflections on, **1**. 91, **10**. 157, **23**. 367–8

HW thinks most detestable passion, **35**. 355–6

HW thinks, should be attribute of youth, not old age, **23**. 351

Pitt's verses disclaim, **23**. 387

useless unless combined with ability, integrity, and power, **36**. 249

Voltaire considers, as natural as love, **7**. 370

*Ambitious Stepmother, The.* See under Rowe, Nicholas

Amblimont, Comtesse de. *See* Chaumont de Quitry, Marie-Anne de

Amboise, Georges d' (1460–1510), cardinal: pity he had no bastard puppies, **33**. 386

Amboise (France):

Choiseul, Duchesse de, establishes chapter, college, and manufactures at, **4**. 437

couriers between Paris and, **5**. 243

doctor from, called to Chanteloup, **5**. 254

Amborssa; Ambrae. *See* Ambrose

Ambrogi, Paolo Antonio, Inquisitor at Florence:

Greek letters on seal mistaken by, for masonic symbols, **30**. 12

HW calls, 'holy blockhead,' **30**. 12

Stosch's correspondence interrupted by, **30**. 11–12

Ambrogi, Casa, at Florence:

Arno flood confines Gray and HW in, **13**. 237

Bouverie, Clephane, Fuller, and Trapp to stay at, **17**. 67, 146

Chute and Whithed occupy, **17**. 146, 154, **18**. 386

(?) Chute ill at, **19**. 216

Chute writes from 'terrazzino' of, **35**. 27

HW describes, **37**. 68

HW longs to stop at, **43**. 234

Mann houses HW and Gray in, **13**. 237n, **37**. 68

—— to call on Whithed at, **18**. 109

—— to reoccupy, temporarily, **17**. 381

(?) terrace of, enjoyed by Anne Pitt, **24**. 6

Ambrogiana, Villa dell':

(?) Stampa occupies, **20**. 116n

Ambrose, ——, of Trinity Hall, Cambridge:

'blind' verses said to be written by, **13**. 146

Ambrose, John (d. 1771), Capt.:

Genoa squadron commanded by, **19**. 55

Genoese and Spaniards harassed by, **19**. 37

inactive at Toulon, **19**. 25

Osborn succeeded by, **19**. 12n

Rowley to send, to England under arrest, **19**. 55

squadron under, from Vado, to aid Leghorn, **19**. 2n

Ambrosebury. *See* Amesbury

Ambrosi; Ambrosio, Casa. *See* Ambrogi, Casa

Ambrosia:

HW jokes about eating, **31**. 67

Ambrosian Library:

MS at, **18**. 421–2

*Ambuscade,* the, British ship:

Gwynn brings prizes to Leghorn in, **21**. 123n

—— captain of, **21**. 273n

prizes captured by, **21**. 273n, 288n, **33**. 272n

ship to be convoyed by, **21**. 132

Amelia, Empress. *See* Wilhelmine Amalie

Amelia (1783–1810), Ps, dau. of George III:
HW to entertain, 39. 510
Amelia Sophia Eleanora (1711–86), Ps, dau. of
George II ('Ps Amalie'; 'Ps Emily'):
Adolf Fredrik expected to marry, 18. 275,
277–8, 303–4, 305
Ailesbury, Cts of, drives, in small chaise,
31. 146
Aix treaty provides no marriage for, 9. 57
armchair refused by, 9. 337–8
Bath and Tunbridge acquaintance the only
topic of, 38. 344
Bedchamber ladies of, 10. 313n, 338, 12. 240,
19. 389n, 20. 34, 24. 242n, 35. 189n
Bedford's relations with, 20. 201n, 38. 567
Bedford, Ds of, congratulated by, on hus-
band's becoming grandfather, 38. 397
Bedford House has gallery for, 32. 411, 33. 2
Bedford House to be visited by, 9. 324
Bird bars, from his property, 20. 322–3
birthday of, HW promises ode on, 39. 441
Bolingbroke's relations with Cts of Suffolk
discovered by, 31. 420
brewhouse preferred by, to peerage, 33. 268
Brooke not allowed Richmond Park key by,
9. 135
Buckingham residents come to Stowe to see,
10. 314
burial of, at George III's expense, 33. 535
Bute jokingly suggested as husband for, 9.
209–10
Bute's and Gloucester's Garter installations
not attended by, 22. 79
Charles, P., rumoured to wed, 18. 278n
Chesterfield offers house to, 9. 314
Christian VII and HW entertained by, at ball
and fireworks at Gunnersbury, 23. 48
Clermont, Cts of, rebuked by, for bad manners, 35. 533
Coke, Lady Mary, accuses HW of repub-
licanism before, 31. 188
—— corresponds with, 23. 534n, 553, 556
—— helps HW receive, at SH, 31. 147
—— unable to exclude HW from card-table
of, 31. 186
—— with, at Park Place and Stowe, 31. 146
commerce played by, 39. 441
Compton, Lady Margaret, hears news of
Morice from, 33. 357
Conway talks with, 9. 334
court of, 10. 57n
crowds entertained by, 9, 337
Cumberland, D. of, dissuaded by, from Newmarket, 38. 444, 445
—— not tenderly regarded by, 38. 567
——'s bequest to, 33. 535n
deafness causes, to abandon Court and
Drawing-Rooms, 31. 153
death of: expected, 36. 241; to be wished,
39. 444
Devonshire said to have lent Burlington
House to, 9. 316
Drawing-Room of, attended by HW, 38. 494

Drawing-Rooms held by sisters and, in London, 30. 22
dresser to, 19. 427n
Duncannon's note to, 25. 368
Ferrers's trial not attended by, 9. 280
Finch, Elizabeth, presented to, 19. 389
fireworks watched by, 20. 48, 56
flattery pleases, 10. 315
Fox talks with, 9. 334
Francis III says his diamonds are bigger than
those of, 20. 57, 75
George II found dead by, 9. 311, 21. 443
—— greeted by, 18. 341
——'s bequest to, 9. 317, 21. 450, 33. 535n,
38. 79
——'s birthday ball opened by, 17. 183n
——'s will opened in presence of, 21. 450n
—— would have been shocked by infor-
mality of, 9. 369
George III notified by, of George II's death,
9. 311, 21. 443
——'s request about servants' voting rejected by, 25. 489n
——'s correspondence with, 9. 311, 313
——'s statue ordered by, 28. 472n
George IV entertained by, at Gunnersbury,
35. 533
(?) Grafton's relations with, 30. 27
Gunnersbury fire alarms, 38. 527
Gunnersbury house of, 9. 169n, 31. 163, 33.
337, 404, 406, 463, 517, 535, 35. 237n
HW accompanies, to Handel rehearsal, 25.
647–8
HW a member of circle of, 3. 45, 4. 430–1,
431–3, 29. 193
HW amuses, 39. 128
HW and Lord Waldegrave informed by, of
legacies, 33. 534
HW apologizes to, 10. 50
HW asked by, about Hertford's Irish post,
38. 536, 537
HW asked to visit, 3 nights a week, 34. 393
HW attends levee of, 9. 330
HW attends weekly parties of, since her
father died, 25. 647
HW avoids party of, 31. 188
HW by his cheerfulness tells, that Conway
spoke well, 38. 501
HW calls: 'our Princess,' 31. 153; 'vulgar,'
9. 334
HW carries candle before, at Hertford's
party, 31. 133
HW declines invitation of, to dine with
George IV, 39. 439n, 42. 160
HW does not mention, 7. 173
HW does not see, because of nephew's death,
32. 411n, 38. 358
HW gives medallion to, 4. 302n
HW gives portrait of Henri IV with verses
to, 4. 187, 189, 201
HW gives snuff-box to, 10. 328n, 31. 141
HW hears news at card-table of, 25. 368
HW inquires about, at Kensington, 9. 315

HW is Polonius to, 39. 127
HW jokes about gait of, 10. 315
HW jokes about Lady Mary Coke and, 31. 163
HW mentions, 9. 164, 23. 442, 38. 113
HW not recognized by, 9. 330
HW not summoned by, to Gunnersbury, 35. 346
HW not to wed, 10. 310, 32. 65
HW plays cards with, 6. 137, 9. 334, 337, 36. 156
HW praised by, 9. 334
HW presented by, to George IV, 25. 647
HW receives note from, 39. 442, 42. 160
HW questioned by: about Hertford's plans, 38. 536; about politics, 10. 49, 50
HW scolded by, for wit, 10. 49, 50
HW's correspondence with, 39. 442, 42. 160, 166, 167
HW's dancing at Park Place, surprises, 31. 146
HW sees Stuart Mackenzie at house of, 22. 579
HW's Historic Doubts entertains, 31. 138
HW's opinion of, 10. 313
(?) HW's verses satirize, 20. 141
HW's verses to, at Stowe, 4. 432, 435, 10. 308, 315–16, 31. 147, 39. 127–8
HW's verses to, on Gunnersbury, 33. 517–18, 39. 441–2
HW's verses to, with snuff-box, 10. 328
HW teased by, about mystery of Hertford's plans, 38. 536
HW's visitors' rules approved by, 42. 96
HW thanked by, for verses, 42. 167
HW told by: about Catherine of Braganza's faro winnings, 19. 494–5; of Augusta, Ps of Wales's health, 23. 360; to tell Hertford of Lady Massereene's gratitude, 38. 343
HW to tell story of, 32. 29
HW treated graciously by, 9. 331
HW treats, respectfully, 9. 331
HW wants copy of portrait owned by, of her grandmother, 42. 180–1
HW wonders about reaction of, to Bubb Dodington's diary, 39. 414
Hampton Court chapel attended by, in riding-clothes with dog, 37. 339, 341
Hampton Court rangership accepted by, 20. 29
Hardwicke denied key to Richmond Park by, 9. 135
health of: 31. 153; bilious fever, 23. 265, 31. 153; bled, 10. 10; blistered, 10. 10; cold, 33. 104; deafness, 10. 50, 21. 443; ill, 10. 10; purblind, 21. 443, 33. 164; rheumatism, 21. 443; strong, 10. 315; suffers, 39. 444
Henri IV admired by, 31. 141
Hertford makes HW's excuses to, 39. 274
—— makes peace with, 39. 248
—— sends regrets to, about her fire, 38. 532
——'s letter from, mentions HW's Paris visit, 38. 408

—— summoned to, by Lady Isabella Finch, 38, 81
Hesse, P. of, advised by, to take house for winter instead of using hers, 39. 262
—— visits, 32. 277n
Hesse, Ps of, death of, shocks, 31. 167
horses ordered by, to Dover, for D. and Ds of Gloucester, 36. 155n
houses of, to be sold, 33. 535
Howard, Lady Anne, accompanies, to Stowe, 10. 313–16
income of, from government, 33. 535n
jewels of, left to Ds of Brunswick, 33. 535
La Fayette's journey to America known to, 6. 445
last of George II's children, 23. 375
legacies left by, 33. 534–5
Leigh, Miss, insulted by, in Drawing-Room, 34. 258
Leveson Gower, Hon. William, called chaplain to, in HW's newspaper parody, 9. 129–30
London Evening Post prints memorial to, 20. 322
London house of, 23. 7n, 32. 65, 33. 267, 455, 535
loo-playing of, 9. 337, 369, 412, 10. 49, 20. 34, 253, 25. 368, 31. 20, (?)52, 138, 153, 38. 81, 344, 39. 273n
Lyttelton's house to be taken by, 9. 316
Marlborough House, scene of party for, 39. 377, 383
Middleton, Catharine, accompanies, to Stowe, 10. 313–16
Mirepoix, Mme de, congratulated by, on leaving off rouge, 20. 89
mob forces house of, to be illuminated, 23. 7
Monday the 'day' of, 33. 400
Montagu hopes, saw china closet at SH, 10. 84
Montpensier, Mlle de, jokingly compared to, by Montagu, 9. 332–3
name of, corrected, 43. 81
Newcastle complains of ill-usage by, 20. 120n
New Park privileges denied by, to people, 9. 135, 20. 322–3
New Park (Richmond) rangership reversion of, 9. 135n, 20. 29, 125, 233
New Park's stone lodge completed by, 20. 455n
New Park visited by, 18. 449
newspapers vilify, 33. 535
Nivernais's Jardins modernes given to, 12. 260
no longer handsome, 18. 278
Northumberland, Cts of, thanked by, 9. 334
Orford succeeded by, as ranger and keeper of Richmond Park, 9. 135n, 20. 29n, 125n
Park Place visited by, 10. 310, 311, 31. 146
Pelham told by, of North's appointment, 20. 203n
Pigot's gambling losses at house of, 39. 238
Portland, Lady, governess to, 34. 260
portrait of, 10. 338

[Amelia Sophia Eleanora, *continued*]
presentations to, **31**. *52*
Riccardi asks Mann about, **18**. 289
Richmond's fireworks attended by, **9**. 81
Rodney's alleged intrigue with, **9**. 106n
Rouen merchant to forward parcel of trees to, **38**. 279, 339–40, 345, 358, 366, 373, 379
rumoured sponsor to Ps Sophia Matilda, **32**. 129n
sacrament for rangership taken by, at St Martin's Church, **30**. 29n
Scott, Lady Jane, offended by, **31**. 147
Selwyn's joke about, **9**. 318
servants of, limited to 4 for visit to SH, **42**. 96
social relations of, with: Ailesbury, Cts of, **31**. 138, **33**. 104, 463; Ashburnham, **32**. 307; Barrymore, Cts of, **33**. 517, **38**. 379; Bedford, Ds of, **9**. 363, **33**. 104, 267, 268, 272, **38**. 344; Bedford, D. of, **9**. 363; Christian VII, **23**. 48; Clermont, Cts of, **33**. 517, **35**. 533; Coke, Lady Mary, **31**. 138, 141, 146, **32**. 164, 285, 307, **33**. 164–5; Compton, Lady Margaret, **32**. 307, **33**. 104; Conway, H. S., **33**. 463; Delmé, Lady Elizabeth, **33**. 104; Dillons, **33**. 104; Edgcumbes, **33**. 104; Finch, Lady Isabella, **38**. 397; George IV, **33**. 416, 517, **42**. 160; HW, **4**. 430, 432, 435, **9**. 330, 337, 412, **10**. 49, 310, 311, 313–16, **22**. 247, **23**. 48, **25**. 221, **31**. 138, 141, **32**. 65, 279, 285, 307, **33**. 11, 104, 159, 267, 272, 313, 333, 337, 346, 394, 400, 404, 406, 416, 455, 461, 517, **35**. 338n, 456, **36**. 156, 217, **39**. 127–8, 133, 441, **42**. 160–1; Harcourts, **33**. 463; Hertford, Cts of, **31**. 133, **33**. 104; Hertford, E. of, **31**. 133, **32**. 307, **33**. 104; Holdernesse, Cts of, **9**. 324, **32**. 307, **33**. 104, 164; Holdernesse, E. of, **32**. 307; Howard, Lady Anne, **32**. 307, **33**. 104; Howe, Mrs, **32**. 307, **33**. 104, 463, 517; Marlboroughs, **39**. 377, 383; Massereene, Cts of, **38**. 343; Mecklenburg, P. of, **33**. 517; Morice, **32**. 307, **33**. 104; Mount Edgcumbes, **33**. 463; Norfolks, **9**. 331, 337; Northumberlands, **9**. 334; Orford, 2d E. of, **20**. 29; Pelhams, **33**. 104; Spencer, Lord and Lady Robert, **32**. 307; Temple, E. and Cts, **4**. 430, 432–3, 435, **10**. 310, 311, 315–16, **22**. 247, **31**. 133, 146–7, **35**. 338n, **39**. 127–8; Weymouths, **32**. 307
society avoided by, **9**. 334
SH visited by, **9**. 331, **10**. 82, 84, **12**. 225, **31**. 147, **35**. 227, **42**. 96
strength of, that of Brunswick lion, **10**. 315
summer spent by, at St James's Palace, **18**. 218
Sussex, Cts of, Bedchamber lady to, **10**. 338
Temple builds arch to, at Stowe, **10**. 315–16
Temples' house-party for, at Stowe, **4**. 432, 435, **10**. 308, 310, 311, 313–16, **22**. 247, **31**. 146–7, **35**. 338n, **39**. 127–8
to deny rumoured match of P. of Mecklenburg, **32**. 65
Tunbridge visited by, **32**. 7

vulgarism not understood by, **11**. *265*
Walpole, Sir Robert, fishes with, **18**. 449
wealth of, exaggerated, **33**. 535
William, P., visits, **33**. 406
Yertzin, Mme de, turns back upon, at Birthday, **38**. 401
York, Edward, D. of, gives ball for, **22**. 270, **38**. 475, 476
Young Margaret, receives tip from, **10**. 82
Amelia. *See also* Amalia; Amalie
'Amelie, Lady.' *See* Darcy, Lady Amelia
'Amélie, Ps.' *See* Amelia Sophia Eleanora
Amelot, Antoine-Jean (d. 1795), Marquis de Chaillou; Mme du Deffand's relative:
Court post of, **6**. *310*, 311
(?) Du Deffand pension signed by, **8**. 38
Maurepas, unlike Turgot, wants, to succeed Malesherbes, **24**. 207n
relatives of, **6**. 315
ridiculed as secretary for the interior, **7**. 129
Amelot, Noël-Marie-François (d. 1786):
(?) attends session of parliament of Paris, **8**. 173
Amelot de Chaillou, Jean-Jacques (1689–1749), French minister of foreign affairs:
Amezaga, Marquise d', widow of, **7**. 291
Bestuchev seizes letters of, **18**. 495n
dismissal of, **18**. 409n
formerly minister of foreign affairs, **6**. 315
son of, **6**. 315
Tencin's intrigues may upset, **18**. 280
Thompson told by, of French declaration of war against England, **18**. 422
Young Pretender's departure known to, **18**. 379n
Amelot de Chaillou, Mme Jean-Jacques. *See* Vougny, Marie-Anne de
Amelot de Chaillou, Marie-Louise (b. ca 1734, living 1809), m. (1752) Claude-Sibylle-Thomas-Gaspard-Nicolas-Dorothée, Marquis de Roncherolles, 1752:
biographical information about, corrected, **43**. 86
brother of, **6**. 315
Craufurd's correspondence with, **6**. 73, 76, 88
——'s friendship with, **5**. 285, 286, 288, 362, 374, 413, **6**. 82, 221, 482, 489
Du Deffand, Mme, expresses opinion of, **3**. 363, **5**. 269
——'s relations with, **5**. 288, **6**. 315
Dijon visited by, **6**. 82
Fontainebleau visited by, **6**. 221, 223, 484, 485
HW visits, **32**. 258
house on Richmond Green taken by, **11**. *221*
social relations of, with: Caramans, **5**. 269; Craufurd, **3**. 363, **5**. 268–9, 288, **6**. 223, **7**. 352–3; Du Deffand, Mme, **5**. 269, 285, 301, **6**. 220, 278, 483, **7**. 344–5, 347–9, 351; (?) Ussons, **5**. 269
'turgotin,' **6**. 278
Amerani. *See* Hamerani
'America.' *See under* Jenyns, Soame

*America* (American ship):
(?) building of, **24**. 386
*America* (Russian ship):
Cocuffsoff commands, **33**. 214n
America, continent of (North America) [*see also* America, English colonies in; America, United States of (after 1776)]:
*Anecdotes* concerning, *see under* Hornot, Antoine
Bedford compels Louis XV to surrender, **38**. 188
Boscawen's laurels from, **21**. 297
boundaries in, **7**. 286
campaigns in, depend on Quebec's capture, **21**. 335
colonization in, **33**. 349
conditions in, may make Tortola lands worthless, **24**. 206
England at war with a quarter of, **33**. 295
England conquers, in Germany, **22**. 1, **24**. 120
England has lost most of, **24**. 287
England intends to subdue French colonies in, **21**. 261, 335
England now controls, **21**. 438
English disagreements hinder progress of war in, **17**. 207
English expect much from operations in, **21**. 306
English fleet in, dispersed by storm, **21**. 153
English-French negotiations could proceed peaceably except in, **20**. 488
English laurels in, blighted, **20**. 495
English stronger than French in, **20**. 524, **21**. 101
English want good news from, **21**. 195
Estaing's squadron in, to be reinforced, **24**. 397
European animals said to degenerate when taken to, **25**. 47
European settlers in, cruel and villainous, **35**. 240–1
Europe may be replaced by: as centre of civilization, **23**. 210, **25**. 47; as producer of genius, **24**. 149
Falkland Islands near, **23**. 239
Florentine cavalieri ignorant about, **21**. 236
Forbes's success in, **21**. 270
forts in: fought over by French and English, **20**. 506; menaced by France, **20**. 448
France may attempt coup in, **20**. 524
France may start offensive in, **20**. 504
France's territorial claims upon, **20**. 468n
France to send reinforcements to, **20**. 541
French fleet said to have sailed to, **20**. 474
French may send expedition to, **20**. 536–7
French war may break out in, **20**. 448
George III's possessions in, may all be gone, **24**. 137
glory irreconcilable with barbarism of, **21**. 290
HW cannot remember map of, **24**. 98
HW-Mann correspondence covers, **24**. 363
HW reads histories and travel accounts of, **35**. 186–7, 240–1

*History* of, *see under* Robertson, William
Indians in, start war, **22**. 177
James I did not lose, **35**. 364
Jephson should write about new empires and customs in, **42**. 292
Jesuits in, George III's aid asked for, **22**. 233
'juvenile continent,' **34**. 218
La Condamine visits, **22**. 147n
La Motte takes convoy to, **20**. 562n
Mann hopes for good news from, **17**. 35, 207, **20**. 499
maps of, **20**. 497
military operations in, difficult, **21**. 421
navigation on Great Lakes of, **9**. 308
'pitiful' continent, **31**. 21
Pitt says, may be conquered in Germany, **23**. 551, **24**. 187, **38**. 558
plunder from, **10**. 202
Sicilian paintings show world before discovery of, **35**. 409
Spanish conquests in, less cruel than slave trade, **20**. 126
thoughts of death might reduce everybody to primitive state of, **24**. 103
troops diverted from, **21**. 13
uninhabited because nobody expects to find mines there, **25**. 545
Vespucci's return from, depicted in Florentine show, **24**. 514
America, English colonies in:
agitation over, **23**. 43, 216, **24**. 67, 81, 87, 106, 114, 117, 121
Americans demand repeal of all Parliamentary acts concerning, in George III's reign, **39**. 227
Amherst won reputation in, **25**. 297n
armed rebellion in, rumoured, **24**. 45
Ashburnham-Lincoln feud may be cemented by crisis in, **35**. 246
Beckford's speech refers to freedom in, **38**. 499
Birmingham petitions Parliament to enforce acts against, **24**. 77
Board of Trade may have control of, **20**. 249, **21**. 488n
Boscawen to protect, **20**. 487n
Buckinghamshire prefers taxing, to increased land tax, **22**. 494n
Bute joins Bedford and Grenville in wanting troops sent to, **22**. 401
Campbell, Lady William, born in, **25**. 263n
Campbells, not camels, arrive in, **15**. 331
Canada invaded by, **24**. 132, 138, 156, 161, 229
Canada may be ceded to France by, in return for aid, **24**. 133
Canada said to have joined, **24**. 161
Canadians not to fight against, **41**. 312n
charters of, disregarded by England till France supported them, **24**. 401
chiefs from, throng St. James's St, **21**. 518
conciliation and force both to be used upon, **24**. 148
convicts no longer transported to, **25**. 316

[America, English colonies in, *continued*]
Conway hears news from, of war with French, **37.** 501-2
—— joins friends concerning import duties for, **41.** 82
——'s friendship to, **43.** 377
—— should humour, since they welcome Rockingham administration, **39.** 24
cost to England of losing, **25.** 255
customs posts for, held by non-residents as sinecures, **40.** 293
disputes with, to be settled by Parliament, **22.** 407, 408
Dowdeswell and George Grenville quarrel over, **22.** 566
Draper's plans for pacifying, **39.** 221
England almost ready to fight with, **22.** 401, **39.** 40
England can afford to lose, **23.** 561
England can settle in, if she loses her own island, **21.** 301
England does not try pacification with, **24.** 74
England encouraged by news from, **24.** 215
England expects critical news from, **24.** 55
England has little hope of accommodation with, **24.** 108
England imitated by, in scandal and abuse, **42.** 501-2
England may see wisdom of taxing, **24.** 208
England now hindered rather than helped by, against France, **24.** 213, 484
England passes winter in preparing punishment for, **24.** 92
England's chief hope is, **21.** 229, **37.** 556
England sends troops to, **20.** 448, 545, **21.** 56, **24.** 5, 74, 175, 193, 197, **35.** 230, **39.** 183, 197, 247
England should continue robbing Indies instead of fighting, **24.** 120
England's Indian depredations may be praised by, in future, **23.** 210
England's loss of provinces in, **2.** 84, **15.** 188
England's preparations against, **24.** 178
England's recovery of, not obtained by North administration, **25.** 259
England's relations with, serious, **39.** 40
England's sovereignty over, in dispute, **23.** 568
England's sugar colonies in West Indies seek to continue trading with, **41.** 315n
England's taxation attempts upon, **22.** 395, 494n, **23.** 550, **24.** 208, **31.** 94, **35.** 571, **38.** 508-9, **39.** 99, 108, **41.** 82
England to enslave or butcher, **41.** 347
England treats Ireland like, **39.** 325
England tries to muster a great army in, **24.** 175
England unable to cope with, even before they were aided, **39.** 330
England undone whether it enslaves or loses, **39.** 289
English army buried in, **19.** 69
English commands may not be obeyed in, **22.** 525

English conquests in, **9.** 251
English country gentlemen in Parliament probably bribe constituencies to present addresses against, **24.** 132
English defeated by, at Concord, **24.** 110, 112
English fleet could hardly control, **24.** 46
English-French war adjourned to, **35.** 222
English ministry provokes, instead of intimidating, **24.** 137
English policy towards, disliked by HW, **35.** 352 and *passim*
English politicians busy with, **24.** 92
English refugees from Charles I made, 'Old England,' **32.** 404
English slow in campaigns in, **35.** 290-1
English trading towns present addresses against, **24.** 132
English troops insufficient to reconquer, **24.** 138
English tyranny shocks, **24.** 124
English unpopularity of, **24.** 92
Fox, H. E., goes to, with regiment, **24.** 5
France and Spain may give underhand aid to, to baffle England, **24.** 124, 139
French dare not aid, for fear of Pitt, **30.** 216
Gage to seize magazine of, **24.** 98
George II strikes Mordaunt's, Cornwallis's, and Conway's names from staff for, **21.** 165n
George III's speech mentions rebellion in, **39.** 225
George IV the future 'emperor' of, **35.** 472
grain sent by, to French colonies and to Leghorn, **22.** 486
Grenville, George, opposes, **22.** 542, 567, **39.** 46n
HW jokes about pamphlets concerning, **31.** 97
HW lacks knowledge of, **24.** 38, **38.** 490, **39.** 212
HW's visions of future greatness of, **23.** 209
HW wishes success to, **24.** 125
Harley reproaches North ministry for boasting of returning zeal of, **39.** 375
Hillsborough secretary of state for, **22.** 571, **23.** 423
Holmes and Saunders sail to, **21.** 306n
Hopson and Hay to take expedition to, **21.** 56
Howe, Richard, sails to, **24.** 98
Howe, Sir William, may include men from, in army, **24.** 306
independence declared by, **39.** 288
Indians overwhelm western strongholds of, **38.** 213, 268
Italian merchants hope to get grain from, **23.** 430
Jews may be naturalized after 7 years' residence in, **21.** 341n
Kingston, Ds of, eclipses, by her trial, **24.** 191
leaders of, will not easily retire to private life, **24.** 213
Lee favours cause of, **24.** 128
Lexington battle enrages and encourages, **41.** 402

lies coined about, **24**. 198

London and Bristol merchants petition for reconciliation with, **39**. 247, 248

London merchants dealing with, to convene, **39**. 231

London mob should have sympathy of, **23**. 292

Loudoun commander-in-chief of forces in, **19**. 102n

Lyttelton changes attitude towards, **24**. 151

Methodism in, **17**. 477

news from: awaited, **24**. 226; bad, **24**. 81; Congress not mentioned in, **24**. 61; dubious, **24**. 185; encouraging, **24**. 215; stocks affected by, **39**. 250; the chief topic in England, **24**. 121

newspaper accounts of, confusing, **24**. 220

North administration never inclined towards, **24**. 143

—— ministry has lost, **39**. 326

Northumberland to be 'Vice-Adm.' of, **38**. 492, 497

O'Brien has Ordnance post in, **39**. 138

Parliamentary bill to encourage iron imports from, **20**. 135n

Parliamentary Opposition dear to, **41**. 305

Parliament's attention absorbed by, **24**. 46, 513, **38**. 490

Parliament should settle disputes with, **22**. 390

patriots from, at Leghorn, **24**. 87–8

Penn attempts mediation in, **24**. 128

Pitt (Chatham) attacks Parliament for taxing, **22**. 395

—— excludes Conway from service in, **37**. 533n

——'s chief support is from, **22**. 396

—— unlikely to allay rebellion in, **39**. 227–8

Raynal questions HW about, **39**. 212

rebellion begins in, **24**. 97, **39**. 99

regiments from Ireland sail to, **37**. 434, **39**. 247

remonstrances from, **39**. 108

'Repeal, The,' shows shipments to, **22**. 400

residents of, carried on their servants' shoulders, **23**. 240–1

Rockingham ministry's firmness against George III saves, **22**. 401, 407, 408

royal governors of, assured by Hillsborough that further taxes will not be imposed, **41**. 315n

Scotch and Irish go to, **23**. 569

secretary of state, southern department, almost severed from, **22**. 444

settlement of, will be thorny problem, **22**. 508

Seven Years' War made for, **21**. 369

ships from, reach Lisbon, **20**. 498

ships in, to be destroyed by new Parliamentary bill, **24**. 158

situation in: causes irregular dissolution of Parliament, **24**. 44; grows gloomy, **24**. 34;

pacified, **22**. 540; quiet, **23**. 78; said to be bad, **24**. 56; serious, **24**. 13

soldiers and seamen raised by, **24**. 81

Stamp Act opposed in, **31**. 94

taxation attempts upon, **22**. 395, 494n, **23**. 550; **24**. 208, **31**. 94, **35**. 571, **38**. 508–9, **39**. 99, 108, **41**. 82

tea rejected by, **23**. 550

trading towns present addresses against, **39**. 270

tranquillity of, due to English ministry, **22**. 573

transports sailing to, **35**. 230

unfashionable topic, **35**. 254

Walpole, Sir Robert, believed in conciliating, **24**. 513–14

—— did not tax, **28**. 416

—— foresaw foreign readiness to interfere in England's quarrels with, **24**. 523

Whigs in, called three millions by Chatham, **39**. 246

Whitefield returns from, **20**. 52n

America, United States of:

accounts from, mostly lies, **32**. 303

agents from, *see under* Agent

allies of, cannot be reverenced by Franklin, **25**. 338

ambassadors from and to, *see under* Ambassador

Amsterdam's negotiations with, **33**. 243n

Arbuthnot to convoy recruits to, **24**. 472

army of: Arnold rises in, and betrays it, **25**. 241n; Boston besieged by, **24**. 158; Carleton repulses, at Quebec, **24**. 215; Clinton said to have repulsed, **24**. 331; Crown Point burnt by, **24**. 261; defeated at Long Island, **24**. 248; Dunmore's clash with, **24**. 157; English defeated by, **24**. 109; Halifax said to be captured by, **24**. 138; Howe defeats, **24**. 246; Howe said to have defeated, **24**. 352; New York might be captured by, **24**. 347; reduced and unable to get recruits, **24**. 306; Rhode Island quitted by, **24**. 419; said to be besieged in Ticonderoga, **24**. 261; said to revolt but will not surrender to Clinton, **25**. 135; *see also under* War, American-English; Washington, George

battle in, falsely reported, **7**. 346

Beauchamp's arguments for Irish independence apply just as well to, **39**. 394–5, 396

bishops want 'blood and victory' in, **35**. 587

Burgoyne sails to, **24**. 98

Byron sails to, **24**. 387

campaign in: disappoints North administration, **24**. 141; looks less rosy, **24**. 282; seems to be over, **24**. 278

Canada asks for union with, **33**. 32

Canadian news from, brought by Burgoyne, **32**. 286–7

cannot be recovered, **29**. 152

capital of, will receive spoils from Henley bridge, **33**. 524

[America, United States of, *continued*]

Carlisle and Eden stay in, to make peace, **24.** 419–20

Carlisle was former commissioner to, **25.** 365n

cause of, popular in Paris, **6.** 417

caution observed by English troops in, **24.** 223

Charles III may have received mercantile agents from, **24.** 476

Charles X wants to serve in, **33.** 399n

Charleston's capture encourages English hopes about, **25.** 74

Chatham may join in debate on, **6.** 38, 138–9, 139

—— offers bill on, **32.** 234–5

Clinton said to have support of, **39.** 333

—— sails to, **24.** 98

——'s rash proclamation in, **24.** 426

colonies of: falsely reported to revolt against Congress, **25.** 321; want peace, **24.** 392

commissioners to: expected, **24.** 387; fail, **28.** 409–10; Johnstone's 'clumsy success' as, **24.** 465; leave England, **28.** 382; sent, **41.** 316; to bring North's conciliatory plan, **24.** 358

condemned to fire and sword by men afraid of crackers, **33.** 93

confiscation of property in, **33.** 50–1

Congress of: expected to be aggressive, **39.** 204; to convene, **39.** 207–8; *see also* Congress, American

constitution of, able to select best parts of various governments, **33.** 381

Conway's motions for peace with, **25.** 244, 251

——'s resolutions on, **35.** 616

Cornwallis has not yet subdued, **39.** 374

—— may succeed better against Holland than against, **33.** 256

—— sails to, **24.** 482

——'s campaigns in, *see under* Cornwallis, Charles (1738–1805)

Court party still demands subjugation of, **29.** 63

Dalrymple's news implies loss of, **25.** 88

defeat of, rumoured in Europe, **24.** 343

dependence on France as well as on England should be shaken off by, **25.** 285

distressed clergy in, **28.** 254–6

Du Deffand, Mme, disapproves of English policy towards, **7.** 78

—— disturbed by affairs in, **6.** 250, 261–2, 354, 385

—— mentions, **4.** 30, **6.** 243, 283

—— more interested than HW in, **6.** 215

—— royalist in affairs of, **6.** 386, 392, 472, 492

——'s interest in news from, **6.** 348, 356, 364, 480, 482, 495, 498

Dutch commercial agreement with, **25.** 91n

Eden's conciliatory policy towards, **33.** 243

enfranchisement of, capital feature of new era, **25.** 237

England at last gasp in, **25.** 201–2

England begs France not to dabble in, **33.** 119

England cannot maintain, if she conquers it, **24.** 336

England can spare more ships for, **25.** 72

England discusses, more fully than Europe, **25.** 116–17

England has no more men to send to, **33.** 264

England has lost, **2.** 84, **28.** 217, 277, 411, **33.** 116, **35.** 363

England has sent no troops to, lately, **24.** 448

England hopelessly alienated from, **24.** 324

England lacks news from, **25.** 78

England loses, **28.** 411

England makes head against, only by sufferance of Eastern powers, **25.** 201

England may get France to mediate with, **24.** 324

England may lose, **28.** 277

England might as well expect to rule France as, **24.** 525

England not satisfied with persecuting, **25.** 7

England not strong enough to use force in, **24.** 365

England not yet free from visions of, **24.** 525

England ruined by loss of, **39.** 409

England's conciliation of, unpopular, **24.** 359

England's defeat by, **15.** 157

England's experience with, makes her cautious in Ireland, **25.** 520

England's failure in, explained by Mann, **25.** 76

England's frenzy over, **33.** 232

England should know that France would foment any quarrel with, **24.** 523

England's insults to, shameful, **24.** 446

England's loss of, will be sufficient revenge for France, **24.** 384

England's new administration favours independence of, **25.** 285

England's provisional treaty with, signed, **25.** 347

England's quarrel with, opposed by C. J. Fox, **34.** 253

England still in suspense over, **24.** 331

England still persists in trying to recover, **25.** 99

England's troops will seldom return from, **24.** 485

England's war with, hopeless, **39.** 356

England to send more troops to, **24.** 419

England to send no more troops to, **24.** 367

England totally in the dark about, **24.** 327

England unable to replenish army in, **39.** 330

England wants commerce with, according to North's peace terms, **24.** 354

England will be hated by, even after the war, **24.** 287

England will lose other possessions in trying to recover, **33.** 290

English army and fleet in, cannot be maintained, **28.** 365

English army in, overestimated, **33.** 76

English commanders should attempt bold stroke in, **24.** 522

English connections with, great enough for a reconciliation, **24.** 329

English-French peace would not seem sincere to, **24.** 465

English-French war may save, **24.** 268

English frenzy to conquer, may be spurred by temporary success, **24.** 535

English generals declare impossibility of conquering, **24.** 474

English losses in, **29.** 90

English military measures concerning, **6.** 138, 139–40

English mistakes in, must not be pursued in Ireland, **24.** 525

English opulence may be terminated by, **24.** 228

English peace efforts with, to be forestalled by France, **24.** 369

English peace terms virtually permit independence of, **24.** 354

English policy towards, confusing, **24.** 357

English reverses in: alleged, **25.** 69–70; supported by French, **24.** 250, 345

English ships destroy coastal towns in, **24.** 161

English troops extended to, **24.** 485

European usurpation avenged by, **25.** 109

events in: not to be expected every day, **24.** 347; unimportant in London, **24.** 385

firmness with, unavailing, **33.** 173

Fitzpatrick goes to, **6.** 413, **32.** 346

fleet of, Jamaica-men captured by, **24.** 229

France aids, and trades with her, **24.** 254

France can no longer aid, **25.** 285

France does not frown upon, **24.** 262

France may assume naval superiority in, **24.** 381

France not thought to have treaty with, **7.** 4

France's advantages from, might be repeated in Ireland, **39.** 430

France's aid to, may precipitate war, **24.** 316

France said to have signed treaty with, **24.** 348

France sends stores and officers to, **24.** 309

France's relations with, **7.** 12

France thinks, disposed to return to England, **24.** 504

France will not let England reconquer, **24.** 256

Franklin and Washington should govern, **33.** 418

Franklin has not yet persuaded France to aid, **24.** 273

——'s son seized by, **24.** 230

freedom of England and, will keep earth from vassalage, **25.** 263

French alliance with, offends Maria Theresa, **24.** 396

French amazed at English sacrifice of, **32.** 257

French debt caused by aid to, **42.** 252

French fleet in, must receive decisive defeat, **25.** 83

French invasion of England would not please, **24.** 392

French naval ships supposedly gone to, **25.** 181

French negotiations would be difficult for, if England were totally crushed, **24.** 393

French officers and men to be sent to, **7.** 212

French protection for, not heard of by Mme du Deffand, **6.** 237

French rumours concerning, **6.** 366, 427, 452

French treaty with: **24.** 354; announced to Weymouth by Noailles, **24.** 363–4; does not exclude England from American trade, **24.** 364; four ships carry news of, to Congress, **24.** 369; Noailles to avow, to England, **24.** 369; not known in detail, **24.** 369; signed at Versailles, **24.** 362, **28.** 358–9

Gates joins insurgents after second trip to, **25.** 92n

——'s victory may open up northern part of, **24.** 345

gazettes optimistic over, **24.** 306

genius does not progress in, **25.** 47

George III allegedly offered bribe from, **32.** 227–8

—— 'late king of,' **32.** 224

——'s affairs in, go badly, **24.** 287

——'s obstinate refusal to appease, brought Spanish war on, **24.** 492

——'s speech pessimistic about, **33.** 106

—— wants commerce with, to be of convicts only, **35.** 535

Germain demands unlimited submission of, **24.** 282

—— might conquer, but not in Germany, **24.** 187

——'s resignation shows loss of, **33.** 325

Grenville caused loss of, **34.** 48

Grosley's remarks on, **6.** 259

HW against sending army and fleet to, **33.** 14

HW believes England will not recover, **32.** 364

HW believes nothing in newspapers about, **32.** 363

HW does not understand disputes of, **32.** 222

HW favours freedom of, **32.** 400–1, **33.** 381

HW hopes for conquest of, **32.** 325

HW in sympathy with, **34.** 163

HW knows no more of, than ministers do, **32.** 389

HW longs for poetry from, **28.** 160

HW might be going to, instead of France, **32.** 252

HW proposes neutrality, allowing France to aid, **39.** 302

HW questions possibility of reconquering, **33.** 132

HW regards, as lost, **2.** 84, **24.** 355, 481, 490, 519, **25.** 362, 559, **28.** 217

HW rejoices in freedom and independence of, **39.** 327

[America, United States of, *continued*]
HW's reflections on fate of, 32. 272, 328
HW wishes better to, than to Scots, 33. 302
HW would go to, were he young and heroic, 33. 304
HW writes of, 6. 412
Harcourt should vote for independence of, 35. 528
Hertford despairs of, 39. 354
high cost of dependence of, 33. 307
Holland and Russia may ally with, 33. 332
hot weather in, dangerous: to both armies, 24. 406; to English troops, 24. 185
Howe, Lord, returns from, 33. 65
independence of: Charles III recognizes, 24. 459n; Chatham against, 28. 379; England still protests against, 29. 118; HW welcomes, 28. 202, 262, 351; not recognized by Spain, 33. 60; recognition of, will be forced by European powers, 29. 29; Rockingham favours, 28. 349; Spain may recognize, 28. 376, 448
Ireland almost as estranged as, from England, 25. 267
Ireland favours, 32. 296
Ireland imitates, 24. 473
Ireland may now get trade of, 39. 330
Ireland would be more useful than, to France, 25. 481
Johnstone, Gov., returns from, 33. 65
La Fayette sails for, 6. 427, 435n, 445
Lauzun told he will be king in, 6. 283
Lee may be court-martialled by, 24. 215, 286
liberty of, the source of England's greatness, 24. 485
liberty still exists in, 33. 92
'lost and settled in a republic,' 34. 53
Louis XVI gracious about, 7. 33
loyalists in: abandoned by Cornwallis, 29. 168; abandoned by England, 25. 365, 369, 33. 388-9; greatly overestimated, 39. 374
majority of, said to favour England, 24. 484
Markham's views on, 2. 99
merchants from, numerous in London, 24. 116
military reverses of, 7. 158
ministers from and to, *see under* Minister
ministry no longer gives up, as lost, 24. 348
naval forces of, 7. 158
navy of, half-starves West Indies, 24. 229
news from: 6. 200, 368, 386, 387, 409, 415, 417, 424, 452, 470, 472, 497, 500, 7. 2; Mann expects, will be bad, 24. 403; Mann impatient for, 24. 189, 313, 318; Mann thanks HW for, 24. 237; Mann would not rely on, without HW's authority, 24. 270; slow and unreliable, 32. 367, 387-8, 392, 396, 397, 33. 3
North administration hates Bourbons for making England lose, 39. 333
—— administration not afraid of, 32. 405
—— administration raves against independence of, 35. 528

—— is blamed for loss of, 28. 222
——'s peace terms for, 24. 354
not submissive, 28. 178
only topic to be talked of, 32. 236
Opposition joined by Conway, only on question of, 35. 619
pacification of, 32. 206
Paine proposes Louis XVI's banishment to, 34. 180n
Parliamentary addresses on accommodation with, 25. 352
Parliamentary discussion of, 6. 138-9, 140, 145-6
Parliament eagerly promotes war with, 24. 81
Parliament fulminates against, 24. 85
Parliament may send virtual war declaration to, 24. 75
Parliament proposes negotiations with, 24. 141
Parliament's ambiguous treatment of, 28. 179
peace overtures from, unlikely, 24. 387
peace overtures may be rejected by, 24. 362
peace with: awaited in England, 29. 276-7; more important than domestic politics, 33. 342; would make HW happy, 25. 252
Pitt's followers alone acknowledge sovereignty of, in Parliament opposition, 24. 371
'Presbyterian parson' elopes with, 32. 245
Priestley to go to, 31. 386
privateers from, infest English and Scottish coasts, 24. 315
reconquest of: hopeless, 24. 302, 456, 25. 86, 259; still remote, 25. 78, 141
regiments from Ireland may go to, 32. 248
rumour of English defeat in, 6. 364
Russian troops may be transported to, 24. 127, 138, 324
St John may go to, 32. 251
Scotland's rejection of Roman Catholicism will please, 24. 439
Scots unintentionally responsible for independence of, 24. 377-8
Selwyn on concern with, 6. 151
ships of, burnt on the Delaware, 24. 386, 394
sixteen-year-old lass from, at Florence, 24. 260
smuggling vessel might sail under colours of, 33. 24
something new may come from, 5. 356
sovereignty of, assured, 24. 367
Spain may aid, 24. 459
Spain may send fleet to, 24. 224
Spain should not protect, 7. 152-3
Spain's policy towards, 33. 60
Spanish gold and French promises support, 33. 199
Spanish treaty with, rumoured, 24. 366
suspense about, 36. 152
Ternay's ships said to arrive at, 25. 70
Toulon fleet goes to, 24. 381, 386
trade of, not the only one to be lost by England, 24. 287
troops in, are in winter quarters, 24. 349

victory of, assured, **24.** 89

Winchilsea volunteers for service in, **32.** 308

Wright, Mrs, arrives from, **32.** 98

York, D. of, had never visited, **7.** 365

*See also* American Revolution; Congress; War: American-English

*Américaine, L'* (?Dutch ship):

Prudente, La, captures, **33.** 272n

American; Americans:

agent from, *see under* Agent

Amsterdam gentlemen correspond with, **29.** 89n

Burgoyne's terms from, **35.** 597

cabinet ministers will be frightened into their senses by, **28.** 213

Carleton reported to be captured by, **31.** 186

Coke, Lady Mary, calls, cruel, **31.** 186

conduct of, contradicts reputed cowardliness, **28.** 211, 217, 227, 357, **29.** 162

feather bonnets from, **17.** 357

Fort Edward abandoned by, **28.** 327–8

Gloucester, Ds of, supports, **31.** 187

HW admires, **28.** 217

HW asks if Halifax and Sandwich regret opportunity to plunder, **10.** 202

HW consigns Shakespeare to, **35.** 597

HW hopes Lady Ossory's daughters will marry, **32.** 406

HW imagines, re-discovering England, **28.** 234

HW prefers, to Scots, **33.** 302

HW's sympathy for, **31.** 187

leg of Benedict Arnold to be buried by, with military honours, before hanging him, **25.** 241–2

Opposition too spiritless to encourage, **28.** 337

Rochambeau's approach encourages, **25.** 70

Romans and Cromwellians imitated by, **32.** 248

Scots being driven out by, **28.** 270

ships of, not yet taken, **28.** 282

Stony Point captured by, **24.** 519

successes of, **28.** 321–3

temperate, **34.** 111

American Commissioners Bill *and* American Declaratory Bill. *See under* Parliament: acts of

American Revolution:

dancing-masters and, **32.** 391–2

HW's opinion of, **32.** 400–1

HW upholds, against Lady Ossory, **33.** 305

hostilities in, *see under* War: American-English

peace negotiations and proposals concerning, *see under* War: American-English

rational, **39.** 478

*Unconnected Whig's Address* discusses, **32.** 383

Amersham, Bucks:

Drake rector of, **12.** 107n

road through, **1.** 37

Ames, Joseph (1689–1759), antiquary:

Byrom's verses mention, **2.** 162n

*Catalogue of English Heads* by: **43.** 46; Cole indexes, **1.** 54–5; Granger's 'new edition' of, **1.** 56

copperplate illustrations in *Birth of Mankind* noticed by, **40.** 306n

HW's sponsor at Antiquarian Society, **13.** 28n

*Typographical Antiquities* by, **1.** 54n, 271, **16.** 145, 156, **40.** 255, **43.** 46

Amesbury, Wilts:

Cornbury portraits from, **12.** 152n, **33.** 541

Rose founds charity school at, **42.** 45

Amethyst; amethysts:

George II gives, to maids of honour, **20.** 112

intaglio of Apollo on, **21.** 457n

Amezaga, Marquise d'. *See* Vougny, Marie-Anne de

Amfreville, Chevalier d'. *See* Davy d'Anfreville, Charles-Bernardin

Amfrye de Chaulieu, Guillaume (1639–1720), writer:

Du Deffand, Mme, talks to Mme de Genlis of, **8.** 64

Voltaire alludes to, **6.** 248

Amherst, Bns. *See* Cary, Elizabeth

Amherst ('Amhurst'), Jeffrey (1717–97), K.B., 1761; cr. (1776) Bn Amherst; commander-in-chief of the army 1778–82, 1793–5:

Berrys' cousin gets ensigncy from, **12.** 88

Botetourt's quarrel with, **35.** 328–9

Canadian invasion prepared by, at Oswego, **21.** 421n

Chatham works begun by, **28.** 455

commands forces quelling riots, **29.** 70

Conway's predecessor as commander-in-chief, **25.** 296

—— succeeded by, as lt-gen. of Ordnance, **36.** 83n, **39.** 164

Crown Pt occupied by, **21.** 336n

defence plans of, **28.** 458n

Dutch war to be averted by, **33.** 156n

Eliott's and Murray's dispatches to, **25.** 136n

English army must be reinforced by, before French reassemble, **21.** 338

express arrives at Whitehall house of, **25.** 110n

fame of, **31.** 20

force under, **9.** 308n

Gage not to be superseded by, **23.** 44

Germain will not be subordinate to, **29.** 177n

Gordon examined before, **25.** 71n

HW belittles military ability of, **11.** 230

HW calls, dotard, **28.** 453

HW unable to understand, **33.** 171

hero for a moment, though 'a log of wood,' **25.** 297

Hessian troops to be conducted from Holland to Scotland by, **20.** 526n

house of, **33.** 192

inquiries about, **21.** 421

London celebrates Montreal's capture by, **21.** 437

Louisbourg approached by, **21.** 204n

——'s surrender announced by, **21.** 232n

[Amherst ('Amhurst'), Jeffrey, *continued*]
Murray's conduct to be reported to, by Pringle, **25.** 200

name of, corrected, **43.** 121

not arrived at Quebec, **21.** 336

one of 'our old ladies,' **33.** *121*

peerage and Quebec coal mines requested by, **23.** 48–9

pension and regiment resigned by, for not becoming gov. of Virginia, **23.** 44–5, **35.** 329

Pitt complains of treatment of, **23.** 61

Quebec's capture causes, to abandon move on Canada, **21.** 336n

reputation gained by, in America, **25.** 297n

Stormont asks, for Light Horse to guard Caen Wood, **33.** 184n

stupidity and incapacity of, **25.** 276, 297

Ticonderoga, Crown Pt, and Montreal objectives of, **21.** 301n

'Ticonderogicus' should be name of, for posterity, **35.** 294

Townshend, Roger, killed when looking for spy-glass of, **9,** *248*

West's painting of George III includes, **29.** 33n

wife of, **11.** 230n, 260n

Wilkes eclipsed by, **23.** 58

Wolfe recommended to, for Quebec command, **21.** 267n

Amherst, John (?1718–78), naval officer:
news of Louisbourg's surrender brought by, **21.** 232n

Amherst. *See also* Amhurst

Amhurst, Nicholas (1697–1742), poet; political writer:
*Craftsman's* editor, **13.** 119n, **18.** 20n

*Terræ filius*, echoed by Pinkerton's play, **16.** 253–4

Walpole, Sir Robert, attacked by, **18.** 20n

Amicis, ——, actor:
burletta performed by, in Dublin, **9.** 414–15

HW asks about English visit of, **10.** 4

Amicis, Anna Lucia de (b. ca 1740), m. (1771) —— Buonsollazzi; singer:
burletta performed by, in Dublin, **9.** *414–15*

HW inquires about English visit of, **10.** 4

Amiens, Bp of. *See* Dorléans de la Mothe, Louis-François-Gabriel

Amiens, Vct. *See* Stratford, Edward Augustus

Amiens, Vcts. *See* Herbert, Barbara (1742–85)

'Amiens, Monsieur':
should be restricted to one suit of clothes, **35.** 36

Amiens (France):
balloon ascent from, **25.** 543n

Bunbury, Lady Sarah, may be escorted to, **3.** 231

cathedral at: **7.** 259; Cole pleased with, **1.** 101, 103; 'good Gothic piece,' **37.** 41

HW buys great-coat at, **7.** 408

HW writes from, **3.** 2, 7, **7.** 381, **35.** 123, **39.** 7–8

inn at, *see* Aux Bons Enfants; Duc de Bourgogne

La Ferrière governor of, **4.** 285

Minden victory may open, to English army, **35.** 292

pie from, **13.** 175

suitable for over-night stay, **37.** 40

visitors to: Douglas, Ds of, **39.** 8, 9; Elliots, **6.** 420; Gray, **13.** 162n; HW, **7.** 259, 314, 324, 333, 334, 371n, **13.** 162n, **35.** 123, **39.** 7–8, 9

Amiger. *See* Armiger

Amigoni, Jacopo (1675–1752), painter:
London visited by, **20.** 341n

Walpole of Wolterton family painted by, **20.** 341–2

Amis, Aphra (1640–89), m. —— Behn; novelist:
Cowley, Mrs, apes indelicacy of, **33.** 544

*Love-Letters between a Nobleman and his Sister*, **18.** 220

*Oroonoko* by, recalled by story of Anamabu princes, **20.** 40

Ricardos, Antonio, compared to hero of comedy by, **12.** 40

Theodore of Corsica's life deserves pen of, **18.** 249

Amis, Judith, widow of Rev. Thomas Amis; m. 2 (after 1759) —— Phillips:
witness against Ds of Kingston, **24.** 195, **28.** 264

Amis, Rev. Thomas (d. 1759), Vicar of Sparsholt; Rector of Lainston, Hants:
Chudleigh, Elizabeth, married by, to Augustus Hervey, **24.** 195, **28.** 264

—— gets back certificate from, **23.** 93

*Amis à l'épreuve*, play. *See under* Pieyre, Pierre-Alexander

*Amitié, De l'. See under* Darlus, Marie-Geneviève-Charlotte

*Amitié scythe, L', ou histoire secrète de la conjuration de Thèbes:*
Du Deffand, Mme, buys, **3.** 228–9

Amity Hall, Jamaica:
Goulburn of, **12.** 79n

Ammon, god of Thebes:
George IV compared with, **32.** 305

Louis XVI represented as, **33.** 582

Ammone of Sorrento, Cavaliere di Malta:
Mann gives indigestion to, **20.** 369

San Severino to be accompanied by, to England, **20.** 369

Ammonians:
Bryant discusses, **28.** 146

HW mentions, **29.** 130

Ammunition:
for muskets, **17.** 66

France buys, from Holland, **25.** 9

HW sees carriages of, moving westward, **28.** 460

'made-up,' destroyed, **24.** 209n

Protestant Ireland lacks, **21.** 373

Prussians throw, into Moldau, **18.** 543

Spaniards receive, **18.** 296

Amoeneburg:
cannonading at, **22.** 86
*À Monsieur de Voltaire sur l'A, B, C. See under*
Saurin, Bernard-Joseph
*À Monsieur le Chancelier de Maupeou. See
under* Voltaire
*À Monsieur Marmontel. See under* Voltaire
Amor, Don Theodore Diamato:
captured at Velletri, **18.** 493, 505
*Amores. See under* Ovid
Amoretti, Signora Giustina:
actress in burlettas in London, **43.** 265
Amorevoli, Signora, wife of Angelo Amorevoli:
husband writes to, **17.** 197, 222
Mann to tell, how to write to husband, **17.**
171
Amorevoli, Angelo (1716–98), opera tenor:
Beard mimics, **17.** 435
Calais visited by, **17.** 141, **30.** 19
Chiaretta abandoned by, in his illness, **17.**
197
——'s London visit to please, **18.** 31–2
Conway, Bns, to have, sing at assembly, **17.**
334
correspondence of, in London with Italy, **17.**
148, 164, 165, 171, 197, 222, 334, 398
Dresden visited by, for summer, **17.** 478
Feroni, Mme, wants to hear, **17.** 81
HW called on by, **17.** 170
HW glad his sister is not in love with, **17.** 487
HW has, to sing at entertainment, **17.** 274
HW hears his Italian compared by, to Mann's,
**17.** 141
HW meets, at Calais, **30.** 19
HW mentions, **17.** 475
HW travels with, **17.** 141
has not sung yet, **17.** 191
health of, fever, **17.** 185, 190, 191
Holdernesse entertains, **18.** 131
London opera retains, **17.** 358, **30.** 5
Mann asked by Mme Suares to write letter of
introduction for, to HW in England, **17.**
101, 112
—— asks about, **17.** 208
—— entertains, **17.** 104
—— prefers Babi to, **18.** 526
—— receives postscript from, **17.** 240
—— writes letter of introduction to HW for,
**17.** 132
may sing in England, **30.** 5
opera directors fear, may not return to London, **17.** 478
opera ill-adapted to voice of, **17.** 79–*80*
popular in England, **17.** 211
salary of, **17.** 191
sings in Mann's garden, **17.** 240
Suares, Mme, brings, to Mann, **17.** 101
successor to, **18.** 342
too ill to sing in *Alexander in Persia*, **37.** 116
Townshend, Vcts, to entertain, **17.** 211
Vaneschi's wife kept by, **18.** 210

Venetian airs sung by, to Mann, **17.** 101, 240
yacht visited by, **17.** 141
*Amorum Troili et Criseidæ. See under* Kynas-
ton, Sir Francis
Amour; amours:
HW's reflections on, **36.** 210
*Amour diable, L'. See under* Legrand, Marc-
Antoine
Amphion, Theban prince:
Thebes's walls raised by lyre of, **39.** 505
Amphitheatre; amphitheatres:
Astley establishes, in Southwark, for riding
and rope-dancing, **25.** 451n
at Ranelagh, **20.** 47
in Boboli Gardens, **25.** 586
Roman, near Dorchester, **37.** 491
Amphitrite:
goldfish offering worthy of, **39.** 404
HW's name for Q. Charlotte, **32.** 130
mourning for, **32.** 238
*Amphitryon. See under* Dryden, John; Molière;
Plautus
Amphlett, Christina *or* Christian, m. William
Wilkinson:
Lyttelton's party with, at Epsom, **24.** 537, **28.**
480n
Amphlett, Elizabeth, m. Col. Andrews:
Lyttelton's party with, at Epsom, **24.** 537,
**28.** 480n
Amphlett, Rev. Joseph (1715–80):
(?) West has supper with, **13.** 173–4
Amphlett, Margaret, m. 1 John Perrot Noel;
m. 2 Henry Andrews; m. 3 John Gwinnell:
Lyttelton's party with, at Epsom, **24.** 537, **28.**
480n
Ampthill, Beds:
church at, has painted glass, **33.** 249
cross at, in memory of Catherine of Aragon:
**2.** 1, **32.** 53, 130, **33.** 81, 256, **34.** 112, **43.** 56;
cost of, **1.** 338n; Essex designs, **1.** 226n, 232,
235, 236, 240, 242, 296, 299, 322, 338, 339;
HW proposes, **1.** 225–6; HW's verses on,
**1.** 241, 242, 296, **32.** 146
'gentry' of, and dancing-master's daughters,
**32.** 391
manor of: a joint manor of the queens of
England, **33.** 351; Bedford holds, **38.** 433–4;
Bute has reversion of, **38.** 433–4
vestry at, as important as Parliament, **33.** 106
Ampthill-Houghton, Beds. *See* Houghton Park
House, Beds
Ampthill Park, Beds; E. of Upper Ossory's seat:
Ampthill-Houghton distinguished from, **33.**
256
'Ampthilliana,' **32.** 223
amusements at, **34.** 41
Brown landscapes, **32.** 82n
bullfinch buried under rose-tree at, **29.** 312
carpenter's shop at, **34.** 5n
coach to, **33.** 167
conveyance to, safer than to Farming Woods,
**34.** 127

[Ampthill Park, Beds, *continued*]
daughters of, have no crooked legs, **34.** 4
fire at, **33.** 583–5, 588, **34.** 4, 5
former tenants of, **33.** 249
gallery at, **32.** 70
Gibbon declines invitation to, **32.** 141
good fires at, **32.** 64
ground plan of, **33.** 256
HW an unentertaining correspondent at, **32.** 279
HW 'a retainer of the honour of,' **34.** 147
HW assumes Lady Ossory is at, **33.** 288
HW envisages Scipio at his, **33.** 552
HW not to visit, in Lord Ossory's absence, **32.** 320
HW receives present and verses from, **41.** 282
HW recommends possible treasures for, **32.** 70
HW relieves anxiety at, **32.** 396
HW's allegiance to, **32.** 130
HW's ghost will walk at, **33.** 282
HW's impromptu verses on visit, to, **32.** 368, 373–4
HW to identify pictures at, **32.** 51
HW to keep all at, in suspense, **32.** 227
HW to visit, **1.** 256, **2.** 1, **31.** 199, **32** *passim*, **33** *passim*, **35.** 482–3
HW unable to visit, **32–33** *passim*
HW uncertain if Lady Ossory is at, **33.** 120, 288
HW would like to range books at, **33.** 477
habit-maker at, in love with Lady Ossory, **33.** 139
history of, not clear, **33.** 350
Houghton 'cousin' of, **34.** 87
house at: altered by John Thorpe, **33.** 248–9; 'good,' **39.** 140
in HW's couplet, **33.** 96
letters of HW and Lord Macartney delivered at, **33.** 216, 220, 221
lines addressed to HW from, **33.** 324
Montagu fails to see, **10.** 170
'most agreeable place in the world,' **32.** 83
new library at, **33.** 476
open house at, suggested by HW, **33.** 204
Ossory, Lady, at, **28.** 326n
—— at Farming Woods instead of, **33.** 527
—— has not mentioned return to, **34.** 80
—— leaves Plymouth for, **33.** 216
—— leaving, **32.** 113
—— may have left, **33.** 32
—— reluctant to leave, **32.** 352
—— should not bury herself at, **32.** 355
—— to go to, **34.** 49
Ossory, Lord, returns to, **33.** 74
——'s seat, **1.** 226, **3.** 122n
Ossorys catch cold at, **32.** 57–8, 64
—— to remain at, till after Christmas, **33.** 429
park at, beautiful, **39.** 140
plan for garden at, suggested by HW, **32.** 57
plans of, **43.** 353–4
poetical production of, **32.** 222
post to, **33.** 7–8

seems to HW far away, **16.** 236n, **33.** 318
Selwyn unable to visit, **32.** 103, 108
sumach from, **34.** 44
theatrical activities at, **33.** 508, 552, 585, 586, **34.** 1
Vernon, Miss, will be cared for at, **33.** 241
Vernons would be missed at, **32.** 374
visitors to: Catherine, Q., **33.** 256; Dorset, D. of, **32.** 178; Fitzpatrick, Hon. Richard, **32.** 360; HW, **2.** 1, 4n, **5.** 82n, **6.** 257, 262, **23.** 313, **24.** 174, **28.** 99, 326, **30.** 268, **32.** 83, 290–1, 368, 455, **33.** 573 and *passim*; Reynolds, Sir Joshua, **33.** 571; Selwyn, **32.** 395; Tavistocks, **10.** 170; Vernon, Misses, **32.** 347; Waldegrave, Capt., **33.** 323; Warwick, Lady, **34.** 203
weather at, not sultry, **33.** 334
Ampulla:
part of Coronation regalia, **14.** 78
Amputation:
highwayman prefers death, to, **22.** 147
Amsterdam:
Ailesbury, Cts of, buys drawings at, for HW, **38.** 129, 130, 142
American negotiations with, **33.** 243n
Barthélemy compares Chanteloup to, **8.** 207
citizens of, incited by England to attack Van Berckel, **29.** 124
Fliess, Mme de, from, **12.** 242
Fox, C. J., has partisans at, **25.** 495
gazette of, *see Gazette d'Amsterdam*
gentlemen of, correspond with Americans, **29.** 89n
Gordon, Lord George, at, **36.** 246n
HW has not heard who is to burn, **33.** 256
HW unable to afford commissions to, **38.** 90
Huquier's auction at, **38.** 130n
Jonson van Ceulen's death at, **16.** 149
lie given to English concerning complaints of conduct of, **25.** 142
Pensionary of, *see* Berckel, Engelbert François van
people of, friendly to France, **25.** 3
Pichegru enters, **12.** 121n
politics expressed at, by case-knives, **25.** 496
reported insurrection at, **29.** 128
riots in, **29.** 124n
Stadthuis at, seen by Conway and wife, **37.** 286
trade with France desired by, **33.** 155
Amsterdam Gazette. *See Gazette d'Amsterdam*
Amulet; amulets:
in Middleton's collection, **15.** 16
of St. Hubert, said to cure hydrophobia, **20.** 509
Amulius, legendary king:
herdsmen of, **9.** 3–4
Amurath. *See* Murad
Amusement; amusements:
HW's reflections on superiority of, to friendships with ungrateful people, **10.** 174
*Amusement philosophique sur le langage des*

*bêtes. See under* Bougeant, Guillaume-Hya-cinthe

Amwell, Herts:
Scott, John, tries to immortalize, in verse, **28.** 257–8

*Amwell. See under* Scott, John

Amyand, Claudius (d. 1740), surgeon:
Ashton, Mrs, daughter of, **14.** 236
HW probably inoculated by, **13.** 3n
son of, **9.** 138n

Amyand, Claudius (1718–74), M.P.; commissioner of customs:
Ashton, Mrs, sister of, **14.** 236
Casley deputy to, **14.** 109n
HW called on by servant of, **9.** 138
HW might be informed by, about Cts of Ailesbury's commission, **39.** 130
marriage of, expected, **9.** 401
Richmond, Ds of, gets report from, about contraband imports, **38.** 124, 130

Amyand, Harriet Maria (1761–1830), m. 1777 James Harris, cr. (1788) Bn and (1800) E. of Malmesbury; K. B., 1779:
marriage of, **32.** 183n

Amyand, Judith (1732–?*post* 1803), m. (1760) Thomas Ashton:
marriage of, **14.** 236

Amyatt, Peter (d. 1763), chief of English factory at Patna:
deputy beheaded by Nabob, **38.** 310

Anabaptism:
HW's witticism on, **33.** 539
Leyden, John of, leader of, **29.** 217
sabbatarianism of, **31.** 436
weapons of Presbyterians used by, **31.** 435

*Anacharsis. See* Barthélemy, Jean-Jacques: *Voyage du jeune Anacharsis*

Anacreon, Greek poet:
carving of, at Horton, **10.** 334
Cowley's translation of, quoted, **12.** 108
HW lacks joviality of, **15.** 133
HW's reasons for not printing edition of, **16.** 275, (?) 276
humming old catches of, **1.** 177
'the only sensible philosopher,' **33.** 286

Anagram; anagrams:
Choiseul, Duchesse de, sends, to HW, **4.** 67
HW compared to, **3.** 55, 63, **4.** 31
knotting verses superior to, **33.** 263

Anak:
sons of, noted for height, **34.** 227, **39.** 379

Analeptic pills:
James's, **36.** 260

*Analysis of Beauty. See under* Hogarth, William

Anamabu ('Anamaboes'), Africa:
'caboceer' of, *see* Corrantee, John
'princes' of: fashionable in English assemblies, **20.** 40; *Oroonoko* resembles accounts of, **20.** 40; Richmond's fireworks attended by, **9.** 81, **20.** 56; *see also* Sessaracoa, William Ansah

Anana. *See* Pineapple

Ananias and Sapphira:
HW resembles, **28.** 103
painted glass picture of, **2.** 48

Anarchy:
attempts towards, in England, **11.** 194
despotism in hands of mob, **11.** 239
France's tyrannic, makes despotism preferable, **34.** 163
France will see acceleration of, **34.** 109
French tend towards, **31.** 329
HW's reflections on, **15.** 237–8
More, Hannah, disapproves of, **31.** 329

Anatolia:
Turkish fleet near coast of, **23.** 234

Anatomy:
Cocchi's son lectures on, in his place, **21.** 152

Ancarville (d'Hancarville). *See* Hugues, Pierre-François

Ancaster, Ds of. *See* Brownlow, Jane (d. 1736); Layard, Mary Anne (1743–1804); Panton, Mary (d. 1793); Pitt, Harriot (1745–63)

Ancaster, D. of. *See* Bertie, Lord Brownlow (1729–1809); Bertie, Peregrine (1714–78); Bertie, Robert (1756–78)

Ancaster, Dukes of:
seat of, *see* Grimsthorpe, Lincs

Ancel, ——, at the Treasury:
Astle addressed in care of, **41.** 119

Ancel. *See also* Ansell

Ancestor; ancestors:
Chesterfield's witticism about, **15.** 334
computation of, by Gray, **9.** 100, 103, **43.** 115–16
HW's reflections on, **15.** 4, **20.** 64–5, **25.** 133
Leicester's passion for, **15.** 330, 334
protected by descendants, **15.** 86, 102, 130, 134

Ancezune, Marquise d'. *See* Colbert de Torcy, Françoise-Félicité

Ancezune de Caderousse, André-Joseph d' (1696–1767), Marquis d'Ancezune:
death of, **3.** 354
wife of, **7.** 215n

Anchevilliers. *See* Angiviller

Anchin:
Lanti's French benefice, **43.** 275

'Anchises' in Virgil's Æneid:
carried out of Troy, **33.** 108

Anchor: anchors:
frigate driven from, **23.** 192
in frieze, **35.** 80
iron, made by Crowley family, **16.** 76

Anchovy; anchovies:
sauces of, **19.** 357n

Ancient; ancients:
thought lightly of death, **15.** 22

*Ancient and Modern History of . . . Rippon, The. See under* Gent, Thomas

*Ancient and Present State of Gloucestershire. See under* Atkyns, Sir Robert

*Ancient and Present State of the County and City of Cork. See under* Smith, Charles

*Ancient Funerall Monuments. See under* Weever, John

*Ancient Scottish Poems. See under* Pinkerton, John

Anckarloo, David, capt. of Swedish ship: (?) news from, **25**. 9

Anckarström, Jacob Johan (1762–92), assassin: bust of, wanted by Condorcet for National Assembly, **34**. 174–5
Condorcet praises, **15**. 237
crooked nails used by in gun, **34**. 175
forgotten, **12**. 117
Gustav III assassinated by, **12**. 6n, **31**. 375n, **34**. 139n, 175
one of worst men of 18th century, **34**. 179

Ancona (Italy):
Austrian consul at, *see* Pironi
Austrians seize magazines at, **18**. 419
English fleet reported at, **21**. 135n
Modena, Ds of, visits, **18**. 222
Neapolitan privateers at, threaten Lobkowitz, **18**. 502n
route to, from Foligno, **17**. 265n

Ancram, Cts of. *See* Darcy, Lady Caroline (d. 1778); Hobart, Lady Henrietta (1762–1805)

Ancram, E. of. *See* Ker, Sir Robert (1578–1654); Ker, William Henry (ca 1710–75); Ker, William John (1737–1805)

Ancre, Maréchal ('Marquis') d'. *See* Concini, Concino (d. 1617)

Ancre, Maréchale d'. *See* Dori, Leonora

Ancus:
quotation about, from Horace, **42**. 272

Andelot. *See* Andlau

Anderby, Lincs:
Purkis rector of, **1**. 361n

Anderson, ——:
Florence visited by, **18**. 479

Anderson, ——:
HW mentions, **37**. 425

Anderson, ——, painter:
Richard III's portrait may be restored by, **41**. 132

Anderson, Francis Evelyn (1752–1821), M.P.; army officer:
at Hampton, **11**. 57
Parliamentary membership of, corrected, **43**. 140
SH visited by, **12**. 244
wife of, **11**. 23n, 237n

Anderson, Mrs Francis Evelyn. *See* Johnston, Caroline Georgina

Anderson, James (1662–1728), numismatist:
*Selectus diplomatum et numismatum Scotiæ thesaurus*, spared by Pinkerton, **16**. 304n

Anderson, James (?1680–1739), genealogist:
*Genealogical History of the House of Yvery* compiled by, **17**. 272n
*Royal Genealogies*: **43**. 155; Aragon, Q. of, in, **41**. 445; HW jokes about reading, with Lady Mary Coke, **31**. 163; (?) Vendôme mentioned in, **35**. 509

Anderson, James (1739–1808), economist; editor:
*Bee, The*: Buchan's account of Brown and Runciman in, **15**. 189; HW's letter in, **15**. 178

Anderson, John (1726–96), professor of natural philosophy at Glasgow:
Parker's letter from, **16**. 296n
Pinkerton's letter from, **16**. 373–6
professorship of, corrected, **43**. 231

Anderson, Lt Jonathan, of 83d Foot:
express from Jersey brought by, **25**. 110n, **39**. 357n

Anderson, Mary, m. (1585) Andrew Jamesone:
George Jamesone's mother, **40**. 263n

Anderson, William (fl. 1781), woolen draper:
to convey MS to Cole, **2**. 262

Anderson Pelham, Charles (1749–1823), cr. (1794) Bn Yarborough:
brother of, **11**. 23n, 237n

Andigné de la Chaise, Joseph-François (d. 1806), Bp of St-Pol-de-Léon 1763–72, of Châlons 1772–81:
(?) social relations of, with Comte and Comtesse de Maurepas, **7**. 285

Andirons:
brazen, of Q. Elizabeth, at Beddington, **32**. 111
silver, at Ham House, **10**. 306
Ussé bequeaths, **5**. 276

Andlau, Comtesse d'. *See* Helvétius, Geneviève-Adélaïde

Andlau, Mme d'. *See* Polastron, Marie-Henriette de

Andlau, Antoine-Henri (1746–1820), Comte d':
(?) England visited by, **25**. 409

Andlau, Jeanne-Françoise-Aglaé d' (1746–1826), m. 1 (1768) Hardouin de Chalon, called Comte de Chalon; m. 2 (1795) Marie-François-Henri de Franquetot, Duc de Coigny:
England visited by, **25**. 408

Andouillé, Jean-Baptiste, surgeon:
Louis XV attended by, **6**. 48

Andover, Hants:
Butler at, **14**. 101
election candidates at, **21**. 484
HW to visit, **38**. 25
Portsmouth influential in borough of, **21**. 484n

Andrási, Adam Johann Josef (ca 1698–1753), Baron von; army officer:
Velletri attacked by, **18**. 488–9
Walpole, Bns, discusses Newton and Voltaire with, **18**. 555

Andrault, Charles-Claude (1720–92), Marquis de Maulevrier-Langeron:
made lt-gen., **7**. 147

Andrault de Langeron, Marie-Louise-Aglaé (1759–1827), m. (1779) Joseph-François-Louis-Charles, Comte de Damas:
Brienne, Comtesse de, related to, **7**. 124
finances of, **7**. 124
marriage of, **7**. 124

SH visited by, **4.** 236n

André, John (1751–80), Maj.; English spy:
Americans capture, **29.** 124n
execution of, probably precipitated by Cornwallis's cruelty, **25.** 98, **33.** 239–40

André, Pierre-Nicolas (1754–1815), called Murville:
*Adieux d'Andromaque et d'Hector, Les,* by, wins Académie prize, **6.** 354
Voltaire eulogized by, **7.** 172

Andrea, St. *See* Corsini, St Andrea

*Andrea Doria,* American brig:
*Glasgow's* battle with, **24.** 216

Andreani, Andrea (fl. 1584–1610) of Mantua:
wood engravings by, **16.** 96

Andreasi. *See* Andrasi

Andreoni, Giovanni Battista (d. 1797), singer:
(?) acts in Florentine opera, **19.** 454
(?) chairman's quarrel with, over fare, **17.** 248
(?) Conway dislikes, **37.** 50
(?) first man in *Andromache,* **18.** 128
sings at cathedral in Lucca and operas at Venice, **17.** 248n

Andrew, St:
cross of, worn in button-hole, **23.** 225
day of: favourite with Jacobites in Florence, **33.** 260; Young Pretender gets drunk on, **25.** 100
in Bagot's painting, **41.** 430

Andrewes, Lancelot, (1555–1626), Bp of Chichester, 1605, of Ely, 1609, of Winchester, 1619:
quoted, **33.** 340

Andrews, Mrs. *See* Amphlett, Elizabeth; Amphlett, Margaret

Andrews, ——:
Chute designs house of, near Donnington Castle, **35.** 642

Andrews, Bridget (ca 1698–1783), m. Philip Southcote:
death and will of, **31.** 210

Andrews, Francis (ca 1719–74), provost of the University of Dublin:
Montagu describes house of, **9.** 391
Paris traversed by, to south of France with Rigby, **38.** 427

Andrews, Lancelot, of Edmonton:
daughter of, **2.** 371n

Andrews, Mary (d. 1776), m. (1753) Edmund Keene, Bp of Chester:
Keene proposes to, through Bp of Lincoln, **20.** 347

Andrews, Miles Peter (d. 1814), dramatist:
SH visited by, **12.** 231
SH visitors sent by, **12.** 234

Andrews, Capt. Thomas (d. 1756):
French fleet attacked by, **20.** 484

*Andria. See under* Terence

Andrié, Jean-Henri d' (1693–1762), cr. (1749) Baron de Gorgier in the canton of Neuchâtel; Prussian minister to England 1738–47:
Anglo-Prussian convention signed by, **19.** 95n

Frederick II's *Rescrit* published by, **30.** 68

Osborne's *Rescrit* ordered printed and distributed by, **18.** 500n

Andrienne:
Vitelli, Mme, to wear, with lace head, **18.** 334

Andrione. *See* Andreoni

Androgeus:
Chatham calls, mayor of London in Cæsar's time, **23.** 209n

Andromache:
HW's name: for Ds of Kingston, **24.** 6, **32.** 149; for wolf of Gévaudan's widow, **31.** 61

*Andromache,* English frigate:
Cumberland, D. of, sails on, **25.** 645n
Manners dies on way home in, **25.** 278n

*Andromache. See under* Feo, Francesco

*Andromaque. See under* Racine, Jean

Andromeda:
Chudleigh, Elizabeth, resembles, **20.** 49

*Andromeda,* English ship:
William IV commands, **25.** 684n

Andronicus:
carving of, at Horton, **10.** 334

Androuet du Cerceau, Jacques (ca 1510–85):
HW has rare publications by, **41.** 258
Hôtel de Carnavalet built by, **7.** 305n, **28.** 196n, **41.** 258

Anecdotes:
not to be trusted to panegyrists, **22.** 24

*Anecdotes américaines. See under* Hornot, Antoine

*Anecdotes de la cour et du règne d'Édouard II. See under* Guérin, Claudine-Alexandrine, Mme de Tencin; Morin-Dumesnil, Anne-Louise, Mme Élie de Beaumont

*Anecdotes des Reines de France. See under* Dreux du Radier, Jean-François: *Mémoires historiques*

*Anecdotes historiques, militaires . . . [to] 1748. See under* Raynal, Abbé Guillaume-Thomas-François

*Anecdotes littéraires. See under* Raynal, Abbé Guillaume-Thomas-François

*Anecdotes of Eminent Painters in Spain. See under* Cumberland, Richard

*Anecdotes of Painting in England,* by HW:
additional lives for, *see Additional Lives*
additional prints to, given by HW to Mariette, **41.** 99
advertisement for, Gray sees, **41.** 121
Agincourt reads, for monuments to write about, **41.** 103
——'s observations on, **41.** 102–3
——'s praise of, **42.** 65n
Algarotti ignorant of, **14.** 165–6
Bannerman's plates for, **43.** 188
Barrington takes, to Montagu, **10.** 15
Bathoe sells, **15.** 92n
Beauchamp thanks HW for, **38.** 150–1, 152–3
book mentioned in, **41.** 467
Borlase praises, **40.** 288
Bowle could supply data for, on sculptors, **40.** 306

[*Anecdotes of Painting*, continued]
—— encouraged by HW to indicate errors or omissions in, **40.** 301–2
—— sends additional material for, to HW, **42.** 42–5
(?) Bridges mislays his copy of, **41.** 131
Bromfield borrows, from Winterton, finding variants, **40.** 325
—— criticizes HW's use of foreign words in, **40.** 316
—— gives HW corrections and additions to, **40.** 313–17, 319–20, 325–6, 327
Bull extra-illustrates, **2.** 273
—— informed by, that HW lacks Pass's print, **42.** 458
Bunbury praised in, **41.** 429
Burton to bring, to Montagu, **10.** 13
Bute thanks HW for, **40.** 209–10
Cambridge University library wants, **2.** 246, 248
*Catalogue of Engravers* more faulty than, **42.** 302
*Catalogue of Engravers* often mis-named as 4th vol. of, **41.** 236
Cave points out error in inscription in, **41.** 236
Charlemont and Bp of Derry only ones able to appreciate, in Ireland, **10.** 17
Charles I more favourably revealed in, than by his apologists, **16.** 151
Chatterton offers HW materials for, **16.** 101, 124
cited by HW, **1.** 244
Cole's comments on, **1.** 1–11, 15–22, 27, 36, 52, 54, 63, 72, 73n, 78, 79n, 81–3, 129, 150, 162, 317, **2.** 44
completion of: Lort glad to hear of, **16.** 160; may be long delayed, **16.** 70–1
Coucy monument not included in, **41.** 103–4, 106
*Critical Review* discusses, **10.** 248
Cromwell's funeral in, derived from Vertue's notes, **42.** 127
Cullum's inquiries resemble those in, **41.** 103
Cumberland mentions, **2.** 321–2, 324, 326
Custodis's painting of Elizabeth Brydges mentioned in, **41.** 252
Dalrymple's corrections of, **15.** 92
—— sends notes for 3d vol. of, **40.** 321
——'s missing letters concerning, **15.** 99, 101
Dassier described in, **16.** 300
Davidson thinks Hilliard was omitted from, **40.** 250
Delany, Mrs, praised in, **42.** 179
Dixon described in, **41.** 96
Dodsley reprints, **29.** 252, 253
duplicates of prints in, for Kerrich, **2.** 83, 84, 85–6, 90, 108, 111, 112, 118
Edwards writes continuation of, **42.** 71n
*Essay on Modern Gardening* first printed in, **28.** 29n, **41.** 405
Eyre's comments on, **1.** 35, 36
Farmer points out mistake in, **2.** 330

first and second volumes of: editing and printing of, **1.** 12; not given to King's College, **2.** 249, 250–1; publication of, **1.** 1n
Fitz-Othes in, **42.** 87
fourth edition of, **42.** 179, 181
fourth volume of: **10.** 307, 309; advertised, **33.** 227, 229; Bell cheated HW on, **34.** 35; Bell has not seen, **41.** 236; Cole asks for, **1.** 126–7, 139; 'completed,' **1.** 206, **15.** 133; dedicated to Richmond, **29.** 84–5, 238n; 'finished and printed,' **1.** 316, 317, **15.** 133, **23.** 266, **33.** 246–7; HW may publish no more after, **33.** 90; HW plans, **1.** 150; HW sends, to Mrs Hogarth, **41.** 416–17; HW withholds, for 9 years, **42.** 122; omission in, **33.** 246; plates for, **1.** 198, 201, 203, 207; praised by Cole, **2.** 241; printed but undistributed, **41.** 236, 405, **42.** 122; published, **2.** 233, 237, 254; reasons for delay of, **1.** 207, **2.** 235, **28.** 149, 166, 222, **29.** 83, **41.** 239; received by Hillier, **16.** 71–2, 93; reviewed, **2.** 267, 270; sale of, **2.** 248, **29.** 101; sent to Cole, **2.** 233, 235, 236–7; six hundred copies of, printed, **33.** 246–7; to be printed, **1.** 198, 201, 203; to be published, **35.** 508; Zouch eager to see, **16.** 35
frontispiece to, HW seeks stained glass portraits for, **9.** 326
Garrick to borrow, from Hawkins, **40.** 229
Gaynsborough inscription sought for, **40.** 234
Granger sends errata for, **41.** 186–8
Gray collects artists for, **14.** 117
—— desirous of interleaving his copy of, **14.** 121
—— enthusiastic about, **9.** 326
—— mentions, **14.** 166
—— sends HW passage for new edition of, **14.** 175
Guilford and Frederick Montagu like, **10.** 20
HW about to print, **9.** 326
HW accused of starving the illustrators of, **43.** 195
HW and Hogarth discuss, **9.** 365–6
HW apologizes for, **15.** 141–2, **42.** 209
HW asks about Cts of Lincoln's portrait for, **40.** 174
HW asks Dalrymple to correct, **15.** 75, 85
HW at work on, **13.** 33, 34, 35–6, 37, 46
HW avoids offending descendants of artists mentioned in, **40.** 352, 354
HW begins, **16.** 27, 32, 36–7
HW belittles, **16.** 51–2
HW continues to annotate, without reprinting it, **42.** 254
HW corrects Montagu's mistake about, **9.** 416
HW dedicates, to Bns Hervey, **31.** 24, 416, 428
HW discusses materials for, with Zouch, **16.** 26, 29, 35–7, 40, 41, 42, 45–52
HW does not care about minor errors in, **2.** 300
HW does not think about new edition of, **42.** 72, 107
HW explains omissions from, **40.** 310

HW gives, to: Bibliothèque du Roi, **41**. 58n; Bute, **41**. 209; Chute, **41**. 419; Coke, Lady Mary, **31**. 201, 297; Cole, **1**. 127, 129, **2**. 233, 235, 236–7; Cowslade, **41**. 420; Delany, Mrs, **42**. 179, 181; Ducarel, **40**. 212; Forcalquier, Mme de, **7**. 415; Gray, **14**. 121, 122, 133; Hamilton, Mary, **31**. 214; Harcourt, **35**. 493; Hawkins, **40**. 227; Hertford, **38**. 323, 328; Hillier, **16**. 93, 94; Hogarth, Mrs, **41**. 416; Holland, **34**. 92; Lincoln, **30**. 165; Lort, **16**. 142; Lucan, Lady, **41**. 418; Mann, **22**. 10, 20, 49; Montagu, **9**. 415, **10**. 11, 13, 15, 17, 20, 145, 146; Ossory, Lady, **32**. 41, **33**. 237; Ratcliffe, **40**. 236; Stanislas II, **42**. 162–4; (?) Vorontsov, **40**. 308–9; Zouch, **16**. 45, **43**. 184, 217

HW has slender hope of success for, **15**. 75

HW has to pay high price for copy of, for Stanislas II, **36**. 238, 281

HW inserts print of Cts of Exeter in, **1**. 150, **43**. 53

HW might have included Gunter in, **42**. 107

HW might include (?) Böhm's compliments as testimonial in, **38**. 359

HW needs Bacon's portrait for, **40**. 193–4, 196–7

HW offers copy of, to Scottish society of antiquaries, **15**. 158

HW often fails to remember things in, **16**. 207

HW reprints, **1**. 373, **16**. 53, **40**. 324, **41**. 455

HW's aim in, **2**. 300

HW's copy of 1st edn of, **1**. 150, **2**. 248n, **43**. 154

HW's progress on, **15**. 72, **16**. 40

HW to continue annotating without reprinting it, **42**. 254

HW too old to revise, **42**. 305

HW tries not to offend descendants of artists mentioned in, **40**. 352, 354

HW uses magnifying glass in compiling, **16**. 299

HW writes, **9**. 292, 304, **38**. 59

HW writes, at night, **38**. 94

(?) Hardwicke wants, **41**. 284

Hawkins thanks HW for, **40**. 227

Henry VI's picture in, compared with Fenn's drawing, **42**. 98, 100, 105

Hillier searches, for mention of Greenwich Palace, **16**. 71–2

Hogarth's article in, to be revised in new edition, **41**. 450–1

—— 's fame established by, **42**. 153

—— wants to correct, **9**. 365–6

Holbein's responsibility for painting at Basle questioned in, **16**. 146

Hutchins given extract from, **41**. 205

in the press, **16**. 41

Irish would not appreciate, **10**. 20

Jamesone's life to be inserted in, **40**. 260, 269

Jamisone hopes for second edition of, **40**. 285–6

*Journal encyclopédique* reviews, **3**. 138

Lely's portrait in, **41**. 98

Lort's remarks on, **16**. 159

Malone sends notes on Van Dyck for, **41**. 465

Mariettte translates, **7**. 269, **41**. 99n

Masters's comments on, **1**. 22–6, **28**. 247n

Mason refers to, **25**. 195n, **28**. 4, 465, **29**. 80, 125n

Maty's notice of, in *New Review*, **35**. 514

Montagu may have, bound in Ireland, **10**. 13

—— to show, to Charlemont and Bp of Derry, **10**. 17

—— unable to purchase, **10**. 142

Montagu, Charles, said to have borrowed, **10**. 66

new edition of, **1**. 373, **10**. 142, 145, 146, 248, **14**. 175, **23**. 266, **29**. 150, **33**. 573–4, **41**. 450–1, 455; *see also* second edition of; third edition of

*New Oxford Guide* quotes, **35**. 462n

number of copies printed of, corrected, **43**. 72

obscure artists necessarily included in, **15**. 86

painter's bill in, **16**. 133

painters of various reigns mentioned in, **42**. 442

Panton sends to HW items from Wynn's accounts, naming people in, **41**. 160

Parkin sends information for, **40**. 222–3

pays for itself, **28**. 23n

Petitot article in, **40**. 238

Ponz questions account in, of Raphael cartoons, **16**. 169

Pope's mother mentioned in, **29**. 279

popular, **10**. 15, 142

popular topics avoided in, **9**. 326

Presbyterians offended by passage in, **15**. 109

price of, **2**. 246, 282, 284, 319, **10**. 66, 146, **15**. 98

printer of, runs away, **9**. 411, 416–17, **15**. 76

printing of, **31**. 154, **43**. 39, 126, 132, 217

publication of: expected but delayed, **9**. 398, 416–17, **10**. 10, **15**. 76, **16**. 45; will elicit new information, **40**. 220

rarity of, **10**. 66, **33**. 573–4, **36**. 238, 281

Reeve offers aid for, **40**. 230–1

Richardson conveys, to Zouch, **16**. 45

Roscommon's portrait attributed in, to Maratti, **42**. 159

second edition of: **16**. 106, **23**. 266, **29**. 150, **40**. 367–8, **43**. 49; too far advanced for further corrections, **40**. 324

Sharp sends remarks on, **40**. 253

Simon brothers omitted from, **40**. 238

size of, **15**. 103

size of editions of, **2**. 248

Smith, John, corrects, **1**. 167

social customs in, **40**. 209–10, 220

third edition of, **2**. 280, 282, 319, 326, **15**. 158, **41**. 450–1, 455, **42**. 20, **43**. 74

third volume of: **1**. 53, 57–8, 61, 65, **14**. 130, 132, 133, **15**. 94, 198, **43**. 132; published, **1**. 53, **15**. 92, **16**. 53, 54, 157, 160, **28**. 2–3; (?) second edition of, **43**. 47

[*Anecdotes of Painting*, continued]
Thornhill article in: sent to Hutchins, **41.** 205; to appear later, **40.** 310, 381
Thorpe added to, **42.** 20
Tyson's corrections for, **1.** 169–72, 175
Vertue's materials for, arranged by HW, **15.** 72, **16.** 133, 299, **40.** 288, 309, 354
Walker thanked by HW for notes on, **42.** 305
Warburton is incensed by passage in, **13.** 38–9, **40.** 228
West compliments HW on, **40.** 311–12
Wren article in, criticized by grandson, **40.** 345–54
Wright, Michael, mentioned in, **32.** 52
Zouch eager to see specimen of, **16.** 35
—— makes too generous a return for, **16.** 54
'Anecdotes of Painting in Scotland':
Kirgate transcribes, from *Weekly Magazine*, **42.** 72n
*Anecdotes of Polite Literature*:
booksellers' compilation, **15.** 93
HW abused by, for defending father, **1.** 57
*Anecdotes of the Late Samuel Johnson. See under* Salusbury, Hester Lynch, Mrs Piozzi
'Anecdotes of the Streets of London and other places,' by HW:
Cole sends notes for, **1.** 137–8, 148
HW plans, **1.** 134, 194
*Anecdotes sur la révolution de Russie. See under* Rulhière, Claude-Carloman de
*Anecdotes sur la vie de Mme du Barry. See under* Pidansat de Mairobert, Mathieu-François
*Anello del Piscatore* (Pope's ring):
Chute's witticism about, **21.** 52
Anemone:
HW mentions, **21.** 113
Anfossi, Pasquale (1727–97), composer:
*Viaggiatori felici, I*, seen by HW, **25.** 242, **33.** 322
Anfreville, Chevalier d'. *See* Davy d'Anfreville, Charles-Bernardin
Angara. *See* Lángara
Angel; angels:
cannot get pensions and salaries in France, **39.** 143
choristers sing like, **38.** 87
Du Barry, Comtesse, saves, **31.** 157–8
fallen, Milton's description of, **37.** 92
HW's reflections on, **10.** 291, **33.** 523–4
'Angel,' the, in John St in the Minories:
Shuter performs at, **32.** 244n
Angelelli, Angelo:
Malvezzi's son adopted by, **22.** 374n
Angelelli, Marchese Roberto (d. 1784), Bolognese *maestro di camera* to Cardinal York:
servant of, sent to Young Pretender, **22.** 374
York, Cardinal, arrives at Bologna house of, **20,** 332n
Angeli family:
art collection of, at Rome, **23.** 570n
Angelini Bontempi. *See* Bontempi

Angélique, Mme de Choiseul's femme de chambre. *See* Corbie, Mme (?)Angélique
Angelis, Cesare Crescenzi de (ca 1705–65), Bp of Segni 1755–65:
Clement XIII sends, to Corsica, **21.** 393, 411
Angelo, Michael. *See* Buonarroti, Michelangelo
Angennes, Catherine-Henriette d' (1634–1714), m. (1652) Louis de la Trémoïlle, Comte d'Olonne:
anecdote about, **3.** *169*
marriage date of, **43.** 83
Petitot's miniature of, **6.** 96–8, 102, 111, 116, 119, 125, 128, 129, 140–2, 150, 153, 168, 181, 215, 217, 239, 245, 247, 251, 254, 255, 258, 260, 262, 263, 266, 267, 269, 271, 274–5, 280, 282–3, 288, 368, **7.** 269, **14.** 146, **32.** 282, **39.** 198, 208, 215
Angennes, Julie-Lucine d', Mlle de Rambouillet:
Montausier gives 'Guirlande de Julie' to, **42.** 93n
Angennes, Madeleine d' (1629–1714), m. (1655) Henri de St-Nectaire, Maréchal-Duc de la Ferté:
anecdotes of, **3.** *169*, **7.** 275–6
Fiesque lover of, **7.** 275
Longueville son of, **7.** 275
Staal, Mme de, informed by, of her always being right, **39.** 11
Angers (France):
Brancas family to visit, **5.** 79
Chapelle de St-Bernardin in, misnamed by Montfaucon, **14.** 69
Churchills to visit, **5.** 60, 65, 79, 80, 83
tomb at, of Ds of Lorraine, **35.** 163–4
Angerstein, Mrs John Julius. *See* Lucas, Mrs
Angeul. *See* Plumard de Dangeul
Angharad:
mother of Cadwaladr, **13.** 225n
Anghiari:
battle at, **11.** 250n
Angiers. *See* Angers
Angioletta, Mme:
Galli, Mme, entertains, **17.** 239
Angiviller, Comte d'. *See* Flahaut, Charles-Claude
Angiviller, Comtesse de la Billarderie d'. *See* La Borde, Élisabeth-Josèphe de
*Anglais à Bordeaux, L'. See under* Favart, Charles-Simon
Angler:
fish caught by, **25.** 464
Anglesey, Cts of. *See* Darnley, Lady Katherine
Anglesey, E. of. *See* Annesley, Arthur
Anglesey, M. of. *See* Paget, Henry William
Anglesey (Wales):
Plas Gwyn in, **41.** 160
*Angleterre, Éléments de l'histoire d'. See under* Millot, Claude-François-Xavier
*Anglia resurges*:
medal of, **21.** 189, 201
*Anglicæ historiæ. See under* Vergil, Polydore

Angling:
Strafford, Cts of, avoids, **35.** 335
Angliviel de la Beaumelle, Laurent (1726–73):
Du Deffand, Mme, attributes attack on Voltaire to, **5.** 79–80
epigram on Voltaire and, **28.** 253
*Examen de la nouvelle histoire de Henri IV* by, **4.** 94–5, 158–9, 163, 171
*Mémoires pour servir à l'histoire de Mme de Maintenon*, **5.** (?) 190, **8.** (?) 32, **14.** 62n, **35.** 276
verses on, **6.** 274, 277
Voltaire's controversy with, **5.** 79–80, **28.** 253, **35.** 283–4
Anglo-Indian clergyman:
coloured print of, **28.** 57, 60, 61, 63
Anglomania ('Anglomanie'):
Boufflers, Comtesse de, cures, by visiting England, **22.** 270
France loses, **41.** 7
French, extends from customs to persons, **35.** 369
Frenchman's witticism about, **22.** 113
in Paris, **35.** 126
Marchais's, **24.** 266
*Anglomanie, L'. See under* Saurin, Bernard-Joseph: *Orpheline léguée, L'*
*Anglomanie, L':*
Mann hopes to see, **22.** 113
published in France, **22.** 105
*Anglo-Norman Antiquities. See under* Ducarel, Andrew Coltee
Anglo-Saxon; Anglo-Saxons. *See* Saxon; Saxons
Anglo-Saxon language:
HW abhors, **42.** 230
*Angola. See under* Rochette de la Morlière, Jacques
'Angola, P. of':
Hertford to be called on by, **38.** 404–5
Angora cats. *See* Cats, Angora
Angosse, Marquise d'. *See* Usson de Bonac, Louise-Pétronille d'
Angosse, Bernard-Hippolyte d' (ca 1777–9):
death of, **7.** 140
Angosse, Claude-Alexandre-Casimir (1779–1838), Comte d':
birth of, **7.** 140
Angosse, Jean-Paul (1732–98), Marquis d':
Béarn to be visited by, **7.** 140
deaths in family of, **7.** 139–40
Du Deffand, Mme, gives opinion of, **7.** 140
——'s social relations with, **7.** 131, 140, 431, 432, 460
leaves Paris, **7.** 422, 433
returns to Paris, **7.** 431, 455
Angosse, Louise-Pauline-Pétronille-Charlotte-Léontine d' (1770–79):
death of, **7.** 140–1
Angoulême, Duc d'. *See* Bourbon, Louis-Antoine d' (1775–1844)
Angoulême, Duchesse d'. *See* Diane (1538–

1619); Louise de Valois (d. 1696); Marie-Thérèse-Charlotte (1778–1851)
Angoulême, Marguerite d'. *See* Marguerite
Angoulême (France):
Ruffec near, **5.** 402
Angoumois (France):
Broglie to go to Ruffec in, **6.** 358, 363
Gourville in, **4.** 44
Angran d'Alleray, Denis-François (1715–94), procureur général du grand-conseil:
(?) attends session of parliament of Paris, **8.** 172
(?) Keller, Rose, appeals to, **4.** 58
Angran d'Alleray, Madeleine (d. 1814), m. César-Henri, Comte de la Luzerne:
(?) SH visitors sent by, **12.** 235
Angri, Principe d'. *See* Doria, Gian Carlo
Anguish, Catherine (1764–1837), m. (1788). Francis Godolphin Osborne, styled M. of Carmarthen 1761–89; 5th D. of Leeds, 1789:
Carmarthen's engagement to, angers Lady Mary Coke, **31.** 288
Holdernesse, Cts of, friend of, **31.** 288
'vulgarly joyous' at wedding, **31.** 288n
Anguish, Thomas (d. ?1786), master in Chancery:
family ill-provided-for by, **31.** 288n
Angus, E. of. *See* Douglas, Archibald (ca 1490–1557)
Angustine. *See* Angerstein
Anhalt-Bernburg, Karl von (1723–1806), Prinz, 1772:
Conway replaces, **21.** 516n
Anhalt-Dessau, D. and P. of. *See* Leopold III (1740–1817) (Leopold Friedrich Franz)
Anhalt-Dessau, P. of. *See* Leopold II (1700–51); Leopold III (1740–1817) (Leopold Friedrich Franz)
Anhalt-Zerbst, Ps. of. *See* Catherine II (1729–96) of Russia; Johanna Elisabeth (1712–60) of Holstein-Gottorp-Oldenburg
Aniello, Tommaso (1620–47), called Masaniello; Neapolitan demagogue:
ghost of: Mann should appeal to, **23.** 5; may alarm Neapolitan court, **17.** 501
Gordon, Lord George, resembles, **33.** 189
revolt of, compared to reign of French mob, **11.** 42
Rigby may be, in Ireland, **9.** 263
Wilkes compared with, **23.** 5, 317–24, **24.** 535–6
*Animadversions on the Present Government of the York Lunatic Asylum. See under* Mason, William
Animal; animals:
at Horton, **10.** 334
at SH, **9.** 51, 77, 134, 155, **10.** 94, 108, 127
Bentley draws, well, **35.** 243
Cardigan, Cts of, protects, **9.** 94
compassion not felt by, **7.** 360
cruelty to, **40.** 257
Damer, Mrs, models well, **25.** 576

[Animal; animals, *continued*]
dying, HW hides himself like, **39.** 198
English painters paint, well, **24.** 93
European, said to degenerate when taken to America, **25.** 47
HW plays with, at SH, **38.** 94
HW said by Mme du Deffand to prefer, to people, **4.** 222
HW's childhood pets, **36.** 1
HW's reflections on, **35.** 377–8
hunting a persecution of, **35.** 387
La Fontaine brings out characteristics of, **41.** 28–9
'medicine themselves,' **33.** 166
Montagu, D. of, mentions, in will, **9.** 94–5
Noah and Moses preserved and distinguished, **20.** 71
pet, provision for, **2.** 271
pictures of, at Newstead Abbey, **9.** 299
Straffords lose, **35.** 377–8
torture of, HW's aversion to, **15.** 70
Walpole, Sir Robert, enjoys, **36.** 9
*See also*: Alligator; Ant; Antelope; Ass; Bantam; Barbette; Bat; Bear; Bee; Beetle; Bloodhound; Boar; Buck; Bug; Bull; Bullock; Calf; Camel; Cat; Caterpillar; Cattle; Chimpanzee; Cockatoo; Cow; Cricket; Crocodile; Deer; 'Diane'; Doe; Dog; Dormouse; Dragon; Dromedary; Eel; Elephant; Elk; Ermine; Fawn; Flea; Fox; Foxhound; Frog; Game; Game-animals; Gelding; Goat; Goose; Greyhound; Grub; Guinea hen; Hare; Hart; Hippopotamus; Hog; Horse; Hound; Hyena; Insect; Jackass; Jerboa; Kangaroo; Kitten; Lamb; Lapdog; Leopard; Lion; Lizard; Lobster; Mare; Marten; Mastiff; Menagerie; Monkey; Moose-deer; Mouse; 'Mufti'; Mule; Opossum; Orignal; Ostrich; Ox; Padnag; Panther; 'Patapan'; Pig; Pointer; 'Ponto'; Pony; Porcupine; Pug; Puppy; 'Puss'; Rabbit; Raccoon; Rat; 'Raton'; Reindeer; Rhinoceros; 'Rosette'; Salamander; Scorpion; Sea-horse; Serpent; Sheep; Snail; Snake; Sow; Spaniel; Squirrel; Stag; Tiger; Toad; 'Tonton'; Tortoise; 'Tory'; Turkeyhen; Turtle; Vermin; Wasp; Weasel; Whale; Wolf; Worm; Zebra
Animal magnetism. *See under* Hypnotism
'Animaux malades de la peste, Les.' *See under* La Fontaine, Jean de
Aniseikonia (retinal disparity):
(?) HW has, **43.** 165–6
Anjorrant de Tracy, Claude-Nicolas-Étienne (d. 1781):
(?) attends session of parliament of Paris, **8.** 173
Anjou, Duc d'. *See* René I
Anjou, Margaret of. *See* Margaret (?1430–82) of Anjou
Anjou, Yolande d' (1412–40), m. François I, Duc de Bretagne:
husband of, **14.** 72n

Anjou, Rue d', Paris:
Rue Dauphine near, **4.** 442n
Ankarström. *See* Anckarström
'Ankerstrom, Mrs.' *See* Johnston, Caroline Georgina
Ankerwycke:
Jodrell of, **11.** 176n
Ankle; ankles:
HW sprains, **37.** 66
*See also* Swollen ankle
Ankram. *See* Ancram
Anlezy, Comte d'. *See* Damas, Jean-Pierre
Anlezy, Comtesse d'. *See* Gassion, Madeleine-Angélique de (1712–94); Le Veneur de Tillières, Michelle-Pétronille de (b. 1741)
Ann, Mrs, George Montagu's housekeeper:
HW glad he does not know, **10.** 172
HW regarded by, as half her master, **10.** 169
HW's letter given to Montagu by, **10.** 160, 169
Montagu feared by, to have read of HW's illness, **10.** 160
*Ann*, English fire ship:
Mathews sends, to burn *Real Felipe*, **18.** 413–14
Anna, Czarina of Russia. *See* Anne
Anna (1757–9), Ps, of Russia:
(?) Peter III disowns, **22.** 57, **35.** 314
Anna *or* Anne of Mecklenburg-Schwerin, Ps of Brunswick-Wolfenbüttel. *See* Elizabeth (1718–46) of Mecklenburg-Schwerin
Anna Amalie (1723–77) of Prussia, Abbess of Quedlinburg, 1755:
(?) Cumberland, D. of, may wed, **18.** 62
Anna Amalie (1739–1807) of Brunswick-Wolfenbüttel, m. (1756) Ernst August II, D. of Saxe-Weimar:
(?) George III to wed, **20.** 494
Anna Charlotte Amalie (1710–77) of Nassau, m. (1727) Friedrich, Margrave of Baden-Durlach:
death of, **32.** 388
Annadale. *See* Annandale
Anna Ivanova. *See* Anne (1693–1740)
*Annales. See under* Camden, William; Tacitus; Worcester, William
*Annales de la république française*:
(?) Louis XVI's alleged phrase in, **34.** 179n
*Annales del Emperador Carlos V. See under* López de Gómara, Francisco
*Annales ecclesiastici. See under* Baronio, Cesare
*Annales of England. See under* Stow, John
*Annales ordinis S. Benedicti. See under* Mabillon, Jean
*Annales patriotiques*:
(?) Louis XVI's alleged phrase in, **34.** 179n
*Annales politiques. See under* Linguet, Simon-Nicolas-Henri
*Annales rerum Anglicarum. See under* Worcester, William
*Annales rerum Anglicarum et Hibernicarum regnante Elisabethæ. See under* Camden, William

*Annalium. See under* Hoveden, Roger de

*Annals of Agriculture*:
Orford's treatise in, **34.** 85

*Annals of Horsemanship. See under* Bunbury, Henry William

*Annals of Italy. See under* Muratori, Lodovico Antonio

*Annals of Scotland. See under* Dalrymple, Sir David

Annaly, Bn. *See* Gore, John

Anna Maria Luisa (1667–1743) de' Medici, m. (1691) Johann Wilhelm, Elector Palatine; 'Electress':
Berrue reports to, **17.** 215–16
Bianca Cappello's portrait excluded by, from those of Medici grand duchesses, **20.** 399, 414, **21.** 561n
coach of, has long traces, **19.** 370
Costa, Rosa, 'virtuosa' of, **30.** 14n
couch of, 'broken,' **35.** 35
courtiers of, **17.** 237
Craon, Mme de, shows to, HW's gifts, **17.** 424
Craon, Prince de, converses with, **18.** 134
death of, **18.** 159–60, 171–3, 177, 178, 184, 353, **19.** 23, **25.** 215n
devout, **18.** 139
Elector's death touches, **18.** 139
Eleonora, Ps, has bastard under very nose of, **18.** 39
English Court to mourn for, **18.** 201
fortification plans for Florence opposed by, **17.** 198
Francis I's family convention with, safeguards Medici art treasures at Florence, **20.** 466n
Francis I tells, to give up her gems, **17.** 236–8
funeral of, **18.** 173
Gavi inquiry pressed by, **17.** 225
godmother by proxy, **17.** 473
goes out on Epiphany after illness, **18.** 134, 148–9
guard of, **17.** 198
HW calls on, **17.** 225, **42.** 190, 191n
health of: bleeding, **18.** 172; fever, **18.** 139; ill, **18.** 113; illness minimized by *London Gazette*, **35.** 35; oppression on breast, **18.** 139, 172; sore leg, **18.** 139
jewels of, **17.** 428, **18.** 170, 171, 173, 175, 236–8
Kaunitz gets snuff-box from, **17.** *48*
Lorraine guards sent to Leghorn at demand of, **17.** 198n
Mann calls on, **17.** 83
—— congratulates, on 75th birthday, **18.** 10–12
Maria Theresa sends Hungary water to, **18.** 139
masks hated by, **18.** 178
Modenese princess cannot arrange ceremonial with, **17.** 65, 99
mourning for, **18.** 175, 190–1, 206
Old Pretender left ring by, **17.** 173, 175, 191
Panciatichi godson of, **18.** 121

pensions left by, to be taxed after recipients' deaths, **19.** 23
Poggio Imperiale desired by, **20.** 415
Quiete, the, retreat of, **17.** 65, 83, 428
relatives acknowledged by, after her death, **18.** 170–1, 173, 177
resurrection of, not wanted, **18.** 369
Richecourt's relations with, **17.** 225, **18.** 10, **20.** 268
sacrament given to, **18.** 160, 173
San Lorenzo chapel finished by gifts of, **18.** 113, 171–2
Serristori, 'Joan,' proxy for, at baptism, **17.** 473
Urbino property of, **18.** 169
Walpole, Sir Robert, to hear of affair of, **17.** 241
Walseck calls on, **17.** 130
wealth of, falsely reported, **18.** 205–6
will of, **18.** 168–73, 176–7, 205–6
would shudder at Galluzzi's history and Leopold II's sale, **25.** 215

Annandale, M. of. *See* Johnston, George (1720–92)

Annapolis, Md:
French to relieve Lafayette at, **25.** 150n
Newcastle's ignorance of, **30.** 146n

Anne (1693–1740), Empress of Russia 1730–40:
ale kills, **40.** 43
Biron, favourite of, **10.** 39n, **18.** 467n
death of, **13.** 236, 237, **40.** 43
French hated by, **17.** 20
HW and Montagu contemporary with, **10.** 39
La Chétardie supposedly imprisoned by, **13.** 217, **17.** 20
Vernon would be prized by, **37.** 83

Anne (1366–94) of Bohemia, m. (1382) Richard II of England:
comes to England, **9.** 67n
dead before *Richard II* begins, **42.** 139
headdress introduced to England by, **7.** 359, **9.** 68, 78
Lancerona, maid of honour to, **9.** 68

Anne (Neville) (1456–85), (?) m. 1 (1470) Edward, P. of Wales; m. 2 (1472) Richard III of England:
barrenness of, **14.** 179
death of, **15.** 177n
HW's print of, **1.** 133
Manchester's pedigree includes, **35.** 607, **41.** 134
portraits of, **1.** 133, **14.** *177–8*, **15.** 123–4

Anne (Boleyn) (1507–36), m. (1533) Henry VIII of England:
arms of, on looking-glass, **32.** 323
axe for beheading of, in Tower of London, **17.** 233
coronation of, **2.** 365
father of, **2.** 165
HW would be pleased by, **41.** 290
Henry VIII and, at Wolsey's ball, **42.** 421
Henry VIII determined to wed, **1.** 82
—— gives clock to, **9.** 304, **29.** 40n

[Anne (Boleyn), *continued*]

——'s alleged comment on beheading of, 11. 97

Howard, Catherine, and, 32. 364

letter of, a forgery, 41. 270

not vindicated by Q. Elizabeth, 34. 229

Parker chaplain to, 40. 159

picture of, 1. 171, 41. 451n

portrait of, could not be Anne Vane, 41. 451

Prinknash visited by, 1. 342n

Rochford, brother of, 1. 357, 28. 191, 42. 381

SH walk named after, 35. 142

uncle of, 2. 31n

Wyatt's relations with, 1. 261, 270

Anne (1515–57) of Cleves, m. (1540) Henry VIII of England:

HW's witticism on proxy wedding and divorce of, 9. 99

Holbein's portrait of, 12. 111, 125, 43. 154

husband calls, Flanders mare, 37. 531

tomb of, 2. 77, 185

Anne (1574–1619) of Denmark, m. (1589) James VI of Scotland (later James I of England):

furniture of, at Somerset House, 32. 324–5

Herbert's relations with, 10. 134

letter from, to Buckingham, 15. 74

monument to, 1. 174

steward of, 33. 350

Van Dyck's grant from, 16. 35

Anne (1665–1714), Q. of England 1702–14:

ballads of time of, 32. 200, 33. 557

Bedford pardoned by, 2. 357

Bolingbroke says Old Pretender not to be introduced at end of reign of, 20. 60

Burnet clerk of the Closet to, 41. 332

'Church's wet-nurse,' 28. 387

Clarendon's anecdotes of, 15. 149

costumes of time of, 18. 95

Cromarty's dedication to, 15. 29–30

Dalrymple's *Memoirs* reveal stupidity of, 32. 105

Dartmouth secretary of state to, 20. 208n

end of reign of, momentous, 20. 222

farthing of, 33. 436

Fitzpatrick's *Dorinda* might have been written in time of, 28. 208

formality of era of, copied in France, 22. 218

gardeners to, 2. 200n

goddaughter of, 11. 56n

HW calls 'silly woman,' 25. 8

HW imitates, by signing letter 'Morley,' 31. 235

HW remembered half the Court of, 25. 558

HW's erroneous reference to, 13. 248

head of, on ale-house signs, 35. 58

heart of, entirely English, 32. 60n

Jacobites devoted to, 32. 130

Jacobitism of last years of, 20. 60

judge commended by, for defending Richard Cromwell, 33. 443n

letter-endings of time of, 14. 43

Limerick, Vct, wants to revive law of, against secular priests, 37. 426

maid of honour to, 10. 203n

Marlborough and Godolphin would not have sacrificed, 28. 389

Marlborough the great general of, 29. 309n

Marlborough, Ds of, publishes letters of, 17. 357

Masham, Lady, convivial with, at Windsor Lodge, 32. 305

medal of, for repulse of Scottish invasion, 21. 357n

Methodism would be defended by, 20. 41

Old Pretender preferred by, as her successor, 20. 76, 23. 329, 33. 439n

painting of, 12. 111n

Pope's lines about, 37. 8

Prior examined about ministry of, 13. 186n

reign of, treated in King's *Works,* 32. 310

secret committee inquires into last administration of, 22. 26

statue of, at Gloucester, 40. 44

Strawbridge, Mrs, surpasses, 34. 262

Swift's journal of last years of, 10. 219, 21. 184–5, 25. 8 (*see also under* Swift, Jonathan)

Walpole, Sir Robert, wrote speeches for, 22. 26

war of, 24. 482, 40. 25, 26

war's end in 1762 like last years of, 38. 173

Whigs in reign of, try to bribe Emperor's ministers, 7. 354

wigs large in reign of, 25. 609n

Windsor guide mentions, 9. 18n

Wyndham chancellor of Exchequer under, 25. 68n, 39. 179n

Anne (1476–1514) of Brittany, m. 1 (1491) Charles VIII of France; m. 2 (1499) Louis XII of France:

looking-glass of, 7. 305

prayer book of, 7. 359

Anne (1601–66) of Austria, m. (1615) Louis XIII of France:

called 'Dame Anne' in the Fronde, 11. 109

Chevreuse, Duchesse de, attached to, 15. 266n

Ennery has medallion of, 7. 325

Mazarin intimate with, 9. 343n

Anne (1475–?1511) (Plantagenet), m. (1495) Lord Thomas Howard:

Papal bull omits, 42. 208n

Anne (1709–59), Ps, of England, m. (1734) William IV of Orange:

appearance of, extremely ugly, 37. 289

Augusta's marriage to P. of Brunswick follows precedents set by, 38. 288

Conway and wife see, in bed with family, 37. 287, 289

death of, 7. 354, 21. 260, 266, 268, 38. 5–6, 8

Ferdinand's retort to, 21. 221–2

George II anxious to avoid suspicion of, 20. 283n

Griffin, Miss, maid of honour to, 10. 139n, 23. 269n

health of, bad, **20.** 279
Holdernesse ill-received by, **20.** 283n
Hop brings Holdernesse a letter from, **21.**
  260n
Louis XV refused as husband for, **7.** 354
name of husband of, corrected, **43.** 257
Orford, Cts of, to visit Court of, **19.** 49
Portland, Lady, governess to, **34.** 260
portrait of, **10.** 338
(?) print of, **40.** 237
Regency of, may terminate with husband's
  death, **20.** 279
son born to, **19.** 469
Sussex, Cts of, lady of Bedchamber to, **10.** 338
temper of, **20.** 279
Willoughby's verses on marriage of, **16.** 21
Anne (d. 1432) of Burgundy, m. (1423) John
  of Lancaster, D. of Bedford:
tomb of, **7.** 271, **39.** 201
Anne (1439–76) Plantagenet, m. 1 (1447)
  Henry Holand, D. of Exeter (divorced); m.
  2 Sir Thomas St Leger:
birth of, **1.** 320
Hardinge descended from, **35.** 610n
husband divorced by, **2.** 365
'Anne, Lady.' See Fitzpatrick, Lady Anne (1768–
  1841); Wentworth, Lady Anne
'Anne, Lord.' See Hamilton, Lord Anne
*Anne,* English galley:
*St Isidore* pursued by, **18.** 189
Anne-Charlotte (1714–73) of Lorraine, Ps:
Tuscan court mourns for, **23.** 533
Tuscany may be governed by, **19.** *49,* 207, **20.**
  29, 178, 210, 355
Anne-Charlotte (1755–86), Princesse de Lor-
  raine. See Lorraine, Anne-Charlotte de
Annecy, Bp of. See Biord, Jean-Pierre
*Année littéraire, L'. See under* Fréron, Élie-
  Catherine
Annesley, Cts of. See Darnley, Lady Katherine
Annesley, Arthur (1614–86), cr. (1661) E. of
  Anglesey:
Belsham attacks HW's criticism of, **15.** 147n,
  **31.** 293–4
—— descendant of, **31.** 294, 296
Kippis's answer to HW's remarks on, **2.** 92–3
Annesley, Arthur (1744–1816), 8th Vct Valentia,
  cr. (1793) E. of Mountnorris; titular E. of
  Anglesea:
Echlin, Lady, escorted by, at masked ball at
  Paris, **38.** 514–15
Elliott, Lady, elopes with, **24.** 15, **35.** 422
Annesley, Catherine (d. 1770), m. (1760)
  Arthur Saunders Gore, styled Vct Sudley; 2d
  E. of Arran, n.c., 1773:
Florence visited by, **20.** 149
Maria Louisa plays whist with, **23.** 203
Pisa and Florence visited by, **23.** 203
Annesley, Hon. Charles Henry:
father of, elopes, **24.** 15
Annesley, Hon. George (1771–1844) styled Vct

Valentia 1793–1816; 2d E. of Mountnorris,
  1816:
father of, elopes, **24.** 15
Annesley, James (1674–1702), 3d E. of Anglesey,
  1690:
wife of, **9.** 244n, **28.** 389n
Annesley, Hon. Juliana Lucy (ca 1772–1833),
  m. (1789) John Maxwell-Barry, 5th Bn Farnham, 1823:
father of, elopes, **24.** 15
Annesley, Hon. Thomas Lyttelton:
father of, elopes, **24.** 15
*Annette à l'âge de quinze ans:*
verses to air of, **5.** 186
*Annona. See under* Rome
*Anno santo:*
Benedict XIV announces, **20.** 43–4
—— tells Roman Catholic princes to respect,
  **20.** 98
England's jubilee to surpass, **20.** 71
*Annotazioni. See under* Redi, Francesco
*Annual Register:*
account of Gothic architecture in, **1.** 148
fountain tree described in, **10.** 155
HW praises, **22.** 41
HW reads, in post-chaise, **10.** 155
HW recommends articles in, **28.** 101
HW sends, **22.** 49
Mann requests, **22.** 36
preferments listed in, **28.** 274
quotation from, **11.** 39n
source of HW's death-notices, **7.** 372
verses attributed to C. J. Fox in, **32.** 382
Annuitants:
Mann, Horace II, sets no money aside for,
  **24.** 36
Annuity; annuities:
**1.** 233, **6.** 225, 234, 401, 403, **7.** 11, 184, 191
Chute thinks of buying, **24.** 210
Clive gives up, for *jagir,* **38.** 275
Cole's, **1.** 243n, 303n, 306n
Conti's, **4.** 419
Craon's, **6.** 141
Du Deffand, Mme, has, **4.** 386–7, **6.** 38–41,
  43–4, 46, 187–90
Electress leaves, to servants and courtiers, **18.**
  169–70, **19.** 23–4
Fane gives, to Sandwich, **20.** 258
for: Du Deffand servants, **4.** 365–6, 387, **8.**
  39–41, 43–4; Denis, Mme, **7.** 49; Lauzun,
  **7.** 33; Maillard, Mme, **7.** 252, **8.** 6, 9–10;
  Talmond, Princesse de, servants of, **5.** 438
Fox, C. J., sells, **39.** 157
Frederick II gives, to Muzell (Stosch), **25.** 651
Geoffrin, Mme, leaves, **6.** 484
Gray buys, for aunt, **1.** 233n
HW does not advise, **23.** 134
HW offers, to gardener, **32.** 567, **35.** 480n
Lucchi, Angiola, entitled to, **20,** 238, 312n,
  **22.** 266, 278–9
Mann considers, **23.** 129, 134

[Annuity; annuities, *continued*]
—— makes Linton over to Horace Mann II in return for, **24.** 257, 259
——'s, to servants, **25.** 667
——'s money invested in, **24.** 183
—— to receive, in case of losing position, **21.** 38n, **23.** 51, **24.** 183
Mann, Edward Louisa, leaves, to daughter, **24.** 160, 168, 176
Molesworth gives, to brother, **22.** 140
money to be raised by, **24.** 361n
Montagu's, on father's lands, **21.** 472n
Norfolk's, to niece, more suitable to housekeeper, **32.** 384n
Parliament settles, on Earldom of Chatham, **24.** 382
Pitt's, **38.** 132, 135
Pompadour, Mme de, had, **38.** 164
'ravishing' effects of, **30.** 164
sold for 10 times more than HW can ever pay, **24.** 310
Valentinois, Mme de, leaves, **6.** 72
Walpole, Sir Edward, leaves, to Anne and Margaret Clement, **36.** 156n
Young Pretender might buy, by selling pawned jewel, **25.** 526
Annuity and Lottery Bill. *See under* Parliament: acts of
Annunziata, church of, at Florence:
Craon, Mme de, walks from, to San Lorenzo, **18.** 196
faithful to visit, 15 times during jubilee, **20.** 220n
Grifoni, Signora, attends, **17.** 433
HW used to drive to, in heat of day, to look at buildings, **25.** 558
Sansedoni visits, **20.** 228n
Te Deums at, **17.** 100, 433n
Virgin's 'holy picture' in: completed by 'angels,' **18.** 227n; Craon, Mme de, prays to, **18.** 216; exposition of, **17.** 100; uncovered for Ds of Modena, **18.** 227
Annunziata, Piazza della SS.:
Grifoni, Mme, of, **35.** 52
'Anodyne Stars and Garters':
Newcastle to dispense, in HW's newspaper parody, **9.** 130
Anquetil, Louis-Pierre (1723–1806), priest:
*Esprit de la Ligue, L':* Du Deffand, Mme, criticizes, **6.** 84; Du Deffand, Mme, owns, **8.** 31, **43.** 97
Villars's life edited by, **33.** 439n
Anquetin de la Chapelle de Saint-Jean. *See* Saint-Jean
Ansart, Jean-Baptiste:
*Henriette* by, (?) Du Deffand, Mme, owns, **8.** 34
Ansbach, Margrave of. *See* Christian Friedrich Karl Alexander (1736–1806), Karl Wilhelm Friedrich (1712–57)
Ansbach, Margravine of. *See* Berkeley, Lady

Elizabeth (1750–1828); Friederike Luise (1714–84)
Ansbach. *See also* Brandenburg-Ansbach
Ansbach (Germany):
academy at: founded by Bns Craven, **35.** 538–9; HW to be enrolled in, by Bns Craven, **36.** 250–1
Gloucester, D. and Ds of, visit, **25.** 413n
Karl Alexander to visit, **20.** 376
Williams leaves, **20.** 90n
Anseaume, Louis (1721–84), dramatist:
*École de la jeunesse, L',* by, **7.** 272
*Tableau parlant, Le,* by, **7.** 331
Ansell, ——, lawyer:
law chambers of, burnt, **20.** 321n
Ansell, Robert:
(?) sale of pictures of, **23.** 299
Ansell. *See also* Ancel
'Anselmo, Signore':
Pertici acts, **20.** 357
Anson, Bns. *See* Yorke, Elizabeth (1725–60)
Anson, Lady. *See* Dickenson, Louisa
Anson, ——, capt. of English merchant ship:
*Hibernia* ship of, **21.** 16n
Anson, Hon. (Lady) Elizabeth. *See* Yorke, Elizabeth (1725–60)
Anson, George (1697–1762), cr. (1747) Bn Anson; naval officer; M.P.:
Acapulco ship captured by, **18.** 463, 478n, **30.** 53–4
acrostic mentions, **12.** 261
Admiralty appointments of, **9.** 211, **18.** 550, **20.** 259, **21.** 103
Beauclerk resigns from Admiralty on appointment of, as vice-adm., **20.** 80
becomes privy councillor, **20.** 135
Bedford forsaken by, to follow Hardwicke, **20.** 135
Bedford, Ds of, told by, of war prospects, **35.** 220
Boscawen quarrels with, **20.** 113, 259
Brest fleet evaded by, **18.** 463
buys Moor Park, **9.** 285n
Byng ill-treated by, **21.** 23, 55n, 65
——'s trial and condemnation to be prepared by, **20.** 578n
Cape Finisterre scene of victory of, **19.** 402–3, 410–11, **20.** 38
captains at Leghorn not adherents of, **21.** 123
*Centurion* carries, from Canton, **18.** 463n
Charlotte, Q., transported by, to England, **21.** 528, **38.** 116, 118–19
*Charlotte* commanded by, **21.** 525n
circumnavigation of, mentioned in verses, **30.** 126
'continence' of, **9.** 55, **37.** 535
Cumberland, D. of, may be replaced by, on street signs, **37.** 272–3
destination of, in doubt, **37.** 531
death of, **10.** 35
diamonds and gold captured by, off Panama, **18.** 478

docks visited by, with Beauclerk and Sandwich, **20.** 80

dying at Bath, **22.** 33

English invasion of France commanded by, **21.** 204, **37.** 535

English naval preparedness a credit to, **20.** 483

Evans draws up impeachment articles against, **21.** 23

fleet of, sails towards Brest, **21.** 210

George II agrees to sacrifice, **21.** 12n

'gravelled,' **37.** 479

HW calls: 'Admiral Almanzor,' **35.** 284; 'Admiral Amadis,' **37.** 550

HW's ridicule of, offends Cts of Pembroke, **37.** 538

Halifax succeeds, as first lord of Admiralty, **22.** 42n

Hardwicke asks navy treasurership for, **21.** 93

—— asks Newcastle to put, in Privy Council, **20.** 135n

—— communicates anti-Byng evidence to, **21.** 23n

—— might get Rochester title for, **35.** 170

health of, poor, **10.** 27

impotence of, suspected, **9.** 54–5, 90, 285, 410, **20.** 13, **21.** 66n, 528n, **35.** 288, **37.** 527

incompetence of, **30.** 141

Keppel accompanies, **20.** 459n

La Jonquière's battle with, **40.** 284

letter received by, about Kunersdorf battle, **30.** 156–7

marriage of, **9.** 54–5

*Monitor, The,* attacks, **21.** 39n

naval defences strengthened by, **21.** 306n

Navy Bill largely the work of, **20.** 33, 38

negligence of, alleged, **9.** 236

peerage granted to, **19.** 414, **37.** 273

Pitt quarrels with, **9.** 236

—— selects, for Admiralty, **21.** 104n

——'s reference to, as 'great and respectable name,' **38.** 545

——'s Spanish war proposal opposed by, **38.** 131n

resignation of, **21.** 17

Rochefort expedition planned by, **21.** 117n

'romantic delicacy' of, **30.** 270

Sandwich replaced by, **9.** 115n

Sawyer may excel, in wealth, **22.** 44

seamen do not envy expedition leadership of, **21.** 223

sea piece painted for, **20.** 38

Selwyn's witticism about, **35.** 261

ships sent to Ireland by, **21.** 374

son not begotten by, **35.** 229

Spanish captives of, **9.** 55

Temple succeeds, as Admiralty's first lord, **21.** 18, 25

Townshend, Charles, jokes about 'miscarriage' of, **37.** 527

Townshends cite, as reason for their leaving London, **21.** 104

Tripoline ambassador calls, 'his Majesty's

chief eunuch,' **21.** 528, **35.** 206, 312, **38.** 116

unpopularity of, grows, **20.** 38

verses attack, **30.** 126

*Voyage around the World, A,* by, **9.** 55, 90, **18.** 463n, **35.** 284, **43.** 114

Warren richer than, **20.** 33

Wichnor flitch of bacon envied by, **9.** 294

wife of, **20.** 13, 121n, **21.** 66

Anson, Thomas (ca 1695–1773), M. P.:

estate bought by, near Wichnor, **9.** 294

*Anson,* English ship:

captain of, killed, **25.** 278n

Anspach. *See* Ansbach

Anstaing, Château d':

Conway stationed at, **37.** 175–7

Anstey, Christopher (1724–1805), poet:

*Election Ball, An,* **28.** 242

HW praises, **1.** 310, **10.** 218

Hamilton's quarrel with, **33.** 527

*Heroic Epistle* attributed to, **28.** 75, 77, **32.** 101

Macaulay, Mrs, satirized by, **33.** 84–5

Millers championed by, **32.** 221n

*New Bath Guide, The,* **1.** 310n, **10.** 218, 238, **28.** 75n, **30.** 229, **32.** 101, 196, **33.** 85, 527, **42.** 230, **43.** 134

*Patriot, The,* **1.** 310, **14.** 161, **35.** 561

*Priest Dissected, The,* **28.** 170, **32.** 196

'Winter's Amusement' by, at Batheaston, **33.** 84–5

Anstey, James (1714–42), Fellow of King's College, Cambridge; HW's tutor:

HW's correspondence with, **40.** 24–6

HW's tutor, **13.** 5

Malpas's tutor, **40.** 24n

Anstey, John:

father's *Poetical Works* published by, **42.** 230n

Anstey. *See also* Ansty

Anstis, John (1669–1744), Garter King-of-Arms:

Buckingham, Ds of, summons, for burial instructions, **18.** 192–3

death date of, corrected, **43.** 115

HW the equivalent of, at Newmarket, **32.** *142*

*Observations . . . on the Knighthood of the Bath,* **1.** 246

(?) royal visitors to Richmond's fireworks would please, **9.** 81

Anstis, John (ca 1709–54), Garter King-of-Arms:

Ansbach, Margrave of, receives Garter from C. H. Williams and, **30.** 320

birth date of, corrected, **43.** 115

HW the equivalent of, at Newmarket, **32.** 142

Mann pedigree delayed by, **20.** 96

rebuked by Lord Pembroke, **1.** 330

(?) royal visitors to Richmond's fireworks would please, **9.** 81

Anstruther, Sir John (1718–19), 2d Bt:

*Rolliad* contributor, **25.** 613n

SH visited by, **12.** 234

Anstruther, Philip (ca 1680–1760), army officer; M. P.:

[Anstruther, Philip (ca 1680–1760), *continued*]
Bedford orders regiment of, assembled, **21.** 373n

biographical information on, corrected, **43.** 249

Churchill, Gen., solicits Sir Robert Walpole for, **30.** 289n

Edinburgh's demolition advocated by, **20.** 230

Erskine and the Scotch attack, **20.** 229–30

Erskine ill-treated by, in Minorca, **20.** 230

——'s affair with, languishes, **20.** 240

Mann may send painting to, at Port Mahon, for shipment, **18.** 144

regiment of, **9.** 196n, **17.** 300n, **20.** 373n, 474n

Anstruther, Philip (b. 1747). *See* Leslie, Philip

Ansty, Mrs (fl. 1765), of Stall St, Bath:
Cole, Jane, visits, **1.** 93

*Answer to Mr Horace Walpole's late Work, An.* *See under* Guidickins, Frederick William

*Answer to Part of Dr Middleton's Late Treatise, An:*
Middleton's attack on Sherlock provokes, **15.** 300

*Answer to the Latter Part of Lord Bolingbroke's Letters on . . . History. See under* Walpole, Horatio (1678–1757)

*Answer to the Letter to Dr Waterland, An:*
Middleton answered in, **15.** 295

*Answer to the Reverend Dr Middleton's Grand Objection, An:*
Middleton's attack on Sherlock provokes, **15.** 299

Ant; ants:
HW imitates, **21.** 368

Voltaire mentions, **35.** 413

Antæus:
Mendip, Lord, compared to, **12.** 148

Antaldi, Lavinia, m. (ca 1735) Conte Ludovico Ubaldini:
(?) affair in Mann's garden reported by, **19.** 497–9, 502n

(?) Papal States banish, **19.** 497

Antechapel:
to Vyne chapel, **35.** 639, 642

Antelminelli. *See* Salvetti Antelminelli

*Antelope,* English ship:
Brodrick, Byng, and Fowkes board, for England, **20.** 573n

Byng and West reach Spithead in, **20.** 583n

Gibraltar destination of, from Portsmouth, **20.** 562n

Hawke and Saunders arrive on, **20.** 573n

involved in war, **18.** 469, 476, 506, **19.** 207, 232, 234, 236, 292

off Ajaccio, **19.** 207n

Vanbrugh commands, **19.** 232n, 276n

Antelope; antelopes:
on staircase in SH hall, **20.** 381

Antenori. *See* Antinori

Ant-hill:
Messina's devastation might be regarded as that of, **35.** 374

'Tonton' might drown, **33.** 367

*Anthologie françoise ou chansons depuis le 13° siècle jusqu'à présent:*
(?) Montagu's opinion of, **10.** 186

Anthony (1195–1231) of Padua, St:
Lanfranco's painting of, *see under* Lanfranco

pig of, **13.** 145, **43.** 176

speech of, to fishes, **37.** 312

temptation of, painted by Teniers, **7.** 335

Anthony Abbas, St:
early oil painting of, **42.** 66

Anthony Victor Joseph Johann (1779–1835), archduke:
birth of, **24.** 530n

living, **25.** 549

Anthropophagi. *See* Cannibals

Antibes (France):
Austrians and Sardinians threaten, **19.** 323

Biot near, **19.** 336

bombarded but uncaptured, **19.** 352–3

*Catalogue of French Books* mentions, **18.** 53

couriers from, **19.** 345

Diodati to compliment Montemar at, **17.** 207

feluccas near, **18.** 116

Fort Quarré at, to be Curzay's prison, **20.** 354

French and Spanish troops may be transported from, to Genoa, **23.** 469

French fleet's movements reported from, **17.** 309

French may try to cross from, to Corsica, **20.** 588

French said to embark at, **17.** 323

governor of, **19.** 353

not captured, **19.** 352, 358

Philip, Don, marches towards, **18.** 395

—— to embark from, **17.** 361–2, 380, 388

Spanish couriers to receive French letters at, **18.** 412

visitors to: Boufflers, Chevalier de, **8.** 137; Francis III, **19.** 313–14; Gloucester, D. of, **23.** 370; HW, **13.** 11; Montemar, **17.** 198; Murray, **25.** 271; Philip, Don, **17.** 361–2, 380, 388, **19.** 313–14; Young Pretender, **18.** 385

*Antichità di Ercolano exposte. See Pitture antiche di Ercolano, Le*

Antici, Tommaso (1731–1812), Polish minister to Rome; cardinal, 1789:
Stanislas II warned by, of Young Pretender, **23.** 352

*Anticipation. See under* Tickell, Richard

Antier, Marie (ca 1687–1747), actress:
anecdote of, **4.** 217

Antigny-Damas, Marquis d'. *See* Damas, Jacques-François de

Antigny-Damas, Marquise d'. *See* Rochechouart, Zéphirine-Félicité de

*Antigone,* opera:
Hesse, P. of, sees, at Haymarket, **19.** 265n, **43.** 260

Antigua, West Indies:
English forces at, **19.** 69n

hurricane at, **20.** 331n
ship from, **24.** 229n
Young has estates in, **20.** 331n
*Anti-Jacobin, The*:
Gifford edits, **12.** 62n
'Anti-Lactilla, Miss.' *See* More, Hannah
*Anti-Lucretius. See under* Polignac, Melchior
de
Antimonial medicine:
Orford takes, **23.** 460, **36.** 332
Antimony:
Ward's drop and pill contain, **21.** 358n
Antin, Duchesse d'. *See* Montmorency-Luxem-
bourg, Gillette-Françoise de
Antin, Marquis d'. *See* Pardaillan de Gondrin,
Antoine-François de
Antin, Marquise d'. *See* Carbonnel de Canisy,
Marie-Françoise-Renée de
Antinori, Mme. *See* Capponi, Teresa Maria
(1715-55); Gaddi, Maria Gaetana (1722-82)
Antinori, Luigi:
daughter discussed by, at Craon's, **20.** 36
Antinori, Maria Maddalena (1725-1802), m.
(1744) Domenico Andrea Bocchineri:
Acciaioli's affair with, **19.** 497, 502, **20.** 432,
448-9, **35.** 65
Bocchineri to marry, **18.** *435*, **35.** 53
child born to, **35.** 53
Chute knows, **20.** 447, **35.** 53
Craons entertain, **20.** 36, 447
English lovers preferred by, **20.** 36
English visitors catch diseases from, **20.** 447
famous for singing and dancing, **20.** 447
father boasts of strength of, **20.** 36
HW knew, **20.** 36, 447
Hobart knows, **20.** 36
'pitchcaia,' **35.** 53
procaccia's affair with, arouses husband's
jealousy, **20.** 447
Regency relegates, to Prato, **20.** 447
Watson's relations with, **20.** 36, 447
Antinori, Maria Maddalena (1744-1811), m.
(1765) Francesco Maria Gioacchino Buon-
delmonti:
birth of, **18.** 406
name of husband of, corrected, **43.** 253
Antinori, Ruberto (1742-1808), canon:
birth of, **17.** 499
Antinori, Vincenzo Baldassarre (1689-1757),
senator:
Craon, Mme de, accompanied by, to Artimino, **18.** 329, 521
——'s relations with, **17.** *203*, 313, 413, 463,
**18.** 318, 353, 485-6
Mann entertains, **18.** 17, 353
*Museum Florentinum* directed by, **18.** 391
Antinori Calderini, Mme. *See* Gaddi, Maria
Gaetana
Antinori Calderini, Cavaliere Gaetano (1705-
63), Regency member:
Botta's second letter to Pitt shown by, to
Mann, **21.** 197n
death of, **22.** 124

Eszterházys entertained by, **20.** 350
(?) Frescobaldi, Mme, probably not content
with, **17.** 136
Mann presents memorial to, **20.** 276n
—— talks with, **17.** *120*
Regency member, **20.** 350, **21.** 107n, **22.**
124
Richard, gentleman of the office of, **21.** 114n
secretary at war, **22.** 124
Tuscany ruled by, as sole Regency member,
**21.** 85, 90, 107
Vienna neglects, **21.** 107
Antinori Calderini, Niccolò (1698-1775), archdeacon:
sister-in-law's letter shown by, **22.** 334-5
Antinous (d. 122), favourite of Emperor Hadrian:
Albani's bas-relief of, at Rome, **20.** 86n
bronze of, **15.** 17
busts of: HW's, **15.** 12; Rockingham buys,
at Mead sale, **35.** 217
drawing of, for Middleton's *Monumenta*, **15.**
21
medallion of, bought by HW, **26.** 7
statue of, in Vatican, **11.** 338n
'Antiochus':
character in Racine's *Bérénice*, **41.** 154
Antiochus Evergetes:
bust of, destroyed in Uffizi fire, **22.** 68n
Antiope:
Fitzroy, Lady Caroline, compared with, **37.**
235
in Cumberland's *Calypso*, **2.** 150
Antiquarian; antiquarians:
Jacobite sympathies of, **35.** 146-7
Zouch condemns use of, as noun, **16.** 50-1
*See also* Antiquary
Antiquarian books. *See under* Book
*Antiquarian Repertory*:
cited, **2.** 255-6, **43.** 72
Antiquarian Society. *See* Antiquaries, Society of
Antiquaries, Society of:
*Archæologia's* account of, **2.** 347
archiepiscopal seat of folly and knavery, **24.**
284
Arundel's medals probably mentioned in
registers of, **16.** 160
Clarence's attainder may have been printed
by, **15.** 176
Cole disparages leaders of, **1.** 299
Cooke echoes HW's opinion of, **1.** 340
Cosway can have letters on ring explained
by, **42.** 187
Cowdray paintings published by, **16.** 211
dinners by, or in honour of, **1.** 259, 306n, 307,
307-8, 360, **2.** 271
Edward I's tomb opened by, **1.** 384, **15.** 149n
Felton's Roman coins exhibited at, **34.** 10n
Foote ridicules, **1.** 265, 267, 270, **13.** 47,
**28.** 40
Gough director of, **1.** 290, 311
—— may be disgusted with, **2.** 290
Granger wants to join, **1.** 205

[Antiquaries, Society of, *continued*]
HW a member of, 43. 55
HW expects more attacks from, 28. 239
HW quits, 1. 266n, 270, 324, 327, 2. 264,
 13. 47, 15. 155, 24. 284, 28. 40, 212, 213,
 32. 84, 195, 35. 539, 43. 57, 73, 173, 294
HW refers to, 15. 176
HW's contempt for, 1. 206, 218–19, 265, 266n,
 270–1, 279, 293, 304, 330, 384, 2. 2, 116,
 119, 164, 186n, 250, 258, 261, 298, 366
HW's Hentzner dedicated to, 13. 28
HW's memorandum on, 14. 120
HW's pun may amuse, 39. 207
HW visits, in Chancery Lane, 38. 371
hawking a topic interesting to, 34. 146
Hillier exhibits intaglio to, 16. 69
—— shows Hollar's print to, 16. 74
Hollar prints of, said to be taken from Lady
 Fitzwilliam's pictures, 16. 78
King's paper the best published by, 42. 35
library of: has print of Nonsuch, 40. 254;
 may have print of Cromwell's funeral, 42.
 127–8
Lort may exhibit MS account of Henry VI's
 Bury visit to, 16. 188
—— quotes minute book of, 16. 166
Lyttelton, Charles, a fellow of, 41. 385n
——, president of, 10. 148, 16. 74n
Masters's *Some Remarks* dedicated to, 1. 290
members of: Barnard, 16. 95; can decipher
 old texts but cannot read, 42. 187; HW,
 13. 28, 16. 69n; Hillier, 16. 69n; Hollis,
 2. 189n; Kippis, 2. 72, 196; Pond, 2. 189n;
 West, 20. 371n
Milles president of, 28. 429
minute book of, 16. 176
minutes of, 43. 59
new apartments of, 2. 255
papers read at, 1. 8, 217, 218, 268
prints engraved for, 1. 299, 2. 8, 11, 128,
 277n, 308, 16. 73, 78, 166
proposed presidents for, 2. 245, 247, 250
Richmond Palace print published by, 16. 73
ring inscriptions can be explained by, 42. 187
Roman remains investigated by, 15. 179
Rose Tavern painting and, 2. 7, 8
statue decided by, not to be Henry VII, 1. 279
Tyson's drawing of diploma for, 16. 181
*Vetusta monumenta* by, 37. 349n
Vertue's historical prints republished by, 2.
 8, 11, 16. 166
Vertue, Mrs, makes gift to, 2. 8
Whittington and cat discussed by, 1. 265, 270
'Whittingtonians,' 1. 267, 293, 295
Antiquaries of Scotland, Society of the:
Buchan enrolls HW in, 35. 539
—— founds, 15. 138n
—— notifies HW of membership in, 29. 107
—— tells HW about, 33. 363
error in memoirs of, 33. 368
HW declines to send copy of jewel to, 15.
 233

HW honorary member of, 2. 261, 264, 15.
 150–1, 154–5, 29. 107
HW offers copies of his works to, 15. 157–8
memoirs of, sent to HW, 15. 164, 165
Nivernais's *Jardins modernes* given to, 12. 260
opposition to charter of, defeated, 15. 178–9
'Temple of Caledonian Fame' proposed for,
 by Buchan, 42. 13n
Antiquary; antiquaries:
always turn into fools, 29. 118, 120
Caligula's bust formerly owned by, 22. 528
classical, HW ridicules, 11. 358
Cocchi's salary as, 21. 194
Cole on, 1. 5, 359, 2. 91, 148
communal spirit among, 32. 53
Court costumes designed by, 32. 102
HW as, diverted by mystery, 32. 224
HW a superannuated, 34. 224
HW bored by friend who is, 32. 94–5
HW corresponds with, over Richard III, 32.
 281
HW on, 1. 5n, 12, 29, 258, 292–3, 2. 7, 31,
 238, 240, 259, 300
HW recognized as, 32. 297–8
HW's comments in his capacity of, 32. 78
HW's indebtedness from, 38. 151
HW's reflections on, 15. 252, 254
HW's 'Tom-Hearnality' as, 32. 297
Hawkins's *History of Music* a delight to,
 32. 333
Jacobite, at Rome, 20. 174
modern, discover nothing, 24. 62
pleasure of being, 33. 349
preferable to a salamander, 35. 415
proper end for, 32. 317
ridiculed for recovering trifles, 25. 146
Storer becomes, 35. 359
Antique; antiques. *See* Antiquities
*Antiquité expliquée et représentée en figures
 (Antiquitas explanatione et schematibus
 illustra)*. *See under* Montfaucon, Bernard
 de
*Antiquités étrusques, grecques, et romaines.*
 *See under* Hugues, Pierre-François
Antiquities:
Arundel's taste for, 42. 422
Devonshire's passion for, 32. 139
English, HW the first to introduce taste
 into, 28. 213
export of, from Rome and Florence forbid-
 den, 18. 161, 20. 465
George III likes, 21. 449, 451–2
Gothic, 2. 204
Gough's book on, 15. 334–5
Gray's catalogue of, 28. 56–7
HW criticizes study of, 32. 8
HW less fond of, 1. 247
HW's: discussed with Stanley, 30. 71; dis-
 paraged by Mme du Deffand as uncomfor-
 table, 7. 173; offered to Middleton for his
 use, 15. 11–15, 22
HW's and Gray's later correspondence on,
 28. 28

HW's love of, **1**. 292, 293

HW's reflections on best ways to write of, **16**. 307

Hamilton's collection of, **32**. 70–1

Indian, negative value of study of, **15**. 212

insufficient occupation for HW, **7**. 65

Ionian, ridiculed by HW, **11**. 358

Italian, Conway knows little of, **37**. 73

Middleton's collection of, **15**. 15–17, 22

Roman, **1**. 212, 368, **2**. 116, 204, 208, **15**. 179, 202, **37**. 324

Saxon, HW does not care for, **1**. 163, **2**. 116, 301

Scottish, Haddington's collections concerning, **15**. 29

study of, **1**. 375, 377–8, **2**. 116

taste for, flourishes, **28**. 40

truth the sole merit of, **16**. 234

*Antiquities and Scenery of the North of Scotland. See under* Cordiner, Charles

*Antiquities of Furness. See under* West, Thomas

*Antiquities of Herculaneum. See Pitture antiche di Ercolano*

*Antiquities of Leicestershire. See under* Burton, William

*Antiquities of Scotland. See under* Grose, Francis

Antiquity:

advantages of study of, **32**. 349

Conway venerates, **37**. 59

institutions hampered by, **7**. 363

*Antiquity, Evidence and Certainty of Christianity Canvassed. See under* Bayly, Anselm

'*Antiquus urbis,*' bull. *See under* Benedict XIV

Antiscorbutics:

Hénault takes, **4**. 5, 7, 13, 182

'Anti-Sejanus.' *See* Scott, James (1733–1814)

Antoine, Jean-François (b. 1724), Chevalier de St-Louis:

(?) Gévaudan beast killed by, **22**. 289n

*Antoinette. See under* Linguet, Simon-Nicolas-Henri

Anton Ulrich (1714–74), D. of Brunswick-Wolfenbüttel:

death of, rumoured, **17**. 256

imprisoned for life, **34**. 3

Antonia Minor (d. A.D. 38), dau. of Marcus Antonius:

HW's bust of, **15**. 12

'Antonines, the Two.' *See* Antoninus Pius (86–161); Marcus Aurelius (121–80)

*Antonini itinerarium:*

villages named in, **2**. 204, **10**. (?) 274n

Antonino (1389–1459) Pierozzi, Saint; Abp of Florence:

women ordered by, to uncover breasts in church, **21**. 292

Antoninus (Caracalla), itinerary of. *See Antonini itinerarium*

Antoninus Pius (Titus Aurelius Fulvus Boionius Arrius Antoninus) (86–161), Roman emperor:

England has the arts and fustian of, **23**. 212

good emperor, **15**. 50–1, **35**. 127

HW praises, **33**. 479

Louis XVI compared with, **34**. 179

Voltaire mentions, **35**. 413

'Antonio, St':

faction of, at Pisan Battle of the Bridge, **20**. 473, **25**. 582

'Antonio, Dom.' *See* Rodriguez, P.F. Antonio Giuseppe

Antonio, Dom (1714–1800) legitimated Portuguese prince:

alleged plot by, **21**. 475, 476n

Antonio, Marc. *See* Antonius, Marcus (ca 83–30 B.C.); Raimondi, Marcantonio (1480–ca 1534)

Antonius, Lucius (fl. 41 B.C.):

statue of, at Holkham, **16**. 300

Antonius, Marcus (Mark Antony) (82–30 B.C.):

Augustus's alliance with, eliminating Lepidus, **39**. 406

Cicero's son prides himself on out-drinking, **21**. 57

daughter of, **15**. 12n

Grenville called, by HW, **10**. 272

HW admires, as hero, **32**. 28

medals of, **6**. 54, **15**. 13–14, **42**. 262

Octavius's struggle with, over Lepidus, **21**. 79

slung into Cleopatra's monument, **32**. 147

toasts Cleopatra in bumper of pearl, **11**. 295

Antony:

character in *Ballet de la Paix*, **18**. 495–6

Antony, Mark. *See* Antonius, Marcus

*Antony and Cleopatra. See under* Shakespeare, William

Antrim, co. (Ireland):

Conway M.P. for, **37**. 74n

(?) election in, **38**. 343

Hertford's estates in, **37**. 74n

Antrobus, Anne (1677–1758), m. (1710) Jonathan Rogers; Gray's aunt:

cottage leased by, **14**. 25n

Gray questioned by, **14**. 59n

—— visits, **14**. 32, 59

Gray, Mrs, lives with, at Stoke, **14**. 25n

husband of, **13**. 105n

Antrobus, Dorothy (1685–1753), m. (1709) Philip Gray; Thomas Gray's mother:

dying, **14**. 25, 66

family of, **43**. 190

Gray dreads death of, **13**. 141

——'s letter to, **28**. 96

recovering from illness, **14**. 59

sisters live with, at Stoke, **14**. 25n

Antrobus, Dorothy (b. 1734), m. Richard Comings; Thomas Gray's cousin:

Gray's bequest to, **1**. 231, 232–3

husband of, **1**. 231, **2**. 39

Antrobus, Jane (1681–1771), m. William Olliffe:

Gray buys annuity for, **1**. 233n

—— questioned by, **14**. 59n

Antrobus, Mary (1683–1749), Thomas Gray's aunt:
  buried at Stoke Poges, 14. 66n
  Cole overlooks note on, 1. 353n
  Gray, Mrs, lives with, at Stoke, 14. 25n
  milliner, 13. 95n
Antrobus, Mary (b. 1732), Thomas Gray's cousin:
  Gray attended by, in last illness, 1. 234
  —— attended by, to grave, 1. 230
  ——'s bequest to, 1. 231, 232–3
  sister of, 1. 231n
Antrobus, Rev. Robert (1679–1730), vicar of Burnham; assistant at Eton College; Thomas Gray's uncle:
  Gray encouraged by, to study medicine, 28. 186n
  ——, nephew of, 43. 190
  sister inherits lease of Cant's Hall from, 13. 106n
Antrobus, William (1688–1742), assistant at Eton:
  nephew under tutorship of, 43. 190
Antwerp:
  Arundel family group at, by Van Dyck, 41. 168
  Bladen tariff commissioner at, 17. 336
  Buckingham retires to, in Rebellion, 16. 154
  ——'s pictures sent to, 16. 154n
  capture of, by French, 19. 209, 255, 261n, 37. 249
  Dutch army said to approach, 37. 154
  Dutch-English reinforcement goes from, up Scheldt, 37. 205
  English may take over, 37. 295
  English secure, 37. 205
  Hoostman of, 1. 3n
  Jamesone studies at, with Van Dyck under Rubens, 40. 263
  Mitchell later commissary at, 20. 209n
  Portland, Ds of, buys views of, at Schaub sale, 21. 200n
  retreat of Allied armies near, 12. 101n
  Van der Borcht dies at, 1. 24n
  visitors to: Ancrams, 37. 119; Conway, 37. 119
  Wade stores plate at, 37. 154
Anus, fistula in. See under Fistula
Anville, Duc d'. See La Rochefoucauld d'Ánville, Louis-Alexandre de
Anville, Duchesse d'. See La Rochefoucauld, Marie-Louise-Nicole-Élisabeth de
Anville. See also Bourgignon d'Anville
Apamea, Abp of. See Assemani, Stefano Evodio
Apella, the Jew:
  Horace's reference to, 11. 151
Apelles (fl. 4th cent. B.C.), painter:
  HW calls Reynolds England's, 28. 250
  Protogenes criticized by, 34. 243
Apennines:
  Florence near foot of, 30. 294
  Giogo part of, 17. 257n, 20. 180n
  HW and Gray to cross, 13. 195

HW dreads recrossing, 13. 238, 22. 332, 340
Apethorpe Hall, Northants; E. of Westmorland's seat:
  Fane family inherits, from Mildmay heiress, 41. 364–5
  HW never saw, 33. 419
Aphrodisiacs. See Cantharides
'Apicius':
  HW's letter signed, 40. 257
Apis. See Bull
Apocalypse; Apochrypha. See under Bible
Apocolocyntosis. See under Seneca
Apollo:
  bust of, in Nuneham garden, 35. 484n
  Craven, Lady, runs to, not from, 34. 44
  Darwin's Botanic Garden mentions, 42. 267
  Frederick II's letters to Voltaire often mention, 34. 33
  HW an, in Lady Craven's verses, 32. 245
  HW favoured by, 37. 52
  HW is Lady Ossory's, 32. 88–9
  HW praises, as god of medicine, 32. 210
  intaglio of, 20. 99, 21. 457n, 24. 15, 26. 56
  Mason 'licenser of the press' to, 35. 494
  Masucci's copy of, from Guido's 'Aurora,' 21. 88
  Minerva's rivalry with, 37. 52–3
  never gave recipe in rhyme, 31. 241
  Phaeton must have taken curricle of, closer to earth, 39. 472
  Pope alludes to, 32. 372
  statues of: at Stowe, 10. 315, 31. 146–7; at Rome, see Apollo Belvedere; at Florence, see Apollo Medicis
  stockings of, 11. 292
Apollo, English frigate:
  Ross goes to Plymouth with, 25. 25n
Apollo Belvedere (statue at Rome):
  Astley resembles, 25. 451
  Berry, Mary, describes, 11. 338n
  comparisons with, 36. 238
  Darwin's Botanic Garden mentions, 42. 267
  graceful, 16. 272, 35. 37
  HW to appear in dream like, 32. 88
  Indian idol inferior to, 35. 602
  Milton's characters comparable to, 16. 270
  not derived from archaic statues, 33. 479
  passion expressed by, 35. 445
  Raphael figure compared with, 35. 37
  symptoms of anger in, 11. 338
  travel enhances, 39. 195
Apollo Medicis (statue at Florence):
  Mann to get gesso of, for Lyttelton, 20. 539, 547
Apologie de Shakespeare . . . à la critique de M. de Voltaire. See Robinson, Elizabeth: Essay on . . . Shakespear
Apologue:
  Bacon's, 34. 107
Apology for a late Resignation:
  Marchmont supposedly wrote, 20. 5–6
Apology for the late Mr Pope. See under Spence, Joseph

*Apology for the Life of Colley Cibber, An. See
under* Cibber, Colley
*Apology for the Life of George Anne Bellamy.
See under* Bellamy, George Anne
*Apology for the Life of Major-General G——*:
mentioned, 11. 185n
*Apology for the Life of Mrs Shamela Andrews,
An. See under* Fielding, Henry
*Apophtegmes . . . des anciens. See under* Perrot
d'Ablancourt, Nicolas
Apoplectic lethargy. *See* Lethargy, apoplectic
Apoplexy:
  epileptic fit resembles, 25. 627
  faintings may indicate possibility of, 18. 254
  fits of, 20. 192, 22. 90, 24. 371, 35. 80, 38. 419
  gout in the head confused with, 38. 419
  HW might have, if he cured his gout, 25. 402
  HW not dead of, 38. 236
  merchant writes postscript to letter    after
    being struck by, 24. 239
  Montfort's tendency to, 35. 201
  occurrences of, 9. 101, 10. 347, 19. 277n, 461,
    20. 298, 444, 463n, 476n, 21. 81, 149, 197,
    22. 530n, 23. 455, 24. 228, 25. 272, 495,
    28. 262, 379, 32. 308, 35. 308, 38. (?)419,
    39. 418n
  Poulett's lost Parliamentary motion compared
    to, 35. 224
  rumour of, 17. 211
  Young Pretender's fits may lead to, 24, 245
  —— thought to have had, 25. 467
  *See also* Fit, apoplectic; Palsy; Paralysis;
    Stroke
Apostle; apostles:
  portraits of, at Dulwich College, 11. 289
  pyx box represents, 40. 259
  Quin jokes about, 10. 150
Apostle-spoons:
  1. 313, 316, 319, 2. 13, 14
Apostoli, Santi. *See* Santi Apostoli
Apostolical Chamber, at Rome:
  cardinal's salary from, 23. 118
  Charles III not to burden, with Jesuits' up-
    keep, 22. 516n
  Lepri case dismissed by, 25. 587n
  omission of funeral oration for Old Pretender
    would save expenses by, 21. 391
  Valenti to be indemnified by, for loss of
    abbeys, 18. 55
  Young Pretender's allowance from, 24. 244
Apothecary; apothecaries:
  advises using force on HW's ward, 11. 307
  at Exeter, Patch apprenticed to, 23. 275n
  at Kingston, 31. 10
  at Leghorn, provides drugs for D. of Glou-
    cester, 23. 393
  at Rome, HW's purchases from, 26. 4, 7
  attempted suicide attended by, 31. 339
  Bentley needs surgeon instead of, 35. 221
  bootikins at first praised but later condemned
    by, 24. 71
  draught from, given to E. of Orford, 24. 372

  English weather benefits trade of, 25. 582
  French invasion of England to include, 21.
    311
  genuine spirits cannot be conveyed by, 35. 376
  HW attended by, 11. 316, 12. 194
  HW gets peppermint-water from, 33. 412
  HW's, *see* Gilchrist, Stirling
  HW sends for, 34. 199
  HW told by, that weakness on the breast is
    caused by bootikins, 24. 80
  impertinence of, 42. 335
  in London, give noxious drugs under name of
    James's powders, 24. 71
  in St Alban's Street, 34. 130
  La Cour's prescriptions should be filled by
    confectioner instead of, 35. 108
  Lobkowitz attended by, 18. 564
  Louis XV's, *see* Le Lièvre
  Montrose, Ds of, attended by, 33. 296
  Orford's, 24. 294, 32. 350, 36. 125, 335
  organ made by, from glister pipes, 36. 8
  port wine as nauseous to HW as anything
    from, 12. 38
  shop of, containing empty pots, 34. 9
  'vehicle' used by, in administering medicine,
    35. 263
  Walpole, Sir Edward, talks like, 36. 145
  Walpole of Wolterton, Bns, spends money on,
    for first time at 86, 25. 385
  witnesses Miss Gunning's oath, 11. 205
  *See also* Allen, ——; Garney, ——; Gilchrist,
    Sterling; Graham, Daniel; Guernier, ——;
    Hallifax, Robert; Livett, John; Lucas, ——;
    Plunket, ——; Skrine, William; Yonge, ——
Apothecary's shop:
  London as nauseous as any drug in, 35. 375
  tarwater popular in, 18. 452
Apothecary's wife:
  HW gives, as instance of provincial ill-
    breeding, 19. 234
*Apothicairerie:*
  at St-Cyr, 10. 294
*Appaltatori* (tax farmers):
  Tuscany said to be governed by, 19. 23
*Appartement; appartementi* (state receptions):
  gala, at Tuscan Court, 25. 301
  *See also* Drawing-Room; Gala
Appeal, Commissioners of, for prizes:
  prize ships adjudged by, 21. 287n
*Appeal from the Old to the New Whigs. See
under* Burke, Edmund
*Appeal to the Jockey Club, An. See under* Fitz-
gerald, George Robert
*Appeal to the Serious and Unprejudiced. See
under* Church, Thomas
*Appel à toutes les nations. See under* Voltaire
Appendicitis. *See* Inflammation of the bowels
*Appendix, Containing some Observations upon
. . . the Poems Attributed to Rowley. See
under* Tyrwhitt, Thomas
Apperley, ——:
  Mann escorted by, 23. 6on

Appian Way:
'costly and durable,' but 'uneasy,' **42.** 51
might be paved with diamonds, **11.** 295
Romans drag prisoners along, **21.** 367
Velletri approached by, **18.** 488
Apple; apples:
cooked, eaten by Mme du Deffand, **6.** 132
floods might compel people to live on, **35.** 384
given to children, **33.** 21
HW expects, to ripen early, **28.** 162
inedible for the toothless, **33.** 533
lady carries, in pocket, **37.** 22
Mann's house stocked with, **18.** 132
Marchais, Mme de, gives, to Mme du Deffand, **6.** 251, 259
more exuberant than their leaves, **34.** 8
'old store-pippin' withers, **37.** 124
orchards of, **32.** 359
roasted, sputtering of, **9.** 200
stewed, **17.** 218
*See also* Pippin
Apple blossoms:
at Little Strawberry Hill, **11.** 251
Appleby, Westmorland:
Bentley's remark about, **37.** 126
election at, contested, **20.** 435, 456n, **37.** 429
Pembroke, Cts of, rejects Williamson's candidate for, **9.** 125, **35.** 133
Appleby Castle:
Percy visits, **10.** 185
portraits at, **10.** 185
Applegirth:
Jardine of, **12.** 62n
Apple pie and cheese:
Mason wanted to invite HW to dine on, **28.** 273
Apple trees:
bent down with fruit, **35.** 397
in bloom, one of HW's spring delights, **33.** 334
lanes overhung by, near Worcester, **35.** 152
on Amiens-Clermont road, **7.** 259
Appleyard, Mary (1727–88), m. Kenrick Prescott:
away from Cambridge, **2.** 22–3, 26
*Appollon,* French ship of India Co.:
captured off Cape Finisterre, **19.** 410
Appraisers:
furniture at Little Strawberry Hill appraised by, **42.** 306–7
Apprentice; apprentices:
Bedlam inmate rebukes, **38.** 453
Brownrigg, Mrs, murders, **30.** 252
coachmaker's, brings news of house-breaking, **23.** 286
English, all in arms, **21.** 347
'flirt to Epsom in a timwhiskey,' **39.** 106
Gordon rioters mostly composed of, **25.** 62, 67, **33.** 189, 190, 192
HW compares D. of Grafton to, **39.** 100
Hogarth's idle and industrious, **33.** 393, **36.** 209

Porter takes, to church, **16.** 217
Twickenham churchyard thronged with, **34.** 115
Apprius. *See under* Godart de Beauchamps, Pierre-François
Apps Court, Walton parish, Surrey:
Charlemont imitates, **9.** 391
Knox from, **12.** 239
Apraxin, Stephan Feodorovich (1702–58), Russian field marshal:
Bestuchev orders, to retreat after defeating Prussians, **21.** 159n
death of, after trial, **21.** 159n
Siberian exile of, for retreat, **21.** 159
succeeded by Fermor, **21.** 172n
victory of, at Gross-Jägersdorf, **21.** 144n
Apremont, Comtesse d'. *See* Mérode, Josephine-Monique-Mélanie
Apremont, Henri-Ange, Comte d':
(?) social relations of, with Marquise de Coislin, **7.** 297
Apremont (in Piedmont):
Las Minas forces surrender of, **18.** 143n
*Apremont. See also* Aspremont
Apricot; apricots:
frost should reduce quantity of, **23.** 200
infant, may succumb to frost, **2.** 149
peaches and, sugared and chilled, **3.** 405–6, **4.** 3n
Apricot trees:
deal of the 'influenza,' **33.** 335
Apriment. *See* Linden, Apriment
Apron; aprons:
black, St-Cyr pensioners wear, **10.** 293
blue, waiters wear, **20.** 209
falbala, quoted from Cibber's *Careless Husband,* **38.** 208
leather, carpenter wears, **9.** 133
midwife presents child in, for baptism, **33.** 208
Salins, Mme de, wears, **20.** 75n
white: executioner wears, **19.** 300; Queensberry, Ds of, wears at fireworks, **9.** 82; worn at Marlborough House assembly, **39.** 383n
Young, Margaret, carries dead fawn in, **33.** 208
young girl's costume, **17.** 174
Apse Court Farm, Walton, Surrey. *See* Apps Court
Apsley, Bn. *See* Bathurst, Henry (1714–94)
Apsley, Bns. *See* Scawen, Tryphena
Apsley House, London:
guarded during Gordon riots, **33.** 184
near Ossory's, **32.** 236
Apthorp, George (b. ?1744):
Mann's correspondence with, over Tortola lands, **24.** 169, 200, 220
Apthorp, John:
(?) Foote, Mrs, summons, to reading of E. L. Mann's will, **24.** 159
Apthorp, Mrs John. *See* Mann, Alice (1739–63)

Apthorp, Sarah:
  (?) grandmother's watch given by, to robber, 25. 343–4
Apthorp. *See also* Apethorpe; Apthorpe
Apthorpe, Anne (d. 1782), Cole's niece:
  death of, 2. 315, 317, 329
Apthorpe, Rev. East (d. 1816):
  Gibbon replies to, 33. 84
Apthorpe, Rev. Stephen (?1708–90), Cole's half-brother:
  at Eton, 1. 38, 348, 349n
  Bryant admired by, 1. 370
  —— dines with, 1. 349n
  Cole gives box to, 1. 260n
  ——'s visits to, 1. 35, 38, 78, 332n, 348, 381
  daughter of, dies, 2. 315n, 317
  death of, falsely reported, 2. 181, 184n
  HW called on by, 1. 85
  Nell Gwynn's letter owned by, 1. 348–51
  remains in living of Burnham, 1. 106
  Worplesdon living acquired by, 1. 331n
Apthorpe. *See also* Apthorp
Apthorpe, Northants:
  Mildmay of, 14. 113n
Apthorpe Hall. *See* Apethorpe Hall
Aqua:
  Austrians break camp at, 18. 534
Aquano di Sinopoli. *See* Sinopoli
Aqua Pendente:
  Spaniards intercept courier at, 18. 515
Aquapulca. *See* Acapulco
'Aquatinta':
  Gilpin wants method of, 29. 103, 112, 127–8
  plates in Gilpin's *Observations on the River Wye* are in, 29. 277–8
  Sandby experiments with, 29. 71, 101
*Aqua vitæ. See* Brandy
Aquaviva. *See* Acquaviva
Aquedotto Carolino, at Caserta:
  Vanvitelli designs, 21. 379n
Aqueduct:
  at Caserta, 21. 379
  for Westminster, 40. 223
Aqui:
  Spaniards march towards, 19. 225
Aquila (Italy):
  Castropignano reaches, 18. 3n
  Lobkowitz's detachment reaches, 18. 454
  Neapolitan army at, 18. 325
  Neapolitan Court may flee to, from plague, 18. 302
Aquila, Albergo d', Florentine inn:
  Modenese princess at, 17. 68n
Aquila degli Abruzzi:
  Spanish troops reach, from Naples, 17. 265
*Aquila del Nord*, Russian war ship:
  (?) Leghorn left by, without Ds of Kingston's treasure, 24. 404, 409–10
Aquilaja. *See* Aquileia
Aquila Nera, inn at Florence:
  faro played at, 17. 68
Aquilar, Baron d'. *See* Pereira, Ephraim Lopez

Aquileia (Italy):
  Benedict XIV negotiates with Maria Theresa and Venice over, 20. 173n
  —— quarrels with Venice over, 20. 160–1, 163, 176
  —— suppresses patriarchate of, and sub-divides it, 20. 173n
  France proposes sub-division of, 20. 191n
  patriarchate of, to be abolished, 20. 191, 206n
*Aquilon*, English frigate:
  Augustus, P., sails on, 39. 503n, 504n
Aquinas, St Thomas (1225–74):
  quotation from, 4. 214n
Aquino, Francesco d' (1736–95), Principe di Caramanico; Neapolitan envoy to England 1780–5:
  Acton displaces, as Maria Carolina's favourite, 33. 242n
  England to be visited by, 33. 241–2
  Lunardi secretary to, 25. 528n, 543n
  Maria Carolina of Naples said to favour, 33. 242
Aquitaine, Grand Prior of. *See* Foucault de St-Germain-Beaupré, Armand-Louis-Joseph
Aquitaine:
  HW does not want, for England, 12. 4
  HW thought as much of losing duchy of, as Canada, 38. 56
Ara, sepulchral. *See* Altar
Arab; Arabs:
  English caravan captured by, 24. 510
  in East and West Indies, 39. 168
  robberies by, 11. 358
Arabia:
  Conway imagines deserts of, full of tigers, bears, and wolves, 37. 130
  perfume of, 32. 325
  SH flowers are from, 39. 299
Arabian; Arabians:
  acacias worshipped by, 10. 156
Arabian horses:
  pure breed of, 15. 201
Arabian jasmine. *See under* Jasmine
*Arabian Nights*:
  Berry, Mary, reads, 11. 20
  Birthday celebrations exceed splendour of, 38. 88
  Cagliostro's legend more absurd than anything in, 25. 654
  Ceylon called 'Isle of Serendip' in, 25. 277
  'delineator' makes pictures as magical as, 28. 329
  East Indies compared with, 32. 328
  Fitzpatrick, Lady Anne, should like 'Squire of Low Degree' as well as tales from, 32. 194
  HW praises, 11. 20, 22
  HW refers to Princess in, 17. 278
  HW's copy of, 43. 139
  HW's gout reminds him of, 41. 343
  HW's letter might have been written in time of, 25. 15
  HW's letters filled with tales from, 34. 97

[*Arabian Nights*, continued]
HW's stories rival, **29.** 101
La Borde's house resembles entertainment in, **31.** 80
newspapers as untrustworthy as, **33.** 536
popular power rising like black cloud in, **34.** 102
Stanley's poem drawn from, **29.** 8
truffle palace in Darwin's *Botanic Garden* resembles saloon in, **31.** 293
*See also Mille et une nuits,* 'Scheherazade,' and *under* Pétis de la Croix, François

Arabian tales:
Du Deffand, Mme, prefers, **6.** 400
HW wants invisible architect from, at SH, **20.** 372
magic of, **21.** 313

Arabic:
HW's handwriting resembles characters in, **12.** 204–5

Arabic language:
diversity of terms in, **31.** 247–8
'jerboa' derived from, **37.** 467

Arabic numerals:
not used in Edward IV's reign, **16.** 242

Arabin, William John (ca 1751–1828), army officer; amateur actor:
acts in East's and Mrs Hobart's theatres, **33.** 369
Murphy's *Way to Keep Him* acted by, at Richmond House, **33.** 563n

Aragon, K. of. *See* John I (1350–95); Pedro IV (1319–87)

Aragon, Q. of. *See* Sibilia (d. 1406) de Forciá

Aragon, Catherine of. *See* Catherine (1485–1536) of Aragon

Aragon, Yolande d', m. Louis II, Duc d'Anjou:
daughter of, **14.** 72n

Aragon (Spain):
arms of, **1.** 242, **2.** 5
Bayeu from, **16.** 170
HW imagines intrigues of, at Rome, **35.** 222

Araia, Francesco (b. ca 1700):
*Ceffalo e Procri* by: almost deserted, **43.** 244; performed but never printed, **17.** 434n

Aranda, Conde de. *See* Abarca de Bolea, Don Pedro Pablo

Aranjuez (Spain):
Charles III flees to, **7.** 312, **39.** 64
'king of,' HW's term for Charles III, **22.** 414
views of, engraved, **16.** 170

Aranjuez, Treaty (Convention) of:
arranged at Madrid, **20.** 294–5, 320
Charles III recognizes United States by, **24.** 459n
Genoa's agreement under, **18.** 509n, 554n
Gibraltar's return to Spain stipulated by, **24.** 484n
Keene promotes, **21.** 166n
Mann ignorant of, **24.** 476n
provisions of, **17.** 216n

Ararat, Mt:
flood and, alluded to, **32.** 291
HW calls Prospect House, **12.** 121, 133
HW jokes about balloon from, foundering in hurricane, **39.** 425
SH compared to, **35.** 228

Araujo de Acebedo, Antonio de (1752–1817), Portuguese statesman:
SH visited by, **12.** 233

Arbalet. *See* Ponte d'Albaret

Arbermarle. *See* Albemarle

Arblade, Comtesse d'. *See* Helvétius, Élisabeth-Charlotte

Arblay, Mme d'. *See* Burney, Frances

Arblay, Alexandre-Jean-Baptiste-Piochard d' (ca 1753–1808), Comte d':
dines at Windsor Castle, **12.** 204
wife of, **12.** 73n

Arbor vitæ:
Chinese: HW admires, **9.** 176; HW can supply Montagu with, **9.** 177
Royal Society receives mock dissertation on, **24.** 290

Arbour:
druid distributes verses in, to ladies, **39.** 330

Arbuthnot, Mrs:
Florence visited by, **20.** 327

Arbuthnot, Charles (1767–1850), diplomatist:
wife of, **12.** 102n

Arbuthnot, Mrs Charles. *See* Lisle, Marcia Mary Anne

Arbuthnot, Dr John (1667–1735), physician and wit:
Bathurst's correspondence with, said to be burnt, **28.** 239
Charteris's immorality celebrated by, **19.** 148n
correspondence among Bolingbroke, Swift, Pope, and, published, **30.** 24
*Gulliver's Travels* not written by, **34.** 259
Italian opera attacked by, **13.** 64n
Jervas and, **15.** 144
Lindamira and Indamora attributed to, **20.** 214
*Memoirs of Martin Scriblerus* by Pope and, **28.** 61n, **30.** 24–5, **43.** 247
Pope's *Epistle* to, **28.** 436
portrait of: **15.** 164; belongs to E. of Bristol, **42.** 12
whore rebuked by, for absurdities, **18.** 70

Arbuthnot, Marriot (ca 1711–94), naval officer:
account of naval actions of, not understood by Mann, **25.** 150
Ailesbury, Cts of, said by, to be coming to Italy, **20.** 285
Charleston captured by Clinton and, **7.** 233n, **33.** 198n
Clinton's correspondence with, about attack on Rhode Island, **25.** 99n
convoy to be joined by, at Torbay, leaving force to protect Channel Islands, **39.** 320
Conway's intention unknown to, when at Port Mahon, **20.** 284–5

Estaing said to have blockaded, **24.** 528
fleet of, windbound at Torbay, **24.** 482n
Gambier succeeded by, **28.** 467n
HW expects French to capture fleet of, **28.** 474
Jersey attack learned by, when about to take recruits to America, **24.** 471n, 472n
*London Gazette's* news of, **29.** 137
Mann's correspondence with, **20.** 285
Minorca hastily left by, in haste to see wife in Italy, **20.** 284–5, **37.** 314
*Nightingale*, ship of, **43.** 269, 270
recruits to be convoyed by, to America, **24.** 472
sails to relieve Jersey, **24.** 472
seven ships of, at New York, **33.** 126
*Triton*, former ship of, **43.** 270
victory of, over inferior squadron, **25.** 145–6
Arbuthnot, Mrs Marriot:
Florence visited by, with sister, **43.** 270
husband hastens to Italy to see, **37.** 314
Arbuthnot family:
'Fitz-Arbuthnot' parrot in picture at Ampthill, **32.** 51–2
Arbutus:
HW admires, **9.** 176
Arc, Chevalier d'. *See* Saint-Foix, Philippe-Auguste de
Arcade:
niches of, closed at Livry, **10.** 212
Arcadia:
Campbell's match with Ds of Hamilton worthy of, **21.** 267
England more rural than, **10.** 298
HW an elderly Arcadian, **32.** 114
HW imagines, at Eton, **9.** 3
'nymphs and swains' of, **32.** 147
Shenstone's ballad, **32.** 244
Stowe house-party worthy of, **10.** 314
*Arcadia. See under* Berry, Agnes; Sidney, Sir Philip
Arce, Don Antonio de; Spanish lt-gen.:
Orvilliers joined by fleet of, **24.** 496n
Arch; arches:
builder of, *see* Jadot
'great,' at Park Place, **35.** 395
of Francis I, at Florence, **18.** 272, **21.** 343
of Sissinghurst stables, **35.** 144
of SH library bookcases, **35.** 157, 164, 200
pedestal of column used as part of foundation of, **21.** 343
pointed, Young's theory about, **42.** 305
rude, in grounds at Whiteknights, **35.** 71
Temple erects, to Ps Amelia, at Stowe, **10.** 315
triumphal: at Horton, **10.** 334; at Mereworth, **35.** 143; for Old Pretender's funeral, **21.** 424
*Archæologia*:
account in, of Society of Antiquaries, **2.** 347
answers to HW in, **2.** 5
article on freemasons for, **1.** 293, 295
Caley's essay in, on Jews in England, **12.** 262, **33.** 569

Cole has not seen, **1.** 203
——'s comments on, **2.** 162
——'s contribution to, **2.** 162
Gough's preface to, **43.** 77
HW comments on, **2.** 163–5
HW is scolded in 3d volume of, **28.** 212–13
HW mentions, **42.** 103n
HW reads, as penance, **29.** 309
HW's copy of, **43.** 58
HW's low opinion of, **33.** 353
HW's resignation from Society of Antiquaries blamed on, **43.** 73
King's and Marsh's essay in, on Barberini Vase, **42.** 268
King's *Observations on Ancient Castles* in, **28.** 320, **33.** 353, **42.** 35
Lort's 'Observations on Celts' in, **16.** 172
Masters's 'Remarks' in, on *Historic Doubts*, **1.** 268, 290, 334, **2.** 197, **13.** 49, **28.** 58
Moira, Lady, author of letter in, **33.** 474
Nash's article in, with print, about disinterment of Q. Catherine Parr's corpse, **43.** 385n
'old women's logic' in, **28.** 239, 319, **33.** 477–8
'or *Old Women's Logic*,' **1.** 218–19, 270, 304
vol. I of: account in, of Society of Antiquaries, **2.** 347; Cole has not seen, **1.** 203
vol. II of, published, **1.** 302
vol. VI of, in press, **2.** 277
*Archæologia Græca. See under* Potter, John
*Archæological Epistle to . . . Jeremiah Milles, An. See under* Mason, William
Archangel, Father. *See* Forbes, Hon. John; Lesley, George
Archangel; archangels:
cannot get pensions and salaries in France, **39.** 143
of Philadelphia, **32.** 394
Archbishop; archbishops:
Cabinet Council appoints, for Armagh, **22.** 275–6
Chute would not be, **35.** 32
HW mistakes Lady Mary Coke for concubine of, **39.** 7
*See also under* names of sees
'Archbishop of Saint Promontory':
character in 'Sequel to Gulliver's Travels,' **32.** 72–3
Archdall (until 1728, Montgomery), Nicholas (d. 1763), M.P. Fermanagh:
speech by, **37.** 410
Archdeacon ('Archdeakon'), Mr:
SH visited by, **12.** 245, 250
Archdeckne, ——:
Mann escorted by, at Florence, **23.** 60n
'Archduchess, the.' *See* Maria Christine (1742–98); Maria Ricciarda Beatrice (1750–1829)
'Archduchess, the second.' *See* Maria Anna (1718–44)
'Archduke, the.' *See* Ferdinand Karl Anton Joseph (1754–1806)
'Archduke, the little.' *See* Joseph II

Archduke; archdukes:
  Botta's remark about dignity of, **24**. 23
  names of, **11**. 265
  Tuscan, arrested for fighting each other at
    Pisa, **25**. 569
Archer, Bns. *See* West, Sarah
Archer, Lady Elizabeth. *See* Montagu, Lady
    Elizabeth (d. 1789)
Archer, Henry (1700–68), M.P.:
  genealogy of, **10**. 280n, 352
  HW calls, fool, **30**. 164
  Onslow's pension urged by, **30**. 164
  wife of, **10**. 280n
Archer, John:
  print of, **40**. 236
Archer, John, Dublin bookseller:
  *Mysterious Mother* published by, **42**. 301,
    309n, 324n
Archer, Thomas (1695–1768), cr. (1747) Bn
    Archer:
  brother of, **10**. 280n
  HW and Hertfords entertained by, **9**. 121
  Hertford entertained by, at Umberslade, **38**.
    69
  long dinner at Northumberland House ex-
    ceeds day at house of, **38**. 530
  peerage granted to, **19**. 419
Archer. *See also* (?) Huber, Rev. Mr
Archery:
  popularity of, **11**. 25n
Arches, Court of:
  dean of, *see* Bettesworth, Dr John; Lee, Sir
    George
Archiac de St-Simon, Comte d'. *See* Desmier,
    Louis-Étienne
'Archibald, Lady.' *See* Hamilton, Lady Jane
'Archimage, Dr':
  HW refers to Milles as, **35**. 522
Archimedes:
  Voltaire mentions, **35**. 413
Archinto, Alberigo (1698–1758), nuncio to Tus-
    cany 1739–46; cardinal, 1756:
  Acciaioli assured by, that Clement XIII will
    not change Benedict XIV's Jesuit policy,
    **21**. 340n
  becomes vice-chancellor of Santa Chiesa, **20**.
    590
  Borromeo ordered by, to break off map sale,
    **21**. 192
  HW's inscription for Benedict XIV's profile
    to be shown by, to Benedict XIV, **21**. 124,
    127
  leaving Florence, **18**. 288
  Richecourt often sees, at Florence and Leg-
    horn, **17**. *489–90*
  too young to be pope, **21**. 216–17
Archinto, Maria (d. 1762), m. 1 (1715) Mar-
    chese Carlo Giorgio Clerici; m. 2 Principe
    Antonio Gallio-Trivulzio:
  Wachtendonck courts, **17**. 489–90
  —— relinquishes pictures of, at priests' urg-
    ing, **17**. *109*
  ——'s mistress, **18**. 251n

Archipelago. *See* Greek Islands
Architect; architects:
  England's, described by HW, **24**. 93
  'Gothic,' *see* Essex, James (1722–84)
  liable to criticism because they are public,
    **40**. 354
  Salisbury Cathedral choir spoiled by, **41**. 420
Architecture:
  Agincourt's project on monuments of, **42**. 103
  ancient, pictures of, **40**. 217
  at Houghton, **34**. 237
  at Kenilworth, 'degenerate,' **32**. 356
  at Osterley, **32**. 127, **34**. 237–9
  Attic, or Roman, **35**. 37
  bad, at Florentine villas, **20**. 191
  Bentley draws, well, **35**. 243
  book of designs of, **35**. 412
  by royalty, HW dislikes, **39**. 182
  ceilings: decoration of, **31**. 88; design for
    Anne Pitt's, **31**. 99, 106, 110
  Chatterton forges, **16**. 131, 221
  Chinese: Bateman's at Vcts Townshend's, **40**.
    52; Bedford, D. of, wants house in, **35**. 177;
    Bentley's plan for, for HW, **35**. 177–8;
    garden seat half Gothic and, **35**. 143; HW
    admires, **20**. 127; HW converts Bateman
    to Gothic from, **35**. 359; HW does drawing-
    room in, for Rigby, **20**. 166; HW suggests
    galleries in style of, at Mistley, **30**. 87;
    Hallet's, at Latimers, 'mongrel', **35**. 233;
    Radnor's summer house in, **20**. 382; temples
    and bridges of, in English landscape effects,
    **20**. 166; Westwood represents, **40**. 14;
    Wroxton landscape has, **35**. 74
  Chinese, Gothic, Greek, Italian, and Roman,
    'inlaid upon one another,' **35**. 241
  Chute's taste in, **21**. 363
  Conway wants books on, **38**. 198
  cornices, decoration of, **31**. 88
  Doric, pillars and frieze of, at Mereworth
    church, **35**. 144
  Drummond ascribes misfortunes of James
    III's reign to love of, **37**. 262, 263
  Dutch: Bulstrode exemplifies, **35**. 233
  earliest, was of twisted rods, **16**. 46
  Elizabethan, HW's opinion of, **9**. 64, 297
  English: as classic as Rome's, **23**. *313*; be-
    comes perishable, **23**. 257; formerly made
    to keep out cold winds, **32**. 359
  English houses have a single staircase, us-
    ually wooden, **22**. 143
  French: antique style influences, **31**. 106; at
    Boughton, **10**. 340; Carnavalet hôtel un-
    like, **31**. 50–1; chimneys in, low and strad-
    dling, **31**. 88; doors in, rounded at corners,
    **31**. 88; fashions in, ephemeral, **31**. 99;
    Grecian influence on, **22**. 218, 270, **23**. 158;
    HW wishes to see villas of, **10**. 167; house
    of Bns Hervey imitates, **31**. 416; in room
    at Florence, **33**. 286; interior decoration
    in, **30**. 265, **31**. 49, 55–6, 80, 87–8, 99, 106;
    revived by the French, **35**. 425; taste in, in-
    ferior, **25**. 635; town houses in, resemble

each other, **31.** 49; *see also under* France: houses in

George III fond of, **16.** 42, **21.** 460

Gothic: account of, in *Annual Register*, **1.** 148; Andrews's house a chaste specimen of, **35.** 642; at Bristol, **10.** 232; at Burghley House, **10.** 344; at Lee Priory, **11.** 59, **12.** 134, **31.** 342; **35.** 635; at Lord Holland's at Kingsgate, **12.** 112, 124–5; at Netley Abbey, **35.** 251; at Oxford, good when not altered, **35.** 155; at St George's Chapel, Windsor, **11.** 362; at Sandleford Priory, **31.** 321; at SH, **2.** 150, 370; at Sudeley Castle chapel, **42.** 113; at the Vyne chapel, **35.** 641; at Welbeck, **35.** 271; at Wentworth Castle, **11.** 66–7; barn for Lady Suffolk, **35.** 102, 644; Barret's and Wyatt's compared, **35.** 635; Barrett Lennard's, at Belhus inferior to SH, **35.** 183–4; bastard, at Kippax Park, **35.** 270; Bentley alone can combine, with Grecian, **21.** 250; Bentley and workmen did not study, before building SH, **42.** 220; Bentley to copy market cross in, for Wentworth Castle's menagerie temple in woods, **35.** 267, 279–80, **38.** 72; Bentley to introduce, at (?) Aston and Chalfont, **9.** 285; Bentley to introduce, at Roel, **9.** 138, 146; bridge at Tunbridge in, **35.** 135; bridge in, at Ferrybridge, **35.** 269; Brooke attempts, at Warwick, **9.** 121; chapel on Wakefield Bridge, **35.** 270; church in, as stage scenery, **39.** 133; Chute 'exquisite' in, **35.** 641–2; Croyland Abbey beautiful example of, **16.** 195; degenerate, at Kenilworth, **32.** 356; English more florid than French, **42.** 305; Essex's projected treatise on, **1.** 184, 190–2, 203–4, 205–6, 206, 209, 284–5, 286; Essex's skill in, **1.** 208; Exchequer House gallery roof in, **37.** 454n; Fairfaxes show gleam of, at Leeds Castle, **35.** 145; Fingal's Cave an example in, **1.** 329; French consider, not *solide* enough, **22.** 270; Frenchmen ascribe all English houses to, **23.** 312; garden seat half Chinese and, **35.** 143; garden seat in, at Wroxton, **35.** 74; gate at SH in, **11.** 283; Gloucester bishop's house restored to, **35.** 153; good, at Newstead Abbey, **35.** 305; Grecian has less variety than, **11.** 362; HW absorbed in antiquities of, **35.** 106; HW and Thomas Pitt bring Gothic trowels to, **40.** 288; HW avoids, in garden, **20.** 372; HW converts Bateman to, from Chinese, **35.** 359; HW defends, **20.** 127; HW does not believe in Moorish, Saracenic, or Saxon origins of, **42.** 305; HW hopes to interest Lord de Ferrers in, **2.** 146, 148; HW introduces, at Bateman's, **10.** 43; HW likes, **9.** 64 and *passim*; HW on, **1.** 190–2, 339–40; HW searches history of, **16.** 27; HW's quarrel with Warburton arises from Warburton's note on, **13.** 39; HW suggests spires in style of, at Mistley, **30.** 87; HW to build

columbarium in, **36.** 39; HW wants Bentley to paint ruins in, **35.** 208; in tapestry, **1.** 169; Italy has few specimens of true taste in, **20.** 372; James I's period in, at Belhus, **35.** 184 (*see also* Architecture: Jacobean); Kent adheres to, at Rousham, **9.** 290; Kent misuses, in Gloucester Cathedral screen, **35.** 154; King's College Chapel described by Mary Berry, **11.** 22n; lacking, at Hardwick Hall, **35.** 304; Langley's, at Latimers, 'bastard,' **35.** 233; lock designed in, **42.** 223; Mann disparages, though admitting it is fashionable, **20.** 119; Mann supposes that SH garden will be in, **20.** 368; Mann tells architect to seek in Rome some ornaments in, **20.** 368–9; Mason to introduce, at (?) Aston, **9.** 285; Matthew trained in, by Wyatt, **42.** 220; 'menagerie' temple in, **38.** 72; Mereworth lures HW away from, **35.** 143; Methodist chapel windows in, **35.** 118; Miller's ruined castle at Hagley, **35.** 148; Miller's Wroxton church tower, **35.** 74; monument to Galfridus Mann in, **35.** 644; Norfolk, D. of, to restore Arundel Castle in style of, **12.** 205; perfection of, at time of Ely's completion, **16.** 49; Pitt, Thomas, draws ornaments in, for SH, **22.** 25; plate designed in, **16.** 84; Pomfret, Cts of, has house of, **2.** 135; popularity of, in landscape effects, **21.** 418; Pownal's 'observations' on, **1.** 293n; Pratt's house at Bayham Abbey, **35.** 136; proportions of, **1.** 226n; restoration of, in Worcestershire, **35.** 150; Rockingham Hall in, by Miller, **35.** 149; SH Cloister in, **35.** 110; SH Cottage not to be designed in, **10.** 168; SH more in style of, after explosion, **32.** 75; SH's pretensions in, **20.** 362; Temple of Liberty in, at Stowe, **35.** 77; temples and bridges of, in English landscape effects, **20.** 166; towers in, at W. G. Hamilton's house, **33.** 82; Tyson collecting specimens of, **1.** 161n; Venetian and mosque influences in, **35.** 77; Vyne chapel walls to be painted to imitate, **35.** 640; Warton could see pictures of, at SH, **40.** 255; Warton's account of, more thorough than HW's, **40.** 254; Warwick Castle better than new tower of St Mary's Warwick, **32.** 356–7; Winchester Cathedral and its tombs in, **35.** 250; windows in, at the Vyne, **35.** 640; Worksop farm in, **37.** 566, 572, 579; Wren's Tom Tower as good as Bentley in, **35.** 154; Wroxton chapel newly built in, **35.** 73; York Minster's best part done in Henry IV's reign, **16.** 49; Yorkshire quarries good for, **35.** 266; Young traces, **42.** 305; *see also* SH

Gothic and Greek styles in, seldom gracefully combined, **21.** 250

Gothic paintings in convent at Agrigento, **35.** 409

[Architecture, *continued*]

Gothic Saracen mosaic, **35**. 408–9

Grecian (Greek): admits less variety than Gothic, **11**. 362; Aubeterre thinks that Doric fret comprises, **23**. 158; Bentley alone can combine, with Gothic, **21**. 250; Chiswick House a model of, **20**. 362; Chute 'exquisite' in, **35**. 641–2; French styles show influence of, **22**. 218, 270; HW's opinion of, **20**. 127; Jones, Inigo, progressed to purity in, **1**. 191; of Stowe temple, **35**. 76–7; Paris buildings in style of, said to be copied from Pantheon frieze, **23**. 158; Wyatt's, **35**. 635

Greek's grace in, **16**. 270

Greeks set standards for, **33**. 479

HW considered excellent judge of, by Cole, **10**. 332

HW discusses, with Stanley, **30**. 71

HW may get aid in treating history of, when he has finished that of painting, **16**. 37

HW on, **1**. 190–2, 339–40, **20**. 127, 146, 361–2, **21**. 250, **25**. 177

HW shows fancy and genius in, with whim and foppery, **35**. 648

HW's influence on, at Mistley, **9**. 88

history of, planned by Warton, **15**. 169

importance of structural elements in, exaggerated, **42**. 274

Ionic, in Belhus chimney-piece, **35**. 184

Ireland's, improves, **42**. 305

Italian, in French garden, **32**. 57

Jacobean, HW dislikes, **9**. 64, 297

Kent's, **21**. 250, **24**. 93

Mann's ideas on, **20**. 119, 146

medieval, HW's strictures on, **40**. 209n

modernization of, incongruous, **33**. 419–20

Moorish, **2**. 150–1, 152, **16**. 180

of London town houses, **18**. 316

of Parisian hotels, admits of no variety, **23**. 312

of Somerset House, discussed, **16**. 187–8

Palladian: at Mereworth, almost converts HW from Gothic, **35**. 143; briefly fashionable in Paris, **31**. 99; French china and costume affected by, **31**. 99; HW calls, 'true architecture,' **31**. 99

Parisian, recommended by HW, **35**. 429

Roman: HW suggests porticos in style of, at Mistley, **30**. 87; theatre in, at the Vyne, **35**. 640; urn on tomb in, **35**. 149

ruins of, make one regret not seeing it intact, **42**. 507

Saracen shrine, **35**. 409

'Saxon': at Kirkstall Abbey, **35**. 270; at Roye, **7**, 315; HW's distaste for, **15**. 203

Tuscan: Botta claims to know more than inventors of, **22**. 254; order of, appropriate for seats of old families, **41**. 361

Vanbrugh's ridiculed, **24**. 93

Wentworth Castle's new front considered most perfect by HW, **35**. 361, 407

Wren's, **40**. 345–54

Wyatt's, praised, **24**. 93

Archives, Jesuits'. *See under* Jesuit

Archivio, Florentine. *See* Florence: Archivio

Archon. *See* Le Michaud d'Archon

Arckenholtz, Johann (1695–1777):

*Mémoires concernant Christine*, **9**. 117, **15**. 30, 29. 120n, **43**. 117

Arclais de Montamy, Didier-François d' (1702–65):

fire-proof colours for enamel discovered by, **7**. 262

Arçon, Chevalier d'. *See* Le Michaud, Jean-Claude-Éléonore

Arconville. *See* Tiroux d'Arconville

Arcos, Duque de. *See* Ponce de Léon y Spinola, Antonio (1726–80); Ponce de Léon y Spinola y Maqueda, Don Joaquín

Arcot, Nawab of. *See* Muhammad 'Ali K͟han (1717–95), Wālājah

Arcot:

Clive takes, **29**. 35n

Arcoussy. *See* La Recousse

Arctic Circle:

Catherine II travels around, **33**. 562

Arcueil (France):

scene of Sade's attack on Rose Keller, **4**. 58

Arcy, d', family of. *See* Darcy

Ardagh, Bp of. *See* Wetenhall, Edward

Arden, Bn. *See* Perceval, Charles George

Arden, Bns. *See* Wilson, Margaretta Elizabeth

Arden, Richard Pepper (1744–1804), solicitor-gen.; M.P.; cr. (1801) Bn Alvanley:

(?) Hardinge opposes, in Norwich trial, **35**. 633n

Kenyon succeeded by, as Master of the Rolls, **34**. 9n

Macdonald succeeds, as attorney-general, **34**. 9n

opinion by, in Powell's case, **25**. 407n

Pitt administration's more respectable member, **36**. 222

Arden, Robert (d. 1643):

owned roll of Earls of Warwick, **1**. 147

*Ardent*, English ship:

Mulgrave reported lost on, **32**. 367n

sunk by the French, **24**. 511

*Ardent*, French ship:

English capture, **7**. 426, **25**. 278

Ardfert, Dean of. *See* Hoby, Sir Philip

Ardkingloss, Argyllshire:

Campbell of, **11**. 107n

Ardoch:

Stirling of, **11**. 165n

Ardres (France):

HW at, **7**. 315

Ligonier, Vcts, boards with Benedictines at, **30**. 256n

—— joins marching regiment at, **30**. 255

Aremberg. *See* Arembourg; Arenburg

Arembourg [?Arenberg], Lt-Gen.:

captured at San Lazaro, **19**. 267

Arena, G.:
Alexander in Persia by, **17.** 184n
Arenberg, Count:
descent traced by, from Adam, **20.** 195
Arenberg, Duc d'. See Ligne, Léopold-Philippe-Charles-Joseph de (1690–1754)
Arenberg, Duc d':
Van Dyck's portrait of, **35.** 594
Arenberg, Princesse d'. See La Marck-Lumain, Louise-Marguerite de
Arenberg ('Aremberg'), Charles-Marie-Raymond (1721–78), Duc d'; Duc d'Arschot and de Croÿ:
Ranelagh visited by, **35.** 342
son of, **32.** 264
title of, corrected, **43.** 363
Arenberg, Louis-Engelbert-Marie-Joseph-Augustin (1750–1820), Duc d'; Duc d'Arschot and de Croÿ:
biographical information on, corrected, **43.** 349
eyes of, said to be shot, **32.** 264
Arenberg, Louise Franziska (1764–1838), Ps of, m. (1781) Ludwig Joseph Max, P. of Starhemberg:
SH visited by, **12.** 252
Areopagite:
Wilkes has phlegm of, **22.** 182
Are These Things So? See under Miller, James
Arethusa, English ship:
Abercromby returns in, to Portsmouth, **12.** 213n
La Belle Poule's combat with, **7.** 52, 54, **24.** 394–5
success of Mme du Deffand's remark about, **7.** 54
Thurot pursued by, from Portsmouth, **21.** 374n
Aretino, Pietro (1492–?1556), Italian satirist:
princes bribe, **22.** 13
Thomas dedicates work to, **1.** 271n
Areton, Sir William:
faro banker, **39.** 377n
Arezzo, Bp of. See Franceschi, Angelo (d. 1806); Inghirami, Giacomo Gaetano (d. 1772)
Arezzo (Italy):
Albergotti ordered to retire to, **17.** 163
Austrian artillery arrives at, **18.** 541
bishopric of, Clement XIV disputes with Leopold about, **23.** 504
Du Châtelet's army may approach, **18.** 174
Leopold returns to Florence by way of, **24.** 343
Montemar and Castellar at, **18.** 44n
nobles of, to be enrolled in two classes, **20.** 192n
route through, from Foligno, **17.** 265n
Spaniards to approach Lombardy through, **17.** 341, 350
Spanish army threatens approach from, to Tuscany, **17.** 289
Arf, Johan Gerhard (1723–81), Danish naval officer in Russian service:
Russian fleet left by, **23.** 326
Russian squadron under, **23.** 222n
Turkish fleet said to be burnt by, at Lemnos, **23.** 319
Argens, Marquis d'. See Boyer, Jean-Baptiste de
Argenson, Comte d'. See Voyer, Marc-Pierre de (1696–1764); Voyer, Marc-René de (1722–82)
Argenson, Marquis d'. See Voyer, René-Louis de
Argenson, Marquise d'. See Rosen-Kleinroop, Sophie de
Argental, Comte d'. See Ferriol, Charles-Augustin
Argental, Comtesse d'. See Bosc du Bouchet, Jeanne-Grâce
Argentan, point d' (lace):
men's ruffles of, **39.** 264, 267
Argenteau. See Mercy-Argenteau
Argenteuil (France):
Watelet's villa near, **28.** 215n
Argentile and Curan. See under Mason, William
Argentré, Du Plessis d'. See Du Plessis d'Argentré
Argenville. See Dezallier d'Argenville
Argenvillier, Baron d'. See Froment-Fromentes de Castille, Gabriel-Joseph de
Arget, d'. See Darget
Argilliers. See Argenvillier
Argo, Dutch ship:
Feilding captures, **25.** 3n
Argo, legendary ship:
not arrived, **32.** 394
Argomento:
of Italian opera books, **23.** 281
Argonne, Noël (or Bonaventure) d' (1634–1704), called 'M. de Vigneul-Marville'; Carthusian:
Mélanges d'histoire et de littérature, **1.** 9n, **2.** 159, 176, **16.** 205
Argonne (France):
Château de Nubecourt in, **38.** 495
'Argosie':
Shakespeare's term, **18.** 202
Argouges, Michel d', Marquis de Gouville:
wife of, **15.** 187n
Argout, Robert (d. 1780), Comte d', governor of the French Leeward Islands:
career of, **6.** 403
Argument of the Divine Legation of Moses, The. See under Towne, John
Argus:
backward eyes of, are his best, **25.** 563
eyes of, mentioned, **32.** 330
Argyle. See Argyll
Argyll, Cts of (1st):
Jamesone's portrait of, **42.** 265
Argyll, Ds of. See Gunning, Elizabeth (1733–90); Warburton, Jane (ca 1683–1767)
Argyll, D. of. See Campbell, Archibald (1682–1761); Campbell, George William (1768–1839); Campbell, John (1680–1743); Campbell, John (ca 1693–1770); Campbell, John (1723–1806)

Argyll, E. of. *See* Campbell, Archibald
Argyll Buildings, Argyll St:
    Chute's residence, **14**. 82n, **35**. 84n
    Hamilton, Ds of, lives in, **23**. 7
Argyll (Campbell) family:
    Damer, Mrs, visited by, **12**. 96
    HW has no connection with, **11**. 187
    Mrs Gunning's silence on, **11**. 225
Argyll House, London:
    confidential junto at, **11**. 197
    Gunning, Miss, banished from, **11**. 199
    Spencer, Lord Henry, called to, **11**. 198
Argyllshire:
    militia of: at Culloden, **37**. 240; at Strath-
    bogie, **37**. 229; piper of, **14**. 115
Argyll St, London:
    Argyll Buildings in, **23**. 7n
Ariadne:
    HW's term for Mary Anne Drury, **38**. 57
    Hénin, Princesse d', compared to, **12**. 30
    Luxborough, Lady, compared to, **11**. 66
Ariel:
    Ramsay, Amelia, quick as, **31**. 59
    sleep brought to HW by, **34**. 105
Arimanius. *See* Ahriman
Ariosto, Lodovico (1474–1533), poet:
    bawdry of, **29**. 256
    Conway wants to read, **37**. 73, 151
    Este's remark to, **21**. 253n
    Gudin's poem in style of, **4**. 243
    Hayley imitates, **31**. 266n
    La Fontaine's story taken from, **6**. 102n
    *Orlando Furioso* by: Harington's translation
    of, **11**. 68, **28**. 193; Hoole translates, **15**.
    261; 'Marfisa' in, **11**. 68; moon allusion in,
    **3**. 194; Rinaldo in, **38**. 126
Arisaig, Scottish island:
    Young Pretender escapes from, on French
    vessels, **19**. 270n
Aristides:
    Akenside deserts, for Bute, **35**. 566
    Conway compared to, **37**. 523
    justice of, **37**. 37
Aristippus:
    Conway mingles Diogenes with, **37**. 259
    London loved by, **37**. 258
Aristocracy:
    HW not a partisan of, **33**. 342
Aristophanes, Greek dramatist:
    Brumoy translates, **21**. 52
    HW calls, blackguard, **16**. 272
    HW compares Foote to, **28**. 218
    Molière and Regnard better than, **41**. 155
    Socrates ridiculed by, **41**. 55
Aristotle, Greek philosopher:
    Conway does not read, **37**. 576
    Du Deffand, Mme, quotes, **4**. 214
    French authors and, cannot regularize English
    authors, **40**. 379
    medal of, **42**. 64
    More, Hannah, disparages followers of, **31**.
    290

Patin cites, **39**. 157
    question about, in *giuoco della sibilla*, **20**. 477
    *Robinson Crusoe* (pantomime) would not be
    approved by, **33**. 361–2
    rules of: bards did not follow, **15**. 69; for
    eloquence, **35**. 574; HW calls, ridiculous,
    **29**. 369; Harris, James, follows, **29**. 139;
    letter-writing not regulated by, **32**. 385
Arithmetic:
    Cambridge bursar poor in, **33**. 19
    Du Deffand, Mme, has poor opinion of, **4**. 247
    HW poor in, **31**. 331, **33**. 365
Ark; arks:
    English should live in, in bad weather, **35**. 474
    HW, after flood, may sail to Jersey in, **35**. 228
    HW's Gallery at SH may become, **35**. 316
    Noah's: Conway compares bilander to, **37**.
    118; goat on, eats fig-leaves, **39**. 294; SH
    has enough land to populate, **37**. 270
    Thames floods may necessitate, **35**. 279
Ark of the Covenant:
    David prances naked before, **30**. 302n
Arkwright, Sir Richard (1732–92), manufac-
    turer:
    spinning mill of, destroyed by workers, **31**.
    325n
Arland, James Anthony (1668–1746):
    Bretherton's engraving of, **14**. 190n
Arlandes de Salton, François-Laurent (1742–
    1809), Marquis d'; aeronaut:
    balloon ascent of, **25**. 450
*Arlequin Phénix*:
    (?) Du Deffand, Mme, cites, **3**. 247
*Arlequin sauvage*. *See under* Delisle de la
    Drévetière, Louis-François
Arles, Abp of. *See* Du Lau, Jean-Marie
Arles (France):
    visitors to: Boufflers, Comtesses de, **6**. 349,
    355, 379, 430; Grille, **7**. 422; Pomme, **6**.
    349, 355
Arlington, E. of. *See* Bennet, Henry
Arlington St, Westminster:
    Cock Lane near, **10**. 282
    Conway respects Sir Robert Walpole as much
    in, as in Downing St, **37**. 184
    damage in, by hurricane, **2**. 135, 137
    'Female Coterie' has house in, **32**. 67n
    HW lists noted residents of, **10**. 271, **18**. 231,
    349, **21**. 167, **33**. 340
    HW sees Patty Blout in, **33**. 511
    HW's furniture in: **23**. 284–8; beds, **10**. 160,
    193, 207; books, **2**. 199; bronzes, **37**. 258;
    cabinet, **10**. 204; (?) candlesticks, **9**. 295;
    (?) commodes, **10**. 207; couch, **10**. 160;
    flowers, **10**. 204; pictures, **10**. 57, **16**. 54,
    **20**. 407, **37**. 258; portraits, **35**. 228; taken
    to SH, **10**. 43, 193; Vespasian's bust, **19**.
    420n
    HW's house in: **1**. 245, 286, 331; adjoins
    father's house, **17**. 334n; Bedford to call on
    HW in, **40**. 86; Bianca Cappello's portrait
    in, **20**. 407; broken open, **1**. 213, **5**. 52–3, 54,

55, 57; **14**. 189–90, **23**. 284–8, 295–6, 301;
Brown calls on HW in, **1**. 275n; Chatterton
to write to HW at, **16**. 106; Chute at, **20**.
234; Cole calls on HW in, **1**. 185, 306n, 335,
347, 378, 381, **2**. 79; dining-room of, **20**. 188;
dressing-room in, **36**. 39; Ewin to call at,
**1**. 298; Favre at, **1**. 96, 100, **40**. 381; finances
concerning, **33**. 62; fine young ladies come
to, when HW is ill, **23**. 454; Gray dines at,
**20**. 234; HW and father return to, **28**. 470n;
HW arrives at, from Paris, **7**. 314, 324, 333,
342, 353, **10**. 297, **39**. 67; HW calls meeting
at, of Walpole heirs, **36**. 93; HW finds no
fire or dinner at, **40**. 151; HW hopes, will
not be carried to Paris, **35**. 235; HW hopes
to find Cellini chest at, **23**. 425; HW invites
Chute to visit him at, **35**. 66–7; HW keeps
father's portrait at, **41**. 234; HW leaves, for
Paris, **7**. 258, 315, 324, 333, 342; HW not
settled in, **32**. 216; HW removes from, **7**.
96n, **29**. 140; HW spends Christmas at, **10**.
241; HW takes furniture from, to SH, **10**.
43, 193; HW tells Montagu to send letters
to, **10**. 172, 283; HW to be addressed at,
**1**. 85, 86, 124, 225, 229, **30**. 140, 262; HW
writes in shady back room of, to keep cool,
**24**. 407; hearth of, marble, **24**. 71; Hillier
sends covers to, for franking, **16**. 71; Lort
calls at, **2**. 132, **16**. 161, 162, 178, 180; maid
at, **9**. 191, **10**. 40, 296, **35**. 229, **39**. 162 (*see
also* Mary); Mann, Galfridus, at, **20**. 234;
Mason writes from, **28**. 1; Montagu contrasts Rockingham lodging with, **10**. 214;
Montagu hopes HW received Hertford in
back parlour of, **10**. 165; Montagu leaves,
with regret, **10**. 209; Montagu may send
books to, **10**. 172; Montagu occupies, **10**.
189, 193, 195, 198–200, 207, 214; Ossory,
Lady, does not send letters to, **33**. 71; Ossory, Lady, shy of, **33**. 125; painted, **10**. 43;
picture to be sent to, **1**. 83; Riccardi's gems
in closet of, **19**. 273; skylight demolished
at, **33**. 81–2; Walpole, Sir Robert, leaves,
to HW, **13**. 15, **19**. 32n; Walpole, Sir Robert, rents, for HW, **18**. 137; Walpole, Sir
Robert's payments for, incomplete, **36**. 163n

**Hardinge's St Giles address inferior to, 35**. 601
*Hermione* treasure passes end of, **22**. 66
ministerial levees in, **18**. 349
ministers inhabit, **10**. 271, **18**. 231, 349, **21**.
167, **33**. 340
mob in, on King's Birthday, **18**. 96
noisy, **10**. 271
paving of, **10**. 199
resemblance of, to Tyre and Sidon, **20**. 469
residents of: Beauclerk, **10**. 270, 271; Bethel,
**33**. 511; Campbell, Lord Frederick, **11**.
265n, **34**. 46n; Carteret, **18**. 96, 231, 349,
**21**. 167n; Cholmondeley, **19**. 340n; Grafton,
D. of, **33**. 125, 340; Granville, Cts, **18**. 521n,
**19**. 133n; Hamilton, W. G., **33**. 82; Holdernesse, **28**. 1n; Kildare, **19**. 340n; Lincoln,

E. of, **24**. 420n, **35**. 199; Morgan, **10**. 270,
271; Pelham, Henry, **18**. 231, 349, 523n, **21**.
167n, **35**. 199; Pirner, **28**. 297n; Pomfret,
Cts of, **2**. 135, **33**. 82; Romney, **23**. 286
rowers pass through, **32**. 237
Selwyn should write to HW at, **30**. 140, 262
straw strewn in, during accouchement, **31**.
189
Walpole, Sir Robert, house of, in: HW born
in, **13**. 3, 12, **28**. 469; HW catches cold by
returning to, before it is aired, **18**. 546; HW
describes, **18**. 137; HW's 'warm little apartment' in, **18**. 136; Mann asks about, **18**. 114;
Walpole, Sir Robert, dies in, **22**. 27; Walpole, Sir Robert, formerly had, **17**. 478; Walpole, Sir Robert, retires to, **13**. 12, **17**.
478

**Arlus**, Marie-Geneviève-Charlotte d' (1720–
1805), m. (1734) Louis-Lazare Tiroux d'Arconville:
*Vie de Marie de Médicis, La*, by, **6**. 84
**Arm; arms:**
broken, Gustav III exercises, on pumps at
Pisa baths, **25**. 442
Conway breaks, **25**. 89, 111, 115, **39**. 363n, 365
—— might lose, in battle, **37**. 181
HW might lose, when hunting, **37**. 185
rheumatism in, **25**. 432
sacred relics, **37**. 320
Salimbeni breaks, **17**. 116
**Armada, Spanish:**
bicentennial of destruction of, **34**. 31n
Elizabeth, Q., gives thanks at St Paul's for
defeat of, **12**. 33
——'s medal on defeat of, **21**. 357
England may again be attacked by, **32**. 239
French fleet compared with, **34**. 229
HW suggests, as scene for historic picture,
**42**. 421
poem mentions, **40**. 26
tapestry depicting, **1**. 10–11, 13, **23**. 242,
**34**. 84–5
**Armagh, Abp of.** *See* Boulter, Hugh (1672–
1742); Newcome, William (1729–1800); Robinson, Richard (ca 1708–94); Stone, George
(ca 1708–64); Stuart, Hon. William (1755–
1822); Ussher, James (1581–1656)
**Armagh, Ireland:**
archbishopric of: candidates for, **10**. 145;
offered in England, **22**. 275–6
election at, **35**. 158
**Armaments:**
England prepares, **20**. 538
English and French ports prepare, **20**. 483
peace not augured by, **25**. 354
Turkey prepares, **21**. 493–4
**Armandiers, Rue d', Paris:**
house in, bequeathed to Scots College, **15**.
108n
**Armano**, Federico Gaetano Gustavo, Tuscan
consul at Algiers, 1759–63:
ill-treated, **22**. 259
**Arm-chairs.** *See under* Chair

Armenia:
　Wortley Montagu visits, **22.** 113n
Armenian robe. *See under* Robe
'Arménien, l.' *See* Rousseau, Jean-Jacques
Armentières, Maréchal d'; Marquis d'. *See* Conflans, Louis de
Armentières, Maréchale d'; Marquise d'. *See* Senneterre, Marie-Charlotte de
Armes d'Angleterre, hotel at Turin:
　poor accommodations at, **11.** 143n
Armet, ——, notary:
　contracts passed before, **8.** 38, 39, 41, 44
　Du Deffand, Mme, summons, for codicil to her will, **7.** 461
　(?) —— works with, **5.** 28n, **7.** 442
　Luynes estate settled before, **8.** 36–7
'Armida':
　painting of, by Gennari, **10.** 346
　*See also under* Tasso, Torquato
*Armida* (opera):
　HW has not seen, **32.** 216
　(?) reference to garden in, **33.** 61
　*See also under* Sacchini, Antonio
*Armide. See under* Gluck, Christoph Willibald; Lulli, Jean-Baptiste; Quinault, Philippe
Armiger, Mrs Robert. *See* Bunbury, Elizabeth
Armine, Lady, *See* Talbot, Mary
Armine, Sir William (1593–1651):
　wife of, **1.** 181n
*Arminio. See under* Salvi, Antonio; Scarlatti, Alessandro
Armitage. *See* Armytage
Armoire; armoires (furniture):
　La Borde's, **31.** 80
　Sévigné letters supposedly found in, **35.** 393
Armour:
　Æneas's, **32.** 220
　bishop wears, in portrait, **10.** 337
　brass, exchanged for gold, **35.** 553
　Brooke wears, in portrait, **35.** 411
　Buckingham wears, in portrait, **40.** 226
　Charles I and Cromwell portrayed in, **30.** 370
　Clifford wears, in portrait, out of compliment to Charles II, **35.** 148
　figure of man in, at Horton, **10.** 333
　François I's (alleged): acquired by HW for SH, **1.** 243, 245, **5.** 260n, **12.** 168, **23.** 350, **29.** 303, **31.** 234, **35.** 421, **43.** 56, 93; arrival of, **5.** 139, **32.** 66; HW pleased with, **5.** 146; HW sees, **7.** 373; HW will 'wear into battle,' **32.** 160; HW wishes for, in Gordon Riots, **33.** 186; history of, **34.** 235; price of, **5.** 115n, 185, 233, **7.** 412; purchase of, **5.** 109–17, 119–20, 121, 123, 128, 147, 156, **8.** 185; transportation of, **5.** 121, 124, 139, 141, 143, 145, 233
　Gramont wears, in portrait, **42.** 157
　HW directs painting of, for *Count of Narbonne*, **33.** 310
　HW's, at SH, **20.** 381, **31.** 26
　HW's servant mistakes chimney-back for, **20.** 396
　*Hamlet* ghost wears, **20.** 209

　in Eccardt's painting of Conway, **37.** 234
　in painting at Rose Tavern, **1.** 382
　in stained glass, **40.** 225
　Leopold transfers, from Fortezza to Uffizi, **25.** 531n
　Ligonier buckles on, **21.** 305
　Medici collection of, sold, **25.** 230n
　Newcastle sells, at Halland, **10.** 287
　rusty, HW hopes to have, **20.** 372
　saint wears, in painting, **41.** 431
　suit of, used at battle of Hastings: Durham, Bp of, saves, from braziers, **10.** 287; Durham, Bp of, gives, to Montagu, **10.** 301
　worn: at masquerade, **17.** 339; in Battle of the Bridge at Pisa, **22.** 515n
　*See also* Gauntlet; Helmet; Mail, coat of; Spur
Armoury:
　at SH, *see under* SH
　in Tower of London, **17.** 233
*Armoury of Nobility. See under* Cook, Robert
Arms (weapons):
　HW collects, at SH, **20.** 372
　must be carried by Londoners at night, because of footpads, **25.** 316–17
　small, English and French engaged with, **37.** 191
Arms, heraldic:
　at Hinchingbrooke, **40.** 283, 284
　Beauclerks', in tower at SH, **28.** 318
　Chatterton forges, **16.** 131
　Chandos, Ds of, displays escutcheon of pretence, **28.** 446
　Chaucer arms, **13.** 108–9
　Cole copies MS of, **2.** 29
　——'s, **1.** 93
　——'s MS of, **2.** 148, 222
　Conway thought, were Latimer's, **37.** 306
　Damer, Mrs, asks about her right to, **35.** 494–5
　for Cts of Orford's monument, **25.** 226–7, 239–40
　found locked up in Jacobite household, **19.** 107
　'gules' and 'sable' probably not used except in, **16.** 343
　HW sends, to Mason, for stained glass by Peckitt, **6.** 202, **28.** 213, 216
　Howard family's, **16.** 86
　Hyndford's, **18.** 107
　in Bagot's painting, **41.** 431
　in Dugdale, probably authentic, **14.** 81–2
　in MS for Gough, **2.** 232
　in painting in Rose Tavern, **1.** 380, 382–3, **2.** 2, 7
　in windows at SH, **1.** 254, 377, 378
　Kendal, Ds of, had, **41.** 451
　Northampton's, on Trinity Hospital plate, **16.** 84, 91
　of Cappello and Medici families, **20.** 407, 415
　of James V and Mary of Guise, **15.** 112
　of Museum Minervæ, **16.** 151

of Nassau family, Cowper not allowed to use, **24.** 370

of Sweden and Denmark, **15.** 112

on altar doors from Bury, **2.** 32, 35–6, 220, **16.** 184, 185, 186

on monument in Trinity Hospital, Greenwich, **16.** 88

on Palgrave's chaise, erroneous, **29.** 365

Prussian consul at Leghorn has, over his door, **21.** 112

William of Hatfield's, **28.** 308

Wolsey's set above Henry VIII's, **16.** 47

Armstrong, ——, Maj. Gen.:

regiment of, **17.** 300n

Armstrong, Mrs:

Conolly, Lady Anne, visits, **11.** 56

HW to inquire about, **11.** 69

Teddington house to be vacated by, **11.** 56, 58, 60, 61, 62, 68n

timorous about health, **11.** 61

Armstrong, Bigoe, Col. of Irish regiment:

regiment of, to leave Cork for Portugal, **22.** 23n

Armstrong, John (1709–79), M.D.:

*Art of Preserving Health* by, fashionable but now forgotten, **37.** 262, 263

Armstrong, Sir Thomas (?1624–84):

print of, **1.** 181

Army; armies:

mere soldier thinks all life confined to, **37.** 129

Army, English:

American locations of, in 1745, **19.** 69n

Americans fire on, at Concord, **24.** 100, 112

Americans to support Boston against, **39.** 226

America to be station of regiments of, from Ireland, **32.** 248

anti-Court officers may be dismissed from posts in, **38.** 239–40, 244, 246, 253–5, 488

at Boston, **24.** 119–20, 137–8, 158, 161, 204, **28.** 217–18

at Havana, sickly, **38.** 173n, 178

at Roucour, **30.** 107–8

Austrians separate from, in Flanders, **18.** 124

Baldwyn gets ensigncy in, from Conway at HW's request, **37.** 432

camps of: healthy in damp but not in hot weather, **33.** 481; prepared, **20.** 505; toured by Conway, **37.** 476

chaplains' leaves from, **40.** 91

chaplains of, in India do not preach liberty, **31.** 284

Chatham wants, recalled from Boston, **32.** 228

clothing supplied to, by Galfridus Mann, **9.** 182

colonelcy of the Blues the best post in, **23.** 246

commissions in, bought, **13.** 244

contracts diseases in Flanders, **19.** 78

Conway commander-in-chief of, **35.** 434

—— enters, **37.** 31

——'s appointment to command of, an advantage to England, **25.** 276

——'s distinction in, **20.** 264–5

——'s Parliamentary voting might disqualify him for command in, **40.** 328–42

—— tends debarkation of, **37.** 516

—— to supervise embarkation of, from Flanders, **38.** 191

—— would have ruined himself had he remained at head of, **39.** 408

Cope's, at Dunbar, **30.** 97

Crown Pt the objective of, **20.** 512, **21.** 233, 326

Cumberland, D. of, a tyrant to, **20.** 73n

——'s rôle in, **18.** 217, 327, **19.** 19, 39, 166–7, 173–4, 177, 178, 179, 185, 186, 199, 204, 208, 213–14, 222, 233, 239–40, 242, 273–4, 285, 299, 340, 389, 409, 424, 495, **20.** 73, 100, 117, 119, 136, 145, 146, 150, **22.** 163

debentures of, Pulteney attacks Sir Robert Walpole about, **37.** 91

Dettingen exploits of, belittled at Vienna, **35.** 40

disbanded regiments in, mutinous, **25.** 406

disbanding of, will increase robberies, **33.** 382

discontented, **19.** 464

Dutch aid for, **18.** 402, 407, 416, 423–4, 429, 449, 457, 466, 478, **19.** 52, 103, 104, 109, 131, 134, 240, **20.** 526, 538, **37.** 145–6, 159

England raising, for America, **24.** 175, 193–4, 197, 348

England will not have, to defend her, **24.** 349

enlistments in, occur only from drunkenness, **37.** 125

Erskine dismissed from, **37.** 429

fights American compatriots while lacking food and medicine, **41.** 313

Flanders to be invaded by, **19.** 346, **37.** 163, 295

Flemish butchers bicker with, over beef, **18.** 30

Flemish campaigns of, *see under* Flanders

Fletcher's promotion enrages, **38.** 432n

Fox's official correspondence regarding, **30.** 103

freezing weather inconveniences, **9.** 268

French armies superior to, **21.** 279, **37.** 265, 272, 282

French conquest of Flanders would release, **30.** 49

furloughs in, **9.** 85–6

George II's leadership of, **18.** 102, 229, 247, 250, 258–60, 265–6, 297, 327

George III meets opposition in wanting to renew, **33.** 433

German arrival of, **37.** 555

Gloucester, D. of, not intended by George III to be head of, **36.** 85

Gower proposes that nobles recruit men for, **37.** 446

Granby does not interfere with Irish establishment of, **39.** 110–11

—— resigns command of, **23.** 175

greater than ever, **20.** 524

[Army, English, *continued*]

HW jokes about Lady Mary Coke's raising, in Germany, 31. 25

HW one of few Englishmen who are not in militia or, 21. 344

Hanoverian and Hessian troops aid, 18. 209, 259, 19. 240, 255

Hanover orders, not to engage the French, 18. 250

Hertford to appoint Fitzgerald to ensigncy in, 31. 113

House of Commons should resist corruption in, 26. 15

'Hyder Ali' (Haidar 'Alī) attacks, 25. 141

in America: barbarities of, described by Burke, 28. 354; besieged in Boston, 28. 217–18; buried, 19. 69; cannot be replenished, 39. 330; desertion from, 39. 183; frequent sailings to, 32. 303; HW traces retreat of, 28. 411; losses of, 28. 415, 434; overestimated, 33. 76; size of, 24. 347n

increase in: discussed by Parliament, 17. 410; ordered, 23. 250, 32. 228–9

independent companies for, 35. 91

in Flanders: 39. 527; Austrians join, 37. 204; retires, 37. 201; sickness in, 37. 291; to be enlarged, 35. 63

in Ireland, not paid, 28. 454

in New York, lacks provisions, 33. 44

in Scotland, 26. 32

in summer quarters, 22. 256

Irish Catholics considered too dangerous for, 18. 566

Irish staff officer's salary in, 9. 257

Jacobites pursued by, from Preston to Lancaster towards Carlisle, 37. 213

Lepell, Mary, gets cornetcy in, 34. 256

London occupied by, in Gordon Riots, 35. 504

Lorient abandoned by, 19. 319n

Louis XV extols bravery of, at Fontenoy, 37. 194

Maria Theresa wants, at Mainz, 18. 102

Martinique casualties of, slight, 22. 43

Mawhood quits, from ridicule, 39. 250

may go abroad, 37. 225–6

Minden victory may open Amiens and Paris to, 35. 292

Mons's siege by French may be relieved by, 37. 188

morale of, in Germany, 37. 136

New York the station of, 24. 246–7, 255–6, 261–2, 336, 393, 405–6, 33. 44

not ready, 38. 15

of observation, 21. 73n

Onslow describes dangers of, 9. 143

—— votes against (?) augmentation of, 30. 301n

Ostend ineffectually reinforced by, when England is inadequately defended, 30. 96

Ostend the theatre of, 18. 456–7, 19. 78

Paris might be attacked by, 19. 91, 21. 228, 352

Parliamentary discussion of, 17. 343, 410, 18. 123, 191, 382–3, 19. 4–5, 26. 10, 13–19, 37. 420, 38. 498–501

Parliamentary members of, *see under* Parliament: army officers in

Parliamentary Opposition's triumph must surmount attacks from, 35. 617

Parliament debates estimates for, 38. 498–501

Parliament denies Charles I pay for, till priest is hanged, 42. 235

Parliament's members turn to, instead of racing, 24. 384

paymaster of, *see* Fox, Henry; Rigby, Richard

Peterborough hunts for, in Spain, 18. 180, 24. 482

Philadelphia the theatre of, 24. 282, 336, 338–9, 342, 393

Pitt proposes subduing, by breaking officers of court martial, 21. 165n

plunders convents and villages near Quimperlé, 19. 319n

popularity of raising regiments for, 9. 264, 268

private raising of regiments irritates, 19. 153–4, 26. 13–15

recruits awaited by, at Lessines, 19. 52

reduction plan for, 42. 54–5

reforms in, 19. 340

regiments of: raised by Gordons, 15. 153–4; remain in London after Gordon Riots, 29. 65; Scottish, mutiny, 33. 484

regulations of, keep Conway from aiding Lambert Walpole, 36. 211

Rhine crossings by, 18. 209, 290, 293, 37. 143–4, 43. 250

Saxe's army opposed by, 18. 481, 496, 526

Saxon troops to join, 19. 240, 255

Scheldt crossed by, 18. 448, 481

Scottish clans would join George II if convinced of strength of, 19. 130

sickness in, 37. 291

small, in Canada, 24. 336

Stair a 'mad captain' of, 18. 224

—— commands, in Flanders, 17. 373, 19. 191, 37 *passim*

—— expects, to capture Paris, 19. 91

—— liked by, 18. 400

—— to accompany, to Mainz, 18. 102

—— to keep Wade from command of, 19. 127

standing, militia supposed to obviate need for, 35. 286

Stanley comes from 30. 71

Townshend, George, to be kept from bad companions in, 36. 6–7

troops from: in Flanders, not yet arrived in England, 30. 98; land near Cherbourg, 30. 146

Tyrawley to command, in Portugal, 22. 43

used to return to London in winter, 21. 362

veterans of, Dalrymple's plan to aid, 38. 205

volunteers in, under age and fond of bird-nesting, 38. 34

widows of officers from, get India spoils through Clive, **22**. 540

Willemstadt may provide escape route for, **18**. 457

winter quarters for, may again be necessary, **38**. 190

*See also*: America; Artillery; Brigade; Cavalry; Cornetcy; Deserters; Dragoons; Flanders; Foot Guards; Foot soldiers; France: English invasion of; Germany: English troops in; Guards; Holland: English troops in; Horse Guards; Militia; Officer; Regiment; Royal Horse Guards; War

Armytage, Sir John (1732–58), 2d Bt; M.P.:
death of, **21**. 245, **37**. 571

Howe, Mary, engaged to, **21**. 245

—— mourns for, **9**. 264

in English invasion of France, **21**. 204

'son' of, **37**. 530

Arnaldi, Antonino (1732–1809), Marchese:
agent for father and uncles, **21**. 208n

collection of: Mann buys pictures from, for Hoare, **21**. 208, 231; Mengs visits Florence to see, **20**. 331n; sale of, leaves few good paintings available, **21**. 478

prices obtained by, would seem small compared to English ones, **21**. 232

Arnaldi, Bonaventura, Abate:
nephew agent for, **21**. 208n

Arnaldi, Maurizio:
nephew agent for, **21**. 208n

Arnaldi, Teresa Maria, m. (1711) Balì Leonardo Rinaldi:
Craons entertain, **17**. 217–18

Arnaldi, Tommaso (fl. 1728–49); Marchese (1740) di Carniana e Poiago; Genoese art collector:
ball given by, **17**. 56

Cignani painting sold to Court of Dresden by, **21**. 208n

son agent for, **21**. 208n

Arnaldi Palace, Florence:
Pallavicini collection housed at, **17**. 56n

Arnaud, François (1721–84), abbé; editor:
Aiguillon ruins, **5**. 93, **7**. 341

Barthélemy offended at, **6**. 366

*Gazette* taken from, **5**. *93*, **7**. 340n

Harcourt makes no complaint against, **5**. 93, **7**. 341

Louis XV angered by article by, **5**. 92–3

*Variétés littéraires*: **8**. 32; *Éloge de Richardson* in, **6**. 251

Arnauld, Antoine (1612–94), theologian:
(?) *Logique, La*, by, owned by Mme du Deffand, **8**. 33n

Arnauld, Simon (1618–99), Marquis de Pomponne:
death date of, corrected, **43**. 84

letters of Mme de Sévigné to, about Fouquet's trial: **3**. 187–8, 190, 212, 387, **4**. 24, **5**. 380, 420, **41**. 259; copied by Wiart, **3**. 193, 200

tomb of, **7**. 282

Arnay-le-Duc:
Louis XVI's aunts stopped at, **11**. 208n

Arne, Susannah Maria (1714–66), m. (1734) Theophilus Cibber; actress:
Clive, Mrs, resents aspirations of, **18**. 124n

Conway's dream about, **37**. 17

death of, **7**. 397

*Foundling* well acted by, **19**. 465

Garrick's epilogue to Crisp's *Virginia* spoken by, **35**. 167n

Gray not inclined to see, **13**. 96

plays acted by, **19**. 342, 465n

voice of: (?) inadequate, **18**. 180; needed for *Pigmalion*, **28**. *183*

Arne, Thomas Augustine (1710–78), composer; Mus. D.:
adaptation of *Elfrida* by Colman and, deplored by Mason, **28**. *53–5*

*Alfred* composed by, **16**. 296n

*Caractacus* composed by, **28**. 277n

Colman's *Fairy Prince* has music by, **32**. 66n

*Comus* composed by, **11**. 65n, **13**. 153n

(?) *Guardian Outwitted, The*, deplored by HW, **10**. 138, **43**. 132

Ireland visited by, **37**. 412

operas accompanied by, on harpsichord, **37**. 412n

*Rosamond*, Norfolk heiress sings song from, **18**. 317

Arno, river:
Berry sisters near, **11**. 234, 246

cats to be drowned in, **17**. 452, 482

cocchiata on, **22**. 158

dry in summer, **17**. 452

floods on, **13**. 237, **17**. 109n, **18**. 120, **19**. 131, 155, **30**. 3

Florentine mills fail because of low water in, **25**. 318

frozen in several places, **24**. 434

HW's gallery overlooks, **13**. 228n, **37**. 68, 72

HW's 'Patapan' mentions, **30**. 294

HW to forsake, for Parliament, **37**. 93

Lorraine Guards embark on, **17**. 182n, 199n

Mann's little house on, *see* Ambrogi, Casa

Maria Louisa travels on, in gondola from Pisa, **25**. 393n

skating on, **33**. 95

Thames compared with, **37**. 49, 72

Arnold, Benedict (1741–1801), Gen.:
arrives in England, **25**. 241

Burgoyne defeated by, **32**. 393, 399, *see also* Saratoga

Cornwallis joined by, in Virginia, **25**. 167

depredations of, **29**. 163

HW calls: 'atrocious villain,' **33**. 239; 'double Arnold,' **29**. 161–2; 'Mohock,' **29**. 188

Howe and Clinton now equalled by, **41**. 401

Lake Champlain fleet of, defeated, **24**. 261n

leg of, injured in American service, to be cut off and buried with honours by Americans before hanging him, **25**. 241–2

[Arnold, Benedict, *continued*]
money that purchased treachery of, wasted, 29. *124*
said to have died of wounds, 24. 341
treason of, 25. 98, 141, 241n, 33. 239–40
Wooster relieves, at Quebec, 24. 215n
Arnold, Mrs Benedict. *See* Shippen, Elizabeth
Arnold, Samuel (1740–1802), composer:
music by, for O'Keeffe's *Agreeable Surprise*, 12. 151n, 16. 256n
Arnold, Rev. William (d. 1802), Bp Hurd's chaplain; canon of Windsor; precentor of Lichfield:
Jackson replaced by, as sub-preceptor to George III's two eldest sons, 43. 285
Arnoldi. *See* Arnaldi
*Arno Miscellany*:
HW gives true authorship of, 25. 517n, 26. 46
HW inquires about, 25. 506–8, 517
Mann knows, 25. 522
Ramsay contributes to, 15. 47n, 25. 540
—— sends, to HW, 25. 517n, 522, 523, 633
Arnould, Madeleine-Sophie (1744–1803), singer:
Conti, Princesse de, answered by, 7. 369
Lauraguais's affair with, 38. 351n
Arnoult, Antoine-Remy (b. 1734), Jesuit:
(?) Beauchamp asks HW about position for, in London, 38. 349
*Arnoux,* French ship:
ships captured by, near Leghorn, 21. 264n, 274n
Arosteghi. *See* Clemente de Arostegui
Arouard du Beignon, ——:
Paris visited by, 7. 447
Arouard du Beignon, Anne-Suzanne, m. (1764) Denis-François-Marie-Jean de Suarez, Marquis d'Aulan; Mme du Deffand's niece-in-law:
Aulan devoted to, 7. 72, 116
bouquet given to, 7. 425
bouquet of, 7. 425
brother of, arrives, 7. 447
Du Deffand, Mme, buys dress for, 7. 432
(?) —— given purse by, 7. 447
(?) —— gives present to, 7. 439
——'s arrangement with, 7. 116, 122–3, 126, 132, 133, 182; satisfactory, 7. 135, 136, 138, 140, 141, 150, 167; unsatisfactory, 7. 212
——'s opinion of, 7. 116, 167, 219
HW advises against company of, 7. 235
habits of, 7. 136
health of, 7. 429, 430
Juilly visited by, 7. 450
Montrouge to be visited by, 7. 94, 123, 132
—— visited by, 7. 132, 422, 423, 428
Paris visited by, 7. 132
Plombières to be visited by, 7. 219
—— visited by, 7. 235, 454
relatives of, in Paris, 7. 123
social relations of, with: Champrond, Abbé de, 7. 427, 431; Du Deffand, Mme, 7. 132, 138, 198, 223
to leave Paris, 7. 219, 225, 227, 230

to live in Paris, 7. 71, 72, 84–5, 94, 115–6, 120, 126
to return to Avignon, 7. 126, 133, 219, 225
Arouet, François-Marie. *See* Voltaire
Arpajon, Chevalier d'. *See* Noailles, Louis-Marc-Antoine de
Arpajon, Marquis d'. *See* Noailles, Philippe de (1715–94)
Arpajon, Anne-Claudine-Louise d' (d. 1794), m. (1741) Philippe de Noailles, Marquis d'Arpajon, Comte de Noailles, later Duc de Mouchy and Maréchal de France:
balls given by, 5. 191
breaks arm, 7. 179, 428
Chanteloup visited by, 8. 207
daughter of, placed at Court, 3. *240*
Du Deffand, Mme, gives opinion of, 7. 179
follows Court, 4. 351–2
HW saw, 39. 214
Marie-Antoinette attended by, 6. 104
social relations of, with: Hénault, 3. 369, 7. 307; Louis XVI and Marie-Antoinette, 6. 104
verses on bulletins about, 7. 179
Arquebusade-water. *See* Harquebusade
Arrack water punch. *See under* Punch
Arragon. *See* Aragon
Arragon House:
Twickenham's manor-house, 42. 417n
Arran, Cts of. *See* Crewe, Elizabeth (ca 1679–1756)
Arran, E. of. *See* Butler, Charles (1671–1758); Gore, Sir Arthur (1703–73); Gore, Arthur Saunders (1734–1809); Gore, Charles (d. 1773)
Arran, isle of:
Boyd flees to, after Culloden, 19. 285n
Arranda (Aranda). *See* Abarca de Bolea
Arras, Bp of. *See* Conzié, Louis-François-Marc-Hilaire de
Arras (France):
court to be held at, 5. 30n
gates of, 7. 315
Hôtel d'Artois at, 5. 289n, 7. 342
post halts at, 3. 343
visitors to: Bunbury, Lady Sarah, 3. 234; Conway, 39. 536; Craufurd, 5. 289; Cumberland, D. and Ds of, 23. 349; HW, 5. 90, 92, 7. 315, 342, 394; Lauzun, 3. 234; Scott, 39. 536
Arras lace. *See under* Lace
Arras-makers (*see also* Tapestry):
Montagu, D. of, places, on Great Wardrobe payroll, 20. 79
Arrêt; arrêts:
France issues, daily, 35. 126
of 1762, caused by excommunication of Parma, 23. 398–9
of 1768, suppressing papal brief about Parma, 23. 4, 10
*See also under* Louis XV; Louis XVI; Parliament of Paris

Arria:

Pætus and, **32**. 230

Arrigoni, Carlo (1697–1744), composer:

concert promoted by, **18**. 12

dates of, corrected, **43**. 246

Gray collects works of, **13**. 233n

(?) Mann, Mary, studied with, **17**. 101n

Arrogenes. *See* Aragon

Arrow, Mrs. *See* Jordan, Elizabeth

Arrow, Warwickshire:

church at: Conway buried in, **39**. 513n; Hertford buried in, **39**. 509n; Hertford, Cts of, buried in, **33**. 371n; Seymour-Conways buried in, **43**. 371

Arrow; arrows:

Charles III shoots, at tapestries, **23**. 238

Chinese, HW's, **31**. 26

from long-bows, **35**. 137

Gordon boys, as Cupids, shoot, at Stanislas II, **35**. 82

HW buys, at Mrs Kennon's sale, **37**. 439n

HW's, at SH, **11**. 25, **20**. 375, 381, **31**. 26, **37**. 439n

HW speculates about aerial battles with, **39**. 425

pandours carry, **37**, 142

servants intercept, from sovereigns' bosoms, **36**. 245

toy, George IV shoots E. of Bath with, **38**. 365

Arrundel. *See* Arundell

Arruntius, Lucius (d. A.D. 37):

columbarium belonging to, **13**. 207n

'*Arsame.*' *See* Choiseul-Stainville, Étienne-François de

Arsenal; arsenals:

at Paris, Maréchale du Muy's house at, **6**. 218

at Venice, *see under* Venice

Arsenic:

elderly prelates averse to, **24**. 75

Jesuits' weapon, **24**. 51

Arson:

Jobbins and Lowe hanged for, **34**. 98

*Ars poetica. See under* Horace

Art; arts:

Bristol, E. of, buys dregs of, in Italy, **25**. 651

classical: deficiencies of, **35**. 443–5; lacks perspective and passion, **35**. 444–5

comparative progress of, in Europe and the East, **15**. 211–12

decline of, in Florence, after extinction of the Medici, **25**. 93

export license required for, in Italy, **20**. 465, **21**. 208

French revolutionists destroy, **35**. 447

German Count bores HW with talk on, **11**. 250

HW comments on history of, **1**. 368

HW comments on progress of, **15**. 202–3

HW patron of, which humanize mankind, **37**. 172

HW prefers ornamental part of, to scientific, **15**. 332

HW to write treatise or panegyric on, **37**. 292–3

Mann's advisers in, *see* Chambers, Sir William; Vierpyl, Simon; Wilton, Joseph

materials for history of, in 15th-century England, scanty, **15**. 169

mystery in, proceeds from unskilfulness, **21**. 561

new reign does not encourage, **15**. 97

westward course of, **28**. 166, 217

*See also* Artists; Drawing; Illumination; Mosaic; Painting; Pastel; Portrait; Print; Seapieces; Statue; Water-colour; *and under names of artists*

Artaguette d'Iron, Jeanne-Victoire-Marie d', m. (1740) Louis-Nicolas, Marquis de Pérusse:

(?) social relations of, with Mme de Praslin, **7**. 349

*Artamène ou le Grand Cyrus. See under* Scudéry, Madeleine de

'Art and science travel west':

HW paraphrases, **24**. 154

*Artaserse*, opera:

ballets to, **25**. 360n

*Artaxerxes. See under* Hasse, Johann Adolph

Art dealers:

English in Italy, cheat, **20**. 352

*Art de former les jardins moderns, L'. See* Whately, Thomas: *Observations on Modern Gardening*

*Arte de los metales. See under* Barba, Alvaro Alonso

Artemino. *See* Artimino

Artemisia:

HW's name for Lady Caroline Fitzroy, **37**. 196

mausoleum raised by, **9**. 7

*Arte of English Poesie. See under* Puttenham, George

Artfulness:

HW calls 'filigraine of a little mind,' **33**. 549

Arthur, King:

HW alludes to legend of, **11**. 347, **12**. 82

HW jokes about, **10**. 148

in HW's verses on destruction of French navy, **38**. 50

'Rowley' the reverse of, **2**. 105

—— will be as abandoned as, **16**. 228

Arthur (b. 1186), P.:

HW praises, in *King John*, **41**. 294, 373

Arthur (1486–1502), P. of Wales:

Catherine of Aragon's marriage to, **40**. 198

Elizabeth of York crowned after birth of, **14**. 79

Mabuse's picture of, **40**. 317

painting of Catherine of Aragon and, given to HW by Myddelton, **42**. 215

(?) stained-glass figure of, at Copt Hall, **9**. 92

tomb of, at Worcester, **35**. 150

Arthur, Lucile (b. ca 1780):

jewelry presented by, to national fund, **34**. 66–7

Arthur, Mary, m. (1761) Robert Mackreth:

marriage of, **28**. 173n

Arthur, Robert (d. 1761), proprietor of White's Club:
George III removes, as clerk of the wine-cellar, **9.** *318*
HW told by, of postponed ridotto, **20.** 135
Rumbold perhaps related to, **25.** 141n
—— supposedly employed by, as waiter, **29.** 88, 122
White's Club called Arthur's after, **25.** 483n, **35.** 313
Arthur's. *See* White's
Arthy. *See* Arty
Artichoke; artichokes:
Du Deffand, Mme, would compare HW to rosebush rather than, **6.** 334
on monument at Easton Mauduit, **10.** 339
*Articles of Charge . . . against Warren Hastings. See under* Burke, Edmund
Articles of Confederation:
American colonies adopt, **24.** 354n
Articone, Erasmo, canon:
Theodore of Corsica calls, traitor, **18.** 156
Articulating:
young English have different style of, **25.** 22
Artillery:
at Naples, **17.** 154
Austrian, **18.** 163, 541, **19.** 401, 406
Braddock drags, in America, **20.** 492
brass pieces of, rewards offered for capture of, **24.** 122
Brown's and Castellar's, **19.** 236
Catherine II uses, to dethrone husband, **10.** 38
Cuneo to be taken with supply of, **18.** 502
difficulty of transporting, in winter, **17.** 204, **19.** 7–8
English: at Culloden, **37.** 239; cost of, **18.** 457; HW jokes about sending, to London, **37.** 181; Jersey should not divert, from English defence, **39.** 335; lacking, for recapture of Minorca, **20.** 588; Pitt sends, against St-Malo, **21.** 213
English fleet negligent in capturing, **18.** 296, **19.** 100, 147, 150–1
English lose, at Prestonpans, **19.** 117
English ships keep Gages from getting, **19.** 51
Frederick II awaits, **21.** 95, 102
—— captures, at Prague, **18.** 511
——'s, **17.** 316, **22.** 12
French: **19.** 318; at Fontenoy, **36.** 11
galleys to convey, to Glimes, **17.** 501
Genoa aids Spanish army with, **19.** 64
Genoa to turn over, to Austria, **19.** 306
George II has right to, when captured, **19.** 151
heavy, arrival of, awaited by enemy at Minorca, **25.** 196
Jersey should not divert, from English defence, **39.** 335
lacking, for recapture of Minorca, **20.** 588
Lobkowitz discards, **18.** 529
—— endangers, **18.** 542

Modena to receive, from Mantua, **17.** 464
Pitt sends, against St-Malo, **21.** 213
rebels lack, **19.** 134
Royal Regiment of, to be reviewed, **32.** 195n
Sardinian, **18.** 151, 436
Spaniards abandon, at Algiers, **24.** 121–2
Spaniards lack, for Tuscan invasion, **19.** 38
Spaniards receive, despite English fleet, **18.** 296, **19.** 30
Spanish, **18.** 27, 244, 257, **19.** 35–6, 147
Spanish ships bring, from Barcelona to Italy, **17.** 286
Swedish, captured, **17.** 155
transports from Naples escape with, **19.** 82
Young Pretender lacks, for siege, **19.** 109
*See also* Cannon; Field piece; Fire-arrows; Mortar
Artillery Ground, Moorfields, London:
cricket at, **18.** 48n
meat roasted by sun in, **21.** 121
stores in, seized by Gordon rioters, **33.** 185
Artimino, Grand Duke of Tuscany's villa:
Craon rents, **20.** 116
Craon, Princesse de, returns from, **19.** 466
Craons supply furniture for, **20.** 116
visitors to: Antinori, **18.** 329, 521; Antinori, Mme, **19.** 145; Craon, Princesse de, **18.** 324, 329, 521, **19.** 145, 455, 466; Mann, **19.** 145; Salviati, **19.** 145
Artimiso:
Lobkowitz attacks mountain of, **18.** 488
Artisan; artisans:
Nova Scotian lands granted to, **20.** 40n
Artist; artists (*see also* Painter):
*Anecdotes of Painting* may be useful to, **42.** 254
Cole on, **1.** 298
English, HW does not value, as much as Onslow does, **40.** 309
HW's reflections on impertinence of, **9.** 259
modern, 'too feeble to paint anything but fan-mounts,' **25.** 247
Neapolitan, unemployed, **35.** 433
Piozzi, Mrs, comments upon, **9.** 259n
*Art of English Poetry. See under* Bysshe, Edward
*Art of Painting, The. See under* Mason, William; Piles, Roger de
*Art of Political Lying, The:*
Townshend, George, attacked by, **21.** 78, 90, **37.** 473n
*Art of Politics. See under* Bramston, James
*Art of Preserving Health. See under* Armstrong, John
*Art of Sinking in Poetry. See under* Pope, Alexander
Artois, Comte d'. *See* Charles X of France
Artois, Comtesse d'. *See* Marie-Thérèse (1756–1805)
Artois, 'Évêques d'. *See* Conzié, Joachim-Fran-

çois-Mamert de; Conzié, Louis-François-Marc-Hilaire de

Artois:

*Comte d'Artois* paid for by, **7.** 241

Conzié brothers important in, **5.** 197

*Art póetique, L'. See under* Boileau-Despréaux, Nicolas

Arts and Sciences, Society of. *See* Royal Society of Arts; Society for the Encouragement of Arts, Manufactures, and Commerce

Arty, Mme d'. *See* Guillaume de Fontaine, Marie-Anne

Arundel, Cts of. *See* Adeliza (ca 1103–51); Mordaunt, Lady Mary (ca 1661–1705); Talbot, Lady Alathea (d. 1654)

Arundel, E. of. *See* Aubigny, William d' (d. 1176);Fitzalan, Henry (1512–80); Howard, Charles (1746–1815); Howard, Henry Frederick (1608–52); Howard, Philip (1557–95); Howard, Thomas (1585–1646)

Arundel Castle, Sussex, D. of Norfolk's seat:

'a nothing on a fine hill,' **34.** 127

Cordell chaplain at, **9.** 96n

Cromwell besieges, **9.** 97, **12.** 205

Fitzalan chapel in, monuments in, **9.** 97, **12.** 205

ghost of giant walks among ruins at, **12.** 206

HW tells Conway about, **39.** 310

Norfolks build apartment at, **9.** 96, **12.** 205

painted glass window at, **12.** 205n

picture removed to, **1.** 192n

scenes worthy of commemoration at, **42.** 420–2

visitors to: Berry, Mary, **12.** 205; Chute, **9.** 96; HW, **9.** 96, **12.** 205, **34.** 127; Ossory, Lady, **34.** 127

Arundel Collection:

Raphael in, **2.** 169n

Richardson acquires miniature of Catherine Howard from, **40.** 366n

sale of, **1.** 192n, **15.** 114

Arundel family:

Brébeuf family wish genealogical connection with, **38.** 555

Norfolk, D. of, despises, for not being dukes, **12.** 209

Arundel House, London:

seat of 14th E. of Arundel, **1.** 186n, **15.** 114n, **43.** 55

Arundel Marbles:

Salisbury's letter on, in *Gentleman's Magazine,* **16.** 182–3

Arundel. *See also* Arundell

Arundell, Bns. *See* Slingsby, Barbara (ca 1669–1721)

Arundell, Lady Frances. *See* Manners, Lady Frances (d. 1769)

Arundell, Henry (1740–1808), 8th Bn Arundell:

Booth the Jesuit governor of, **21.** 339

devout Roman Catholic, **21.** 339

Santini's watch brought by, to Italy, **21.** 339

Wardour Castle, seat of, **21.** 339n

wife of, **1.** 6n

Arundell, John (1649–98), 2d Bn Arundell:

son of, **25.** 178n

Arundell, Hon. Richard (ca 1696–1758), M. P.:

biographical information about, corrected, **43.** 267

government posts of, **18.** 551, **19.** 256

HW satirizes, **13.** 14

Irish pension awarded to, **9.** 181, **20.** 517

Pembroke's last conversation with, **20.** 108–9

Shelley to succeed, as Clerk of the Pipe, **21.** 26

statues at Wilton 'adorned' by, **25.** 178

treasurer of the Chambers, **9.** 33, **20.** 108n, 517

Arundell, Thomas (?1560–1639), 1st Bn Arundell of Wardour:

refers case to Palavicini, **1.** 5

Arvillars, Abbé d':

social relations of, with: Choiseul, Duchesse de, **7.** 307, 330; Du Deffand, Mme, **7.** 322; Rochfords, **4.** *15*; Souza, **7.** 318, 321; Viry, Contessa di, **7.** 350

Arzac de Ternay, Charles-Henri-Louis d' (ca 1722–80); Chevalier; naval officer:

fleet of: Clinton and Arbuthnot want to destroy, **25.** 99n; La Fayette allegedly predicts success for, **25.** 70; Minorca to be attacked by, **25.** 48n, 58n

Newfoundland captured by, **22.** 52n

*As,* Roman coin:

in Middleton's collection, **15.** 16

Asafoetida:

bottle of, revives fainting lady, **37.** 22

Thomas prescribes, for Chute, **24.** 210

Asaf-ud-daulah (ca 1750–97), Nawab-Vazir of Oudh:

weak, **25.** 13n

Ascanio, Père Salvator Maria (ca 1655–1741), Spanish minister to Tuscany:

death of, **17.** 86

Vernaccini secretary and successor to, **17.** 207n

Ascension, the:

De Wet's painting of, at Glamis Castle, **42.** 347n

festival of, at Venice. *See under* Venice, Ascension at

in window at Trinity Hospital, Greenwich, **16.** 86

*Ascents of the Soul, The. See under* Loredano, Giovanni Francesco

Aschaffenburg:

Montagu, D. of, jokes about organist at, **18.** 342

Ascham, Roger (1515–68):

*Rogeri Aschami epistolarum libri quatuor* prints Somerset's letter, **16.** 5

*Scholemaster, The:* Lady Jane Grey's learning mentioned in, **16.** 365; Wyatt mentioned in, **1.** 261

Asciotti, ——:

HW and Bateman buy painted glass from Flanders from, **9.** 146n, **20.** 199n

marriage of, to a Fleming, **20.** 199n

Ascoli:
  Lobkowitz's men to cross the Tronto at, 18. 438
Ascot:
  races at, 19. 298n, 38. 435
Ascow, d'. See Dashkov
Asgill, Sir Charles:
  house of, on the Thames, 32. 317n, 318n
Asgill, John (1659–1738), eccentric writer:
  denies necessity of dying, 32. 82
Ash, John, nurseryman and seedsman:
  Brydson employed by, 12. 251
  mother and sister of, see robbery near his nursery, 11. 283, 284
  Sherriff employed by, 12. 252
  Twickenham resident, 42. 487
Ash, John (1723–98), M. D.:
  HW confers with, about HW's nephew, 16. 314, 42. 335
  Orford attended by, at Houghton, 42. 332, 335
  ——'s executors liberally pay, for attendance on him, 42. 355
Ash or Ashe, Thomas, nurseryman at Twickenham:
  (?) HW quotes, about 'poetical' trees, 35. 157
  (?) HW wants melon seeds for, 20. 170
  Pope served by, 35. 157n
  Twickenham resident, 42. 487
Ash. See also Ashe
Ash (tree):
  at SH, 10. 108
  France lacks, from lopping, 35. 336
  grotesques probably imitated from curling branches of, 42. 240–1
  mountain, at Wharncliffe Lodge, 35. 268
Ash: ashes:
  English suits should be made of sackcloth and, 37. 437
  'pale as,' 32. 75, 78
Ashbourne, Derbyshire:
  Hodgson of, 11. 33n
  rebels leave cannon and sick at, 19. 179n
Ashbroke. See Ashbrook
Ashbrook, Vct. See Flower, Henry (d. 1752); Flower, William (1744–80)
Ashbrook, Vcts. See Ridge, Elizabeth (1746–1808); Tatton, Elizabeth (d. 1759)
Ashburnham, Cts of. See Crowley, Elizabeth (ca 1728–81)
Ashburnham, Elizabeth Sophia (1786–1879):
  mother of, dies, 11. 244n
Ashburnham, George (1760–1830), styled Vct St Asaph; 3d E. of Ashburnham, 1812:
  Mann hears news from, 25. 314
  SH visited by, 12. 241
  wife of, dies, 11. 244
Ashburnham, Lady Jemima Elizabeth (1762–86), m. (1785) James Graham, styled Bn Graham, later 3d D. of Montrose:
  death of, 33. 527
  Fawkener abandons, 29. 305

Graham to wed, 36. 232
  marriage of, 25. 562, 604n
  miscarriage of, 25. 604
  pretty and amiable, 25. 562
Ashburnham, John (1687–1737), 3d Bn Ashburnham, 1710: cr. (1730) E. of Ashburnham; M. P.:
  Boughton Park sold by, to Strafford, 35. 279n
  Walpole, Sir Robert, moves to house of, 28. 470n
Ashburnham, John (1724–1812), 2d E. of Ashburnham, 1737:
  Amelia, Ps, entertains, 32. 307
  Ashburnham House of, 25. 562n, 33. 554
  Bedchamber appointment expected by, 19. 419–20
  Bexhill window procured by, for SH chapel, 1. 244, 32. 197
  Chichester, Bp of, anecdote about, told by, 12. 109
  children of, 33. 184
  Clark twits, on jealousy of Argenson's son, 19. 454
  dances at Robinson's ball, 37. 115
  Dashkov, Ps, warns, 29. 60
  daughter of, 25. 562, 604n, 29. 305
  extravagance of, 21. 200
  family misfortune of, 25. 414
  George III saves, after overthrow of government, 25. 273
  Gordon rioters tear, from chariot, 33. 175
  Gordon rioters threaten, 33. 184
  HW and Chute well know the character of, 19. 453–4
  HW entertains, at SH, 38. 276
  HW expects, at SH, 32. 197
  HW's Customs place sought by, 40. 145n
  Huntingdon may succeed, as ranger, 22. 113n
  Le Despenser succeeded by, in Great Wardrobe, 22. 311
  Lincoln's quarrel with, over cook, 35. 246
  marriage of: 16. 76n; witticism on, 37. 438, 450
  may become George III's governor, 20. 345
  Newcastle believed in by Lincoln and, 21. 97, 43. 274
  —— considers, for cofferer, 20. 518n
  ——'s favourite, 35. 246
  offices resigned by, 30. 167
  Parks rangership resigned by, 36. 37
  Pomfret succeeded by, in Park posts, 9. 153
  resigns as Groom of Stole, from failure to receive Garter, 25. 273
  Rome not visited by, for fear of imprisonment, 19. 454
  Selwyn's witticism on, 9. 153
  summer suit made by, in vain, 19. 420
  to be Groom of the Stole, 24. 142
  wife and children of, 33. 184
Ashburnham, John (1789–1810), ensign:
  mother of, dies, 11. 244n

Ashburnham, Sophia (1788–1807):
mother of, dies, 11. 244n
Ashburnham, Sir William (1710–97), 4th Bt,
1762; Bp of Chichester, 1754:
ghost appears to, 12. *109*–10, 116
St Paul's deanery to go to, 22. 324n
Ashburnham House, (London):
in Dover St, 25. 562n, 33. 554n
Ashburton, Bn. See Dunning, John
Ashburton, Bns. See Baring, Elizabeth
Ashburton (Devon):
borough of: candidates at, 36. 47; contested
election for, 30. 169; Lucas tends, for Or-
ford, 25. 462; Orford compromises, 36. 47;
Orford chooses Boone for, 24. 47; Orford,
Cts of, should have entrusted, to her agents,
24. 67; Orford, Cts of, to assign to HW
her interest in, 23. 548; Parliament's disso-
lution blamed for neglect of, 24. 57
HW's burgage-tenures at, offered to Trefusis
and refused to Lisburne, 42. 376–8
Orford heir to maternal estates at, 30. 169n
Platel perhaps vicar of, 29. 331n
Ashby, Rev. George (1724–1808), antiquary:
Cole led by, to correspond with Pennant, 2. 20
——'s acquaintance with, 1. 107n
Granger corresponds with, 1. 269n
HW receives prints from, 1. 195
HW tries to answer query of, 16. 206–8
MS sent by, to HW through Lort, 16. 203–4,
209
*Miscellaneous Antiquities* commented on by,
1. 300, 303, 304
refuses to read petition that Fellows might
marry, 1. *107n*
sends notes on Baker, to Cole, 2. *344*
Ashby. See also Asheby
Ashdon, Essex:
Lagden, Mrs, Quaker at, 1. 363
Ashdown Park, Berks:
Craven's seat, 11. 361n
Ashe, Elizabeth, m. 1 (1751) Edward Wortley
Montagu; m. 2 (1761) Robert Faulknor; 'the
Pollard':
Chute satirizes, 20. *140*
cosmetics of, 9. 106
daughter of, 12. 33n
husband deserts, in HW's newspaper parody,
9. 129
joke commented upon by, 9. 110
Kilmorey, Vcts, tells scandal about, 20. 278
Maclaine visited by, 20. 169
of St Martin's-in-the-Fields, 20. 289n
Petersham, Lady Caroline, accompanied by, to
theatre, 37. 433
—— entertains, 9. 106–10
—— quarrels with, 9. 112–13
—— takes, to supper at tavern with Hérault,
35. 222–3
(?) Selwyn jokes about Lyttelton and, 35. 195
Vauxhall visited by, 9. 106–10

Wortley Montagu thought to have married,
20. 289
Ashe, Capt.(?)T. S., actor:
*Hamlet* acted by, at Margate, 12. 129n
Ashe, William Wyndham:
comptroller of D. of Cumberland's house-
hold, 20. 208n
Ashe, Devon:
Drake of, 10. 197n
Ashe. See also Ash
Ashe A'Court. See A'Court
Asheby, Elizabeth, m. Henry Naunton:
stained-glass portrait of, at Letheringham,
35. 248
Asheton. See Ashton
Ashfeild. See Ashfield
Ashfield, Edmund (d. 1700), painter:
miniature by, of Lady Herbert, 10. 346
Ashford Common:
Conway reviews regiment at, 35. 365
Ashley, Dorothy (d. 1761), m. 1 Charles Pit-
field; m. 2 Hon. Felton Hervey:
death of, expected, 9. 401
Ashley. See also Astley
Ashmole, Elias (1617–92), antiquary:
*Antiquities of Berkshire* by, 16. 78n
HW a 'contemporary' of, 33. 456
Hillier thinks Richmond Palace print was in
book by, 16. 78
Hollis's diary as anile as that of, 29. *19*
*Institution . . . of . . . the Garter*, Gray men-
tions, 14. 96
*Memoirs of the Life of . . . Elias Ashmole*, 12.
258
Ashmolean Museum, Oxford:
Huddesford keeper of, 1. 255n
—— sends transcripts from, 38. 157–9
Ashmore, Mrs, of Richmond:
SH visited by, 12. 237
Ash Park, Roscommon:
Kirwan of, 11. 198n
Ashridge, Bucks:
HW condemns Selwyn for sending him to,
30. 120
Ashridge College, Bucks:
Cole's account of paintings in, 1. 312, 326n
'Ashtaroh':
HW calls Mrs Montagu, 29. 116, 121, 126
Ashton, Alpress (d. 1808):
buried at St Ives, 13. 116n
Ashton, Charles (1665–1752), D. D.; master of
Jesus College, Cambridge:
consulted about Cornwallis's fellowship, 13.
155
Ashton, Francis (1688–ca 1758), usher of Lan-
caster grammar school:
Ashton, Thomas, son of, 13. 177n, 14. 234
Ashton, Hugh (d. 1522), divine:
archdeacon, not dean, 2. 342
Ashton, John (1721–59), Fellow of Trinity Col-
lege, Cambridge; Thomas Ashton's brother:

[Ashton, John (1721–59), *continued*]
Aldingham living to be transferred to, **43**. 189
Ashton presents Gray as, **13**. 161
Ashton, John (d. 1768), marshal (1749–66) of King's Bench:
Theodore of Corsica's release signed in presence of, **40**. 191
Ashton, Mat, painter:
Laroon's caricature of, **42**. 282
Ashton, Rev. Thomas (1715–75), HW's correspondent:
Aldingham living sought for, by HW, **40**. 37, 39–40
at Mrs Lewis's, Hanover Sq., **43**. 180
*Character of the Life and Administration of the Late . . . Earl of Orford*, **14**. 234; **19**. 29, 40
chaplaincy of, redated, **43**. 189
Clive, Mrs, admires sermons of, **9**. 72
Conway sends compliments to, **37**. 260
costume of, **9**. 29
*Dissertation on 2 Peter, A,* **14**. 43–4, 236, **15**. 300
epitaphs by: on himself, **14**. 236; on West, **17**. 468–9, 470, 491, **28**. 119–20, 124, 130
Eton College fellow, **18**. 470n, **20**. 164n, **37**. 258
fellow-commoner of St John's, Cambridge, attacks, **15**. 302
Gray alludes to, as 'bishop,' **14**. 12
— quarrels with, **28**. 124
— requests letter from, **13**. 103
— sends greetings to, **13**. 112, 115, **14**. 8
—'s letter from, **13**. 99
— tells HW to ask, about West's MSS, **14**. 16
HW asks for preferment for, **17**. 430n
HW calls, Christian philosopher, **37**. 258
HW mentions, **37**. 175
HW no longer abuses, **30**. 176
HW promises letter to, **13**. 206, 209
HW promises West a letter from, **13**. 250
HW's correspondence with, **13**. 138, 176, 214, 219, 246, **40**. 66, **43**. 179, 182
HW's *Epistle* to, **13**. 22, **15**. 9n, **28**. 124, 130, **34**. 35
HW's illness alarms, **13**. 246–7
HW's memoir of, **14**. 234–6, **43**. 189
HW's neighbour at Windsor, **37**. 258
HW's pride deplored by, **13**. 82
HW's quarrel with, **5**. 345n, **14**. 32–3, **20**. 164–5, 178, 215, 218, **28**. 124
HW to be told by, of crowded coach from Cambridge, **37**. 21
HW to hear sermon by, **9**. 44
HW with: at Eton, **9**. 43; in London, **40**. 37
health of: ague, **9**. 59; apoplexy, **14**. 236
Hetherington recommended to, by HW, as Eton fellow, **40**. 66
King's College attended by, **13**. 78
King's College fellow, **13**. 140, **15**. 303, **40**. 39–40

Lincoln's grant to Spence witnessed by HW and, **30**. 32
'long ungainly mortal,' **13**. 78
Mason avoids mentioning, **28**. 124
Middleton's death not caused by, **20**. 167
—'s *Examination* attacked by, **20**. 179n
—'s quarrel with, **20**. 164, 215
Montagu to be aided by, in preparing HW's Windsor house, **9**. 44
— to be kept informed by, **9**. 48–9
— to hear about Twickenham gun-firing from, **9**. 74
motto to be given to, **20**. 178
Naylor to receive resignation of, **40**. 40
nicknames of, and circle, **13**. 55
'of Lancaster,' **40**. 37
Peterhouse scholars stare at, **13**. 60
portrait of, HW's inscription on, **20**. 164–5
psalms paraphrased by, **14**. 234–5
rector of St Botolph's, Bishopsgate, **20**. 164n
St Ives visited by, **13**. 116
sermons printed by, **14**. 234, 236
*Some Observations on a Book Entitled an Essay,* **15**. 303, **43**. 212
Tonson's book store sells few books by, **20**. 165
tutor to E. of Plymouth, **13**. 153, 156, 161, **20**. 164n
unsuccessful attempt by, to turn Buondelmonti's verses into Greek, **13**. 235–6
Walpole, Sir Edward, intimate with, **20**. 215, 218
West's relations with, **13**. 101, 109, 110, 118, 127, 132, 198
Whitaker's attack on, **15**. 301
Ashton, Mrs Thomas. *See* Amyand, Judith
Ashurst, Henry (d. 1680):
establishes family fortune, **9**. 63n
Ashurst, Thomas (d. 1765):
Hedingham Castle owned by, **9**. 63
new house built by, **9**. 63
Ashurst, Sir William Henry (1725–1807):
commissioner of the Great Seal, **15**. 216n
Ashurt. *See* Ashurst
Ash Wednesday:
Carnival's ending embittered by, **19**. 364
HW invited to supper party on, **41**. 2
not dreaded, after bad Carnival, **20**. 219
Ashwell, Mr, of Barnes:
SH visited by, **12**. 242
Asia:
assassins, sect of, supposed to exist in, **12**. 54
Bragança's acquaintance with, **7**. 9
British fight Tippoo Sahib in, **11**. 186
Catherine II and, **34**. 146
climate of, **32**. 241, **33**. 97, 212
Clive subdues, **38**. 188
Coke, Lady Mary, unlikely to visit, **31**. 162
England discusses, more fully than Europe, **25**. 117
England's government worthy of, **33**. 97, 212
Europe's intercourse with, **15**. 212

HW's correspondence with Mann covers, **23.**
363
oppression in, **31.** 284
peace in, not to be based on Saunders-Godhue
treaty, **21.** 527n
rhinoceros from, **20.** 127n
St Martin's parish said to include, **23.** 551
world's youthful vigour exhibited in, **25.** 47
*Asia,* English ship:
arrival of, with American news, **32.** 394
Boston to be reinforced by, **39.** 197n
Asiatic; Asiatics:
fortune's pranks among, **37.** 221
reincarnation of, in geese and turkeys, **21.** 7
Asiatic distemper:
occurrence of, **33.** 5n
Asiatic poets:
Jones's translations of, **28.** 35–6
Askew, Mrs. *See* Holford, Elizabeth
Askew, Anthony (1722–74):
HW identifies, **28.** 187n
Askew. *See also* Ayscough
'Asmodeo.' *See* Le Sage, Alain-René: *Diable
boiteux, Le*
Asoph. *See* Azov
Asp:
poison of, in the church, **25.** 245
Aspasia, Pericles's mistress:
fame of, **31.** 21
Montagu, Mrs, called, **34.** 70
Aspinwall, Rev. Dr Edward (ca 1678–1732):
Bower denies attending, in last illness, **21.** 46n
Roman Catholicism attacked by, **21.** 46n
Aspremont, —— (d. 1743), Graf von; Sardinian
general; Conte:
Spaniards capture, **18.** 154
wounded at Campo Santo, **18.** 164
Aspremont. *See also* Apremont
Aspuru. *See* Azpuru
Ass; asses:
Balaam's, Cholwick compared with, **35.** 30
ears of, **10.** 118
fable about, **9.** 270
HW jokes about, of patriarchs, **37.** 290
jawbone of, **33.** 304
lion kicked by, **16.** 379
milk of, medicinal, **2.** 317, 318, 320, **10.** 164,
**20.** 520, **21.** 418n, **22.** 348, **31.** 62, **33.** 254
ox and, should be spared labour, **31.** 328,
365, 435
Wilkes refers to Biblical rôle of, **22.** 184–5
Assalto, Conde dell', capt.-gen. of Barcelona:
Mann entertains, **25.** 435n
Assassin; assassins:
HW chooses his favourite victims for, **35.** 525
HW's reflections on, **25.** 202
sect of: Crusaders believed existence of, in
Asia, **12.** 54; HW comments on, **12.** 117
Assassination:
Dimitri, Abp, thinks, a less affront to Heaven
than 3 Lutheran churches, **38.** 164
French profess, **34.** 158, 161, 164, 177

French revolutionists offer rewards for, **31.**
373n, **35.** 446
grows contagious, **34.** 169
Assassination Plot:
Somers's papers about, **20.** 321–2
Assemani, Stefano Evodio (1707–82), Abp of
Apamea:
Agdollo hears from, of Louis XV's support
of Young Pretender, **17.** 114
*Bibliothecæ apostolicæ Vaticanæ codicum
manuscriptorum catalogus,* **17.** 48n
Craon, Mme de, tells, to negotiate about eti-
quette with Modenese princess, **17.** 60
Kaunitz acquires stone snuff-box from, **17.** *48*
Sade's verses translated into Latin by, **17.** 46n
Assemblée nationale, French. *See* National As-
sembly
Assembly, The (building at Paris):
French royal family imprisoned at, **31.** 372n
Assembly; assemblies:
abbés and canonici not to attend, **21.** 224
Albizzi, Mme degli, gives, **18.** 329
Amherst, Lady, has, **33.** 215
at Canterbury, **40.** 4
at Chichester, **39.** 80
at Dublin, inferior to those in Paris, **39.** 39
at Hôtel de Beaupréau in Paris, **39.** 37
at Northumberland House, **38.** 400, 401
at Siena, for D. of York, **22.** 224
balls in theatre as grave as, **20.** 464
Belturbet girls fit to appear at, in York or
Chester, **37.** 336
Chesterfield gives, at new house, **20.** 302–3
Cobham, Vcts, gives, **20.** 123–4, 145, **26.** 29
Conway, Bns, to give, **17.** 334
Cornelys, Theresa, has, **23.** 271
Craon, Princesse de, gives, **17.** 16, **35.** 8
Devonshire, Ds of, gives, **37.** 341
Dublin's, surpass those at Bath, **37.** 412
eccentric Englishwoman attends, in *pet en
l'air,* **24.** 260
English: Anamabu 'princes' fashionable at,
**20.** 40; HW dislikes, **31.** 93
Feroni, Mme, gives, **17.** 33–4
Ferrers and wife meet at, in country, **21.** 395
Gloucester, D. and Ds of, go to, in evenings,
**33.** 582
Grandison, Vcts, gives, **10.** 206
Granville, Cts, gives, **18.** 537, 562
Guerchy's, **10.** 139
HW gives, for great-nieces, **39.** 316
HW's at SH, **10.** 102, 106, 107, **33.** 61–2
HW tells Mann not to renew, in garden, **20.**
169–70
HW to attend, **17.** 25
HW unable to jump into, from post-chaise,
**39.** 167
HW will not attend, at Windsor, **19.** 298
Harrington, Cts of, gives, **38.** 234
Hertford, Cts of, gives, **25.** 123n
Holman, Mrs, gives, **20.** 142, **35.** 196
Lincoln, Cts of, gives, at Exchequer House,
**37.** 453–4

[Assembly; assemblies, *continued*]

Lorenzi presents Frenchmen to Mann at, **20.** 489

Mann breaks off, **19.** 501

—— gives: for Bns Spencer, **22.** 180; for Brand, **20.** 471; for Contessa Acciaioli, **19.** 501; in his garden, **18.** 332; in his garden for Mrs Barrett and Signora Capello, **20.** 174, 191; on Thursdays in garden, **19.** 115; well attended by court officials, **22.** 350; will be enjoyed by D. of York, **22.** 236

——s, criticized by Bns Holland, **22.** 467n

——'s conversazione resembles English card-, **20.** 427

——'s garden illuminated for, **18.** 485

—— to hold, on special occasions only, **20.** 191

—— to recommence, **18.** 462, **19.** 277

Masserano's, **10.** 138–9

Mirepoix, Mme de, and Mrs Nugent attend, **20.** 131

Naylor, Mrs, gives, on Sundays, **20.** 136

Northumberland, Ds of, gives up, on Ps of Orange's death, **38.** 8

Petroni's, **19.** 85

politics less dignified than, **21.** 542

Richecourt gives, every Thursday night at Imperialino, **20.** 446

Roman, attended by D. of Gloucester, **24.** 163

Seilerns', daughter's death does not prevent, every Tuesday, **10.** 138, **38.** 510

Strafford, Lady, gives, **34.** 257

tiresome, in Florence, **19.** 311

vast, attended by HW, **35.** 213

Vitelli, Mme, gives, **18.** 541

Assembly-room:

Almack's, **10.** 138

of Theresa Cornelys, **10.** 138

*Assendelft*, Dutch ship:

Holland to send, **18.** 458

Assheton, Lady Catherine. *See* Gordon, Lady Catherine

Assheton, Christopher, of Fyfield, Berks:

wife of, **15.** 121n

Assiento, Treaty of:

England and Spain to renew, **19.** 480

Seville treaty renews, **20.** 198n

Assietta (Col de l'Assiette):

French defeated at, **19.** 417n

Assignats, French:

Burke jokes about value of, **11.** 151

depreciation in value of, **12.** 148, **31.** 357, **34.** 183

prolific coinage of, **31.** 359

*See* Money, paper

Assizes:

at Carrickfergus, **37.** 74

at Hertford, **21.** 184

at Huntingdon, **10.** 92

at Norwich, *see under* Norwich

at Warwick, **38.** 16

at Winchester, **20.** 237

Aylesbury and Buckingham clash over, **19.** 449n, 470–1, **20.** 112

in Bucks, transferred, **13.** 20

Parliament no more discussed than, **24.** 278

Waldegraves busy with, **36.** 240

Association; associations:

county: Du Deffand, Mme, doubts success of, **7.** 202; fashionable, **25.** 66; increasing, **25.** 20; Mann distrusts, **25.** 23; Mason should not revive, **35.** 377; Opposition tries to shift Parliamentary power to, **25.** 29; people raised by, to a frenzy, **25.** 32; petitions from, **25.** 18; Powys calls, 'Quintuple Alliance,' **25.** 401n; seems to doze, **25.** 47; serious for North ministry, **7.** 210; turbulence of, has subsided, **25.** 406; *see also* Yorkshire Association

Association for Preserving Liberty and Property:

HW approves of, **15.** 235, **34.** 172

Nares elected to committee of, **15.** 234–5

zeal of, must be increased, **15.** 243

Association for the Preservation of Game:

Chaworth active in, **38.** 503

Assomption, Filles de l'. *See* Filles de l'Assomption

Asson, Comtesse d'. *See* Wassenaer, Marguerite-Élisabeth-Barbe de

Asson, Philippe-Joseph (fl. 1769–75), Comte d':

wife of, **7.** 92n

Assumption, Church of (London):

Haszlang's chapel becomes, **25.** 55n

Assyria:

kings of, not hinted at, **35.** 78

Assyrian Empire:

uncertain boundaries of, **7.** 358

Aste *or* Asti, Prince Maurice d':

palazzo of, collapses, **22.** 17n

Aster; asters:

HW sees: at Chantilly, **7.** 260; at Hôtel de Biron, **7.** 263

'Astérie,' character in Voltaire's *Lois de Minos*:

Du Deffand, Mme, praises, **8.** 191

Asterisks:

hack writers delight in, **42.** 502

Asthma:

Fox does not have, **30.** 235

lap-dog catches, from mistress, **35.** 16

occurrences of, **18.** 65, 117, **20.** 108, 433, 522–3, 540, 543, 549, 551, 554, 564; **21.** 152, 292, **22.** 243, 259, **23.** 83, 91, 303, 348, 355, 369, **24.** 31, 244, 360, **25.** 112, **28.** 94, **32.** 245, **35.** 442–3, **36.** 246n

Asti (Italy):

capture of, **19.** 226, 227, 231

HW and Gray at, **13.** 192n

Asti, Palazzo, at Rome:

fall of, **22.** 17

Astle, Thomas (1735–1803), antiquary; F.S.A.; F.R.S.:

*Antiquarian Repertory* edited by, **2.** 255n

Buckingham inherits MSS of, **42.** 280n

Clarence's attainder printed by, **15.** 177

HW asks, about auction prices of Edmund Crouchback's seal, **42.** 266

HW asks, for copyist for copying inscription, **41**. 144

HW called on by, **2**. 7

HW directs that SH be shown to, **41**. 399

HW invites: to dine and sleep at SH, **41**. 95; to call at SH, **42**. 148

(?) HW is plagued with letters from, concerning Richard III, **15**. 243

HW 'left off' by, **2**. 2

HW receives coronation roll and attainder from, **2**. 2, **43**. 64

HW recommends Pinkerton to, (?) **42**. 279–80

HW refers Cosway to, for explanation of ring, **42**. 187

HW's correspondence with, **2**. 2, 3, 5–6, **28**. 238–9, **41**. 95, 119–22, 144, 322–4, 399, **42**. 145, 147–8, 223, 266, (?) 279–80

HW thanks: for Alfred's will and royal lock, **42**. 223; for aid in Fitzwilliam's law suit, **42**. 147–8; for attainder of D. of Clarence, **41**. 322

HW to be helped by, with old handwriting, **14**. 178

HW to call on, **42**. 223

paper shown by, to HW, **41**. 322, 356

Scottish charters and documents owned by, **42**. 280

son of, **12**. 231

SH visited by, **12**. 225, 231

subscribes to Mrs Penny's poem, **16**. 182n

Walpole, Sir Robert, papers of, said by, to be owned by Duane, **41**. 119

Astley, Lady, *see* Milles, Anne (d. 1792)

Astley, Miss:
SH visited by, **12**. 227

Astley, Alicia (1716–91), m. (1742) Charles Bennet, 3d E. of Tankerville:
Karl Wilhelm Ferdinand offers seat to, at opera, **38**. 289

Astley, Anne (fl. 1775–1832), m. —— Agnew, Mrs Delany's 'own woman':
Delany, Mrs, leaves clothing and candlesticks to, **33**. 497n
inspects house at Windsor, **33**. 497

Astley, Arabella (1719–85), m. 1 (1748) Anthony Langley Swymmer; m. 2 (1761) Sir Francis Vincent, 7th Bt:
(?) beauty of, **20**. 376
birth date of, **43**. 271
(?) Florence and Rome visited by, **20**. 376n

Astley, Sir Edward (1729–1802), 4th Bt, 1760; M.P.:
'gentleman in Norfolk,' mentioned in *Anecdotes of Painting*, **1**. 175
Parliamentary proposal by, to make Grenville's election bill permanent, **32**. 189n
son of, captured by pirates, **25**. 480

Astley, Edward John (1761–1806), Col.:
equerry to D. of Cumberland, **12**. 263
(?) Rome visited by, **25**. 480

Astley, Sir Jacob Henry (1756–1817), 5th Bt, 1802; M.P.:

(?) Rome visited by, **25**. 480

Astley, John (1730–87), painter:
Guercino painting copied by, **20**. 313–14
HW and Galfridus Mann see pictures by, **20**. 341
HW misses seeing, in London, **20**. 324
HW recommends, to Cardinal Albani, **43**. 270
Mann's great room hung with copies by, **20**. 313
——'s portrait by, **20**. 309–10, 313, **23**. 267, **26**. 56
—— wants HW to be painted by, **20**. 313
Rome visited by, **20**. 310n
Walpole of Wolterton family portrayed by, **20**. 341
Young's alleged Titian to be examined by, **20**. 331

Astley, John (ca 1767–1821), 'young Astley'; equestrian performer:
balloons will eclipse popularity of, in France, **25**. 451
HW sees acrobatics of, **33**. 418
Marie-Antoinette summons, to Paris, **25**. 451, **35**. 375
minuets danced by, on galloping horses, **25**. 451, **35**. 375
pantomimes at amphitheatre of, **34**. 71n

Astley, Philip (ca 1742–1814), equestrian performer:
amphitheatre of, in Southwark: Churchill family visits, **12**. 196–7; for riding and rope-dancing, **25**. 451n; HW visits, **35**. 375
equestrian feats of, **33**. 317
monkey of, 'General Jackoo,' **33**. 515
training abilities of, **33**. 418

Astley, William Coke (1769–89):
pirates capture, on *Great Duchess of Tuscany*, **25**. 480

Aston, Bns. *See* Talbot, Barbara

Aston, Lady. *See* Pye, Elizabeth

Aston, ——:
Mann presents, at Tuscan Court, **24**. 251n

Aston, Anthony:
Bracegirdle, Mrs, called Diana by, **25**. 74n

Aston, Catherine, m. Hon. Henry Hervey:
husband of, **14**. 38n

Aston, Henry Hervey. *See* Hervey Aston, Henry

Aston, Mrs Henry Hervey. *See* Dicconson, Catherine

Aston, Mary (1706–ca 1765), m. (1753) David Brodie:
HW's correspondence with, **40**. 75

Aston, Mary (1743–1805), m. (1766) Sir Walter Blount, 6th Bt:
(?) proposed marriage of, **32**. 65

Aston, Sir Richard (d. 1778), Kt, 1765; judge of the Court of King's Bench:
Bathurst to receive Great Seal from, **23**. 269n
lord chancellor's seals in commission to, **23**. 179n
Wilkes to appear before, **23**. 12

Aston, Sir Willoughby (ca 1715–72), 5th Bt:
Beaufort entertains, at Paris, **7**. 271

Aston, Sir Willoughby (ca 1748–1815), 6th Bt, 1772:
Cholmondeley and, lose to C. J. Fox and Fitzpatrick at Brooks's, 39. 368–9
Aston, Yorkshire:
Alderson rector of, 28. 43n
(?) Bentley's Gothic room to be executed at, 9. 285, 40. 180n
HW sends letters to Mason at, 28. 3, 21
HW visits, 1. 264n, 28. 36–7, 39
manor of, sold by Holdernesse, 28. 91, 112, 172, 231
Mason rector of, 13. 55n, 29. 349n
Mason's house at: 43. 301; Byron and Lady Conyers stay at, 28. 472, 483, 484–5, 29. 20, 29; Mason does not wish to leave, for London, 28. 32; praised by Markham, 28. 317; wind damages slates of, 28. 484–6
(?) plan for Gothic room at, 40. 180
seven miles from a turnpike, 28. 4, 29. 20n
Aston family:
Standon abandoned by, 40. 198
Aston Hall, Warwickshire:
Dacre wants Mrs Wettenhall to get drawing of, 9. 362
Astracan. See Astrakhan
Astræa:
Switzerland may yet be cherished by, 35. 583–4
wise to forsake earthly affairs, 25. 27
Astræa. See under Urfé, Honoré d'
Astrakhan lamb. See under Fur; Lamb
Astrology:
Humphrey might have written about, 16. 15
Astronomer; astronomers:
Beauclerk keeps, 39. 293
Du Deffand, Mme, hires, to show comet, 10. 290
HW quotes, on annihilation of stars, 19. 71, 21. 85
HW's verses mention, 38. 89
responsibility of, for French Revolution, 31. 385
Astronomy:
Boyle, Charlotte, knows, 31. 251n
HW's ignorance of, 15. 188, 20. 120, 21. 368, 33. 477, 569
HW's reflections on, 28. 160–1, 33. 360–1, 364–6, 474–5, 477, 569–70
HW takes to, 33. 364
Herschel's discoveries in, 25. 614
human events no longer explained by, 33. 404–5
Hume Campbell studies, 20. 5
Humphrey unlikely to have written about, 16. 15
Orford's letters on, 34. 85
Perelli, professor of, 21. 348
See also under Herschel, Sir William
Astrua, Giovanna (1730–57), singer:
biographical information about, corrected, 43. 263
Neapolitan cantata to include, 19. 438

Asturias, P. of the. See Charles IV (1748–1819); Ferdinand VI (1713–59); Louis I (1707–24)
Asturias (Spain):
Charles of Naples may become prince of, 19. 307
Jardine consul in, 12. 62n
mines of: 35. 349; Gage and Lady Mary Herbert meet in, 7. 288, 30. 215; Pope's Moral Essays mention, 35. 349n
Asturies, Hôtel des (Paris):
Aulan lives at, 8. 11
'Asylum, The':
Eton locality, named by HW, 9. 3
As You Like It. See under Shakespeare, William
Atabalipa. See Atahuallpa
Atahuallpa (or Atabalipa) (ca 1502–33), last Inca of Peru:
biographical information on, corrected, 43. 307
HW can cipher like, 33. 263
HW mistakes, for Guatemotzin, 43. 154
in 'bed of roses,' compared to Marie-Antoinette's sufferings, 12. 120
Jephson might attempt story of, 41. 292
sufferings of, confused with Aztec emperor's, 29. 102n
Atalanta. See under Handel, George Frideric
'Atalantis':
Albany, Cts of, compared with, 25. 538
Atalantis, The New. See under Manley, Mary de la Rivière
Ath:
Conway encamped at, 37. 190–2
'Athaliah,' northern. See Catherine II
Athalie ('Athaliah'). See under Racine, Jean
'Athanais.' See under Lee, Nathaniel: Theodosius
Athanasius (ca 298–373), St:
creed of, 11. 15
Gibbon characterizes, 29. 98
HW rejects, 2. 100
Athawes, Mrs Mary (ca 1729–1817) of Barnes Green, Surrey:
(?) SH visited by, 12. 248
Atheism:
French: avowal of, 34. 142, 176, 177; HW and Gray shocked at, 14. 144, 147; has not infected people of quality, 14. 149; of French Revolutionists, 31. 329, 377, 381–2, 383, 391–2, 401
Gray calls, a 'vile dish,' 14. 187–8
HW's reflections on, 28. 72
More, Hannah, attacks, 31. 329, 381–2
suicides attributed to, 6. 1
Atheist; atheists:
French, 12. 56; see also under Atheism: French
Secker president of club of, 30. 304n
Warburton once headed club of, 39. 104–5
Athelard, John (fl. 1350), painter:
Edward III employed, 1. 153
Athelwold. See under Hill, Aaron

'Athenæ Cantabrigienses':
Cole's MS of, 1. 370, 2. 134, 43. 63
*Athenæ Oxonienses. See under* Wood, Anthony
Athenry, Bn. *See* Bermingham, Francis (1692–1750)
Athenry, Bns. *See* Agar, Ellis (ca 1709–89)
Athens, Dukes of:
Acciaioli family descended from, 20. 116
Athens (Greece):
Acropolis at, 28. 393, 42. 507
Cato might have lived comfortably in, 39. 409
Damer, Mrs, spends mornings in sculpture as at, 35. 437
England resembles, in fondness for the stage, 24. 435
HW alludes to Theoric fund in, 28. 393
HW and Voltaire on taste in, 4. 129, 8. 142, 41. 155
HW unlikely to see revival of, 35. 392
HW would like to restore, 28. 257
history of, paralleled by modern occurrences, 22. 186
ladies of, never kept their words, 33. 328
men of taste in, fewer than those in Paris, 41. 155
Paris excels, in comedy and tragedy, 41. 155
politics in, 35. 215
Propylæum of, 32. 126
scarce bigger than Brentford, 33. 479
visitors to: Craven, Lady, 25. 654n, 42. 176n; Pars, 26. 48
world will see, no more, 35. 127
Atherley, Lady Louisa. *See* Ker, Lady Louisa
Atherton, Mr:
SH visited by, 12. 223, 245
Athis (France), country seat of Duchesse de Rohan-Chabot:
La Vallière, Duchesse de, visits, 4. 265
Athleague, Roscommon (Ireland):
Lyster of, 11. 199n
Athlone (Ireland):
(?) Conway to go to, 37. 360
Conway writes from, 37. 375–6
Atholl, Ds of. *See* Frederick, Jane (ca 1693–1748); Ross, Mary (d. 1767)
Atholl, D. of. *See* Murray, James (1690–1764); Murray, John (1729–74); Murray, John (1755–1830)
Atholl, Dukes of:
Man, Isle of, formerly owned by, 33. 390
Atholl (Scotland):
Jacobites deserted by men of, 37. 237
Atholl Highlanders (regiment):
mutiny of, 25. 362n
Athos, Mt:
storms reach, 32. 364
Athronree. *See* Athenry
Atkin, Lady Anne. *See* Mackenzie, Lady Anne
Atkins, Lady. *See* Stonehouse, Penelope
Atkins, ——, actor and singer:
Smith's *Fairies* acted by, 35. 209

Atkins, (?) Christopher, capt. of the *Actæon*:
acquitted at court martial, 24. 236n
Atkins, Sir Henry (ca 1707–28), 4th Bt:
daughter of, 11. 96n
family of, 30. 328n
HW mistakenly calls, Sir Robert, 30. 328n
Atkins, Penelope (ca 1725–95), m. (1746) George Pitt, cr. (1776) Bn Rivers:
beauty of, 20. *49*, 58, 21. 548, 23. 451, 24. 131, 30. 328
biographical information on, corrected, 43. 143
blindness threatens, 23. 451
children of, not allowed to communicate with her, 23. 451
Cumberland, D. of, in love with, 9. 94, 20. 58
deafness of: beauties and good nature threatened by, 23. 451; compensated by her sagacity, 23. 456; makes her society troublesome, 24. 131
family of, 30. 328n
Florence left by, for Rome and Naples, 23. 447
Florence revisited by, 24. 131
French Amazons described by, 11. 96–7
HW given commission by, at Holdernesse's, 38. 461
HW receives Sévigné letter from, 34. *81*
HW's *Beauties* praises, 21. 548n, 30. 328
HW's *Epistle to Eckardt* mentions, 23. 451n
haymaking party given by, at Wandsworth Hill, 38. 400, 401
house of, near Lyon, 34. 81n
husband's relations with, 20. 58, 21. 548, 23. 451
husband to be accompanied by, to Turin, 21. 548
Italy to be visited by, 20. 58, 21. 548
Lyon visited by, 11. 96, 34. 81n, 121
Mann admires and pities, 23. 456
minuet danced by, at Florentine theatre, 23. 456
mobbing of, in park, 9. 94
Parliament attended by, after opera, 38. 318
Pitt visits, at Wandsworth Hill, 22. 572
Richmond's fireworks attended by, 9. 81
social relations of, with: Beaufort, Ds of, 23. 456; HW, 38. 494–5; Mann, 23. 447; Pelham, Frances, 10. 72–3
son's letter from, 34. 121
Stonehouse family beauty inherited by, 30. 328
subscription masquerade attended by, 20. 49
threads needle by candlelight to mend ruffle, 23. 456
Atkins, Sir Richard (1728–56), 6th Bt:
Murray, Fanny, given money by, 9. 80
sister of, 20. 58n, 21. 548n, 23. 451n
Atkins, W.:
print of, 40. 237
Atkins. *See also* Atkyns
Atkinson, ——, attorney:
Thurlow, Bp, saved by, from mob, 33. 174n

Atkinson, Richard (1738–85), M. P.; contractor:
contracts of, 28. 192, 33. 269
E. India Co. directorship of, corrected, 43. 354
Mure associated with, 28. 437n
Atkinson, Rev. William (1757–1846):
rector of Warham All Saints, 15. 217n
Atkinson. See also Achesoun
Atkyns, Anne (1683–1761), m. (1699) John
Tracy:
(?) Gray sends compliments to, 14. 18
sons of, 14. 95n
Atkyns, John Tracy (d. 1773), barrister; John
Chute's nephew:
breach between Chutes inflamed by, 14. 201
Chute, Anthony, commends, 14. 201
HW pictures, bringing will for Anthony
Chute to sign, too late, 35. 84, 85
Pratt prefers, at HW's request, 41. 182
wife of, 14. 199n
Atkyns, Mrs John Tracy. See Lindsey, Katherine
Atkyns, Richard (1615–77), author:
Original and Growth of Printing, The, HW
and Lort correspond about, 16. 150–1, 158,
160
Atkyns, Sir Robert (1647–1711), Kt, historian:
Ancient and Present State of Gloucestershire:
2. 179, 204; Rudder continues, 42. 115;
Stuarts praised in, 35. 146–7
Atkyns family:
Chute inheritance may be claimed by, 9. 161
Atkyns. See also Atkins
Atlantic Ocean:
Banks searches for islands in, 25. 451
England interested only in things across, 24.
82
England not strong enough to use force on
other side of, 24. 365
European animals said to degenerate after
crossing, 25. 47
genius may be revived on other side of, 24. 387
HW glad that liberty survives on one side of,
24. 448
HW knows nothing of politics across, 24. 34
horrible metropolis will arise on other side
of, 24. 154
next Augustan age will dawn on other side
of, 24. 62
peace desired on only one side of, 24. 354
Scotland, as monotonous as, 37. 250
Atlantis. See under Manley, Mary de la Rivière
Atlas:
Hercules replaces, 33. 364
unsuited to London traffic, 11. 249
Atlas (of maps):
Muzell tries to sell, to Ferdinand VI, 21. 434
see also Map
Atlas, Mt:
'an ant-hill,' 11. 358
Atlas historique. See under Châtelain, Nicolas
Atlas nouveau. See under Sanson, Guillaume
and Nicolas
'Atquavivians.' See under Acquaviva, Trajano

Atri, Duchessa d'. See Salviati, Laura
Atrisco, Don Solis y Sante (d. 1744), Duque d':
Monte Rotondo to be attacked by, 18. 443
Attaignant. See L'Attaignant
Attainder, acts of. See under Parliament: acts of
'Attainder of George, Duke of Clarence.' See
under Rotuli Parliamentorum
Attelage:
Craon, Mme de, goes about in, 17. 60
Francis I's, 18. 196
Mann's, at Cascine gardens, 18. 100
Attempt to Prove à Priori that in Gen. iii. 15
Jesus Christ is Particularly Foretold, An:
Middleton's attack on Sherlock provokes, 15.
302
Attempt towards an Apology for his R. H. the
Duke, An. See under Bentley, Richard (1708–
82)
Attems, Karl Michael (1710–74), Graf von; Bp
of Mannito, 1750; of Pergama, 1750; of Goerz,
1752:
Venice resents Benedict XIV's appointment
of, at Maria Theresa's request, to Aquileia,
20. 160–1
Atterbury, Mr, of Teddington:
SH visited by, 12. 239
Atterbury, Francis (1662–1732), Bp of Roches-
ter 1713–23:
Boyle, Lord, may have visited, 20. 66n
Dalrymple publishes Jacobite correspondence
of, 29. 293–4
Epistolary Correspondence of: 43. 139; disparaged by HW, 33. 416; published by Nichols,
29. 292–5; Wynn's letter in, 43. 172
epitaph on, by Cadogan, 33. 112
funeral sermon by, on Bns Cutts, 9. 261
gentleman courts, in France, 20. 66
HW declines publishing letters of, 15. 98
HW quotes remark, 29. 156–7
Kelly in the Tower for plotting with, 19. 153n
Old Pretender to have been proclaimed by,
20. 60
on Burnet's history, 2. 60
poems by, 15. 111
Pope sends Persian and Turkish Tales to,
11. 20
preface to Clarendon's history attributed to,
16. 8
Private Correspondence of, sent to HW, 15.
110, 117, 118, 43. 196
Scots College has box of papers by, 7. 359,
42. 287
speech of, supposedly borrowed by Wynne, 13.
32–3, 15. 110–11
translation attributed to, 42. 18
turbulence and ambition of, 29. 293
witticism by, on Pope, 20. 66
Atterbury, Rev. Lewis (ca 1631–93), D.D.:
father of Bp Atterbury, 29. 293
Atterbury, Mary (d. 1729), m. William Morice:
son of, 13. 33n
Atterbury. See also Adderbury

Attercliffe:
  turnpike at, **29**. 84n
Attica:
  Pomfret, Lady, mistakes, for Utica, **20**. 579
Atticus, Titus Pomponius (110–33 B.C.):
  Cato might have lived comfortably like, **39**. 409
  Cicero's letters to: collected by Atticus, **35**. 561–2; Du Deffand, Mme, reads, **6**. 332
  Conway resembles, **37**. 92
  HW compares, to Ralph Allen, **9**. 394
Attila (d. 453), chieftain:
  as innocent as Cæsar and Clive, **25**. 142
  HW alludes to, **29**. 295
  HW does not want, as gardener, **35**. 473
  HW's term for Frederick II, **25**. 613
  Jackson's prints seem coeval with, **20**. 381
*Attilio Regalo. See under* Jomelli, Niccolò; Metastasio, Pietro
Attitude; attitudes:
  Heinel, Mlle, copies, from classics, **35**. 343
Attonville. *See* Bourbon-Hattonville
Attorney, attorneys:
  Bayond's: tells Fanny Burney to pay servant's money to Bayond, **42**. 290; to get offer from Fanny Burney for dividing money, **42**. 298
  Bedlam actuated by, **25**. 316
  Mann, Horace II, retains Hull as, **24**. 78
  passengers in coach, **37**. 21
  Scottish, **35**. 622
  void of sensibility, and can only be foiled by another attorney, **25**. 298
Attorney, power of:
  Chatham executes, to wife, **39**. 89, 95
  HW jokes: about Conway sending, to claim bacon flitch, **38**. 71; about nephew bringing, to Conway, **38**. 73
  HW's, to Charles Bedford, **34**. 13n
  Mann receives and returns, **21**. 71, **24**. 205, 219
  Mozzi sends, to Sharpe, **25**. 137, 144
Attorney-General:
  changes in post of, **9**. 413, **10**. 109, 110
  Charlotte's, Hussey resigns as, **23**. 180–1
  Fuller prosecuted by, **16**. 366
  Irish, *see* Fitzgibbon, John; Tisdal, Philip; Yelverton, Barry
  Macdonald succeeds Arden as, **34**. 9n
  Wedderburn becomes, **39**. 136n
  Yorke said to succeed Norton as, **22**. 263, 268, **38**. 468, 471
  *See also* Arden, Richard Pepper; De Grey, Sir William; Henley, Robert, 1st E. of Northington; Kenyon, Lloyd; Lee, John; Macdonald, Sir Archibald; Murray, William, E. of Mansfield; Norton, Sir Fletcher; Ryder, Sir Dudley; Thurlow, Edward; Wallace, James; Yorke, Charles
Atys:
  busts of: Damer, Mrs, does, **12**. 273; infant, **35**. 437
*Atys. See under* Lulli, Jean-Baptiste; Quinault, Philippe

Au, Joseph Wiellinger von der:
  Charles Albert's claims get reply from, **17**. 151n
Auber. *See* Huber
Auberge Royale, hotel at Turin:
  Berrys find, full, **11**. 143n
Aubespine. *See* L'Aubespine
Aubeterre, Marquis ('Vicomte') d'. *See* Bouchard d'Esparbez de Lussan, Henri-Joseph
Aubeterre, Marquise d'. *See* Bouchard d'Esparbez de Lussan, Marie-Françoise
Aubigné, Françoise d' (1635–1719), Marquise de Maintenon, 1678; m. 1 (1652) Paul Scarron; m. 2 (1684) Louis XIV:
  apartment and furniture of, at St-Cyr, **7**. 330, **10**. 292–3
  Bath, Cts of, and Mrs Cleland argue about, **35**. 94
  compared with: Delany, Mrs, **33**. 497–8; Jersey, Lady, **12**. 155; Newcome, Mrs, **1**. 280n
  death of, at St-Cyr, **10**. 292
  Du Barry, Mme, contrasted with, **7**. 369
  Du Deffand, Mme, discusses, **4**. 60, **5**. 299, 330, **6**. 50, 434
  —— quotes, **4**. 237, **5**. 253
  —— to reread, **5**. 190
  grandfather of, **28**. 35n
  grave of, at Saint-Cyr, **10**. 293
  HW comments on, **4**. 55, **10**. 295
  HW has letter of, **6**. 144–5, **7**. 330, **34**. 82
  HW prefers earlier tastes of, **31**. 43
  HW visits St-Cyr to see relics of, **6**. 144–5, **7**. 330, **10**. 292–3, **34**. 82
  Jekyll, Lady Anne, imitates, **9**. 201
  letters of: in St-Cyr archives, **10**. 294; to Cardinal and Duc de Noailles, **5**. 258, 266, 283; to her family, **5**. 299, 330; to (and from) Princesse des Ursins, **4**. 44, 46, 55, 62, 68–9, 74, 81, 88, 108, 111, **5**. 258, 266, 283, 299, 320, 326, 327, 330, **17**. 1n
  *Lettres* of, **14**. 62, 98, **35**. 276–7
  Louis XIV calls, 'Votre Solidité,' **30**. 257n
  —— intends St-Cyr apartment for, **10**. 293
  ——'s marriage to, **22**. 270n, **33**. 514
  —— subject of witty complaint by, **42**. 489, 490
  Mary of Modena said to visit, **9**. 244
  *Mémoires* of, **35**. 276–7; *see also under* Angliviel de la Beaumelle, Laurent
  niece's injury by populace feared by, **38**. 38
  Noailles's account of, **6**. 434
  Orléans, Duchesse d', censures, **34**. 16
  Peter the Great sees, at Saint-Cyr, **10**. 292
  Piozzi, Mrs, mentions, **12**. 93n
  pope's gift to, **10**. 294
  portraits of, at St-Cyr and SH, **10**. 4n, 54, 293–4, **34**. 472
  proverbs of, St-Cyr pensioners act, **10**. 294
  royal rank of, implied by texts, **10**. 293
  St-Cyr abbess sees, **10**. 294
  Sévigné, Mme de, almost rivalled by, in letter-writing, **35**. 276

Aubigné, Françoise-Charlotte-Amable d' (d. 1739), m. (1698) Adrien-Maurice, Duc de Noailles:
Ferdinand's portrait of, **10**. 294

Aubigné, Marie-Joséphine-Marguerite d' (1746–1805), m. (1765) Jean-René-Hippolyte, Marquis de Toulongeon:
social relations of, with Comtesse de la Marche, **7**. 298

Aubigné, Théodore-Agrippa d' (1552–1630), man of letters:
Mrs Scott's life of, **28**. 35

Aubigny (de Albini), William d' (d. 1176), 1st E. of Arundel:                                      ,
marries Henry I's widow, **12**. 205, **42**. 422

Aubigny ('Aubigné'):
game sent from, **6**. 395n
HW not to visit, **31**. 79, **39**. 31
Leinster, Ds of, may visit, **30**. 267
Lennox family may be at, **31**. 127
Louis XIV confers seigneury of, on Ds of Portsmouth, **40**. 28n
Richmond, D. of, may have gone to, **6**. 312
—— occupies, **6**. 349, 356, 365, **31**. 79, **35**. 337, **39**. 34
——'s claim to duchy of: **4**. 287, 296–7, 298–9, 413n, 417–18, 423, 424, 427–8, 435, **6**. 327, 333, 347, 349, 368, 454, **39**. 119–20; granted, **6**. 455, 456
——'s inheritance of, corrected, **43**. 363
Richmond, Ds of, followed to, from Paris, by sick servant, **40**. 28
visitors to: children of Ds of Leinster, **6**. 333; Leinster, Ds of, **6**. 333, 337, 338, 342, 421, **7**. 56, 58, 61, 71, 129, 160, 171; Lennox, Lord George, **39**. 61; Ogilvie, **6**. 421

Aubigny, Castle of:
paintings in, **15**. 158, 182

Aubigny. *See also* Aubigné

Aubonne, Bn d'. *See* Tavernier, Jean-Baptiste

Aubray, Marie-Marguerite d' (d. 1676), m. (1651) Antoine Gobelin, Marquis de Brinvilliers:
poisonings by, **7**. 119n, **30**. 218

Aubrey, John (1626–97), antiquary:
Hollar's letters to, **40**. 367
*Natural History and Antiquities of . . . Surrey*, **16**. 78, 197

Aubrey, Sir John (1739–1826), 6th Bt, 1786:
(?) HW's social relations with, **7**. 268
Verney's petition against, **25**. 572n

Aubusson, Pierre d' (1423–1503), cardinal:
Bonhours' *Life* of, **1**. 249

Aubusson (France):
furniture from, **4**. 457, **5**. 233
goods from, **5**. 3
HW's tapestry coverings from, **4**. 428, 437, 439, 452, 454–5, 457, 459, 472, **5**. 121, 161, 182, 233, **7**. 181

Aubusson de la Feuillade, Françoise-Catherine-Scholastique d' (b. 1733), m. (1752) François-

Henri d'Harcourt, Comte de Lillebonne:
Brunswick flirted with, by, **3**. 42
social relations of, with: Bentheim, Mme de, **7**. 302; Du Deffand, Mme, **4**. 75; HW, **7**. 312; Harcourt, Earl, **7**. 312; Maurepas, Comte and Comtesse de, **7**. 285

Auch, Abp of. *See* Chabillard de Montillet de Grenaud, Jean-François d'

Auchenames (Scotland):
Craufurd of, **3**. 6n, **5**. 153n, **12**. 197n, **31**. 91n
spelling of, corrected, **43**. 93

Auchmedden, Aberdeenshire:
Baird of, **40**. 267

Auckland, Bn. *See* Eden, William (1744–1814)

Auckland. *See also* Bishop Auckland

Auction; auctions:
Abercorn, Cts of, attends, **17**. 477
at Baldwins, **10**. 76–7
at Canons, **36**. 246n
at Christie's, **32**. 124n, 249n, 289, **35**. 428
at Holland House, **32**. 279–80
Ayliffe's, **40**. 305
Bateman's, **32**. 241, 242n
Batt's, **37**. 460n
Beauclerk's library, **32**. 122n
Bedford, Ds of, wishes HW to buy bust of Faustina for her at, **42**. 452
Bever's, of Orford's horses, **32**. 134n, 159n, **36**. 95n
Brand's, **38**. 340n
Canaletto 'copies' sold at, **23**. 299
Caylus's, **39**. 32, **43**. 106
Colebrooke's, **23**. 569
collectors know their things will end at, **25**. 604
Cottrell Dormer's, **15**. 92, **38**. 340n
Dayrolles attends, for Grafton and Richmond, **19**. 403
Duane's, **25**. 572n
for damsels, at Minorcan ball, **37**. 311
Franceschi's, **17**. 121–2
Frankland, by Christie, **42**. 125n
French, Mrs, has, **11**. 221
Furnese's, **21**. 172–3
Germain, Lady Elizabeth's, **23**. 286
Greville's, **33**. 249n
HW has no money for, **10**. 54
HW's attendance at, **7**. 302, **9**. 187, **10**. 43, 54, 76–7, 187, 267, **17**. 477, **21**. 368, **31**. 36, 339, **37**. 465–6, **38**. 312, 340
HW's pedestal will look well at, **21**. 514
Hamilton's, **26**. 46
Hindley's, by Skinner, **33**. 105, 180, 183
Hogarth's, **32**. 114
Huquier's, **38**. 130
Irish, Conway buys books at, **37**. 422
Ives's, **42**. 246n
Joseph II's, at Brussels, **33**. 486–7
Julienne's, **22**. 523
La Vallière's, **36**. 216n
Lethieullier's books, **40**. 221
library, of Sir Simeon Stuart, **32**. 323n

Lovibond's, sold by Skinner, **32**. 294n
Malpas's, **38**. 346n
Mariette's, **32**. 281–3, **35**. 428
Martin's, **42**. 246n
Martin's orange trees, **21**. 121
Mead's, **20**. 165, 185n, 470, **35**. 196, 216–17
of books, **38**. 167
of china, at Twickenham, **21**. 122
of prints, **7**. 302
Orford (2d E.), pictures, **20**. 261n, 268, **24**. 441
Orford (3d E.), horses, **32**. 134, 159n
Ossory's, **32**. 215n
Ottoboni's, **15**. 12
Oxford, E. of, **17**. 357–8, 373–4, 378
Paisley attends, **17**. 477
Pelham's plate, **35**. 220–1
Pesters's, **37**. 465–6
Portland, Ds of, **25**. 597, **33**. 518, **36**. 236–7
(?) Pritchard, Mrs, at Christie's, **32**. 124n
(?) St John's, **17**. 477
Schaub's, **21**. 199–201
Sheldon's, **33**. 292n
Squibb's room for, **11**. 101
Strafford's, **11**. 283
SH may soon be put up at, **35**. 516
stuffed birds, **23**. 210
Talman's, **42**. 458
Thoresby's museum, **38**. 340n
Villiers's, **32**. 370n
Waddes's, **38**. 371n
White's, of Cole's books, **33**. 575n
Zenón gets furniture bought at, **18**. 253
*See also under* Godfrey, Elizabeth; Howard, Hon. Anne; Pelham-Holles, Thomas, D. of Newcastle; Waldegrave, James
Auctioneer; auctioneers:
hammer of, 'going and going,' **22**. 257
methods of, described by HW, **25**. 337
'rowwagon' a term used by, **38**. 87
*See also* Christie, James; Hutchins, ——; Langford, Abraham; Prestage and Hobbs; Skinner; Sotheby
Audebert:
Bèze's poem to, **40**. 100
Audenarde. *See* Oudenarde
Audinot, Nicolas-Médard (1732–1801):
Du Deffand, Mme, praises theatrical troupe of, **8**. 208n
Auditor of the Exchequer. *See under* Exchequer
Auditor of the Imprest:
Burke's list of sinecure offices omits, **39**. 388
Mount Stuart appointed as, **10**. 65
Audlem, Cheshire:
(?) church window at, to be designed, **10**. 11, 18
Audley, Bn. *See* Tuchet, James
Audley, Bns. *See* Delaval, Elizabeth (d. 1785)
Audley, Edmund (d. 1524), Bp of Salisbury:
SH Chapel copied from chapel of, at Salisbury Cathedral, **41**. 420n
tomb of, **2**. 370n

Audley Chapel, St George's, Hanover Sq.:
Northampton's marriage at, **35**. 295n
Audley End ('Audley Inn'), Essex:
demolitions at, **10**. 30
escutcheon in church at, **10**. 30
HW bids for book on, **35**. 196–7
HW describes, **10**. 30, **13**. 88
HW visits, **43**. 127
Audley Inn. *See* Audley End
Audley Square, London:
residents of: Keppel, Adm., **24**. 443n, **33**. 92n
Audley Street, London:
residents of: Bute, **23**. 7; Mount Stuart, **25**. 354n; Portuguese embassy, **20**. 74n
*See also* North Audley St; South Audley St
Audouard, ——:
Louis XV suppresses plea made by, **8**. 174
Audran, Karl *or* Charles (1594–1674), engraver:
Joyeuse's portrait engaved by, **30**. 217n
Auersperg, Fürstin. *See* Neipperg, Marie Wilhelmine Josephe
Aufrere, Anthony (1756–1833), of Hoveton Hall:
wife of, **12**. 196n
Aufrere, Mrs Anthony. *See* Norris, Anna
Aufrere, Rev. George John (1769–1853):
mother seeks Crostwick living for, **42**. 441–2
Aufresne. *See* Rival, Jean
Augean stables:
Harcourt not expected to clean, **35**. 507
Auger, Nicolas (d. 1783), actor:
acts part of 'Lucas' well, **3**. 289
Auget, Antoine-Jean-Baptiste-Robert (1733–1820), Baron de Montyon; philanthropist:
Bastard replaced by, **7**. 442
chancellor to Comte d'Artois, **7**. 442
social relations of, with Mme du Deffand, **4**. 415
Augsburg (Augsbourg):
Berrys visit, **11**. 359, 364, 367, 371, 372
congress to be held at, to conclude peace treaty, **9**. 353, **21**. 498
Egremont was to have had post at, **21**. 540
may be scene of war council instead of peace treaty, **21**. 511
Niccolini may be at, **20**. 2, 7
Orford, Cts of, takes letters of credit on, **19**. 49
'Augur,' Ossory's horse:
'Prophet's' foal, wins race, **32**. 133n
August III, K. of Poland. *See* Frederick Augustus II
August (1747–1806) of Saxe-Gotha:
Bernis's dinner for, **23**. 389n
Bute recommends, to Mann, **23**. 328
August (month):
best month for French invasion of England, **21**. 307, 317–18
Greenwich, Bns, enlivens, with speaking trumpet, **39**. 251
August Wilhelm (1715–81), D. ('Prince') of Brunswick-Bevern:

[August Wilhelm (1715–81), *continued*]
Austrians defeated by, **21**. 88
defeat of, at Breslau, **21**. 158n
Frederick II informs, of armistice, **22**. 14n
—— orders, to Böhmisch-Brod to observe Daun, **21**. 95n
road block by Austrians near Reichenberg dislodged by, **21**. 88n
Stettin governed by, **21**. 88n
Swedes defeated by, **21**. 247n
troops of, at Fischbach, **21**. 2n
August Wilhelm (d. 1731), D. of Brunswick-Wolfenbüttel:
pensioned for suppressing George I's will, **2**. 124, 125, **43**. 68
August Wilhelm (1722–58) of Prussia:
wedding of, **17**. 315
Augusta (1719–72) of Saxe-Gotha, m. (1736) Frederick Louis, P. of Wales:
ballad against, **23**. 217
ball opened by, **13**. 36n
Bathurst preferred by, as George III's governor, **20**. 345
Bedford and Halifax oppose inclusion of, in Regency Bill, **10**. 152n
Bedford, Ds of, throws 'first stone' at, **38**. 548
Bedfords ignore, but Gower courts her, **38**. 534
—— may triumph over, **38**. 561
Bentley's picture of, and her family, **35**. 261
bird of paradise symbolizes, at ball, **38**. 204
birthday ball of, **10**. 186
birthday of, **38**. 473
Bootle compliments, on alleged confinement, **9**. 58
brother of, visits England, **17**. 331
Bubb Dodington excluded by, **20**. 263
Bute may find, regent, if George III and Charlotte go to Hanover, **38**. 355
——'s alleged affair with, **9**. 202n, 237, 305, 338, 343n, **12**. 262, **16**. 350, **21**. 6n, 104, 487, **38**. 206, 315–16, 438–9, 462
—— told by, to tell Mann of P. of Saxe-Gotha's approach, **23**. 328
Champigny and, **36**. 8
Charlotte, Q., received by, **21**. 529
child born to, **9**. 104, **18**. 341, 358, **19**. 175, **20**. 155
Christian VII visits, at Carlton House, **35**. 326–7
Chudleigh, Elizabeth, retorts to, about Bute, **9**. 338
Clerk favoured by, **37**. 582
Coke, Lady Mary, offended by, **31**. 108
consent of, to be asked for Mann to be K.B., **22**. 318
costumed as Mary, Q. of Scots, **17**. 338, 343
Court ball attended by, **9**. 406
Cresset favourite of, **20**. 247, 323n
Cumberland, D. of, urged by, to linger on George III's wedding night, **21**. 530
daughter begs, to let her act in *Cato*, **21**. 327
daughter summoned by, **23**. 379, **32**. 68

death of: **5**. 183, 189, **23**. 374, 379, 388, 389, **31**. 164
departure of, a reproach to England, but may be wise, **23**. 221
Drawing-Room of, **10**. 242
Egmont declines treasurership procured by, **35**. 195n
Essex, Cts of, may be suspected by, of designs on D. of York, **21**. 54
'evil' brought by, into royal family, **22**. 275n, **25**. 406, 412n, 413n
Ferrers's trial avoided by, **9**. 280
Finch, Elizabeth, received by, **19**. 389
fireworks watched by, **20**. 48
Fox, Henry, disliked by, for attachment to D. of Cumberland, **9**. 209, **20**. 412, 502n, **21**. 6n
—— with Lyttelton coolly received by, **9**. 179
George II's relations with, **17**. 337, 343, **20**. 233, 239, 245, 246, 249, 348n, **25**. 413n
George III and Charlotte talk to, just before her death, **23**. 379
George III's relations with, **9**. 313, 320–1, **20**. 449, 562, **21**. 461, 517n, **22**. 581, **23**. 345, 385, **31**. 285
—— urged by, to give Bath order to Mann, **22**. 581
—— visited by, at Richmond, **23**. 345
German subsidies and royal matches with Germans disliked by, **35**. 255
German visit by, **4**. 419–20, 421, **23**. 217, 221
Gloucester, D. of, distressed by illness of, **23**. 355, 358, 377, 395
godmother to George IV, **38**. 174
Greenwich visited by, by water from Tower, **17**. 451
Grenville ministry stigmatizes, **22**. 396
HW calls, 'dowager Lady Prudence,' **35**. 254
HW does not know, **31**. 1
HW entertained by, **10**. 242
HW jokingly calls Fox chamberlain to, **9**. 209, **35**. 281
HW mentions, **9**. 402, 403, **38**. 167
HW praises, **20**. 248–9
HW presented to, **17**. 386
HW's duty to, **40**. 185
HW's opinion of, **31**. 108
(?) HW's relations with, **10**. 284
HW's verses on 'fuction' of, **21**. 7n
HW to attend reception of, after her delivery, **18**. 358
HW thanked by, **39**. 116
Halifax adjourns House of Lords before friends of, arrive, **22**. 297n
—— and possibly Sandwich force George III to propose omitting name of, from Regency Bill, **22**. 297n
Harcourt ill-treated by, **20**. 344
Hayter's tutorship attacked by, **20**. 344
health drunk to, at Leghorn, **19**. 152
health of, bad, **5**. 131, **9**. 56, **23**. 345, 349, 358, 360, 363, 364, 375, 379, **31**. 108, 164, **32**. 68
Hertford, as lord chamberlain, to supervise burial of, **23**. 381

Home given income by, **9.** 207
household of: Bloodworth, **20.** 245; Butler, John, **20.** 344; Chudleigh, Elizabeth, **9.** 338, **21.** 487, **24.** 196, 203, **30.** 328n; Cresset, **9.** 144n, **20.** 247, 323n; Drax, Elizabeth, **18.** 441, **30.** 326n; Granville, Hon. Elizabeth, **34.** 255; Hales, **20.** 347; Hamilton, Elizabeth, **17.** 279n; Hamilton, Lady Archibald, **19.** 62, 361n; Hussey, Richard, **38.** 241; Irby, **9.** 209; Lee, **17.** 220n, 242n, **20.** 245, 412, **21.** 104–5, 110; Martin, **22.** 183n, **21.** 105n; Middlesex, Cts of, **19.** 62; Pitt, Anne, **23.** 451n, 558n, **31.** 1n; Pitt, Elizabeth, **20.** 507n; Potter, **19.** 449n, **20.** 247; Rochford, Cts of, **17.** 431n, **20.** 58n; Stone, **23.** 538n; Thomas, **21.** 105n; Walkinshaw, Catherine, **25.** 516, **26.** 46, **33.** 442; Young, Lucy, **17.** 431n
husband keeps, waiting when she fetches him from Kew, **20.** 122
husband leaves, in hackney coach, **30.** 94–5
husband mentions, in ballad, **19.** 45
husband's death witnessed by, **20.** 232
husband's followers support Regency Bill from kindness to, **20.** 257
husband's papers burnt by, **20.** 239
jewels borrowed by, for masquerade, from Frankz, **17.** 343
Karl Wilhelm Ferdinand and Ps Augusta dine with, at Kew, and call at Leicester House, **22.** 197
Kew seen by, only when breakfasting with George III, **39.** 116n
Kingston, Ds of, at trial cites former protection by, **24.** 196, 203
Latin poem mentions, **40.** 26
Leicester House home of, **9.** 321; *see also under* Leicester House
Lennox, Lady Sarah, feared by, as George III's lover because of connection with Fox, **21.** 517n
London opposes, **9.** 320–1, 325, **23.** 196, 203
Mann ships statues to, **20.** 314
marriage of, **9.** 1, **13.** 7n, 102n
mob's insults to, cruel, **23.** 203
monument to Stephen Hales erected by, **20.** 347n
mother-in-law may be equalled by, **19.** 62
Musgrave charges, with taking bribes, **7.** 367n
newspaper epigrams on doves and parrots given to Bute by, **38.** 462
obelisk to, in tableau, **38.** 204
opera attended by, **35.** 80
Parliamentary friends of, **37.** 416
Pelhams have made, regent, **20.** 249
person of, in danger, **23.** 196
Pitt, Anne, blames Ds of Kingston for mentioning, **24.** 203
Pitt, William (Chatham), denounces as 'secret influence,' **23.** 195
Pomfret, Cts of, compares, with Lady of Loreto, **17.** 343, 368, 370
pregnant, **19.** 161, **20.** 233

presentations to, **31.** 52
Queens Isabel and Margaret compared to, **22.** 53
Ranelagh attended by, **17.** 434, **20.** 57n, **30.** 57
reception by, after son's christening, **19.** 175
Regency Bill omits, **22.** 294, 297–8
Regency may be headed by, **9.** 113n, **20.** 239, 249, 257n, **31.** 1–2, **38.** 541–5, 547–50, 553, 568–9
Regency restrictions probably irksome to, **20.** 249, 257
rides daily in coach to spare her numb legs, **23.** 364
Robson bookseller to, **40.** 326
St James's palace not occupied by, **9.** 313
satiric print of, **9.** 338, **21.** 487
satiric writings, especially Wilkes's abuse, **23.** 340n
Selwyn's witticism on, **9.** 202
sensible, **20.** 243
sits at Court ball, **9.** 406, **38.** 144
social relations of, with: Norfolk, Ds of, **17.** 338, 343; Robinson, Sir Thomas, **35.** 179; Stanhope, **19.** 175
'stigmatized,' **22.** 303
Stone and Scott countenanced by, in dispute over George III's tutorship, **20.** 323
SH to be visited by, **39.** 116
Stuart Mackenzie not treasurer to, **21.** 104–5, 110
takes the air, though dying, **23.** 375, 379
Templars attempt to kiss, **30.** 95
theatre attended by, **17.** 222n, **19.** 469
Tosier, Grace, called on by, **17.** 451
Townshend charges that House of Commons is influenced by, **23.** 289
Vansittart, Miss, said to lend sedan chair to Bute for visits to, **38.** 462n
(?) verses attack, **30.** 126
*Whisperer* and *Parliamentary Spy* denounce, **23.** 196, **39.** 124
*World*, by HW, may hint at Bute's affair with, **37.** 438–9
York, D. of, told by, not to make himself common, **21.** 57
Augusta (1737–1813), Ps, m. (1764) Karl Wilhelm Ferdinand, P. and D. (1780) of Brunswick-Wolfenbüttel; George III's sister:
Amelia, Ps, leaves legacy to, **33.** 535
bird of paradise symbolizes, at ball, **38.** 204
birth of eldest son of, **1.** 106
brother borrows Dorléans's book from, **20.** 344
brothers and fiancé attend opera with, **38.** 289
*Cato* acted by, **21.** 327
Charlotte, Q., assisted by, **21.** 529, **38.** 117
Coke, Lady Mary, going to, **39.** 8
Conway dines with, at Brunswick, **39.** 537
Court displeases, by neglecting fiancé, **38.** 288
Covent Garden play attended by, with family, **22.** 199
dowry voted for, **38.** 249
England visited by, **31.** 57, 164, **32.** 16, 68

[Augusta (1737–1813), *continued*]

Ferrers's trial attended by, **9.** 278, 280, 280n

fireworks watched by, **20.** 48

George III and Charlotte snub, at Carlton House, **23.** 379n

—— opens ball with, at Kew, **35.** 229n

—— says fortune of, will please Opposition, **38.** 291

Gower explains to, about lack of gunfire at her wedding, **38.** 288

HW jokes about balls for, on English visit, **31.** 57

health of, smallpox, **18.** 341n

Hervey's letters to, **30.** 223n

husband of: to take her away soon after nuptials, **22.** 195; to visit Italy alone, **32.** 17

lively, **22.** 342

marriage of, **10.** 118n, **22.** 94, 189, 197, **38.** 179, 286, 288

mother entertains, at Kew, **22.** 197

mother's illness, **32.** 68

mother summons, **23.** 379

mother to visit, **4.** 420

probably in Germany, **22.** 205

Rich, Sir Robert, mistaken by, for Sir Robert Walpole, **18.** 219

safely landed at Hellevoetsluis, **38.** 321–2

St James's Palace visited by, **22.** 342

shipwreck of, rumoured, **38.** 311, 312, 313, 321–2

sings and plays on the harpsichord, **38.** 101n

sister visited by, **23.** 426

Stewart, Lady Susanna, lady of the bedchamber to, **38.** 143n

Witham to be visited by, **38.** 292

younger brothers dance with, at private ball, **38.** 143

'Augusta':

Vernon's name for river in West Indies, **17.** 175

*Augusta*, English ship:

loss of, **24.** 339

Townshend, Augustus, capt. of, **19.** 277n

Augusta Sophia (1768–1840), Ps:

Cheltenham visited by, **34.** 12n

father requests provision for, **24.** 371–2

(?) HW visited by, at SH, **39.** 510–12

Augustan age:

America may have, **24.** 62

England in, **28.** 40–1, 193, **29.** 220

Auguste, Mlle, dancer:

HW mistakes, at Conti's levee, for Comtesse de la Marche, **7.** 292, **35.** 116

Auguste, Robert-Jacques (*or*-Joseph) (1725–1805), goldsmith to Louis XVI:

snuff-box for HW sought at shop of, **6.** 302, 303

Augustenberg, P. of:

Danish troops commanded by, **22.** 49n

Augustine (354–430), St, of Hippo:

Augustinians follow Epicurus instead of, **37.** 314

controversies of, **41.** 386

Du Deffand, Mme, quotes, **3.** 5, 242, **5.** 25

Ghent would fulfil HW's idea of paradise of, **37.** 127

Augustine (d. 604), St, Abp of Canterbury:

Pius VI may send another, to England, **33.** 209

sent to convert British, **2.** 162

Augustinians:

Epicurus followed by, **37.** 314

France reduces, **39.** 147

Greenwich establishment of, **16.** 80

Leghorn church of, falls, **17.** 307

monastery of, on Minorcan mountain, **37.** 314

Paris church and convent of, *see* Grands-Augustins

Augustins, Quai des:

Grands-Augustins' convent in, **7.** 276n

Le Clerc lives in, **8.** 25, 31

*Augustinus, seu doctrini. See under* Jansen, Cornelius

Augustus (63 B.C.–A.D. 14) (Octavius), Roman Emperor 27 B.C.–A.D. 14:

Antony's struggle with, over Lepidus, **21.** 79, **39.** 406

burial places of *liberti* of, **13.** 207

cameo of, **33.** 485n

Cofano, K. of, supposedly crowned by, **37.** 67

courtiers of, could be taught farming by Virgil, **16.** 269

Damer, Mrs, copies head of, **12.** 271

drunken sailor incompatible with, **41.** 154

English too frivolous to imitate, **10.** 239

fame of, **21.** 31

Fitzwilliam not likely to be, **25.** 294

Horace celebrates, **33.** 517

laurels of, bloom in odes, **42.** 166

Pitt called, by HW, **10.** 272

rhinoceros exhibited by, at Rome, **20.** 128

Trojans condole with Tiberius on death of, **36.** 280

tyranny of, **15.** 70

*Augustus Cæsar*, English merchant ship:

French capture, **19.** 13

Augustus Frederick (1773–1843), cr. (1801) D. of Sussex:

appearance of, **39.** 503–4

at Göttingen, **11.** 145n

birth of, celebrated, **32.** 96n

Eastbourne visited by, **33.** 232n

father requests provision for, **24.** 371–2

health of: asthma, **35.** 442–3; Lisbon trip needed for, **39.** 503

Naples visited by, **35.** 442

punished for wearing Keppel colours, **33.** 226n

Rome to be visited by, **35.** 442

travels of, **34.** 213

York, Ds of, visits, at Windsor Castle, **12.** 9

'Aujourd'hui Bacchus et l'amour':

Pont-de-Veyle's verses, **8.** 124–5

Aulan, Bailli d'. *See* Suarez, Henri de

Aulan, 'le petit d'.' *See* Suarez d'Aulan, Étienne-Anne-Marie-Bernard-Régis de

Aulan, Marquis d'. *See* Suarez, Denis-François-Marie-Jean de

Aulan, Marquise d'. *See* Arouard du Beignon, Anne-Suzanne; Vichy, Anne de (1706–69)

Aulcester. *See* Alcester

Aulic Council:
chamber of: formality of, **31**. 150; HW peevish at Conway being in, **39**. 180
councillor of, Ellis, Welbore, as active as, **33**. 326
HW does not belong to, **36**. 227
Maria Theresa has Frankfurt fined by, for aiding Prussia, **21**. 28
matrons of, may report as jury to Maria Theresa, **21**. 258
mémoire about, **21**. 102
Nuremberg to be punished by, for Prussian recruiting, **21**. 29

*Aulicus coquinariæ. See under* Sanderson, Sir William

Aulla (Italy):
Lobkowitz to protect, **19**. 36

Aulnay, Marquise d'. *See* Lamoignon, Olive-Claire de

Aulne, Baron de l'. *See* Turgot, Anne-Robert-Jacques

Aulnoy, Baronne de. *See* Le Jumel de Barneville, Marie-Catherine

Aumale, D. of. *See* Edward (d. 1415)

Aumale, Marie-Jeanne d' (1683–1756):
aunt fears for safety of, **38**. 38

Aume, ——:
Mann presents, at Tuscan Court, **24**. 251n

Aumerle. *See* Aumale

Aumont, Jean d' (1522–95), Maréchal de France:
Henri IV and Biron sing trio with, **39**. 217

Aumont, Jeanne-Louise-Constance d' (1731–1816), m. (1747) Gabriel-Louis-François de Neufville, Duc de Villeroy:
Boufflers, Comtesse de, not adored by, **3**. 213–14
Clairon, Mlle, acts for, **3**. 75, 146, 159, 213, 224, 231, 254, 268–9, 282–3, 294, **4**. 154
comedies given for, **3**. 213, 229, 234, 254, 281, 285, 289, 294, 385, **4**. 46–7
Du Deffand, Mme, curries favour with, **3**. 213
—— gets news from, **5**. 123, 161
——'s opinion of, **3**. 229, 281
—— wagers with, **4**. 203
HW mentions, **3**. 342
HW sends mezzotints to, **5**. 172, **7**. 416
HW welcome at comedies of, **3**. 269
L'Isle tells, of HW's cattle, **4**. 267
Molé benefit urged by, **3**. 230
Pont-de-Veyle asks, why Mme du Deffand was not invited to comedy, **3**. 229
social relations of, with: Aiguillon, Mme d', **7**. 309, 326, 337; Brunswick, **3**. 75; Bunbury, Lady Sarah, **3**. 224, 231; Christian VII, **4**. 154; Damas, Mme de, **7**. 338; Du Deffand, Mme, **3**. 213, 342, **7**. 316; Flamarens, Mme

de, **7**. 333; Forcalquier, Mme de, **3**. 213; HW, **7**. 316, 337; Hénault, **7**. 321; La Vallière, Mme de, **6**. 7, **7**. 349; Maurepas and wife, **7**. 337; Pont-de-Veyle, **3**. 75, **7**. 337; Senneterre, Mme de, **7**. 337; Ussé, **7**. 337
tragedies given for, **3**. 75, 224, 231, **4**. 18, 22
wants HW to bring her a cow, **4**. 267

Aumont, Louis-Alexandre-Céleste d' (1736–1814), styled Duc de Villequier; Duc d'Aumont, 1799:
arrives in England, **11**. 259, **34**. 110
Beaumarchais's letter to, **33**. 536–7
first gentleman of the Bedchamber, **4**. 191n, **11**. 259

Aumont, Louis-Marie-Augustin (1709–82), Duc d':
attends session of parliament of Paris, **8**. 172
first gentleman of the Bedchamber, **4**. 191n
garden of, at Guiscard, **16**. 190
Monaco, Ps of, wanted by, to sign son's marriage contract, **6**. 460
Richelieu differs with, in actors' quarrel, **38**. 538n
Stormont asked by, to send Sutton to Louis XV, **24**. 2n
Ussé bequeaths music stand to, **5**. 276

Aumont, Louis-Marie-Guy d', Duc de Mazarin:
wife of, **3**. 357n

Aumont, Hôtel d' (Paris):
HW visits and describes, **7**. 353

Aumont de Mazarin, Louise-Félicité-Victoire d' (1759–1826), m. 1 (1777) Honoré, Duc de Valentinois, later P. of Monaco:
brought up at Bellechasse, **4**. *438*
marriage of, **6**. 460
Monaco, Ps of, uses, as pretext, **4**. 438
(?) rival suitors of, **33**. 515–16

Aumont de Rochbaron, Louis-Marie-Céleste d' (1762–1831), Marquis d' Aumont; Duc de Piennes, 1780; styled Duc d' Aumont, 1799:
arrives in London, **11**. 256, **34**. 109

Aungier, —— (b. ca 1671):
at Ely, **1**. 162n

Aunoy, Conte and Marchese d'. *See* Desarmoises, Antonio-Bernardo

Aurangzíb A'lamgír (1618–1707), Emperor of India:
England to take the place of, **28**. 293
HW costumed as, **17**. 339
successors of, **23**. 212

Auray (France):
letters of Mme de Sévigné from, **7**. 87

Aurelius, Abraham (1575–1632), French Protestant pastor in London:
engraving of, by (?) Vorsterman, **16**. 64

*Aureng-Zebe. See under* Dryden, John

Auretti, ——, dancer:
rivalry between the Barberina and, **16**. 280n

Auretti, Janneton, French actress:
parties for, **18**. 131

Auriculas:
potted, at Ranelagh, **20**. 47

Auriel, Mrs:
SH visited by, **12**. 239
Auriol, Henrietta (d. 1773), m. (1749) Hon.
Robert Hay Drummond, Abp of York:
East India Co.'s election turns on vote of,
**38**. 371n
Auroille (?Auvoille), Monsieur (?Count) d':
SH ticket not used by, **12**. 238
*Aurora,* English frigate:
loss of, **23**. 282
*Aurora,* English ship:
Tobago's capture reported by, **25**. 172n
'Aurora.' *See under* Guido Reni
*Aurum potabile:*
George III, Thurlow, and Pitt will swallow,
**25**. 685
Aurung-Zebe. *See* Aurangzíb
Ausbourg; Ausburgh. *See* Augsburg
Ausonius (Decimus Magnus Ausonius) (309–
ca 394):
epigram attributed to, imitated, **30**. 25
Austin, St. *See* Augustine, St
Austin, —— (fl. 1769), carpenter at Fulbourn:
buys Palavicini house, **1**. 170
Austin Canons:
community of, at St Osyth's, **9**. 88n
Austin Friars, London:
Cazalet merchant in, **39**. 306n
Chauncy writes from, **41**. 145
Australia:
Cook and Banks in, **28**. 94
Austrasia:
Karl Theodor may become king of, **36**. 233
Austrasie, regiment of:
captured, **7**. 445
prisoners from, **7**. 213
Austria, Archduchess of. *See* Maria Ricciarda
Beatrice (1750–1827)
Austria, Archduke of. *See* Ferdinand Karl Anton
Joseph (1754–1806); Karl Ludwig (1771–
1847)
Austria, D. of. *See* Leopold V (1157–94)
Austria, Emperor of. *See* Charles VI; Francis I;
Francis II; Joseph II; Leopold I; Leopold II
Austria, Empress of. *See* Maria Theresa
Austria:
Albani may arouse sympathizers of, at Rome,
**19**. 114
Albert II's deed about Bavaria denied by,
**24**. 403
ambassadors from and to, *see under* Ambassador
Aranjuez treaty between Spain, Sardina, and,
**20**. 294n
army of: Abruzzo overrun by, **18**. 460; Antibes
threatened by, **19**. 523; at La Cattolica, **18**.
335; at Viterbo, **18**. 527; Bavarian-French
army to oppose, at Prague, **19**. 194; Bavarian operations of, **7**. 2n, **18**. 230, 234,
289, **19**. 37, 41; Berlin menaced by, **21**. 332,
444; Bevern said to have defeated, **21**. 88;
Bisagno the theatre of, **19**. 417; Bocchetta

the theatre of, **19**. 297, 304, 359; Botta leads,
towards Genoa, **19**. 297; Broglie to be driven
by, from Moravia, **17**. 401n; camp of, near
Rome, **18**. 530–4; Campo Morone reached
by, **19**. 359; Campo Santo battle of, **18**.
153–4, 161, 163–5; Cannes and Grasse
reached by, **19**. 323n; Časlau defeat of, **17**.
429–30, 433, 464; Charles Emmanuel III's
relations with, **18**. 444, 461, **19**. 120, 269,
431; Charles of Naples delivered from, **18**.
519; Civitella and Pescara to be captured
by, **18**. 460; corruption in, **19**. 409; council
of war held by, at Tuchomirschitz, **21**. 95n;
Daun's army to include, **21**. 266; deserters
from, **19**. 23; destitute in Piedmont, **19**.
431n; Dettingen exploits of, overvalued at
Vienna, **35**. 40; Dresden receives, coolly, **21**.
332; Dresden trees cut down by, **21**. 361n;
Empire troops joined but not emboldened
by, **21**. 304; England may be invaded by,
from Flemish coast, **21**. 19; English defeat,
at Korbitz, **38**. 32; English joined by, in
Flanders, **37**. 204; English separate from,
in Flanders, **18**. 124; estimated, **37**. 265;
Faenza the theatre of, **18**. 65; Faiola and
Faioletta the theatres of, **18**. 454; Ferdinand, P., cuts to pieces, **21**. 285; Fivizano
seized by, **19**. 36; Flanders left by, **37**. 296;
France encourages Genoa to resist, **19**. 417;
France must send troops to Germany to
defend, **21**. 90; Frankfurt to be subdued
by, from Flanders, **21**. 29; Frederick II's
hostilities with, **17**. 400–1, **18**. 547, **21**. 137n,
158, 258, 400–1, 453–4, 520; French armies
oppose, in Flanders, **12**. 89; French force,
to retire across Rhine, **39**. 508n; French
regiments demolish, at Metz, **11**. 27; Gages's
hostilities with, **19**. 119, 236, 253; Gavi
threatened by, **19**. 297, 304; Genoese operations of, **19**. 58, 312–13, 333, 417; geographical ignorance of, **19**. 401; Hohenfriedberg
defeat of, **19**. 58n; Holland opens dykes
against, **25**. 543n; Hungary and Transylvania approached by, **37**. 295–6; hussars of,
**17**. 289, **18**. 460, 530, **21**. 319n; in Lombardy, estimated, **17**. 291; invalids of, sent
to Civita Vecchia, **18**. 519; Joseph II sends,
towards Holland, **25**. 541; La Roque to
rescue, **19**. 344–5; Lobkowitz brings, to
Monte Rosi, **18**. 525; Lobkowitz joins, **18**.
302; magazines seized by, at Ancona and
Loreto, **18**. 419; Mann calls, 'horse-eaters,'
**21**. 446; Mann hopes Dauphiné or Provence
will be invaded by, **19**. 306; Mannheim and
Frankfurt report victories of, costly, **12**. 88–
9; marches away without informing D. of
Cumberland, **37**. 295–6; Marseille threatened by, **19**. 323; Mathews accused of not
aiding, **18**. 452–3; Maubeuge defeat of, **12**.
39; may aim at Naples, **18**. 336; may retire
to Lombardy, **18**. 413; miquelets of, **18**. 100,
531; Montemar forced back by, **35**. 29;

Munich threatened by, 17. 289; Nemi the theatre of, 18. 454; Novi and Pavia the theatres of, 19. 58n; Panaro the theatre of, 17. 432, 464, 489; Piacenza the theatre of, 19. 276; Pilsen approached by, 17. 456n, 18. 58; Prague's capture reported by, 17. 466, 472, 488, 18. 58; Provençal defeat of, blamed on English, 19. 423; Provence to be invaded by, 19. 306, 333; Prussians said to be defeated by, in Moravia, 17. 372; Recanati hospital seized by, 18. 419; reinforcements from Germany expected by, 19. 30, 36; retreats, 15. 227; Rimini the theatre of, 18. 335; Russian troops restrain, 21. 444; Sade captured by, 19. 18; St Pierre d'Arena the camp of, 19. 312; Sardinians' junction with, 19. 323n, 431–2; Saxony to be recovered by, 21. 137n; Schulenberg in charge of, 19. 41, 119; Serbelloni to be joined by, in Saxony, 21. 229n; Simbach victory of, 18. 230, 234, 249; Spaniards captured by, at Ripalta, 19. 262; Spanish troops to cut off, 18. 65–6; strong, 37. 556; successes of, may encourage Richecourt, 17. 477; Tanaro and Pavon e Moncastello the stations of, 19. 84; Te Deum sung at headquarters of, 21. 246n; to embark at Trieste for Naples, 18. 3; Tronto crossed by, 18. 419; Tuscan troops to join, 21. 15; Var, the theatre of, 19. 334, 336, 374, 436; Ventimiglia the theatre of, 19. 409; victories of, 12. 177; Vilshoven captured by, 17. 288; Wentworth hated by, for favouring Piedmontese, 19. 451; Wentworth to spur on, 19. 406

artillery, of, 18. 163, 541, 19. 401, 406
Bavarian elector to be archduke of, 17. 151
Belgian convention signed by, 39. 484n
Benedict XIV inclined towards, 18. 56
brutality in, disgusts Chute and Whithed, 19. 279
campaign in, slow, 34. 217
campaign of, against Turkey, 35. 392
Charles, P., appointed by, in Flanders, 19. 288
Charles Emmanuel III's relations with, see Austria: Sardinian relations with
Charles of Naples may lead army against, 18. 419
Choiseul's fall may be disliked by, 23. 259
convents abolished in, 34. 53
Conway visits, to see its army, 6. 61n, 24. 38, 39. 537–8
Coromandel scheme of, to offend English and Dutch, 20. 146
Cours de l'Europe satirizes, 17. 177
Court of, obstinate, 17. 168
Daun told to protect, 21. 95
—— will probably be punished by, 21. 240
Dutch peace with, 39. 437
eagle of, turns vulture, 24. 55
eagle symbolizes, 30. 126
East India Co.'s trade will not be destroyed by, 20. 101–2

England may be surpassed by, in maritime power, 25. 541
England's relations with, 17. 168, 250, 288, 18. 250, 311, 390, 447, 19. 238, 20. 101–2, 570–1, 21. 18–19, 28, 135n, 462–3, 24. 437, 35. 36
English ships transferred to service of, at Leghorn, 20. 162
envoys from and to, see under Envoy
Florentines do not favour, 20. 9
France and, renew Treaty of Westphalia with Treaty of Versailles, 21. 96n
France and Prussia might combine with, for Dutch partition, 39. 429
France may aid Turkey against, 25. 360
France may be diverted from Flanders by, 19. 306
France may order Charles Emmanuel III to restore territory to, 20. 576
France may pay Holland's indemnity to, 39. 437
France may secretly be courted by, 17. 160
France might join Frederick II to crush, 21. 141
France must back Holland against, 25. 545, 39. 428–9
France offers subsidy or troops to, 20. 589n
France resents increased Italian power of, 20. 394
France's alliance with, not disapproved, 20. 582
France's ancient and natural rival, 21. 125
France's boundaries with, 23. 143
France's treaty with: Bernis's disgrace might be caused by, 21. 262n; enrages England, 20. 570
France's war with, see War: Austrian-French
France to defend Holland against, 25. 545
France will allow, to rule Germany, 21. 112
Frederick II's relations with, see Austria: Prussian relations with
French alliance with, 20. 582
French and Spaniards abandon Genoa to, 19. 306
French and Spaniards may be resisted by, in Lombardy, 23. 474
French attack on England from Flanders may be joined by, 21. 19
French cardinals not supported by, in opposing Clement XIV, 21. 219n
French presumption may be checked by, 24. 396
French seizure of Corsica injures, 23. 137
French treaty with, 20. 565, 578, 584, 21. 262n
French troops must aid, 20. 588–9, 21. 90
generals of, to negotiate with Charles Emmanuel III through Wentworth, 19. 401
Genoa's hatred of, 22. 41
Genoa's peace terms from, 19. 305–6
Genoa the objective of, 19. 75, 297, 305–6, 312–13, 333, 374, 376, 393, 400, 406, 409, 417

[Austria, *continued*]

George II's relations with, *see* Austria: English relations with

Germany's enslavement considered by, as her right, **21.** 469

Guasco brothers enter service of, **22.** 529

HW expects partition of France by, **12.** 4

HW would be glad to see revolution in, **32.** 184

Holland's clash with, over Scheldt, **25.** 539, 541, 554, 556, 561, **39.** 428–9

Jesuits' wealth in, **23.** 473

Louis XV persuaded by, to leave Don Philip at Parma despite Aix treaty, **21.** 323n

—— quells, by negotiating with Turks, **18.** 543

Maria Theresa not to demand reversion of Parma to, **21.** 280n

Mathews at odds with, **18.** 228–9, 476

Maximilian, Archduke, wanted by, as K. of Poland, **25.** 45n

Maximilian Joseph may dispute succession of, **19.** 5

ministers from and to, *see under* Minister

ministers of, want Mann to have Mathews help them, **18.** 453

Modena's treaty with, **20.** 393–4, 395–6, 400

must be contemptuous of western warfare, **25.** 201

Naples and Sicily given up to Charles III, and Parma to Don Philip by, **21.** 280n

Naples threatened by, **18.** 419–20, 443–4, 461, 502, 508, **19.** 41, 306, 423

navy to be built by, **20.** 102

Netherlands may be restored to, **11.** 131n

neutral, **20.** 571

Newcastle's devotion to, **20.** 38n

offensive should be launched by, in Italy, **19.** 478

Parma may be coveted by, **22.** 379

peace delegates of, at Paris, **21.** 498

peace with, expected, **29.** 118

perfidy of, **19.** 320

Peter III's dethronement may aid, **22.** 62–3

Polish claims of, **24.** 11–12

Prussia compared with, as England's ally, **42.** 496

Prussia's relations with, **17.** 121, **21.** 73n, 141–2, **24.** 454, **25.** 359–60, 399, 409

Prussia's war with, *see* War: Austrian-Prussian

quota of, against France should be demanded, **21.** 28

Ratisbon, Diet of, forbidden by, to aid Frederick II, **21.** 28n

Rivera scorns ingratitude of, **19.** 312

Roman adherents of, **19.** 113–14

royal progeny of, **15.** 188

Russian relations with, **21.** 2n, 53n, **25.** 359–60, 399, 409, **34.** 153

Russia urged by, to continue war, **21.** 360n

Sardinia, Naples, and Parma guarantee possessions of, in Italy, **20.** 294n

Sardinian relations with, **17.** 342, **18.** 228, **19.** 223, 400–1, 436–7, 478, **20.** 576, **22.** 55

Scott, David, tours, **39.** 537–8

Silesia's recovery sought by, **20.** 528, **21.** 360

Spain guaranteed her European possessions by, **20.** 294n

Spain's war with, *see* War: Austrian-Spanish

Spanish prisoners held by, **18.** 174n

squadrons of, invade Poland, **23.** 145

subsidies to, may not produce the promised offensive, **19.** 478

Te Deums sung in, for Zorndorf 'victory,' **21.** 246

Turkish relations with, **25.** 359–60, 399, 409

Tuscan independence of, would please England, **18.** 2

Tuscany dominated by, but knows little about Dutch quarrel, **25.** 554

Tuscany's monetary accumulations forgotten by, **21.** 102

Tuscany to become appendix to, like Milan and Brussels, despite treaties, **25.** 505

verses refer to projected alliance of Spain, France, and, to restore Old Pretender, **30.** 126–7

Williams, C. H., seeks aid of, in case of Anglo-Prussian rift, **30.** 321

*See also*: Austria, house of; Francis I; Joseph II; Maria Theresa; Vienna, Court of

Austria, House of:

Bourbons' contest with, over Spain, **21.** 200

England wants Empire kept in, **20.** 178n, 187n

France against aggrandizing, **21.** 187, **24.** 389

Frederick II wants to make house of Brandenburg equal to, **18.** 543

German Electors want to keep imperial crown in, **42.** 494

HW calls, 'detestable,' **19.** 128

ingratitude of, **21.** 240

Leopold no longer needs to give heirs to, **22.** 526

Maria Louisa provides many heirs to, **23.** 171, 214

Modena may be inherited by, **20.** 400

princes of the Empire need Prussia to offset power of, **24.** 450

'Austrosards' (Austrian-Sardinian army):

new word in Florence, **17.** 426–7

Auteroche, Jean Chappe d'. *See* Chappe d'Auteroche

Auteuil (France):

Boufflers, Comtesse de, has English garden at, **28.** 222, **32.** 259

—— sorry to quit, **34.** 80

Boufflers, Comtesses de, have house at, **6.** 67, 72, 75, 81, 185, 211, 345, 349, 459, 469, 472, **7.** 153, 162, 165, 166, 168, 176, 218, 230, 347, 422–30, **31.** 183

mentioned, **7.** 161

visitors to: Beauvau, **7.** 422; Coke, Lady Mary, **7.** 347, **31.** 183; Du Deffand, Mme, **6.** 72, 81, 346, 353, 459, 466, 469, 472, **7.** 155, 162, 166, 178, 347, 422–30, **31.** 183; Gibbon, **6.**

459, 469, 472; HW, **7.** 347, **31.** 183; Holdernesse, **6.** 185; Lauzun, Mme de, **7.** 162, 347; Luxembourg, Mme de, **6.** 211, 345, 347, 348–9, **7.** 162, 178, 218, 347; Mirepoix, Mme de, **7.** 427; Sanadon, Mlle, **7.** 347; Ségur, Vicomte de, **7.** 348; Shuvalov, **7.** 347; Toulouse, Abp of, **7.** 422

*Authentic Papers Relating to the Expedition against the Charibbs . . . in the Island of St Vincent*:
HW's copy of, **28.** 142n

*Author, The*. *See under* Foote, Samuel

'Author,' Mann's. *See* Leopold II

Author; authors:
absurd compliments to, **32.** 372
ancient, unreliable on countries other than their own, **15.** 227
at Holbach's, bore HW, **30.** 208
booksellers should supply, with rare books for their researches, **40.** 306, 307
Cambridge finds, vain and troublesome, **28.** 250–1
classic, include Hannah More, **31.** 271
dedication to Conway useless in opinion of, **37.** 544
Du Deffand, Mme, compares all, to Abp of Granada in *Gil Blas*, **5.** 409
—— not fond of readings by, **7.** 236
English dismiss, to their colleges, **41.** 55
every Frenchwoman has, planted in her house, **39.** 12
female: HW criticizes English, **31.** 271; More, Hannah, criticizes English, **31.** 273–4; suspected of vanity, **31.** 311
French: dictatorial pertness of, **33.** 543; HW does not pay homage to, **39.** 12
gentlemen, civilly treated if they do not write nonsense, **31.** 269
grave, not immediately read, **15.** 239
great, will in time be read only by good judges, **28.** 46
Greek and Latin, unpublished at Naples, **31.** 278–9
HW jokes about unreliability of resolutions of, **30.** 152
HW not ashamed of being, **28.** 24
HW's reflections on, **15.** 106, 125, **28.** 25, 29. 295, *see also* HW: aversions to
impartial, make poor reading, **4.** 406
literary disputes among, ridiculous strivings for publicity, **41.** 47, 51–3, 55–6
Louis XIV's, had merit; Louis XV's, pretensions, **7.** 364
modern, Gray's opinions on, unsuitable for publication, **28.** 28, 119
modern German, delicacy of, not so great as that of English and French, **25.** 206
only survivors of Louis XIV's glory, **35.** 345
printers to make overtures to, **35.** 410
profession of, trifling, **25.** 584
self-importance of, **15.** 196
vain, **3.** 201
Walpole, Sir Robert, employed bad, **30.** 314

Authorship:
HW done with, **2.** 85, 245–6, 303
HW repents of, **35.** 539
HW's aversion to, **30.** 152
HW's reflections on, **1.** 207, 309, 337, **2.** 110, 143, 337

Autichamp, Marquis d'. *See* Beaumont, Jean-Thérèse-Louis de

Autographs:
noblemen's, HW leaves paper of, with Fenn, **16.** 231

'Automaton, The':
public attention absorbed by, **35.** 381

Autopsy; autopsies:
on: Castromonte, **4.** 367; Chauvelin, **5.** 428; Fitzjames, Maréchale de, **6.** 464; Marie Leszczyńska, **4.** 93; Saulx, **4.** 118; Townshend, Charles, **39.** 90–1; Waldegrave, George, 4th E., **37.** 264–5; Walpole of Wolterton, **4.** 136

'Autumn':
HW suggests Rigby should be drawn as, **30.** 93

Autun, Bp of. *See* Marbeuf, Yves-Alexandre de (1732–99); Roquette, Gabriel de (1623–1707); Talleyrand-Périgord, Charles-Maurice de (1754–1838)

Autun (France):
Condé's corps attacks, **6.** 498n

Auvergne, Antoine d' (1713–97), director of Opéra:
director of Opéra, **6.** 28–9
in country, **6.** 51

Auvergne (France):
Bouillon governor of, **3.** 68n

Auvergne, La Tour d'. *See* La Tour d'Auvergne

Auverquerque, Lady Frances Nassau d' (ca 1700–72), m. (1737) Capt. (later Lt-Col.) William Elliot:
Bramston, Mrs, left paltry legacy by, **23.** 416
father's bequest to, reverts to Cowper, **35.** 195n
Grantham's co-heiress, **24.** 360n
HW glad to see, **10.** 208
Montagu desired by, to live at Twickenham, **10.** 252
Morice acquires Grove House after death of, **33.** 274n
to entertain Chute, Vcts Grandison, George and Charles Montagu, **10.** 206

Auverquerque, Lady Henrietta d' (d. 1747), m. (1732) William Cowper, 2d E. Cowper:
family of, **24.** 353, 360n, **25.** 78n
insanity confines, **30.** 22

Auverquerque, Henry d' (ca 1672–1754), cr. (1698) E. of Grantham:
Cowper sends for plate and jewels of, **23.** 449
daughter of, **10.** 206n, **24.** 360n, **25.** 78n
dies rich, vacating pension, **35.** 195
drawing-teacher reminds Conway of, **37.** *103*
Morice bought the Grove of, at Chiswick, **25.** 298n
Tyrawley comments on tiptoe walk of, **18.** 104

[Auverquerque, Henry d', *continued*]
William III compels, to take name of Auver-
querque instead of Nassau, **24.** 360
—— does not allow, to use Nassau arms, **24.**
370
Auverquerque ('Overkirk'):
Cowpers to have as title, **24.** 353
family of, object to Cowper's assuming their
name, **24.** 370
principality of, an Iricism, **24.** 360
*See also* Ouwerkerk
Auvoille. *See* Auroille
Aux Bons Enfants, Amiens inn:
(?) HW and Ds of Douglas at, **39.** 8
HW dislikes, **35.** 123
HW stays at, **7.** 334, 370–1, **35.** 123
Auxerre, Bp of. *See* Champion de Cicé, Jean-
Baptiste-Marie
Auxerre (France):
Burke places son at, **32.** 103n
Chitry near, **5.** 83n
*Aux mânes de Louis XV. See under* Gudin de la
Brenellerie, Paul-Philippe
Auxy de la Grange de Monceaux, Anne-Made-
leine-Françoise-Émilie d' (1721–1803), m.
(1736) André-Hercule de Rosset de Rocozel
de Pérignan:
imprisonment of, **12.** 79
Avalos, Ferdinando Francesco d' (ca 1489–
1523), Marchese di Pescara:
to appear in Robertson's *Charles V*, **15.** 46
Avaray, Marquise d'. *See* Mailly-Nesle, Angé-
lique-Adélaïde-Sophie de
*Avare, L'. See under* Molière
'Avarice.' *See under* Le Chauvelin
Avarice:
canonizes crime, **3.** 300
destroys taste and sentiment, **4.** 242
'orthodox vice,' **20.** 134
Voltaire considers, as natural as love, **7.** 370
Aveiro, Duque de:
limbs of, broken alive, **21.** 267n
Ave Maria:
Boufflers's paraphrase of, **6.** 249
HW says, to Lady Mary Coke, **39.** 7
Ave Maria Lane, London:
Law, bookseller in, **16.** 238
*Aventures d'Abdalla, Les. See under* Bignon,
Jean-Paul
Avenue; avenues:
at Mistley, bad and ill-placed, **30.** 87
Avenza:
Francis III makes new port at, **37.** 320
Averdy. *See* Del 'Averdi
Averne, Mme d', mistress of the Regent of
France, 1721:
Du Deffand, Mme, at fêtes with, **14.** 144n
hôtel of, in Rue St-Honoré, **22.** 245n
Aviary; aviaries:
at Hinchingbrooke, **10.** 80
HW's, **30.** 93
*See also* Menagerie

Aviation:
HW expects, **22.** 333, **39.** 425
*See also under* Balloon
'Avidien.' *See* Wortley Montagu, Edward (1678–
1761)
Avignon, Abp of. *See* Manzi, Francesco Maria
de' (d. 1774)
Avignon (France):
abbey near, **9.** 116
Aiguillon may not relinquish, to papacy, **23.**
527
atrocities at, **11.** 78, **15.** 237, **31.** 373, **34.** 95,
120, 157, 158, 161, 181
Aulan, Marquis d', hanged at, **11** 76, 84
Aulan family move between Paris and, **3.** 376,
**4.** 65, 229, **7.** 79, 84–5, 126, 132, 133, 219,
225, 440, 459, 461
Benedict XIV urges Young Pretender to leave,
**20.** 22n, 35n
Buondelmonti vice-legate to, **17.** 8n
Celestins' convent at, René's portrait in, **31.**
143n
Chesterfield and Ormond confer at, **17.** 133n,
232n, **19.** 68–9
Clement XIII unlikely to recover, **23.** 38
—— would sacrifice, to his brief, **23.** 10
Coke, Lady Mary, should visit, **31.** 143
Dunbar may go to, **19.** 376, 378
Durini to govern, **23.** 11
France may offer, to Clement XIV if Jesuits
are suppressed, **23.** 306
France may punish, for sheltering Young
Pretender, **20.** 23
France threatens to bring Young Pretender
by force from, **20.** 23n
France to seize, **23.** 24
Old Pretender may visit, **19.** 94, 97
Ormond sends courier from, to Old Pre-
tender, **19.** 85
out of the way for travellers, **20.** 27
Papacy to regain, **23.** 473
restitution of: Clement XIV's prerequisite,
for Jesuits' suppression, **23.** 447n; delayed,
**23.** 527; not settled, **23.** 518
Rome hopes to induce Young Pretender to
leave, **20.** 22
Sheridan takes charge of Young Pretender's
effects at, **20.** 9n
vice-legate at, **20.** 44n; *see also* Acquaviva,
Pasquale
visitors to: Carlisle, Cts of, **7.** 84; Elliots, **6.**
385; Grave, **4.** 310; Hardinge, **35.** 579; Inverness, Ds of, **17.** 28n; Montagu, Lady
Mary Wortley, **7.** 281, **20.** 235n; Palazzi,
Conte, **20.** 235n; Sheridan, Michael, **20.**
9n; Stafford, Henry, **20.** 9n; Toulouse,
Abp of, **4.** 310; Trudaine de Montigny, M.
and Mme, **4.** 310; Young Pretender, **19.**
140, 368, 376, 377, **20.** 27, 35, 44, 84n, 508
York, Cardinal, may be legate of, **19.** 416
—— may visit, **19.** 97
Young Pretender's presence at, may keep

Parliament from ratifying peace treaty, **20**. 27

Avocat-général. *See* Séguier, Antoine-Louis

*Avocatoria:*
disappear from Nuremberg's streets before von Mayr's arrival, **21**. 102n

Avoglio, Christina Maria:
sings in Handel's *Samson*, **18**. 180n
sings in *Temistocle*, **43**. 249

Avon, river:
cascade of, at Warwick, **9**. 121
dirty, at Bristol, **10**. 232
HW calls, 'dirty ditch,' **31**. 130
Millers' house overlooks, **10**. 233, **39**. 240
paltry enough to be Seine or Tiber, **39**. 76
Thames compared with, **31**. 131

Avranches, Bp of. *See* Huet, Pierre-Daniel (1630–1721)

Awnings:
on boats at Richmond regatta, **32**. 317n

Axbridge, Somerset:
Prowse of, **9**. 398n

Axe; axes:
Balmerinoch tries edge of, **19**. 281n
brought from Tower, to trial of rebel lords, **19**. 282
for beheading Anne Boleyn, **17**. 233
red velvet covers handle of, at peers' trial, **19**. 281n

Ayat, Mme d'. *See* Morphy, Marie-Louise

Aydie, François-Odet d' (1703–94), abbé:
(?) Du Deffand, Mme, corresponds with, **7**. 442
Gennevilliers visited by, **4**. 469
social relations of, with Mme de Choiseul, **4**. 469

Ayen, Comte d'. *See* Noailles, Jean-Louis-François-Paul de

Ayen, Duc d'. *See* Noailles, Jean-Louis-François-Paul de (1739–1824); Noailles, Louis de (1713–93)

Ayen, Duchesse d'. *See* Aguesseau, Henriette-Anne-Louise d'

Ayla, Baron d':
commander of Maestricht, receives orders for surrender, **19**. 480n

Aylesbury, Frances (1617–67), m. (1634) Edward Hyde, 1st E. of Clarendon:
daughter, when married, treated respectfully by, at dinner, **20**. 408

Aylesbury, Bucks:
Buckingham clashes with, over assizes, **13**. 20, **19**. 449n, 470–1, **20**. 112, **26**. 25–8
meeting at, **7**. 367
on road between Bletchley and SH, **1**. 2n, 37–8
races at: Grenvilles move, to Buckingham, **9**. 72; to be attended by Henry and George Grenville, Margaret Banks, and Rigby, **9**. 72
Wilkes's letter to electors of, **38**. 484

Aylesbury. *See also* Ailesbury

Aylesford, Cts of. *See* Seymour, Lady Charlotte (1730–1805); Thynne, Louisa, (1760–1832)

Aylesford, E. of. *See* Finch, Heneage (1649–1719); Finch, Heneage (ca 1683–1757); Finch, Heneage (1715–77); Finch, Heneage (1751–1812)

Aylett, ——:
witness at Mrs Cornelys's trial, **23**. 272n

Aylett, Edward, attorney:
Parliament commits, to Newgate, for prevaricating in prosecuting a J.P., **23**. 74

Ayliffe, John (d. 1759), Fox's steward:
Churchill mentions, in *The Duellist*, **38**. 290n

Ayliffe, John (ca 1733–59), forger:
(?) Bowle buys Q. Elizabeth's MS at sale of, **40**. 305

Ayliffe family:
arms of, in glass, **30**. 136n

Aylmer, Mr and Mrs, of Whitton:
SH visited by, **12**. 227, 229, 234, 246

Aylmer, Henry (1718–66), 3d Bn Aylmer, 1754:
Bower said to have met mistress while in family of, **20**. 532n

Ayloffe, Sir Joseph (1709–81), F.S.A.; 6th Bt:
*Accounts of Some Ancient Monuments in Westminster Abbey, An*, **2**. 215
commissioner for 'methodizing' state papers, **28**. 238n
Edward I's exhumation described by, in *Archæologia*, **24**. 4n
paintings described by, **28**. 212n

Aylsbury. *See* Ailesbury; Aylesbury

Aylsford. *See* Aylesford

Ayre. *See* Eyre

Ayrolles, d'. *See* Dayrolles

Ayr River, Yorks:
Ferrybridge on, **28**. 321n

Ayrshire:
Craufurd estates in, **5**. 153n
HW's pun on, **33**. 73

Ayscough, Rev. Dr Francis (1700–63), D.D.; Dean of Bristol:
George III converses with, at P. of Wales's death, **20**. 240
—— to benefit by replacement of, **20**. 203n
not to remain as George III's tutor, **20**. 239
(?) speech for George III written by, **9**. 89

Ayscough, George Edward (d. 1779), dramatist:
Lyttelton's *Works* edited by, **28**. 104n
*Semiramis*, witticism on, **32**. 342–3

Ayscough, Samuel (1745–1804), librarian:
appointed assistant librarian in the British Museum, **16**. 312n
*Catalogue of the Manuscripts Preserved in the British Museum, A*: **2**. 332, 334, **43**. 76, 198; no great treasures listed in, **15**. 164–5

Ayscough, William (d. 1450), Bp of Salisbury, 1438:
Henry VI's confessor, **43**. 184
——'s marriage performed by, **43**. 183–4

Ayston, Rutland:
Brudenell of, **9**. 184n, **14**. 2n

Ayton, William (d. 1800) of Macclesfield:
HW's kindness to, after SH visit, 15. *338*
(?) Nivernais's *Jardins modernes* given to, 12. 260
SH editions collected by, 15. 338
SH visited by, with Sandby and Ireland, 15. 338, 42. 175n
Ayton, Berwickshire:
Fordyce of, 11. 250n
Ayton, Yorks:
Skottowe of, 41. 245n
Aytoun. *See* Ayton
Azara y Perera, José Nicolas de (1730–1804), Marquis de Nibbiano:
Mengs's biographer, 16. 170n
Azémar de Montfalcon, Jean-Balthazar d' (1731–91), Comte d'Adhémar; ambassador to England 1783–7:
Adhémar title taken by, 5. 207–8
England left by, 39. 448, 449
expected soon in England, 25. 398
Fox, C. J., aided by voting instructions of, to Westminster tradesmen, 25. 496n
HW does not know of appointment of, 25. 363
Liancourt said to succeed, 39. 450
marriage of, 5. 145n, 207–8
returns to England as ambassador, 36. 237
social relations of, with Mme du Deffand, 5. 208, 210
SH visited by, 12. 221, 33. 403
Azincourt. *See* Seroux d'Agincourt
Azov:
Catherine II to retain, 23. 212
Russians seize, 23. 116
Azpuru y Jiménez, Tomás (1713–72), auditor of the Rota; Spanish minister to Rome 1765–72:
Aiguillon tells Bernis to support efforts of, 23. 373n
Clement XIII asked by, for audience, 23. 10, 15
—— persecuted by, to acknowledge Young Pretender, 22. 386
—— told by, to discard Torreggiani, 23. 35–6
Clement XIV assures, of Palafox's canonization, 23. 123–4
—— importuned by, 23. 214n
confers with French and Neapolitan ministers, 23. 10
courier to, announces Jesuits' expulsion, 22. 517n
Mann's bullying of, may please Pitt, 22. 441
Old Pretender acknowledged by, as king, 22. *369*, 374
Spanish Court tells, to disavow Young Pretender, 22. 399
Azraël, angel of death:
Lincoln to be conducted by, 18. 167–8, 30. 36
Aztec; Aztecs:
Dee's 'black stone' mirror made by, 43. 389n
Azzaloni, Giuseppe:
confessor to Bernardina Rienzi, 24. 29n
Azzi. *See* Degli Azzi

**B**

B.,A.:
HW's emissary to give charity in name of, 40. 308
'B ——, Dom.' *See under* Gervaise de la Touche, Jean-Charles
B ——, Lady:
St-Germain intimate with, 26. 20
'B ——,' Mr:
'a second Cosmo Gordon,' 33. 117
B ——, Sir B ——. *See* Bridges, Sir Brook
Baalbek:
Pantheon resembles, 23. 298
HW's reflections on Robert Wood and, 9. 349
St Paul's will resemble ruins of, 24. 62
Wood's tombstone should stress achievements at, 41. 247, 248
*See also under* Wood, Robert
Babbi, Gregorio (fl. 1732–77), opera singer:
dies at Cesena, 18. 527n
duo and trio to include, in Neapolitan cantata, 19. 438
Grand Duke of Tuscany's 'virtuoso,' 18. 526n
sings at Leghorn and Florence, 18. 525–6
Babedoglie, ——, French financier in Tuscany:
dismissal of, 20. 327
Babel:
confusion at, 10. 211
languages of, audible from SH visitors, 35. 531
tower of, 33. 474
unintelligibility at, 33. 269
Baberham. *See* Babraham
'Babes in the wood':
Townshend, Vcts, covered with laurel like, 35. 297
*Babillard, Le. See under* Boissy, Louis de
Babington, Gervase (?1550–1610), Bp of Llandaff, 1591; of Exeter, 1595; of Worcester, 1597:
confused with Abbot Babington, 2. 38
Babington, William (d. 1453), abbot:
connection of, with Bury abbey, 2. 32, 36, 38–9
portrait of Cardinal Beaufort mistaken for, 2. 31
Bablot, ——, Paris hotel-keeper:
HW offered quieter lodging by, 6. 81, 209, 210
HW's host, 6. 81
HW to reoccupy former lodgings with, 6. 210
Baboczai, Col.:
Austrians under, to join Sardinian army at Nice, 19. 323n
Baboon; baboons:
in shrine of Indian temple, 24. 433
*See also* 'Pug'
Babraham, Cambs:
Cole's native parish, 1. 2n
——'s family buried at, 1. 363n
Palavicini's estate and house at, 1. 2–3, 3n, 5, 170, 2. 181n
Palavicinis in parish register of, 1. 3

Baby-houses:
Frederick, P. of Wales, builds, **20.** 187
HW compares his family affairs to play in, **25.** 133
'Babylon, Princess of.' *See under* Hamilton, Anthony: *Mémoires de Grammont; see also* Burgh, Lady Margaret de
Babylon:
betrayed to Darius, **34.** 41
HW compares Rome and Turkey to, **23.** 212
'Madam of': HW's term for Pius VI, **24.** 162, **35.** 397; HW's term for Rome, **24.** 255
'Old Mother,' HW's term for Clement XIII, **22.** 420
probably stared at its own downfall, **24.** 228
tirewomen of, **35.** 249
waters of, **10.** 228, **18.** 466, **30.** 213, **31.** 347, **32.** 76, 145, **35.** 60
'whore' of, **33.** 173, **34.** 19, **35.** 397
Winchilsea built like, **40.** 5
Bac, Rue du, Paris:
Le Droit, Mme, lived in, **3.** 359n
Bacallar y Sana, Vicente (ca 1669–1726), Marqués de San Felipe:
biographical information on, corrected, **43.** 197
*Commentarios* by: Strafford prefers, to Torcy's, **35.** 283; superseded, **15.** 137
Baccalan, Joseph, president of Parliament of Bordeaux:
social relations of, with: Aiguillon, Mme d', **7.** 278; Hénault, **7.** 303
Baccano (Italy):
refugees flee towards, **18.** 532, 534
Baccelli, Gianetta (*or* Giovanna) (d. 1801), dancer; D. of Dorset's mistress:
dances at Pantheon fête, **39.** 330–1
Garter insignia worn by, while dancing in Paris, **31.** 268
housekeeper at Knole perhaps dresser of, **29.** 78
name of, corrected, **43.** 307
Pembroke, E. of, pursues, **10.** 15n, **43.** 291
Bacchante:
bronze of, **15.** 17
Bacchus:
Aylesford's marriage serves, instead of Venus, **36.** 205
bronze of, **15.** 17
by Sansovino, **22.** 67
Cipriani did not copy figure of, **19.** 48
gesso of, Mann can send, to Lyttelton, **20.** 547
idol of 'Noble Jeffery,' **32.** 85
Luxborough, Lady, consoles herself with, **11.** 66
Mann to procure gesse of, for HW, **19.** 34
mentioned in verses, **12.** 269
painted by Lady Diana Beauclerk, **33.** 473
statue of, sitting, destroyed in Uffizi fire, **22.** 68n
triumph of, by Carracci, Mann to get copy of, **20.** 328
Venus shares empire with, in Ireland, **37.** 35

Wilton's statue of, for Tylney, **20.** 397–8
*Bacchus*, English ship:
involved in war, **18.** 438n, 485n
*Bacchus and Hegemone. See* Leclerc de la Bruère, Charles-Antoine: *Bacchus et Erigone*
Bach, Johann Christian (1735–82), composer:
*Adriano in Siria*, opera by, **38.** 504
symphonies of, executed from MSS at an *accademia*, **18.** 13n
*Zanaida*, opera by, **38.** 201
'Bacha, le.' *See* Montmorency-Luxembourg, Charles-Anne-Sigismond de; Vignerot du Plessis-Richelieu, Emmanuel-Armand
Bachaumont. *See* Le Coigneux de Bachaumont, François (1624–1702); Petit de Bachaumont, Louis (1690–1771)
Bache, Benjamin Franklin (1769–98):
Paris visited by, **6.** 383
Bachois de Villefort, ——, lieutenant criminel:
St-Vincent, Mme de, interrogated by, **6.** 157
Bachycraig, Flintshire:
Salusbury of, **11.** 21n
*Baciamano:*
Tuscan Court function for those admissible to antechamber only, **43.** 280
Back. *See* Pain in back
Backer, Georges de (early 18th c.), printer and bookseller:
*Dictionnaire des proverbes françois,* (?) owned by Mme du Deffand, **8.** 25
Backgammon:
Cosby, Mrs, plays, **10.** 166
Backwell, Edward (d. 1683), goldsmith; banker; M.P.:
biographical information on, corrected, **43.** 137
print of, **10.** 301, 303
Backwell, Messrs, London bankers:
Mann's arrears from, for Lucchi annuity, **22.** 279
Backwell. *See also* Bakewell; Blackwell
Bacon, Anthony:
Birch publishes papers of, **33.** 256n
Bacon, Edward (?1712–86), M.P.:
Speaker's position rumoured for, **38.** 136
Walpole, Horatio (1678–1757), not to set up Thomas Walpole against, as M.P. for Norwich, **21.** 56n
Bacon, Sir Francis (1561–1626), Kt, 1603; cr. Bn Verulam, Vct St Alban:
apologue favoured by, **34.** 107
brother of, **40.** 193
Chesterfield places Hardwicke in company of, **28.** 303
despicable as magistrate, **7.** 354
Dryden's tribute to, **35.** 569
Du Deffand, Mme, wants print of, **4.** 241, 266
Elizabeth, Q., entertained by, at Twickenham Park, and receives sonnet entreating Essex's pardon, **42.** 488, 489
Essex gives Twickenham Park to, but is later opposed by him, **42.** 489
Fuller cites, on Cts of Desmond's age, **40.** 112n

[Bacon, Sir Francis, *continued*]
HW quotes, 12. 155, 18. 30
HW's query about, 2. 3n
HW's unflattering remarks on, 14. 166n
*Historie of the Raigne of King Henry VII* by: apology for a tyrant, 15. 177, 184, 41. 126; HW criticizes, in *Historic Doubts*, 41. 126
Mallet's edition of: 15. 78; mentions Lambert Simnel, 42. 255n
*Novum Organum*, HW's new, on plan of, 34. 171
political life of, weakened by flattery, 35. 569
Pope's lines on, 32. 50
portraits of, 1. 180n, 40. 194
'prophet of arts,' 33. 418
Shaw says, had art of inventing arts, 37. 294
Sidney compared with, 40. 136
Taylor prefers pagan philosophers to clarity of, 34. 83
Twickenham resident, 42. 488
Bacon, Jane (ca 1731–1819), m. (*ante* 1753) James Nares:
Nares, Robert, anxious about, 15. 231, 234
Bacon, John (1740–99), R.A.:
Gray's monument by, 2. 101n, 28. 439n, 41. 387
Bacon, Sir Nathaniel (1547–1622), Kt (uncle of painter):
HW confuses with nephew, 1. 23n, 40. 193n
monument and bust of, 1. 23
Bacon, Sir Nathaniel (1585–1627), K.B., 1625; painter:
birth and death dates of, 43. 44
HW wants copy of portrait of, 40. 193, 196
monument and bust of, 1. 23, 25
Bacon, Sir Nicholas (1509–79), Kt; lord keeper:
arms of, 1. 378
contributor to building Corpus Christi College chapel, 1. 378
Bacon, Sir Nicholas (ca 1540–1624), cr. (1611) Bt:
bust of, 40. 193
Bacon, Thomas Sclater. *See* Sclater, Thomas
Bacon:
ditchers' diet, 37. 172
flitch of: at Dunmow, 11. 14, 16, 31. 209; at Wichnor, 9. 294, 38. 70–1
for SH dinner, 41. 366
HW does not want, 18. 366
Ireland to send, to Lisbon earthquake victims, 37. 423n
Mann has, with beans for dinner, 21. 10
price of, lowered, 22. 460n
refugees from fire take, to Sir Robert Walpole's, 17. 496
rioters seize, in warehouses, 22. 460n
'Bacon, Save one's':
Bessborough misunderstands, 38. 88
Bacton, Norfolk:
living of, 42. 441
Badajoz:
Damer, Mrs, writes from, 11. 237n

Spanish army at, 40. 240
Badcock, Rev. Samuel (1747–88):
Milles reviewed by, 29. 225n
Baddeley, Rev. Mr:
Gloucester, D. and Ds of, allegedly married by, 36. 62n
Walpole, Sir Edward, mistakes, for Dr Morton, 36. 62–3
Baddow, Little, Essex:
Tyson visits, 2. 175
Baden, Grand Duke of. *See* Karl Friedrich (1728–1811)
Baden:
Richecourt may visit baths of, 17. 95
Baden-Durlach, Margrave of. *See* Karl Friedrich (1728–1811)
Baden-Durlach, Margravine of. *See* Anna Charlotte Amalie
Badesley Clinton and Packwood, Warwickshire:
Noble, vicar of, 42. 133n
Badge; badges:
of knighthood, Gunter's designs for, 42. 107n
waterman's, 39. 142
Badger, Salop:
Chelsum, rector of, 42. 209n
Badger Weller, Jane (ca 1747–1818), m. (1767) Sir Thomas Spencer Wilson, 6th Bt, 1760:
SH visited by, 12. 239
Badia di Grotta Ferrata:
Benedict XIV tells Guadagni to confer, on Cardinal York, 19. 433
Badingham, Suffolk:
Derehaugh and Burwell families of, 1. 376–7
Badini, Carlo Francesco (d. *post* 1808), author:
Duncan, Lady Mary, clashes with, over tickets, 11. 307–8
lampoon by, signed 'Vittorio Nemesini,' 11. 308n
Badiote, ——:
Cardini may be reached at house of, in Haymarket, 25. 309n, 42. 37
Badminton, Glos, D. of Beaufort's seat:
Boscawen, Mrs, to visit, 31. 348
Dodd and Whaley visit, 40. 11
HW and Chute not to visit, for fear of meeting Beaufort, 10. 228
Baeffa, Giuseppe. *See* Baesa e Visentelo, Don Giuseppe
Baesa e Visentelo, Don Giuseppe (d. ?1770), Conte di Cantillana; (?) Marchese di Castromonte; Neapolitan ambassador to Sardinia and to France:
(?) death of, 4. 366–7
social relations of, with: Bentheim, Gräfin von, 7. 265, 312; Brancas, Marquis de, 7. 298, (?) 317; Brancas, Marquise de, 7. (?) 317; Caraman, Comte and Comtesse de, 7. 304
Bag; bags:
cloak: HW to take, to Houghton, 18. 498; stolen from courier, 19. 334
counters in, 30. 50
Du Deffand, Mme, carries, 4. 201

flannel and fur, Mann uses, for gout, **25.** 248

green: Holdernesse has, **20.** 346; used by secretaries of state and Lord Treasurer, **18.** 225

hair worn in, **19.** 299, **38.** 221

leather and silk, contain Great Seal, **25.** 481n

sweet: Du Deffand, Mme, wants iris roots for, **23.** 323; lying on velvet tables at Knole, **35.** 132

Bagard, (?) Nicholas, councillor of finances at Florence:

(?) dismissal of, ordered by Vienna, **17.** 368, 406

Gavi's prosecution pressed by, **17.** 368

Bagarotti, Mlle, dame d'honneur to dowager Princesse de Conti:

Viry, Contessa di, resembles, **5.** 404–5

Bagdad:

caliphs of, as uninteresting to England as the Conclave is, **24.** 82

Baggage:

Conti's, sent by P. Charles, **37.** 137

Conway's, thought lost, **37.** 152

English take, on retreat, **37.** 191

servant must see, sealed and registered in book of coach, **37.** 39–42

*See also* Portmanteau; Trunk

'Bagnal, Mr':

Mann's code name for Leopold of Tuscany, **25.** 43, 58

Bagnani, M.:

Guido's illness prevents, from singing, **18.** 12

Bagnano, Guido:

ill, **18.** 12

opera not to be given by, **17.** 56

Bagnara (Italy):

earthquake account mentions, **25.** 376

Bagnères de Luchon:

Belsunce, Mme de, dies at, **4.** 381n

Bagnesi, Signora. *See* Vitelli, Agnese

Bagnesi, Cosimo (d. ca 1743), governor of Grossetto:

governor of Grossetto, **17.** 65n

(?) Modenese princess gives presents to, **17.** 65

Bagnesi, Francesco Maria (1681–1759):

(?) Modenese princess gives presents to, **17.** 65

(?) Strozzi applies to, **18.** 133

Bagnesi, Marchese Ippolito Giuliano (1717–1802):

(?) HW liked, **18.** 148

(?) Strozzi fights duel with, over debt, **18.** 133–4

Bagneux (France):

Henry Benedict (Stuart) takes house at, **19.** 177n

Bagni della Porretta:

German troops reach, near Pistoia, **18.** 98

Bagnio; bagnios:

Cerretesi lodges in, in London, **17.** 459

Francis III gets wife from, **22.** 148

future dukes will pop out of, **20.** 155

Hamilton frequents, **20.** 155

in Covent Garden, **17.** 505

nuns visit, in disguise, **20.** 464

Wilkes and Mme du Barry both emerged from, **23.** 152

*See also* Cardigan's Head

Bagnolese Pinacci, Anna M.:

*Andromache* acted by, **18.** 128

costume of, **18.** 128, 134

Mann disparages elocution of, **17.** 284

second rôle played by, in opera, **17.** *239–40*

Bagnolet (France):

Orléans 'hunts' at, **8.** 127–8

Bagnolles. *See* Du Gué Bagnolles

Bagnolo, Duca di. *See* Strozzi, Filippo (1700–63); Strozzi, Lorenzo (d. 1802)

Bagot, Bns; Lady. *See* St John, Hon. Elizabeth Louisa

Bagot, Lewis (1740–1802), D.C.L.; Bp of Bristol, 1782; of Norwich, 1783; of St Asaph, 1790:

becomes Bp of Bristol, **29.** 188

dozes over Clarendon's *History*, **29.** 149

*Letter to the Rev. William Bell, A,* Hoadly is called Socinian in, **29.** 125

Newton, Thomas, succeeded by, **29.** 186n

orthodoxy of, **29.** 198

Bagot, Mary (1645–79), m. (1664) Charles Berkeley, Vct Fitzhardinge; 1st E. of Falmouth:

diamond ring worn by, despite insolvency, **10.** 1

Bagot (after 1783, Howard), Richard (1733–1818), Northampton's secretary at Venice:

Northampton, Cts of, accompanied by, to Rome, **22.** 142

Venice reached by, with news of Cts of Northampton's death, **22.** 150n

Bagot, Sir William (1728–98), 6th Bt, 1768; cr. (1780) Bn Bagot; M.P.:

barony conferred on, **25.** 86

dozes over Clarendon's history, **29.** 149

HW's correspondence with, **41.** 430–1

(?) Montagu to be visited by, at Greatworth, **9.** 291

peerage for, **36.** 173, 174

picture owned by, **41.** 430–1

Bagpipe; bagpipes:

dance music by, **20.** 121n

German flute imitates, **9.** 131

Middleton's bronze of man playing on, **15.** 16

Bagshot Heath:

Cumberland's lodge spoiled by, **10.** 44

Baguette:

HW brings sample of, for Cts of Ailesbury's cabriolets, **39.** 146

Bag-wig; bag-wigs:

Parliament members stripped of, by rioters, **25.** 54

Baiae (Italy):

Twickenham to rival, **35.** 234

Baiardi, Ottavio Antonio (1694–1764), Abp of Tyre; scholar:

[Baiardi, Ottavio Antonio, *continued*]
Charles of Naples dismisses, **21**. 143n
—— generous with *Prodromo* of, **21**. 142
Bailas. *See* Francesco
Baile Cliet. *See under* Dublin
Bailey, John, barrister:
Mrs Rudd's counsel, **24**. 153n
Bailey, Nathan (d. 1742), lexicographer:
(?) print of, **40**. 237
*Universal Etymological English Dictionary,
An*, by, thumbed by schoolboys, **35**. 31
Bailey *or* Bailie. *See also* Baillie
Bailey *or* Baily, Old. *See* Old Bailey
Bailie. *See* Bayly
Bailies, Mr, fortune-teller at Bath:
(?) in Westminster, **31**. 280n
Bailiff; bailiffs:
La Condamine's landlady dresses chairmen
as, **22**. 146–7, 151
*See also* Westminster, High Bailiff of
*See also under* Servant
Baillie *or* Balli, painter or engraver:
HW knows nothing about, **42**. 395
Baillie, Col.:
Haidar 'Alī Khān defeats, **25**. 141n
Baillie, Mr, of Bedford Sq.:
Ealing Grove sold to, **11**. 8n
Baillie, George (ca 1663–1738) of Jerviswood:
family of, **21**. 301n, **24**. 67n, **34**. 256
Baillie, Griselda, wife of George Baillie:
family of, **24**. 67n
Mann's dream interpreted by, at Paris, **25**. 2
Baillie, Griselda ('Grizel') (ca 1691–1759), m.
(1710) Sir Alexander Murray, 3d Bt:
Bristol, Cts of, friend of, **34**. 259
career and death of, **21**. 301
Grey, Arthur, her footman, tries to ravish,
**19**. 450n, **34**. 256
Mellerstein, seat of, in Scotland, **21**. 301n
Montagu, Lady Mary Wortley, makes ballad
on, **34**. 256, 259
Baillie, Joanna (1762–1851), dramatist:
star of, had not risen in unpoetical age,
**11**. 67n
Baillie, Matthew (1761–1823), M.D.; anatomist:
HW inquires about, **15**. 245
Hunter leaves collection in trust for, **15**. 181n
Baillie, Rachel (1696–1773), m. (1717) Charles
Hamilton, styled Bn Binning:
book carried by, to Edinburgh, **15**. 101
family of, **24**. 67n, **34**. 256
Naples visited by, when Mann is there, **21**.
301n
sister attends, in illness, **21**. 301
Baillie family:
Mann knew, **24**. 67
Baillie. *See also* Bailey; Bailly
Baillif. *See* Le Baillif
Baillon, Jean-Baptiste, French watch-maker:
Du Deffand, Mme, leaves watch made by, to
Mlle Couty, **8**. 27
Baillou, Guillaume de (1538–1616), physician:
rheumatism defined by, **22**. 451n

Bailly, Jean-Sylvain (1736–93), astronomer;
mayor of Paris 1789–91:
compared to lord mayor of London, **11**. 210
responsibility of, for French Revolution, **31**.
385
Bailo; baili:
from Venice to Turkey, *see* Corraro, Pietro
(1707–68)
title of Venetian ambassador to Turkey, **20**.
177n
Baily. *See* Bailey; Baillie; Bailly
Baines. *See* Baynes
Baird, Lady. *See* Dalrymple, Janet
Baird, Mr, of Auchmedden, Aberdeenshire:
Jamesone painting owned by, **40**. 267
Baireuth. *See* Bayreuth
Baisly *or* Beasly, ——, messenger:
(?) sent to Paris for duplicate of lost dis-
patches, **25**. 619
Baize. *See* Bays
Bajazet I (1347–1403), Ottoman sultan:
HW expects another, in chains, **23**. 224
Bajazet II, sultan 1481–1512:
Charles VIII contemporary with, **4**. 243
'Bajazet':
Barthélemy compares headache to that of,
**8**. 201
*Bajazet*. *See under* Racine, Jean
Baker, Mr:
SH visited by, **12**. 249
Baker, David Erskine (1730–67):
*Biographica dramatica*: Broughton a contrib-
utor to, **42**. 3; Henderson saves HW's
scenes from being in. **42**. 5; Mason's polit-
ical activity mentioned in, **29**. 252, 253;
*Mysterious Mother* noted in, **33**. 578n, **42**.
319n; revised by Reed, **43**. 202
Baker, Sir George (d. 1667), Kt:
epitaph of, **2**. 353
Baker, Sir George (1722–1809), M.D.; cr. (1776)
Bt:
Charlotte, Q., scolds, for not telling her of
George III's illness, **25**. 680n
drawing of, by Tyson, **1**. 142
Edgcumbe, Emma Sophia, attended by, **12**.
*134*
George III sent by, to Cheltenham, **34**. 6n
——'s illness declared by, to have ceased, **25**.
682n
HW urges Mary Berry to consult, **12**. 182, 183
Baker, George, collector:
Edwards sends HW's sketch of SH, to, **42**. 71n
Baker, Henry (1698–1774):
HW's sponsor at Antiquarian Society, **13**. 28n
Baker, James ('Sir James of the Peak'):
Gay and Pope use name of, **18**. 317n
(?) HW quotes, **18**. 317–18
Baker, Sir John (d. 1558), chancellor of Ex-
chequer to Q. Mary:
Sissinghurst built by, **35**. 144
Baker, Dr (?John ca 1700–82), physician at
Richmond:

Mann, Galfridus, consults, **20**. 523, 525–6
Baker, Martha (1747–1809), m. (1767) Henry
Swinburne:
Albany, Cts of, visits, **11**. 258
friend of queens, **11**. 258
letter of, from France, not reliable, **11**. 52
Maria Theresa presented Order of La Croix
Étoilée to, **25**. 128
SH visited by, **12**. 226
Baker, Sir Richard (1568–1645), Kt:
*Chronicle of the Kings of England* by: HW
consults, **15**. 83; HW disparages, **20**. 142,
**23**. 21; lists of casualties in, **32**. 76, **33**. 335,
355
George III's reign would be thought well-
omened by, **9**. 313
'Sir Roger de Coverley' reveres, **35**. 562
Baker, Robert:
Twickenham resident, **42**. 485
Baker, Samuel (ca 1712–78), bookseller:
auctions by, **1**. 12n, 172n, **42**. 239n
Baker, Thomas (1656–1740), antiquary:
aid given by, to: Fiddes, **2**. 355; Strype, **2**.
349; Willis, **2**. 351
birth of, **2**. 350
books given by, to St John's College, **2**. 347,
351
Burnet does not support, **2**. 98, 343, 348–9, 350
Cole encloses letter to HW with materials on,
**43**. 66, 77
costume of, **2**. 351–2
Crew's connection with, **2**. 98, 99, 344–6
death of, **2**. 350
Eglisham's pamphlet extracted by, **14**. 133
ejected from fellowship, **2**. 98, 341, 343, 344,
346–7
Ely seldom visited by, **2**. 361
epitaphs by, **2**. 353, 354
Fisher's *Funeral Sermon of Margaret Countess
of Richmond* edited by, **1**. 42–3, **2**. 69n,
341, 353
friendships of, **2**. 348
godfather to Cole's uncle, **2**. 351
HW admires, **2**. 98, 99, 100
HW suggests a life of, **2**. 59
Hearne's books have extracts relating to, **2**.
355–6
'History of the College of St John the Evan-
gelist,' **2**. 53, 56–7, 59–61, 62, 63, 69, 86,
230, 231, 347–8, 349–50
incorporated at Oxford, **2**. 354
Jortin's attack on, **2**. 93, 342, 352–3
King's College records cited by, **1**. *18*
Le Clerc censured by, **2**. 342, 352–3, 361
life of, and comments on, in *Biographia Britannica*, **2**. 71–2, 73, 78, 80, 82, 87–8, 93,
106, 129, 341–4, 346–7, 348, 350, 353
life of, by HW, **2**. 61–2, 63–4, 65, 67, 68–9,
70–3, 75, 82, 87–90, 91, 94–5, 98, 100–1, 102,
103, 104, 106, 107, 118, 129–30, 131, 132–3,
134–5, 137, 138–9, 139–40, 141, 142–3, 144–5,

186n, 226–7, 229, 230, 231–2, 235, 237, 296,
297–8, 358–61, 362, **13**. 51
life of, by Masters, **2**. 63–4, 231
life of, Cole's list of materials for, **2**. 341–57
loyal to James II, **2**. 343, 344–6
MSS of, **1**. 56n, 58, 62, **2**. 349–50
Middleton praises, **2**. 355
not a guest at Wimpole, **2**. 144–5, 361
notes and comments of, on: Erasmus, **2**. 352–
3, 361; Gunning, Bp, **2**. 59–60, 63; *London
Gazettes*, **2**. 130, 344–6; Wood's *Athenæ*, **2**.
348, 353–4; Wyatt, **1**. 269
plate of his portrait, **2**. 354, 361
Prior does not support, **2**. 87–8, 90, 91, 96, 98,
341, 343–4, 361
proposed *Athenæ Cantabrigienses* of, **2**. 98,
114–15, 342, 347–8, 350
*Reflections upon Learning*, **2**. 59, 64, 352,
361, **43**. 66
Strype's letters from, **2**. 144–5, 358
Vertue commissioned to portray, **2**. 144, 352,
361
Watson's correspondence with, **2**. 64, 353
welcome at Wimpole, **2**. 348
Baker, Sir William (1705–70), Kt, 1760; M.P.:
Grenville attacked by, over navy bills, **38**. 307
office refused by, **30**. 201
Pitt criticized by, **21**. 553n
Baker; bakers:
compelled to bake after Leghorn earthquake,
**17**. 304
letter ascribed to, **42**. 504
Penthièvre has, in his entourage, **20**. 466
Baker and Leigh, auctioneers:
Ives's library sold by, **2**. 30n
Baker Holroyd, John (1735–1821), cr. (1781,
1783, and 1802) Bn Sheffield, (1816) E. of
Sheffield; M.P.:
Berry, Mary, identifies, **1**. 353n
French travels of, troubled, **11**. 335
Gibbon's MSS published by, **12**. 99n
Gibbon visited by, at Lausanne, **11**. *335*
Gordon, Lord George, prevented by, from
speaking, **33**. 181
HW cannot satisfy curiosity of, about por-
trait, **42**. 206
light dragoons of, **25**. 34n
Parliamentary motion by, defending North,
**25**. 29n
peerage of, **25**. 433
SH visited by, **12**. 229
ungenerous to Gibbon's memory, **15**. 331
wife of, **11**. 114n, **28**. 447n
Bakewell, Derbyshire:
Haddon Hall near, **42**. 35n
Bakewell (*or* Backwell) family:
Tyringham House the seat of, **41**. 252n
Balaam:
Sainthill compared with, **35**. 30
sword of, **35**. 33
Balagna (Corsica):
Theodore of Corsica's manifesto from, **18**. 158

Balagny, Seigneur de. *See* Monluc, Damien de
Balainvilliers. *See* Bernard de Boulainvilliers
Balam, Anthony (d. 1737):
　HW succeeds, in Customs, **13.** 7n
Balance of power:
　used as excuse for war, **22.** 39
'Balancing Captain':
　ballad about, *see Late Gallant Exploits, The*
Balandino, Eustachius, ensign:
　captured at Velletri, **18.** 493
Balbani, Lucrezia, m. (1759) Marchese Paolino
　Santini:
　name of husband of, corrected, **43.** 275
　Santini to wed, **21.** 293
Balbases; Balbasos. *See* Los Balbasos
Balbastre, Claude-Louis (1729–99), organist;
　clavecin-player:
　brings piano to party, **4.** 452n
　composes airs for Duc and Duchesse de
　　Choiseul, **6.** 115
　to play pianoforte for Mme du Deffand's
　　Christmas party, **6.** 115
Balbe-Berton, Louis-Alexandre-Nolasque-Félix
　(1742–1806), Marquis de Crillon:
　Du Deffand, Mme, corresponds with, **7.** 457,
　　459
　Gibraltar entrenchments left by, with defence
　　army, **25.** 344n
　regiment rejoined by, **7.** 455
　social relations of, in Paris, *see index entries
　　ante* **8.** 234
Balbec. *See* Baalbek
Balbedas, ——, French Revolutionist:
　Barère denounced by, **12.** 86n
Balbi, Comtesse de. *See* Caumont-La Force,
　Anne-Jacobé
Balbi, Anna, m. Giuseppe, Marchese di Brig-
　nole-Sale:
　(?) expected in Florence, **17.** 151
　(?) Francis III admires, **17.** *44*
　(?) HW mentions, **17.** 43
Balbi, Costantino (d. 1740), Doge of Genoa
　1738–40:
　HW calls, 'a dear Doge,' **30.** 1
Balbis-Simeone di Rivera, Giovanni Battista (d.
　1777), Conte; diplomatist:
　Albani's circular letter about Catherine II
　　enrages, **22.** 76
　Austrian ingratitude scorned by, **19.** 312
　Chute and Whithed hear accusations by, **19.**
　　*142*
Balcarres, E. of. *See* Lindsay, Alexander (1752–
　1825)
Balchen, George (d. 1745), Capt., 1740:
　entertained at Florence, **18.** 98, 99
　HW wrongly attributes intimidation of
　　Naples to, **23.** 506
Balchen, Sir John (1670–1744), Kt; naval of-
　ficer:
　expected to defeat Brest squadron off Lisbon,
　　**30.** 69
　Hardy succeeded by, **18.** 458

loss of, on the *Victory*, **18.** 521
Balcony; balconies:
　in Palace Yard, Westminster, **9.** 386
Baldacchino:
　Young Pretender wants, over his theatre
　　boxes, **25.** 536
Baldini, Carlo:
　Mann's annuity and legacy to, **25.** 667n
Baldinotti, P., theologian:
　Clement XIII consults, **23.** 38
Baldinucci, Filippo (ca 1624–96), writer:
　Francavilla's life by, **21.** 479, **22.** 583
　Frederick, P. of Wales, gets works of, **21.** 481,
　　**22.** 583
Baldocci, Signora. *See* Guadagni, Settimia
Baldocci, Nunziato (1696–1767), deputy intro-
　ducer of ambassadors; master of ceremonies:
　Mann informed by, of gala for Joseph II's
　　birthday, **18.** 182
　(?) —— invited by, **18.** 173
　—— will recommend, as grand master of
　　ceremonies and introducer of ambassadors,
　　**18.** 146
　Sassoferrato painting owned by, **18.** *94*
　sister-in-law entertained by, **19.** 461
　Strozzi's deputy, **18.** 146, 182
　Tripoline ambassador escorted by, **20.** 128
Baldung, Hans (?1480–1545), painter:
　altar-piece by, with Howards, **2.** 44
Baldwin, ——:
　name of, as donor, on window in Addington
　　Church, **10.** 343
Baldwin, Ann (fl. 1698–1711), bookseller:
　*Ladies Companion* published by, at the Ox-
　　ford Arms, **9.** 138n
'Baldwin, Sir Charles' (in Chatterton's Rowley
　poems):
　Cole questions, **2.** 104
Baldwin, Henry (ca 1734–1813), printer:
　House of Lords orders arrest of, **23.** 77
　*Yearly Chronicle for 1761*, (?) Montagu men-
　　tions, **9.** 332
Baldwin, John (fl. 1777):
　testimony by, **28.** 288n
Baldwin. *See also* Baldwyn
Baldwins, Great, Stoughton, Hunts; Conyers's
　seat:
　Conyers of, **10.** 76n
Baldwyn *or* Baldwin, Charles (d. after 1775),
　army officer:
　Conway gets ensigncy for, at HW's request,
　　**37.** 431–2, 440
　ensigncy must disappoint dreams by, of
　　riches, **37.** 440–1
Bale, John (1495–1563), Bp of Ossory:
　*Brefe Chronycle* by, misleads HW, **16.** 4n
　'foul-mouthed,' **1.** 273n
　Rowley not mentioned by, **2.** 105, 106
　*Scriptorum illustrium Maioris Brittaniæ*
　　cited, **1.** 16, 250, 262, 273
Bale, Rev. Sackville Spencer (ca 1724–93):
　Oxford servant mistreated by, **19.** 387
Bale. *See also* Bayle

Bâle. *See* Basle

Balf, ——, London printer:
arrested for printing *North Briton*, **38.** 199n
testimony by, **38.** 199n

Balfour, Capt., of the *Bienfaisant*:
Dunn confined by, **38.** 265n

Balfour, Sir James (1600–57) of Denmilne and Kinnaird:
collection of, in Advocates Library, **15.** 86n

Balfour, Mrs William Townley (d. 1789), 'votre Irlandaise':
(?) acts part, to fool HW, **3.** 299, 302
(?) Narbonnes equal to, in provincialism, **4.** 104
(?) social relations of, with Mrs Clive, **3.** 298–9

Balgonie, Lady. *See* Thornton, Jane

Balgonie, Lord. *See* Leslie, Alexander

Balgoony. *See* Balgonie

'Balì, the.' *See* Suares de la Concha, Balì Baldassare

Balie. *See* Baillie

Balincourt, Marquise de. *See* Polignac, Henriette-Zéphyrine de

Balio. *See* Bailo

Baliol, John (d. 1269) and 'Dervorguilla' [Dervigilde]:
prints of, **40.** 236

Baliol College. *See* Balliol College

Balkan Mountains:
Rumiantzev cuts off Grand Vizir's retreat through, **24.** 33

Balkis (Belkis). Q. of Sheba:
Arundel Castle window depicts, **12.** 205n

Ball, Mrs. *See* Hall

Ball (*or* Balle), Thomas (d. 1749):
Edgcumbes visit, at Mamhead, **30.** 66–7
perversity of, **30.** 67

Ball, Rev. Thomas (ca 1734–89), D.D., 1777; rector of Eriswell, Suffolk:
doctor's title prized by. **24.** 293n
HW argues with, over removing E. of Orford, **36.** 118
(?) HW employs, to live with E. of Orford, **16.** 171
Orford hires parsonage of, **24.** 293, **28.** 306n

Ball; balls:
abound when weather is too hot for them, **37.** 352
Adhémar cancels, **39.** 450
after dinner, **5.** 322
after midnight on Mardi Gras, **17.** 311
Aiguillon's, for Mme du Barry, **5.** 324
Albani's, for D. of York, **22.** 234
Amelia, Ps, gives, for Christian VII, **23.** 48
Antinori, Mme, gives, for Eszterházys, **20.** 350
Arnaldi's, **17.** 56
at Aberdeen, **37.** 225
at Almack's, **38.** 512n
at Bath, *see under* Bath
at Bedford House, **9.** 232, 363, **19.** 464, **32.** 7, **35.** 225

at Belturbet, **37.** 336
at Blenheim, **38.** 462
at Buckingham House, **38.** 290
at Carlton House, **9.** 58
at Casa Incontri, **18.** 60, 65
at Chester, for Hertfords, **39.** 18
at Compiègne twice a week, **13.** 178
at Court, **6.** 148, 162, **9.** 406, **22.** 197, **35.** 189
at Dublin, **9.** 400, **37.** 412
at Florence, **18.** 386, **19.** 8, 14, 364, **20.** 219, 464, **22.** 237n, 486, **23.** 458n, **37.** 78; *see also* Ball; balls: masked
at Fontainebleau, **38.** 221
at Gloucester House, **29.** 356
at Hampton Court, **10.** 166
at Hatfield, **33.** 322
at Haymarket, Blackstone's, and Pantheon, **23.** 476n
at Holland House, **37.** 352, **43.** 262
at Kew, **35.** 229
at London Pantheon, **5.** 230, 235, 239
at Naples, **24.** 280n
at Norfolk House, **9.** 338
at Palazzo Vecchio, for newly-wed girls, **22.** 491
at Paris, early because of short carnival, **38.** 477, 485
at Paris Opéra, **4.** 154
at Paris vauxhalls, **38.** 404
at Pisa, **23.** 171, 191, 262, **25.** 581
at Ranelagh, **19.** 265n
at Reggio fair, **13.** 242
at Richmond Castle, for D. of Clarence's birthday, **11.** 342
at St James's, **22.** 197, **32.** 343n
at Siena, for D. of York, **22.** 224, 232
at Sion House, **35.** 330–1
at Soho: opposed by bishops, **23.** 193; subscription, **4.** 371, 375
at Venice, for doge's election, **17.** 76–7
at Versailles, **32.** 254–6, **39.** 244n, 256
(?) at Villa Patrizi, Rome, **37.** 63
at Welbeck, **35.** 330
at Windsor: on P. of Wales's birthday, **29.** 149, **32.** 316n; young men refuse invitations to, **11.** 329–30

Aylesford, Lady, gives, **33.** 283

Bardi's, **18.** 60

Bath Knights give: at Haymarket, **39.** 322; at installation, **23.** 414

Beaufort's, in Paris, **22.** 365

Beckford gives, for Opposition, **23.** 200

Bedford's, **37.** 54

Bedford, Ds of, asks HW to give, at SH, **38.** 335

—— enjoys, at 5 A.M., **33.** 477

—— gives, **19.** 464

Bolton's, for D. and Ds of Gloucester, **7.** 212, **25.** 22

Boodles Club's, at Ranelagh, for George III's recovery, **39.** 465n

Boothby, Mrs, gives, **17.** 278

[Ball; balls, *continued*]

Borghese and Corsini give, to D. of York at Rome, 22. 229

Boyle Walsingham, Mrs, gives, at Thames Ditton, 35. 391

Bridgwater's, 21. 278

Brodrick's, 10. 14

Capello, Signora, gives, at Rome, 37. 324

Caraman's, at Roissy, 32. 260

Cardigan, Cts of, gives, 36. 41, 38. 357

Carmarthen gives, at Beverley, 28. 471

Charlotte, Q., gives: for Augusta and P. of Brunswick, 22. 197; for P. of Wales, 29. 108

——'s, exclusive, 33. 325

——'s birthday, 32. 343n, 39. 274

Chartres's, weekly, 38. 505

children's, 7. 442

Chudleigh, Elizabeth gives, 10. 73, 75, 76, 35. 299–301, 38. 203–5

Clarence, D. of, gives, at Almack's, 39. 465n

Clement XIII allows, for D. of York, 22. 229

Conway and others to give, 37. 50

Conway does not envy HW's, 37. 358

——'s aversion to, 37. 232, 358

corn-factor at Twickenham gives, 33. 298

Corsi's, 17. 122, 137, 20. 350

Corsini's, 25. 50

Cossé, Duchesse de, gives, 6. 162

costume: 3. 217, 5. 179, 6. 148, 154, 32. 102, 110–12; popular in England, 5. 348

Court: at Versailles under Richelieu's care, 38. 465; quadrilles at, 6. 148

Cowper's, 22. 393, 23. 64

Craons', 17. 56, 416

Croÿ prepares, at Calais, 38. 211

Cumberland, Henry, D. of, gives, 23. 351

Cumberland, William, D. of, gives, 9. 38, 42, 19. 234n, 37. 276

Dal Borgo's, 18. 84–5

Danish, masked, 23. 373n

Delci's, 18. 60

Del Campo's, at Ranelagh, for Q. Charlotte, 39. 465n

Devonshire, Ds of, does not dance at, when pregnant, 36. 233n

Dick gives, at Leghorn, for D. of York, 22. 221

*di giuoco*, 18. 60

Du Châtelet's, at Leghorn, 18. 78

during Florentine carnival, 13. 201, 19. 8, 364, 20. 219, 464, 22. 486

Egmont, Comtesse d', gives, at Versailles, 38. 505

Englefield, Lady, sees Berrys at, 12. 46

English, do not interest Mme du Deffand, 6. 190

Essex, Cts of, gives, for D. of York, 21. 54

Estrées, Maréchale de, may give, for Karl Wilhelm Ferdinand, 30. 220

Ferdinand of Naples gives, at Caserta, 23. 191

Florentine academy gives, for Francis I's election, 19. 115

Fontainebleau lacks, 38. 451

for Christian VII, 4. 154, 159, 35. 407

for Churchill, Mary, 5. 26–7

for George II's birthday, 17. 176, 183, 185, 18. 95n, 37. 113, 116

for George III's birthday, 23. 125–6, 25. 284

formal, at Florence, 13. 234

for Maximilian, Archduke, 6. 148

for P. and Ps of Brunswick, 31. 57

for Q. Caroline at Sir Robert Walpole's Chelsea house, 15. 333

Fox, Henry, gives, 19. 397, 37. 352

French officers shoot holes in hats to show off at, 20. 159

Furnese, Lady Anne, gives, 35. 80

George III declares, are private functions, 23. 126

—— gives, for Christian VII, 23. 57

——'s, for wedding, 21. 525, 531

George IV entertained at, 36. 232

——'s, 25. 476

Gloucester, D. of, frequents, 21. 67

—— to have been entertained at, in Pisa, 23. 357

Granville's, 37. 352

Granville, Cts, to give, 18. 565

Guines's, 5. 348, 32. 96, 100, 101–2, 106, 109–12, 33. 256

HW attends, 5. 230, 235, 239, 7. 300, 25. 22, 32. 115, 33. 171, 285, 35. 213, 299, 37. 63

HW expects no more, till the French have landed, 39. 331

HW has not danced at, 37. 352

HW's, for nieces, 28. 445–8

HW to leave, before supper, 25. 22

HW will miss, unless he reaches Paris before Lent, 38. 505

Harley to give, for Christian VII, 23. 57–8

Hertford gives, for P. of Wales, 33. 565, 39. 447, 449

—— introduces English visitors to, in Paris, 38. 222

—— unable to give, 38. 337

Hobart, Mrs, gives, 33. 285–6

Holdernesse's, 32. 89, 35. 162, 213

hours of, 3. 219, 4. 409, 415, 6. 265

in Haymarket theatre, 37. 50, 54

in honour of Artois's marriage, 5. 421, 425

in London: 17. 331, 19. 464, 25. 502, 32. 192, 35. 407; plentiful, 38. 379

in Paris: 13. 171; frequent, 38. 337; masked, end at carnival, 38. 514

Italian opera subscribers to have, 10. 138

Keppel's election celebrated by, at Chichester, 39. 80

Ladies Club gives, 32. 89, 232

ladies to dance barefoot at, 37. 412

La Luzerne's, for Q. Charlotte, 39. 465

Leopold attends, 22. 486, 23. 171

Lord Mayor's, 17. 183, 185, 208, 23. 200

Lorenzi to give, for prince's birth, 20. 191, 276

Louis XV's, for Dauphin's marriage, 4. 409–11

Louis XV should let Richelieu give, 38. 469

Lucchese minister at Florence to give, for D. of York, **22.** 171

Mann frequents, **17.** 25

—— gives: at his investiture, **23.** 60, 63; for Vorontsovs, **22.** 204

——'s servants forbidden to go to, after his death, **25.** 670

Marie-Antoinette's, **4.** 488, **6.** 142, 154

Martelli, Signora, gives, **18.** 435, 438

masked, **4.** 371, 375, **5.** 348, 421, 427, **7.** 29, 145, 300, **19.** 265n, 398, 464, **22.** 237n, **23.** 353, 373n, 456, 458n, 476n, **25.** 50, 645, **32.** 256, **38.** 505, 514, **39.** 256; HW fond of, **38.** 505

Massereene's, in Paris, **30.** 211

Mercy-Argenteau's, **4.** 409, 415

Milton's, **38.** 295

Mirepoix may give, **20.** 117

modern Camillus now to be found at, **24.** 86

Monaco, P. of, gives, **4.** 159

mothers attend daughters at, **28.** 403

mourning prevents, at Dublin Castle, **39.** 49

Niccolini to give, for D. of York, **22.** 171

Norfolk, D. and Ds of, give, **37.** 50, 55, 352, 454

officers give, in Via della Pergola, for Francis I's election, **19.** 115

old woman describes, of Charles II's time, **37.** 55

Orlandini to give, **18.** 435, 438

Orléans, D. of, gives, **4.** 154

Ossory, Lady, attends, but not HW, **33.** 222

—— gives, **33.** 571

Panciatichi's house unsuitable for, **17.** 122

Parliament and war do not disturb, **20.** 469

Petersham, Lady Caroline, gives, **35.** 223

Pitt, Anne, gives, **24.** 16, **32.** 48, 52, **38.** 335, 475–6

Pitt, George, gives, **20.** 367

Poix's, **7.** 113

politics less dignified than, **21.** 542

politics replaced by, **23** 476

postponed at Rome till after Easter, **23.** 95

private, at Court, **38.** 143

public: at Minorca, **37.** 311; Tylney to give, at Naples, **24.** 280–1

Queensberry, Ds of, gives, **19.** 28, **20.** 226, 235–6, **23.** 299, **38.** 341, 342–3

Riccardi, Cosimo, forbids, **17.** 122

—— gives, **17.** 164

Riccardi's, for Archduke and Archduchess, **25.** 51

Richecourt gives, **20.** 432

Richmond, Ds of, to give, **18.** 442

Richmond, D. of, gives, **21.** 67

Ridolfi's, **18.** 60

Rinaldi's, **18.** 85

Robinson, Sir Thomas, gives, **17.** 174, 183–4, 208, 221–2, **37.** 55, 113–15

Rochford, Cts of, gives, **21.** 57

Russians give, at Pisa, **24.** 84n

Sandwich gives, for D. of Cumberland, **20.** 121–2

Santa Croce's, **17.** 20

Selwyn, John, should not be allowed at, **37.** 56

servants', **9.** 295

Shannon, Lady, gives, **19.** 398n

Soubise said to attend, on eve of battle, **22.** 47n

Stanhope, Sir William, gives, **19.** 485

Strozzi's, **18.** 60

Suares, Mme, to give, **17.** 56

subscription: at Carlisle House for P. of Brunswick, **38.** 289, 291, 296; masquerade, **4.** 371, 375; Pantheon, **24.** 481; Ranelagh, **18.** 464; Theresa Cornelys's, **23.** 271

suppers followed by, **35.** 213

Susa gives, for English captains, **18.** 360

Tempi's, **18.** 435, 438

Townshend, Vcts, gives, **19.** 18

Tylney's: at Naples, **24.** 280–1; at Wanstead, **21.** 417

Villars's, at country house, **22.** 553

violinist at, **34.** 173

Viry's, masked, **32.** 256

Wales, P. of (George IV), gives, **25.** 476

Wales, Ps of, gives, **10.** 186

Wolsey's, masked, **42.** 421

York, Edward, D. of, frequents, **21.** 67

—— gives: at Cherbourg, **21.** 232; for Ps Amelia, **22.** 270, **38.** 475, 476; in London, **38.** 94

York, Frederick, D. of, gives, **34.** 8n

Young Pretender's, quiet, to amuse daughter, **25.** 549n

See also Masquerade

Ball; balls (projectile):

Conway and D. of Cumberland struck by spent, **37.** 191

Ball (spheroid):

blue, Cappello family probably add, to arms, after Medici alliance, **20.** 415

Italian game of, called *calcio*, **22.** 423

See also Cannon ball; Tennis ball

Ballad; ballads:

against E. of Bath, **18.** 71–5, 90–1

against Ps of Wales, **23.** 217

at Vauxhall, **33.** 501

Bubb Dodington's, on Mrs Strawbridge, **33.** 556, **34.** 262–3

collection of, from Queen Anne's time, **32.** 200

Dalrymple plans collection of, **15.** 63

Estcourt's, on D. of Marlborough, **33.** 215

Frederick, P. of Wales, makes, **19.** 44–6

French fondness for, **25.** 373

George II attacked in, **17.** 187–9

——'s dismissal of Sir Robert Walpole attacked in, **19.** 80–4

gondoliers sing, in Venice, **20.** 177

HW does not understand, **30.** 124

HW has not seen, **38.** 187

HW recommends, to ridicule French Revolution, **15.** 232

HW's, Conway refers to, **37.** 72

HW sends, to Selwyn, **30.** 124

illustrations to, **17.** 358

[Ballad; ballads, *continued*]
in Ireland: on Sackville family and Stone, 20. 316; tolerable, 37. 450
Jacobite, 18. 356
Lyttelton's, to Delia, 33. 501
Montagu to sing, 10. 191
Montagu, Lady Mary Wortley, writes, on Arthur Grey and Mrs Murray, 34. 256, 259
'O Bessy Bell and Mary Gray,' 12. 147, 153
on HW and Maclaine, 20. 188
on Joseph and Mary, 32. 330
on Lord Hervey's wedding to Mary Lepell, 34. 256
on quadrille, 32. 96
on Queen Eleanor, 32. 348
Opposition too dull to produce, 22. 110
Percy's collection of, 1. 89–90, 92, 15. 106; *see also* Percy, Thomas: *Reliques*
Pulteney (E. of Bath), repeats, 35. 94
——'s, parodying Newcastle's speech, 19. 106
Rowe's, on Mrs Strawbridge, 35. 237
satirical, in Paris, 32. 49
Scotch, Methodists sing hymns to tunes of, 35. 118
sung at Vauxhall and Mary-le-Bone, 39. 182
to Duc de Chartres, 33. 45–6
Walpole, Sir Robert, sings, 18. 68
Wharton's, 42. 10
yacht captain demands, 17. 141
*See also* 'Chevy Chace'; 'Christ's Kirk of the Green'; 'Dragon of Wantley'; 'Henry and Emma'; 'Phoebe is Gone'; 'Queen Eleanor's Confession'; 'Rising in the North'; 'Vicar of Bray'; 'Wind in the East'
'Ballad of Lady Hounsibelle and Lord Lovel': HW sends, to Percy, 40. 374–6
'Ballad on Quadrille, A.' *See under* Gay, John
Ballenden *or* Ballandine. *See* Bellenden
Ballet; ballets:
at French Court, 6. 148, 157
Hilverding, maître de, 19. 293n
in Buckingham's *Rehearsal*, 35. 213
Noverre's, 35. 363n
*Ballet de la Paix*:
HW sees, in Paris, 18. 495–6
Ballintate, co. Armagh:
Synnot of. 12. 88n
Balliol College, Oxford:
HW admires windows at, 9. 289n
Parker fellow of, 15. 298
Savage's history of, 2. 231
Balloch, Scotland:
hall and dais chamber of, 40. 265
Balloon; balloons:
'aerial Quixotes,' 33. 447
'a sort of folly' HW does not admire, 33. 467
astronomical observations may be made by, 25. 614
Blanchard's, visible, 35. 631, 632, 39. 423–4
'Brobdignag kites,' 33. 446
Channel crossed by, 33. 458–9
Chartres, Duc de, ascends in, 25. 517

Deeker, maker of, 25. 596n
England gets rage for, from France, 25. 449
Fitzpatrick's ascent in, 25. 591, 33. 468, 469, 474
France may try to annihilate English Channel with, 25. 590
French, perishable, 11. 128
French dancer's daughter makes ascent in, 25. 575
guinea charged for sightseers for, 25. 528
HW imagines aerial warfare by, 39. 425n
HW jokes about French invasion arriving in, 12. 27
HW jokes about future newspaper references to, 39. 425
HW mentions, 11. 233, 355, 12. 85
HW might send Jerningham home in, 42. 109–10
HW sees, 25. 579, 35. 631, 632, 39. 418–19, 423–4
HW's reflections on, 25. 527–8, 579, 590, 591, 33. 446–7, 458–9, 467–8, 39. 425
HW would prefer, to packet-boat, 33. 459
human passions form, 25. 532
inflammable air in, 33. 475
life seldom risked in, 39. 419
Louis XVI orders statues made of pioneers in, 25. 450
Lunardi's profits from, 25. 543
Lunardi the first to ascend in, in England, 25. 528
Mann considers, puerile amusements, 25. 593
Necker a 'great air-balloon,' 34. 73
Orford, E. of, encourages ascent in, 25. 596
Pilâtre's fatal accident in, 25. 590, 593, 596, 33. 467, 468
popularity of, 25. 449, 517, 543, 596, 35. 381
post offices might be settled in, in the air, 42. 176
prohibited in Florence for fear of igniting the town, 25. 593
Robert brothers to cross Channel in, 25. 517n
Sadler's flights in, 25. 579, 591
ships may be replaced by, 39. 425
Stockholm Castle imitated in, at Paris, for Gustav III, 39. 419
topic of, exhausted, 35. 384
Windham ascends in, 25. 579
Ballot:
HW opens, at Mme du Deffand's, 7. 320
Bally. *See* Baylies
Ballymoyer, co. Armagh:
Synnot of, 12. 88n, 124n
Balmerinoch (Balmerino), Bn. *See* Elphinstone, Arthur (1688–1746); Elphinstone, James (1675–1746)
Balmerinoch, Bns. *See* Chalmers, Margaret
*Balneum mariæ*:
Du Deffand, Mme, asks meaning of, 3. 187
Balsam; balsams:
Friar's, used for Mary Berry's injured nose, 11. 243

monks of St Mark make, **18.** 177n

Balsamo, Giuseppe (1743–95), self-styled Conte Alessandro di Cagliostro:
discussion of, spoils conversation, **31.** 242
England entertained by stories of Rohan and, **36.** 236, 238
Ferdinand, P., believed in, **33.** 508
Fitzgerald might employ, to raise the dead, **25.** 639–40
HW could not be resuscitated by, **33.** 507
Loutherbourg believes in, **34.** 51n
Marie-Antoinette accused of persecuting, **39.** 451n
*mémoire* about, **25.** 631
released instead of being punished and imprisoned, **25.** 653n, 654
Soubise supposedly cured by, **33.** 507n

Balthazar, K. of Cofano:
Mead acquires painting of, **37.** 67
Radicofani the shrine of, **37.** 66–7, 73

Baltic Sea:
England may send fleet to, to sustain Danzig's freedom of trade, **23.** 466n
English pursue Dutch fleet to, **25.** 311
English rich ships from, arrive, **25.** 320
English ships to be sent to, **11.** 227, **23.** 401n
Milbanke's squadron returns from, **35.** 521
neutrality in, **39.** 369n
Pitt might like to send squadron to, **10.** 39

Baltimore, Bn. *See* Calvert, Charles (1699–1751); Calvert, Frederick (1731–71)
Baltimore, Bns. *See* Egerton, Lady Diana
*Baltimore*, English ship:
American news brought by, from Halifax to Portsmouth, **37.** 501n
French ships engaged by, **37.** 246
Owen, Capt., arrives from Halifax in, **21.** 130n

Balue. *See* Magon de la Balue

Balustrade:
to Hinchingbrooke stairs, **40.** 283

Balzac, Jean-Louis Guez de (ca 1597–1654), writer:
'Messieurs ses livres,' **32.** 372
neighbour's compliment to, **32.** 372

Balzac d'Entraigues, Catherine-Henriette de (1579–1633), Marquise de Verneuil; Henri IV's mistress:
Doumenil has portrait of, **7.** 313

Bambara:
Capona abbess dreams of playing, **20.** 429

Bamberg, Bp of. *See* Seinsheim, Adam Friedrich von (d. 1779)

Bamberg (Germany):
Henry, P., captures, **21.** 294n

Bambi *or* Bamdi, Michele; Mann's cook:
dinner at Meggitt's inn dressed by, for D. and Ds of Cumberland, **25.** 644
Mann's annuity to, **25.** 667n

Bamffe. *See* Banff

Bampfylde, Sir Richard Warwick (1722–76), 4th Bt; M.P.:

Devonshire electors instruct, to oppose Cider Tax, **38.** 459n
peerage rumoured for, **38.** 326, 328

Bampton, Oxon:
Amphlett vicar of, **13.** 173n

Banbury, E. of. *See* Knollys, Thomas Woods (1727–93); Knollys, William (1547–1632)

Banbury, Oxon:
Buccleuchs and Montagu see play at, **10.** 266
chimney-piece from Steane said to be at, **9.** 156
election at, North and Montagu to attend, **10.** 256, **43.** 135
Miller's chimney-piece at, **43.** 118
North the representative of, **24.** 187
—— to get jobs for constituents at, **9.** 262
postage from, **10.** 251n

Banbury Castle:
capture of, **2.** 76n

Bancal des Issards, Jean-Henri (1750–1826):
named commissioner, **12.** 1n

Bance, John (ca 1694–1755), M.P.:
bank directorship of, corrected, **43.** 245
voted for, as commissioner, **17.** 437

Banchi, Via de', at Florence:
Giambologna's 'Hercules' at junction of, **22.** 124n

Bancroft, Edward, Deane's secretary:
British agent who sent American-French treaties to England, **24.** 355n

Bancroft, Richard (1544–1610), Abp of Canterbury:
epitaph on, **35.** 26

Bancroft, Rev. Thomas, of Chester:
Shrewsbury's portrait owned by, **42.** 313n

Band; bands (costume):
clerical, Kent, E. of, wears, **10.** 338
Niccoli wears, **19.** 49
red, of Anglo-Indian clergyman, **28.** 63

Band; bands (instrumental):
regimental, of Cheshire militia, plays at Pantheon, **24.** 481n

Bandage; bandages:
after cataract operation, **41.** 110n
English troops lack, in America, **41.** 313

Bandalore, toy:
Englefield plays with, **11.** 114–15
HW wonders, whether Turkish or Moorish, **11.** 115

Bandbox; bandboxes:
clandestine letter put in, **35.** 230
embroidered linings for, **35.** 36
murdered infant thrown into pond in, **37.** 179n
(?) riddle about, **28.** 102–3n
tax on, proposed, **35.** 36

*Bande. See* Militia

Bandi, Giancarlo (1700–84), Bp of Imola 1752–84:
(?) Pius VI writes to, **24.** 107

Bandi, Giulia, m. Francesco Braschi, grandmother of Pius VI:
(?) consumed by internal fire, **24.** 467

Bandini, Alessandro (fl. 1743–53), cr. (1753) Marchese; postmaster:
    Old Pretender's underling escorted by, through Tuscany, 18. 380, 389
Bandini, Angelo Maria (1726–1803), canon; librarian:
    Ἐπιθαλάμιον by, 18. 510, 521–2, 545, 43. 255
*Banditti, The,* opera:
    opening of, postponed because of *Count of Narbonne,* 41. 464n
Banditti:
    deserting soldiers form body of, 13. 221
    in Houghton cottages, 39. 172
    Monte Santa Maria inhabited by, 20. 424, 428
    Papal States infested by, 17. 29n
Band of Pensioners, *See* Yeomen of the Guard
Banff, Bn. *See* Ogilvy, Alexander
Banff (Scotland):
    minister of, doubts antiquity of Ossian, 29. 37
    St Andrew's chapel at, 29. 37n
Bangalore, India:
    Cornwallis captures, 11. 350
Bangor, Bp. of. *See* Caducanus (d. 1241); Ewer, John (d. 1774); Herring, Thomas (1693–1757); Hoadly, Benjamin (1676–1761); Hutton, Matthew (1693–1758); Moore, John (1730–1805); Pearce, Zachary (1690–1774); Sherlock, Thomas (1678–1761); Warren, John (1730–1800)
Bangor, co. Carnarvon:
    Hughes of, 16. 181n
    letter postmarked at, 41. 160n
Bangorian controversy:
    Hoadly causes, 2. 291
Banian:
    worn by dancers in quadrille, 32. 116
*Banishment of Cicero. See under* Cumberland, Richard
Bank; banks:
    cost of building, in London, 23. 210
    Cowper's plate and jewels deposited in, in England, 23. 449
    failures of, at Bath and Bristol, 31. 382, 384
    Florentine, seizure of, feared, 17. 239
    Hertford does not use Selwin's and Foley's in Paris, 31. 32
    modern, unknown to Greeks and Romans, 15. 49
    plate kept in, 23. 449, 25. 561
    Scottish, fail, 23. 498
    Spanish officers deposit effects in, 17. 427
    *See also* Banker; Banking; Bank of England; Bankruptcy; Currency; Stocks
Bank-bills:
    discarded at Newmarket, 20. 53
    Order of the Bath revived as succedaneum to, 22. 381
    Ponsonby gambles with, 21. 7
Banker; bankers:
    at Bologna, 17. 228
    at Paris, HW uses Foley as, 40. 387; *see also under names, below, of bankers*
    bankruptcies of, 23. 418
    Cowper's at Florence, to receive plate, 25. 661
    Craven, Lady, does not name, for her address, 42. 176
    for faro, in Paris, 38. 398
    HW's, *see* Crofts, Devaynes, Dawes, & Noble
    HW to put E. of Orford's funds in hands of, 36. 94
    Italian dancers and singers hired through, 17. 191
    Mann's: in Florence, *see* Orsi, Donato and Giusto; in London, *see* Croft, Richard
    Paris hotel taken by, for D. of York, 38. 440
    Portuguese, at Rome, *see* Rosa, Lopez
    *See also* Alexander, Alexandre; Backwell, Messrs; Belloni, Girolamo; Biddulph, Francis; Busoni; Cantillon, Richard; Cocks, James; Cocks, Thomas Somers; Colebrooke, James; Compagni and Libri; Croft, Richard (d. 1793); Foley, Sir Robert Ralph; Fordyce, Alexander; Hoare, Henry; Ironside, Edward; Knight, Robert; Le Gros and Le Cras; Mazzoli; Minores and Boldero; Neal, James, Fordyce, and Down; Orsi, Donato and Giusto; Panchaud, Isaac; Sassi; Selwin, Charles; Waters, John; Wolters, Dirk
Bankes, Henry (1700–76), M.P.:
    commissioner of customs, 24. 177n, 41. 327
Bankes, Henry (1756–1834), M.P.:
    North opposed by, in debate over East India Co., 39. 380–1
Bankes, Mrs William. *See* Meredith, Elizabeth
Bankes. *See also* Banks
Banking:
    foreign exchange, 1. 97, 98
Bank-notes:
    for five pounds, to be issued, 23. 498
    HW keeps, at Arlington St, 23. 284
    Rudd, Mrs, gives, to mercer, 24. 153–4
    Scots issue, 23. 419
    Townshend, Vcts, robbed of, by her servants, 30. 224
Bank of England:
    currency regulated by, 23. 498n
    directors of, 17. 411, 22. 279n
    endangered, 19. 186
    Gordon rioters at, 29. 56, 57n, 58, 33. 187–8, 191, 35. 354
    Scots provoke, by issuing own bank-notes, 23. 418–19
    Scottish finance regulated by, 23. 420
    specie brought to, from France, 11. 350
    stock of, 21. 74n, 497n, 22. 38n
    Temple says John the Painter was to set fire to, 28. 287
    Walpole, Hon. Thomas, appeals to, for allowance, 36. 204n
    Wilkes safeguards, 25. 63n
*Bankrupt, The. See under* Foote, Samuel

Bankruptcy; bankruptcies:
  Cole's tenant's, 1. 15, 213
  Conway expects, 37. 113
  in England, 17. 296n, 23. 418–19, 420, 426, 455, 35. 378
  in Florence, 17. 61–2, 65–6, 413n
  Jones's, 2. 35
  Raynal's *Histoire* tells how to make, 39. 167
  Terray dispenses, 39. 144
  war will produce, in France, 21. 122–3
Banks, Capt.:
  HW mentions, 21. 263
  (?) Northampton's steward, 21. 272
Banks, Lady. *See* Hugessen, Dorothy
Banks, Miss:
  sister of Sir Joseph Banks, 16. 381n
Banks, John (ca 1653–1706), playwright:
  *Albion Queens, The*, Mrs Porter acts in, 13. 96
  biographical information on, 43. 175, 243
  *Earl of Essex, The*, imitations of, 41. 293–4
  *Unhappy Favourite, The*, Frederick, P. of Wales requests, 17. 336; HW wants, 36. 2; plays based on, 41. 293–4n
Banks, John (1709–51):
  Prior's works dedicated by, to Oxford, 13. 187n
  supposed editor of *Old England*, 13. 18n
Banks, Sir Joseph (1744–1820), cr. (1781) Bt:
  as secretary to Dilettanti society, can distribute Knight's book only by society's order, 42. 193n
  Beriea discovered by, 31. 162
  birth date of, corrected, 43. 59, 220
  Blagden friend of, 11. 275n
  Cook sails with, in *Endeavour*, 32. 111n, 122n, 127n
  disbelieves in Ireland's MSS, 15. 321
  Edward IV's hair given by, to HW, 11. 6n
  forgotten, 24. 21
  George III informs, of plan to return to Cheltenham, 34. 47
  HW called on by, 16. 295
  HW dines with, 32. 122
  HW informs, of portraits of Mary, Q. of Scots, 42. 320–2
  HW's correspondence with, 16. 294, 42. 193–5, 212–13, 320–2
  HW sneers at explorations of, 23. 436n, 25. 451
  HW tells: to ask Knight for print of Ceres, 42. 193–4; to thank Knight and Dilettanti for book, 42. 194
  HW visits, 11. 214
  HW writes to, in Pinkerton's behalf, 16. 294, 42. 212–13
  Hamilton gives *Collection of Engravings* to, 35. 442n
  ——'s letters to, on Vesuvius, 33. 509n
  Hawksworth receives £1000 from, for book about voyage, 28. 86
  Iceland visited by, 23. 436n, 29. 31n

inscription by, 29. 340n
list of subscribers includes, 29. 322n
literary receptions of, 11. 153n, 214
Lort and HW meet at house of, 16. 202
Lysons, S., accompanies, to Kew, 12. 198
Pacific islands exposed by, 39. 459
Pennant's *Tour* has contributions by, 1. 329, 336
Pinkerton's correspondence with, 16. 326n
Pinkerton to receive compliments of, 16. 381n
Solander accompanies, 11. 12n
SH visited by, 12. 226, 243
travels of, 32. 127, 33. 361
voyages of, 2. 225
Banks, Margaret Eleanor ('Peggy') (d. 1793), m. (1757) Hon. Henry Grenville:
  (?) at Chesterfield's assembly, 37. 327
  Berry, Mary, identifies, 11. 128n
  Berrys attend party of, 11. 2
  Chute's town house coveted by, 35. 105
  Clifford St house selected by, 35. 108
  (?) Conway visited by, at Park Place, 37. 380
  correspondence of, 6. 231
  Craufurd to bring, to Mme du Deffand, 6. 225, 410
  Cumberland, D. of, gives ball for, 9. 38, 42, 19. 234n
  Du Deffand, Mme, drops, 6. 254, 271, 282
  —— sends package through, 6. 239
  ——'s opinion of, 6. 226, 235
  forehead of, bare, 9. 82
  HW accompanies, to theatre, 7. 347
  HW asks, about bandalore, 11. 115
  HW's social relations with, 11. 48, 88, 128, 187, 317, 39. 259
  HW's verses mention, 20. 141
  Leroy to be near, 6. 228
  Mann encloses letter to, 23. 38
  Montagu, D. of, adds couplet concerning, to HW's *Beauties*, 30, 329n
  —— in love with, 30. 101n, 329n
  —— protests absence of, from HW's *Beauties*, 9. 38n
  Nancy acquaintances of, 6. 254
  Orford, Cts of, and Wray thank, after conversation at opera, 19. 234
  Paris visited by, 6. 225, 226, 235, 239, 254, 276, 282, 30. 264, 39. 259
  sings at Richmond's fireworks, 9. 81
  social relations of, in Paris, *see index entries ante* 8. 234
  SH visited by, 12. 235
  SH visitors sent by, 12. 240
  unacquainted in Paris, 6. 254
  Vauxhall scene of ball given for, 9. 42
  Viry, Mme de, entertains, in Paris, 39. 259
Banks, Robert. *See* Hodgkinson, Robert
Banks, Thomas (1735–1805), sculptor:
  SH visited by, 12. 236
Banks. *See also* Bankes
Bankside, Southwark:
  brothels licensed in, 1. 137n

Banner; banners:
blue, in Gordon riots, **33.** 177
George II's, at Garter ceremony, **22.** 79n
of Santa Maria and St Antonio, at Pisa festival, **20.** 473
Bannerman, Alexander (fl. 1762–72), engraver:
Cole asked to supervise, **1.** 212
HW displeased with, **14.** 188, 190, **15.** 133n
prints made by, for HW, **15.** 96n, **43.** 188
proposal of, **1.** 246, 247
(?) SH visited by, **12.** 225, 241
(?) SH visitors sent by, **12.** 227
to work on *Anecdotes* vol. iv, **1.** 198, 201, 203, 207, 210
Walker's portrait of Lambert engraved by, **42.** 280n
Bannister, Henrietta Maria (1750–96), m. (1771), Brownlow North:
foreigners entertained by, at Farnham Castle, **39.** 449
takes three hours to undress, **28.** 391
Bannister, Mrs James. *See* Seton, Barbara Cecilia
Bannister, John (1760–1836), actor:
*Children in the Wood, The,* performed by, **12.** 78
HW's favourite, **12.** 78
*No Song, No Supper* acted by, **12.** 78–9
Bannockburn:
rebel army assembles for battle at, **19.** 201n
Young Pretender's amour at, **25.** 512n
Banns:
reading of, before marriages, **37.** 361
Banquet; banquets:
at Cambridge, for Newcastle's installation, **20.** 71, 83
at Versailles, for Ps of Piedmont's wedding, **39.** 256
city, in London, attended by Wilkes, **23.** 208
for Bath installation, **23.** 341
for Mozzi's wedding, **25.** 535
London to give, for Keppel, **24.** 445
Stanhope, Lord, to give, on Bastille Day, **11.** 89
Viry's, for Ps of Piedmont's wedding, **39.** 256
Banqueting House, Whitehall, London:
Van Dyck's project for painting at, **9.** 223
Banqueting house in garden:
Wood's house compared with, **31.** 136
Bantam, king of:
England might be bolstered by support from, **33.** 60
Montagu compares self to, **10.** 188
Pitt compared with, by HW, **10.** 153
Bantam; bantams. *See under* Poultry
Banti, Mme. *See* Georgi, Brigitta
Banti, Zaccaria, dancer:
wife of, **12.** 99n
Bantry Bay:
French ships in, flee, **34.** 228
Baptism; baptisms:
Corsi's, **20.** 432
Cowper's, **24.** 199, 206, 209, 219, 238–9

Florentine, Lorenzi's greatest treat, **20.** 92
French abbé's, with rose water, **17.** 62–3
George III seldom attends, in person, **24.** 199
George IV's: anticipated, **32.** 8; performed, **38.** 171, 174, 180–1
HW attends frequently, **11.** 264
HW unable to attend Lady Maria Waldegrave's, **33.** 416
illegitimacy mitigated by, **43.** 365
Mann to be George III's proxy at, **24.** 199, 206, 209, 219, 238–9
of Catharine Mann, **18.** 31
of George Seymour-Conway, **38.** 209
of Henry Frederick, D. of Cumberland, **19.** 174
of P. William of Gloucester, **36.** 115–16
of Townshend, Thomas Charles, **37.** 550, 553
of Walpole, Horatio (1783–1858), **25.** 418
Panciatichi's, **18.** 121
Poussin depicts, **33.** 539
Rinuccini child's, **17.** 417
Seymour-Conway, Lady Isabel Rachel, absent at start of, **37.** 428, 430
Sophia of Gloucester's, **32.** 129–30
Townshend, T.C., has three godfathers, **37.** 550
Vossius on, **33.** 494
William V's, **37.** 283
Baptiste, flower painter (fl. ca 1683):
flower pieces by, at Boughton House, **10.** 341
Baptistery, gates of, at Florence:
Patch's engravings of, **23.** 429–30, 435
Bar, D. of. *See* René I
Bar, Confederacy of:
Young Pretender may head, **5.** 111
Bar, duchy of:
Stanislas I rules, **7.** 356n
*Bara* (litter for dead bodies):
Salimbeni carried in, **17.** 116
Barabbas:
Gordon, Lord George, called, **34.** 76
Barail. *See* Du Barail
Barailh, ——, French naval officer:
Brest fleet under, to cover Dunkirk crossing, **18.** 398n
(?) Conway to settle cartel with, **21.** 261n
Baral, Mlle du. *See* Barral, Louise-Françoise de
Baralipton:
'rude rumbling' of, **35.** 575
Barataria. *See under* Cervantes
*Baratariana:*
(?) dinner in, **33.** 73
Grattan's 'Character' of Chatham in, **32.** 177–8, 179
Baratynski, Russian army sergeant:
plot exposed by, **23.** 440n
Barazza, Signore, Roman merchant:
formerly English, rents lodging at Rome to D. of York, **22.** 228n
Barb; barbs. *See* Horse: Barbary
Barba, Alvaro Alonso (fl. 1640), metallurgist; curate:
*Arte de los metales,* Sandwich translates, **16.** 6

Barbados:

Brest fleet, may sail to, **18**. 382

Codrington's estates on, **35**. 178

Cuninghame's misconduct at, **33**. 265n, 357n

Frere of, **30**. 76n

governor of, vindicated, **33**. 357

Grenville governor of, **11**. 2n, **13**. 19n

hurricane in: **29**. 90; benefit for sufferers from, **25**. 134; devastation from, **33**. 259, 263, 265; slaves witness casualties caused by, **25**. 109

Robinson made governor of, **17**. 301

——'s friends unlikely to accept invitations to, **37**. 127

Robinson, Lady, 'ironmongress' from, **9**. 140

Selwyn clerk of the Crown and peace, and registrar of Court of Chancery at, **30**. 154n

Sessaracoa sold as slave at, **20**. 40n

ship from, **24**. 229n

William IV at, **25**. 684n

Barbados water:

HW drinks, **17**. 44

Barbaggi, Giuseppe, Corsican rebel:

Segni, Bp of, welcomed by, **21**. 412n

Barbaggio (Corsica):

capture of, **23**. 46

Barbançon, Marie de (d. 1601), m. (1587), Jacques-Auguste de Thou, Baron de Meslai:

tomb of, **7**. 282

Barbantane, Marquis de. *See* Puget, Hilarion-Paul-François-Bienvenu de (1754–1828); Puget, Joseph-Pierre-Balthazar-Hilaire de (1725–ca 1800)

Barbantane, Marquise de. *See* Du Mesnildot de Vierville, Charlotte-Françoise-Élisabeth-Catherine

'Barbara':

character in Pinkerton's play, **16**. 253, 256

Barbarians:

HW's reflections on, **34**. 177

Barbarigo, Pietro, mayor of Verona, 1740:

Barzizza succeeds, as mayor, **17**. 196n

son of, **17**. 196

Barbarigo, Pietro (b. 1708 or 1717):

Walpole, Bns (Cts of Orford) said to have affair with, **17**. 196

'Barbarina.' *See* Campanini, Barbara

Barbarini. *See* Barberini

Barbarossa, Frederick. *See* Frederick I (?1123–90)

'Barbarossa':

HW's name for George II, **20**. 494

*Barbarossa. See under* Brown, John (1715–66)

Barbary corsairs:

Mann calls, 'teasing wretches,' **25**. 416

Barbary horses. *See under* Horse

Barbary states:

piratical, **15**. 46

traveller in, alluded to, **33**. 236–7

Tuscany may no longer pay tribute to, **22**. 259

Tuscany's only official enemy, **21**. 349

vessel leaves Leghorn to buy corn in, **21**. 330n

*See also* Algiers; Morocco; Tripoli; Tunis

Barbauld, Mrs Rochemont. *See* Aikin, Anna Letitia

Barbazan. *See* Barbantane

Barbé-Marbois, François (1745–1837), Marquis de:

*Lettres de Mme la Marquise de Pompadour* by, **5**. 300, 307, 310

Barbentane. *See* Barbantane

Barber; barbers:

'boy' of, may want to drive HW to Epsom, **30**. 86

French furnish: to England, **37**. 499; to the age, **22**. 15

HW not to rival, as a gossip, **34**. 22

HW rails like, **23**. 499

repellant put by, in window, **11**. 29

shop sign for, **7**. 357

Townshend accompanied by, **21**. 138

Barberie, Jacques-Dominique de (ca 1697–1767), Marquis de Courteille; ambassador to Switzerland 1737–49:

Switzerland alarmed by, **18**. 290

Barberie de Courteilles, Marie-Mélanie-Henriette de, m. (1764) Aimeri-Louis-Roger, Comte de Rochechouart:

social relations of, in Paris, **7**. 312, 341, 342, 428, 434

Barberie de St-Contest, François-Dominique de (1701–54), diplomatist:

ministry of, **28**. 365n

Puisieux succeeded by, as secretary of state for foreign affairs, **20**. 286

Barberin de Reignac family:

mentioned, **7**. 113n, **10**. 71n

Barberina. *See* Barbarina

Barberini, Bonaventura (1674–1743), Abp of Ferrara:

receives Conclave votes though not a cardinal, **13**. 212

Barberini, Cornelia (ca 1711–97), m. (1728) Giulio Cesare Colonna, Principe di Carbognano and Duca di Bassanello:

art sold by, to pay gaming debts, **33**. 485n

(?) Cumberland, D. of, entertained by, **23**. 566n

daughter seen with, by Hamilton, **35**. 434

paintings sold by, **21**. 533

Barberini, Urbano, Principe di Palestrina:

chariot of, **19**. 428

Barberini collection:

HW's bust from, **11**. 29n

Barberini Colonna, Maria Felicità, m. Bartolommeo Corsini, Principe di Sismano:

(?) Mann dines with, at Pisa, **22**. 424

name of, corrected, **43**. 281

Barberini Colonna di Sciara, Giulio Cesare. *See* Colonna, Giulio Cesare (1702–87)

Barberini Palace, at Rome:

Guido's Magdalen at, **21**. 533

La Trappe marble floor surpasses that of, **20**. 54n

Barberini Vase:
Darwin's *Botanic Garden* mentions, **42**. 267
Hamilton buys, **12**. 273, **32**. 70
Portland, Ds of, owned, **33**. 485–6, 489–90
*See also under* Vase; vases
Barbette (dog):
Ailesbury, Cts of, has, **38**. 132
Barbezieu. *See* Rigaut de Barbezieu
Barbiano de Belgioioso, Lodovico Carlo Maria (1728–1801), Conte di, Austrian ambassador to England 1770–82:
biographical information on, corrected, **43**. 92, 146
Brussels said to be escaped from by, in a tub, **39**. 455–6
expects Austrian-Prussian war, **24**. 393
HW mentions, **5**. 75
HW prefers, to Seilern, **31**. 152
HW to entertain, at SH, **23**. 311, **43**. 283
Joseph II accompanied by, at Necker's, **6**. 443
—— dines with, **6**. 440
Kennedy, Polly, corresponds with, **11**. 195
member of Ladies' Club, **31**. 152
mistake of, in writing English, **11**. 195
Barbiellini, Carlo:
*Raccolta di lettere sulla pittura* by, **7**. 355, **43**. 107
Barbier, ——:
attends session of parliament of Paris, **8**. 173
Barbier, Louis (d. 1670), Abbé de la Rivière:
Gaston d'Orléans sold by, **9**. 228
HW compares, with Rigby, **9**. 228
*Barbier de Seville, Le. See under* Beaumarchais, Pierre-Augustin Caron de
Barbieri, Giovanni Francesco (1591–1666), called Guercino. *See under* Guercino
Barbolani, Contessa. *See* Lorenzi, Luisa Elisabetta
Barbolani da Montauto, Isabella (1710–95), m. (1727) Piergannozzo Mozzi:
Orford, Cts of, abused by, for obstructing son's marriage, **25**. 130
Barbot:
anchovy sauce with, **19**. 357n
Barbour, John:
*The Bruce*, edited by Pinkerton, **16**. 326n
Barbuda, West Indian island:
Codrington's plantations on, **35**. 178n
Barbut. *See* Barbauld
Barcaroles:
Venetian, **23**. 249
Barceló, Don Antonio, Spanish naval officer:
Gibraltar blockaded by, **24**. 501n
Spanish expedition against Algiers led by, **25**. 416n, **39**. 421n
Barcelona, capt.-gen. of. *See* Assalto, Conde dell'
Barcelona (Spain):
armaments prepared at, **24**. 98n
cannon embarked at, for attack on St Philip's, **25**. 229
Cornish ordered to, **18**. 414
fleet preparing at, **23**. 474

French and Spanish fleets said to go to, **17**. 324
Haddock to keep Spanish squadron in, **17**. 259, 290, 380–1
Hayley's play laid at, **34**. 37
Jesuits shipped from, **22**. 516n
Lorenzi's news from, **21**. 193
Mann, Horace II, and Lady Lucy, travel to, **24**. 222, 225, 233, 239, 247
Montemar at, **17**. 182
Spanish expeditions from, **17**. 179, 182, 192, 286, 290, 312, 361, **18**. 106, **28**. 460n
Toulon squadron reaches, **17**. 190
Barcelonetta:
French to invade Piedmont by way of, **19**. 417
Barck, ——:
Swedish envoy to Austria, **21**. 280n
Barclay, Cornelia, m. Stephen de Lancey:
SH visitor sent by, **12**. 245
Barclay, James:
witness, at trial of rebel peers, **18**. 283n
Barclay, John (1582–1621), scholar and writer:
Dalrymple's life of, **15**. 181
*Bard, The. See under* Gray, Thomas
Bardi, Contessa. *See* Malaspina, Margharita
Bardi, Carlo (d. 1795), Conte di Vernio:
ball given by, upon marriage, **18**. 60
Bardi, Geronimo (1685–1761), cardinal, 1743:
Conclave left by, because of ill health, **21**. 217
promotion of, to cardinal, **18**. 302n
Bardi, Maria Costanza (1691–1717), m. (1710) Camillo Pandolfini:
dowry of, **17**. 137
Bardi, Conte Vincenzo (1682–1762):
Electress leaves money and silver to, **18**. 169
Electress's courtier, **17**. 237
Bardi, Via de', at Florence:
Ambrogi, Casa, in, **13**. 237n, **17**. 67n, **37**. 68
Mann and Hugford live in, **18**. 91
Palazzo Manelli in, **11**. 154n
Bardo (N. Africa):
blockaded, **20**. 319n
Bardon, ——, scribe:
Simiane, Mme de, favours, **5**. 423n
Barducci Cherichini, Vittoria, m. 1 (1738) Francesco Carnesecchi; m. 2 (1744) Donato Maria Dal Borgo:
marriage of, **18**. 439
Bardville, Joan, m. Thomas Frowyk, Kt, 1502:
epitaph on tomb of, **12**. 104
Barefoot, John:
Granger misplaces, in list of prints, **40**. 322
Barèges (France):
Bute given escort to, **7**. 367
Choiseul to visit, **6**. 64
visitors to: Bute, **7**. 367, **23**. 42n, 152n, 161n; Choiseul-Beaupré, Comtesse de, **5**. 183, 350, 353, 363, 403; Gramont, Duchesse de, **4**. 407, 421, 444–5, 450n, **6**. 64, 71; Mirepoix, Bp of, **6**. 187
water route to, **5**. 350, 352–3

Bareil. *See* Du Barail

'Bareith,' Margravine of. *See* Anna Charlotte Amalie

Bareith. *See also* Bayreuth

Barentin, Charles-Louis-François de Paule de (1738–1819), advocate general:
(?) mentioned by Mme du Deffand, **6.** 168

Barère de Vieuzac, Bertrand (1755–1841), legislator; author:
French Revolution discussed by, **12.** *66*
HW calls, 'Moloch,' **12.** 86
passport given by, to friend, **12.** 66
Robespierre gives up defence of, in Jacobin Club, **12.** 86
Vendée, La, destruction of royalists in, announced by, **12.** 66, 71

Baretti, Giuseppe Marc'Antonio (1719–89), writer:
Cholmondeley, Mrs, friend of, **4.** *230*, 230–1, 232
Du Deffand, Mme, sends letters and pamphlets to England by, **4.** 230, 232, 233, 237
Gray's Italian letter might be shown to, **28.** 97, 99
*Guide through the Royal Academy* by, **29.** 139
*Journey from London to Genoa* by, **28.** 191n
Piozzi, Mrs, would have been told by, about her indiscretions, **42.** 245
suggests customs officials might open packet of HW's letters, **4.** 230–1

*Barfleur* (ship):
Aix island captured by, under Graves, **37.** 506
expected at Port Mahon, **17.** 285

Barford, William (1719–92), D.D.; scholar and divine:
Brand's tutor, **1.** 198n
fellow of King's College, **15.** 311

Barfort, Chevalier de. *See* Jerningham, Charles

Barge; barges:
at Richmond regatta, **32.** 317n
at Thames regatta, **32.** 237
Christian VII brought in, from Whitehall to the Temple, **23.** 58n
consul's, at Leghorn, **25.** 665n
embankment at Richmond for drawing, **29.** 69
Ferdinand of Naples reprimands pilot of, **25.** 581
from Henley, **39.** 133
George II and Ps Amelia occupy, at Richmond's fireworks, **20.** 56
goldsmith company's, **33.** 47, **39.** 311
HW sighs for view of, on the Thames, **23.** 491
Holbein Chamber at SH has view of, **10.** 168
London builds at Richmond facilities for horses for, **33.** 207
musicians', **37.** 289
of Frederick, P. of Wales, **37.** 289
on Thames at Richmond's fireworks, **22.** 149
Petersham, Lady Caroline, takes party to Vauxhall in, **9.** 108

tax on, **25.** 254n
visible from SH, **20.** 380, **37.** 269

Bargellini, Santi. *See* Santi Bargellini

Bargello, the, Florentine chief constable:
Dumesnil visits, to procure valet's release, **17.** 225
Gavi lodged with, **17.** 239
Pepi bribes, **17.** 444
—— taken to prison of, **17.** 137
Strozzi jewels to be sought by, **19.** 350
*See also* Chelotti

Bargello of Cortona. *See* Mengozzi, Bernardo

Bargeman; bargemen:
at Windsor, riot, **22.** 79n
English, asks money to drink Frederick II's health, **21.** 238
liveries made for, on Clement XIV's ship, for D. of Gloucester, **23.** 566
on ferry-boat, **41.** 278

Bargrave, Isaac (1586–1643), divine:
print of, by James Cole, **1.** 142

Bari, Comtesse de. *See* Frotier-de-la-Messalière, Marie-Élisabeth; Urre de Aiguebonne, Anne-Marie d' (ca 1633–1724)

Bariatinsky, Ps. *See* Holstein-Sonderburg-Beck, Katharine von

Bariatinsky, Ivan Sergeievitch (1738–1811), Prince; Russian minister to France:
social relations of, in Paris, **7.** 346, 347–9, 428–30

Barigioni, Filippo (1690–1753):
mausoleum for Ps Sobieska designed by, **21.** 391n

Barillon d'Amoncourt, Paul (ca 1630–91), Marquis de Branges; French ambassador to England 1677–89:
letter of, relating to Sidney, perhaps forged, **28.** 75–6, 78
letters of, from England, **34.** 113
Sidney traduced by, **28.** 66n

Barillon de Morangis, Antoine-Marie:
(?) attends session of parliament of Paris, **8.** 173

Baring, Elizabeth (1744–1809), m. (1780) John Dunning, Bn Ashburton, 1782:
SH visited by, **12.** 232

Baring, Sir Francis (1740–1810), cr. (1793) Bt; London merchant:
East India Co. director, **25.** 490
(?) SH visited by, **12.** 235

Barini, Giuseppe; Cts of Orford's master of the household:
Lady Orford's declaration signed by, **43.** 288
——'s legacy to, **25.** 122

Barjot, Paul-Jean-Baptiste-Alexis, Comte de Roncée:
wife of, **5.** 361n

Bark (medicinal):
ague treated by, **21.** 222n, **38.** 138
Chute takes, **35.** 96
Cole takes, **1.** 159, 371, **2.** 338
difficult to have, genuine, **2.** 337
English troops lack, in America, **40.** 313

[Bark (medicinal), *continued*]
forbidden during gout, **1.** 371, **2.** 338
HW advises people to take, against earthquakes, **20.** 135
HW takes, **1.** 301, **2.** 7, 9. 227, 271, 275, **24.**
521, 532, **28.** 468, **29.** 311, **33.** 419, **35.** 376
Jamaican and Peruvian varieties of, **43.** 76
Newcastle, D. of, takes, **22** 579n
Orford, 2d E. of, not saved by, **20.** 233, 238
remedy for fever, **17.** 164, **18.** 268n
rheumatism treated by, **35.** 376
Selwyn improved by, **37.** 89
tumour or boil treated by, **2.** 337
used by D. of Gloucester, **32.** 274
Walpole, Sir Edward, takes, to restore ap-
petite. **25.** 463
Bark, barks (naval):
Charles of Naples sends, to Adriatic, **19.** 220
convoy of, for Genoa, **19.** 409–10
Eliott sends, to Mann, **25.** 339
English capture of, **19.** 51, 56–7, 82
Francis I's, tows plague ship, **18.** 262
French, at Leghorn, **17.** 179, 407–8
French, intercepted, **19.** 383n
from Savona, reaches Leghorn, **19.** 434
from Sicily, **18.** 252
Genoese and Neapolitan, captured by English under suspicion of smuggling supplies
to Spanish army, **19.** 56–7
Genoese send, to keep bishop out of Corsica,
**21.** 394
governor of Savona sinks, **19.** 81
on lake at Stowe, **10.** 314
Osborn pursues, at St Andrea, **18.** 28
*padrons* of, repulsed by Genoa for carrying
disguised Jesuits, **22.** 546
plague refugees flee in, **18.** 256
Spanish, **17.** 262, 350, 433, **18.** 288
weather keeps, from Leghorn, **19.** 360
Bark, tanner's:
sugar and water raised in, **35.** 473
Barker, ——, bookseller at (?) East Dereham:
book to be forwarded to, for Fenn, **16.** 239
Barker, ——:
SH visited by, **32.** 208
Barker, Lady. *See* Hallowes, Anne
Barker, Mrs, of Richmond:
SH visited by, **12.** 232, 250
Barker, Edward, Carmelite friar in Italy:
*A New and Easy Grammar* by, dedicated to
Mann, **22.** 438
Barker, John, capt. of the *St Quintin*:
ship commanded by, **17.** 279n
to stay at Genoa, **17.** 302
Barker, John (?1727–1808), master of Christ's
College, Cambridge:
vice-chancellor, **2.** 241n
Barker, Mrs John. *See* Conyers, Caroline
Barker, Rev. Robert (d. 1796):
print of, **1.** 362
Barking Church. *See* All Hallows, Barking

Barking Hall, Suffolk:
Sturt of, **11.** 142n
Barkley (*or* Berkley), Samuel (1714–*post* 1750),
Eton, and King's College, Cambridge:
appointed orator, **13.** 116
Bar-le-Duc (France):
Boufflers dies in chaise accident near, **20.**
236n
family of Margaret of Anjou take leave of
her at, **14.** 72
François II received René I's picture at, **16.**
159
René I's self-portrait at, seen by Montaigne,
**16.** 143
Bar-le-Duc château de:
Old Pretender occupies, **19.** 108n
Barley, Robert. *See* Barlow, Robert
Barley:
abundance of, in England, **12.** 142
Cole raises, **1.** 276
HW tired by talk about, at Houghton, **23.**
122
Barley bread:
for breakfast, **33.** 138
Barley sugar:
Beauvau, Prince and Princesse de, send, to
HW, **6.** 368, 370
Craufurd says HW does not want, **6.** 487
Du Deffand, Mme, sends, to HW, **5.** 297, **6.**
120, 125, 239
good for chest, **4.** 297, **6.** 239
Moret sends, **7.** 425–6
Barley water:
Loutherbourg prescribes, for patients, **34.** 51
Barlocci, ——, singer:
opera sung by, **18.** 302
Barlow, Catherine (d. 1782), m. (1758) Sir
William Hamilton:
Agincourt visits HW at SH at recommenda-
tion of, **42.** 102
Ailesbury, Cts of, tells, of HW's visit to
France, **22.** 354n
—— writes to, **40.** 383
Conway to tell, of HW's hospitality to Agin-
court, **39.** 291
Conways visited by, at Park Place, **23.** 339,
**37.** 527
death of, **25.** 321
Drummond physician to, **24.** 199n
Du Deffand, Mme, sees, **6.** 350
Florence visited by, on way to Rome and
Naples, **23.** 448, **24.** 337
fortune of, in land, **25.** 321
HW discussed English climate with, **23.** 339
HW exchanges compliments with, **30.** 241,
**35.** 408, 410, 412, 415
HW invited by, to Naples, **40.** 383
HW sure that husband's antiquarianism is
preferred by, to his volcano researches, **35.**
415
HW tells, to buy fruit and plumes for fashion-
able headdress, **35.** 428

HW to receive Girifalco story from, **35**. 433–4

HW unable to visit, at Naples, **35**. 73

HW visited by, at SH, **23**. 339, **35**. 411, 429

health of: asthma, **22**. 243, 259; English climate affects, **23**. 339; Neapolitan air removes all complaints, **40**. 384

husband to tell, about celestinette, **35**. 423

husband would be aided by, in musical history, **35**. 420

Leghorn visited by, as result of storm, **22**. 259

Mann recommends Mrs Gibbs and Miss Steavens to, **24**. 337n

Mann visited by, in Florence, **22**. 259

musical, **22**. 243, **26**. 46, **35**. 425

Naples may be left by, **35**. 427

Paris visited by, **6**. 345

Rome visited by, **24**. 337

silhouettes by, **26**. 46, **43**. 96

suffers much in journey from Vienna, **23**. 448

Vesuvius's eruption must try the nerves of, **39**. 339

Barlow, Francis (1626–1702), painter:

chimney boards of birds by, at Burghley House, **10**. 345

Barlow, Robert (d. 1533):

wife inherits property of, **9**. 298, **40**. 182

Barlow, Mrs Robert. *See* Hardwick, Elizabeth

Barlow, Thomas:

Little Marble Hill, Twickenham, occupied by, **42**. 484

*Barmécides, Les. See under* La Harpe, Jean-François de

Barming, Kent:

Noble, rector of, **42**. 133n, 425n, 447n

Barming Parsonage:

Noble writes from, **42**. 447

Barn, Mr:

money to be paid back by, to (?) Waldegraves, **36**. 328

Barn; barns:

at Battle Abbey, **35**. 140

at the Vyne, to have spire, **35**. 640

Clive, Mrs, pulls down, to open views, **37**. 348

plays in, by strolling companies, **24**. 371, **39**. 493

Suffolk, Cts of, advised by HW in gothicizing, **35**. 102

Barnabas, Père:

cane of, blossoms in France, **39**. 254

'Barnabas, Béquille du Père':

tune of, cited, **33**. 534

Barnabiti (religious order):

Domenichino painting in church of, **14**. 20

Pitt, Elizabeth, embraces Roman Catholicism in, **20**. 416n

Barnabotti (impoverished Venetian nobles):

votes not sold by, **17**. 75

Barnacchi. *See* Bernacchi

Barnard, Bn. *See* Vane, Gilbert (1678–1753); Vane, Hon. Henry (ca 1705–58)

Barnard, Bns. *See* Holles, Lady Elizabeth (ca 1657–1725)

Barnard, ——:

SH visited by, **12**. 227

Barnard, Commodore. *See* Barnett, Curtis

Barnard, Anna (d. 1792), Quakeress:

Charlotte, Q., seeks cow from, and is offered a bull, **33**. 568

SH visited by, **12**. 227

Barnard, Dr Edward (1717–81), D.D.; provost of Eton:

Eton at its height under, **22**. 84

Eton students weep at departure of, **10**. 189

(?) HW not in awe of, **28**. 134

headmastership of Eton kept by, till holidays, **10**. 189

Hertfords invite HW to dine with Hunter and, **39**. 351–2

Montagu calls on, **10**. 43

—— rejoices at appointment of, as provost, **10**. 183

——'s opinion of, **10**. 183, 189

position of, gets him invitations from all ranks, **10**. 56

provost of Eton, **10**. 183

Villiers aided by, **10**. 43

Waldegrave's illness arouses concern of people visited by, **10**. 56

Barnard, Frederick Augusta (ca 1743–1830), K.C.H., 1828; King's Librarian:

HW imagines conversation by, **33**. 319

Barnard, Sir John (ca 1685–1764), Kt, 1732; M.P.; lord mayor of London:

absent from presentation of City of London's petition, **20**. 585n

Admiralty post may be gained by, **17**. 333

army increase supported by, in Parliament, **17**. 410

Ashton might curse, for falling rents, **13**. 138

biographical information on, corrected, **43**. 176, 241, 294

Blackerby given respite at instance of, **17**. 252

bust of, at Stowe, **35**. 76

Chesterfield tries to establish as wit, at Tunbridge, **19**. 404

death of, **22**. 252, **38**. 436

election of, **19**. 425n

Exchequer post refused by, **19**. 212

financiers detest, **20**. 111

former lord mayor of London, **22**. 252n

HW's indifference to Sir Robert Walpole's resignation offends, **28**. 48

last survivor of old Opposition, save Egmont, **35**. 196

Maria Theresa's subsidy voted by, **17**. 390

Onslow humiliates, over trade bills, **20**. 135

——'s character sketch of, **17**. 252n

Parliamentary speeches by: defending Granville, **26**. 10; on merchants' petition, **17**. 354; on Regency Bill, **20**. 257

Pelham influenced by, **20**. 111

Pitt answered by, **26**. 10

Secret Committee lists include, **17**. 383

Secret Committee not attended by, **17**. 401

[Barnard, Sir John, *continued*]
  unpopularity of, **20**. 585–6
  Walpole, Sir Robert, opposed by, **22**. 252n
Barnard, John (d. 1773), P. of Wales's page:
  (?) Wales, P. of, attended by, **20**. 232
Barnard, North Ludlow. *See* Bernard, North
  Ludlow
Barnard, Thomas (1719–81), divine:
  collection of, **1**. 155
Barnard, Thomas (ca 1728–1806), D.D.; Dean
  of Derry; Bp of Killaloe, 1780; of Limerick,
  1794:
  Beauclerk, Topham, visited by, **32**. 292
  (?) disbelieves in Ireland's MSS, **15**. 321
  SH visited by, **12**. 243
  verses of, admired by HW, **32**. *288*
  'Verses to Sir Joshua Reynolds and Co.' by,
  **43**. 350
Barnard, Thomas Allen (d. 1788), hop mer-
  chant:
  copy of Northampton's portrait left by, in
  HW's care, **16**. 97
  Harding employed by, to copy portrait, **16**.
  95
  —— taken by, to Hillier's house, **16**. 96–7
Barnard, Dr William (1697–1768), Bp of Rap-
  hoe, 1744; of Derry, 1747:
  Montagu to show *Anecdotes of Painting* to,
  **10**. 11, 17
Barnardiston, Lady. *See* Winn, Catherine
Barnardiston, Mr:
  SH visited by, **12**. 251
Barnardiston, John (1718–78), Master of Corpus Christi ('Benet') College, Cambridge:
  Brown dines with, **1**. 283
  Cole dines with, **2**. 11, 12n, 70n, 283
  ——'s friend, **1**. 189n
  death of, **2**. 94n, 137n
  last illness of, **2**. 82
  Orford, E. of, seen by, at Houghton, **1**. 347,
  348
Barnardiston, Thomas (1706–52), serjeant-at-
  law:
  family property of, **1**. 189n
  print of, **1**. 188, 190
Barnard's Inn, London:
  burnt in Gordon Riots, **29**. 56, **33**. 190
Barnave, Antoine-Pierre-Joseph-Marie (1761–
  93), revolutionist:
  'butcher' of the National Assembly, **12**. 86,
  **42**. 373
  compared with Malachowski, **34**. 159
  France will be gutted by, **39**. 486–7
  guillotined, **12**. 86
  negotiation of, with Comtes d'Artois and de
  Provence, **11**. *345*
Barnborough, Yorks:
  Eyre, Mrs, dies at, **2**. 23n
  seat of More family, **16**. 49n
Barne, Miles (1718–80), M.P.:
  birth date of, corrected, **43**. 266
  Florence visited by, **20**. 78

Barnes, Surrey:
  Herbert Lodge near, **39**. 285
Barnes Terrace:
  house of Lady Derby at, **11**. 310n
Barnet, Herts:
  races at, inconvenience HW, **28**. 42
  road through, **1**. 38
Barnett, Capt. Curtis (d. 1746):
  Caylus defeated by, **18**. 15
  Montagu, Lady Mary Wortley, rewards, with
  'emerald' ring for ship passage, **21**. 473
  Spanish and French ships captured by, in
  East Indies, **19**. 92n
Barnewall, Vcts. *See* Daly, Honora (d. 1784);
  Hamilton, Mary (d. 1736)
Barnewall, Nicholas (1668–1725), 3d Vct Barne-
  wall of Kingsland, 1688:
  wife of, **42**. 89
Barnewall, Nicholas (1726–1813), later 15th Bn
  Trimlestown:
  Browne, Lady, knows, **7**. 358
Barnewall family:
  HW unable to obtain portraits from, **5**. 222
Barney, Tom, HW's servant:
  (?) Bath visited by, instead of Houghton, to
  repair health, **18**. 498
  (?) HW hears from, about his pets, **36**. 1
  (?) HW mentions, **35**. 65
  income of, more than necessary, **37**. 171–2
  Mann knew, **20**. 396
  Mary known to, **17**. 101
  room of, in Mann's house, **20**. 370
  successor to, **20**. 396
Bärnklau. *See* Pernklö
Barnwell, Northants:
  head of Henry III from, **2**. 275, **16**. 192n, **43**.
  73
  HW asks about church of, **2**. 275, 277n
Barnwell Abbey, Cambs:
  founding of, **2**. 115
Barometer:
  quicksilver in, **37**. 13
'Baron, le.' *See* Gleichen, Carl Heinrich
Baron; barons:
  Charles II's warrant for coronets of, **30**. 153
  Commons dispute with, **9**. 149
  Ferdinand of Naples sends orders to, after
  earthquake, **25**. 376
  garb of, **1**. 149
  German: makes naive remark to Clement XII
  at Rome, **20**. 546; SH visited by, **39**. 440;
  to be reinstated as gentleman after desert-
  ing family and becoming a common soldier,
  **21**. 510
Baronage:
  privately-raised regiments will help restore,
  **26**. 15
*Baronage of England, The. See under* Dugdale,
  Sir William
*Baronagium genealogicum. See under* Edmondson, Joseph
*Baron d'Albikrac, Le. See under* Corneille,
  Thomas

*Baron de la Crasse, Le. See under* Poisson, Raymond

*Barone di Torre Forte, Il. See under* Piccinni, Niccolò

*Baronetage. See under* Wotton, Thomas

Baronius, Cæsar (1538–1607), cardinal, 1596; ecclesiastical historian:

*Annales ecclesiastici*, Montagu's reply to, **16.** 146

Gibbon contrasts Middleton with, **41.** 393

'Barons' Wars':

Miller's castle has 'true rust' of, **35.** 148

Barowe *or* Barrow, Thomas (d. ?1497), Master of the Rolls; Keeper of the Great Seal:

Richard III's benefactions to Cambridge University through, **43.** 51

Barracks:

at Leghorn, **17.** 293, **22.** 418, 423

Barral, Claude-Martin-Joseph de (d. 1803) Bp of Troyes:

social relations of, with Mme du Deffand, **7.** 432

Barral, Louise-Françoise de (b. 1720):

(?) social relations of, with Mme du Deffand, **7.** 433, 435–6, 452

Barral, Pierre (d. 1772), abbé:

*Dictionnaire portatif et historique*, (?) owned by Mme du Deffand, **8.** 25

*Sévigniana* owned by Mme du Deffand, **8.** 33n

Barral de Montferrat, Louise-Jacqueline-Sophie de (b. 1713), m. (1731) Jean-Emmanuel de Guignard, Vicomte de St-Priest:

(?) Pitt, Anne, acquainted with, **31.** 58

Barras, Comte de:

fleet of, reaches Chesapeake from Rhode Island, **33.** 306n

Barrataria. *See* Barataria

Barre. *See* La Barre

Barré, Isaac (1726–1802), M.P.; politician:

American taxes opposed by, in Parliamentary speech, **38.** 508

annual grant obtained by, **39.** 404n

biographical information about, corrected, **43.** 279, 282

Bostonians deserted by, **28.** 142

Burke's speech acclaimed by, **28.** 354, 356

Burke succeeds, in Pay Office, **25.** 407

Chatham (Pitt) gets apologies from, for attack, **38.** 321

—— should be subject of oration by, **38.** 255

——'s substitute, **38.** 508

—— would give essential post to, **28.** 377

Clive goes to Bengal instead of, **38.** 378

Cust does not restrain speeches of, **23.** 175n

dismissed for joining Opposition, **22.** 189, **38.** 254

Dowdeswell opposed by, in Parliamentary debate on naval estimates, **38.** 496

Florence visited by, **22.** 327

Fullarton prevented by, from traducing Shelburne in House of Lords, **29.** 13

HW meets, in Paris, **22.** 365

HW mentions, **4.** 311

HW satirizes greediness of, **33.** 394, 412

HW sends letters by, **7.** 377

Hertford not sorry for, **38.** 260

—— said to be having, as secretary, **22.** 327n, 365n

'honest,' **33.** 348

House of Commons forsaken by, **23.** 289, 291

hurries home, **22.** 327

Irish vice-treasurership refused by, **22.** 365

Johnstone clashes with in Parliamentary inquiry, **39.** 325

likely to resign, **23.** 65

North attacked by, **23.** 186

——'s witticism to, on their blindness, **33.** 585

Paris visited by, with intent to observe French sea-coasts, **38.** 413n

Parliamentary activity of, on Regency Bill, **38.** 547, 552

Parliamentary éclat of, over Newfoundland dispute, **38.** 528

Parliamentary motions by, **24.** 205n, 474n, **33.** 20n

Parliamentary speeches by, **22.** 283–4, 286, **23.** 186, 248, **33.** 348n, **38.** 321

pension of, **29.** 264–5, 269, **33.** 345n, 348

Sandwich's taunt from, in Parliament, **38.** 513

Shelburne advised by, against marquisate, **25.** 554n

—— obtains pension for, **33.** 345n, 348n

——'s friend, **23.** 65

social relations of, with Craufurd, **7.** 272

speechless in Parliament, **39.** 126

Townshend, Charles, benefits by absence of, in debate, **38.** 552

—— quarrels with, **30.** 244

treasurer of the Navy, **25.** 264n

vice-treasurer of Ireland, **22.** 443

Barré. *See also* Du Barry

Barreau de Girac, François (1732–1820), Bp of St-Brieuc:

Châtillon visited by, **7.** 331

social relations of, in Paris, **7.** 291, 308, 316, 319, 320, 325, 331

Barrell, William (d. 1749), army officer:

regiment of, **18.** 449n, **19.** 248, **37.** 239

Barrells, Warwickshire:

Luxborough estate of, **28.** 233n

Luxborough, Lady, retires to, **11.** 65n

Barrère. *See* Barère de Vieuzac

Barret, ——:

HW rejects gauze lace of, **9.** 358

Barret, Mr:

social relations of, with HW in Paris, **7.** 325

Barret, Thomas (d. 1757), of Lee, Kent:

bids against HW's agent at Mead sale, **35.** 197

biographical information about, corrected, **43.** 361

Barret, Thomas (?1743–1803), M.P.; of Lee Priory:

Berrys visit, at Lee Priory, **12.** 111, 125, 126, 134, 136, 137

[Barret, Thomas (?1743–1803), *continued*]
biographical information about, corrected, **43.**
    72, 141, 295, 307, 343, 353, 358
(?) Bridges's neighbour, **41.** 132
Cole's copy of 'Des. of SH' bought by, **33.** 576n
father of, bids against HW's agent at Mead
    sale, **35.** 197
Gothic plans of, approved by HW, **35.** 635
HW asked by, to let Matthew see SH, **42.** 220
HW cancels visit to, **11.** 59
HW gives *Mysterious Mother* to, **41.** 428
HW praises house of, **11.** 98
HW's correspondence with, **42.** 220–2, 362–4
HW's friendship with, **12.** 135, 136
HW visited by, at SH, **12.** 203
HW visits, **2.** 237, **11.** 93, 97, **12.** 105, 109n, **29.**
    77, **31.** 199, 342, **33.** 220
'Mabuse' painting acquired by, for Lee Priory,
    **42.** 362
Nicholls visits, **11.** 109
Nivernais's *Jardins modernes* given to, **12.** 259
quite like his house, **29.** 78
sale of, **15.** 191n
stands for Dover, **28.** 80
SH visitor sent by, **12.** 238
*See also under* Lee Priory
Barret. *See also* Barrett; Barrett Lennard
Barrett, Mrs. *See* Lennard, Anne (1684–1755);
    Pratt, Anna Maria (d. 1806)
Barrett, James (1710–79), Col.; of Concord,
    Mass.:
affidavit by, **24.** 112
Barrett, William (1733–89), historian:
argument by, defending Chatterton's good
    faith, **16.** 220–1
Bristol's history being written by, **16.** 115, 116
Chatterton asked by, to have HW return
    Rowley papers, **16.** 115, 116
—— gave no poetical MSS to, **16.** 362
—— not supposed to have brought 'Battle of
    Hastings' to, **16.** 361
—— said to have told HW that MSS were
    owned by, **16.** 113n, 358
——'s MSS revised by, **16.** 107n
——'s poems in hands of, **16.** 126, 242n
——'s unsent answer to HW in hand of, **16.**
    175
—— tells, that MSS were owned by another,
    **16.** 176
Dacre borrows Rowley parchments from, **16.**
    228n
death of, attributed to criticism of his *History*,
    **31.** 331
deceived but not intentionally deceitful, **16.**
    223
foolish credulity of, **15.** 201, **16.** 117
HW identifies, as possessing 'the fund of
    Rowley's poems,' **43.** 231
HW understands Chatterton to claim that
    Rowley papers belonged to, **16.** 128
*History and Antiquities of . . . Bristol, The*:

**16.** 115, 116, **43.** 203; Chatterton's forgeries
    used in, **6.** 223; Chatterton's letters to HW
    printed in, **16.** 219–20, 222, **31.** 326, **34.** 150;
    Glynn encourages publication of, **16.** 224–5,
    227; HW advised to contradict, concerning
    Chatterton, **31.** 331; HW scoffs at, **15.** 201,
    **16.** 227, **31.** 325–6; partisans of Chatterton
    should be disillusioned by, **16.** 222, 227;
    spurious prints in, **31.** 326
ignorance of, **31.** 326
Lort receives copy of Bristol Castle print from,
    **16.** 223
—— sees Chatterton MSS in possession of,
    **16.** 174–6
name of, corrected, **43.** 221
originals of Rowley poems should be pro-
    duced by, **16.** 356
Barrett Lennard, Anne Barbara (1740–9):
mother recovers from death of, **20.** 92
Barrett Lennard, Barbara (b. 1766):
father's wife cares for, **36.** 236
Barrett Lennard, Richard (d. 1696):
Mildmay's grandfather, **10.** 150n
Barrett Lennard, Thomas (1717–86), 17th **Bn**
    Dacre of the South, 1755:
Aylesford entertained by, **10.** 7
Bath visited by, **10.** 187, 207
Bayham Abbey recommended by, **35.** 136
bishop acquired by, **35.** 572
Blayney to see, **9.** 415
Capell patronized by, **35.** 599
carried about, though health no worse, **24.**
    103
Chute and HW visit, at Belhus, **35.** 183–4
Chute not well acquainted with, **20.** 100
—— (?) receives ring from, **21.** 52
—— responsible for Mann's attentions to,
    **20.** 84, 173
——'s correspondence with, **20.** 87
——'s relationship to, **20.** 100n
——'s social relations with, **10.** 4, 6, 7
—— to have sent Mann's pedigree through,
    **20.** 78
Cocchi advises, to leave off drugs and medi-
    cines, **20.** 94–5
Cole visits, **2.** 212
correspondence of, with Nicholas Hardinge,
    **35.** 606
Court attendance prevents, from visiting
    Chute, **35.** 89
Davis, Mrs, calls, 'Barrett's folks,' **20.** 174
death of, **33.** 509, **36.** 236, 241
Essex to be visited by, **41.** 185
Florentine amusements missed by, **20.** 92
footman of, kills the butler, **38.** 193
Giberne's prospects not to be told to, **20.** 91
Glover described by, **37.** 19
Gothic of, not up to that of SH, **35.** 183
Gough's *British Topography* lent by, to HW,
    **2.** 237
HW accustomed to temper of, **20.** 204
HW admires house of, **9.** 164

HW and Thomas Walpole, jr, entertained by, **36**. 212

HW announces visit from, to Chute, **35**. 90

HW consulted by, on improvements to Belhus, **41**. 360

HW known by, through Montagu, **20**. 78

(?) HW plans to visit, at Belhus, **20**. 443n

HW pleased by Mann's liking for, **20**. 96

HW returns books and MSS to, **42**. 459

HW's friendship with Hardinge owing to, **35**. 620

HW's correspondence with, **40**. 197–200, **41**. 185–6, 359–61, 392, **42**. 72, 459

HW's social relations with, **7**. 326, 327, 328, 330, **9**. 231, **10**. 4, **24**. 103

HW thanks, for print, list of Scots painters, and hospitality at Belhus, **42**. 72

HW to hear from, about sending ruffles to Montagu, **10**. 1

HW to receive compliments of, **35**. 591, **37**. 6

HW to recommend nephew of, to Conway, **41**. 185

HW visits, **9**. 369, **20**. 317, 443n, **24**. 117, **32**. 239, **39**. 402–3

Hardinge announces marriage plans to, **35**. 591

—— apologizes to, **35**. 581

—— impresses, with wife's royal lineage, **35**. 610

—— sees correspondence of, with Nicholas Hardinge, **35**. 366

Hardinge family honoured by, **35**. 576

health of, **10**. 187, 207, 290, 296, **20**. 92, 94, 105, **24**. 103, **41**. 392

house taken by, at Florence, **20**. 75

hypochondria of, **20**. 84, 100, 105, 175, **35**. 121

lodgings of, in Paris, near HW's, **10**. 290

Lyttelton initiates, at Cambridge, into College of Arms, **35**. 184

Mann asks, to live with him, **20**. 159, 165

—— coolly treated by, **20**. 173

—— declines to meet, at Montopoli, **20**. 194

—— gets house for, in Florence, **20**. 75

—— gives garden assembly for, **20**. 191

—— likes, for Chute's sake, **20**. 84

—— may invite, to Fiesole, **20**. 194

—— not invited by, to Pisa baths, **20**. 194

——'s attentions to, **20**. 87, 94

——'s life after departure of, **20**. 98

——'s opinion of, **20**. 84, 105, 173, 175, 180

—— to accompany, to Pisa Baths, **20**. 84, 86

Mann, Galfridus, urged by, to come to Italy, **21**. 564

Miller aids, in remodelling Belhus, **35**. 183n, 184n

Montagu's correspondence with, **9**. 376

—— sends compliments to, **10**. 296, **20**. 87

—— sends message to, by HW, **9**. 362

Montagu, John, to be entertained by, **10**. 4

Naples visited by, **20**. 92, 105

Niccolini entertains, at dinner, **20**. 174

Nivernais's *Jardins modernes* given to, **12**. 260

one of HW's oldest friends, **33**. 509

Paris visited by, **10**. 290, **35**. 121

Pisa visited by, **20**. 91–2

Pomme, Dr, consulted by, **35**. 121, **43**. 137

portrait of, at the Vyne, **35**. 639

print of Vallombrosa owned by, **20**. 317

Rowley parchments borrowed by, **16**. 228n

social relations of, in Paris, **7**. 326, 327, 328, 330

spaniel bitch of, miscarries, **22**. 534

spaniels promised by, to HW, **22**. 479

statuary and Siena marble liked by, **35**. 184

Trevisani's portrait of Vendôme owned by, **35**. 509

Tunbridge Wells left suddenly by, for **Paris**, **10**. 290

Wettenhall, Mrs, to have drawing done for, of Holte's house, **9**. 362

wife may not be permitted by, to stay in same house with Mann, **20**. 194

will of, **36**. 236, 241

Barrett Lennard, Thomas (b. 1762):
father's wife cares for, **36**. 236

Barrett Lennard, Mrs Thomas. *See* Pratt, Anna Maria (d. 1806)

Barri. *See* Barry; Du Barry

Barrier; barriers:
at border of Tuscany, to keep plague out, **18**. 270

at Paris entrance, HW's chaise attacked at, **7**. 325

Barrière, Dom Jean de. *See* La Barrière, Dom Jean de

Barril. *See* Barrell

Barrimore. *See* Barrymore

Barrin, Roland-Michel (1693–1756), Marquis de la Galissonnière, French naval officer:
Byng clashes with, **35**. 277n

—— to get from Admiralty extract of letter by, **20**. 561n

embarkation orders received by, **20**. 541n

journal of, on Minorca expedition, **20**. 552

Machault asked by, for more ships, **20**. 572n

rumoured disgrace of, after English fleet's escape, **20**. 561–2

squadron of, returns to Toulon, **20**. 587n

wife of, **3**. 19n

Barrington, Mrs. *See* Vassal, Elizabeth

Barrington, Vct. *See* Barrington, John (1678–1734); Barrington Shute, William Wildman (1717–93)

Barrington, —— (d. 1779):
Arabs attack, near Suez, **24**. 510

Barrington, Hon. Daines (1727–1800), lawyer; antiquary; naturalist:
*Archæologia's* articles by, **2**. 164

(?) Arundel marbles discussed by, **16**. 182–3

calls HW 'ingenious and learned,' **33**. 479

father of, expelled, **2**. 121

*Observations on the Statutes*, **2**. 203

possible president for Society of Antiquaries, **2**. 245, 247, 250

Barrington (formerly Shute), John (1678–1734), 1st Vct Barrington:
*Essay on the Several Dispensations, Rights of the Protestant Dissenters*, and *Miscellanea sacra* by, 40. 156–7
HW omits, from *Royal and Noble Authors*, 33. 469–70
son asks HW to omit, from *Royal and Noble Authors*, 33. 470, 40. 175
Walpole, Sir Robert, said to have expelled, from House of Commons, 2. 121–2, 15. 147–8, 33. 470
works by, 16. 370
Barrington, Hon. John (d. 1764), army officer:
(?) at Chesterfield's assembly, 37. 327
Basseterre abandoned by, for Grand Terre, 21. 289n
battalion of, going abroad, 38. 49n
commander at Guadeloupe, 21. 289n
death of, 38. 361
Portsmouth destination of, to join West Indies expedition, 37. 580
White's Club rejects, in HW's newspaper parody, 9. 127
Barrington, Hon. Samuel (1729–1800), naval officer:
Admiralty reached by, with Byron's dispatch, 24. 515n
Byron joined by, 24. 466n
command of Navy refused by, on Hardy's death, 29. 47, 36. 172
Dominica's capture reported by, 24. 421n
Estaing defeats, 24. 515
George III's instructions to, about D. of Cumberland, 23. 50n
Grenada clash with d'Estaing reported by, 33. 122n
Hotham joins, for attack on St Lucia, 24. 424n, 447n
retired, after disputes, 35. 358
success of, against Brest fleet, 25. 273
Barrington, Hon. Shute (1734–1826), Bp of Llandaff, 1769, of Salisbury, 1782, of Durham, 1791:
Adultery Bill brought by into House of Lords, 24. 455n
appointed to see of Durham, 11. 288
Bath and Wells diocese may go to, 32. 168n
HW does not know, 42. 258
inserts father's life in *Biographia Britannica*, 33. 470
judge in House of Lords' appellate division, 35. 622
social relations of, with Hannah More, 31. 258
SH visited by, 12. 240
wife's estates in the south, 11. 288
Yearsley, Mrs, befriended by, 31. 222n, 33. 463n
Barrington, Mrs Shute. *See* Guise, Jane
Barrington Shute, William Wildman (1717–93), 2d Vct Barrington; M.P.:
Address debated by, 37. 415

Admiralty post given to, 17. 436n
army strength estimated by, in House of Commons, 21. 76n, 24. 347n
Beckford and Sawbridge provoked by speech of, in Parliament, 39. 125n
Bertie's flattery of, 35. 568
Bradshaw patronized by, 35. 350n
Bristol, E. of, said to have given bond into custody of, 24. 196
Clare may succeed, as secretary at war, 39. 93
Conway longs for dispatch from, ending Sluys negotiation, 38. 11
—— reports to, 38. 3n
death of, 34. 197
declines to give evidence at Ds of Kingston's trial, 28. 265, 267
Exchequer chancellorship may go to, 21. 486, 38. 553, 39. 93, 94
father not vindicated by, 15. 148
Fowke ordered by, to send Gibraltar troops to Minorca, 20. 560n, 35. 92n
Garter may be obtained by, 32. 168
George II discusses Newcastle's ambition with, 21. 74n
George III forbids, to go to D. of Gloucester, 36. 77
German war supported by, in debates on foreign estimates, 21. 553n
Gloucester elects, 33. 227n
HW asked by, to omit his father from *Royal and Noble Authors*, 33. 470, 40. 175
HW mentions, 9. 211
HW's account of, 2. 122
HW's correspondence with, 7. 378, 30. 214
HW sends *Anecdotes of Painting* through, to Montagu, 10. 15
HW sent snuff-boxes to Mme de Guerchy through, 30. 214
HW used to shock, 32. 191
Hanoverian troop bill supported by, 19. 241
Harrington, Cts of, accompanies, 9. 265
—— has intrigue with, 9. 265
Hillsborough accompanies, 9. 265
House of Commons informed by, of George II's order for Mordaunt's arrest, 21. 163n
—— informed by, of Sackville's arrest, 21. 374n
Indemnity Bill examination seconded by, 17. 436
Legge replaced by, as chancellor of Exchequer, 21. 490
Mason does not identify, 28. 188n
master of the Great Wardrobe, 17. 436n
name of, corrected, 43. 197
Navy Bill brought in by, 20. 33n
Navy treasurership rumoured for, 22. 37n
Newcastle does not want Legge to be superseded by, in Exchequer, 21. 486n
Newcastle probably responsible for transfer of, 30. 196
Parliamentary debate by, on privately raised regiments, 26. 13, 14, 15, 16, 17, 18
Parliamentary speech by, 18. 440n

Pitt proscribes, **22**. 161
Price nephew of, **9**. 335
retirement announced by, **28**. 402
secretary at war, **20**. 502, **21**. 104, 109, 490, **35**. 253–4
Selwyn's joke about, **9**. 265
Townshend, Vcts, has affair with, **38**. 127
Treasury post may be given to, **9**. 72
Barrocio:
'Repose' by, **43**. 275
Barron, William Augustus (living 1813):
painting by, of Gray's tomb, **28**. 196n
Barrow, Sir Charles (1707–89), cr. (1784) Bt; M.P.:
Gloucester elects, **33**. 227n
Barrow, Joseph Charles (d. *post* 1802), painter:
drawings by, **9**. 299n, **11**. 82n
SH visited by, **12**. 222, 234
SH visitors sent by, **12**. 242, 244
Barrow, Thomas. *See* Barowe *or* Barrow, Thomas
Barrow, Suffolk:
Ashby at, **2**. 344, **16**. 203
Williams rector of, **2**. 350n
Barrow; barrows:
at Bradford Peverell, **37**. 491
letters better than, for history, **42**. 100
Barrowfield:
Walkinshaw of, **12**. 43n
Barrowghe. *See* Barowe *or* Barrow
Barry, Miss —— Smith (b. 1747). *See* Smith Barry
Barry, Mr, farrier:
(?) opinion expressed by, on Agnes Barry's mare, **12**. 15
Barry, Anne (d. 1767), m. (1753) John Irwin, K.B., 1775:
death of, **7**. 397
Barry, Hon. Augustus (1773–1818):
birth of, **32**. 139
Barry, Lady Caroline (b. 1768), m. (1788) Louis Pierre Francis Malcolm Drummond, Comte de Melfort:
acts in *The Beaux' Stratagem*, **11**. 101
Barry, Elizabeth (1678–1713), actress:
clogs worn by, to theatre, **17**. 435
Barry, James (1667–1748), 4th E. of Barrymore:
Argyll receives Old Pretender's letters through, **17**. 479
arrested, **18**. 408, 426, 433
Old Pretender's 'general,' **17**. 479, **18**. 408
Traquair talks with, about Young Pretender's affairs, **19**. 381
Barry, James (1741–1806), painter:
*Account* by, of his pictures, **29**. 301
'Distribution of Premiums' by, **29**. 296, 297
'Elysium' by, **29**. *292, 296, 299, 300, 301, 303*
HW attributes *The Exhibition* to, **16**. 186
HW describes paintings of, **29**. 299–301
HW laughs at paintings of, **32**. 234
HW misrepresented by, **2**. 189
HW's reply to, **34**. 243–4
HW to tell story of, **32**. *229*

*Inquiry into the . . . Arts in England*, ridicules HW, **32**. 234
Lort agrees that *The Exhibition* may be by, **16**. 187
'Venus Rising from the Sea,' HW laughs at, **29**. *298*, **43**. *70*
Barry, Jane (?ca 1724–6—? after 1777), m. (1767) Robert Jephson:
older than fiancé and has no fortune, **39**. 50
Barry, Lady Penelope (ca 1707–86), m. Hon. James Cholmondeley; 'Lady Pen':
elopement of, **37**. 1–2
Florence to be visited by, **18**. 308–9
good will of, for HW, **30**. 28
HW describes scene at house of, **17**. 152
HW's correspondence with, **30**. 21, 28
husband does not mention, in will, **23**. 362n
Barry, Dr Peter:
arrest of, **19**. 288
Barry, Richard (1745–73), 6th E. of Barrymore:
Compiègne visited by, **35**. 344
death of, **32**. 139, **35**. 415
Du Barry acknowledged by, as relative, **11**. 206, **23**. 116
Du Barry, Mme, said to reward, for claiming relationship to her, **32**. 55n
HW mentions, **5**. 75
slender build of, **32**. 144
Stanhope, Lady Amelia, to marry, **31**. 125
Barry, Richard (1769–93), 7th E. of Barrymore:
acts in *The Beaux' Stratagem*, **11**. 101
Delpini dances with, **31**. 345
dances and acts in pantomime at Richmond, **35**. 399
Du Barry, Mme, may not acknowledge, **11**. 207
Squibbs's in Savile Row bought by, **43**. 143
theatre interest of, **11**. *95, 101, 207, 216n*
Barry, Spranger (1719–77), actor:
Gray describes, in *Othello*, **14**. 6–7
HW identifies, in Chatterton's poem, **16**. 345
(?) Hertford visited by, at Ragley, **39**. 85
loses teeth, **28**. 277
plays acted by, **19**. *342, 465*
Quin surpassed by, in expressing tenderness and sorrow, **14**. 7
—— urged by, to play ghost in *Hamlet*, **20**. 209
Richmond theatre attended by, **9**. 74
Barry, Mrs Spranger. *See* Street, Ann
Barry. *See also* Du Barry
Barrymore, Cts of. *See* Davys, Hon. Margaret (d. 1788); Stanhope, Lady Amelia (1749–80)
Barrymore, E. of. *See* Barry, James (1667–1748); Barry, Richard (1745–73); Barry, Richard (1769–93)
Barsham, Suffolk:
Suckling rector of, **9**. 153n
Barsine, wife of Alexander the Great. *See* Statira
Bartenstein, Johann Christoph (1689–1767), Freiherr von:
Vienna letters patent signed by, **19**. 215n

Barthélemy, François (1747–1830), cr. (1800) Comte and (1815) Marquis de; secretary to French embassy in England; displomatist:
Adhémar succeeded by, **39.** 450n
Barthélemy, Abbé, awaits, **6.** 183–4
Chanteloup to be visited by, **6.** 184
comments on d'Éon's accent, **33.** 510
Cosway, Mrs, entertains, **33.** 510–11
Gustav III talks with, of Mme du Deffand, **5.** *96*
(?) Napoleon orders, to get Bolognese pictures, **34.** 217n
Nivernais's *Jardins modernes* given to, **12.** 260
Paris visited by, **6.** 184, 198, 200
SH visited by, **12.** 228
successful in Swedish post, **6.** 198
Venetian post of, **6.** 184, 198
Barthélemy, Jean-Jacques (1716–95), abbé; antiquarian; numismatist; writer; secretary of Swiss Guards; 'Sénèque':
Affry aids, **5.** 168
Arnaud has offended, **6.** 361, 366
Barthélemy, Marquis de, holds, in Paris, **6.** 183–4, 198
Chanteloup visits of, **3.** 297, 312, **4.** 234, 240, 254, 261, 263, 406, 431, **5.** 6, 63, 152, 168, 173, 240, 245, 404, **6.** 184, 212, 291, 295, 332, 348, 349, 353, 441, 476, **7.** 424, **41.** 194, 196
Choiseul appoints, secretary of Swiss Guards, **4.** 9–10, 16, **5.** 155
Choiseul, Duchesse de, accompanied by, **3.** 359, **4.** 254, 261, 338, 431, 450, **5.** 412, **6.** 167, **41.** 193, 194, 195, 196
—— aided by, **4.** 372, **5.** 170
—— fails to write to, **4.** 286
—— inspires devotion of, **34.** 79
—— reads to, HW's letter concerning him, **41.** 110
——'s correspondence with, **7.** 151
——'s relations with, **3.** 302, 337, 359, 372–3, **4.** 110, 202, 238, 251, 342, 350, 359; **5.** 25, 49, 169, 327, 338, 412, **6.** 15, **7.** 151, **41.** 193
collar-bone broken by, **5.** 275, 276, 297
Cook's *Voyages* recommended by, to Mme du Deffand, **7.** 52
Cotte offered books by, **6.** 40
curator of medals in Bibliothèque du Roi, **5.** 108
Delos festival described by, **7.** 114–15, 121
disturbed, **4.** 286
Du Deffand, Mme, aided by, in writing song, **4.** 302
—— and, count up living authors of tragedies, **6.** 42
—— attributes mistake to, **5.** 88
—— cites, **5.** 21
—— dissuaded by, from supping with Mme de Choiseul, **4.** 362–3
—— gives unexpired subscription to *Bibliothèque des Romans* to, **6.** 400
—— has no letter from, **4.** 85, 86
—— hears from, about Mme de Choiseul's health, **4.** 287–8
—— hopes, will not go to Compiègne, **4.** 256
—— lends Mme de Jonzac's medal to, **7.** 445
—— mentions, **3.** 159, 239, **4.** 74, 151
—— offered escort of, **5.** 108, 109
—— received by, at Chanteloup, **5.** 240
—— receives letter through, **7.** 450
——'s correspondence with, *see index entries ante* **8.** 236
—— sends HW's letter to, **7.** 441
—— sends letter of, to HW, **6.** 142
——'s offer of a lodging to HW approved by, **4.** 391, 398
——'s opinion of, **3.** 255, 280, 302, 337, **4.** 39, 244, 251, 263, 342, 369, 372, **5.** 25, 49, 164–5, 412, **6.** 361, **7.** 35, 151
——'s relations with, **4.** 165, 359, 388, **5.** 43, 44, 137, 150, 243, 255, 343, 404, 426, **6.** 66, 361, 426–7
—— summons, to warn Choiseuls, **41.** 194
—— suspicious of, **4.** 355
—— swears, to secrecy about visit to Chanteloup, **5.** 237–8, 240, 241
—— talks with, about Mmes de Gramont and de Choiseul, **5.** 401
—— talks with, about HW and Voltaire, **4.** 97, 113, 117, 117–18
—— to be helped by, in giving proverbs, **4.** 278
—— wagers with, on Mme du Barry, **4.** 203–4
English of, weak, **7.** 213
*Entretiens sur l'État de la musique grecque,* **7.** 24, 35, **28.** 374n, **43.** 103
finances of, **5.** 159
Fontainebleau visited by, **4.** 289, 291
forwards pencils to Chanteloup, **7.** 154
Gatti justified by, in smallpox cases, **4.** 321
gay, **4.** 238, **5.** 426, **7.** 66
Gennevilliers visited by, **4.** 450, **7.** 326, 328, 332
Gustav III inquires after, **5.** 96
HW admired by, **3.** 21, 62, 256, **4.** 275, 276, 304, **6.** 54, 246, 247
HW asks, to describe Mme de Choiseul's health, **41.** 100
HW fears opinion of, on *Mysterious Mother,* **5.** 316
HW inquired after by, **7.** 26
HW inquired after by, though he seized letters from bequest to HW, **36.** 215–16
HW offered information by, on medals, **6.** 40
HW recommends, to Conway, **39.** 236
HW's absence regretted by, **6.** 146
HW's book to be sought by, **6.** 81
HW's commission executed by, **7.** 197, 199, 200, 203–5
HW's correspondence with, **4.** 23, 25, **7.** 213, 386, 444
HW's defence of Shakespeare inquired about by, **6.** 268

HW sends messages to, **5**. 253, **6**. 66, 125, 247, 378, **7**. 26, **36**. 55

HW sent messages by, **5**. 243, **6**. 200, 224, 391

HW's *Gramont* to be given to, **5**. 315, 317

HW's health concerns, **6**. 129

HW's letter to Mme de Choiseul charms, **4**. 38

HW's letter to Mme du Deffand read to, **5**. 162

HW's medal of Antony and Octavia interests, **6**. 54, 60, 140–1, 142, 150–1

HW spoken of by, **6**. 289

HW's portrait desired by, **3**. 360, **4**. 23

HW's relations with, **6**. 378

HW's verses on Mme du Deffand read to, **4**. 275

HW ungratefully treated by, **16**. 281

HW wants Mme du Deffand's correspondence with, **36**. 184, 190

health of, **4**. 286, **5**. 352, 358, 360, 426, **6**. 75, 87, **7**. 66

jokes of, **5**. 426

jokes with Mmes du Deffand and de la Val-lière, **4**. 70–1

leaves Paris, **7**. 424

makes researches for HW, **4**. 6

Mariette gives book to, **5**. 242–3

Mirepoix, Mme de, talks to, at Mme du Deffand's, **5**. 61, 62

Muzell asks, to forward letter to Winckel-mann, **21**. 418n

*Othello* pleases, **6**. 287–8

Paris visited by, **5**. 59, 61, 144, 163, 228, 231, 234, 237–8, 330, 401, 403, 404, **6**. 348, **7**. 438

*Pater*, mock by, **4**. 343

pension of, **5**. 167–8, 173

political entanglements of, **5**. 108

Provençal; author, keeper of King's medals, **41**. 193

proverbs acted by, **7**. 331

remains in Paris: **7**. 151; to cheer Mme du Deffand, **36**. 55

St-Simon's memoirs done up by, **5**. 81

secretary of Swiss Guards, **4**. 9–10, 16, **5**. 155, 167–8, 173

Shakespeare admired by, **6**. 288–9, **28**. 258–9

social relations of, *see index entries ante* **8**. 237

SH Press book wanted by, **3**. 268, 272, 293n, 295, 297, 312

suggests that HW live in Paris, **3**. 358, 359

to leave Paris, **6**. 289, 426

to return to Paris, **4**. 200, 253, 264, **5**. 130, 137, 158, 224, 343, 395, **6**. 22, 66, 75, 87, 121, 240

uncertain about going to Chanteloup after Choiseul's disgrace, **5**. 1

Versailles visited by, **4**. 6, 9, 169

verses by, on Mme du Deffand, **3**. 289–90, 293

*Voyage du jeune Anacharsis* by: **28**. 374n, **43**. 104; 'Arsame' in, portrays Choiseul, **34**. 78; Damer, Mrs, admires, **34**. 70; HW's

criticism of, **34**. 40, 41–2, 70–1, 79; Ossory, Lady, on, **34**. 42, 70; tedious, **34**. 79

Bartholemy. *See* Bartholomew

Bartholomew, St. *See* St Bartholomew's Day

Bartholomew Fair:
George III's coronation compared to, **9**. 389
Walpole, Horatio (1678–1757) behaves like clown at, **19**. 169

Bartholomew-tide:
Villiers to spend, with Charles Montagu, **10**. 81

Bartoli, Pietro Santo (ca 1635–1700), artist:
*Admiranda romanarum . . . vestigia* illus-trated by, **42**. 268n

Bartolini Baldelli, Signora. *See* Serristori, Maria Luisa

Bartolini Baldelli, Anton Vincenzo (1691–1766), cavaliere:
Rinuccini, Signora, cicisbea of, **17**. 40, 53
Serristori's sister to wed, **17**. 40, 53

Bartolini Salimbeni, Signorita:
sister sacrifices dowry to, **25**. 498

Bartolini Salimbeni, Maria Luisa (1766–1813), m. (1784) Conte Giulio Giuseppe Mozzi:
marriage of, **25**. 498, 512, 527, 535, 539

Bartolommei, Marchese Ferdinando (1678–1748), Tuscan envoy to Austria; Tuscan and Hungarian minister to Sardinia:
Austro-Sardinian convention negotiated by help from, **17**. 196n
Florentines expect news from Turin from, **17**. 342
Francis I could not be instructed by, about Tuscan affairs, **17**. 406
Ginori may replace, **17**. 395, 406, 490
Maria Theresa sends, to Turin, **17**. *195–6*
Piacenza visited by, **17**. 392n
Regency member, **17**. 195n

Bartolommeo della Porta, Fra (1472–1517), painter:
HW once regarded, as Raphael's equal, **23**. 465
HW saw pictures by, at Florence, which Patch should engrave, **23**. 267, 268
HW's 'standard for great ideas,' **11**. 154
Patch's engravings from, **23**. 276–7, 362, 371–2, 465, 468–9
Raphael's 'parent,' **23**. 267

Bartolozzi, Francesco (1727–1815), engraver:
Buchan mentions, **15**. 189
Bunbury's 'Robin Gray' engraved by, **33**. 401n
'Death of Chatham' engraved by, **29**. 185n
drawing of Lady Diana Beauclerk's daughter engraved by, **29**. 71
engravings by, **11**. 247n, **25**. 528n, **28**. 413n, 421n, **33**. 322n, 401n, **42**. 322n, 375n
fit only to illustrate *Il Pastor fido*, **33**. 547
Harcourt a better engraver than, **35**. 459
Henshaw a pupil of, **1**. 291n, **28**. 59n
—— interests, **1**. 301, 306n, 314, 321, 388
Hollis's *Memoirs* decorated with cuts by, **29**. 19

[Bartolozzi, Francesco, *continued*]
  Italy visited by, 1. 306n
  Mann encloses letter to, 23. 459
  Ogborne and Van den Berghe pupils of, 16.
    323n
  portrait of Ds of Devonshire engraved by,
    28. *386*
  portrait of Mary Queen of Scots, in Drapers'
    Hall, engraved by, 42. 322
  portraits for Johnson's *Poets* engraved by,
    28. 413n
  Sherwin, a pupil of, 2. 8n
  SH visited by, 12. 252
Barton, Capt.:
  *Thomas* commanded by, 24. 334n
Barton, Cutts (ca 1707–80), D.D., rector of St
    Andrew's, London:
  refuses to pray against earthquakes, 20. 155
Barton, Frances (1737–1815), m. (1759), James
    Abington; actress:
  as Lady Teazle, 33. 87, 564
  Burgoyne's *Maid of the Oaks* acted by, 32.
    216n
  coiffure of, 32. *216*
  Cooke's *Capricious Lady* could be redeemed
    only by acting of, 41. 403
  epilogue delivered by, 33. 182n
  Garrick's jealousy of, 33. 88
  HW calls on, and is asked to see her in South-
    ampton St, 41. 215–16
  HW declines invitation by, 42. 450–1
  HW mentions, 7. 142
  HW's correspondence with, 41. 215–16, 413,
    42. 449–50
  HW to invite, to SH, 42. 450
  HW to sup with, 39. 323
  HW to suspend visitors' rules for SH in
    favour of, 41. 413
  Hobart, Mrs, entertains, 33. 428n
  Hôtel Turenne the Paris address of, 41. 215
  Jekyll's epilogue read by, 29. 44
  limitations of, 33. 564
  marriage information about, corrected, 43.
    104, 306, 348, 377
  *School for Scandal* well acted by, 41. 363
  speaks epilogue to Craven's *Miniature Pic-
    ture*, 33. 182
Barton, Matthew (ca 1715–95), naval officer:
  George III's remonstrance from, for Keppel
    trial, 24. 432n
Barton, Rev. Philip (1717–86):
  Cole asks, to convey parcel, 1. 117
Barton Hall, near Newmarket; Bunbury's seat:
  Boufflers, Comtesse de, visits, 32. 14n
  Bunbury of, 9. 152n
Barton Hall, Bristol:
  Browning of, 16. 176n
Bartoni [?Batoni]:
  miniature by, 9. 304n
Barton Mills, Suffolk:
  'Bull' inn at, 28. 306
  HW writes from, 24. 292, 32. 349, 36. 117,
    122

Barzizza, Vincenzo Carlo:
  Barbarigo succeeded by, as mayor of Verona,
    17. 196n
Bas, Le. *See* Le Bas
Basan (Bassan), Pierre-François (1723–97),
    engraver:
  biographical information on, corrected, 43. 99
  collection of, seen by HW, 7. 282
  *Dictionnaire des graveurs* by, 1. 155, 43. 53
  HW buys through, 6. 238, 245
  HW calls on, 7. 349
  HW's purchases at sale of, 7. 402
  HW told by, of Mariette's sale, 32. 282–3
  Presle not to outbid, 6. 231, 238
  social relations of, with HW, 7. 352, 353
  Torré described by, 6. 269
*Bas Bleu, The. See under* More, Hannah
Baschi-St-Estève, Comtesse de. *See* Riquet de
  Caraman, Émilie-Rose-Marguerite de
Basel. *See* Basle
Bashaw; bashaws:
  England will be ruled by, 4. 200
*Basilicon Doron. See under* James I
Basilowitz. *See* Ivan IV
Basin; basins:
  HW fishes with, 9. 155
  of Chelsea china, 22. 180, 191
  of goldfish, do not inspire HW to poetry,
    30. 100
  of Turkish earthenware, given to HW by
    Fitzwilliam, 42. 52–3
  of water, housekeeper at Castle Howard gives,
    to 'Rosette,' 30. 258
  silver, ecclesiastical, 35. 497
  Suffolk, Cts of, holds, for Q. Caroline's hand-
    washing, 31. 420n
Basingstoke, Hants:
  Cowslades live near, 9. 251n
  sermon preached at, 15. 302
  Vyne, the, near, 9. 251n, 35. 640
Basire, Claude (1761–94), Danton's friend:
  opposes Reign of Terror, 12. 71n
Basire, Isaac (1704–68), engraver:
  print by, of Morell, after Hogarth, 43. 184
  print by, to *Funeral Sermon*, 16. 66n
Basire, James (1730–1802), engraver:
  engraving for Lodge being made by, 15. 209
  plates for Gough's *Sepulchral Monuments*
    engraved by, 42. 169n
  prints by: 2. 8n, 175n, 15. 160n, 16. 194n, 29.
    19n; 'Champ de drap d'or, Le,' 1. 299, 2.
    277n; 'Embarkation of King Henry VIII,'
    2. 277n; Gray, 1. 361, 367, 28. 141n; Lee,
    Sir Henry, 42. 199n; of Richmond Palace,
    16. 73–5, 78; of William Bowyer, 42. 21n;
    picture at Cowdray House, 2. 8n, 128; seal
    of Q. Henrietta Maria, 2. 129; 'Siege of
    Boulogne,' 16. 211; Stuart, Arabella, 42.
    313
Baskerville, John (1706–75), printer:
  Bible and Prayer Book the printing projects
    of, 40. 275

Cambridge University's grant to, **40.** 275

editions of, HW would send, to Albani, **21.** 262

HW a subscriber to *Paradise Lost* printed by, **40.** 276n

HW's correspondence with, **40.** 274–6

HW's patronage solicited by, **40.** 274–6

printing of, excelled by Norden's book, **9.** 414

Pope's works said to be at press of, **40.** 276

*Select Fables of Esop* printed by, **31.** 58n

type of, **29.** 165

Warburton asks, to print edition of Pope, **13.** 38n

Basket; baskets:

bantams to come in, by coach from London, **38.** 345

Chinese and Indian, HW buys, at Mrs Kennon's sale, **37.** 439, 439n

Coke, Lady Mary, carries, in garden, **31.** 138

evergreens sold in, from nursery, **9.** 176

of provisions, **30.** 276

of shell flowers, **42.** 307

*See also* Work basket

Basket-woman:

Grenville in rage resembles, **38.** 500

Huntingdon, Cts of, resembles, in print, **35.** 346

Basking Ridge, N. J.:

Lee captured at, **28.** 282n

Basle; Basel:

Austrian-French peace at, fabricated to manipulate stocks, **34.** 213n

Benedict XIV's death reported at, from Rome, **21.** 44n

Berrys visit, **11.** 356, 359

canton of, prepares to resist Prince Charles, **18.** 290

HW addresses letters to, **11.** 347, 351, 371

Holbein drawings from, **40.** 231

Mechel of, **12.** 242, **15.** 96n, 281

Meyer, mayor of, **14.** 166n

Necker visits, **11.** 36n, 45

painting at, of 'Dance of Death,' **16.** 144, 145–6, **40.** 254

Polignac family visit, **34.** 67n

sketch of Holbein painting in, **16.** 48n

Basquiat de la Houze, Mathieu de (1724–94), Baron de la Houze; Chevalier; secretary of Swedish legation at Rome:

Swedish *coup d'état* instigated by, **23.** 439

Bas relief; bas reliefs:

Beauclerk, Lady Diana, models, in wax, **35.** 425

Breton designs, for Wolfe's tomb, **21.** 436

classical, inexpressive, **35.** 445

Damer, Mrs, does, **12.** 272–4, **43.** 167

—— might design nymphs in, **42.** 272

Delineator, The, may aid copying of, **41.** 366

Donatello's, of St John, at SH, **23.** 450, 453, 456, 459, 463, 464, **24.** 15, 499

in SH cloister, given to HW by Cole, **43.** 61

ivory, HW buys, at Mrs Kennon's sale, **37.** 439n

marble, at La Borde's, **31.** 80

medallions in, **39.** 254

Nicholson incident represented in, **11.** 363

of Leonora d'Este, sent by Hamilton to HW, **35.** 409, 412, 429

wax, of Benedict XIV, *see* Benedict XIV: HW's inscription for wax bas-relief of

Bass. *See* Bass-viol; Double-bass; Thorough-bass

*Bassa, l'illustre. See* Scudery, Madeleine de: *Ibraham*

Bassan, ——, collector and curio-dealer. *See* Basan, Pierre-François

Bassan; Bassano, painter. *See* Ponte, Jacopo da

Basse, ——, Paris grocer:

Du Deffand, Mme, has receipt from, **8.** 41

Bassenge (*or* Bassange *or* Bassanges), Paul (b. ca 1742), Paris jeweller:

Rohan's revenues should be sequestered to pay, **25.** 654

Basset, Lady. *See* Coxe, Frances Susanna

Basset, Sir Francis (1757–1835), cr. (1779) Bt, (1796) Bn de Dunstanville, (1797) Bn Basset:

English peerage declined by, **33.** 430n

haying on island of, at Twickenham, **11.** 351

Hindley's Twickenham house bought by, **33.** 183n

Radnor House, Twickenham, occupied by, **42.** 480

SH visited by, **12.** 222, 225, 229

SH visitors sent by, **12.** 224

Basset, Harvey:

Selwyn's deputy at the Mint, **30.** 154n

Basset, Isabel (fl. 14th cent.):

Leicester's claim of descent from, **15.** 330n, **34.** 28

Basset, John Prideaux (1744–56):

Faber's print from Ramsay's portrait of, **40.** 287

Basset, Hon. Ralph (d. ca 1335):

Leicester's claim of descent from, **34.** 28

Basset, Ralph (ca 1335–90), 3d Lord Basset of Drayton:

Leicester's collateral descent from, **15.** 330

sister of, **15.** 330n

Basset (game):

deep, played by men at Stanhope's, **19.** 485

Basset, barony of:

Leicester considers claiming, **15.** 330

Basseterre, Guadeloupe:

English fleet captures, **21.** 277n

Bassett. *See* Basset

Bassingbourne Church, Cambs:

Butler monument in, **1.** 7

Cole's visit to, **1.** 7n

*Bassoio* (tray):

Uguccioni gives, to Granvilles, **18.** 553

Bassompierre, Marquise de. *See* Beauvau, Charlotte de

Bassompierre, François (1579–1646), Bn de, Marquis d'Harouel:

[Bassompierre, François, *continued*]
  HW seeks portrait of, **31.** 78
  Lasne's print of, owned by HW, **31.** 78n
Bassoon; bassoons:
  imitation of, **9.** 131
Basso relievo. *See* Bas-relief
Bass viol:
  imitation of, **9.** 131
  Middleton plays, **15.** 293
  Walpole, Sir Edward, plays, **9.** 14
Bastard, François (d. 1780), seigneur de La
    Fitte:
  death of, **7.** 441
  (?) hearing granted to, **7.** 439
  Montyon replaces, **7.** 442
Bastard, John Pollexfen (1756–1816), M.P.:
  Pitt's Parliamentary motion amended by, **25.**
    629n
Bastardella *or* Bastardina, La. *See* Aguiari,
    Lucrezia
Bastia, governor of. *See* Mari
Bastia (Corsica):
  batteries to be raised at, by French engineer,
    **20.** 573n
  Corsican rebels compelled to abandon, **20.**
    386
  Curzay displeases Corsican chiefs at, **20.** 353n
  English fleet blockades, **21.** 140n
  French and Genoese recapture, **19.** 437
  French not to take over, **20.** 588
  Genoa reserves, **20.** 273
  Genoa said to have recaptured, **19.** 215
  Jesuits in ships near, **22.** 526, 532
  Marbeuf wants communication between San
    Fiorenzo and, **23.** 46
  Rivarola captures, **19.** 162–3
  Scipioni from, **20.** 206n
  Townshend almost destroys, **19.** 156–7, **162,**
    169, 190
Bastiano da Pistoia:
  master gunsmith, **18.** 232n
Bastie. *See* La Bastie
Bastille, at Paris:
  'affair' of, **39.** 267n
  anniversary of capture of: English celebration
    of, **11.** 88–9, **31.** 361–2, **35.** 399n; French
    celebration of, **11.** 91, 94, 95, 96, 98, 99, 109,
    **31.** 340, 343; out of fashion, **11.** 319; to
    draw money, **39.** 477; will be forgotten in a
    year, **34.** 117
  burning of, **34.** 144, 152, 158
  Bussy ill at, **5.** 190
  Du Deffand, Mme, mentions, **3.** 327
  Dunn said to be imprisoned in, **20.** 9
  Edward, D. of York might capture, **21.** 228
  Éon probably fears, **38.** 238
  firing of cannon from, **11.** 36, **39.** 467–8
  Gourville sent to, **4.** 44
  Gouvernet in, **4.** 33–4
  Gray, cutler, almost sent to, **33.** 497
  HW fears, more than the Tower, **30.** 141

  HW jokes about, **10.** 201
  Hervey, Bp, threatened with imprisonment
    in, **25.** 454
  La Chalotais in, **3.** 188, 190
  Launey governor of, **11.** 40n
  Malesherbes releases prisoners from, **28.** 226
  mentioned, **3.** 44, **32.** 349
  Morton imprisoned in, **19.** 341
  number of prisoners in, **11.** 233, **34.** 152, 158
  pantomimes of horrors of, **34.** 71
  Richelieu in, **6.** 38
  Rohan confined in, **25.** 603, **33.** 494
  Royer de Surbois committed to, **6.** 112
  Sauvè, Dame, taken to, **20.** 287n
  seizure of, **11.** 40
  seven prisoners in, **43.** 147
  Sigorgne committed to, **4.** 407
  'Tonton' to be in, **39.** 258
  Tower of London no longer resembles, **22.**
    312
  Tower of London said by Temple to resemble,
    **38.** 199
  Wilkes should be sent to, **22.** 198
  *See also under* Paris
Bastin, John:
  HW's agent at Mrs Kennon's sale, **37.** 439n
Basville, Marquis de. *See* Lamoignon, Chrètien-
    François de
Bat; bats:
  and balls, HW's nephews and nieces might
    as well talk of, **34.** 231
  cricket, **40.** 6
  Temple, Cts, mentions, in verses, **10.** 115
Batailhe de Francès, Mlle ——, m. (?Louis-
    Augustin) Blondel:
  breaks arm, **7.** 428
  HW sees letter from, **11.** 99
  Joseph II calls on, to see Turgot, **6.** 443
  social relations of, with: Craufurd, **7.** 352;
    Damas d'Antigny, Mme de, **7.** 338; Ville-
    gagnon, Mme de, **7.** 352
Batailhe de Francès, Jacques (ca 1724–88),
    French chargé d'affaires (with rank of min-
    ister) 1769–ca 1771 in London:
  Argyll, Ds of, gets regrets from, for party,
    **39.** 135
  Blondel, Mme, sister of, **6.** 443n
  Choiseul's fate said by, to depend on his
    making peace, **39.** 135
  Craufurd introduces, to Mme du Deffand, **5.**
    267
  ——'s correspondence with, **5.** 317, 327, 335,
    362
  ——'s friendship with, **5.** 280, 317
  Du Deffand, Mme, hears war rumour from,
    **5.** 352
  —— likes, **5.** 267
  —— may send parcel by, **4.** 10
  England asked by, for satisfaction for insult
    to French ship, **32.** 39n
  England visited by, **3.** 275n

English ways known to, **6.** 11
Éon in England for same reason as, **33.** 511
HW entertains, at SH, **43.** 85
HW hears description by, of fireworks disaster, **23.** 217–18
HW receives canvas and silk from, **32.** *53*
HW sends letter by, **5.** 18, **7.** 392
HW's *Gramont* given to, **5.** 306, 315
HW told by, of Alfieri's account of Lady Ligonier's affair, **30.** 256
has not yet returned to Paris, **5.** 301
health of, **4.** 336, 344
London visited by, **3.** 237, 278, **4.** 42
*Mysterious Mother* may be translated by, **5.** 306, 320
seeks translator for Mme du Deffand, **5.** 325
silent at Hertford's, after Choiseul's fall, **39.** 136
sister of, marries T. Walpole, **33.** 587
social relations of, with: Mme du Deffand, **5.** 267, **6.** 278, 483; HW, **7.** (?) 322, 337
'turgotin,' **6.** 278
watches may be sent to, from Paris, **39.** 117–18

Batailhe de Montval, Jeanne-Marguerite (1731–1821), m. 1 (1755) —— Durand, Marquis de Villegagnon; m. 2 (1787) Hon. Thomas Walpole; 'Mme de Villegagnon-Walpole':
Berry, Mary, identifies, **11.** *97n*
biographical information on, corrected, **43.** 91, 143
Craufurd's friendship with, **6.** 221
goes to her ill brother, **4.** 336
HW likes, **4.** 336
HW sees, in London, **11.** *96*
second marriage of, **33.** 587, **36.** 248
shows HW's letter from Paris, **11.** 99
social relations of, with: Blondels, and Craufurd, and Malesherbes, **7.** 352; HW, **7.** 332, 352, **10.** 278–9, **11.** 97, 108, **39.** 271; Malesherbes, **39.** 271
SH visited by, **4.** 236n, **10.** 278–9

Batavia:
Tobia dies at, **31.** 162
Townshend Augustus, dies at, **9.** 32n, **19.** 277n

Bate, George (1608–69), M.D.:
*Dispensatory* of, *see* Salmon, William: *Pharmacopœia*

Bate, Rev. Henry. *See* Dudley, Sir Henry Bate

Bate, Rev. Julius (1711–71):
*Use and Intent of Prophecy, and the History of the Fall, The*, by, **15.** 299

*Bâteaux plats à vendre*:
HW's translation of, **38.** 35

Bateman, Vcts. *See* Spencer, Lady Anne

Bateman, Anne (d. 1802), m. (1744) Samuel Dashwood:
death date of, **43.** 253
marriage of, **18.** 451

Bateman, Lady Anne. *See* Spencer, Lady Anne

Bateman, James (d. 1758):
daughter's marriage not sanctioned by, **18.** 451
death date of, **43.** 254

Bateman, John (1721–1802), 2d Vct Bateman; M.P.:
Admiralty appointment of, **9.** 180–1, **20.** 517, **21.** 25
Berkeley succeeded by, as treasurer of the Household, **21.** 25
HW's correspondence with, **7.** 395
Macartney, Mrs, and Miss Gardiner in scandal with, **30.** 226n
sells Richard Bateman's things, **1.** 325, 328, **32.** 241–2
white stick received by, as treasurer of the Household, **37.** 481

Bateman, Nathaniel (d. 1761), Ps Amelia's equerry and gentleman usher:
Amelia's inquisitiveness at SH disliked by, **35.** 227

Bateman, Richard (ca 1705–73), collector:
Asciotti sells Flemish glass to, **9.** 146n, **20.** 199n
auction of, affects HW, **32.** 241
chairs of, bought by HW, **1.** 90, 93, 325n, **9.** 384, **10.** 43, **32.** 242, 245
cloister of, at Old Windsor, **1.** 90, 325, **10.** 43
HW and, to visit Ilchester at Redlynch, **40.** 249
HW entertains, at SH, **10.** 306
HW may visit, at Old Windsor, **31.** 120
HW passes day with Lady Hervey at house of, **30.** 253
HW's correspondence with, **21.** (?) 219, **38.** 167
HW sends compliments to, **31.** 36
HW sends Milles's packet to, **41.** 102
heir of, sells his things, **1.** 325, 327, 328, **32.** 241–2
house of, at Old Windsor: a 'kingdom of flowers,' **31.** 36; HW changes, from Chinese to Gothic, **10.** 43, **35.** 359; Montagu visits, **10.** 42
offices of, at Old Windsor, altered by Bentley, **35.** 644
social relations of, with Lady Hervey and Ilchester, **31.** 36–7
Townshend, Vcts, has Chinese architecture by, at her house, **40.** 52
Williams, C. H., describes love of, for Ds of Manchester, in 'Isabella,' **30.** 317

Bateman, [?Richard], Lt; engineer:
captured by the French, **24.** 476–7

Bateman, William (?1695–1744), cr. (1725) Vct Bateman; M.P.:
birth date of, **43.** 285
George I's witticism about, **24.** 227
homosexuality of, **30.** 309
wife separated from, by her brother, **30.** 309n

Bates, Henry:
  *Flitch of Bacon* by, acted at Haymarket, **11.** 14n
Bates, Mrs Joah. *See* Harrop, Sarah
Bates, William, customs official:
  Manchester orders, to submit accounts for customs place, **42.** 47
Bates. *See also* Bate
Bath, Bns. *See* Pulteney, Henrietta Laura
Bath, Bp of. *See* Bath and Wells, Bp of
Bath, Cts of. *See* Gumley, Anna Maria (ca 1694–1758); Pulteney, Henrietta Laura (1766–1808); Russell, Lady Elizabeth (d. 1605)
Bath, E. of. *See* Bourchier, Sir Henry (ca 1587–1654); Pulteney, William (1684–1764)
Bath, Marchioness of. *See* Bentinck, Lady Elizabeth Cavendish (1735–1825); Byng, Hon. Isabella Elizabeth (1773–1830)
Bath, M. of. *See* Thynne, Thomas (1734–96); Thynne, Thomas (1765–1837)
Bath, Somerset:
  abbey church at, **10.** 232–3
  Abbey Green in, **15.** 270n
  Amelia, Ps, talks about acquaintances at, **38.** 344
  Anstey's guide to, *see under* Anstey, Christopher
  balls at, **31.** 130, 131
  bank failures at, **31.** 382, 384
  Batheaston near, **5.** 189n
  Bedford, Ds of, unlikely to prefer, to political eminence, **30.** 186
  Bedfords the subject of satiric verses at, **38.** 462
  Bertrand, Mrs, keeps toy-shop at, **9.** 83
  Braddock, Fanny, gambles away fortune at, **20.** 492
  Bristol, E. of, dies at, **24.** 86
  Bristol contrasted with, **40.** 10
  Buxton Wells compared with, **40.** 16
  childless ladies visit, **18.** 239
  Chute to persuade HW to go to, **10.** 48
  Cole, Jane, lives at, **1.** 78, 93, 235
  disturbance at, during Gordon Riots, **2.** 224, **25.** 62, **33.** 196
  Du Barry, Vicomte, killed at, **33.** 71–2
  Dublin's assemblies, theatre and music surpass those of, **37.** 412
  Du Deffand, Mme, mentions, **3.** 152
  duel at, **33.** 71–2
  *Earl Goodwin* performed at, **11.** 254n
  earthquake at, **20.** 133n
  earthquake fits to be cured at, **37.** 424
  Ellis writes verses at, **35.** 369
  epigram on Pitt's gift from, **21.** 87
  expansion of, **11.** 287
  fortune-tellers from, **31.** 280n
  Gabriel, preacher at, **11.** 23n
  General Hospital of, **15.** 268n
  Gloucester abbot would divert visitors from, **1.** 346
  gout-sufferers at, **10.** 141

  Guilford's health improves at, **10.** 268, 308
  HW alone at, **10.** 232
  HW has not seen, **9.** 293
  HW knew Millers at, **10.** 233, **24.** 197, **32.** 196, **39.** 240–1
  HW may go to, for health, **1.** 286–7, **10.** 47–8, 62–3, **14.** 158, **22.** 110, 451, 454, 461, 492, **24.** 272, **30.** 139–43, 150, **31.** 125, 127, 128, **32.** 192, **33.** 152, **37.** 408, 412, 514
  HW no longer benefited by waters of, **10.** 231
  (?) HW's *Account of the Giants* written at, **31.** 132
  HW sees Wesley at, **3.** 159n
  HW's health improved after leaving, **10.** 232
  HW's health restored by, **30.** 235
  HW's opinion of, **3.** 151, **10.** 228, 229, 231, **15.** 268, **30.** 235, **31.** 130, 131, **32.** 200
  HW stays near Cross-Bath at, **10.** 228
  HW to be accompanied to, by: Chute, **10.** 227; Montagu, **10.** 48
  HW to leave, **10.** 231
  Hamilton's house in Crescent at, **33.** 527
  Henderson the actor is from, **28.** 326
  'heroine' at, **33.** 257
  Hoare, Miss, makes drawing at, **33.** 512
  Huntingdon, Cts of, builds chapel near, **10.** 179
  Lackham near, **10.** 229
  ladies 'ordered' to go to, when needing diversion, **19.** 26
  Lansdowne suggested as master of ceremonies at, **33.** 468
  Lansdown Road, Hamilton writes from, **42.** 88
  loo played at, in circle, **39.** 79
  Lort catches cold at, **16.** 201
  Lysons, D., may try, **12.** 144, 149, **15.** 265, 267–8
  Mann, Galfridus, to visit, **20.** 537, 544, 549
  Mary, Ps, to drink waters at, **19.** 295
  master of ceremonies elected at, **9.** 188n
  mayor of, *see* Wright, Henry
  memorandum on, **15.** 14
  Miller, Mrs, at, *see under* Batheaston
  Milsom Street in, **15.** 270n
  mob may visit, to protest food prices, **35.** 320
  Montagu's opinion of, **10.** 234
  Montagu to accompany Guilford to, **10.** 264
  Montagu, D. of, gives dinner at, **33.** 554
  nerves cured at, **20.** 389
  new buildings at, look like hospitals, **39.** 76
  Norfolk, D. of, arrested at, **12.** 206n
  Osbaldeston, Mrs, dies at, **12.** 74n
  Pitt and Bedford negotiate at, **30.** 236
  Pitt and Legge receive freedom of, **21.** 77n, 87
  Pitt unable to visit, for gout, **21.** 261
  Polignac, Mme de, looks as if presented to Bladud at, **39.** 449
  Pomfret, Cts of, dies on road to, **9.** 412, **21.** 560

post between London and, 3. 138
Pump Room at, avoided by HW, 10. 228, 31. 130
raffle held at, 10. 187
rakes repentant at, 10. 141
riot at, 43. 71
rioters said to have burned, 33. 196
Roman Catholic chapel near St James's Parade at, 25. 63n, 33. 196
St James's Church at, 32. 146n
Selwyn would be better diverted at London than at, 30. 145
sharper at, quoted, 35. 584
Skrine apothecary at, 20. 145
Stall St at, 1. 93, 114
telescope at, 33. 360
temperature at, 4 above zero, 22. 579n
Tyson master of ceremonies at, 33. 572n
Venner practised at, 1. 180n
visitors to: Ailesbury, Cts of, 35. 408, 37. 360; Amelia, Ps, 31. 420, 38. 343, 344; Ansbach, 33. 136; Anson, 22. 33; Barney, Tom, 18. 498; Bathurst, 37. 87; Beauclerks, 6. 390n, 32. 341; Bedfords, 10. 229, 30. 236, 35. 120, 320, 38. 433n, 460, 39. 76, 41. 41; Bingham, 11. 37n; bishops, 31. 131; Brown, Lady, 40. 89–90; Buccleuchs, 10. 266; Calder, 11. 119n; Calonne, 11. 36n; Camden, 10. 229, 31. 130, 35. 319, 39. 76, 95; Camden, Bns, 35. 319n; Caroline, Ps, 19. 234; Chamberlayne, 9. 208n; Chatham (Pitt, William), 10. 229, 21. 540, 22. 425, 449, 461, 462, 472, 479, 483, 488, 492, 567, 30. 236, 240, 31. 125, 130, 35. 120, 199, 263, 319, 39. 76, 41. 35, 41; Charlemont and family, 42. 311n; Chesterfield, 19. 463, 35. 258; Christian VII, 23. 41; Churchill, Charles, 19. 62n; Chute, 10. 227, 14. 95, 24. 210; Clive, 24. 60n, 32. 218n; Coke, 14. 87; Coke, Lady Mary, 31. 132; Cole, 15. 309; Conway, 39. 317; Craufurd, 3. 234, 24. 210, 30. 242; Dacre, 10. 187, 207; Devonshire, 22. 96; Dodd, 40. 8, 10–11; Egremont, 22. 96n; Élie de Beaumont, 38. 461; Fox, C. J., 34. 37n; George III, 34. 47n; Gibbon, 29. 106; Gleichen, 5. 359; Gloucester, D. of, 33. 2n, 136; Gloucester, Ds of, 33. 2n; Glynn, 2. 107; Gower, 18. 89; Guilford, Cts of, 10. 169, 173, 178; Guilford, E. of, 10. 169, 173, 178, 264, 266, 268, 308; HW, 1. 119, 120, 3. 136, 138, 139, 149, 153, 159, 160, 164, 170, 9. 293, 10. 47, 48, 62, 63, 227–9, 231–3, 15. 108, 22. 461, 466, 24. 197, 30. 235, 238, 31. 130, 35. 89, 118–20, 319–20, 39. 76–80, 41. 35, 36, 38, 39, 43. 196; Hardinge, 35. 633; Hartley, Mrs, 28. 362; Herschel, 33. 360, 365; Hervey, 18. 89, 96; Holdernesse, 28. 150; Hotham, 11. 237n; Ibbot, Henry, 42. 94; Jekyll, Lady Anne, 10. 169, 173, 178; Johnson, Bp, 39. 220; Johnstons, 11. 350, 352; judges, 31. 131; Keppel, Bp, 36. 156n;

Keppel, Mrs, 33. 2n; Kingston, Ds of, 32. 146; Lambert, 16. 123n; Lort, 16. 174n, 201; Lysons, D., 12. 144, 149; Malpas, Vcts, 16. 126, 39. 76; Mann, Sarah, 21. 503; March, 30. 242; Massereene, Cts of, 38. 343; Montagu, Frederick, 9. 247; Montagu, George, 10. 48, 141, 173, 178, 264; Moravian baron, 35. 258; More, Hannah, 31. 364, 374; Morice, 25. 191, 195, 202, 213, 216, 220, 235, 33. 300; Muzell, 21. 461; Newcastle, Ds of, 22. 567n; Newcastle, D. of, 22. 566–7, 579n; Norfolk, D. and Ds of, 9. 397, 40. 89; Northington, E. of, 10. 229, 30. 236, 31. 130, 131, 35. 319, 39. 76; Northumberland, Ds of, 38. 143; Nugent, Lord, 30. 236, 33. 136; Paoli, 23. 150; Powis, E. and Cts of, 31. 130, 35. 319, 39. 76; Pulteney (E. of Bath), 18. 24, 89; Quin, 10. 150, 187; Rich, Mary and Sir Robert, 39. 76; Richmond, Ds of, 38. 384; Rockingham, Marchioness of, 31. 130, 35. 319, 39. 76; Scarbrough, Cts of, 31. 130; Selwyn, 30. 145, 242, 32. 341; (?) Sherard, Lady Lucy, 10. 229, 231; Sillery, Mme de, and Pamela, 34. 138n; Spencer, E. and Cts, 31. 130–1, 35. 319; Suffolk, E. of, 24. 450; Taylor, 29. 112; Thanet, Cts of, 37. 87; Thurlow, 33. 173n; Townshend, 2d Vct, 36. 41n; Townshend, 3d Vct, 38. 319, 346; (?) Trevor, Grace, 10. 229, 231; Vane, Vcts, 10. 228, 31. 131; Waldegrave, Cts of, 35. 530n; Waldegrave, 4th E. of, 33. 374, 36. 258, 260; Warburton, 10. 150; Wesley, 35. 118–19; Whaley, 40. 8, 10–11; William IV of Orange, 24. 53n; Williams, C. H., 18. 104; Williams, G. J., 30. 125, 150, 238, 35. 89n; York, D. of, 22. 437n; Zouch, 16. 54
'warm spot,' 10. 47
waters of: Cope drinks, from lady's hand, 14. 87; effect and season of, 3. 128, 134, 151, 5. 76; 'gilding' qualities of, 31. 128, 364; HW drinks, at Cross-Bath, 31. 130; HW finds, agree with him, 31. 130; jaundice cured by, 31. 364; March benefits from, 30. 242; More, Hannah, favours, 31. 350, 364; proper use of, 15. 268
Williams, G. J., may meet HW and Selwyn at, 30. 125, 150
Wilmington, E. of, to visit, 18. 135
Bath; baths:
Beauclerk, Lady Diana, returns from, 6. 460
HW takes, cold, 17. 452
Harwich salt-baths, 35. 247
hot, not approved of in Florence, as relaxing the nerves, 24. 280
Mann benefited by, at Pisa, 19. 486–7
—— makes, on his ground floor, 20. 357
—— to take: 17. 73; to cure headache, 20. 377
Modenese princess takes, 17. 65

[Bath; baths, *continued*]

Montaigne's *Journal* much concerned with, **24**. 16

near Venice, **4**. 428

of Lisbon, **34**. 146

Richecourt to take, at Plombières, **21**. 62

therapeutic, **3**. 349, 368, **5**. 183, **6**. 482

warm, eruption to be promoted by, **38**. 429

*See also* Abano; Aix-la-Chapelle; Aix-les-Bains; Bath; Bathing; Bath-tub; Bourbonne; Luxen; Malvern; Mud-baths; Pisa; Pougues; St-Amand-les-Eaux; Sea-bathing; Spa; Syringe-bath

Bath, Order of the:

absurdity of old usages of, **1**. 79

appointments to: **17**. 497, **18**. 451, 501; **19**. 117, 414, **20**. 39–40, 311, **21**. 24, 174, 370, 490, 507, **22**. 323, 380, 381, 383, 390, **23**. 14, 272, 358–9, 364, 387, **24**. 81, 215n, 249, **25**. 367, **29**. 251, **39**. 179

ball given by, at Haymarket, **39**. 322

Bateman not awarded, because no gentleman, **24**. 227

Bolton's suicide may make room for Mann in, **22**. 312

Bubb Dodington encourages Mann's hopes for, **22**. 235, 314, 317

Burgoyne may be offered, **32**. 380

Catherine II invests Gunning with, **23**. 508

Clive gets, ahead of Draper, **22**. 242–3, 318, 323, 503, 581

Conway helps Mann's aspirations to, **22**. 309, 339, 359n, 577, **23**. 52, **25**. 129

Coronation dinner for knights of, **38**. 133

Cowper and Rosenberg congratulate Mann on getting, **23**. 9

Dick takes, to Mann, **23**. 41, 47, 52, 55, 367

—— unlikely to get, **24**. 85

Downe, in robes of, **35**. 72

Draper's assurances of getting, **22**. 236, 323, 344, 383

esquires of, and their exemptions, **24**. 146

George III gives uncle's place in, to second son, **22**. 578, **23**. 341

—— promised, to Mann, **22**. 344, 509, 515, 580, 587, **23**. 3, 5, 9, 41, 52

Gloucester, D. of, promised to get, for Dick, **24**. 85

Grafton corresponds with Cowper about Mann's getting, **22**. 339, 469, 546

Grand Mastership of, coveted by D. of Cumberland on D. of Montagu's death, **20**. 120n

HW cautions Mann against striving too hard for, **22**. 509

HW presses Mann's campaign for, **22**. 323, 358–9, 363, 366, 381

HW remembers his father's reviving, **22**. 381

HW's brothers said to esteem, **22**. 390

HW surprised that Sir Edward Walpole should accept, **22**. 381

HW unable to aid Mann towards, **22**. 363, 480

HW writes about: to Conway, **22**. 332, (?) 363; to Edward Louisa Mann, **23**. 45

Harley does not receive, **23**. 21, 32

Hillsborough hopes Mann will receive, **22**. 495, 502, 540

Huntingdon may aid Mann towards, **22**. 314, 581

insignia of: foreigner at Paris wears, **24**. 361, **25**. 572; lost, **32**. 346

installation of: **20**. 71, **23**. 341, 414–15, **30**. 67, 78, 81, 82, 83, **39**. 322; deferments of, **23**. 341, 354, 364, 417; George III to make, magnificent, **23**. 407; knighthood expenses for, **23**. 411; Mann's choice of proxy for, in question, **23**. 326–8, 340–1, 346, 350, 353–4, 356, 357, 359, 362, 364, 366, 371, 379, 383, 385, 388, 389–90, 407–8, 410–11, 414–15, 417, 418; 'institution' of, see *Procession and Ceremonies . . . of . . . the Order of the Bath*

Leopold, Grand Duke, to invest Mann into, **23**. 59

Lyttelton a member of, **19**. 189n, **20**. 33n, **23**. 240

Mann disclaims excessive longings for, **22**. 335, 376, 390, 407, 486, 502, 546, 580–1

—— may get, by aping Pitt's hauteur, **22**. 441

—— may get, through Edward, D. of York, **22**. 226, 235, 241, 245, 309, 314, 317–18, 383, 390, 402, 417, 425, 429, 521, 581

—— may get, through Stuart Mackenzie, **22**. 235–6, 314, 317, 469, 486, 579–80, 581, 587, **23**. 1, 3, 4, 5, 41, 49, 52

—— mentions his aspirations to, to Beauchamp, **22**. 502

—— persists in desiring, **22**. 390, 396–7

——'s aspirations to, might antagonize any new Grenville ministry, **22**. 397, 433–4

——'s delay in getting, **22**. 439, **23**. 22, 36–7, 40, 52–3

——'s investiture in, **23**. 47, 57, 63–4, 70

——'s portrait in robes of, **23**. 48, 155; *see also under* Maron, Anton von

——'s promotion might prevent his getting, **22**. 341, 352–3, 376

Mordaunt's death makes vacancy in, **29**. 87

Newcastle, D. of, might recommend Cambridge college head to, **22**. 332

nominations to, still uncertain, **30**. 164

plumes of, in George III's coronation procession, **38**. 122

Proctor and Lloyd said to receive, **20**. 136

red ribbon of: **9**. 56; HW considers, a plaything, **22**. 381

revived as succedaneum to bank-bills, **22**. 381

Rockingham unable to aid Mann towards, **22**. 359n

Stanhope's protest when table of, is removed from Coronation banquet, **9**. 389

vacancies in, **22**. 314, 332, 577–8, **23**. 240

Walpole, Sir Edward, has, **17**. 209n, **22**. 27, 390, **25**. 426n

Walpole, Sir Robert, member of, **22**. 26, 381n

—— promised, to C. H. Williams, who received it from Pelham, **30**. 311

Washington probably would not accept, **32**. 380

Williams, Sir C. H., received, from Pelham on old promise of Sir R. Walpole, **30**. 311

'Bath, Wife of.' *See* Gumley, Anna Maria; *Wanton Wife of Bath, The*

Bathampton:

Holder of, **10**. 228n

Bath and Wells, Bp of. *See* Beadon, Richard (1737–1824); Foxe *or* Fox, Richard (ca 1448–1528); Ken, Thomas (1637–1711); Kidder, Richard (1633–1703); Montagu, James (ca 1568–1618); Moss, Charles (1711–1802); Welles, Edward (d. 1773)

Bath and Wells:

bishopric of, vacant, **32**. 168

Bath coach:

joke on Pulteney and, **17**. 485

Batheaston, Somerset:

Anstey's verses at, **33**. 84–5

Conway escapes visiting Millers at, **39**. 317

Millers' 'Parnassus' at, **5**. 189n, **10**. 233, **24**. 197, **32**. 196, 221, **39**. 240–1

miscellany from, dull, **32**. 224–5

Montagu, Lady Barbara, lives at, **10**. 165n, 234

visitors to: HW, **10**. 233, **24**. 197, **32**. 221, **39**. 240–1; Rich, Mary, **39**. 240–1

*Bath Guide. See* Anstey, Christopher: *New Bath Guide, The*

Bathiani. *See* Batthyáni

Bathing:

Mann tired of, **17**. 73, 78

Morice overdoes, **25**. 220

piles necessitate, **17**. 78

Walpole, Horatio (1678–1757), and wife dislike, **17**. 47

*See also* Bath; Bath-tub; Mud-bath; Seabathing

Bathoe, Mrs Mary (d. 1772), bookseller; (?) widow of William Bathoe:

Bell succeeds, at shop near Exeter Change in the Strand, **23**. 418n

Bathoe, William (d. 1768), bookseller:

catalogue of royal collection published by, **42**. 354

Chauncy sends Sunderland's etchings to HW by, **41**. 145

Dalrymple to receive from: HW's volumes, **15**. 94; Nanteuil's prints, **15**. 92, 95, 100, **40**. 320

HW's *Anecdotes of Painting* sold by, **14**. 121n, **22**. 10n

HW's correspondence with, **10**. 102, (?) **14**. *120*, **40**. 290

Hillier receives information from, **16**. 63n

Nanteuil's prints investigated by, **15**. 92, 95, 100, **40**. 320

shop of: Chatterton MSS conveyed by, to HW, **16**. *123*; HW corrects misspelling of name of, **16**. 358

(?) SH Press may be examined by, for stolen copies after Pratt left, **30**. 17n

*See also* Bell, John

Bathsheba:

Pompadour, Mme de, called, **22**. 4

Bath-tub:

HW imagines Mrs Cavendish in, **39**. 139

Bathurst, Cts. *See* Lennox, Georgiana (1765–1841); Scawen, Tryphena (1730–1807)

Bathurst, Capt.:

Villinghausen news brought by, **21**. 516n

Bathurst, Allen (1684–1775), cr. (1712) Bn and (1772) E. Bathurst; M.P.; lord chancellor:

Augusta, Ps of Wales, prefers, as George III's governor, **20**. 345

Bath's quarrel with, **20**. 38

Beefeaters said to be assigned to, **17**. 457

Bolingbroke recommends George Lewis Scott through, **20**. 203n

bust of, at Stowe, **41**. 6n

Carteret, Bns, attended by, **18**. 483, 501, **30**. 63

correspondence of, said to have been burnt by son, **28**. 239

Cromwell, Richard, replies to, **33**. 443

death of, **7**. 398, **23**. 268

Frederick, P. of Wales, mentions, in ballad, **19**. 46

Gentlemen Pensioners to be headed by, **17**. 492

George III appoints, to examine D. of Gloucester's marriage, **36**. 92

Hobart succeeds, in Gentlemen Pensioners, **18**. 551

Montagu, Lady Mary Wortley, writes poetical epistle to, **14**. 242

*New Ode, A*, satirizes, **18**. 50

not dishonest, but prejudiced against Sir Robert Walpole, **25**. 7–8

park of, at Cirencester, **40**. 11

reversion of Guilford's place said to go to, **32**. 176

son to become lord chancellor on death of, **23**. 268

Suffolk, Cts of, vainly asks George III for earldom for, **34**. 259

Swift's correspondence with, **25**. 6, 7

Thanet, Cts of, retorts to remark by, about Sir Robert Walpole, **37**. 87

Walpole (Sir Robert)'s head said to be in pocket of, **37**. 87, 91

Bathurst, Charles (ca 1709–86), bookseller:

in Fleet St, **1**. 201n

Bathurst, Henry (1714–94), cr. (1771) Bn Apsley; 2d E. Bathurst, 1775; M.P.:

[Bathurst, Henry (1714–94), *continued*]
agreeable, **32.** 236
bankruptcies enrich, **28.** 401
biographical information on, corrected, **43.** 265
bust of, at Stowe, **10.** 155n
Chatham's son's provision opposed by, **29.** 248
Cornwallis, Mrs, has, at soirées, **11.** 217n
Dodd's attempt to bribe, for St George's living, **32.** 185
father's correspondence said to be burnt by, **28.** 239
Frederick, P. of Wales's attorney, **20.** 5, 32
'fuddled,' **29.** 58n
George III sends, to examine proofs of Cumberland and Gloucester royal weddings, **23.** 483, **36.** 92
Gordon examined before, **25.** 71n
Gordon rioters attack, **33.** 176
Gower succeeded by, as president of the Council, **24.** 534
Guines's ball attended by, **32.** 117, **33.** 256–7
HW calls: 'old woman,' **29.** 38; 'wig-block,' **28.** 239
HW mentions, **28.** 49, **29.** 70, 128
HW's Glastonbury chair copied by, **33.** 209n
HW wishes, to dance at Guines's ball, **33.** 256–7
house of, guarded during Gordon Riots, **33.** 184
Huber might not be appreciated by, **32.** 307
Kingston, Ds of, attacked by, **24.** 150
—— may be protected by decree of, **24.** 123
——'s trial to be conducted by, **28.** 245n, 262
lord chancellor, **24.** 534n, **39.** 136n
lord chancellor's seals in commission to, **23.** 179n
lord keeper and future lord chancellor, **23.** 268
lord keeper's post may go to, **23.** 251, 259
lord presidency of the Council may go to, **28.** 469n, **33.** 134
'Lord President Jenkins,' **33.** 326
Murray, John, acquitted by, **28.** 322
Opposition aided by, **20.** 32
Ossory's neighbour, **32.** 236
Parliamentary debate by, on privately-raised regiments, **26.** 17
'Peach in Brandy' alludes to, **32.** 60–1
publication of Chesterfield's letters permitted by, provisionally, **28.** 144–5
resignation of, as lord chancellor, **7.** 49
reverses himself in debate on literary property, **28.** 138
Royal Marriage Act passes as work of, **36.** 84–5
ruling by, for Court of Chancery, **24.** 118n, 123n
SH visited by, **12.** 221
studies astronomy and lives on roots, **20.** 5
Thurlow succeeds, as lord chancellor, **7.** 47n, **24.** 385

Wilkes freed by, **38.** 200–1
——'s retort to, on becoming lord mayor, **39.** 207
Württemberg, D. of, gets invitation in bad French from, **28.** 262
Bathurst, Henry (1762–1834), 3d E. Bathurst, 1794:
Seymour-Conway, Lord and Lady Hugh, visit, in Sussex, **36.** 288
Bathurst, Miss (? Margaret) (d. 1777):
death of, **36.** 143, 151
Bathurst, Peter (ca 1688–1768):
Fielding, Henry, fed by, **9.** 84
son of, **9.** 84
Bathurst, Peter (ca 1724–1801), army officer; M.P.:
attempted assassination of, **9.** 84
Fielding, Henry, visited by Rigby, and, **9.** 84
wife of, **30.** 329n
Bathurst, Mrs Peter. *See* Evelyn, Elizabeth
Bathurst, Lady Selina. *See* Shirley, Lady Selina (ca 1701–77)
Baton; batons:
on Fiennes arms, **35.** 139
Wolfe's, shown on design of his monument, **21.** 422
Batoni, Pompeo Girolamo (1708–87), painter:
Cholmondeley, 4th E. of, to be painted by, **23.** 349, 371, **43.** 284
English visitors' portraits painted by, **20.** 490
(?) miniature by, of Young Pretender, **9.** 304n
Northumberland's commission for Italian paintings to be copied by, **20.** 352, 490, 507n, **21.** 88
promises never kept by, **22.** 255
York, Cardinal, painted by, **21.** 467n
York, D. of, painted by, for Mann, whose nephew gives it to George III, **22.** 255, **25.** 673, 676
Batsford, Edward (d. 1800), parish clerk and sexton at Fulham:
Pinkerton's letter from, **16.** 382
portrait of James IV belongs to, **16.** 321n
Batson, Stanlake (fl. 1783–1808):
buys Horseheath, **2.** 113n
Batt, Rev. Charles William (ca 1761–91), divine:
death of, **11.** 322
*Dissertation on the Message from St John the Baptist* by, **11.** 322n
Batt, Christopher:
art collection of, sold, **37.** 460n
Batt, John Thomas (1746–1831), attorney:
approves of HW's settling Little Strawberry Hill on Berrys, **11.** 263, 309
Berrys inquired about by, **11.** 211, **12.** 49
——' plan of going abroad told by, **11.** 110n, 141, 189, 224
—— praised by, **11.** 309
biographical information on, corrected, **43.** 139
*Bishop Bonner's Ghost* given to, **31.** 310, 313
brother of, dies, **11.** 322

Cambridge, R. O., visited by, **12**. 49
Campbell, Lord Frederick, to be visited by, **11**. 322
Garrick, Mrs, entertains, at dinner, **11**. 310
HW and Hannah More friends of, **31**. 310
HW drinks tea with, **11**. 33
HW entertains, at dinner, **11**. *17*, 309
HW reads *Reminiscences* to, **11**. 309, 311
HW visited by, **11**. 186
London left by, **31**. 313
never inquires about HW, **11**. 183
prospective inheritance of, **11**. 322
SH visited by, **12**. 232n

Batt, William (ca 1714–92) of Nunton and New Hall, Wilts:
partiality of, to younger nephew, **11**. 322

Batteley, Nicholas (1648–1704), antiquary:
*Antiquities of Canterbury* by, **2**. 349n
opinion of, about Strype, **2**. 349

Batteley. *See also* Battely

Battely, Rev. John (1647–1708):
. . . *Antiquitates S. Edmundi Burgi* cited, **2**. 39, 222

Battering-ram; battering-rams:
Conway thinks soldier's heart should be like, **37**. 224
HW mentions, **43**. 181

Battersea:
Bolingbroke dies at, **20**. 291n
Church, Thomas, vicar of, **15**. 298
(?) HW and Conway visit Jackson at, **20**. 362
Hay lives at, **33**. 59n
King's Road from Chelsea to, **31**. 273n
snuff-box from copper-plate process at, for enamelling, **35**. 252

Battersea Rise:
Astle addressed at, **41**. 399, **42**. 266

Battery; batteries:
at Sion House, for Quebec celebration, **38**. 60
balloons compared with, **25**. 450
English, at Fontenoy, **36**. 11
French: at Toulon, **21**. 303; destroyed by Murray, **25**. 207; ineffective at Minorca, **20**. 572; may be put in Corsican ports, **20**. 573–4
French and Spanish, opened on Minorca, **25**. 233–4, 269
not yet erected for Minorca siege, **25**. 196
rioters seize, in Genoa, **19**. 338
Spanish, in Italy, **17**. 306, 311, **18**. 335
Spanish floating, against Gibraltar: criticized by Bolognese professor, who invents a better one, **25**. 323; demolished, **25**. 326, 329–30, 331, 339, **39**. 394; in place at Gibraltar, **25**. 324, **33**. 358; loss of, blamed by Charles III on engineers, **25**. 329–30; opened, **25**. 318; reported destroyed by shore batteries, **25**. 325; Spanish confidence in, misplaced, **25**. 334

Batteux, Charles (1713–80), abbé:
Alembert defeats, for secretary of Académie française, **5**. 222
death of, **7**. *240*

Batteville. *See* Buisson, Pierre de, Chevalier de Beauteville

Batthyáni, Karl Joseph (1697–1772), Fürst von; general:
army command refused by, from dislike of Pallavicini, **19**. 50
army in Flanders led by, **19**. 240
Austrian army estimated by, **37**. 265
Cumberland, D. of, expects to relieve, **19**. 446n
Genoese insurrection belittled by, **19**. 346
health of, gout, **37**. 283
Lobkowitz to be replaced by, **19**. 23
Maria Theresa suspends orders to, to invade Venetian territory, **20**. 173n
not yet defeated, **37**. 249
retreat of, to Breda, **19**. 255
Schulenburg to command Austrian army till arrival of, **19**. 41

Battie, William (1703–76), M.D.; physician:
biographical information on, corrected, **43**. 153, 284, 351, 367
died worth £100,000, **32**. 315
HW hears lectures by, at Cambridge, **13**. *6*, **36**. 123n
HW prevents, from separating Martha Turk from E. of Orford, **42**. 336
Orford, 3d E. of, attended by, **1**. 298, **23**. 461, 467, 471, 482, 489, 505, 537, **28**. 126n, **32**. 175, 179, **42**. 336, **43**.
—— pronounced incurable by, **23**. 537, **25**. 126
——'s recovery confirmed by, **23**. 540–1, 546, 552, **36**. 123–4, 334
Poulett Lodge built by, **12**. 74n
Twickenham resident, **42**. 481
Williams, C. H., treated by, at Kensington, **30**. 322, **33**. 78n, **41**. 290n

Battista della Porta, Giovanni (ca 1538–1615), natural scientist:
Plat imitates, **28**. 275

Battle, Sussex:
HW writes from, **35**. 131
inn at, **35**. 137
St. Mary's Church at, **35**. 140

Battle; battles:
grow to victories, **12**. 268
mere lists of burials, **35**. 367

Battle Abbey, Sussex, Webster's seat:
Chute and HW visit, **35**. 131, 137–40
Hurstmonceaux near, **39**. 309
landscape effects at, **35**. 140
Montagu writes to, **9**. 328
Webster of, **11**. 331n
window at, **16**. 110

Battle-axe; battle-axes:
Hertford, Cts of, escorted by men with, at Dublin, **39**. 73

Battlements:
at Hurstmonceaux, **35**. 137
at SH: **9**. 149, **35**. 161; HW may mount pop-guns on, **21**. 311; Gothic shield and SH both have, **35**. 421
SH will rear, **20**. 199

*Battle of Hastings, The. See under* Cumberland, Richard

Battle of the Bridge. *See under* Pisa

Battlesden, Beds:
Page, Mrs, dies at seat at, **33**. 205n

Battoni. *See* Batoni

Batty. *See* Battie

Bauble; baubles:
HW sees no new fashions of, in Paris, **30**. 264
Smithson, Lady Elizabeth, wears pyramid of, on head, **20**. 49

Bauderon, Brice (ca 1540–1623), physician:
engraving of, **16**. 66
*Pharmacopœa* and *Praxis medica* by, **14**. 126

Bauffremont, Marquise *and* Princesse de. *See* Courtenay, Hélène de

Bauffremont, Charles-Roger de (1713–95), Chevalier de Listenois; Prince de Bauffremont, 1769; 'l'incomparable':
arrives in Paris, **4**. 278, 351
becomes Prince de Bauffremont, **4**. 238
Boisgelin, Mme de, to visit, **6**. 281
Boufflers, Marquise de, accompanied by, **5**. 86, 100, 122, 130, 150, 152, 163, 170, 225, 298, **6**. 168, 189, 212, 281
—— to be accompanied by, to Lorraine, **6**. 168
brother of, dies, **4**. 234–5, 238
Chanteloup to be visited by, **4**. 411, **7**. 448, **41**. 197–8
—— visited by, **4**. 71, **5**. (?) 268
Choiseul, Duchesse de, described by, **5**. 152
—— friend of, **41**. 193
—— visited by, **5**. 152
circle of, **5**. 86
Du Deffand, Mme, accompanied by, from Mme de Choiseul's, **41**. 196
—— accompanied by, to Sceaux and Montrouge, **4**. 442–3
—— allots suit to, **6**. 258
—— befriended by, **36**. 180
—— conveys, home, **4**. 369
—— entertains, **41**. 194, 196
—— given spaniel by, **5**. 422
—— has no letter from, **4**. 85
—— likes, like bread, **4**. 254, 256
—— mentions, **5**. 101
—— proposes to join, at Versailles, **4**. 362
—— sends HW's chain to Mme de Choiseul by, **4**. 365
—— sends letter by, **7**. 448
——'s opinion of, **4**. 64, 71, 254, 256, 351
——'s 'portrait' of, **4**. 236
epitaph by, for himself, **4**. 236
Franche-Comté estate of, **7**. 246
—— to be visited by, **4**. 254, 256, **6**. 189, **7**. 246
HW mentions, **6**. 258
HW met, at Mme du Deffand's and Mme de Choiseul's, **41**. 415
HW need not send Gramont to, **5**. 268
HW's correspondence with, **41**. 415–16

HWs correspondence with Voltaire approved by, **4**. 117–18
HW will not find, in Paris, **6**. 212
HW would like, **4**. 254, 256, 351
*Hamlet* attended by, **4**. 281
Le Val visited by, **7**. 457
Lorraine may be visited by, **5**. 225, **6**. 168
Marly visited by, **4**. 447
Mirepoix, Mme de, to visit, **6**. 281
permission to visit Duc and Duchesse de Choiseul sought by, **5**. 45
Praslin visited by, **7**. 426
Rueil visited by, **4**. 443, **7**. 337
St-Florentin a close friend of, **4**. 354
St-Sauveur aided by, **7**. 246, **36**. 180
Scey-sur-Saône occupied by, **5**. 97, **6**. 281
social relations of, in Paris, *see index entries ante* **8**. 238
Soyres recommended by, to HW and D. of Richmond, **25**. 518
Swedish princes talk with, of Mme du Deffand, **5**. 26
to return to Paris, **5**. 163
undecided about marrying, **4**. 351
Vaugirard, Rue de, the address of, **41**. 415

Bauffremont, Joseph de (1714–81), Prince de Listenois:
made vice-admiral, **6**. 403

Bauffremont, Louis (1712–69), Prince de:
death of, **4**. 234–5, 238

Bauffremont, Louise-Françoise-Bénigne-Octavie-Marie-Jacqueline-Laurence de (1750–1803), m. (1762) Joseph de Bauffremont, Prince de Listenois:
social relations of, with Hénault, **7**. 270

Baulas; Baulle. *See* Francesco

Baume, La. *See* La Baume

Baume, Friedrich (d. 1777), Lt-Col. of Brunswick dragoons:
army of, defeated at Bennington, **24**. 340, **32**. 393n

Baume de vie (medicine):
HW mentions, **38**. 516
Keppel, Lady Sophia, wants, **38**. 511, 514, 525
Le Lièvre prepares, at Paris, **38**. 511

Baumgarten, John:
HW's copy of Wood's *Essay* probably bound by, **40**. 306

Bausset, Comtesse ('Marquise') de. *See* Gérente d'Orgeval, Félicité-Justine de

Bausset, —— (d. 1767), French minister to Russia:
successor to, **23**. 127n

Bausset, Nicolas-Jean-Baptiste-Gabriel (1752–89), Marquis de:
Bausset, Comtesse de, not the wife of, **5**. 370n

Bausset de Roquefort, Emmanuel-François de (d. 1802), Bp of Fréjus, 1766:
HW does not know, **6**. 219
social relations of, with Mme du Deffand **6**. 219

Bauwell. *See* Bouwel

Bavaria, Cardinal of. *See* Johann Theodor (1703–63)

Bavaria, Ds of. *See* Maria Anna Charlotte Amalie

Bavaria, Elector of. *See* Charles Albert (emperor, as Charles VII) (1697–1745); Karl Theodor (1724–99); Maximilian Joseph (1727–77)

Bavaria, Ps of. *See* Louisa Hollandina (1623–1709); Maria Anna (1693–1751)

Bavaria:
Albert II's deed about, denied by Austria when Frederick II claimed under it, **7.** 2, 24. 400–1, 403, **33.** 9n, 14n, 35n
army of: at Linz, **17.** 315; Austrian army to be reinforced from, **19.** 41; Austrians defeat, **18.** 230, 234; commit outrages against church in Austria, **17.** 201n; said to be visible at Venice, **17.** 108
army of France and: Austrian army to oppose, at Prague, **17.** 194; driven back to Prague, **17.** 205
Austrians invade, **17.** 289
Austrians to evacuate, **19.** 37
Conti's army defeated in, **37.** 137
Conway and Scott tour, **39.** 538
*Cours de l'Europe* satirizes, **17.** 177
England and Holland at Treaty of Hanover grant subsidy to, **20.** 212n
England's new ally, **42.** 494, 497
France negotiates treaty with, **20.** 510n
French alliance with, **42.** 494
French evacuate, **18.** 250
French-Spanish treaty with, reported, **17.** 183
German troops may march to, **17.** 154
Holy Roman Empire's 'vicar' and 'most material elector,' **42.** 496
hostilities in, **17.** 446
imperialist aggressors at Dettingen, **18.** 259
impudent force may decide succession to, **24.** 365
Ingolstadt, Braunau, and Schaïdingen to be restored to, **19.** 37n
Maillebois to stop at, **18.** 32
Maximilian Joseph secures, by renouncing imperial claims, **19.** 37–8
ministers from and to, *see under* Minister
neutrality said to be proclaimed by, **37.** 189
peace said to be concluded by, **19.** 34
Saxony's relations with, **42.** 495
towns in, burned by defenders, **18.** 241
Versailles treaty guarantees troops of, to France, **21.** 147n

Bavarian chapel, London:
Gordon rioters pillage, **25.** 54–5, **29.** 52

Bavaro (cloak *or* cloak cape):
pun on, **17.** 351–2

Bavaroise:
for catarrh, **3.** 306

*Baviad, The. See under* Gifford, William

Bavière, Maximilien-Emmanuel-François-Joseph (1695–1747), Comte de:
death of, at Laeffeld, **9.** 50, **19.** 426n

*Bawdy Guardian, The. See under* Chute, John

Bawdy-house. *See* Bagnio; Brothel

Bawtree, W.:
Capoccio shrine engraved by, **35.** 406n

Baxter, Richard (1615–91), Presbyterian divine:
*Reliquiæ Baxterianæ*, **2.** 64, 72, 93

Bayardi. *See* Baiardi

'Bayes.' *See under* Villiers, George, 2d D. of Buckingham: *Rehearsal, The*

Bayet:
battle at, **12.** 84n

Bayeux, Bp of. *See* Albert de Luynes, Paul d' (1703–88); Odo (d. 1097)

Bayeux:
Broglie's army at, **7.** 47, 68, 72
tapestries at, **40.** 213, 221

Bayeux. *See also* Bayond

Bayeu y Subias, Francisco (1734–95), of Aragon; painter:
Spanish king's painter, **16.** 170

Bayfordbury, Herts:
Baker of, **11.** 57n

Bayham, Vct. *See* Pratt, Hon. John Jeffreys (1759–1840)

Bayham, Vcts. *See* Molesworth, Frances (before 1766–1829)

Bayham Abbey:
Chute and HW visit, **35.** 136–7

Bayle, Pierre (1647–1706), lexicographer:
*Anti-Lucretius* attacks ideas of, **9.** 52n
Choiseul, Mme de, praises, **8.** 148
Frederick II's poetry more harmful than writings of, **21.** 408
*General Dictionary* of: **43.** 154–5; cited against Whitelocke, **40.** 131; Conecte's attack on 'piked horns' described in, **9.** 78; HW cites, **15.** 87; HW cites, mistakenly, **40.** 138; HW quotes, **9.** 77n, **37.** 293n; Scaliger and Scioppius enshrined in, **41.** 52; Warburton's *Critical and Philosophical Inquiry* quotes, **16.** 368; wearing of looking-glasses described in, **9.** 78–9
HW's commonplace book on, **43.** 115
'pedantic bawdy' of, **14.** 62
Voltaire defends, against Spinoza, **3.** 113n

Baylens, Charles-Léonard-Bernard de (d. 1781), Marquis de Poyanne:
carabineers commanded by, **4.** 330, **6.** 78
daughter of, dies, **5.** 273
Malherbe's social relations with, **7.** 311
model for letter to Orléans sent to, **8.** 183
party at Livry includes, **10.** 211n
St-Germain second choice of, **6.** 228
second in command at Paris, **6.** 185

Baylens de Poyanne, Henriette-Rosalie de (ca 1750–72), m. (1767), Maximilien-Alexis de Béthune, Duc de Sully:
death of, **5.** 273
Poix, Princesse de, devoted to, **5.** 273

Baylies, William (1724–87), M.D.:
Frederick II's retort from, about killing people, 39. 259
Bayly, Lady. *See* Paget, Caroline
Bayly, Anselm (d. 1794), theologian:
*Antiquity, Evidence and Certainty of Christianity, Canvassed, The,* by, 15. 301
Bayly, Caroline (d. 1786):
sister of, 38. 575
Bayly, Dorothea (1738–64), m. (1759) George Forbes:
marriage and death of, 38. 575–6
Bayly, Gertrude (d. 1761):
sister of, 38. 575
Bayly (after 1770, Paget), Henry (1744–1812), 10th Bn Paget, 1769; cr. (1784) E. of Uxbridge:
children of, act in Lady Craven's play, 29. 235n
Hervey, Bp, rents St James's Sq. house to, 25. 455n
opposes bill providing for Chatham's son, 29. 248
son's marriage to Ds of Rutland forbidden by, 11. 244
Bayly, Louisa Augusta (b. 1750):
sister of, 38. 576
Bayly, Mary (d. 1790):
sister of, 38. 575
Bayly. *See also* Bailey; Baillie
Baynes, Mrs, of Kingston:
SH visited by, 12. 248
Baynes, John (1758–87), fellow of Trinity College, Cambridge; lawyer and writer:
*Archæological Epistle* attributed to, 2. 311n, 29. 244
Coney Court, Gray's Inn, the address of, 42. 10
HW's correspondence with, 29. 249–50, 252, 42. 10–11
intermediary in publication of: (?) *Heroic Epistle,* 28. 82, 128; Mason's later satires, 29. 247
Mason sends query by, to HW, 42. 10
Baynes, Roger:
secretary to Cardinal Allen, 42. 64n
Bayning, Bn. *See* Townshend, Charles (1728–1810)
Bayntun Rolt, Sir Edward (1710–1800), cr. (1762) Bt; M.P.:
biographical information about, corrected, 43. 243
petition against, 17. 318
Bayond, Peter:
Colomb cousins suspect, of forging Jacob Colomb's will, 42. 294
Colomb, James, does not want cousin's money paid to, 42. 290
—— tied with, as Jacob Colomb's executor, 42. 298
Bayonet; bayonets:
Conway busy with, 37. 358
Gordon Rioters repelled with, 33. 192

Pitt has, in Gorgon's head, 35. 262
used by English at Culloden, 37. 239
Bayonne (France):
Du Deffand, Mme, receives hams from, 7. 448
Bayreuth, Margrave of Ansbach-. *See* Friedrich Wilhelm (1711–63); Karl Alexander (1736–1806)
Bayreuth, Margravine of Ansbach– . *See* Berkeley, Lady Elizabeth (1750–1828); Friederike Sophie Wilhelmine (1709–58)
Bays (baize):
passage at Westminster Hall hung with, 37. 454n
scaffold rails draped with, 19. 300
Bays. *See also* Laurel
Bazett, Sarah (ca 1761–1838), m. 1 Edward Stephenson; m. 2 (1786) George Capel Coningsby, styled Vct Malden; 5th E. of Essex, 1799:
Boyle, Miss, to accompany, to Italy, 11. 238
SH visited by, 12. 233
Bazin, Jacques-Gabriel (b. 1725), Marquis de Bezons:
(?) Du Deffand, Mme, cites, 4. 169
marriage of, 3. 159n
Bazzicalupi, Pietro:
payment to, for services as courier, 17. 114
Beach, John, mate of the *Surprize*:
imprisoned at Dunkirk, 24. 302n
Beach, Mary (ca 1647–1725), Pope's nurse:
burial of, at Twickenham, 18. 36n
Pope's alleged affair with, 18. 35
Beacon; beacons:
France will hang out alms-boxes instead of, 21. 238
Beaconsfield, Bucks:
Burke's address, 42. 300
visitation at, 15. 300
Waller of, 19. 347n
Beacroft. *See* Beecroft
Bead; beads:
Africa trade employs, 31. 248
of lapis lazuli, 18. 447
rosary, discovered in D. of Cumberland's baggage, 19. 242
Turkish, HW buys, 22. 523n
'wooden' or 'woolen,' 43. 47
Beadle; beadles:
rural, in England, drive vagabonds into next parish, 22. 573–4
Beadon, Richard (1737–1824), Bp of Gloucester; of Bath and Wells; Public Orator:
Cole mentions HW's life of Baker to, 2. 69n, 230
—— receives MS from, 2. 53n, 69n, 230
—— receives print from, 1. 281n
Walpoles complimented by, 1. 312, 316
'Beadsman':
HW refers to himself as, 10. 127
HW signs himself as, 35. 454
Bead-work:
Magdalen House inmates make, 9. 274

Beagham. *See* Beaghan

Beaghan, ——

Venturini courts, 18. 392

Beaghan, ——, m. Leonardo Venturini:

marriage and Florentine visit of, 18. 391–2

sister of, 18. 392, 424

Beaghan, Edmund Hungate (1703–55), M.P.:

biographical information on, corrected, 43. 241

Doneraile's competitor in election, 17. 251

Beaghan, Katherine (d. 1756), m. (1725) George Bubb Dodington; 'Mrs Begham':

biographical information about, corrected, 43. 248, 358

Bubb Dodington entertains, at Eastbury, 40. 9

——'s marriage to, 18. 104–5, 424, 33. 556

death of, 21. 39, 49

Florence visited by, 18. 392

husband kept, as his mistress, 18. 392

sisters of, 18. 391–2, 424

Beagle. *See under* Dog

Beaker; beakers:

china, might adorn great rooms at Ragley, 39. 47

Beale, Charles (b. 1631), of Walton:

HW gets water-colours by, after Van Dyck and Lely, 15. 191n, 32. 294n

HW to get transcript, from Warton, of 'pocket-book' of, 40. 367

Lely and other painters deal with, to obtain colours, 40. 367n

Beale, Mrs Mary. *See* Cradock, Mary

Beale family:

coat of arms of, 10. 338

monument to member of, at Easton Mauduit, 10. 339

Beamore, co. Meath:

Balfour of, 3. 299n

Bean; beans:

Cole raises, 1. 276

Du Deffand, Mme, tempted by, 4. 244, 247, 252, 5. 371

frost said to have killed, in England, 23. 200

HW's, parched, 39. 499

Lyttelton thinks, are bought by the load, 40. 88

Mann has, for dinner, with bacon, 21. 10

Montagu eats, at Bp of Durham's, 10. 211

planting of, 1. 106

poison thought to be as plentiful as, in racing stables, 41. 6

Pythagorean associations of, 10. 211

Bear; bears:

Ailesbury, Cts of, sees, at Tower, 37. 396

Arabian deserts thought to have, 37. 130

clumsiness of, 16. 271

Conway compares country gentlemen to, 37. 178

English resemble, when gamboling, 35. 364

new term in finance, 21. 559

Orpheus would tolerate, if it danced to his music, 20. 427

tournament of, Milbanke prominent in, at Hanover, 20. 200

Bearcroft, Philip (1696–1761), D.D.; Master of the Charterhouse:

Morton may succeed, 31. 427

Beard, Lady Henrietta ('Harriot'). *See* Waldegrave, Lady Henrietta

Beard, John (ca 1716–91), actor:

acts at Covent Garden, 9. 265

Amorevoli imitated by, in *Miss Lucy in Town*, 17. 435

*Case Concerning the Late Disturbances* by, 22. 121n

diction of, admirable, 28. 347

marriage of, 9. 265, 25. 571n

rioters' demands upon, 22. 120–1

'Samson' in Handel's *Samson*, 18. 180n

sings in *Atalanta*, 13. 102n

Smith's *Fairies* acted by, 35. 209

voice of, inadequate, 18. 180

Beard, Mrs John. *See* Rich, Charlotte

Beard; beards:

double white, on man in portrait, 30. 371

Gordon, Lord George, has, 33. 587–8

Liotard wears, down to his girdle, 20. 362

royalists let grow, till Restoration, 29. 135

Wortley Montagu has, 22. 113

Beardmore, Arthur, attorney; Temple's man of business:

Monument's illumination abandoned by, after Pitt's earldom, 30. 234

Bear Garden:

bruisers of, 18. 538–9, 30. 331

English theatre is, 41. 404

opera attendants hired from, 17. 166

suppression of, 15. 70

Bear Key *or* Quay, London:

prices at, 34. 39

Béarn, Comtesse de. *See* Achard des Joumards, Angélique-Gabrielle

Béarn, Mlle de. *See* Galard de Béarn, Angélique-Marie-Gabrielle de

Béarn (Switzerland):

Angosses to return to estate in, 7. 140

censorship in canton of, 10. 192–3

HW's joke about officer of justice of, 10. 192–3

'Bears':

(?) HW's nickname for Russians, 9. 227

'Bears and bear-leaders':

Pitt, Anne, will indemnify Mann for 30 years of, 24. 16

Bearskin; bearskins:

HW and Gray are swathed in, crossing Alps, 13. 189

man in, worried by dogs, 37. 340

official: divides former allies, 38. 195–6; in Francis I's state box at Leghorn opera, 17. 259

Beartie, John (d. 1768):

murder of, 23. 34n

Beaston, Devonshire:
  Hussey dies at, **42**. 255
Beatifications:
  Benedict XIV deals with, **19**. 171n
'Beat knaves out of doors':
  HW alludes to, as children's game, **19**. 5
Beaton, David (1494–1546), cardinal; Abp of
  St Andrews:
  life of, in *Biographia Britannica*, **2**. 188
  print said to be of, **2**. 20–1
Beaton, James (1517–1603), Abp of Glasgow
  1552–1603; founder of Scots College in Paris:
  James I's letters to, **7**. 359
  Mary Stuart's letters to, **7**. 359
  prayer book of, **7**. 359
  Scots College founded by, **15**. 108n
'Beatrice.' *See* Shakespeare, William: *Much Ado
  about Nothing*
Beattie, James (1735–1803), poet, essayist,
  moral philosopher:
  *Dissertations Moral and Critical* by, disliked
    by HW, **29**. 309–10, **33**. 416
  Gray's consent obtained by, to publish poems,
    **14**. 172n
  ——'s letters to, excellent, **28**. 64
  HW's impression of, **11**. 291
  London, Bp of, entertains, **11**. 291
  may know where truth is, **34**. 43
Beauchamp, Bn. *See* Seymour, Edward (1561–
  1612); Seymour, Henry (ca 1626–54)
Beauchamp, Vct. *See* Seymour, Edward (ca
  1500–52); Seymour, George (1725–44); Sey-
  mour-Conway, Francis (1743–1822)
Beauchamp, Vcts. *See* Ingram Shepheard, Isa-
  bella Anne (1760–1834); Windsor, Hon. Alice
  Elizabeth (1749–72)
Beauchamp, ——
  SH visited by, **39**. 453n
Beauchamp, Anne (ca 1426–92), m. (1434)
  Richard Neville, cr. (1450) E. of Warwick;
  she was cr. (1450) Cts of Warwick, s. j.:
  Richard III could not have maltreated, **35**.
    607–8
Beauchamp, Guy de (ca 1271–1315), 10th E.
  of Warwick, 1298:
  figure might be misidentified as, **42**. 247
  HW quotes vow of chastity by wife on death
    of, **43**. 112
Beauchamp, Margaret (d. ca 1482), m. 1 Sir
  Oliver St John; m. 2 (ca 1442) John Beaufort,
  1st D. of Somerset; m. 3 (ca 1447) Leo Welles,
  6th Bn Welles:
  family of, **16**. 233n
Beauchamp, Lady Margaret (1404–67), m.
  (1425) John Talbot, 7th Lord Talbot; cr.
  (1442) E. of Salop, known as E. of Shrewsbury, (1446) E. of Waterford:
  biographical information on, corrected, **43**.
    183
  in Margaret of Anjou's escort, **14**. 73, 74
  portraits of, **10**. 336–7, **41**. 220, 251
  print of, in Pennant's *Journey*, **42**. 16n

Beauchamp, Philip, of Twickenham:
  (?) SH visited by, **12**. 222, 226, 228
Beauchamp, Philippe de. *See* Ferrers, Philippe
  de
Beauchamp, Richard (1382–1439), 13th E. of
  Warwick:
  daughter of, **10**. 337, **14**. 73n
Beauchamp Chapel, Salisbury. *See under* Salis-
  bury: cathedral
Beauchamp Chapel, Warwick. *See under* War-
  wick: St Mary's Church
Beauchamp family:
  arms of, **1**. 28, **33**. 350
  badge of, **9**. 122
  chapel of, at St Mary's, Warwick, **9**. 121–2
  genealogy of, **15**. 267
  HW praises, **18**. 357
  Warwick Castle haunted by, **32**. 352
Beauchamps. *See* Godart de Beauchamps
Beauclerc. *See* Beauclerk
Beauclerk, —— (d. 1758):
  funeral of, **21**. 172
Beauclerk, Aubrey (1740–1802), 2d Bn Vere,
  1781; 5th D. of St Albans, 1787; M.P.:
  appearance of, **10**. 343
  Drayton may be inherited by, **10**. 342
  Drayton visited by, **10**. 342–3
  family of, **10**. 342
  Grafton to return, as M.P. for Thetford, **31**.
    18
  HW and Cole entertained by, at Drayton,
    **10**. 342–3
  HW meets, at Drayton, **10**. 90, 342–3
  HW visits, at Hanworth, **33**. 294
  Hanworth trees cut down by, **11**. 287
  lives abroad, from debt, **33**. 294n
  Lowick parish estate held by, **10**. 342
  Mann has seen, **25**. 191
  marriage of, **10**. 342
  M.P. for Thetford, **10**. 342, **31**. 18
  Penn, Lady Juliana, not congenial with, **11**.
    23
  picture sent by, to Lady Elizabeth Germain,
    **10**. 342
  Sackville carries, into opposition, **38**. 311
  SH visitors sent by, **12**. 228
  'the new Veres,' returned to England, **33**. 293
  title inherited by, **25**. 191
Beauclerk, Aubrey (1765–1815), 6th D. of St
  Albans, 1802:
  grandfather's bequest to, **33**. 294n
Beauclerk, Caroline (d. 1769), m. (1756) Sir
  William Draper, K.B.:
  (?) Granby makes love to, **9**. 108
  (?) Lloyd, Mrs Gresham, deplores bad com-
    pany of, **9**. 108
  (?) mother entrusts, to Lady Caroline Peter-
    sham's chaperonage, **9**. 107
  (?) Petersham, Lady Caroline, includes, in
    Vauxhall party, **9**. 107–10
Beauclerk, Lady Catherine. *See* Ponsonby, Lady
  Catherine (1742–89)

Beauclerk, Charles (1670–1726), cr. (1676) E. of Burford, (1684) D. of St Albans:
Charles II conveys Burford House to, 1. 350n
Gwynn, Nell, writes of, 1. 350
sons of, 9. 85n, 10. 342, 33. 387
Vere, 1st Bn, younger son of, 25. 191n

Beauclerk, Charles (1696–1751), 2d D. of St Albans:
brother of, 20. 80n
Burford House, Windsor, owned by, 20. 42n
pictures of, at Burford House, Windsor, 37. 242
stiffness of, inherited by son, 37. 309
Walpole, Sir Edward, notifies, not to expect his help against Fox, 20. 42

Beauclerk, Hon. Charles (d. 1775), army officer:
death of, 7. 398

Beauclerk, Charles George (1774–1846):
Farington mentions, 15. 320
Hardinge to deliver HW's note to mother in absence of, 35. 632
wife of, 11. 118n

Beauclerk, Mrs Charles George. See Ogilvie, Emily Charlotte

Beauclerk, Lady Diana. See Spencer, Lady Diana

Beauclerk, Diana (1741–1809):
at private Court ball, 38. 143
Charlotte, Q., said to include, in Household, 9. 377, 38. 96
HW mentions, 9. 402, 403

Beauclerk, Elizabeth (ca 1767–93), m. (1787) George Augustus Herbert, styled Bn Herbert; 11th E. of Pembroke and 8th E. of Montgomery, 1794:
Bartolozzi engraves drawing of sister and, 29. 71
illness of, 33. 334
marriage of, 15. 320
peerage of husband of, corrected, 43. 324
Trevor, Miss, reportedly gives legacy to, 30. 275

Beauclerk, George (1730–86), styled E. of Burford 1730–51; 3d D. of St Albans:
Brussels the retreat of, because of debts, 21. 172
Chancery decree to be passed by, 22. 267
Conway made by, deputy lieutenant of Berkshire militia, 37. 567–8
father's stiffness inherited by, 37. 309
HW has copy of portrait owned by, 10. 54
Mastership of the Horse coveted by, 20. 183n
Paris visited by, 37. 309
sumptuous public funeral for illegitimate child of, 21. 172

Beauclerk, Lord Henry (1701–61), army officer; M.P.:
children of, 9. 332
Cumberland, D. of, persecutes, 9. 86
death of, 9. 331–2
Dicks' letters to, may mention Mann, 21. 10
mother's funeral at Windsor attended by, 17. 295

regiment of, 18. 449n
resignation of, 9. 85–6
wife of, 9. 331n

Beauclerk, Lady Henry. See Lovelace, Hon. Martha

Beauclerk, Lord James (1702–87), Bp of Hereford, 1746:
Albemarle, Lady, may now mourn for, 33. 387

Beauclerk, Mary (b. 1743), m. (1762) Lord Charles Spencer:
mother's bequest to, 33. 295n
royal ball for Christian VII attended by, 23. 57n

Beauclerk, Mary (1766–1851), m. (ca 1795) Graf Franz von Jenison zu Walworth:
Bartolozzi engraves drawing of sister and, 29. 71
elopement of, with her half-brother, 34. 56, 35. 636
Farington mentions, 15. 320
illegitimate children of, 43. 213
illness of, 33. 334
(?) marriage of, rumoured, 35. 630
Trevor, Miss, reportedly gives legacy to, 30. 275

Beauclerk, Lord Sidney (1703–44), M.P.:
birth date of, corrected, 43. 242
Finch, Hon. William, succeeds, as vice-chamberlain, 17. 493–4
Germain, Lady Elizabeth, pays, to avoid marrying him, 34. 258–9
handsome but no wit, 34. 258
mother's funeral at Windsor attended by, 17. 295
prevented from entering House of Commons, 17. 299
son of, 24. 524n

Beauclerk, Topham (1739–80), friend of Dr. Johnson:
absence of, in Brighton, 7. 73
acute in argument, 15. 320
Adelphi house of, 32. 170n
astronomer kept by, 39. 293
bad temper of, 15. 320
Bateman's auction attended by, 32. 241
Beauclerk, Lady Diana, suffers because of, 6. 79, 286
—— will be consoled for death of, 7. 214
Boufflers, Comtesse de, interested in, 6. 367, 7. 218
—— little moved by death of, 7. 218
death of, 7. 214, 218, 42. 490
dirt of, 30. 272
(?) Draycott, Anna Maria, rejects, 10. 14
Du Deffand, Mme, compares, to Diogenes, 6. 367
—— inquires after, 6. 390
—— inquires if, is in London, 6. 384
—— thinks HW will not regret, 7. 214
gambles, 3. 27
Garrick reads Cumberland's ode backwards, at request of, 28. 237–8

[Beauclerk, Topham, *continued*]
Goldsmith's letter intercepted by, **32.** *112*
HW buys cup and saucer for, **7.** 414
HW does not mention, **7.** 173
HW gives *Mysterious Mother* to, **33.** 578
(?) HW inspects house of, for Montagu, **10.** 271
HW's correspondence with, **7.** 396, **41.** 308–10
HW sorry, not in as much danger as Bolingbroke, **30.** 269
HW's receiving all visitors surprises, **32.** 406
HW thinks, insane, **30.** 269
HW trusts, will return from Bath in week, **32.** 341
HW visited by: at SH, **6.** 334n, **39.** 276; with news of Palliser, **33.** 96
HW would be pleased by death of, **30.** 267
health of, improved, **32.** 365
Houghton visit contemplated by, **32.** 313, 319
house of: in Great Russell St, taken by Mansfield, **33.** 255n; (?) under repair, **10.** 270
laudanum taken by, **15.** 320
library built by, in Great Russell St, **33.** 136
library of, **6.** 373
lousiness of, **15.** 320, **30.** 275
Lucans given commissions by, **6.** 373
marriage of, **5.** 392n, **14.** 141n, **22.** 567
Muswell Hill seat of, **32.** 122, 241, **41.** 308
observatory and library of, at Muswell Hill, **32.** 122n
opium will not kill, **33.** 107
Paris visited by, **7.** 270
Rigby confused with, **31.** 68
Selwyn's letter to HW carried by, **30.** 203
servant inherits clothes of, **36.** 192
social relations of, in England, *see index entries ante* **34.** 282
social relations of, in Paris, *see index entries ante* **8.** 239
son of, **11.** 118n
suits of, at Le Duc's in Paris, **36.** 192, 196
wife of, **5.** 392n, **9.** 377n, **11.** 82n, **15.** 270n, **16.** 280n, **22.** 148n, **24.** 524n, **28.** 244n, **42.** 490
wife's relations with: patched up for the present, **30.** 269; reported smooth at Brighton, **30.** 272
Beauclerk, Lady Vere. *See* Chambers, Mary (d. 1783)
Beauclerk, Lord Vere (1699–1781), cr. (1750) Bn Vere of Hanworth:
Admiralty post of, **17.** 356, **18.** 550
Admiralty post resigned by, **20.** 80
Argyll, Ds of, retorts to, **9.** 368
Baltimore resents precedence given to, **18.** 565
death of, **25.** 191
docks visited by, with Anson and Sandwich, **20.** 80
dog of, **23.** 442
Dorset and Lady Elizabeth Germain secure post for, **17.** 356
Dorset entertains, **9.** 368
father of, **33.** 387

George II makes, Baron, **20.** 135
Gothic lantern at SH coveted by, **9.** 151
HW mentions, **37.** 337
HW sent by, to settle Lady Elizabeth Germain's auction, **23.** 286
HW visits, **9.** 62
house of, in St James's Sq., **25.** 191n
mother's funeral at Windsor attended by, **17.** *295*
Pelhams solicit peerage for, **20.** 135
Pomfrets entertain, **17.** 169n
protest of, **22.** 7
robbed, **35.** 315
Sandwich's quarrel with, causes his resignation, **20.** 135
shoulders of, covered with powder, **30.** 270
son of, **10.** 342
SH visited by, **9.** 151
Sykes said to have been waiter to, **29.** 122n
Vernon publishes letters from, **19.** 459n
wife of, **10.** 342
will of, not known at Twickenham, **33.** 294
Windsor borough should be resigned by, to D. of Cumberland, **31.** 18–19
Beauclerk, Lady William. *See* Werden, Charlotte
Beauclerk, Lord William (1766–1825), 8th D. of St Albans:
grandfather's bequest to, **33.** 294n
Beauclerk Closet. *See under* Strawberry Hill
Beau Desert, Uxbridge's seat:
HW wishes to see, **39.** 435
Beauford. *See* Beaufort
Beaufort, Duc de. *See* Vendôme, François de
Beaufort, Duchess of. *See* Berkeley, Elizabeth (ca 1719–99); Boscawen, Elizabeth (1747–1828); Capel, Mary (1630–1715); Leveson Gower, Lady Charlotte (1771–1854); Scudamore, Hon. Frances (1711–50)
Beaufort, Duke of. *See* Somerset, Charles Noel (1709–56); Somerset, Henry (1684–1714); Somerset, Henry (1707–45); Somerset, Henry (1744–1803); Somerset, Henry Charles (1766–1835)
Beaufort, Daniel Augustus (1739–1821), LL.D.; topographer:
(?) SH visited by, **12.** 236
Beaufort, Edmund (ca 1406–55), cr. (1448) D. of Somerset:
daughter of, **16.** 234n
Beaufort, Edmund (ca 1439–71), titular D. of Somerset 1464–71:
Burgundy's army followed by, **35.** 256
Beaufort, Henry (ca 1375–1447), Bp of Lincoln, 1398, of Winchester, 1404; cardinal, 1426:
Bury Abbey's connection with, **2.** 32, 36, 38, 222
chantry and effigy of, **35.** 250
Henry VI gives jewel to, **14.** 75
——'s ambitious uncle, **16.** 183n
image on tomb of, **14.** 68n
portraits of: **2.** 31, 219, 221, **42.** 247; on Bury altar tables, **16.** 184

possible retainer of, **2**. 220
probably not shown in HW's picture, **14**. 75
Reynolds's picture of death of, disparaged by HW, **15**. 206
Beaufort, Henry (ca 1436–64), 5th E. and 2d D. of Somerset:
son of, **16**. 233n
Beaufort, Jane, Q. of Scotland. *See* Jane (d. 1445)
Beaufort, John (ca 1371–1410), cr. (1397) E. and M. of Somerset; M. of Dorset:
ancestor of Henry VII, **16**. 233n, **41**. 114
legitimated son of John of Gaunt, **15**. 172n, **41**. 114
(?) print of, **40**. 236
Beaufort, John (ca 1404–44), 3d E.; cr. (1443) D. of Somerset:
(?) print of, **40**. 236
Priory procured by, for Pembroke Hall, **2**. 257
wife of, **16**. 233n
Beaufort, Lady Margaret, m. 1 (ca 1454) Humphrey Stafford, styled E. of Stafford; m. 2 (after 1455) Sir Richard Darell:
grandson of, **16**. 234
Beaufort, Lady Margaret (1443–1509, m. 1 (1455) Edmund Tudor, E. of Richmond; m. 2 (1482) Thomas Stanley, 10th E. of Derby:
death date of, corrected, **1**. 39
*Funeral Sermon* on, **1**. 42–3, **2**. 69
half-brother of, **1**. 227n
mother of Henry VII, **2**. 364n, 365n, **14**. 163n, **16**. 233n
portraits of: at St John's College, Cambridge, **14**. 114; in painted glass, **1**. 31
position of, at Henry VIII's Court, **2**. 363
Beaufort, Thomas (d. 1426), D. of Exeter:
buried at Bury Abbey, **2**. 38, 39, 222
died at Greenwich Palace, **16**. 80
distinction of white and red rose unknown at time of, **16**. 233
Fenn's unidentified portrait probably is not, **16**. 232
Beaufort, Dukes of:
Worcester, E. of, ancestor of, **16**. 233
Beaufort, house of. *See* Beaufort family
Beaufort Buildings, Strand:
Sisson of, **43**. 275
Voelcker's address, **23**. 56
Beaufort family:
arms of, **1**. 28
doubly illegitimate, **33**. 454
Morgan an enemy of, **23**. 174
*See also* Lancaster, house of
Beaufort St, Chelsea:
Lindsey House at Cheyne Walk and, **20**. 359n
'Beau-frère,' HW's. *See* Churchill, Charles (?1720–1812)
Beaufront, Northumberland:
Errington of, **12**. 149n
Beauharnais, Mme de. *See* Mouchard, Marie-Anne-Françoise
Beauharnais, Alexandre (d. 1794), Vicomte de:
aunt of, **6**. 428n
Beauharnais, Claude de (1717–84), Comte des Roches-Bartitaud:
wife of, **6**. 428n
Beaujeau, ——:
Quebec's relief attempted by, **24**. 215n
Beaujolais, Comte de. *See* Bourbon d'Orléans, Louis-Charles de (1779–1808)
Beaulieu, Bn and E. of. *See* Hussey, Edward (ca 1721–1802)
Beaulieu, Bns and Cts of. *See* Montagu, Isabella (d. 1786)
'Beaulieu, Lord':
Queensberry, Ds of, calls Cardigans' son, by mistake, **38**. 342
Beaulieu, Hants:
Warbeck surrenders at, **42**. 255n
Beaulieu River:
Yorke, Caroline, etches, from mother's drawing, **42**. 237n
Beaumanoir. *See* Du Rozel de Beaumanoir
Beaumarchais, Pierre-Augustin Caron de (1732–99), dramatist:
accused of bribery, **6**. 19n
*Barbier de Seville, Le*, by, **6**. 21, 162, 167–8, 407, **28**. 250n
carriage of, upsets, **6**. 499
Choiseul and Praslin write to Vergennes about, **7**. 439
Du Deffand, Mme, criticizes, **6**. 21, 53
*Eugénie*, by, **3**. 252
*Folle journée ou Mariage de Figaro*, **31**. 255, 256n, **33**. 536–7, 542–3, 544, 545, **36**. 249
Goëzmann affair of, **6**. 19–23, 26, 28, 30–2, 35, 53, 162, **43**. 96
HW and Cambridge will avoid, while he is in England, **28**. 250–1
HW's opinion of, **6**. 31, 53
health of, **6**. 499
'Jack-pudding,' **33**. 537
Kehl edition of Voltaire directed by, **7**. 130n, **36**. 242, **39**. 385–6
*Mariage de Figaro* by, never seen by HW, **31**. 255n, 256n
*Observations sur le Mémoire justificatif de la cour de Londres*, protests against, **7**. 195
popularity of, **6**. 21, 35
proposed, jokingly, for minister of marine, **7**. 129
sends ships to America, **6**. 360n
social relations of, with P. of Monaco, **6**. 21, 22
*Tarare* by: **31**. 255, **39**. 448, 451–2; France should produce more of, **36**. 249
Beaumelle. *See* Angliviel de la Beaumelle, Laurent
Beaumont, Lady. *See* Willes, Margaret
Beaumont, Charles-Geneviève-Louis-Auguste-André-Timothée de (1728–1810), Chevalier d'Éon:
absconds, **22**. 263, **38**. 467, 469
account by, of French economy, **38**. 356n, 369

[Beaumont, Charles, *continued*]
armed against attack, 38. 378
arrested for misbehaviour at Halifax's, and discredited by French and English courts, 22. *190*–1, 217
Bastille probably feared by, more than madhouse, 38. 238
Boisgelin, Comtesse de, owed money by, 4. 368
Botta asks Mann to return compliment to Lorenzi on visit of, to Florence, 22. 282
Brissac connected with letters of, 7. 277
Burgundian accent of, 33. 510
convicted but not yet sentenced, 22. 247–8
Court of King's Bench sentences, 22. 263, 38. 467, 469
Du Deffand, Mme, diverted by accounts of, 5. 77
England revisited by, 25. 631
*Essai historique* by, 38. 507n
foreign ministers at London unite with Guerchy against, 38. 377–8
France refuses to reimburse, 38. 356n, 369
French consider, mad, 38. 238
French Court hurt, by misconduct of, 38. 360
George III orders Norton to prosecute, 22. 227, 38. 377–8
Guerchy and Nivernais partly responsible for rôle of, 22. 273
Guerchy and Nivernais wronged by, 36. 40
Guerchy said to have sent Vergy to cut throat of, 22. 262
——'s money retained by, 22. 191
——'s secretary, 22. 217
—— the object of indictment procured by, 38. 522–3
Guerchy, Mme de, called Mme de Pompadour's successor by, 22. 239
HW calls, 'hen-dragon,' 'Herculean hostess,' 11. 68
HW entertains, at SH, 10. 70–1
HW has no taste for, 34. 37
HW has to ask Hertford for news of, 38. 274
HW meets, at Mrs Cosway's, 33. 510–11
HW meets, but will not visit 'her,' 36. 237
HW mentions, 38. 216
HW reminded of, by verses, 11. 68
HW suggests that fishwomen be headed by, 34. 73
Halifax forces, to promise not to fight Vergy, 38. 244
Henley rules against expulsion of, from England, 38. 392
heroes inferior to, as news, 36. 238
hides at Mme Dufour's, after leaving Eddowes' house in Scotland Yard, 38. 467–8
jokingly proposed as minister of foreign affairs, 7. 129
La Condamine, Camus, and de Lalande presented by, to George III, 22. 146n
letter attributed to, 5. 80

letters no longer safe when example is set by, 38. 356–7
*Lettres, mémoires et négociations* by: 22. 216–18, 272, 36. 40, 38. 356–7, 365–6, 372, 39. 14, 43. 141
Louis XV's relations with, 38. 238n, 239
Lovaine, Lady, provokes indelicate reply from, 33. 548
*Mémoires pour servir à l'histoire générale des finances*, 38. 507n
Mount Edgcumbe calls, 'her own widow,' 11. 279, 12. 266
Musgrave's address answered by, 7. 367
Nivernais's secretary, later minister plenipotentiary, 22. 190, 216
*Note remise à son Excellence . . . de Guerchy* by, 22. 190, 227, 230, 239
*Nouvelles lettres du Chevalier d'Éon*, (?) Hertford asks about, 38. 507
opera attended by, looking like Bedlam, 38. 378
Paris visited by, 6. 472
peace negotiations of, give him delusions of grandeur, 38. 243–4
pension of, 6. 474
*Pièces relatives aux lettres . . . du chevalier d'Éon*, (?) Hertford asks about, 38. 507
Praslin gives post to, under Guerchy, 22. 217
——'s letters published by, 22. 217
rumoured to be ordered to Tonnerre, 6. 474, 476
sex of, doubtful, 4. 494, 6. 472, 474
unpaid for treaties carried from St Petersburgh, 22. 217
Vergy attacked by, 22. 190
—— liberated by, from debtors' prison, 22. 262
——'s affidavit in behalf of, 38. 467
——'s *Lettre* might be partly by, 22. 272
Beaumont, Elizabeth (d. 1671), m. (1619) Robert Maxwell, 9th Bn Maxwell, 1613; cr. (1620) E. of Nithsdale:
Jamesone's portrait of, 40. 285
Beaumont, Francis (1584–1616), dramatist, and John Fletcher (1579–1625), dramatist:
Cooke's version of *Scornful Lady* by, criticized by HW, 41. 403
Grandison's verses said to be in edition of, 16. 27
*Humorous Lieutenant* by, 37. 196
Jephson imitates, 41. 369
metaphoric diction of, should not be imitated, 41. 372
*Philaster* by, 22. 176n
*Scornful Lady* by, returned by HW to Bns Craven, 41. 403
Beaumont, Sir George Howland (1753–1827), 7th Bt; painter:
Berry, Mary, mentions, 11. 220
HW sees ash tree at place of, 42, 240–1
SH visited by, 12. 227, 233, 243
wife of, 11. 220n

'Beaumont, Sir Harry.' *See* Spence, Rev. Joseph

Beaumont, Jacques-Abraham (b. 1743), Marquis de:
grandes entrées obtained by, **6.** 52

Beaumont, Jean-Thérèse-Louis de (1738–1831), Marquis d'Autichamp:
(?) Condé's duel witnessed by, **7.** 439
(?) ——'s écuyer, **5.** 301

Beaumont, Mary (ca 1570–1632), m. 1 George Villiers; m. 2 (1606) Sir William Rayner; m. 3 Sir Thomas Compton; cr. (1618) Cts of Buckingham, s. j.:
portrait of, at Boughton House, **12.** 341

*Beaumont*, French ship from India:
capture of, **21.** 524

Beaumont (France):
Maria Theresa cedes, to France, **21.** 117n

Beaumont. *See also* Élie de Beaumont; Moreau de Beaumont

Beaumont de Péréfixe, Hardouin de (1605–71), Abp of Paris:
*Histoire du Roy Henry le Grand*, HW wants Bentley to depict scene from, **35.** 243–4
*Tartuffe* banned by, **18.** 63

Beaumont du Repaire, Christophe de (1703–81), Abp of Paris, 1746–81; Duc de St-Cloud:
Aiguillon supported by, **5.** 213
Cholmondeley daughter's expulsion demanded by, **4.** 400
Coke, Lady Mary, looks like concubine of, **39.** 7
Conti visited by, on deathbed, **6.** 344–5
date of archbishopric of, corrected, **43.** 270
dispensation refused by, **7.** 204
Gaultier's relations with, **7.** 21
Gisors, Mme de, defends, **14.** 154
Jesuits defended in *Instruction pastorale* by, **38.** 303
La Vauguyon regretted by, **5.** 179
Louis XV gives hospitals to, **20.** 293n, 294
——'s letter to, **21.** 502n
Maria Theresa asks, to send nuns to Vienna, **20.** 333–4
Marmontel persecuted by, **8.** 150
Mocenigo's ball opposed by, **6.** 277
(?) Monaco, Ps of, permitted by, to visit Bellechasse, **4.** 438
new parliament's passing regretted by, **6.** 118
opposes Mme Louise's desire to join Carmelites, **4.** 399
Orléans, Bp of, suspects sudden death of, **3.** 361
parliament of Paris attended by, **8.** 172
parliament of Paris to act on letter of, **7.** 284
pastoral charge expected from, **8.** 177
Piron's remark to, **28.** 326
priest's license taken away by, **7.** 284
sells Princesse de Talmond's burial garments for charity, **5.** 438
Te Deum ordered by, for Condé's victory, **22.** 90n
Voltaire invokes, **8.** 152

Beaumont Lodge, Old Windsor; Sir Charles Montagu's seat:
HW visits, **1.** 236
Montagu, Charles, ill at, **10.** 268
Montagu, John, to visit, **10.** 320

Beaumont St, London:
Ramsay, 'Mrs K.', dies at house in, **25.** 523n

Beaunay, Mme Charles-Abraham-Laurent de. *See* Desmier d'Archiac de St-Simon, Louise-Antoinette

Beaune, Mme de:
social relations of, with Mme du Deffand, **7.** 424

Beaune, Vicomte de. *See* Montaigu-Bouzols, Joachim-Charles-Laure de (1734–1818)

Beaune, Rue de, Paris:
Du Deffand, Mme, lived in, **8.** 52
Villette, Marquis and Marquise de, have house in, **7.** 17

Beaupoil, François-Joseph de (1643–1742), Marquis de Ste-Aulaire:
song by, on Newton and Descartes, **7.** 202

Beaupré, ——:
statue by, of George III in Berkeley Sq., **28.** 472n

Beaupréau, Hôtel de, Rue de l'Université, Paris:
(?) Berkeley, Cts of, gives assemblies in, **39.** 37
Hume and Mme du Châtelet lived in, **7.** 267
name of, corrected, **43.** 106

Beaurepaire, Rue, Paris:
Vermond of, **33.** 318n

'Beau Richard.' *See* Richards, Fitzherbert

Beauséjour, seigneur de. *See* Chauvelin, Jacques-Bernard

Beau Séjour, Fort:
capture of, **20.** 506n, **35.** 240

Beaushini *or* Brianchini, Giuseppe; Mann's butler:
ices sent by, to D. and Ds of Cumberland, **25.** 644
Mann's annuity to, **25.** 667n

Beausset, —— de, French naval leader:
squadron leader under Orvilliers, **24.** 484n
squadron under, at Cadiz, may be augmented, **25.** 48n

Beauteville, Chevalier de. *See* Buisson, Pierre de

*Beauties, The*, by HW:
beauties in, all arrant vestals, **32.** 32
Cooper publishes folio edition of, **19.** 333n
epistle on, **23.** 451n
'Flora' in, Rigby insists identity of, be left doubtful, **30.** 101
Fox, Henry, praises, and threatens to publish it, **30.** 102, 103
Gray, Sir James, sends, to Mann, **19.** 326
Gray, Thomas, admires, **14.** 37
HW disparages, **19.** 332
HW includes only those he thinks beauties in, **30.** 101
(?) HW promises, to Montagu, **9.** 39

[*Beauties, The*, continued]

HW's choices for inclusion in: Egremont, Cts of, **25**. 68n; Evelyn, Elizabeth, **30**. 101; Lennox, Lady Emelia, **30**. 100, 102; Pitt, Mrs George, **21**. 548n, **23**. 451n

HW sends, to Henry Fox, **30**. 100–1

(?) HW sends, to Montagu, **9**. 43

HW's objections to publication of, **30**. 104–5

HW writes, for Lady Caroline Fox, **30**. 100–1

HW wrote, in less than three hours, **30**. 105

in Dodsley's collection, **13**. 21–2

Montagu, D. of, protesting Margaret Banks's omission, adds lines to, praising her, **9**. 38n, **30**. 329n

printings of, **13**. 16, **30**. 324n

Rigby insists that HW send, to Fox, **30**. 100

—— suggests different set of characters for, **30**. 100–1

text of, **30**. 324–9

Beauties, Hampton Court. *See* Hampton Court: 'beauties' at

Beauties, Windsor. *See* Windsor Castle: 'beauties' at

Beauty:

of present age, superior to future, **32**. 117

taste in, changes, **25**. 308

Beauvais, Abbé de:

Philip, D. of Parma's funeral sermon by, **31**. 111n

Beauvais, Bp of. *See* La Rochefoucauld-Bayers, François-Joseph de; Potier, Étienne-René

Beauvais (France):

Devreux, Mlle, lives with son at, **3**. 166n

tapestry from, at Hôtel de Soubise, **7**. 283

Beauvau, Chevalier de. *See* Beauvau, Ferdinand-Jérôme de (1723–90)

Beauvau, Prince de. *See* Beauvau, Charles-Just de (1720–93); Beauvau, Marc-Étienne-Gabriel de (1773–1849)

Beauvau, Princesse de. *See* La Tour d'Auvergne, Marie-Sophie-Charlotte de (1729–63); Rohan-Chabot, Marie-Sylvie de (1729–1807)

Beauvau, Alexandre (1725–45), Comte de:

death of, **19**. 54, 59, 70, **35**. 59–60

Beauvau, Anne-Agnès de (1699–1743); m. (1717) Agésilas-Gaston de Grossolles, Marquis de Flamarens:

Aiguillon, Mme d', jealous of, **3**. 143–4

Du Deffand, Mme, friendly with, **3**. 257, **8**. 51

Hénault's 'portrait' of, **8**. 97–100

reason's priestess, **8**. 51

Beauvau, Anne-Louise-Marie de (1750–1833), m. (1767) Philippe-Louis-Marc-Antoine de Noailles, Prince de Poix:

acts at Chanteloup, **5**. 382n

birth of, **20**. 116n

Bordeaux visited by, **7**. 428

Chanteloup to be visited by, **3**. 317

Du Deffand, Mme, has, at her chaise longue, **39**. 271

——'s neighbour, **6**. 308

family of, **22**. 341n

HW meets, at Mme de Mirepoix's, **22**. 342

HW's praise of Poix to be told to, **6**. 424

husband of, **12**. 14n

illumination for wedding of, **7**. 319

Lauzun, Duchesse de, joins, **6**. 214

L'Isle's verses on, **5**. 186

Marly to be home of, **7**. 424

—— visited by, **4**. 447

marriage of, **3**. *323*

pregnant, **6**. 468

Saint-Amand-les-Eaux visited by, **6**. 214

social relations of, in Paris, *see index entries ante* **8**. 240

son born to, **5**. 27, **6**. 472

Sully, Duchesse de, cared for by, **5**. 273

Beauvau, Anne-Marguerite de (b. 1719):

(?) Maria Theresa sends for, **20**. 326, 334

Beauvau, Anne-Marguerite-Gabrielle de (1707–91), m. 1 (1721) Jacques-Henri de Lorraine, Prince de Lixin; m. 2 (1739) Gaston-Charles-Pierre de Lévis de Lomagne, Duc de Mirepoix; Maréchal de France:

acts, **5**. 117, **6**. 466, **7**. 350, 351

agreeable when not at cards, **39**. 212

Ailesbury, Cts of, charms, **6**. 101, 104, 115, 117

Amelia, Ps, compliments, on her leaving off rouge, **20**. 89

'Archiduchesse,' **3**. 89

arrival of, in England, **9**. 95

Artois celebrations avoided by, **5**. 421

Auteuil visited by, **7**. 427

ball given by, **3**. 212n, 214, 217, 219, 221

Barthélemy talks with, at Mme du Deffand's, **5**. 61, 62

Bauffremont to be visited by, **6**. 281

Beauvau, Prince de, aided by, **5**. 49, 105

—— at odds with, **3**. 323, **4**. 298, 447, **23**. 144

—— discussed by Mme du Deffand and, **5**. 99–100, 105

—— may visit, in England, **20**. 15

—— recommends HW to, in letter, **20**. 87

—— reconciled with, **6**. 50–1, 53

Beauvau, Princesse de, hates and is hated by, **3**. 173, 182n, 323, **4**. 298, **5**. 105, 269, 353, **6**. 26–7, 53, 261, **23**. 144

—— reconciled with, **6**. 53, 59, 60

Bedford, Ds of, precedes, after dispute at Sandwich's ball, **9**. 338, **20**. 122, 144

Bellevue visited by, **3**. 27, **5**. 142

biographical information about, corrected, **43**. 81, 252

Boisgelin, Comtesse de, has apartment with, **6**. 349, **7**. 11, 24

Bolingbroke and HW invited by, to dinner, **20**. 225

Boufflers, Chevalier de, verses of, on sending of hair of, to Nivernais, **6**. 418, 419, 426

Boufflers, Comtesse de, hated by, **3**. 19

Boufflers, Marquis de, brother-in-law of, **20**. 250

Boufflers, Marquise de, visits, at Port-à-l'Anglois, **6**. 92

Boulevard visited by, **7.** 336

Broglie, Comte de, aided by, **5.** 51

Bussy, Marquise de, retorts to, about Louis XV's gift, **7.** 369

Caraman, Comte and Comtesse de, at odds with, **6.** 270

Caraman, Comte de, nephew-in-law of, **10.** 156, **38.** 520, 523–4

—— proposes building house for, **5.** 209, 219

cat of, **31.** 55

Chaillot visited by, **6.** 357

Chantilly visit avoided by, **4.** 447

—— visited by, **3.** 127, **4.** 257

children's ball given by, **7.** 442

Choiseul, Duc de, at odds with, **3.** 152, 214, 283, **4.** 298, 300, 339, **6.** 261

—— praised in mot of, **4.** 381

Choiseul, Duchesse de, admired by, **3.** 111

—— in opposing camp to, **6.** 261

Choisy visited by, **4.** 15, 243, 258, 472, **5.** 421

Churchill, Mary, liked by, **5.** 56

—— 's marriage pleases, **6.** 468

—— to be given ball by, **5.** 26–7

Compiègne visited by, **3.** 319, **5.** 264, 394

conduct of, reprehensible, **3.** 152, 160, 214, **4.** 60

Conway liked by, **6.** 115, 117, **39.** 218

—— takes letter of, to HW, **6.** 165

Cornbury's retort to Fontenelle retold by, **20.** 213–14

Court accompanied by, **6.** 11

Court not always accompanied by, **4.** 472

Craon's debts to be partly paid by, **6.** 141

—— disappoints, **6.** 134

Craon, Princesse de, has apartment with, **6.** 349

—— occupies attention of, **5.** 402

Damer, Mrs, charms, **5.** 260, 263, **6.** 101, 104, 115, 117

—— welcomed by, **5.** 259–60, 263

does not preside at her own entertainments, **20.** 280, 285–6

Du Barry, Comtesse, accepted by, **4.** 250, 258, **5.** 110, 322, **23.** 144, 169

—— little influenced by, **5.** 380

—— solicits grant for, **4.** 339

—— tells, that Mme du Deffand should not visit Choiseuls, **5.** 43–4

Du Deffand, Mme, aided by, in getting permission to visit the Choiseuls, **5.** 43–4

—— attends Opéra-Comique with, **3.** 345

—— dislikes company of, **4.** 252–3

—— disparaged by, **7.** 295

—— has no news of, **5.** 386

—— lends money to, **3.** 123

—— mentions, **3.** 267, **4.** 139, 272, **6.** 197

—— not greatly older than, **7.** 173

—— old friend of, **41.** 192

—— pities, **5.** 27, 29–30

——'s correspondence with, **5.** 259, **7.** 425

—— sends to, for news, **4.** 458

——'s informant, **5.** 61, 161

——'s opinion of, **3.** 47, **4.** 80, 109, 381, **5.**
30, 49, 434, 435, **6.** 67, 134, 149, 441, **7.** 5, 7, 11, 14, 221

——'s 'portrait' of, **8.** 64, 78–9

——'s relations with, **3.** 19, 59, 214, **4.** 335, 339, 458, 491, **5.** 5, 27, 122–3, 269, 353, **6.** 6, 100, 103, 149, 164–5, 183, 261, 301, 349, 353, 375, 386, 391, **7.** 7, 11

—— to visit, at Port-à-l'Anglois, **5.** 73

—— urged by, to visit Chanteloup, **5.** 237–8

—— warned by, of Choiseul's impending fall, **41.** 193–4

England to be husband's station, as ambassador, **20.** 13, 15

English manners and costume aped by, **20.** 89

family likeness of, **20.** 87

faro loved by, **20.** 106, **38.** 337, 517, 525

father recommends HW and St Leger to, **20.** 55–6, 64, 87

Ferney to be visited by, **6.** 281

finances of, **3.** 101–2, 122–3, **4.** 60, **5.** 30, 169–70, 434, **6.** 16, 134, 136–7, 141, 149, **7.** 3, 7, 8–9, 10–11, 14

Fontainebleau may be visited by, **4.** 472, **5.** 120

—— visited by, **5.** 137, **38.** 217

Forcalquier rumour not mentioned by, **6.** 19

(?) Fox, Lady Mary, liked by, **5.** 219

France visited by, to occupy tabouret, **20.** 280

Franche-Comté to be visited by, **6.** 281

Frederick, P. of Wales, praises HW's paper on D. of Cumberland to, **20.** 73n

French Court avoided by, after second marriage, because of lost tabouret privilege, **20.** 28, 92, 116

French translation of *Castle of Otranto* owned by, **3.** 270n

gambles, **3.** 13, 18, 27, 101–2, 122, 127, **6.** 67. 134, 168, 393, **20.** 106, **31.** 55, 89, **32.** 298, **38.** 337, 517, 525, **39.** 212

gambles less in Paris than in London, **38.** 267

Gramont, Mme de, avoids and is avoided by, **5.** 363, **6.** 18, 26–7

Gramont, Marie-Élisabeth de, known to, **9.** 119

grandes entrées obtained by, through Mme du Barry, **4.** 330, 339, **20.** 169

Greville, Mrs, friend of, **3.** 124, 163, **5.** 323

HW accompanies, to theatre, **7.** 351, **32.** 266–7

HW aided by, in Lady Fenouilhet's behalf, **5.** 372–3, 375, 379–82, 398–9, 402, 405, 408

HW aids, in financial matters, **5.** 434, **6.** 2, 6, 11, 12–13, 13, 16, 19, 24, 27, 36, 38, 43, 45, 136–7, 141, 149, 168

HW converses with, **41.** 5

HW describes, **14.** 152, **20.** 87, 92, 106

HW discusses Beauvau's dismissal with, **7.** 340

HW dreads playing faro with, till 11 A.M., **38.** 525

HW likes, **40.** *387*

[Beauvau, Anne-Marguerite de (1707–91), *continued*]

HW meets Beauvau's daughter at house of, 22. 342

HW plays faro with, 20. 106, 32. 298

HW praised by, 5. 292

HW's anecdotes of, 28. 290

HW's arrival awaited by, 5. 83, 85

HW's break compared by, to *Castle of Otranto*, 5. 54

HW's civilities from, 31. 47, 55, 93

HW's conversation with, about dinner invitations, 20. 225

HW's correspondence with, 3. 273, 5. 259, 421, 434, 6. 11, 164–5, 168, 7. 382, 41. 230

HW sends compliments to, 7. 174, 221, 36. 242, 38. 215

HW sends preserves to, 6. 247, 259, 261

HW sent messages by, 3. 26, 6. 468

HW's proposed present from, 6. 391, 401

HW's proposed present to, 3. 83, 86, 89, 7. 416, 417, 22. 534

HW's relations with, 3. 186, 5. 219, 263, 264, 382, 434, 6. 13, 19, 216, 7. 176, 226

HW sups at house of, 32. 261

HW thanked by, for sending kettle, 5. 172

HW 'toasted' by, in tea, 39. 7

HW to see, in Paris, 10. 172

HW wants introduction to, 20. 13, 45–6

has nothing to do, 6. 371

health of, 3. 186, 5. 46, 49, 56, 66, 79, 198, 339, 434, 6. 270, 7. 101, 226

(?) Hénault's 'portrait' of, 8. 64

Hénin's wedding clothes chosen by, 3. 123

Hertford announces HW's approach to, 38. 504

—— knew, in England, and meets her often in Paris, 38. 337

Hertford, Cts of, asks about, 39. 21, 37

—— attended by, on visits and at Versailles, 38. 237

—— directed by, 38. 216–17

(?) —— liked by, 5. 219

—— orders wallpaper from London sent to, by Dr Hunter, 39. 37, 49

—— told by, she will not expect HW in Paris till he reaches Calais, 38. 481

Hertfords have faro for, 38. 517

influence of, small, 5. 30, 45, 169, 380

Isle-Adam trip abandoned by, for Mme du Deffand's sake, 6. 100

journeys of, 4. 256

(?) Leinster, Ds of, and family introduced by, to Caramans, 7. 150

Le Val visited by, 7. 454, 457, 459

Lévis introduced by, to Mme du Deffand, 8. 65

likes fresh air, 6. 192, 237

London left by, for Spa and Lorraine, 20. 116n

Lorenzi's remarks to, about Lincoln's gesse and her diamond ring, 20. 106–7

Louis XV gives carpet to, 5. 170

—— gives money to, 7. 369

—— includes, in new côterie, 4. 256n

——'s friendship with, 3. 101–2, 31. 47, 55

——'s summer parties with, 38. 389

—— tells anecdote about Ps of Orange to, 7. 354

Luxembourg, Mme de, hated by, 3. 18, 19, 173, 182n

Mann tries to dictate her father's letter to, 20. 77

Maynard presents letter from, to her father, 18. 371

Meudon apartment occupied by, 6. 349

misfortunes of, 3. 186, 6. 134

Molière's plays acted by, 5. 117, 6. 466, 7. 350, 351

Monconseil, Marquise de, at odds with, 3. 152

Montesquieu's 'portrait' of, 8. 64, 78

Montesson, Mme de, visited by, 6. 102, 211 (*see also under* Ste-Assise: visitors to)

mother of: dies, 5. 264; found by her in deplorable state, 20. 213

Nicolet attended by, 7. 66

Nugent, Mrs, frightens, at assembly by calling *voleur*, 20. 132

Orléans visited by, at Raincy, 6. 224, 228

parents to be visited by, in Lorraine, 20. 116

parents to tell, about HW, 20. 23

Parisian patter lacking in, 20. 87

Paris residences of, 5. 98–9, 105, 140, 145, 170, 209, 431, 435, 436, 6. 11–12, 42, 67, 7. 3, 5, 7, 8–9, 10–11, 14, 24, 31. 49, 55, 99

—— to be visited by, 5. 142, 259, 412

—— visited by: 5. 127, 137, 142, 163, 260, 421, 6. 29, 493; to see HW, 32. 253

Pitt, Anne, discussed by, 5. 292

—— to be brought by, to Mme du Deffand, 5. 295

Port-à-l'Anglois, le, occupied by, 5. 66, 69, 73, 97, 264, 370, 396, 6. 53, 92

—— taken by, 4. 472

'portraits' of, by: Du Deffand, Mme, 8. 64, 78–9, (?) Hénault, 8. 64; Montesquieu, 8. 64, 78

Putney the residence of, 20. 87

relative of, shoves Lady Echlin, 38. 514–15

relatives of, 3. 123n

repeats plays from memory, 7. 351

Richelieu and Mme du Barry leagued with, against Choiseul, 41. 192

Richelieu killed first husband of, 7. 369

—— reconciled to, 7. 369

Roissy visited by, 6. 56, 81, 84, 86, 7. 66, 454, 460

Rueil visited by, 7. 335

sad, 4. 362, 5. 27

Ste-Assise to be visited by, 6. 368

—— visited by, 6. 211, 236, 237, 491

—— visit of, interfered with, 6. 102, 103

St-Hubert to be visited by, 5. 421

St-Ouen visited by, 3. 122–3, 127

'salle-en-stuc' in house of, 7. 417

Scey-sur-Saône to be visited by, 6. 281

Selwyn gives tea to, **4**. 39

sister of, **42**. 90

social activity of, **6**. 149, 305, **7**. 11, 13

social relations of, in Paris, **5**. 145n, 31. 183, **41**. 195; *see also index entries ante* **8**. 242–3

Soubise a close friend of, **4**. 447

Spa to be visited by, **20**. 116n

spreads tale of a letter by Mme de Choiseul, **4**. 298

Stormont's aid for, enlisted by Mme du Deffand, **6**. 11

Sunday suppers of, **6**. 127

suppers given up by, **6**. 441

Switzerland to be visited by, **6**. 281

Taaffe estate pays sum to, **6**. 136

——'s aid asked by, **5**. 434

——'s correspondence with, **5**. 231, **6**. 16, 19

tabouret denied to, **20**. 28, 92, 116

tabouret regained by, **20**. 280

tea-kettle and lamp for, **5**. 160, 162, 177, 211

tea procured for, **4**. 39, **6**. 134, **7**. 226

Thellusson, Mme, takes house of, **7**. 8–9, 10–11, 24

Thiard's verses for, **3**. 129–30

to leave Paris, **6**. 29

to lodge at Assomption convent, **7**. 3, 7, 11

Trianon visited by, **5**. 98

Versailles to be visited by, **5**. 49, 51, 421

—— visited by, **5**. 198, 260, **20**. 280n

—— visit of, cancelled, **5**. 51

Walpole, Hon. Thomas, brings tea to, **7**. 226, 233, 234, **36**. 168

wishes to give present to HW, **5**. 160

Wortley Montagu and Taaffe, faro-bankers to, **20**. 288

York's misunderstanding about, **3**. 333

Beauvau, Charles-Just de (1720–93), Prince de Beauvau:

Académie française admits, **5**. 34–5, 37

—— 's deputation to Voltaire headed by, **7**. 18

——'s discussions shared by, **5**. 354

——'s meeting attended by, **6**. 232, **7**. 458

—— speech delivered by, **5**. 34, 46, 52, 54, 57

amiable qualities lost by, in Versailles meanness, **23**. 142

armour viewed by, **5**. 119

Auteuil visited by, **7**. 422

away from Paris, **7**. 65

Bavarian-French army includes, **17**. 194

Beauvau, Princesse de, first wife of: inherits property, **19**. 426; related to Young Pretender, **19**. 262

Beauvau, Princesse de (second wife) attached to, **3**. 47

—— does not seem seriously ill to, **6**. 16

—— dominates, **3**. 245, **6**. 417

—— joins, at Bayeux, **7**. 68

—— may have harmed, **5**. 47–8, 118, 138, 169

—— reconciliation of, with Mme de Mirepoix, pleases, **6**. 60

Belle-Isle's aide-de-camp in Bohemia, **17**. 194n

Bordeaux visited by, **22**. 341

Boufflers, Chevalier de, makes verses for, **4**. 123–4, **5**. 354

——'s verses on M. de Vaux and, 39. 212

Boufflers, Marquise de, jealous of Mme du Deffand and, **5**. 123

—— visits, at Le Val, **7**. 241

Bourbonne to be visited by, **7**. 220

bread dispensed by, to Versailles rioters, **24**. 102, 112n

Bressei, Capt., fights duel with, **18**. 432n

Brest fleet said to have sailed with, **24**. 484

Brisson waters to be taken by, **7**. 427

Broglie, Comte de, corresponds with, **7**. 341

Broglie, Duc de, accompanied by, to coast defences, **7**. 53

brought up in Florence, **23**. 142n

Bulstrode to accompany, **17**. 11

Castries expected by, to be minister, **7**. 326

——'s promotion incenses, **4**. 340

Chanteloup to be visited by, **5**. 34, 169, 256, 345, 380, **6**. 3, 82, 212, 214

Chanteloup visited by, **5**. 37, 45, 48, 391, **6**. 417

child expected by, **20**. 116

Choiseul, Duc and Duchesse de, visited by, in exile, **5**. 30, 32, 45, 48

Choiseul, Duc de, friendly with, **41**. 192

—— gives promotion and restores seniority to, **4**. 340

Choiseul, Duchesse de, mentions, **4**. 103

Cholmondeley, Mrs Robert, to be placed by, at Dauphin's marriage festivities, **4**. 402, 407

chooses Mme du Deffand's books, **5**. 276n

Comédie-française attended by, **7**. 458

Compiègne visited by, **3**. 114, 118, 319

Condé at odds with, **4**. 447

cousin of, escapes from Prague, **17**. 69

Craon's debts to be partly paid by, **6**. 141

Delille's election to Académie française defended by, **5**. 234

disgrace of, **5**. 91, 104–5, 118, 127, 138, 214

Du Barry, Comtesse, not unfriendly with, **23**. 144

Du Châtelet's maître d'hôtel given commission by, **6**. 173

Du Deffand, Mme, allots suit to, **6**. 258

—— and Mme de Mirepoix discuss, **5**. 99–100, 105

—— compares Ossory and, **7**. 111

—— consults, on French usage, **5**. 319

—— discusses Mme du Barry's presentation with, **4**. 192

—— entrusts her legacy for HW to, **8**. 7–8

—— fears for, **5**. 47–8, 50, 74, 76

—— given game by, **7**. 431

—— has, at her chaise longue, 39. 271

—— has no news of, **5**. 123

—— hears Court and political news from, **4**. 288, **7**. 38, 63

[Beauvau, Charles-Just de, *continued*]
—— hears from, of: Mme de Choiseul's illness, 4. 286, 292, 5. 327; Princesse de Beauvau's illness, 4. 195
—— leaves punch-bowl, books, and mantel ornaments to, 4. 7n, 38n, 248n, 369n, 5. 276n, 350n, 6. 7, 26, 50n, 84n, 251n, 8. 7, 26
—— may not have loyalty of, 41. 4
—— mentions, 4. 275, 6. 450
—— misses, 7. 239
—— reads story recommended by, 7. 107
—— relies on, for Court matters, 7. 65
—— scolds, for neglect of HW, 7. 323
——'s correspondence with, 3. 5, 4. 88, 286, 303, 417, 5. 81, 6. 295, 434, 461, 7. 38, 54, 426–8, 432, 447–50, 453–5, 457–60, 8. 187–9
—— sends to HW a letter received by, 7. 55
——'s executor, 29. 306n
——'s finances arranged by, 4. 97, 103, 5. 269n, 280–1, 297
——'s friendship with, 3. 133, 225, 4. 256, 491, 5. 6, 51, 353, 6. 3, 33, 48, 60, 82, 100, 142, 183, 191, 192, 259, 266, 391, 417, 470, 472, 492, 7. 15, 36, 102, 110, 190, 205, 208, 212–13, 231
——'s MSS copied by, 4. 182n, 5. 1, 7. 59n
——'s opinion of, 5. 101, 138, 234, 292, 6. 50, 259, 7. 110–11
——'s papers will be purged by, of compromising matter, 41. 423
——'s pension continued at request of, 4. 97, 103
——'s picture sent to HW by executors of, 4. 35n, 8. 216, 12. 14, 15
——'s quarrel with Mme de Forcalquier known to, 4. 391
——'s will permits, to copy her MSS, 3. 5n, 4. 182n, 5. 1, 7. 59n, 8. 8
—— sympathizes with, 5. 101
—— to pay debts of, to HW, 3. 324
—— to secure bowl for, 6. 164
—— unable to write to, 41. 199
duties of, as capt. of the bodyguard, 5. 47
England to be visited by, 40. 31, 38
family of, 34. 77–8
father may be induced by, to sympathize with France, 18. 513
father to inform, about HW's civilities, 40. 39
father worries over fate of, 19. 267
finances of, 5. 105, 151, 169, 214, 220, 225
Fontainebleau visited by, 5. 120, 123, 137, 6. 221, 224, 232, 368
French army service of, 17. 11
French expeditionary force said to be led by, 39. 328, 329
Gennevilliers visited by, 7. 327
gets up behind Louis XV's chaise, 3. 291–2
grandee of Spain, 19. 1
HW aided by, in Mme de Fenouilhet's behalf, 5. 371, 372, 374, 379, 380
HW allows, to keep Boufflers's letters, 4. 305n

HW has not seen, 31. 89
HW inquires about, 18. 62, 69, 267, 432, 19. 70
HW may see, in England, 19. 501, 503, 20. 15, 87
(?) HW mentions, 3. 342
HW offers book to, 7. 9
HW praises, 5. 297
HW probably forgotten by, 38. 215
HW's controversy with, through Hon. Thomas Walpole, over Mme du Deffand's MSS, 3. xliv–xlv, 12. 14, 33. 235, 292, 567, 36. 183, 185–6, 188–94, 196, 202, 204
HW's correspondence with, 6. 452n, 266, 270, 425, 36. 185, 188–90, 40. 31–2, 41. 330–2, 357–8, 423
HW sends excuses to, 6. 266
HW sends information for, 6. 171, 175
HW sends preserves to, 6. 247, 259, 41. 330–2
HW sent barley sugar by, 6. 368
HW sent parcel by, 6. 408
HW's extraordinary conversation with, 7. 341
HW's *Gramont* may be given to, 5. 304
HW signs himself *le survivant de*, 12. 19
HW's offers to, 40. 38
HW's relations with, 6. 259
HW talks with, 17. 11, 23. 142
HW thanked by, for civilities to son-in-law, 41. 357–8
HW to be cared for by, 6. 215
HW to be placed by, at Versailles theatre, 32. 257
HW to give Bn Walpole's *Case* to, 7. 417
HW to send letter through, to Mann at Florence, 17. 22–3
HW writes about, from Italy, 37. 53
health of, 5. 350, 352, 358, 360, 6. 244, 492, 497, 7. 3, 5, 8, 9, 186, 190, 219–20, 225, 231, 235, 239, 451, 453, 454
Hénault eulogized by, 5. 34
—— succeeded by, in Académie française, 4. 489n
Hénin's marriage displeases, 3. 123
Hénin, Princesse d', brings bequest from, to HW, 12. 14
holds Estates of Languedoc, 31. 89
honey water desired by, 6. 13, 14, 16, 19, 27, 28
horse meat eaten by, 18. 61
James's powders desired by, 3. 110, 247, 253, 259
Joseph II's letter about Paoli quoted by, to HW, 23. 142, 154
La Borde's correspondence with, 8. 188
Languedoc government taken from because he supported Parliament of Paris, 7. 340, 23. 321–2
—— visited by, 4. 341
La Tuilerie visited by, 7. 345
leaves Paris, 7. 425, 449, 458
Le Boulingrin exchanged by, for Le Val, 6. 397

letter to, about Cholmondeley's passport, **8.** 211

Le Val occupied by, **7.** 176, 186, 235, 239, 429, 431, 446, 458, 460

lives well, at camp, **7.** 72

Lorraine visited by, **4.** 273, 445, **5.** 264, 296, 345, 403, **6.** 417, **40.** 31

Louis XV accompanied by, on hunt, **5.** 47, 50

—— asked by, for grant, **5.** 169

—— attended by, **5.** 169, 208, 225, 256, 345, 358, **6.** 33, 50

—— compliments, on marriage, **19.** 1

—— does not mention Académie speech to, **5.** 52

——'s correspondence with, **7.** 340

Louis XVI asked by, for La Chalotais's release, **24.** 10n

—— attended by, **6.** 55, 194, 417, **7.** 36, 186, 219–20, 235

—— to be attended by, **6.** 270, 272, 281, 419

Lunéville visited by, **18.** 267n, 432n, **40.** 31

Mann drinks health of, **17.** 155

—— hopes that Francis I will spare, **17.** 481

—— to entertain, at dinner, **19.** 501

marriages of, **19.** 1, **22.** 341n, **40.** 53

Mirepoix, Mme de, aids, **5.** 49

—— at odds with, **3.** 323, **4.** 298, 447

—— may be visited by, in England, **20.** 13

—— reconciled with, **6.** 50–1

—— reconciled with wife of, **6.** 60

—— told by, in letter, about HW, **20.** 87

model for letter to Orléans sent to, **8.** 183

Montpellier visited by, **3.** 186, **4.** 310

mother anxious about, **18.** 1–2, 61

mother informs, of HW's friendship, **40.** 31

mother of, **5.** 264n

mother's correspondence with, **40.** 38

mother visits Florence to be with, **19.** 502

Naples visited by, **17.** 11, 16

Nice visited by, **18.** 448

not on military service, **7.** 186

Old Pretender visited by, **17.** 11

parents visited by, at Petraia, **19.** 500

Paris may be visited by, **5.** 350

—— to be visited by: **3.** 225, 354, 356, **4.** 17, 341, **5.** 137, 412, **6.** 234, 358, 363, 467, 470, **7.** 235; weekly, **7.** 219–20

—— visited by, **3.** 237, 240, **5.** 296, **6.** 11, 365, 472, **7.** 422, 423, 426, 454, **19.** 426n

pension of, **5.** 220, 225

Philip, Don, to be joined by, **19.** 54

Piedmont said to be station of, **19.** 70

Plombières visited by, **6.** 461, **7.** 427

Poix asked by, to bring Linguet's letter to Vergennes, **6.** 416

—— to have reversion of captaincy of, of guards, **6.** 59, 61

Port-à-l'Anglois, le, visited by, **6.** 53, 54

Port Mahon scene of military prowess of, **20.** 579

portrait of, **5.** 392n

printer's error found by, in HW's *Gramont*, **5.** 313

Raincy visited by, **7.** 440

regiment reorganized by, at Lunéville, **18.** 432n

(?) removal of, predetermined, **7.** 340

Richelieu said to be accompanied by, in French army, **20.** 545

——'s army joined by, **20.** 545n

Roissy visited by, **7.** 454, 455

Rome visited by, **17.** 11, 16, 22

St-Antoine, Abbess of, sister of, **7.** 346

Ste-Assise visited by, **7.** 432

St-Esprit, Ordre du, awarded to, for storming Fort St Philip, **20.** 579n

St-Lambert's patron, **4.** 216–17

St-Louis cross won by, with Louis XVI's approval, **18.** 216

St-Priest greatly liked by, **3.** 237

Schelestadt command of, **6.** 322, 324–5

—— to be visited by, **6.** 324–5, 331

Selwyn aided by, in disagreeable affair, **7.** 110, 184, 189

——'s passport secured by, **7.** 36

Sévigné letters talked of by, **5.** 301

Sinzendorf not introduced by, **17.** 11–12

sister of, **5.** 100n

social relations of, in Paris, *see index entries ante* 8. 244–5

Soubise at odds with, **4.** 447

Spa not visited by, **7.** 453

Stormont's maître d'hôtel given commission by, **6.** 173

Suard's election to Académie française defended by, **5.** 234

submissive husband and does not see his sister, **23.** 144

Suin, Mme, recommended by, to Mme du Deffand, **6.** 237

Tissot attends, **7.** 235, 453

—— deserts, **7.** 241

to move to Rue Bergère, **5.** 140

Versailles visited by, **4.** 404, **5.** 210, 350, **6.** 434, **7.** 219, 451, 454

Walpole, Hon. Thomas, gets letter from, **36.** 191

will of, quoted, **12.** 15

wishes to rent house to Caracciolo, **5.** 140

Beauvau, Charlotte de (1717–87), m. (1734) Léopold-Clément, Marquis de Bassompierre: Abbess of Poussai, **19.** 467n

social relations of, with Mme de Mirepoix, **7.** 350

Beauvau, Élisabeth de (b. 1722):

(?) Maria Theresa sends for, **20.** 326, 334

Beauvau, Élisabeth-Charlotte de (1705–87), m. (1723) Charles-François-Ferdinand de la Baume de Montrevel, Marquis de St-Martin: lodges at convent of Filles de l'Assomption, **7.** 3

Beauvau, Ferdinand-Jérôme de (1723–90), Chevalier de Beauvau; later Prince de Craon:

[Beauvau, Ferdinand de, *continued*]
Carteret's supposed civilities to, **18.** *286*, 312
Conway to intercede for, **18.** 286
debts of, **6.** 134, 141
detachment of, repulsed near Rittersbude, **21.** 177n
Du Deffand, Mme, accompanied by, to Sceaux and Montrouge, **4.** 443
—— has unfavourable opinion of, **5.** 292n
English capture, **18.** 286
father may be induced by, to sympathize with France, **18.** 513
flees to Malta, to escape arrest for debt, **6.** 134, 141
Hanau visited by, **18.** 286
knight of Malta, **18.** 286, 298n
marriage of, **5.** 314n, **6.** 134
Mirepoix, Mme de, lacks influence to aid, **5.** 30
mother of, **5.** 264n
parents not fond of, **18.** 298
'parts' of, not natural, **39.** 212
proposed marriage of, broken off, **5.** 170
release of, **18.** 298
social relations of, in Paris, *see index entries ante* **8.** 245
wounded, **18.** 286
Beauvau, François-Vincent-Marc de (1713–42), Primate of Lorraine:
Chute's joke on death of, from smallpox, **17.** 480, 498, **35.** 28, 32
death of, **17.** 456, 463, 468, 480, 481, **35.** 28, 32, **40.** 38
father's correspondence with, **17.** 328
HW called on by, **17.** 125
HW's opinion of, **17.** 468
HW to send letter through, to Mann at Florence, **17.** 22–3
leg of, injured, **17.** *12*, 17
Richecourt's banishment rumoured by, **17.** 125n
——'s toes kicked by, to stop story, **17.** 490
Rome visited by, **17.** 12, 17, 22–3
'Ruspantism' engages, **17.** 273
Stafford hears witticisms by, **17.** 273–4
—— would please, **17.** 135
Stone, Abp, compared with, **20.** 316, **22.** 269
Vincent ruined by, **18.** 111
Beauvau, Gabrielle-Charlotte de (1724–1806), Abbess of St-Antoine:
Beauvau's sister, **7.** 346
Caraman entertains, **7.** 346
contributes church plate to Revolution, **34.** 77
family of, **34.** 77
Roissy visited by, **7.** 346, **34.** 77
rudeness of, to HW, **34.** 77–8
Beauvau, Gabrielle-Françoise de (1708–58), m. (1725) Alexandre d'Alsace-Hénin-Liétard, Prince de Chimay:
canoness of Poussai, **42.** 90
relatives of, **3.** 123n
Beauvau, Henri (d. 1684), Marquis de:

*Mémoires* by, owned by Mme du Deffand, **8.** 34
Beauvau, Henriette-Augustine de (b. 1716):
(?) Maria Theresa sends for, **20.** 326, 334
Beauvau, Louis-Antoine de (1715–44), Marquis de:
escape of, **18.** 68
rumoured report of, on quarrels of Belle-Isle, **18.** 69n
Beauvau, Louis-Charles-Antoine (1715–44):
(?) French envoy to Charles Albert, **17.** 152n
Beauvau, Marc de (1679–1754), Prince de Craon; president of council of Regency to Grand D. of Tuscany 1737–49:
age of, mistaken by HW, **35.** 6on
Artimino and Petraia occupied by, **20.** 116
Austrian army in Lombardy estimated by, **17.** 291
Azzi often played with, in HW's company, **17.** 488
ball in honour of, **13.** 217n
ball may be given by, **17.** 56
Betange and Cocchi discuss, **35.** 16
Bocchineri, Mme, and her father entertained by, **20.** 36
Botta compared with, **21.** 178
—— to have been subordinate to, **19.** 23
Braitwitz angry with, for spreading Spanish news, **17.** 84
cannon firing at Modena may be heard by, **17.** 443
cards preoccupy, **17.** 259, 416–17, **18.** 101
Castello shown by, to visitors, **18.** 1
Charles VI creates, prince, **18.** 298n
Chute and Guadagni play ombre with, **17.** 416
Chute constantly invited by, to play quadrille, **18.** 101
——, Mann, and Whithed to visit, at Petraia, **35.** 28
Chute's letter from, on son's death, **35.** 59–60
—— to be entertained by, **18.** 372
—— told by, that his painter makes him look too young, **18.** 263
Cocchi summoned by, for excuse to visit Pisa baths, **17.** 342
Conway has not seen, **37.** 318
cook of, asks guests if they stay to supper, **18.** 122
Corsi entertains, at ball, **17.** 137
costume of, indoors in unheated room, **18.** 109
councils held in house of, **17.** 195
country sojourn of, **18.** 513
daughters of, **18.** 371, **20.** 23, 55–6, 64, 87, 116, 122n, **22.** 270n
death of: **20.** 418; may be followed by wife's remarriage, **20.** 116, 126
Del Fantasia's letter to, about Leghorn earthquake, **17.** 307–8
denies attempt to seize Crowe's effects, **20.** 2
departure of, from Tuscany, chief concern of, **20.** 14
dinners given by, **17.** 155, **18.** 348

Dumesnil quarrels with, **17**. 225–6

Electress's legacy to Old Pretender explained by, **18**. 175

—— talks with, **18**. 134

England accused by, of alliance with France and Spain, **17**. 180–1

English captains entertained by, **18**. 98

epitaph by, **17**. 153, 169

Eszterházys lodge in former house of, **20**. 350

family of, **34**. 77–8

fires not provided by, in winter, **18**. 109

Florence to be visited by, to entertain Vorontsov, **19**. 184

Francis I gives pension and invitation to Vienna to, **20**. 25–6

—— keeps, in ignorance, **17**. 214–16

—— orders: to aid Richecourt, **17**. 407, 490; to send news to Mann in exchange for information, **17**. 315

——'s birthday celebrated by, **17**. 217, **18**. 113, 115, 348

——'s consent to Spanish invasion suspected by, **17**. 195

——'s correspondence with, **17**. 281, 287–8, 327–8

——'s list of effects exhibited by, **19**. 58–9

——'s thanks conveyed by, to Mann, **18**. 67

—— to be told by, of Mann's messages, **18**. 259

French, in sympathy, **18**. 427

French letters to: mention peace rumours, **19**. 218; on Jacobite successes, **19**. 257

Gastin de Paris reports believed by, **19**. 197

Gerini plays piquet with, **17**. 61–2

Ginori's and Neri's resignations predicted by, **17**. 236

Goldsworthy, Mrs, called on by, **17**. 314

grandchild expected by, **20**. 116

guests, *see index entries ante* **26**. 112

guests overflow accommodations of, **20**. 387

HW amused by misinformation of, **18**. 305

HW and St Leger named by, in letter to daughter, **20**. 55–6, 64, 87

HW desired by, to send him presents, **17**. 152, 169, 194, 222, 255

HW discusses La Chétardie with, **17**. 20

HW enjoys hearing of economies of, **18**. 148

HW gets condolences from, on father's death, **40**. 53

HW has seen, receive homage for Francis I, **22**. 427

HW jokes about congratulating, on Francis I's failure at Prague, **30**. 34

HW regrets departure of, from Florence, **20**. 34

HW's correspondence with, **17**. 409, 413, 422, 435, 488, 505, **18**. 15, **19**. 38, 53, 59, **40**. 38–9, 53

HW's presents to, **17**. 324n, 413–15

HW's regards and thanks to, **17**. 24, **18**. 432

HW suspects loyalty of, to Mann, **17**. 419

HW to visit, at Petraia, **37**. 69

HW well treated by, at Florence, **34**. 77

Haddock's letter to, to be shown to Regency, **17**. 380

Hamilton taken by, to Abbess of Poussai, **42**. 90

health of: indigestion, **19**. 293; itch, **17**. 95, 100, 109, 122, **35**. 8; very ill, **20**. 92

horse race encouraged by, despite son's death, **17**. 456

Houghton plan disliked by, **17**. 443

house of, at Florence, *see* Craon, Casa

Jadeau asks, for satisfaction for Ginori's affronts, **17**. 226

jewels and plate may be pawned by, **18**. 134

Kaunitz attracts visitors to house of, **17**. 36–7

Leghorn may be visited by, **18**. 27, 38, 503

Leopold of Lorraine ejects, from wife's bed, **18**. 298n

lodge of, Mann watches race from, **17**. 79

Lorenzi does not invite, to Te Deum for Dauphin's marriage, **19**. 14

Lorraine archives secured by, **17**. 199

—— may be revisited by, **19**. 467, **20**. 24, 25–6

Madame Royale mourned by, **19**. 1

Mann and Rinuccini discuss war rumour with, **18**. 44

Mann asked by, about English-French neutrality, **17**. 181

—— borrows money for, from Whithed, **18**. 134

—— called on by, **17**. 53, 314, 326–8, **18**. 120–1

—— calls, 'Knee-buckles,' **17**. 195

—— calls on, **17**. 36–7, 178, 179–81, 203, 205, 217, 259, 463, **19**. 500

——, Chute and Whithed constantly invited by, to play quadrille, **18**. 101

Mann, Chute and Whithed invited by, to Castello and Toppaja, **17**. 443

Mann discusses Electress's cabinet with, **18**. 207

—— discusses Spanish war aims with, **17**. 214, 216

—— embraced by, **17**. 83, 259

—— entertained by, **17**. 155, 194, **18**. 98, 109, 115, 132, 545

—— entertains, **18**. 17, **19**. 501

—— hears complaint by, about Mrs Bosville, **18**. 286

—— not to sup with, till winter is over, **18**. 132

—— remonstrates with, on opening of Bns Walpole's cases, **17**. 224

——'s correspondence with, **17**. 380, **18**. 427, **20**. 116

—— sends news of HW's illness to, **17**. 51

—— serves chocolate to, **17**. 259, 413, 424

—— shunned by, **18**. 179

——'s innocence of sonetto authorship asserted by, **19**. 498

——'s visits embarrass, **19**. 197

[Beauvau, Marc de, *continued*]

—— tells: of George II's orders to Haddock, **17.** 259, 282; of HW's wish to meet Mme de Mirepoix, **20.** 45

—— tells HW to condole with, on son's death, **19.** 54

—— to be called on by, **17.** 342

—— to denounce 'Onslow' to, **19.** 506

—— to entertain, **18.** 78, **19.** 501

—— to give steel articles to, **17.** 302

—— told by: about son-in-law's appointment, **20.** 15, 28; about Stair's defiance of George II, **18.** 289, 310, 324; of fellow-sufferers from piles, **17.** 59–60; of Francis I's willingness to expel Bns Walpole, **17.** 326–7, 359; of French grief over Laeffeld battle, **19.** 426; of French minister expected at Vienna, **17.** 151; of Old Pretender's pardon for D. of Marlborough, **20.** 332; of Viennese affairs, **17.** 154–5; of wood shortage in Florence, **18.** 270; that Spaniards threaten Florence, **35.** 22

—— tries to dictate letter of, introducing HW, **20.** 77

—— visited by, in illness, **18.** 110

maxim by, of things arranging themselves, **20.** 387, **21.** 95

Maynard introduced to, by Mann, **18.** 367, 371–2

may retire, **17.** 236, 283

meals at house of, 'farmed out,' **17.** 122

medals not discussed by, **17.** 342

Montemar asks, for passage through Tuscany, **17.** 226, 280, 289–90, **18.** 46

Old Pretender entertains, **17.** 9, 16

—— gets Spanish grandee's rank for, from Philip V, **17.** 10n

—— lived with, in Lorraine, **19.** 108n, **20.** 132n, 332

—— said to be avoided by, **17.** 11

——'s resignation of pretensions reported by, **17.** 19n

——'s sons may be helped across Tuscany by, **17.** 15

opera attended by, **19.** 439

Osborn criticized by, **18.** 477

Palio carried to house of, **17.** 79

Paris post brings letters of condolence to, **17.** 463

Petraia summer residence of, **17.** 390n

—— supplied by, with furniture, **20.** 116

—— visited by, **17.** 95, 100, 109, 122, 463, **18.** 1, 17, **19.** 498, 500

Pfützchner's correspondence with, **17.** 287, 472

Philipps avoids, **17.** 81

pictures collected by, for sake of frames, **18.** 115

Pisa baths to be taken by, **17.** 342

promises regarded by, as 'politesses,' **23.** 53

pronunciation of, **20.** 387

Regency Council headed by, at Florence, **17.** 189n, **23.** 142n

religion of, makes him hope for Old Pretender's success, **18.** 427

retiring hour of household of, after one o'clock, **17.** 21

Richecourt blamed by, **20.** 268

—— converts, in Regency Council's discussion of Leghorn suicide, **20.** 14

—— employed by, despite wife's warning, **20.** 220

—— may replace, **20.** 29

—— mortifies, **17.** 189n

—— opposes departure of, for fear of Stampa coming, **20.** 24

——'s appointments increased to equal those of, **20.** 392n

——'s enemy, **17.** 327, 407

——'s return with Francis I's orders alarms, **17.** 236

—— supersedes, **21.** 178n

—— torments, to disavow his enmity to Ginori, **18.** 216

Rome visited by, **17.** 9–20

Sade and others play quadrille with, **18.** 329

Sade blames Mann's illness on cold house of, **18.** 110

—— dissuades, from Leghorn trip, **18.** 38

—— lends money to, **18.** 38–9, 62

St John prepares suppers at house of, **21.** 533

St Leger promised letter of introduction by, **20.** 77

Sarrazin, Mme, banished by, from quadrille médiateur, **18.** 329

—— dismissed by, **18.** 361–2

Scarlatti *vestimento* attended by, **17.** 53

servants of, **17.** 9, 122, **18.** 122

sonnet by, on Lady Sophia Fermor, **30.** 12–13

son not a favourite of, **18.** 298

son of, **17.** 273n, 456, 463, **18.** 54, 298, **19.** 54, 59, 70, **22.** 269n, 341, **23.** 142n

son's correspondence with, **17.** 328

son's death saddens, **35.** 28, 59–60

son's fate at San Lazaro worries, **19.** 267

son's future marriage pleases, **19.** 1

sons may induce, to sympathize with France, **18.** 513

son's success pleases, **18.** 216

son visits, at Petraia, **19.** 500–2

Spanish invasion fears of, decrease, **17.** 197, 214

Spanish not understood by, **17.** 280

Stainville may succeed, **20.** 29, 45, 84

Stanislas I favours, **19.** 467, **20.** 236

tax to be levied on, for daughter-in-law's fortune, **19.** 23

Tesi receives banishment notice from, **18.** 521

*toison d'or* awarded to, **17.** 11, 16, 20

transplanting of teeth discussed by, **18.** 324

Traun's letter to, **18.** 164–5

Tuscan post may be taken from, **18.** 310

Venetian trip proposed to, by wife, **17.** 25

Venice to be visited by, at Ascension, **20.** 29

Vernaccini presents memorial to, on allodials, **18**. 177

—'s correspondence with, **17**. 241–2, 280

— to receive packet through, from Vienna, **19**. 292–3

Vernon 'adored' by, **20**. 305

Walpole, Bns, entertained by, only on most public occasions, **17**. 462

Whithed's servant's case supported by, in Regency council, **18**. 10

Whithed to be entertained by, **18**. 37

(?) —— visits, at Petraia, **18**. 1

wife and Stanislas I watch, constantly, **20**. 92

wife called 'm'amie' by, **18**. 298

wife compels, to leave her after cards and go home to bed, **24**. 23

wife forces, to refuse Richecourt's request for certificate, **18**. 216–17

wife not pacified by, at opera, **19**. 440

wife's age admitted by, **22**. 324

wife's children resemble Leopold of Lorraine, **18**. 298n

wife told by, that her hair is too thin for Tesi's coiffure, **18**. 263

Young Pretender's arrest displeases, **20**. 22

—'s execution feared by, **19**. 262

—'s landing in Scotland announced to, from Paris, **19**. 86

Beauvau, Marc-Étienne-Gabriel de (1773–1849), later Prince de Beauvau:

Archiac, Comte d', visited by, **6**. 349

birth of, **5**. *402*

emigrates to England, **4**. 328n

Beauvau, Marie-Françoise-Catherine de (1711–86), m. (1735) Louis-François de Boufflers, Marquis de Remiencourt; 'Marquise de Boufflers'; one of the 'oiseaux de Steinkerque'; 'la Dulcinée':

Bauffremont's attendance on, **5**. 86, 100, 122, 130, 150, 152, 163, 170, 225, 298, **6**. 168, 281

— to accompany, to Lorraine, **6**. 168

Beauvau's attentions to Mme du Deffand arouse jealousy of, **5**. 123

— visited by, **7**. 241

Boufflers's letters shown by, to Mme du Deffand, **4**. 289, 292, 305

Boufflers, Comtesse de, not to be confused with, **22**. 270n

Cambis, Vicomtesse de, at odds with, **4**. 368, 381, **5**. 270

cheats at cards, **4**. 381

Cholmondeley, Mrs, consults, on Comtesse de Boisgelin's debt, **4**. 360, 368

— cordially treated by, **4**. 477

— in danger from, **4**. 326, 327

— paid debt from Comtesse de Boisgelin by, **4**. 423

Churchill, Lady Mary, acquaintance of, **5**. 23

Craufurd liked by, **5**. 280

—'s correspondence with, **5**. 298, 317, 374n

death of son of, **6**. 92

Du Deffand, Mme, accompanied by, to Sceaux and Montrouge, **4**. 442

— agrees with HW's cautions against, **4**. 273–4, 324, 326, 327

— desires fan for, **5**. 157

— hears recitation by, **5**. 117

— lent by, letters of Chevalier de Boufflers, **4**. 292

— mentions, **4**. 310, 342, **5**. 21

—'s correspondence with, **5**. 239

— sees and hears nothing of, **4**. 277, 281–2

—'s opinion of, **4**. 286, 322, 326, 334, 381, 461, **5**. 260

—'s relations with, **4**. 322, 334–5, **5**. 120, 122, 130, 137, 152, 154, **41**. 195

— to see less of, **4**. 295

Dunkirk visited by, **7**. 332

family of, **41**. 193

Ferney to be visited by, **6**. 281

Fitzpatrick and Fox will be missed by, **5**. 8

Franche-Comté may be visited by, **5**. 225

friend of both d'Aiguillon and Choiseul factions, **5**. 13

gambles, **4**. 316, 317, 326, 328, 337, 367, 381, 461, **5**. 140, **6**. 168

Greville, Mrs, at odds with, **5**, 323, 362

HW admired by, **4**. 287

HW's *Gramont* given to, **5**. 305

health of, **5**. 159, 163, 164, 170

Huber charms, **5**. 298

husband's supposed death, **20**. 236, 250

Lénoncourt, Marquise de, friend and relative of, **4**. 338

Le Val visited by, **7**. 241, 457

Lorraine visited by, **5**. 23, 225, **6**. 168, 189

Luxembourg, Mme de, visited by, at Montmorency, **4**. 319

Marly visited by, **4**. 447

marriage date of, corrected, **43**. 86

Mazarin, Hôtel de, visited by, **7**. 332

Mirepoix, Mme de, visited by, at Port-à-l'Anglois, **6**. 92

Monaco friend of, **5**. 86

mother jealous of, **22**. 243

mother may displace, in Stanislas I's affections, **20**. 26

Nancy residence of, **7**. 241

Nicolet attended by, **7**. 336

Rueil visited by, **7**. 337

Scey-sur-Saône visited by, **6**. 281

social relations of, in Paris, **41**. 195; *see index entries ante* **8**. 246

Spencer, Lord Robert, in clutches of, **5**. 150

— plays trictrac with, **5**. 120

— will be missed by, **5**. 8

Stanislas I ridiculed by, in letters to her husband, **20**. 236

—'s favourite, **20**. 236, **22**. 270n

—'s witticism about La Galaizière's affair with, **22**. 244

Switzerland to be visited by, **6**. 281

to move, **5**. 150

[Beauvau, Marie-Françoise de, *continued*]
verses by: **5.** 284n, 353; on gambling, **5.** 226; on Mme du Deffand's tonneau, **4.** 289–90
verses by Chevalier de Boufflers for, **4.** 123–4
verses on Broussin recited by, **4.** *284*, 295
Beauvau family:
Belle-Isle inspires, with anglophilia, **19.** 501
Beauvau, Hôtel de, at Paris:
Du Deffand, Mme, entertained at, **7.** 431
Leinster, Ds of, takes house near, **7.** 24
Beauvenir:
Selwyn and Mme du Deffand engaged to Princesse at, **7.** 145n
Beauvert, Comte de:
SH visited by, **12.** 249
Beauvillier. *See* Beauvilliers
Beauvilliers, Charles-Paul-François de (1745–1828), Comte and (1765) Duc de Buzançais; Duc de St-Aignan, 1811:
Nassau fights duel with, **5.** 175
Beauvilliers, François-Honorat de (1610–87), Duc de St-Aignan:
second marriage of, **6.** 342
sons of, **6.** 342
Beauvilliers, Paul (1648–1714), Duc de; the Dauphin's governor:
brother of, **6.** 342
Beauvilliers, Paul-Étienne-Auguste (1745–71), Duc de:
Mesdames scratch name of, from party list, **23.** 115–16
Beauvilliers (*or* Beauvillier), Paul-Hippolyte de (1684–1776), Duc de St-Aignan; French ambassador to Rome 1730–40, and to Spain:
Académie seat of, goes to Colardeau, **6.** 274, 284
birth date of, corrected, **43.** 234
Burgundy's governor, **17.** 12n
Craon, Mme de, takes, through Corso in phaeton, **17.** 83
—— entertains, **17.** 78
death of, **6.** 274
Du Deffand, Mme, tells about, **6.** 342
Imperial Court asked by, to let him join Albani faction in Conclave, **37.** 70
lodges at Collins's, **17.** 78
Lorenzi receives presents from, **17.** 95–6
Mann calls on, **17.** 78
—— receives recommendation from, of surgeon, **17.** 81
Rome entered by, **17.** *12*
Rome residence of, **17.** 81
son's marriage with opera girl broken up by, **30.** 59
wife of, **6.** 342n
Beauvilliers, Paul-Louis-Victor de (b. 1714), abbé of Lagny, 1733:
marriage of, to opera girl, dissolved by family, **30.** 59
Beauvoir, Mrs. *See* Sharpe, Mary
Beauvoir, Osmond (d. 1781), packet-boat captain:

mail thrown by, into the sea, **24.** 504
Beauvoir, Osmund (ca 1720–89), D.D.:
wife younger than, **31.** 360
Beauvoir. *See also* Belvoir; Virieu-Beauvoir
Beauvoir de Grimoard, Louis-Claude-Scipion de (ca 1678–1752), Comte du Roure:
wife of, **3.** 379n
Beauvoir de Grimoard du Roure, Louise-Sophie de (b. 1762), m. (1780) Claude-Louis-Joseph, Marquis de Saisseval:
marriage of, **7.** 453
Beauvoisin, Pont de. *See* Pont-de-Beauvoisin
*Beaux' Stratagem, The. See under* Farquhar, George
Beaver, Mr (fl. 1684):
Nell Gwyn sends for, **1.** 350
Beaver, Mrs:
SH visited by, **12.** 239
Beaver:
coat of, **19.** 445
hat of. *see* Hat: beaver
under-petticoat of, **18.** 333
Beavor, Edmond (d. 1745), capt. of the *Fox*:
Young Pretender's offers to, repulsed, **19.** 168
Beazley, Mr, of Christchurch, Surrey:
SH visited by, **12.** 231
Beazly. *See* Baisly
Bec, Anthony de. *See* Bek, Antony, I
Bec, Abbey of:
*History* of, **2.** 159–60, 163
print of, **2.** 159
Beccaria, Marchese di. *See* Bonesana, Cesare
Bec-Crespin. *See* Du Bec-Crespin
Beccuto. *See* Orlandini del Beccuto
Bechameil, Louis de (d. 1703), Marquis de Nointel; superintendant of buildings under Louis XIV:
Voltaire alludes to, **4.** 52
Beck, Anthony. *See* Bek, Antony, I
Beckenham, Kent:
Burrell of, **11.** 255n
Becket, ——, trunkmaker in Haymarket:
craws exhibited by, **33.** 571n
Becket, Isaac (1653–ca 1700), engraver:
print of, in HW's *Catalogue of Engravers*, **1.** 74
Becket, Thomas à (ca 1118–70), Abp of Canterbury; St:
Barrett Lennard descended from murderer of, **35.** 184
illumination depicting murder of, **42.** 68n
Otterbourne's mention of, **14.** 78–9
Becket, Thomas (fl. 1760–76), bookseller:
*Correspondents, The*, published by, **32.** 240n
Donaldson, Messrs, prosecuted by, for pirating, **28.** 135n
Hume instructs, about translation of *Exposé succinct*, **41.** 61
——'s *Concise and Genuine Account* published by, **22.** 465n
*Present Crisis* published by, **28.** 180n

Becket, Thomas, and P. A. De Hondt, book-sellers at Tully's Head, near Surry St, Strand:
imitation of Voltaire's *Candide* published by, 21. 514n
London edition of Hume's *Exposé* printed by, 41. 26n, 50n

Becket, Berks; Barrington's seat:
Conway visits, 39. 106

Beckford, Elizabeth (1725–91), m. 1 (1745) Thomas Howard, 2d E. of Effingham; m. 2 (1776) Field Marshal Sir George Howard, K.B.:
away from Chatham, 38. 33
Bedchamber post to Q. Charlotte given to, 21. 518, 38. 96
dances much, at private Court ball, 38. 143
daughters of, 23. 57n
death of, 11. 367

Beckford, Julines (?1717–64), M.P.:
Address may be opposed by, 20. 510n

Beckford, Peter (?1739–1811), sportsman; M.P.:
*Thoughts on Hunting*, HW comments on, 29. 147, 33. 274
wife of, 11. 268n

Beckford, Mrs Peter. *See* Pitt, Louisa

Beckford, Richard (1712–56), M.P.:
Address may be opposed by, 20. 510n

Beckford, William (1709–70), lord mayor of London, 1762, 1769; M.P.:
Address debated by, 37. 414, 415
Address may be opposed by, 20. 510n
alderman of London, 22. 39n
ball and dinner given by, for Opposition, 23. 200
Barrington's speech provokes, in Parliament, 39. 125
behaviour of, insolent, 23. 219
Bentley's *Patriotism* satirizes, 43. 131
biographical information about, corrected, 43. 361
Bribery Bill moved by, 22. 584n
Chatterton on death of, 2. 288
death of: deprives Pitt of support, 23. 246; stops political disturbances, 23. 221, 223, 224–5
Delaval's alleged encounter with, at Shaftesbury, 35. 171
Dresden treaty opposed by, 20. 299n
East India Co. inquiry opened by, 22. 471n, 41. 65n
Fonthill seat of, burnt but will be rebuilt by him, 35. 211
Frederick II called 'king of resources' by, 21. 257, 258
from Jamaica, 22. 39n
George III's coronation attended by, 9. 389
gold from Mexico might be remitted by, 38. 120
HW jokes about belligerence of, 31. 29
HW jokes about funeral of, 10. 310
HW mentions, 9. 164, 31. 431

Harley's clash with, in Parliament, 39. 125
Hogarth's 'Rake's Progress' etc. bought by, at auction, 32. 114n
house of, in Soho Sq., labelled 'Liberty,' 23. 205
Knowles attacked by, in Parliament, for misconduct in Jamaica, 37. 432
London council instructs, 21. 546
London council thanks, 38. 333–4
London election candidate, 23. 5–6
London remonstrance avowed by, 23. 198
London remonstrance presented by, to George III, 23. 196
lord mayor's feast of, attended by Temple, 39. 119
money kept by, in drawer, 35. 211
newspapers overrate, 35. 339
officers' dismissals denounced by, in Parliament, 38. 499
Parliamentary speeches by: on Draper's letter about Manila ransom, 38. 487; on Dresden treaty, 42. 496
Parliament may punish, for remonstrance, 23. 198
'patriotism' shown by clamour of, for conquests and high prices, 22. 39
petition presented by, for livery of London, 23. 132
Philipps favoured by, at Horn Tavern conclave, 35. 216n
Pitt (Chatham) answers speech of, 21. 345n
—— confers with, 22. 160
—— desires, to lay East India Co.'s plans before House of Commons, 22. 493
—— makes, lord mayor, 38. 183
—— quarrels with, 9. 325
——'s business in Parliament conducted by, 22. 506–7
——'s example recommended to, by Common Council, 21. 546
——'s friend, 22. 39n, 23. 132
——'s pension and peerage may embarrass, 38. 132
——'s politics reported by, 22. 382n
*Protester, The*, supported by, 13. 22n
re-elected lord mayor, 7. 368
*Remarks upon the Situation of Negroes in Jamaica* by, 31. 280n
Rockingham faction's desertion alarms, 23. 199
sister of, 11. 367n
son of, 25. 507n
speech added by, to London's new remonstrance to George III, 23. 215
stepdaughter of, 11. 280n
sugar price interests, 22. 39
Talbot gets complaint from, about City's treatment at Coronation banquet, 9. 389
Temple discouraged by death of, 35. 339
'thirty children' of, 35. 211
Townshend, Hon. Charles, accused by, of 'diarrhœa of words,' 38. 499

[Beckford, William (1709–70), *continued*]
tranquillity demanded by, at time of Wilkes's release, 23. 205
violence of, in presenting petition of livery of London, 39. 115
wife of, 11. 132n
Beckford, William (1760–1844), M.P.; novelist:
HW disparaged by, for starving his artists, and lauding 'splendid scribblers,' 43. 195
HW wrongly attributes *Arno Miscellany* to, 25. 507–8, 517n
half-sister of, 11. 132n, 34. 89n
Jupiter Serapis bought by, 11. 29n
just returned from Italy, 25. 508
writes music for Lady Craven's play, 29. 235n
Beckford, Mrs William. *See* Hamilton, Maria
Beckley; Becksley. *See* Bexhill
Beckwith, Thomas (d. 1786), painter; F.S.A.:
(?) encaustic painting practised by, 28. 300, 307
(?) Mason mentions, as 'picture-cleaner,' 29. *164*
Beconsfield. *See* Beaconsfield
Bécu, Jeanne (1743–93), m. (1768) Guillaume, Comte du Barry; mistress of Louis XV:
accepted by few, 4. 249, 250, 298, 5. 30
Adélaïde, Mme, refuses to receive, 23. 87
Aiguillon aids and is aided by, 4. 169n, 196–7, 339–40, 5. 45, 69, 285, 39. 144
——gives ball for, 5. 324, 338
—— often visits, 23. 321
—— on good terms with, 4. 372
—— patent of, carried to, 7. 370
—— said to have betrayed, 24. 12
—— tells his mother to visit, 23. 338, 41. 193
—— wishes to use, 4. 339–40
Aiguillon, younger Duchesse d', visited by, 6. 48
*Anecdotes sur la vie de, see under* Pidansat de Mairobert, Mathieu-François
apartment of, in palace, given to Thierry, 6. 57
Barrymore said to be rewarded for claiming, as relative, 32. 55n
Beauvau not on bad terms with, 23. 144
—— refuses to see, 4. 250n
Beauvau, Princesse de, hates, 5. 63
—— refuses to see, 4. 250n
Breteuil's appointment at mercy of, 5. 48, 50, 51
Brissac lover of, 34. 181n
Broglie, Castries, and Mme de Mirepoix get favours from, 23. 169
Broglie, Comte de, wishes to use, 4. 339–40, 23. 169
Caracciolo avoids, 5. 110
—— refuses homage to, 23. 338
Castries not aided by, 4. 340–1, 341
Chantilly visited by, 4. 447
Choiseul braves, to please Mmes de Gramont and de Beauvau, 23. 264
—— calls on, but is obdurate, 23. 144

—— contrasts, with Mme de Maintenon, 7. 369
—— may fall, by provoking, 23. 143–4
—— not favoured by, 4. 169n, 185–6, 297–8, 300–1, 381, 447
—— opposed by, 4. 305n, 464n, 7. 329n, 23. 75, 84–5, 28. 51n, 41. 192
—— probably dreads Pitt more than, 23. 134
——'s administration strangled by, 23. 258
—— seems to triumph over, 23. 125
——'s friends banned by, 5. 48
—— should be replaced by, 23. 130
—— unwise in treatment of, 4. 372
Choisy visited by, 4. 243, 472
Clement XIV influences Louis XV through, 23. 372
—— to tell, to influence Louis XV against Charles III, 23. 431
Condé's reconciliation not ascribed to, 5. 296
Corsica might be saved by, 23. 75, 81, 87, 90, 96, 107, 124
Cossé favoured by, 5. 107
Court factions during ascendancy of, 28. 290–1
death of, rumoured, 24. 18
deprived of liberty, 24. 18
discourtesy to, at theatre, 4. 437n
Du Barry, Françoise-Claire, accompanies, at Mass at Versailles, 10. 292
Du Barry, Vicomtesse, given diamonds by, 5. 378
—— thought less beautiful than, 5. 425
Du Châtelet courts, 39. 141
—— secures increase for Choiseul from, 5. 166
Du Deffand, Mme, finds application to, in Griffet's book, 4. 343
—— mentions, 4. 166n, 169n, 177n, 249
(?) —— mentions Choiseul and, 4. 188
—— might have pension stopped by, 5. 249n
——'s opinion of, 4. 234, 339, 372, 373, 5. 29, 30, 45
——'s visit to Choiseuls not approved by, 5. 43–4
—— transfers 'dame de Bordeaux' to, 4. 218
England unlikely to have counterparts of, 23. 403
English scrupulously treated by, 5. 379
English-Spanish war averted by, 23. 298, 304
exiled from Court, 6. 52
fame of, would never have been predicted, 23. 152
family relationships of, 6. 57
fête given by, 5. 338
French people curse, 23. 320
Fuentes avoids, 5. 108, 110, 23. 320–1, 338
gains ground, 23. 133
gains ground at Fontainebleau visit, 23. 151
George III snubs at Windsor, 34. 127
George IV entertains, at dinner, 11. 248
Gramont, Duchesse de, hates, 5. 63
grandes entrées obtained by, 7. 340

HW admires hospitality of, to refugees, **34.** 181

HW calls, 'Abishag,' **23.** 258

HW detests, **23.** 128

HW has not yet seen, **35.** 121

HW jokes about ecclesiastical interests of, **31.** 157–8

HW mentions, **4.** 256n, **6.** 64n

HW sees, at Mass at Versailles, **7.** 330, **10.** 292, **11.** 294

HW talks with, about Choiseul, **11.** 341

HW wishes Lady Ligonier would replace, **30.** 256

HW wishes to see, **10.** 291

health of, **5.** 179

Jesuits might be restored by, **23.** 87, 94, 316

jewels of, stolen and recovered, **11.** 206, 210

known as 'Mlle l'Ange,' **23.** 75

ladies make epigrams and vaudevilles against, **39.** 143

ladies will soon want to sup with, **39.** 144

ladies with, **4.** 256–9, 472, **5.** 97, 285, 322, **6.** 48

La Muette visited by, on eve of Dauphin's marriage, **4.** 406

'late Queen of France,' **11.** 294

La Vauguyon a chief supporter of, **23.** 87

—— notifies Mme Adélaïde of presentation of, **23.** 85n

*Lettres originales* purporting to be by, **7.** 183, 190

liberties of Gallican Church upheld by, **23.** 81

life of, in danger, **12.** 61

L'Isle's verses about, **6.** 411

London visited by, **11.** 206, 216, 244

lord mayor entertains, at dinner, **11.** 210, 216, 270

Louis XV and Maupeou almost alone with, at Versailles, **23.** 298

Louis XV can still enjoy, despite war, **23.** 253

—— influenced by, **23.** 320, 414

—— reproaches, for 'mauvais ton,' **8.** 181–2

—— reproves, for making faces at Choiseul at whist, **23.** 157

—— said to be kept diverted or drunk by, **23.** 270

—— sends away, during smallpox, **6.** 48

——'s face powdered by, **23.** 85

—— still devoted to, **4.** 373

——'s vacillations caused by, **23.** 284

—— would undo Paoli by expelling, **23.** 90

Louis XVI releases, **23.** 99

—— should release, **24.** 35

Louise, Princesse, contends with, for Louis XV, **23.** 399

Louveciennes pavilion built by, **5.** 97

Luxembourg, Mme de, jokes about, **4.** 447–8

made comtesse, **7.** 372

Maillebois wishes to use, **4.** 339–40

Mann curious about, **23.** 90, **24.** 10

Marie-Antoinette gets pension for, and leave to live at Louveciennes, **24.** 10n

—— ignores, **23.** 321

Marly visited by, **4.** 233, **23.** 115

marriage of, **23.** 75

Mirepoix, Mme de, on good terms with, **4.** 250, 257, 339, **5.** 30, 269n, 380, **6.** 51n, **7.** 369, **23.** 144, **41.** 192

Nantes, les boutiques de, revenue from, granted to, **4.** 339, **7.** 370

'noble-minded' and 'generous,' **12.** 61

not a fixed star, **23.** 83

not to be feared, **4.** 341, 464

nuncio and ambassadors wait on, **23.** 320

oranges tossed by, **23.** 85

Paoli might be saved by, **23.** 75, 81, 87, 90, 124

papacy might be bolstered by, to oppose Choiseul's opposition to it, **23.** 117

Pont-aux-Dames left by, to buy Château de St-Vrain, **24.** 99n

portrait of, exhibited at Louvre, **35.** 121

power of, **4.** 380, **5.** 29, 45, 48, 285

presentation of, at Court, after delays, **4.** 182, 185–6, 187, 189, 191–6, 198, 200, 203–4, 204, 210, 218, 223–5, 230, **23.** 78–9, 85, 94, 107, 115

Princes may be reconciled with, **5.** 214

(?) print of, desired by HW, **6.** 344–7, 368

Queensberry, D. of, takes, to Windsor, **34.** 127

—— visited by, at Richmond, **34.** 121

Queensberry House visited by, **11.** 341

restoration of, suggested, **32.** 266

retires to Aiguillon's at Rueil, **6.** 48, 51, **24.** 2

Richelieu advises Mme Adélaïde to receive, **23.** 87

—— and Mme de Mirepoix leagued with, against Choiseul, **41.** 192

—— loses to, at cards, **4.** 250

——'s quotation applied to Louis XV and, **4.** 250–1

Rue Tire-Boudin assigned to, in joke, **8.** 181

St-Hubert visited by, **4.** 242–3

salon attended by, **4.** 233

sent to convent of Pont-aux-Dames, **6.** 52

Seymour, Henry, lover of, **20.** 216n

Shuvalov calls, 'Mme Barbari,' **6.** 51

social relations of, in Paris, *see index entries ante* **8.** 247

song about, **41.** 199–200

supper given by, for Choiseul's enemies and for Richelieu, **23.** 115

Terray at feet of, **4.** 371

verses on, **5.** 70, **6.** 94

Bed; beds:

Adam to design for SH's Round Drawing-Room, **41.** 39

Anne of Denmark gives, to 'lady of the sweet coffers,' **32.** 325

at Castle Ashby, given by Q. Elizabeth, **10.** 337

at Drayton, spangled, **10.** 90

at Hardwick, **9.** 297

at Hurstmonceaux, scanty, **35.** 138

[Bed; beds, *continued*]

at Letheringham, with ivory pillars, 35. 247

at Osterley Park, 28. 413, 34. 237, 238

at St-Cyr infirmary, white linen, 10. 293

at SH: chintz in Blue Bedchamber, 35. 173; chintz, in Red Bedchamber, 39. 285; Hardinge, Mrs, to be measured for. 35. 598; tapestry, (?) procured from Paris, 5. 111, 113, 116, 121, 128, 134, 139, 143, 146, 148, 151, 156, 182, 184, 193, 198, 224, 28. 42, 446, 31. 169, 179; will be ready for Selwyn, March, and Contessa Rena, 30. 166

Blandford, Lady, has two, under one tester, 31. 180

blue or red damask, in every Paris hotel, 23. 312

brown watered tabby, 10. 337

Charlotte's, placed in Drawing-Room for christening, 38. 174

Cocchi calls, 'only good climate' in Tuscany in winter, 20. 216

Coventry, Cts of, never opens curtains of, on deathbed, 21. 451

curtains for: 17. 171, 21. 451, 23. 207, 394; not permitted by E. and Cts of Bath in maids' rooms, 30. 89–90; ring of, used as wedding ring, 20. 303

damask, bought for Zénon, 18. 253

embroidered: at Knole, 35. 132; at Norfolk House, 37. 438

Favre to air, for Montagu, 10. 193

field, used by Mann, 17. 95

green velvet, 34. 237, 238

HW and Anne Seymour Conway are in separate, 37. 334

HW carried from, to couch, 36. 90

HW confined to, 30. 192, 35. 330

HW has only two, in Arlington St house, 10. 193, 207

HW in illness had, made three times a week, 32. 42

HW jokes about offering part of, to Lady Mary Coke, 37. 563

HW lies in, longer than the lark, 38. 73

HW not to wrong Lincoln's, 30. 37

HW pleased with, 5. 224

HW receives cabinet and foreign ministers in, 31. 39

HW's, to be heated like oven and shared with 'Tonton,' 39. 420

HW sits on, 39. 4

HW under tester of, 39. 127

HW writes on, when ill, 10. 160

Hamilton's difficulty in finding, for visitors to Newport, 37. 503

Handcock, Mrs, would prepare for HW in Mrs Vesey's closet, 31. 235

Hardinge occupies, at SH, 35. 591

Henrietta Maria does over, in French fashion, 32. 325

Hertford's boys will share, 39. 284

horse caparison made into, 32. 325

in Italian inns, lack testers, 18. 315

ivory, inlaid with gold, 11. 295

maid to make, 36. 319

Mann makes, of damask, 21. 447

Mann's: inconvenient to write in, 20. 218; occupied by HW, belonged to Mann's landlord, 21. 447; Mann writes in, 20. 216, 25. 547, 555

Marchais, Mme de, surrounds, with mirrors, 30. 265

Montagu, Lady Mary, soils, in Roman lodging, 30. 8

Naylor, Mrs, has two in bedchamber, 20. 136

Northumberland, Ds of, shares, with chambermaid, 32. 128–9

of Mme de Maintenon, at St-Cyr, 10. 292

of silk and gold tapestry at Mereworth, 35. 143

only one vacant, at Rotherbridge inn, 35. 137

paid for, in French inns, 37. 41

parson's children lie at foot of, 35. 186

Plymouth prefers, to other amusements, 23. 378

recommended for cold sufferers, 20. 216

red velvet, at Hinchingbrooke, 40. 283

refugees from fire take, to Sir Robert Walpole's, 17. 496

Rinuccini gives, to the poor, 19. 461

Rucellai supervises making of Bns Walpole's, 17. 107

seven children burnt to death in, 25. 242

silver tubes used to ventilate, 20. 203

state, of P. and Ps of Orange, 37. 287

straw, Henri IV lies on, 35. 244

travelling, Young Pretender orders, 17. 13–14

twin, not customary for married couples, 20. 136

Walpole, Bns, gives, to Richecourt's abbé-secretary, 17. 107

Walpole, Sir Robert, snores behind curtains of, 17. 171

washing, Hertford's at Taplow, 38. 26

Bedchamber; bedchambers:

at Mamhead, has only one chair, 30. 67

family, two-coloured brocatelle suitable for, 21. 468

French, decoration in, sparse, 31. 87

HW adds, to SH, 21. 238

HW confined to, 30. 280

HW's: improper place to receive Lady Holland, 30. 280; up two pair of stairs, 30. 280

Townshend, Vcts, displeased with, at Brompton, 30. 70

Bedchamber, royal (Austrian):

Francis I's, includes Folco Rinuccini, 19. 251

Bedchamber, royal (English):

Albemarle, Cts of, treats her maids as ladies of, 25. 564

Amelia's: members of, robbed, 35. 189n; Vernon, Lady Henrietta, lady of, 24. 242n

Amelia's and Caroline's: Finch, Lady Isabella, in, 19. 389n; Hastings, Lady Elizabeth, rejected for, 20. 34

at Hanover, **20**. 184n

Augusta, Ps of Wales's: members of, **19**. 62–3; Walkinshaw, Catherine, woman of, **25**. 516, **26**. 46

Caroline's, members of, **17**. 165n, 346, **20**. 111n, 114n, 389, **22**. 543n, **23**. 94n

Charles II's, Hamilton groom of, **42**. 89

Charlotte's: appointments to, **21**. 518; Berry, Mary, does not want to be in, **12**. 126, 127–8; candidates for, **38**. 96–7; Dalkeith, Cts of, excluded from, **38**. 142n; ladies of the, at St James's, **32**. 19; ladies of the, cannot attend her at Kew in evening for fear of highwaymen, **24**. 47; members of, **21**. 518, **25**. 68n, 338n, **34**. 110n, **41**. 342n; vacancy in, **11**. 367

Cumberland, D. of: includes Albemarle in, **20**. 459n, **22**. 366n; includes Felton Hervey in, **18**. 69n

Frederick, P. of Wales's: members of, **17**. 251n, **18**. 8n, 159, **19**. 360, **20**. 32; Pitt resigns from, **19**. 27

George II's: appointments to, **20**. 246n, 470, **35**. 281; Brudenell wants post in, **37**. 386, 387; changes in, **17**. 493, **18**. 143, 166, **19**. 397, 420, **21**. 25, **37**. 530; Churchill, groom of, **17**. 221n; Conway becomes groom of, **21**. 75; Conway offers to send Sluys hat to gentlemen of, **38**. 11; Conway's attendance as groom of, **37**. 547, 552, 553, 558, **38**. 27n, 74; Conway wants post in, **37**. 385–6, 387–8; Cornwallis active in, **9**. 145, **37**. 202n; Cornwallis groom of, **19**. 177n; Finch groom of, **17**. 493; Hertford's attendance as lord of, **38**. 55, 61, 62, 76; members of, **9**. 323–4, **20**. 246n; Poulett resigns from, **20**. 469–70; Rockingham and Coventry eager to resign from, **21**. 99

George III's: appointments to, **9**. 323–4, 329, **10**. 14n, 46, **20**. 247, **21**. 460, **23**. 44n, **38**. 143; Carnarvon resigns from, **38**. 417–18; Cholmondeley may succeed Orford in, **25**. 266n; Conway expelled from, **22**. 238, **38**. 375, 376; Cornwallis dismissed from, **38**. 435n, 470; Coventry resigns from, **23**. 174; dissension in, **38**. 118; exclusions from, **38**. 118; George III tells, to vote against India Bill, **25**. 512; Harcourt prefers not to be in, **35**. 512; Hertford hints that HW might be in, **38**. 171; members of, **20**. 247, **22**. 97, **23**. 152, **26**. 46; Orford and Bolingbroke still in, though mad, **36**. 187; Orford resigns from, **25**. 266, **39**. 389; Orford's duties as lord of, **25**. 226; Peachey, Schutz, and Digby grooms of, **20**. 247; Pomfret's appointment to, astonishes the French, **36**. 187; Queensberry dismissed from, **34**. 127; resignations from, **37**. 530, **39**. 122; Richmond resigns from, **38**. 80; Waldegrave, 3d E., denied place in, **38**. 433

Gloucester, D. of, has grooms of, **38**. 468

Gloucester, Ds of, attended in, by: Carpenter, Lady Almeria, **25**. 638n; Heywood, Mrs, **24**. 323n

Groom of the Stole directs, **31**. 85

HW jokingly threatens to enter, **9**. 332

Harcourt mistaken for lord of, **33**. 463

Monro should be in, **25**. 11

York, D. of: has St John as groom of, **22**. 553n; has Wrottesley as groom of, **22**. 554n

Bedchamber, royal (French):
first gentlemen of, take years of service in turn, **31**. 64n
lord of, in waiting, is equivalent to English lord chamberlain, **38**. 451
Louis XV's, Fleury as lord of, curbs amusements, **38**. 451

Bedchamber, royal (Modenese):
Modena, Ds of, has Mme Pucci in, **18**. 25n

Bedding:
county gaol lacks, **40**. 308n
Francis I's, sold, **17**. 53n

Beddington, Surrey:
HW visits, **28**. 455
Scawen Park near, **33**. 111
seat of Sir Nicholas Carew, **33**. 111

Bede (673–735), the Venerable:
church of, **16**. 103
HW alludes to, **13**. 89n
painting may have been introduced by, **16**. 35

Bedeau, Julien (d. 1660), actor; 'Jodelet':
HW confuses, with Étienne Jodelle, **4**. 292

Bédée. See Botherel de Bédée

Bedell, William (1571–1642), Bp of Kilmore and Ardagh, 1629:
Sarpi urges, to have Wotton present James I's *Premonition* to Venetian senate, **20**. 198n

Beden, Treaty of:
Treaty of Utrecht followed by, **35**. 276n

Bedesman; bedesmen:
at Hurstmonceaux, **35**. 139

Bedford, Cts of. See Carr, Lady Anne (1615–84); Harington, Hon. Lucy (1581–1627)

Bedford, Ds of. See Anne (d. 1432) of Burgundy; Egerton, Anne (d. 1762); Leveson Gower, Hon. Gertrude (1715–94); Wydevill, Katharine (b. ca 1458)

Bedford, D. of. See John (1389–1435); Russell, Francis (1765–1802); Russell, John (1710–71); Russell, Lord John (1766–1839); Russell, William (1616–1700); Russell, Wriothesley (1680–1711); Russell, Wriothesley (1708–32); Tudor, Jasper (ca 1430–95)

Bedford, E. of. See Russell, Francis (1527–85); Russell, Francis, (1593–1641); Russell, John (ca 1485–1555); Russell, William (1616–1700)

Bedford, ——, child of Grosvenor Bedford:
illness of, **42**. 456

Bedford, Miss ——:
HW thanks, **40**. 206

Bedford, Charles (ca 1742–1814), HW's deputy in the Exchequer:
career and family of, **42**. 491–2

[Bedford, Charles, *continued*]
'Catchem' not found by, at Houghton or Eriswell, **39**. 489–90
commissioners of accounts send for, **42**. 32
examination of, **14**. 256–7
Exchequer, the, address of, **42**. 198
(?) Farington finds, at HW's, **15**. 322
father succeeded by, **34**. 13n
HW condoles with, on family troubles, **41**. 421
HW directs, to furnish Rose with stationery accounts, **42**. 29–30, 32–3, 34, 57
HW gives *Mysterious Mother* to, **41**. 428n
HW hopes, will be kept at Exchequer, **42**. 58
HW informed by, of Rowe's transactions, **41**. 206
HW's bequest to, **15**. 336, **30**. 359
HW's coach tax to be paid by, **41**. 432
HW's correspondence with, **7**. 396, **41**. 384, 387, 421, 432, 433, **42**. 29–30, 34, 198
HW's deputy, **28**. 75n
HW sends SH admission ticket to, **43**. 163
HW's servant tax to be paid by, **41**. 432, 433
HW tells: to investigate and relieve a needy case, **41**. 384; to see if Gray's monument is unveiled in Abbey, **41**. 387
HW thanks, **40**. 206
HW zealously served by, **41**. 208
illness of, **42**. 456
Martin asks, value of HW's place, **28**. *71*
——'s interference with, **34**. 13, 264–5
Nivernais's *Jardins modernes* given to, **12**. 260
Robinson to be supplied by, with prices paid for articles procured, **41**. 358–9
sons of, **12**. 229
SH visited by, **12**. 229, **43**. 163
Bedford, Mrs Charles. *See* Page, Mary
Bedford, Grosvenor (d. 1771), HW's deputy in the Exchequer:
aunt of, **10**. 276n, **13**. 220n
career and family of, **42**. 491
death of, **5**. 132n, *133*, **23**. 343
Du Deffand, Mme, asks about, **4**. 123, 131
HW consults, about place tax on his Exchequer place, **40**. 153–5
HW inquires about illnesses of family of, **42**. 456
HW offers Exchequer house to, **40**. 86
HW receives Gibbons's carved cravat from, **10**. 278n
HW refuses to give place of, to O'Brien, **41**. 209
HW's anonymous advertisement to be conveyed by, to *Public Advertiser*, **42**. 455–6
HW's charities distributed by, **40**. 308
HW's correspondence with, **7**. 377, 378, **40**. 41, 84, 86–7, 117–18, 142, 155, 203–5, 206, 258–9, 270, 308, 344–5, 380–1, 387–8, **41**. 172, 206–7, 208, 209, **42**. 453–6
HW sends his verses to Conway to, for *Public* or *Daily Advertiser*, **40**. 118
HW sends paper for, **7**. 378

HW takes leave of, to go to Paris, **40**. 380–1
HW tells: not to come to town, **40**. 203; not to connive at clerk's irregularities, **41**. 206–7, 208; to buy watchcoats of Mann, not Jackson, **40**. 344–5; to copy 'Garland,' **40**. 203–4; to get paper for printing, also McArdell's mezzotint of HW, **40**. 117; to inquire at Somerset House about Wimbledon's portrait, **40**. 142; to insert verses in newspaper, **40**. 118; to investigate appeals for needy persons and give money to each, **40**. 270, 345; to pay tax, **40**. 153–5; to turn in accounts without Palmer's, **41**. 172
HW thanks, for hospitality at Coronation, **40**. 206
HW to send, to collect MS from Ducarel, **40**. 120
health of: distemper, **40**. 388; gout, **42**. 454
house of, in Palace Yard, **9**. 380n, **21**. 534, **38**. 123
Le Gros and Le Cras to be paid by, for HW, **40**. 87
Philadelphia sinecure of, taken away, **40**. 291–3
son succeeds, **34**. 13n
Swinburn to be succeeded by, as deputy usher of the Exchequer, **40**. 84
Walpole, Sir Robert, appoints, to Philadelphia customs sinecure, **40**. 291
Bedford, Mrs Grosvenor:
HW notifies, **40**. 203
HW sends compliments to, **40**. *84*, 87
illness of, **42**. 456
Bedford, Grosvenor Charles (1773–1839):
career and family of, **42**. 492
(?) illness of, **41**. 421n
(?) SH to be visited by, **43**. 163
Bedford, Henry (? ca 1782–?1844):
family of, **42**. 492
(?) illness of, **41**. 421n
(?) SH to be visited by, **43**. 163
Bedford, Henry Charles (d. 1879):
family of, **42**. 492
Bedford, Hilkiah (1663–1724), noncomformist divine:
Baker related to, **2**. 357
——'s letter to, **2**. 353
*Hereditary Right of the Crown of England Asserted, The*, edited by, **2**. 356–7
Bedford, Horace Walpole (ca 1776–1807):
career and family of, **42**. 492
(?) illness of, **41**. 421n
(?) SH to be visited by, **43**. 163
Bedford, Thomas (1673–1710), Chancery clerk:
family of, **42**. 491
Bedford, Thomas (d. 1773), historian:
*Symeoneonis monachis Dunhelmensis libellus* by, **2**. 356
Bedford, Mrs Thomas. *See* Grosvenor, Elizabeth
*Bedford*, English ship:
expected at Port Mahon, **17**. 285

Howe to be joined by, 24. 411
involved in war, 19. 292, 325
Mann directs, 19. 42
Townshend captain of, 19. 42
—— takes, to England, 19. 374n
Bedford, Beds:
Bedford, D. of, defeated at, 7. 367
petition drawn up by meeting at, 34. 209
Swan Inn at, 34. 188n
Bedford Arms, Covent Garden (tavern):
Damer's suicide at, 24. 234–5, 32. 314, 39. 281–2
Bedford Church:
Ossory, Lady, might canvass for election at, 32. 210
Bedford Coffee-House, Covent Garden:
Hackman at, 33. 110
Bedford faction. See Russell, John, 4th D. of Bedford: faction of
Bedford family. See Russell family
Bedford Head, Covent Garden (tavern):
Board, the (Jacobite Club) meets at, 20. 50n, 25. 12n, 43. 249
Whithed entertains at, 17. 211
Bedford House, London; D. of Bedford's town house:
Amelia, Ps, entertained at, 9. 324, 369
ball and supper at, 35. 225
ball at, 9. 232, 363, 32. 7
Bedford and Rockingham meet at, 22. 542n
Cumberland, D. of, plays hazard at, 35. 225
Fox, Henry, abused at, 30. 183, 191
gallery at, for Ps Amelia, 32. 411, 33. 2
George II's set frequents, 9. 324
Gower deals at silver faro in, 35. 217
guests at, 20. 57, 135, 303, 22. 17, 33. 139
HW sups at, 35. 217
HW thinks Bedford-Grenville union no longer popular at, 30. 236
Marlborough, D. of, receives warrant from, for brother, 38. 327
Newcastle, D. of, goes to, 22. 556
new Paddington Road will make dust behind, 37. 453, 457n
Northumberlands insulted at, 38. 562–3
one of London's few surviving palaces, 12. 254
rioters threaten, 30. 181n
Temple's reconciliation with Grenville may not please, 38. 566
triumph of inhabitants of, 10. 153
'twilights' at, 33. 200
'Violette' visits, 9. 28
weavers' mob attacks, 38. 559–60
'Bedford-Hussars.' See under Russell, John, 4th D. of Bedford
Bedford Level Corporation:
debt of, 31. 5n
Bedford Level River:
Cole's farm flooded by, 1. 121–2
Bedford Row, London:
Duane's house in, 25. 568n

Fenn writes from Frere's house in, 42. 97
Bedfordshire:
Bedford, D. of, cannot be influenced about, 38. 434
conversation in, a change for Lady Ossory, 33. 128
ebony cabinet in, 1. 94, 96
election in: 10. 235, 32. 209n, 215n, 33. 225, 226, 43. 135; Ongley's defeat in, 36. 177
epidemics in, 33. 412–13
fire in, 33. 413
Giberne's prebendal estates in, 20. 82n
HW begs for a cutting of truth from, 33. 133
HW hopes province of, will stay close to home, 33. 204
HW visits Ossorys in, 24. 174, 39. 138; see also under Ampthill
husband in, refuses to see Mrs Siddons without his wife, 33. 396
lord lieutenancy of, Ossory's only government appointment, 32. 216n
militia of, 7. 44, 9. 248, 32. 123, 301, 33. 13, 20, 27, 34–5, 38, 49, 56, 204, 292, 372, 34. 202, 205
Militia Bill riots in, 21. 137n
Montagu visits, 10. 169, 263
Northampton clashes with, over Turnpike Bill, 20. 112
Pitt, Thomas, in, 10. 57
riots in, over Militia Bill, 35. 285n
wagon from, 32. 208
Bedford Square, London:
Hardinge writes from, 35. 600, 603, 605
Bedford St:
Reader of, 12. 249
Bedford Turnpike. See Parliament: acts of: Turnpike Bill
Bedinfield. See Bedingfield
Bedingfield, Lady. See Jerningham, Charlotte Georgiana
Bedingfield, Fr Charles Bonaventure (fl. 1762–70):
on Markham tapestries, 1. 6n
on Crane's burial place, 1. 19
Bedingfield, Edward (1730–post 1795), of York; Mason's friend and correspondent:
Mason's inscription revisited by, 28. 98n
seal given by, to Gray, 1. 233–4
text of memoirs of Gray to be revised by, 28. 163
Bedingfield, Elizabeth (d. 1689), m. Thomas Whetenhall:
Baronetage praises, 9. 118–19
'la blanche Whitnell,' 9. 118, 161, 174
Wetenhall, Edward, related to, 9. 174
Bedingfield, Sir Henry Arundell (ca 1685–1760), 3d Bt, 1704:
Lyttelton exposes alleged Bower letters owned by, as forgeries, 20. 532–4
most bigoted Papist in Norfolk, 20. 532
Bedingfield, Sir Richard (1726–95), 4th Bt:
brother of, 1. 234

Bedingfield family:
praise of, in *Baronetage*, to offset ridicule in Gramont's memoirs, **9.** 118–19
*Bedlam, a Poem on His Majesty's Happy Escape*:
HW to send, to Mann, **17.** 187
Bedlam (Bethlehem) Hospital, London; for the insane:
Annandale 'out-pensioner' of, **17.** 486
attorneys actuate, **25.** 316
Coke, 'out-pensioner' of, **19.** 457
Coke, Lady Mary, may go to, **24.** 179
De la Warr's trooper sent to, **20.** 137
Éon looks like, **38.** 378
Gordon, Lord George, should be sent to, **33.** 181
HW jokes about reservation of apartments at, for beginning of Parliamentary session, **30.** 23
HW's letters about England compared to annals of, **23.** 94
HW's plans to confine the sane in, **33.** 163, **36.** 187, **43.** 368
inmate of, rebukes impertinent visitor, **38.** 453
(?) Lawman may be sent to, **14.** 54
Lee confined in, **41.** 290n
lunatics in, were to be loosed in Gordon Riots, **33.** 197
Monro physician at, **17.** 168n, **19.** 210n, **25.** 11n
'out-pensioners' of: **11.** 217, **12.** 166, **17.** 486, **19.** 457, **32.** 184; outnumber the inmates, **2.** 156, **35.** 386–7
Queensberry, Ds of, 'out-pensioner' of, **32.** 184
revolutionists in France would kill keepers of, **31.** 332
Rousseau wants to be sent to, **33.** 39
Bednal Green. *See* Bethnal Green
Bedoart *or* Bedouart, ——:
social relations of, with Mme du Deffand, **7.** 429, 430
Bed-pan; bed-pans:
Q. Elizabeth's, with her coat-of-arms, **32.** 324
'Bedreddin,' Mme du Deffand's dog:
HW's love for his dogs not equalled by Mme du Deffand's for, **3.** 365
mourned, **4.** 25
Bedwell Park, Hertfordshire:
Gideon's art collection later at, **20.** 261n
*Bee, The. See under* Anderson, James
Bee; bees:
busyness of, **30.** 9
HW's letter on keeping, **40.** 256–7
HW's verses mention, **31.** 96
Irish, **35.** 80
killing of, Rider's almanac discusses time for, **30.** 34
Lyttelton's improper conversation on generation of, **15.** 330
Beech; beeches:
at Knole, cut down, **33.** 224

at Penshurst, **35.** 141
Gray's lines on, **43.** 175
groves of, at Park Place, too big for small deer, **37.** 347
Beecroft, John (d. 1779), bookseller:
Essex with, **2.** 81
Beef:
buttock of, West dines on, **13.** 174
Clement XIII might allow, in Lent, if fish is scarce, **22.** 101
eaten at Cambridge banquet, **20.** 83
England sends barrels of, to Portugal, **20.** 512n
English, exported to Calais inn, **20.** 13
English farmer's diet consists of pudding and, **31.** 66
English fear disease from, **19.** 174
English troops bicker over, with Flemish butchers, **18.** 30
'forbidden fruit' to Chute, **35.** 46
France tries to buy, from Ireland, **37.** 423n
Goldsworthy makes profit by sale of, to English ships, **18.** 107
HW compares eloquence to, **39.** 408
HW eats, *bouilli*, **31.** 66
Ireland sends, to Portuguese earthquake victims, **37.** 423
Lorenzi thinks venison as good as, **20.** 89
Mann's English guest rejects, **18.** 162
Mathews's taste for, ridiculed by HW, **18.** 79
Porter's apprentices have, for Sunday dinner, **16.** 217
raw, Bruce's anecdotes about eating, in Africa, **30.** 260
roast: Mann, Robert, demands, **20.** 301; Norfolk squires are 'mountains' of, **35.** 42–3, 46; 'of old Germany,' **38.** 2; on spit, sold to buyer of estate, **36.** 152n
royal family allows only 4 lbs of, for soup, **38.** 434
salted, Dick procures, for Minorca, **20.** 537n
sirloin of, a 'remove' for soups, **19.** 357n
Beefeaters:
assigned to Falmouth but promised to Cowper, **19.** 397
Bathurst to command, in place of Bolton, **17.** 457
Bristol, E. of, revived by prospect of, **22.** 450
George III aided by, **34.** 11n
Beefsteak; beefsteaks:
Africans said to eat living, **33.** 237
Bentley's mock heroics on the art of broiling, **35.** 643
Queensberry, Ds of, recommends, to Lady Sophia Thomas, **9.** 82
Beefsteak Club, Covent Garden:
HW hopes not to belong to, **35.** 539
Sandwich expelled from, for blasphemy, **10.** 111
Beelzebub:
Devil's name as physician, **24.** 71
HW refers to Wilkes as, **23.** 170
HW's name for Duc d'Orléans, **34.** 175

'President of Physicians,' **33.** 230
Robespierre compared to, **12.** 86
Beer:
brewed for army camps, **33.** 57
butt of, Germans would sell picture for, **18.** 323
English, Mann serves, to Vorontsov family, **22.** 193
Leopold's comptroller serves, to Cowper and Tylney, **22.** 379
mob forces Northumberlands to dispense, **23.** 7
Northumberland, D. of, would have drenched populace with, **33.** 93
Rowley sends, to Mme de Craon, **19.** 9
small: at Dover Inn, **18.** 315; English addiction to, **19.** 272; HW as weak as, **39.** 402–3; Mann procures, from fleet for Mme de Craon, **18.** 228
strong: hogsheads of, given to people at Powis Castle, **32.** 302n; Mason recommends, **29.** 170; Pigot should exchange diamond for glasses for, **31.** 159
tax on, **25.** 254n
verdigris contaminates, **40.** 257
Walpole, Sir Robert, granted pension charged to the excise on, **18.** 465n
writing under sign recommends, **30.** 24
Beerlegem (Flanders):
Conway encamped at, **37.** 155–60
Beeston (or Berston), Frances (fl. 1727–31), m. 1 (1727) Peter Le Neve; m. 2 (1731) Thomas Martin:
Humphrey's portrait owned by, **42.** 246
marriages of, **2.** 30, **16.** 185, **42.** 246n
Beetle; beetles:
Conway's green fruit eaten by, **39.** 418
Beevor, John (1727–1815), M. D., of Norwich:
Jebb's return for consultation requested by, **36.** 120–1
Orford, E. of, attended by, at Eriswell, **24.** 293, **32.** 349–50, **36.** 120–2, 125, 335
Befana (fairy puppet show):
on Epiphany, with horn concert, **18.** 134, 149
Beggar; beggars:
at Dublin Castle, **39.** 48
child gives farthing to, in Paris, **10.** 209
mutilated limbs thrust by, into coaches, **10.** 201
Richecourt's departure awaited by, **21.** 80
rise late, in London, **7.** 258
women, Irish, **20.** 358
*Beggar on Horseback, A. See under* O'Keeffe, John
*Beggar's Opera. See under* Gay, John
*Beggar's Pantomime. See under* Woodward, Henry
Begham, Mrs. *See* Beaghan, Katherine
*Bégueule, La. See under* Voltaire
Beguine; beguines:
Flemish picture of, **40.** 226
Begums of Benares. *See under* Benares
Behan. *See* Beaghan

Beheading; beheadings:
holding up the severed head a disused custom at, **37.** 267
Béhic, Monsieur:
SH visited by, **12.** 238
Behn, Mrs. *See* Amis, Aphra
Beignon. *See* Arouard du Beignon
Beinheim (Germany):
Charles of Lorraine's army re-crosses Rhine at, **18.** 505n
Beira, P. of. *See* José Francisco Xavier
Beira, Ps of. *See* Maria I (1734–1816); Maria Francisca Benedetta (1746–1829)
Beirlegem. *See* Beerlegem
Bek, Antony, I (d. 1310), Bp of Durham:
titles of, **2.** 178, 182
Bekel, Monsieur de:
SH visited by, **12.** 222
'Bel and the Dragon':
Johnson, Dr Samuel, heard story of, as a boy, **33.** 494
story of, alluded to, **34.** 16
Bélanger, Mlle de:
dies in fire, **4.** 54
Belardi, Francesco (b. 1696):
columbaria discovered by, **13.** 207n
Belasyse, Bns. *See* Brudenell, Anne
Belasyse, Lady Elizabeth (1770–1819), m. 1 (1789) Bernard Edward Howard, 12th D. of Norfolk, 1815 (divorced, 1794); m. 2 (1794) Hon. Richard Bingham, 2d E. of Lucan, 1799:
Piozzi, Mrs, comments on, **10.** 228n
Belasyse, Thomas (1627–1700), E. Fauconberg:
wife of, **1.** 182n
Belasyse, Thomas (1699–1774), 4th Vct Fauconberg; cr. (1756) E. Fauconberg:
earldom granted to, **20.** 563
George III removes, from Bedchamber, **9.** 324, **21.** 460
Sterne patronized by, **15.** 66
Belchier, William (d. 1772), M.P.:
Durdans, seat of, destroyed by fire, **35.** 211
Belcour. *See* Bellecourt
*Bel'Endroict, Les. See under* Drouin, Daniel
Bélesta, Marquis de. *See* Varagne-Gardouch, François de
Belfast, E. of. *See* Chichester, George Augustus
Belfast (Ireland):
dissenters of, support Roman Catholic emancipation, **34.** 166n
French threaten, **21.** 372
Moore, M.P. for, **13.** 179n
Rutland rejects petition from, **25.** 529n
Belfield, Bn and Vct. *See* Rochfort, Robert
Belfield, Bns and Vcts. *See* Molesworth, Hon. Mary
Belford, William (1709–80), army officer:
Sackville objects to, as court-martial member, **21.** 367
——'s court martial avoided by, **21.** 366n, 367n

Belforte, D. of:
(?) *Omaggio poetico* by, **7**. 264
Belfour, ——, Maj.:
New York news brought by, to Germain, **24**. 255n
Belfry; belfries:
flag flies from, at Leghorn, **21**. 278
Belgioioso. *See* Barbiano di Belgioioso
Belgium:
Austria, Britain, Holland, and Prussia sign convention to confirm Leopold II's rule of, **39**. 484n
independence of, declared, **34**. 87n
Leopold II's terms accepted by provinces of, **39**. 484
Patriotic Committee in, **39**. 456n
visitors to, Conway and David Scott, **39**. 537
*See also* Brabant; Flanders
Belgrade:
Mahmud I regains, by Treaty of Belgrade, **18**. 53n
Belgrade, Treaty of:
France guarantees, **25**. 415n
peace made at, **18**. 53n
Belgrado, Abate Conte Jacopo [Giacomo] (1704–89), Jesuit scientific writer; rector of the college of St Lucia, Bologna:
Malvezzi's orders resisted by, **23**. 486–7
Belgrave, Vct. *See* Grosvenor, Robert
Belhaven, Bn. *See* Hamilton, John
Belhouse. *See* Belhus
Belhus ('Belhouse'), near Avely, Essex; seat of T. Barrett Lennard, Lord Dacre:
Barrett Lennard's improvements at, **35**. 183–4; HW consulted about, **41**. 360
HW admires, **9**. 164
HW hears from Dacre at, **41**. 359
Hardinge apologizes to occupants of, **35**. 581
—— writes from, **35**. 590
Miller, Sanderson, Gothicizes, **9**. 156n, **35**. 183n, 184n
visitors to: Chute, **35**. 183; HW, **20**. 443n, **32**. 239, **35**. 183, **39**. 402–3, **40**. 197–8, **41**. 360–1; Hardinge, **35**. 610
Beliardi, Augustin (1723–living, 1791), abbé:
social relations of, with Mme du Deffand, **6**. 115
'Belief.' *See* Creed
*Bélisaire. See under* Marmontel, Jean-François
*Belisarius. See under* Clarke, Richard
'Bell.' *See* Seymour-Conway, Lady Isabel Rachel
Bell, Mrs:
SH visited by, **12**. 246
Bell, Beaupré (1704–45), of Upwell:
daughter of, **1**. 10n
Bell, Francis (b. 1704), 'Norfolk monster':
print of, **1**. 183, 216
Bell, John (1745–1831), bookseller; printer:
*Anecdotes of Painting* (last vol.) published by, **33**. 247, **34**. 35, **35**. 508, **41**. 236
HW cheated by, **34**. 35

HW's 'Epistle . . . to Thomas Ashton' reprinted by, **34**. 35
HW's *Miscellaneous Antiquities* published by, **13**. 48n, **29**. 37n, **41**. 256
(?) HW to give orders to, about Mann's request for maps, **23**. 418
*Morning Post* published by, **32**. 332n
Bell, Joseph (d. 1760), Col.:
released, **17**. 502–3
Bell, William (1731–1816), D.D., latitudinarian divine:
*Attempt to Ascertain and Illustrate the Communion, An*, by, **29**. 125, 134
Bagot's *Letter* to, **29**. 125
Bell; bells:
Aiguillon forbids ringing of, lest English prisoners be mortified, **21**. 251
at SH gate, **24**. 211, **35**. 331, **38**. 418, **39**. 176
church: installation of, at Santo Spirito near Mann's house, **18**. 227; mottoes on, **25**. 224, **33**. 305
earthquake rings, **20**. 130
'general's health' drunk by, after victory, **12**. 57
HW listens for announcement of victory by, **12**. 73
HW rings, for candles, **25**. 563
HW's silver, for inkstand, attributed to Cellini and acquired from Rockingham, **15**. 316, **23**. 383, **28**. 38, **35**. 478
in HW's bedroom, **35**. 373
Italian churches regulate days with, **17**. 32n
jangling of, keeps HW awake on night before coronation, **21**. 534
London prepares to ring, for Opposition victory, **38**. 324
London rings: for celebrations, **38**. 106n; for Torgau victory, **21**. 452n; for victories, **9**. 250–1; for Warburg victory, **38**. 69
silver, soothes teething, **30**. 308
tolled for George II's funeral, **9**. 322
wire attached to, **23**. 392
*See also* Doorbell; Handbell
Bell, The, inn at Windsor:
prices at, exorbitant, **19**. 298n
Bellacourt:
Humphrey, D. of Gloucester, builds, **16**. 71n
Bellamont, Cts of. *See* Fitzgerald, Lady Emily Mary Margaretta
Bellamont, E. of. *See* Coote, Charles
Bellamy, Mr:
SH visited by, **12**. 224
Bellamy, George Anne (ca 1731–88); actress:
*Apology* by: Boswell's advertisement compared with that of, **33**. 462; compared with Lady Craven's letter, **35**. 538; HW reads, but does not believe it, **33**. 479; number of volumes of, **33**. 465
Wray mentioned supposedly by, **33**. 465n
Bellanger, Antoine-Louis (ca 1719–86):
(?) daughter of, **4**. 54n
Bellanger, Mlle (d. 1768):
burnt in convent fire, **4**. 54

Bellardire, Geronimo Gabriele de:
press of, **18.** 421
Bellarmino, Roberto (1542–1621), cardinal:
Benedict XIV's researches lead to beatification of, **21.** 216n
Cavalchini supports canonization of, **21.** 216
HW calls, 'Mother Bellarmine,' **25.** 224
Paul V induced by, to refuse dispensation to James I, **25.** 224
Bella Vista (Italy):
Feroni, Mme, sends cedrati from, **17.** 317
Belle, Baron de:
social relations of, with Mme du Deffand, **7.** 428
Bellechasse, convent of canonesses of the Holy Sepulchre, Rue St Dominique:
Monaco, Ps of, takes refuge in, **4.** 438
Bellecour. *See* Colson, Jean-Claude-Gilles
Bellecourt, Mlle. *See* Le Roy de la Corbinaye, Rose-Pétronille
Bellecourt. *See also* Bellecour
Belle-Île (France):
Bussy to demand surrender of, **38.** 97n
capture of, **21.** 505, 511, 513, 516, 519
Conflans may attack ships at, **21.** 358n
—— tries to escape behind, **21.** 351
English expedition against: **9.** 364, 366, **21.** 438n; not to be commanded by Conway, **38.** 76; not yet successful, **38.** 90, **40.** 199; stopped, **21.** 466n, 474n
France to regain, **21.** 526–7, **22.** 76n
Young Pretender sails from, to Scotland, **19.** 85n
——'s ship gets escort at, **19.** 87
Belle-Image, La; inn at Versailles:
Franklin writes from, **32.** 337n
Belles-Isle, Chevalier de. *See* Fouquet, Louis-Charles-Amand
Belle-Isle, Comte de. *See* Fouquet, Charles-Louis-Auguste
Belle-Isle, Duc de. *See* Fouquet, Charles-Louis-Auguste
Belleisle, Hôtel de, Rue de Lille:
Louis XV offers, to Hertford, **38.** 305, 314n
Belle-Isle, Maréchal de. *See* Fouquet, Charles-Louis-Auguste
Belle-Isle, Marquis de. *See* Fouquet, Nicolas (1615–80)
Bellenden, Hon. Sir Henry (d. 1761), Kt, 1749:
acts in theatre at Queensberry House, **19.** 468n
(?) Argyll, D. of, visited by, **9.** 60–1
biographical information on. corrected, **43.** 114
Campbell, Lord Frederick, inherits house at Petersham from, **43.** 347
Coke's duel with, **9.** 59–60
death of, from drink, **9.** 359, **38.** 84
Gentleman Usher of the Black Rod, **9.** 357
Lorne may inherit villa of, **9.** 360
Middlesex's verses on, **9.** 359
Montagu not to imitate drinking of, **9.** 357
Sunninghill visited by, **9.** 60

Tuftons reconciled by, **9.** 359
Bellenden, Jacomina Caroline, m. (1749) Thomas Orby Hunter:
daughter said to have returned to, **22.** 19
Bellenden, Hon. Mary (1685–1736), m. (1720) John Campbell, 4th D. of Argyll, 1761:
brother of, **9.** 59n
Campbell marries, secretly, **31.** 419
George II's passion for, **31.** 419
Bellenden, William (d. ca 1633):
*De tribus luminibus Romanorum* by, Parr accuses Middleton of plagiarizing from, **15.** 8n
*Bellendenus. See under* Parr, Samuel
*Belle Poule, La*, French frigate:
*Arethusa's* battle with, **7.** 52, 54, **8.** 209
Du Deffand, Mme, comments on, **7.** 54
Keppel eluded by, **28.** 405n, 410
——'s clash with, **24.** 390, 394–5
Bellevue (France), bought by Louis XV from Mme de Pompadour:
anecdote of lady dining at, **7.** 121
fireworks at, **20.** 338n
Louis XV countermands Court visit to, **20.** 500n
—— occupies, **4.** 169
Mesdames leave, **11.** 207n, 208n
visitors to: Choiseul, Duchesse de, **4.** 137; Mirepoix, Mme de, **3.** 27, **5.** 142
Bellew (?Pellew), C.:
SH visited by, **12.** 228
Bellhouse. *See* Belhus
Belli, Valerio. *See* Vicentino, Valerio
Belling, —— von; Prussian general:
Bossi captured by, **24.** 404n
Bellingham, Lady. *See* Cholmondeley, Hester Frances
Bellingham, Charles:
name of, corrected, **43.** 299
Plat's relative and editor, **28.** 275n
Bellingham, Elizabeth (ca 1711–83), m. (1725) Sir Robert Echlin, 2d Bt:
Anglesea escorts, at masked Paris ball, when she is dressed as a man and insulted, **38.** 514–15
Bellingham, Sir William (ca 1756–1826), cr. 1796) Bt:
wife of, **4.** 217n
Bellingham, Mrs William. *See* Cholmondeley, Hester Frances
Bellisle, Vct. *See* Gore, Sir Ralph (1725–1802)
Bellisle, Vcts. *See* Gore, Catharine (d. 1771)
Bellman; bellmen (public criers):
HW compares night fever to, **10.** 109
Ossory, Lady, must think HW is, **33.** 43
reward for runaway slave cried by, **31.** 340
verses by, **13.** 146, 29. 312
*Bellona*, English ship:
news of Martinique from, **21.** 277
*Vestal* brought by, into Portsmouth, from Martinique, **21.** 277n
*Bellona* (or *La Bellone*), French war ship:
*Ardent* capture due to **24.** 511

[*Bellona* (or *La Bellone*), continued]
English ships engage, off Scotland, **37.** 246
Jacobites escape to France in, **19.** 254, 270
Belloni, Giovanangelo, banker at Rome:
Charitable Corporation's scandal threatened with exposure by, **43.** 258
Belloni, Girolamo (d. 1761), Marchese; banker at Rome:
*Dissertazione sopra il commercio* by, **17.** 23n
HW to receive letters forwarded to, **17.** *23*
'Onslow' to receive money from, **19.** 506
Shuttleworth's escape facilitated by, for vengeance against Parliament, **19.** 77
Belloni, Don Pietro, scagliola artist:
Hugford's disciple, **20.** 93n
Mann employs, to make tables, **20.** 93n, 194n
Bellori, Giovanni Pietro (1615–96), antiquary:
*Admiranda romanarum . . . vestigia* by, **42.** 268n
Bellotto, Bernardo (1720–80), called Canaletto, landscape painter:
views of Verona by, **23.** 299
Bellosguardo, Villa. *See* Michelozzi, Villa
Bellows:
at Drayton, enamelled, **10.** 90
at Ham House, filigree, **10.** 306
Bellows-blower:
organist and, **35.** 565
Belloy. *See* Buyrette de Belloy
Bell pull:
Charles III's, at Leghorn, **23.** 238
*Bell's Classical Arrangement of Fugitive Poetry.*
*See under* Bell, John
Bell Tavern, London:
Hogarth shows, in print, **15.** 142n
Belluga y Moncada, Luis (1662–1743), cardinal, 1719:
Louis XV wants French candidate elected by, **17.** 20–1
Belmore, Bns and Vcts. *See* Hobart, Lady Henrietta
Beloe, Rev. William (1756–1817), miscellaneous writer:
*British Critic* edited by Nares and, **15.** 238n
Combe's *Thames* disparaged by, **15.** 319
dedication by, of translation of Aulus Gellius, declined by HW, **15.** 255, 256–8
Farington finds, at HW's, **15.** 319
*Free Translation of the Preface to Bellendenus* by, owned by HW, **34.** 45n
HW declines offers of, to compliment SH, **15.** 228, 229–30
HW receives news of Nares from, **15.** 231
HW recommends, for living of Warham All Saints, **15.** 217
HW's dinner considered scanty by, **15.** 226n
learning of, **15.** 217, 223
*Miscellanies: Consisting of Poems, Classical Extracts, and Oriental Apologues* by, **15.** 228n, **43.** 205
*Sexagenarian, The,* by, **15.** *215n,* 216, 217n
SH visited by, **12.** 242, 243, **15.** 241n

translation of Aulus Gellius by, **15.** 223, 229, 254–5, 257–8, 296
See also *British Critic*
Beloe, Mrs William:
(?) SH visited by, **12.** 243
Belombre (at St-Geneis near Marseille):
Simiane, Mme de, buys, from Bp of Belsunce, **34.** 85n
Beloste. *See* Bélesta
Belot, Mme. *See* Guichard, Octavie
Belphegor:
French revolutionists resemble, **34.** 176
Sandwich will return like, **22.** 312
Belsay Castle:
Middleton of, **10.** 313n
Belsham, William (1752–1827), political writer; historian:
Anglesey ancestor of, **31.** 294, 296
HW calls, 'gentleman-essayist,' **31.** 293
*Memoirs of the Kings of Great Britain* by, HW has not seen, **34.** 203
More, Hannah, doubts critical ability of, **31.** 296
'Strictures on Walpole's *Catalogue of Royal and Noble Authors*' by: HW criticized in, **31.** 293–4; More, Hannah, has not heard of, **31.** 296
Belshazzar:
Montagu jokes about amanuensis of, **10.** 158
Belsies:
Seton of, **11.** 19n
Belsunce, Bp of:
Simiane, Mme de, buys Belombre from, **34.** 85n
Belsunce, 'Comtesse' de. *See* Sublet d'Heudicourt, Charlotte-Alexandrine
Belsunce, Marquise de. *See* Hallencourt de Drosménil, Adélaïde-Élisabeth de (1746–70); Vergès, Marie-Madeleine de (1762–1837)
Belsunce, Antonin-Armand de (fl. 1737), Marquis de Castelmoron:
wife of, **3.** 346n
Belsunce, Antonin-Louis de (1741–96), Marquis de Castelmoron; called Marquis de Belsunce:
(?) dances at ball for Dauphin's marriage, **4.** 410
grandes entrées granted to, **6.** 52
second marriage of, **7.** *109*
social relations of, with Mme de Forcalquier, **4.** 317
wife of, **4.** 381n
Belsunce (France):
dragoon of, **6.** 1n
Belt; belts:
broad, on figure in stained glass, **40.** 224
buff, **37.** 332
Conway busy with, **37.** 358
officers', captured at Dettingen, **18.** 261
pandours wear, **37.** 142
See also Marine belt

Belton, Tyrconnel's seat:
HW sees, **35.** 266
Belturbet, co. Cavan (Ireland):
Conway writes from, **37.** 335–6
Irish parliament has members from, **37.** 336
Belvedere; belvederes:
at Esher, **10.** 73
at Waldershare, **40.** 5
in Vatican, **12.** 10
Belvidere, Cts of. *See* Molesworth, Hon. Mary
Belvidere, E. of. *See* Rochfort, Robert
Belvoir Castle, Leics; D. of Rutland's seat:
Brown's plans for improving, **33.** 218
Dodd and Whaley to visit, **40.** 17
HW sees, **35.** 266
priory at, **2.** 281
rebuilt, **2.** 281n
Belzebub. *See* Beelzebub
Belzer de Berensberg, Annette-Marie-Thérèse
de (1747–94), m. 1 Charles-Léopold, Cheva-
lier (later Marquis) de Jaucourt; m. 2 (1790)
Antoine-Adolphe de Seiglière de Belleforière
de Soyecourt de Pas de Feuquières, Marquis
de Feuquières:
social relations of, with Comtesse de Broglie,
**7.** 444
Belzunce. *See* Belsunce
Bembo, Pietro (1470–1547), cardinal; writer:
HW quotes, **20.** 287
notes by, on Vatican MS, **21.** 169
Bembridge, Charles (d. 1794):
Burke restores, to Pay Office after dismissal,
**25.** 407, 408
Bemerton, Wilts:
Herbert buried in church at, **1.** 70
Benacre, Suffolk:
Gooch rector of, **1.** 354n
Benares:
Sheridan's speech on Begums of, **35.** 391n,
392
treaty of, **25.** 13n
Bénavent. *See* Froment de Bénavent
Bench; benches:
around HW's bowling green, **39.** 403
at Little Strawberry Hill, **35.** 306
back-to-back in alehouse fashion, **38.** 335
HW mentions, **38.** 157
in chimney-niches, **35.** 71
in Cordon's chapel, **25.** 55
in House of Lords, women stand on, **30.** 164
in theatres, **22.** 120n
Bencraft, James (d. 1765), manager of Covent
Garden Theatre:
rioters' demands upon, **22.** 120n
Bender, ——, Austrian field marshal:
Austrians under, occupy Brussels, **39.** 484n
Bender:
Russians soon to capture, **23.** 155, 160, 245
Russian victory at, **23.** 231n
Benedetta Ernestina (d'Este) (1697–1777), Ps,
of Modena:
appearance of, **33.** 531

Bologna visited by, after family rupture, **22.**
144
Braitwitz praises, **19.** 257
Charles Emmanuel III said to pension, **18.**
223
Chute and Whithed see, at Bologna, **19.** 257
Fermor, Lady Sophia, informed by, about
HW, **43.** 169
HW hospitably treated by, **17.** 44
HW sends compliments to, **19.** 257, 272–3
HW's old friend, **22.** 144
house at Bologna rented by, **18.** 223
Modena, Ds of, must be bored by, **18.** 237
Philip V's match with, broken off by father,
**13.** 242–3
St Crispino and Venice on route of, from
Modena, **17.** 442
sister hastens back to, **17.** 65
sister not allowed to wed before marriage of,
**17.** 55n
Benedetti, ——, Ensign:
captured at Velletri, **18.** 493
'Benedick.' *See* Shakespeare, William: *Much
Ado About Nothing*
Benedict XIII (Pietro Francesco Orsini) (1649–
1730), pope:
cardinals created by, **13.** 212n, 215–16, **17.**
22n
Palafox's canonization begun by, **23.** 123n,
**43.** 282
priests fined by, for wearing wigs, **24.** 107n
Sobieska, Maria Clementina, receives furniture from, **25.** 525n
Benedict XIV (Prospero Lambertini) (1675–
1758), pope 1740–58:
Acquaviva asks, to let Don Philip have Parma
and Placentia, **17.** 201
—— blessed by, **19.** 329
—— discusses Neapolitan invasion with, **17.**
110
——'s conversation with, about Austrian defeat, **17.** 465
——'s recovery deplored by, **19.** 339
advisers impel, towards Spain despite his
Austrian leanings, **18.** 56
Albani and Franchini complain to, **19.** 114
Alberoni recalled by, **18.** 199n
Almada denounces Jesuits to, **21.** 217n
*anno santo* announced by, **20.** 43, 98
'Antiquus urbis' of, authorizes repairs to
Pantheon, **21.** 37n
Austrian ambassador summoned by, **19.** 157
Avignon vice-legate tells, about Young Pretender, **19.** 368
beatifications and canonizations occupy, **19.**
171n, **21.** 216n
Belloni rewarded by, **17.** 23n
benediction by, from balcony at Easter, **21.**
103
Bolognese vainly appeal to, **18.** 99
Bossu notifies, that Young Pretender has
turned Protestant, **20.** 333n

[Benedict XIV, *continued*]

brief to be published by, against Venice, **20.** 161

bull by, jokingly proposed for legitimating (?) Lady Mary Walpole, **17.** 139

'bull' signed by, against Jesuits, **21.** 217

Bussy sent by, to Gages to threaten Spaniards with excommunication, **18.** 56

Canillac disliked by, **35.** 59

cardinals assembled by, when Atrisco threatens Rome, **18.** 444

cardinals' congregation to be held by, **19.** 416

cardinals consulted by, about bringing Young Pretender to Rome, **20.** 22

cardinals created by, **17.** 10n, **18.** 302

cardinals impatient for death of, **21.** 37

cardinals may soon be created by, **18.** 288

cardinals not created by, **18.** 183

Castro and Ronciglione embarrass, **17.** 204

'cazzo' the favourite epithet of, **19.** 492

Charles III agrees with, to restore commerce with Malta, **20.** 406n

—— meets, at Monte Cavallo, **23.** 389n

—— received by, at Quirinal, **18.** 533

Charles Albert's letter to, **17.** 351

—— thanks, for influencing imperial election, **17.** 351, 372

Charles Emmanuel III asks permission of, to invade Bologna, **17.** 482

——'s manifesto to, claiming Milan, **17.** 323n

Charles of Lorraine and Maria Anna get marriage dispensation from, **18.** 330n

churches and theatres furbished up by, **20.** 98

Chute compliments unworldliness of, **21.** 138

Clarelli and Ferretti chosen by, to meet Montemar at Viterbo, **17.** 214–15

Clement XIII to welcome D. of York in manner worthy of, **22.** 227

'coglione' the favourite epithet of, **19.** 492

Cologne, Elector of, not well received by, **20.** 508–9

Colonna holds public dispute with, **19.** 114

—— made vice-chancellor by, despite Old Pretender's opposition, **20.** 589

—— speaks to, about giving vice-chancellorship to Cardinal York, **20.** 590

consistory to be called by, **19.** 157

death of: **21.** 196; rumoured, **21.** 44n

Del Monte family invades territory of, **20.** 423, 428, 430–1, 435, 442, 445

Dumesnil consecrated by, despite Migazzi's opposition, **19.** 492–3

eagle, carved, might be kept by, from leaving Rome, **19.** 149

election of, as pope, **13.** 203n, 227n, **17.** 4n, **21.** 206–7

Electress leaves painting to, **18.** 171, 207

enemies of, **21.** 124, 132

extreme unction administered to, **21.** 37, 81

Ferrara's condition worries, **17.** 379

Florentine bishops accused by, of fearing Vienna, **20.** 305n

France may hesitate to antagonize, over Young Pretender, **20.** 23

Francis I acknowledged by, despite French, Spanish, and Jacobite opposition, **19.** 113–15, 157, 183

—— should complain of, to college of cardinals, **19.** 114

—— should keep, on bad terms, **20.** 431

—— will not be permitted by, to send troops against Del Monte family, **20.** 428

Frangipani major-domo of, **19.** 416n

freemasons suppressed by Maria Theresa at instigation of, **18.** 208

French, Spanish, and Jacobite cabals terrify, **19.** 157–8

Frescobaldi rebuked by, for slovenliness, **21.** 224

frigate of, cruises with Tuscan ships, **20.** 473n

Gavi's removal from church permitted by, **17.** 239

'great dog' of, **35.** 61

Guadagni pressed by, to aid Cardinal York, **19.** 433, 435

—— prevented by, from aiding Borghese, **19.** 433

HW laments supposed death of, **21.** 44–5

HW mentions, **9.** 211

HW pleased that Clement XIII does not eclipse, **21.** 238

HW sends joking regards for, **17.** 487

HW's fondness for, **21.** 27, **23.** 195

HW's inscription for wax bas relief of: **2.** 78, **3.** 114–15, **21.** 44n, 105–6, 113, 124, 125–7, 132, 138, **37.** 488, **43.** 66; Benedict XIV's letter about, to Bologna friend, **21.** 125–6, 127, 196, 204; Latin translation of, **22.** 88, 126

HW wishes that Chute, Whithed, and eagle were safe from, **19.** 161

Hamerani medallist to, **17.** 18n

health of: almost out of danger, **21.** 37; apoplexy suspected, **18.** 254; better, **21.** 113; faintings, **18.** 254; holds out, **21.** 69; much recovered, **21.** 124; not well, **20.** 442; recovered, **20.** 103; recovered though in bed, **21.** 59; relapse and recovery, **21.** 81; relapsed, **21.** 108; very ill, **21.** 21

Hobart encloses speech of, **40.** 58

Hope asked by, about Young Pretender, **20.** 508

Hugford wants to give scagliola table to, **18.** 87

'imbecility' of, **19.** 114

interference in French affairs regretted by, **21.** 59

Italian towns look to, as their only resource, **18.** 344

Jansenist when cardinal, **21.** 59

Jesuit policy of, not to be changed, **21.** 340n

Jesuits not favoured by, **21.** 340, **23.** 514n

—— would have been suppressed by, **21.** 308

João V receives title of *'fidelissimus'* from, **20.** 44n

jubilee ordered by, **18.** 295

jubilee will probably disappoint, **20.** 98

lapis lazuli beads and gold medal usually presented by, **18.** 447

Laurenti goes to Castel Gandolfo on learning illness of, **20.** 442n

Leghorn squadron may investigate relations of, with Charles of Naples, **18.** 67

Lercari, Abbé, banished by, **20.** 332n

letter from England shown to, **19.** 142

Livizzani's death lamented by, to Sersale, **20.** 429

Lobkowitz has audience with, **18.** 446–7

—— permitted by, to approach Naples through Monte Rotondo, **18.** 437

——'s gifts from, **18.** 447

Lorenzi corresponds with, **17.** 206

Louis XV's letter from, **21.** 59–60

——'s son avows subservience to, **21.** 44

Maffei's *Del impiego del denaro* censured by, **17.** 150n

Maltese-Neapolitan dispute shunned by, **20.** 406

Mann translates English addresses to show to, **19.** 144

—— wants English to punish, for supporting France, Spain, and Pretenders, **19.** 131, 158

—— wonders whether to call 'His Holiness' in dispatches, **18.** 301

Mardi Gras exempted by, from jubilee restrictions, **20.** 220

Maria Theresa may dismiss nuncio of, if Valenti is still upheld, **18.** 56

—— may quarrel with, over seizure of Valenti's abbeys, **18.** 55–6

—— persuades, to appoint Attems, **20.** 160–1

—— promises support to, **20.** 173n

——'s correspondence with, **18.** 55

—— told by, not to attack Venice, **20.** 177

Mathews accuses, of favouring Spaniards, **18.** 300–1

—— to punish, by demolishing Civita Vecchia, **18.** 314

measures against plague taken by, **18.** 252

medals of, HW gets, **11.** 271, **21.** 203–4, 215, 231, 242, 272, 278, 299, **26.** 3, 5

Medici estates at Urbino bought by, through St-Odile, **20.** 306n

Muzell tries to sell Stosch's maps to, **21.** 186, 192

Neapolitan troops may try to intimidate, into opposing Francis I, **19.** 144

Neapolitan troops not permitted to go through dominions of, **17.** 145n

Nemi convent entertains, **19.** 416n

niece of, visits Pisa baths, **19.** 487

officers of, at Ponte Molle battle, **18.** 532

Old Pretender asked by, to be reconciled to son, **20.** 332

—— receives money and indulgences from, **19.** 170

—— said to have asked, for money, **19.** 90, 96

——'s letter unanswered by, **20.** 590

——'s pension secured by, to Cardinal York, **22.** 368

——'s quarrel with, reminiscent of Henry VIII's with papacy, **21.** 8 ,

—— told by, of Cardinal York's cardinalate, **19.** 415n

Palazzo Madama bought by, from Francis I, **20.** 264n

pasquinades against, **20.** 189

Passionei drafts brief for, against Jesuits, **21.** 217n

Peggi's letter from, **21.** 125–6

Pironi's imprisonment enrages, **18.** 254

Pontano's arrest disavowed by, **18.** 55–6

Querini at odds with, **20.** 190n, 464

returns from Castel Gandolfo, **20.** 442

Richecourt prayed for by, **21.** 60n

Riva nun transferred by permission of, **18.** 86

Roman borders closed by, **18.** 270

Roman Catholic princes told by, not to disturb *anno santo*, **20.** 98

Ruffo's complaints ridiculed by, **19.** 416

Sabbatini employed by, **9.** 81n

Sacchetti collection bought by, **26.** 8n

St John wants to urge, to unite Anglican and Roman Churches, **19.** 358

St Peter's 'Holy Gate' opened by, for jubilee, **20.** 105n

saints' canonizations please, **19.** 171

Saldanha appointed visitor and reformer of Portuguese Jesuits by, **21.** 217n

sbirri of, arrest Pontano, **18.** 56

Schaffgotsch not recognized by, as coadjutor of Breslau, **20.** 269n

Serbelloni told by, to negotiate with Francis I about Monte Santa Maria, **20.** 428

Spain indemnifies, for right to appoint to its benefices, **21.** 437

Spanish-Austrian campaign enrages, **18.** 200

Spanish xebecs received by, **18.** 291

Spanish xebecs repelled by, **18.** 287–8, 296, 300–1

special license required by, for celebrating mass in a wig, **24.** 107n

speech by, on consecrating Cardinal York, **19.** 422

Spinelli's audiences with, about Old Pretender, **20.** 590

states of, *see* Papal States

Stosch's collection might have been bought by, for Instituto at Bologna, **21.** 434

——'s maps not to be bought by, **21.** 192

successor's ineptitude makes, more amiable, **21.** 304

takes air in a chair, **21.** 124

Tencin assures, that France will support rebellion in England, **19.** 170n

[Benedict XIV, *continued*]
—— friend of, **20.** 255n
——'s retirement to Lyon forbidden by, **20.** 255
Thun communicates news to, **17.** 282
——'s audience with, **17.** 201
——'s memorial to, fictitious answer to, **17.** 445–7
Tron's dismissal from Vienna depends on parley of, with Rezzonico, **20.** 190n
Tuscan borders closed by order of, **18.** 270
Tuscan disputes to be settled by, with St Odile, **20.** 305
Tuscan reconciliation with, to be marked by prosecution of Del Monte brothers, **20.** 446
Unigenitus bull unworthy of, **21.** 44
Valenti governs, **19.** 158
—— guides, **19.** 114
—— indemnified by, for loss of abbeys, **18.** 55
—— keeps close to, **19.** 330
—— said to betray, to France and Spain, **19.** 492
——'s secretary of state, **18.** 55, **19.** 144
Venice's quarrel with, **20.** 160–1, 163, 165, 173, 176–7, 189, 190–1, 198, 206
verses on, **18.** 334–5
Virgin might have been exiled by, to Albano with Stuarts, **22.** 227
virtues of, make Roman prelates less criminal, **22.** 66
Walpole, Horatio (1678–1757), contrasted with, **21.** 52
witticisms of: HW hears, **21.** 27; HW wants Mann to collect, **21.** 27; on Cardinal Landi's death, **21.** 69–70; on Choiseul's delayed entry, **20.** 589; on Frescobaldi's slovenliness, **21.** 224; to Ponzio who hurt him with syringe, **17.** 37
York, Cardinal, given pension by, **21.** 391, **22.** 368
—— honoured by Senate's visit at request of, **19.** 428
—— might be made perpetual legate of Bologna by, **20.** 332
—— reluctantly allowed by, to become priest, **19.** 499
York, D. of, would have been correctly welcomed by, at Rome, **22.** 227
Young Pretender asks blessing of, **19.** 85, 90
—— asks money from, **20.** 27
—— might be made martyr by, **19.** 131
—— said to be furnished by, with money and briefs, **18.** 427
——'s conversion said by, to be rumoured by Old Pretender, **20.** 333n
——'s whereabouts unknown to, **20.** 84, 508
—— urged by, to leave Avignon lest English bombard Civita Vecchia, **20.** 22n, 35n
Benedict, Ps, of Modena. *See* Benedetta Ernestina (d'Este)

Benedictine; Benedictines:
at Paris, petition Parliament to let them doff habits and rules, **22.** 325, **39.** 2
cardinals of, Porcia's quarrel with, **17.** 22
Caxton perhaps belonged to, **16.** 3–4
cloisters of, for ladies, near Capua, **20.** 429n
English, at Paris. *See* English Benedictines, church of
France reduces, **39.** 147n
Ligonier, Vcts, boards with, at Ardres, **30.** 256n
monk of, depicted: on gateway at Peterborough, **10.** 347; on monument at Easton Mauduit, **10.** 339
Benediction:
Benedict XIV gives, from Vatican balcony, **21.** 103
*in articulo mortis*, priests never give, when recovery seems possible, **22.** 14
Benefice; benefices:
Spanish, right of appointment to, **21.** 437
Venetians refuse to send money for, to Rome, **20.** 173
Benefit performance; benefit performances:
for Gluck, **19.** 234
Mann proposes, for impresario's widow, **20.** 298
Porter, Mary, has, **17.** 336
Benet College, Cambridge. *See* Corpus Christi College
Benet. *See also* Bennet; Bennett
Benevento, P. of. *See* Talleyrand-Périgord, Charles-Maurice de
Benevento (Italy):
Clement XIII unlikely to recover, **23.** 38
—— would sacrifice, to his brief, **23.** 10
Naples to seize, **23.** 24
restitution of: Clement XIV's prerequisite for Jesuits' suppression, **23.** 477n; delayed, **23.** 518, 527; promised, **23.** 473
'Benevolence, A':
'long-obsolete but now revived,' **41.** 381
Benevolent activity:
HW's reflections on, **31.** 208–9
*See also* Charity
Benevoli, Antonio (1685–1756), surgeon:
Albizzi operated on by, **17.** 481
Cocchi recommends, **17.** 77
Florentine malice against, **17.** 95
Florentines ask examination by, for fear of piles, **17.** 112
Mann attended by, **17.** 52, 77, 81, 97, 100, 104, 106, 362, 368, 369, 381
—— operated upon by, **17.** 88, 89, 90, 100, 340–2
—— talks with, **17.** 66
punctuality of, **17.** 341
surgical instruments lacked by, **17.** 89, 341
Benfield, Paul (1741–1810), M.P.:
alleged Parliamentary agent for Nawab of Arcot, **25.** 117, **33.** 244n

HW calls, rascal, 29. 123
investigation of, at India House, 25. 117
Markham votes for, 29. 102, 123
Parliament members said to be bribed by, 25. 117–18, 33. 244n
Pigot deposed by, 29. 103
Bengal (India), governor of, *see* Clive, Robert (1725–74); Vansittart, Henry (1732–?70); Verelst, Harry (d. 1785)
Bengal, Nawab of. *See* Mīr Ja'far 'Alī Khan (1691–1765); Mīr Qāsim 'Alī Khan (d. 1777); Najam-ud-Dowlah (ca 1747–66)
Bengal:
capital of, 28. 45n
Clive fortifies, 22. 540
—— instead of Barré goes to, 38. 378
—— made gov.-gen. of, by East India Co., with jagir restored, 38. 344
—— made president of, 22. 211
—— makes Mīr Ja'far Nawab of, 21. 279n
—— makes Najam-ud-Dowlah Nawab of, 22. 416
—— proposes financial restrictions on governorship of, 22. 540n
—— secures, from Great Mogul, 22. 416
Council at, sends deputation to Nawab in opposition to governor, 38. 310
diamonds of, 11. 125, 269–70, 29. 122
East India Co.'s depredations in, 23. 400, 35. 429
England may be conquered in, 23. 551
——'s revenue from, 22. 416
—— to dictate to, 11. 227
Englishmen return from, encrusted with gold and diamonds, 25. 400
famine and pestilence in, 23. 282, 387
governor of, Clive reduces salary of, 22. 540
HW expects French to capture, 28. 324
HW hopes, will not rebel, 32. 388
HW might do good in, 16. 132
HW would buy peace with, 33. 14
merchants of, 17. 277
Mill to organize Austrian exploitation of, 19. 407n
natives of, not enlightened by army chaplains, 31. 284
Pactolus dry in, 32. 184
plunderers of, alone can afford to pay engravers' fees, 35. 429
*Princess Amelia* sails from, 11. 251n
supervisors for, lost in shipwreck, 23. 282
Tuscany cannot draw on, 23. 134
Ben-hadad, K. of Assyria:
Rich, Lady, does not allude to, 35. 78
Benham Place, Berks; Craven's seat:
Brandenburg-Ansbach dies at, 11. 100n
Craven's seat, 11. 361n
*Miniature Picture, The*, performed at, 39. 372n
*Sleepwalker, The*, acted at, 28. 443n
Bening *or* Benninck, Levina (?1483–1576), m. George Teerlinc; miniature-painter:
biographical information on, 43. 391

Gray sends name of, to HW, 14. 117
Bening (*or* Benninck), Simon, of Bruges:
daughter of, 14. 117n
Benino. *See* Del Benino
Benislawski, Jan (1735–1814), titular Bp of Gadara, 1784; coadjutor of Mohilov:
Catherine II sends, to Pius VI, 25. 389
'Benjamin, Don.' *See* Keene, Benjamin
Benlowes, Edward:
*Theophila* by, quoted by HW, 43. 129
Benn. *See* Du Benn
Bennet, Lady Annabella (d. 1769), m. William Powlett:
daughter of, elopes, 9. 154
Bennet, Lady Bridget (1696–1738), m. (1716) John Wallop, cr. (1720) Vct Lymington, (1743) E. of Portsmouth:
(?) child of, attributed to Nugent, 9. 104
Bennet, Lady Camilla (d. 1785), m. 1 (1754) Gilbert Fane Fleming; m. 2 (1779) —— Wake, apothecary at Bath:
biographical information on, 43. 239
'Camilla' the swan in HW's 'Patapan,' 30. 295
exhibitionist frightens, 17. 399
father of, 30. 295n
Robinson entertains at ball, 17. 184, 37. 114
Bennet, Lady Camilla Elizabeth (1747–1821), m. 1 (1764) Count Dennoff *or* Dunhoff of Poland; m. 2 (1778) Robert Robinson:
Cumberland, D. of, linked with, in *Town and Country Magazine*, 32. 121n
Grosvenor's relations with, 32. 120
Bennet, Charles (1697–1753), 2d E. of Tankerville:
daughter of, 30. 295n
Jamaica governorship given to, 19. 296
Bennet, Charles (1716–67), styled Vct Ossulston; 3d E. of Tankerville, 1753; army officer:
commission resigned by, 9. 86
Bennet, Sir Henry (ca 1620–85), cr. (1665) Bn Arlington, (1672) E. of Arlington:
Euston built by, 18. 255
life of, in *Biographia Britannica*, 2. 187–8
rogue, 28. 72
Bennet, Lady Isabella (1668–1723), m. 1 (1672, remarried 1679) Henry Fitzroy, cr. (1672) E. of Euston and (1675) D. of Grafton; m. 2 (1698) Sir Thomas Hanmer, 4th Bt; Cts of Arlington, s. j.:
birth date of, corrected, 43. 325
Fitzroy, Lady Caroline, descended from, 30. 326n
Kneller's portrait of, 30. 326
second husband of, 30. 302n
Bennet, Rev. James (ca 1731–92), vicar of Aldeburgh, Suffolk:
Fonnereau charges, with corruption, 22. 585
Bennet, Levina (living, 1819), m. (1762) John Luther:
(?) drawings by, 42. 107
husband separates from, 38. 331n, 348
name of, corrected, 43. 375

Bennet, Mary (ca 1703–63), m. (1725) Francis Capper:
Capper employs, as copyist, 14. 221
—— informed by, of Chute interview, 14. 216–17
HW alludes to, 14. *211*
mentioned in Capper's statement, 14. 231–2
Walpole, Mrs, calls on, 14. 222
Bennet, Philip (d. 1761), M.P.:
Parliamentary debate by, on privately-raised regiments, 26. 17
Bennet, Thomas; bookseller:
daughter of, 14. 211n
Bennet, Thomas (d. 1764), Master in Chancery:
Chute attends conference at house of, 14. 226
hearings before, to end soon, 14. 227
Nicoll affair is referred to, 14. 201–2, 231
Bennet. *See also* Benet; Bennett
Bennet College, Cambridge. *See* Corpus Christi College, Cambridge
Bennett, Richard Henry Alexander (?1742–1814), M.P.:
birth date of, corrected, 43. 59
Bull's stepson, 1. 313n
estate of, large, 24. 499
House of Commons entered by, 1. 313n
marriage of, 24. 499
Bennett, Mrs Richard Henry Alexander. *See* Burrell, Elizabeth Julia
Bennett, William (d. 1790), Capt. of the *Æolus*:
London reached by, from Gibraltar, 23. 148n
Benninck. *See* Bening
Bennington, Vermont:
battle at, 24. 331n, 335n, 340
Benoist, Mme. *See* Puzin de la Martinière, Françoise-Albine
Benoît-Maurice-Marie (1741–1808), Duc de Chablais:
birth of, 17. 84
Benserade, Isaac de (1612–91):
Bussy's correspondence with, 5. 181
Bensley, Robert (1742–1817), actor:
performance of, in *Elfrida*, poor, 28. 109
Bensley, T., bookseller:
Italian edition of *Castle of Otranto* published by, 35. 436n
Benson, Catharine (d. 1748), m. (1725) Rev. Thomas Secker:
Clement, Dorothy, rescued by, from dust-cart, 43. 111
Benson, Harriet (1705–71), m. (1731) George Fox (afterwards Fox Lane), cr. (1762) Bn Bingley:
Giardini's threat frightening only to, 38. 209
(?) Pomfret's ears boxed by, for fondling her, 38. 88
son of, inherits her father's estate, 28. 336n
Benson, Jane (ca 1752–1826), m. (1776) Charles Agar, Abp of Cashel, 1779, of Dublin 1801–9, cr. (1795) Bn Somerton, (1800) Vct Somerton, (1806) E. of Normanton:
created Bns Somerton, 12. 164

Guilford, Lady, and daughters visit, 12. 164
HW calls, 'Mrs Arch-Cashel,' 12. 164
SH visited by, 12. (?) 202, 249
Benson, Martin (1689–1752), D.D.; Bp of Gloucester 1735–52:
bishop's house at Gloucester restored by, 35. 153
small chapel of, 1. 20–1
Benson, Robert (ca 1676–1731), cr. (1713) Bn Bingley:
Burgoyne said to be illegitimate son of, 28. 336
Goodricke, Sir John, heir to, 28. 375
peerage of, corrected, 43. 301
widow of, 20. 141n
Benson, William (1682–1754), surveyor-general of the works; M.P.:
bribe by, to get Wren's position, 40. 346
Benthagen (*or* Benthacken *or* Benthaken), Anna Catharina, known as Støvlet-Katrine and Frau Maes:
Christian VII's affair with, 35. 327
Bentham, James (1708–94), antiquary:
account by, of Henry VII's statue, 1. 278–9
brother of, 1. 178n
*History of Ely Cathedral*: 43. 45, 55, 56; advertisement of, 1. 201; Cole's involvement in, 1. 31, 135–7, 141n, 143, 178n; publication of, 1. 160n, 202n, 216; slow progress of, 1. 157, 159–60, 162, 164–5, 202–3, 205, 210, 212, 214
HW hopes for visit from, 1. 196
in London to present book to bishop, 1. 216
Bentham, Rev. Jeffery (1719–92):
Cole dines with, 1. 216
Bentham, Joseph (1710–78), mayor; printer:
Cole drinks tea with, 1. 299
—— goes to town hall with, 1. 362n
—— means to give glass to, 2. 48n
—— to receive books left with, 1. 260, 264–65, 266, 295
—— visits, 1. 201
death of, 2. 88, 90, 138n
HW's compliments to, 1. 183, 192, 196, 201
HW visits, 1. *178*, 185
writes to Cole of floods, 1. 121n
Bentham, Mrs Joseph. *See* Reste, Ann
Bentheim, Gräfin von. *See* Bournonville, Marie-Lydie de
Bentheim, Mlle de:
HW calls, 'Mlle Bleue et Jaune' in dream, 39. 4
Bentheim, Friedrich Karl Philipp (1725–1803), Graf von:
Estrées restores territory to, 21. 88n
George II given territory by, in return for pension, 21. 88n
(?) HW mentions, 3. 341
marriage of, 4. 11n
social relations of, with: HW, 7. 263; Hénault, 3. 363–4, 7. 321, 323
*Triomphe de l'amitié, Le*, read to, 3. 364
woeful, 39. 16

Bentheim, county of:
French seize, from George II, **21**. 87–8
Bentinck, Mr:
social relations of, in Paris, **7**. 293, 294, 298,
299, 301
Bentinck, Lady Anne. *See* Bentinck, Lady Isabella
Bentinck, Lady Charles. *See* Elliott, Georgina
Bentinck, Lord Charles (1780–1826):
wife of, **11**. 255n
Bentinck, Lord Charles Edward Cavendish
(1744–1819):
brother too compassionate for, **33**. 486n
dancing of, at Guines's ball, **32**. 111
Fitzherbert, Mrs, sups with, **34**. 41n
HW's correspondence with, **7**. 393
mother's executor, **33**. 484n
riches of, unstable, **33**. 486
social relations of, in Paris, **7**. 282, 289, 292,
294, 299, 312
to convey letter for HW, **1**. 229
Bentinck, Lady Elizabeth Cavendish (1735–
1825), m. (1759) Thomas Thynne, 3d Vct
Weymouth, 1751, cr. (1789) M. of Bath:
Amelia, Ps, entertains, **32**. 307
at Mrs Boyle Walsingham's ball, **42**. 222n
Bedchamber post to Q. Charlotte given to,
**21**. 518, **38**. 96, **41**. 342n
daughter born to, **38**. 143
Delany, Mrs, leaves Petitot self-portrait to,
**42**. 254n
HW reminded by, of failure to give to Mme
de Viry Mason's memoir of Gray, **41**. 342
husband flees for debt, leaving her mother
to care for, **38**. 567
Malmesbury mentions, **10**. 7on
marriage of, **9**. 236
mother's executrix, **33**. 484n
Bentinck, Lord George (1715–59); M.P.; army
officer:
does not subscribe to Middleton's *Life of
Cicero*, **15**. 7n
HW's contemporary at Eton, **17**. 264n
Paris visited by, **13**. 166
regiment of, from Ireland to be augmented,
**20**. 474n
Stosch receives offer from, for Gladiator, **17**.
264
Bentinck, Hans Willem (1649–1709), cr. (1689)
E. of Portland:
French portraits brought by, to England,
**10**. 4
second wife of, **34**. 260
William III gives Charles I's pearl to, **9**. 114n
Bentinck, Lady Henrietta (1737–1827), m.
(1763) George Harry Grey, styled Lord Grey
1739–68, 5th E. of Stamford, 1768:
Charlotte's bridesmaid, **21**. 529
illumination at house of, **10**. 204
mother's executrix, **33**. 484n
Bentinck, Lady Isabella (d. 1728), m. (1714)
Evelyn Pierrepont, E. of Kingston; cr. (1716)
D. of Kingston-upon-Hull:

daughter of, **20**. 434n
family of, **34**. 256
Kingston's courtship of, **14**. 243
Bentinck, Lady Sophia (d. 1748), m. (1729)
Henry Grey, 12th E. of Kent, cr. (1706) M.
and (1710) D. of Kent:
death of, **30**. *115*
Old Windsor residence of, **30**. 304n
portrait attributed to, **9**. 4
Remenham bequeathed by, to mother and
then to daughter, **30**. 115
Williams, C. H., makes witticism on Secker's
relations with, **30**. 304n
Bentinck, William (1649–1709), 1st D. of Portland. *See* Bentinck, Hans Willem
Bentinck, William (1704–68), Count:
Aix preliminary treaties signed by, **19**. 479n
Newcastle to meet with, **19**. 485n
Bentinck, William (1709–62), 2d D. of Portland:
Bute succeeds, in Order of the Garter, **22**. 37n
daughter of, **21**. 530, **41**. 342n
expected at Welbeck, **35**. 271
Le Moine chaplain to, **15**. 302
son called back to England by, **21**. 543, 550–1
son of, **1**. 229n
steward cuts passage for, through oak, **35**. 271
wife of, **9**. 114n, **16**. 157n, **25**. 596n
Bentinck, William Henry Cavendish (1738–
1809), styled M. of Titchfield; 3d D. of Portland, 1762; M.P.:
administration of: HW's prophecy about
shortness of, fulfilled, **25**. 399n; insecure,
**33**. 398; should show strength in Parliament, **33**. 429
Amelia, Ps, entertains, **33**. 416n, **35**. 533n,
**39**. 441
becomes prime minister, **25**. 391, **29**. 261, 265,
271, 330n, **33**. 390, 393, **36**. 208–9
begins Parliamentary speech but is frightened, **38**. 248
Burke's *Reflections* admired by, **34**. 99n
Bute and Dyson considered the sole enemies
by, **39**. 100
candidates of, in Cumberland election, **10**.
273
Carlisle supports candidates of, **39**. 96n
Cavendish family wants, to be prime minister,
**33**. 342n
Chatham the object of protest by, **22**. 471n
Cheshire Whigs viewed with suspicion by,
**43**. 305
Clermont, Cts of, rebuked by Ps Amelia for
passing snuff-box to, **35**. 533
Court offends, by appointing another person
to treat with him, **25**. 380
Cumberland, D. of, entertains, **36**. 199
expenses of, in Carlisle election, **30**. 250
father summons, back to England, **21**. *543*,
550–1
fortune of, depleted by mismanagement and
compassion for brother, **1**. 229n, **33**. 486n

[Bentinck, William H. C. (1738–1809), *continued*]

Fox, C. J., prefers, as Rockingham's successor, **25.** 295

—— talks with, about Paris embassy secretaryship, **42.** 73

George III and North differ with, about cabinet posts, **25.** 381

George III confers with, at Buckingham House, **25.** 387n

—— does not easily stomach, as minister, **25.** 418

—— does not object to, as prime minister, **33.** 391n

—— does not tell, of disapproval of India Bill, **25.** 458n

—— nearly discharges ministry of, **25.** 418

—— orders North to form new administration headed by, **25.** 387, 390–1

—— rejects Rockingham faction's choice of, as prime minister, **35.** 517n

—— reluctant to accept, as prime minister, **25.** 386n

—— tells, through North that his arrangement is accepted, **25.** 391

George IV (Prince of Wales)'s establishment urged by, **25.** 418n

—— sups with, nightly, **34.** 41n

HW calls, a cipher, **25.** 381

HW communicates with, about Orford's boroughs, **39.** 193

HW learns anecdotes of Pratt and Pitt from, **30.** 197

(?) HW's correspondence with, **42.** 414n

HW wishes well to ministry of, **35.** 380

lord chamberlain, **15.** 160n

Lowther's contest with, **23.** 58, **34.** 242

marriage of, **22.** 465

masquerade given by, at Welbeck on son's birth, **35.** 408

member of committee to restore freedom of Parliament, **2.** 208n

mother's collection partly to be retained by, **33.** 484

mother's wealth inherited by, **25.** 596–7

name of, corrected, **43.** 368

North and C. J. Fox propose, as first lord of the Treasury, **25.** 377, 379

Newcastle urges, not to resign, **22.** 442n

Newcastle House meeting attended by, **22.** 541n

North confers with C. J. Fox and, **25.** 387n

portrait of Lady Arabella Stuart owned by, **15.** 160, 163

Powys tries to reconcile Pitt and, **25.** 476n

Privy Council attended by, during Gordon Riots, **33.** 188

proclaims restoration of Ireland's rights, **29.** 253n

resignation of: as lord chamberlain, **22.** 471, **30.** 234, **41.** 67n; as prime minister, **25.** 460n, **35.** 519

Richmond answers, in House of Lords, **25.** 458n

Rockingham's possible successor, **25.** 289, 372

Shelburne succeeded by, as prime minister, **36.** 208–9

Thurlow's dismissal demanded by, **25.** 381

Torrington indebted to, **33.** 210n

unmarried, **10.** 29

vase bought by, at mother's sale, **39.** 442

violence of, towards Bute, abated, **30.** 187

voting shunned by, **22.** 508n

Waldegrave, Cts, pursued by, **38.** 351, 357

windows of, illuminated for Wilkes's release, **23.** 205

witticism on, as block to hang Whigs upon, **36.** 209

Bentinck, William Henry Cavendish Scott (1768–1854). *See* Cavendish Scott Bentinck

Benting. *See* Bentinck

Bentivoglio, Signora. *See* Bonaventuri, Pellegrina

Bentivoglio, Cornelio (1668–1732), cardinal, 1719; nuncio to France, 1712:
Aguesseau's conversation with, **7.** 276–7

Bentivoglio, Elisabetta (ca 1696–1771), m. (1716) Marchese Leonardo Tempi:
Franceschi cicisbeo to, **17.** 61

Bentivoglio, Guido (1579–1644):
authorities not cited by, **40.** 141–2

Bentivoglio, Ulisse (d. 1618), of Bologna:
marriage of, **20.** 414

Bentley, Miss:
Montagu's god-daughter, **9.** 281–2

Bentley, Misses, daughters of Richard Bentley (1708–82):
(?) SH visited by, **12.** 248

Bentley, Elizabeth, m. 1 Humphrey Ridge; m. 2 Rev. James Favell, D.D.:
Bentley may have intended ormer shells for, **35.** 175

Bentley, George, publisher:
Mann's letters published by, **26.** 41–2, 44

Bentley, James, of Oulton, Yorks:
half-brother of Dr Richard Bentley, **13.** 173n

Bentley, Joanna (d. 1775), m. (1728) Rev. Denison Cumberland, D.D.; Bp of Clonfert and of Kilmore:
brother may give ormer shells to, **35.** 175

brother's correspondence with, **35.** 188–9

marriage of, **29.** 9n

Bentley, Dr Richard (1662–1742), Master of Trinity College, Cambridge:
Appleby, subject of remark by, **37.** 126

Atterbury's controversy with, **29.** 294

biographical information on, corrected, **43.** 194

buried at Trinity College, Cambridge, **15.** 19

Campbell to correct genealogy of, in *Biographia Britannica*, **35.** 204

Casley deputy to, **14.** 109n

Conway mentions, **37.** 468

Cornwallis's fellowship brought to attention of, **13.** 155

Cumberland is grandson of, **35.** 644

*Dr. Bentley's Proposals for Printing a New*

*Edition of the Greek Testament* by, **15**. 294
Greek epigram on 'sons of heroes' given by, to son, **9**. 227
HW prints notes by, on Lucan, **1**. 35n, **2**. 188, **15**. 59, 72, **16**. 22, 364, **43**. 72
(?) HW quoted by, for list of unengraved portraits, **16**. 234–5
HW's opinion of, **9**. 105
letter reaches, with 'England' as sole address, **25**. 609
life of, in *Biographia Britannica*, **29**. 9
Master of Trinity College, Cambridge, **20**. 368n, **21**. 120n, **23**. 365n
Middleton's controversy with, **15**. 294
misuse of 'antiquarian' condemned by, **16**. 50–1
Montagu hopes that son's profits will equal fame of, **9**. 333
nephew of, **13**. 173
notes of, on Lucan, praised, **15**. 72
Pope mentions, in *Dunciad*, **1**. 227n
preyed on by vultures, **15**. 59
proposals by, for new edn of Greek Testament, **15**. 294
son despised by, **9**. 105
son of, **14**. 51n, **16**. 25, **20**. 368n, 554n, **21**. 120n, 239n, **23**. 365n, **24**. 277, **23**. 131n
son will be abused as much as, **9**. 373
Warburton resembles, **40**. 228
——'s controversy with, **7**. 354, **13**. 39n
Bentley, Richard (1708–82), HW's correspondent; 'Cliquetis':
Alpine taste of, **35**. 268
appearance of: dirty, old, and poor, **10**. 203; La Borde resembles, **7**. 280
architecture not studied by, **42**. 220
Armagh, Abp of, tells stories about, to Montagu, **9**. 393–4
*Attempt towards an Apology for his R. H. the Duke, An*, by, **35**. 643
banished, **9**. 172n
bantams and goldfish to be sent to, **35**. 182
Bateman's house remodelled from drawings by, **10**. 42n
——'s offices at Old Windsor altered by, **35**. 644
Buckingham to be visited by, **9**. 193
Bute makes, commissioner of the Lottery, **10**. 72, **35**. 645
——'s resignation may harm, **10**. 66
'cascade scene' by, **43**. 361
Casley deputy librarian to, **14**. 109n
Cassiobury Park should be designed by, **35**. 177
chairs to be designed by, for HW, **14**. 60, **35**. 182
Chalfont to be visited by, **9**. 249
Challis to share income of Customs place with, **24**. 277
Charlotte, Q., complimented by, in *Wishes*, **9**. 383
children of, to receive fund HW invested for them, **33**. 372

chilliness of, **9**. 210, 211, 214, 239–40
chimney-piece by: in SH Blue Bedchamber, **35**. 174; Strafford to have design for, **35**. 214
Chinese plan of, for HW, recommended by Williams to D. of Bedford, **35**. 177–8
Chute's correspondence with, **35**. 177, 256
——'s design for SH Cloister examined by, **35**. 110
——'s wit praised by, **24**. 212
Cole's account of, **2**. 47n
colours carelessly chosen by, **28**. 195
Conway does not need, at Park Place, **37**. 329
costume of: dirty linen, **10**. 158; milk-white coat with blue cape, **9**. 373; purple and gold, **10**. 158; rags, **10**. 158
Court aspirations of, **9**. 345
credit preferred by, to money, **9**. 333
cul-de-lampe by, for HW's *Entail*, **35**. 208
Cumberland contrasted with, **10**. 187
—— nephew of, **11**. 103n, **28**. 233n
——'s *Brothers* possibly influenced by, **10**. 301, 302
——'s failure with the *Summer's Tale* may disappoint, **10**. 196
——'s pamphlet to, attacking Garrick, **35**. 645
——'s parcel sent to, by HW, with seeds and books, **35**. 198
—— to convey apologies of, to Hampden and Bp of Durham, **9**. 343
Cumberland, D. of, does not employ as architect, **35**. 161
decline of, after leaving SH, **10**. 243
designs by, at Hinchingbrooke, **9**. 267
designs by, for: Chalfont stable, **9**. 285; Galfridus Mann's monument, **13**. 29, **21**. 128n, 157, 250, **35**. 644; Holdernesse's room, **9**. 285, **40**. 180n; Montagu's mantel-piece, **9**. 151; ostrich plumes for SH bedchamber, **20**. 375n; Ragley, **9**. 121, 223; Roel, **9**. 146; Strafford's temple in the menagerie, **9**. 295, **11**. 67, **35**. 279–80, 306; SH, **1**. 379n, **35**. 157, 158, 164, 171; SH lantern, **9**. 150
*Designs by Mr R. Bentley for Six Poems by Mr T. Gray*, **9**. 116, 134, 143, **13**. 24, **14**. 59–66, 172, **20**. 368, 386, **35**. 185, 238–9, 643
Dodsley's correspondence with, about Lucan's *Pharsalia*, **40**. 148–9
drawing (drawings) by: as finished as engravings, **14**. 59, 65; Bedford, Ds of, notices, **35**. 225; for Gray's odes, **28**. 271; HW has not received, **35**. 181, 206; HW praises, **35**. 157; of SH, (?) sent to Montagu, **9**. 212, 213, 217; of the Vyne, (?) to be sent to Montagu, **9**. 212; owned by Montagu, **35**. 644; shown to Worsley, **9**. 343; to be copied by Müntz for Chute, **35**. 232
drawings by, of 'Mabland,' show he has seen Winchester, **35**. 249–50
Drury Lane attended by, **9**. 382
Eccardt's portrait of, **9**. 207n, **35**. 174, 639
engravings of SH chimney-pieces from drawings by, **43**. 72

[Bentley, Richard (1708–82), *continued*]

*Epistle to Lord Melcombe* by: **9.** 408–10, 411, 416, **10.** 16, 57, 61, **35.** 645; printed in *St James's Magazine,* **10.** 57

extravagance of, **10.** 303

Farmer's agreement witnessed by, **40.** 165

father of, abused, **9.** 373

father's opinion of, **9.** 105, 227

father tells, that 'sons of heroes are loobies,' **9.** 227

finances of, **9.** 158, 172, 195, 261, 262, 302, 303, 333, **10.** 69, 75, (?) 113, 203, **35.** 191–2, 219–20, 221, 227, 231–2

Fleet Prison predicted as next abode of, **9.** 303

forests thrive in letters but not in landscapes of, **35.** 205

'foundling hospital' of, **9.** 201, **43.** 119

Frederick II predicted by, to inhabit Somerset House, **21.** 319–20, 332

*Full and True Account of the . . . Earthquake, A,* **35.** 643

Garrick admires, **35.** 242

—— satirized by, in *The Wishes,* **9.** 383

George III complimented by, in *The Wishes,* **9.** 383

—— pays, for *The Wishes,* **9.** 373, **35.** 645

goldfish carried by, in decanter, **9.** 155

Gothic building to be designed by, for Strafford, **35.** 267

Gothic taste of, as good as Wren's, **35.** 154

Granville grants apartment in Jersey to, **35.** 161

Gray chooses gruesome subject for sketch by, **9.** 143–4

—— mentions, **14.** 51

—— praises and scolds, alternately, **14.** 66

——'s *Bard* should be illustrated by, **35.** 252

—— sends compliments to, **14.** 58

——'s poems illustrated by, **9.** 116, 134, 143, **13.** 24, **14.** 59–66, 172, **20.** 368, 386, **35.** 185, 643, **43.** 191

——'s sketch of Stoke Manor improved by, **35.** 185

Grecian and Gothic graces can be combined only by, **21.** 250

HW advises, to eschew wild schemes and develop his talents, **35.** 190–1

HW always dedicates his travels to, **35.** 266

HW and carpenter want visit from, at SH, **35.** 177

HW asks amount of debts of, for compounding them, **35.** 219–20

HW asks Montagu to solicit pension for, through North, **9.** 261, 262

HW calls 'Cliquetis,' **9.** 172, **35.** 85

HW encourages, to draw while awaiting pigments, **35.** 243

HW gets no bricks for Strafford's menagerie temple by, **35.** 282

HW has shown, inscription for Lady Walpole's monument, **35.** 178

HW hopes Selwyn will often meet, **30.** 154

(?) HW jokes about, as 'Cycnus,' **10.** 38

HW jokes about plans of, for Roel, **43.** 118

HW knows no architecture but from Chute and, **35.** 103

HW laughed at by, **35.** 244

HW mentions, **10.** 232, **14.** 103, **37.** 489

(?) HW not to be attended by, **35.** 131

HW praises, **21.** 120, 239

HW promises place to, in Customs, but misfortunes prevent acceptance, **24.** 277

HW quotes, **9.** 253

HW's account of, **35.** 643–5

HW's antiqarian tastes described by, **9.** 250

HW's antiquarian tastes praised by, as furnishing matter for future antiquarians, **21.** 140

HW scolds: for advancing money to Müntz, **35.** 226–7; for pursuing visionary projects, **35.** 190–1, 231–2, 240

HW's conversation with, about sects and parties, **35.** 167n

HW's correspondence with, **9.** 162, 179–80, (?) 302, **35.** 131–272 *and passim,* **36.** 313, **37.** 379

HW's design for Roger Townshend's monument drawn by, **40.** 167

HW's dispute with, over picture in Gibbons frame, **35.** 174

HW's friendship for, **15.** 59

HW's generosity to, **9.** 302, 303

HW's gifts from: granite fragment, **35.** 172; Guernsey lilies, **35.** 185; Johnson's life of Gray, **29.** 117, **35.** 272; myrtles, **35.** 214; plants, **35.** 263; shells and roots, **35.** 258; shells, trees, cones, and landscape, **35.** 207

HW's gifts to: books, **35.** 214; cloth and paints, **35.** 264; French writings, **35.** 263–4; goldfish, **35.** 205, 221; *Sir Charles Grandison,* **35.** 168; trees, **35.** 204; *World, The,* **35.** 257, 258

HW shows to, Mann's account of Papal-Portuguese quarrel, **21.** 428

HW's opinion of, **9.** 105, 227, **10.** 113

HW's procurement of granite through, **35.** 172, 175, 178, 182

HW's rift with, **9.** 301–2, 303

HW's scoldings hurt, **35.** 239–40

HW suggests, as deputy to Selwyn, **30.** 154

HW's Swiss boy mentions, **20.** 554

HW tells anecdote about 'Gracchus' and, **9.** 397

HW tells: not to draw Louis XV when he has not drawn Henri IV, **35.** 257; to come to SH and not be taken prisoner to France, **35.** 226; to paint more in oils, **35.** 208

HW thanks: for paintings of Mt Orgueil, Elizabeth Castle, and Hercules, **35.** 243; for partridges, **35.** 260

HW thanks Selwyn for promising a position to, **40.** 163

HW to be visited by, **9.** 203, **35.** 177

HW to carry, to SH in chariot, **35.** 69

HW to inform, of Chute's inheritance, 35. 85
HW to send to: eagle prints, snuff-box, and Müntz's directions, 35. 252; fish and fowls, 35. 182; glasses, proverbs, and goldfish, 35. 192; paints, brushes, and oil, 35. 252; seeds, 35. 185; Sévigné letters, shrubs, 35. 196, 197
HW treats, as a child, 35. 221
HW visited by, 9. 105, 134
HW wants drawings from, 35. 197, 206, 231, 239–40, 241, 243, 261, 263, 264
HW wants Dublin editions of, 10. 20
HW will send wallpaper to, if wanted, 35. 196
Halifax, E. of, may be visited by, 9. 134
—— may aid, 10. 69
——'s 'Gartering' witnessed by, 10. 125
——'s 'shoes licked by,' 10. 125
Hardinge meets, at Griffin's, and hears of HW's kindness, 35. 608
——'s error about, 35. 610
*Harlequin's Mouth Opened* by, 35. 644
health of: fever, 14. 99; fever and sore throat, 9. 198, 216; inflammation of the bowels, 9. 216; relapse, 9. 217; sweating sickness, 35. 100
Henri IV not drawn by, and he should not draw Louis XV, 35. 257
—— sketching among his soldiers should be depicted by, 35. 243–4
Hentzner's *Itinerarium* translated by, 13. 28, 35. 643
——'s *Journey* to be prepared by, for SH Press, 35. 99
Holt Castle inhabited by, with Montfort's permission, 35. 201n
house of, in Abingdon Street, 33. 372n
imagination of, Pindaric, 10. 20
income anticipated by, in Jersey, 35. 232
(?) indifference of, to heroes, 10. 113
'infantas' confined with, 9. 198, 201, 203
Ireland not visited by, 9. 393
Jersey refuge of, to escape creditors, 9. 158, 172, 195, 35. 78, 79, 157–252
landscape painting by, 35. 207–8
letters of, praised by HW, 35. 157, 261, 264
literary ambitions of, 9. 417
lives much with HW, 20. 554n, 21. 120, 239
*London Chronicle*'s letter from, on cruelty to dogs, 35. 644
London to be visited by, 9. 302, 303
Lucan edition annotated, introduced and illustrated by, 35. 644
—— printed at SH for benefit of, 9. 333, 28. 24n, 29. 10
Mall visited by, 9. 373
marriage of, 9. 411
Mason's Gothic design to be corrected by, 9. 285
merit and misfortunes of, 30. 154
Miller's castle almost worthy of, 35. 148
money from Ely for, 35. 188
Montagu given mantel-piece design by, 9. 151

—— godfather to daughter of, 9. 281–2
—— invites, to Hawkhurst, 9. 105
—— never told by, about future marriage, 9. 303
—— regrets inability to get favours for, 9. 267
——'s correspondence with, 9. 148–9, 151, 162, 167, 261–2, 281, 35. 177, 205
—— sends cider to, 9. 277, 281
—— sends compliments to, 9. 197, 209, 211, 245, 248, 253, 258, 282
—— sends messages to, 35. 261
——'s opinion of, 10. 158
—— to be visited by, at Greatworth, 9. 193, 194
—— to have received Gothic designs by, for Roel, 9. 146
—— to meet, at SH, 9. 112
—— wishes Cumberland would manage finances of, 10. 75
Montagu, Charles, meets and describes, 10. 203
Müntz found in Jersey by, 21. 239
—— might work on designs of, 35. 185
—— orders cloths for, 35. 263
—— recommended by, to HW, 9. 259
——'s abusive letter to, 9. 259
—— sends directions to, 35. 252
—— to bring, to SH, 9. 216
not noted for cleanliness, 28. 195
ode by, *On the Sonatas of Bendall Martyn*, 10. 17, 35. 645
odes by, distrusted by HW, 10. 20
Osborn, Sir Danvers, subject of postscript by, 9. 149
Oxford friend of, forwards Johnson's life of Gray, 35. 272
paintings by, HW criticizes figures in, 35. 243
*Patriotism* by, 10. 128, 154, 187, 196, 14. 134, 139, 31. 69n, 35. 645, 43. 131, 186
pension desired by, 9. 261–2
*Petition to the R. H. Mr Pelham in Favour of Mr Maclean, A*, by, 35. 643
*Philodamus* by, 9. 409, 414, 10. 242–3, 29. 9–10, 35. 645, 43. 126
pictures painted by, in Jersey, 35. 644
plates of designs by, reported to be worn out, 14. 172
post-office post received by, 10. 128
*Reflections of the Different Ideas of the French and English in Regard to Cruelty* by, 13. 29–30, 21. 289, 35. 644
return of, from Jersey, arranged, 9. 187
Rochester, 'cousin' of, 9. 409, 410, 411
St-Simon admires designs of, for Gray's odes, 35. 238–9
schemes of, for finding longitudes and philosopher's stone, 35. 190–1
silver service said to be reward of, for sycophancy, 9. 308–9
sister's correspondence with, 35. 188–9
sketch by, for Gray's 'Bard,' 43. 292

[Bentley, Richard (1708–82), *continued*]
sonnet by, *To the Printingpress at Strawberry hill*, 9. 212, 217, **43**. 120
Strafford's menagerie temple designed by, 9. 295, **11**. 67, **35**. 279–80, 306
SH Blue Bedchamber will show Rigby that HW can design without aid from, **35**. 174
SH hall design of, to be used in library, **35**. 171
SH library bookcases designed by, but rejected, **35**. 157
SH library chimney-piece to be designed by, to frame picture, **35**. 158, 164
SH library ceiling to be designed by, **35**. 164, 171
SH view by, **20**. 368, 379–80
Tory by principle, **29**. 220
town-house at St Helier designed by, **35**. 241
tragedy proposed by, 9. 373
*True and Faithful Account of . . . Munpferdt the Surprising Centaur* by, **35**. 643
Vavassor, Miss, pursues, **35**. 181 (?) 219
Vyne, the, should be visited by, **35**. 185
wallpaper at SH painted under direction of, 9. 150, **35**. 191
wallpaper scheme of, discouraged by HW, **35**. 196
weather joked about by, 9. 210
wife involves, in debt, 9. 172
wife of, said to have written part of *The Wishes*, 9. 373
wife tries to discover hiding-place of, 9. 158
wife, second, of, on Jersey shore with him, **43**. 123
Winchester Cathedral probably seen by, **35**. 249–50
*Wishes, The*, by, 9. 372–3, 381–3, 402, 405, 409, 411, **10**. 1, 13, 18, **29**. 218–20, 222, **35**. 644–5, **38**. (?) 104
witticisms by: **35**. 262; about abuses being freeholds in England, **23**. 365; on Lady St John, **28**. 239–40
*World* contribution by, 9. 195
Wren equals, in Tom Tower, **35**. 154
Bentley, Mrs Richard, wife of Richard Bentley (1708–82); 'Hannah Bernard'; 'Hannah Cliquetis':
Court aspirations of, 9. 345, 373
HW attributes bad parts of *Wishes* to, 9. 382
HW dislikes, 9. 301–2
HW negotiates with, for husband's return, 9. 172
HW thanks, for partridges, **35**. 241
husband attributes part of *Wishes* to, 9. 373
husband enamoured of, 9. 301–2, 303
husband of, to return, 9. 172, 187
husband's hiding-place sought by, 9. 158
husband uses, as character in *Philodamus*, 9. 414
London to be visited by, 9. 302
marriage of, 9. 411

Montagu attributes Bentley's relationship to Rochester to, 9. 409
—— hopes daughter will resemble, 9. 282
—— jokes about, 9. *308–9*, 346, **10**. 196
—— never heard about, till after marriage, 9. 303
—— receives compliments of, 9. 281
——'s story of, about diving and white man, 9. 72
(?) on Jersey shore with Bentley, **43**. 123
*Wishes* attended by, 9. 382
—— said to be partly written by, 9. 373, 382
Bentley, Richard (1794–1871), publisher:
advertisements by, about HW's MSS, **36**. 314n, 315n, 316n
HW's letters owned and published by, **26**. 36, 40–1, 43
HW's MSS acquired by, **36**. 315–16, **43**. 139, 192, 232–3
Bentley, Richard (1854–1936):
HW's MSS owned by, **36**. 316, **43**. 139, 233
Mann's letters sold by, **26**. 42, 44
Bentley, Samuel:
*Excerpta historica* by, reprints Mountjoy's letters to Henry VIII, **40**. 134n
Bentley, Thomas (ca 1691–1742), LL.D.:
West advises HW to consult, **13**. 173
Bentley, Thomas Richard (ca 1759–1831), lawyer:
HW to transfer money in funds to, **33**. 372
Bentley family:
Campbell to correct genealogy of, in *Biographia Britannica*, **35**. 204
Benwell, Mrs William. *See* Loveday, Penelope
Beorn, D. of. *See* Richard
*Béquille du Père Barnabas*:
blossoms in France, **39**. 254
tune of, cited, **33**. 534
Ber. *See* Le Ber
Beraargard (*or* Berargard), Mme de. *See* Bünau, Henrietta Frederica von
Beranger. *See* Berenger
Béraud de la Haie de Riou, Charlotte-Jeanne (1738–1806), m. 1 (ca 1754) Jean-Baptiste, Marquis de Montesson; m. 2 (1773) Louis-Philippe de Bourbon, Duc d'Orléans:
ball given by, **7**. 443
Chanteloup visited by, **7**. 124, 150, 153
Du Deffand, Mme, gives bootikins to, for Orléans, **6**. 66
——'s relations with, **6**. 86
*Femme sincère, La*, by, **6**. 284
Gourgue, Présidente de, leaves jewels to, **5**. 369
—— mourned by, **5**. 369
Lauzun, Duchesse de, visits, **6**. 329
Luxembourg, Mme de, visits, **6**. 102, 329, 330, **7**. 183 (*see also under* Ste-Assise: visitors to)
marriage of, to Duc d'Orléans: **5**. 354, 356–7, 359, 386, **6**. 63–4, **23**. 480n; Louis XV regulates, **36**. 207

Mirepoix, Mme de, visits, **6**. 102, 211 (*see also under* Ste-Assise: visitors to)

Orléans, Duc d', accompanied by, **5**. 369, **6**. 163, **7**. 126

pious, **7**. 124

Ste-Assise (St-Port) bought by, **5**. 386

—— occupied by, **6**. 102, 163, 211, 329, 330, **7**. 124, 183

sings, **7**. 296

social relations of, in Paris, **6**. 86, 284, **7**. (?) 296, (?) 451

to return to Paris, **7**. 124

visitors to, at Ste-Assise, *see under* Ste-Assise

Berceau. *See* Cradle

Berch, Carl Reinhold (1706–77), Keeper of Q. of Sweden's Cabinet of Medals:

Ducarel copies letter by, mentioning HW, **40**. 214

Berchény, Comte de. *See* Bercsény, Ladislas-Ignace de

Berchény, Nicolas-François de (1733–62): wife of, **4**. 134n

Berchény, Mme Nicolas-François de. *See* Berthelot de Baye, Agnès-Victoire de

Bercher, Mme. *See* Crépé, —— (d. 1798)

Bercher, Jean (1742–1806), called Dauberval; dancer:

England visited by, without leave, **38**. 477

Hertford to ask Fleury for permission for, to rejoin London opera, **38**. 460, 477

—— told by, that Ds of Ancaster and Lady Rockingham patronized him, **38**. 483

imprisoned for refusing to act, **38**. 538n

London opera needs, **38**. 467

Berckel, Engelbert François van (1726–96), Pensionary, 1762, of Amsterdam:

(?) Dutch defeats to be blamed on, **25**. 283

England accuses, of befriending America, **29**. 124

house of, reported destroyed, **29**. 128n

Yorke demands punishment of, **25**. 142n

Bercsény, Ladislas-Ignace de (1689–1778), Maréchal and Comte de Berchény:

Maximilian's social relations with, **6**. 156

Bercy (France):

Chartres rents house at, **7**. 219

Genlis, Mme de, accompanies Orléans princesses to, **7**. 219

Orléans, Princesses d', inoculated at, **7**. 451

Bereavement:

Mann's reflections on, **21**. 512

Berecynthia:

HW lives like, surrounded by nephews and nieces, **39**. 300

Berenclau. *See* Pernklö

Berenger, Moses:

Furnese clerk to, **18**. 51n

Bérenger, Raymond, V (1205–45), Count of Provence:

Richard I at Court of, **40**. 115

Berenice (b. A.D. 18):

HW alludes to Titus and, **31**. 155

*Bérénice. See under* Racine, Jean

*Berenice* (opera):

crowded, **38**. 503–4

Berenikov, ——, governor of Schlüsselburg:

Ivan VI said to be murdered by, **22**. 253n

Beresford, Rev. Benjamin (ca 1750–ca 1819):

Hamilton, Sidney, sued by, in France, **33**. 363–4

Ossory, Lady, gives 'orders' concerning SH and, **33**. 60

Beresford, Mrs Benjamin. *See* Hamilton, Sidney

Beresford, Lady Elizabeth, m. Thomas Cobbe: daughter of, **12**. 201n

Beresford, Hon. Louisa (d. 1851), m. 1 (1806) Thomas Hope; m. 2 (1832) George de la Poer Beresford, 1st Vct Beresford:

painter insults, **9**. 259n

Beresford, Marcus (1694–1763), cr. (1746) E. of Tyrone:

daughter of, **12**. 201n

Berg (Germany):

Conway and Scott visit, **39**. 536

Hanoverian troops may go to, **18**. 142

Stair invades, **18**. 191

Bergamasco, The (Italy):

Montagu, Lady Mary Wortley, said to be imprisoned in, **20**. 272

Bergamo (Italy):

gentleman from, resembles Harlequin's mask, **11**. 365

Bergamote; bergamotes:

HW jokes about statues of himself in, **31**. 100

Berganzo, Marchese. *See* Botta-Adorno, Giuseppe

Bergavenny, Bn. *See* Nevill, Henry (after 1527–1587)

Bergavenny, Bns. *See* Tatton, Katherine

Bergen, near Frankfurt (Germany):

French army retires to, **38**. 176

French claim victory at, **21**. 287

Bergen-op-Zoom ('Bergopzoom'):

casualties at siege of, **19**. 470

French capture of: **37**. 278, **43**. 113; Cibber's ode alludes to, **30**. 111; Mann surprised by, **19**. 440

French convoy captured en route to, **19**. 469

French lose heavily in attacks on, **19**. 434

French siege of, **37**. 276

French still resisted by, **19**. 428

French threaten to explode mines under forts of, **19**. 482

HW knows only what gazettes say about, **19**. 448

Mann not fully informed about details of, **19**. 444

treachery at, **19**. 440, 442, 444

Bergerac, Cyrano de (ca 1620–55):

*Pédant joué, Le*, **28**. 39n

Bergère, Rue (in Paris):

Mirepoix, Duchesse de, lives in, **5**. 98–9, 105, 170, 209, 435

—— moves from, **7**. 7n

—— moves to, **5**. 140n

*Bergère des Alpes, La. See under* Fouques, François-Georges; Marmontel, Jean-François
Berghe. *See* Van den Berghe
Berghem, Nicolas (1620–83), painter:
Loutherbourg's paintings in style of, **7.** 317
paintings by, at Julienne's, **4.** 287
Berghen. *See* Bergen
Bergier, Nicolas-Sylvestre (1718–90), abbé:
Voltaire's *Conseils* to, **4.** 94, 101, 135
Bergonzi, Marchese:
Ferdinand of Parma's governor, **23.** 17n
Bergue, M. de:
house of, at Calais, **5.** 398
Bergue. *See also* Berg
Berham. *See* Derham
Beriea. *See* Tevahine
Béringhen, Henri-Camille (ca 1693–1770), Marquis de; premier écuyer de la petite écurie:
Clanbrassill intimate with, **4.** 16
death of, **4.** 362
Berkeley, Bns. *See* Clivedon, Katharine (d. 1385); Temple, Jane Martha (1672–1751)
Berkeley, Capt. *See* Berkeley, Hon. George Cranfield
Berkeley, Cts of. *See* Drax, Elizabeth (ca 1720–92)
Berkeley, Lady. *See* Lennox, Emilia Charlotte
Berkeley, Augustus (1716–55), 4th E. of Berkeley:
Barrington hints at regiment-raising by, **26.** 13
cousin of, **17.** 459
daughter of, **11.** 100–1n
house of, in Spring Gardens, **17.** 210n
marriage of, **18.** 441
Vane, Vcts, kept by, **17.** *210*
wife of, **1.** 343n, **30.** 326n
Berkeley, Charles (d. 1665), Vct Fitzhardinge, 1st E. of Falmouth; ambassador to France:
(?) Emperor gives diamond ring to, **10.** 1
Berkeley, Charles (1649–1710), 2d E. of Berkeley; M.P.:
daughter of, **10.** 341
Berkeley, Hon. Charles (d. 1765):
(?) HW sends 'my hate' to, **40.** 252
Berkeley, Lady Elizabeth (1680–1769), m. (1706) Sir John Germain, Bt:
age and failing faculties of, **10.** 342
Arundelian marbles given by, to Lord Charles Spencer, **42.** 204n
'at home' in London, **9.** 15
Beauclerk, Lord Sidney, paid by, to avoid marriage to him, **34.** 259
Beauclerk, Lord Vere, owes Admiralty post to, **17.** 356
brother of, **17.** *221*
charity of, **10.** 342
Chute and Holdernesse entertained by, **19.** 372
clock presented to HW by, **2.** 334n, **29.** 40n
Cole's opinion of, **10.** 341, 342
death of, expected, **31.** 144, **32.** 38

Dee's black stone owned by, **23.** 286, **33.** 324, **43.** 389
Drayton owned by, **9.** 287, **10.** 341, 342
—— religiously preserved by, **10.** 90
—— rumoured to be left by, to Aubrey Beauclerk, **10.** 342
family of, **10.** 341, 342
HW mentions, **37.** 467
HW reveals painting to, **10.** 92, 342
(?) HW sends regards to, **31.** 81
HW visits, **10.** 90n
HW visits seat of, in Northants, **30.** 171
home of, on road to Horton, **10.** 85
husband leaves fortune to, **10.** 342
husband of, **9.** 287n, **33.** 277–8
husband on death-bed persuaded by, to take Sacrament, **33.** 278n
income from Drayton spent by, on hospitality, **10.** 342
Knole's associations with, **33.** 224
marriage of, **10.** 342
Mason alludes to, as proper recipient for old-fashioned verses, **28.** 208
(?) Milton, Bns, and Cts Temple entertained by, at dinner, **38.** 358
nephew of, **36.** 12
niece of, **15.** 92n
Peterborough collection partly dispersed by, **23.** 286
Sackville inherits estates of, **23.** 256n, **28.** 235n
St James's Sq. residence of, **31.** 81
servants of, old retainers, **10.** 90
Suffolk, Cts of, defended by, against Swift, **10.** 218
Swift's correspondence includes letters from, **9.** 62n, **10.** 218, **22.** 524n
Vere asks HW to help auction off effects of, **23.** 286
wealth of, **10.** 342
will of, **4.** 324, **32.** 38
Berkeley, Elizabeth (ca 1719–99), m. (1740) Charles Noel Somerset, 4th D. of Beaufort, 1745; 'Dowager Duchess Plantagenet':
air of youth displayed by, on return to England, **24.** 46
Albemarle, Cts of, and Lady Mary Coke entertained by, **33.** 484n
brother of, **21.** 313n
Carlisle, Cts of, writes to, **23.** 508
children of, lost by consumption, **23.** 372
Court partisan, **25.** 564n
daughter of, to marry, **24.** 120–1, 148
family of, **25.** 564n
Florence to be visited by, **23.** 397
HW hears Mann's praises from, **24.** 46, 54
HW jokes about dignity of, **31.** 284, 309
HW reassures, in Gordon Riots, **33.** 184–5, 186, 189, 192
HW sees, and hears inquiries about Mann, **24.** 148
HW's social relations with, **7.** 334, **25.** 165, **33.** 278–9

HW visited by, **25.** 165

Holland, Bns, writes to, about sons' ingratitude, **24.** 30

house of, next door to HW's in Berkeley Sq., **25.** 563–4, **33.** 184n

'in great spirits,' **39.** 266

Leopold and Maria Louisa of Tuscany befriend, **23.** 372

loo party made by, to resemble Quaker meeting, **39.** 208

Lymington visited by, **11.** 86–7

Mann discussed by HW and, **25.** 165

—— praised by, **24.** 46, 54

—— praises, **23.** 397

——'s house in Pisa borrowed by, **23.** 372

——'s letter from, about Ds of Kingston, **23.** 567

manner of, more unpinioned, **24.** 54

Maria Louisa often accompanied by, **23.** 429

More, Hannah, calls 'Plantagenet Dowager Duchess,' **31.** 320

—— visits, at Stoke, **31.** 281, 320, 335

Naples visited by, **23.** 449

not as lively as a boat-race, **11.** 87

person of, as stately as ever, **24.** 54

Pisa visited by, with daughter, **23.** 372, 397

Pitt, Mrs, entertained by, **23.** 456

powder now worn by, in well-preserved brown hair, **24.** 54

stiffness of, **11.** 250, **34.** 39

SH visited by, **33.** 278–9

style of, **31.** 320

Tuscan Court favours, at Florence, **23.** 406

'upright,' **33.** 278

Williams, Sophia, lives with, **31.** 333n

—— may be with, at Stoke, **31.** 333

windows of, broken by mob, **25.** 563–4

Berkeley, Lady Elizabeth (1750–1828), m. 1 (1767) William Craven, 6th Bn Craven; m. 2 (1791) Christian Friedrich Karl Alexander, Margrave of Brandenburg-Ansbach:

adventures of, kept secret by HW, but will be published by Spencers, **25.** 632

Ailesbury, Cts of, to be visited by, at Park Place, **39.** 500

beautiful and talented, **29.** 43

Berry, Mary, writes to Mrs Damer about, **11.** 342n

biographical information on, corrected, **43.** 95, 299

brother sends address of, to HW, **42.** 177–8

Catherine II and Joseph II friends of, **42.** 183

Circassians might be freed by crusade by, **42.** 184

conduct of, **11.** 219

cottage of, to be visited by HW, **41.** 404

*Country Eclogue* by, sent to HW, **41.** 336–8

Court presentation not achieved by, **11.** 340

dairy blended by, with library, **36.** 251

Drury Lane performance of *Miniature Picture* attended by, **29.** 43–5

eccentricities of, **34.** 27–8

England may be revisited by, **42.** 231

England visited by, with Margrave of Ansbach, **11.** 342

family of, **34.** 36

Ferdinand of Naples sees, **11.** 274

Florence visited by, **11.** 274

French writings by, **42.** 231

Guines's affair with, **5.** 358, 360

Gunnings to be superseded by, **11.** 366

HW and, exchange verses, **28.** 247

HW calls, 'fiancée du Roi de Garbe,' **42.** 176

HW discourages, from visiting Greek islands, **42.** 507

HW gives merely compliments and good advice to, **25.** 633

HW has not seen poetry of, **32.** 92

HW receives drawing of Otranto from, **35.** 435

HW recommends, to Mann at Florence, **25.** 611

HW returns Beaumont and Fletcher's *Scornful Lady* to, with criticism, **41.** 403

HW's correspondence with, **25.** 611, 616, 654, **35.** 538, **36.** 250–1, **41.** 336–8, 403–4, **42.** 176–8, 181–4, 228–32, 507, **43.** 292

HW sees performance of pastoral opera by, **29.** 235

HW's friendship with, **29.** 365

HW's letter shown by, to Stanislas II at Warsaw, **25.** 632–3

HW's opinion of, **5.** 360

HW stops corresponding with, **25.** 615, 655, **35.** 538

HW thought, to be in Paris, **25.** 611

HW visited by, **33.** 241

Hamilton's affair with, **35.** 435n

Harcourt's correspondence with, **29.** 360–1, **35.** 538

Hart, Emma, too prudish to visit, **11.** 274

identification of, **43.** 67

indiscreet, **25.** 611

invites herself and party to SH, **31.** 181

itinerary of, **25.** 632, 654–5, **42.** 176

Joseph II gives private audience to, at Vienna, **42.** 184n

journal of her travels kept by, **42.** 181–2

Mann, Horace II, quarrels with, **25.** 615, 616

Marlborough, Ds of, offered play by, sent to Blenheim, **34.** 27

marriage of, left-handed, **11.** 342, **34.** 132–3

*Miniature Picture, The,* by, **29.** 43–5, **33.** 182, **39.** 372

*Modern Anecdotes* by, dedicated to HW, **2.** 198, 203, 206, **29.** 7, **33.** 165–6, 167, **43.** 70

Montagu, Lady Mary Wortley, discredited by, **42.** 183

mother visited by, in London, **42.** 176n

(?) newspapers abuse, for amour with servant, **36.** 210

'one of our Camillas,' **11.** 274

Paris friends of, may not give her time to write, **42.** 181–2

[Berkeley, Lady Elizabeth (1750–1828), *continued*]

*Philosophe moderne, Le,* by, owned by HW, 42. 231n

portrait of, in Blue Room at SH, 29. 45, 362

Portugal, Q. of, to be notified of marriage of, 11. 361

pretty and good-humoured, 33. 39

quadrille danced by, at Guines's ball, 32. 110

runs to Apollo, not from, 34. 44

second marriage date of, corrected, 43. 150, 151

*Silver Tankard, The,* by, 33. 241, 248, 39. 372

sister corresponds with, 42. 176n

*Sleep-Walker, The (Somnambule),* translated by, printed at SH, 2. 111, 112, 119, 28. 443, 33. 39, 41. 422

social relations of, with: Beaufort, 7. 271; HW, 12. 88, 31. 181, 33. 241; Massereene, 7. 294

Strafford calls, HW's 'Sappho,' 29. 279

'Travels' (*Journey through the Crimea*) by, 34. 28, 35, 36–7, 41, 44

Vernon has adventures with, 25. 632

—— 'knight' of, 25. 616

—— said to be cousin of, 25. 632

verses of, pretty, 32. 244–5

widow though wife, 11. 100

youth and vivacity of, make her drop 'old superannuated' HW, 42. 229

Berkeley, Frederick Augustus (1745–1810), 5th E. of Berkeley, 1755:

Florence to be visited by, 22. 285, 25. 611n

George III to visit, 34. 47n

Gloucester mayor entertained by, at dinner, 39. 183

highwayman shot by, 12. 25, 24. 57

militia of, mar HW's visit to Berkeley Castle, 28. 167

Paris visited by, 31. 79

Patch paints, 26. 45

refuses to recognize sister's marriage, 11. 342

seat of, 1. 343, 28. 167

sister of, 11. 342, 361n, 25. 611n

social relations of, in Paris, 7. 277, 294

travels improve, 31. 79

Whig meeting attended by, 29. 261

Berkeley, George (ca 1627–98), 14th Bn Berkeley, 1st E. of Berkeley:

daughter of, 16. 12n

*Historical Applications:* HW owns, 16. 8, 43. 215; letter by Cts of Warwick at end of, 16. 138

'Lady Harmonia' of, 16. 138

print of, 1. 181

Berkeley, George (1685–1753), Bp of Cloyne:

HW perhaps echoes line written by, 9. 263n

newspapers print verses on tar-water of, 18. 505

*Siris:* popularity of, 18. 452; Trinity and tar-water discussed in, 18. 452, 464–5, 29. 282

Berkeley, Hon. George (?1692–1746); M.P.:

birth date of, corrected, 43. 240

Dorset influenced by, 17. 221

Hedon election contested by, 35. 20n

petition of, charging bribery, granted, 17. 220n

Pulteney's follower, 17. 220n

relatives of, 31. 420, 427

Suffolk, Cts of, makes request in name of, 31. 427

—— wife of, 3. 75n, 9. 60n, 13. 160n, 15. 152n, 22. 543n, 31. 420

Berkeley, George (d. 1746), naval capt.:

Gardiner brought by, to Mann, 18. 507

Theodore of Corsica's identity not revealed by, 18. 145n

Berkeley, Hon. George Cranfield (1753–1818), naval officer; M.P.:

HW gets Lady Craven's address from, 42. 177–8

Keppel's messenger, 28. 408

Berkeley, Mrs George Cranfield. *See* Lennox, Emily Charlotte

Berkeley, George Monck (1763–93):

cousin of, 10. 28n

Berkeley, Lady Georgiana Augusta (1749–1820), m. 1 (1766) George Forbes, styled Vct Forbes; 5th E. of Granard, 1769; m. 2 (1781) Rev. Samuel Little:

Forbes elopes with, 38. 577n

marriage of, impending, 33. 233

name of, corrected, 43. 106

social relations of, in Paris, 7. 271, 294

Berkeley, Lady Henrietta (ca 1664–1710):

brother-in-law's intrigue with, 18. 220

(?) letters to, 16. 12

'Sylvia' nom-de-plume of, 18. 220

Berkeley, Henry (d. 1745), army officer:

killed at Fontenoy, 17. 459n, 19. 43, 36. 12, 37. 192

Berkeley, Isabel de (d. 1362), m. 1 (1328) Robert de Clifford, Bn Clifford; 2 (1345) Sir Thomas Musgrave:

owner of Clifford's Inn, 1. 148

Berkeley, James (d. 1736), 3d E. of Berkeley:

brother of, 22. 543n, 31. 420

Berkeley, Jane (ca 1715–91), m. (1749) William Craven, 5th Bn Craven, 1764:

(?) Hertford visits, at Coventry, 39. 85

(?) Hertford, Cts of, friend of, 39. 85

Berkeley, John (ca 1697–1773), 5th Bn Berkeley of Stratton, 1741; M.P.:

Buckinghamshire succeeded by, as Capt. of the Pensioners, 21. 25

Carteret's disciple, 18. *143*

HW fails to give character of friend to, 30. 170

HW sends *Fugitive Pieces* to, through Fox, 30. 152

HW's writings requested by, 30. 152

Pensioners position to be granted to, 18. 143

portraits left by, 1. 344

regiment raised by, 19. 128n

Treasurer of the Household, 20. 518, 21. 25

Berkeley, Mary, m. Thomas Perrot; Henry VIII's mistress:
reputed son of, **1.** 182n, 375n
Berkeley, Mary (d. 1737), m. (1703) Walter Chetwynd, cr. (1717) Vct Chetwynd:
verses on picture of, **16.** 48
Berkeley, Mary (d. 1755), m. (1744) Charles Morton:
husband of, **31.** 427
niece of Lady Elizabeth Germain, **15.** 92n
Berkeley, Lady Mary, m. Thomas Chamber:
family of, **10.** 342
Berkeley, Maurice de (ca 1331–68), 4th Bn Berkeley, 1361:
daughter of, **1.** 148n
Berkeley, Norborne (? 1717–70), 4th Bn Botetourt, 1764; M.P.: gov. of Virginia:
Address moved by, in House of Lords, **38.** 489
Amherst's quarrel with, **35.** 328–9
Botetourt barony claimed by, in House of Lords, **22.** 219n, **38.** 159n, 354, 368
Bute attends House of Lords at peerage of, **36.** 40n
Court favourite but financially ruined, **23.** 44
France to be conquered by, without changing clothes, **35.** 102
French campaign entered by, with scanty shirts, **37.** 530
George III's Groom of the Bedchamber, **21.** 460, **23.** 44n
HW's *World* gives story of sinking of, in Woburn Park, **35.** 199
Hillsborough suggests, as governor of Virginia, **23.** 44
niece supplied by, with dowry, **21.** *313*
St-Malo attempt by, satirized by HW, **35.** 288
sister of, **11.** 86n, **21.** 313n, **25.** 564n
supper given by, **37.** 530
Tory, **21.** 460
Virginia's new governor, financially ruined, **21.** 313n, **39.** 104
Berkeley, Thomas de (? 1292–1361), 3d Bn Berkeley:
conspirator, **1.** 344
wife of, **15.** 204n
Berkeley, William (d. 1741), 4th Bn Berkeley:
amour of, with Mrs Coke, **14.** 243n
Berkeley Castle, Glos:
Edward II carried to, **1.** 341
HW visits, **1.** 343–4, **6.** 83n, **28.** 167, **30.** 150, **39.** 179, 183
militia regiment at, **39.** 183
Berkeley Chapel, London:
Kidgell preaches at, **22.** 187n
Berkeley family:
tombs of, **1.** 344
Berkeley of Stratton, Bns. *See* Temple, Jane Martha
Berkeley Sq., London:
alderman might be chosen for, **35.** 335
Berkeley St another name for, **30.** 355
Bishopsgate St remote from, **2.** 259
'chalk-pits' in, **33.** 516
Chute's house in: **10.** 126; Chute offers to lodge Montagu in, **9.** 358; Chute takes, **9.** 330
Coke, Lady Mary, disputes with Herbert over property in, **9.** 368
Conway meets P. of Wales in, **12.** 44
HW calls, M. of Lansdowne's demesnes, **31.** 235
HW jokes about spending night under oak in, **31.** 235
HW's house in: 'a little coffee-house in the morning,' **25.** 371; Beaufort, Ds of, next door to, **25.** 563–4; being redecorated, **15.** 242–3, **33.** 124; cheerful, **39.** 342; dealer may bring pictures to, **16.** 285; Damer, Mrs, charmed with, **39.** 342; dining room in, redecorated, **12.** 17, 41, 47; Du Deffand, Mme, asks about, **7.** 82, 92, 167, **30.** 272; Du Deffand, Mme, comments on furnishings of, **7.** 173, 181; Fenn calls at, **16.** 236, 246–7, **42.** 97; gout brings HW to, **16.** 287; HW acquires, **2.** 177n, **7.** 82n, 96n, **24.** (?)447, 521, 532, **28.** 453n, **31.** 189, 191, 193, **33.** 62–3, 65, 67, 68, 108, 115–16, 118, 124, 125, **36.** 166, 201, **39.** 316; HW avoids, in hot weather, **33.** 410; HW calls, his 'Penates,' **42.** 202; HW invites Beloe to, **15.** 238, 258; HW leaves parcel at, for Lort, **16.** 196; HW opens window of, on the Square, **25.** 392; HW's MSS in, **36.** 310–12; HW's removal to, **7.** 96, **28.** 468–9, 472, **30.** 272, **31.** 193, **33.** 124–5, **39.** 342; HW's servant at, gets letter too late, **25.** 57; HW tells Pinkerton to call at, **16.** 288, Hillier sends to, to get painting, **16.** 97; Holcroft to call at, **42.** 228; illuminated for Rodney, **25.** 280; lease and contents of, bequeathed to Waldegraves, **30.** 355–6; Lort sends picture to, **16.** 202; Lort sends print or book to, **16.** 195–6; Lort to call on HW at, **16.** 193; mentioned, **11.** 129, **12.** 207, 215n, **29.** 140, 276, 359; mob orders candles lit in, for Westminster election, **25.** 563; 'my garrison' in Gordon Riots, **33.** 186; 'my own coffee-house,' **33.** 396, 460, **34.** 37, 107, 180; Oxford, Lady, letter of in, **12.** 80; pictures in, landscapes by Gaspar Poussin, **30.** 354; pictures in, list of, **30.** 370–1; Pinkerton calls at, **16.** 287, 311; prints in trunk at, to be sent to SH after HW's death, **30.** 373–4; screen out of place in, **33.** 273; (?) Selwyn to get key to, **30.** 276; staircase of, to be clean, **30.** 272; Stavely portraits to be left at, **42.** 289–90; suit in Chancery over, **28.** 453, **33.** 108, **34.** 250–2, **35.** 602, **43.** 104; 'vast nursery' in, **33.** 68; Walpole family papers at, to be sent to Houghton after HW's death, **30.** 372, 377; windows in, broken by mob, **25.** 343, **33.** 374
HW lives more at home, now he is comfortably lodged in, **2.** 178
HW travels between SH and, **33.** 318

[Berkeley Sq., London, *continued*]

Herbert alters house in, 9. 368

Lansdowne's house faces HW's in, 31. 235n

Ossory, Lady, says, is wholesomer than the country, 34. 145

residents in: Ancaster, Dowager Ds of, 11. 255n, 34. 108n; Beaufort, Ds of, 25. 563–4, 33. 184n; Bisshopp family, 35. 300n; Chaworth, 38. 503; Chute, 9. 330, 358, 10. 126; Clermont, 6. 282n; Clive, 23. 530n, 24. 60n, 32. 218n, 35. 418n; Coke, Lady Mary, 9. 368, 29. 74n, 31. 22; Cosways, 11. 285n; Dwerrihouse, 30. 377; Egerton, Mrs, 12. 107n; Herbert, 9. 368; King, Dr, 30. 283; Lambton, Lady Ann, 12. 188n; Orford, Cts of, 19. 72n; Pitt, Anne, 31. 98; Shelburne, 29. 193n, 31. 235, 33. 6n, 129, 340; Shelburne, Lady, 33. 125; Spencer, Lord Robert, 42. 490

Shelburne's gates in, 33. 340

'Shelburne Square,' 33. 129

statue of George III in, 28. 472

Berkeley St. *See* Berkeley Sq.

Berkenhout, John (ca 1730–91), M.D.; physician and author:

anecdotes of HW requested by, 28. 101

*Biographia Britannica*, HW's life needed for, 41. 255–6

*Biographia literaria* by, 28. 101n

biographies to be written by, 32. 122

HW's correspondence with, 41. 255–6

Berkenroode, Matthys Lestevenon van (1719–79), Dutch ambassador to France:

Choiseul warned by, of Dutch intervention if Pretender is involved, 21. 298n

Richmonds' social relations with, 7. 290

Berkley. *See* Barkley; Berkeley

Berkshire, Cts of. *See* Graham, Catherine

Berkshire, E. of. *See* Howard, Henry Bowes

Berkshire:

Donnington Castle near 'Spinhamlands' in, 35. 642

HW in, 42. 175

militia of, 33. 184, 37. 567–8, 572–3

More, Hannah, to visit Mrs Montagu in, 31. 281

Park Place called 'House of Riddles' in, 37. 411

——'s view of, 39. 550

Sandleford Priory in, 31. 321

Berlan (game):

Conti and guests play, 7. 302

HW mentions, 30. 221

Holland, Bns, describes, 30. 221n

played, 17. 179

Berlichingen, Johann Friedrich:

cuirassiers of, 17. 214n, 266n

Berlin (Germany):

ambassadors from and to, *see under* Ambassador

Austrians and Russians capture, 9. 313, 21. 441, 444–6

Austrians and Russians fail to take, 21. 332

Barbarina's debut in, 17. 358n

book printed at, 3. 138

Chatham said to be next envoy to, 25. 314

Cholmondeley may be envoy to, 33. 336

—— resigns appointment to, 25. 319–20, 324, 333

Chute and Whithed to visit, 19. 279

Conway sees war games at, 39. 537

crime moves to, 24. 154

Elgin minister at, 11. 272n

England cordial with Court of, 20. 523

—— unlikely to send a minister to, 19. 448

English-French accommodation being arranged at, 20. 541

English ministry powerless at, 20. 348

Fawkener said to become minister at, 11. 247, 256, 19. 456, 457–8

Flanders mail brings letters from, 21. 91n

Frederick II attends wedding feast at, 17. 315

—— said to have lost, 21. 319

——'s death will elicit no condolence from HW to, 33. 524

—— to defend, 18. 547

—— would be avoided by HW if in, 39. 185

Gray, Sir James may go to, 19. 444, 448, 453

Harris becomes English representative to, 32. 183

Legge goes to, as envoy extraordinary, 19. 457–8

—— leaves, 20. 16n

——'s negotiations at, 42. 496

—— takes Osnabrück negotiations out of hands of George II's agent at, 20. 39n

letters from, do not convince Botta, 21. 241–2

Mann, Horace II, writes from, 24. 389

Mitchell resident at, 22. 323n

Nivernais arrives at, 20. 542n

opera house at, 20. 329n

postmaster of, sends incorrect account of Kunersdorf, 21. 319n

Richecourt's brother posted at, 18. 107

Roman Catholic church at, Querini sends ornaments to, 20. 329

royal academy of, Sloane's museum offered to, 20. 358

Russians will sack, 21. 441

Sandwich suggests himself for post at, 19. 456n

Stuart Mackenzie sent from, at Hyndford's request, 30. 58–9

Swedish troops threaten, 21. 247

treaty of, 17. 151n

Villiers refuses post at, 19. 458

visitors to: Conway, 39. 537; Croix de Frechapelle, 20. 184n; Holland, Bn, 12. 191; Shuvalov, 8. 205; Williams, Sir Charles Hanbury, 20. 186n; York, D. of, 11. 257

Wilkes to visit, 22. 272

Williams, Sir C. H., has diplomatic post at, 19. 341, 30. 319, 320, 38. 393

Young Pretender may visit, 20. 35, 44

Berlin (carriage):
Du Deffand, Mme, has, **5.** 238, 239, **8.** 12
—— travels in, to Chanteloup, **5.** 239
French officer and wife travel in, **10.** 283
Old Pretender has, **19.** 135
Penthièvre travels in, **20.** 466n
*See also* Carrosse
Berlin Gazette:
George IV reported by, to have married Mrs Fitzherbert, **25.** 628
Bermingham, Francis (1692–1750), 14th Bn Athenry:
Beauvau asks about family of, **41.** 331
Bermondet, Philippe-Armand (1730–1806), Chevalier de; later Marquis de Cromières:
HW mistaken by, **7.** 266
Bermuda:
*Constant of Teneriff* captured off, **17.** 276n
Craufurd governor of, **4.** 283n, **11.** 90n
Deane poses as merchant from, **24.** 253n
English forces at, **19.** 69n
Bern. *See* Berne
Bernacchi, Antonio (1685–1756), singer:
'broken-bellied,' **35.** 16
chief actor in opera, **17.** 239
Mann criticizes, **17.** 284
Bernard, St (1091–1153):
English might as well be led by, **33.** 9
Bernard, Lady. *See* Weldon, Anne
Bernard, ——:
Florence visited by, **18.** 479
Bernard, ——, painter:
Simiane, Mme de, favours, **5.** 423n
Bernard, Mr and Mrs (? Mrs Richard Bentley's relatives):
notes drawn on HW in names of, **40.** 87
Bernard, Anne-Gabriel-Henri (1722–98), Marquis de Boulainvilliers:
daughter of, marries, **7.** 109
social relations of, with Marquis de Brancas, **7.** 347
'Bernard, Hannah.' *See* Bentley, Mrs Richard
Bernard, Jean (fl. 16th century):
*Dicours des plus memorables faits des rois et grands seigneurs d'Angleterre*, HW's interest in, **6.** 76, 77, 80
Bernard, Jean-Frédéric (d. 1752):
*Recueil des voyages au Nord*, (?) read by Mme du Deffand, **5.** 184
Bernard, Louise-Olive-Félicité, m. Nicolas-Hyacinthe de Montvallat, Comte d'Entragues:
social relations of, with Mme de la Vallière, **7.** 336
Bernard, North Ludlow (d. 1766), Maj.:
death of, **7.** 397
(?) Dyve, Miss, walks with, **37.** 320
Pembroke, Cts of, weds, **9.** 270n, **20.** 281, **37.** 320
Bernard, Pierre-Joseph (1710–75):
*Castor et Pollux*, given for Joseph II, **6.** 439, 443
social relations of, with Mme Geoffrin, **7.** 317

*Surprises de l'Amour, Les,* **7.** 322
Bernard, Sir Robert (?1739–89), 5th Bt, 1766; M.P.:
election of, **23.** 206
genealogy of, **10.** 352
member of committee, **2.** 208n
Bernard, Samuel (d. 1739), financier:
illegitimate daughters of, **38.** 480n
Bernard. *See also* Barnard
Bernard de Boulainvilliers, Anne-Marie-Louise (d. 1781), m. (1779) Gaspard-Paulin, Vicomte de Clermont-Tonnerre:
appearance of, **7.** 109
Franklin admires, **7.** 109
marriage of, **7.** 109
Bernardi, Francesco (ca 1680–ca 1750), called Senesino, castrato singer:
English nobility court, but Siena countess will not sit at table with him, **22.** 170
HW and Gray have encounter with, **13.** 205
Bernardi, Gaetano:
Mann's annuity to, **25.** 667n
Bernardi, Theodore:
frescoes attributed to, **9.** 99n
Bernardin, Franziska von (1748–1811), m. 1 Baron Friedrich von Leutrum; m. 2 (1785) Karl Eugen, D. of Württemberg; cr. (1774) Reichsgräfin von Hohenheim:
English Court receives, while D. of Württemberg's mistress, **28.** 253
Bernardines:
abbey of, at Picquigny, **7.** 259
convent of, at Poblet, **16.** 6
Voltaire buried in church of, **7.** 48
Bernardini, Francesco Paolino, Lucchese ambassador to the Empire, to Modena, to Parma:
Eszterházys invited by, to Lucca, **20.** 351
'Bernardino.' *See* Riccardi, Bernardo
Bernardins, Rue des, Paris:
St-Nicolas-du-Chardonnet in, **7.** 274
Bernardiston. *See* Barnardiston
Bernardoni, Capt. ——:
wounded at Fierenzuolo, **18.** 101
Bernasconi, Andrea (1706–84), composer:
*Tamerlane* by, **18.** 280, 294
Gray collects works of, **13.** 233n
Bernclau. *See* Pernklö
Berne (Switzerland):
Artois goes to estate near, **11.** 39n
Villettes will be more welcome than Burnaby at, **20.** 76
(?) Young Pretender at, **22.** 90n
Berne Gazette. *See* Gazette de Berne
Berners, Juliana (b.? 1388):
*Boke of St Albans*, HW well read in, **34.** 146
Berners St (London):
Udny lives in, **42.** 165
Berneville, Marie-Catherine-Jumelle de (d. 1705), Comtesse d'Aulnoy; 'Mme Danois':
*Chatte blanche, La*: **13.** 200n; magic filbert in, **28.** 329
*Contes de fées,* **1.** 90, **28.** 329n, 357

[Berneville, Marie-Catherine de, *continued*]
(?)Du Deffand, Mme, adopts style of, 4. 392
—— owns, 8. 32
fairy tales of, 24. 14n
HW a composite of Anthony à Wood and, 2. 269
*Nain jaune, Le,* HW refers to, 18. 238
Bernin, Mlle:
appropriates and distributes brother's effects, 5. 287
Lisieux, Bp of, keeps, 5. 287
Maurepas given books by, 5. 287
Bernin, Louis-Sébastien (1696–1772), Marquis d'Ussé:
Guérin to operate on, for stone, 4. 300
Hénault's 'portrait' of, 8. 107–8
Lespinasse, Mlle de, championed by, 5. 276
Maurepas's verses sung by, 7. 283
Pont-de-Veyle's parody sung by, 7. 283
sister appropriates and distributes possessions of, 5. 290
social relations of, in Paris, *see index entries ante* 8. 250
will of, 5. 276
Bernini, Giovanni Lorenzo (1598–1680), architect and sculptor:
Brutus's bust by, 35. 268
Charles I patronizes, 41. 191
Damer, Mrs, models like, 25. 184
Laocoön restored by, 11. 338n
Louis XIV's bust by, 7. 290
Bernis, Cardinal de. *See* Pierre de Bernis, François-Joachim de
Bernklau. *See* Pernklö
Bernouilli, Daniel:
La Condamine's *Lettres* to, 22. 150n
Bernstorff, Greve Andreas Peter (1735–97):
Frederik VI's thanks to HW promised by, 36. 282
Bernstorff, Johan Hartvig Ernst (1712–72), greve; Danish prime minister:
blue ribbon of Order of the Elephant worn by, 43. 88
Christian VII accompanied by, 23. 42, 43, 35. 329
——'s mentor, 4. 159
——'s near-sightedness admitted by, 23. 43n
—— treats, like a slave, 35. 328
Du Deffand, Mme, criticizes, 4. 132, 156, 159, 163
HW's opinion of, 4. 128, 10. 265
Hanoverian, 23. 43
Hertford, Cts of, entertains, 10. 265
London visit of, 10. 265
Paris furiously admires, 4. 130, 132
'Puffendorf,' 4. 130
servility of, to Christian VII when he might be living on own estate in Mecklenburg, 23. 43
social relations of, in Paris, 4. 153, 154, 156, 164
Berridge, Rev. John (1716–93):
Methodist activities of, 1. 126, 134

Berriman, Rev. William (1688–1750), fellow of Eton:
death of, 20. 121
Berrisford. *See* Beresford
Berrue, ——, Braitwitz's adjutant:
Braitwitz sends, to Florence, 17. 179
Electress given report by, 17. 215–16
Empress Elizabeth gives chocolate to, on receiving him at Gratz, 17. 205
Francis I revisited by, 17. 205
information from, said to be too vague, 17. 229
Königseck visited by, 17. 205
orders awaited from, 17. 199
Pressburg visited by, 17. 205
Prussian officer talks with, 17. 206
stories by, may be inventions, 17. 215
troop movements by Croats reported by, 17. 206
Berry, Duc de. *See* Charles (1686–1714) de Bourbon; Louis XVI (1754–93)
Berry, Duchesse de. *See* Bourbon d'Orléans, Marie-Louise-Élisabeth de
Berry, Agnes (1764–1852), HW's correspondent (*see also* Berry, Agnes and Mary, and Vols 11–12):
Berry, Mary, hopes to see, married, 12. 127
——'s fall affects, 11. 235
——'s health reported by, 11. 245, 324, 334, 12. 181
——'s letters to, 12. 199
——'s love affair not suspected by, 12. 171
balcony of, at Little Strawberry Hill, 12. 162
bower of, at Little Strawberry Hill, 12. 194
cat of, 12. 101
Cheltenham visited by, 12. 99, 101, 103n, 147
coy, 11. 16
Darells visited by, 12. 175
enchanted with mosaic near Rodborough, 15. 251
fortune, lack of, lamented by, 11. 158–9
girl asks, if she is aristocrat or democrat, 34. 173
HW calls: 'Martha,' 11. 322; 'sister' and 'my Strawberries,' 31. 325
HW franks letters for, 12. 114, 121
HW's affection for, 11. 22, 37, 46, 71, 102, 12. 100
HW's correspondence with: vols 11–12, *passim*; MSS of, 36. 314
HW visited by, 12. 174, 175, 194, 15. 318, 326
HW visits, 12. 195
HW wishes to serve, 12. 126, 127, 132, 199
health of: Berry, Mary, worries about, 12. 23, 46; Cheltenham benefits, 12. 103, 134; cold, 12. 19; delicate, 12. 179; HW pleased with, 11. 77; HW recommends James's powder for, 11. 327; HW teases about, 11. 104; HW worries about, 11. 112, 140, 248, 12. 8, 15, 16, 17, 22, 50, 68, 100, 168; improved, 11. 102, 149, 374, 12. 21, 35; improves slowly, 31. 343; poor, 11. 89; rosy cheeks of, 11. 261; satisfactory, 11. 168; Scarborough benefits, 12. 26, 30; swelled

face, **12**. 195; teeth, **11**. 129; worse, **12**. 16
horse of, **11**. 179
letter-writing disliked by, **11**. 52, **12**. 35, 76, 100
mare of, **12**. 15, 19, 20, 26, 33, 35, 57, 74
paintings and drawings of: **34**. 24–5; 'Arcadia,' **11**. 112; 'Death of Cardinal Wolsey,' **11**. 111, 113–14, 121, 125, 248, 304, 344, **12**. 268; HW encourages, **11**. 46, 125, 139, 261, 344–5, **12**. 153; pencil idle, **11**. 248; SH Little Parlour furnished with, **11**. 112; superior to Mary Berry's, **11**. 267–8
Pinkerton to receive compliments of, **16**. 381
Raphael, Flora, visited by, **12**. 175
Scarborough visited by, **12**. 30
servant problems of, **12**. 211–12
Seton, Barbara Cecilia, visits, **12**. 198
shy, **11**. 210
SH shown by, **12**. 247
SH visited by, **12**. 174, 175, 194, 230, 237
SH visitors sent by, **12**. 241
Udny's concert attended by, **12**. 198
Berry, Agnes and Mary (see Vols 11–12 passim):
Albany, Cts of, fails to remember, **11**. 304
Bernis meets, **11**. 4n
Blagden inquires about, **12**. 77
Cambridge family interested in, **12**. 159
Channel crossing of, **43**. 144
Court positions not wanted by, **12**. 127, 128
dance reels at Florence, **11**. 287
Farington invites, to exhibition, **15**. 322
——'s description of, **15**. 317
Foldsone, Miss, to paint, **42**. 292
fortune lacked by, **11**. 158n, 282
Gloucester, Ds of, jealous of, **15**. 336
HW desolate at departure of, **39**. 474–5
HW finds house for, at Teddington, **31**. 325
HW first sees, at Lady Herries's, **12**. 5
HW gives house to, **13**. 44n, **15**. 320
HW is carried to see, **15**. 333
HW is rumoured to have proposed marriage to, **29**. 364–5
HW loved by, **12**. 47
HW offers financial aid to, **11**. 134, 221, 224, 330
HW promises Little Strawberry Hill to, **42**. 317–18
HW refuses to accept sacrifices from, **11**. 192
HW regrets absence of, **11**. 13, 23, 48, 60, 112–13, 233, 367, **12**. 10, 13, 15, 23, 76, 83, 85, 88, 103, 108, 133, 134, 147, **15**. 269
HW remains at SH to be near, **34**. 85
HW's account of, **34**. 24–6, 141
HW's affection for: 'children,' **11**. 110, 118; gossip about, **12**. 5; HW's 'ribs,' **34**. 49; 'honeymoon,' **11**. 7, 14, **12**. 16; 'husband,' **11**. 7, 18, 21, 41, 48, 51, 66, **12**. 103; 'mes amours,' **11**. 37; not a lover's, **11**. 193, **12**. 5; 'wives,' **11**. 12, 14, 19, 38, 48, 50, 51, 61, 67, 69, 72, 97, 110, 128, 242, 243, 261, 266, 326, 350, **12**. 4, 10, 32, 37, 104, 155, **15**. 266, 269, 271, **31**. 325, 328, 364–5, **39**. 474

HW's bequests to, **15**. 335, 336, 337, **29**. 343n, 30. 363–4, 373, 374, **36**. 311
HW's constant attendance by, **15**. 333, 335, **29**. 343n
HW's correspondence with, not to be published, **15**. 338
HW's 'intentions' towards, **43**. 151
HW's invitation from, **12**. 89
HW's invitations to, **11**. 58, 71, 304, **12**. 99
HW's obligations to, **11**. 51–2, 377
HW's verses to, **34**. 26–7
HW takes house at Teddington for, **31**. 325, **34**. 68
HW will not interfere with, **11**. 189–90
HW wishes happiness for, **11**. 330–1, 354, **12**. 137
HW wishes to remain with, **11**. 22
HW wishes to serve, **11**. 158, **12**. 131
HW worries about, **11**. 16, 17, **12**. 17, 18, 23, 116
health of: Cheltenham benefits, **12**. 158–9, 162, 167; delicate, **11**. 113, 173, **12**. 6; good accounts of, **11**. 172, 374, **12**. 46; good weather will benefit, **11**. 50; HW toasts, **12**. 9; HW worries about, **11**. 41, 42, 73, 77, 129, 134, 210, 356–7, **12**. 9, 16, 33, 50, 57, 68, 134; improved, **12**. 35, 41, **31**. 343; Italian journey does not benefit, **11**. 209, 324; Italian journey to benefit, **11**. 144, 146; paleness, **11**. 77; riding improves, **11**. 50, 180, 211, **12**. 15, 57, 68, 74, 124; Scarborough to benefit, **12**. 33; sea air helps, **11**. 77, 113; sea-bathing improves, **11**. 69; travel to benefit, **12**. 6, 32, 103; verses on, **12**. 157; writing bad for, **11**. 115–16, 125
houses (attempts to find, renting, etc.), **11**. 26, 30, 31, 42, 47, 50, 54, 55, 56, 58, 60, 61, 62, 71, 72–3, 103; see also Little Strawberry Hill; North Audley St; Somerset St; Teddington
Italy returned from by, **11**. 351, 374, **34**. 117, 125
Italy to be visited by, **11**. 74, 77, 89, 90, 91, 102, 103, 110–11, 146, 330, 334, **31**. 325, 341, 343, 359–60, 402, **42**. 292
Lally-Tollendal inquires about, **12**. 41
Lawrence, Sir Thomas, introduced to, **15**. 334
Lysons, S., visits, **15**. 337
More, Hannah, inquires for, **31**. 340, 359, 376
—— jokes about, **31**. 328
—— might envy, **31**. 370
(?) —— recommends Law's Serious Call to, **31**. 399
—— sends regards to, **31**. 390
name of, word-plays on, **11**. 1–3, **31**. 325, **34**. 49, 68
one of HW's 'ribs,' **34**. 49, 117, 125
Ossory, Lady, sends HW a transcript of letter on, **34**. 41
Park Place visited by, **39**. 474
portraits of, by Miss Foldsone, **11**. 77, 133–4, 145, 193, 219, 350

[Berry, Agnes and Mary, *continued*]
  Smith, Sydney, discusses, 43. 138
  SH visitors sent by, 12. 247
  Teddington to be left by, for London, 34. 85
  Twickenham residents, 42. 480, 484, 486
  virtues of, 11. 17, 23, 51–2, 59, 60, 62, 110–11,
    171, 364, 12. 5, 74, 145
  Yorkshire visits of, 12. 6, 8, 10, 35, 47, 34.
    49, 68, 194
  *See also* Berry, Agnes; Berry, Mary
Berry, Christopher (fl. 1781–90), bookseller:
  catalogue of books for sale by, 2. 282
Berry, John (d. 1789), bookseller:
  catalogue of books for sale by, 2. 282
Berry, Mary (1763–1852), HW's correspondent
    (*see also* Berry, Agnes and Mary, and Vols
    11–12):
  agitation of, over newspaper notice, 11. 375–7
  Benwell, Elizabeth, has letter from, about
    HW's death and will, 43. 157–9
  Berry, Agnes, causes concern to, by ill health,
    12. 21–2, 23, 35, 46
  Blenheim visited by, 12. 100
  Bognor Rocks base for excursions by, 12. 204
  bust of, by Mrs Damer, at SH, 43. 155
  Cheltenham mineral water to be drunk by,
    12. 147
  Cholmeley, Mrs, gets criticism by, of Hannah
    More's *Strictures*, 31. 390n
  constancy of, 11. 322
  continental journey (first) of, 11. 30n
  Court attendance agreeable to, 12. 123
  Damer, Mrs, does bust of, 12. 144, 274
  devotion of, to father, sister, and HW, 12. 127
  drawing of: at Bognor Rocks, 12. 199, 204;
    perspective studied, 11. 267; Prospect House
    sketched, 12. 128
  early life of, reflections on, 11. 30n
  Edwards sends fragment of Roscoe's *Life of
    Lorenzo de' Medici* to, 42. 400n
  'erudite,' 12. 200
  Farington's landscape praised by, 15. 322
  fortune lacked by, 12. 127
  French proficiency of, 11. 163, 34. 24
  geography known to, 12. 92
  HW appoints, executrix, 13. 55n
  (?) HW asks Harcourt for ticket for, for
    Hastings's trial, 35. 541
  HW calls: 'Latian nymph,' 34. 27; 'Queen
    Mary,' 11. 333; 'Sultana Maria,' 11. 72
  HW hopes that Pinkerton will know, better,
    16. 316–17
  HW praises understanding of, 12. 129
  HW receives anonymous letter advising him
    to marry, 15. 335
  HW's affection for, 11. 102, 235, 12. 131, 184,
    210, 211
  HW's correspondence with: vols 11–12,
    *passim*; MSS of, 36. 314; not to be pub-
    lished, 15. 338
  (?) HW's cup and saucer later given to, 7. 414
  HW's friendship from, disinterested, 11. 375
  HW's letters edited by, 26. 38, 39

HW's MSS left in charge of, 13. 55n, 15. 337,
    36. 310–16
HW's verses from, 11. 2–3, 22, 34. 27
HW's verses to, Dec. 1789, with her reply and
    his reply, 43. 141–2
HW to leave handsome bequest to, 15. 335
HW visited by, 15. 318
HW wants to serve, 12. 126, 127, 130
health of: bad, 11. 231n, 12. 189; Cheltenham
    to improve, 12. 145, 154; cold, 11. 231,
    12. 170, 212–13; delicate, 15. 322; fever, 11.
    326, 327, 328, 330, 334, 335, 336, 357, 362;
    HW teases about, 11. 104; HW worries
    about, 11. 25, 26, 12. 213–14; headaches, 12.
    113, 159, 183, 211; illness, 11. 324, 325, 12.
    178–9, 181, 182; improved, 12. 50; indif-
    ferent, 15. 317; nose injured, 11. 234–362
    *passim*, 31. 365; rheumatism suspected, 12.
    182; sea-bathing benefits, 12. 199, 204, 208,
    31. 402; stomach-ache, 12. 146; writing bad
    for, 11. 140, 281, 283, 12. 8–9, 19, 159, 199,
    204
interests of, numerous, 11. 267–8
Jerningham's lines for, 12. 270
Knight family met by, in Italy, 34. 167–8
Latin known by, 11. 164, 12. 161, 34. 24
More, Hannah, converses with, about religion,
    31. 390
—— corresponds with, 31. 401–2
—— expects to meet HW at house of, 31. 296
—— prays that eyes of, may be opened to
    Christianity, 31. 390n
note by, not written by HW, 43. 98
Nuneham visited by, 12. 100
O'Hara's engagement to, 12. 171–3, 184, 210,
    211, 29. 43n
Oxford visited by, 12. 100
Pinkerton's gift to, 16. 316, 381
——'s letter from, 16. 381
proud, 11. 376, 12. 127
punctual, 11. 25
Russell, Lady Mary, life of, written by, 20.
    283n
'Sketches of Italian Peasants' by, 43. 147
specimen of Roscoe's book brought to HW
    by, 15. 249
SH shown by, 12. 242, 244, 250
SH visited by, 12. 230, 237
SH visitors sent by, 12. 231, 240, 241, 246, 248
verses by, 34. 27, 43. 139
Berry, Robert (d. 1817), father of Agnes and
    Mary Berry:
  daughters of, get Little Strawberry Hill from
    HW, 15. 317
  dines with HW, 34. 186
  expected from Italy in October, 34. 117, 125
  HW called royalist by, 11. 77
  HW compares himself to, 11. 354
  HW leaves his MSS to, for daughters, 15. 337
  HW's account of, 34. 24, 25–6
  HW's correspondence with, 11. 174, 317, 322

HW's papers bequeathed to, **15**. 337, **30**. 373, **36**. 311

HW's regard for, **11**. 7, 9, 19, 31, 73, 158, 355, 360

HW to meet, at Park Place, **11**. 48

HW uses coach of, **11**. 134

HW visited by, at SH, **12**. 100, 175, 194, **15**. 318

health of, **11**. 168, 378

horse of, sold, **11**. 160, 162

house of, at Teddington, **11**. 62, 73

house of, in North Audley St, **30**. 363, 373

house sought by, in Twickenham, **11**. 7, 9, 19

Marchant told by, about edition of HW's works, **15**. 338

mentioned, **11**. 58, 235, 304, 319, 325, 335, 353, **12**. 32, 49, 159, 171, 183

news interests, **11**. 75, 120, 124, 127, 231, 239, 242, 251, 357, **12**. 12, 66, 70, 120

Pinkerton to receive compliments of, **16**. 381

rick of, **12**. 163

SH visited by, **12**. 230

Twickenham resident, **42**. 480, 484, 486

uncle disinherits, **11**. 111n, 375

virtues of, **11**. 282

well-meaning, **15**. 337

Yorkshire visited by, **34**. 194

Berry, Mrs Robert. *See* Seton, Elizabeth

Berry, William. *See* Ferguson, William Berry

Berry, Hants:
Conway, Hugh, has estate of, **11**. 262n

Berry (France):
Aubigny in, **4**. 287n

Berry; berries:
ivy, wood pigeon eats, **16**. 190

'Berryana,' collection of bons mots:
HW contributes to, **12**. 140, 142

Berryer, Nicholas-René (1703–62), ministre de la marine:
inexperienced, **21**. 263
protégé of Mme de Pompadour, **21**. 263n

Berry House, Hants:
Marshall's seat, **33**. 269n

Bersin, Claude-Louise-Angélique, m. (1747) Anne-Emmanuel-François-Georges de Crussol d'Uzès d'Amboise d'Aubijoux, Marquis de Crussol d'Amboise:
social relations of, with Duchesse d'Aiguillon, **7**. 307

Berston. *See* Beeston

Bertaut, Françoise (ca 1621–89), m. (1639) Nicolas Langlois de Motteville; writer:
Arckenholtz's *Mémoires concernant Christine* attacks, **9**. 117
Burney, Frances, to be transformed into memoirist like, **33**. 518
name of husband of, corrected, **43**. 117

Bertellet, ——, Chevalier de; French consul at Leghorn 1766–79:
fishing boat sent by, **24**. 476

Bertet de la Clue Sabran, —— (ca 1696–1764), French naval officer:

accounts from, of naval battle, **21**. 188
Boscawen burns flagship of, **21**. 326n
—— defeats, **21**. 352, **35**. 294n
Ireland to have been object of, **21**. 328
Toulon reached by, **21**. 197
West Indies the probable destination of, **21**. 318

Berthelot, Étienne (1720–85):
(?) attends sessions of parliament of Paris, **8**. 173

Berthelot de Baye, Agnès-Victoire de (b. 1741), m. (1757) Nicolas-François de Berchény, lady of honour to Louis XV's daughters:
Montbarey's retort to, **4**. 134
social relations of, with Mme de Monconseil, **7**. 297

Berthelot de Baye, Étienne-Louis-Alexandre (b. 1707):
marriage of, **4**. 284n
Prie, Marquise de, sister of, **7**. 273
(?) social relations of, in Paris, **5**. 95, **7**. 273, 282, 299, 323

Berthelot de Baye, Mme Étienne-Louis-Alexandre. *See* Compagnolt, Marie-Anne-Louise-Charlotte de

Berthelot de Pleneuf, Agnès (1698–1727), m. (1713) Louis, Marquis de Prie:
Berthelot brother of, **7**. 273
Bourbon, Duc de, takes, as mistress, **4**. 284n, **7**. 273, 275
Du Deffand, Mme, has picture of, **7**. 289
——'s anecdote of, **7**. 275
——'s verses for, **7**. 214
—— with, in exile at Courbépine, **7**. 214
La Touche, Mme, not sister to, **43**. 98
mother of, **6**. 423
portrait of: given by Mme du Deffand to Conway, **6**. 129–30, 136; HW hopes to get, **6**. 136, 140, 197, **39**. 243; to be shown by Mme du Deffand to Conway, **39**. 215, 234, 243
suicide of, **7**. 275
uncleanly, **7**. 275

Berthelot de Pleneuf, Mme Jean-Étienne. *See* Rioult de Douilly, Agnès

Berthier de Sauvigny, Mme. *See* Durey d'Harnoncourt, Louise-Bernarde

Berthier de Sauvigny, Louis-Jean (1709–88), intendant de Paris:
(?) Silhouette succeeded by, as controller-general, **21**. 349n
wife of, **4**. 422n

Berthon de Maisonneuve, Louise-Adélaïde (1746–1823), called Mlle Doligny; actress:
Collé's *Partie de Chasse* acted by, **39**. 217
*Fausse Agnès* acted by, **7**. 275

Berti, Giovanni Lorenzo (1696–1766), theologian:
anti-Jesuit champion, **21**. 475

Bertie, Albinia (ca 1738–1816), m. (1757) Hon. George Hobart, 3d E. of Buckinghamshire, 1793:

[Bertie, Albinia, *continued*]

acting of, at Richmond House, 33. 580n, 586, 34. 1

acts well, 33. 368–9

agility of, in dancing, 32. 111, 117

biographical information about, corrected, 43. 104

(?) coiffure of, distracts HW from balloon, 39. 419

Conway's prologue spoken by, at Richmond House, 33. 563n, 39. 448n, 546

cotillion danced by, 10. 259

'Dame Cowslip' played by, 12. 151

Damer, Mrs, pre-empts part of, 34. 1

fancy dress of, for quadrilles, at Guines's ball, 32. *102*, 111

faro table of, 11. 273, 34. 190n

'fat grandmother,' 11. 290

fêtes of, at Ham Common, 34. 143

Frederick II compared with, 33. 286

guests of, 33. 285, 428n

HW calls, 'a spangle-pudding,' 32. 111

HW did not attend plays given by, 33. 428

HW invited by, to play at Ham Common, 33. 368

HW mentions, 7. 142

HW not invited by, to fête, 33. 285

'Inis' not acted by, at Richmond House, 34. 4n

Jordan, Mrs, writes to, 34. 143

now a Countess, 34. 190

rural breakfast of, 11. 290, 294

SH visited by, 12. 229

toothache of, 33. 286

villa of, Sans Souci, 33. 285–6

*Wonder, The,* acted by, at Richmond House, 34. 1n

Bertie, Lady Brownlow. *See* Layard, Mary Anne (1743–1804)

Bertie, Lord Brownlow (1729–1809), 5th D. of Ancaster, 1779; M.P.:

brother disinherits, 24. *499*

nephew's bequest to, 24. 494, 33. 110n

Waldegrave, Lady Anna Horatia, told by, that nephew would have married her, 24. 494, 33. 114

wife of, 9. 263n, 11. 255n

Bertie, Charles (1734–80):

pictures of, 1. 171

Bertie, Diana (d. 1754), m. (1751) George James Williams:

message cards of, 9. 29

Bertie, Lady Elizabeth (ca 1724–1804), m. Giovanni Andrea Battista (called John) Gallini, cr. Papal Kt:

husband of, 25. 431n

mesalliance of, 38. 367, 43. 291

Bertie, Georgiana Charlotte (1764–1838), m. (1791) George James Cholmondeley, 4th E. of Cholmondeley, 1770; cr. (1815) M. of Cholmondeley:

'charming over the way,' 33. 108

England returned to, by, 12. 44

father entails estate on, 24. 499

Florence visited by, 25. 618n

France visited by, 11. 255n

Houghton visited by, 15. 326

lady of Bedchamber to Q. Charlotte, 12. 108n

marriage of, 11. 241, 251, 255, 33. 108, 110

mother of, dies, 12. 43–4

to winter in France, 2. 235

Wales, P. of, to include, in household, 12. 115, 123, 128

Wales, Ps of, visits, 12. 200n

Bertie, Lady Mary (d. 1774), m. (1748) Samuel Greatheed:

Guy's Cliff improved by, 32. 353

Lindsey House inhabited by, 20. 10n

Bertie, Peregrine (1686–1742), 2d D. of Ancaster:

daughter lives in house of, after his death, 20. 10n

death of, reported, 17. 197

steward of, dies, 17. 197n

Bertie, Hon. Peregrine:

natural daughter of, 9. 29n

Bertie, Peregrine (1714–78), 3d D. of Ancaster:

Christian VII not received by, due to Lincolnshire visit, 35. 325

daughter of, 11. 241n

death of: leaves mastership of the Horse vacant, 24. 407; verses on, 29. 7n

De La Warr succeeds, as Q. Charlotte's Master of the Horse, 22. 473

estate entailed by, on his daughters after his son, 24. 499

Garter promised to, but never given, 33. 11n

George III appoints, Master of the Horse to Q. Charlotte, 22. 473, 30. 186

Grimsthorpe, seat of, 1. 172

HW hates to ask, for ticket, since he does not know him, 40. 202

housemaid of, wounded, 37. 9n

Piozzi, Mrs, comments on, 9. 280n

regiment of, 19. 128n

Somerset, D. of, buys house of, 20. 11

wife of, 2. 235n, 9. 377n

will of, set aside, 24. 494

Bertie, Peregrine (1723–86), M.P.:

Philipps opposed by, at Horn Tavern conclave, 35. 216n

Bertie, Lady Priscilla Barbara Elizabeth (1761–1828), m. (1779) Peter Burrell, 2d Bt, 1787, cr. (1796) Bn Gwydir; she was Bns Willoughby de Eresby, s.j., 1780:

appointed Bedchamber lady to Ps of Wales, 12. 193n

dances at Guines's ball, 32. 116

father entails estate upon, 24. 499

health of, out of danger, 33. 203

husband is Lord Great Chamberlain by right of, 39. 334

husband of, 33. 206

Lady Great Chamberlain of England, 24. 499

marriage of, 11. 255, 24. 499, 33. 84, 95

to winter in France, **2.** 235

Waldegrave, Lady Anna Horatia told by, that brother would have married her, **24.** 494, **33.** 114, 164

Wales, Ps of, dines with, **12.** 200n

Bertie, Robert (1582–1642), 1st E. of Lindsey: portrait of, **1.** 171

Bertie, Lord Robert (1721–82), M.P.; army officer:

aide-de-camp rebukes, for blowing nose beneath D. of Cumberland's window, 19, *464*

(?) appointment of, as Groom of the Stole, unlikely, **30.** 162–3

Barrington's flattery of, **35.** 568

Byng requests, as witness, **21.** 3n

council of war signed by, **35.** 92

(?) Court ball attended by, **9.** 402

Dover Castle occupied by troops of, **35.** 91

Drawing-Room attendants told by, of sister-in-law's message from Ds of Gloucester, **33.** 114n

drinks New Year's toast to Montfort, **35.** 202

Fitzroy, Lady Caroline, quarrels with, **37.** 228

Fowke ordered to receive women and children of regiment of, **20.** 586n

Furnese, Selina, dismisses, **9.** 85

George III met by, at Petersfield, **32.** 129

Gibraltar resolution signed by, **20.** 560n

HW mentions, **37.** 339

lord of the Bedchamber to George III, **20.** 247

marriage of, expected, **10.** 14

Portugal to be visited by, **14.** 120n

Sackville's court martial to include, **21.** 366n

testimony of, in Byng's favour, **21.** 51

White's club rejects, in HW's newspaper parody, **9.** 127

Bertie, Robert (1756–79), 4th D. of Ancaster, 1778:

Barrymore, Cts of, said to be mistress of, **32.** 144n

death of, **11.** 255n, **24.** 498, **33.** 110, **39.** 334

drinking and rioting of, **24.** 498

had presentiment of death, **33.** 165

heirs of, **2.** 235n

turbulent nature, fine figure, and ignoble manners of, **24.** 499

Waldegrave, Lady Anna Horatia, to have married, **24.** 494, 498, **25.** 75, **33.** 107n, 114

will of, **24.** 494, **33.** 110

Bertie, Lord Vere:

Boston mob breaks windows of, **21.** 137n

Bertie, Willoughby (1740–99), 4th E. of Abingdon, 1760:

buffoon speech of, in House of Lords, **35.** 381

Dashwood to be supported by, **9.** 320

Hardinge might get introduction to Huber through, **35.** 580

may have attended Markham's dinner, **28.** 334, 337

Parliamentary motion by, on legality of troop levy, **28.** 352

protest by, against Germain's elevation, **29.** 178n

*Thoughts on the Letter of Edmund Burke,* **28.** 330, 334

Bertie family:

duchesses of, **24.** 499–500

Bertier, Louis-Bénigne-François:

(?) attends session of parliament of Paris, **8.** 171

Bertier de Savigny. *See* Berthier de Sauvigny

Bertin, ——, Choiseul's major-domo:

(?) death of, **6.** 110

ill, **6.** 97

Bertin, François-Jacques:

(?) attends session of parliament of Paris, **8.** 173

Bertin, Henri-Léonard-Jean-Baptiste (1720–92), chancellor; secretary of state; controller-general of finance:

advises on choice of controller, **4.** 326

anecdote of, and Monclar's pension, **4.** 285

birth date of, corrected, **43.** 90

Du Barry, Mme, adds, to her circle, **4.** 302

Du Deffand, Mme, fears influence of, **4.** 234

Forcalquier, Mme de, cites, **4.** 382

foreign affairs temporarily assigned to, **6.** 60, 61

resigns because unpopular with parliament of Paris, **38.** 261–2

retirement of, rumoured, **7.** 192

retires, **7.** 452

Vergennes given departments of, **7.** 452–3

Bertini, Maddalena, m. (1721) Franchino Franchini:

son tells lies in letters to, **21.** 510

Bertoldo di Giovanni (ca 1420–91), sculptor:

pupil of, **14.** 117n

Bertoli, Conte Antonio Daniele (1678–1743), painter:

Maria Theresa studies drawing and painting under, **18.** 139n

Berton, Pierre-Montan (1727–80), director of Opéra:

Bishop sent to, **6.** 55

*Daphnis and Chloe* augmented by, **32.** 259n

director of Opéra, **6.** 28–9

in country, **6.** 51

Berton. *See also* Breton

Berton de Balbe, Louis de (1718–96), Duc de Crillon; cr. (1783) Duc de Mahon:

bulletin by, on Minorca, more sensible than that of Spain, **25.** 188–9

Charles III orders, to assault Gibraltar, **25.** 300

commands expedition against Minorca, **25.** 174

Eliott's letter to, **25.** 340

floating batteries opposed by, **25.** 329n

HW hopes Mann may feast on heart of, **25.** 327

in Spanish service, **29.** 151n

merchandise taken at Minorca said by, to equal that taken at St Eustatius, **25.** *189*

Minorca's surrender expected by, to come from garrison's weakness, **25.** 429

[Berton de Balbe, Louis de, *continued*]
Moñino informed by, of troops going into winter quarters, **25**. 340
Murray praised by, **25**. 263-4
—— quarrels with, after accepting apartment, **25**. 269
—— refuses bribe from, **25**. 207-8, 213, 229, 263n, 269
——'s prudence approved by, **25**. 189
—— surprised by, **25**. 198
—— writes jocosely to, welcoming general assault, **25**. 229
St Philip's to be starved rather than assaulted by, **25**. 249-50
sure of taking St Philip's, **25**. 180
Bertoni, Ferdinando Giuseppe (1725-1813), composer:
*Ezio* by, costumes seen at, **35**. 363
'Bertram, Mr.' *See* Bedford, Charles
Bertrand, Mrs. *See* Deard, ——
Beru. *See* Berrue
Bérulle, Pierre de (1575-1629), cardinal:
tomb of, **7**. 280
Berwick, Bn. *See* Hill, Thomas Noel
Berwick, Ds of. *See* Bulkeley, Anne (d. 1751); Silva, Maria Teresa de (1716-90); Stolberg-Gedern, Karoline Auguste of (1755-1829)
Berwick, D. of. *See* Fitzjames, Charles-Bernard-Pascal-Janvier (1751-87); Fitzjames, James (1670-1734); Fitzjames, James Francis Edward (1718-85); Fitzjames, James Francis Stuart (1696-1738)
Berwick, Mrs:
SH visited by, **12**. 239
Berwick, John:
execution of, **19**. 287n
Berwick, Joseph (d. 1798), banker:
Farington visited by, **15**. 321
Berwick:
Conway and Cornwallis visit, **37**. 220
Cope escapes to, **19**. 117
Craufurd M.P. for, **9**. 307n
petition from, **20**. 453n
volunteers at, **26**. 13
Wade sends Handasyde from, **19**. 159
Watson, Thomas, of, dies, **7**. 397
*Berwick*, English ship:
damaged in storm, **33**. 245
*Poder* recaptured by, **18**. 415n
Berwick regiment (French):
Fitzjames, Comte de, commands, **19**. 208n
Berwickshire:
election in, **17**. 294
Berwick St, Soho (London):
Decker, balloon-maker in, **25**. 596n
Beryl:
glass of, **32**. 323
Berzichelli, Maria Leopolda (1704-82), m. 1 (1726) Bindo Peruzzi; m. 2 (1742) Conte Antonfrancesco Pecori:
marriage of, **18**. 150

Besançon (France):
Cumberland, D. and Ds of, to meet at, **25**. 645
explosion near, **11**. 52
Louis XVII and counter-revolution supported by, **12**. 13
parliament of: dissolved, **35**. 126; reformed, **23**. 320; revived after suppression, **35**. 344
reported revolt at, **12**. 15
Besborough. *See* Bessborough
Besenval, Jean-Pierre-Victor (1721-91), Bn de:
Artois allowed visits of, in exile, **7**. 32
(?) Beauvau, Princesse de, takes, to theatre, **7**. 344
Chanteloup visited by, **5**. 238, 243
Chartres's arrival announced to Orléans by, **8**. 127
Choiseul consulted by, on troops, **5**. 32
(?) La Tuilerie visited by, **7**. 345
Marie-Antoinette accompanied by, in quarantine, **7**. 129
social relations of, in Paris, **6**. 404, **7**. 32, 325, (?) 345
verses for, at Mme de Luxembourg's supper, **6**. 406
Besenval, Théodore-Élisabeth-Catherine de (d. 1777), m. (1733) Charles-Guillaume-Louis, Marquis de Broglie:
HW sends message to, through Selwyn, **30**. 251
pimpernel seeds for, will be carried by Fox and left at Panchaud's, **30**. 251
Selwyn will see, at Hénault's, **30**. 251
social relations of, in Paris, **7**. 270, 297, 311, 313, 316-17, 321, 323, 325, 332
Besey, Mrs John. *See* Cobb, Anne
Besford Court:
Sebright of, **9**. 133n
Bésiade, Charles-Antoine de, Marquis d'Avaray:
wife of, **4**. 259n, **5**. 194n
Besné, Du Chaffault de. *See* Du Chaffault
Besozzi, Gioacchino (1679-1755), cardinal, 1743:
Benedict XIV makes, cardinal, **18**. 302n
Bessborough, Cts of. *See* Cavendish, Lady Caroline (1719-60); Spencer, Lady Henrietta Frances (1761-1821)
Bessborough, E. of. *See* Ponsonby, Brabazon (1679-1758); Ponsonby, Frederick (1758-1844); Ponsonby, William (1704-93)
Bessuéjouls, Jean-Armand de (1721-1818), Comte de Roquelaure; Bp of Senlis:
Paradis de Moncrif succeeded by, in Académie, **4**. 489n
Best, James (fl. 1762-89), under-secretary of the Court of Exchequer; Montagu's deputy:
HW to receive funds from, for plate, **10**. 286
North mentions, **10**. 249n
Bestucheff. *See* Bestuzhev-Ryumin
Bestuzhev-Ryumin, Count Alexei Petrovich (1693-1768), Grand Chancellor of Russia:
Apraxin ordered by, to retreat, **21**. 159n

Catherine II recalls, **22**. 59
HW imagines Biron passing, on road to Siberia, **10**. 39
(?) letters seized by, **18**. 495n
Peter III allegedly placated by, in relaxing war on Prussia, **21**. 144n
—— vainly expected by, to succeed Czarina Elizabeth, **21**. 159n
Vorontsov could never live near, **22**. *11*
—— should have been replaced by, **22**. 62
Beswick, Lavinia (ca 1708–60), called Fenton, m. (1751) Charles Powlett, 3d D. of Bolton:
*Beggar's Opera* acted by, **21**. 365n
biographical information on, corrected, **43**. 122
deathbed will of, disinherits sons in favour of Irish surgeon, **21**. 365
death of, **9**. 271–2
Betange, ——:
Cocchi discusses Craons with, **35**. 16
(?) dismissal of, ordered, **17**. 368
in despair, **17**. 282
turned out for being Richecourt's enemy, **17**. 490
Betham, Rev. Edward (1709–83):
Cole agrees with, for house at Milton, **1**. 155
Exeter Cathedral's ornament described by, **1**. 146–7
Bethell, Hugh (1689–1747), M.P.:
asthma of, cured at Venice, **18**. 117
biographical information about, corrected, **43**. 314, 357
Blount, Martha, visits, **33**. 511
death of, at Venice, of asthma, expected by Mann, **18**. 65
Moyser accompanies, to continent, **17**. 408n, **43**. 244, 247
sisters of, **30**. 105n
Bethell, Priscilla (b. 1690) or Bridget (b. 1692):
(?) HW's suggestion for beautifying, **9**. 139
(?) HW surpasses, in thinness, **35**. 218
name of, corrected, **43**. 314
(?) Paris opinion of, to be influenced by Lady Mary Churchill, **9**. 139
(?) Selwyn jokes about sharp features of, **9**. 41, **43**. 112
(?) sepulchral aspect of, fashionable, **9**. 183
(?) 'ugliest woman in England,' **30**. 105
Bethell, Slingsby (1695–1758), lord mayor of London; M.P.:
biographical information about, corrected, **43**. 119, 314
election of, **19**. 425n
house of, on Tower Hill, **19**. 299n, **43**. 261
instructions by, to Parliamentary members, **9**. 201
sisters of, **30**. 105n
Bethesda:
pool of: cripples suitable only at, **24**. 187; Parliament resembles, **38**. 226
*Bethia*, English ship:

*Arnoux* captures, near Leghorn, **21**. 274n
Béthisy, Comtesse de. *See* Du Deffand, Adélaïde-Charlotte-Marie-Octavie
Béthisy, Eugène-Eustache (1739–1823), Comte de:
social relations of, with Egmont family, **7**. 299, 301
Béthisy, Eugène-Marie (d. 1721):
wife of, **6**. 213, **10**. 291n
Béthisy, Henri-Benoît-Jules de (ca 1744–1817), Bp of Uzès, 1779:
Uzès, see of, given to, **7**. 435
Béthisy, Jules-Jacques-Éléonor (1747–1816), Vicomte de:
wounded, **7**. 438
Béthisy de Mézières, Catherine-Éléonore-Eugénie de (1707–57), m. (1722) Charles de Rohan-Guéménée, Prince de Montauban:
mother of, **37**. 353
Béthisy de Mézières, Henriette-Eugénie de (1710–87), m. (1729) Claude-Lamoral-Hyacinthe-Ferdinand, Prince de Ligne:
Askew, Mrs, resembles, **30**. 214, **39**. 215
Chanteloup visited by, **5**. 243, 245
Colmant forwards letter by, **5**. 240
cousin of, **3**. 333
HW hears comment of, on his Rousseau letter, **39**. 44
(?) HW mentions, **3**. 341
HW visits, at Luxembourg Palace, **31**. 100
mother of, English, **39**. 44
Orléans, Bp of, visited by, at Meun, **5**. 239–40
social relations of, in Paris, *see index entries ante* **8**. 251
Béthisy de Mézières, Marie-Catherine de (ca 1714–94), Abbess of Panthémont:
age of, joked about, **10**. 290–1
biographical information on, corrected, **43**. 90, 137
Cholmondeley, H. F., not inquired after by, **4**. 374
Cholmondeley, H. M., denied return to Panthémont by, **4**. 400
HW calls on, **10**. 290–1
HW does not send kiss to, **36**. 55
HW refuses to call on, **8**. 58
social relations of, in Paris, **7**. 325, 328, 458
Bethlehem Hospital, London. *See* Bedlam Hospital
Bethnal Green:
Gerbier's academy at, **1**. 23
Béthune, Comtesse de. *See* Crozat de Thiers, Antoinette-Louise-Marie
Béthune, Marquise de. *See* Boullongne, Marie-Edmée de (1725–53); Crozat de Thiers, Louise-Marie-Thérèse
Béthune, Armand-Joseph de (1738–1800), Duc de Charost; Gov. of Calais; economist and philanthropist:
attends session of parliament of Paris, **8**. 172
Coke, Lady Mary, detained by, at Calais, **31**. 25, 27

Béthune, Armand-Louis (1711–90), Marquis de:
daughter of, **5.** 147
HW to buy armour from wife of, **5.** 112
marriages of, **5.** 109n, 147

Béthune, Catherine-Pauline de (b. 1752), m. (1770) Louis-Jean-Baptiste-Antonin Colbert, Marquis de Seignelay:
sister of, **5.** 147

Béthune, Joachim-Casimir-Léon (1724–69), Comte de:
social relations of, with Duchesse de Choiseul, **7.** 297
wife of, **5.** 109n

Bethune, John Drinkwater:
Gibraltar's siege described by, **25.** 300n, 325n

Béthune, Louis-Joseph de (1681–1709), Marquis de Charost:
estate of widow of, settled, **8.** 37

Béthune, Maximilien de (1559 or 1560–1641), Baron de Rosny, Duc de Sully, minister of Henri IV:
birth date of, corrected, **43.** 186, 290
Du Deffand, Mme, has print of, **4.** 254
—— sends china group of Henri IV and, to HW, **4.** 302, 304–5, 307, 311–12, 315, 316, 323, 331, 336, 338, 385
Galluzzi too severe upon, **25.** 225
HW contrasts Colbert and, **5.** 407
less objectionable than Necker, but needed Henri IV's support, **25.** 159
*Mémoires*: Gray refers HW to, **14.** 127; re-read by Mme du Deffand, **5.** 146, **6.** 189
Séguier cites, **41.** 346
Turgot compared to, **6.** 95

Béthune, Paul-François de (1682–1759), Duc de Charost:
anecdote of losses of, **6.** 73
Du Deffand, Mme, cites, **7.** 159
Praslin succeeds, as chef du conseil des finances, **39.** 65

Béthune (France):
visitors to: Conway, **39.** 536; Craufurd, **5.** 294; HW, **3.** 343n, **7.** 315, 343; Scott, **39.** 536
wretched inn at, **7.** 343

Béthune-Chabris, Armande-Jeanne-Claude de (b. 1753), m. (1772) Félicité-Jean-Louis-Étienne, Comte de Durfort:
relatives of, **5.** 147
rumour of proposed marriage of, **5.** 147

'Betier, Le':
HW borrows 'thought' from, for 'Patapan,' **30.** 300n

Bétizy, Rue:
Louis XVI assigned to, in joke, **8.** 181

Bets, Daniel. See Veers, Daniel Diederick

Betterton, Thomas (ca 1635–1710), actor:
Argyll prefers Garrick to, **17.** 435
*Dioclesian* by, **18.** 565
HW did not admire, **23.** 265
portrait of, at Knole, **35.** 134

Bettes, John (d. ?1570), engraver:
print by, of K. Alfred, **1.** 172

Bettesworth, Dr John (d. 1751), Dean of the Arches Court of Canterbury; judge of the Prerogative Court of Canterbury:
Beaufort's potency witnessed by, **18.** 185

Betti, Domenico:
Lady Orford's will probated by, **43.** 288

Bettina. See Lapier, Bettina

'Bettina' (dog):
death of, **17.** 45, 53
epitaph for, **17.** 112
HW mentions, **17.** 43, 418
Mann sends regards to, **17.** 41

Betts, Thomas:
glass shop of, **10.** 224, **31.** 159
HW takes glass and pattern to, for Selwyn, **30.** 242

'Betty,' fruit vendor. See Munro (or Neale), Elizabeth

Betuwe (Holland):
deputies of, complain about Prince Ferdinand's crossing the Rhine, **21.** 222n

Betz. See Lallemant de Betz

Beugo, John (1759–1841):
Seton's portrait of Hailes engraved by, **42.** 432n

Beurnonville, Marquis de. See Riel, Pierre de

Beuvron, Marquis de. See Harcourt, Anne-François d'

Beuvron, Marquise de. See Rouillé, Marie-Catherine

Beuvron, M. de. See Harcourt de Beuvron, Marie-François d'

Bevan, Mr:
HW desires Boyce to be succeeded by, in Windsor Castle post, **40.** 173–4
HW recommends, to Hertford, for keeping courts in Suffolk, **38.** 25–6

Bevan, Arthur (ca 1688–1743), M.P.:
(?) son of, **38.** 25, **40.** 174n

Bevan, Henry, of Twickenham:
Cambridge House occupied by, **11.** 31n

Bever, ——, auctioneer:
Orford's horses sold by, **31.** 174n, **36.** 95n, **41.** 266n
pedigrees of horses to be sent to, **32.** 134

Bevere, Claines, Worcs:
Nash's address, **42.** 17n

*Beverlei. See under* Saurin, Bernard-Joseph

Beverley, Cts of. See Burrell, Isabella Susanna

Beverley, E. of. See Percy, Lord Algernon

Beverley, John à. See John of Beverly

Beverley, John (1743–1827), esquire bedell:
marriage of, **1.** 363

Beverley, Mrs John. See Thornhill, Susannah

Beverley, Yorkshire:
address from, to George III, **41.** 311n
Anderson, M.P. for, **11.** 23n
anti-American address from, **24.** 132n, **39.** 270n
Byron to remove recruiting party to, **28.** 485
Carmarthen gives ball at, **28.** 471
Gothic rebuses at, **34.** 224
HW to visit, **28.** 37, **35.** 333
minster at, **34.** 224, 225, 227

Beverly, Robert de:
charter mentions, **40**. 224
Bevern. *See* Brunswick-Bevern
'Bevil':
character in comedy, **19**. 465
Bevois Mount, Hants, Edward Horne's (formerly, Peterborough's) seat:
Berry, Mary, does not mention, **11**. 80
Conway writes from, **37**. 514
HW passes, **35**. 250-1
HW suggests Lady Ossory should visit, **33**. 42-3
visitors to: Ailesbury, Cts of, **37**. 516; Conway, **37**. 514-16, 519
Bévy, Charles-Joseph (1738-1830), historian:
*Histoire des inaugurations* by, **16**. 181, 184, 185
Bewdley, Worcs:
Roberts of, **28**. 3n
Whaley visits and describes, **40**. 42
Winnington M.P. for, **10**. 49n
Bewick, Thomas:
quoted, **15**. 44n
Bewley, William (ca 1726-83), surgeon; apothecary:
apothecary at Great Massingham, **16**. 349
author of *Monthly Review*, **16**. 349
Burney's correspondence with, **43**. 64-5, 218, 351, 367
death of, at Burney's house, **16**. 351
HW invites, to SH, **42**. 457
HW's correspondence with, **2**. 85, 87, 90, 92, 102, 104, 107, 109, 114, 132, 133, **16**. 121-34, **42**. 457
Orford E. of, attended by, at Eriswell, **36**. 118, 119
Bewley. *See also* Beaulieu
Bexhill, Sussex:
window from, at SH, **1**. 244, 245, **2**. 370, **9**. 326, **43**. 56
Bexley, Kent:
HW visits, **13**. 3-4
Thorpe of, **40**. 213
Trinity Hospital has estates at, **16**. 91
Bexley Heath:
Selwyn meets Scots officer on, **18**. 524
Beylon, Jean-François (1717-79), Swiss reader to Q. of Sweden:
report by, on Q. of Sweden's medals, **40**. 214
Beyton, Suffolk:
Nesling vicar of, **1**. 51n
Bezançon. *See* Besançon
Bèze, —— de:
attends session of parliament of Paris, **8**. 171
Bèze, Théodore de (1519-1605), French reformer:
*De sua in Candidam et Audebertum benevolentia* by, **40**. 100
Bezons, Marquis de. *See* Bazin, Jacques-Gabriel
Bezons, Marquise de. *See* Briqueville, Anne-Marie de
Bezval. *See* Besenval

Bianchette, Convent of:
Albany, Cts of, takes refuge in, **25**. 102, 108n
Bianchi, Antonio, Mann's doorkeeper:
(?) Leghorn messenger to be admitted by, at any hour, **25**. 9
Bianchi, Francesco (1752-1810), composer:
*Réduction de Paris, La,* by, **32**. 267n
*Semiramide* by, **12**. 99n
Bianchi, Giovanni Battista, composer:
*Omaggio, L',* opera by, **39**. 382
Bianchi, Giuseppe (b. ca 1727), keeper of the Uffizi gallery, 1753;
stove of, for washing linen, **22**. 67n
Uffizi ignited by, and robbed of a gold foot, **25**. 65
Bianchi Buonavita, Giovanni Francesco (1670-1752), keeper of the Uffizi gallery:
Chute dreams of, **35**. 55
Conway presented to, by Mann, **20**. 290
friend of, to sell Hermaphrodite, **17**. 213
Bib:
young girl's costume, **17**. 174
Bibbiena:
Niccolini's villa at, **23**. 459n
Bibiena, Antonio Galli (1700-74):
Accademia degli Intronati rebuilt by, after fire, **20**. 391n
Bibiena, Jean Galli de:
*Triomphe du sentiment, Le,* by, **37**. 435
Bibikov, Alexander Ilich (1729-74), soldier, diplomatist:
marshal of the diet, **28**. 476n
Bible:
Aaron's rod in, **39**. 254
Abraham and Methusaleh in, compared to Mann and HW, **25**. 417
Acts, quotations or allusions, **33**. 550, **34**. 166, **35**. 355
Adam in, **35**. 531
Apocalypse (Revelation), **32**. 367, 393, **33**. 227, 238, **34**. 124
Apocrypha: Dr Johnson had not read, **33**. 494; quoted, **32**. 113; spurious poetry called, **33**. 317; *see also* 'Bel and the Dragon'
ark in, bilander resembles, **37**. 118
Ashton's epigram drawn from, **14**. 234
ass's rôle in, **22**. 184-5
Assyrian kings in, **35**. 78
Balaam and the ass in, **35**. 30
Baskerville prints, in folio, at Cambridge, **40**. 275
belief is better than demonstration as rule of faith, despite, **35**. 624
bigots think, is always on their side, **32**. 310-11
bishop's thumb worn flat by page-turning in, **37**. 35
Chapone, Mrs, to make fashionable, **28**. 197
Chesterfield's witticism about faith moving mountains in, **24**. 91, **38**. 155
Churchill asks Cts of Coventry a question about, **20**. 367

[Bible, *continued*]

Chute puns on 'zeal of thine house' in, **35.** 29–30

'coals of fire' in, **35.** 190

Conway paraphrases, about man living by bread alone, **37.** 124

Cooke wants novel edition of, without punctuation, **15.** 301, **20.** 185–6

Corinthians: Markham's text from, **29.** 157; quoted about law, **35.** 573

Daniel: Conway refers to, **37.** 106; HW quotes from, **23.** 236

daughters of Zion in, **39.** 379

draught of fishes in, **35.** 301, 464, 522

Du Deffand, Mme, cites, **3.** 88, 128, 332, **4.** 36, 112, 274, **5.** 89, **6.** 347

—— quotes, **4.** 48, 124, **5.** 223, **7.** 207, 214

—— recommends, to HW, **6.** 447

—— to read, **6.** 116

Ecclesiastes in, **4.** 48

English clergy often read, in services, with no regard to punctuation, **20.** 186

epistles, quoted or alluded to, **32.** 43, 385, **33.** 154, 305, 379

Esdras, quoted by Hillier and Conway, **43.** 217

Exodus: HW alludes to, **30.** 275; Mason gives list of gems set in ephod as described in, **28.** 273

Ezekiel: Chesterfield finds prophecy in, **35.** 218–19; Hardinge quotes, **35.** 563

footman's misreading of, **32.** 268

Fox, H., thinks, enjoins forgiveness, **37.** 363

furnishes texts for every sect, **3.** 155

Genesis: figleaf and Babel in, **35.** 531; flood in, imitated by HW, **35.** 228; HW alludes to, **30.** 72, 309; HW does paraphrase from, **28.** 220, **30.** 207; HW jokes about goat on ark in, **39.** 294; Joseph in, **40.** 246; parodied in *New Lesson for Pope*, **18.** 34–6; quotations and allusions, **32.** 94–5, 208, **33.** 237, 469, **34.** 116, 138, 199, **35.** 335, 520, 531; *see also* Adam; Eve; Methusaleh; Noah

Good Samaritan, Mason's altar-piece of, **35.** 527

gospels: deists do not know, **42.** 448; parchment MS of, owned by Jamesone, **40.** 285; quoted or alluded to, **32.** 35, 166, 304, **33.** 38–9, 149, 278, 319, 457, **34.** 43, 214, and *passim*; *see also* Luke; Mark; Matthew

Gothic paintings have scenes from, **35.** 409

Gray alludes to, **13.** 229, **14.** 14, 22, 25, 129

Gunning, Miss, wants to swear innocence on, **11.** 201

Gustav III takes oaths on, **23.** 436

HW alludes to, **12.** 47, **13.** 90, 250

HW alludes to lions and lambs, doves and serpents in, **33.** 395

HW alludes to loaves and fishes in, **38.** 335

HW calls, Mason's law-book, **29.** 273

HW does not imitate Jeremiah in, though English imitate the Jews, **24.** 484

HW mentions, **12.** 47

HW paraphrases: about driving money-changers from the temple, **23.** 511; about trusting in princes, **23.** 349; genealogies in, **23.** 400; verse in, **25.** 262

HW parodies, **17.** 491–3, **18.** 148

HW prays for peace of Jerusalem but fears Pharisees and Sadducees in, **25.** 27

HW quotes, **9.** 102, 297, **10.** 228, **15.** 129, **17.** 209, 495, **18.** 248, 466, **21.** 261, **23.** 236, 531, 555

HW's allusions to: cripple who takes up bed and walks, **22.** 311; Egyptians and Red Sea, **39.** 342; Egypt's plagues, **25.** 582, **39.** 418; Elijah's mantle, **24.** 455; E. L. Mann's mistresses as Rachel and Leah, **22.** 242; gifts of Magi, **23.** 320–1; guiding star, **25.** 409, 417; Joshua and walls of Jericho, **37.** 543; Palm Sunday, **25.** 640; pool of Bethesda, **24.** 187, **38.** 226; seals of book in Revelation, **25.** 106; Sermon on the Mount and money-changers, **25.** 287; stone, casting of the first, **23.** 158

HW's mock sermon parodies, **31.** 423–6

HW will swallow, if guilty, **33.** 159

Habakkuk, misquoted, **32.** 163, **35.** 560

Herodias and John the Baptist in, **35.** 163

Hillier quotes, from Vulgate, **16.** 92

Holdernesse, Cts of, swears on, **32.** 70

Hutchinsonians seek ties in, between Old and New Testaments, **35.** 156

Israelites and golden calf in, resembled by England, **24.** 481

Jeremiah; HW paraphrases, **31.** 11; HW quotes, **43.** 245

Johnson, Dr, does penance by reading 200 verses of, **33.** 493

Joshua's grapes and tribe of Isaachar in, **32.** 207–8

Judges alluded to, **33.** 25, 304

Kings, alluded to, **34.** 123

*London Gazette* is, to Mann, **24.** 216, 249

Luke: (?) misquoted by Mann, **43.** 260; quoted by Chute, **35.** 62

Magdalen and Pharisee the most beautiful story in, **33.** 38

Mann mentions HW's superior knowledge of, **18.** 9

—— paraphrases sentence in, about sinner that repenteth, **25.** 23

miracle in, of walking on the sea now equalled, **22.** 333

Mark: HW paraphrases parable of sower in, **39.** 173; HW quotes, **39.** 14

Matthew: HW alludes to passages in, **28.** 72, **29.** 198, **31.** 402; HW paraphrases, **11.** 15, **30.** 45; HW paraphrases passage in, on camel and needle's eye, **39.** 174; HW refers to fish and stone in, **38.** 100

Montagu quotes, **10.** 80, 178, 197

More, Hannah, wishes HW would study, **31.** 399

morocco binding for, **31.** 399

Moses's rod in, **35.** 256

New Testament: Bentley's proposals for new Greek edition of, **15.** 294; Luther aimed to restore, to good sense in essentials, **31.** 435; Porter, Stephen, translates passage from, **16.** 224

oath on: **12.** 47; footman ready to take, as witness, **33.** 298; HW will take, **34.** 225; Ossory, Lady, may take, **32.** 385; Stone and Murray take, **20.** 361

Old Testament: Dr Johnson writes in spirit of, **15.** 149–50; Gray's allusions to, **28.** 169; patriarchal families in, with flocks and animals, **37.** 289–90

Oxford, E. of, collects prints from, **17.** 358

Patapan does not read, **35.** 48

Paul, St, accused of madness, **35.** 462

Peter, quoted by Mason, **29.** 39

prodigal son and fatted calf in, **35.** 225

Proverbs: **32.** 191; HW misquotes, **23.** 198

Psalms: Ashton paraphrases, **14.** 234–5; Chute quotes, **35.** 60–1; HW alludes to, **30.** 213, **35.** 79; HW falsely attributes quotation from Matthew to, **30.** 45; HW paraphrases, **18.** 466, **25.** 20, **28.** 206, **29.** 208, **31.** 23, 306, 347, **32.** 145, **33.** 105, 445, 447; HW puns on, **35.** 308; HW quotes, **12.** 262, **28.** 380, **35.** 348; Mason paraphrases, **29.** 119; Mason quotes, **29.** 258; Montagu quotes, **43.** 133; More, Hannah, quotes, **31.** 211; reading-glass used by HW's grandfather to begin, **37.** 181; scraps of, on Glastonbury chair, **35.** 106; Twickenham choir squalls, **34.** 115; Vernon quotes, **17.** 76n

Revelation, book of: beasts in, **31.** 52–3; **35.** 322; foretells present era, **23.** 169; HW paraphrases, **18.** 129–30; see also Apocalypse

Ruth in, **35.** 14

Samson in, **35.** 558

Samuel: HW alludes to Philistines and Dagon in, **35.** 617; HW quotes, **38.** 558

scripture histories from, depicted in bow window, **32.** 75

Septuagint in, **35.** 79

Solomon and the lilies of the field in, **35.** 461

sons of Anak in, **18.** 248, **39.** 379

style of, well imitated by Billingsgate, **30.** 33

Surrey's versions of Psalms and Ecclesiastes from, **42.** 368

Ten Commandments: Fourth, interpreted by HW, **31.** 261, 434–7; HW's reflections on, **31.** 365

texts from: at St-Cyr, **10.** 293; on Castle Ashby's balustrades, **10.** 336

Vernon quotes, **35.** 29–30

Voltaire demolishes, **31.** 92

—— may be trying to show the likeness between fable and, **5.** 411

Vyne's stained glass has scenes from, **35.** 641

Wager quotes, **17.** 333

Waldegrave, Cts, quotes, **36.** 286

weeping and wailing in, **35.** 32

widow's mite in, **40.** 322

Wilson's edition of, given by HW to Hannah More, **31.** 399

Ximenes's, in Pinelli sale, **42.** 240

See also: Adam; Adam and Eve; Aholah and Aholibah; Ananias and Sapphira; Ashtaroth; Dagon; Greek Testament; Hezekiah; Jeremiah; Jezebel; Job; Medes and Persians; Paul; Samson; Second temple; Tubal

Bible, Court. See 'Red Book'

*Bibliotheca Britannico-Hibernica. See under* Tanner, Thomas

*Bibliothecæ apostolicæ Vaticanæ . . . catalogus. See under* Assemani, Stefano Evodio

*Bibliothecæ Cantabrigiensis ordinandæ methodus quædam. See under* Middleton, Conyers

*Bibliotheca eruditorum præcocium. See under* Klefeker, Johann

*Bibliotheca Maphæi Pinelliana. See under* Morelli, Jacopo

*Bibliotheca Ratcliffiana:*

Christie's sale catalogue of John Ratcliffe's library, **40.** 236n

*Bibliotheca Stoschiana:*

appearance of, at Lucca and Florence, **21.** 151n, 187n

*Bibliotheca topographica Britannica,* ed. John Nichols:

Cole's opinion of, **2.** 272

HW corrects note in, on his alleged picture of Bosworth Field, **42.** 289

HW's copy of, **43.** 73

HW's genealogical reference to, **12.** 267

HW wishes Stavely portraits from, **42.** 289–90

Peterborough's poem on Cts of Suffolk printed in, **42.** 87

Bibliothèque (table). *See under* Table

*Bibliothèque de Cour:*

owned by Mme du Deffand, **8.** 35

*Bibliothèque des génies et des fées. See under* La Porte, Joseph

*Bibliothèque des romans. See Bibliothèque universelle des romans*

Bibliothèque du Roi (King's library in Paris):

Barthélemy curator of medals in, **5.** 108

—— secures MS from, to copy miniature for HW, **7.** 199

books from SH Press given to, **3.** 72, 260n, 262–3, 263, 268, 297, **36.** 280–1, **41.** 57–9, 64, **43.** 84–5, 370

Duclos leaves vacancy in, **5.** 209

fires not permitted in, **15.** 108

HW and Mariette visit, **7.** 311

HW and Selwyn visit, **7.** 323

HW stays in, till after dark, scanning prints and medals, **39.** 236

keepers of, **3.** 262n

La Vallière treasures bought for, by Louis XVI, **42.** 93

Magnan clerk in, **18.** 548n

[Bibliothèque du Roi, *continued*]
Maupeou borrows MS trial from, **39**. 151
medals in, **5**. 108n
Ormesson claims to have seen an old Horace Walpole in, **36**. 283
—— thanks HW for gift of SH editions to, **42**. 357
prints and medals in, **7**. 358
St-Simon's *Mémoires* may be at, **5**. 88
Bibliothèque Nationale. *See* Bibliothèque du Roi
*Bibliothèques françaises de la Croix du Maine et du Verdier. See under* Grudé de la Croix du Maine, François
*Bibliothèque universelle des romans*:
*Amadis de Gaule* in, **25**. 487n
Du Deffand, Mme, advises HW to subscribe to, **6**. 308, 316
—— no longer subscribes to, **6**. 396, 400
—— reads, **7**. 107
——'s opinion of, **6**. 396, 400, 471, **7**. 111, 180
HW's set of, **7**. 10, 229, **43**. 100, 101, 368
HW to have numbers of, **6**. 399–401, 408–11, 415, 436, 439, 453, 454, 456, 471, 473, 476, 481, 494, 496, **7**. 5, 8, 10, 14, 16, 18, 38, 43, 58, 60, 63, 67, 69, 70, 75, 82, 91, 97, 108–9, 121, 126, 128, 151, 171, 180, 183, 196, 203, 213, 227–31, 250, 253, 451, **36**. 195, 207, 214, 220, 223, 242
story of Eleanor of Aquitaine in, **28**. 477–8
Tressan continues, **7**. 121, 126
Bibreck. *See* Biebrech
Bicester:
Mason to visit, **29**. 84n
Bicêtre, Paris mad-house:
'Angola, P. of,' put in, **38**. 405n
Bichi, Marchesa. *See* Corsini, Anna Maria; Lanci, Hieronyma (d. 1743)
Bichi, Marchese Francesco (b. 1676):
Mann tells, that churches are conducive to colds, **20**. 228
Sansedoni lives with, **20**. 228
Bickerstaffe, Isaac (ca 1735–?1812), dramatist:
*Hypocrite, The*, Hertford asks HW about licensing of, **39**. 113
*Lionel and Clarissa*, 'Oldboy' in, **43**. 181
*Love in a Village*: at Covent Garden, **33**. 98, 100; performed, **2**. 156n
*Love in the City*, altered by Lloyd to *The Romp*, played by Mrs Jordan, **34**. 51
Bickerton, Jane (1644–93), m. Henry Howard, 6th D. of Norfolk:
message from Nell Gwyn to, **1**. 350
Bickerton, Sir Richard, naval officer:
*Terrible* commanded by, **39**. 307
Bickerton, Sir Richard (1727–92), army officer:
captures reported by, **24**. 464n
Bickham, George (?1684–1769), 'George Johnson'; engraver:
Cole calls attention to, **1**. 45
(?) print by, of Langton, **1**. 176
Bickham, George, jr (d. 1758), engraver:
print by, of Barnardiston, **1**. 188

Bicknell, Alexander:
Bellamy's *Apology* said to be edited by, **33**. 462n
Bidault, Jean-Baptiste (d. 1788), lawyer:
(?) judgment on, in Goëzmann case, **6**. 23
*Biddeford*, English ship:
Barnett captain of, **18**. 15n
Biddel, Thomas, P. of Wales's coachman:
(?) son forbidden by, to marry maid of honour, **18**. 232
Biddulph, ——:
Meget's inn, at Florence, visited by, **25**. 612n
Biddulph, Francis (d. 1800), banker in Charing Cross:
subscription with, for relief of French prisoners, **42**. 453n
Biddulph and Cocks:
banking firm of, **42**. 453
Bīdpaī ('Pilpay'), collection of Hindu stories:
HW refers to, **14**. 169
Biebrech:
Conway encamped at, **37**. 143–4
Bieganski, ——, Marie Leszczyńska's confessor:
banished by parliament but may return, **38**. 339
Bielitz, Ds of. *See* Mnizech, Louise (b. 1745)
Bielitz, D. of. *See* Sulkowsky, August Casimir (1729–86)
Bienassise, Antoine-Charles-Jacomel de (1712–99), commandant at Calais, 1773:
house of Lady Fenouilhet desired for, **5**. 366, 372, 373, 398
*Bienfaisant*, English ship:
American news brought by, from Halifax, **32**. 397
Dunn a lieutenant under Capt. Balfour of, **38**. 265n
Ross goes to Plymouth with, **25**. 25n
Bientina, Lake (Italy):
Regency to make, overflow into Lucca, **20**. 515
Bièvre, Marquis de. *See* Mareschal de Bièvre, Georges-François
Bifleet. *See* Byfleet
Bigamy:
Kingston, Ds of, may be burnt in the hand for, **24**. 25, 31, 123, 196
—— undoubtedly guilty of, **24**. 193
Walpole, Sir Robert, refuses to have Nugent prosecuted for, **17**. 271n
*See also under* Chudleigh, Elizabeth
Bigby, Mrs:
funds for appeal of, **23**. 264n
Bigendian heresy. *See under* Swift, Jonathan: *Gulliver's Travels*
Biggin, ——:
Orford, E. of, said to entertain, at High Beech, **25**. 596n
Biggs, John:
arrested for riot, **23**. 74
Biggs, Robert, naval officer:
*Lively* commanded by, **39**. 308
Bighouse, Sutherlandshire:
Mackay of, **14**. 115n

Bigio, F. *See* Francabigio, Francesco

Biglia, Antonio (ca 1708–55), Abp of Corinth, 1754; nuncio to Florence, 1754:
appointment of, **20.** 445, 446
edicts of, to curb clerical licentiousness, **20.** 458
Florence reached by, **20.** 445n
Mann to call, 'Signor Biglia,' **20.** 446
Richecourt entertains, **20.** 446
Santo Spirito convent the lodging of, **20.** 446
secretary of, **20.** 465

Bignon, Armand-Jérôme (1711–72), King's Librarian:
(?) HW keeps, till dark, when seeing Bibliothèque du Roi, **39.** 236
leaves vacancy in Académie française, **5.** 234

Bignon, Jean-Paul (1662–1743), Abbé:
*Aventures d'Abdalla, Les,* owned by Mme du Deffand, **8.** 33

Bigod, Hugh (d. ca 1177), cr. (1140 *or* 1141) E. of Norfolk:
(?) HW quotes verses by, **37.** 406

Bigod, Hugh (fl. ca 1220):
(?) HW quotes, **37.** 406

Bigod family:
HW does not forget, **42.** 422

Bigot; bigots:
HW's reflections on, **32.** 310–11

Bigot de Morogues, Sébastien-François (1706–81), army officer:
invasion plans made by, **21.** 264n

Bilander; bilanders (Flemish boat):
Conway conveys released English prisoners in, **37.** 208
—— travels in, **37.** 118
Dutch troops in, lost, **37.** 205

Bilboquet (game):
HW tries to replace whist with, **18.** 204
out of fashion in Paris, **40.** 385

Bile:
Chute's, observed by doctor at Marseille, **35.** 25

Bilious attack:
occurrence of, **39.** 507

Bilious cases:
occurrences of, **33.** 321, 449, **36.** 258, 259, 262, 263, 328, **42.** 395

Bilivelt, Jacques:
ebony coffer by, **23.** 407n

Bill; bills, Parliamentary. *See under* Parliament: acts and bills of

Billard du Monceau, ——; caissier des fermes des postes:
bankruptcy of, **4.** 356, **5.** 190–1
execution of sentence on, **5.** 190
Grisel's connection with, **4.** 402
Jesuits expected to protect, **5.** 190

Billarderie. *See* La Billarderie

Billaud-Varenne, Jacques-Nicolas (1756–1819):
National Convention addressed by, **12.** 27n

'Billebaude':
hunting term, used by Conflans, **21.** 357

Billeraye, M. de, valet-de-chambre:
news received by, **28.** 461n

Billerey, ——, French chargé d'affaires at Florence:
(?) courier leaves orders with, **24.** 369
(?) French Court orders, to avoid Mann, **24.** 375n
(?) French naval news through, **24.** 408
name of, corrected, **43.** 286
(?) Piccolomini gets threatening French order from, **24.** 508n
(?) threat conveyed by, to Leopold, **24.** 505

Bill Hill, Hurst, Berks; Cts Gower's seat:
Leveson Gower, Adm., dies at, **31.** 374n
Mason visits Cts Gower at, **33.** 407n
Montagu, Mrs Charles, visits, **10.** 306

Billiard; billiards:
at Goodwood, **32.** 204
Dorset engrossed by, in Paris, **36.** 215n
played, **6.** 161
Poix, Princesse de, plays, **5.** 186

Billiard room:
at Crewe Hall, **10.** 96
at the Vyne, **35.** 639
La Borde's house has, **31.** 80

Billiard sticks:
HW's, with which Sidney played with Cts of Pembroke, **39.** 294

Billingford, Rev. Richard (d. 1432), Master of Corpus Christi College:
print of, on his tomb, **1.** 188, 190

Billingford, Norfolk:
Tindal rector of, **15.** 253n

Billingham, Charles (fl. 1653):
*Garden of Eden* published by, **28.** 275n

Billingham Manor, Southend, Blackheath:
Falkland's home, **41.** 298n

Billingsgate (place):
Marlibrunus dwelt at, **1.** 317, 321, 323
oyster women of, **11.** 89

Billingsgate (style of invective):
author of additions to HW's *Lessons for the Day* writes in, **30.** 33
Biblical style well imitated by, **30.** 33
Dart writes, against Cromwell and regicides, **35.** 146
Dublin orators excel in, **35.** 379
French transmit memorial in, **37.** 429
HW will scold like, **33.** 47
in new *Morning Post,* **32.** 332
Kingston, Ds of, uses, **24.** 126
Parliamentary dialogue in, **25.** 27
philippics reminiscent of, **35.** 262
Pitt and Temple probably used, to each other, **30.** 226
Scaliger and Scioppius use, **41.** 51–2
used by fishwomen of Paris, **34.** 72
Yorke, Charles, cannot be victim of, **23.** 179

Billingsley (Billingsly), Mr:
SH visited by, **12.** 224, 225

Billingsley, S.:
*Trial of . . . Earl Ferrers* published by, **21.** 407n

Bill of exchange; bills of exchange:
 Compagni and Libri to furnish, **17**. 422–3
 Conway will return with, **39**. 181
 tax on, **25**. 254n
Bill of health; bills of health:
 required before entry into Florence, **18**. 288
 Young Pretender gets, **18**. 376
Bill of Lading; bills of lading:
 captains of men-of-war never give, **18**. 234
 Cosby, Mrs, signs, for portraits, **10**. 103
 for Aleatico and Verdea wine, **23**. 215, 279
 for Bianca Cappello's portrait, **20**. 398
 for Chute's altar painting, **20**. 529
 for Cocchi's books, **20**. 438
 for Fox's vases, **21**. 118, 123, 132, 134
 for Fox's wine, **21**. 164, 187, 189, 304, 309
 for gesse figures, **19**. 34, 66, 79
 for HW's cases: **26**. 5–6; Mann sends, to Oswald, **17**. 31
 for HW's drams, **19**. 238, 246, 353
 for HW's liqueurs, **21**. 220, 225, 231, 309
 for HW's pamphlets, **18**. 354
 for Herculaneum and Caserta volumes, **21**.
  324, **22**. 547, 555, 559, 561, 562, **23**. 109
 for Hertford's drams, **21**. 69, 133
 for Lyttelton's vases and gesso statues, **20**.
  539, 577, 582
 for Patch's engravings from Masaccio, **23**. 276
 for Patch's views and iris roots, **23**. 333
 for pedestal, Medici prints, and burlettas,
  **21**. 521, 533, 538
 for Santini's watch, **21**. 322
 for Van Dyck's alleged painting of Clinton,
  **25**. 501
 HW encloses, **17**. 302
 HW expects, **18**. 210
 HW had better give, to James Mann, **21**. 164
 HW should carefully guard, **21**. 225
 Mann has examined, **17**. 68
 —— to send, to Cts of Holdernesse, or Hobart, **19**. 438
 —— warns HW against loss of, **21**. 220
 Tuscan merchants' names on, **21**. 269
Bill of mortality; bills of mortality:
 verses in style of, **9**. 11
 Windham declaims about, **30**. 56
Bill of rights:
 supporters of, **23**. 92n
'Billy.' *See* William Augustus, D. of Cumber-
 land
Bilton:
 Blackburne prebendary of, **29**. 19n
Binding; bindings:
 cost of, **1**. 35
 Florentine, **25**. 507
 gilt, HW removes, for postal purposes, from
  Bonducci's translation, **17**. 64
 HW's, uniform for his copies of SH editions,
  **41**. 467
 Irish, **9**. 418, **10**. 13, 16, 18
 of *Ædes Walpolianæ*, **9**. 89

Ormesson admires, on HW's gifts to Bibliothèque du Roi, **42**. 357
 red turkey leather, **18**. 126–7
 *See also* Bookbinding, Irish
Bindley, James (1737–1818), collector; commissioner:
 album formerly owned by, **43**. 106
 believes in Ireland's MSS, **15**. 321
 collection of modern medals sold by, **16**. *301*
 HW allows, to bring 5 to SH, **41**. 440–1
 HW asks, for medal of Czarina Elizabeth, **41**.
  350
 HW's correspondence with, **41**. 349, 350,
  440–1
 HW thanks, for print of Mme de Bury, **41**.
  350
 HW to lend *Wits Commonwealth* to, **41**. 350
 (?) HW to show ample materials to, **41**. 349
 lives at Somerset House, **16**. 301
 Nivernais's *Jardins modernes* given to, **12**. 259
 Pinkerton might ask, about medal, **16**. 301
Bindley, John (d. 1786), M.P.:
 HW confuses, with brother, **16**. 301n
Binet, Gérard (ca 1711–80), Baron de Marchais:
 *anglomanie* of, **24**. 266
 at Versailles, **6**. 49, 56
 death of, **7**. 456
 Louis XV's valet-de-chambre, **6**. 49
 Louis XVI attended by, **6**. 299
 ——'s valet-de-chambre, **24**. 266
 marriage of, **6**. 43n
Binfield, Berks:
 Macaulay, Mrs, lives at, **42**. 63n
Bingham, Lady. *See* Smith, Margaret (d. 1814)
Bingham, Hon. (later Lady) Anne (1767–
 1840):
 birth date of, **43**. 147
 engagement of, broken, **11**. 243
 mother teaches, **24**. 417
Bingham, Sir Charles (1735–99), 7th Bt; cr.
 (1776) Bn, and (1795) E. of Lucan:
 at Hampton Court, **43**. 345
 attends play at Ham Common, **33**. 370
 baron's patent expected for, **32**. 293
 Beauclerk gives commissions to, **6**. 373
 Berkeley, Cts of, talks with, about Nugent,
  **24**. 418
 created earl, **12**. 152
 daughter of, **11**. 243n, **12**. 202n, **25**. 104, 613n,
  632n
 (?) daughter resembles, **25**. 104
 Du Deffand, Mme, given concerts by, **6**. 356–
  7, 363, 366
 —— receives letter through, **7**. 423
 —— sends letter through, **7**. 157, 159
 ——'s opinion of, **6**. 330, 356, 358, 363, 371
 —— sorry, is not to come to Paris, **7**. 32
 ——'s relations with, **6**. 366, 371, 373, 375
 family of, revisit Florence to see Mann, **24**.
  462
 Florence visited by, **24**. 417

HW entertains, at breakfast at SH, **39**. 390

HW persuaded by, to write epilogue to *Braganza*, **32**. 233

HW prints *Muse Recalled* to please, **35**. 362

HW's affairs interest, **6**. 373

HW's neighbourhood visited by, **24**. 517

HW's old acquaintance, **24**. 417

HW's relations with, **24**. 475

HW to talk with, **6**. 373

house of, in Charles St, Berkeley Sq., **33**. 138n

Italian purchases not to be sent home by, till peace, **24**. 462

Italy to be visited by, **6**. 373

leaves Paris, **7**. 423

Mann praised by, **24**. 517

—— to entertain, at dinner, **24**. 462–3

mistake made by, concerning Dance's portrait of HW, **15**. 318

niece's fortune nursed by, **33**. 506n

Paris may be visited by, **7**. 13, 28

—— not to be visited by, **7**. 71

—— visited by, **7**. 157, **32**. 293

races attended by, **6**. 366

(?) sarcophagus from Rome to be presented by, to HW, **24**. 462

social relations of, in England, **33**. 246, 253, 254, 264, 370

social relations of, in Paris, **6**. 330, 335, 371

son to be left by, at Neufchâtel, **24**. 462

son to be visited by, in Paris, **36**. 192

to leave Paris, **6**. 371, 372, **7**. 157, 159

to return to Paris, **6**. 373

Voltaire's *Mémoires* brought by, from Paris to HW, **39**. 414

Walpole, Hon. Thomas, might send things from Paris by, **36**. 192

wife of, **11**. 37n, 29. 104n

wife's leadership followed by, **24**. 475

Bingham, Lady Elizabeth. *See* Belasyse, Lady Elizabeth

Bingham, Hon. Lavinia (1762–1831), m. (1781) George John Spencer, styled Vct Althorp 1765–83; 2d E. Spencer, 1783:

Althorp, Lord, dines at table with, **33**. 254

arrives in England, **25**. 632

artistic talents of, **24**. 417, **25**. 613

bistre used by, in drawing, **41**. 119n

charms of, **33**. 253–4

engagement of, **25**. 104, 108

(?) father resembles, **25**. 104

Florence visited by, **24**. 417, **25**. 620

HW entertains, at breakfast at SH, **39**. 390

HW's nuptial ode for, **33**. 260–1

Hamilton, William Gerard, leaves bequest to, **12**. 202

Italy visited by, with husband, **25**. 613n

Jones, William, writes nuptial ode for, **33**. 287–8, **35**. 362n

Mann receives Sèvres piece from, **25**. 645

—— saw, with her mother and cousin, **25**. 620

(?) Marie-Antoinette chooses miniature of, **6**. 349

marriage of, **25**. 632n, **33**. 249–50

mother recommends, to HW as artist, **41**. 419

mother teaches, **24**. 417

music studied by, **24**. 462

not handsome but well qualified, **25**. 108

singing of, **33**. 138–9

(?) sings for Mme du Deffand, **6**. 357, 363, 366

verses not by, **34**. 131

Vesuvius ascended by, **33**. 509

Bingham, Hon. (later Lady) Louisa (d. before 1803):

Althorp, Lord, dines at table with, **33**. 254

mother teaches, **24**. 417

singing of, **33**. 138–9

Bingham, Hon. (later Lady) Margaret (1767–1839), m. (1784) Thomas Lindsay:

artistic taste of, **24**. 417

mother teaches, **24**. 417

music studied by, **24**. 462

(?) sings for Mme du Deffand, **6**. 357, 363, 366

Bingham, Hon. Richard (1764–1839), styled (1795) Lord Bingham; 2d E. of Lucan, 1799:

father to leave, at Neufchâtel, **24**. 462

father to see, in Paris, **36**. 192

Marie-Antoinette chooses miniature of, **6**. 349

measles attack, **36**. 192

mother of, **12**. 76n

rustic schoolboy, **24**. 462

Bingham family:

Florence revisited by, to see Mann, **24**. 462

HW sends compliments to, but does not want their gifts, **24**. 475

HW's nuptial ode for, **33**. 260–1

HW's praises from, may not be sincere, **24**. 422

HW surprised by early arrival of, at Florence, **24**. 422

Bingley, Bn. *See* Benson, Robert (ca 1676–1731); Fox Lane, George (ca 1696–1773)

Bingley, Bns. *See* Benson, Harriet (ca 1705–71); Finch, Lady Elizabeth (ca 1679–1757)

Bingley, William (ca 1738–99), bookseller in the Strand:

prosecuted as Wilkes's publisher, **23**. 29

*North Briton* of, **15**. 128n

Binks, Mr, a Quaker:

advances of Mrs Tracy to, **14**. 202

Binning, Bn. *See* Hamilton, Charles

Binning, Bns. *See* Baillie, Rachel (1696–1773); Hope, Sophia (1759–1813)

Binns, Anne (ca 1681–1777), m. (1725) Sir John Shadwell, Kt:

Conway meets, **37**. 46

death of, **24**. 282–3

HW meets, at Court, **17**. 185

Mann knew, in Florence, **24**. 283n

Biographer; biographers:

HW suggests conciseness to, **33**. 466

*Biographia Britannica*:
account of Pope in, **29.** 278
Bentley genealogy to be corrected in, **35.** 204
Boyle's writings listed in, **15.** 26–7
Chatterton's life in, **16.** 212–14, 360, **31.** 326
Codrington's life in, (?) read by HW, **35.** 178
first edn of: account of Browne Willis in, **1.** 263; HW censures, **2.** 92–3, 98, 187–8; Kippis censures some articles in, **2.** 187–8, 353
Gray finds, uneven, **14.** 62
HW calls, 'Vindicatio Britannica,' **15.** 147
HW comments on Hayley's life of Crashaw in, **15.** 201–2
HW denies accusation against his father in, **15.** 147–8
HW's copies of, **43.** 66
Holles's trial inaccurately reported in, **40.** 187
Kippis threatens to be severe on Sir Robert Walpole in, **15.** 147
second edn of: attack on Church of England in, **2.** 190n; article on Sir Robert Walpole in, **2.** 117; Baker's life and comments on him in, **2.** 71–2, 73, 78, 80, 82, 87–8, 93, 106, 129, 341–44, 346–7, 348, 350, 353; Barrington's life in, **33.** 470; blunder in, **2.** 202–3; Cole on, **2.** 190, 190n, 195–7; Cole refuses to aid Kippis in, **2.** 11, 12, 71–2, 73, 93, 191, 196; HW on new articles in, **2.** 120–2, 186–8; note to life of Dr Bentley in, mentions Gray, **29.** 9; remarks on Walpoles in, **2.** 88, 92–3, 95, 96, 98, 187, 190n, 343; reviewed in *Gentleman's Magazine*, **2.** 108
*Biographia dramatica. See under* Baker, David Erskine
*Biographia literaria. See under* Berkenhout, John
*Biographia Scotica. See under* Erskine, David Steuart
*Biographical and Literary Anecdotes of William Bowyer. See under* Nichols, John
*Biographical Anecdotes of William Hogarth. See under* Reed, Isaac; Steevens, George
*Biographical History of England. See under* Granger, Rev. James
*Biographical Memoirs of Extraordinary Painters*:
reviewed in *Gentleman's Magazine*, **2.** 229
Biography:
HW's reflections on, **15.** 179–80
Biord, Jean-Pierre (d. 1785), Bp of Annecy (Geneva), 1764:
Voltaire thought by Mme du Deffand to have been excommunicated by, **7.** 46
Biot:
Brown assembles forces at, **19.** 336
Birabi. *See* Biribi
Birback *or* Birkback, English agent at Marseille:
Mann sends letters in care of, **22.** 166n, 170n
Birch, Mrs:
SH visited by, **12.** 245
Birch, Edward (d. 1772), convict:
hanged at Tyburn, **32.** 73

Birch, Rev. Thomas (1705–66), D.D.; antiquary; historian:
agrees with HW about Robertson, **15.** 62n
biographical sketches by, **15.** 96n
Bower's alleged perfidy proclaimed by, **20.** 533
death of, **1.** 107, **7.** 397
HW's correspondence with, **9.** 227n, **40.** 127, 134, 356–9, 360
HW's materials from, for *Lord Herbert of Cherbury*, **40.** 356–9, 360
HW's opinion of, **2.** 186, 196, 332
HW visited by, to discuss *Royal and Noble Authors*, **40.** 127
Hardwicke's letter from, **43.** 170
Hatton's dancing mentioned in Anthony Bacon's papers published by, **33.** 256n
*Heads of Illustrious Persons of Great Britain* by, **1.** 207n, **16.** 324, **40.** 365, **43.** 47
*Life of . . . Dr John Tillotson* by, **2.** 359, **14.** 62, **20.** 282n, **28.** 30
*Life of Henry Prince of Wales*, **16.** 140, **33.** 416–17
Oglethorpe thought by, to be ignorant of his profession, **19.** 321n
preferment of, **1.** 107
Swift's MS of *Four Last Years* thought by, to be in Swift's hand, **21.** 185n
zealous but simple, **20.** 533
Birch, William (1755–1834), enameller and engraver:
SH visited by, **12.** 244
Birch, pendulous:
HW mentions, **21.** 113
Bircham, Norfolk:
living of, **23.** 510, **32.** 141, **36.** 95
Birch-bark:
Dalrymple's elegy printed on, **15.** 58
Birckmann, Arnold:
designs by, for 'Dance of Death,' **42.** 432n
Bird, Mr:
Amelia, Ps, barred from property of, **20.** 322–3
Caroline, Q., given ground by, at Richmond Park, **20.** 323
Bird, Lt–Col. John:
Peekskill expedition of, **24.** 306n
Bird, William (fl. 1657–87), stonecutter:
method of colouring marble invented by, **16.** 35–6
Bird, William (d. 1743), keeper of St Martin's roundhouse:
acquittal of, **17.** 504n
Bird, William (b. 1755):
lent money by Ewin, **2.** 35
Percy, Bns, has affair with, **24.** 378n
Bird; birds:
aeronauts resemble, **33.** 458
attracted by special trees and shrubs, **16.** 190
cardinal, Duchesse de la Vallière's, **5.** 245
chimney boards depicting, by Barlow, **10.** 345
Cibber compares Pope to, **30.** 310n
Clermont's paintings depict, **35.** 79n
concert of, **40.** 283

eggs of, *see under* Egg
HW goes 'a-birds'-nesting,' **32**. 66
HW likes, **31**. 68
HW prefers, to men, **5**. 346
HW's, **3**. 76, 80, 105, **4**. 77, **31**. 36
HW sends, to Duchesse de la Vallière, **5**. 123, 125, 126, 128, 129, 134, 141, 151–2, 155–6, 159, 160, 171, 211, 215, 220, 224, 229–30, 234, 236, 245, 342, 346
in Kensington Gardens, **10**. 206
in menagerie at Osterley, **32**. 126–7
ivy to be torn from tower to repel, **35**. 135
Johnston, Lady Cecilia, has, **35**. 474
Lort wants, in garden, **16**. 190
Montagu feeds, **10**. 111
nests of, **32**. 329
owl described as sacred, **37**. 52
painting of, by Bogdány, **10**. 334
singing, at Cts of Strafford's, **35**. 275n
stuffed: auction of, **23**. 210; Tylney collects, **24**. 312n
tapestry, used as targets, **23**. 254
transportation of, **5**. 129, 134
wild, at Horton, **10**. 334
*see also* Aviary; Bantam; Bird of paradise; Blackbird; Bluebird; Bullfinch; Canary; Cock; Cockatoo; Cormorant; Crane; Crow; Cuckoo; Cygnet; Dabchick; Didapper; Dove; Eagle; Falcon; Finch; Fowl; Game; Goldfinch; Goose; Grouse; Hawk; Hen; Heron; Humming-bird; Kite; Lark; Luri; Macaw; Martin; Nightingale; Ostrich; Owl; Parakeet; Parrot; Partridge; Peacock; Pelican; Perroquet; Pewit; Pheasant; Phœnix; Pigeon; Poultry; Pullet; Quail; Raven; Robin; Sparrow; Stork; Swan; Thrush; Turkey; Turkey-cock; Turkey hen; Turtle-dove; Vulture; Woodcock; Wood-pigeon
Bird-cage:
in Gloucester Cathedral pew, **35**. 154
Bird-cherry. *See* Cherry
Bird-nesting:
young army volunteers take to, **38**. 34
Bird of paradise:
Augusta, Ps of Wales's, and Ps Augusta's emblem, **38**. 204
fables about, **11**. 22
Biribi; biribis (game):
fashionable in Paris, probably of Italian origin, **38**. 267
HW plays, at Reggio, **17**. 46
played in Paris, **6**. 388, **7**. 302
Birkback. *See* Birback
Birkett, Isabella (ca 1631–1703), m. John Shorter:
HW's great-grandmother, **28**. 24n
Birkhead, Mrs. *See* Dixon, ——
Birmingham, Warwickshire ('Birgingham'):
Albany, Countess of, at, **11**. 343n
Baskerville editions from, **21**. 262
—— writes from Easy Hill at, **40**. 274
big enough to be a European capital, **11**. 288

Boulton and Westwood of, **39**. 552
counterfeit coinage from, **31**. 277, **33**. 528
Croft writes to, about plated silver for Mann, **24**. 27
Gordon, Lord George, arrested at, **33**. 588n
HW visits, and finds it 'swarms with people and trade,' **35**. 147
Hill, Robert, tailor at, **21**. 289n
iron prices might be raised by, **38**. 101
Mann writes to Munro at, about plated silver, **24**. 32
Mason to travel through, **28**. 429, **29**. 259
millers and engrossers riot at price of wheat at, **20**. 585n
Parliament urged by, to enforce American acts, **24**. 77
Presbyterian hotbed, **34**. 182
Priestley's house at, burnt, **31**. 385
(?) ——'s 'warehouse' at, **42**. 304
'Repeal, The,' indicates American trade of, **22**. 400
Revolution Society at, **31**. 385n
riots at, **11**. 313n, 314–15, 317–20, 345, **15**. 244, **31**. 361
steel industry of, competes with Woodstock, **17**. 302n
Warburton proposes edition of Pope to be printed at, **13**. 38
wishes war with colonies because of arms trade, **6**. 146, **24**. 77
withering of, **36**. 257
Wolverhampton near, **40**. 42
Birmingham shilling. *See* Birmingham: counterfeit coinage
Biron, Comte de. *See* Gontaut, Armand-Louis de (1747–93); Gontaut, Charles de (1562–1602)
Biron, Comtesse de. *See* Boufflers, Amélie de
Biron, Duc de. *See* Gontaut, Armand-Louis de (1747–93); Gontaut, Charles de (1562–1602); Gontaut, Louis-Antoine de (1700–88)
Biron, Duchesse de. *See* Boufflers, Amélie de (1751–94); La Rochefoucauld de Roye, Pauline-Françoise de (1723–94)
Biron, Maréchal de. *See* Gontaut, Louis-Antoine de
Biron, Maréchale de. *See* La Rochefoucauld de Roye, Pauline-Françoise de
Biron, Ernst Johann (1690–1772), D. of Courland; Anne of Russia's favourite:
Catherine II restores, to Courland duchy, **22**. 118
HW compares Sir Robert Walpole to, **18**. 467, 481, **30**. 63
HW curious about fate of, **22**. 59
HW imagines Bestuzhev passing, on way to Siberia, **10**. 39
HW jokes about, as Houghton neighbour, **17**. 495
Poland interested in restoration of, **22**. 118–19
son of, in Bastille, **4**. 7

Biron, Karl Ernst (1728–1801):
in Bastille, 4. 7
Biron family:
French Revolution swallows up, 11. 86, 39. 475
'Biron voulut danser':
to be played at Guines's ball, 32. 102
Birrell, A.:
engravings by, 15. 139n
Birt, Samuel (d. 1755), bookseller:
(?) anecdote about Chapman and, 33. 247
Birth:
HW's reflections on, in relation to merit, 30. 131
Birtha, Bp of. See Talbot, James (1726–90)
Birthdays, royal: balls on, regulated by lord chamberlain, 39. 322; see also under names of monarchs, princes, etc.
Birth of Mankind:
Raynalde publishes, with copperplate cuts, dedicated to Q. Catherine, 40. 306
Birtles, John (d. ?1765), English consul at Genoa 1740–60:
consul at Genoa, 20. 283n, 364
Corsican purchase expected by, 18. 229, 240
England receives naval news from, 18. 540
Genoa assures, of friendship to George II, 20. 575
—— reassures, about safety of English merchants there, 19. 65
Genoese courier to be sent by, to Turin, 18. 375
Genoese plea to France reported by, 20. 429
HW and Lincoln to be entertained by, 17. 92
HW does not believe information from, 20. 283
Haddock informed by, of Spanish invasion, 17. 305
Leghorn visited by, 19. 76
Mann hears from, of mission to Genoa, 20. 283n
—— quotes letter from, 19. 237
——'s correspondence with, 17. 103, 19. 65, 20. 277
—— sends letters through, to HW, 17. 94, 96–7
(?) ——'s letter detained by, 17. 100
—— told by, of French demands on Genoa, 20. 277
Mari presented with memorial by, 18. 546n
Montagu, Lady Mary Wortley, dislikes, 17. 98, 103–4
Rowley tells, to leave Genoa when it gives aid to Spanish army, 19. 65
Spanish fleet's arrival reported to, 17. 306
Stone said by, to have betrayed dispatches, 20. 364–5
Villettes's correspondence with, 19. 65
Bisagno (Italy):
Austrian artillery fortifies, 19. 401, 417
Bisagno, valley of:
Genoese mob joined by people of, 19. 343

Biscay, Bay of (Gulf of Gascony):
British arm withdraws from, 7. 158
French ships from, captured by English, 19. 411
Orvilliers approaches, 7. 158
Biscay province, France:
privileges of, for Newfoundland fishing, demanded by Spain, 38. 120
Biscuit; biscuits:
Du Deffand, Mme, eats, 7. 243
England sends bags of, to Portugal, 20. 512n
HW serves, at SH parties, 10. 69, 33. 530, 39. 447
Louis XVI takes, with lemonade, 31. 372n
rebels send, to Carlisle, 37. 211
Selwyn sups on, 6. 132
served at Versailles ball, 32. 256
Spanish army lives on, 19. 35
See also Naples biscuit
Biscuit porcelain:
HW jokes about statues of himself in, 31. 100
Bisham, Berks:
Hoby monuments in church at, 9. 101
Bisham Abbey, Berks:
Cholmondeley rents, 9. 101
HW visits, 9. 100, 43. 116
Montagu visits, 9. 100
Salisbury, Earls of, buried at, 9. 100
Bishop, ——:
Kingston, Ds of, has, as proctor, 24. 193n
Bishop, (?) Edward, actor; dancer:
arrives in Paris, 6. 55
Du Deffand, Mme, aids, at HW's request, 6. 28–9, 31n, 45, 46, 51, 55, 77, 160, 36. 105–7
health of, mended by Dr Jebb and bark, 36. 105
Pont-de-Veyle aids, 6. 29, 31, 46, 51, 55
social relations of, with HW, 7. 344
success of, 6. 160
Walpole, Sir Edward, solicits favour towards, 6. 28n, 36. 105–7
See also Bisshopp
Bishop; bishops. See under Church of England; Church of Ireland; Church of Scotland; Roman Catholic Church
Bishop Auckland, Durham; Bp of Durham's seat:
(?) Bentley's designs for, 35. 644
Manchester visits, 9. 310
Trevor, Dr Richard, alters, 9. 310
Bishop Bonner's Ghost. See under More, Hannah
Bishopp. See Bishop; Bisshopp
Bishop Parker's History. See under Parker, Samuel
'Bishoprick':
Caroline, Q., makes malapropism about, 23. 313n
Bishopsgate:
St Botolph's Church in, 20. 164n
Bishopsgate St, London:
Black Bull Inn, in, 2. 47n, 260n

Cambridge wagon leaves from, **1**. 262, 263, **2**. 47, 259, 260n, 262

HW mentions, **20**. 397

Le Gros and Le Cras merchants in, **40**. 87

London Tavern in, **23**. 114n

Macaronies will adjourn to, **35**. 334

St James's Church in, **2**. 198n

Bishopthorpe Palace, York:

Markham, Bp, invites Mason to, **28**. 316

Bishopwearmouth:

Bland rector of, **13**. 4n

Bisset, Maurice George (ca 1757–1821), army officer:

Worsley, Lady, leaves husband for, **25**. 228

Bissextile:

Grifoni, Mme, frightened by, **18**. 405

Bisshopp, Anne (ca 1729–1803), m. (1759) Hon. Robert Brudenell:

'beauty daughter,' **35**. *300*

Cardigan's marriage disappoints, **11**. 241–2

Charlotte's Household to include, **9**. 377, **38**. 97

engagement of, **9**. 140

(?) HW calls Sabbatini's attention to, **9**. 82

HW's nephew not to marry, **9**. 140

(?) Richmond's fireworks attended by, **9**. 82

(?) Spencer loves, **37**. 359

subscription masquerade attended by, in vast beauty, **20**. 49

Bisshopp, Catherine (1744–1827), m. 1 (1767) Sir Charles Cope; m. 2 (1782) Charles Jenkinson, cr. (1786) Bn Hawkesbury, (1796) E. of Liverpool:

'beauty daughter,' **35**. 300

Bisshopp, Sir Cecil (d. 1778), 6th Bt, 1725; M.P.:

children of, **9**. 82n, 140n, 269n, 377n, **11**. 242n, **28**. 453n, **33**. 68, **35**. 300

HW buys house of, **33**. 65, 68, **34**. 250–2

Spain never visited by, **35**. 300

Bisshopp, Charlotte (ca 1731–62), m. (1751) Sir William Maynard, 4th Bt:

'beauty daughter,' **35**. *300*

Edward Augustus favours, **9**. 269

French ballads sung by, at Rochford's, **9**. 269

(?) HW calls Sabbatini's attention to, at Richmond's masquerade, **9**. 82

Bisshopp, Edward (d. 1792):

HW's suit over Berkeley Sq. house of, **34**. 250–2, **35**. *602*

Bisshopp, Frances (d. 1804), m. (1764) Sir George Warren, K.B.:

at private court ball, **38**. 143

(?) 'beauty daughter' at Chudleigh ball, **35**. *300*

Charlotte, Q., may include in Household, **9**. 377, **38**. 97

HW mentions, **9**. 402, 403, **10**. 7

marriage of, **38**. 233

Bisshopp, Harriet (d. before 1825), m. 1 (1766) Thomas Dummer; m. 2 (1790) Nathaniel Dance (later Holland), cr. (1800) Bt:

'beauty daughter,' **35**. *300*

(?) Chudleigh ball attended by, **35**. 300

Bisshopp, Hugh:

money left to, **34**. 250–2

Bisshopp, Susanna Sophia (b. ca 1759):

money left to, **34**. 250–2

Bisshopp, Col. Thomas (ca 1737–1805):

HW's suit with, over Berkeley Sq. house, **33**. 109, **34**. 250–2, **35**. 602

Bisson, ——, draper in Paris:

Du Deffand, Mme, has receipt from, **8**. 41

Bissy, Comte de. *See* Thiard, Claude de (1721–1810)

'Bistina.' *See* Uguccioni, Giovanni Battista

Bistre:

Beauclerk, Lady Diana, draws in, **35**. 426, 41. 322

Bingham, Hon. Lavinia (Cts Spencer) draws only in, **41**. 419n

Bitcher, ——:

Mann corresponds with Tempi about Maria Meroni's affair with, **20**. 219n

Bitonte, Duc de. *See* Carrillo de Albornoz, Duque de Montemar

Bitonto:

Montemar's return from, **17**. 427

Bizzarri:

Mann entertains, **17**. 104

Blachford, John (d. 1759), sheriff of London and Middlesex 1745–6:

inquiry into Maidstone affair and triennial Parliaments requested by, **21**. 12n

Kilmarnock's speech to, **19**. 300

Black, John (d. 1761), chaplain of Hampton Court Palace and of Conway's First Dragoons:

death of, in Germany, **38**. 104n

Mirepoix plays chess with, and gets him chaplaincy, **38**. 104n

'Blackacre, Widow.' *See under* Wycherley, William

'Black-and-All-Black,' horse:

HW alludes to, **32**. 131

Blackberry; blackberries:

constellations like, **33**. 569

'Black Bess' (?Dick Turpin's mare):

sent to Newgate, **42**. 503

Blackbird; blackbirds:

HW deprived of, by bad summer, **32**. 359

Lort wants, in garden, **16**. 190

sing at SH despite eclipse, **38**. 362

Twickenham militia learning exercise on, **33**. 8

*Black-bird's Tale and Black-bird's Song*:

in book of ballads, **32**. 200n

'Black Book of Taymouth':

excerpt from, **40**. 264–5

Blackbourne, Bishop (nonjuring):

Rawlinson consecrated by, **42**. 239n

Blackbourne, Capt.:

news brought by, **32**. 387n

Blackbrook Farm, Weeford, Staffs:

Wyatt, James, born at, **41**. 323n

Black Bull Inn, Bishopsgate St, London:

Cambridge wagon sets out from, **2**. 47, 260n

Blackburn, Lancs:
  Hilton vicar of, 1. 223n
  vicarage of, 1. 223
Blackburne, Rev. Francis (1705–87), latitudi-
    narian; editor of Hollis's *Memoirs*:
  apparently a dissenter, 29. 23, 28
  *Remarks on Johnson's Life of Milton*, Mason
    mistakenly thanks HW for, 29. 143, 144
  simpler than Hollis, 29. 18
Blackburne, Lancelot (1658–1743), Bishop of
    Exeter, 1717; Abp of York 1724–43:
  anecdotes of, 15. 142–3
  buccaneer in West Indies, 7. 368
  Caroline, Q., and, 31. 421
  death of, 18. 201
  George I's will said to be in keeping of, 2. 127
  Hayter said to be natural son of, 20. 246, 43.
    197
  sailors hear sermon by, 7. 369
  sub-deanery at Exeter resigned by, from
    scandal, 20. 246n
Blackburne, Mrs Lancelot. *See* Talbot, Cath-
  erine
'Black cap':
  Frederick, P. of Wales, sends, to dismiss
    Vaughan, 20. 122
Black Castle, Bristol:
  HW describes, 10. 232
Blackerby, Nathaniel (d. 1742), J.P.:
  punishment proposed for, for calling soldiers
    to election, 17. 252
Blackett, Anne (d. 1783), m. 1 John Trenchard;
    m. 2 Thomas Gordon:
  Cole's account of, 15. 311
  friend of Mrs Middleton, 15. 293
  Harris disparages, 20. 167n
  Middleton marries companion of, 20. 167
Blackett, Lady Barbara. *See* Villiers, Lady Bar-
  bara
Blackett, Sir Edward (1719–1804), 4th Bt; M.P.:
  Parliamentary motion by, against denial of
    Parliament's validity, 39. 126
Blackett, Mary Dawes:
  *Suicide* by, inscribed to Cosway, 43. 231
Blackett, Sir Thomas. *See* Wentworth, Sir
  Thomas
Blackett, Sir Walter (1707–77), 2d Bt; M.P.:
  Dresden treaty opposed by, in Parliament, 20.
    299n, 42. 496
Blackett, Sir William (ca 1657–1705), Bt:
  Trenchard, Mrs, daughter of, 15. 311
Blackett, Sir William (1690–1728), 2d Bt; Jaco-
    bite; M.P.:
  birth date of, corrected, 43. 212
  brother of Mrs Trenchard, 15. 293
  wife of, 9. 345n
Blackett, William, sea captain:
  *Great Duchess of Tuscany* commanded by, 25.
    473
  ship of, captured by pirates, 25. 479–80
Blackett, Mrs William (b. ca 1766):
  Slavonian pirates capture, 25. 480
Blackford. *See* Blachford

Blackfriars, London:
  Shakespeare's deed to gatehouse in, 42. 210n
Blackfriars Bridge, London:
  Albion Mills by, 11. 212
  Lord Mayor lays cornerstone of, 21. 449
  Paterson built, 32. 153n
  toll-houses on, pillaged in Gordon Riots, 29.
    56, 33. 188
'Black Friday':
  London's alarm on, 19. 178n
*Black Giles, the Poacher*:
  in 'Cheap Repository Tracts,' 31. 396n
Blackheath, Kent:
  Allen, Vcts, gives dinner at, 35. 94
  Berry, Mary, avoids, 12. 134
  Cardigan, Cts of, lives at, 31. 57, 35. 234
  Falkland writes from, 41. 298
  George II reviews foot regiments at, 17. 410n
  Gloucester's house at, 33. 125, 137
  hanging prevalent on, 20. 65
  Lambarde mentions, 16. 80
  Page's art collection at, 33. 137
  Q. Margaret at, 14. 71
  Stanhope stops at, to call on Chesterfield, 22.
    164
  Tozier's tavern at, 17. 451n
  visitors to: George III, 11. 258n; HW, 35. 234;
    Stanhope, 22. 164
  waters at, curative, 38. 406n
  Whitefield preaches at, 13. 250n
'Black Joke,' tune:
  Catley, Miss, should have sung, 28. 110
  Craon's sonnet on Lady Sophia Fermor to be
    sung in part to, 30. 13
Blackleach, Abraham (d. 1639):
  tomb of, at Gloucester, attributed to Van
    Dyck, 35. 153
Blackleach, Mrs Abraham. *See* Elton, Gertrude
Blacklegs:
  Ossory, E. of, trips up, 33. 502
'Black Lyon,' Salisbury Court, Fleet Street:
  Ward printer at, 17. 83n
Blackman. *See* Blakman
Blackman Street, Southwark, London:
  Horseshoe Inn in, 23. 20n
  King's Bench Prison in, 29. 55n
Blackmore, Sir Richard (d. 1729), physician
    and writer:
  Johnson praises, 29. 97, 111
  William III knighted, 41. 191
Blackmore, Robert, King's Messenger:
  Wilkes arrested by, 38. 197
Black Mountain, Wales:
  visible from Hagley, 35. 148
Black Prince. *See* Edward (1330–76), P. of
  Wales
Black Rod. *See* Gentleman Usher of the Black
  Rod
Black Sea:
  British ships may be sent to, 11. 221, 227
  Catherine II's aggression on, 11. 221, 230
  La Condamine visits, 22. 147n

Russo-Turkish negotiations over navigation on, **23**. 469

Blacksmith:
HW exults as much as, at good news, **38**. 106–7

Blackstock Hill, N.C.:
Tarleton's victory at, **29**. 110n

Blackstone, Mr:
SH visited by, **12**. 229

Blackstone, Sir William (1723–80), judge; Kt; D.C.L.; legal writer:
*Commentaries*, **29**. 36n, **35**. 557
HW ridicules, **29**. 36
Hackman tried by, **24**. 459n
Oxford scholars tried by, **20**. 6n
Salisbury may have quoted, on Arundel Marbles, **16**. 182–3
Tories led by, against expellers of James II, **35**. 613

Blackstone's Warehouse, York St, Covent Garden:
masked ball in, **23**. 476n

Black Swan, Paternoster Row:
Scott, bookseller at, **10**. 349

Black Watch, the:
Sempill's regiment, reaches London, **18**. 236n

'Black Wednesday':
during Gordon Riots, **2**. 224–6

Blackwell, Alexander:
landscaping by, at Cannons, **30**. 61n

Blackwell, Thomas (1701–57), the younger, classical scholar:
life of, in *Biographia Britannica*, **2**. 186, 196

Blackwell & Co., bankers (*see also* Backwell):
draft on, **38**. 259n

Blackwell Grange, Durham:
Allan's private press at, **41**. 351n, **42**. 214n

Blackwood, ——:
Sandwich gives Lely painting to, later bought by HW, **10**. 79

Blackwood, Adam (1539–1613):
poem by Mary Q. of Scots printed in *Works* of, **15**. 107n

Blacow, Rev. Richard (d. 1760), Canon of Windsor:
HW identifies, **28**. 188n

Bladder:
stone in, **37**. 543n, 547n, 549

Bladen, Barbara (b. ca 1733), m. (1771) Col. (afterwards Gen.) Hon. Henry St John:
abigails of, **33**. 224
husband to be accompanied by, to America, **32**. 251
'Mrs St Jack,' **32**. *251*
'porpoise covered with flowers and feathers,' **28**. 403
Selwyn's witticism on 'breastwork' of, **32**. 251

Bladen, Harriet (ca 1735–1821), m. (1767) William Anne Holles Capel, 4th E. of Essex:
Essex to wed, **30**. 241
fortune of, **30**. 241
March and G. J. Williams praise, **30**. 241n
sister of, **28**. 403n

Bladen, Martin (? 1680–1746), Lt-Col.; M.P.:
birth date of, corrected, **43**. 243
Board of Trade member, **37**. 299
*Cæsar* by, Bedford, D. of, used to study, at Blandford, **21**. 374
commissioner for the tariff at Antwerp, **17**. 336
impeachment of, drawn up, **17**. 336
Mathews's friend, **19**. 33n
Parliamentary debate by, on privately-raised regiments, **26**. 14
Walpole, Horace (1678–1757) praises, as 'Hercules,' **26**. 16

Bladen, Col. Thomas (ca 1698–1780), M.P.; deputy governor of Maryland 1742–6:
daughter of, **28**. 403n
daughter to inherit fortune from, **30**. 241
Glastonbury Abbey owned by, **33**. 208

Bladon, Samuel (d. 1799), printer:
arrested, **23**. 280

Bladud, K.:
Polignac, Mme de, might have been presented to, in dirty gown, at Bath, **39**. 449

Blagden (Bladdon; Blagdon), Sir Charles (1748–1820), M.D.; Kt, 1792:
Boswell censured by, **11**. 275
Devonshire, Ds of, visited by, **12**. 214
Farington finds, at HW's, **15**. 319
finds HW worse, **15**. 336
(?) HW dictates letters to, **12**. 184–5
HW visited by, **12**. 92, 198, **15**. 335
illness of, **12**. 59, 77
Italy visited by, **12**. 59, 77
More, Hannah, calls, 'new bluestocking,' **31**. 258
social relations of, with Mrs Montagu, **31**. 258
SH visited by, **12**. 198, 246

Blagnac. *See* Blaignac

'Blagrave, Mrs.' *See* Blague, Mrs

Blagrave, John (? ca 1713–?1787):
wife of, **10**. 266n

Blagrave, Mrs John. *See* Cobb, Anne

Blague ('Blagrave'), Mrs:
Jane Shore's friend, **24**. 162

Blaignac, Comte de. *See* Durfort, François-Aimery de

Blair, Col.:
SH visited by, **12**. 231

Blair, Mr:
Conway's chemist, **39**. 551

Blair, Mr:
SH visited by, **12**. 235

Blair, Rev. Hugh (1718–1800), D.D.; professor of rhetoric:
agrees with HW about Robertson's treatment of Mary, **15**. 62n
Caldwell's engraving of, sought by HW, **42**. 56
*Lectures on Rhetoric and Belles-Lettres*, **33**. 416
letters of, on Erse recitation, **29**. 239
Macpherson's *Fragments* sponsored by, **15**. 69

Blair, Robert (1741–1811), of Avontoun, lawyer:
(?) counsel in House of Lords appellant juris-
diction, 35. 622
Blair, William (d. ca 1781), undersecretary:
(?) at Chesterfield's assembly, 37. 326
Mann gets letter from, from Hanover, 19. 99
——'s tribute from Cts of Orford told to him
by, 19. 99, 119
Blair, William (d. 1841), of Blair, Col.; M.P.:
(?) SH to be visited by, 15. 199
wife of, 11. 250n
Blair, Mrs William. See Fordyce, Magdalene
Blair, Scotland:
rebels raise siege of, 37. 237
Blair Castle, Atholl:
Atholl alters, 19. 106
Young Pretender at, 19. 106
Blake, Lady. See Bunbury, Annabella
Blake, ——:
might order a live sheep for supper at Al-
mack's, 24. 21
Orford, E. of, said to entertain, at High
Beech, 25. 596n
ship sunk by, to see if man can live under
water, 24. 20
Blake, Capt.:
SH visited by, 12. 250
Blake, Andrew, of St Kitts:
daughter of, 1. 240n
Blake, Daniel (ca 1744–63), Dacre's footman:
hanged for murder, 38. 193
Selwyn elicits confession from, 38. 193–4
Blake, John, attorney:
Cross Deep Lodge, Twickenham, occupied by,
42. 481, 43. 363
(?) HW to leave book with, for Bowle, 42. 45
law firm of, 12. 180n, 42. 348n
Shirley builds house to spoil view of, 35. 358n
SH visited by, 12. 237, (?) 240
Blake, Mrs (?) John:
SH visited by, 12. 221
Blake, Joseph:
Carolina plantations of, 33. 51n
Blake, Mary Anne (d. ca 1830), m. Thomas
Bromley, 2d Bn Montfort:
birth of son to, 1. 311n
drives out with Cole, 1. 335
late hours of, 1. 311n
marriage of, 1. 237n, 240
takes Cole to and from Ealing, 1. 311n
Thomas, Sophia, visits, 1. 287
wishes to see SH, 1. 311n
Blake, Patrick (ca 1730–84), 1st Bt; M.P.:
marriage of, 1. 237n, 240
sister of, 1. 237n
Blake, Robert (1599–1657), admiral; M.P.:
Sandwich compared to, 28. 110, 119, 120
winter weather not braved by, 9. 268
Blake, Robert, attorney in Essex Street:
(?) consults HW about executorship, 11. 282
(?) Eriswell and Houghton visited by, seeking 'Catchem,' 39. 489–90, 43. 378–9

(?) HW consults, about Little Strawberry
Hill, 11. 114
HW expects, at SH, 12. 184
HW has business with, 12. 180
HW's correspondence with, 42. 438
HW's lawyer, 12. 180n, 15. 337, 42. 348, 43.
156
HW's will and codicil witnessed by, 15. 337n,
30. 368, 369
HW told by, that Dashwood wants to hunt on
Norfolk estates, 42. 348
(?) SH visited by, 11. 240
SH visitor sent by, 11. 240
Blakeney, J., of Twickenham:
SH visited by, 12. 224
Blakeney, William (1672–1761), cr. (1756) Bn
Blakeney; Lt-Gen.; M.P.; governor of Mi-
norca:
birthday of, 21. 171
Conway permitted by, to sail to Italy on
Nightingale, 37. 313–14
Court attended by, in hackney coach attended
by foot soldier, 21. 24
Dick ordered by, to supply Minorca with salt
provisions, 20. 537
England may yet save, from capture, 20. 570
French attack anticipated by, 20. 529
French transport carries, 20. 581n
gout of, 20. 583, 21. 24
Minorcan roads blocked by, and cattle re-
moved, 20. 567
Minorca's defences confidently described by,
20. 550n
peerage granted to, for losing Port Mahon,
21. 52
red ribbon and barony conferred on, by
George II, 21. 24
said to be confined to his bed during siege,
20. 570n, 21. 24
statue of, in Dublin, 9. 391
Blakiston, Mr:
SH ticket misused by, 12. 226n
SH visited by, 12. 228
Blakiston, Sir Matthew (ca 1702–74), Kt, 1759;
cr. (1763) Bt; lord mayor of London 1760–1:
alderman of London, 20. 261n
Blackfriars Bridge cornerstone laid by, 21. 449
Charlotte, Q., greeted by, 21. 531
independent grocer, 20. 261
Walpole, Sir Robert, pardons, for smuggling,
20. 261n
Walpole pictures bought by, 20. 261, 268
Westminster independent electors led by, 20.
261n
Blakiston. See also Blackstone
Blakman, John (fl. 1436–48), fellow of Merton
College, Oxford:
account of Henry VI by, 14. 78
Blamire, Richmond (d. 1797), stationer:
Gilpin's book to be obtained from, 29. 278
Blamont, François Collin de (1690–1760), com-
poser:

(?) *Caractères de l'amour* by, parodied by Pont-de-Veyle, 14. 151
Blanc, Le. *See* Le Blanc
Blanchard, Mrs:
SH visited by, 12. 239
Blanchard, Jean-Pierre (1750–1809), aeronaut:
birth date of, corrected, 43. 356
flight of, in balloon over English Channel, 25. 527n, 33. 458–9
Lunardi's rival, 25. 543
Orford said to entertain, at Blackheath, 25. 596n
visible in balloon, 35. 631, 39. 423–4
Blanchard. *See also* Blanshard
Blanchefort de Créqui, François de (ca 1624–87), Maréchal de France:
tomb of, 7. 281
Blanckart, Marie-Antoinette-Charlotte de (ca 1732–ca 1790), m. (1774) Louis-Nicolas-Victor de Félix, Comte du Muy, later Maréchal de France:
Du Deffand, Mme, gives account of, 6. 96
finances of, 6. 218
marriage of, 6. *96*
pensions of, 6. 218
Blancmange:
sculptures in, for dessert, 37. 442
Blancmesnil. *See* Lamoignon de Blancmesnil
'Bland, Lady' (possibly a joke):
Rigby would defeat, at whist, with little ceremony, 30. 54
Bland, Miss:
HW shows SH Press to, 9. 215–16
Bland, Anne (ca 1718–86):
survives brothers, 9. 215n
Bland, Dorothy (1761–1816), called 'Mrs Jordan'; actress; William IV's mistress:
acts at Richmond theatre, 34. 51
Clarence, D. of (William IV), keeps, 11. 368, 12. 142, 151
Ford, Richard, acknowledges, as wife, 11. *352, 368*
HW has not seen, 33. 507
HW will not talk much of, 33. 514
Hobart, Mrs, gets letter from, 34. 143
poorly cast in *Richard Cœur de Lion*, 33. 546
proposed performance of, at Richmond, 12. 142, 151
rôles of, 43. 357
Bland, Elizabeth:
survives brothers, 9. 215n
Bland, Henry (d. 1746), D.D.; Dean of Durham; headmaster and provost of Eton:
Anstey's epigrams to be shown by, to Sir Robert Walpole, 40. 25
chaplain to Chelsea Hospital, 18. 245n
deanship of, 43. 45
Eton headmaster and dean of Durham, 42. 18
Nichols to cite HW on, 42. 21
son of, 13. 4, 36. 3n
translations by, 1. 52, 42. 18
Walpole, Sir Robert, called on by, 18. 244

Bland, Henry (ca 1703–68), D.D.; prebendary of Durham:
HW at Eton refused extra tasks set by, 37. 161
HW's tutor, 13. 4–5
Walpole, Lady, corresponds with, 36. 3, 4
—— gets account of Conway from, 36. 3
Bland, Humphrey (ca 1686–1763), Gen.:
battalions led by, at Fort Augustus, 37. 249n
Conway transmits D. of Cumberland's orders to, to attack rebels, 19. 233n
George II receives, 18. 556
*Military Discipline* by, Bedford, D. of, used to study, at Blandford, 21. 374
rebels dislodged by, at Strath Bogie, 37. 229–30
Bland, Sir Hungerford (ca 1726–56), Bt:
sisters survive, 9. 215n
Bland, Sir John (1722–55), 6th Bt; gambler; M.P.:
(?) at Chesterfield's assembly, 37. 326
birth date of, corrected, 43. 271
Coventrys entertained by, at dinner in Paris, 20. 338
daughter of, 9. 215n
(?) Furnese given dinner by, in lieu of gambling debt, 30. 84
gambles at Twelfth Night, 35. 204
George II honours, 35. 204
HW jokes about affectations of, 30. 86
HW's opinion of, 9. 173
intemperance of, 30. 84
Kippax Park laid out by, without looking at plans, 35. 269–70
letter of, 9. 247
Montfort's bet with, at White's, 35. 258
O'Brien wins fortune from, at hazard, 35. 208–9
Petersham, Lady Caroline, receives candlesticks from, 9. 106–7
Rigby puts, to bed, 30. 84
sisters survive, 9. 215n
suicide of, 9. 172–3, 35. 25, 37. 405
Young, Mr, hired by, 30. 84
Blandford, Marchioness of. *See* Jong, Maria Catherina de (1695–1779); Stewart, Susan (1767–1841)
Blandford, M. of. *See* Spencer, George (1739–1817); Spencer, George (1766–1840)
*Blandford*, English ship:
French capture, 20. 500, 35. 251
return of, from France, 20. 513n
Blandford, Somerset:
army camp at, 37. 476n
Bedford, D. of, studies military books at, 21. 373–4
incident at, 11. 32n
Blandford. *See also* Blandford-Forum
Blandford-Forum, Dorset:
Ayliffe of, 40. 305
rebuilt after fire, 40. 9

Blandy, Francis (d. 1751):
    daughter murders, 20. 312
    Henley disturbed by alleged ghost of, 35. 71
Blandy, Mary (ca 1717–52):
    execution of, 20. 317, 37. 342
    father murdered by, 20. 312, 314
    forfeited property of, goes to Gislingham
        Cooper, 9. 142, 37. 348
    Henley disturbed by alleged ghost of, 35. 71,
        37. 348
Blaney. See Blayney
Blanford. See Blandford
Blanket; blankets:
    Ferdinand of Naples tosses Florentines in, 23.
        254
    fustian, 32. 193–4
    HW uses portmanteaus and saddles for, 18.
        315
    Orford suggests tossing Lucas in, 25. 322, 328
    Parliament members wrapped in, 38. 326
Blankett, Capt. John:
    Thetis commanded by, 25. 480n
Blank verse:
    metaphysical poems in, fashionable, 37. 261
Blanshard, Wilkinson (1734–70), M.D.:
    Cambridge doctor, with Yorkshire estate, 38.
        442
    HW recommends, to Hertford, 38. 442, 447,
        40. 364
    Hertford to see, in Paris, 38. 465, 466
Blaquiere, Lady. See Dobson, Eleanor
Blaquiere, John (1732–1812), Col.; cr. (1784)
    Bt, and (1800) Bn de Blaquiere; secretary of
    British embassy in Paris:
    courier of, reports on HW's birds, 5. 229
    Du Deffand, Mme, compares Stanley with, 5.
        137
    —— hears of Hon. T. Walpole from, 5. 109
    —— may send letter through, 5. 110
    —— sees no other Englishman than, 5. 153
    —— sends letter through, 7. 40
    ——'s opinion of, 5. 137, 189, 212. 7. 16
    duel of, 5. 334
    Gazette article on Cts Waldegrave discussed
        by, 5. 92–3
    Guines's affairs discussed by, 7. 341
    HW informed by, about Mrs Abington, 41.
        215
    HW mentions, 5. 324
    HW to receive parcel through, 5. 264, 266
    Harcourt's letter from, 5. 87n, 43. 92
    name of, corrected, 43. 92
    opens Irish budget and mentions absentee
        tax, 32. 161
    social relations of, in Paris, 5. 91, 92, 95, 98,
        101, 6. 496, 7. 16, 26, 341, 342
    son born to, 7. 16
Blaquiere, Mrs John. See Dobson, Eleanor
Blaquiere, William (1778–1851), 3d Bn de
    Blaquiere, 1844:
    birth of, 7. 16

Blaru, Marquis de. See Tilly, François-Bonaven-
    ture de
Blasini, English vice-consul at Leghorn:
    Crowe's trunks sealed by, 20. 1n
Blassac, Comtesse de. See Chauvelin, Louise-
    Philippe de
Blast upon Blast. See Roome, Edward: Dean
    Jonathan's Parody
'Blatant Beast.' See under Campbell, Caroline
    (1717–93), Cts of Ailesbury
Blathwayt, William (d. 1717), William III's
    secretary of state:
    Dyrham Park built by, 40. 11n
Blathwayt, William (1688–1742):
    Dyrham Park, seat of, 40. 11
Blavet, Abbé Jean-Louis (1719–1809):
    Dalrymple's memoirs translated by, 6. 316n
Blaxham. See Bloxam
Blaye, government of:
    St-Germain declines to ask for, 6. 251
    vacant through Lorges's death, 6. 251
Blayney, Bns. See Cairnes, Mary (d. 1790)
Blayney, Cadwallader (1720–75), 9th Bn
    Blayney:
    Dacre to see, 9. 415
    England visited by, from Ireland, 9. 415
    HW may send parcels to Montagu by, 9. 415,
        10. 1
Bleak (fish):
    unsuccessful angler catches, but nobody will
        touch it, 25. 464
Blecheley; Blechley. See Bletchley
Blechinden, Lydia (ca 1712–43), widow of
    Thomas Blechinden:
    (?) HW glad to serve Bedford because of,
        40. 41
Bleeding (medicinal):
    by leeches, 17. 48
    Du Deffand, Mme, made more ill by, 6. 105
    during confinement, 7. 95
    Egremont resorts to, to counteract overeating,
        22. 158–9
    Electress's death probably caused by, 18. 172
    Eyre rejects, 18. 201
    following concussion, 4. 248
    foot lanced for purpose of, 24. 79
    for: bump on the head, 3. 56; cold, 2. 207,
        5. 179, 7. 15, 18. 200, 213; cough, 2. 317,
        318; fever, 3. 10, 371, 372, 4. 206, 369, 374,
        6. 100, 472–3, 17. 463, 18. 200, 213, 321, 19.
        247, 357; fit, 18. 109; gout, 3. 125, 6. 134,
        232, 233; hemorrhage, 3. 372; influenza, 25.
        297; insanity, 33. 166; palsy, 21. 15; rheu-
        matism, 19. 250; throat trouble, 3. 99
    gout might be brought on by, 24. 188, 190
    HW cured of cold without recourse to, 22. 42
    HW tells Mann to have, on brother's death,
        22. 237
    harmful when used for miliary fever, 19. 467
    Mann avoids, 18. 139, 24. 188, 190
    —— cured by, 20. 56

—— uses, to induce gout in feet, **24.** 457
not a gouty symptom, **25.** 570
not recommended in gout, **2.** 317
performed 7 times in 6 days, **7.** 101
Rider's almanac discusses time for, **30.** 34
treatment of illnesses by, **1.** 76, **2.** 317, 318,
    **3.** 10, **4.** 369, 374, 381, **6.** 180, **10.** 10, 147,
    **12.** 202, 214, 271, **14.** 84, **17.** 340, **18.** 109,
    200, 213, 321, **19.** 357, **20.** 56, 237, **21.** 62,
    **22.** 42, 288, 313, 331, 413, 430, 466, **23.** 91,
    215, **24.** 193, 442, **25.** 102, 112, 280, 297,
    317–18, 547, 560, **28.** 179, 348, **29.** 249, **31.**
    82, **36.** 116–17, **38.** 334, 363, **39.** 525
White's gamblers oppose, for dying man, **20.**
    185
wholesome in spring, **35.** 220
Bleeding:
    from breast or stomach, **25.** 560, 567, 570
    from foot, **3.** 330, **4.** 50, **7.** 95
    *See also* Blood, effusion of
Bleinheim. *See* Blenheim
Blemwell, Mr (fl. ca 1645), painter:
    Lely's friend, **1.** 372
Blencowe, John (ca 1720–77):
    (?) geldings preferred by, to antiquities, **10.**
        76
    (?) hay crop of, **9.** 194
    (?) Montagu not to tell HW's plans to, **10.** 76
    (?) —— often rides to visit, **10.** 111
    (?) —— to accompany, to Cheshire, **9.** *194*
*Blenheim*, English privateer:
    *Novum Aratrum* captured by, **21.** 288n
*Blenheim*, English war ship:
    Dodd and Whaley visit, at Spithead, **40.** 8
Blenheim, battle of:
    Conway and Scott visit site of, **39.** 538
    eagles of, on Marlborough's teaspoons, **21.** 221
    Hostun captured at, **18.** 563n
    Jersey victory worth more than, to HW, **25.**
        111
    Marlborough at, **11.** 105n
    obsolete, but country tales survive, **21.** 295
    standards of, hung in Westminster Hall, **25.**
        337
    SH remote from, **39.** 196
    Tallart captured at, **21.** 381n
    Tories' situation altered by, **40.** 12
Blenheim Palace, Oxon, D. of Marlborough's
    seat:
    Austrian Archduke and Archduchess ill-
        treated at, **33.** 531
    Beauclerk, Lady Diana, ill at, **32.** 77
    Bedford, Ds of, not invited to, by daughter,
        **38.** 177
    Berry, Mary, admires, **12.** 100
    bridge at, **9.** 289, **10.** 309
    Brown's landscaping at, **39.** 435
    cascade at, **10.** 309
    Cerretesi taken to, by Venetians, **18.** 166
    Craven, Lady, sends play to, **34.** 27
    ——'s epilogue spoken at, **32.** 92n

furniture of, **9.** 289
gardeners at, **10.** 309
HW compares to auctioneer's palace, **9.** 289
HW dislikes, **39.** 435
HW passes, without stopping, **9.** 120
HW to visit, **9.** 285
inscriptions at, **9.** 289
Kirtlington Park near, **11.** 201n
landscape effects at, **9.** 289, **29.** 285n, **39.** 435
maids at, perform as dancers, **38.** 462
Marlborough summons brother to, **38.** 327
mentioned in connection with Gunning affair,
    **11.** 197–9, 201, 220
Montagu does not see, **10.** 309
—— to inspect house near, **9.** 239
observatory at, **33.** 531n
Pope should prescribe what to say at, **40.** 12
tapestry at, **9.** 18, 18n
theatre at, **34.** 4
Vanbrugh might use Francavilla statues at,
    **21.** 480n
—— predicts 'glorious ruins' from, **40.** 350
visitors to: Austrian Archduke and Arch-
    duchess, **33.** 531; Beauclerk, Lady Diana,
    **32.** 77; Bedford, Ds of, **33.** 522n; Berry,
    Mary, **12.** 100; Cerretesi, **18.** 166; Christian
    VII, **23.** 57n; Dodd, **40.** 12; Élie de Beau-
    mont, **38.** 461; HW, **9.** 6, 289; Hardwicke,
    **10.** 309; Mason, **28.** 44–5; Montagu, **10.**
    309; Orange, P. and Ps of, **12.** 203; royal
    family, **36.** 246n; Spencer, Lord Henry, **11.**
    198n; Whaley, **40.** 11–12
York, D. of, entertained at ball at, **38.** 462
Blenheim St, London:
    Bond St near, **10.** 159
    Wilmot, Mrs, lives in, **10.** 158–9
Blennerhassett, William (d. ?1765), writer:
    (?) Ducarel told by, that HW was coming
        to town, **40.** 259
    *New History of England* by, **40.** 259n
Bletchley, Bucks:
    Benson rector of, **1.** 20n
    Cartwright of, **1.** 54
    Cole has living of, **1.** 1n, 106, 334, **2.** 378
    —— joins HW at, **10.** 88n
    —— leaves, **1.** 121–2
    ——'s garden at, **2.** 320
    drought at, **1.** 14–15
    HW and Chute to visit Cole at, **10.** 84
    HW invited to, **1.** 86
    HW unable to visit, **1.** 88–9
    HW visits, **10.** 332
    near Fenny Stratford, **10.** 84
    Newport Pagnell's distance from, **10.** 332
    routes to, **1.** 37–8, **10.** 85
    snowfall in, in May, **2.** 320
    Tyson in, **2.** 285
    Wood family of, **1.** 242
Bletterie. *See* La Bletterie
'Bleu et Jaune, Mlle':
    HW calls Mlle de Bentheim, in dream, **39.** 4

Blickling, Norfolk:
Buckinghamshire leaves, to daughters, **34.** 190n
church at, **2.** 163, 176
Harbord inherits, **12.** 5
letter more appropriate to, than to SH, **42.** 233
seat of Boleyns and Hobarts, **2.** 32, 163, 165, 176
Bliecastle (Germany):
military actions at, **12.** 26n, 86n
Bligh, Edward (1715–47), 2d E. of Darnley:
Court party joined by, **18.** 159
Woffington, Mrs, kept by, **17.** 176, **30.** 52
Bligh, Hon. John (1719–81), 3d E. of Darnley, 1747, M.P.:
(?) Chiaretta's London visit to please, **18.** 32
daughter of, **11.** 215n
death and will of, **16.** 197, **43.** 220
mausoleum of, **16.** 197
Parliamentary vote by, on privately-raised regiments, **26.** 19
Bligh, John (1767–1831), 4th E. of Darnley, 1781:
witticism by, on armorial supporters on Fitzgerald's chariot, **34.** 177
Bligh, Lady Mary (1768–91), m. (1789) Lawrence Palk, 2d Bt, 1798:
death of, **11.** 215
HW not acquainted with, **11.** 215
Bligh, (naval) Capt. (?) Richard Rodney:
West Indies news brought by, **25.** 220n
Bligh, Lt-Gen. Thomas (1685–1775), Irish M.P.:
Ancram to be associated with, in expedition against France, **37.** 547–8
carelessness of, **9.** 226n
Cherbourg's capture by, **21.** 225–6, 238
Clerk quartermaster-general to, **37.** 574n
Conway's troops perform before, **37.** 336
dragoon colonelcy for, leaves regiment for Sackville, **37.** 220n
expedition against France to be commanded by, **37.** 549
Ferdinand, P., might join, at Paris, **37.** 555
German command no longer goes to, **37.** 547–8
letter from, on St-Malo attempt, **37.** 570
nephew not to be preferred by, **37.** 570
regiment of, **17.** 450n, **40.** 55
Sackville resents army for Germany being commanded by, **37.** 545n
St-Lunaire landing reported by, **21.** 243n
Blincourt. See Hocquart de Blincourt
Blindman's buff:
English keep warm with, **32.** 360
Holdernesse plays, **9.** 145, **20.** 346
Juliana wants to play, **16.** 253
troops must have been playing, **37.** 573
Blindness:
HW's, temporary, in one eye, **30.** 268
occurrences of, **21.** 292, **25.** 385, 562n, 604n,

**36.** 151n; see also under Vichy-Champrond, Marie de, Mme du Deffand
Pitt, Mrs George, threatened with, **23.** 451
Blind people:
gayer than deaf people, **21.** 177
visual descriptions by, **41.** 292
Blisset. See Bisset
Blissmore Hall (Clanville Lodge), Hants:
Seymour-Conway, Hon. Mr and Mrs Hugh, to retire to, **39.** 443
Blister; blisters (medicinal):
application of, **10.** 10, **20.** 551, **25.** 113
complexion improved by, **19.** 31
fever to be eased by, **37.** 94
for gout in face and ears, **37.** 451
for palsy, **21.** 15
George II has, to back of head to aid eyes, **21.** 222n
George III has, for cold, **22.** 42
Gordon has, **17.** 298
Marlborough, Ds, resists, **17.** 235
Medley recovers senses by application of, **19.** 433
Blockade:
French and English rules for enforcing, against neutral ships, **21.** 273–4
HW mentions, **20.** 569
Blockhead:
charade on, **33.** 508, 509, 510
Block Island:
British fleet off, **24.** 229n, 419n
Bloemaert, Abraham (1564–1651), painter:
Poelenburg's first master, **7.** 355
Bloemaert, Cornelius (1603–80), engraver:
father of, **7.** 355
Blois, Bp of. See Lauzières de Thémines, Alexandre
Blois, Cts of. See Adela (ca 1062–1137)
Blois (France):
Burke's son to enter school at, **32.** 103n
court to be held at, **5.** 30n
Du Deffand, Mme, stays in Bishop's palace at, **5.** 240
—— to stay at, **5.** 251
Pezay near, **6.** 499n
Blome, Mme de:
social relations of, with Mme du Deffand, **7.** 431
Blome, Otto (1735–1803), Baron von:
social relations of, with Mme du Deffand, **7.** 429, 430
SH visited by, **12.** 229
Blomefield, Francis (1705–52), topographer:
*Essay towards a Topographical History of . . . Norfolk, An,* by, **1.** 75, 375, **2.** 222, **16.** 4, **20.** 381n, **43.** 47
Blomefield (Blomfield), Capt. Thomas (1744–1822), cr. (1807) Bt:
(?) SH visited by, **12.** 221
Blonay, Louis (fl. 1741–57), Baron de, Sardinian diplomatist:

Charles Emmanuel III sends, with Villettes, to English fleet off Genoa, 19. 64

Bloncal, George, ensign:
captured at Velletri, 18. 492

*Blonde*, French frigate:
in Thurot's squadron, 21. 372

Blonde (lace):
SH does not indulge in, 10. 133
*See also under* Lace

Blondel, ——:
attends session of parliament of Paris, 8. 173

Blondel, David (1591–1655):
Nanteuil's print of, 15. 100

Blondel, Louis-Augustin (1696–living 1760), minister to Austria 1749–51:
(?) Joseph II uses, as pretext to see Turgot, 6. *443*
(?) social relations of: with Mme de Damas, 7. 338; with Mme de Villegagnon, 7. 352
wife of, 11. 99n

Blondel, Mme (?Louis-Augustin). *See* Batailhe de Francès, ——

Blondel de Gagny, Augustin (1695–1776):
sale of effects of, 6. 377

Blondot, Catherine-Thérèse-Élisabeth-Améline (1690–1753), m. (1704) Séraphin Rioult de Douilly, Marquis de Curzay:
Du Deffand, Mme, gives account of, 6. 423–4

Blood, Andrew, army officer:
execution of, 19. 287n

Blood:
circulation of, HW's simile about, 15. 237
HW's cleared by gout, 25. 370
Henry VIII's wives mostly lacked, when buried, 42. 117
issue of, 19. 226
Mann coughs up, 25. 547

Blood, effusion of:
occurrences of, 25. 560, 567

Blood, spitting of:
occurrences of, 22. 520, 25. 322, 30. 55, 59

Bloodhound; bloodhounds:
humans dressed as, for stag-hunt, 37. 340

Bloodstone:
Gray's father's, given to HW by Mason and Brown, 41. 233
'Torcy' of, 35. 86

Blood vessel:
breaking of, 25. 353

Bloodworth (*or* Bludworth), Margaret (d. 1786):
Charlotte, Q., to include, in Household, 9. 377, 38. 97

Bloodworth, Thomas. *See* Bludworth

Bloody flux. *See under* Flux

'Bloom of her wrinkles':
Mann's phrase for Bianca Cappello's portrait, 20. 398

Bloomsbury, London:
Russell St in, 20. 74n

Bloomsbury Sq., London:
Bedford, D. of, gives assembly in, 20. 56n
duel in, 15. 180n
Mansfield's house in, 29. 57n, 35. 505
Wager dies at his house in, 18. 245n
Wilmot in, 29. 268

Blooteling. *See* Bloteling

Blosius, C. (d. 132 B.C.) of Cumes:
Du Deffand, Mme, cites, 3. 85

Blosset, Paul (1728–after 1780), Marquis de, French diplomatist:
ambassador to Portugal, 6. 90
Denmark, not Tuscany, to be post of, 6. 90, 22. 445–6
Lorenzi might be succeeded by, in Tuscany, 22. 346n
social relations of, in Paris, 7. 282, 299

Blot, Baron de. *See* Chauvigny, Gilbert de

Blot, Baronne de. *See* Charpentier d'Ennery, Marie-Cécile-Pauline

Bloteling, Abraham (1640–90):
print in style of, 29. 301n

Blouet, Pierre (ca 1666–1753), Comte de Camilly; French naval officer:
Brest left by, supposedly for Mediterranean, 18. 443

Blouin, Louis (1706 *or* 1710–ca 1775), called Dubois; French actor:
actors refuse to act with, despite Louis XV's order to take him back, 38. 538

Blouin, Marie-Madeleine (1746–79), called Mlle Ainée Dubois:
Fronsac's alleged mistress, 38. 538n
Richelieu induced by, to force her father into theatre, 38. 538–9

Blount, Lady. *See* Aston, Mary

Blount, Col.:
SH visited by, 12. 246

Blount, Sir Edward (d. 1758), 4th Bt, 1717:
Mawley Hall fitted up by, 40. 42
Roman Catholic, 40. 42

Blount, Henrietta (ca 1709–82), m. 1 Peter Proli; m. 2 (1739) Philip Howard:
(?) social relations of, with Lady Blandford, 31. 168

Blount, Martha ('Patty') (1690–1763), Alexander Pope's friend:
Bethel visited by, 33. 511
blue eyes of, 32. 32, 33. 511
death date of, corrected, 43. 293
HW sees, after Pope's death, 33. 511
lack of poetry in Twickenham since death of, 32. *31*
petticoats of, pinned up in rain, 33. 511
Pope's alleged affair with, 32. 32n
——'s letters published by Dodsley not addressed to, 28. 17
——'s poetry addressed to, 32. 32
——'s verses in imitation of Horace allude to, 37. 8

Blount, Mary (ca 1702–73), m. (1727) Edward Howard, 9th D. of Norfolk:
apartment built at Arundel Castle for, **9.** 96
(?) at Chesterfield's assembly, **37.** 326
balls given by, **37.** 50, 352, 454
Bath visited by, **9.** 397, **40.** 89
Bedford, Ds of, talks with, **9.** 338
Brown, Lady, consigns pane of glass for HW to, **40.** 89
Cambridge's elegy written in assembly-room of, **28.** 91
Conway and brother attend supper given by, **37.** 54–5
death of, **5.** 361, **23.** 485
Fuentes, Condessa de, not invited by, **9.** 338
HW and Strafford permitted by, to see Worksop, **35.** 270
HW glad he was not consulted by, about Gothic farm, **37.** 572, 579
HW's correspondence with, **41.** 167–8
HW sends picture to, **41.** 167–8
HW's 'humorous' hair treatment to be used by, **9.** 140
HW's remark to, about mourning desired by her servants, **21.** 165
house of, burnt, **9.** 397
Howard, Charles, of Greystock, on bad terms with, **30.** 241
Lovat's trial may involve, **19.** 381
Mann related to, **20.** 138
marriage of, corrected, **43.** 95
masquerade given by, **17.** 331, 337, 338–9, 343, 368, 370
new house in St James's Sq. opened by, **37.** 438
Norfolk possessions reassembled by, **15.** 114
proposal of, for marriage within family, **32.** 65
rebellion criticized by, in letters shown by Ds of Richmond, **19.** 176
Rockingham's witticism about the fears inspired by, **37.** 438
Roman Catholicism of, prevents her being Ps Louisa's mourner, **34.** 240
royal family entertained by, **17.** 337
social relations of, in England, **9.** 331, 337–8
Strafford avoids third visit to, **37.** 578–9
Sutton, Lord Robert, entertained by, to divert from arsenal, **9.** 97
Terrick might have been ungrateful to, **30.** 209
three Tuesdays to be given by, **37.** 438
Tunbridge visited by, **35.** 270, 280
Worksop's improvements urged by, **37.** 566
Blount, Mountjoy or Montagu (ca 1597–1666), cr. (1628) E. of Newport:
painting of, at Kimbolton, **10.** 78
portrait of, with Goring, at Knole, **35.** 133n
print of, **1.** 181
Blount, Thomas (1618–79), writer:
(?) Boscobel by, **10.** 105n

frontispiece to Academie of Eloquence by, **1.** 179
Blount, Walter (d. 1474), cr. (1465) Bn Mountjoy:
wife of, **14.** 75n
Blount, William (ca 1478–1534), 4th Bn Mountjoy, 1485:
Birch tells Jortin about writings of, **40.** 134
Blow, John (1648–1708), composer:
portrait of, **1.** 149n
Blowes, Mrs:
SH visited by, **12.** 239
'Blowzabel,' song:
popular in Italy, **13.** 201
Bloxam, Rev. John (d. 1519), chaplain:
tomb of, in Addington Church, **10.** 343
Bloxholme; Bloxome. See Broxholme
Bluck, William:
print of, **40.** 236
Bludworth ('Bloodworth'), Thomas (d. 1773), M.P.:
Augusta, Ps of Wales, has, as Master of the Horse, **20.** 245
biographical information on, corrected, **43.** 269
Bludworth. See also Bloodworth
Bluebird; bluebirds:
HW hopes Conway's canary is with egg by, **39.** 103
Blue Boar Inn, at (?) Henley:
flitch of bacon, might be left at, **38.** 71
Bluecoat boys:
Ailesbury, Cts of, might get news of her husband from, **37.** 509
English behave like, **30.** 26
Pentycross was, **2.** 18
Blue Nuns' School, Paris:
Browne, Miss, enrolled in, **9.** 152n
'Blues, the.' See Royal Horse Guards
Bluestocking; bluestockings:
HW is, **34.** 20
HW's dinners for, **33.** 406
Lucan, Lady, has gathering of, **29.** 104, 116
Mason satirizes, **29.** 287
parties for, **31.** 213, 214–15, 223, 227–8, 243
'Bluffe, Capt.' See Congreve, William: Old Batchelour
Blundell, Hon. Mary, m. 1 (1741) Robert Raymond, 2d Bn Raymond; m. 2 (1762) Lord Robert Bertie:
house of, in Berkeley Sq., unroofed, **10.** 14
marriage of, expected, **10.** 14
Blundell, 'Nanny':
'Plato' is said to be in love with, **13.** 173
Blundell, Nicholas (d. 1737), of Crosby Hall:
niece of, **13.** 173n
Blunderbuss; blunderbusses:
footpads carry, **35.** 365
HW carries in chaise, **32.** 249, **39.** 300
HW sends for, **33.** 296
HW's servant armed with, **31.** 234, **35.** 367

HW to arm himself with, for journey, 9. 118

Ham Common play audience armed with, 33. 369

Jones, Henry, pursues burglars with, 9. 133

lawyer fires, at thieves, 32. 77

Maclaine steals, from Eglintoun, 20. 168

'Blunderer':

nickname for Sir Robert Walpole, 17. 234

Blunt, Richard (ca 1706–63), distiller; sheriff of London, 1763:

Cheapside riot described by, 38. 256

Common Council defeats motion to thank, 38. 262

House of Lords hears testimony by, about riot, 38. 257

mobbed, 22. 187

Blyth, F., Cornhill bookseller:

Pentycross's poem published by, 32. 298n

Blyth, Yorkshire:

waiting-woman near, murders bastard, 37. 179n

Blythe, Mr:

Turin visited by, 43. 178

Boadicea (d. 62 A.D.), Q. of the Iceni:

did not mind being tanned, 33. 22

heroines as much forgotten as, 11. 280

name applied to Lady Ossory, 33. 49

Yearsley, Ann, might attribute Dutch tiles to dairymaid of, 31. 326

*Boadicea. See under* Glover, Richard

Boar; boars:

Chinese, with sow, sent by HW to Conway, 37. 345, 347, 349

Florentine, Chute compares, with HW's eagle, 19. 121–2

French princes hunt, 40. 387

German princes hunt, 25. 364

Louis XV shoots, 38. 408

statue of, unhurt in Uffizi fire, 22. 67

wild: HW would roast, alive, without hurting him, 37. 293; hunt for, arranged for D. of York, 22. 221; hunt for, at Diester near Hanover, 20. 200n

*See also* Boar's head

Board, the, Jacobite club:

Gower succeeds Lichfield as president of, 18. 186

meeting places of, 43. 249

moves from Bedford Head, Covent Garden, to St Alban's tavern, to Cocoa Tree, 20. 50n

Board; boards:

Richard III's painting on, 41. 131–2

Board of Trade:

America may be controlled by, 20. 249

American appointments may be shifted from, to secretary of state, 21. 488n

appointments in, 9. 181, 10. 60, 21. 489, 33. 314

Bladen of, 37. 299

Burke's bill would annihilate, 25. 26–7

Dartmouth resigns from, 22. 444

first lord of: Dowdeswell refuses, despite promise, 30. 232–3; Halifax may be succeeded by Dupplin as, 21. 104, 111; Hillsborough becomes, 22. 167; Nugent becomes, 22. 473

Granville may be president of, 20. 249

Halifax resigns from, 30. 135n

——'s salary from, 9. 213

Hamilton a member of, 21. 73–4

Jenyns commissioner of, 15. 331

lord of: Dyson becomes, 38. 377; Germain succeeds Dartmouth as, 32. 276n; Gibbon becomes, 35. 615; Pitt, John, is, 19. 458n; Rice, George, becomes, 21. 489, 490; Robinson, Sir Thomas, becomes, 20. 17; Talbot, Jenyns, and Rigby succeed J. Grenville, T. Pitt, and Edgcumbe as, 20. 517; Thomas, Sir Edmund, becomes, 21. 490; Yorke, John, becomes, 21. 490

Montagu said to be connected with, 9. 105

Montagu, Charles, may have been favoured by, 9. 258–9

Newcastle negotiates with Pitt to regain Halifax for, 21. 111n

North rumoured to succeed Halifax in, 9. 340

plantations might be put under, 20. 259

president of, 20. 249; *see also* first lord of

registers of exports in, searched, 32. 242

returns to former insignificance, 21. 489

Sandys may be head of, 9. 341

—— succeeds Halifax in, 21. 489

Selwyn said to be engrossed in, 33. 136

Shelburne to be head of, 22. 130

Stone commissioner of, 17. 6n

Storer succeeds Walsingham in, but must pay him part of salary, 33. 314

Talbot may succeed Halifax in, 21. 486

Yorke's resignation from, 10. 110

Board of Works:

book owned by, 14. 110

Brown succeeds Harris as paymaster of, 17. 487n

Coronation prepared by, 38. 90n

Selwyn fears for his post in, 33. 169

—— succeeds Onslow as paymaster of, 9. 181, 20. 518

Worsley becomes master of, 21. 460, 24. 428n

Boar's head:

Ford, Ann, gives history of, 9. 338–9

laurels cover, at Christmas, 21. 301, 35. 289, 38. 462

Boat; boats:

army's bridge of, across Rhine, 18. 209n

at Horton, 10. 334

at Richmond, 11. 342, 32. 317n

at Thames regatta, 32. 237, 317n

at Twickenham, 11. 86

Conway cleans his, 32. 314

——'s troops in, on way to French shore, 37. 515

[Boat; boats, *continued*]

Coke, Lady Mary, and Lady Betty Mackenzie take, to SH, **31.** 129

Dutch captains invited to supper in, **37.** 208

Dysart, Cts of, takes HW and his great-nieces in, at Ham House, **39.** 311

flat-bottomed: at Havre-de-Grâce, **21.** 305; August the best month for launching of, for French invasion of England, **21.** 307, **38.** 34, 35; France does not send, against England, **21.** 300; French assemble, at Dunkirk, **20.** 506–8; in Normandy, **21.** 293n, 296n; Rodney burns, **21.** 309; to be disarmed and laid up, **21.** 352n

Florentines use, in flood, **19.** 131

HW and Montagu to take, to SH, **10.** 118

HW tells Mann to go out to sea in, for gout cure, **24.** 311

near Prospect House, **12.** 122

open: for drums and trumpets, **37.** 289; Young Pretender in, **37.** 251

rebels cross Cromarty Firth in, **37.** 232

small, at Liverpool, **38.** 108

statues in, **35.** 55

visible from SH, **20.** 380

Watelet's bridge supported by, **28.** 215

*See also* Barge; Bark; Cockboat; Ferry; Hoy; Packet-boat; Privateer; Ship; Sloop; Wherry; Xebec; Yacht; *and cross-references at end of* Ship *entry*

Boat (utensil):

frankincense ship, **32.** 324

Boatman; boatmen:

at Lerici, refuse to put to sea, **23.** 552

manifest for box at Leghorn brought by, to Mann, **17.** 183

Venetian, abuse Benedict XIV, **20.** 177

Boat race; boat races:

at Richmond, **11.** 337, 341–2, **43.** 150

at Twickenham, **11.** 86–7

Dutch merchants at Leghorn give, for Tuscan Court, **22.** 418, 423

Bobbins:

HW brings, from Paris for Lady Ossory, **32.** 270, 272

of gold, for Lady Ossory's tambour, **32.** 250

Bob cherry walk:

in Mann's garden, **19.** 277

Boboli Gardens, Florence:

amphitheatre in, fête in, for Ferdinand of Naples, **25.** 586

church to be built in, for Pitti palace, **22.** 258

Hewet beats his wife in, until sentinel separates them, **24.** 204

Joseph II has key to back door of, **23.** 112

—— received at, by Leopold and Maria Louisa, **23.** 108

Leopold and Maria Louisa walk in, **22.** 340

Mann escorts Karl Alexander to, **20.** 376

—— frequents, **17.** 77

people prefer, to seeing Mann, **17.** 97

Walpole, Bns, to make door into, from Franceschi's house, **18.** 391

Wright admires ivy in, **21.** 457

Bob periwig. *See under* Wig

Bob wig. *See under* Wig

Boca Chica:

capture of, **17.** 71n

Walpole, Sir Robert, makes joke about, **9.** 235

Bocage. *See* Boccage; Fiquet du Boccage

Bocard. *See* Boccard

Boccaccio, Giovanni (1313–75), 'Boccace':

*Decameron* by, **1.** 248n, **33.** 410, **40.** 374n

long sentences of, **35.** 558

Orford, E. of, appreciates, **25.** 555n

Boccacieca. *See* Boca Chica

'Bocca della verità.' *See* Santa Maria in Cosmedin, Church of

Boccage, Mme du. *See* Le Page, Anne-Marie

Boccage. *See also* Fiquet du Boccage

Boccalini, Traiano (1566–1613), satirist:

HW might have, as proctor, **11.** 21

HW wishes, were alive, **18.** 480

Boccaneri. *See* Bocchineri

Boccano. *See* Baccano

Boccapadugli gardens, at Rome:

marble eagle found near Caracalla's baths in, **19.** 66n

Boccapaduli (Boccapaduglio), ——, faro banker at the Borghese's:

HW jokes about, **30.** 6

Boccard, François-Jean-Philippe de (1696–1782), Swiss officer in French service:

Swiss regiment of, **40.** 92

Bocchetta, La, pass in Italy:

Austrian operations near, **19.** 297, 304, 359

discouraging to travellers, **13.** 230

Gages's drive through, **19.** 58n

Genoese mob seizes, **19.** 343

HW counts mules on, **17.** 91

Bocchineri, Signora. *See* Antinori, Maria Maddalena (1725–1802)

Bocchineri, Domenico Andrea (1712–76):

Antinori daughter to marry, **18.** 435

marriage of, **35.** 53

(?) Strozzi's duel with, prevented, **17.** *111*

wife's affair with procaccia exposed by, to Regency, **20.** 447

Bochart, Jean-Baptiste-Gaspard:

attends session of parliament of Paris, **8.** 171, 172

Bocland, Maurice (d. 1765), army officer:

battalion of, going abroad, **38.** 49n

Boconnoc, Cornwall:

Pitt, Thomas, writes from, **40.** 328, 338

Boconock. *See* Boconnoc

Bocton Malherbe. *See* Boughton Malherbe

Bode, Johann Elert (1747–1826), astronomer:

Uranus named by, **15.** 188n

Bodens, Col. [?Charles (d. 1762)]:

family of, **41.** 241

Bodens, Mrs. *See* Myddelton, Althemia

Bodens, Molly [?Meliora], companion to Lady Burlington:

Hartington asked by, about ministry, **35.** 165

perhaps Meliora Boden, **43.** 361

Bodens. *See also* Bowden
Bodice; bodices:
laced, worn by Lady Mary Wortley Montagu, **22**. 3
Bodie *or* Bode, (?) James, Capt. in Turkish service:
news brought by, to Malta, **23**. 227, 232
Bodiham, Sussex:
Beckley near, **9**. 326
'Bodkin, bare':
Shakespeare's use of, **41**. 295, 373
Bodleian Library, Oxford:
catalogue of, **1**. 249, **16**. 140
Charles I's and Christ's portraits in, **9**. 114, 34. 179
Du Deffand papers at, **36**. 312
Elizabeth, Q., author of MS at, **40**. 296–7
HW asks if *Licia* is in, **40**. 301
HW gives *Anecdotes* to, **2**. 248n
Owen persuades Bowle to give Q. Elizabeth's MS to, **40**. 305
Rawlinson's bequests to, **42**. 239n
Saxon book in, **40**. 248
transcript of Thomas's MS in, **1**. 271n
Bodley, Sir Thomas (1545–1613):
Haistwell's etching of, **42**. 53n
Stone's monument to, **1**. 7n
Bodoni, Giambattista (1740–1813), Italian printer:
Berry, Mary, describes, **11**. 150n
*Castle of Otranto* edition printed by, **11**. 150, 15. 212–13, **31**. 369, **35**. 436
Bodrhyddan, Flintshire:
Stapleton of, **41**. 253n
Body-coach:
HW jokes about Onslow's, **37**. 378
Boehm, ——:
balloon lands in field of, near Sunbury, **39**. 424n
Boehm, Edmund (ca 1702–81), merchant:
address carried by, in riot, **10**. 273
(?) 'Buckhorse' feared by, **10**. 273–4
East India director, **25**. 490
(?) merchants' address carried by, **43**. 136
Nando's coffee-house shelters, in riot, **10**. 273
Boehm, (? Thomas, d. 1770), merchant:
(?) merchants' address carried by, **43**. 136
mob attacks, **23**. 99
Boehme, Jakob (1575–1624), mystic:
engraving of, **16**. 66
Boehmer. *See* Böhmer
Bœotia:
Chancery Lane worthy of, **35**. 557
quotation from Horace about, **24**. 62
Boerhaave, Hermann (1668–1738), medical professor:
Hoffmann a predecessor of, **36**. 140
Boethius, Anicius Manlius Severinus (ca 475–525), philosopher:
*De Consolatione philosphiæ*, Preston's translation of, **16**. 14
Boetié, La. *See* La Boetié

Boetzelaer, Jacob Filips (1711–81), Baron van den; Dutch ambassador to England, 1744:
Dutch troops hurried away by, **18**. 457
English position criticized by, **19**. 408n
English proposal to be presented to, **18**. 458n
Holland sends, to England, **19**. 189
Bogdani. *See* Bogdány
Bogdanov, Maj.:
Turks attacked by, **23**. 469n
Bogdány, Jakob (d. 1724), painter:
painting by, of birds, **10**. 334
Boggust, Rev. Thomas (Peter) (1765–92), fellow of King's College, Cambridge:
Waldegrave, Cts, puts sons in Eton house of, **36**. 283–4
Waldegraves meet, at Scarborough with Bn Holland, **36**. 284
Bogle, George (1746–81):
Hastings's envoy to Tibet, **25**. 14n
journal of, **25**. 16n
Bognor Rocks, Sussex:
Berry, Mary, sketches, **11**. 268n
—— visits, with Mrs Damer, **12**. 193, 195, 200, 204, **31**. 402
Devonshire, Ds of, to visit, **12**. 202n
Jersey, Lady, visits, **12**. 204
Bohea (tea):
for breakfast, **13**. 67
Bohemer. *See* Böhmer
Bohemia, K. of. *See* Frederick V (1596–1632)
Bohemia, Q. of. *See* Elizabeth (1596–1662) of England
Bohemia, Anne of. *See* Anne (1366–94) of Bohemia
Bohemia:
affairs in, may interfere with Leopold's plans, **24**. 95
Bavarian elector to be king of, **17**. 151
bread shortage in, **24**. 105
Carlsbad in, **38**. 473
Charles, P., enters, **18**. 528
—— forced to retreat to, **18**. 505
—— may drive Frederick II from, **18**. 526
Conway and Scott visit, **39**. 537, 538
Daun retires to, **21**. 355
forces in, oppose Frederick II, **21**. 327
Francis I's troops may march to, **21**. 10
Frederick II could gallop from, to Danzig, **25**. 190
—— invades, **18**. 499, 504–5
—— recalled from, to defend Berlin, **18**. 547
—— recalls his outposts from, **22**. 63
—— retains parts of, **21**. 116
—— said to be leaving, **18**. 543
—— said to send troops into, as Maria Theresa's auxiliaries, **17**. 206, 215
——'s campaigns in, **21**. 4, 14–15, 95, 147
——'s retreat from, leaves Maria Theresa free to dispense with French aid, **21**. 229
French to be driven from, **17**. 472
hostilities in, **17**. 446

[Bohemia, *continued*]
insurrections in: **24.** 113; to be crushed by Joseph II, **24.** 105

Joseph II not content with state of, **24.** 278n

Maximilian Joseph to acknowledge vote of, **19.** 37

military action expected in, **21.** 72

peasants in, declaring themselves Hussites or Moravians, want religious freedom, **24.** 95n

political decisions about, **6.** 394n

Törring commands relief force from, **17.** 289

Bohemian glass. *See under* Glass

Böhm, Andreas (1720–90):
(?) HW writes to, disclaiming mathematical knowledge, **38.** 359

*Metaphysica* by, (?) presented to HW, **38.** 359

Böhmer, Charles-Auguste (b. ca 1735), Paris jeweller:
Rohan's revenues should be sequestered to pay, **25.** 654

Böhmisch-Brod:
Frederick II orders Bevern to, to observe Daun, **21.** 95n

Bohun, Humphrey de (? 1309–61), 6th E. of Hereford:
claim of, to authorship, **2.** 291

Bohun. *See also* Boone

Bohun family:
scene of, re-enacted, **22.** 303

Boil; boils:
bark for, **2.** 337
dispiriting, **2.** 336
occurrences of, **2.** 335–8, **20.** 233, 413, **22.** 498

Boileau-Despréaux, Nicolas (1636–1711), poet:
alluded to, **4.** 290
ancients copied by, too slavishly, **16.** 271

*Art poétique, L'*: quoted by Mme du Deffand, **4.** 228; Voltaire praises, **41.** 155

*Épître au Marquis de Seignelay*, quoted by Mme du Deffand, **6.** 285

*Épître au roi*, quoted by Mme du Deffand, **6.** 292

*Épîtres*, cited by Mme du Deffand, **3.** 403

French abandon, **31.** 43

HW compares: to a dog, **16.** 271; to Mason, **28.** 81

HW not to be linked with Perrault by, **37.** 293

HW would not emulate, **28.** 166

*Lutrin, Le*: ancients not imitated in, **16.** 271–2; HW alludes to, **13.** 215; Hayley calls, an epic poem, **29.** 256; standard of grace and elegance, **16.** 257, 272; Whaley quotes, **40.** 43

mature tastes pleased by verse of, **41.** 28

Molière trusts housekeeper's judgment more than that of, **41.** 372

Nivernais's dialogue of Horace and, **28.** 84–5

——'s translation of Milton as good as poetry of, **42.** 129

odes of, unsuccessful, **28.** 276

*Œuvres*, owned by Mme du Deffand, **8.** 32

Pinkerton depreciates, **33.** 492

Racine praised by, **41.** 155

Voltaire's epistle to, **32.** 35–6

Boines. *See* Bourgeois de Boynes

Boisdale, loch, in Hebrides:
Young Pretender hiding at, **19.** 269n

Bois de Boulogne, Paris:
race at, **1.** 110
royal château at entrance to, **3.** 122n

Bois de la Motte. *See* Du Bois de la Motte

Boisgelin, Comte de. *See* Boisgelin de Cucé, Louis-Bruno de

Boisgelin, Comtesse de. *See* Boufflers, Louise-Julie de

Boisgelin, Jean-Baptiste, Vicomte de:
(?) gambling losses of, **4.** 54

Boisgelin de Cucé, Jean-de-Dieu-Raymond de (1732–1804), Bp of Lavaur 1765–70; Abp of Aix 1770–90:
Académie elects, **6.** 260
Châtillon visited by, **7.** 331
Du Deffand, Mme, receives diocesan charge of, **7.** 436–8
——'s opinion of, **3.** 68
HW quotes, **31.** 386
Marie-Josèphe's funeral oration by, **7.** 318
praised, **3.** 76
social relations of, in Paris, **3.** 86, 368, 374, **5.** 92, 105, **6.** 71, **7.** 282, 308, 310, 311
Stanislas I's funeral oration by, **3.** 68, 69, 71, 74, 76, 86, 93, **22.** 403n, **31.** 111n

Boisgelin de Cucé, Louis-Bruno de (1733–94), later called Comte de Boisgelin; (?) 'Marquis de Cucé'; diplomatist:
Boisgelin, Comtesse de, income of, limited by, **5.** 150
Du Deffand, Mme, makes inquiry of, **4.** 5
—— sends books by, **4.** 37
—— talks with, about HW and Craufurd, **4.** 88–9
England visited by, **4.** 54
HW admired by, **4.** 89
made member of Ordre du St-Esprit, **7.** 14
marriage of, **4.** 316n
master of the wardrobe, **7.** 14
recalled to Paris because of Court squabble at Parma, **23.** 330
social relations of, in Paris, **4.** 88–9, **7.** 302, 307, 308
(?) SH visited by, **12.** 237

Boislecomte. *See* Martin de Boislecomte

Bois-le-Duc (France):
French may march by, **37.** 282

Boismont, Nicolas-Thyrel de (1715–86), abbé:
funeral oration by, on Louis XV, **6.** 80, 81, 83
social relations of, with M. and Mme Necker, **6.** 442

Boismontier, ——, surgeon:
Simiane, Mme de, favours, **5.** 423n

Bois Prévu, Prie's villa near Rueil:
HW visits and describes, **35.** 115–16
Prie entertains at, **7.** 293

Boisset de Randon. *See* Randon de Boisset

Boissier, M. de:
SH visited by, **12.** 231
Boissière, Mme Jean. *See* Poupardin d'Amanzy,
Marie-Louise-Anne-Constance
Boissière. *See also* La Boissière
Boissy, Louis de (1694–1758):
*Babillard, Le,* silly, **7.** 265
*Homme du jour, L'* (*Les Dehors trompeurs*):
liked by HW, **6.** 44; translated by Conway,
**31.** 263n, **35.** 391n
Boiston, Joseph (fl. 1789–90), sculptor:
Brutus's bust by, given to National Assembly,
**34.** 175
Boit, Charles (1662–1727):
Cooper's miniature of Cromwell copied in
enamel by, **41.** 263n, **42.** 125
HW's enamel by, **9.** 412n
Boitard, Louis Peter (fl. 1750), engraver:
print by, of gowned ass, **2.** 214n
Boitard, Louis-Philippe (fl. 1738–63):
plates by, **15.** 20n
*Boke of St Albans. See under* Berners, Juliana
Bolby. *See* Bouldby
Boldre, Hants:
Gilpin vicar of, **11.** 66n, **29.** 80n
Bolena, Caterina. *See* Boleyn, Catherine
Boleyn, Alice (d. 1538), m. Sir Robert Clere,
Kt:
marriage of, **2.** 163, *176*
Boleyn, Anne. *See* Anne (Boleyn) (1507–36)
Boleyn, Catherine (fl. 1540?), aunt (?) of Q.
Elizabeth:
print of, **1.** 181, 188, 189
Boleyn, George (d. 1536), 2d Vct Rochford:
HW's version of alleged poem by, **42.** 382–3
madrigal supposedly by, **28.** 191, **42.** 381
verses by, **1.** 357–8, **40.** 373
Boleyn, Sir James (d. 1561):
death of, **2.** 32n
Boleyn, Sir Thomas (ca 1478–1539), E. of Wilt-
shire:
Blickling owned by, **2.** 165
tomb of, at Hever, **35.** 142
Boleyn, Sir William (d. 1505), K.B.:
daughter of, marries, **2.** 163, 176
Boleyn family:
arms of, **2.** 32, 163, 176, 178, 220, 222, 225
Bolinbroke. *See* Bolingbroke
Bolingbroke, Vct. *See* St John, Frederick (1734–
87); St John, George Richard (1761–1824);
St John, Henry (1678–1751)
Bolingbroke, Vcts. *See* Collins, Charlotte (d.
1803); Des Champs de Marcilli, Marie-Claire
(1675–1750); Spencer, Lady Diana (1734–
1808)
Bolivia:
silver discovered in, **23.** 562n
Bollan, Arthur, American agent in London:
Congress's petition presented by, to Dart-
mouth, **39.** 231n
Middleton notifies, about Congress, **24.** 85n
'Bolledit, Jean':
in Margaret of Anjou's escort, **14.** 73

Bolney Court, near Henley:
Villiers stages *Provok'd Husband* at, **32.** 342n
Bologna, Abp of. *See* Malvezzi, Vincenzo (1715–
75)
Bologna, legate of. *See* Boncompagni, Ignazio
(1743–99)
Bologna, vice-legate of. *See* Molinari, Giovanni
Carlo (ca 1717–63); Spinola, Girolamo
Bologna, John of. *See* Boulogne, Jehan, called
Giambologna
Bologna:
Acquaviva keeps Roman-Neapolitan com-
munications open, in order to communi-
cate with army in, **18.** 270
Algarotti writes from, **21.** 271
Angelelli from, **22.** 374
Austrian cavalry enters, **18.** 197n
banker at, **17.** 228
Beauchamp (Francis Seymour-Conway) to go
to, **22.** 336
Beauchamp (George Seymour) dies at, **18.**
510
Benedict XIV the 'old doctor' of, **20.** 189
—— vainly appealed to by people of, **18.** 99
Bentivoglio of, marries Bianca Cappello's
daughter, **20.** 414
Borsini keeps Pellegrino inn at, **22.** 232n
Casa Ratta at, contains Domenichino paint-
ing not seen by HW, **17.** 267n, **35.** 19
Charles Emmanuel III and Traun threaten,
with army, **17.** 500
Charles Emmanuel III asks Benedict XIV's
permission to invade, **17.** 482
—— reaches, **18.** 7n
——'s troops to assemble at, **18.** 55
—— wants Austrian army at, **18.** 461
Chute and Whithed to visit, **17.** 228, 312–13,
**19.** 48, **35.** 22
Chute sees HW's copy of Guido's 'Pallione'
at, **35.** 5
Conway to visit, **20.** 304
courier leaves, for Modena, **19.** 156
Creti's copy of picture at, **17.** 118
dialect of, heard at Reggio fair, **13.** 242
Domenichino's sibyl at, **17.** 264n, 267–8, *313*
Dominican church at, **13.** 193–4
Fantuzzi da Trento at, **16.** 96n
Franciscan church at, **13.** 193
French plunder, **34.** 217
Gages may be forced to give up, to Traun,
**18.** 108
—— refused provisions by, **18.** 108
gazette of, *see* Bologna Gazette
Germans advance in territory of, **18.** 98
Giogo between Florence and, **20.** 180n
gonfaloniere at, *see* Caprara, Count
Graftons to visit, **22.** 34
HW mentions, with regard to Gray, **17.** 50
HW prefers art of: **34.** 217; to that of Rome,
**15.** 332
HW probably at, **17.** 31
HW writes from, **30.** 16–17

[Bologna, *continued*]

Instituto at, interested in getting Stosch's map collection, **21**. 187, 434

Jesuits' college at, to be dissolved, **23**. 486–7

Joseph II may be asked by, to aid in dispute with Pius VI, **25**. 85

—— takes other road from, **23**. 104

Karl Alexander to visit, **20**. 376

Lee barred from, by Cardinal Legate, **20**. 364

legation in: Clement XIV gives Jesuits' revenues in, to the city under Malvezzi, **23**. 494

Leopold to meet Maria Carolina at, **23**. 15

letters from, expected at Florence, **18**. 151

Lobkowitz moves army to, **18**. 322

Lorraine archives may go to, **17**. 199n

magistrates shut gates of, against fleeing Spaniards, **18**. 154

Mann does not hear from, about picture, **17**. 199

—— may have to wait at, **17**. 196

—— plans for Sir Robert Walpole's visit to, **18**. 211–13

—— receives Domenichino painting from, **18**. 57

—— sends to, for drams, **19**. 200, **21**. 49

—— to confute gazetteers of, **19**. 205

melon seeds sent to, **17**. 34

Modenese princesses rent house at, **18**. 223

Molinari's uncle vice-legate of, **18**. 138

Montemar leaves, **17**. 427

—— takes baggage from, **17**. 455

mountains of, untenable for Francis I's troops, **18**. 77

Mugello near borders of, **19**. 11

news from, of battle, **18**. 154

opera singer ill at, **18**. 302

Orford, Cts of, to visit, **19**. 50

Palazzo Monti at, **21**. 173n

Palazzo Zambeccari at, Domenichino painting in, **17**. 167, 257n, 267–8

Peggi at, **21**. 126, 196

Pellegrino at, **20**. 304

Penny at, to secure Domenichino painting for HW, **17**. 227–8, 241, 267–8, **35**. 17

Pitt, Thomas, intends to visit, **21**. 543

Poggelini's civilities at, **11**. 364–5

posts from, to Florence, **17**. 32, 47, **19**. 462

Prati della Masone near, **17**. 424

professor at, invents a better floating battery, **25**. 323

Pucci, Mme, may stay at, with Giovanardi, **17**. 158, 171

Ratisbon to be balanced by confederation at, **21**. 494n

Richmond, Mrs, may visit, **19**. 49, 50

Riva nun and Moroni live at, **23**. 86

roads to: from Florence, unsafe, **18**. 13; Leopold and Maria Louisa travel, to escort Ferdinand and Maria Amalia to Naples, **25**. 2; picketed, **18**. 100; Salimbeni has accident on, **17**. 116; snow on, **25**. 2

Sale sends paper from, to Mann, **19**. 226

Sampieri collection at, *see under* Sampieri

Sauveterre performs at, **17**. 463

senate of: disputes with Papal legate and Pius VI, **25**. 85; honours D. of York, **22**. 236

Sisson less learned than a professor of, **21**. 407

snow on mountains of: in September, **21**. 435; towards Florence, **25**. 22

Spaniards at, **18**. 76

—— may advance on, **18**. 45, 55

—— move from, **18**. 175, 199

—— retreat towards, **18**. 163

—— starve inhabitants of, **18**. 99

—— unexpectedly to avoid, **17**. 341, 350

—— unlikely to approach, **18**. 58

Spanish army threatens Tuscany from, **17**. 289, **18**. 76–7

Spanish baggage sent to, **17**. 432

Spanish courier intercepted on borders of, **18**. 85

Strange buys paintings at, for Dundas, **21**. 478n

—— draws from paintings at, **22**. 108n

taxes at, **18**. 344

third city in Italy for pictures, **13**. 195

Traun and Charles Emmanuel III prepare army at, **18**. 55

Traun's army to approach, **17**. 350, **18**. 199

Via Emilia leads from Rimini to, **17**. 289n

visitors to: Berrys, **11**. 128, 149n, 150n, 155, 325n, 351n, 363, 364–5; Bolognetti, Contessa, **18**. 65; Cholmondeley, **23**. 349; Chute, **17**. 228, 235, 240, 241, 268, **19**. 257, **30**. 16, **35**. 5, 13, 22; Cologne, Elector of, **20**. 508n; Conway, **20**. 297n; Craon, Princesse de, **22**. 537; Doria, Cardinal, **20**. 332–3; Elcho, **30**. 16; Franchini, **18**. 111; Francis III, **20**. 75; Frescobaldi, Mme, **18**. 65; Graftons, **22**. 34n; Gray, **13**. 9, 192, 195, 241n; HW, **13**. 9, 192, 195, 241n, **35**. 19; Hervey, George William, **30**. 16; Huntingdon, E. of, **23**. 447; Karl Wilhelm Ferdinand, **22**. 457n; Lee, Charles, **20**. 363n; Legge, Mrs, **11**. 359–60; Mann, **18**. 273, **20**. 75; Marlborough, D. of, **21**. 512n; Modenese princesses, **22**. 144; Montemar, **17**. 314; Montgomery, **20**. 363n; Penny, **18**. 334, **35**. 16, 17, 18; Philipps, Sir Erasmus, **17**. 67n; Pitt, Anne, **24**. 381; Reynolds, **35**. 19n; Rochfords, **20**. 376n; Spencers, **22**. 173; Spencer, Lord (?) Charles, **21**. 512n; Strange, **21**. 478n, **22**. 108n; Suares family, **17**. 444; Tripoline ambassador, **20**. 128; Velluti, **17**. 314; West, James, **20**. 379n; Whithed, **17**. 228, 235, 240, 241, **19**. 257, **30**. 16, **35**. 5, 13, 22; York, Cardinal, **20**. 332; York, D. of, **22**. 232, 236; Young Pretender, **20**. 318

Walpole, Sir Robert, wants to see, **18**. 202

wounded Spanish officers at, **18**. 154

York, Cardinal, may become perpetual legate of, **20**. 332

Young Pretender may visit, **20**. 15, 22n, 35n, 44

Zambeccari at, **17**. 281

Bologna Gate, at Florence:
Mann hears that Lady William Campbell has passed, **25**. 272
Bologna Gazette:
authority of, in Florence, **22**. 19
calls George II Elector of Hanover and Young Pretender Prince of Wales, **19**. 205
contents of, might come from same source as Pannoni's gossip, **17**. 417
Mann often sees, **21**. 281n
—— to confute, **19**. 205
Peter III said by, to be fighting for Maria Theresa, **22**. 19
report in, from St. Petersburg, **21**. 247
Wilkes's separation from mistress reported in, **22**. 305
Bologna sausage. *See under* Sausage
Bolognese school of art:
HW admires and Chute understands, **18**. 284
HW's favourite, **11**. 365, **34**. 217
Bolognetti, Contessa. *See* Acciaioli, Faustina
Bolognetti, Conte Giacomo:
(?) fête by, **17**. 16n
(?) *Sea Horse* restored to master through, **17**. 8n
Bolognetti, Mario (1691–1756), cardinal, 1743:
Benedict XIV makes, cardinal, **18**. 302n
Bolognetti, Palazzo, at Rome:
fête at, **17**. 16n
Bolsano (Italy):
Maria Louisa met at, by Riccardi and Mme Antinori, **22**. 334
Bolsena (Italy):
sarcophagus at, described by Addison, **15**. 22
Bolsover, Thomas (ca 1704–88):
silver plating invented by, **9**. 295
Bolsover, Derbyshire:
Bess of Hardwick builds, **9**. 298, **40**. 182
Bolster; bolsters:
clergy wear, supposedly to ape Richard III's deformity, **41**. 223, 225
HW's, shaken by earthquake, **20**. 130
Ilchester strains neck while adjusting, **31**. 84
jewelled, for Ds of Devonshire, **32**. 194
Bolt; bolts:
Le Brun designs, for Louvre gallery, **35**. 344
Bolton, Bn. *See* Orde, Thomas
Bolton, Ds. of. *See* Beswick, Lavinia (ca 1708–60); Crofts, Henrietta (d. 1730); Fenton, Lavinia (ca 1708–60); Lowther, Katharine (ca 1736–1809); Vaughan, Lady Anne (d. 1751)
Bolton, D. of. *See* Powlett, Sir Charles (1661–1722); Powlett, Charles (1685–1754); Powlett, Charles (ca 1718–65); Powlett, Lord Harry (1720–94)
Bolton, Rev. Robert (1572–1631):
Payne's engraving of, **16**. 65
Bolton, Sam:
print of, **40**. 236
Bolton. *See also* Boulton

Bolton Abbey:
Hartington acquires, by marriage, **20**. 66n
Bolton-le-Sands, Lancs:
Ashton baptized at, **13**. 108n
Bolton Row, London:
Pitt, George, has house in, **22**. 2n
Vesey, Mrs, lives in, **32**. 229n
Bolton St, London:
Dickensons in, **31**. 367n, 400
Bomb; bombs:
Conway tries burning glass on, **21**. 155
Cooper's, at Savona, **35**. 63
English ships try to fire, at Genoa, **19**. 76
English shoot, at San Remo, **19**. 120–1
French army practises firing, **38**. 410
French use, against Lérins islands, **19**. 406
from Edinburgh Castle, threaten Holyrood House, **19**. 126
Genoese rioters shelled with, **19**. 338
Gibraltar shelled by, **25**. 156
in English invasion of France, **21**. 204
Mann wants, used sparingly on Corsica, **19**. 163
Medley may be unable to use, against Genoa, **19**. 385
Piacenza bombarded with, **19**. 276
Russians use, against Turks, **23**. 228
shell of, boats overturned by, **21**. 309
used in allied war against France, **34**. 182
Voyer and Paulin take, past Lyon, **20**. 536
Bombardier; bombardiers:
Warren, colonel of, in Tuscany, **17**. 66
Bombardment:
HW deplores, as bad example to enemy, **21**. 306
Bombay, Governor of. *See* Hornby, William
Bombay:
account of hurricane from, **20**. 113n
president and council of, report to East India Co., **21**. 523n
Scott commissioner of police at, **2**. 112n
Bombelles, Comtesse de. *See* Gaudion de la Mannerie, Marie-Jeanne-Armande
Bomb-ketches:
Rodney uses, to burn Havre-de-Grâce, **21**. 305
Bomb-ship; bomb-ships:
Charles III threatened by, **18**. 32, **23**. 506
Civita Vecchia to have been demolished by, **18**. 314
Cooper's, shattered by their own discharges, **19**. 81
Corsica to be attacked by, **19**. 146
English, bombard Antibes, **19**. 352
Fermor commands, **18**. 509
in Spanish fleet, **17**. 286
Mathews adds, to Nettuno fleet, **18**. 473, 475, 476
Naples threatened by, **18**. 15, 469–71, 473, 475
ready at Toulon, **23**. 474
Saunders awaits, for attack on Cadiz, **22**. 12
Townshend's, **19**. 207, 325

Bomluer, —— de, commandant de la marine du roi:
Lauzun receives order from, 4. 136n

Bompar, Maximin (d. 1773), Comte de; governor of 'Îles-sous-le-Vent,' 1750; Lt-Gen., 1764:
Conflans waits for squadron of, to be equipped, 21. 358n
court martial condemns, for not destroying Moore's squadron, 43. 275
squadron of, to fight Moore's at Martinique, 21. 297

Bomporto (Italy):
Sardinian garrison and artillery at, 18. 151
Spaniards gain victory at, 18. 189
Spaniards to go to, 18. 151
Traun at, 18. 66

'Bomston, Lord Edward.' See Rousseau, Jean-Jacques: Julie

Bona, St (ca 1156–1208):
HW's account of, 13. 88–9

Bonac, Abbé de. See Usson de Bonac, Jean-Louis d'

Bonac, Marquis de. See Usson, François-Armand d'

Bonaccorsi. See Buonaccorsi

Bona Dea:
Roman matrons addicted to mysteries of, 20. 41

Bonaichi, ——, Agdollo's secretary:
Venice sought by, after quarrel with Agdollo, 17. 148

Bonaparte, Napoleon (1769–1821):
assassination of, attempted, 12. 121n
Austrians defeated by, 12. 191n
Bolognese pictures plundered by, 34. 217n
letters of Mme du Deffand censored by, 5. 235n
mentioned, 12. 88n
Sémonville protected by, 12. 191n

Bonarelli, ——, Papal officer:
at Ponte Molle battle, 18. 532

Bonaventuri, Pellegrina (b. 1564), m. (1576) Ulisse Bentivoglio of Bologna:
marriage of, 20. 414

Bonaventuri, Pietro (d. 1572):
giovane di banco at Venice before fleeing to Florence with bride, 20. 414
Ricci family murder, at Francesco I's instigation, 20. 414

Bonbons:
Ailesbury, Cts of, gives to HW, 38. 87
children receive, when well-behaved, 41. 108

Boncerf, Pierre-François (ca 1745–94):
Inconvénients des droits féodaux, Les, Voltaire's letter about censorship of, 6. 287, 8. 197–8

Boncifort, ——, Corsican intendant-general at Pisa:
Panettien's letter to, 24. 437n

'Boncœur.' See Berkeley, Norborne

Boncompagni, Anna Maria (1697–1752), m. (1719) Antonio Maria Salviati, Duca di Giuliano-Salviati:

Craon, Princesse de, entertains, 19. 145
—— served by, 17. 4
name of, corrected, 43. 233

Boncompagni, Gaetano (1707–77), Duca di Sora, 1739; Principe di Piombino, 1745; Neapolitan ambassador to Spain 1735–7, 1746:
Ferdinand VI refuses to accredit, 19. 307
iron mines of, 23. 131
Rosenberg keeps, waiting, 23. 104n

Boncompagni, Ignazio (1732–99), cardinal, 1775; legate of Bologna, 1775:
Bologna senate quarrels with, 25. 85

Boncompagni, Maria (1686–1745), m. (1702) Antonio Boncompagni; Ps of Piombino; Duchessa di Sora, s.j.:
biographical information on, corrected, 43. 247
Marciana belongs to, 18. 28

Bond, Elizabeth (1715–80), m. (1736) Gabriel Hanger, cr (1762) Bn Coleraine:
Mann shocked by sons' cruelty to, 24. 240
sons summon, to London to show her to Jews, 24. 236
sons wheedle, out of her money to pay their debts, 24. 235
Windsor, Vcts, supports, 24. 235–6

Bond; bonds:
Bristol said to have given, to Barrington, 24. 196
East India: Crassus's death did not affect value of, 21. 558; Ferrers has, 21. 397
Orford, E. of, gave, to Horace Mann II, 23. 78

Bondelmonti. See Buondelmonti

Bondeno (Italy):
Spaniards cross Panaro at, 17. 464, 472
Spanish army remains at, 17. 489

Bondi. See Bondy

Bondigli, ——, Monsignore, finance minister of Modena:
Francis III's art collection sold by, 19. 314n

Bond Stables. See under Fetter Lane

Bond St, London:
Blenheim St near, 10. 159
Chute writes from, 35. 65
Frankland, Sir Thomas, has house in, 33. 334
Grafton's house in, 38. 441
Lort's lodgings in, 1. 313n, 2. 16
mentioned, 12. 79n
Montagu to dine in, 9. 275
Pitt's town house in, 22. 472n, 31. 86n
Schaub in, 9. 88n
Stapleton lives in, 32. 361n
West dates letter from, 13. 235

Bonducci, Abbé:
Bouverie buys Guercino drawings from, 18. 116
Buondelmonte's Lettera sopra la misura sold by, 20. 117n
Gray taught Italian by, 25. 507n
HW confuses, with Buondelmonte, 25. 507n
HW sees Guercino sketch brought by, 18. 91–2
HW unable to aid, 18. 210

Mann asked by, for recommendation to HW as Vaneschi's successor, **18.** 198

probably dead years ago, but his buffoonery survives, **25.** 507

*Riccio rapito, Il:* **13.** 231n; HW's compliments on dedication of, **17.** 73; HW to receive, **17.** 64; translation of, **18.** 210n

satire probably translated by, **17.** 462

Bondy (France):

forest of, **10.** 167n

Livry in forest of, **10.** 211

Bone; bones:

fish-hooks of, **25.** 451

HW jokes about his, **35.** 524, 535

martyrs' tabernacle made from, **20.** 489

old, may be dug up near Dorchester, **37.** 491

Bone Bridge. *See* Bourn Bridge

Bonechi, Giuseppe (fl. 1767–95), Tuscan chargé d'affaires and secretary of legation at Naples:

Ferdinand of Naples would have tossed, in blanket, **23.** 254

*Bonefoy,* French ship:

capture of, **24.** 420n

Bonesana, Cesare (1738–94), Marchese di Beccaria:

*Trattato dei diletti e delle pene,* **3.** 173, **43.** 83

*Bonetta,* English sloop:

Carolina reached by, with Cuban news, **38.** 169–70

loyalists evacuated from Yorktown to New York in, **25.** 211n

Bonfire; bonfires:

at alehouse in Sion Lane, for Quebec's recovery, **38.** 60

at Edinburgh, for Wilkes's recovery, **38.** 268

at Hampton, for Keppel's election, **36.** 178

at Venice, for Doge's election, **17.** 76

Dublin lacks, on Hartington's arrival, **37.** 393

Florentine poor people celebrate birth of Cowper's son by, **24.** 232

for capture of Cape Breton, **19.** 79

for Cartagena victory, **17.** 93

for celebrations, HW mentions, **11.** 342, **12.** 90, 98

For Culloden anniversary, **37.** 266

for Dettingen victory, **35.** 39

for Frederick II's birthday, **21.** 171

for Frederick II's victory, **21.** 452

for George II's return, **18.** 340

for Minden victory, **21.** 314

for Montreal's capture, **21.** 437

French love to treat English mob with subjects for, **38.** 106

Gordon rioters cautious in building, **25.** 63

HW jokes about, to burn Mordaunt and D. of Cumberland, **30.** 142

HW might light, to celebrate peace, **31.** 29

in Garrick's *Coronation,* **38.** 133

in Gordon Riots, **33.** 178

in London, **17.** 196, 253, 319, 337, 390, **18.** 340, **21.** 171, 314, 437, 452, **38.** 106n

in London streets, **9.** 246

lacking, on Vernon's return, **18.** 135

London mobs given money for, **17.** 390

London's: for Ferdinand's victory, **35.** 101; for Opposition victory, **38.** 324

pope's effigy paraded at, **10.** 254

(?) Townshend, Vct, makes, of wife's portraits, **30.** 81

Bonfoy, Nicholas (d. 1775), serjeant-at-arms to House of Commons, 1762:

death of, **7.** 398

Devonshires entertain, at Chatsworth, **9.** 295

Gray probably visits, **14.** 51n

lord mayor committed to, **23.** 290

(?) Paris visited by, **13.** 166

subscriber to Middleton's *Cicero,* **43.** 177

*Bonhomme Richard,* American ship of French origin:

Jones allows, to sink, **28.** 467n

Boniface VIII (1235–1303), pope 1294–1303:

(?) HW would like to imitate, in consecrating Harcourt's gifts, **35.** 477

inscription referring to, at Siena, **13.** 205

jubilee customs different from time of, **20.** 83n

Bonifacio ('Bonifazzio'), Corsica:

Corsican rebels to besiege, **19.** 163

Corsicans blockade, **19.** 171

English may try to capture, **20.** 553

France sends engineer to, to raise batteries, **20.** 573n

Genoa reserves, **20.** 273n

Jesuits land at, **22.** 526n, 545n

Spanish munitions to be deposited at, **18.** 271

'Bon mariage payera tout':

Mozzi cannot be consoled by, **25.** 512

Bonmischetto:

Jesuits' villa at San Remo, **19.** 123

*Bon mot; bons mots:*

Betty's, **30.** 208

HW's reflections on, **28.** 193

history often depicted by, **21.** 459

Parisian, non-existent, **30.** 208

*See also under* Selwyn, George Augustus; Townshend, Hon. Charles

Bonnaire, ——, maître des requêtes:

attends session of parliament of Paris, **8.** 171

Bonnay, Charles-François (1750–1825), former Marquis de; president (twice) of National Assembly, 1790:

Du Deffand, Mme, relies on, **5.** 147

——'s correspondence with, **8.** 185

HW's purchase of armour aided by, **5.** 119, 121, 147, **6.** 185

Louis XVI accompanied by, to National Assembly, **11.** 96

Thiers sale investigated by Mme du Deffand and, **5.** 147–8, 154

Bonnel, Mr and Mrs, of Whitton:

SH visited by, **12.** 229

Bonner, Edmund (ca 1500–69), Bp of London 1539–49, 1553–9:

bench of, in walk at Fulham Palace, **11.** 33

burnings during episcopacy of, **31.** 319

[Bonner, Edmund, *continued*]
'chair' of, **31.** 313, **34.** 54, **43.** 342
English admirers of French Revolution should
be curbed by, **31.** 343
Wyatt accused by, **42.** 379n
——'s abuse of, unfashionable, **28.** 66
*See also* More, Hannah: *Bishop Bonner's
Ghost*
Bonnet; bonnets:
'aristocrate' with fleur-de-lis, **34.** 142
beaver, HW and Gray wear, in crossing Alps,
**13.** 189
feather, Americans present, to Q. Elizabeth,
**17.** 357
green, Primate of Lorraine wears, **17.** 17
Henry VIII's black, **40.** 225
Naunton wears, **35.** 248
Scott, Lady Caroline, wears, **32.** 338
Bonnet de Martanges, —— (1722–1806), maréchal de camp:
made secretary of Swiss Guards, **5.** 173
Bonneval, Claude-Alexandre (1675–1747), Comte de:
HW asks if Wilkes imitates, by turning Mos-
lem, **22.** 290
Bonnier de la Mosson, Anne-Josèphe (d. ca
1787), m. (1734) Michel-Ferdinand d'Albert
d'Ailly, Duc de Chaulnes:
social relations of, with Mme de Rochefort,
**7.** 270
Bonnières, Mlle:
Mozart composed concerto for, **43.** 98
Bonnières, Adrien-Louis de (1735–1806), Comte
and (1776) Duc de Guines; French ambassador to England, 1770:
ambassadorship of, **4.** 380n, 416, **5.** 50, 111,
121, 134, 139, 143, 146, 151, 169, 215, 365,
380n, 388, 434, **6.** 7, 11, 68, 89, 192, 196;
ended, **6.** 263, 264, 290, **24.** 178; may be
resumed, **25.** 363n
Argyll, Ds of, gets regrets from, for party,
**39.** 135
balls given by, **5.** 348, **32.** 96, 100, 101–2, 106,
109–12, 116–17, **33.** 256–7
Blaquiere gives bad account of affairs of, **7.**
341
Boyer steward of, **4.** 461
carriage of, broken, **6.** 274
Choiseul, Duchesse de, would be eagerly
served by, **5.** 23
contraband not desired by, **4.** 439
Conway invited by, to military review at
Metz **39.** 178
courier of, **5.** 11, **7.** 392
Craven, Bns, affair of, with, **5.** 358, 360, 365
daughters of: **33.** 403; dowered by Louis XVI,
**7.** 53; marriage of, **7.** 53, 62
Du Deffand, Mme, interested in arrival of, in
London, **6.** 198, 199
—— may send packages by, **5.** 320, 419, **6.** 11
—— mentions, **6.** 66
—— sends letter through, **5.** 3
—— sends pamphlets through, **6.** 198–9

—— sent copy of Louis XVI's letter to, **6.**
313–14
——'s money may be sent by, **6.** 196
——'s opinion of, **4.** 483, **6.** 129, 160, 172,
177, 179, 265, 283, 290
—— suggests that HW send packages through,
**5.** 20, 23
—— to hear, play his flute, **6.** 363
enemies of, **6.** 271, **24.** 178
England assured by, that French fleet will not
attack Russia, **5.** 348
—— liked by, **4.** 492
English gardens admired by, **23.** 313
English ways not well known to, **6.** 11
English weather evokes remark by, **28.** 30
flautist, **6.** 363, 405–6
George III bids Harcourt prevent recall of,
**39.** 141
Gourgue, Présidente de, friend of, **5.** 369
HW asks Conway to remember him to, **39.**
215
HW called on by, but not received, **41.** 340
HW does not mention, **5.** 215
HW mentions, **5.** 75
HW praises, **31.** 152
HW regrets the recall of, from embassy, **41.**
339
HW's correspondence with, **41.** 339–40, 423–6
HW sends compliments to, **6.** 430
HW sends letter by courier of, **7.** 392
HW's furniture and tapestries sent with bag-
gage of, **4.** 424, 425, 428, 430, 435, 439, 457,
461, 472, 481
HW's furniture may be sent by, **5.** 139, 143,
146, 148
HW's opinion of, **4.** 492, **5.** 348
HW takes, to Pantheon, **23.** 298
HW told by, about Mme du Deffand's be-
quest, **36.** 193
HW to receive commission through, **5.** 162,
164, 173
Hertford regrets probable recall of, **39.** 141
Le Texier's reception by, disapproved of, **6.**
254
Louis XV favours, **5.** 93
Louis XVI dowers daughter of, **7.** 53
—— gives title of Duc de, **6.** 311, 313–14, 315,
**24.** 208
—— said not to favour, **6.** 265
—— sees, **6.** 277, 290
—— slow to give audience to, **6.** 284, 290
—— thanks, **24.** 208
Malesherbes urges Marie-Antoinette to abandon, **6.** 299, 321, **24.** 207
Marie-Antoinette accompanied by, in quarantine, **7.** 129
—— protects, **6.** 299
*Mémoire pour le comte de Guines*, **6.** 158
Mirepoix, Mme de, might be aided by, **5.** 434
Mozart composed concerto for, **43.** 98
Necker pleased by news of, **8.** 214
not protected by ministry, **6.** 178
Paris to be left by, **4.** 424, 481, **5.** 3

—— to be visited by, **6**. 263, 270–1, 272

—— visited by, **6**. 274, 276–7

Parliamentary proceedings astonish, **23**. 256–7

pendant mirror used by, to reflect dancers, **32**. 115

Pezzana recommended by, to HW, **36**. 193, **41**. 423

regulations sent to, **6**. 251

*Réplique pour le comte de Guines*, **6**. 166, 168, 171–3, 175

royalist in American affairs, **6**. 386

social relations of, in England, *see index entries ante* **34**. 288

social relations of, in Paris, *see index entries ante* **8**. 255

SH visited by, **23**. 311–13, **35**. 369–70, 531

SH visited by family of, **33**. 402–4

style of, admired by Mme du Deffand, **6**. 178

supper given by, **32**. 277

to return to London, **4**. 134, 159, 161, 163, 172

Tort de la Sonde's law-suit with, **6**. 24, 39, 129, 143n, 158, 160, 166–8, 171–3, 175–9, 181, 183, 185–7, 192, 195–6, 198–9, **24**. 90, 100; judgment in, **6**. 196, 200; judgment in appeal of, **6**. 421, 422, **8**. 200; mémoires in, voluminous, **30**. 263

—— 's *Premier mémoire* against, **6**. 160, 175

—— 's second mémoire about, **6**. 168, 173, 179, 181

Versailles visited by, **6**. 274, 277, 283, 284, 290, **41**. 423

verses for, at Mme de Luxembourg's supper, **6**. 405–6

verses on, **5**. 365, **8**. 193

Bonnières de Guines, Marie-Louise-Charlotte de (d. 1792), m. (1782) Charles-Philibert-Gabriel Le Clerc, Comte (later, 1807, Marquis) de Juigné:

SH visited by, **33**. 403–4, **35**. 369–70, 531

Bonnières de Guines, Marie-Louise-Philippine de (d. 1796), m. (1778) Armand-Charles-Augustin de la Croix, Comte de Charlus, later Marquis and Duc de Castries:

Louis XVI dowers, **7**. 53

marriage of, **7**. 53, 62

name of, corrected, **43**. 104

SH visited by, **33**. 403–4, **35**. 369–70, 531

Bonnot de Condillac, Étienne (1715–80), abbé:

*Cours d'étude pour l'instruction du Prince de Parme*, **6**. 285

Bonomi, Signora. *See* Florini, Rosa

Bonomi, Giuseppe (1739–1808), architect:

Adam, Robert and James, invite, to England, **42**. 101n

Agincourt's letter to be delivered by, to HW, **42**. 101

HW to entrust packets to, **42**. 104

marries and settles in England, **42**. 101

rooms designed by, **11**. 290n

Bonrepos, Mme de. *See* Maupeou, Marie-Catherine-Charlotte de

Bonrepos, seigneur de. *See* Riquet, Jean-Gabriel-Amable-Alexandre de

Bons Enfants, Amiens inn. *See* Aux Bons Enfants

Bonstetten, Charles-Victor de:

Albany, Cts of, writes to, **24**. 94n

Bontempi, Giovanni Andrea Angelini (1624–1705):

*Historia musica* by, **21**. 467, 477, 482, 492

Bontempi, Padre Giuseppe:

Clement XIV's food prepared by, **23**. 136

—— 's sole confidant, **24**. 49–50

*Bon ton*:

HW's reflections on, **23**. 364

Bonus, (?) Richard, picture-cleaner; 'old Bonus':

biographical information on, corrected, **43**. 65, 109, 220

Bury St. Edmunds altar tablets left by HW at Oxford St shop of, for repair, **2**. 30–1, 219, 220, **16**. 184, 186

business to be lost by, because of lemon treatment of mildew, **10**. 261

Erasmus's portrait whitewashed by, **10**. 285

HW sends to, for picture of Barnaby Fitzpatrick, **32**. 140

(?) HW to see, **8**. 162

Leicester portraits not to be cleaned by, **10**. 256

Montagu dislikes methods of, **10**. 285

son of, **21**. 429n, **33**. 55

Bonus, Richard, picture-cleaner:

Guise's pictures at Oxford spoiled by, **21**. 429n, **33**. 55

Bonville, Sir William (1393–1461), cr. (1449) Lord Bonville of Chewton:

in Margaret of Anjou's escort, **14**. 73

Bonvoust de Prulay, Mlle (d. 1783):

(?) Du Deffand, Mme, corresponds with, **7**. 459

(?) —— gives cup to, **7**. 450

(?) —— receives purse from, **7**. 428, 450

(?) —— 's social relations with, **7**. 425, 426, 428, 429, 444

(?) returns to Paris, **7**. 436

Bonzi, Pierre de (1631–1703), cardinal; Abp of Narbonne:

Pennautier 'étoile' of, **3**. 64

Boodles Club, London:

George IV drunk at, **39**. 465

Book; books:

Ailesbury, Cts of, and Mrs Damer know which, HW wants from Paris, **39**. 198

antiquarian, HW to redeem from reputation of being ill-written, **38**. 152

architectural: HW and Thomas Pitt have all, **38**. 198; wanted by Conway, **38**. 198

auction of, **38**. 167, 341

burning of: by hangman, **21**. 412, 476–7, **22**. 187–8, 328; Louis XVI said to prefer burning of authors to, **24**. 10

case of, sent by Mann to Horace Mann II and left unopened at latter's London house, **25**. 304, 504

[Book; books, *continued*]

catalogue of, amuses HW, **12.** 58

Churchill, Gen., never read one entire, **30.** 289n

Conway buys, at auction, **37.** 422

—— lacks, **37.** 420

—— leaves, for Lady Mary Churchill, **37.** 189

—— may be denied use of, **37.** 119

—— offers to send, to HW, **37.** 24

—— reads, **37.** 112–13

Conway, Anne Seymour, shall never run after, **37.** 334

cupboard for, in Gloucester pew, **35.** 154

Du Deffand, Mme, offers to leave, to HW, **36.** 181

dummy, **19.** 414

Edgcumbe talks to, **30.** 37

England and France lose the art of making, **33.** 147

English: Firmian collects, **21.** 282, 339; sent to K. of Poland, **11.** 243

French: HW to send amusing, to Fox, **30.** 203; HW will not read, **12.** 58

HW 'almost done with,' **41.** 278

HW and Montagu 'tumble over,' in Wroxton library, **35.** 72

HW asks C. H. Williams to bring, to Houghton, **30.** 64

HW busy publishing or revising, **38.** 312

HW, in winter, content with fire, candle, and, **36.** 285

HW lacks, in London, **33.** 81

HW likes to arrange, **33.** 477

HW orders, for Mann, **22.** 49

HW passes time with, **24.** 91

HW's: at SH, **20.** 382; stolen in Paris, **39.** 17

HW sends half-dozen, from Houghton to London, **37.** 181

HW's resumption of, shows his recovery, **35.** 529

HW suggests, for gallery at Wentworth Castle, **35.** 267

HW thanks Conway for, **37.** 421

HW to get, from Paris, **39.** 198

HW to take, to Houghton, **18.** 498

heretical and bawdy, earthquake a judgment against, **20.** 134

Hertford returns, to HW, **39.** 431

high price of, in England, **23.** 466

Inquisition bans, **22.** 204

Ireland's scarcity of: Conway complains of, **37.** 420; HW jokes on, **10.** 16; Hamilton jokes on, **10.** 11

Jones, Inigo, threatened with sequestration of, **40.** 207, 208n

Kildare, Cts of, sends, to Cts of Ailesbury, **37.** 435

large sums paid for, **16.** 42

man in portrait has hand on, **30.** 371

Mann asks HW to get, **22.** 36

—— sends, to Conway, **20.** 329

morocco binding of, **31.** 399

new: appear slowly in Ireland, **37.** 421; lacking in France, **39.** 144

of plays, borrowed by Conway from HW, **37.** 189

quarto, written about emerald dish, **37.** 320

religious, fortify Cts Waldegrave's composure, **36.** 271

sales of, **38.** 340n, 341

scarce, at Ghent, **37.** 119

talk of, distracts loo players, **31.** 138

Townshend, Vcts, carries, to Brompton lodging, **30.** 70

White to buy, for HW, at La Vallière's sale, **36.** 216–17, 218, 223

Wren's, sold, **40.** 348

*See also* Criticism, literary; French books; Library; Literature; Opera book; Reading

Bookbinder, HW's. *See* Baumgarten, John

Bookbinding, Irish:

HW wishes specimen of, **9,** 418, **10.** 13, 16, 18

Bookcase; bookcases:

Bentley and Chute design, for SH library, **35.** 157, 164, 200

in garret gallery, **35.** 301

Book-collecting:

HW's comments on, **33.** 573–5

Booker, Holden, high constable of Westminster:

warrant for arrest of vagabonds issued by, **17.** 504n

*Book of Christian Prayers, A*:

Ames's *Typographical Antiquities* mentions, **16.** 145

HW points out probable error in, **16.** 156

*Book of Common Prayer*:

Baskerville prints, **40.** 275

creed in, **17.** 3

HW paraphrases, **23.** 376, **33.** 395

HW quotes: collect for peace from, **32.** 348; *Gloria* from, **25.** 642; 'noble army of martyrs' from Te Deum in, **25.** 52; versicle from, **25.** 546

Mann calls Mozzi 'Gloria in Excelsis' from, **21.** 70

Sydenham's mind dominated by, **30.** 292n

Trail's rendition of, criticized, **38.** 352

'Book of Materials,' HW's:

correction about, **43.** 46, 49, 66, 124, 143, 185

HW starts entering anecdotes of streets of London in, **1.** 134n

Book of Meditations:

Jerome's, **40.** 225

Book of Sports:

objects of, praiseworthy, **31.** 436

Bookseller; booksellers:

arguments of, for Robertson's writing history of William III will outweigh HW's objections, **28.** 390

authors should be supplied by, with rare books for research, **40.** 306, 307

Baskerville not encouraged by, **40.** 274

book sales benefit, **16.** 42

circulating libraries kept by, **28**. 148

copyright lost by, **28**. 149–50

English, Mann sends Pitti Gaddi catalogues to, **24**. 80

Faithorne and Hollar worked for, **16**. 371

Florentine, lack *Illustri fatti Farnesiani*, **25**. 412

French, at Florence, *see* Bouchard, Giuseppe

Gray too generous to, **28**. 22

HW approves of Mason's censure of, **28**. 24

HW calls, rascally, **31**. 306–7

HW not ashamed of being, **28**. 24

HW's: at Cambridge, **37**. 19; French, *see* Bosse, Joseph de; in London, *see* Bathoe, William; Bell, John

HW satisfies, by buying pamphlets on Sackville, **38**. 35

HW suffers from tricks of, **15**. 98, 99

HW's writings collected by, for edition, **16**. 259

Hamilton's: to get Italian translation of *Castle of Otranto*, **35**. 438; to send HW Hamilton's *Collection of Engravings*, **35**. 443

Johnson's agreement with, for *Rasselas*, **29**. 179–80

piracy practiced by, **28**. 150, 311

profit the only interest of, **40**. 307

relative integrity of English and Scottish, **28**. 135

Scotch, monopolistic practices of, **28**. 86–7, 310–11

shops of: Chinese in, **34**. 22; Galluzzi's book to be kept secret until put on sale at, **25**. 81

spurious works published by, **31**. 277–8

threaten publication of HW's *Mysterious Mother*, **29**. 139–40, 141

trash commissioned by, **15**. 93

*See also*: Barker, ——; Bathoe, William; Bathoe, Mrs William; Becket, Thomas; Bell, John; Bowen, T.; Cadell, Thomas; Davies, Thomas; Dodsley, James; Dodsley, Robert; Elmsley, Peter; Evans, Thomas; Fielding, John; Harrod, William; Jacob, James Rutland; Law, Bedwell; Merrill, Joseph; Merrill, Thomas; Prince, Daniel; Richardson, Joseph; Robinson, George; Stringer, ——; Walker, John; Ward, Cæsar; Ware, (?) Catharine; Whiston, John; White, Benjamin; White, R.

Boone, Mrs:

SH visited by, **12**. 234

Boone, Charles (?1729–1819), M.P.:

Ashburton may be borough of, **36**. 47

birth date of, corrected, **43**. 317

Callington election may be entered by, from obligations to Orford, **35**. 416–17

elected M.P., **32**. 212

HW asks favour for, from Cts of Orford, **24**. 82, 292

HW mentions, **10**. 7

HW's correspondence with, **38**. 168

HW to notify, to succeed him at Castle Rising, **33**. 34

HW to write to, about E. of Orford, **32**. 355

health of, gout, **24**. 47

Hertford sees Moone and, about Orford's interest at Callington, **39**. 192

marriage plans denied by, **10**. 32

Orford, E. of, chooses, to represent Ashburton borough, **24**. 46–7

——'s only grateful friend, **24**. 292

Selwyn's joke to, about marriage, **10**. 32–3

Boone (? 'Bohun'), Daniel (1710–70), of Rook's Nest, Surrey; M.P.:

(?) Cholmondeley abuses, **30**. 31

Fox has, to supper, **30**. 56n

(?) HW defends, **30**, 31

Huxley succeeded by, as commissary-general of the musters, **17**. 494

Parliamentary debate by, on privately-raised regiments, **26**. 15

Parliamentary membership of, corrected, **43**. 313

Parliamentary speech by, on renewing regiments, **40**. 50

(?) reputation of, based on two speeches allegedly composed by others, **30**. 31

wife of, **30**. 329n

Boone, Thomas:

Müller encloses letter to HW in one to, **41**. 353n

Boorde *or* Borde, Andrew (ca 1490–1549), physician:

*Fyrst Boke of the Introduction of Knowledge, The*, **15**. 122

Booshala:

Banks describes, **1**. 329n

Boot; boots:

a boy's first, when mounting cock-horses, **10**. 321

Conway busy with, **37**. 358

Cumberland, D. of, preserved by, from horse's kick, **37**. 382n

Danvers wears, **35**. 70

Heathcote scolds son for wearing, in the house, **20**. 80n

heel piece of Charles I's, declined by HW, **28**. 338, 339

jockeys wear, tight, **31**. 108

man wears, to London theatre, **17**. 172

North, Hon. George, dances in, **33**. 284

people wear, to D. of Cumberland's levee, **37**. 291

spy hanged in, **19**. 201

Vorontsov wears, to dinner table, **21**. 248

Booth, Barton (1681–1733), actor:

Hamilton and guests discuss, at Bushy Park, **9**. 380

older generation could talk of, **23**. 351

Booth, Charles (1707–91), S.J.; head of English College at Rome:

Arundell, his pupil, not permitted by, to travel in Italy on All Souls Day, **21**. 339

[Booth, Charles, *continued*]
death of, at Arundell's seat, Wardour Castle, **21**. 339n

Booth, Edward, lawyer:
papers saved by, from fire, **20**. 321n

Booth, Frederick, attorney:
Hackman's brother-in-law, **33**. 99

Booth, George (1675–1758), 2d E. of Warrington:
Lort may allude to, **16**. 370n

Booth, Lady Katherine. *See* Clinton, Lady Katherine

Booth, Lady Mary (ca 1703–72), m. (1736) Harry Grey, 4th E. of Stamford:
unattractive at Coronation, **38**. 127

Booth, Peniston (1681–1765), Dean of Windsor:
death of, **7**. 396
Garter records shown by, to Montagu, **9**. 100
Keppel succeeds, **10**. 182, **43**. 134

Booth, Sarah, m. 1 Samuel Salmon; m. 2 (ca 1742–7) Sir Thomas Robinson, 1st Bt; 'Barbadoes ironmongress':
husband hopes to survive, **9**. 140

Booth; booths:
at Sadler's Wells, **39**. 266

Boothby, Sir Brooke (1743–1824), Bt:
painting owned by, **16**. 324n
Rousseau's dialogue published by, **29**. 48n

'Boothby, old.' *See* Clopton, Anne

'Boothby, Prince.' *See* Boothby Skrymsher, Charles

Boothby, Mrs Thomas. *See* Clopton, Anne (d. 1776)

Boothby, Sir William (1721–87), 4th Bt, ca 1740; army officer:
dances at Robinson's ball, **37**. 115
HW mentions, **10**. 7
HW sees, **20**. *142*
health of, out of order, **22**. 231
Mann grateful to, **20**. 151
—— praised by, **20**. 142
—— praises, **22**. 223
—— writes to, to Minorca, **22**. 166
Mann, Edward Louisa, suggests, as Horace Mann's proxy at Bath installation, **23**. 356, 362, 373, 379, 385, 389
Mann, James, told by, of D. of York's intended Italian journey, **22**. 165
York, D. of, accompanied by, on Tuscan tour, **22**. 220
—— announced by, **22**. 213

Boothby Skrymsher, Anne (ca 1737–1814), m. (1758) Hugo Meynell:
biographical information on, corrected, **43**. 102, 137
(?) Brussels to be visited by, **6**. 460
club at Almack's founded by, **10**. 305
(?) Du Deffand, Mme, has seen little of, **6**. 460
HW has not seen, **32**. 124
(?) HW sends fan to Mme du Deffand by, **6**. 455

HW sups at house of, **28**. 391
house of: formerly occupied by Ossorys, **32**. 192; leased for another year, **32**. 114
illness of, prevents Paris visit, **43**. 102
Ossory, Lady, will see on visit to SH, **32**. 114
SH visitors sent by, **12**. 241
talks of calling on Lady Ossory on way to Derbyshire, **32**. 132

Boothby Skrymsher (Clopton after 1792), Charles (ca 1740–1800):
Acciaioli, Contessa, in tears at departure of, from Tuscany, **21**. 481–2
biographical information about, **43**. 157
Carlisle might ask, about shoe-buckles of, **35**. 359
Douglas, Lady Mary, said to be marrying, **38**. 207
Mann sends patterns and letters to HW through, **21**. 481, 497, 501
might hate to be alderman, **35**. *335*
mother of, was cousin of HW's mother, **21**. 497
passport to be obtained by, at Venice, **21**. 482
Siddons, Mrs, admired by, **33**. 359
Walpole, Sir Edward, recommends, to Mann, **21**. 431, 482
Walpoles related to, **21**. 482

Boothby Skrymsher, Mrs Thomas. *See* Clopton, Anne

Bootikin; bootikins (mittens or foot-coverings for gout sufferers):
apothecary says that weakness on the breast is caused by, **24**. 80
Chute uses, **23**. 76, 252, 310
Du Deffand, Mme, mentions, **4**. 151, **5**. 286
—— thinks, may cause weakness, **6**. 203
exchanged for glove, **32**. 154, **34**. 188
'flannel glove,' **32**. 43
for Colmant: **6**. 409; cancelled, **6**. 415, 418
for hand, has no fingers, **39**. 235
for Orléans, **6**. 61–6, 68, 69, 133
gout shortened but not prevented by, **39**. 229–30
HW and Cole correspond about, **1**. 356, 360, 366, 369, 372, 373, **2**. 1, 3–4, 68, 70, 292
HW calls, post-horses, **39**. 235
HW praises, **23**. 76, 231, 246, 252, 310, 450, **24**. 66, 67, 70–1, 72, 76, 80, 268, 272, 281, 421, **25**. 149, 242
HW recommends, to Mann, **23**. 450, **24**. 67
HW sends, to Hénault, **3**. 236, 237, 277
HW sends, to Mann, **24**. 463, 494, 518
HW's gout deferred by, for three weeks, **39**. 206
HW's instructions for use of, **24**. 494
HW thinks he has sent, to Mann, **23**. 231
HW to teach use of, to Horace Mann II, **24**. 479
HW trusts in, **39**. 199
HW uses, **4**. 462, **6**. 7, 124, 131, 133, 137, 196–7, 203, **10**. 245, 266, 320, **31**. 168, **32**. 89, 210, 341, 343, **33**. 148, 154, 375, 379, **34**. 188, **39**. 157

HW uses, on hand, for rheumatism in shoulder, **24.** 463

HW wants to send, to Mann, **23.** 241, **24.** 71

HW writes with, **39.** 235

Hervey, Bns, used, **23.** 76

Mann attributes weakness of the feet to, **24.** 72, 79, 80, 280

—— glad to keep, as a curiosity, **23.** 239

—— in no hurry for, **24.** 79

—— may be weakened by, but HW is not, **24.** 281

—— not relieved by, **23.** 464, **24.** 72, 79

—— was probably helped by, without knowing it, **24.** 80

Mann, Edward Louisa, does not believe in, **24.** 71

—— helped by, **23.** 231

many Englishmen dislike, **24.** 72

method of using, **1.** 366

of oilskin, **23.** 464

Orford, Cts of, offers to take, to Mann, **23.** 231

physicians and apothecaries at first praise, later condemn them, **24.** 71

physicians scorn, **23.** 76, **41.** 281

rheumatism in arm not aided by, **33.** 129

sting prevented or extracted by, **39.** 226

to promote perspiration, **2.** 166

wonders done by, **39.** 244

Bootle, Sir Thomas (1685–1753), Kt, 1745; chancellor and keeper of the great seal to Frederick, P. of Wales; M.P.:

Court visited by, to compliment Ps of Wales on her rumoured confinement, **9.** 58

dirt and slovenliness of, **30.** 95n

Frederick, P. of Wales, and Breton visit, in Inner Temple, **30.** 94

Frederick, P. of Wales's chancellor, **17.** 234, **20.** 183

—— visited by, at Cliveden, **20.** 184

gold brocade nightgown of, **20.** 184

guardian of Lady Frances Seymour, **20.** 183

love letter of, widely circulated, **20.** 183

on circuit, **20.** 245

Pulteney employs, in 'dirty causes,' **17.** 234n

——'s follower, **18.** 72n

rumoured to be chief justice, **17.** 486

Somerset, D. of, leaves half a borough to, **20.** 11

Somerset, Ds of, wooed by, **20.** 183

speech of, scorned by Sir Robert Walpole, **17.** 234

taxing of Lady Frances Seymour's bills advocated by, **20.** 183

washerwoman told by, to send news of George II's death, **20.** 245, 254

Williams, Sir, C. H., satirizes, **18.** 320

Boquet River:

Burgoyne camps on, **28.** 354n

Borbón, Luis Antonio. *See* Luis Antonio

Borbone del Monte. *See* Del Monte

Borbonius, Matthias (1566–1629):

Latin motto by, **38.** 567n

Borcht, Henry van der, father and son (fl. 16th–17th centuries):

Masters's note on, **1.** 24

Borda, Jean-Charles (1733–99), mathematician:

social relations of, with Mme Geoffrin, **7.** 294

Borde, Charles (1711–81), author:

*Docteur Pansophe, Le,* **3.** 178–9, 190

*Prédiction tirée d'un ancien manuscrit sur 'La Nouvelle Héloïse,'* **3.** 93, 110

Secondat friend of, **3.** 110

Voltaire's friend, **1.** 114n

Borde. *See also* La Borde

Bordeaux, Abp of. *See* Rohan-Guéménée, Ferdinand-Maximilien-Mériadec de (1738–1813)

Bordeaux:

Baccalan from, **7.** 278

Borde from, **3.** 110

Clugny intendant at, **6.** 300

'dame de,' transferred by Mme du Deffand to Mme du Barry, **4.** 218

document about Windsor dated at, **40.** 220

epigram on Louis XV for statue at, **17.** 125

Gloucester, D. and Ds of, may visit, **7.** 28–9, **24.** 360

HW plays upon name of, **4.** 194, 203, 205, **6.** 5

*Histoire de la ville de, see under* Agneaux, Charles-Jean-Baptiste d'

insurrection at, over militia levy, **39.** 66

La Fayette sails from, **6.** 427

Louis XV's statue at, by Lemoyne, **17.** 125n

Mouchy commands at, **7.** 179

Shelburne to visit, **6.** 352, 354, 355

ship arrived at, with American news, **21.** 344

Townshend to visit, **6.** 352, 354, 355

visitors to: Aiguillon, **7.** 366; Beauvau, **32.** 341; Duras, Marquise de, **7.** 428; Noailles, Vicomtesse de, **7.** 428; Poix, Princesse de, **7.** 428; York, D. of, **7.** 365

Bordeaux, Parliament of:

arrêts from, against Aiguillon, **4.** 449n

edicts not registered by, **38.** 301

reformed, **5.** 105–6, **23.** 320

Richelieu intimidated by, **23.** 329

'Bordel':

HW's play on Bordeaux and, **4.** 194, 203, 205, **6.** 5

Bordeu, Théophile (1722–76), physician:

Lespinasse, Mlle, attended by, **6.** 296

Louis XV attended by, **6.** 47

Bordier, Jacques (1616–84), artist:

Petitot's medallions completed by, **7.** 325

Bordoni, Faustina (1700–81), m. (1730) Johann Adolph Hasse:

first arrival of, **34.** 258

racehorse as valuable as, **23.** 571

Boreas:

HW mentions, **11.** 113

*Boreas,* English frigate:

news received by, **24.** 242n, (?) 246, **32.** 321

Boredom:

reflections on: by HW, **6.** 477; by Mme du Deffand, **3.** 288, 293, 302, **4.** 324, 429, 450,

[Boredom, *continued*]
471, 496, **5.** 60, 67, 189, 318, 325, 415, 432, **6.** 197, 285, 477, **7.** 180, 216; by Mme de Maintenon, **4.** 237

Boreel, Anna Maria (1739–81), m. (1764) François Fagel:
(?) social relations of, with Comtesse d'Usson, **7.** 329

Boreel, Jacob (1711–78), Dutch deputy to England, 1759; ambassador 1761–2:
attack on Dutch convoy does not enrage, **22.** 71
English mission of, **21.** 290
nephew of, **22.** 71
(?) social relations of, with Comtesse d'Usson, **7.** 329

Borgherini, Signora. *See* Gaetani, Vittoria

Borgherini, Vincenzo (1683–1757), cavaliere:
corn embezzled by, **19.** 473

Borghese, Principessa. *See* Colonna, Agnese (1702–80)

Borghese, Principe:
Cumberland, D. of, entertained by, **23.** 566n
Rosenberg keeps, waiting, **23.** 104n
villa of, **23.** 23

Borghese, Camillo (1552–1621), *see* Paul V

Borghese, Camillo (1693–1763), Principe:
Gray's anecdote of, **13.** 210
HW calls, 'nasty foul thing,' **30.** 5
wife's attentions to Lincoln may have been curtailed by presence of, **30.** 6

Borghese, Francesco (1697–1759), cardinal, 1729:
death of, **21.** 304
Guadagni wants to alleviate bankruptcy of, **19.** 433
Spanish orders not to celebrate Francis I's election obeyed by, **19.** 183–4
valet of, drowns himself in Tiber, **19.** 444

Borghese, Don Paolo:
England visited by, **22.** 228
York, D. of, escorted by, at Rome, **22.** 228
—— receives mosaic from, **22.** 233n

Borghese, Scipione (1734–82), cardinal, 1770; maestro di camera, 1766:
Young Pretender notifies, of his return, **23.** 406

Borghese, Casa, at Rome:
cortège of, does not greet D. of York, **22.** 228

Borghese family:
expedient of, **22.** 226–7
York, D. of, to be entertained by, at ball, **22.** 229

Borghese, Villa, at Rome:
Leopold, Maria Louisa, and Maria Carolina dine at, **23.** 23
Young Pretender at, **17.** 13n

Borghese, Villa ('little') at Frascati:
HW's china room has ceiling copied from, **21.** 471

Borghesi, Domenico Antonio (ca 1686–after 1752), governor of Pitigliano:

Spanish invasion reported by, **17.** 178, 179

Borgia, Cesare (1475–1507):
cardinals murdered by, **22.** 254
character of, will appear better, at Day of Judgment, **32.** 146
Maupeou would have served, **24.** 35
modern crimes make those of, more plausible, **22.** 65
motto of, **31.** 156, **43.** 244
(?) Titian's portrait of, **9.** 414
Voltaire questions poisonings by, **22.** 253n

Borgia, Roderigo. *See* Alexander VI, Pope

Borgia family:
Rome the soil of, **24.** 154

Borgo, Dal. *See* Dal Borgo

Borgognissanti, Via, Florence:
Gavi's house in, searched, **17.** 217n

Borgognone, Ambrogio Stefani da Fossana (ca 1450–ca 1524), called; painter:
Furnese has pictures by, **21.** 172n

Borisov, ——, Russian Rear-Adm.:
squadron under, goes to Mediterranean, **25.** 60n

Borlase *or* Burlace, Edmund (d. ca 1682), physician; historian:
HW knew nothing of, **16.** 16

Borlase, Rev. William (1695–1772), antiquary:
HW praised by, to Lyttelton, for *Anecdotes of Painting*, **40.** 288

Bormida, Italian river:
Charles Emmanuel III crosses, **19.** 262

Bormida, Valle di:
Charles Emmanuel III marches by, **19.** 297

Born, (?) Abbé:
Mann receives apologies from, **19.** 339

Boromean Islands. *See* Borromean Islands

Borough, Sir John (d. 1643), Kt, 1624; Garter king-of-arms 1634–43:
*Burrhi impetus juveniles* by, **16.** 151n
coat of arms granted by, to Museum Minervæ, **16.** 151

Borough; boroughs, English Parliamentary:
admirals fight over, **21.** 484
Cornish: Boscawen 'manages,' **17.** 346n; Bubb Dodington influential in turning, against Sir Robert Walpole, **30.** 292n
country, instructions of, have pro-Jacobite flavour, **21.** 12
North accused by Luttrell of buying, **25.** 29
Orford's: lost by not trusting HW, **24.** 308; Orford, Cts of, leaves, to son's care, **24.** 46–7; Sharpe recommends sale of, **24.** 52; tended by Lucas, **25.** 462; *see also* Ashburton; Callington; Castle Rising; Hedon; King's Lynn
Wilkes wants more equal representation of, **24.** 187

Boroughbridge, Yorkshire:
Cholmley M.P. for, **28.** 491n
Wilkinson of, **10.** 49n

Borough-jobbers:
House of Commons punishes, **22.** 584

Borough town:
  Cowper regales Florentine mob as if he lived in, **24**. 242
Borra, Giovanni Battista (fl. 1747–86):
  Grecian temple at Stowe ornamented by, **35**. 77n
Borré de la Chavanne, Joseph, Comte de la Chavanne:
  Aix and Breda conferences attended by, **19**. 440n
  Charles Emmanuel III sends instructions to, for Aix congress, **19**. 446n
  Gorsegno told by, of ruptured peace negotiations, **19**. 440
  refuses to sign Aix treaty, **19**. 480
Borrodale, John:
  Vernon, Caldecott, and, partners in Ludgate St, **20**. 361n
Borromean Islands:
  Mann, Horace II and James II, to see illumination at, **25**. 586
  Mann, Horace II, to visit, **24**. 129
  to be illuminated for visit of K. and Q. of Naples, **25**. 586
Borromée, Charles. *See* Borromeo, Carlo
Borromeo, Carlo (1538–84), saint:
  church of Barnabiti dedicated to, **14**. 20
  festival of, **20**. 451, **21**. 148–9, **22**. 355
  old woman hails canonization of, because he had seduced her, **28**. 152
Borromeo, Vitaliano (1720–93), Abp of Thebes; cardinal; nuncio to Tuscany and the Empire:
  Archinto orders, not to get Stosch's maps, **21**. 192
  Mann disputes with, **21**. 235
Borry, Jacques:
  (?) attends session of parliament of Paris, **8**. 171
Borsini, ——, keeper of Pellegrino inn at Bologna:
  York, D. of, lodges with, **22**. 232n
Bosanquet, Jacob:
  Monson sells Broxbournbury to, **42**. 219n
Bosarno. *See* Rosarno
Boscarcuff, Capt.; Russian naval officer:
  Russian ship commanded by, **33**. 214
Boscawen, Anne (1744–1831), maid of honour:
  genealogy of, **10**. 352
  Trevor, Margaret, attended by, in last illness, **10**. 302
Boscawen, Hon. Anne Evelyn (1791–1871), m. (1810) Sir George Warrender, Bt:
  'pretty babe,' **31**. 390n
Boscawen, Charlotte (d. 1829):
  genealogy of, **10**. 352
Boscawen, Hon. Edward (1711–61), Adm.; M.P.:
  Admiralty does not hear from, **20**. 511
  —— includes, **20**. 259
  ——post retained by, **21**. 25, 73
  Anson has, sent to Pondicherry, **20**. 113
  —— resented by, **20**. 259
  ——'s quarrel with, at Cape Finisterre, **20**. 113

—— 's 'victory' really due to, **20**. 38
brother prefers, as Truro candidate, **17**. *451*
Byng's execution eagerly sought by, **21**. 55n
Clevland's letters from, **21**. 326n, 332n
disgraced for refusing to serve under Hawke, **21**. 120
dissatisfaction of, explained, **21**. 130
fame of, **31**. 20
fleet of: arrives with prize, **21**. 511; cruises off Toulon, **21**. 297; France threatens invasion to get Admiralty to recall, **20**. 579n; goes to Gibraltar for supplies, **21**. 307; sails from Plymouth, **20**. 480n, 487n
Florentines deplore illegality of victory of, **21**. 334
French captains captured by, **35**. 235
French fleet burnt by, on Portuguese coast, **35**. 294
French fleet defeated by, **15**. 134n
French fleet escapes, **9**. 168n
French fleet missed but two ships captured by, **35**. 235
French frigates at Toulon destroyed by ships of, **21**. 303
French man of war captured by, **20**. 511
French privateers not captured by, in *Royal George*, **21**. 120n
French ships seized by, **29**. 8n
French transports to be 'swallowed up' by, **20**. 483
George II coldly receives, as Admiralty lord, **37**. 481
HW and Hon. Mrs Osborn do not mourn death of, **9**. 332
HW mentions, **21**. 128
HW procures scarlet spider from, **9**. 114
Hocquart surrenders only when ship of, joins attackers, **20**. 489
Howe ordered by, to attack French fleet, **20**. 113
hurricane injures fleet of, **20**. 113
Hyères reached by, **21**. 292
La Clue could not easily be attacked by, **20**. 511
——'s flag-ship *L'Océan* burnt by, **21**. 326n
Lagos, Battle of, reported by, **21**. 326n
La Motte's fleet not intercepted by, on way from Louisbourg, **21**. 145n
Louisbourg captured by, **21**. 232n, **30**. 148, **35**. 103
—— may be attacked by, **20**. 511
Mann awaits news of, **20**. 487, **21**. 318
——'s congratulations on victory of, **21**. 332
Martinique fleet to be intercepted by, **20**. 579
Mauritius not captured by, **20**. 113n
Mediterranean laurels unlikely to be added to American ones of, **21**. 297
name of, Cornish for 'obstinacy,' **20**. 259
*Namur* commanded by, **20**. 38n
——, ship of, lost in hurricane, **20**. 113n
old tar's alleged letter to, about Port Mahon's capture, **21**. 52
Pitt selects, for Admiralty, **21**. 104n

[Boscawen, Hon. Edward, *continued*]
Pondicherry not taken by, **20.** 113n
Portsmouth visited by, to command fleet, **20.** 468n
Portuguese pardon to be asked for La Clue's defeat by, in Portuguese waters, **21.** 352
Santini's watch might be sent by courier to, **21.** 302
severely wounded off Cape Finisterre, **20.** 113n
taciturnity of, **30.** 148
Toulon fleet demolished by, **21** 326, 330
—— fleet may be engaged in battle by, **21.** 318
—— fleet may drive, away, **21.** 302–3
—— fleet to be bottled up by, **21.** 292
victories expected from, **21.** 230
wife of, **11.** 34n, **14.** 119n, **32.** 335
Boscawen, Edward (1787–1841), 4th Vct Falmouth; cr. (1821) E. of Falmouth:
'pretty babe,' **31.** 390n
Boscawen, Mrs Edward. *See* Glanville, Frances Evelyn
Boscawen, Elizabeth (1747–1828), m. (1766) Henry Somerset, 5th D. of Beaufort:
HW and Chute afraid of, **10.** 228
Boscawen, Hon. Elizabeth (1785–1816), m. (1808) Lord Arthur Somerset:
'pretty babe,' **31.** 390n
Boscawen, Frances (b. 1746), m. (1773) John Leveson Gower:
SH visited by, **12.** 231, 247
Boscawen, Hon. Frances (d. 1794):
'pretty babe,' **31.** 390n
Boscawen, Hon. George (1712–75), army officer; M.P.:
at Bruges, **37.** 151
Boys, Commodore, sends invasion report to, **21.** 305n
Cumberland, D. of, angry with, about court martial, **9.** 93
daughter of, **10.** 302n
death of, **23.** 98
Dover Castle commanded by, **21.** 305n
genealogy of, **10.** 352
HW to entertain, at SH, **9.** 161
Harcourt hears from, of Montagu's possible ranger's post, **10.** 199
son of, **10.** 295n
wife of, **9.** 12n
Boscawen, George (b. 1745), army officer; M.P.:
biographical information about, corrected, **43.** 137
drinks claret and gambles at quinze at Adderbury, **10.** 297
genealogy of, **10.** 352
HW regrets reading by, of *Mysterious Mother*, **10.** 298
Montagu's youth restored by, **10.** 296–7
—— visited by, at Adderbury, **10.** 295–6
*Mysterious Mother* acted by, at Adderbury, **10.** 297, 300
Boscawen, Mrs George. *See* Trevor, Anne
Boscawen, George Evelyn (1758–1808), 3d Vct

Falmouth, 1782:
mistress of, **32.** 138n
Boscawen, Hugh (ca 1680–1734) cr. (1720) Vct Falmouth:
son of, **9.** 93n, **23.** 99n
wife of, **9.** 141n
Boscawen, Hugh (1707–82), 2d Vct Falmouth, 1734:
Beefeaters assigned to, **19.** 397
brother of, **17.** 451, **20.** 113n, 484n
Byron's acquittal voted by, **38.** 535
Cornish boroughs 'managed' by, **17.** 346n
death of, **25.** 241
Dorset, D. of, succeeds, as capt. of Yeomen of the Guard, **25.** 241
dying, **36.** 205
Frederick, P. of Wales, quarrels with, over Truro elections, **17.** 451
Opposition's Cornish failure due to switch of, to Administration, **43.** 243
regiment raised by, **19.** 128
Townshend's witticism on stomach of, **37.** 429
Boscawen, Mrs Hugh. *See* Godfrey, Charlotte (ca 1679–1754)
Boscawen, Hon. John Evelyn (1790–1851):
'pretty babe,' **31.** 390n
Boscawen, Lady Margaret. *See* Clinton, Lady Margaret
Boscawen, William (1752–1811), barrister; translator:
birth of, **9.** 141
genealogy of, **10.** 352
Bosc du Bouchet, Jeanne-Grâce (1703–74), m. Charles-Augustin Ferriol, Comte d'Argental:
death of, **6.** 116
Du Deffand, Mme, gives opinion of, **6.** 116, 120
Pont-de-Veyle's death desired by, **6.** 116, 120
Boschi, Giovanni Carlo (1715–88), cardinal, 1766:
Bourbon Courts would exclude, from Papal councils, **23.** 16, 35
(?) Clement XIII summons, to advisory congregation, **21.** 308n
Boscobel House, Staffs, Richard Penderel's seat:
(?) HW compares, to Meeke's house, **10.** 105
Bošković, Père Rudjer Josif (1711–87), Jesuit explorer:
Cortona and Florence visited by, **43.** 281
Royal Society agrees to California trip of, **22.** 527
Bosnia:
Mahmud I regains part of, **18.** 53n
Bosse, Joseph de, HW's French bookseller:
books bought from, **31.** 245
Bosselman de Bellemont, ——:
*Maintenoniana*, **6.** 50, 103, 110–11, **43.** 97
Bossi, Col.:
Austrian defeat blamed on, **24.** 404n
Bossier, La. *See* La Bossier
Bossiney, Cornwall:
election at, **43.** 137

mayor of, **17.** 233n
petition over election in, **17.** 233, 247
spelling of, corrected, **43.** 131
'Bossu, Cardinal,' of Alsace:
Benedict XIV told by, that Young Pretender
has turned Protestant, **20.** 333n
Bossu. *See also* Bussy; Le Bossu
Bossuet, Jacques-Bénigne (1627–1704), Bp of
Condom, 1669; of Meaux, 1681:
Académie hears eulogies of, **6.** 189
Burigny's life of, **7.** 277
Du Deffand, Mme, gives opinion of, **6.** 435
HW's opinion of, **5.** 12
hermitage might be entered by, to annoy
Fénelon, **28.** 221
*Histoire des variations des églises, L'*, by, **20.**
510, **34.** 20
Necker, Mme, praises eloquence of, **32.** 260
Bossut, Charles (1730–1814), abbé:
office to be given to, **6.** 155
Bostock, Mr:
notes on Oulton and Starkey families by, **1.**
251
Boston, Bn. *See* Irby, Frederick (1749–1825);
Irby, Sir William (1707–75)
Boston, Lincs:
mob at, break Bertie's windows, and menace
Lincoln races, **21.** 137n
Boston, Massachusetts:
American army shows spirit in siege of, **24.**
158
American troops in, **28.** 206
Barré deserts people of, **28.** 142
'Boston Massacre' at, **23.** 209
Bunker Hill 'victory' at, **24.** 119
Burgoyne to bring good news from, **32.** 286
Canadians are expected to help conquer
people of, **28.** 216
cargoes of ships at sea to be sold to benefit
poor of, **39.** 227
Chatham moves for evacuation of, **24.** 75n,
**32.** 227n, 228, **39.** 245–6
Cincinnati society taken for canonization at,
**33.** 431
colonies to support, against English troops,
**39.** 226
Conway, unlike Germain, does not threaten,
**39.** 239
custom house at, endangered by rebellion,
**39.** 100n
England threatens, **23.** 561
English army may withdraw from: to England, **28.** 210–11; to Halifax, **24.** 161
English army withdraws from, **24.** 204, **28.**
268–9, 411
English have lost, **24.** 336, **28.** 227
English may abandon, **24.** 137–8
English officer expects to be in prison in, **33.**
279
English troops sail to, **24.** 197n, **32.** 248, 380,
**39.** 197n
Estaing gets supplies from, **7.** 75n
—— said to be in harbour of, **33.** 34

famished, **24.** 175, **28.** 294
Fox, Hon. Henry, stationed in, **41.** 273n
France to have ships built at, **24.** 386
Gage fortifies, **39.** 204n
—— general at, **23.** 44n
——'s army an asylum for magistrates of, and
security for port, **39.** 232
HW fears, is lost, **28.** 227
HW imagines Earls of, **33.** 421
Howes said to have sailed to, **24.** 327, **28.** 327,
**32.** 370
Howe's troops eat pickles at, **28.** 294
Howe supposed to have blockaded d'Estaing
in, **24.** 418
—— withdraws from, **28.** 268–9, 411
Mann wants to hear of Gage's reception by,
**24.** 11
minute-men raised by, **39.** 239–40
news of destruction of, would be welcome in
England, **28.** 174
new Thucydides may be produced by, **24.** 62
New York imitates opposition of, to tea, **24.**
13
Parliamentary acts about, *see under* Parliament: acts of
Parliament deliberates over, **23.** 568
regiment at, said to mutiny, **39.** 240
riots at, mentioned in Grenville's speech, **22.**
566n
Scottish firms send supplies to English army
in, **41.** 312n
ship from, in Jacobite service, **37.** 237
store ships for, seized at New York, **41.** 303
Stowe not to enshrine patriots of, **31.** 94
'tea party' at, **23.** 550, **24.** 13
Toulon squadron may go to, **24.** 386
transports to, are expensive, **41.** 313
turbulent temper of, **23.** 66
'Boston Castle,' Yorks, Lord Effingham's lodge:
Mason not qualified for membership in club
at, **28.** 208
*Boston Gazette*:
Gage's misconduct said to be reported in,
**39.** 240
Boston Port Act. *See under* Parliament: acts of
Bosville, Godfrey (1717–84), 'Nikin'; 'Nykin':
answer by, about his lack of children, **18.** 264
HW enjoys hearing of, **18.** 298
heir wanted by, **35.** 41
Mann called on by, **18.** 238–9
——'s opinion of, **18.** 242, 251
—— to entertain, **18.** 275
naval captain lodges with, **18.** 251
red coat donned by, **18.** 309
Traun's army may be joined by, **18.** 309
wife advised by, to leave Florence with Prole,
**18.** 286
wife freed by paper of, granting separation,
**18.** 309
Bosville, Mrs Godfrey. *See* Wentworth, Diana
Boswell, James (1740–95), biographer:
*Account of Corsica, An* ('histoire de Paoli'):
Boswell presents, to HW, **41.** 138; Choiseul

[Boswell, James, *continued*]

has translation made of, 4. 113, 124, 126; complimentary letters about, 41. 138–9n; Du Deffand, Mme, and, 4. 60, 82, 109; Gray's remarks on, 2. 161n, 14. 174; HW discusses, 14. 170–1; Wiart translates, 4. 82, 87, 92, 106, 109, 113, 124–5, 126

books of, can readily be taken up and laid down, 42. 273

Booth approached by, for visit to Hackman in prison, 33. 99n

Burke, Richard, mistaken for, 33. 466

Calder's witticism on Dr Johnson and, 43. 166

contemptible for practice of flattery and humility, 11. 275

'Corsican fairy' seen by, 29. 95n

*Critical Strictures* by, ridicules Mallet's assumed name, 43. 195

Cunynghame friend of, 12. 154n

Davies introduces, to Johnson, 1. 151n

*Decision of the Court of Session upon . . . Literary Property* by, 28. 135n

dines at Shakespeare Tavern, 11. 319n

dines with Beloe at Wilkes's, 15. 246n

discussions of Johnsonian writings of, spoil conversation, 31. 242

Donaldson's counsel, 28. 135n

Eglintoun friend of, 6. 357n

Gibson's hanging attended by, 1. 135n

Gray discussed by HW and, 11. 276

HW alludes to, in verses, 12. 258

HW apologizes to, for missing his visits, 41. 1–2

HW calls: 'jackanapes,' 25. 634; 'Johnson's biographical zany,' 25. 638; 'quintessence of busybodies,' 29. 144; 'sot,' 33. 509

HW complains of having been attacked by, in newspapers, 14. 170

HW considers, a classic compared with Hayley, 33. 509

HW converses with, about Corsica, 41. 2n, 138

HW gives account to, of Theodore of Corsica, 14. 170

HW mentions, 6. 297

HW's conversation with, 29. 144–5

HW's coolness to Johnson explained by, 11. 276

HW's correspondence with, 41. 1–2, 138

HW's 'elegant writings' please, 41. 138

HW's epigram on Johnson and, 33. 509n

HW silent in company of, 33. 466n

HW visited by, 7. 296, 11. 276

Hesse-Cassel visited by, 9. 42n

Hessenstein met by, in Genoa, 22. 292n

incapable of inventing anything, 14. 174

Johnson, Dr Samuel, exposed by, 36. 236, 241, 249

——'s faults aped by, without his sense, 39. 438

——'s *fidus Achates*, 11. 275

*Journal of a Tour to the Hebrides* by, 25. 634, 39. 437–8, 43. 292

*Letter to the People of Scotland, A*, advertisement for, ridiculed by HW, 33. 462

*Life of Johnson*: Beauclerk favourably pictured in, 15. 320n; HW awaits, 33. 466; HW gently treated in, 11. 275–6; HW's opinion of, 11. 275; Mrs Damer's copy of, 43. 148; publication of, 11. 272

Malone (and sisters) and Courtenay accompany, to SH, Hampton Court, Bushy Park, and Pope's grotto, 42. 143n

Mann described by, as 'neat-talking minister,' 17. 313n

Mason's conversation with, 16. 263n, 29. 358

——'s exchange of letters with, about Temple's character of Gray, 28. 209

——'s *Gray* the model for, 28. 185n

Montagu, Mrs, disparaged by Johnson according to, 25. 634, 640

monument for Dr Johnson, HW asked by, to subscribe to, 11. 276

Morell's preaching heard by, 1. 8n

Murray, Fanny, knows, 9. 80n

Ossory, Cts of, sends 'Three Vernons' to, 34. 59n

Paoli accompanied by, 23. 142n

——'s panegyrist, 12. 63

'Paolists' led by, 23. 31n

Piozzi, Mrs, disavows, 25. 634, 640

possible contributor of collection of characters, 28. 489n

Reynolds breakfasts with, 33. 486n

Rudd, Mrs, mistress of, 11. 208n, 28. 192n

*St James's Chronicle* letter probably not by, 43. 188

San Gillio, Contessa di, mentioned by, 20. 309n

satiric prints of, 25. 641

Seward friend of, 16. 189n

SH visited by, 12. 223

Waters, banker of, in Paris, 19. 507n

Wilkes met by, at Naples, 22. 292n

Wolcot ridicules, 25. 638, 640–1, 643

wrote when mad or drunk, 33. 462

Bosworth Field, battle of:

bas-relief of, 9. 64–5

battle of, 14. 165n

Brackenbury dies at, for Richard III, 41. 113

HW wrongly alleged to own picture of, on jewel, 42. 289

Henry VII's actions after, 14. 79

Norfolk, D. of, slain at, 33. 505

Botanical garden:

at Chelsea, 18. 183, 216

*See also under* Landscape effects

Botanical Society, Florence. *See under* Royal Botanical Society, Florence

*Botanic Garden, The. See under* Darwin, Erasmus

Botany:

Bute's fondness for, 39. 61

Fitzpatrick, Richard, interested in, 34. 123

French, Mrs, devoted to, 42. 271

HW jokes about Charles III and Squillace discussing, **39.** 61
HW's lack of, **31.** 267
lettuce gone to seed confuses HW's, **37.** 292
Botany Bay, Australia:
*Guardian* sails for, **11.** 92n
Gunning, Miss, may be sent to, **11.** 208
Boteler, Lady. *See* Butler, Lady Eleanor
Boteler, Mrs:
SH visited by, **12.** 242
Boteler, Lady Eleanor. *See* Butler, Lady Eleanor
Boteler, Philip (d. ?1787), Capt.:
French capture, on the *Ardent*, **24.** 511
Boteler, Sir Ralph (d. 1473), 6th Lord Sudeley:
documents witnessed by, **14.** 76
son of, **1.** 304n
Boteler, Sir Thomas (15th century):
marriage of, **1.** 304n, **15.** 171n
Botetourt, Bn. *See* Berkeley, Norborne (1717–70)
Botetourt, barony of:
Berkeley's claim to, discussed in House of Lords, **38.** 354, 368
Bothal and Shipwash, Northumberland:
Smallridge rector of, **14.** 203n
Bothenar. *See* Bothmar
Botherel de Bédée, Françoise-Jacquette-Charlotte-Antoinette (d. 1788):
Aiguillon, Mme d', has social relations with, **7.** 334
Du Deffand, Mme, gives opinion of, **4.** 299
——'s social relations with, **4.** 299, **5.** 183, **7.** 340
Rueil visited by, **4.** 443
Bothmar, Johann (or Hans) Caspar (1656–1732), Graf von:
George I gives house to, **13.** 11n
Hanoverian minister to England, **18.** 110n
letter of, quoted, **2.** 357
(?) Nomis related to, **18.** 110n
print of, **40.** 236
Bothmar, Sofia Eleanora Dorotea, m. (1712) Marchese Benedetto Nomis:
of Hanover, **18.** 110n
name of, corrected, **43.** 248
son of, **18.** 110
Bothmer, Hans Caspar von (1727–87), Count of the Empire; Danish minister to England:
Selwyn's joke to, at Bute's levee, **10.** 35
Bothwell, E. of. *See* Hepburn, James
Bothwell (Scotland):
pictures removed to, **11.** 152n
Botoner, William. *See* Worcester, William
Botot, Marie-Anne (1714–96), called Mlle de Dangeville; actress:
HW mentions, **30.** 26
Bott, Johann (1670–1745), Prussian architect:
Frederick II's *Mémoires* mention, **35.** 266
Wentworth Castle designed by, **35.** 266
Botta Adorno, Antonietto *or* Anton Otto (ca 1688–1774), army officer; imperial commissary in Italy:

Accademia celebration could be substituted by, for Drawing-Room, **22.** 367
Affry's plan to invade England announced to Mann at house of, **21** 297–8
altered Court ceremonies at Florence explained by, **22.** 378–9
always thinks of his soldiers, **22.** 124
anti-French and pro-Austrian, **22.** 22
architectural and artistic boasts of, **22.** 254
audiences given by, **21.** 148, 151
Austrian-Prussian peace not believed by, **22.** 118
Austrians led by, towards Genoa, **19.** 297
autumn opera desired by, at Florence, **22.** 166
believes that Ferrers must have been stripped of rank before execution, **21.** 410
boys in streets ridicule, **2.** 334
Brussels dispute over precedence settled by, **22.** 44
burletta to be permitted by, on Emperor's birthday, **22.** 171
cardinals avoid Florence during régime of, because of ceremonial, **22.** 28
chair models imported by, from France, **21.** 557
Charles Emmanuel III complains to, about Genoese peace terms, **19.** 312
—— may give troops to, to chastise the Genoese, **19.** 352
circular letter of, to Regency and foreign ministers on Peter III's overthrow, **22.** 63
close room of, heated by German stove, **21.** 370
coaches and horses prepared by, for Leopold, **22.** 123, 157
Cobentzl replaces, as first minister of Austrian Netherlands, **20.** 320n
commands troops in Tuscany for Francis I, **21.** 471n
Coote's victory belittled by, **21.** 441
courier awaited by, for news of battle, **21.** 361
courtyard of: French horns play in, to celebrate victories, **21.** 317, 441, 445, 456, 463
Craon alone to have been superior to, **19.** 23
——'s house occupied and altered by, **21.** 134, 468, 557
death of, expected, **21.** 12–14, 18
Del Monte advised by, about receiving D. of York, **22.** 166
Deux Ponts's resignation rumoured at house of, **21.** 304
dignity of, hurt by insults to Francis I's flag, **21.** 269–70
English brig's release deplored by, **21.** 334
Englishman's huzza startles, **21.** 445
English restitution of Dutch ship announced to, **21.** 287–8
English secret expedition not believed by, **21.** 446
equipage and equerry of, **21.** 179
explanation by, of José Manoel's escape from assassin, **21.** 276
extreme unction administered to, **22.** 13, 14

[Botta Adorno, Antonietto, *continued*]
Flanders and Genoa hate, **20.** 320
floods prevent return of, **21.** 510
Florentine festivities by, for Joseph II's coronation, **22.** 237n
Florentine good weather ascribed by, to Madonna della Impruneta, **21.** 276
Florentine opponents of, fail to undermine his good credit in Vienna, **22.** 254
Florentines' repugnance for inoculation shocks, **22.** 150
foreign ministers rebuffed by, till they get new credentials, **22.** 345
Francis I and Maria Theresa hoped, would be influential at Florence, **22.** 448
Francis I orders, to accredit young Pucci as minister to England, **22.** 180
—— orders, to have Te Deum sung for Kunersdorf battle, **21.** 317n
—— represented by, at St John's festival, **21.** 302
——'s death notified by, **22.** 329n
——'s deputy in command of Florence, **21.** 178n
——'s favours to, **22.** 338
——'s plan to acquire Corsica denied by, **22.** 157
——'s plea from, in Gravier case, **22.** 266–7
—— to receive account of Stosch's collection from, **21.** 149n
Francis III forbids daughter-in-law to see, since she must yield precedence, **22.** 201–2
Frederick II's defeat believed by, **21.** 241
Gavi and Novi approached by, **19.** 297
Genoa's negotiations with, **19.** 312, 314–16, 337
Genoese mob to be subdued by, **19.** 359
Genoese revolt and Provençal failure blamed on, **19.** 344, 364
George II's health misrepresented by, **21.** 202
Gorsegno accuses, of responsibility for Genoa's revolt, **19.** 344
Grafton calls on, **22.** 28
Grand Ducal title not permitted by, until Leopold II's appointment is announced, **22.** 335
Grub St reports in Vienna court gazette read aloud at house of, **22.** 178
HW does not approve of wall-hangings of, **21.** 471
HW wants more news of, **21.** 178
illness of, leaves Mann's the only reception on gala day, **22.** 15
impartial, **21.** 307
Incontri, Abp, pleased by audience with, **21.** 151
Joseph II irritated at opposition by, to demands on Tuscany, **22.** 447n
——'s plenipotentiary, **22.** 330
Karl Wilhelm Ferdinand to be received by, **22.** 454n
Leopold II's and D. of York's approach keep, busy, **22.** 166–7

Leopold II's decision not to have a Te Deum distresses, **22.** 334
——'s disapproval of, **22.** 337, 379, 398, 454
——'s *grand maître*, **22.** 246
—— to be met by, at Pietra Mala, **22.** 334
Liechtenstein, P. of, next to, in knowledge of Court procedure, **22.** 153–4
Lorenzi brings book to, on Kloster-Zeven convention, **21.** 235
—— criticized by, for attentions to Wilkes, **22.** 282
—— exasperates, with complaints, **21.** 275n
—— may inform, of English secret expedition, **21.** 446
—— reprimanded by, **21.** 475
Lorraine faction discredits, to Francis I, **22.** 13
—— faction hopes for fall of, **21.** 424
major's plan for church at Pitti palace approved by, **22.** 258–9
Malta may be visited by, as volunteer defender, **21.** 494n
Mann advised by, to quit house when D. of York occupies it, **22.** 170
—— advises, about placing statues, **22.** 124
—— a favourite with, for not insisting on precedence, **22.** 44
—— calls on, at Poggio Imperiale, **22.** 40–1
—— complains to, of Austrian incivilities to English, **21.** 462
—— declares Louisbourg's capture at house of, **21.** 235
—— defends Bristol's dealing with Spain to, **21.** 564
—— discusses things with, **21.** 329, 343–4, **22.** 282
—— does not visit, on Francis I's birthday, **22.** 173–4
—— must not be frightened by, **21.** 313
—— no longer represents all Ireland in presence of, **21.** 371
—— persuades, to ask Francis I to yield to English demands, **22.** 266–7
—— presents his credentials to, **22.** 377n
—— presents Strathmore and Tavistock to, **21.** 564
—— prevented by headache from taking George III's letter to, **21.** 464
——'s advice from, about D. of York, **22.** 176, 193
——'s conferences with, invented by Lorenzi, **21.** 356
——'s debates with, over Protestant girls' conversion, **22.** 249
——'s French horns will exceed those of, **21.** 326
——'s opinion of, **21.** 148–9, 202
——'s retort to, enjoyed by HW, **22.** 2
—— talks with Firmian at house of, **21.** 339
—— tells, of Martinique conquest, **22.** 22
—— tells, that England will continue war in Germany, **21.** 456

—— tells Niccolini and, about insignificance of Carrickfergus, **21**. 381

—— to ask, when to pay homage to new court, **22**. 327

—— told information by, **21**. 271, 280, 302, 307, 329, 333, 469, **22**. 30, 41, 63, 74, 87, 89, 345, 356

—— to show Vienna Court Gazette to, and Frederick II's account, **21**. 463

—— unable to see, after Francis I's death, **22**. 330

—— will not get such high talk from, **21**. 315

Maria Isabella's death excuses, from entertaining Vorontsovs, **22**. 194

Maria Louisa will probably not approve of taste of, **22**. 335

masks forbidden by, **21**. 435

Mediterranean war preparations observed by, **21**. 494

Modena, Ps of, entertained by delegates of, at Pietra Mala, **22**. 202

Neapolitan ministers tell, to observe strict neutrality, **21**. 271

nephew of, from Pavia, disappointed by uncle's recovery, **22**. 14

Neri, Pompeo, intimate with, **21**. 125n

never stirs before hearing mass, when commander-in-chief at Genoa, **21**. 329

Newcastles and Nuncio placed by, at Brussels dinner, **22**. 44

news expected by, from Germany, **21**. 308

Niccolini tells, of Mann's coming promotion, **22**. 317–18

nuncio disputes with Mann at house of, **21**. 235

Onorati deprived by, of precedence, **22**. 44

palace, coaches, and plate prepared by, for Leopold II, **22**. 123

people get little information from, about Leopold's arrival, **22**. 333–4

Peter III's overturn announced by, with French horns at Poggio Imperiale, **22**. 63

pink of Court breeding, **22**. 438

Pitti palace ignorantly rearranged by, **21**. 557, **22**. 123–4, 157, 178–9, 206, 246, 290–1, 337

Pitt's attention to Regency flatters, **21**. 503

—— to receive letter from, **21**. 180

post of major-domo regarded by, as degradation, **22**. 454

prides himself on tawdry taste, **21**. 557

Pucci's credentials botched by, **21**. 197

recovers, **22**. 14

Regency members' visits not returned by, **21**. 148

Regency to be headed by, **21**. 107

remark by, about dignity of archdukes, **24**. 23

retires to Pavia as imperial plenipotentiary, **22**. 448, 454

returns to Florence in political triumph, **21**. 435

Richecourt could not endure, as military chief in Tuscany, **19**. 23

Rosenberg to replace, as major-domo and first minister, **22**. 447–8, 453–4

Russian victory announced to, by express, **21**. 317

Sackville's retention of rank incomprehensible to, **21**. 411

satisfaction of, over Louisbourg's capture, puzzles HW, **21**. 244

Schulenburg replaces, in Austrian command, **19**. 363n

Siena assembly ordered by, for D. of York, **22**. 224

Siena inn cleaned up by order of, for D. of York, **22**. 223

Spaniards attacked by, **19**. 291

Stampa to be succeeded by, as commissary-general in Italy, **20**. 320

Thurn at odds with, **22**. 398

Townshend and Villettes complain to, about peace terms, **19**. 312

troops reviewed by, **21**. 179

Tuscan succession to be arranged by, **22**. 87

Tuscany to be governed by, **21**. 107, 125

unpopular because of food shortage, **22**. 206, 337, 448

Vienna rejects proposals of, **22**. 13

—— to be visited by, **21**. 424, **22**. 87

—— visited by, **21**. 424, **22**. 245n, 246, 454n

Viviani's credentials to, **22**. 349

Vorontsov asks, to get house in Florence for 50 people, **22**. 180

war against Algiers advocated by, **22**. 259

would be a Prussian sympathizer if not in Austrian service, **21**. 463

York, Cardinal, evades, **22**. 250

York, D. of, exchanges visits with, **22**. 213

—— urged by, to stay at Florence, **22**. 232

Botta Adorno, Giuseppe (1725–99), Marchese; Austrian field marshal:

(?) Coke, Lady Mary, sees, at Lerici, **23**. 552

(?) uncle's succession to be claimed by, **22**. 14

Botta Adorno, Jacopo (1729–1803), Marchese; Austrian field marshal:

(?) Coke, Lady Mary, sees, at Lerici, **23**. 552

(?) uncle's succession to be claimed by, **22**. 14

Bottarelli, Giovanni Gualberto (fl. 1741–79), librettist:

Lauraguais's epistle to, **32**. 92

*Motezuma* by, **24**. 90

*Zanaida*, opera by, **38**. 201

Bottari, Giovanni Gaetano (1689–1775), Monsignore; librarian of the Vatican:

'ablest man in Rome,' **21**. 475n

(?) anti-Jesuit champion, **21**. 475

Mariette writes to, of attempt to translate *Anecdotes of Painting*, **41**. 99n

notes by, on Fabretti's prints, **22**. 233n

Patch's engravings criticized by, **23**. 469

*Raccolta di lettere sulla pittura* by, sent by Mann to HW, **23**. 265–6, 276, 315

Bottesham. *See* Bottisham

*Bottetourt*, English ship:
St Vincent's capture reported by, **24.** 503n
Bottetourt. *See also* Botetourt
Botteville. *See* Buisson, Pierre de
Bottisham, Cambs:
Smith vicar of, **2.** 354n
Bottisham Hall, Cambs, Soame Jenyns's seat:
Cole dines at, **2.** 53
Jenyns of, **14.** 38n
Bottle; bottles:
Bland's guests pelt 'mob' in Pall Mall with, **30.** 84
earthen, HW buys, at Mrs Kennon's sale, **37.** 439n
liquor: English ministers settle affairs over, **23.** 157–8; HW calls, 'country interpreter,' **30.** 34; HW uses, as means of conversing with Norfolk neighbours, **30.** 34
of boiling water, to warm D. of Gloucester, **36.** 139
of purple glass, bought by HW, **39.** 32n
quart, deceives people, **20.** 29
salts in, **30.** 84
square, **43.** 58
*See also* Hunting-bottle
*Bottoncino*:
Chute buys essence of roses in, **18.** 214
Boucault, Mme. *See* Moreton de Chabrillan, Jeanne-Marie-Thérèse-Tècle de
Bouchard, Giuseppe, French bookseller at Florence:
(?) book ordered by, **20.** 117
Locke's works sold by, **20.** 117n
Bouchard d'Esparbez de Lussan, François-Pierre-Charles (b. 1714), Marquis de Jonzac; Hénault's nephew:
Du Deffand, Mme, gives opinion of, **4.** 131, 486, **5.** 56, **6.** 7–8, 34
——'s social relations with, **4.** 137, **5.** 101, **7.** 331
—— told by, about Hénault's will, **4.** 486
extravagant, **5.** 61
Hénault's social relations with, **7.** 293, 300, 332–3
marriage of, **3.** 3n
niece of, **5.** 422n
settles on Hénault, **4.** 131
wife of, **3.** 3n
wife's relations with, **4.** 486, **5.** 56, 61
wife taken out by, **4.** 131
wife to accompany, to Jonzac, **5.** 56, 61
Bouchard d'Esparbez de Lussan, Henri-Joseph (1714–88), Marquis ('Vicomte') d'Aubeterre; French ambassador to Rome:
arrival of, awaited at Paris, **4.** 259
audience with Clement XIII demanded by, to protest against treatment of Parma, **23.** 10, 15–16
Bristol, E. of, wants equal diplomatic rank with, **21.** 195n
Choiseul selects, to treat Court of Rome with high hand, **22.** 384

Clement XIII persecuted by, to make him acknowledge Young Pretender, **22.** 386
—— tells, that he will acknowledge Young Pretender if Louis XV does, **25.** 526
—— told by, to discard Torreggiani and 3 others, **23.** 35
French Court disavows partiality of, for Young Pretender, **22.** 399
Guasco excluded by, **22.** 575
HW hears remark from, about Greek architecture in Paris, **23.** 158
Jesuits' plot denounced by, **23.** 89
Mann's contest with, over Young Pretender, **22.** 441, **25.** 526
marriage of, **3.** 11n
Old Pretender acknowledged by, as king, **22.** 374
Portuguese minister to be ruled by, in opposing Clement XIII's brief, **23.** 26–7
recalled from Rome, **4.** 244
recent ambassador to Vienna, **6.** 157n
Richmond told by Conway to counteract efforts of, for Young Pretender, **22.** 369n
social relations of, in Paris, **6.** 156–7, **7.** 325, 326, 332, 336
Spanish and Neapolitan ministers at Rome confer with, **23.** 10
wife of, **3.** 11n
York, D. of, uncivilly treated by, at Rome, **22.** 229–30, 384
Young Pretender's claims as king supported by, at Rome, **22.** 384, 386, 399, **25.** 526
Bouchard d'Esparbez de Lussan, Marie-Françoise (1720–72), m. (1738) Henri-Joseph Bouchard d'Esparbez de Lussan, Marquis ('Vicomte') d'Aubeterre; Hénault's niece:
absent from Paris, **3.** 130
Aix-la-Chapelle visited by, **4.** 259
Comédie attended by, **4.** 275
court of 'Roi Guillemot' of, **3.** 11, 14, 130
Du Deffand, Mme, asks HW to send message to, **3.** 190
——'s opinion of, **4.** 72n
HW sends compliments to, **41.** 29
Houdetot, Mme d', meets Mme Verdelin through, **3.** 214n
sings, **7.** 293
social relations of, in Paris, *see index entries ante* **8.** 257
to return from Rome, **4.** 244, 259
Bouchard d'Esparbez de Lussan, Marie-Louise-Françoise (d. 1804), m. (1780) Denis-Gabriel Adhémar, Vicomte de Polastron:
marriage of, **7.** 453
Bouchardon, Edmé (1698–1762), artist:
drawings by, of *Cries of Paris*, at Caylus's sale, **7.** 275
Bouche, La:
edict for reform of, **7.** 460
Boucher, François (1703–70), painter:
collection of, seen by Carburi, HW, and Mme Geoffrin, **7.** 304

paintings by, over doors in French houses, 31. 88

social relations of, with Mme Geoffrin, 7. 283

tapestries made by, 28. 413n

Boucher, Jacques (d. before 1787):
(?) attends session of parliament of Paris, 8. 171, 172

Bouchet, Du. See Du Bouchet

Bouchier. See Bourchier

Boudot, (?) Étienne-Edmé, procureur at the Châtelet; councillor to the Comte de Provence:
Valentinois, Comtesse de, leaves annuity to, 6. 72

Boudot, Pierre-Jean (1689–1771), abbé; librarian:
Bourbonne visited by, 8. 178
HW's letter of thanks from, 43. 370
Hénault and Mme de Jonzac friends of, 8. 178
L'Isle to pay respects to, 8. 178
negligent about HW's gift of books, 3. 262, 263, 36. (?)280
social relations of, with Hénault, 7. 323

Boudret, Mme. See Radix de Ste-Foix, Marie-Geneviève

Boufflers, Comtesse de. See Campet de Saujon, Marie-Charlotte-Hippolyte de (1725–1800); Puchot des Alleurs, Amélie-Constance (ca 1750–1825)

Boufflers, Duchesse de. See Montmorency, Marie-Anne-Philippine-Thérèse de (d. 1797); Neufville, Madeleine-Angélique de (1707–87)

Boufflers, Marquise de. See Beauvau, Marie-Françoise-Catherine de (1711–86)

Boufflers, Amélie de (1751–94), m. (1766) Armand-Louis de Gontaut, Comte (Duc, 1788) de Biron; Duc de Lauzun, 1766; one of 'les Luxembourgs':
Amant bourru, L', attended by, 6. 469
arrested and imprisoned, 12. 30
Artois's marriage to be attended by, 5. 412
Auteuil visited by, 6. 67, 72, 75, 81, 7. 162, 347
Boufflers, Chevalier de, compliments, 6. 249
—— verses of, sung by, 7. 200, 221
Boufflers, Comtesse de, friendly with, 3. 241
—— visited by, 6. 67, 72, 75, 81, 7. 162
Brest visited by, 7. 182, 433
Choiseul, Duchesse de, attends wedding of, 10. 198
Choiseuls visited by, 5. 7, 231, 238, 243, 426–7, 6. 441
comes to England, 34. 75
does not dance at ball for Dauphin's marriage, 4. 411
Du Deffand, Mme, has, at her chaise longue, 39. 271
—— mentions, 4. 106
—— plays games with, 7. 435
——'s opinion of, 3. 241, 7. 33, 183, 200
——'s relations with, 7. 102

family of, 8. 83n
father-in-law of, 6. 406
finances of, 7. 5–6
Fleury, Duchesse de, imprisoned with, 12. 30
HW entertains, at dinner, 11. 104, 108
HW glad that Conway likes, 39. 233
(?) HW mentions, 3. 342
HW's Gramont given to, 5. 305, 308
HW visits, 34. 80, 109
Haussonville, Comtesse d', not very fond of, 7. 107
health of, 6. 67, 72, 75, 81, 7. 428
house of, 7. 6
husband to join, in London, 3. 237
inoculation of, 6. 67, 72, 75, 81
Isle-Adam visited by, 5. 403, 6. 324
La Harpe's play at Gonesse seen by, 4. 445
La Tuilerie visited by, 7. 345
London revisited by, 11. 175
Luxembourg, Mme de, aids, 7. 6, 33
—— attended by, in illness, 7. 206
—— corresponds with, 7. 183
—— shelters, 5. 394, 7. 33
——'s relations with, 7. 33
marriage of, 7. 299, 300
Montesson, Marquise de, visited by, 6. 329
penknife given by, to La Fayette, 11. 175–6
Poix, Princesse de, joined by, 6. 214
Richmond, D. of, houses, at Goodwood, 39. 492–3
Richmond Green house taken by, 11. 221
St-Amand-les-Eaux visited by, 6. 214
St-Cloud to be visited by, 6. 441
Ste-Assise visited by, 6. 329
showered with missiles in Paris theatre, 11. 175
social relations of, in Paris, see index entries ante 8. 258
SH visited by, 12. 235
Switzerland to be visited by, 11. 291
to return to Paris, 7. 183

Boufflers, Charles-Joseph (1731–51), Duc de:
daughter of, 11. 104n
death of: falsely reported, 20. 236, 250; Genoa scene of, 8. 83n
Luxembourg, Mme de, mother of, 8. 83n
marriage of, 3. 58n
not Mme de Mirepoix's brother-in-law, 20. 250

Boufflers, Charles-Marc-Jean (1736–74), Marquis de:
Choiseuls may be visited by, in exile, 5. 30
death of, at Chanteloup, 6. 92, 94, 97
social relations of, in Paris, 4. 196, 456, 7. 338

Boufflers, Emmanuel de (1785–1858):
father takes leave of, 11. 88

Boufflers, Joseph-Marie (1706–47), Duc de, army officer:
French troops commanded by, 17. 451n
Genoese encouraged by, 19. 400, 406
wife of, 3. 12n, 14. 155n

Boufflers, Louis-Édouard (1746–94), Comte de:
Florence to be visited by, **22.** 434, 435, 445
friends of, could not share his honours at Tuscan Court because no minister presented them, **22.** 474
HW recommends, to Mann, **22.** 434, 435, 445, **41.** 14, 32
letter of, from France, **11.** 88
Mann's attentions to, at Florence, **3.** 172, **22.** 458, 463
marriage, **4.** 58–9, 168, 171
Rueil visited by, **4.** 130
(?) social relations of, with Choiseuls, **7.** 331
travels of, **4.** 58
Trouillet accompanies, to Florence, **22.** 474–5
wife of, **4.** 58n
Boufflers, Louis-François de (1714–51), Chevalier de; Marquis de Remiencourt:
brother-in-law of Mme de Mirepoix, **20.** 250
death of, **20.** 236
wife of, **3.** 347n
wife's letters to, **20.** 236
Boufflers, Louise-Julie de (1741–94), m. (1760) Louis-Bruno Boisgelin de Cucé, Comte de Boisgelin, one of the 'oiseaux de Steinkerque'; (?) 'Mme de Cucé':
anecdote by, of lady at Bellevue, **7.** 121
apartment of, with Mme de Mirepoix, **6.** 349, **7.** 11, 24
Bauffremont friend of, **5.** 86, **6.** 281
Beaumont owes money to, **4.** 368
Caramans visited by, **6.** 86
Chaillot visited by, **6.** 357
Cholmondeley, Mrs, befriended by, **4.** 327, 477
—— in danger from, **4.** 326, 327
—— owed money by, **4.** 360, 366, 368, 369, 377–8, 423
—— repaid for debt to, by Marquise de Boufflers, **4.** 423
Churchill, Lady Mary, acquainted with, **5.** 23
Du Deffand, Mme, desires fan for, **5.** 157
(?) Du Deffand, Mme, mentions, **4.** 310, 342
(?) —— receives Chevalier de Boufflers's letters from, **4.** 305
(?) ——'s opinion of, **4.** 286, 322, 326, 381, 461
——'s relations with, **4.** 324, 327, **5.** 152, **7.** 102
Duras, Marquis de, owes money to, **4.** 368
Ferney to be visited by, **6.** 281
finances of, **4.** 368, **5.** 150
Franche-Comté to be visited by, **6.** 281
friend of both d'Aiguillon and Choiseul camps, **5.** 13
gambles, **4.** 316, 317, 367, 461
(?) HW admired by, **4.** 287
HW's *Gramont* given to, **5.** 305
Lénoncourt, Marquise de, friend and relative of, **4.** 338
Lorraine visited by, **5.** 23
Monaco, P. of, friend of, **5.** 86, 150, 163, 170
recites for Mme du Deffand, **5.** 117, **6.** 466
Roissy visited by, **6.** 84, 86, 209, **7.** 455
Scey-sur-Saône to be visited by, **6.** 281

social relations of, in Paris, *see index entries ante* **8.** 258
Switzerland to be visited by, **6.** 281
(?) verses by, on Mme du Deffand's tonneau, **4.** 289–90
Boufflers, Stanislas-Jean de (1737–1815), Chevalier de Boufflers; Marquis de Remiencourt:
Ailesbury, Cts of, collects and quotes bons mots of, **39.** 218–19
—— sups with, **39.** 208
Antibes visited by, **8.** 137
Chanteloup visited by, **5.** 238, 245
Choiseul's correspondence with, **4.** 60, **8.** 137–8
Choiseul, Mme de, may be visited at Chanteloup by, **4.** 431
Corsica to be visited by, **8.** 137
'Couplets du vieillard' by, **8.** 126
Du Deffand, Mme, mentions, **3.** 56, **4.** 74
—— proposes to take, to Versailles, **4.** 362
——'s opinion of, **3.** 13, 77, **5.** 410, **6.** 237
—— to ask, to write verses, **6.** 497
'Envoi de Milord Chesterfield à Mme la M. du Deffand,' **6.** 462, 465
gambles, **4.** 381
Gennevilliers visited by, **7.** 327
HW admires work of, **6.** 137
HW had already heard bons mots of, **39.** 224
HW to get a Hogarth for, **7.** 415
letters of: **4.** 289, 292, 305, **5.** 103, **7.** 307; copied by Mme du Deffand, **4.** 292, 305
'Lettre en monosyllabes,' **5.** 226, 232
*Lettres de M. le chevalier de Boufflers pendant son voyage en Suisse à madame sa mère,* **5.** 108, **6.** 285, **16.** 200, **43.** 220
Ligne would like to resemble, **3.** 333–4
Lorraine to be visited by, **8.** 138
Louis XVI refuses regiment to, **6.** 305
Mirepoix, Mme de, tête-à-tête with, **3.** *13*
'Oculist,' **7.** 264
*Œuvres* of, printed, **39.** 196
Paoli to be visited by, **8.** 137
Paris visited by, **5.** 206, 226, 410, **6.** 213, 237, **7.** 454
Porquet tutor to, **4.** 325n
prediction of, concerning writings on religion, **4.** 92
regiment given to, **6.** 412
regiment joined by, **6**, 213, 462
social relations of, in Paris, *see index entries ante* **8.** 259
style of, compared to Voltaire's by Mme du Deffand, **4.** 289, 303
talked of, at Gustav III's supper, **5.** 40
trained for priesthood, **4.** 296
verses by, **5.** (?)353, **8.** 123; cited by Mme du Deffand, **3.** 117; for Beauvau, **4.** 123–4, **5.** 354; for Mme du Deffand in Chesterfield's name, **6.** 462, 465; for Mme du Deffand's Christmas Eve party, **6.** 127, 138; for Mme du Deffand to give to Choiseuls, **39.** 236; gathered by Mme du Deffand, **3.**

69, 71, **4**. 281, 283–4; left to HW by Mme du Deffand, **36** 182; on chestnuts, **4**. 370; on embassy from Stanislas I to Ps Christine, **3**. 40, 53, **4**. 277, **5**. 40, 39. 212, 215; on Mme de Mirepoix's sending of hair to Nivernais, **6**. 418, 419, 426; on pale, **4**. 20; on Pigalle's statue of Voltaire, **5**. 354; on Voltaire and Tonton, **7**. 2; sent by Mme du Deffand to HW, **3**. 40, 43, 53, 64, 71–2, 77; sung by Duchesse de Lauzun, **7**. 200, 221; sung by Vicomtesse de Cambis, **7**. 96–8; to accompany Mme du Deffand's gifts to Mme de Luxembourg, **6**. 3–4, 249, 252, 260; to accompany Mme de Luxembourg's gifts to Mme du Deffand, **6**. 127, 137, **7**. 2, 97–8, 200, 221; when chided by Stanislas I, **4**. 361; written at St-Sulpice, **4**. 360
verses wrongly ascribed to, **4**. 168n, 216, 218
wife of, **5**. 269n
wit and bouffonerie of, **39**. 211–12
witticisms by, on the Virys, on chewing tough mutton and on Stanislas I's picture, **39**. 219
witty, **41**. 193
Boufflers, Mme Stanislas-Jean. *See* Jean de Manville, Françoise-Éléonore de
Boufflers family:
Du Deffand, Mme, entertains, **7**. 449
HW mentions, **22**. 239
Boufflers-Rouverel, Comtesse de. *See* Campet de Saujon, Marie-Charlotte-Hippolyte de (1725–1800); Puchot des Alleurs, Amélie-Constance (ca 1750–1825)
Boufflers-Rouverel, Édouard (d. 1764), Comte (Marquis, 1751) de:
death of, **22**. 270, **38**. 480
wife of, **3**. 12n, **10**. 70n, **11**. 76n, **14**. 153n, **28**. 222n
*Bouffon*, French ship:
capture of, **21**. 523
Bouffons, les, theatrical troupe:
Barthélemy tells Mme du Deffand to visit, **8**. 208
Bouflers. *See* Boufflers
Bougainville, Louis-Antoine de (1729–1814), navigator; writer:
(?) HW attends theatre with, **7**. 303
*Voyage autour du monde*, HW to get, for Conway, **39**. 148
Bougeant, Guillaume-Hyacinthe (1690–1743), writer:
*Amusement philosophique sur le langage des bêtes*, Ashton runs away with, **13**. 175
Bouget, Maria Magdalena Theresa de (d. 1796), m. (1750) Charles Knowles; divorced, 1757; remarried, 1764:
Gambier's affair with, **38**. 278n
remarriage of, after divorce, **38**. 278
Bougheleen Bawins. *See* Whiteboys
Boughrood, Radnor:
Powell of, **1**. 364n, **14**. 31n
Boughton, Mrs. *See* Greville, Mary (d. 1786)

Boughton, Elizabeth (d. 1823), m. (1769) Clotworthy Upton, cr. (1776) Bn Templetown:
Amelia, Ps, leaves legacy to, **33**. 534
Hertford's note about Ps Amelia answered by, **39**. 444
Boughton, Northants:
avenue to, from Boughton House, **10**. 340
distance from, to Drayton, **10**. 341
HW has seen, **33**. 233
Boughton House, Northants, Cardigan's seat:
armorial bearings on stairs at, **10**. 89, 340
avenues from, **10**. 340
Cardigans and Manchesters dispute ownership of, **10**. 89, 340
Cardigans avoid, during law suit, **10**. 89
—— stop at, **10**. 89, 340
Cole's visit to, **10**. 89, 340–1
frescoes on ceilings at, **10**. 89, 341
furniture at, **10**. 341
HW and Cole leave, hastily, to avoid Cardigans, **10**. 340
HW visits, **10**. 86, 89, 340–1
landscape effects at, **10**. 340
pictures at, **10**. 340–1
Boughton Malherbe, Kent:
Chute and HW visit, **35**. 145
Foote, Rev. Francis Hender, rector of, **11**. 81n, **20**. 308n
Mann, Galfridus, buys, **13**. 29n, **20**. 166
Wotton and Chesterfield once owned, **20**. 166
Boughton Park, Staffs, E. of Strafford's house:
Ashburnham sells, to Strafford, **35**. 279n
HW sees copy of SH tower at, **35**. 279
Strafford entertains Conway and D. of Cumberland at, **37**. 212
Bouhours, Dominique (1628–1702), Jesuit scholar:
*Life of the Renowned Peter d'Aubusson, The*, **1**. 249
*Manière de bien penser, La*: Du Deffand, Mme, owns, **8**. 33n; HW translates dialogue from, **9**. 7–8; Piozzi, Mrs, comments on, **9**. 7n
Bouillé, François-Claude-Amour (1739–1800), Marquis de; French army officer:
bravado of, in letter to National Assembly, **11**. 336
dines with Lord Rawdon, **34**. 175–6
Dominica taken by, **24**. 421n
Louis XVI's escape aided by, **11**. 301n
St Eustatius captured by, **25**. 235n, **29**. 191
St Kitts captured by, **25**. 263n
son of, **34**. 175
Tobago captured by, **25**. 172n, **33**. 295n
two battalions of, said to have laid down their arms, **34**. 113
Bouillé, François-Guillaume-Antoine de (1770–1826 *or later*), Comte de; army officer:
(?) dines with Lord Rawdon, **34**. 175–6
Bouillé, Louis-Joseph-Amour de (1769–1850), Marquis de:
(?) dines with Lord Rawdon, **34**. 175–6

Bouilli:

soup to be relieved by, at Florentine dinner, **19.** 357

Bouillon, Chevalier de. *See* La Tour d'Auvergne, Charles-Godefroy-Louis de

Bouillon, Duc de. *See* La Tour d'Auvergne, Charles-Godefroy de (1706–71); La Tour d'Auvergne, Frédéric-Maurice de (1605–52); La Tour d'Auvergne, Godefroy-Charles-Henri de (1728–92), La Tour d'Auvergne, Godefroy-Maurice de (1641–1721)

Bouillon, Duchesse de. *See* Hesse-Rheinfels-Rotenburg, Maria Hedwige Eleonore Christine von (1748–1801): Lorraine, Louise-Henriette-Gabrielle de (1748–84); Sobieska, Maria Carlotta

Bouillon, Mlle de. *See* La Tour d'Auvergne, Marie-Sophie-Charlotte de

Bouillon (France):

Bouillon, Duc de, has seat at, **21.** 298n

*Journal encyclopédique* published at, **3.** 119n

Weissenbruch at, **6.** 27n

Young Pretender at, **21.** 298n, **22.** 389, 393, **43.** 280

Bouillon (soup):

Du Deffand, Mme, offers, to invalid, **4.** 368, 369

—— takes, **3.** 280, **6.** 223, **7.** 243, 247, 249; at noon, **4.** 332, **6.** 220, 240, 244; by HW's orders, **6.** 219, 221, 224, 240, 242, 244, 270

HW suggests, in place of tea, **6.** 133

medicine given in, **4.** 196

Pomme prescribes, **3.** 367–8, **4.** 127, **5.** 183

Bouillon, Hôtel de:

HW visits, **7.** 317

Bouillon family:

Talmond, Prince de, belongs to, **8.** 57

Bouilly, Jean-Nicolas (1763–1842):

*L'Abbé de l'Épée* by, based on story of Joseph, **7.** 134n

Boula, ——:

attends session of parliament of Paris, **8.** 171

Boulainvilliers, Mlle de (ca 1687–1776):

death of, at convent of St-Joseph, **6.** 323

Boulainvilliers, Marquis de. *See* Bernard, Anne-Gabriel-Henri

Boulainvilliers, Marquise de. *See* Caumont, Marie-Françoise de

Boulainvilliers, Henri de (1658–1722), Comte de St-Saire:

*Vie de Mahomet*, Gray denies borrowing, from Chute, **14.** 41

Boulainvilliers, Henri-Claude de (1753–76), Chevalier:

(?) social relations of, with Marquis de Brancas, **7.** 347

Boulainvilliers. *See also* Bernard de Boulainvilliers

Bouldby, Lady Mary. *See* Brudenell, Lady Mary

Boulderson, Capt.:

*Halifax* commanded by, **24.** 156n

Boule, André-Charles (1642–1732), furniture carver:

Aumont, Hôtel d', has cabinets by, **7.** 353

Julienne has cabinets by, **7.** 286

Presle has carvings by, **7.** 346

Boulevard, the, at Paris:

HW and Mme du Deffand drive on, till 2 A.M., **35.** 121

New: HW and Mme du Deffand visit, **7.** 336, 349, **32.** 267

Old, described by HW, **32.** 261

visitors to: Churchills, **7.** 334; Du Deffand, Mme, **7.** 327, 336, 338, **10.** 289, **35.** 121; HW, **7.** 314, 316, 317, 327, 334–6, 338, **10.** 289, **35.** 121; Lennox, Lady George, **7.** 314; Mirepoix, Mme de, **7.** 336

Boulingrin, Le. *See* Le Boulingrin

Boullongne, Bon de (1649–1717), painter:

paintings by, at Invalides, **7.** 265

Boullongne, Jean-Nicolas de (1726–87), later Comte de Nogent-sur-Seine:

sister of, **5.** 147

social relations of, with Choiseul, **6.** 441

spoken of, to succeed Terray, **5.** 35

wife of, **5.** 112n

Boullongne, Mme Jean-Nicolas de. *See* Feydeau de Brou, Louise-Julie

Boullongne, Louise-Élisabeth de (1721–67), m. (1736) Paul-François Galluccio, Marquis de l'Hôpital:

death of, **3.** 354

social relations of, with Comtesse de la Marche, **7.** 301

Boullongne, Marie-Edmée de (1725–53), m. (1746) Armand-Louis, Marquis de Béthune:

relatives of, **5.** 147

Boulogne, Jehan de (1529–1608), called Giambologna:

*Bronzo* by: *Ædes Walpolianæ* mentions, **20.** 69n; Mann gives to Sir Robert Walpole, **18.** 177, 298, 303, 312–13

Centaur by, **22.** 124

figure carved by, at Pratolino, **35.** 42

Francavilla's master, **21.** 480

Henri IV's statue by, **31.** 99n

Mann might attribute coffee pot to, **18.** *116*

Boulogne. *See also* Boullongne

Boulogne-sur-Mer (France):

American news via, **6.** 366

Caligula played with cockle-shells at, **16.** 211

cathedral at, **37.** 41

English House at, **31.** 117

English outlaws at, **17.** 140n

English outlaws no longer congregate at, **25.** 632

exchange at, **1.** 98

French transports gather at, **19.** 193n

goods sent by, **5.** 184

HW mentions, **11.** 88, 116

HW's expenses from, to Paris, **7.** 399

Lion d'Or inn at, **7.** 258

Lort to visit, for sea-bathing, **16**. 211

pharos at, **16**. 211, **37**. 41

siege of, **35**. 641

stained glass of Vyne chapel taken from, **20**. 485n, **35**. 641

suitable for overnight stay, **37**. 40

Venturini meets future wife at inn at, **18**. 392

visitors to: Bulstrode, **17**. 140; Cazalet, **39**. 306n; Churchill (poet), **22**. 261; Couty, **6**. 234; Gray, **13**. 162n; HW, **3**. 14, **7**. 258–9, 314, 324, 333, 353, 399, **10**. 283, **13**. 162n, **17**. 140, **31**. 117, **39**. 8; Hertfords, **38**. 211; Shrewsbury, **17**. 140; Stormont, **24**. 365, **28**. 376; Talbot family, **17**. 140; Thistlethwayte, **30**. 89n; Wilkes, **22**. 261

Boulogne-sur-Seine:

Forcalquier, Mme de, entertains at, **3**. 155, **7**. 326, 331

—— to stay at, **4**. 267, 270

François I's Madrid castle at, **5**. 116, **7**. 307

Marie-Antoinette and Mme Necker attend theatre at, **7**. 424

visitors to: Boucault, (?) Mme, **7**. 331; Du Deffand, Mme, **3**. 155, **7**. 326, 331; Greville, Mrs, **3**. 155; HW, **7**. 326, 331; Irwin, **7**. 331; La Fare, Comtesse de, **7**. 326; Pont-de-Veyle, **7**. 326; Walpole, Hon. Robert, **7**. 326

*See also* Boulogne, Bois de

Boulogne, Bois de:

Artois and Bourbon fight in, **7**. 30

Comtesse de Boufflers's garden adjoins, **28**. 223

Cornbury dies from fall from horse in, **5**. 193n

Boulter, Hugh (1672–1742), Bp of Bristol, 1719; Abp of Armagh, 1724:

nymph toasted by, **37**. 35

Boulton, Henry Crabb. *See* Crabb Boulton

Boulton, Matthew (1728–1802), engineer:

Conway's experiments can be judged by, **39**. 552

ormolu invented by, **23**. 211–12

Bound Brook, N.J.:

artillery captured at, **24**. 309n

Bouquet, Col. Henry:

battle of, at Edge Hill, **22**. 177n

Bouquet, Rev. Philip (ca 1671–1748), D.D.; fellow of Trinity College:

bawdy verses by, **13**. 147

Bouquet, bouquets:

Lennox, Lady Emilia, appears from behind vast, at Robinson's ball, **37**. 114

'Bouquet, The.' *See* Bocchetta, La

Bourbon, Abbé de. *See* Bourbon, Louis-Aimé de

Bourbon, Duc de (16th century):

leaves France, **1**. 383n

Bourbon, Duc de. *See also* Bourbon, Louis-Henri de (1692–1740); Bourbon, Louis-Henri-Joseph de (1756–1830)

Bourbon, Duchesse de:

portrait of, at Hinchingbrooke, **40**. 284

*See also* Bourbon d'Orléans, Louise-Marie-Thérèse-Bathilde de (1750–1822)

Bourbon, Anne-Geneviève de (1619–79), m. (1642) Henri d'Orléans, Duc de Longueville:

Du Deffand, Mme, resembles, **4**. 78

Bourbon, Anne-Louise-Bénédicte de (1676–1753), m. (1692) Louis-Auguste de Bourbon, Duc du Maine:

Biron has hôtel and garden of, **7**. 263

Clermont's painting of, with court of monkeys at Sceaux, **7**. 322, **8**. 57, 114

conspiracy of, **7**. 278, **8**. 114

Du Deffand, Mme, cites, **6**. 228, 401

—— guest of, **3**. 367n

—— quotes, **4**. 496, **6**. 95

—— 's 'portrait' of, **8**. 56, 113–14

—— talks to Mme de Genlis of, **8**. 64

death of, **8**. 52, 114

gambler, **13**. 165n

HW describes vanity of, **8**. 56–7

HW's 'portrait' of, **8**. 114

Sandwich, Cts of, disparages, **7**. 283

Sceaux the seat of, **6**. 145n

Staal, Baronne de, attached to, **3**. 78n

—— 's 'portrait' of, **8**. 56, 111–13

tomb of, **7**. 322

Troy's portrait of, at Sceaux, **7**. 322

Vernon presented to, by Bolingbroke, **17**. 126

verses composed for, **8**. 114

verses by, on Noailles and Law, **6**. 432

Bourbon, Armand de (1655–1732), Marquis de Miremont:

French exile at Somerset House, **34**. 257

Bourbon, Charles (1490–1527), Duc de; constable of France:

to appear in Robertson's *Charles V*, **15**. 46

Bourbon, Charles de (1523–90), cardinal:

proclaimed king as Charles X, **25**. 482, 520

York, Cardinal, compared with, **25**. 482

Bourbon, Charles de (1700–60), Comte de Charolais:

Louis XV takes dogs from, for shooting Président's dog, **20**. 340

Bourbon, Élisabeth-Alexandrine de (1705–65), Mlle de Sens:

French Court mourns, **38**. 537n

Bourbon, François-Claude-Fauste de (b. 1771), Marquis de Bourbon-Removille; Marquis de Bourbon-Conti, 1815:

SH visited by, **12**. 237

Bourbon, François-Louis de (1664–1709), Prince de Conti:

elected K. of Poland, **4**. 214n

Bourbon, François-Louis-Antoine de (1722–95), Comte de Bourbon-Busset:

(?) Choiseul's support lost by, **5**. 349

father-in-law of, **5**. 349

(?) Gramont, Duchesse de, no longer supports, **5**. 349

grandes entrées granted to, **6**. 52

marital relations of, **5**. 350

marriage of, **5**. 342n, 344–5, 347, 349

[Bourbon, François-Louis de (1722–95), *continued*]
social relations of, with Mme de Forcalquier, **5**. 349
wife of, **4**. 130n
Bourbon, Françoise-Marie de (1677–1749), m. (1692) Philippe de Bourbon, Duc d'Orléans; Regent of France:
daughter's and granddaughter's relations with, **18**. 385–6, **33**. 531
Bourbon, Henri de (1552–88), Prince de Condé:
(?) Autun escapes attack from, **6**. 498
wife of, **5**. 187n
Bourbon, Louis de (1621–86), Prince de Condé; 'the Great Condé':
Du Deffand, Mme, cites, **5**. 302
—— reads war dispatches of, **7**. 238
pictures of battles of, at Chantilly, **7**. 260
Ripault Desormeaux's life of, **3**. 69
Sévigné, Mme de, writes letter about, **5**. 423
statue of, at Chantilly, **7**. 260
tomb of, at Jesuits' church, **39**. 203
Turenne would be little regarded if he died a subordinate to, **38**. 182
(?) witticism by, about fancies of unmarried girls and unmilitary men, **24**. 414
Bourbon, Louis de (1703–52), Duc d'Orléans:
affair of Mrs Knight cut short by, **17**. 126
bust of, at Ste-Geneviève, **7**. 305
(?) Du Deffand, Mme, cites, **3**. 185
Magnan teaches Russian to, **18**. 564
Russian princess might marry, **18**. 564
Ste-Geneviève scene of last years of, **7**. 305
Bourbon, Louis-Aimé de (1762–87), Abbé de Bourbon:
Louis XV's son by Mlle de Romans, **7**. *371*, **38**. 350, 374
St-Germain abbey taken from, **6**. *404*, 410
Vendôme dukedom rumoured for, **7**. 371
Bourbon, Louis-Alexandre de, Comte de Toulouse:
wife of, **3**. 92n
Bourbon, Louis-Alexandre-Joseph-Stanislas de (1747–68), Prince de Lamballe:
death of, **4**. 77
health of, **3**. *112*, 114, **4**. 63
marriage of, **3**. 225, 227, 229, 231, 245
wife of, **12**. 61–2n, **15**. 219n
Bourbon, Louis-Antoine de (1775–1844), Duc d'Angoulême:
aide-de-camp to Lord Moira, **12**. 156
birth of, **32**. 226n, 264, **33**. 310
Moira, Lord, visited by, at Donington Castle, **12**. 156
wife of, **11**. 298n
Bourbon, Louis-Armand de (1695–1727), Prince de Conti:
wife of, **3**. 330n
Bourbon, Louis-Auguste de (1670–1736), Duc du Maine; son of Louis XIV:
château of, **3**. 367n
death of, **8**. 52
portrait of, by Troy at Sceaux, **7**. 322

sons of, **3**. 363n, **5**. 155n
tomb of, **7**. 322
wife of, **4**. 496n, **13**. 165n
Bourbon, Louis-Auguste de (1700–55), Prince de Dombes:
Malézieu secretary of Swiss Guards under, **5**. 155
wounded at Dettingen, **18**. 265
Bourbon, Louis-Charles de (1701–75), Comte d'Eu:
always hunting, **8**. 114
asked to permit drawings of cabinet at Sceaux, **3**. 363, 367, 373, 375
death of, **6**. 214
Du Deffand, Mme, permitted by, to show Sceaux to HW, **8**. 114
Louis XV entertained by, **13**. 178
Malézieu secretary of Swiss Guards under, **5**. 155
Montglas, Mme de, mistress of, **3**. 375, **6**. 23
Montglas, M. de, secretary of, **6**. 23
Montpellier assembly presided over by, **6**. 23
wounded at Dettingen, **18**. 265
Bourbon, Louis-François de (1717–76), Prince de Conti; Grand Prior of Order of Malta; 'l'Altesse Sérénissime'; 'l'Idole'; 'Apollon':
(?) Adélaïde, Mme, allegedly married to, **32**. 329n
Aligre, Mme d', friend of, **3**. 395–6
Arty, Mme d', his first mistress, visited by, **38**. 480
Boufflers, Comtesse de, loved by, on public couch, **38**. 221
—— mourns, **6**. 345, 346, 347
—— provided for by, **7**. 218
——'s relations with, **3**. 15n, 41n, 118n, **4**. 19n, **5**. 357, **6**. 473, **7**. 218, **14**. 153, **22**. 135, 270, 434, **38**. 470, 477–8, 480
Boufflers-Des Alleurs festivities not attended by, **4**. 168
Bourbon visited by, **3**. 330, 334
Bunbury, Lady Sarah, favoured by, **3**. 224
Charles, P., defeats, at Deggendorf, **18**. 249, **37**. 137
—— returns baggage of, **37**. 137
Chauvelin's friendship with, **5**. 431
Choiseul's reconciliation with, **4**. 177, 182, (?) 188, 202n, 203
Clermont's executor, **5**. 84
climate of, differs from Choiseuls', **4**. 121
collection and sale of, **43**. 101
commissioners named with, **6**. 265n
Condé family neglects, in illness, **6**. 345
Conti, Princesse de, seeks return of, to Court, **6**. 51–2
Conway meets, at Montmorency, **39**. 231
Cumberland, D. of, in similar situation to that of, **5**. 144
death of, **6**. 344–5, 347, 355
drinks waters, **32**. 14
Du Deffand, Mme, alludes to years of, **4**. 189
—— asks for news of, **3**. 344

—— mentions, 3. 229, 4. 139, 159, 269n
—— occupies theatre box of, 3. 236–7, 7. 285, 317
——'s opinion of, 5. 256
——'s relations with, 3. 117, 231, 267, 4. 16
—— will not give *Cornélie* to, 4. 100
exile of, may be ended, 6. 51–2, 67
Fel, Mlle, sings at supper of, 7. 302
finances of, 4. 419, 6. 195
Fontainebleau visited by, omitting levee, 38. 221
Forcalquier, Mme de, favoured by, 3. 229
—— not of the society of, 3. 214n
Francis I's alleged defeat of, 19. 68, 70n, 71
garrulity of, equals D. of York's, 30. 214
gave up house, 4. 355
good-looking but ill-dressed, 38. 221
HW jokes with, about Mme du Deffand, 31. 91
HW mentions, 4. 64n
HW not disapproved by, 3. 283
HW occupies theatre box of, 7. 285, 317
HW offends, by letter to Rousseau, 14. 156, 22. 434, 31. 101, 35. 117, 39. 231
HW ought to like, 39. 48
HW pleased not to see, 31. 136
HW presented to, at levee, 35. 116
HW to receive compliments of, 41. 15
HW to sup with, at the Temple, 30. 215
HW will know much of, at Paris, 32. 20
health of, 3. 385, 4. 100, 419, 6. 67, 226, 240, 265, 280, 324, 339
Herbert, Lady Mary, supported by, 7. 288, 289n, 30. 215
Hertford told by, of Tavistock's arrival, 38. 359–60
Holland, Bns, and sisters entertained by at Isle-Adam, 38. 556
Hume's acquaintance with, 3. 100
hunts, 4. 179
impoliteness of, at Lamballe wedding, 3. 225, 227, 231, 245
inheritance of, 6. 195
Isle-Adam occupied by, 3. 41n, 56, 127, 285, 292, 303, 330, 338, 389, 5. 51, 31. 136
Jéliotte sings at supper of, 7. 302
La Borde exhorts, 6. 344–5
La Marche, Comtesse de, at odds with, 3. 330, 334
levee of, 7. 292, 298
Louis XV's exclusion of princes from Orléans controversy protested by, 8. 166
Louis XVI's retort from, 23. 304
Luxembourg, Mme de, attentive to, 6. 339
—— occupies theatre box of, 7. 285
Malta may be visited by, as volunteer defender, 21. 494n
marriage intentions of, rumoured, 3. 329–30
Maupeou's retort from, 23. 298
Mercœur sold by, 4. 419
missing after battle, 18. 436

Montmorency visited by, 3. 191, 338, 385, 389, 4. 243
mother attended by, in illness, 6. 102, 102–3
natural son of, 11. 45n
Olonne portrait bidden for by, 6. 245
opera by, for Duc de Chartres, 4. 217
Orléans family neglects, in illness, 6. 345
Paris, Abp of, visits, on deathbed, 6. 344–5
parliamentary party led by, 37. 446
parliament of Paris asserted by, to be sole house of peers, 38. 539–40
parliament of Paris attended by, 6. 265, 272, 280
parliament of Paris commissions, to examine edicts, 6. 265
Philip, Don, to join, in Provence, 18. 371n
Polish throne sought by, 4. 214, 217, 42. 494
political ambitions of, 5. 296
Pompadour, Mme de, not attended by, in illness, 38. 338
Pont-de-Veyle attached to, 3. 245, 321
—— visits, 3. 321
Pougues visited by, 3. 303, 308–9, 311, 319, 330, 4. 106, 253, 5. 225, 256
prevented from volunteering, 18. 62
returns to Paris, 3. 191, 334, 365, 385, 389
restrictions added by, to etiquette for Princes of the Blood, 38. 245
Richards and Italian lady entertained by, 38. 507
Rousseau aided by, 3. 310, 31. 89
—— does not wish to see, 4. 434
—— never mentioned by, 3. 301
sacraments refused by, 6. 344–5
sale of effects of, 6. 377
Sartine's search of, at the Temple, 23. 453
Selwyn visits, 38. 452
Senonches sold by, 4. 419
social relations of, in Paris, 31. 45, 38. 359, 452, *see also index entries ante* 8. 261
society of, 5. 226n
Tavistock entertained by, at the Temple, 38. 359
Temple, the, residence of, 3. 41n, 245
Turin menaced by, 18. 504
Bourbon, Louis-François-Joseph de (1734–1814), Comte de la Marche; Prince de Conti, 1776:
(?) Adélaïde, Mme, allegedly married to, 32. 329n
attends session of parliament of Paris, 8. 172
behaves well towards dying father, 6. 345
Condé's reconciliation negotiated by, 5. 296
Conti, Princesse de, leaves life use of Paris house to, 6. 195
HW presented to, 7. 300
HW sorry for, 21. 221
lit de justice attended by no princes except, 5. 61
marriage of: 3. 118n; said to be unconsummated because of previous match with Mme Adélaïde, 32. 329n
parliament of Paris's recall not asked by, 5. 47, 296

[Bourbon, Louis-François de (1734–1814), *continued*]

Seilly, Mme de, bears son to, 32. 329n

SH visited by sons of, 12. 237

verses on, 5. 297

wife of, 3. 118n

Bourbon, Louis-Henri (1692–1740), Duc de:

chair of, at Chantilly, 31. 46

Chantilly kept as in time of, 7. 260

continues Palais de Bourbon, 4. 270n

disgrace of, 7. 214n

Hervey, Bns, writes to, 18. 518

house and gardens of, at Chantilly, 7. 260, 37. 41

Prie, Mme de, mistress of, 6. 130n, 7. 273, 39. 215, 234, 243

sister of, 31. 416

Bourbon, Louis-Henri-Joseph de (1756–1830), Duc de; Prince de Condé, 1818:

absent from ball, 7. 343n

Artois, Comte d', fights with, over insult to Duchesse, 7. 29–31, 30, 32

banished, 33. 582

Crillon to be accompanied by, at Gibraltar, 25. 300

dances at ball in honour of Dauphin's marriage, 4. 410

foolish jaunt made by, to Gibraltar, 25. 320

HW hopes Mann can feast on leg of, 25. 327

Louis XV reconciled with, 5. 303, 304

Louis XVI exiles, to Chantilly, 7. 31

ridiculous flippancy of, 25. 337

verses on, 5. 299–300, 304

Vibraye captain of guards to, and second in duel, 7. 30

Voltaire's *Irène* attended by, 7. 30

Bourbon, Louis-Jean-Marie de (1725–93), Duc de Penthièvre; grandson of Louis XIV:

apartment of, at Hôtel de Toulouse, 7. 302

Choiseul at house of, 3. 360

*Couronnement d'un roi* banned by, 6. 153

daughter of, 4. 217n

Du Deffand, Mme, asks Mme de Forcalquier about, 4. 393

father of Princesse de Lamballe, 4. 77n

Florence visited by, 20. 466

Forcalquier, Mme de, exchanges visits with, 4. 68, 7. 317

Louis XVI writes to: authorizing letters of marque, 39. 306n; on naval operations, 7. 60, 8. 209–10

Meinières, Mme de, praises, in account of Jacqueline and Jeanneton, 3. 362, 364

seat of, 4. 68n, 28. 223

son of, 3. 112n

Bourbon, Louis-Joseph de (1736–1818), Prince de Condé:

abandoned house of, 7. 260

Agoult's duel with, 7. 438

Aiguillon's opposition from, 5. 5, 45 .

attends session of parliament of Paris, 8. 172

Autichamp écuyer of, 5. 301

ball at Versailles attended by, 32. 255

Beauvau at odds with, 4. 447

Bourbon, Duchesse de, tells, of Artois's insults, 7. 29

Chamfort given position by, 6. 374

Chantilly occupied by, 1. 98n, 5. 15, 6. 163

Choiseul opposed by, 5. 45

——'s command of the Swiss coveted by, 23. 265n

——'s restrictions conveyed by, 41. 200

Choiseul-Meuse, Comte de, made capt. of the guard by, 7. 441

Clermont's executor, 5. 84

counter-revolution may soon be led by, 11. 295

dances at ball in honour of Dauphin's marriage, 4. 410

disgraced for espousing parliament's cause, 5. 15, 39. 143n

Escouen château of, 7. 260

French army expects to be covered by, on retreat, 22. 50n

French nobility under, slaughtered, 12. 51

game of, destroyed, 11. 207n

Karl Wilhelm Ferdinand defeated by, at Friedberg, 22. 90n

—— entertained by, at Chantilly, 41. 19

letters of, repeated by Mme du Deffand, 5. 300, 301–2, 303

Louis XV influenced by, 23. 265

——'s rift with, later healed, 5. 15, 45, 296, 297, 299–300, 301–2, 23. 453

Louis XVI summons, to Versailles to settle Artois quarrel, 7. 29

made infantry general, 7. 448

Maillé in service of, 3. 373

Maillebois aided by, 23. 283

marriage of, 3. 61n

Monaco, Ps of, aided by, 5. 14n

—— loves, 5. 297

——'s separation from husband caused by, 5. 14n

Monteynard chosen by, for ministry of war, 5. 5

Pompadour, Mme de, watched by, at night, 38. 338

power of, 5. 45

Ste-Hermine given reversion of captaincy of guard by, 7. 441

social relations of, with Mme du Barry, 4. 288

Terray head of council of, 4. 325, 326

Versailles visited by, 7. 438

verses on, sent by Mme du Deffand to HW, 5. 296–7, 299–300, 303–4, 6. 15, 20

Villinghausen battle includes, 21. 519n

wife of, 3. 61n, 14. 156n

wounded in duel, 7. 438

Bourbon, Louis-Philippe de (1725–85), Duc de Chartres; Duc d'Orléans, 1752:

ancestors of, 8. 125

appeal to, to secure recall of parliament, 5. 40, 48

art collection of: almost equalled by Sir Robert Walpole's, **24**. 304n; badly cleaned and varnished, **3**. 344–5

attends session of parliament of Paris, **8**. 172

banished: for refusal to recognize new parliament, **6**. 64n, 77, 39. 143n; from Court for refusing to attend Louis XV's catafalque, **24**. 26, **32**. 201

Barbantane, Mme de, loved by, before he married Mme de Montesson, **23**. 480n

Beauvau, Princesse de, has influence with, **5**. 296

—— visits, **5**. 269

Benedictines' petition presented by, to Louis XV, **22**. 325n

Bingham, Lady, given room by, **32**. 298

Boufflers, Comtesse de, talks with, **3**. 396

Chanteloup visited by, **7**. 124, 150, 153

Court forbidden to, **32**. 201

Court regards, with disfavour, **32**. 264

daughter of, **22**. 554n

Du Deffand, Mme, gets bootikins for, **6**. 61–6, 86

——'s opinion of, **6**. 63–4

——'s relations with, **6**. 86

etiquette for Princes of the Blood would be relaxed by, **38**. 245

guests of: at Raincy, *see under* Raincy: visitors to; at Villers-Cotterêts, *see under* Villers-Cotterêts: visitors to

HW recommends bootikins to, **6**. 133

health of, **6**. 61, 66, 226, **32**. 264

Hertford calls on, **38**. 245

La Marche, Comtesse de, entertains family of, **4**. 352

—— to visit, **3**. 330

Louis XV forbids, to attend parliamentary discussion of d'Aiguillon, **4**. 429–30, **8**. 166

——'s letter from, sent by Mme du Deffand to Craufurd, **5**. 305–6, 307

——'s reconciliation with, contemplated, **5**. 297

Luxembourg, Mme de, may visit, at Raincy, **5**. 431

marriage of, impending, **17**. 126

marriage of, to Mme de Montesson: **5**. 354, 356–7, 359, 386, **6**. 63–4; Louis XV regulates, **36**. 307

mistress dismissed by, **8**. 127–8

model petition for French nobility to send to, **8**. 183–4

Montesson, Mme de, accompanied by, **5**. 369, **6**. 163

mother-in-law of, ill, **6**. 102, 103

parliamentary party led by, **37**. 446

pious, **7**. 124

Pompadour, Mme de, watched by, at night, **38**. 338

Pont-de-Veyle's verses to, **8**. 125

Powerscourt's wager with, on Fontainebleau-Paris race, **35**. 190n

Raincy occupied by, **5**. 269, **6**. 29

riding accident of, **4**. 248

Ste-Assise visited by, **6**. 163, **7**. 124

social relations of, in Paris, **3**. 241, **4**. 154, **6**. 29, 86, **7**. 451

son of, **25**. 243n, 517n

son restrains, from being reconciled at Court, **23**. 453

son's touching scene with, **3**. 159, **8**. 127–8

Stormont supposed to have quarrelled with, **24**. 50

to return to Paris, **7**. 124

Tronchin called to Paris by, **3**. 114n

verses from fête of, **3**. 121

Bourbon, Louis-Philippe-Joseph de (1747–93), Duc de Chartres, 1752; Duc d'Orléans, 1785; 'Égalité'; 'Monsieur Capet':

abolition of titles accepted by, **11**. 76

absent from ball, **7**. 343n

Agincourt's print of, **42**. 64

allegedly made *Chef de la République*, **31**. 386

attends session of parliament of Paris, **8**. 172

ballad addressed to, **33**. 45–6

balloon ascent by, **25**. 517

banished: for refusal to recognize new parliament, **6**. 77; for refusing to attend Louis XV's catafalque, **24**. 26, **32**. 201, **33**. 582; parliament of Paris's objection to, **34**. 2n

Brest fleet under, supposedly sails to Cadiz, **24**. 383n

Brighton visited by, **11**. 85

Brossard's list headed by, **11**. 79n

Bunbury, Lady Sarah, admired by, **3**. 199n, 205, 231, 251n

Cadiz visited by, **32**. 301

Choiseul declines visit of, **5**. 333, 340–1

——'s acquaintance with, **5**. 340

——'s correspondence with, **5**. 336, 338, 340–1

—— to be visited by, **5**. 331, 340

Choiseul, Mme de, not mentioned by, **5**. 338, 341

Cholmondeley invited to dine by, **25**. 348

Constantinople visited by, *pour apprendre à être grand seigneur*, **25**. 243

Conti's fête for marriage of, **4**. 217

Conti, Princesse de, remembers, in her will, **6**. 195

Conway sups with, **29**. 308

crimes of, **31**. 379

cynosure, **3**. 221

dances at ball in honour of Dauphin's marriage, **4**. 410

dances at Mirepoix ball, **3**. 217, 221

Du Chaffault joined by, at Cape St Vincent, **24**. 224n

'Égalité,' **12**. 61, **34**. 164, 176

Elliott, Mrs, mistress of, **24**. 15n

English visits of, **11**. 104, **25**. 403, 408, 517, **29**. 302, **33**. 399, 483, **36**. 232

États addressed by, **11**. 91–2

execution of, **12**. 61, 63, 66, 72, 86, **15**. 248n, **31**. 397

[Bourbon, Louis-Philippe de (1747–93), *continued*]

express received by, about Breton unrest, **35.** 392n

father of, **3.** 121n

father restrained by, from becoming reconciled at Court, **23.** 453

father's marriage to Mme de Montesson opposed by, **5.** 356

father's reconciliation with Louis XV opposed by, **5.** 296

father's touching scene with, **3.** 159, **8.** 127–8

Ferdinand pleased by, at Naples, **21.** 417

fishwomen stop, **31.** 332

Fox, C. J., praised by, **25.** 495n

French fleet may be commanded by, **24.** 224

French ladies never mention, **34.** 80

Genlis, Comte de, capt. of the guard to, **7.** 448

Genlis, Comtesse de, educates daughters of, **7.** 219

—— made governess of sons of, **29.** 181

—— protected by, **34.** 97

George IV visited by, at Brighton, **25.** 517n

Gramont, Duchesse de, acquainted with, **5.** 340, 341

greatness not to be expected from, **39.** 468

HW calls: 'foul wretch,' **12.** 66; 'monster,' **34.** 174; 'quondam *Prince du Sang*,' **11.** 305

HW compares, to sea-monster, **12.** 27

HW considers, of no consequence, **34.** 80

HW doubts Cosway's story of, **15.** 335

HW's contempt for, **11.** 303, 305

HW's opinion of, **31.** 332, 386

health of, **6.** 472–3

horse race of, **39.** 270

horses' and dogs' copulations displayed by, on buttons at dinner with Vcts Duncannon, **25.** 409, 417, **29.** 302, **43.** 311

house; houses of: adjoining Bellechasse, **7.** 219; in Portland Place, London, **33.** 483; rented at Bercy, **7.** 219

Hunolstein, Comtesse de, has affair with, **32.** 255n

hunts, **4.** 179

inflammatory genius of, **34.** 65

insults to, **11.** 104

Italy toured by, as Comte de Joinville, **42.** 64

Lansdowne compared to, **11.** 78

La Woestyne capt. of the guard to, **7.** 448

Leopold II slighted by, **25.** 417

literary ability lacked by, **34.** 7

London pantomimes to amuse, **34.** 71n

Louis XVI has interview with, **11.** 99

——'s death plotted by, **34.** 175

—— summons, **25.** 517n

Louis XVIII does not invite, to Brunoy fête, **6.** 365

Malesherbes's *Discours* to, **4.** 190

Marie-Antoinette's alleged letter said to be forged by, **34.** 179

marriage of, **4.** 217, 223

miscarries on three elements, **25.** 517

money of, gains him influence, **34.** 110

National Assembly addressed by, **11.** 92n

natural brother might have been murdered by, **34.** 175–6

(?) natural daughter of, **12.** 62n, **33.** 490

naval career of, over, **24.** 408–9

Newmarket not to be visited by, **6.** 294

—— races attended by, with George IV, **25.** 485n

—— to be visited by, **24.** 186

newspapers will lie about English visit of, **36.** 232

one of worst men of 18th century, **34.** 179

Paris revisited by, **11.** 78, 91

pictures of, to be sold, **11.** 85

plan of, to make son king, **12.** 213

political ambitions of, **5.** 296

possible triumph of, **34.** 164

proletarian leanings of, **34.** 97

regency renounced by, **11.** 305

rumoured to be French ambassador to England, **25.** 363

runs under stern of d'Orvilliers's ship, **24.** 402

social relations of, in Paris, **3.** 241, **8.** 127

squadron of, **24.** 179n, 413n

SH visited by, **12.** 235, **33.** 402, **35.** 531

Toulon to be visited by, **6.** 294

trousers worn by, to show he is *sans culottes*, **34.** 164

twin daughters of, **7.** 165n

warned not to embark for France, **11.** 85

weekly balls by, **38.** 505

witticism by, on Du Barry's alleged death, **23.** 116

Bourbon, Louise-Françoise de (1673–1743), m. (1685) Louis, Duc de Bourbon:

Palais de Bourbon built by, **4.** 270n

toilette of, **35.** 601

Bourbon, Louise-Françoise de (1707–43), called Mlle du Maine:

Clermont's painting of, with court of monkeys, at Sceaux, **7.** 322, **8.** 57, 114

Bourbon, Louise-Marie-Adélaïde de (1753–1821), m. (1769) Louis-Philippe-Joseph de Bourbon, Duc de Chartres; Duc d'Orléans, 1785:

attendants of, **6.** 293, **7.** 448

dances at ball in honour of Dauphin's marriage, **4.** 410

daughters, twin, born to, **6.** 469

Genlis, Comtesse de, attends, **6.** 293

Italy hurriedly toured by, in plumes, **24.** 222

Lamballe, Princesse de, related to, **34.** 17

Louis XVIII's wedding festivities not attended by, **5.** 77

marriage of, **4.** 217

Pius VI refuses to treat, like Archduchess Maria Christine, **24.** 222n

Toulon visited by, **6.** 294

Bourbon, Marie-François-Félix de (b. 1772), Chevalier de Bourbon-Hattonville; Chevalier de Bourbon-Conti, 1815:

SH visited by, **12.** 237
Bourbon, Philippe de (1640–1701), Duc d'Orléans, 1660; Louis XIV's brother:
father of, **32.** 387
Bourbon, Philippe de (1674–1723), Duc d'Orléans; Regent; nephew of Louis XIV:
Dal Pozzo, Mme, mistress of, **17.** 80n, **22.** 84n
*Daphnis et Chloé* by: **7.** 288–9; Pont-de-Veyle adapts, **14.** 151
daughters of, **6.** 424n, **7.** 289, 345n, **13.** 242, **18.** 237, **22.** 134n
daughters too familiar with, **33.** 531n
Du Deffand, Mme, cites, **3.** 47
—— former mistress of, **14.** 144, **30.** 204
—— quotes, **4.** 374, **7.** 41
Frederick, P. of Wales, writes songs in imitation of, **2.** 215n, **19.** 45
grandson of, **8.** 125
HW's dream of, **32.** 74
James II invests money in time of, **22.** 385
Magnan employed by, to teach Russian to his son, **18.** 563–4
Mann quotes remark by, **24.** 532
Matignon subject of witticism by, **3.** 277–8
mother of: **35.** 394; letters by, **34.** 12
Noailles's memoirs of, **28.** 295
people said by, to be fools or rogues, **4.** 374
Pitt diamond bought by, **9.** 2n, **29.** 4n
St-Simon a favourite of, **34.** 29
sister's jealousy not encouraged by, **18.** 298n
son of, **19.** 355
wife of, **15.** 191n
Zanetti employed by, to buy pictures, **21.** 562n
Bourbon, dynasty of. *See* Bourbon family
*Bourbon*, French ship:
involved in Mediterranean war, **19.** 222
Bourbon, French watering-place. *See* Bourbon-l'Archambault; Bourbonne-sur-les-Bains
Bourbon, house of. *See* Bourbon family
*Bourbon, Histoire de la maison de. See under* Ripault Desormeaux, Joseph-Louis
Bourbon, Île de. *See* Île de Bourbon
Bourbon, Palais de:
noise of building of, **4.** 270
Bourbon, Rue de, Paris:
Chauvelin house in, **5.** 435
Hôtel de Praslin in, **3.** 55n
Bourbon-Busset, Comte de. *See* Bourbon, François-Louis-Antoine de
Bourbon-Busset, Comtesse de. *See* Clermont-Tonnerre, Madeleine-Louise-Jeanne de (1722–69); Moreton de Chabrillan, Jeanne-Marie-Thérèse-Tècle de (d. 1812)
Bourbon-Charolais, Marie-Marguerite de (b. 1752), m. (1769) Denis-Nicolas, Comte du Puget:
(?) dances at ball in honour of Dauphin's marriage, **4.** 410
Bourbon-Condé, Anne-Louise-Bénédicte de. *See* Bourbon, Anne-Louise-Bénédicte de
Bourbon-Condé, Louis de (1709–71), Comte de Clermont:

attends session of parliament of Paris, **8.** 172
accusations by, against Richelieu, **21.** 195
Contades succeeds, in Rhine command, **21.** 227n
death and will of, **5.** 84
Drumgold aide-de-camp to, **40.** 302n
English try to divert troops from army of, **21.** 221
Ferdinand defeats, at Crefeld, **21.** 193n, 220n
France claims credit for naming, to army post, **21.** *176*
Marie-Josèphe's funeral oration attended by, **7.** 318
Rhine may be crossed by, **21.** 193
Bourbon-Condé, Louise-Adélaïde de (1757–1824), Mlle de Condé, later Princesse de Condé, and (1786) Abbess of Remiremont; 'Mademoiselle':
appearance and dancing of, **32.** 255
brother reassures, **43.** 103
Clermont's legacy to, **5.** 84
ill, **7.** 459
Bourbon-Condé, Louise-Anne de (1695–1758), called Mlle de Charolais:
gambler, **13.** 165n
Hervey, Bns, friend of, and has apartment in each of her palaces, **31.** 416, 43.
Bourbon-Condé, Louise-Élisabeth de (1693–1775), m. (1713) Louis-Armand de Bourbon, Prince de Conti:
(?) anecdote of guest of, **7.** 121
auction attended by, **7.** 369
Bagarotti, Mlle, *dame d'honneur* to, **5.** 404n
Clermont's legacy to, **5.** 84
Conti's return to Court requested by, **6.** 51–2
—— with, **6.** 102, 102–3
death of, **6.** 194
garden of, **4.** 351n, **7.** 327
health of, **6.** 102, 103
Hôtel de Conti of: Brienne, Comte and Comtesse de, buy, **6.** 250; St Joseph's convent overlooks, **4.** 351n
Isle-Adam to be visited by, **3.** 330, 338
mourning for, **32.** 255
Orléans, Duc d', with, **6.** 102, 103
will of, **6.** 195
Bourbon-Condé family:
paintings of, at Sceaux, **7.** 322
Bourbon-Conti, Louise-Henriette de (1726–59), m. (1743) Louis-Philippe de Bourbon, Duc de Chartres; Duc d'Orléans, 1752:
Barbantane, Mme de, in household of, **23.** 480n
(?) Polignac, Marquise de, lady of honour to, **28.** 354n
Bourbon del Monte. *See* Del Monte
Bourbon de Malauze, Charlotte de (ca 1658–1732), called Mme de Malauze:
French exile at Somerset House, **34.** 257
Bourbon d'Orléans, —— (1777–82), called Mlle d'Orléans:
Bercy visited by, **7.** 451

[Bourbon d'Orléans, ——, *continued*]
birth of, **6.** 469
Genlis, Mme de, governess to, **7.** 165, **33.** 483, 490
inoculated, **7.** 451
Bourbon d'Orléans, Anne-Marie-Louise de (1627–93), Duchesse ('Mlle') de Montpensier; niece of Louise XIII:
Arckenholtz's *Mémoires concernant Christine* attacks, **9.** *117*
house built by, **3.** 122n
*Mémoires* of: Du Deffand, Mme, owns, **8.** 32; Montagu reads, **9.** 332; mention Marguerite-Louise of Tuscany, **25.** 214n; style of pleases Mme du Deffand, **4.** 482, **5.** 47
Petitot's miniature of, **39.** 32n
projected marriage of, **10.** 310n
Bourbon d'Orléans, Antoine-Philippe de (1775–1807), Duc de Montpensier:
Joseph II mourned by, **34.** 97
Bourbon d'Orléans, Charlotte-Aglaé (1700–61), Ds of Modena. *See* Charlotte-Aglaé
Bourbon d'Orléans, Élisabeth-Charlotte de (1676–1744), m. (1698), Léopold, Duc de Lorraine:
brother does not encourage jealousy of, **18.** *298n*
Carnival might be spoiled by death of, **18.** 352
Commercy the château of, **18.** 352n
Craon, Princesse de, maid of honour to, **17.** 17n
Craons mourn, **19.** 1
death of: **18.** 558, **19.** 1, **20.** 211; at beginning of Carnival, puts Florentines in mourning, **19.** 1; feared, **18.** 369
grave of, may still be disturbed by grandchildren's education, **20.** 334
husband's amours arouse jealousy of, **18.** 298n
husband's mistress will cause, to shiver in her coffin, **20.** 326
mourning for, **19.** 8, 14
Paris visited by, **18.** 298n
recovery of, **18.** *367*
son not wished by, to give up Lorraine for Tuscany, **37.** 97n
Bourbon d'Orléans, Louis-Charles de (1779–1808), Comte de Beaujolais:
Joseph II mourned by, **34.** 97
Bourbon d'Orléans, Louise-Élisabeth de (1709–42), m. (1723) Louis I, K. of Spain:
sister to occupy apartment of, **18.** 222
Bourbon d'Orléans, Louise-Marie-Adélaïde-Eugénie de (1777–1847), called Mlle de Chartres; m. Baron Athelin:
Bath and London visited by, **34.** 138n
Bercy visited by, **7.** 451
birth of, **6.** *469*
death date of, corrected, **43.** 102
father of, **29.** 302
Genlis, Comtesse de, governess of, **7.** 165, **33.** 483, 490
inoculated, **7.** 451

Bourbon d'Orléans, Louise-Marie-Thérèse-Bathilde de (1750–1822), m. (1770) Louis-Henri-Joseph, Duc de Bourbon:
Artois reconciled with, **7.** 30
——'s fight with husband of, over insult to her, **7.** 29–31
Barbantane, Marquise de, accompanies, to convent, **22.** 554
—— dismissed as governess to, **23.** 480n
dances at ball in honour of Dauphin's marriage, **4.** 410
inheritance of, from Princesse de Conti, **6.** 195
Louis XVI reprimands, in Artois affair, **7.** 29–30
——'s and Marie-Antoinette's social relations with, **6.** 104–5
Louis XVIII's wedding festivities not attended by, **5.** 77
Voltaire's *Irène* attended by, **7.** 30
Bourbon d'Orléans, Marie-Louise-Élisabeth de (1695–1719), m. 1 (1710) Charles, Duc de Berry; m. 2 (1716) —— von Rioms:
anecdote of, and lover, **4.** 22–3
father too familiar with, **33.** 531n
Bourbon family:
Angoulême, Duc d', descended from, **12.** 156
Artois, Comte d', revives, **32.** 264
Austria's contest with, over Spain, **21.** 199–200
cardinals of: awaited at Conclave, **23.** 95; control Conclave, **23.** 96; formerly opposed by Pius VI, **24.** 86n; party of, at Conclave of 1774, **24.** 59n, 73n; subjects of complaint by Conclave, **24.** 79
Charles III exemplifies, **21.** 442
Clement XIII's death ends his defiance of, **23.** 88–9
——'s temporal possessions menaced by, **23.** 24
—— terrified by family compact of, **23.** 38
Clement XIV unlikely to disappoint, by not suppressing Jesuits, **23.** 135–6
Conclave must decide between kings of, and Jesuits, **24.** 75
Courts of, placated by Clement XIV, **23.** 147
England may be at war with all members of, **20.** 488
—— must be curbed by, **24.** 300n
Europe should not tolerate, as rulers of the ocean, **24.** 520
fall of, in France, precipitate, **34.** 55
family compact of: Aiguillon and ambassadors uphold, **5.** 214; Brussels gazette announces, **21.** 544n; Charles III will not compel Ferdinand of Naples to sign, **22.** 6; cited, **5.** 214; devised by Choiseul, **23.** 259; English-Spanish war would have riveted, **23.** 274; forces Charles III to join France, **24.** 495; France and Spain make, **21.** 539, 563; France manages Spain in, **22.** 4; Grimaldi gets cordon bleu for promoting, **21.** 560n; HW not curious about, **38.** 213,

216; Louis XV's reluctance to aid Charles III weakens, 23. 277; may be laid aside, 24. 375n; Pitt said to have paid £4,000 for copy of, 21. 539n; Portugal's seizure of Rio Grande may lean towards, 36. 47n; said to include Sardinia, 23. 465; should alarm Maria Theresa, 21. 565; should be crushed, 23. 38; Spain may desert, 25. 74; Spain's losses by, 22. 95; would require France to aid Spain in war, 23. 244

fleets of: menace British West Indian fleet, 24. 501; unite in West Indies, 25. 73–4; see also France: fleet of Spain and ('combined fleet')

Francis III of Modena should join, against Clement XIII, 23. 35

George III promises Pitt to strengthen alliances against, 30. 188

humiliation of, 42. 251

Italian relatives of, may be forced to declare against England, 24. 505

Jesuits' destruction to be accomplished by, through Clement XIV's election, 23. 118

—— stripped by, 23. 472

Kaunitz inclines Viennese Court towards, 23. 54

Mediterranean control achieved by, 23. 36

ministers of: at Rome begin to press Clement XIV to dissolve Jesuits, 23. 214; at Rome, treat Almada with contempt, 23. 221; pleased with Clement XIV's election, 23. 118; urge Clement XIV to suppress Jesuits, 23. 306

monarchs of, will be angry and frightened by Clement XIV's murder, 24. 51

North administration hates, for making England lose America, 39. 333

old mistresses readily married by, 22. 270

Orléans, Duc d', descended from, 11. 76

Parma, D. of, supported by, in quarrel with Clement XIII, 23. 10

playing with fire, 33. 116

princes of, make foolish jaunt, 25. 320

restoration of, 36. 280

Sardinia, K. of, surrounded by, 17. 290

Spain may desert family compact of, 25. 74

Spanish branch of, excluded from France by treaties, 34. 66n

Bourbon-Hattonville, Chevalier de. See Bourbon, Marie-François-Félix de

Bourbon l'Archambault (France), watering-place:

Montespan, Mme de, dies at, 4. 445

visitors to: Conti, 3. 330, 334; Pont-de-Veyle, 3. 334

Bourbonnais:

Moulins in, 6. 94n

Bourbonne-les-Bains (France), watering-place:

visitors to: Beauvau, 7. 220; Boudot, 8. 178; Châtillon, Duchesse de, 5. 256, 260, 6. 67, 211; Choiseul, 6. 198; Damas d'Antigny, Marquise de, 8. 177; Du Châtelet, Comtesse,

4. 468–9, 8. 177; Gramont, Duchesse de, 6. 184, 198; L'Isle, 4. 468, 8. 177

Bourbon-Penthièvre, Louise-Marie-Adélaïde de (1753–1821). See Bourbon, Louise-Marie-Adélaïde de

Bourbon regiment:

Cipriani, col. of, 18. 493

Bourbon-Removille, Marquis de. See Bourbon, François-Claude-Fauste de

Bourcet, Pierre-Joseph (1700–80), Lt-Gen.:

retreat across the Po planned by, 19. 291n

Bourchier, Eleanor (d. 1474), m. (1424) John de Mowbray, 3d D. of Norfolk, 1432:

letter of, in Paston letters, 33. 559

Bourchier, Elizabeth (d. 1665), m. (1620) Oliver Cromwell:

Cooper's portrait of, 12. 270

print of, 1. 216

Bourchier, Henry (1404–83), 1st Vct Bourchier:

received into fraternity of Bury Abbey, 2. 38

Bourchier, Sir Henry (ca 1587–1654), 5th E. of Bath:

Dionysius may be published by, 16. 11

Bourchier, John (d. 1495):

received into fraternity of Bury Abbey, 2. 38

Bourchier, John (1467–1533), 2d Bn Berners:

Froissart translated by, 32. 251n

HW's life of, 16. 2n

Bourchier, Thomas (ca 1404–86), Abp of Canterbury, 1454; cardinal, 1467:

commission of, to Edward IV's executors, for funeral expenses, 41. 124

'constitutions' of, enclosed by Garnett, 41. 222–3, 224

Henry VII crowned by, 14. 79

Henry VIII said to have been married and crowned by, 16. 47

Henry, Robert, does not explain conduct of, 15. 173

life of, in Biographia Britannica, 2. 197n

register of, 2. 257, 41. 123–4

translations of, from sees of Worcester and Ely, 2. 258

Bourchier family:

Wrey descendant of, 19. 238

Bourdaloue, Louis (1632–1704), Jesuit preacher:

sermons of, more interesting than works of philosophes, 18. 311

Bourdeaux, —— (ca 1754–73), dragoon of Belsunce:

suicide of, 6. 1, 4, 6, 32. 183

Bourdeaux. See also Bordeaux

Bourdeille, Charles de (1614–74), Comte de Mastas or Matta:

(?) Beaumont called on by, 43. 106–7

conversations of, with Senantes in Mémoires de Gramont, 34. 17

remark by, to Maréchale d'Albret, 30. 220

Bourdeille, Pierre de (ca 1540–1614), Abbé and Seigneur de Brantôme:

'always assents,' 41. 7

birth date of, corrected, 43. 77

[Bourdeille, Pierre de, *continued*]
court-lovers remind HW of, 22. 365–6
François I's Court depicted in drawings owned by, 7. 307
HW buys portraits formerly owned by, 32. 282
HW compares himself to, 29. 108
HW gossips like, 2. 365
HW signs himself as, 32. 53
HW would like to write in manner of, 32. 281
heroines of, virtuous, 34. 220–1
life of Don Carlos by, 12. 24n
portraits owned by, 2. 9n
Bourdic, Gaston (d. 1793), Vendean royalist:
HW wishes success to, 34. 183
Bourdieu, James de (d. 1768):
(?) HW sends letter by servant of, 7. 396
Bourdon, Sébastien:
paintings by, in Colebrooke's sale, 23. 569n
Bourdonnais. *See* Mahé de la Bourdonnais
Bouret, Étienne (1710–77), fermier général; administrateur des postes:
(?) Du Deffand, Mme, inquires of, about parcel, 4. 22
Mailly, Comtesse de, furnished with money by, 7. 279
(?) terrein to, 7. 370
Veri's anecdote about, 7. 274
Bourgeois de Boynes, Pierre-Étienne-François (1718–83), secretary of state for the marine:
appointed secretary of state, 5. 5n, 59
dismissed from office, 6. 77, 32. 200
duties of chancellor may be given to, 5. 214
made minister of the marine, 5. 82n
Sorba's social relations with, 5. 83
Turgot replaces, 24. 26
*Bourgeois gentilhomme, Le. See under* Molière
Bourges, Abp of. *See* Chastenet, Jean-Auguste de (1740–1815); La Rochefoucauld, Frédéric-Jérôme de (1701–57); Phélypeaux d'Herbault, Georges-Louis (1729–87)
Bourget, Dom. John (1724–76), Benedictine monk:
translation of history by, of abbey of Bec, 2. 159–60, 161, 163, 166, 43. 69
Bourgevin, ——:
attends session of parliament of Paris, 8. 173
Bourgh, Capt. Charles:
captured at Velletri, 18. 492
Bourgh. *See also* Bourke; Burke
Bourgogne, Duc de. *See* Charles (1433–77) the Bold; Jean (1371–1419); Louis (1682–1712); Louis-Joseph-Xavier (1751–61); Philippe III (1396–1467)
Bourgogne, Duchesse de. *See* Margaret (1446–1503) (Plantagenet); Marguerite (d. 1423); Marie (1457–82); Marie-Adélaïde (1685–1712) of Savoy
Bourgogne, André-Joseph:
(?) attends session of parliament of Paris, 8. 173

Bourgogne, *Histoire des ducs de. See État de la maison des ducs de Bourgogne*
Bourgogne, Hôtel de, Rue Mauconseil, Paris:
Opéra-comique (Comédie italienne) in, 31. 46n
Bourgogne. *See also* Burgundy
Bourgoin (France):
Berrys' trunks ransacked at, 11. 137–9, 143, 158
Bourgoyne. *See* Burgoyne
Bourguignon d'Anville, Jean-Baptiste (1697–82), map-maker:
Schuma not included in maps of, 24. 29
Bourk. *See* Bourgh; Bourke; Burk
Bourke, Hon. Bridget (d. 1770), m. Col. John Gunning:
Bedford House visited by, with elder daughter, 20. 303
Bourke (after 1752, De Burgh), John Smith (1720–82), 11th E. of Clanricarde:
Beauvau asks about family of, 41. 331
Bedford's letter from, 38. 79
Bourke, Richard (ca 1572–1635), 4th E. of Clanrickarde, 1601; cr. (1628) E. of St Albans:
HW describes, 32. 15
Bourke, Theobald (ca 1706–42), 7th Vct Mayo, 1741:
Beauvau asks about family of, 41. 331
Bourke, Mrs Theobald. *See* Agar, Ellis
Bourn Bridge, Cambs:
HW alludes to, 13. 88
inn and turnpike at, 1. 363, 2. 307
Bourne, Kent:
Mann, Horace II, writes from, 25. 659
Bournonville, Marie-Lydie de (1720–91), m. (1746) Friedrich Karl Philipp, Graf von Bentheim:
HW dreams of seeing, in Paris, 39. 3–4
HW makes Selwyn's compliments to, 30. 213
(?) HW mentions, 3. 341
HW's civilities from, 31. 47, 69, 39. 15–16
HW thanked by, 5. 172
HW writes name of, on Selwyn's lottery ticket, 30. 251
house and garden of, 30. 56
illumination for Poix wedding seen by, 7. 319
lacks common sense, 4. 83–4
Selwyn reports to HW about, 39. 4
——'s business affairs with, 4. 11
social relations of, in Paris, *see index entries ante* 8. 264–5
Bournonville. *See also* Beurnonville
Bournpaddock:
cricket matches at, 25. 312n
Bourrée, ——:
attends session of parliament of Paris, 8. 172
*Bourru bienfaisant, Le. See under* Goldoni, Carlo
Boursault, Edmé (1638–1701), dramatist:
*Mercure galant, Le*, 7. 322

Bousquet de St-Pardoux, Chevalier; Mme Élisabeth's attendant:
Élisabeth's identity would have been revealed by, to mob, 31. 372, 379
Boussières (France):
Rothe, Comtesse de, canoness of, 7. 204
Bouteiller, Monsieur:
SH visited by, 12. 238
Boutet de Monvel, Jacques-Marie (1745–1813):
*Amant bourru, L'*, by: 43. 102; attended by Mme du Deffand, 6. 469; Berrys see, 11. 140n
Bouteville. *See* Buisson, Pierre de
Bouthillier, Gabrielle-Pauline (living, 1810), m. 1 (1752) Joseph-Ignace-Come-Alphonse-Roch, Marquis de Valbelle; m. 2 (1772) Jean-Balthazar d'Azémar de Montfalcon, Comte d'Adhémar:
appearance of, 5. 207
cavagnole weekly at house of, 5. 372
circle of, 5. 370
finances of, 5. 207–8
second marriage of, 5. 207–8
social relations of, in Paris, *see index entries ante* 8. 265
Bouthillier de Chavigny, Louise-Françoise (ca 1634–1722), m. Philippe Clerembault, Comte de Palluau:
(?) Du Deffand, Mme, quotes, 5. 391
Bouthillier de Chavigny, Marie (1646–1728), m. 1 (1669) Nicolas Brulart, Marquis de la Borde; m. 2 (1699) César-Auguste, Duc de Choiseul; Mme du Deffand's grandmother:
Bussy's affairs told to Mme du Deffand by, 5. 188
death of, 8. 102
Du Deffand, Mme, nicknames Duchesse de Choiseul 'grand'maman' after, 41. 192
—— taken by, to see Mme de Coulanges, 41. 259
estate of, shared, 8. 35–6
family relationships of, 5. 207n, 391n, 8. 54
Bouthillier de Rancé. *See* Le Bouthillier de Rancé
Boutigny. *See* Le Vayer de Boutigny
Boutin, Simon-Charles (d. 1794):
English garden of, at Paris: HW ridicules Conway for liking, 39. 213; HW visits and describes, 7. 336, 32. 55–6, 35. 125–6
(?) Le Texier's surety, 6. 378
(?) Montagu, Mrs, sends censers to Mme du Deffand through, 6. 486
(?) —— sends letter through, 8. 203
social relations of, in Paris, 7. 304, 344, 345
Terray's correspondence with, 8. 161
Boutonnière of roses:
flower woman provides, at half-guinea a day, 23. 210
Boutray, ——, quartenier de Paris:
Du Deffand, Mme, has contract with, 8. 41
*Bout rimé; bouts rimés*:
Anstey's, 32. 196

Coke, Lady Mary, would have been coupled with Louis XIV in, 31. 21
Leneve, Isabella, makes, 37. 112
Millers introduce, at Batheaston, 32. 222, 39. 241
Boutteville, Chevalier de. *See* Buisson, Pierre de
Bouvard de Fourqueux, Adélaïde-Agnès-Élisabeth (b. 1745), m. (1758) Étienne Maynon d'Invault:
Châtillon visited by, 7. 331
sister of, 4. 189n
social relations of, with Mme de Choiseul, 7. 331
Bouvard de Fourqueux, Anne-Marie-Rosalie (d. 1776), m. Jean-Charles-Philibert Trudaine de Montigny:
Châtillon visited by, 7. 331
circle of, 4. 100, 6. 363
Clairon, Mlle, acts for, 4. 30
controller-general brother-in-law of, 4. 189
death of, 6. *363*
Du Deffand, Mme, gives opinion of, 4. 77, 100
—— wishes HW to know, 4. 266
HW's correspondence with, 4. 74, 77, 7. 387
HW's *Gramont* may be given to, 5. 268, 299
*Historic Doubts* given to, 4. 31
journeys to Lyon, Avignon, and Montpellier, 4. 310
leaves Paris, 4. 253
pregnant, 3. 57
remarks of, precise, 3. 214
social relations of, in Paris, *see index entries ante* 8. 265
Stormont devoted to, 6. 68, 82
Bouvard de Fourqueux, Michel (d. 1789), conseiller d'état:
appointed to committee on finance, 6. 457
Bouvard. *See also* Bouvart
Bouvart, Michel-Philippe (1717–87), physician:
Craufurd attended by, 5. 280, 290
Du Deffand, Mme, allots suit to, 6. 258
—— attended by, 3. 33–4(?), 6. 219, 221, 222, 224, 229, 240, 241, 255, 445, 7. 243–6, 248, 33. 229–30, 36. 176, 178–9
—— saved by, once, 33. 230
James's powder withheld by, from Mme du Deffand, 7. 248, 33. 229–30, 36. 176, 178–9
Pomme joked about by, 5. 183
'Pompom' attended by, 6. 409
social relations of, in Paris, *see index entries ante* 8. 265
Bouverie, Hon. Edward (1738–1810), M.P.:
Beauclerk, Lady Diana, called on by, 42. 451n
—— entertains, at breakfast, 11. 341
boat race prizes given by, 43. 150
family of, 11. 163n, 341n
Florentine great lady discards, 22. 88
HW mentions, 5. 75
HW's letters to be obtained by, from Strathmore, 22. 88

[Bouverie, Hon. Edward, *continued*]
watches boat race, 11. 341
wife of, 11. 163n
Bouverie, Hon. Mrs Edward. *See* Fawkener, Henrietta
Bouverie, Elizabeth (ca 1726–98):
HW sends Stratford's *Fontenoy* to, through Mrs Garrick, 42. 40
More, Hannah, to visit, in Kent, 31. 294
Bouverie, Harriet (1736–77), m. (1775) Sir James Long, 7th Bt:
jewels given to, by Lord Tylney, 25. 144
Tylney accompanied by, 24. 312
Bouverie (formerly Des Bouverie), Sir Jacob (1694–1761), 3d Bt; cr. (1747) Vct Folkestone; M.P.:
baronetcy of, corrected, 43. 113
HW sees house of, 38. 25
Jacobite, 19. 419
Mann's intended purchase of pictures for, countermanded by Hoare, 21. 479
relative of, 17. 70
Society for the Encouragement of Arts, Manufactures and Commerce elects, president, 21. 173n
Yarmouth, Cts of, procures peerage for, when bribed, 9. 51, 19. 419
Bouverie (later Pleydell Bouverie), Jacob (1750–1828), 2d E. of Radnor:
alleged Correggio bought by, 32. 70n
Bouverie, John (ca 1722–50):
art purchases by, 18. 116
Chute's fan disliked by, 17. 117
Clephane, Fuller, and Trapp travel at expense of, 17. 70
*Common Sense* taken by, 17. 83
Florence visited by, 17. 63, 67, 70, 83, 116–17
Holdsworth's disciple, 19. 196
Holt, Monro, and Phelps accompany, 19. 191, 196
languages not known by, 17. 70
Mann entertains, 17. 70, 116–17
—— ridicules, 17. 116–17
——'s little house occupied by, 17. 67, 146, 154
Old Pretender's faction frequented by, in Rome, 19. 191, 400
Pisa visited by, 17. 67
punishment rumoured for, in England, 19. 400
Rome visited by, 17. 154, 19. 191, 196
silent, 17. 67, 70, 116
Turner's capture concerns, 17. 153–4
Bouverie, Hon. William (1725–76), 2d Vct Folkestone, 1761; cr. (1765) E. of Radnor, M.P.:
American conciliatory bills opposed by, 24. 359n
brother of, 11. 341n, 22. 88
Fawkener, Henrietta, rumoured to wed, 38. 394n
paintings bought by, 1. 170

Parliamentary activity by, on Regency Bill, 38. 544
Bouvier de Lamotte de Cépoy, Marguerite-Françoise (1767–1808), m. 1 (1784) Georges-Louis-Marie Leclerc, Comte de Buffon; m. 2 (1799) Julien-Raphael Renouard de Bussierre:
mistress to Duc d'Orléans, 11. 303n
sets out for Paris, 11. 85
Bouwel (Flanders):
Conway encamped at, liable to French attack, 37. 272–3
Bouwers, Jacoba Johanna (1741–93), m. (1758) Willem August Sirtema van Grovestins:
Gloucester, D. of, rumoured to have affair with, 5. 430, 32. 93n
—— sees, 43. 95–6
Scott, Lady Jane, friend of, 32. 92
Bouzols, Chevalier de. *See* Montaigu, ——
Bouzols, Comte de. *See* Montaigu-Bouzols, Anne-Joachim de
Bouzols, Marquis de. *See* Montaigu-Bouzols, Joachim-Charles-Laure de
Bouzols, Marquise de. *See* Fitzjames, Laure-Anne
Bovi, Marino (1758–*post* 1805), engraver:
Bartolozzi's pupil, 15. 189n
Bow (town). *See* Stratford-le-Bow
Bow (porcelain):
HW owns, 6. 429n
Bow (instrumental):
celestinette played with, 35. 423
Bow; bows (weapons):
Charles III shoots with, at tapestries, 23. 238
Chinese, HW's, 31. 26
Gordon boys as Cupids shoot with, 35. 82
HW imagines aerial battles with, 39. 425
HW's, in Armoury at SH, 11. 25
India, with arrows, HW buys, 37. 439n
long, at SH, 20. 381
Bowater, Edward (1752–1829), Adm.:
SH visited by, 12. 221
Bowater, Mrs Edward. *See* Lane, Louisa
Bowden, Col., brother of Jane Bowden. *See* Bodens, Charles
Bowden *or* Bodens, Mrs, mother of Jane Bowden. *See* Myddelton, Althemia
Bowden, Jane (ca 1690–1716), m. (1709) Francis Seymour Conway, cr. (1703) Bn Conway:
daughter of, 17. 274n
relatives of, 41. 241
Bowdler, ——, Capt.:
*Lowestoft* commanded by, 19. 82n
Bowdler, John (1746–1823), author:
(?) SH visited by, 12. 237
Bowdler, Thomas (1754–1825), M.D.; 'Bowdlerizer':
(?) Florence visited by, with Gore family, 25. 352
(?) More, Hannah, learns news of HW from, 31. 376

Bowels:
ancestors', sent to the Holy Land, **25.** 578
Cameron's, to be burnt after his execution, **20.** 384
paralysis in, **35.** 460
*See also* Diarrhœa; Disorder in stomach and bowels; Flux; Inflammation of the bowels; Pain in bowels; Purging
Bowen, Capt. Essex (d. *post* 1800), army officer:
affidavit of, **11.** 197n
forgery revealed by, **11.** 200
Gunning, Miss, confronted by, **11.** 201
Gunning, Mrs, libels, **11.** 225, 228, 229
letter for Miss Gunning copied by, **11.** 199
letter from, to Gen. Gunning, **11.** *198–9*
*Statement of Facts, in Answer to Mrs Gunning's Letter, A*, HW's comments on, **11.** 252
Bowen, Mrs Essex. *See* Lyster, Lizetta Margaret Kirwan
Bowen, T., bookseller:
prosecuted, **23.** 29
Bowen's paper. *See under* Paper
Bower, Archibald (1686–1766), writer:
alleged letters of, published, **20.** 532, 580, **21.** 46; reply to, **21.** 46
Aspinwall not attended by, in last illness, **21.** 46n
Brown invests money for, **20.** 533–4
Douglas exposes, **28.** 430
earthquake predicted by, **20.** 157
HW tells, he was foolish to trust Jesuit, **20.** 534
*History of the Popes* by: **20.** 531; HW admires, **20.** 580; HW criticizes, **20.** *157*; HW subscribes to second volume of, **20.** 157n
Italian adventures of, **20.** 580
Lyttelton angers Moore by favouring, **35.** 176
—— obtains government post for, **20.** 533, **35.** 176
Mann pleased by story about, **20.** 542
—— to make inquiries about, in Italy, **20.** 580
Millar angry at, for want of patronage, **20.** 533
mistress of: said to have borne a child to him, **20.** 532; said to have received him at her brother's London house, **20.** 532n
Pelham consults, about earthquake, **20.** 157
reply of, mentions falsehood about Aspinwall, **21.** 46
Roman Catholicism deserted by, **20.** 157
Sheldon's alleged letters from, **20.** 532
Bower, Edward (17th century):
paintings by, **16.** 65n, **28.** 28n
Bower, George (fl. 1664–89):
medal made by, **16.** 301n
Bower; bowers:
in Nuneham Courtenay garden, **35.** 484
*Bower and Tillemont Compared. See under* Douglas, John

Bowes, Andrew Robinson (Stoney before 1777) (1747–1810), army officer; M.P.:
biographical information about, corrected, **43.** 357
Irish peerage declined by, **33.** 430n
wife beaten by, **33.** 539–40
Bowes, John (ca 1690–1767), cr. (1758) Bn Bowes of Clonlyon; Irish chancellor, 1757:
Dublin rioters have oath administered by, **9.** 266
Bowes, John (1769–1820), 8th E. of Strathmore, 1776:
Tyrconnel, Cts of, has affair with, **34.** 8n
Bowes, Mary Eleanor (1749–1800), m. 1 (1767) John Lyon (from 1767, Bowes), 7th E. of Strathmore, 1753, m. 2 (1777) Andrew Robinson Bowes (before 1777, Stoney):
eloped with two maids, **33.** *460*
house of, in Grosvenor Sq., **33.** 460n
husband's barbarities to, **33.** 539–40
'veteran madwoman,' **33.** 461
Bowet, Henry (d. 1423), Abp of York:
York Minster and Cawood Castle partly built by, **16.** 49
Bow Hills:
rebels may enter Wales at, **19.** 160n
Bowier, Simon:
petition to Abp Parker in favour of, **1.** 223
Bowl; bowls:
scalloped, HW buys, at Mrs Kennon's sale, **37.** 439n
Bowlby, Lady Mary. *See* Brudenell, Lady Mary
Bowlby, Thomas (1721–95), M.P.:
biographical information about, corrected, **43.** 270
Mann receives commission through, to get paintings, **20.** 328
Sion House visited by, **38.** 429
Bowle, Rev. John (1725–88), scholar:
*Don Quixote* edited by, **40.** 296n, **42.** 43n
Douglas's *Milton Vindicated* acknowledges aid of, **40.** 305
HW asked by, for writings on Chatterton to bind with *Anecdotes of Painting*, **42.** 42
HW invites, to call on him in London, **40.** 307
HW's correspondence with, **40.** 296–302, 305–7, **42.** 42–5
HW supplied by: with additions to *Anecdotes of Painting*, **42.** 42–5; with additions to *Royal and Noble Authors*, **40.** 296–302
Owen induces, to give Q. Elizabeth's MS to Bodleian, **40.** 305
Bowles, Anna Maria (d. 1780), m. Nathaniel Heywood:
dying of fever, **24.** 360
Gloucester, Ds of, does not see, for 3 weeks, **24.** 323
—— has, as Bedchamber woman, **24.** 323n
Bowles, Carrington, engraver:
Mason and Mrs Montagu satirized in 'Abelard and Eloisa' by, **43.** 298

[Bowles, Carrington, *continued*]
   prints by: of Cts of Huntingdon, **35**. 346; of
      goitres, **33**. 571n
Bowles, William (1686–1748), M.P.:
   Indemnity Bill supported by, **17**. 429
   named in Secret Committee list, **17**. *383*, 386
Bowling:
   Cloué engaged in, **30**. 91n
   Conway and wife engaged in, **37**. 548
   HW alludes to terms in, **42**. 178
Bowling-green; bowling-greens:
   at Putney, **20**. 169
   at Wentworth Woodhouse, **35**. 267
   Briscoe's, **35**. 372
   HW's, at SH, **35**. 177, **39**. 403
   orders posted at, about dancing, **19**. 471
   Young Pretender never saw, in Scotland, **19**.
      106n
Bowman, Walter (d. 1782), antiquary; Hert-
   ford's and Beauchamp's tutor:
   biographical information on, corrected, **43**.
      122
   Conway brothers and sister to be accompanied
      by, **37**. 63
   Conway writes to, at Geneva, of sister's death,
      **37**. *30–1*
   'Directions' by, for HW's tour, **37**. *39–42*
   HW misses call from, **38**. 215
   HW's presentation copy of Lucan to, **43**. 374
   Hertford, Cts of, invites HW to dine with,
      **38**. 77
   Hôtel de Bretagne, the Paris address of, **37**.
      41
   (?) house of, in Kent, **9**. 30
   inquiry to be made by, about Cts of Hert-
      ford's things seized at Dover, **38**. 355
   Magdalen House visited by, **9**. 273–4
Bowood Park, Wilts, Shelburne's seat:
   magnificence of, **33**. 129
   Ossory, Lady, visits, **30**. 274, **33**. 216
   Shelburne's seat, **29**. 24n
Bow St, Covent Garden:
   E. O. tables burnt in celebration at, **35**. 101n
   Fielding's house in, **29**. 58n
   Ford chief magistrate at, **11**. 368n
   police court in, **22**. 138n
   Rickaby, printer in, **43**. 390n
   rioters examined in, **33**. 179n
Bowstring; bowstrings:
   English, unlike Mohammedans, do not kill off
      unwanted princes with, **20**. 494
   English ministries as changeable as if termi-
      nated by, **35**. 281
Bow window. *See under* Window
Bowyer, Mr:
   Bertie ladies to be attended abroad by, **2**.
      235
Bowyer, Mr, of Willoughby, Lincs:
   wife of, **2**. 235n
Bowyer, Frances (b. 1685):
   (?) Coislin, Mme de, resembles, **30**. 215
   (?) Selwyn will remember, **30**. 215

Bowyer, George, naval capt.:
   Derby tells, to take shelter in Ireland, **25**.
      183n
Bowyer, William (1699–1777) the younger;
   printer:
   HW a better printer than, **40**. 106
   HW to beg print of, **42**. 21
   Lyttelton's *Henry II* printed by, **40**. 106
   Nichols's *Biographical and Literary Anec-
      dotes of*, **2**. 332, 333, **42**. 21
   ———'s partner, **2**. *182*
   ———'s predecessor, **29**. 293
   Wood's *Essay* printed by, retaining annotated
      copy, **41**. 176n
Bowyer. *See also* Boyer
Box; boxes:
   at Elizabeth Chudleigh's, **9**. 277
   Catherine II gives, to Chesterfield, **23**. 376
   Conway may have locked HW's notes in, **37**.
      389
   Florentine, HW enumerates among Mann's
      presents, **24**. 15, **26**. 56
   for HW's letters to Mme du Deffand, **3**. 27,
      33, 58, 68, 126, **4**. 229, 231
   gold: Bath Common Council presents, to
      Pitt and Legge, **21**. 77n; freedom of city
      given in, **21**. 77; Hartington receives, in
      Ireland, **37**. 400; Leopold gives, to Gatti,
      **24**. 7; should go to English 'discoverers' of
      French coast, **37**. 536; Wilkins, Bp, might
      receive, for flying, **37**. 551
   HW presents, to Mme Suares, **35**. 29
   HW's papers sealed in, **26**. 36–44, **30**. 373,
      **36**. 310–16
   hard stone, for essences, present by Mann,
      through Stuart Mackenzie, to Q. Charlotte,
      **22**. 241, 243
   heart of oak: **33**. 95n; Exeter gives, to Pitt
      and Legge, **21**. 87n
   Hotham, Henrietta, finds, at Cts of Suffolk's,
      **10**. 113
   jewelled, Catherine II gives, to Rutherfurd,
      **24**. 453
   La Malle plan enclosed in, **10**. 196
   Mann receives, from HW, **17**. 413
   milliner's, **10**. 218
   of deal, **36**. 168, 169
   packing of HW's, at Paris, **10**. 201
   Pandora's, **9**. 1
   patch: Craon, Princesse de, shows, to Elec-
      tress, **17**. 424; of mocoa, given by HW to
      Princesse de Craon, **17**. 414; Sackville
      should get, for his laurels, **37**. 536
   pimpernel seeds sent in, **30**. 251
   red leather, velvet-lined, **35**. 477n
   ring, in Stosch's collection, **21**. 189
   silver, Conway receives, in Ireland, **37**. 400
   *See also* Pill box; Snuff-box
Box; boxes, theatre. *See under* Opera; Theatre;
   *and names of individual theatres*
Boxing:
   HW does not want to engage in, **31**. 305
   Pembroke an addict of, in youth, **20**. 109

Boxing match:
HW describes, between two ladies at theatre, **11**. 9
HW may be invited to, **30**. 86
Box-keeper; box-keepers:
at theatre, **39**. 252
Gray, Sir James, started as, **20**. 409
Boy; boys:
negro, given by Orlov to Dick and Mann, **23**. 228
'Boy bishop':
Latin lines on, might apply to Bp of Osnabrück, **38**. 369
Boyce, —— (d. 1759):
HW wants Bevan to succeed, in Windsor Castle post, **40**. 173–4
Boyce, William (1710–79), composer:
anthem by, at George II's funeral, **9**. 322
Boycott, Harriet (1805–68):
aunt confused with, **11**. 195n
Boycott, Louisa Victoria Maria Sobieski Foxhunter Moll (1778–1849), m. (1807) Walter Smythe:
baptism of, **11**. 195
Boycott, Maria:
sister confused with, **11**. 195n
Boycott, Thomas (1734–98), sportsman:
family of, **11**. 194–5
Boycott, Thomas (1771–1856):
family of, **11**. 195n
Boycott, Salop:
Boycott of, **11**. 194n
Boyd, Col.:
Ferdinand, P., sends to England, with campaign news, **22**. 46n
Boyd, Hon. Charles (1728–82):
father accompanied by, in rebel army, **19**. 285
Boyd, Rev. Hannington Elgee, Percy's curate:
Percy aided by, in editing Surrey, **42**. 367n
Boyd (afterwards Hay), James (1726–78), styled Bn Boyd; 15th E. of Erroll, 1758; high constable of Scotland:
father pleads services of, in D. of Cumberland's army, **19**. 285
George III's coronation attended by, **9**. 388
——'s wedding attended by, **9**. 388
HW admires appearance of, at coronation, **9**. 388
HW mentions, **10**. 7
Lennox, Lady Sarah, refuses, **9**. 406
marriage of, **9**. 406n
mother pained by disobedience of, **37**. 218
(?) Saturday Club and, **43**. 185
succeeds to title, **9**. 41n
Boyd, Sir John (1718–1800), cr. (1775) Bt; East India Co. director:
withdraws at East India Co. election, **38**. 378n
Boyd, Mark Alexander (1563–1601):
Dalrymple publishes life of, **15**. 181n
Boyd, Sir Robert (1710–94), K.B., 1785; army officer:
appointed governor of Gibraltar, **11**. 119

officer in Minorca garrison, **20**. 584
passes from St Philip's to fleet and back again, **21**. 3
SH visited by, **12**. 230
Wilhelmsthal victory reported by, to England, **38**. 161
Boyd, William (1704–46), 4th E. of Kilmarnock:
aunt forces, to join Pretender's followers, **9**. 41
Balmerinoch advises, **9**. 41, 45
—— fears the behaviour of, at trial, **9**. 38
capture of, **19**. 248, **37**. 240
clergy attend, at Tower of London, **19**. 301n
Cumberland, D. of, cool to plea of, **9**. 46
earldoms of, **19**. 283
execution of, **19**. 254n, 296, 299–300, 311
Hamilton pleads for, **9**. 46
poverty of, **9**. 41–2, 42, **19**. 283–4
Presbyterian, **19**. 283
shoulders of, droop, **9**. 47
sons of, **9**. 388, **19**. 285
stable boy pretended to be bastard of, **37**. 268
Townshend, Vcts, enamoured of, **9**. 47, **19**. 302
trial of, **19**. 280–6
wife of, **9**. 41n
wife's letters to, **37**. 217–18
Young Pretender said to be betrayed by, **19**. 262
Boyd family, of Erroll:
Jamesone's portrait of young lady of, **40**. 267
Boydell, John (1719–1804), engraver; publisher; lord mayor of London 1790–1:
Bailly compared to, **11**. 210
*Collection of Prints* by, **1**. 207, 210
Faringtons employed by, **15**. 218n
Farington visits HW with, **15**. 322
HW entertains, at SH, **11**. *80*–1, **12**. 236, **15**. 322, **42**. 283
HW receives Combe's *Thames* from Farington and, **15**. 319
hospitality of, to Mme du Barry, **11**. 210, 216, 270
*Houghton Gallery, The*, by, **1**. 385, 388, **32**. 142
Houghton pictures drawn by, **24**. 502n
illustrations to Shakespeare commissioned by, **33**. 546–7, 549
Shakespeare Gallery of, **15**. *206*, 321
subscriptions for Croyland print to be received by, **16**. 194
Boydell, Mrs John. *See* Lloyd, Elizabeth
Boydell, Josiah (1752–1817), painter and engraver:
biographical information on, corrected, **43**. 143
copies pictures at Houghton, **32**. 142, **43**. 63
HW entertains, at SH, **11**. *80*–1, **12**. 236, **42**. 283
Shakespeare edition of, **33**. 546n

Boydell, Mary (d. 1820), m. (1787) George Nicol:
biographical information about, corrected, 43. 143
(?) HW entertains, at SH, 11. 80–*1*, 12. 236, 42. 283
Boyer, ——:
social relations of, with Duchesse de Choiseul, 7. 307
Boyer, ——, Guines's steward:
Guines's baggage looked after by, 4. 461, 472
Boyer, M. de, of Genoa:
Barbantane informed by, 22. 526n
Boyer, Mme:
Clarke, Col., rebuked by, 7. 357
Boyer, Abel (1667–1729), lexicographer:
*Dictionnaire royal français et anglais*, Bathurst uses, to write invitation, 28. 262
Boyer, Alexandre-Jean-Baptiste de (d. 1785), seigneur d'Eguilles:
arrival of, in Scotland, 19. 138
capture of, 19. 248
Boyer *or* Bowyer, Mrs Anna *or* Anne (d. 1726), widow of Capt. (?) John Boyer *or* Bowyer; m. 2 (1659) Sir Thomas Chamber, Kt, 1666:
Beauclerk, Lady Vere, granddaughter of, 9. 62
'black,' 9. 62
HW disapproves of Vere family's alliance with, 9. 67
HW sees portrait of, 9. 62
'Portuguese,' 9. 62, 67
Boyer, Claude (1618–98):
*Judith*, Racine's epigram on, 7. 166
Boyer, Jean-Baptiste de (1704–71), Marquis d'Argens, 1757; novelist and miscellaneous writer:
Frederick II the ape of, 34. 34
Boyer *or* Bowyer, Capt. (?) John (d. 1655):
widow of, 9. 62n
Boyle (later Boyle Walsingham), Mrs. *See* Williams, Charlotte Hanbury
Boyle, Vcts. *See* Ponsonby, Catherine
Boyle, Lady Anne (d. 1741), m. 1 (1696) William Stewart, 2d Vct Mountjoy, 1692; m. 2 (after 1728) John Farquharson:
executor of, 17. 271n
Nugent said to have married, 17. 271n
pocket-book of, reveals payments to Nugent, 17. 271
Boyle, Charles (before 1674–1704), 2d E. of Burlington, M.P.:
Bracegirdle, Mrs, refuses china from, 25. 74
Boyle, Charles (1674–1731), 4th E. of Orrery, 1703:
Atterbury's letter to, 29. 294
*Dr Bentley's Dissertations . . . Examined*, by, 29. 294n
Jacobite leader in House of Lords, arrested for part in Layer's plot, 20. 499n
library of, not left to son, 28. 89
Boyle, Charles (1729–59), styled Vct of Dungarvan:

marriage of, 20. 452
Boyle, Charlotte (1769–1831), m. (1791) Lord Henry Fitzgerald; Bns Ros *or* Roos, s.j., 1806:
ancestry of, 25. 577n
Boyle Farm enhanced by genius of, 42. 197, 203
brother's bust modelled by, 35. 385
chimney-piece sculptures and painted panels by, at Boyle Farm, 35. 390
Damer, Mrs, imitated by, in sculpture, 35. 385
decorations by, at Boyle Farm, 31. *251*
Digby miniatures too difficult for, to copy, 42. 204
engagement of, to Lord Henry Fitzgerald, 11. 266
female companion refused by, 31. 346
Garrick, Mrs, entertains, at dinner, 31. 206, 228, 35. 384–5
—— shows to, Monboddo's proposal, 33. 363n
good taste of, 42. 203
HW visits, 11. 328
Italy to be visited by, 11. 238
marble medallions by, 33. 572–3
marriage of, 11. 238n, 326
More, Hannah, entertains, at dinner, 31. 228
mother cherished by, 31. 346
paints and models, 25. 577
Shannon, E. of, contests inheritance of, 31. 346
SH visited by, 31. 206
suitors of, 31. 346
talents and learning of, 31. 251n
Boyle, Lady Charlotte Elizabeth (1731–54), m. (1748) William Cavendish, styled M. of Hartington, 4th D. of Devonshire, 1755; Bns Clifford, s.j.:
(?) at Chesterfield's assembly, 37. 325
Burlington's bequests to, 20. 545n, 35. 159
husband receives estates through, 20. 66n
Kent escorts, to Robinson's ball, 37. 114
marriage arranged for, 19. 19
mother-in-law avoids, 20. 66
painting descends through, 15. 113n
Richmond's fireworks attended by, 9. 81
Sabbatini inquires about, 9. 81
son born to, 20. 19, 37. 339, 341
Boyle, Lady Dorothy (1724–42), m. (1741) George Fitzroy, styled E. of Euston:
appearance of, 17. 168n, 30. 28
costumed as hussar, 17. 338
Cumberland, D. of, dances with, at Birthday ball, 37. 116
death of, 17. 432
does not dance at Robinson's ball, 37. 115
Fermor, Lady Sophia, handsomer than, 30. 28
HW calls, 'the handsomest woman of this time,' 17. 168n
HW entertains, 17. 274
HW mentions, 35. 24
husband ill-treats, 18. 273
husband's quarrel with family of, mended, 17. 186

marriage of, **17**. 168, 174, **30**. 27, 28

mother's inscription on engraving of her portrait, **18**. 482

Norfolk, Ds of, entertains, **17**. 338

Robinson entertains, **17**. 184

sister-in-law entertains, **17**. 186

sister of, **19**. 19

Boyle, Francis (1623–99), cr. (1660) Vct Shannon:

*Discourses Useful for the Vain Modish Ladies and Their Gallants*, offered by Lort to HW, **16**. 172, **43**. 220

Boyle, Hon. Grace (d. 1763), m. (1744) Charles Sackville, styled E. of Middlesex; 2d D. of Dorset, 1765; mistress of the robes to Augusta, Ps of Wales 1743–63:

fortune of, may be used for husband's opera, **18**. 501

Frederick, P. of Wales, and Breton leave Ps of Wales and, in hackney coach, **30**. 94–5

Frederick, P. of Wales, and Mrs Kennon attend, in miscarriage, **20**. 122

Frederick, P. of Wales, and wife attached to, probably for Miss Granville's sake, **19**. 63

Frederick, P. of Wales, and wife, watch fireworks from house of, **20**. 48

Frederick, P. of Wales, thought to be lover of, **19**. 62n, **20**. 97n

Granville, Hon. Elizabeth, friend of, **19**. 63

HW describes fortune and appearance of, **18**. *481*

Hesse, Landgrave of, may be carousing with, **9**. 28

Lorenzi asks about, **20**. 97

Middlesex to wed, **18**. 481, 501, 523

miscarriage of, **19**. 447, **20**. 122

Mistress of the Robes, **19**. 62–3

pregnant, **19**. 442

Templars attempt to kiss, **30**. 95

wedding of, not announced, **18**. 527

Boyle, Hon. Hamilton (1730–64), 6th E. of Cork and Orrery, 1762:

father addresses, as 'Ham,' **16**. 348

father's letters to, about Swift, **20**. 457

Boyle, Henry (d. 1725), cr. (1714) Bn Carleton:

portrait of Mary, Q. of Scots, bought by, **42**. 321n

Queensberry, Ds of, said to be daughter of, **37**. 357n

Boyle, Henry (ca 1683–1764), cr. (1756) E. of Shannon; speaker of Irish House of Commons; M.P.:

Bath, E. of, resembles, in losing power by accepting earldom, **37**. 462

birth date of, corrected, **43**. 118, 270

burnt in effigy, **37**. 449

Burton challenged by, over estate, **21**. 65n

Carter and Malone oppose, on money bill, **20**. 402n

controls patronage, **10**. 110n

Conway bribes, **37**. 453

—— hopes to regain Exchequer post for, **37**. 400n

death of, **38**. 489

Devonshire's negotiations with, **37**. 448n

Dorset, D. of, and family, opposed by, **20**. 316, 402

Dorset, D. of, and Stone clash with, in Ireland, **9**. 130

Dorset, D. of, differs with, on George II's prerogative over Irish treasury, **20**. 402n

—— removes, at George II's order, **20**. 425n

Exchequer chancellorship not to be restored to, **37**. 398n

Exchequer chancellorship taken from, **20**. 425, **37**. 376n, 400n

Halifax leaves, as lord justice in Ireland to retrieve reputation in England, **38**. 147

Hartington confers with, **37**. 393n

——'s agreement with, **37**. *404*

——'s not leaving Ireland deemed a concession to, **37**. 398n

——'s plan approved by, **37**. 410

——'s policy towards, **37**. 403n

——'s resolutions against, **37**. 399

Ireland risked by, from personal pique, **37**. 406

lord justice in Ireland, **38**. 28n, 147n

members of party of, **20**. 402n

Parliament breaks up without outburst against, **37**. 456

peerage and pension for, **37**. 448n

son of, **10**. 110, **11**. 328n, **30**. 323, **38**. 235

Speaker of Irish House of Commons, **20**. 316n

Stone's struggle with, **9**. 130, 157n, **20**. 505n

Boyle, Henry (d. 1756). *See* Boyle Walsingham, Henry

Boyle, John (1707–62), 5th E. of Cork, 1753; 5th E. of Orrery, 1731:

agent mismanages Irish affairs of, **20**. 545

Atterbury may have been visited by, **20**. 66n

Bolingbroke's intimacy with, **20**. 452

Burlington promises to leave estate to, **20**. 545

death of, **22**. 103

Duncombe's letter from, giving version of Juvenal's satires, **20**. 66n

economy sought by, **20**. 451, 457

Florence visited by, **20**. 451, 456

George II hears misrepresentations about, **20**. 499

HW highly regarded by, **20**. 456

HW obliged by remembrance of, **20**. 461

HW praises, **20**. 454

HW regrets that Mann is losing, **20**. 507

HW's correspondence with, **40**. 161

HW's *Royal and Noble Authors* praised by, **28**. 465, **40**. 161

health of, gout, **20**. 480

Hoare recommends, to Mann, **20**. 452

——'s letters summon, back to England, **20**. 498

in country, **20**. 480

Johnson, Dr Samuel, described by, to Mann, **25**. 643

*Letters from Italy* by, **20**. 451n

*Letters* of, published by Duncombe, **28**. 188–9

[Boyle, John, *continued*]

Mann asked by, to testify to his political principles, **20**. 499

—— discusses Bolingbroke with, **20**. 451–2, 454

—— discusses writings of, **20**. 451

——'s motto discussed with, **20**. 480, 487

——'s old friend, **22**. 103

Pisa to be abandoned by, for Florence, **20**. 451

Pliny's epistles translated by, **20**. 454n

*Remarks on the Life and Writings of Jonathan Swift*: **20**. 454n, 457; Conway belatedly reads, **37**. 360; HW echoes, **24**. 503n; son addressed in, as 'Ham,' **16**. 348

Salkeld employed by, as tutor, **20**. 499n

son's letters from, about Swift, **20**. 457

Swift's history said to be edited by, **21**. 194, 200

——'s reputation endangered by misguided enthusiasm of, **21**. 194

Walpole, Sir Robert, opposed by political connections of, **20**. 456

—— visited by, at Houghton, **20**. 456

Boyle, Lady Lucy (1744–92), m. (1765) George Byng, 4th Vct Torrington:

Brussels the refuge of, **33**. 210n, 291n

daughter of, **12**. 107n

Boyle, Lady Mary (1625–78), m. (1641) Charles Rich, 4th E. of Warwick:

Berkeley's correspondence with, **16**. 138

*Occasional Meditations upon Several Subjects* by, **16**. 138

preparation of father's biography intended by, **16**. 138–9

Walker's funeral sermon on, **16**. 138

Boyle, Richard (1566–1643), cr. (1616) Bn Boyle, (1620) E. of Corke:

daughter considers writing life of, **16**. 138–9

monument to, in St Patrick's Cathedral, **9**. 404

son of, **16**. 172n

*True Remembrances* by, will be mentioned by HW, **16**. 7

Boyle, Richard (ca 1675–1740), 2d Vct Shannon; M.P.:

daughter of, **19**. 62n

Boyle, Richard (1694–1753), 3d E. of Burlington; architect; statesman:

architecture of, mentioned by Green, **14**. 40

birth date of, corrected, **43**. 38

Boyle, Lady Charlotte, inherits Boyle and Clifford family estates from, **20**. 545n

Carleton leaves painting to, **42**. 321n

Chiswick House bought by, **35**. 237n

Cork promised bequest by, **20**. 545

daughter of, **17**. 274n, **20**. 19n

death of, **9**. 157, **35**. 159

Euston challenged by, to duel, **17**. 174

family quarrel of, **17**. 174

father of, **25**. 74

HW imitates, **20**. 361–2

health of, palsy, **37**. 341

houses designed by, **9**. 56, 119n

Lincoln cathedral subject of opinion by, **1**. 10

Monticelli supported by, in action against opera house, **20**. 4n

portrait supposedly of Mary, Q. of Scots, owned by: **15**. 113, 139; engraved by Vertue, **42**. 321n

Pulteney's epigram on illness of, **30**. 24

settles £6,000 on the Violette, **9**. 81n

Thanet to mourn, **35**. 159

Wade's house designed by, **9**. 56

Whitehall plans altered by, **21**. 364

wife of, **9**. 28n

wife to inherit property of, **9**. 157

will of, **35**. 159

Wilton Bridge surpasses architecture of, **20**. 109

Boyle, Richard (1728–1807), styled Vct Boyle; 2d E. of Shannon, 1764:

brother of, **25**. 577n

contests Charlotte Boyle's inheritance, **31**. 346

(?) Conway, Hon, Anne Seymour enraged by kiss of, at Ranelagh, **30**. 87

(?) Kildare friend of, **30**. 87

marriage of, **10**. 110, **38**. 235

Stone, Abp, asks to perform marriage ceremony of, **10**. 110

—— opposes marriage of, **10**. 110

volunteer regiment might be taken from, for voting new taxes, **33**. 158n

Boyle, Richard (1762–88), army officer:

Garrick, Mrs, entertains, at dinner, **35**. 384–5

grandfather resembled by, **35**. 385

(?) mother disowns, **31**. 274–5

sister does bust of, **35**. 385

will of, **31**. 346

Boyle, Hon. Robert (1627–91), natural philosopher:

bust of, in the Hermitage, **14**. 39n, **29**. 34n

*Occasional Reflections upon Several Subjects* resembles sister's writings, **16**. 138

Shaw's alleged preface to, **37**. 294

Boyle, Hon. Robert (1736–80). *See* Boyle Walsingham, Hon. Robert

Boyle, Roger (1621–79), cr. (1628) Bn Boyle, (1660) E. of Orrery:

*English Adventures* by, **34**. 126n

*Parthenissa*, editions of, **15**. 26–7

poetry of, bad, **2**. 188

*Saul* attributed to, **16**. 21

Boyle family:

Burlington leaves Waterford estates of, to Lady Charlotte Boyle, **20**. 545n

Boyle Farm, Surrey; seat of E. of Hertford, Mrs Boyle Walsingham, and Lord Henry Fitzgerald:

Boyle, Charlotte, decorates, **31**. 251, **35**. 390, **42**. 197, 203

Boyle Walsingham, Mrs, lives at, **11**. 41n

—— and daughter will make, a puppet show, **42**. 197

Fitzgerald dies at, **11**. 266n

HW at, hears report of Ds of Portland's death, **31**. 233

Hamilton, Mary, may have visited, **31**. 216

Hertford's house at, bought by Mrs Boyle Walsingham, **39**. 416

More, Hannah, describes, **42**. 204n

visitors to: Clifden, Lady, **11**. 328; HW, **11**. 328, **31**. 233

visitors to ball at, **42**. 222n

Boyle Walsingham, Hon. Henry (d. 1756): widow of, **11**. 328n

Boyle Walsingham, Hon. Mrs Henry. *See* Martin, Lucia

Boyle Walsingham, Hon. Robert (1736–80), naval capt.; M.P.:

apprehensions about, **25**. 79n

Cavendish, Lord Richard, volunteers with, **33**. 38n

daughter of, **11**. 238n, **25**. 577n

family of, **30**. 323

George III gracious to, at levee, despite Gloucester leanings, **36**. 323

hurricane may have killed, **39**. 353

reports on naval situation, **33**. 48

Rodney said to have joined, **25**. 74n, 79

*Thunderer* commanded by, **39**. 307n

wife of, **11**. 41n

Boyle, Walsingham, Hon. Mrs Robert. *See* Williams, Charlotte Hanbury

Boyne, Vct. *See* Hamilton, Gustavus (1710–46)

*Boyne*, English ship:

involved in Mediterannean war, **18**. 396

Medley dies on board of, **19**. 434n

*Teresa* captured by, **6**. 452n

Boyne, Battle of the:

day of, HW hails as 'festival,' **35**. 478

HW's epitaph for Cutts mentions, **10**. 21

Halifax's poem on, **18**. 266

Hamilton, Anthony, fought at, **41**. 270n

Schomberg killed at, **10**. 11n

William III at, **15**. 19n, **28**. 339n

—— hero of, **33**. 153

—— wounded at, **33**. 338

Boyne River, Ireland:

Conway disarms Whiggism on, **37**. 453

Boynes. *See* Bourgeois de Boynes

Boynet, Sir John and Dame Winifred:

alleged tombs of, at Letheringham, **35**. 248–9

Boynet family:

HW unacquainted with coat-of-arms of, **35**. 256

Boys *or* Boyce, Commodore William (d. 1774):

fleet of, returns to the Downs, **21**. 336n

Thurot pursued by, towards Aberdeen, **21**. 346n, 347n, 352n

vessels pursued by, off Deal, **21**. 305n

Bozzini, Michelagelo, Abbate:

(?) Tuscan agent at Venice, **18**. 44

Bozzo, Jacopo (d. 1743), Capt. of *Nostra Signora della Misericordia*:

death of, from plague, **18**. 252n

*Bozzy and Piozzi. See under* Wolcot, John

Brabant, Ds of. *See* Jacoba

Brabant:

Austrian-Prussian peace may sacrifice, **39**. 474

Frederick, D. of York, allegedly offered dukedom of, **34**. 90

Humphrey, D. of Gloucester, said to have married heiress of, **34**. 90

Joseph II revokes constitution of, **34**. 87n

pacification of, may lead to unity against French Revolution, **34**. 102–3

provoked, but may not be emancipated, **35**. 398

revolt in: **11**. 127; said to be promoted by Necker and La Fayette, **34**. 96

troops in English pay in, include no English, **19**. 240n

ultimatum issued to, **11**. 130–1

war seemingly imminent in, **33**. 571

Brabanter; Brabanters:

fury of, **11**. 168–9

HW pities, **11**. 168

Braber *or* Draper, Vcts Townshend's butler:

Townshend, Vcts, robbed by, **30**. 224n

Braber *or* Draper, Mrs Molly, Vcts Townshend's chambermaid:

aunt succeeded by, **30**. 224n

implicated in robbery, **30**. 224n

Bracanza. *See* Bragança; Braganza

Bracci, Antonio, Abbé (fl. ca 1574):

Francavilla made statues for, **21**. 479

Bracci, Antonio (1692–1754):

Francavilla's statues at villa of, **20**. 221, **21**. 479, 482

Mann tries to engage, as agent in Rome to observe Pretender, **20**. 221n

villa of, near Rovezzano and town house in Florence, **20**. 221n

Bracci, Giuseppe, engraver:

Hamilton employs, **35**. 429n

Bracci, Pietro (1700–73), sculptor:

sculptures for Ps Sobieska's mausoleum done by, **21**. 391n

Bracciano, Duca di. *See* Odescalchi, Livio

Bracciano-Odescalchi, Duchessa di. *See* Corsini, Maria Vittoria

*Braccio. See* Brace

Brace (*braccio*):

Florentine, equal to about 23 inches, **21**. 447, **25**. 581n

Bracegirdle, Anne (ca 1663–1748), actress:

Burlington's present returned by, to his wife, **25**. 74

Chute's friend, **17**. 435

clogs worn by, **17**. 435

HW breakfasts with, **17**. 435

HW mentions, **35**. 24

pattens worn by, in humbler days, **17**. 435

'vestal actress,' **25**. 74

Bracelet; bracelets:

Aiguillon, Mme d', wears, with pictures of Christ and Young Pretender, **22**. 325

[Bracelet; bracelets, *continued*]
diamond, Maria Louisa gives, to Comtesse Thurn, **23.** 253
Gévaudan beast's hair may provide, **31.** 61
HW's picture too hideous for, **11.** 183
HW wants to be, on Bns Douglas's arm, **42.** 408
of Elizabeth of Russia's hair, given by Elizabeth to La Chétardie, **18.** 495

Bracey & Co. (? bankers):
Compton has draft on, **38.** 259n

Brachiano, Countess. *See* Paleotti, Adelaide

Brackenbury, Sir Richard. *See* Brackenbury, Sir Robert

Brackenbury, Sir Robert (d. 1485), Kt, (?) 1485, constable of the Tower:
dies at Bosworth for Richard III, and not likely to have been dismissed for not killing princes, **40.** 113

Brackley, Northants:
Greatworth near, **9.** 146n
Mason at, **29.** 84n
Montagu posts letters at, **9.** 334
—— to receive HW's parcels at, **9.** 168
parliamentary representative of, dies, **9.** 171
parliamentary representatives of, **2.** 1, **9.** 110n, 114n, 171n, 319n
postage from, **10.** 251n
Tusmore, Oxon, addressed by way of, **31.** 198, 218n, 286
wagon from, to collect pictures at Uxbridge, **10.** 8

Brackley carrier. *See* Eagles, Ezra

Braco, Bn. *See* Duff, William

Braddock, Maj.-Gen. Edward (1695–1755):
aide-de-camp of, *see* Orme
'Americanus' not yet claimed by, **35.** 245
brutal remark by, on sister's suicide, **20.** 492
Cumberland, D. of, irritated by slowness of, **20.** 491–2
defeat and death of, **20.** 494–7, 498, **35.** 245–6, 254
Dinwiddie blamed by, for poor Indian assistance, **20.** 492n
drunkenness punished by, with lashes, **20.** 492n
France need not envy laurels of, **35.** 90
George II's orders to, **20.** 487n
Gibraltar post of, **20.** 496
Gumley's duel with, **20.** 496
Indians would not have been treated politely by, **35.** 186
Johnson's success emphasizes faults of, **35.** 258
Mann awaits news of, **20.** 487
(?) Montagu, Lady Mary Wortley, mentions, **34.** 260
Upton, Mrs, ill-treated by, for not giving him enough money, **20.** 492–3

Braddock, Frances (d. 1731):
hangs herself after gambling away fortune at Bath, **20.** 492

Bradford, Bn. *See* Bridgeman, Henry (1725–1800)

Bradford estate:
Bath, E. of, recommends Colman to Gen. Pulteney for, **22.** 560

Bradford Peverell, near Dorchester:
Conway at camp at, **35.** 283, **37.** 483, 490, 491

Bradley, John (*alias* Walker):
Wesket's accomplice in robbery, **38.** 473n

Bradley, Derbyshire:
Meynell of, **9.** 240n, **28.** 391n, **29.** 306n

Bradninch, Devon:
Waldegrave steward of, **20.** 246n

Bradshaw, Mrs:
SH visited by, **12.** 226

Bradshaw, Edward, Capt.:
Florence visited by, **18.** 146

Bradshaw, John (1602–59), regicide:
Dart denounces, **35.** 146n

Bradshaw, Lucretia (d. 1766), m. (ca 1714) Martin Folkes:
death of, **7.** 397

Bradshaw, Robert, coachman to P. of Wales:
(?) son forbidden by, to marry a Maid of Honour, **18.** 232

Bradshaw, Thomas (1733–74), M.P.; joint secretary to Treasury:
career and suicide of, **24.** 56, **32.** 214, **35.** 350, **39.** 209, 210
HW calls, 'Marcus Portius,' **32.** 214
*Heroic Epistle* mentions, **28.** 75n
*Heroic Postscript* mentions, **28.** 113
Rigby's agent and a notorious pimp, **34.** 242

Bradshaw, Mrs Thomas. *See* Wilson, Elizabeth

Bradshaw, William (fl. 1700):
*Turkish Spy* adapted by Midgley and, **13.** 70n

Bradwell, Suffolk:
Nicholls rector of, **2.** 132n, **11.** 17n, **28.** 80n

Brag (game):
Francis III plays, at Richmond's fireworks, **20.** 56
London residents play, 10 miles from town to avoid earthquakes, **20.** 137
Methodism almost equals, in popularity, **20.** 41
played, **9.** 90, 108, 115, 126
women addicted to deep play at, **20.** 41

Bragança Sousa Ligne Tavares Mascarenhas da Silva, João Carlos de (1719–1806), Duque de Lafões, 1761:
Du Deffand, Mme, gives account of, **7.** 9
——'s opinion of, **7.** 26
——'s social relations with, and Neckers, **7.** 9
Florence visited by, **22.** 174
to leave Paris, **7.** 26

Bragança, house of:
Villa-Viçosa headquarters of, **4.** 329n

Braganza, Catherine of. *See* Catherine (1638–1705)

*Braganza. See under* Jephson, Robert

Bragelongne, Jean-Baptiste-Claude:
(?) attends session of parliament of Paris, **8.** 173
Bragelongne, Marie-Charlotte de (ca 1703–74), m. (1740) Armand-Henri, Comte de Clermont-Gallerande:
(?) death of, **32.** 258
Bragge, Anne (1720–81), m. Sir John Dick, 5th Bt:
Beauclerk, Lady Henry, will be pleased by Mann's kindness to, **21.** 19
Beauclerks' letters from, may mention Mann, **21.** 10
death of, **25.** 127, 161
Florentine visit of, deferred, **20.** 537
HW pleased by Mann's kindness to, **21.** 19
Kilmorey, Vcts, calls, 'Lady Dyke' to avoid indelicate word, **25.** 108
Leghorn visited by, to break up her house, **24.** 239
Mann expects visit from, **20.** 537, **24.** 240
——'s dinner in garden enjoyed by, **21.** 10
—— visited by, **21.** 10, **22.** 154, **23.** 65, **24.** 233, 251, 289
—— visited by, at Pisa during earthquake scare, **23.** 262
Orlov gives Turkish girls to, **23.** 228
Rome and Naples to be visited by, **24.** 251
Rome to be visited by, for winter, **24.** 240
Rosenberg and Mann to dine with, **23.** 59
to be proxy for dowager Cts Cowper at grandson's christening, **24.** 233, 239
Venice visited by, to see Northampton's entry, **22.** 154
Bragge, Dr Robert (d. ca 1777–8) collector:
HW's copy of catalogue of, identifies a Giorgione as HW's purchase from him, **43.** 252
Walpole, Sir Robert, told by, that Correggio painting at Parma is not original, **18.** 355
Braham, Frances Elizabeth Anne (1821–79), m. 1 John James Henry Waldegrave; m. 2 (1840) George Edward Waldegrave, 7th E. Waldegrave; m. 3 (1847) George Granville Vernon-Harcourt; m. 4 (1863) Chichester S. P. Fortescue, cr. (1874) Bn Carlingford:
HW's MSS bought by, **26.** 40–4, **36.** 316
Braham, John (ca 1774–1856), singer:
daughter of, **26.** 41
Leoni uncle of, **32.** 217n
Brah Visūtra Sundara (Kosā Pān), Siamese ambassador to France:
Louis XIV's medal commemorates visit of, **24.** 469
Brain:
inflammation of, **25.** 467
Braitwitz or Breitwitz, Johann Ernst (ca 1672–1759), Baron von; general:
adjutant of, see Berrue
Botta not to replace, **19.** 23
Charles Emmanuel III and Maria Theresa called 'potences' by, **18.** 524n

Correggio painting to be procured by, **18.** 337, 370
Craon to give news of Campo Santo to, **18.** 163–4
Du Châtelet not to succeed, **18.** 174
—— succeeds, **17.** 182n
English captains entertained by, **18.** 98
example of, frightens Leghorn inhabitants, **17.** 305
financiers stop coach of, **18.** 66
Florentine house, coaches, and horses to be relinquished by, **17.** 195
Florentines like, **19.** 23
Francis I may dismiss, **19.** 51
—— orders: to Firenzuola, **18.** 120; to increase militia, **17.** 288; to keep Spaniards out of Tuscany, **18.** 66, 127–8, 134
—— receives news from, **17.** 179
——'s birthday celebrated by, with dinner party, **18.** 348n
——'s correspondence with, **19.** 3
——'s instructions to, **17.** 229
——'s plans revealed by, to Mann, **18.** 3
friend of, commands hussars, **18.** 338
Genoese news sought by, **17.** 180
health of: fever, **18.** 140; ill, **18.** 174; out of danger, **18.** 179; rheumatism, **18.** 520
Kaunitz receives horses from, **17.** 49
leaves Leghorn for Florence, **17.** 180
Leghorn activities of, at earthquake, **17.** 284, 293, 303
—— garrison not to be weakened by, **18.** 85
——'s resistance predicted by, **17.** 266
—— visited by, **17.** 106, 117, 192
letters to, **17.** 472, **18.** 163–4
Lobkowitz sends courier to, **19.** 11
Mann discusses Spanish expedition with, **17.** 182–3
—— entertained by, **17.** 261, **18.** 98
—— exchanges calls with, **17.** 259, 260, **18.** 144
—— prefers inn to lodging with, **17.** 262
——'s conversation with, **17.** 117
——'s correspondence with, **19.** 170, 257, 310
——'s neighbour, **18.** 353
—— tells George II's reassurances to, **17.** 282
—— to entertain, **18.** 78, 340, 353
—— told by: of Zambeccari's probable arrest, **18.** 257; that Correggio painting will be hard to get, **18.** 370; to trust in England and Holland, **18.** 513
Maricone's correspondence with, **17.** 308–9
Modenese princesses praised by, **19.** 170, 257
money demanded by, **17.** 195
Montemar rejects civilities of, **17.** 214
Moravia may be destination of, **17.** 407
Naples visited by, **20.** 399
Neapolitan invasion discussed by, with Mann, **17.** 110
order of battle of Spanish army communicated by, **18.** 127n
Pistoia to be headquarters of, **18.** 98

[Braitwitz, Johann Ernst, *continued*]
Prato and San Martino to be visited by, **18.** 134
remonstrances of, sent to Vienna, **18.** 128
Riccardi's failure to ask Mann, stirs curiosity of, **17.** 147
Richecourt's opposition to Mann discussed by, with Rinuccini and Tornaquinci, **18.** 10
——'s relations with, **17.** 406, 490, **18.** 66, 120, 144–5, 285
Silva communicates with, **17.** 180
Spanish desertions reported by, **17.** 427
Spanish invasion reported by, to Florence, **17.** 179, 182
Spanish news not heard by, **17.** 84
Theodore aided by, in writing edict, **18.** 151n
Thun engaged through, to secure intelligence about Young Pretender, **18.** 373n
—— hears news from, **17.** 282
——'s correspondence with, **18.** 42
Traun orders: not to obey Francis I's orders, **18.** 128; not to risk battle with Spaniards, **18.** 295; to send troops to San Martino, **18.** 85
—— tells, that Spaniards will invade Tuscany when P. Charles enters France, **18.** 285
Vitelli, Marchesa, has affair with, **18.** 333–4, 351, 353, 364, 520, **19.** 170, 257, **20.** 399
Wachtendonck has meeting with, **17.** 95n
——'s affairs settled by, **17.** 146–7
—— temporarily succeeded by, **17.** 117
Whithed's servant's case supported by, in Regency Council, **18.** 10
Young Pretender's route reported by, at Florence, **17.** 13n
Brambles:
Houghton overgrown with, **23.** 510, **39.** 172–3
Brambridge, Hants:
Smyths of, **11.** 195n
Brampton, Cumberland:
Naworth Castle near, **41.** 250n
Bramson, Mrs. *See* Wither, Henrietta Maria
Bramston, Rev. James (ca 1694–1744), poet:
*Art of Politics* and *Man of Taste* by, **17.** 441n, **43.** 182
epigram by, on Islay's garden at Hounslow Heath, **17.** 441
Gray does not admire, **14.** 36
'Scotch Tast in Vista's' by, prints for, **43.** 245
Bramston. *See also* Bransom
Bramstone, Wither, of Oakley Hall, Hants:
(?) SH visited by, **12.** 229
Bramstone, Mrs Wither. *See* Chute, Mary Lobb
Brancacci Chapel, Florence:
Masaccio's paintings in, **11.** 154n
Brancards:
of Richecourt's litter, **21.** 80
Brancas, Comtesse de. *See* Lowendal, Marie-Louise de
Brancas, Duchesse de. *See* Montmorency, Élisabeth-Pauline de Gand de Mérode de

Brancas, Marquise de. *See* Grandhomme de Giseux, Marie-Anne-Renée-Jacqueline
Brancas, Antoinette-Candide-Pauline de (1756–86), called Mlle de Lauraguais:
proposed marriage of, **6.** 499
Brancas, Bufile-Antoine-Léon de (b. 1735), Comte de Brancas:
marriage of, **1.** 110
social relations of, with Hénault, **7.** 327
Brancas, Louis de (1714–93), Duc de Lauraguais; Duc de Villars-Brancas:
attends session of parliament of Paris, **8.** 172
Brancas, Comte de, son of, **1.** 110n
Craufurd consults, **32.** 267
Lauraguais, Comte de, at variance with, **1.** 110
—— threatened by, with lettre de cachet, **39.** 57
protests illegal parliament, **5.** 61
wife of, **3.** 258n
Brancas, Louis-Bufile de (d. 1753), Comte de Forcalquier:
Du Deffand, Mme, subject of 'portrait' by, **6.** 14n, **8.** 51–2, 59
family of, **8.** 77n, 100n, 114n
marriage of, **3.** 5n
wife of, **3.** 5n, **14.** 144n
Brancas, Louis-Léon-Félicité de (1733–1824), Comte de Lauraguais; Duc de Brancas, 1793:
Arnould, Sophie, has affair with, **38.** 351n
china of, **39.** 32n
Cole sees, **1.** 111n
Craufurd attributes wit to, **3.** 369
——'s friendship with, **5.** 120
Du Deffand, Mme, considers, a fool, **3.** 369–70
England visited by, **3.** *188*, **10.** 219, **30.** 179, **31.** 108, **38.** 531, 535, **39.** 57
English imitated by, **5.** 199
English coachman of: goes to England to buy horses, **39.** 22; takes HW's letters to England, **7.** 377, **39.** 22
epistle of, HW sends, to Lady Ossory, **32.** 92
escape of, from Dijon, **3.** 188–9
flees to England to evade father's lettre de cachet, **39.** 57
Forbes's horse race with, **1.** 110, **7.** 304, **10.** 219, **31.** 107–8, **39.** 57, **41.** 6, **43.** 376
Guerchys fear indiscretions of, **38.** 535
HW calls on, **38.** 535
(?) HW mentions, **3.** 341
HW sends letters by tailor of, **7.** 377
Hertford rents Hôtel de Brancas from, **38.** 351, 531
——'s opinion of, **38.** 351
horse of, poisoned in race: English disgraced by, **30.** 218; HW wishes Mme de Sévigné could write about, **30.** 218; taken ill at race, **39.** 57
in horse race while brother weds, **1.** 110
Louis XV's pun about, **10.** 219
marriage of, **3.** 305n
Maurepas's conversation with, **3.** 370

Pembroke to be visited by, **38**. 531, 535
porcelain manufactured by, **7**. 262
Roux aids and quarrels with, **7**. 262
social relations of, in Paris, **3**. 369, **7**. 262, 290, 303, 322, 369
SH to be visited by, **30**. 179
wife of, **3**. 305n
Brancas, Louis-Paul (1718–1802), Marquis de; later Duc de Céreste:
Angers to be visited by, **3**. 79
Artois, Comtesse d', to be conducted by, **23**. 521n
family of, **8**. 100n, 114n
HW and Brissac dine with, **30**. 205
(?) HW mentions, **3**. 341
HW's correspondence with, **7**. 384
HW sends compliments to, **41**. 21
HW to give Sheffield box to, **7**. 416
hôtel of, **7**. 277
lacks common sense, **4**. 84
social relations of, in Paris, *see index entries ante* **8**. 266
wife of, **5**. 79n
Brancas, Marie-Thérèse de (1716–82), m. 1 (1736) Jean-Anne-Vincent de Larlan de Kercadio, Comte de Rochefort; m. 2 (1782) Louis-Jules-Barbon Mancini-Mazarini, Duc de Nivernais:
always at home on Wednesdays and Sundays, **41**. 214
Du Deffand, Mme, mentions, **3**. 318
——'s relations with, **3**. 257
'enchantress,' **31**. 56–7
England may be visited by, **31**. 68
family of, **8**. 77n, 100n, 114n
Garrick acts with, **7**. 281
HW and Anne Pitt like, **40**. 387
HW consults, about room for Anne Pitt, **31**. 87
HW describes, admirably, **14**. 153–4
HW finds, 'amiable and agreeable,' **32**. 23
HW frequents circle of, **30**. 205, **31**. 69
HW praises, **31**. 53–4, 56–7, 67
HW's correspondence with, **7**. 381, 382, **41**. 21–2
HW's letter to Rousseau approved by, **31**. 101
HW's social relations with, **31**. 54, 67, *see also index entries ante* **8**. 267
health of, **6**. 441
Hénault's 'portrait' of, **8**. 100–2
Louis XV grants apartment to, **40**. 11n
Luxembourg palace the home of, **7**. 266, **8**. 58, **31**. 54, 69, **41**. 21n
'Merlou,' cat of, **31**. 54
Nivernais communicates HW's letter to, **41**. 214
—— later marries, **8**. 58, 77n, 100n, 114n
—— to translate HW's *Fugitive Pieces* for, **41**. 20
—— to visit, at St-Maur, **40**. 19, 21
Pitt, Anne, corresponds with, **31**. 54, 111

—— friend of, **32**. 23
—— neglects, **41**. 22
—— questions, about *corbeilles*, **31**. 54–5
—— recommends HW to, **31**. 53–4
social relations of, in Paris, *see index entries ante*, **8**. 267
witticism by, on bracelet with pictures of Christ and Young Pretender, **8**. 58, **22**. 325
Brancas, Hôtel de, Rue de l'Université, Paris; Hertford's and Richmond's Paris residence:
airy in hot weather, **38**. 403–4
Beauchamp's apartment in, available for HW, **38**. 477, 481
Du Deffand, Mme, mentions, **3**. 18
—— sends to, for news, **3**. 19
garden at, **38**. 361
HW at, **7**. 287, 288, 293, 296–9, 305, 307–10, 312–14, **31**. 87
HW calls, 'Hôtel de Lassay,' **38**. 423
HW declines to stay at, **38**. 485
HW writes from, **39**. 9–10
Hertford takes, **38**. 305n, 351, 359, 361, 373, 387
Mirepoix, Mme de, gives ball at, **3**. 217
proprietor of, **38**. 531
Brancas de Forcalquier, Bufile-Hyacinthe-Toussaint de (1697–1754), Comte de Céreste:
Du Deffand, Mme, gives 'portrait' of, **8**. 114–15
family of, **8**. 114n
relations of, with Comtesse de Maurepas, **5**. 287
Ussé's ring from, **5**. 287
Brancas family:
Lauraguais affronts, by horse race on day of brother's wedding, **43**. 376
Branch. *See* Candelabra
Branchi, Mme. *See* Pinacci, Angela
Branchi, Antonio:
Mann's annuity to, **25**. 667n
Branchi, Niccolò (1723–1810), chemist:
maker of essences, **18**. 177
Branciforte. *See* Reggio e Branciforte
Brand, Lady Caroline. *See* Pierrepont, Lady Caroline
Brand, Caroline (1752–8), child of Thomas and Lady Caroline Brand:
mother of, dies, **20**. 435
Brand, Rev. John (ca 1744–1806):
SH visited by, **12**. 226, **43**. 160
Brand, Nathaniel (fl. 1717–68):
leases Thavies Inn, **13**. 143n
Brand, Sir Thomas, Kt, 1718:
sale of prints and drawings collected by, **38**. 340n
Brand, Thomas (1718–70) of the Hoo; M.P.:
(?) at Chesterfield's assembly, **37**. 327
Bedford coalition opposed by, **41**. 70
Bedford's connection with, **20**. 435
Bedfords entertain, **9**. 233
birth date of, **43**. 55, 177, 194, 239

[Brand, Thomas (1718–70), *continued*]
Florence avoided by, on way to Rome, **20**. 456
Florence visited by, **20**. 471
Gem resembles, physically but not in disposition, **30**. 208
Germany to be visited by, **20**. 434
HW does not hear from, **31**. 112
HW engages, to accompany him to D. of Cumberland's levee, **9**. 330
HW has not yet seen, **20**. 485
HW hopes for arrival of, at Florence, **20**. 461
HW jokes about interests of, **31**. 112
HW mentions, **20**. 292, **37**. 465
HW recommends, to Mann, **20**. 434, 441
HW's correspondence with, **7**. 377, **40**. 186, 384–7
HW to dine with, **37**. 522
HW visited by, **37**. 471
Mann consigns HW's letters to, **20**. 441–2, 456, 471, 485, **26**. 36
—— entertains at assembly, **20**. 471
—— has formerly seen, in Italy, **20**. 434
Newcastle's appearance derided by, in stage whisper, **9**. 233
opera director, **16**. 280n, **17**. 191
'our old schoolfellow,' **1**. 198, 198n, 202
Paris visited by, **13**. 166
Parliamentary minority includes, **42**. 497
peerage suggested for, **30**. 236n
'remarkable laugher,' **40**. 186, 385
Rome to be visited by, **20**. 434
seclusion sought by, **20**. 471
subscribes to Middleton's *Life of Cicero*, **15**. 7, **37**. 98n
Temple hears of Newcastle's embarrassment from, **9**. 233
Uffizi visited by, **20**. 471
wife of, dies, **9**. 150, **20**. 435
Brand, Thomas (1749–94) of the Hoo; M.P.:
mother of, dies, **20**. 435
not mentioned in D. of Kingston's will, **32**. 150
seeks nomination for Parliament, **1**. 198, 198n, 200, 202
Veres leave, behind, **33**. 294
Brand, Mrs Thomas. *See* Roper, Gertrude
Brande, Mr (d. 1783), apothecary:
Pirner partner of, **28**. 297n
'Brandenbourg, M. de.' *See* Frederick II of Prussia
Brandenburg (Germany):
Austrian-Russian atrocities in, **21**. 444n
Burdett's confederate passes for princess of, **20**. 20
Conway and Scott visit, **39**. 537
Frederick II must depend on, to defeat all his enemies, **21**. 327
'Brandenburg, bruin of.' *See* Frederick II of Prussia
Brandenburg, house of:
Frederick II seeks to make, equal with that of Austria, **18**. 543

Brandenburg-Ansbach, Margrave of. *See* Christian Friedrich Karl Alexander (1736–1806)
Brandenburg-Ansbach, Margravine of. *See* Berkeley, Lady Elizabeth (1750–1828); Friederike Karoline (1735–91)
Brandenburg-Bayreuth, Margrave of. *See* Friedrich (1711–63)
Brandenburg-Bayreuth, Margravine of. *See* Sofie Karoline (1737–1817)
Brandenburg House, Hammersmith:
Ansbach acquires, **12**. 88n
theatre at, **12**. 151n
Brander, Gustavus:
*Forme of Cury* given by, to HW, **43**. 71
Brandes, J. C.:
*Der Gasthof* by, adapted by Holcroft, **42**. 226
Brandi, Gaetana (d. 1763), m. (1719) Piero del Vernaccia:
Crudeli's affair with, **18**. *112*
husband wants, released from *le mal maritate*, **18**. 121–2
Karl Friedrich smitten with, **20**. 149
Pitti and Gavi attend, **18**. 112
sent to *le mal maritate*, **18**. 112
Branding:
of Italian criminals, **20**. 144
of slaves, on Codrington's estates, **35**. 178n
on the hand, for bigamy, may be imposed on Ds of Kingston, **24**. 31, 121, 123, 196
Brandon, Cts of. *See* Agar, Ellis (ca 1709–89)
Brandon, Lady. *See* Mason, Anne
Brandon, Charles (ca 1484–1545), cr. (1514) D. of Suffolk:
arras with history of, **32**. 325
'Charles' a rare name in time of, **2**. 104
codpiece of, **35**. 359–60
French queen married by, **15**. 205
portrait of, bought by HW at Granville sale, **10**. 53
Somerset, D. of, lands in Calais with expedition of, **20**. 139n
wife of, **15**. 205n
Brandon, Sir Edward. *See* Brandon, Sir William
Brandon, Lady Frances (1517–59), m. 1 (1533) Henry Grey, 3d M. of Dorset, cr. (1551) D. of Suffolk; m. 2 (ca 1554) Adrian Stokes:
portrait of, by Lukas de Heere, bought by HW at Oxford's sale, **17**. 373–4
Brandon, Gregory, hangman:
son of, **1**. 8n
Brandon, Richard (d. 1649):
Charles I executed by, **1**. 8
Brandon, Sir William (d. 1485), Kt, 1485:
Richard III kills, **41**. 112
Brandon, Suffolk:
Cony instigates Orford's removal from, to Houghton, **42**. 356
HW sends Dr Monro to, to treat E. of Orford, **42**. 355–6
White, Mrs, entertains HW at, **18**. 318
Brandsby Hall, Yorks, Mrs Francis Cholmeley's seat:

Berrys visit, **11.** 35, **12.** 68, 83
Cholmeley of, **2.** 304n, **11.** 29n
HW mentions, **12.** 78
Brandt, Enevold von (1738–72):
arrest of, **23.** 374n, 385
to be executed, **23.** 392 401
Brandy:
Addison said to have died from, **9.** 236
Ancram loves, **37.** 549
cherry: **37.** 22; HW asks for, at Stowe, **10.** 314n
contraband, **9.** 106
Dodd and Whaley armed with, to explore Wokey Hole, **40.** 10
English addiction to, **19.** 272
Ferrers drowns his abilities in, **21.** 395
Fitzwalter consumes 7 bottles of, weekly, **20.** 519
French, tax on, **25.** 254n
(?) gout remedy, **35.** 105
HW tries but dislikes, **14.** 142
HW tries, for gout cure, **22.** 322
Harlequin hears dealer of, **9.** 96,
Kilmarnock, Cts of, requests, with lemons, **37.** 218
Peter III drunk with, **22.** 57
preferable to enthusiasm, **33.** 190
tincture for the eyes infused in, **18.** 365n
Brandy-wine:
Dutch give, to well-behaved soldiers, **37.** 276
Brandywine, Battle of:
England gets news of, **24.** 331n, 334, 338, 339n, 32. 394n, 365n
Branges, Marquis de. *See* Barillon d'Amoncourt, Paul
Branicki, Jan Clemens (1689–1771), grand general of Poland:
competitor for Polish crown, **22.** 249n
Conway will not support Czartoryski and Stanislas II against, **22.** 249
Bransby. *See* Brandsby Hall
Bransom, ——, father of Ann Bransom:
HW's bequest to, **30.** 362
Bransom, Ann, HW's housekeeper at SH, 'Nanny':
HW directs, to show SH to visitors, **43.** 163, 164, 165
HW's legacy to, **15.** 338n, **30.** 362
locks doors at night, **11.** 370
mentioned, **12.** 141
SH shown by, **11.** 25, **12.** 27, 168
talkative, **12.** 168, **15.** 271
Brant. *See* Brandt
Branthwaite, Richard (fl. 1594–9):
buys manor of Stoke, **14.** 59n
Brantôme, Abbé de. *See* Bourdeille, Pierre de
Braschi, Giovanni Angelo. *See* Pius VI
Braschi, Signora. *See* Bandi, Giulia
Braschi Onesti, Luigi (1745–1816), Duca di Nemi; Pius VI's nephew:
Lepri's fortune given to, **25.** 384, 568

Braschi Onesti, Romualdo (1753–1817), cardinal, 1786; Pius VI's nephew:
benefice should have rewarded French mission of, **24.** 470
uncle to provide for, **24.** 479
Brass; brasses:
armour of, **35.** 553
artillery of, **24.** 122
cabinet of, **40.** 283
cannons of, **18.** 455
Chantilly, **37.** 71
Dunstan said to be worker in, **16.** 46
field pieces of, **24.** 309n
figures of, removed from Fotheringhay gravestones, **10.** 344
great, medals of, **23.** 383
guns of, **23.** 228n, **24.** 122n
HW's exchequer chest fastened with, **23.** 285
HW surprised that P. Arthur's tomb is not, **35.** 150
lamp of, **17.** 374
medals of, **18.** 45, **21.** 202, **40.** 221, **42.** 262n
monumental, in Letheringham church, **35.** 248
monument decorated with, at Horton, **10.** 333
pedigree in, on Mereworth tomb, **35.** 144
plated silver turns to, **24.** 27
plates of: for monumental inscriptions, **2.** 234; on gravestone at Fotheringhay, **10.** 344
pots of, **17.** 53
prints of, in Gough's *Sepulchral Monuments*, **34.** 227
sculptured, may be part of Pipwell abbot's cross, **35.** 537
Brassey, Nathaniel (d. 1765), banker:
death of, **7.** 397
Brathwaite, Richard (?1588–1673), author:
*Ar't Asleep Husband? A Boulster Lecture,* frontispiece of, **1.** 174
Bratislava. *See* Pressburg
Braunau (Germany):
battle of, *see* Simpach
restoration of, to Bavaria, **19.** 37n
Braunschweig. *See* Brunswick
Braunston, Northants:
Reynolds, rector of, **1.** 180n
Bravo; bravi; bravos:
Clanwilliam aided by, in castrating rival, **24.** 544
*See also* Miquelet
'Bravo,' E. of Orford's pointer:
Orford's epitaph for, **32.** 179n
Brawn, collar of:
Montagu to eat, for Christmas, **10.** 2
Bray, Mrs:
SH visited by, **12.** 224
Bray, Dorothy (d. 1605), m. Edmund Brydges, 2d Bn Chandos:
arms of, **1.** 342
husband of, **1.** 342n
Bray, Frances, m. Edward Harrison; mother of Vcts Townshend:
falls on stairs, **40.** 52n

Bray, Michael (d. 1797):
lawyer, who will appreciate Mozzi's present, 25. 572
uncle leaves collection to, 25. 571
Bray, Temperance (ca 1581–1619), m. Sir Thomas Crewe:
epitaph for, 35. 74
'Bray, Vicar of.' See Vicar of Bray
Braybrooke, Bn. See Griffin, Sir John Griffin (1719–97)
Braywick, Berks:
Penn proprietor of, 11. 7n
Brazier, Mr:
SH visited by, 12. 222
Brazier; braziers:
Chute needs, at the Vyne, 35. 109
Durham, Bp of, rescues armour from, 10. 287
Brazil:
fleet of, at Lisbon, 20. 520
Jesuits said to endanger Portuguese sovereignty in, 21. 217n
Negro mutiny in, 23. 452
Rio Grande in, attacked by Portuguese, 24. 223
Spaniards take island on coast of, 32. 357–8
Spanish-Portuguese frontier war expected in, 24. 253n
Breach of privilege:
house-painter's arrest of Vcts Townshend is, 38. 502
Bread:
and butter: HW fond of, 30. 19; HW longs for, in France, 39. 7; HW's Parisian breakfast consists of, 30. 19
at St-Malo, composed half of sand, 12. 77
barley, 33. 138
brown, eaten by Henri IV, 35. 244
Cocchi eats, boiled in water, 21. 164
Conway does not live by, but by word from England, 37. 124
Cowper distributes, to poor of 2 Florentine parishes, 24. 232
ditchers' diet, 37. 172
Dodd and Whaley have, at Deane House, 40. 5
floods permit production of, 35. 384
Florentine poor to receive, on P. Charles's wedding day, 18. 364
for breakfast, 30. 19, 132n, 35. 342
Gages orders rations of, prepared at Perugia, 19. 7
HW eats: 31. 66; at Adderbury, 10. 312; for breakfast, 35. 342
HW jokes about invention of, 31. 325
HW should eat, with broth, 22. 114
hour for, 30. 132n
Lorenzi gives, to Florentine poor, 19. 14
Louis XV carries, in pocket, 20. 340
Mann eats, at tea, 17. 104
Mann, Galfridus, has big appetite for, 20. 554
Mestrell's counterfeiting for the sake of, 16. 150
Neapolitan shortage of, 22. 223

of bad quality, in Italy, 22. 446, 452
poultry to get, due to embargo, 35. 320
price of: at Dresden, 9. 268; high, in Florence, 22. 337; in England, rises, 22. 450, 455; in France, 21. 520; to be lowered, 11. 57
Rinuccini gives, to Florentine poor, 19. 461
riots over: about tax and scarcity in Spain, 39. 60–1, 63; French, 6. 184–5, 187, 321; verses on, 6. 192–4
Romans throw, into Clement XIII's coach, 22. 446
Sandwich distributes, at Huntingdon, 10. 151–2
scanty at Leghorn, 17. 304
shortage of: at Naples, 22. 223; at Rome, 22. 223, 229; in Bohemia, 24. 105; in France, 24. 106; in Tuscany, 22. 448, 25. 318
Spanish fleet runs short of, 28. 217
SH visitors eat, 33. 530
veal counterbalanced by, to prevent gout, 35. 21
white, unavailable at Calais, 34. 50
Breadalbane, Cts of. See Grey, Amabel (d. 1727)
Breadalbane, E. of. See Campbell, John (1696–1782)
Bread pudding:
remove for soups, 19. 357n
Breakfast; breakfasts:
Albany, Cts of, often takes, with husband and lady, 25. 101
Albemarle's family at, when news comes of his death, 20. 460
at Stowe, 10. 313
barley bread spread with honey, 33. 138
Bootle wears gold brocade at, 20. 184
Conway's absent-minded behaviour at, 38. 359
——'s hour for, too early for HW, 38. 73
—— takes, at Augustinian monastery, 37. 314
—— to take, at SH with HW, 39. 289
—— to take, with HW on way to Park Place, 37. 558
Craon, Mme de, entertains Mann at, 18. 78
Egremont, Cts of, eats, while husband writes, 22. 159
guests for, at Petersham Lodge, 31. 13–14
HW and Chute take, at SH, 23. 284
HW and Fox take, at SH, 37. 497
HW entertains Élie de Beaumont at, at SH, 30. 176, 38. 461n
HW gives: at SH, 31. 127; to Footes and Lady Herries at SH, 39. 475; to his nieces, 30. 132; to Ps Lubomirska, 42. 196–7
HW goes out to air after, 31. 369
HW invites guests for, but they understand him to say dinner, 38. 402
HW invites Mrs Montagu and Mrs Garrick to, at SH, 42. 83
HW must prepare, for Archduke and Archduchess, 31. 299
HW offers, to Hessenstein, 39. 403
HW's: at SH for Bedford circle, 35. 225; at

SH for D. and Ds of Marlborough, **39.** 418; at SH for D. of Of Newcastle, **38.** 445; for Hon. Henry Seymour-Conway and friends, **39.** 74–5; at SH for Lucans and Althorpes, **39.** 390; Conway appears at, **35.** 361; of bread and butter, attracts flies, **35.** 342; Parisian, consists of bread and butter, **30.** 19

HW takes, with Mrs Bracegirdle, **17.** 435

HW to take, with Horace Mann II, **24.** 493

Hardinge invites HW to, in the Temple, **35.** 575

—— prefers, as time for calling, **35.** 553

hour of, **30.** 132, **31.** 48

in Paris: dinner jostled by, **31.** 48; HW eats, **30.** 19, **31.** 93; Northumberland, Ds of, may give, **31.** 125

London full of, **25.** 502, **32.** 192

Mann and Conway talk Italian during, **20.** 293

Mann, Galfridus, takes, with HW, **20.** 360

meat: Corsi, Marchesa, serves, to Ps of Modena, **22.** 202; HW dislikes, **40.** 386

milk and chocolate for, **23.** 567

newspapers at, **35.** 342

on live oxen, in Abyssinia, **24.** 21

public: at Goodwood, **37.** 484; at Holland House, **25.** 11; Northumberland, Ds of, may give, **31.** 125

Robinson's, for Ps of Wales, **35.** 179

**Breamore, Hants:**

Hulse of, **2.** 239n

**Breast; breasts:**

'complaint' on, **39.** 498

effusion of blood from, **25.** 560, 567

English ladies cover, with gauze protuberances, **25.** 641

inflammation of, **24.** 426, 433, **33.** 318

Mann's cough should clear, **25.** 636

operation on Lady Waldegrave's, **30.** 171

women ordered to uncover, in church, **21.** 292

*See also* Humour on the breast; Oppression on the breast; Pain in head and breast; Pain in breast; Weakness on the breast

**Breast-feeding:**

instances of, **33.** 408, **35.** 532

**Breath:**

like vapour of south-east wind, **7.** 355

*See also* Shortness of breath

**Brébeuf family:**

memorial of, Hertford sends, to HW, **38.** 555, 566

**Breck021nock, Timothy (d. 1786):**

*Droit le Roi* compiled by, **10.** 153, **38.** 333, **43.** 133

**Breconshire:**

Morgan remains lord lieutenant of, **23.** 174

**Breda:**

Batthyány retreats to, **19.** 255

conference at: between Sandwich and Macanaz founders over Spanish demands. **19.** 393n; postponed, **37.** 265

congress may meet at, **21.** 355

Conway rushes to, to prepare for D. of Cumberland, **37.** 281–2

French may march by, **37.** 282

Mann may write to, **19.** 375

peace negotiations at, **19.** 289n

visitors to: Cumberland, D. of, **19.** 446, **37.** 281–2; Sandwich, **9.** 48n, **17.** 231n, **19.** 289n, 351, 375

*Brederode*, Dutch war ship:

Medley's squadron loses, in storm, **18.** 556

**Breeches:**

Adam's, eaten by goat on Ark, **39.** 294

black, *Hamlet* ghost wears, **20.** 209

black silk, **21.** 399n

Broglie loses, **17.** 465

buckskin: **35.** 70; Caroline Matilda wears, **23.** 273; sign of robustness, **30.** 86; worn for hunting, **9.** 240

chairman lets down, **17.** 248

child's eagerness to get into, **39.** 235

chimpanzee to wear, **9.** 127

Conway's letter does not have button on waistband of, **37.** 568

Cumberland, D. of, prepares in, for wedding, **18.** 62

fashion of, to reveal more than they conceal, **15.** 87

green, with silver buckles, worn for boar-hunting, **20.** 200n

Guise's mistress asks price of, as he lets them down, **20.** 481

HW's: black velvet, stolen at Paris, **39.** 17; gold-laced, stolen at Paris, **39.** 17; received from his mother, **36.** 3; Van Dyck style unsuitable for, **35.** 419

Italian ladies wear, **18.** 333

Lorraine, Primate of, does not wear, **17.** 12, 17

nankeen, worn by jockeys, **31.** 108

Naunton wears, **35.** 248

Northumberland, Cts of, wears, **31.** 125

pocket in, **37.** 74

satin, **30.** 211

Scipio's, continent, **24.** 426

velvet, Mme Vitelli wears, **18.** 334

waistband of: **35.** 166; Edgcumbe might break, in glee, **30.** 37

Walpole, Horatio (1678–1757), shrugs, **17.** 484

Young Pretender loses, **19.** 320

**Breeches-strings:**

Newcastle's, burst, **37.** 267

**Breen, François-Xavier, French sea-capt.:**

polacca *Elizabeth* commanded by, **23.** 24n

**Bregançon.** *See* Ricard de Bregançon

**Breglio.** *See* Solaro di Breglio

**Bréhan** (*or* Bréhant), Louis-Robert-Hippolyte de (1699–1734), Comte de Plélo:

verses by, quoted, **12.** 261–2

**Bréhan de Mauron, Jeanne-Marguerite, m. Charles, Marquis de Sévigné:**

[Bréhan de Mauron, Jeanne-M., *continued*]
husband converted by, from pleasure to de-
votion, **41**. 257
Bréhan (*or* Bréhant)-Plélo, Louise-Félicité de
(1726–96), m. (1740) Emmanuel-Armand
Vignerot du Plessis-Richelieu, Duc d'Aiguil-
lon:
Aiguillon's guests entertained by, **5**. 87
aunt of, **6**. 251n
Du Barrys visit, at Rueil, **6**. 48
(?) Louis XV's summer parties with, **38**. 389
Louis XVI and wife dislike, **24**. 10n
Paris visited by, **3**. 302
social relations of, in Paris, *see index entries
ante* **8**. 267
Bréhant. *See* Bréhan
Breitwitz. *See* Braitwitz
Bremen (Germany):
French capture, **21**. 136n, 177
Hanoverians win success near, **21**. 177
Hesse-Cassel, Landgrave and Ps of, flee to,
**37**. 554
Brémond d'Ars, Marie-Louise-Madeleine de (d.
1810), m. (1750) Bernard, Marquis de Verdelin:
Du Deffand, Mme, mentions, **3**. 359, **4**. 59, 215
moral maxims of, **3**. 214
social relations of, in Paris, **4**. 382, **7**. 316, 320–
3, 325–7, 338
Brenellerie. *See* Gudin de la Brenellerie
Brenne de Bombon, Edmée-Charlotte de (ca
1700–56), m. (1720) Marie-Thomas-Auguste
de Goyon-de-Matignon, Marquis de Matignon:
(?) daughter succeeds, in Court position, **17**.
152n
HW admires, and arranges for Lincoln to
meet her, **30**. 21
Lincoln's account of supper of, **30**. 30
(?) quotation from, **17**. 140
(?) rival of, plays trick on her, **17**. 152
Brenner Pass:
shortest route from Italy to England, **17**. 35n
Brennus (fl. ca 389 B.C.), leader of the Gauls:
compared to Mmes Adélaïde and Victoire,
**11**. 222
sword flung into scale by, **34**. 173
Brenta, river:
Patapan not to drown in, **17**. 56
Thames compared to, **19**. 497
Brentano-Cimaroli, Joseph von (ca 1718–64),
Austrian army officer:
Finck encircled by, at Maxen, **21**. 354n
Frederick II attacks, with Russian troops, **22**.
63
Brentford, Middlesex:
Athens scarce bigger than, **33**. 479
Bath, E. of, and Granville the counterparts
of characters from, in the *Rehearsal*, **37**.
221
bells may be ringing at, for victories HW has
not heard of, **12**. 57, 267

chairmen of, represented as killing Clarke,
**23**. 98
coaches can now pass through, without No.
45 on doors, **23**. 360
coach from Park Place passes through, **12**. 36n
election at: **10**. 274; ends, **23**. 104–5; Glynn
and Proctor to contest, **23**. 30; keeps HW
from going to SH, **23**. 73; kept quiet by
Wilkes, **23**. 6; Mann dreads hearing about,
**23**. 110; Newdigate to attend, with Tories,
**18**. 25; riots at, unlikely in summer, **35**.
324; third, **23**. 97; violence at, **35**. 535;
Wilkes and Townshend contend for, **24**. 47;
will make roads unsafe for HW to go to
London, **24**. 47
Florence fouler than, **30**. 3
Fox brothers lead supporters to, **25**. 11
Gray may be fetched from, to Twickenham,
**14**. 32
HW dislikes election mobs on his way
through, **39**. 197
HW sends to, for provisions, **39**. 404
HW to send account to, **41**. 433
high road passes through, **28**. 102
housebreakers at, **42**. 109
justices returning from, mobbed, **33**. 445
London mob blocks roads to, **23**. 6
London to expand to, **11**. 287
mobs at: annoy HW, **23**. 30; said to be hired
by Proctor and D. of Northumberland,
**23**. 79
More, Hannah, jokes about, **31**. 294
Oxford coach passes through, **28**. 338
seditious papers posted in, **38**. 173
Shorter said to have died at, **12**. 267
Spaniards must invade, before HW will call
out Twickenham militia, **24**. 98
Syon Hill near, **35**. 308n
'two kings' of, **18**. 33n, **23**. 34
visitors to: HW, **9**. 154; Mirepoix, **9**. 154
voters going to, halloed by Frederick, P. of
Wales, **20**. 131
walls damaged by storm at, **33**. 81
Wilkes's 'long, lazy, lousy capital,' **35**. 324
windows at, shattered by explosion, **39**. 153
Brentford Butts:
Willet at, **1**. 96n
Brereton, Owen Salusbury (1715–98), antiquary:
disbelieves in Ireland's MSS, **15**. 321
seal owned by, **2**. 129n
Brereton, William, sea-capt.:
misbehaviour of, **21**. 296
Brescia (Italy):
arms ordered from, **17**. 324
cheese trade of, **17**. 324n
gun-manufacturing centre, **17**. 324n, **18**. 232n
linen trade of, **17**. 324n
Montagu, Lady Mary Wortley, lives with
Palazzi at, **20**. 235, 272, 278, 281
Querini, Cardinal, prints at, everything written by or to him, **20**. 190n, 329n
Young Pretender and Dunbar said to visit,
**17**. 113

Breslau, Bp of. *See* Schaffgotsch, Philipp Gotthard, Fürst

Breslau (Germany):
Benedict XIV does not recognize Frederick II's appointment of Schaffgotsch as coadjutor of, **20**. 269n
Bevern defeated at, **21**. 158n
Conway and Scott visit, **39**. 538
Frederick II captures, **21**. 166
—— rests at, **21**. 176
——'s victory at, **21**. 229
treaty of, **17**. 456n, 466n, 483, **19**. 95n; Frederick II agrees in, to take over Silesian mortgages, **20**. 348n; Villiers's witticism about, **35**. 32

Bressei, Capt.:
Beauvau fights duel with, **18**. 432n

Bresson. *See* Bretton

Brest (France):
Anson's fleet sails towards, **21**. 210
Antin died at, **17**. 46n
Aranda and Sartine visit, to reconcile admirals, **24**. 528
armament at, rumoured, **19**. 182n
Bompar returns to, **21**. 297n
Brittany troops to march to, **24**. 355n
Camilly to take ships from, to Mediterranean, **18**. 443
Clancarty made vice-admiral at, **19**. 160
combined fleets expected to sail from, **33**. 131, 133
combined fleets reported at, **33**. 289
*Comtesse de Bentheim* captures *Hanover*, and takes her to, **21**. 75n
Conflans plans to sail from, to conduct French convoys to West Indies, **20**. 579n
—— to leave, in Hawkes's absence, **21**. 336n
counter-revolutionary disturbances reported at, **12**. 40
courier from, **7**. 52
Digby's fleet blockades, **39**. 378
dockyard at, threatened by Breton tumults, **35**. 392
Du Châtelet seems influenced as if by Hawke's threat to, **23**. 164
Dutch convoy intercepted when bringing naval supplies to, **25**. 3
Dutch fleet arrives at, **7**. 441
Dutch fleet may go to, **12**. 189n
Dutch ships bring masts to, **39**. 346
*Elizabeth* forced back to, by the *Lion*, **19**. 87, 91, 95
English attack on rumoured, **7**. 17, **24**. 357n
English fleet said to be near, **24**. 357
English objectives in France should be as important as, **21**. 223
English spy seized at, **19**. 182n
Estaing takes Spanish fleet to, **25**. 3
—— to take ships from, to Cadiz, **25**. 344–5
fleet may sail to Barbados from, **18**. 382
fleet of: **7**. 56, 182, **9**. 33, 168, **19**. 78, **24**. 525, **29**. 122n, **30**. 69; again at sea, **24**. 420; Anson escapes, **18**. 463; appears off Land's

End, **18**. 392–3; Barrington's success against, **25**. 273; Beauvau said to be on board of, **24**. 484; Cadiz said to be destination of, **39**. 313; England was to have been destination of, **21**. 328; English fleet outnumbered by, **39**. 309; enters English Channel, **18**. 463; Feilding fails to seize supplies intended for, **29**. 2; French prepare, **21**. 263–4; Gibraltar might be destination of, **24**. 484, **39**. 329; goes probably to Nova Scotia, **20**. 538; HW mentions, **28**. 422; HW's eagle menaced by, **19**. 274; Hawke and Duff defeat, at Quiberon Bay, **21**. 350–1; Ireland may be destination of, **18**. 392–3, **19**. 261, **21**. 350, **24**. 484, **39**. 329; Keppel captures frigate from, **24**. 394–5; Keppel misses, **24**. 413; Keppel's fleet encounters, **24**. 399–400; Keppel's fleet said to be fighting, **33**. 28, **39**. 313; Keppel still seeks, **24**. 410; Mann feared arrival of, in Mediterranean battle, **18**. 415; Mann made anxious by, **19**. 368; may convey Young Pretender to Scotland, **18**. 375, 378, 393, 404; narrowly misses Jamaica fleet, **18**. 393; near Ireland and Scotland, **18**. 404; Norris may pursue, **18**. 400; Norris misses, **18**. 407; off Sussex coast, **18**. 402; off Torbay, **18**. 398; Philip, Don, to be accompanied by, **17**. 215; preparing to leave, **18**. 360; ready to sail, **33**. 65; returns, **20**. 482–3, **24**. 413; riding in English Channel, **37**. 163; said to be off Spanish coast, **19**. 274; said to have returned, **17**. 46; said to have sailed, **24**. 473; sailed with both white and red cockades, **24**. 483; sails to West Indies, **25**. 220, 221; sails with belligerent orders, **39**. 306, 307, 308; Scotland may be destination of, **18**. 375, 378, 393, 404, **19**. 261; southward voyage of, rumoured, **39**. 315; Spanish fleet may join, **24**. 484, 525, **25**. 16; Spanish fleet not to join, **25**. 72; squadrons from, **28**. 396, 404–5, 414; supply ships for, captured by English privateers, **19**. 230; to attack England, Ireland, or the English fleet, **24**. 383–4; to join Toulon fleet, **18**. 393, 396, 404, 423; to prey on English shipping, **18**. 93; to rectify Jacobites' defeat, **19**. 268; will not engage, **33**. 52; with Spanish fleet may emerge, **24**. 525
France equips men of war at, **20**. 535n
French and Spanish fleets expected to sail from, **33**. 131, 133
French and Spanish fleets reported to have returned to, **25**. 186, **33**. 289
French and Spanish squadrons may go to, **19**. 12
French frigate, safely returned to, would be occasion for triumphant medal, **21**. 357
French ships return to, **12**. 84, 89
French troops march to, **24**. 357
*Gloucester* and *Syrène* arrive at, **21**. 230n
Gordon's espionage at, **4**. 343n, **23**. 183

[Brest, *continued*]

Guay's squadron reaches, **20.** 498n

Hawke's frigates observe French fleet off, **21.** 300n

Hertford would not be permitted to see, **38.** 402

Howe rumoured to have captured French ships from, **12.** 73, 75, 81

Howe rumoured to have received overtures from, **12.** 18

Howe said to have received capitulation of, **39.** 506

invasion troops to embark from, **20.** 474n

Jones, John Paul, solicits ship at, **28.** 467n

Keppel said to have blockaded, **24.** 395

Kersaint de Coëtnempreni sails from, **21.** 101n

*La Belle Poule* returns to, **24.** 395

Louisbourg news seems to come to, **21.** 230

McNamara brings fleet back to, **20.** 482–3, **35.** 230

Macpherson accuses Marlborough of betraying design on, **28.** 387

Mann hears naval news in letter from, **19.** 88

Mathews must pursue French fleet to, **18.** 423

Montcalm sails from, **20.** 541n

Normandy troops move to, **24.** 357n

Orvilliers at, **24.** 516

Perrier de Salvert sails from, to West Indies, **20.** 538n

Picquet de la Motte sets out from, **25.** 160

Pitt suggests attack on, **21.** 213n

registered seamen conveyed to, **24.** 262n

Shelley, Lady, carried to, by privateer, **12.** 132

ship arrives from, **12.** 132n

ships assemble at, for invasion, **21.** 296n

(?) Spanish fleet at, **7.** 182

squadron at: disabled, **33.** 154–5; sails to America, **20.** 474n

visitors to: Bouillon, Duchesse de, **7.** 182, 433; Hénin, Princesse d', **7.** 182, 433; Lauzun, Duchesse de, **7.** 182, 433

Young Pretender said to be at, **19.** 91

——'s escort ship forced to return to, **19.** 88–9

Bret, Antoine (1717–92):

*Mémoires sur la vie de mademoiselle de Lenclos* by: disappoints HW, **39.** 242; Du Deffand, Mme, discusses, **6.** 121, 128–9, 142; HW to have, **6.** 128, 129, 136, 137; HW would like to have, **6.** 125

Bretagne, Duc de. *See* François I (1414–50)

Bretagne, Henri-François de (ca 1685–1746), Comte de Vertus:

wife of, **7.** 6n

*Bretagne, La,* French ship:

Chartres, Duc de, runs under stern of, **24.** 402

Kempenfelt encounters, **25.** 221n, **33.** 315n

Bretagne, Hôtel de, Rue Croix des Petits Champs, Paris:

Conway, Hertford, and Bowman at, **37.** 41

Bretagne, parlement de. *See* Rennes, parliament of

Bretagne. *See also* Brittany

Bretby, Derbyshire, Chesterfield's seat:

Chesterfield searches, for Walpole marriage settlement, **40.** 72n

Breteuil, Abbé de. *See* Le Tonnelier, Élisabeth-Théodose

Breteuil, Bailli de. *See* Le Tonnelier, Jacques-Laure

Breteuil, Baron de. *See* Le Tonnelier, Louis-Auguste

Breteuil, Comtesse de. *See* O'Brien de Clare, Laure

Breteuil, Marquis de. *See* Le Tonnelier, François-Victor

Breteuil, Seigneur de. *See* FitzOsbern, William

Breteuil (France):

suitable for overnight stay, **37.** 40

Bretevile, E. of. *See* FitzOsbern, William

Bretherton, Charles (d. 1783), engraver; printseller:

(?) etching by, of Sir John Fortescue, given by Hardinge to HW, **35.** 628–30

HW commissions, to do engravings, **14.** 190

HW pleased by work of, **14.** 187

portrait engravings by, **43.** 92

prints by, **1.** 313n, **5.** 75n, **14.** 188n

satiric prints published by, **33.** 401n

Bretherton, James (d. 1806), engraver:

Cambridge left by, **1.** 386n

(?) etching by, of Sir John Fortescue, given by Hardinge to HW, **35.** 628–30

(?) HW mentions, **14.** 188–9

name of, corrected, **43.** 331

print of Gertrude More copied by, **1.** 313

promissory note given by, to Cole, **1.** 360

Bretherton, Sarah (fl. 1762–73), wife of James Bretherton:

Cole calls on, **1.** 313

Bretignières, Anne-Charles-René de (d. 1786):

(?) attends session of parliament of Paris, **8.** 171, 172, 173

Bretigny, ——:

social relations of, with: Élie de Beaumont, **7.** 330; HW, **7.** 302

Breton, Luc-François (1731–1800), sculptor:

design by, for Wolfe's monument, **21.** 421–2, 428, 436

Breton, Sir William (d. 1773), Kt, 1761; groom of the Chamber and Privy Purse bearer to Frederick, P. of Wales; M.P.:

Atholl, Ds of, discusses her husband with, **19.** 106

biographical information on, corrected, **43.** 131, 258, 314

Bootle visited by, **30.** 94

Frederick, P. of Wales's household includes, **19.** 106

groom of the Bedchamber, **21.** 460n

HW envies enthusiasm of, for the Court, **10.** 119

snobbishness of, **30.** 101

Breton. *See also* Bretton

Breton; Bretons:
Chilly, Seigneur de, château of, threatened by, **11**. 108–9
Dauphin gives flowers to, **11**. 100
French formerly hated by, **7**. 360
Louis XVI receives homage from delegation of, **11**. 100, 104
march to Paris, **11**. 99

Brett, Miss:
brother's execution may prevent marriage of, **40**. 194

Brett, Anne (d. 1660), m. Lionel Cranfield, cr. (1622) E. of Middlesex:
(?) portrait of, at Knole, **35**. 135

Brett, Charles (ca 1715–99), M.P.; Admiralty lord:
birth date of, corrected, **43**. 306
Chambers asked by, for accounting of Somerset House, **29**. 37–8
resigns from Admiralty, **34**. 9n

Brett, Col. Henry:
wife of, **1**. 181n

Brett, Rev. (?) John (d. 1772):
son of, under sentence of death, **40**. 194–5

Brett, John (d. ?1761):
HW intercedes for, against death sentence, **40**. 194–6

Brett, Sir Piercy (ca 1710–81), Kt, 1753; M.P.: Admiralty lord:
biographical information about, corrected, **43**. 258
*Elizabeth* fights with, **19**. *91*
*Lion* commanded by **19**. 91, 95
made Admiralty commissioner, **22**. 472
resigns as Admiralty lord, **23**. 180, **39**. 122

Brettingham, Matthew (1723–1803), architect:
Albani receives measurements of Northumberland's gallery from, **20**. 329n
Leicester's agent, **20**. 104n
(?) Mann employs, to get sepulchral *ara*, **20**. 352
Norfolk, Ds of, has Norfolk House remodelled by, **37**. 438n
Venuti gives export permit to, to send statues to Leicester from Nettuno, **20**. 104n

Bretton, Enrico (d. 1760), Barone; army officer:
expedition against Del Monte brothers led by, **20**. 430

Brevet:
dukedom by, in France, **24**. 208n

Breviary:
'Sarum' or 'Bedford,' **42**. 93

Brewer; brewers:
dray of, stops runaway horses, **10**. 135
Forth, Samuel, is, in Southwark, **20**. 556n
HW's, see Cole, Stephen
Irish peerage includes, **21**. 24
journeymen, at Twickenham church, **34**. 115
Parsons, Humphrey, is, **17**. 185n
wealth of, **33**. 268

Brewer St, Golden Square:
Hume writes from Miss Elliot's in, **41**. 166

Brewery; breweries:
Whitbread's, **34**. 12n
*See also* Brewhouse

Brewhouse:
at Taplow, **38**. 26

Brewing:
HW avoids, **18**. 8

Brewse, John, Lt-Col.; engineer:
captured by the French, **24**. 476–7

Brewster, Sir David (1781–1868):
Buchan 'adopts,' **15**. 156n

Brézé, Jacques de (ca 1430–94), author:
*Livre de la chasse du grant seneschal de Normandie, Le*, by, **33**. 385–6

Brian, (?) Hertford's servant:
HW's letter to be taken by, to England, **39**. 9

Brian, of Bury. *See* Bryan of Bury

Brian Boirombe, K. of Ireland:
print of, **40**. 236

Brianchini. *See* Beaushini

Briançon, Conte di. *See* Carron di San Tommaso, Giuseppe Gioacchino (d. 1709)

Briançon (France):
Maillebois returns by way of, **19**. 231

Briancourt, Mlle (d. 1768):
dies in fire, **4**. 54

Briar Creek, Georgia:
English victory at, **24**. 464n, **39**. 346

Briatico (Italy):
earthquake account mentions, **25**. 376

Bribery, political:
HW's reflections on, **33**. 389

Bribery Bill. *See under* Parliament: acts of

Brice, Germain (1652–1727):
*Description de Paris*, **7**. 356

Brichanteau, Louis-Armand de (d. 1742), Marquis de Nangis:
(?) mistress's dialogue with, **4**. 22–3

Briche, La. *See* La Live de la Briche

Brick; bricks:
Arundel Castle modernized in, **39**. 310
at Park Place, **39**. 550
HW cannot get, from Prague, for Bentley's constructions, **35**. 282
HW will send, to Mann, **22**. 48
Hurstmonceaux built of, unwhitewashed, **35**. 138
road strewn with, after storm, **33**. 81
SH built of, **20**. 368
staircases should be built of, **22**. 143
tax on, **37**. 445
without straw, **32**. 166, **33**. 523

Brickbat; brickbats:
Carrickfergus defenders use, **21**. 373, 376, 386

Brickenden, Miss, of Newbury, m. Edward Haistwell:
marriage of, **42**. 54n

Brick kilns:
Roman, in England, **15**. 202

Bricklayer; bricklayers:
at Nuneham, **35.** 521
Jones, Henry, apprentice to, **20.** 214n
Osterley Court said to have been built by, in one night, **34.** 238
'Bricklayer Tom,' smuggler:
outlawed, **9.** 105
Brickmaking:
on Twickenham common field, **43.** 155
Briçonnet d'Auteuil, Mme Jacques-Alexandre. *See* Thibert du Martrais, Marie-Madeleine
Bridesmaids:
Q. Charlotte's, **38.** 117
Bridewell, London:
palace of, Henry VIII dates his acts from, **24.** 51
prison of, Guadagni threatened with confinement in, **23.** 272
Bridge; bridges:
at Blenheim, **9.** 289, **10.** 309
at Eton, **9.** 3
at Ferrybridge, **35.** 269
at Florence, *see* Ponte alle Grazie; Ponte a Santa Trinità; Ponte Vecchio
at Hampton Court, **35.** 389
at Henley, **25.** 576, 613, **33.** 485, 524, **34.** 15, **35.** 385, 386, 395, **39.** 386, 461, 549
at Horton, Gothic, **10.** 334
at Livry, wooden, Mme de Sévigné awaits daughter's letters on, **10.** 212
at Park Place, **10.** 104–5, **35.** 331, 395, 428, **39.** 150, 176, 460, 461
at Richmond, **43.** 131
at Sion House, **28.** 108, **35.** 331
at Stowe, Palladian, **10.** 315
at Tunbridge, Gothic, **35.** 135
at Twickenham, lacking, **43.** 130
at Upton, **35.** 152
at Wakefield, has Gothic chapel, **35.** 270
at Wentworth Castle, **37.** 560–1, 578, **38.** 72
at Wilton: **20.** 109; copied in sugar, **9.** 363
at Wroxton, Chinese, **35.** 74
Charles, P., may cross Rhine on, **37.** 144
Conway builds, **39.** 150, 176, 460, 461
Dudley's, over canal, **35.** 389
English build, across Scheldt, **18.** 448
German, destroyed by floods, **25.** 483
Gothic or Chinese, in English landscape effects, **20.** 166
half, for artificial river, **35.** 521
Lobkowitz builds, across Po, **19.** 41
medal of, received by HW, **17.** 11–12
over Tiber, **18.** 437, 525
over Trent, **40.** 43
Ponte Molle, partly wooden, **18.** 444, 531
pontoon: Gages crosses Po on, **19.** 291n; over Rhine at Rees, **21.** 228n
Richmond-Twickenham: not yet started, **39.** 176, 187; ferry-boat runs into, **39.** 187
'rocky' or 'rustic,' *see under* Park Place
scene of, in *King Arthur*, pretty, **39.** 133
to be built across Rhine, **37.** 159

Waldeck said to retreat over, **37.** 146
Watelet's, supported by boats, **28.** 215, 220
*See also* Blackfriars Bridge; Warrington Bridge; Westminster Bridge
Bridge Committee:
Pembroke dies in, **20.** 108
Bridgeman, —— (?) Mrs:
Pomfrets entertain, **17.** 169n
Bridgeman, Henry (1725–1800), 5th Bt; cr. (1794) Bn Bradford; M.P.:
dismissed as clerk comptroller of the Board of Green Cloth, **38.** 377
Bridgeman, Sir Orlando (?1606–74), 1st Bt:
Cole gives print of, to HW, **1.** 61, 63
print of, in Dugdale's *Origines juridiciales*, **1.** 61
Bridgeman. *See also* Bridgman
Bridgen, Edward (d. 1787), F.R.S.; F.A.S.:
picture sold to, **2.** 216n
Bridgen, William (ca 1709–79), lord mayor of London 1763–4:
Bedford attacks, **22.** 188, **38.** 257–8, 263
Common Council vote decided by, against thanking sheriffs, **38.** 262
Rigby tries to blame, for riots, **38.** 258
sea-captain tells, of seeing Karl Wilhelm Ferdinand's yacht, **38.** 312
sits in Guildhall during riots, **38.** 258
Vergy swears affidavit before, **22.** 262n, **38.** 467n
Bridges, Anne (1703–63), m. (1720) Arthur Onslow:
character of 'Isabel' in HW's 'Patapan' not patterned on, **30.** 289n
uncle settles Imber Court on, at her marriage, **40.** 98n
'very homely gentlewoman' with faithful husband, and children, **30.** 289n
Bridges, Sir Brook (1733–91), 3d Bt:
(?) Barret neighbour of, **41.** 132
HW does not understand Mann's allusion to, **21.** 420
(?) HW's correspondence with, **41.** 131–2
pregnant dancing girl nursed by, in obscure Tuscan villa, **21.** 415
Bridges, Mrs Edward. *See* Speke, Philippa
Bridges, Henry:
Mrs Onslow, his niece, receives Imber Court from, **40.** 98n
Bridges, John (1666–1724), topographer:
*History and Antiquities of Northamptonshire* by, **1.** 7, **2.** 277
Bridges, Thomas:
*Dutchman, The*, by, **7.** 417
Bridges. *See also* Brydges
Bridges family, of Kent:
(?) Richard III's portrait owned by, **41.** 132
'Bridget, Lady.' *See* Henley, Lady Bridget
Bridget (1480–before 1513) (Plantagenet), 4th dau. of Edward IV:
Guidickins calls, 'Lady Biddy,' **10.** 255
Papal bull omits, **42.** 208n

Bridgewalter; Bridgewater. *See* Bridgwater

Bridgman, Charles (d. 1738):
Eyre imitates, **42.** 131n

Bridgman. *See also* Bridgeman

Bridgnorth, Salop:
Dodd and Whaley visit, **40.** 14
troglodytes' dwellings hollowed in rock at, **40.** 14
Wynn mostly owns, **40.** 14

Bridgwater, Cts. of. *See* Churchill, Lady Elizabeth

Bridgwater, Ds of. *See* Russell, Lady Rachael (d. 1777)

Bridgwater, D. of. *See* Egerton, Francis (1736–1803); Egerton, John (1727–48); Egerton, Scroop (1681–1745)

Bridgwater, E. of. *See* Egerton, Scroop (1681–1745)

Bridgwater, Somerset:
Poulett writes to mayor of, stirring up opposition, **35.** 225n

Bridle; bridles:
Conway busy with, **37.** 358

Bridlington Bay ('Burlington Bay'):
Dutch troops land at, **30.** 97, **40.** 54n, **43.** 258

Bridport, Dorset:
election at, **19.** 342

Brie (France):
Château d'Éverly in, **4.** 351n

*Brief Chronicle of the Late Intestine Warr in the Three Kingdoms . . ., A. See under* Heath, James

*Brief History of the Life of Mary Queen of Scots, A:*
HW cites, **9.** 83, **43.** 115

Brienne, Comte de. *See* Loménie, André-Louis de (1658–1743); Loménie, Athanase-Louis-Marie de (1730–94)

Brienne, Comtesse de. *See* Fizeau de Clémont, Marie-Anne-Étiennette

Brienne (France):
Brienne, Comte and Comtesse de, spend 8 months of year at, **6.** 250
—— to visit, **6.** 281, **7.** 452, 461
Choiseul to visit, **6.** 174
Gramont, Duchesse de, to visit, **6.** 174, 319

Brienne, Hôtel de, Paris:
Briennes entertain at, **7.** 449, 451, 454, 457–60

Brienne de Conflans, Chevalier de. *See* Conflans, Hubert de

Brietzcke, Catherine, wardrobe-keeper and keeper of Somerset House:
Bedford to ask, about portrait, **40.** 142
Grosvenor, Anne, succeeded by, **43.** 136

Brietzcke, Charles (ca 1738–95), senior clerk in secretary of state's office:
Eliott's and Murray's dispatches to, **25.** 136n

Brièze (France):
Maupeou permitted to return to, **7.** 436

Brig; brigs:
Dutch, with sugar and tobacco captured, **33.** 272n

English: French snow captures, **21.** 334; under repair at Calais, **24.** 365n

Brigade:
Houghton's, at Roucour, **30.** 108

Briges, Marquise de. *See* Radix de Ste-Foix, Marie-Geneviève

Briggs, Sir Humphrey (ca 1670–1734), 4th Bt:
mentioned in Gen. Fitzwilliam's will, **11.** 49n

Briggs, William:
examination of, about Dominica, **24.** 421n

Brighieri, auditor fiscal at Florence:
Onslow's papers examined by, **19.** 507

Bright, Mr:
SH visited by, **12.** 232

Bright, Edward (ca 1720–50):
death of, **20.** 209
dimensions of coffin of, **20.** 208n
print of, **40.** 236
weight of, **20.** 208–9

Bright, Mary (1735–1804), m. (1752) Charles Watson Wentworth, 2d M. of Rockingham:
Bath visited by, **31.** 130, **35.** 319, **39.** 76
Dauberval's patroness, **38.** 483
(?) Giardini connected with, **35.** 323
HW mentions, unflatteringly, **28.** 342
HW speaks to, at Bath, **35.** 319, **39.** 76
half-sister of, **29.** 259n
health of, cold, **38.** 342
House of Commons never left by, in long session, **38.** 317
Methodism perhaps embraced by, **35.** 323
Queensberry, Ds of, rejects tardy answer by, to ball invitation, **38.** 342
weeps at Leicester House for Karl Wilhelm Ferdinand's departure, **38.** 296
Zouch chaplain to, **16.** 1n, **35.** 323n

Brighthelmstone. *See* Brighton

*Brighthelmstone, A Trip to. See* Pilon, Frederick: *Invasion*

Brighton (Brighthelmstone), Sussex:
French men of war seen off, **18.** 402n
HW forgets story of, **33.** 294–5
HW not to go to, **32.** 313, **39.** 282
HW receives card from, in verse, **29.** 151
HW to go to, **32.** 304
Jersey, Lady, does not go to, **12.** 200
—— a fugitive from, **12.** 204
Steine at, **12.** 151
visitors to: Beauclerks, **7.** 73n, **28.** 421, **30.** 272; Berrys, **11.** 111n, 116; Campbell, Lady Charlotte, **12.** 198; Caroline, Ps of Wales, **12.** 142; Chartres, Duc de, **25.** 517n, **33.** 483n; George IV, **12.** 149, **25.** 517n, **33.** 483n; Jersey, Lady, **12.** 142, 204; Lauzun, **25.** 517n; Marlborough, Ds of, **12.** 156n; Montagu, Vcts, **12.** 16; Orléans, Duc d', **11.** 85; Pelham, Mrs, **12.** 201n; Stuart Mackenzies, **12.** 203

Bright's disease:
Chatham may have, **22.** 505n

Brightwalton, Berks:
Eyre rector of, **1.** 36n

Brigittines, Order of:
France suppresses, 39. 147n
'Brignola, The.' *See* Balbi, Anna; Lomellini,
Pellina
Brignole, Marie-Catherine de (1739–1813), m.
1 (1757) Honoré-Camille-Léonor Goyon-de-
Matignon de Grimaldi, P. of Monaco; m. 2
(1808) Louis-Joseph de Bourbon, Prince de
Condé:
Assomption convent the refuge of, 4. 439, 455
beauty of, 3. 72n, 14. 156, 31. 47, 91, 32. 24
Condé contrives marriage separation of, 23.
265n
—— in love with, 5. 14n, 297
Conway should see, 39. 215
Egmont, Comtesse d', can never rival, 39.
45
Grafton, Ds of, not eclipsed by charm of,
32. 18
HW has not seen Petite Maison of, 32. 261
HW hopes Lady Ossory is jealous of, 32. 25
HW plays loo with, 32. 24
HW sees, at theatre, 32. 22
Hertford devoted to, 3. 72, 40. 387
honey-water requested by, 31. 104
may join royal 'voyages,' 5. 323
Monaco, P. of, separated from, 4. 438, 455,
5. 14
—— unwilling to have son's marriage contract signed by, 6. 460
'plus jolie femme de France,' 3. 72
social relations of, with: Du Deffand, Mme,
5. 148; Egmont, Comtesse d', 7. 305
Stainville, Mme de, was to sup with, 3. 217n
tries to unlock Marquise de Beuvron's secretary, 3. 61–2, 63, 72
Brignole palace. *See* Palazzo Rosso
Brignole Sale, Giovanni Francesco (1695–1760),
doge of Genoa 1746–8:
cannon aimed at palace of, 19. 359
Genoese army commanded by, 19. 77n
house of: Mann wants bombs dropped on,
19. 76–7; sacked by mob, 19. 343
Vienna to receive apologetic visit from, 19.
312–13, 315
Brignoli, Mme. *See* Balbi, Anna; Lomellini,
Pellina
Brigstockes, Mrs:
SH visited by, 12. 237
Brill (*or* Bril), Paul (1554–1626), landscape
painter:
HW has painting by, 7. 335, 15. 318
Julienne has paintings by, 7. 287
Louvre has paintings by, 7. 339
Monaco, P. of, has paintings by, 7. 335
Presle has painting by, 7. 346
'Brilliant, Sir.' *See* Edgcumbe, Richard
*Brilliant*, English frigate:
Thurot pursued by, 21. 376
*Brilliant*, French ship:
in Vilaine River, 21. 351
Brilliant; brilliants:
chain of, given by San Vitale to Tesi, 17. 70

dagger and scimitar covered with, 22. 540
*pennino* studded with, 17. 64–5
picture set with, 20. 76
Rumbold carries off, from Mogul's golden
throne, 25. 545
Selwyn, Mrs, suggests earrings of, for Frances
Pelham, 20. 114
sword set with, 22. 62n
*Brilliante*, Spanish galleon:
in Spanish fleet, 17. 286
Brillon, Mme, of Passy:
Burney hears, play on pianoforte, 4. 452n
Brimslade Park, Wilts:
Ernle of, 9. 252n
Brindisi (Italy):
Martin may fetch Spanish artillery from,
18. 27
*See also* Brundusium
Brine, Capt. Robert:
*Lively* commanded by, 25. 620n
Brinet, ——, notary:
Du Deffand, Mme, invests with, 7. 438
Bringhurst, Mrs (b. ca 1682):
at Ely, 1. 162n
Brinvilliers, Marquise de. *See* Aubray, Marie-
Marguerite d'
Brionne, Comte de. *See* Lorraine, Charles-
Louis de
Brionne, Comtesse de. *See* Rohan-Montauban,
Louise-Julie-Constance de (1734–1815)
Briot, ——, medallist:
Simon taught by, 40. 238n
Briqueville, Anne-Marie de (1735–70), m.
(1752) Jacques-Gabriel Bazin, Marquis de
Bezons:
death of, 4. 471
ill, 3. 159
Pont-de-Veyle's devotion to, 3. 159, 4. 471
social relations of, with Mme du Deffand,
7. 275, 291
Brisbane, John (ca 1638–84), Charles II's agent:
MS collection of, 15. 103
Briscoe, John (d. 1809), of Twickenham:
SH visited by, 12. 226, 239, 240
SH visitors sent by, 12. 244
Briscoe, Mrs John. *See* Winthrop, Mary
Briscoe, Sam:
key by, to Buckingham's *Rehearsal*, 33. 159n
Briscoe, Stafford (ca 1713–89), silversmith,
Twickenham resident:
bowling-green of, 35. 372
garden of, adjoins SH, 2. 79n
HW's ball attended by, 28. 447
house of, in Twickenham, 9. 74n, 22. 18n,
42. 480, 487
Brissac, Duc de. *See* Cossé, Jean-Paul-Timoléon
de (1698–1784); Cossé, Louis-Hercule-Tim-
oléon de (1734–92)
Brissac, Duchesse de. *See* Mancini de Nevers,
Adélaïde-Diane-Hortense-Délie
Brissac, Maréchal de. *See* Cossé, Jean-Paul-
Timoléon de

Brissan, waters of:
Beauvau to take, 7. 427
Brisson, Mme la Présidente:
Marseille academy gives prize to, for *Éloge* of Mme de Sévigné, 32. 269n
Brisson, François de (d. 1780):
(?) attends session of parliament of Paris, 8. 173
Brissot de Warville, Jean-Pierre (1754–93), member of National Assembly:
execution of, 12. 72, 86, 15. 248n
Bristle; bristles:
HW compares Elizabeth of Russia's hair to, 18. 495
Bristol, Bp of. *See* Bagot, Lewis (1740–1802); Butler, Joseph (1692–1752); Felton, Nicholas (1556–1626); Fletcher, Richard (d. 1596); Gooch, Sir Thomas (1674–1754); Hume, John (1703–82); Newton, Thomas (1704–82); Secker, Thomas (1693–1768); Smalridge, George (1663–1719); Trelawny, Sir Jonathan (1650–1721); Wilson, Christopher (ca 1714–92)
Bristol, Cts of. *See* Chudleigh, Elizabeth (ca 1720–88); Davers, Elizabeth (1733–1800); Felton, Elizabeth (1676–1741)
Bristol, Dean of. *See* Ayscough, Francis (ca 1702–63); Hallam, John (1728–1811)
'Bristol, Ds of.' *See* Chudleigh, Elizabeth (ca 1720–88)
Bristol, E. of. *See* Digby, George (1612–77); Digby, John (1586–1653); Hervey, Augustus John (1724–79); Hervey, Hon. Frederick Augustus (1730–1803); Hervey, George William (1721–75); Hervey, John (1665–1751)
*Bristol*, English ship:
Campbell, Lord William, aboard, 33. 50n
Charleston harbour entered by, 32. 319n
Lee brought on, 24. 286n
Morris, capt. of, 32. 318n
survives Jamaica hurricane, 39. 353n
Bristol, Glos:
African trade of, 31. 248
air of, 31. 276
anti-American address from, 24. 132n, 39. 270n
antiquities of, 16. 102
artificial stones of, 32. 222
bank failures at, 31. 382, 384
Barrett's history of, *see under* Barrett, William
Bath and Wells contrasted with industry and shipping at, 40. 10
Black Castle at, 10. 232
bridge riots at, 15. 243–4
Broughton, attorney of, 16. 177n
Burke no longer M.P. for, 36. 174
—'s election at, 39. 207
— speaks at, 33. 230
Canynges might have written MSS about, 2. 289
—'s tomb at, 16. 345
castle at, *see* Bristol Castle

cathedral at, *see* Bristol Cathedral
Chatterton easily believed at, 16. 223
—— from, 33. 40
——'s account of painters at, incredible, 16. 124, 214, 222
—— says he got poems from man in, 2. 52
——'s *Miscellanies* published at, 28. 422
——'s poems said to have been found at, 16. 123
—— wrote little after leaving, 16. 224
Chute to visit, 10. 228
coach to, from London, 31. 265n, 313
commercial town, in Henry VI's day, 16. 126–7
concert at, in memory of Chatterton, 16. 351, 363
custom house at, 40. 10
disturbance at, not confirmed, 33. 196
duty on imported china to favour manufacturers of, 32. 270
*Earl Goodwin* performed at, 11. 254n
fanaticism at, 31. 276–7
fire at: attributed to incendiary, 24. 273; John the Painter starts, 28. 284, 286–7
fortune-teller from, 31. 280n
French Protestant chapel at, 25. 518n
George III to visit, 34. 47n
HW compares: to India, 31. 219; to Toulouse, 31. 276–7
HW describes, 10. 232
HW may visit, 10. 228, 22. 110
HW not to go to, 32. 304
HW probably unpopular in, 31. 222
HW sends books to Hannah More at, 31. 229, 231, 313
hot wells at: 42. 54n; Cole recommends, 1. 83–4; Middleton meets his third wife at, 15. 309, 312; Robartes dies at, 15. 312; Thames warmer than, 20. 166
Hudson Bay Co. at, 17. 8n
Irish resent England's commercial favour to, 24. 473
Lambert, attorney of, 16. 123n
literary talent at, 31. 219
London quiet as, 31. 5
Lorenzi to land at, on next visit to England, 20. 114, 285
Lort sees Chatterton MSS at, 16. 174–7
——'s friend at, to investigate Chatterton's letters, 16. 222
'Louisa,' lunatic of, befriended by Hannah More, 33. 490
mail-coach service to, from London, 31. 265n
mayor and aldermen of, send pro-war address to George III but merchants send counter-address, 41. 311n
merchants of, petition House of Commons for reconciliation with America, 39. 247, 248
Methodists practise exorcism at, 31. 276, 279–80, 283–4
*Milford* ordered to pursue Thurot from, 21. 374n

[Bristol, Glos, *continued*]

milkwoman at, *see* Cromartie, Ann (Mrs Yearsley)

More, Hannah, born at, **31**. 277

—— redeems credit of, **31**. 277

—— too good a citizen of, to criticize it, **31**. 325–6

Morgan's duelling challenge at, **40**. 358

Nugent unpopular in, for voting for Jew Bill, **35**. 179

paste of, superior to all but that of Saxony, for porcelain, **25**. 635

Pitt, George, and Stuart Mackenzie to visit, **30**. 59

privateer of, *see* Trial, *The*

proof of authenticity of Rowley poems sought in, **2**. 92, 104, 107

rebels may march to, **19**. 160

regiment of Charles Montagu ordered to, **9**. 190

reported in flames, **32**. 346

Rigby beats up priest at ford of, **30**. 330

Roman Catholic chapel reported demolished at, **33**. 195

St Austin's Church at, **16**. 103–4

St John's Church at: Chatterton mentions, **16**. 102; Chatterton said not to understand Latin epitaph in, **16**. 335

St Mary Redcliff church in: **2**. 44, 92, **10**. 232; Canynges called founder of, **16**. 102; Canynges's donation to, **16**. 176; Chatterton might have found real parchments in, **16**. 355–6; clergy of, must have seen MSS, **16**. 354–5; Hogarth's pictures in, **33**. 246; iron chest in, **16**. 111; Malone suggests shutting Bryant and Milles in, **29**. 176n; MSS supposedly found in, **16**. 24, 174; Vertue transcribed MSS in, **16**. 133

St Nicholas's church at, **10**. 232

school at, Clementina Clerke elopes from, **11**. 253

slave girl escapes at, **31**. 340, 350

Smith at, **2**. 288n

stained-glass painters of, **16**. 113

Trenchard, Mrs, lives near, **15**. 311

visitors to: Desmond, Cts of, **40**. 108; Dodd, **40**. 10; Garrick, Mrs, **31**. 345; HW, **10**. 232; Mann, Galfridus, and family, **14**. 94n, **20**. 551, 556, 563, 564, 569, 574, 586, **21**. 1; Middletons, **15**. 309, 312; Robartes, **15**. 312; Udnys, **12**. 210; Whaley, **40**. 10

watchmen of, Pomfret compares, to Cæsar, **20**. 470

waters of: C. H. Williams and Cts of Essex to visit, **30**. 147; *see also under* hot wells at; *see also* Bristol water

Wilkins, merchant at, **14**. 31n

Worcester, William, native of, writes about Canynges, **2**. 104

Yearsley, Mrs, supported by people of, **33**. 550

zinc factory at, **18**. 184n

Zouch may visit, **16**. 40

*See also under* Barrett, William: *History and Antiquities of the City of Bristol*

Bristol Castle:

prints of, in Chatterton's forgeries, **16**. 221, 223

wrongly depicted in Barrett's *History*, **31**. 326

Bristol Cathedral:

Dicey, prebendary of, **1**. 332n

figure in, of old man playing violin, **16**. 174

Gwyn, Nell, gave window to, **10**. 232

HW calls tombs in, 'pretty,' **10**. 232

wrongly depicted in Barrett's *History*, **31**. 326

*Bristol Journal*. *See under* Farley, Felix

Bristol poems. *See under* Chatterton, Thomas

Bristol stones:

diamonds to be distinguished from, **25**. 386, 449

HW's name for Mrs Yearsley's verses, **31**. 219

Bristol water:

Du Deffand, Mme, advises HW to bring, to Paris, **3**. 234

HW puts out fire with, **21**. 354

Mann, Galfridus, takes, **9**. 194

Montagu orders supply of, **9**. 357

Montagu, Henrietta, to try, **9**. 174

Bristow, Anne Margaret (d. 1788), m. (1761) Hon. Henry Hobart:

(?) coiffure of, distracts HW from balloon, **39**. 419

house of, at Richmond, taken by William IV, **11**. 63

translation dedicated to, **11**. 340n

Bristow, Annie (d. 1774), m. (1728) Francis Howard, 7th Bn Howard; cr. (1731) E. of Effingham:

(?) coiffure of, distracts HW from balloon, **39**. 419

(?) Court ball attended by, **9**. 403

HW disparages appearance of, at George III's Coronation, **9**. 388, **38**. 127

Bristow, Elizabeth (d. 1762), m. (1728) John Hobart, E. of Buckinghamshire:

brother of, **9**. 169n

Bristow, John (1701–68), M.P.:

Bank director, **17**. 411

biographical information on, corrected, **43**. 244

money to be remitted to Jamaica by agreement of, **17**. 411

Secret Committee's investigation of, **17**. 411, 475

Treasury agent, **17**. 411n

Bristow, Robert (1688–1737), M.P.:

son of, **9**. 169n

Bristow, William (d. 1758):

brings seal from Ireland, **14**. 104n

Florence visited by, **20**. 156n

Harrington opposed by, **20**. 156

Irish commissioner, **20**. 157

Mann has seen, in Italy, **20**. 157

'silly mock-virtuoso,' **20**. 156

SH praised by, **9**. 169, **35**. 236, 237

Bristow, William (d. 1770):
(?) HW's correspondence with, 7. 395
'Bristowe Tragedie.' *See under* Chatterton, Thomas
'Britain':
in cantata, 35. 106
'Britannia':
Coke, Lady Mary, compared with, 31. 25
*Britannia*, English ship:
Barrington writes from, 25. 273n
foreign ministers terrified by, 23. 242
*Britannia. See under* Camden, William; Hampden, Robert
Britannica Printing Office:
in Fleet St, 23. 77n
*Britannicus. See under* Racine, Jean
Britard, Jean-Baptiste (1721–91), called Brizard; actor:
*Britannicus* acted by, 7. 277
Collé's *Partie de Chasse* acted by, 39. 217
imprisoned for refusing to act, 38. 538n
*Phèdre* and *Fausse Agnès* acted by, 7. 275
Voltaire crowned by, 28. 385n
Brithnoth (d. 991), D. of Northumberland:
tomb of, in Ely Cathedral: 1. 160, 162, 164; proposed plate of, 1. 160, 162, 164–5
*British Autobiography. See under* Thane, John
*British Champion, The:*
Ralph, James, editor of, 18. 32n
British Coffee-House:
Bedford writes to Scottish peers at, 20. 124
*British Compendium. See under* Nichols, Francis
*British Critic, The* (edited by Nares and Beloe):
HW approves of temper of, 15. 238–9
HW pities Nares for having to read books for, 15. 241
Nash's edition of *Hudibras* reviewed in, 43. 389n
British Empire:
builders of, cut down by 'rapacious foragers,' 24. 287–8
HW's letters the record of the 'mouldering' of, 24. 484
HW's reflections on, 22. 85
Roman Empire compared with, 22. 85, 513, 23. 32
'British Inquisition' (oratory):
Macklin sets up, 35. 200
British Isles:
Bolingbroke 'sells,' to France, 18. 247
*British Journal, The:*
HW refers to, 12. 257
*British Magazine and Review:*
Fox's 'Invocation to Poverty' printed in, 32. 382n
*British Merlin. See under* Rider, Cardanus
*British Monuments. See under* Gough, Richard, *Sepulchral Monuments*
British Museum:
Baker's MSS in, 2. 98

Beauclerk's library envied by, 33. 136
Bedford, Horace W., of, 42. 492
beginning of, 20. 358n
Buckingham's letters in, 15. 85
Burrell bequeaths collections to, 1. 162n
*Catalogue of the Manuscripts . . . in, A,* 2. 332, 334, 15. 164–5
Cavendish trustee of, 9. 184n
Cole's MSS left to, 12. 270
Conway papers deposited in, 15. 73n
Cooper's motion about, 24. 304n
copies of Overbury's letters in, 16. 161
Cottonian MSS in, 1. 271n, 275
Elizabeth, Q., writer of MS at, 40. 296
Exeter gives Homer bust to, 16. 153, 35. 217n
Foley's printed lawsuit should be preserved in, 28. 391
gallstones in, 32. 119
George II presents library to, 1. 271n
governors of, HW should perhaps thank, 40. 129
Gray advises HW to consult, 14. 160, 173
—— mentions King's library in, 14. 109
HW acquainted with librarian of, 15. 92,
HW not a trustee of, but of Sloane's collection which he concurred in transferring to it, 43. 230
HW's MSS at, 36. 310, 314, 315
HW too busy to visit, 40. 288
Hamilton's Etruscan vases in, 26. 46
Harleian MSS in, 1. 156, 15. 59, 221, 222
Houghton pictures might be added to, 24. 302n
James I's letters in, 15. 97–8
King's library in, 1. 271, 14. 109
MS in, about Bury St Edmunds, illustrated, 16. 187
mentioned in memorandum, 12. 258n
Morton librarian to, 31. 427
natural history collection at, 11. 12n
Pinkerton's vain attempt to get post in, through HW, Banks, Lady Diana Beauclerk, and Abp Moore, 16. 294–5, 311–12, 325–6, 327, 42. 212–13
Proctor's tract in, 42. 448
satirical print against Jesuits refused by, 29. 24, 28
Wilkes says, should get Houghton collection and copy of every printed book, 43. 286
Wyatt's MSS in, 42. 370, 379
*See also* Cottonian Library
*British Synonymy. See under* Salusbury, Hester Lynch (Mrs Piozzi)
*British Topography. See under* Gough, Richard
*Briton, The* (periodical, ed. Tobias Smollett):
Bute supported by, 35. 314n
English waste time on, 35. 314
HW tired of, 40. 273
Briton; Britons, ancient:
artistic skill of, 16. 102
HW has haughtiness of, 39. 277

Briton (surname). *See* Breton

Brittany:

affairs of: Burgundian parliament's letter on, **4.** 190; compromised, **7.** 296; Le Prestre's rôle in, **4.** 442

Aiguillon, Duc d', governor of, **11.** 43n, **21.** 221n

—— not to go to, **3.** 370

——'s difficulties with, **3.** 109n, 118, 302, **4.** 197n, 340, 493

Broglie, Maréchal de, commands in, **7.** 45, 47

—— to visit, **7.** 61

butter sent from, **7.** 436

Charles X's expedition to, **12.** 156

Choiseul-Beaupré visits, **7.** 429

Duras removed from government of, **5.** 106, 113, **23.** 322

Dusel des Monts's imprisonment upsets, **4.** 493–4

England not to have, **21.** 214

English expedition to, belittled by French, **19.** 333

English invasion of, *see under* France: English invasion of

English invasion skirts, **21.** 220–1

Fitzjames, Duc de, loses command of, **6.** 173

—— to command, **5.** 106, 113

French forces in, estimated, **37.** 531

French invasion to operate from, **21.** 271n

Grave in, **5.** 268

Jesuits said to have caused troubles in, **22.** 514

Joseph II travels through, **8.** 201–2

Louis XV suppresses pleas and arrêts concerning, **8.** 174–5

—— tries to quell disputes in, **8.** 167

Mann awaits news from, **19.** 330

Montagu discusses weather in, **10.** 158

parliament of, *see* Rennes, parliament of

risings in, **39.** 498–9

Rochers's owner's daughter banished as a result of troubles in, **30.** 213

royal commission in, recalled at insistence of parliament of Paris, **31.** 106–7

royalist victory in, **12.** 33

rumoured dispatch of troops to, **6.** 360

rumour that all officers are to be sent to, **7.** 17

St-Jean, Mme, tells HW that 'tattered scrap' has been in, **30.** 219

Sévigné, Mme de, flees to, to save money, **35.** 198

—— in, **5.** 202

Sombreuil, Vicomte de, accompanies expedition to, **12.** 152

states-general of, **4.** 429

troops in, to march to Brest, **24.** 355n

unrest in, to be quelled by regiments, **35.** 392n

Britton, Thomas (ca 1654–1714), 'musical small-coal man':

Grignion's print of, after Woolaston, **40.** 310

Onslow sends to HW anecdotes about, **40.** 310

Britwell Place, Bucks:

Owen of, **13.** 112n

Britzeke, Catherine. *See* Brietzcke, Catherine

Brivio, Giuseppe Ferdinando (ca 1700–ca 1758), singer and composer:

*Gianguir* has an air by, **18.** 96, 104, **43.** 248

Brixarre, Abbé de:

(?) social relations of, with Mme du Deffand, **6.** 222

Brixham, Devon:

William III lands at, **15.** 296n

Brixton Causeway:

Bedford, Grosvenor, talks with HW at, **41.** 206

—— writes from, **41.** 206

Brizard. *See* Britard, Jean-Baptiste

Broadalbine. *See* Breadalbane

'Broad bottom':

coalition ministry styled as, **17.** 336–7, 355, **18.** 550n

Broadie, Miss:

sings and plays at Mrs Sutton's, **12.** 157

Broadie, *See also* Brodie

Broad St Gyles Church. *See* St Giles-in-the-Fields, London

Broadstairs, Kent:

account of, **12.** 110

Balgonies entertain Berrys at, **12.** 113, 124

gossip at, **12.** 123

Prospect House near, **12.** 104n

storm between Ramsgate and, **12.** 128

*See also* Prospect House

Broad St, London:

Shrewsbury's house in, **1.** 148

Union Court in, **7.** 205n

*See also* Great Broad St; New Broad St

Broadsword; broadswords:

at SH, **20.** 381

Broadsworth, Yorks:

Hay Drummond of, **28.** 491n

Brobdingnag. *See under* Swift, Jonathan: *Gulliver's Travels*

Broc (France):

French forces at, **19.** 336

Brocade:

Carteret, Bns, wears, **18.** 464

coat of, worn with nightcap, **15.** 331

dark green, riding coat of, **22.** 3

gold, Bootle wears, to breakfast at Cliveden, **20.** 184

of fifteenth century, **14.** 78

velvet, **18.** 169

Brocaded silk. *See under* Silk

Brocatelle ('Brocadella'):

HW receives samples of, **21.** 458

HW's attempt to get, for Bedchamber in Round Tower, **21.** 420, 447, 450, 458, 468, 477, 481–2, 497, 501, 514, **22.** 18

Riccardi, Mme, has, in house, **21.** 458

Rinuccini has, specially made in 3 colours, **21.** 468

Rinuccini, Mme, has, in bedchamber, **21.** 458, 468, 481, 497, 501

Brochant, André-Joachim:
(?) attends session of parliament of Paris, 8.
171, 173
Brochon, ——, inn-keeper at Dover:
King's Head kept by, 18. 315n
Brochure; brochures:
HW wants Mme du Deffand's, 36. 190, 192
Brocket Hall, Herts, Vct Melbourne's seat:
fishing eagle taken at, 33. 564n
HW has not seen, 33. 402
Brocklesby, Dr Richard (1722–97), physician:
Chatham attended by, 24. 371n
*Essay concerning the Mortality Now Prevailing among the Horned Cattle*, 19. 174n
Lennox's physician, 11. 202n
Townshend defends, 38. 273
Broderick. *See* Brodrick
Brodrich, Capt. *See* Bodie
Brodie, Mrs David. *See* Aston, Mary
Brodie, Lady Margaret. *See* Duff, Lady Margaret
Brodrick, George (1730–65), 3d Vct Midleton; M.P.:
anecdote of Mordaunt and, 30. 144
death of, 7. 396
HW jokes about, 30. 144
Parliamentary address to George II moved by, 21. 256n
Pembrokes and Miss Hunter attend ball given by, 10. 14
sons of, 7. 349n
Brodrick, Hon. Henry (1758–85), army officer:
Cornwallis's 'courier' to England, 39. 374
(?) HW sails with, 7. 353
name of, corrected, 43. 354
(?) social relations of, with HW, 7. 349–50, 353
Townshend's letter from, from New York, 33. 306n
Brodrick, Thomas (d. 1769), naval officer:
*Antelope* boarded by, for England, 20. 573n
Byng joined by, at Gibraltar, 20. 573
—— should have left Gibraltar on arrival of, 20. 577
Conway sees, about Rochefort expedition, 37. 495
Dick frequently called on by, for news, 21. 249
Gibraltar not yet reached by, 37. 471
—— reached by, 37. 473
Lorenzi urges Regency to expel, from Leghorn, 21. 274
Mann exchanges invitations with, 21. 249
Norfolk gentleman to accompany, to Italy, 21. 206
*Phoenix* commanded by, 18. 392n
(?) print of, 40. 236
squadron of: Campbell's regiment reaches Gibraltar with, 20. 576n; reported off Toulon and Spain, 21. 292n; to be commanded by, off Rochefort, 21. 117n
Brodrick, Hon. Thomas (1756–95), Selwyn's great-nephew:

HW and Dr Gem called on by, at Paris, 30. 262n
HW sails with, 7. 353
HW will be glad to aid, in Paris, 30. 262
Paris visited by, to see things rather than people, 30. 262
Selwyn's letter to HW delivered by, 30. 262
social relations of, with: HW. 7. 349, (?) 350, 353; (?) Viry, Contessa di, 7. 350
Broglie, Comtesse de. *See* Locquet de Grandville, Thérèse-Gilette (d. 1763); Montmorency, Louise-Augustine de (b. 1735)
Broglie, Duchesse de. *See* Crozat de Thiers, Louise-Augustine-Salbigothon (1733–1813); Locquet de Grandville, Thérèse-Gilette (d. 1763)
Broglie, Maréchale de. *See* Crozat de Thiers, Louise-Augustine-Salbigothon
Broglie, Marquise de. *See* Besenval, Théodore-Élisabeth-Catherine de
Broglie, Princesse de. *See* Rosen-Kleinroop, Sophie de
Broglie, Aglaé-Charlotte de (1771–1846), m. (1788) Hugues-François-Casimir de Murat, Marquis de Lens-Lestang:
birth of, 5. 112
Broglie, Charles de (1733–77), Bp of Noyon:
Boufflers, Comtesse de, and Duchesse de, visit, 6. 231
Craufurd inquired after by, 3. 18
Du Deffand, Mme, and, 6. 231
death of, 6. 479
HW inquired after by, 3. 18
health of, 6. 358, 363
Pomme attends, 4. 108, 119, 164
social relations of, in Paris, *see index entries ante* 8. 269
Stanislas II nominates, for cardinalate, 3. 102–3
Broglie, Charles-François (1719–81), Comte de:
Aiguillon's adherent, 23. 283
(?) Aiguillon, Mme d', thought by, to be useful to him, 4. 340
appearance of, 3. 50
Artois, Comtesse d', not to be escorted by, 5. 402, 23. 520–1
—— to be escorted by, 5. 357, 386
'Bastille affair' implicates, 39. 267
Beauvau's correspondence with, 7. 341
Brittany command coveted by, 5. 106
brother aroused by, against Maillebois, 23. 283
brother said to be joined by, 33. 13
busy, 6. 74, 417
Cassel siege lifted, according to, 21. 498n
Compiègne to be visited by, 6. 74
Conti's claim to Polish throne backed by, 4. 214n
Conway may meet, at Mme du Deffand's, 39. 191
Du Barry, Comtesse, obtains *entrées* for, 23. 169
——'s aid sought by, 4. 339–40

[Broglie, Charles-François, *continued*]
Du Deffand, Mme, corresponds with, 3. 358,
7. 430, 431, 436, 438, 439, 450, 457–9
—— sends letter by, 7. 448
——'s opinion of, 4. 340, 6. 71
——'s relations with, 3. 133, 6. 74, 231–2, 7.
102
——'s wagers with, over: lit de justice, 6. 277;
Wilkes, 4. 89, 91, 164, 187, 198
*entrées* granted to, 4. 330, 23. 169
Éon's correspondence with, 22. 191n
exile of: by Louis XV, to Ruffec, 5. 402, 404;
ended by Louis XVI, 6. 64n, 66, 69, 71; may
end, 24. 11n
(?) Forcalquier, Mme de, thought by, to be
useful to him, 4. 340
gala coat worn by, when supping with Hertford, 38. 571
Georgel sued by, 7. 164, 166
Gramont, Duchesse de, avoids, 5. 363, 374
leaves Paris, 7. 427
leg of, injured, 7. 423
Louis XV banishes, for reproachful letter to
Aiguillon over visit to Piedmont to fetch
Comtesse d'Artois, 23. 520–1
Louis XVI gives audience to, 7. 424
Macartney approved by, at Limoges, 33. 126
marriage of, 3. 18n
Metz commands of, 4. 110, 232, 7. 45–6, 53
—— left by, 6. 253
—— to be visited by, 6. 272, 281
—— visited by, 6. 232, 324, 7. 68
Mirepoix, Mme de, aids, 5. 51
opposition of, alluded to, 32. 20
Paris to be visited by, 6. 358, 363
—— visited by, 7. 422, 440, 451
Pitt's inclusion in cabinet interests, 38. 571
political status of, 4. 339–40, 374, 5. 51
quarantines himself with Vassé, 7. 443
recalled, 24. 19
Rueil visited by, 7. 335
Ruffec occupied by, 7. 177, 450, 451
—— to be occupied by, in exile, 5. 402, 23.
521
—— to be visited by, 5. 225, 231, 256, 6. 74,
358
social relations of, in Paris, *see index entries
ante* 8. 269
Stanislas II writes to, 3. 102–3
suit against, 7. 423
Turin may be visited by, to pay court to
Victor Amadeus III, 23. 50
Vergennes suggested by, as ambassador to
Sweden, 23. 264n
Versailles to be visited by, 7. 448
Walpole, Hon. Robert, arouses indignation
of, 4. 374
Broglie, Charles-Louis-Victor (1756–94), Prince
de:
marriage of, 7. 109
Broglie, Charles-Maurice de (ca 1682–1766),
Abbé, of Mont-St-Michel:
death of, 3. 8

Broglie, François-Marie de (1671–1745), Maréchal de France:
army of: retires towards Königsaal, 17. 451n;
retires towards the Rhine, 18. 99
Austrian army to drive, from Moravia, 17.
401n
baggage lost by, 17. 464, 481
blockaded in Prague, 18. 61n
Brissac to report on rumoured tension between Belle-Isle and, 18. 69n
Charles, P., defeats, 17. 464, 481
deprived of his command, 18. 32n
Dresden reached by, 18. 90n
HW indifferent to fate of, 18. 32
Maillebois prevented from joining, 18. 89
Noailles joined by, 18. 267
retreat of, from Frauenberg, 17. 452n
wife's retort to, when taunted with low birth,
33. 392–3
Broglie, Louise-Auguste-Philippine-Charlotte-
Françoise de (1760–1827), m. (1779) Alexis-
Bruno-Étienne, Marquis de Vassé:
social relations of, with Mme du Deffand, 7.
223
son born to, 7. 460
Broglie, Marie-Thérèse de (b. 1732), m. (1751)
Louis-Charles, Comte de Lameth:
social relations of, with Comte de Broglie, 7.
305
Broglie, Victor-François (1718–1804), Duc de;
Maréchal de France:
appointed commander-in-chief of French
army, 11. 27, 28. 396
army of, may aid the Dutch, 25. 545–6
Bayeux to be camp-site for, 7. 68
Belle-Isle notified by, of victory, 21. 287n
Brittany to be visited by, 7. 61
brother arouses, against Maillebois, 23. 283
brother not serving with, 7. 45–6, 53
brother's alleged letters to, 7. 166
brother's alleged sharing of command with,
33. 13
Chaulieu, aide-major-general to, 21. 287n
Choiseul may be succeeded by, 23. 84n
commands seaboard forces, 7. 43–5, 47, 53, 61
daughter born to, 5. 112
Dauphin protects, 21. 519n
——'s *entrée* granted to, 4. 444
defeat of, 21. 362, 515, 518–19
Estrées and Soubise compared with, 22. 47
Estrées' and Soubise's defeat would vindicate,
22. 50
Ferdinand, P., and Conway defeat, at Kirch
Denckern, 38. 105
Ferdinand, P., defeats, 9. 378, 21. 314n
—— opposed by, 21. 419n
——'s defeats of, do not impress English, 38.
128
—— to meet drive of, on Hanover, 21. 306n
French losses estimated by, 21. 518n
HW to buy armour from, 5. 109, 112–13, 119
HW would protect English ministers from,
33. 25

Hanover cannot be captured by, 21. 435
in country, 5. 113
Isenburg defeated by, at Sandershausen, 21. 227n
Karl Wilhelm Ferdinand defeated by, at Corbach, 21. 427n
—— intends to oust, from Hesse, 21. 474n
lawsuit of, 5. 114n
lives high, at camp, 7. 72
Maillebois's appointment protested by, 6. 322-3
Metz command given to, 6. 110
ministry of foreign affairs may be given to, 5. 29
motion not made by, 38. 77
Neckar reached by, near Noailles's army, 37. 140
Necker threatened by, 11. 27
opposition of, alluded to, 32. 20
Paris visited by, 7. 453
pension of, 3. 57
Pitt's inclusion in cabinet interests, 38. 571
print satirizes, 11. 54n
recalled to Paris, 7. 44
reinforcements needed by, 21. 435
retreat of, 21. 362n
St-Germain second choice of, 6. 228
social relations of, in Paris, 3. 8, 100, 6. 156, 7. 312
son of, marries, 7. 109
Soubise's forces blame defeat on, 21. 519
—— waits for, 38. 95n
Stanislas II writes to, 3. 102
Te Deum for success of, 21. 502n
300,000 livres set on head of, 11. 39
Versailles encampment of, 11. 41
wife of, 3. 350n
Württemberg, D. of, warned by, 21. 355n
Broglie, Hôtel de, Rue de Varenne:
Caracciolo at, 5. 140n
Fuentes takes, and offers it to Hertford, 38. 340
Broglie family:
Choiseuls may be succeeded by, in ministry, 22. 227, 38. 380
Piedmontese, 23. 521
Broglio. See Broglie
Brogue, Irish:
Conway, Anne Seymour, not reconciled to, 37. 412
Broker; brokers:
HW's, see Gomes
in Exchange Alley, 11. 213
Brokerage:
Londoners uphold, 21. 549
Bromfield, John (ca 1727-92):
Egerton sells library of, 40. 326n
HW's correspondence with, 40. 313-20, 324-8
HW to receive from, a list of paintings at Petworth, 40. 319, 324, 327
health of: epidemic disorder, 40. 314; long and painful illness, 40. 317

letter of, offends Grenvilles and Ds of Somerset, 40. 327
Petworth visited by, to convalesce amid relatives, 40. 317
Bromfield, William (1712-92), surgeon:
(?) Ancaster dies before arrival of, 24. 407n
attends actors, 13. 113n
Bromich. See Bromwich
Bromley, Hon. Frances (d. 1768), m. (1747) Hon. Charles Sloane Cadogan:
children of, 2. 306
Cole invited by, to Horseheath, 1. 48
father places no bets on marriage of, 35. 202
husband of, 1. 185n
name of, corrected, 43. 361
son of, 1. 199n
Bromley, Henry (1705-55), cr. (1741) Bn Montfort; M.P.:
Allington tomb repaired by, 1. 49
barony of, 9. 51n
Bentley lies at Holt Castle by permission of, 35. 201n
bets by, 20. 74, 35. 201, 202
bets not placed by, on daughter's marriage, 35. 202
Bland's bet with, at White's, 35. 258
Cambridgeshire preferred by, because close to Newmarket, 40. 13
Cole's anecdote of Middleton and, 15. 306
——'s connection with, 2. 153n
Conway, Bn, 'educated' by, 40. 13
cook of, see Joras
cricket matches of, 20. 74
Cromwell portrait acquired by, 1. 9
daughter of, 1. 48n, 185n, 199n, 2. 306n
Demoivre's calculations followed by, 35. 202
footman of, 15. 310n
French not spoken by, 20. 155n
Holt Castle the seat of, 40. 13
Horseheath the seat of, 16. 155
horse-racing bets placed by, through aides-de-camp, 20. 74
Louis XV comments on obesity of, 20. 155-6
Maclaine visited by, with other members of White's, 20. 169
Middleton brought by, to Houghton, 20. 215
—— takes son of, as pupil, 15. 293
(?) Middleton, Miss, likes Lilliputian figure of, 35. 201
parsons brought by, to Richmond Green, 20. 74
Patapan must take precedence of, 17. 76
picture painted for, 28. 252n
suicide of, 9. 173, 20. 461, 35. 201-2, 246
uncle of, 1. 363
Bromley, Henry (1773-1851), 3d Bn Montfort:
birth of, 1. 311n
Bromley, Margaret, m. Sir Richard Newport:
daughter of, 1. 71n
Bromley, Robert (1732-1803):
pedigree sent to, 2. 154

Bromley, Rev. Robert Anthony (ca 1736–1806): (?) Wyvill's manifesto said to have been drafted by, 29. 14

Bromley, Sir Thomas (d. ?1555), judge: Cole's correction concerning, 1. 70

Bromley, Sir Thomas (1530–87), lord chancellor:
pedigree of, 2. 153–4
portrait of, 1. 291, 294n

Bromley, Thomas (1733–99), 2d Bn Montfort:
Cadogan, Mrs, visits, 1. 48
Cambridgeshire election of, 1. 199, 200, 202
—— militia requires pedestal to enable, to lead them, 21. 312
Cole given *Journals of the House of Commons* by, 1. 284n
—— given missal by, 2. 197n
—— informed by, about pictures, 1. 50
—— may go to town with, 1. 277
—— meets Burrell at house of, 1. 162n
—— offered house by, 1. 152n
—— sends packet by his servant, 1. 197
——'s intimacy with, 1. 237n
——'s letter from, 1. 294n
—— taken by, to and from Ealing, 1. 311n
—— to have letter franked by, 1. 194, 296–7
—— visits, 1. 48–50, 152, 185, 287, 295n, (*see also under* Horseheath Hall)
—— warned by, of presence of disagreeable company, 1. 194n
daughter of, 1. 71n
dines in Cambridge, 1. 185
father's cook not retained by, 35. 246
'frolicsome,' 1. 48
Henshaw to copy pictures belonging to, 1. 291
Horseheath sold by, 1. 9n
hours of, 1. 311n
houses of: at Sunbury, 2. 115; in Seymour Place, 1. 308, 311n; *see also* Horseheath Hall
Keene's remarks to, about Cole, 2. 86
marriage of, 1. 237n, 240
Middleton takes, as pupil, 15. 293
obliged to sell his estates, 2. 113, 115
Paris visited by, 1. 381n
pedigree of, 2. 153–4
pictures sold by, 2. 57
profligate ways of, 1. 237n
singularity of, 15. 312
wishes to see SH, 1. 311n

Bromley, William (d. 1729), Capt.:
mistress of, 1. 363

Bromley, Kent:
Chute and HW visit Bp of Rochester's palace at, 35. 131–2
Emmet of, 21. 364n
Hayes near, 22. 277n
horses changed at, 35. 131
Plaistow near, 12. 176n
Trinity Hospital has estates at, 16. 91

Bromley family:
Cole connected with, 2. 153n
pedigree of, 2. 153–4

Brompton, Middlesex ('Brumpton'):
Michael's Grove in, 1. 313n
Townshend, Vcts, visits her lodging in, 30. 69–70, 40. 48
Winnington's 'accidental' visit to Vcts Townshend in, 30. 70
—— walks to London from, 30. 70

Brompton, Yorks:
Berry, Agnes, mare of, to go to, 12. 19, 20
Berrys at, 12. 13, 16, 17, 36n
Cayley, Sir George, has seat at, 12. 13n
High Hall at, 11. 18n
Seton, Mrs, buried at, 11. 19n

Bromwich, Thomas (d. 1787), decorator:
Conway sends, to HW with paper samples, 37. 331
HW hurries, at SH, 35. 173
man of, paints SH wallpaper, 35. 191
Müntz worthy to be employed by, 35. 100
payment to, for ceiling of the Gallery, 40. 312n

Bronze; bronzes:
ancient and modern in Uffizi, 25. 170
at Casa Feroni, 17. 33
at Ham House, 10. 306
at Hôtel de Lambert, Paris, 7. 337
at Wolterton, 18. 47
bull of, owned by Thiers, 7. 373
Caligula's bust in, 22. 523, 26. 56
Damer, Mrs, does bust in, for HW's Jupiter head, 39. 443
funnel of, 39. 15
HW buys, in Italy, 13. 232
HW lists collections of, 15. 12
HW's: 15. 13, 37. 257, 258; of Ceres, 33. 479
HW to buy, at Mead's sale, 20. 470
HW wants cast in, of 'Livia' statue, 20. 98, 22. 107
HW would prefer, to fortune in stocks, 21. 558
Hamilton, Sir William, resembles, 35. 375
Henri IV's statue in, 31. 99n
in Colebrooke's sale, 23. 569n
Knight's, admired by HW, 15. 329
La Borde's, 31. 80
Mann's, for Sir Robert Walpole, 17. 24
medals in, 24. 469n
Middleton's, 15. 16–17
Oxford, E. of, has, 17. 358
statues of, at Kedleston, 10. 230
vase of, 17. 374
Venus statue in, 26. 7

Bronze doré:
medal of, 21. 201

Bronzino. *See* Troti, Angiolo

*Bronzo*, by Giambologna. *See under* Boulogne, Jehan de

Brook, Mrs:
SH visited by, 12. 244

Brook. *See also* Brooke; Brooks

Brook; brooks:
Minorca lacks, 37. 310

Brooke, Bn. *See* Greville, Francis (1719–73); Greville, Sir Fulke (1554–1628); Greville, Robert (1607–43)

Brooke, Bns and Cts. *See* Hamilton, Elizabeth

Brooke, E. *See* Greville, Francis (1719–93); Greville, George (1746–1816)

Brooke, Frances (d. 1690), m. 1 Sir Thomas Whitmore, K.B., 1661; m. 2 Matthew Harvey:
*Mémoires* of Gramont mention, 30. 370
portrait of, by Mrs Beale, 30. 370
print mis-labelled with name of, 16. 323

Brooke, Henry, East India Co. official:
trial of, for deposing Pigot, 25. 13n

Brooke, Henry (ca 1703–83), dramatist:
*Earl of Essex* by, 41. 293n
*Gustavus Vasa* by: called 'dainty' by HW, 13. 171–2; (?) sent by John Selwyn to H. C. Conway, 40. 29

Brooke, John Charles (1748–94), Somerset Herald 1777–94:
account by, of Yorkshire families, 29. 278
Gough's correspondence with, 42. 286n, 313n

Brooke, Margaret (ca 1646–67), m. (1665) Sir John Denham:
portrait of, at Wimbledon, 9. 119

Brooke, Ralph (1553–1625), herald:
*Catalogue and Succession of the Kings . . . of England, A*, cited, 1. 148, 387, 43. 53, 63

Brooke, Selina Elizabeth (d. before 1797), m. (1769) Thomas Vesey, cr. (1776) Vct de Vesci:
More, Hannah, praises, 31. 252
—— visited by, at Cowslip Green, 31. 252
SH visited by, 12. 227

Brooke, Rev. Zachary (1716–88); D.D.:
*Defensio miraculorum*, 15. 297
*Epistle* to, 15. 297
*Examination of Dr Middleton's Free Inquiry*, 15. 299
postscript on, 15. 297
*Second Letter* to, 15. 300

Brookes, H., lawyer:
Selwyn employs, to fight expulsion from Oxford, 30. 93n

Brookes, Henrietta (ca 1676–1769), m. John Pratt:
(?) Mann attends, 18. 65
(?) Turin visited by, 43. 247

Brooklyn, N. Y.:
English victory at, 28. 282n

Brooks's Club, St James's St, London:
Almack's succeeded by, 28. 104n
'beggars' at, despise Indian mines and foreign embassies, 33. 219
Cholmondeley and Aston beaten at faro by C. J. Fox and Fitzpatrick at, 39. 368–9
conversation at, 29. 179
Fox, C. J., at, 35. 520, 615
Gibbon overheard by C. J. Fox at, attacking North administration, 35. 615
Gunnings move next door to, 11. 205
HW calls at, to hear about George IV's duel, 39. 466

oats rare enough to be eaten at, 35. 391
Ossory, Lord, hears news at, 33. 271
—— frequents, 33. 325
prayer-book passage that might have been coined at, 33. 395
Selwyn's witticism about, 29. 185
Siddons, Mrs, receives tribute money from, 33. 377
Skrine loses at cards at, 25. 386n, 36. 210n
Spencer, Lord Robert, keeps faro bank at, 43. 115
Whig Club meets at, 29. 335n
*See also* Almack's

Brook St, Grosvenor Sq., London:
residents in: Abergavenny, Bns, 9. 30; Ossorys, 32. 44, 215; Petershams, 9. 30; Phillips, 38. 18; Pomfrets, 18. 424n

Brook St, Lower:
Ossorys' house on corner of, 32. 215n
residents in: Dickensons, 31. 367n; Hoper, 12. 176n

Brook St, Upper:
Rathbone Place in, 42. 63n
residents in: Brown, Lady, 9. 15; Buller, Mrs, 11. 122n, 219n; Hamilton, 12. 202n; Herbert, 16. 277n, 33. 376n; Molesworths, 22. 138, 38. 201; Nugent, Mrs, 12. 81n

Broom, Capt.:
Villinghausen news brought by, 21. 516n

Broom; brooms:
trees clipped to resemble, in France, 31. 45
*See also* Spanish brooms

Broome, William (1689–1745), translator:
Pope's letter to, on Fenton's death, 2. 259

Broome, Norfolk:
Fowle of 14. 198n
Fowle, Mrs, of, 41. 98

Broschi, Carlo (1705–82), called Farinelli; singer:
Caffarelli brought to replace, 13. 142n
Conti made despondent by, 13. 102n
diamond watches and snuff-boxes collected by, in England, 38. 476
fails to return to London, 17. 478
Monticelli compared with, 17. *190*, 211
print of, 41. 452
Rich, Lady, writes to, 35. 78–9
Saletti tries to imitate, 30. 14
Townshend, Vcts, jokes about alleged escape of, from Spain in English ship to Newfoundland, 18. 119
Young Pretender urged by, to leave Spain, 19. 390n

Broschi, Riccardo (ca 1700–56), composer:
*Idaspes*, Burney sees, 13. 64n

Brossard, Louis:
*Liste des noms* by, 11. 79n

Broth; broths:
Adair brings, to Ds of Gloucester, 36. 142
HW should eat, with bread and herbs, 22. 114
Mann's diet limited to, 25. 547, 560
Montagu takes, for supper, 9. 391

[Broth; broths, *continued*]
Orford, E. of, takes, by force, 23. 505, 36. 333
*See also* Bouillon; Soup
Brothel; brothels:
Almódovar's niggardly fees at, 24. 413
at Covent Garden, 9. 28
in Suffolk St, 17. 331
visitors to, pilloried in newspaper letters, 42. 501
*See also* Bagnio; King's Arms
Brothers, Mr, of Fairfield:
Aitken robs, 28. 284n
Brothers, Richard (1757–1824):
Loutherbourg believes in, 16. 227n, 34. 51n
*Brothers, The. See under* Cumberland, Richard
Brotherton family:
arms of, on monument, 16. 88
Brough, William, marshal of the High Court of Admiralty:
Byng writes to, just before his death, 21. 66n
Brougham, Rev. John (ca 1749–1811) of Ealing:
(?) SH visited by, 12. 245
Brougham, Mary (d. 1812), m. (1767) Richard Meux of Ealing:
SH visited by, 12. 249
Broughton, Lady. *See* Hill, Mary
Broughton, —— (d. 1752), convict:
Newgate turnkey murdered by, 20. 312n
Broughton, John (d. 1801), attorney at Bristol:
Chatterton's *Miscellanies* edited by, 2. 102n, 16. 177n, 28. 422–3, 29. 374, 33. 40, 41. 396n
HW censured by, in Chatterton affair, 2. 102
HW's answer to, 13. 50, 51
Broughton, Sir Thomas:
attainted, 41. 92n
Broughton, Rev. Thomas (1704–74):
*Biographia dramatica* has contribution by, 42. 3
*Hercules* by, the libretto for Handel's opera, 42. 3n
St Mary Redcliff church the cure and burial-place of, 42. 3
Broughton:
Murray of, 9. 40n
Broun, Capt. *See* Brown, William
Brouncker, Henry (ca 1627–88), 3d Vct Brouncker, 1684:
portrait of, at Hagley, 35. 148
Brouncker *or* Brounker, William (1620–84), 2d Vct Brouncker:
HW to look up, in *Philosophical Transactions*, 16. 12
mistress of, 1. 350n
print of, 1. 181
Brounker. *See* Brouncker
Broussin, seigneur de. *See* Brulart, Pierre
Brown, Lady. *See* Cecil, Margaret (ca 1696–1782) (*see also* Browne, Lady)
Brown, Capt.:
(?) drawing by, of Speaker Lenthall, 42. 125

Brown, Capt., in Tuscan service:
prize taken by, 21. 349
Brown, Commodore:
medal of Vernon and, 17. 229n
'Brown, Father,' English Jesuit. *See* Hill, John
Brown, Miss (d. 1755) and her sisters (daughters of Sir Robert Brown):
death of, 9. 170, 35. 236
father haggles with undertaker before death of, from consumption, 25. 609n
footman told to guide, through by-lanes to avoid turnpike fees, 25. 609n
mother might try to marry, to Chute, 35. 86
Brown, Mr:
SH visited by, 12. 238
Brown, Mr:
Isleworth house of, 33. 524n
Brown, Mr:
Pelham, Lady Catherine, might get love-letter from, 35. 166
Brown, Mr, of Egham:
Daye, Carey, cared for by, 43. 149
HW called on by, about bill for Misses Daye, 34. 186–7
Brown, Charles. *See* Booth, Charles
Brown, Rev. Edward (fl. 1690):
*Fasciculus* by, 1. 271n, 273, 274
Brown, Ignatius Michael (d. ?1779) Irish officer:
(?) aide-de-camp to d'Estaing, 19. 217n
arrival of, in Scotland, 19. 138
Louis XV said to have given Croix de St Louis to, for Falkirk news, 19. 217
Brown, Rev. James (ca 1709–84), D.D.; master of Pembroke College, Cambridge:
birth date of, corrected, 43. 56
Cambridge vice-chancellor, 1. 237n, 28. 44
Cole and HW thanked by, for *King Edward's Letters*, 1. 282–3
Cole dines with, 1. 290
—— receives print from, 28. 37
——'s correspondence with, 1. 237n
—— thanks, on HW's behalf, 1. 282
—— told by, of Gray's affairs, 1. 232–3
—— wants *King Edward's Letters* for, 1. 260, 266, 283
good Whig, 14. 90
Gray and Mason ask HW to support candidacy of, 28. 1
(?) Gray asked by, to write tripos verses, 13. 119
—— attended by: in last illness, 1. 234–5; to grave, 1. 230–1
——'s executor, 1. 229n, 230, 28. 18n
——'s goa stone and seal given by, to HW, 1. 275, 283, 41. 233
——'s legacy to, 1. 232, 233
——'s monument erected with help from, 2. 101n, 28. 439n
——'s picture offered by HW to, 1. 237–8
——'s trinket box given by, to Cole, 1. 260, 278

—— supports, as successor to Dr Long, **14.** 89–90, 91–2

HW and Mason thank, for relics of Gray, **28.** 43, 44

HW's correspondence with, **41.** 233

HW thanked by, for Gray's portrait, **28.** 27

HW to receive compliments of, **1.** 291

Masters's *Some Remarks* owned by, **1.** 290, 291

Ramsgate visited by, **2.** 234, 237

Stretham's rector, **1.** 290

Brown, John (b. ca 1642), surgeon:
*Adenochoiradelogia*, given by Gough to HW, **42.** 33

Brown, Rev. John (1715–66), author:
*Additional Dialogues of the Dead, between Pericles and Aristides*, dull, **15.** 69–70

*Barbarossa* by, **20.** 494n, **35.** 198–9

Carlisle, Cts of, entertains, **9.** 219

Cole's opinion of, **2.** 190n, 196

Dodsley given messages by, for Sir Charles Hanbury Williams, **9.** 220

——'s books returned to him by, **9.** 220

—— threatened by, **9.** 220

duelling opposed by, **9.** 220

*Essays on the Characteristics of the Earl of Shaftsbury*, **2.** 196

*Estimate of the Manners and Principles of the Times*: **2.** 187; **15.** 69n; Sir C. H. Williams answers, **9.** 219

'ethic espistles' by, **34.** 35n

Garrick friend of, **9.** 220

Gray dismisses poems of, **14.** 37

HW's opinion of, **2.** 187

insane, temporarily, **9.** 219

Mingotti sings *Stabat Mater* with, **9.** 219

opera condemned by, **9.** 219

profanity of, **9.** 219

suicide of, **14.** 159

Warburton's relations with, **9.** 221

Williams, Sir C. H., threatened by, for disclosures about his profanity, **9.** 219–21

Brown, Lt-Gen. John (d. before 1764):
Burgoyne, Lady Frances, executrix of will of, **10.** 169

(?) HW asks for post under, at Windsor, for Bevan, **40.** 173–4

Jackson's legacy from, **10.** 169

Brown, Maj. John (American army):
Fort Chamblée captured by, **24.** 156n

Brown, John (1752–87), miniaturist and draughtsman:
Buchan recommends, to HW, **15.** 189, 190

——'s account of, in *The Bee*, **15.** 189

drawings by, **15.** 189

*Letters upon the Poetry and Music of the Italian Opera* by, **15.** 189n

Brown, Joseph (ca 1720–1800), painter:
landscape by, **1.** 141, **43.** 49

Brown, Lancelot (1715–83), 'Capability'; landscape gardener; architect:
Chambers's *Dissertation* written in revenge against, **28.** 34

death of, **29.** 285–6, 304, 306, **33.** 385

flippancy of, to D. of Marlborough, **32.** 148, 152

HW compliments, **32.** 82n

HW's epitaph for, **29.** 285–6, 288

'home-brewed rivers' of, **33.** 355

Knight abuses, in *The Landscape*, **29.** 339, 366

'Lady Nature's second husband,' and 'second monarch of landscape,' **33.** 385

landscaping by, at: Ampthill, **1.** 226n, **32.** 82n; Belvoir Castle, **33.** 218; Blenheim, **9.** 289n, **39.** 435; Burghley House, **10.** 344; Moor Park, **9.** 285; Nuneham, **28.** 45n, **33.** 417; Ragley, **9.** 223; Sion House, **35.** 331n; Warwick Castle, **9.** 121; Wrest, **39.** 140

(?) Mason's epitaph for, **29.** 316, 319

(?) social relations of, with HW, **7.** 325, 327

Brown, Lancelot (b. ca 1748, d. ca 1794) the younger:
(?) social relations of, with HW, **7.** 325, 327

Brown, Margaret, Lady. *See* Cecil, Margaret

Brown, Matthew, Wilkes's butler:
House of Commons to hear testimony of, **38.** 292

Brown, Moses:
print of, **40.** 236

Brown, Richard, tobacconist; 'old Richard':
HW asks, about John Montagu, **9.** 392

HW consigns parcel to, for Montagu, **10.** 157

HW mentions, **10.** 124

Louis knows, **10.** 124, 131, 142

Montagu angry with, for giving HW letters to frank, **10.** 31

—— asks, to find lodgings, **10.** 149

——'s correspondence with, **10.** 37, 149

—— told by HW to notify, of changes of address, **10.** 41

—— uses, to transmit articles, **9.** *194*, 226, **10.** 37, 38, 124, 131, 142, 144, 157

Brown, Sir Robert (d. 1760), cr. (1732) Bt; M.P.:
avarice of, **9.** 254, 312, **10.** 68, **20.** 449, **25.** 609

Chute to discuss stocks and actions with, **35.** 86

daughter's funeral bargained for by, **43.** 129

daughters of, all dead, **35.** 236

fortune of, **35.** 236

French financial legislation will injure, **9.** 254

George II's wealth compared to that of, **9.** 317

Gilmour replaces, in paymastership, **17.** *493*

HW compares E. of Bath to, **10.** 68

Harris succeeded by, as paymaster of Board of Works, **17.** 487n

London by-lanes mapped by, to avoid turnpike fees for daughter's rides, **25.** 609n

Scarborough to be visited by, **9.** 16

second-hand wig sold by, to make fortune at Venice, **25.** 609n

undertaker's bargaining with, over consumptive daughter's funeral, **10.** 68, **25.** 609n

widow of, **25.** 246n

[Brown, Sir Robert, *continued*]
wife of: 14. 120n; returns with him from Venice, 25. 609n; to inherit his property, 9. 312; works to re-establish him, in his post, 37. 132
woman kept by, 9. 16

Brown, Rev. Robert (1728–77), Presbyterian divine:
Hume's enemy, 4. 52
Voltaire attacked by, 4. 52

Brown, Robert (d. 1784), mate of *Great Duchess of Tuscany*:
pirates kill, 25. 479

Brown, Thomas (1663–1704), satirist; 'Tom Brown':
HW compares Dr King to, 29. 111
*Letters from the Dead to the Living* by, may mention Mrs Bracegirdle, 25. 74n

Brown, Thomas; sea-capt.:
(?) *Neptune* commanded by, 18. 354

Brown, Ulysses Maximilian (1705–57), Graf von Camus; Austrian field marshal:
achievements of, in Bohemian battle, 21. 5
advantageous situation of, will keep Frederick II in winter quarters, 21. 15
Austrian army under, 9. 206n
Austrian-Genoese agreement signed by, 19. 316
Budin encampment of, 21. 15n
Carteret calls, Irishman, 19. 220
Charles, P., replaces, as commander-in-chief, 21. 95n
Charles Emmanuel III sends cannon to, 19. 252–3
——'s requests not executed by, 19. 436
Daun to be tried for not joining, 21. 96
France invaded by, 19. 336
Frederick II defeats, 9. 198n
Gages escapes from, 19. 291
Leutrum to be reinforced by troops from, 19. 436
*Liverpool* carries, from Genoa to Nice, 19. 323n
Lobositz a 'victory' of, 21. 4–5, 72
Mantua reached by detachment of, 19. 220
Maria Theresa bribes, with *toison* and diamond pictures, 21. 72
name of, corrected, 43. 260, 274
Parma blockaded by, 19. 236
pontoon bridge supervised by, 18. 531
Provence to be invaded by, 19. 323
Prussians to be intercepted according to plan of, 21. 95n
retreat of, across Var, 19. 323n, 363n
Schulenburg succeeded by, in army command, 19. 393
too strongly entrenched to be attacked, 21. 5
troops of, reach Mitteldorf, 21. 14n
Velletri attacked by, 18. 489
Vence the headquarters of, 19. 336n
Viennese court may secretly instruct, not to press the French, 19. 436

Brown, William (d. ?1814), sea-captain:
*Sukey*, express packet, commanded by, 24. 110n
(?) *Tartar* commanded by, 23. 226

Brown. *See also* Browne

Brown (colour):
civilian costume characterized by, 37. 121

Browne, Dr. *See* Brown, Rev. John (1715–66)

Browne, Lady. *See* Fitzgerald, Lady Elizabeth (ca 1528–90); Sheldon, Frances (1714–90)

Browne, Miss:
dances at Robinson's ball, 37. 115

Browne, Mr, merchant:
Jebb's letter to, about D. of Gloucester, 36. 138–9, 141

Browne, Alexander (fl. 1660–77):
mezzotint by, 10. 123n

Browne, Sir Anthony (d. 1548), K.G.:
Battle Abbey said to be built by, 35. 140n
picture of, at Cowdray, 9. 99
portrait at St John's College said to be of, 14. 115
proxy at Anne of Cleves's wedding, 9. 99
tomb of, at St Mary's, Battle, 35. 140
wife of, 11. 154n

Browne, Sir Anthony (ca 1528–92), cr. (1554) Vct Montagu:
HW confuses with father, 35. 140n

Browne, Anthony (1686–1767), 6th Vct Montagu:
Cowdray to be inhabited by, 9. 98

Browne, Anthony Joseph (1728–87), 7th Vct Montagu:
Cowdray the seat of, 2. 8n, 28. 212n
wife of, 12. 16n

Browne, Hon. Catherine (d. 1753):
Acunha, Mme d', lives with, 9. 152
Catholic, 9. 152
death of, 9. 152
Montagu's 'favourite,' 9. 152

Browne, Lady Elizabeth. *See* Fitzgerald, Lady Elizabeth

Browne, Sir George (d. 1754), 3d Bt:
wife of, 10. 252n, 12. 206n, 29. 160n

Browne, George Samuel (1769–93), 8th Vct Montagu, 1787:
drowned in Switzerland, 12. 54
Italy visited by, 12. *16*

Browne, Isaac Hawkins (1705–60), poet:
Gray dismisses poems of, 14. 36

Browne, Isaac Hawkins (1745–1818), D.C.L.; author:
SH visited by, 12. 235

Browne, Mrs Isaac Hawkins. *See* Hay, Henrietta

Browne, Mrs John. *See* Crewe, Temperance (ca 1609–34)

Browne, Mary (ca 1722–95), m. Sir Richard Perryn, Kt, 1776:
SH visited by, 12. 224

Browne, Niel (ca 1660–1740), English consul at Venice ca 1717–40:

Montagu, Lady Mary Wortley, calls, 'old fool,' 17. 98
Browne, Richard, wardrobe keeper to Charles I:
inventory by, 32. 324n
Browne, Robinia (d. 1794), m. (1755) Charles Mordaunt, 4th E. of Peterborough:
(?) bridesmaid to Mrs Harris, 38. 122
comely figure at Coronation, 38. 122
Browne, S.:
children of, playing with musical prodigy, 43. 351
Browne. See also Brown; Browon
Brownhill, Margaret:
(?) Worksop arsenal to have been revealed by, 9. 97
Browning, John (d. 1759), of Barton Hill:
owns account of Canynges's donation to St Mary Redcliffe, 16. 133n, 176
Brownlow, Lady Betty. See Hamilton, Lady Elizabeth
Brownlow, Cts. See Edgcumbe, Emma Sophia (1791–1872)
Brownlow, Isabella (d. 1815), m. 1 George Matthew; m. 2 (1761) Maj. John Forde:
mother's second marriage drives, to England, 18. 117
Brownlow, Jane (d. 1736), m. (1711) Peregrine Bertie, 2d D. of Ancaster:
(?) never sober, 24. 499
Brownlow, Sir John (d. 1754), cr. (1718) Vct Tyrconnel:
Belton the seat of, 35. 266
Brownlow, Mary (1719–85), m. (1743) John Pigott:
mother's second marriage drives, to England, 18. 117
Brownlow, William (1726–94) of Lurgan, Irish M.P.; (?) Lt-Col.:
Armagh election won by, 35. 158
Chute fond of, 19. 472
Florence visited by, 18. 479, 19. 472
(?) Irish address may be carried over by, 25. 453n
Brownlow St, Longacre:
Wibergh's house in, 13. 187n
Browon (?Brown), ——:
Mann presents, at Tuscan Court, 24. 251n
Brownrigg, Elizabeth (d. 1767), wife of James Brownrigg; murderess:
Carlisle suggests that HW vindicate, 30. 252
crimes and punishment of, 30. 252
Broxbournbury, Herts; Monson's seat:
HW negotiates with Monson over pictures at, 42. 218–19
Monson sells, to Bosanquet, 42. 219n
old portraits at, 42. 281
Broxholme, Noel (ca 1686–1748), physician:
Conway, Hon. Catherine, attended by, 37. 28
HW cured by, of fever, 43. 169
Hedges corresponds with, in Latin odes, 9. 66

suicide of, 9. 66
verses attributed to, 37. 82
Winnington consults, 19. 250
Bruant, Jean (d. 1788):
(?) attends session of parliament of Paris, 8. 173
Bruc, Marie-François de (ca 1754–94), Marquis de la Guerche et Montplaisir:
social relations of, with Mme Geoffrin, 7. 302, 332
Bruce, Bn. See Bruce Brudenell, Thomas Bruce (1729–1814); Brudenell Bruce, Charles (1773–1856)
Bruce, Lady. See Clerk, Magdalen (fl. ca 1631)
Bruce, Capt.:
tea ship at Boston commanded by, 23. 550n
Bruce, Miss (b. ca 1720):
(?) Cozens teaches, at Rome, 20. 145n
'great Irishman' marries, 20. 145
studies painting in Italy, 20. 145
Uffizi's pictures offend modesty of, 20. 145
Bruce, Mr:
Mann presents, at Tuscan Court, 23. 527n
Bruce, Mrs:
Conway's play acted by, 35. 391
Richmond House play may not include, 33. 580n
(?) SH visited by, 12. 229
uncle's death prevents, from acting at Richmond House, 34. 1n
Wonder, The, rehearsed by, at Mrs Damer's, 34. 1n
Bruce, Charles (1682–1747), 3d E. of Ailesbury:
daughter of, 11. 245n
dukedom declined by, 21. 26
last earl of his line, 26. 48
Lipyeatt intimate with, 20. 331
widow does not now mourn for, 22. 132
widow to remarry before burial of, 22. 132n
wife of, 2. 199n, 9. 50n, 11. 5n, 12. 160n, 15. 269n, 20. 264n, 30. 327n
Wiltshire and Yorkshire estates of, to go to Bn Bruce, 20. 331n
Bruce, Christian (1595–1675), m. (1608) William Cavendish, 2d E. of Devonshire, 1626:
Donne said to have celebrated, 41. 444
HW's account of, 34. 128
Pembroke, E. of, writes poems to, 41. 443
portrait of, HW asks to borrow, from D. of Bedford, 34. 131
Bruce, Henry:
Derry, Bp of, leaves art collections to, 25. 651n
Bruce, James (1730–94), African explorer:
Abyssinian and Theban musical instruments described by, in Burney's History, 28. 248–9
'Abyssinian Bruce,' 15. 331
camels said to be sent by, to America, 15. 331, 28. 248–9
camels sent to Abyssinia by, 32. 242
(?) HW alludes to, 33. 134

[Bruce, James, *continued*]

HW sceptical about narratives of, **11.** 239, **31.** 255

hyenas described by, **15.** 235

raw beef said by, to be eaten from living animals, **30.** 260

returns from Abyssinia, making Africa fashionable, **24.** 21

Selwyn's witticism about, **28.** 204–5, 250

story by, of Abyssinian king, ridiculed by HW, **28.** 248–9

traveller apes, **33.** 236–7

*Travels to Discover the Source of the Nile*: HW refers to, **11.** 358; HW's scepticism about, **11.** 239; HW sticks at first volume of, **39.** 474, 475–7; ridiculed, **34.** 92–3; story in, **28.** 249n

Bruce, Janet, m. (1601) Thomas Dalziel:

(?) letter mentions, **34.** 189

Bruce, Sir John:

Mathews's friend, **19.** 33n

Bruce, Lewis (1708–79), D.D.:

HW meets at Lady Shelburne's, **32.** 153–4

HW's quarrel with, **32.** 154

Bruce, Lady Marie-Thérèse-Charlotte (1704–36), m. (1722) Maximilian Emmanuel, P. of Hornes:

family of, **26.** 48

marriage of, **11.** 258n

Bruce, Lady Mary (1740–96), m. (1757) Charles Lennox, 3d D. of Richmond:

absent from home, **6.** 470

Ailesbury, Cts of, questions, about Ds of Leinster's marriage, **32.** 204

Albany, Cts of, cousin of, **11.** 258

Amyand reports to, about contraband imports, **38.** 124

Aubigny title of, at French Court, **4.** 418

Aubigny visited by, **31.** 79, **35.** 337

audience of, at Versailles, **7.** 295, **39.** 44

ball, masked, attended by, **7.** 300

Bath to be visited by **38.** 384

better dressed than usual, **38.** 117

biographical information on, corrected, **43.** 83, 157

Bouzols, Marquise de, discusses, **7.** 273

buried in Chichester Cathedral, **34.** 222n

Chichester visited by, from Goodwood, **39.** 80

childlessness of, **32.** 16

Conway and wife write to, of deferred departure from Paris, **39.** 247

Conway's step-daughter, **3.** 39n

Conway, Hon. Henrietta, receives Paris snuffbox from, **38.** 384

Coronation beauty, **9.** 387, **38.** 122, 126

Court presentation of, in France, delayed, **31.** 71, 79

Craven, Lady, attended by, at Drury Lane **29.** 43

Damer, Mrs, half-sister of, **25.** 576n

—— recognized by, in last moments, **34.** 222

—— to accompany, to Paris, **4.** 411

death of, **34.** 221–2

Du Deffand, Mme, asks if, is coming to Paris, **6.** 286

—— at service of, **4.** 297

—— attends Opéra-Comique with, **4.** 274, 275, 276

—— has print of, **6.** 359–60

—— sends messages to, **6.** 201

—— sent tea by, **6.** 317

——'s opinion of, **4.** 274, 276, 277, 278, 292–3, 294, 297

—— will be glad to see, **4.** 343, 411, 413

—— will write to HW by, **4.** 274, 278

Edward Augustus, D. of York, pursues, **9.** 234

—— snubbed by, in talk about *Guardian*, **9.** 234

*Elfrida* moves, to tears, **28.** 110

family of, **11.** 59n

fiancé gives balls for, **21.** 67

Fontainebleau visited by, **39.** 36

HW accompanies in Paris to: opera, **7.** 271, 328; Palais Marchand, **7.** 291; Sèvres, **7.** 271; shops, **7.** 270, 285, 294, 298; theatre, **7.** 271, 272, 297

HW anxious for arrival of, in Paris, **10.** 181, **30.** 202, **31.** 65, **39.** 259

HW asked by, not to mention Chatham's fit, **28.** 379

HW calls: his 'child,' **10.** 172; 'our pretty Duchess,' **30.** 202

HW can talk with, more freely than with her husband, **30.** 230–1

HW describes, **22.** 155

HW discusses Fox's earldom with, **30.** 231–2

HW escorts, on New Year's Eve, **32.** 26

HW expects, **7.** 270

HW expects to see, at Park Place, **35.** 289, **39.** 101

HW hears English gossip about him from, **31.** 73

HW hopes that Cts of Rochford will not efface, as ambassador's wife, **41.** 41

HW inquires for, **31.** 125

HW invited to visit, in Paris, **10.** 163, 172, 181, **32.** 18

HW makes purchases for, **7.** 411

HW may return with, through Holland, **35.** 338

HW mentions, **10.** 7

HW presents *Bishop Bonner's Ghost* to, **31.** 313n

HW receives ring of, at her request, **34.** 222

HW's bequest to, **30.** 354

(?) HW's correspondence with, **42.** 470

HW sees, in London, **39.** 341

HW sends parcel for, **7.** 378

HW's friendship with, **4.** 294, 297, **12.** 125

HW shops with, daily, **31.** 93

HW's interest in Richmond's career through, **3.** 39n

HW's tribute to, **34**. 221–2

HW's verses on Mme du Deffand interest, **4**. 275

HW to accompany, to Versailles for her audience, **39**. 44

HW to spend holidays with, **4**. 323

HW to tell, of her husband's imminent return, **37**. 537

HW will give Cts of Ailesbury's commission to, **39**. 36

HW writes to, for Lady Craven's address, **42**. 177

*Hamlet* avoided by, **4**. 281

health of: better, on Goodwood visit, **38**. 384; bled for fever instead of jaundice, **38**. 334; fever from Parliamentary attendance, **38**. 327, 334; HW's concern for, **12**. 198, 199, 200; illness, **12**. 125, 129, 135, 195, 199, 200; recovered, **12**. 188

Hertford, Cts of, well treated by, in Paris, **38**. 217, 222

Hertfords imagined, to be in London not Paris, **39**. 47

Hervey, Bns, mentions, **31**. 82

House of Commons never left by, in long session, **38**. 317–18

husband of: **9**. 188n; rejoins her, at Goodwood, **37**. 540–1; to be ambassador at Paris, **32**. 16, 18; to rejoin her, **35**. 289, **39**. 526

Keppel's election ball at Chichester attended by, **39**. 80–1

Lennox, Lady Cecilia, awaited by, **4**. 274, 275, 281

Lennox, Lord George, summoned by, in husband's illness, **33**. 77

less beautiful than Ds of Grafton, **32**. 1–2

London to be visited by, at Queen's Birthday, **34**. 1

—— visited by, **22**. 399n, **30**. 242

loo preferred to whist by, at Paris, **32**. 18

Mann compliments Conway on marriage of, **21**. 82

meal man taken in coach by, for backing Wilson in election, **39**. 207n

Merril accompanied by, in his chariot, **43**. 185

mother more beautiful than, **9**. 237, **22**. 67

Newport army camp visited by, **37**. 500

Paris disliked by, **31**. 93

—— may be visited by, **6**. 213, 214, **7**. 6, 26, 28, **10**. 163, 172, **35**. 317, 337

—— visited by, **4**. 114, **7**. 270, 327, **22**. 155, **31**. 125, **32**. 23

Poirier's visited by, **7**. 328

political activity of, **34**. 41n

returns from France, **4**. 313

Richmond's masquerade attended by, as Persian sultana, **22**. 148

(?) Saturday Club of, **14**. 121, **43**. 185

shell bench at SH occupied by, **9**. 237

social relations of, in England, with: Ailes-bury, Cts of, **12**. 135 (*see also* Conway and wife, *below*); Albemarle, Cts of, **37**. 484n, **38**. 400; Bedford, D. of, **38**. 400; Conolly, **9**. 234; Conway and wife, **37**. 483–4, 528, 534, 537n, **39**. 283, 419n, 469, 470, 526; Conway, Hon. Henrietta, **37**. 483–4; Damer, Mrs, **11**. 126, 307, **12**. 76; Fox, Henry and Lady Caroline, **37**. 483–4, 540n; HW, **9**. 234, 237, **11**. 59, 244–5, **12**. 188, **32**. 26, 345, **33**. 93, **35**. 289, **36**. 157, **38**. 400, **39**. 295; Ilchester, **37**. 483, 484n; Keppel, Adm., **33**. 93; Kildare, Cts of, **37**. 484n; Lennox, Ladies Louisa and Sarah, **37**. 484n; Waldegrave, Cts, **38**. 400

social relations of, in Paris, *see index entries ante* **8**. 270–1

Sussex election success pleases, **30**. 242

to return by way of Holland, **4**. 294

wedding of, at stepfather's house, **21**. 67n

*See also under* Goodwood

Bruce, Robert (1274–1329), K. of Scotland 1306–29:

Bruce, Lady Mary, descended from, **21**. 67, **28**. 110n

charter of, **7**. 359, **15**. 159

'Hymn to Liberty' celebrates reign of, **16**. 374

mésalliances of descendants of, **38**. 476

Bruce, Robert (ca 1626–85), 2d E. of Elgin, cr. (1664) E. of Ailesbury:

grandmother's letter to, **33**. 189

Bruce, Robert (d. 1787), of Bloomsbury Sq.:

(?) death of, **34**. 1n

Bruce, Thomas (1656–1741), 2d E. of Ailesbury:

Albany, Cts of, descended from, **25**. 538n, **26**. 48

children of, **11**. 258n, **26**. 48

outlawed, and died in Brussels, **25**. 538n, **26**. 48

Bruce, Thomas (d. 1782), Maj.:

(?) HW sends letters through, **7**. 380

Bruce, Thomas (1766–1841), 7th E. of Elgin; diplomatist:

courier of, brings Mary Berry's letter from Florence, **11**. 272

(?) Leopold II's interviews with, **11**. 262

Menin's recapture reported by, **39**. 505n

Paris left by, **11**. 27n

Bruce Brudenell (later Brudenell Bruce), Thomas Bruce (1729–1814), 2d Bn Bruce, 1747; cr. (1776) E. of Ailesbury, n.c.:

appointed George IV's governor and made E. of Ailesbury, **24**. 217

brother succeeds, as George IV's governor, **24**. 218

Conway and Cts of Ailesbury praised by, **20**. 331

daughter of, **9**. 188n

Florence visited by, **20**. 331, 336

George III adds, to Bedchamber, **21**. 460

HW asked by, to read MS of Knight's *Marcus Flaminius*, **34**. 168

[Bruce Brudenell, Thomas Bruce, *continued*]
Lipyeatt accompanies, **20.** 331
Lucca and Milan visited by, **20.** 336
Mann amazed at behaviour of, **24.** 225
—— to visit, at Siena, **20.** 391
Newcastle, D. of, not told about Bedchamber appointment of, **9.** 328–9
Parliamentary speech by, on Habeas Corpus, **37.** 529
Reynolds caricatures, at Rome, **20.** 331n
Somerset, D. of, may claim part of estate of, **20.** 331
uncle's Wiltshire and Yorkshire estates inherited by, **20.** 331n
wife of, **11.** 270n
wife says she will die if deprived of, **24.** 218
Wiltshire militia commanded by, **35.** 291n
Young's extravagances amuse, **20.** 331
Bruce Castle, Tottenham:
Townsend returns to, **23.** 346n
Bruce family:
arms of, compared with Sidney's, **32.** 47
HW has no partiality for, **32.** 47
mausoleum of, at Maulden, **39.** 139
mésalliances of, since King Robert, **38.** 476
Bruciato, Palazzo, Florence:
Wynn gives dinner at, **23.** 64
Brudenell, Bns. *See* Legge, Anne (d. 1786)
Brudenell, Lady Anna Maria (d. 1702), m. 1 (1659) Francis Talbot, 11th E. of Shrewsbury; m. 2 (before 1677) George Rodney Bridges:
Gramont's *Mémoires* mentions, **32.** 199
sister of, **32.** 199, **34.** 260
Brudenell, Anne (d. 1722), m. 1 (before 1672) Henry Belasyse, 2d Bn Belasyse; m. 2 (1693) Charles Lennox, 1st D. of Richmond:
son of, **19.** 241n
Westmorland, Lady, aunt of, **32.** 199
Brudenell, Catherine (ca 1648–1743), m. (ca 1670) Charles Middleton, 2d E. of Middleton, 1673:
family of, **34.** 260
Hampton Court beauty, **34.** 260
Brudenell, Lady Dorothy (ca 1647–1740), m. 1 Charles Fane, 3d E. of Westmorland; m. 2 (1697) Robert Constable, 3d Vct Dunbar:
died smoking a pipe, **32.** 200
family of, **34.** 260
HW's research on, **32.** 199–200
Twickenham home of, **32.** 199
Brudenell, Lady Elizabeth. *See* Montagu, Lady Elizabeth (1743–1827)
Brudenell, Hon. Frances (ca 1673–1756), m. 1 (1692) Charles Livingston, 2d E. of Newburgh, 1670; m. 2 (1695) Richard Bellew, 3d Bn Bellew; m. 3 Sir Thomas Smythe, 2d Bt, 1697:
'Myra,' **32.** 199, **34.** 260
Westmorland, Lady, aunt of, **32.** 199
Brudenell, Lady Frances, m. (1749) Oliver Tilson:
portrait of, at Boughton House, **10.** 341

Brudenell, George (d. 1732), 3d E. of Cardigan, 1703:
family of, **9.** 273n, **14.** 2n, **34.** 260
house pulled down by, at Kirkstall, **35.** 270
Brudenell (after 1749, Montagu), George (1712–90), 4th E. of Cardigan; cr. (1766) D. of Montagu:
'antiquated Duke,' **33.** 259
Banks, Peggy, added to, by poem, **9.** 38n
Beauclerk, Lady Diana, buys house next to, at foot of Richmond Hill, **42.** 490
Beaulieu, Lady, ill-treated by, **33.** 299
Bedford dislikes rumoured marquisate for, **38.** 392–3
blue ribbon of Garter order conferred on, **20.** 309, 311
Boughton House avoided by, during lawsuit, **10.** 89
—— visited by, **10.** 89, 340
brother of, **11.** 241n, **24.** 217n, **25.** 86n
brother succeeded by, as George IV's governor, **24.** 218
Bute unable to obtain dukedom for, **30.** 247
children of, bear Montagu name, **10.** 341
chimneys of, in Privy Garden, blown down, **24.** 431n
cold dinner brought by, **10.** 89
company of, at regatta, **32.** 237n
Court attended by, **22.** 79n
daughter of, **11.** 121n
deafness of, **32.** 216
death of, **11.** 161n, **42.** 286
Deene Park to be visited by, **10.** 89
dukedom conferred on, **10.** 233, **22.** 462
equipage of, **10.** 89
Garter installation of, **20.** 311n
genealogy of, **10.** 351
George III had not wanted to entail dukedom on children of, by another wife, **24.** 99n
—— saves, after overthrow of ministry, **25.** 273
George IV's birthday celebrated by, in scarlet and gold, **32.** 316
HW and Lysons visit house of, at Richmond, **11.** 105
HW asks, to get Windsor post for Bevan, **40.** 173–4
HW avoids meeting, **10.** 340
HW buys porringer for, **7.** 409
HW condemns renunciation by, of Brudenell names, **10.** 27
HW's correspondence with, **40.** 173–4
HW to meet, at Lady Sophia Thomas's at Hampton Court, **37.** 297
houses of: **11.** 341n; at Kirkstall Abbey, **35.** 270; HW visits, at Blackheath, **35.** 234; in Privy Gardens, has pictures from Holland, **38.** 357; near Richmond, **11.** 341n; scenery of, **32.** 318
may become George IV's governor, **20.** 345
'Mentor,' **32.** *315*
Montagu offered lodge by, in Rockingham forest, **10.** 200

Presle has Rubens landscape like that of, 7. 346

print-framing invented by, 20. 381

Queensberry, Ds of, invites, to ball, 38. 342

remarriage of, probable, 24. 99

Robinson, Sir George, promised Rockingham Forest post by, 10. 200

sets out for Scotland, 29. 68

Shrewsbury papers supposedly owned by, 42. 286

son of, 22. 31n

uncle of, 14. 2n

wife mourned by, in weepers, 32. 315–16

wife of, 9. 28n

wife's bequest to, 24. 99

wife treated deferentially by, 10. 341

wife wants Monthermer title for, 10. 27

Windsor Castle's constable and governor, 40. 173n

Brudenell, George Bridges (1725–1801), of Peterhouse College, Cambridge; M.P.:
candidate for Peterhouse fellowship, 14. 1–2, 4

joke by, on Bute's Treasury appointment, 10. 35

Lowther's legacy to, 9. 184

Brudenell, Hon. James (ca 1687–1746), M.P.:
birth date of, 43. 180

son of, 14. 2n

Brudenell, Hon. James (1725–1811), cr. (1780) Bn Brudenell; 5th E. of Cardigan, 1790; M.P.:
advanced age of, 11. 242

at home in ball-room, 33. 274

barony conferred on, 25. 86

Beauclerk, Lady Diana, visited by, 33. 195

Bedchamber post sought by, 37. 386, 387

biographical information about, corrected, 43. 273

brother of, 11. 241n

can write volumes full of matter, 32. 302

Clare succeeded by, as deputy, 20. 517

George III's Master of the Robes, 9. 291

HW's dancing would make, envious, 33. 282

lethargy of, 'serene house of Brudenel,' 33. 269

Lincoln probably supports Bedchamber candidacy of, 37. 387

marriages of: 11. 241–2; expected, 9. 291; second, 34. 110

may not be laughed at in future reign, 34. 39

Mount Edgcumbe, Lady, entertained by, 12. 164

musicale at Lady Lucan's attended by, 33. 139

peerage of, 25. 86, 33. 235, 36. 174

seat of, in Northamptonshire, 12. 164

son of, 9. 184n

verses perhaps by, 33. 299

White's Club admits, in HW's newspaper parody, 9. 127

Brudenell, Mrs James. See Burton, Susan; Legge, Anne (d. 1786)

Brudenell, James Thomas (1797–1868), 7th E. of Cardigan, 1837:
trial of, decorated in crimson, 19. 280n

Brudenell, John. See Montagu, John (1735–70)

Brudenell, Hon. Mary (ca 1680–1766), m. (1705) Richard Molyneux, 5th Vct Molyneux:
toast of Kit Cat Club, 32. 199

Westmorland, Lady, aunt of, 32. 199

Brudenell, Lady Mary (b. ca 1717), m. 1 (1735) Richard Powys; m. 2 (1754) Thomas Bowlby:
(?) at Chesterfield's assembly, 37. 326

HW mentions, 37. 418

Hertford, Cts of, entrusts genealogical query to, for HW, 38. 476

Hervey, Elizabeth, gets objections from, about bow window, 39. 470n

Sion House visited by, 38. 429

Brudenell, Robert (1607–1703), 2d E. of Cardigan:
arms of, in English Benedictines' church at Paris, 7. 264

Brudenell, Robert (1769–1837), 6th E. of Cardigan, 1811:
disappointed at E. of Cardigan's marriage, 11. 241–2

Brudenell, Hon. Robert (1726–68), army officer; M.P.:
Magdalen House visited by, 9. 273–4

Brudenell, Mrs Robert. See Bisshopp, Anne

Brudenell Bruce, Charles (1773–1856), styled Bn Bruce; 2d E. of Ailesbury, n. c., 1814; cr. (1821) M. of Ailesbury:
imprisoned in Languedoc, 11. 139–40

lives abroad, 11. 139n

Brudenell Bruce, Thomas Bruce. See Bruce Brudenell, Thomas Bruce

Bruère, La. See Leclerc de la Bruère

Bruern Abbey, Oxon, Cope's seat:
Montagu visits, 9. 146

Brueys, David-Augustin (1640–1723), abbé; dramatist:
Grondeur, Le, cited, 3. 194, 309

Théâtre by, owned by Mme du Deffand, 8. 33

Bruffe, co. Limerick:
Hartstonge of, 2. 39n

Bruges, Elizabeth. See Brydges, Elizabeth

Bruges, Giles. See Brydges, Giles

Bruges, William (d. 1449), Garter king-of-arms:
HW asks for plate of, 15. 250

Bruges, Belgium:
Bening of, 14. 117n

Englefield nun in convent at, 37. 118

English army at, 18. 327n, 37. 160

French play given at, 38. 4

French seize, 19. 67

Joseph II and D. of Gloucester confer at, 29. 151n, 33. 275

visitors to: Conway, 37. 118, 151, 152–3, 38. 3–4; Du Barail, 38. 4

Bruhier d'Ablaincourt, Jean-Jacques (d. 1756):
Observations intéressantes sur la . . . goutte

[Bruhier d'Ablaincourt, J.-J., *continued*]
adapted by, from Friedrich Hoffman, etc.,
22. 450n
Brühl, Gräfin von. *See* Carpenter, Alicia Maria
Brühl, Friedrich Aloys (1739–93), Polish official:
rejected as nuncio, 22. 192
Brühl, Hans Moritz (1736–1809), Graf von;
Saxon envoy to England 1764–1809:
birth date of, corrected, 43. 99
Friedrich III's Garter ensigns returned by, to
England, 23. 442n
HW to receive goods through, 6. 252
has print of Mudge engraved, 1. 282, 43. 57
(?) riddle by Mme du Deffand guessed by,
31. 83
stepson's engagement pleases, 33. 205
wife of, 9. 342n, 25. 68n, 28. 286n
Brühl, Heinrich (1700–63), Graf von; prime
minister of Poland and Saxony:
Frederick II abuses, 21. 2
Frederick Augustus's prime minister, 21. 2n,
320n
HW probably informed about, by Sir C. H.
Williams, 21. 320n
Menzel copies dispatches of, for Frederick II,
21. 5n
son of, 22. 192
Stormont, Vct, deep in German feasting at
house of, 37. 472–3
—— requested by, to visit Frederick II at
Torgau, 21. 2n
'tawdry toad,' may re-enter Dresden, 21. 320
Williams, C. H., quarrels with, 30. 322
Bruière, La. *See* Bruyères
Bruise; bruises:
from carriage accident, 10. 135
from fall, 11. 46
from horse's fall, 11. 258
HW's, 11. 19, 25, 70
kick of Conway's horse leaves, on D. of Cumberland's leg, 37. 382
occurrences of, 16. 310, 34. 49, 50, 63–64, 65
Bruiser; bruisers:
from Bear Garden, 18. 538
Vernon accuses Rigby of carrying Sudbury
election by use of, 30. 331n
Brulart, Mme. *See* Ducrest de St-Aubin, Stéphanie-Félicité
Brulart, ——:
mother to live with, at Beauvais, 6. 169
Brulart, Anne, m. (1690) Gaspard de Vichy,
Comte de Champrond:
daughter's scepticism alarms, 8. 54
family of, 4. 284
Brulart, Charles-Alexis (1737–93), Comte de
Genlis; later Marquis de Sillery:
Chartres, Duc de, accompanied by, at Florence, 25. 348n
——'s capt. of the guard, 7. 448
guillotined, 12. 66
La Woestyne announced by, 7. 449
—— ceded captaincy of guard by, 7. 448

social relations of, with Mme du Deffand, 7.
449, 450
wife of, 6 293n, 11. 303n, 29. 181n
Brulart, Jacqueline-Charlotte, m. (1689) André-
Louis de Loménie, Comte de Brienne:
aunt of Mme du Deffand, 3. 28n, 166n
Brulart, Louis-Philogène (1702–71), Vicomte
('Marquis') de Puisieulx:
Argenson replaced by, 19. 429n
(?) behaviour of valet of, 3. 152–3
St-Contest succeeds, as secretary of state for
foreign affairs, 20. 286
Sandwich and, decide on congress at Aix-la-
Chapelle, 19. 430n
—— sends passports to, for peace plenipoten-
tiaries, 19. 446n
social relations of, with Comtesse d'Egmont,
7. 284
Young Pretender ordered by, to leave French
dominions, 20. 8n
Brulart, Marie (ca 1685–1763), m. 1 (1704)
Louis-Joseph de Béthune, Marquis de
Charost; m. 2 (1732) Charles-Philippe d'Albert, Duc de Luynes; Mme du Deffand's aunt:
Champrond pays Mme du Deffand's legacy
from, with annuity, 8. 40, 45
Du Deffand, Mme, has herself painted by
Gobert for, 8. 215
——'s aunt, 8. 55
——'s portrait of, 8. 102–3
Du Roure, Mme, sued, 3. 379
Hénault's letter from, written upon by Queen,
41. 37–8
Marie Leszczyńska's favourite, 8. 55, 41. 37n
——'s service from, rewarded by pension for
Mme du Deffand, 3. 5n, 4. 354, 386
second marriage of, 8. 102
settlement of estate of, 8. 36–7
Brulart, Marie-Anne-Claude (d. 1750), m.
(1687), Henri, Duc d'Harcourt:
grandmother of Comtesse de Guerchy, 3. 114n
Brulart, Nicolas (1627–92), Marquis de la
Borde; president of Parliament of Burgundy;
Mme du Deffand's grandfather:
Bussy's correspondence with, 5. 188
Choiseul, Duchesse de, widow of, 3. 166n,
8. 36
Brulart, Nicolas, bourgeois of Paris:
(?) Devreux, widow of, 8. 40
Brulart, Mme Nicolas. *See* Devreux (?) Louise-
Catherine
Brulart, Pierre, seigneur de Broussin:
Chapelle's friend, 4. 284
(?) verses on, 4. 284
Brulart de Genlis, Caroline-Charlotte-Jeanne-
Séraphine (d. 1786), m. (1780) Charles-
Ghislain-Antoine-François de Paule-Armand
de la Woestyne de Becelaere, Marquis de la
Woestyne:
acts plays written by her mother, 7. 161, 164–5
Chartres, Duchesse de, to make, extra lady in
waiting, 7. 448
marriage of, 7. 448

Brulart de Genlis, Édmée-Nicole-Pulchérie (1767–1847), m. (1784) Jean-Baptiste-Cyrus-Marie-Adélaïde de Timbrune-Thiembronne, Comte de Valence (divorced, 1793):
acts plays written by her mother, 7. 161, 164–5
Brulart de Puisieulx de Sillery, Adélaïde-Félicité (1725–86), m. (1744) Louis-Charles-César le Tellier de Louvois, Maréchal-Duc d'Estrées:
HW dislikes, 40. 387
Karl Wilhelm Ferdinand may be given balls by, 30. 220
mad dog bites, 30. 220
March's 'passion' for, 38. 478, 40. 387
social relations of, with: Du Deffand, Mme, 7. 431; Praslin, Duchesse de, 7. 263
Brull. See Brühl
Brumoy, Pierre (1688–1742):
Aristophanes translated by, 21. 52
'Brumpton, Lady.' See under Steele, Richard: Funeral, The
Brumpton. See also Brompton
Brumstead ('Brunstead'), Norfolk:
HW's will mentions, 30. 368, 369
manor in, see Parkers
Brun, Le. See Le Brun
Bruna, French frigate:
off Leghorn, 25. 199
Brunalleschi ('Brunaleski'), Filippo (1377–1446), architect:
Serchio River's diversion advised by, 20. 514
Brunati, Pierre, Brigadier:
captured at Velletri, 18. 493
Brunau. See Braunau
Brundusium, Italy:
Agrippina's experiences at, might be paralleled by Ds of Gloucester's, 24. 326
See also Brindisi
Brune, P. de (fl. 1650–67), engraver:
print by, of Jacob Hall, 1. 182
Bruneau. See Braunau
Brunehault; Brunehaut; or Brunhilde (ca 543–613), Q. of Austrasia:
death of, 34. 73
HW compares Catherine II to, 22. 64
Brunet, ——, HW's servant in Paris:
(?) hired, 6. 214
wages of, 7. 413
Brunet, Jean:
translates Lady Mary Wortley Montagu's letters, 6. 282n
Brunet, Tressemanes de. See Tressemanes de Brunet
Brunetta, La, Italian fortress:
HW and Gray see, 13. 190
'Brunette,' Conway's dog:
'Patapan' to be saluted by, 37. 158
Bruni, ——, courier:
Henry Benedict (Stuart) accompanied by, to Avignon, 19. 140
Mann's 'little friend' questions, 19. 140
Young Pretender supposedly accompanied by, to Spain, 19. 140–1, 198

Brunier, Pierre-Édouard (d. 1811), physician to Louis XVI's children:
Madame Royale attended by, 34. 180
Brunn, Francesco Saverio. See Breen, François Xavier
Brünn (Germany):
Frederick II threatens, 17. 316
Brunne, Bns of:
pedigree of, 2. 115
Brunne, Robert of. See Mannyng, Robert
Bruno, St (ca 1030–1100):
Le Sueur's paintings of life of, 13. 169, 28. 245
Bruno, Alfonse, Ensign:
captured at Velletri, 18. 493
Brunoy, Marquis de. See Paris de Montmartel, Armand-Louis-Joseph (1748–81); Paris de Montmartel, Jean (1690–1766)
Brunoy, Marquise de. See Pérusse des Cars, Françoise-Émilie
Brunoy, château in France:
Louis XVIII entertains Louis XVI and Marie-Antoinette at, 6. 365, 368
Brunswick, D. of, see Karl Wilhelm Ferdinand
Brunswick, Hereditary P. of. See Karl Wilhelm Ferdinand
Brunswick, P. Alexis of. See Alexis
Brunswick, P. Peter of. See Peter
Brunswick, Ps of. See Augusta (1737–1813)
Brunswick, Ps Catherine and Ps Elizabeth of. See Catherine (1741–1807) and Elizabeth (1743–82)
Brunswick:
china from, 39. 177
Conway and Scott visit, 39. 537
France to restore lands taken from, 21. 526n
HW advises Cts of Ailesbury not to venture to, 38. 84–5
Legard's credentials to, 28. 251
Soubise threatens, 21. 226n
troops from: army of observation contains, 21. 73n; captured with Burgoyne, 24. 345n; England retains, for American war, 24. 175
Brunswick, N. J.:
Cornwallis halts at, 28. 282n
Brunswick, Hôtel de, Paris:
Young Pretender at, 5. 111n
Brunswick, house of:
absent friends never remembered by, 36. 328
Gloucesters' 'babe' of, to be born at Rome, 32. 249
HW's term for English royal family, 28. 417
Hardwick Hall, if built by a duchess of, would not interest HW, 35. 304–5
'immortality' of, 30. 204–5
Newcastle's enthusiasm for, 40. 386
Brunswick-Bevern, P. and D. of. See August Wilhelm
Brunswick-Lunenburg, house of:
memoirs of, see under Belsham, William
Brunswick-Wolfenbüttel, Ds of. See Augusta (1737–1813) of England; Charlotte (1716–1801) of Prussia; Elizabeth (1683–1767) of

[Brunswick-Wolfenbüttel, Ds of, *continued*]
Holstein-Norburg; Elizabeth (1718–46) of
Mecklenburg-Schwerin

Brunswick Wolfenbüttel, D. of. *See* Anton
Ulrich (1714–74); August Wilhelm (d. 1731);
Karl I (1713–80); Karl Wilhelm Ferdinand
(1735–1806)

Brunswick-Wolfenbüttel, P. of. *See* Anton
Ulrich (1714–74); Karl Wilhelm Ferdinand
(1735–1806)

Brunswick-Wolfenbüttel, Ps of. *See* Anna
Amalie (1739–1807); Augusta (1737–1813);
Sophie Karoline (1737–1817)

Brunswick-Wolfenbüttel, Prince Maximilian
Julius Leopold of:
Florence visited by, 24. 113n

Brunton, Ann (1769–1808), m. 1 (1791) Robert
Merry; m. 2 (1803) Thomas Wignell; m. 3
(1806) William Warren; actress:
acknowledged as Mrs Merry, 11. 352
remains on the stage, 11. 352

Brusati, ——, wife of Gianpietro Brusati, m. 2
Barbon, Conte Millerio:
granddaughter to be taken to Lyon by, 7. 77,
133, 135, 317

Brusati, Costanza (d. 1804), m. (1767) Giacomo,
Marchese Fagnani:
daughter not allowed by, to go to England,
7. 148
daughter not to be reclaimed by, 33. 196
daughter to be taken by, to Lyon, 7. 77, 133,
135, 137
daughter used by, to attract Selwyn, 33. 36
Du Deffand, Mme, criticizes, 7. 145
inexplicable conduct of, 30. 269
Selwyn dissatisfied with, 7. 143
—— may be poisoned by, 30. 266

Brusby, Mr:
SH visited by, 12. 266

Brusby, James (d. 1786), consul at Madeira:
(?) ball, masked, attended by, 7. 300
(?) HW accompanies, to shops, 7. 285

Brush; brushes:
HW's economy in, at Houghton, 32. 143
HW to send, to Bentley, 35. 252

Brussels, Archduchess of. *See* Maria Anna
(1718–44); Maria Elizabeth (1680–1741)

Brussels:
Ailesbury, E. of, died at, 25. 538n, 26. 48
(?) Archduke Leopold's gallery at, painted
by Teniers, 40. 5
Austrian appendage, 25. 502
Austrians occupy, 39. 484
banker at, 11. 85n
Botta leaves, for Vienna, 20. 320n
—— seats Newcastles and nuncio at dinner
at, 22. 44
Bulstrode diplomatic representative at, 17.
11n
Cecil marries actress from theatre at, 10. 344
Charles, P., to go to, as administrator, 18. 331
Dillon marries Henrietta Phipps in, 32. 312

Elgin minister at, 11. 272n
English army at, retreats beyond it, 19. 71
English minister at, *see* Gordon, Sir William
French besiege, 19. 209, 215
Gloucester, D. of, said to return from, 33. 275
HW addresses letters to, for Berrys, 11. 367,
371
HW expects Berrys' arrival at, 11. 372
Hanger, Hon. William, may get post at, 24.
236
Joseph II's auction of pictures, jewels, etc.
at, 33. 486–7
—— sends Cobenzl to negotiate at, 34. 87n
La Borde, Mme, from, 7. 280
lace of, 23. 93, 32. 154, 182, 38. 87
letters from: mention Louis XV, 21. 44; un-
authentic, 34. 185
loss of, 19. 218
Montmorency, Mlle de, at convent at, 7. 92
Paris's distance from, 7. 88
peace negotiations at, end in deadlock, 19.
271n
postmaster-general at, receives news, 37. 158
St Albans, D. of, retires to, for debt, 21. 171,
172
tapestries executed at, 16. 157n
Tempi nuncio at, 19. 94
Teniers's views of, 5. 148n, 7. 373
Van der Borchts of, 1. 24n
unsettled state of, 11. 360
visitors to: Ancrams, 37. 119; Breteuil, 11.
36n; Burdett, 20. 20; Chandos, Ds of, 33.
291n; Churchill, Charles (poet), 38. 270n;
Coke, Lady Mary, 33. 292–3; Constable,
23. 244; Conway, 21. 103n, 37. 119, 39. 536;
Craufurd, 32 263; Friedrich Wilhelm of
Hesse, 19 202; Gleichen, 5. 370; Hawley,
19. 202; Joseph II, 33. 291n; Kellie, 33.
299n; Leopold II, 39. 536; Louis XVIII and
wife, 11. 303n; Metternich, 12. 3; Necker,
11. 36n; Piennes, Duc de, 11. 256n; Scott,
David, 39. 536; Spencers, 5. 367; Torrington, Vcts, 33. 210n, 291n; Torringtons, 33.
210n; Windham, 25. 79

Brussels Gazette:
Bourbon family compact announced in 21.
544n
Chesterfield's letter worthy of, 38. 30
Mann often sees, 21. 281n

'Brute, Sir John.' *See under* Vanbrugh, Sir John:
*Provok'd Wife*

Bruté de Lorelle, Abbé:
translates *The Gamester*, 4. 44n,

Bruton St, Berkeley Sq., London:
Cornell, print-seller in, 33. 401n
Dacre lives in, 29. 129n, 41. 392
Sheridan's house in, 11. 321
Townshend, Mary, to welcome HW at, 40. 46
Walpole of Wolterton, Bn, writes from, 36.
162

'Brutus, Dame'; 'Brutus, Old.' *See* Lloyd, Katherine (Mrs French)

'Brutus':
popular signature for letters to newspapers,
42. 500
Brutus, Marcus Junius (85–42 B.C.), conspira-
tor:
Baretti denounces, 29. 139
bust of: by Bernini, 35. 268; by Boiston, re-
ceived by National Assembly, 34. 175
Cæsar's correspondence compared to that of,
41. 305
Cicero's epistles to, deemed spurious by Tun-
stall, 15. 304
compared with justice of the peace, 33. 158
Et tu Brute, applied to Lord Holland, 33. 259
Florence needs a new, 37. 97
Fox, C. J., resembles, 23. 499
HW alludes to, 15. 131, 28. 462, 29. 84
HW alludes to Mann as, 22. 568
HW compares: to Pitt, 10. 272; with justice
of the peace, 33. 158
HW does not want Cæsar for the sake of, 23.
151
HW quotees speech of, from Julius Cæsar, 15.
158
HW refers to Conway as, 23. 180
Harcourt's ring of, 29. 329, 332
Labour in Vain mentions, 18. 119
Livy's lies about, 21. 541
medal of, copied for Lorenzino de' Medici's,
15. 278
More, Hannah, discusses, 31. 249
Nugent's verses mention, 31. 269
Razumovskiĭ not HW's idea of, 22. 456
story of, in The Roman Sacrifice, 32. 409
See also under Middleton, Conyers, Epistles
of Cicero and Brutus
Bruxelles. See Brussels
Bruyère. See La Bruyère
Bruyères (France):
Maupeou exiled to, 6. 87, 32. 205
Bruyers, Capt.:
Mann escorted by, 23. 60n
Bruyn, Mr de:
SH visited by, 12. 242
Bryan, Count, of Bury:
print of, 1. 188, 223, 227
Bryan, Elizabeth, m. (1514) Sir Nicholas Carew:
family of, 38. 125n
Bryan, Barony of:
Somerset, Ds of, inherited, 20. 11n
Bryant, Jacob (1715–1804), classical scholar;
Fellow of King's College, Cambridge:
Address to Dr Priestley by, 2. 212, 43. 71
affable to Cole, 1. 370
antiquity of Rowley poems accepted by, 29.
129
Archæological Epistle attacks, 2. 314
ascribes learning to barbarians, 33. 478
books of, too elevated for Cole, 2. 216
Chattertonian writings of, 2. 294n, 33. 319n,
42. 1–2
Chatterton said by, to lack genius, 16. 332

——'s poems attributed by, to third person,
16. 354
Cole and Apthorpe dine with, 1. 349n
Cole's neighbour at Burnham, 2. 5
——'s opinion of, 2. 291
—— visited by, 2. 172
Conway's opinion of, 33. 317
fêted at Cambridge, 2. 172
HW's letter pleases, 2. 172
HW's opinion of, 2. 314
HW to be visited by, 1. 370
ingenuity of, gives weight to Rowleyans, 42.
13–14
knows of Keene's treatment of Mrs Daye, 2.
373n
mastership of Charterhouse declined by, 2.
172
New System, or an Analysis of Ancient Mythology, A, by, 1. 368, 370, 28. 140, 146, 251,
29. 169n, 43. 63
Observations and Inquiries . . . Ancient History by 1 253
Observations upon the Poems of Thomas
Rowley by, 2. 284, 287–9, 290, 291, 296, 16.
236–7, 239, 333–4, 351–7, 29. 169, 171–2,
176, 183, 186, 195, 206, 33. 316, 35. 522,
43. 74
originals of Chatterton's poems probably not
seen by, 16. 356
'Planetæ sunt habitabiles': sent by HW to
Conway, 37. 18; West's comments on, 13.
128–9
seeks proof of authenticity of Rowley poems,
2. 277–8
Bryant, Robert (d. 1788), 'surgeon-page' and
page of the presence to D. of Gloucester:
death of, 36. 126n
Gloucester, D. of, advised by, to return to
England, 32. 362
—— attended by, 24. 315. 34. 245
letters from, about D. of Gloucester, 32. 379,
35. 472–3, 36. 126, 138, 139
Bryas, Comte de:
Mme du Deffand's picture in collection of,
8. 216
Brydges, Lady Caroline (1730–1804), m. (1755)
James Leigh:
SH visited by, 12. 239, 240, 246
Brydges, Lady Charlotte (b. and d. 1778):
baptism of, 33. 59
Brydges, Edmund (d. 1573), 2d Bn Chandos:
arms of, 1. 342
marriage of, 1. 342n
Brydges, Rev. Edward Tymewell (1749–1807):
dines with Cole, 2. 101
HW not acquainted with, 2. 103
Brydges, Elizabeth (?1575–1617), m. (1603) Sir
John Kennedy, Kt:
Custodis's portrait of, 41. 252
Brydges, Hon. Frances (ca 1580–1663), m. 1
Sir Thomas Smith; m. 2 (1610) Thomas Cecil,
cr. (1605) E. of Exeter:

[Brydges, Hon. Frances, *continued*]
birth date of, corrected, **43.** 53
Faithorne's print of, **1.** 149–50, 150, 154, 179
HW related to, **1.** 149–50, 150
refuses to be buried at husband's left hand, **9.** 7
Van Dyck's portrait of, **1.** 149–50
Brydges, Giles (ca 1548–94), 3d Bn Chandos, 1573:
daughter of, **41.** 252
portraits of: at Woburn, **33.** 322; HW's given to Harcourt, **33.** 322, **35.** 533n
Brydges, Grey (ca 1579–1621), 5th Bn Chandos:
*Horæ subsecivæ* attributed to, **16.** 140
Brydges, Henry (1708–71), 2d D. of Chandos; M.P.:
Canons the estate of, **10.** 77n
chamberlain's post sought by, **10.** 29
death of, delights family, **31.** 164
Hamilton to succeed, as K. B., **23.** 358
unmarried, **10.** 29
Brydges, James (1674–1744), 1st D. of Chandos:
birth date of, corrected, **43.** 73
Canons built by, **2.** 275, **36.** 246n
foreigner prepared landscape plans for, **30.** 61
Van der Myn's portrait of wife and, **30.** 61
Zincke's miniature of, **35.** 477n
Brydges, James (1731–89), styled M. of Carnarvon; 3d D. of Chandos, 1771; M.P.:
daughter of, baptized, **28.** 449n
marriage of, **20.** 238n
Parliamentary bill providing for Chatham's son opposed by, **29.** 248
Parliamentary motion by, for adjournment, **25.** 459n
resignation of, from Bedchamber and lord lieutenancy, on Stanley's appointment to Isle of Wight, **38.** 417–18
resigns as lord lieutenant of Hampshire, **7.** 207
Stuart supported by, in Hampshire election, **38.** 474n
wife of, **14.** 193n, **28.** 446n, **30.** 168n
Brydges, Sir Samuel Egerton (1762–1837), cr. (1814) Bt; editor:
brother of, **2.** 101n
SH visited by, **12.** 240
Brydges. *See also* Bridges
Brydone, Patrick (1736–1818), traveller:
birth date of, corrected, **43.** 98
Keene, Mrs, entertains, **33.** 232
*Tour through Sicily and Malta, A,* by, **6.** 189, **33.** 232
Brydson, Mr, employed in John Ash's nursery:
SH visited by, **12.** 251
Bryll, Count:
Miss Ashe's alleged lover, **9.** 106n
Brytaine. *See* Brittany
Bubb Dodington, George (?1691–1762), cr. (1761) Bn Melcombe; politician; M.P.:
actors familiarly treated by, at play, **9.** 382

Admiralty post may go to, **10.** 35
Argyll supported by, **30.** 292n
Augusta, Ps of Wales, excludes, **20.** 263
—— waiting on by, to take his leave, **20.** 263n
ballad by, **33.** 556–7, **34.** 262–3
(?) Bentley may choose, for hero, **10.** 113
Bentley may write panegyric to, **9.** 417
——'s epistle to, **9.** 408–9, **35.** 645
——'s *Wishes* attended by, **9.** 382
——'s *Wishes* read by, **9.** 373, 382
——'s *Wishes* shown to, by Cumberland and carried to Bute, **35.** 645
biographical information about, corrected, **43.** 241
Bute is called 'Pollio' by, **28.** 242
Byng's pardon advocated by, **21.** 63
Carlton House's first minister, **20.** 96
Catiline imitated by, **30.** 292n
Chamfelt, Countess, subject of joke by, **9.** 167
circle of, **9.** 66n
*Conduct of the Last and Present Ministry* attributed to, **18.** 9
Cornish boroughs turned by, against Sir Robert Walpole, **30.** 292n
coronet loved by, **38.** 130
Court party not joined by, **18.** 118
Cumberland brings Bentley's *Wishes* to, **9.** 373, 381n, **35.** 645
Dashwood and Talbot support, **20.** 39
death of, **10.** 36, **22.** 56, 76
*Diary* of, **25.** 503, **31.** 214–15, **33.** 440, **39.** 411–13, 414, **42.** 123
Eastbury, estate of, goes to Lord Temple, **21.** 39n
——, seat of, **1.** 172, **40.** 9, **43.** 273
Egremont may be succeeded by, as secretary of state, **22.** 17, 23n
*Epistle from John Moore, Apothecary of Abchurch Lane, to L—— C—— upon his Treatise of Worms,* **30.** 316
*Epistle to the Right Honourable Sir Robert Walpole, An,* by, **30.** 292n, 316
'ethic epistles' by, **34.** 35n
Exchequer post refused by, **21.** 74
Fox, Henry, adherent of, **21.** 74
—— clerk of the pells after death of, **21.** 75n
Frederick, P. of Wales, adds, to his party, **20.** 3n
—— disgusted by, **17.** 354
——'s favourite, **18.** 426n, **30.** 292n
——'s hand kissed by, accepting promises, **20.** 245n
——'s offer accepted by, **20.** 39n
—— thanks Mann through, **22.** 583
Fuentes family entertained by, at Hammersmith, **35.** 301–2
George II disgusted by, **17.** 354
Glover's opinion of, **31.** 215
Grenville succeeded by, as treasurer of the Navy, **20.** 517, 518
—— succeeds as treasurer of the Navy, **21.** 25

grows fat after changing sides, **17**. 257–8

HW congratulates, **9**. 344

HW reassures Mann about debts from, **20**. 250

HW's 'character' of, **30**. 292n

HW's 'morsels of criticism' mention flaming pyre of, **31**. 281

HW's opinion of, **31**. 215, **39**. 411–12

HW to visit, at Eastbury, **37**. 202

Halifax told by, he is to be treasurer of Navy, **21**. 74n

. Harrington, Cts of, receives card from, **9**. 344

health of: dropsy, **10**. 36; falls down kitchen stairs, **35**. 308

Hervey, Bns, friend of, **31**. 416

house of: Stanley draws plan of, for HW, **30**. 71; *see also under* Eastbury; Hammersmith

House of Commons avoided by, **20**. 263n

illumination by, **19**. 249

inconsolable at Hammersmith, **20**. 263

Irish Clerk of the Pells, **21**. 75

Leicester House faction not controlled by, **20**. 39

letter of, hints at return to politics, **20**. 521

Lyttelton may supplant, in Navy post, **9**. 72

—— supplants, after being introduced by him, with Frederick, P. of Wales, **30**. 292n

Mann advised by, about new credentials, **21**. 455

—— amused by return of, to old post, **20**. 518, 521

—— arranged with, for Frederick, P. of Wales's purchase of Francavilla statues, **20**. 241, 251, 253, **21**. 479, **25**. 93–4

—— comments on treatment of, **17**. 370

—— condoles with, on wife's death, **21**. 49

—— encouraged by, to hope for Bath knighthood, **22**. 235, 314, 317

—— expects letter from, about P. of Wales's bills, **20**. 241, 251, 263

—— has marble pavement made for, **20**. 54, 255

—— quotes letter of, on P. of Wales's death, **20**. 253, 261

—— reassured by, about commissions, **20**. 253

——'s art purchases for, **24**. 181

——'s correspondence with, **20**. 54–5, 237, 253, 261, **21**. 49, 500, 505, **22**. 235, 314, 317

—— sends to, Marie de' Medici's correspondence with Duchessa Sforza, **25**. 657

——'s letters shown by, to P. of Wales, **20**. 237

—— thanked by, for plants, **20**. 253

—— would like, to be secretary of state, **22**. 23

Mann, Galfridus, sees, **20**. 250

—— told by, of disappointments over P. of Wales's death, **20**. 244

marriage of, **18**. 104–5, 391–2, 424, **33**. 556

meeting held by, of Sir Robert Walpole's opponents, **17**. 364

Mill, James, courts, **20**. 43n

motto on Hanoverian soldiers' caps translated by, **35**. 94

named in Secret Committee lists, **17**. 384, **30**. 292n

naval investigation proposed by, in Parliament, **18**. 399, 427

Navy treasurership resigned by, **9**. 72, **20**. 39, 54–5, **21**. 18, **30**. 319

Navy treasurership to go to, **35**. 263

Niccolini accompanies, on election campaign, **19**. 420

'Ode from Earl Powlett to Francis Fane, Esq.' by, **30**. 316

Opposition refuses to be led by, **20**. 96

Opposition will benefit little by leadership of, **20**. 51

Parliamentary Address debated by, **37**. 414, 415

Parliamentary Address opposed by, **20**. 509n

Parliamentary debates by, on amendment to Address, **26**. 23; on privately-raised regiments, **26**. 14; on Sir Robert Walpole's impeachment, **17**. 354

Patriots, young, headed by, **30**. 292n

peerage granted to, **9**. 344, **21**. 490, 500, 505

poetical epistle by, a faint echo of Pope, **28**. 242

Pope calls, 'Bubo,' **15**. 26

Presbyterians called 'Presbytyrants' by, **31**. 361, **34**. 116

Ralph's *Detection* attributed to, **18**. 464

'relapses into virtue,' **20**. 65, **43**. 266

resignations of, frequent, **30**. 145

Roe may choose, for hero, **10**. 113

Rowe writes ballad on mistress of, **35**. 237

Rushout replaced by, as Navy treasurer, **18**. 551, **30**. 292n

sisters-in-law of, **18**. 391–2

social relations of, with: Bute, **9**. 373; Chudleigh, Elizabeth, **35**. 301; Foote, **9**. 373; HW, **35**. 97, **37**. 202; Hervey, Bns, **9**. 373; Hillsborough, Cts of, **9**. 344; Mansfield, **9**. 373; Willes, **9**. 373

Spanish talked by, to Condessa de Fuentes, **35**. 301

steel machine used by, to pick up his handkerchief, **20**. 203

Strawbridge, Mrs, praised by, in song, **9**. 169n

—— releases, from his bond, **18**. 105n

Temple to inherit fortune of, unless a son is born, **21**. 39

*Test*'s authorship attributed to, **21**. 38

time-serving of, **30**. 292n

title pleasing to, **21**. 505

tossed in a blanket, **9**. 306

Townshend's caricature of, **21**. 77

Trappe, La, villa of, at Hammersmith, **20**. 54n

[Bubb Dodington, George, *continued*]
Treasury post of, **17.** 257n, 384n
trial of, **26.** 23
verse about Anson attributed to, **9.** 90
verse dialogues between Earle and: by C. H.
Williams, **30.** 313; imitation of C. H. Williams, **30.** 314
Walpole, Sir Edward, jokes about, **17.** 258
Walpole, Sir Robert, attacks, **17.** 297
—— deserted by, **30.** 292n, 313
Williams's odes and other writings generally
attributed to, **30.** 315–16
—— satirizes, **30.** 316
widower, **21.** 39
will of, **22.** 76, 80
wit of, **25.** 503n, **30.** 292n, 316
writings of, **30.** 316
Yonge and, **34.** 257
Young, Edward, gets witticism from, on
*Night Thoughts*, **12.** 255
Bubb Dodington, Mrs George. *See* Beghan,
Katherine
Bubble lottery:
Dixon's, in 1698, **41.** 97
Buc, Du. *See* Du Buc
Buc, Sir George. *See* Buck, Sir George
Bucareli y Ursúa, Nicolás (1717–98), Spanish
grandee and army officer; (?) governor of
Buenos Aires:
(?) Byng talks to, at Gibraltar, **20.** 566
(?) Falkland Islands captured by forces sent
by, **23.** 239n, 252n
governor of Cadiz, **20.** 566n
Buccky:
(?) HW mentions, **39.** 171
Buccleuch, Ds of. *See* Montagu, Lady Elizabeth
(1743–1827)
Buccleuch, D. of. *See* Scott, Francis (1694–
1751); Scott, Henry (1746–1812)
Buccleuch House, Richmond Hill:
Cardigans formerly owned, **31.** 2n
Buccleugh; Buccluegh. *See* Buccleuch
Buceli Collection, at Montepulciano:
Etruscan Museum at the Uffizi transferred
from, **25.** 531n
Bucentaur, Venetian state barge:
England may sail forth in, to cuckold America
with her spouse the Atlantic, **24.** 112
Buch, Lt-Gen. Don Felix:
lands at La Musquita, **25.** 189n
Buchan, Cts of. *See* Steuart, Agnes (d. 1778)
Buchan, E. of. *See* Erskine, David Steuart
(1742–1829); Stewart, John (ca 1380–1424)
Buchanan, Elizabeth (d. 1736), actress:
death date of, corrected, **43.** 175
frightened by accident, **13.** 113–14
Buchanan, George (1506–82), poet; historian;
scholar:
epigrams by, on picture of Q. Elizabeth, **16.**
147–8
Buchanan, William:
Ilay's letter to, **21.** 371n

Bucharest:
congress of, breaks up, **23.** 469n
Buck, Catharine (ca 1726–1805), m. (1751) Sir
Henry Englefield, 6th Bt, 1728:
Berry, Agnes, hears from, about gentleman,
**12.** 211
Berrys, account of, by, **12.** *46*
—— entertain, **12.** 210
Churchill, Lady Mary, visited by, **12.** 46, 107
HW always glad to see, **12.** 46
HW receives note from, **12.** 212
HW's will enrages, **15.** 337
SH visited by, **12.** 230
Buck, Sir George (d. 1623), Kt; historian:
HW cites, incautiously, **14.** 186
*History of the Life and Reigne of Richard
the Third, The,* **2.** 153n, **35.** 607, 610, **40.**
110, **43.** 68, 188
life of, in *Biographia Britannica,* **2.** 196
relates Stow's observation on Richard III's
appearance, **2.** 153
Buck; bucks:
Bird asks, as payment, **20.** 323
Bute sends, to Lady Mary Coke, **31.** 179
Waldegrave, Cts, enjoys, **36.** 289
*See also under* Deer
Buckden, Hunts:
HW visits, **1.** 280, **35.** 266
Buckden ('Bugden') Palace:
HW surprised by, **35.** 266
pictures in, **1.** 280, 281
Buckholdt, Johann (ca 1509–36). *See* John of
Leiden
'Buckhorse, Lord.' *See* Smith, John (d. 1772?)
Buckhounds, Master of the. *See* Master of the
Buckhounds
Buckhurst, Bn. *See* Sackville, Charles (1638–
1706); Sackville, Thomas (ca 1536–1608)
Buckinger, Matthew (1674–1737–9), dwarf:
death date of, corrected, **43.** 131
writing by: minute, **10.** 113, 152; without
hands or feet, **32.** 94, **33.** 148, **34.** 211, 217,
**39.** 235
Buckingham, Cts of. *See* Beaumont, Mary (ca
1570–1632) (*see also under* Buckinghamshire)
Buckingham, Ds of: *See* Darnley, Lady Katherine (ca 1682–1743); Fairfax, Mary (1638–
1704); Manners, Lady Katherine (d. 1649);
Nevill, Lady Anne (d. 1480); Percy, Eleanor
(d. 1530); Wydvill, Katharine (b. ca 1448)
Buckingham, D. of. *See* Sheffield, Edmund
(1716–35); Sheffield, John (1647–1721); Stafford, Edward (1478–1521); Stafford, Henry
(1455–83); Stafford, Humphrey (1402–60);
Villiers, George (1592–1628); Villiers, George
(1628–87)
Buckingham, E. of. *See* Stafford, Humphrey
(1402–60)
Buckingham, Marchioness of. *See* Nugent, Lady
Mary Elizabeth (d. 1812)
Buckingham, M. of. *See* Grenville, George
(1753–1813); Villiers, George (1592–1628)

Buckingham (title). *See also* Buckinghamshire

*Buckingham,* English ship:
in squadron at Port Mahon, **17.** 285n
Tyrell, Capt., arrives in, **21.** 277n

Buckingham, Bucks:
Aylesbury clashes with, over assizes, **13.** 20, 19. 449n, 470–1, **20.** 112, **26.** 25–8
Bentley and Müntz to be met at, by Montagu's carriage, **9.** 193
crowds from, at Stowe, **10.** 314
Forester archdeacon of, **2.** 138n
Hill of, **1.** 40n, **28.** 24n
Montagu advises HW to come to Greatworth by way of, **10.** 85
Stowe near, **28.** 45n
Taylor, archdeacon of, **1.** 47n
'White Hart' at, HW to get itinerary at, **10.** 87

Buckingham, county of. *See* Buckinghamshire

Buckingham Gate, London:
Burdett catches ride to, **20.** 21
Pecquigny waits at, to fight Virrette, **38.** 313
Stafford Row in, **42.** 492

Buckingham House, London:
(?) ball and dinner at, by Q. Charlotte, **22.** 197
balls at, **28.** 108, **38.** 290
Bute attends private levee at, **22.** 219n, **36.** 40n, **38.** 354n
—— does not relinquish keys of, to Pitt, **22.** 130
called 'Holyrood House,' **10.** 35, **32.** 8n
Charlotte, Q., lives at, **11.** 227n
council at, during Gordon Riots, **29.** 58, **33.** 188
Cumberland, D. of, waits on George III and Q. Charlotte at, **22.** 288n
drawings after Holbein from, **15.** 95
France sues for peace at gates of, **38.** 188
George III and Q. Charlotte furnish, to live there, **10.** 33
George III and Q. Charlotte stoned on way to, **34.** 212n
George III buys, from Sheffield, **15.** 160n, **22.** 130n
George III receives Christian VII at, **35.** 326
—— receives Pitt at, **38.** 210
——'s conferences at, **25.** 379n, 387n
—— sees Townshends at, **31.** 40n
—— sends pictures to, **15.** 160
George IV to be born at, **32.** 8
Gordon, Lord George, goes to, **33.** 185
Grosvenor Place overlooks gardens of, **32.** 223n
HW buys Sheffield's portrait by More at sale at, **40.** 352
HW expects Chatham to be invited to, **28.** 377
HW would accept post of, if asked, **33.** 393
Harcourt writes at, **35.** 544–5
history of, before its purchase for Q. Charlotte, **32.** 8n
Holbein's drawings at, **41.** 320n

Hugenien authorized to seek Colomb's effects at, **42.** 298n
Kennedy reportedly receives bad representation at, **30.** 254
Nares near, in James St, **43.** 204
Pitt might hobble to, **10.** 112, **28.** 350n
—— visits **22.** 159, **38.** 210
Raphael cartoons in, **16.** 168n
Sandwich may be going to, **29.** 123n
'seraglio' at, **35.** 323
Shelburne summoned to, **29.** 205
Temple and Wilkes unpopular at, **22.** 159

Buckinghamshire, Cts of. *See* Bertie, Albinia (ca 1738–1816); Conolly, Caroline (ca 1755–1817); Drury, Mary Anne (1740–69)

Buckinghamshire, E. of. *See* Hobart, George (1731–1804); Hobart, John (ca 1695–1756); Hobart, John (1723–93)

Buckinghamshire (county):
Chenies in, **35.** 145
grand jury of, thanks Parliament for lowering land tax, **22.** 494–5
HW to visit, **42.** 425
high sheriff of, **22.** 494n
Latimers in, **37.** 299
Le Despenser becomes lord lieutenant of, **22.** 138n
militia of, George III orders Temple to remove Wilkes from, **22.** 138
Parliamentary reform rejected by, **29.** 26
petition from, House of Commons cannot get a committee for, **25.** 572
Temple removed as lord lieutenant of, **22.** 138
Verney's petition against Aubrey's election for, **25.** 572n
Willis's MS on hundreds of, **2.** 336

'Buckingham's Plotting Closet.' *See* Thornbury Castle

Buckingham St, the Strand, London:
Henderson addressed in, **41.** 427, 436, 439, **42.** 4n

Buckland, Mr:
SH visited by, **12.** 236

Buckland, Berks, Throckmorton's seat:
Browne, Lady, at, **31.** 237

Buckland, Devon:
Orford, E. of, presents Paxton to living of, **40.** 39n

Buckland, Dorset, Poulett's seat:
Dobson's portrait may be at, **1.** 171n

Buckland, Herts:
Morell, rector of, **1.** 8n, **14.** 120n

Buckle; buckles:
diamond, offered by Sir Edward Walpole to Mrs Scott, **10.** 329
gold, **30.** 54
Gunter's designs for, **42.** 107n
HW has, of one hero, **37.** 107
jewelled, Niccolini gets, from Bns Walpole, **17.** 134–5
'Pinchbeck,' **30.** 54

[Buckle; buckles, *continued*]
  silver: on shoes, **21.** 399n; worn for boar-hunting, **20.** 200n
  steel: for knees, sent by HW to Craon, **17.** 152, 169, 222, 255, 413; for shoes for Duchesse de Châtillon, **5.** 114, 129, **7.** 416
Buckler; bucklers:
  metal, attributed to Cellini, **23.** 407n
Bucklersbury:
  Margas's china shop near Stocks Market in, **30.** 116n, **37.** 348
Bucknall, Mr:
  SH visited by, **12.** 222
Buckner, John (1734–1824), Bp of Chichester 1798–1824:
  HW persuaded by, to give SH books to library at Paris, **41.** 57–8
  HW shops with, **7.** 303
  HW's social relations with, **7.** 281, 305, 310, 313
  Richmond's chaplain, **7.** 281, **41.** 57–8
  St-Cloud visited by, **7.** 314
Buckram:
  royal velvet and ermine might just as well be actor's, **25.** 624
'Buckskin, Rachael.' *See under* Goldsmith, Oliver
Buckskin:
  breeches of, **23.** 273, **30.** 86, **35.** 70
  hunting costume, **9.** 240
Bucleugh. *See* Buccleuch
Bucquoy von Longueval, Gräfin. *See* Paar, Thérèse
Buda:
  Conway and Scott visit, **39.** 538
Buday, Adam (fl. 1744–52), Lt-Col.:
  Monte Rotondo defended by, **18.** 443
Budd, Dr:
  Craven, Bns, writes to, **42.** 177n
Budé, Jacob de (1737–1818), army officer:
  Anderson, Mrs, will cause trouble for, **12.** 13–14
  HW meets, at Oatlands, **12.** 13
  HW receives note from, **12.** 9
  York, Ds of, accompanied by, to SH, **12.** 11
Budes, Jean-Baptiste (1602–43), Comte and Maréchal de Guébriant:
  wife of, goes to Poland without him, **32.** 209
Budes, Joseph-Marie-Louis (d. 1734), Comte and Marquis de Guébriant:
  (?) Du Châtelet, Marquise, deserted by, **7.** 267
Budgell, Eustace (1686–1737), writer:
  Jeffreys's epigram ascribed to, **2.** 202n
  mistakes in life of, in *Biographia Britannica*, **2.** 202–3
Budgen, John Smith (ca 1740–1805) of Twickenham:
  SH visited by, **12.** 231, 236
Buenos Aires:
  governor of, *see* Bucareli y Ursúa, Nicolás

Spanish armament may be destined for, **24.** 253n
Buer, Jean, Ensign:
  captured at Velletri, **18.** 492
Bufalini, Giovanni Ottavio (1709–82), cardinal, 1766; major-domo:
  York, D. of, receives gifts from, **22.** 229
Buff:
  accoutrements in, **37.** 358
*Buffalo*, English ship:
  Dutch contraband seized by, **25.** 3n
Buffet:
  Montagu's, **9.** 358
Buffon, Comte de. *See* Leclerc, George-Louis
Buffon, Comtesse de. *See* Bouvier de Lamotte de Cépoy, Marguerite-Françoise
*Buffon. See also Bouffon*
Bufo; bufos:
  Batheaston group called 'Bufos and Bufesses,' **32.** 223
  'full-blown,' in quotation from A. Pope, **32.** 372
  unsuccessful in England, **18.** 211
Bug; bugs:
  French inns infested with, **20.** 324
  in French tapestry and needlework, talk of Louis XIV, **35.** 123
  Italian feature, **37.** 73
Bugden, Sophia (d. 1762), m. 1 (before 1729) George Drake; m. 2 (1743) George Morton Pitt:
  biographical information about, corrected, **43.** 121–2
  daughter of, **7.** 397, **9.** 263
  HW accuses, of bigamy, **9.** 264
  HW receives proposals from, through Raftor, **9.** 263–4
  Twickenham resident, **42.** 483
Bugden. *See also* Buckden; Budgen
Bugg, Fr.:
  print of, **40.** 236
Bugle; bugles (ornaments):
  bought by HW's mother, **11.** 212
  gown trimmed with, **18.** 128
  white, worn at Drury Lane by Lady Craven, **29.** 43
Buignon, ——, Swiss tutor:
  *Arno Miscellany* has poems by, **25.** 517n, 523, **26.** 46
  Dawkins's tutor, **25.** 517n, 523, **26.** 46
Buildwas, Salop:
  Whitmore of, **16.** 324n
Buirette de Belloy, Pierre-Laurent (1727–75), dramatist:
  Guerchy receives, coldly, **7.** 261
  HW's social relations with, **7.** 262
  name of, corrected, **43.** 84
  *Siège de Calais, Le,* **3.** 240, **7.** 262, **10.** 150, 151, **28.** 7, **38.** 515, 519, 521–2, 524, 538, **43.** 105, 133, 293
  Voltaire's letter to, **38.** 521–2
  *Zelmire* by, **3.** 240

Buisson, Pierre de (1703–living, 1790), Chevalier de Beauteville:
(?) Chanteloup visited by, 7. 423, 448, 456
(?) Du Deffand, Mme, and Mme de Choiseul joke about wit of, 7. 450
(?) Limoux visited by, 7. 429
(?) Paris left by, 7. 423
(?) —— revisited by, 7. 438, 451
(?) social relations of, in Paris, see index entries ante 8. 272
(?) Tonton likes, 6. 447
Bukaty, Franciszik (1747–97), Polish minister to England 1772–89; ambassador 1789–94:
SH visited by, 12. 231
Bulb; bulbs:
Clive, Mrs, wants, from Montagu, 10. 235
Bulgaria:
Potemkin to be driven out of, 11. 230
Bulgarian; Bulgarians:
in Voltaire's Candide, 38. 473
Bulgarini, Signora. See Chigi Zondadari, Vittoria
Bulkeley, Comtesse de. See Mahony, Mary Anne
Bulkeley, Vcts. See Warren, Elizabeth Harriet (ca 1760–1826)
Bulkeley, Anne (d. 1751), m. (1700) James Fitzjames, cr. (1687) D. of Berwick:
brother of, 18. 429n
Hamilton's 'Mousseline,' 7. 358
Strafford, Cts of, to entertain, 9. 24
Bulkeley, Charlotte, m. 1 (1697) Charles O'Brien, styled 5th Vct Clare; m. 2 (1712) Daniel Mahoney:
Hamilton loved by, 7. 358
——'s 'Clarice' and 'Varice,' 7. 358
Bulkeley, Francis (1686–1756), Comte de Bulkeley; army officer:
Cantillon, Mme, marries, 18. 429n
French regiment commanded by, 18. 429
Hervey, Bns, employs, to inquire for Gramont's portrait, 31. 82
Maubeuge to be defended by, 18. 500n
Bulkeley, Henri- (?) François (1739– ? 1806), Comte de; French minister to Diet of the Empire 1772–5:
Aiguillon, Duchesse d', favours, 5. 134
appointed minister to Diet of Empire, 5. 134
Rueil visited by, 7. 337
social relations of, in Paris, 7. 292, 337, 338, 346
Bulkeley, Henrietta:
Hamilton's Epistle to, 7. 358
Bulkeley, Mrs Henry. See Stuart, Sophia
Bulkeley, Thomas James (1752–1822), 7th Vct Bulkeley, M.P.:
Florence visited by, 25. 618
Welsh revenue reforms opposed by, 33. 82n
Bull, Mr (d. 1775) of Chichester:
death of, 7. 398
Bull, Mrs:
HW's correspondence with, 7. 396
Bull, Frederick (ca 1714–84), M.P.:

elected alderman, but rejected by vote, 32. 40n
elected lord mayor, 23. 520n
elected sheriff, 23. 315n, 32. 52n
poll for, M.P., 24. 48
Bull, George (1634–1710), Bp of St David's 1705–10:
life of, in Biographia Britannica, 2. 202
'Bull, John':
(?) allusion to, 18. 316, 35. 39
apathy of, 35. 616
Hardinge imitates, 35. 584
Bull, Richard (1721–1805), M.P.; collector:
biographical information on, corrected, 43. 57, 198, 355
Carter employed by, 16. 192n
Catherine of Braganza's print given by, to HW, 41. 414
collection of: 1. 287n, 313n; bought by Mount Stuart, 15. 161
Description of SH extra-illustrated by, 43. 109
extra-illustrates HW's Anecdotes, 2. 273
extra-illustrates HW's Royal and Noble Authors, 31. 297–8, 33. 376–7
Grose gives album to, 42. 107n
HW gives Mysterious Mother to, 41. 428n
HW gives Postscript to the Royal and Noble Authors to, 42. 185
HW gives print of Antony and Octavia medal to, 42. 262
HW lends Mysterious Mother to, 41. 414, 415
HW offered prints from, bought at Talman's sale, 42. 458
HW receives Haistwell's engravings from, 42. 53–4
HW receives Laroon's caricature from, 42. 282
HW receives Mrs York's prints from, 42. 237
HW receives Miss Yorke's etchings from, 42. 238
HW receives prints from, and may send him one of 4th E. Waldegrave, 42. 413
HW returns books to, 42. 107
HW's commissions to, for West's sale, 43. 58
HW's correspondence with, 41. 414, 415, 467–8, 469, 42. 49, 53–4, 107–8, 184–5, 237, 262, 282, 413, 458, (?) 43. 382
HW sends Hentzner's Journey to, 42. 49
HW thanks, for game, 42. 184
HW told by, of Morice's illness, 33. 362
HW to show book to, 41. 467
health of: accident, 42. 237; cold, 41. 468; indisposed, 42. 185
houses of, 33. 362n
in Isle of Wight, 42. 127
Lort sees, at West's sale, 43. 58
Nivernais's Jardins modernes given to, 12. 259
North Court, Isle of Wight, visited and later bought by, 42. 127n
note by, 13. 31n
Pennant's correspondence with, 43. 60
print of Cromwell's funeral most likely to be known to, 42. 127

[Bull, Richard, *continued*]
Stratton St address of, **42**. 237
SH *Lucan* bought by, **42**. 107
Strutt's drawings owned by, **43**. 220
Bull, The, inn at Barton Mills:
HW stays at, **36**. 122, 124
*See also* Bull Inn
Bull; bulls (papal):
Benedict XIV's: for *anno santo*, **20**. 43; for legitimatizing Miss ——, **17**. 139
—— signs, against Jesuits, **21**. 217
Clement XIV addresses, to Cardinal York, **23**. 191
—— issues, for suppression of Jesuits, **23**. 506–8
confirming marriage of Henry VII and Elizabeth of York, **42**. 207
Gregory XIII's, to Portugal, **21**. 308n
horns of, blunted, **25**. 85
*in Cœna Domini*, **22**. 582n
Salisbury, Cts of, owns, **9**. 98
*Unigenitus*, **20**. 337, **21**. 44
Bull; bulls:
Barnard, Anna, offers, to Q. Charlotte instead of cow she wanted, **33**. 568
Ceres holds, in HW's bronze, **33**. 479
cock and, *see* Cock and bull
HW's bronze of, **15**. 13
heads of, on coats of arms, **16**. 185, 186
in Greece, copied for coins, **15**. 211–12
Stubb's painting of, **23**. 211n
town, Mann compares town crier with, **17**. 322
winged, symbol of St Luke, **16**. 187
woman gives birth to, with human features, **34**. 201n
'Bull':
new term in finance, **21**. 559
*Bulla aurea*:
in Middleton's *Monumenta*, **15**. 16, 22
'Bull-a-boo, E. of':
character in 'The Peach in Brandy,' **32**. 61
*Bulla in cœna Domini*, Papal:
origin of, **22**. 582n
Bullart, Isaac (1599–1672):
*Académie des sciences et des arts* by, **7**. 371
Bull-baiting:
Mathews's taste for, ridiculed by HW, **18**. 79
Bullen. *See* Boleyn
Bullen tree:
bark of, **43**. 76
Buller, ——:
Kingston, Ds of, has, as counsel, **24**. 193n
Buller, Mrs James. *See* Coxe, Mary
Buller, John (1721–86), M.P., *or* John (1745–93):
Parliamentary motion by, to recruit seamen, **24**. 127n
(?) print of, **40**. 236
Townshend, Hon. Charles, tries to promote, **30**. 193n
Buller, John Francis. *See* Coxe, John Francis Buller Hippisley

Buller, William (1735–96), Bp of Exeter, 1792:
Windsor visited by, **12**. 3–4
Bullet, Jean-Baptiste (1699–1775):
*History of the Establishment of Christianity* by, **16**. 182n
Bullet; bullets:
as treatment for colic, **33**. 147
cannon, straw men shot with, **38**. 410
Conway casts, **39**. 150
—— thinks soldier's head should be like, **35**. 224
(?) Fitzpatrick to give, to HW, **33**. 146–7
hot, floating batteries not proof against, **25**. 330
Ker, Lord Mark, shot in mouth by, **30**. 55
red hot, Preston and Guest threaten Edinburgh with, **19**. 126
*Bulletin des amis de la vérité*:
Condorcet contributes to, **34**. 179n
Bull-fight:
Artois, Comte d', attends, **25**. 337n
George II's preparations worthy of, **18**. 69
Bullfinch; bullfinches:
HW's and Lady Strafford's, whistle tunes, **31**. 127
Lady Blandford's, **41**. 319n
Bull Inn, Bishopsgate St, London:
Cambridge wagon sets out from, **2**. 47, 260n
Bullion:
customs regulations concerning, **10**. 289
Bullion de Fervaques, Jacqueline-Hortense de, m. (1740) Guy-André-Pierre de Montmorency-Laval, Duc de Laval:
admitted to suppers at little château at Compiègne, **4**. 441
Bullioud, Marie-Marguerite-Adélaïde de (d. 1793), m. Louis-François, Comte de Séran:
presents bouquets at Villers-Cotterêts, **3**. 129
Bulloch, Archibald (1730–77), rebel governor of Georgia:
rebellion renounced by, **32**. 346n, **43**. 350
surrender of, **32**. 346n
Bullock, Dr:
HW mentions, **10**. 243
Bullock (later Fetherstonhaugh), Frances:
succeeds to Up Park, **12**. 206n
Bullock, James (fl. ca 1756–76), King's messenger:
Hertford sends dispatches and letters by means of, **38**. 313–14, 494, 521, **39**. 1
Bullock. *See also* Bulloch, Archibald
Bullock; bullocks:
HW sells, from Houghton, **23**. 497, **32**. 142
HW's ignorance of, **36**. 96
Orford's militia consumes, **25**. 12n
Bullrushes:
in ditches, must be Holland's hay, **38**. 90
'Bully.' *See* St John, Frederick, Vct Bolingbroke
Bully, Capt.:
*Sheerness* commanded by, **19**. 173n
Bulmer, William (1757–1830):
Nicoll establishes Shakespeare Press with, **42**. 283n

Bülow, Friedrich Gotthard (1688–1768), Frei-
herr von; Saxon envoy to Prussia 1746–57:
  Frederick II learns Gross's secrets through,
  30. 321
  Williams, Sir C. H., breaks Gross's intimacy
  with, 30. 320
Bulse:
  from India, property of the Crown, 33. 568–9
Bulstrode, ——:
  Beauvau to be accompanied by, 17. *11*
  mismanagement of, 17. 28
  Naples to be visited by, 17. 11
  Shrewsbury's tutor, 17. 140n
  Talbots accompanied by, 17. 140
  (?) unfaithfulness of, 17. 14
  winter to be spent by, at 'court of Boulogne,'
  17. 140
Bulstrode, Sir Richard (1610–1711):
  (?) descendant of, tutor to E. of Shrewsbury,
  17. 11n
Bulstrode Park, Bucks; D. of Portland's seat:
  Delany, Mrs, ceases to visit, after Ds of Portland's death, 33. 497n
  'Dutch and trist,' 10. 104
  fire destroys chapel ceiling at, 35. 233
  French portraits hang in nursery at, 10. 4
  gallery at, 10. 102, 104
  HW describes, 10. 102–4, 35. 233
  portraits at: French, 10. 4; Montagu thinks
  HW would like, 10. 102–3; nameless, 10.
  104
  visitors to: Douglas, Lady Frances, 31. 287;
  HW, 10. 102–4, 35. 233; Montagu, 10. 102–3
Bulwar, John:
  print of, 40. 236
Bumper; bumpers:
  at county election, 35. 9
  at election at King's Lynn, 9. 350
  Conway drinks, with 'stinking freeholders,'
  37. 371n
  excessive, in Ireland, 37. 395
  for Dettingen victory, 35. 39
  HW should not drink, in hot weather, 35. 5
  of ale, at Crewe Hall, 10. 96
Bünau, Henrietta Frederica von (d. 1766), m.
  1 —— de Beraargard; m. 2 (1759) David
  Murray, 7th Vct Stormont:
  brought to bed in flames, 38. 60–1
  death of, 7. 397
  marriage of, 38. 32
Bunbury, Annabella (b. 1745), m. (ca. 1765),
  Sir Patrick Blake, cr. (1772) Bt:
  marriage of, 1. 237n, 240
Bunbury, Sir Charles. See Bunbury, Sir Thomas
  Charles
Bunbury, Elizabeth (1711–65), m. Lt-Gen.
  Robert Armiger:
  death of, 38. 530
Bunbury, Henry William (1750–1811), carica-
  turist:
  *Annals of Horsemanship* by, 42. 316
  at Richmond, 34. 62
  HW has copies of drawings made by, at West-
  minster School, 32. 304n, 34. 84n

  HW pastes prints by, into volume, 32. 304,
  43. 350
  HW's correspondence with, 41. 429, 42. 316–
  18
  HW's praise of, in *Anecdotes*, 41. 429
  HW wants to buy prints by, 42. 318
  lease of Little Strawberry Hill wanted by, 11.
  222–3, 42. 316–18
  'Long Minuet' by, 33. 572
  Richmond Hill drawn by, for HW, 41. 429–
  30, 42. 318
  'Robin Gray' by, 33. 401
  Royal Academy exhibit includes, 41. 429
  SH visited by, 12. 234
  tickets by, for theatre at Wynnstay, 34. 4n
Bunbury, Mrs Henry William. See Horneck,
  Catherine
Bunbury, Louisa (1768–85):
  death of, 31. 238
  Gordon resembled by, 33. 307
  HW sees, at Goodwood, 32. 204
Bunbury, Lady Sarah. See Lennox, Lady Sarah
  (1745–1826)
Bunbury, Susan, m. (ca 1764–65) Henry Soame:
  (?) SH visited by, 12. 230, 43. 160
Bunbury, Susannah (1700–64), m. Col. William
  Handasyd; housekeeper at Windsor Castle
  ca 1756–64:
  HW, Rigby, and Thomas Hervey dine with,
  30. 57
  HW 'sold' to circle of, called 'Bunbury-Bums,'
  37. 157
  misfortunes of, 9. *111–12*
  niece of, 10. 137
  Rigby mentions, 43. 116
Bunbury, Sir Thomas Charles (1740–1821), 6th
  Bt, 1764; M.P.:
  Barton near Newmarket house of, 32. 14n
  'chicken orator,' 22. 8, 19
  Court deserted by, in House of Commons,
  32. 403
  Du Deffand, Mme, gives commissions to, 3.
  224
  —— sends letters, money, and parcels by, 3.
  219, 223–4, 224, 231, 4. 105, 107, 108, 113,
  124
  ——'s good opinion of, 3. 210, 224
  ——'s social relations with, 3. 205, 229
  expected in Paris, 3. 311
  Fox influences, through Lady Sarah, against
  Parliamentary motion, 22. 8n, 43. 185
  Grafton, a Suffolk friend, may be approached
  by, for post, 39. 2
  Grafton, Ds of, takes house of, in Upper
  Grosvenor St, 32. 28n
  Grenville obliging to Hertford about, 38. 329
  HW gives letter of introduction to, for Mann,
  21. (?) 389, 431
  (?) HW hopes wife will not be divorced by,
  and that child is his, 39. 103
  (?) Hertford calls, Weymouth's valet-de-
  chambre, 38. 572
  —— discards, as secretary, 38. 214n
  ——in France without, 38. 214

[Bunbury, Sir Thomas Charles, *continued*]
—— might have, as secretary in Ireland, 38. 536
—— suspicious of motives of, 39. 1–2
house of: at Barton, 32. 14n; in Privy Gardens, 4. 207n; in Upper Grosvenor St, 31. 35n, 32. 28n
Irish peerage declined by, 33. 430n
Irish post expected for, 38. 567, 568, 572
Luxembourg, Mme de, disliked by, 3. 229
Mann's opinion of, 21. 436
marriage of, 3. 199n, 9. 406n, 14. 120, 21. 530n, 22. 8, 19, 32. 6
ministry said to keep, in England to attend Parliament, 38. 222, 235
Palais Royal visited by, 3. 208
Paris post may still be wanted by, 39. 1–2
—— to be visited by, 35. 318
Parliamentary motion against German war not made by, 10. 10, 22. 7–8
removed from Paris embassy, 38. 578
retires out of complaisance to Vct Torrington, 21. 436
Selwyn does not mention, 3. 252
Shelburne's intimacy with, connects him with Fox, 22. 7n
Sillery, Mme de, and family visit, at Barton, 34. 138n
sister of, 1. 237n, 240
Tavistock announces to, his marriage, 22. 243n
wife divorced by, 3. 199n, 4. 221, 21. 530n, 43. 377
wife leaves, 4. 207, 5. 309n
wife loves, 3. 224
wife madly loved by, 3. 224
wife of, 3. 199n, 9. 335n, 43. 185
wife's adorers not objected to by, 3. 208, 231, 239
Bunbury, Rev. Sir William (ca 1710–64), 5th Bt:
Hervey's letter to, proposing duel, 9. 152–3, 30. 121
Bunbury, Cheshire:
Bunbury of, 9. 152n
Bungay, Suffolk:
Norfolk's verses on his castle at, on the Waveney, 37. 406
poor men from, eligible for Trinity Hospital, 16. 90
Soley writes from, 41. 96
Bungay Castle, Suffolk:
HW refers to SH as, 37. 406, 407, 411
Bungerley Hippingstones, Lancs:
Henry VI captured near, 14. 163n
Bunhill Fields:
Cosway's daughter to be buried in, 12. 203n
Bunker Hill, Mass.:
battle of: 7. 346, 24. 119–20, 121, 28. 215, 32. 247; Rawdon wounded at, 12. 66n
Bunyan, John (1628–88):
HW calls Spenser a rhyming, 29. 256
Mason imitates style of, 28. 406

Buonaccorsi, Abbé Ottaviano (1700–70), freemason and author:
marriage promise revealed by, 18. 111
Stosch's will mentions, 23. 149
Buonaccorsi, Simone (1708–76), cardinal, 1763:
Bourbon courts would exclude, from Papal councils, 23. 16, 35
*Buona figliuola, La. See under* Goldini, Carlo; Piccinni, Niccolò
Buonanni, Filippo:
HW owns *Recreatio mentis et oculi in observatione animalium testaceorum* of, 18. 105n
Buonarroti, Michelangelo (1475–1564):
Beauclerk, Lady Diana, surpasses, in style, 29. 272
female nude statue by, destroyed in Uffizi fire, 22. 68n
Gibbon's style more subtle than that of, 28. 243
'Last Judgment,' HW does not see, 14. 240
medal by, 21. 189
Medici chapel of, in Florence, 18. 160
Patch engraves paintings by, 23. 276
St Cecilia by, taken to Paris, 34. 217n
pictures by, in Mariette's sale, 32. 266
torso by, seen by Mary Berry in Vatican, 11. 338n
tripod by, at Julienne's, 7. 287
vellum copies of works by, 22. 233n
Buonaventuri. *See* Bonaventuri
Buoncompagni. *See* Boncompagni
Buoncore, Don Francesco:
Neapolitan physician, 21. 325
Buondelmonti, Signora. *See* Antinori, Maria Maddalena (1744–1811); Rinuccini, Maria Teresa (d. before 1765)
Buondelmonti, Filippo Manente (1691–1741), monsignore; governor of Rome:
Hartington's conversation with, 17. 7–8, 37. 56–7
name of, corrected, 43. 234, 372
Buondelmonti, Francesco Gioacchino (1689–1774), Florentine senator, 1736:
Madonna dell' Impruneta escorted by sons and, 30. 4
name of, corrected, 43. 312
Buondelmonti, Giangualberto (1715–60):
(?) Madonna dell' Impruneta escorted by, 30. 4
Buondelmonti, Giuseppe Maria (1713–57), abbé; writer:
answer by, in *giuoco della sibilla*, to question about French devotion to Louis XV, 21. 48–9
Corsi entertains, 17. 137
Craon, Princesse de, entertains, 17. 414
freemason lodge in Florence attended by, 19. 364n
HW confuses, with Bonducci, 25. 507n
HW had not heard of death of, 21. 79
HW transcribes song by, 13. 231–2
Jadot asks, for subjects of his oration, 30. 9

Lami criticizes *La terra sopra la Misura,* **20.**
117–18

'low mimic,' **13.** 231

Madonna dell' Impruneta escorted by, **30.** 4

Mann entertains, at dinner, **18.** 17

——— serves chocolate to, **17.** 413

Montagu, Lady Mary Wortley, incites, to
satirize the English, **17.** 92

Mozzi's verses on death of, **21.** 70–1, 79

*Museum Florentinum* directed by, **18.** 391

——— given by, to Kaunitz, **17.** *49*

name of, corrected, **43.** 179

oration to be made by, for Charles VI's
obsequies at Florence, **30.** 8

Orford, Cts of, writes to, **19.** 101

Richecourt has, as interpreter at *giuoco della
sibilla,* **20.** 477

West and Ashton unable to turn verses of,
into French and Greek, **13.** 235–6

wit, **21.** 79n, **25.** 507n

Buondelmonti family:

Madonna dell' Impruneta found in lands of,
**30.** 3

Buon Porto. *See* Bomporto

Buonsollazzi, Signora. *See* Amicis, Anna Lucia
de

Buontempi. *See* Bontempi

Buot. *See* Buyot

Buranello. *See* Galuppi

Burch. *See* Birch

Burché, J.:

print engraved by, **15.** 250n

Burchell, William (d. 1800):

Gray, Christopher, succeeded by, in Fulham
nurseries, **9.** 176n

Burchett, Josiah (ca 1666–1746):

*Complete History of the Most Remarkable
Transactions at Sea,* consulted by Mann,
**21.** 223

Burchett, Rev. William (ca 1694–1750), assistant at Eton, (?) Windsor canon:

(?) Good gives supper to, **37.** 14

Burcot, Somerset:

Newcome, Richard, retires to, **2.** 265n

Burdett (Burdet), Charles Sedley (ca 1772–93):

drowned in Switzerland, **12.** 54

Burdett, Sir William Vigors (1715–98), 2d Bt:

career of, at Brussels and Paris, **20.** 20

Castle-Durrow and Rodney cheated by, **20.**
20–1

Penn, Mrs, accompanies, **20.** 20

Bure, Guillaume de:

*Catalogue* by, of La Vallière's library, **36.**
216n

Bureau:

citizen puts money into, **20.** 215

Conway's, HW's notes on debate locked in,
**37.** 389

George II dies after falling against, **9.** 311,
**21.** 443, **35.** 307

——— leaves, to Cts of Yarmouth, **38.** 79

Harrington's, robbed, **38.** 259

Tullie keeps guineas in, **23.** 498

Burford, E. of. *See* Beauclerk, Charles (1670–
1726); Beauclerk, George (1730–86)

*Burford,* English ship:

involved in war, **18.** 396, **19.** 313

Burford, Oxon:

HW visits, **35.** 155

Burford, Shropshire:

Cornwall monuments in church at, **42.** 387n

Burford House, Windsor:

George III buys, **37.** 242n

Nell Gwyn writes from, **1.** 349

pictures at, **37.** 242

St Albans, D. of, owns, **20.** 42n

Burford Priory, Oxon, Lenthall's seat:

Gheeraerts probably did not paint picture at,
**16.** 48

portraits at, **35.** 155

Burgage-tenures:

HW's, in Devonshire, **34.** 184n, **42.** 376–8

purchase of, to secure election, **20.** 435–6

Burgers. *See* Burgersh; Burghers

Burgersh, Maud (ca 1379–1437), m. (ca 1394)
Thomas Chaucer:

daughter of, **14.** 70n

tomb of, shown in print of Geoffrey Chaucer,
**14.** 108

Burges, Capt. in Tuscan service:

prize captured by, **21.** 349

Burges, Lady Margaret Janet. *See* Lindsay, Lady
Margaret Janet

Burgess, Mrs:

(?) listeners of, may die, **9.** 164

Burgess, Helen Maria, m. (1793) John Pinkerton:

Pinkerton marries, **12.** 10n

Burgess, James:

*Lives of the Most Eminent Modern Painters
. . . Omitted by Mons[ieur] de Piles,* Petitot
in, **40.** 238

Burgess, Thomas (1756–1837), D.D.; Bp of St
David's, 1803, and of Salisbury, 1825:

*Considerations on the Abolition of Slavery,*
quotes Dante, **31.** 296

sister of, **12.** 10n

Burgh, Lady. *See* Parr, Catherine

Burgh, Anne, m. (1767) Walter Hussey:

marriage of, **28.** 200n

Burgh, Sir Edward (d. ca 1533), Lord Burgh:

Catherine Parr's husband, **42.** 114

Burgh, Elizabeth (fl. ca 1549), m. Sir Robert
Tyrwhitt, Kt, 1543:

*Lady Eliz. Tirwitt's Morning and Evening
Praiers* presented to Q. Elizabeth in Tower,
**16.** 208

Burgh, Hubert de (ca 1175–1243), cr. (1227)
E. of Kent; chief justiciar:

HW believes, to have been hanged, **20.** 65

Mann's mother's ancestor, **20.** 64–5

titles of, **2.** 178–9, 182

Burgh, Lady Margaret de (d. 1698), m. 1 (ca
1660) Charles Maccarty, styled Vct Muskerry; m. 2 (1676) Robert Villiers, styled Vct
Purbeck; m. 3 Col. Robert Feilding:

[Burgh, Lady Margaret de, *continued*]

Catherine of Braganza, Q., instigated by Miss Hamilton to invite, **20.** 50n

Gramont's *Mémoires* describe, as 'Princess of Babylon,' **20.** 49–50, **35.** 135

Smithson, Lady Elizabeth, resembles, **20.** 49–50

Summer Hill home of, **35.** 135–6, **39.** 310

Burgh, Patrice, Ensign:

captured at Velletri, **18.** 492

Burgh, Patrice, Lt:

captured at Velletri, **18.** 492

Burgh, Thomas, Ensign:

captured at Velletri, **18.** 492

Burgh, Walter Hussey. *See* Hussey

Burgh, William (1741–1808), writer and politician; M.P.; friend of William Mason:

analogue of *Mysterious Mother* translated by, **28.** 363, 366

HW would like, to answer Jenyns, **29.** 200, 203–4, 211

Mason praises intellectual ability of, **28.** 200

Oxford refuses M.A. degree to, **28.** *199–200*

*Scriptural Confutation of the Arguments against One Godhead*, dedicated to Burke and uncomplimentary to George III and Hume, **28.** 199–200

Whig, **28.** 200

writes commentary on Mason's *English Garden*, **29.** 195, 199

Burgh. *See also* Bourgh; Bourke

Burghers, Michael (1653?–1727), engraver:

Holbein woodcut imitated by, **1.** 170

Burghersh, Bn of. *See* Fane, Sir Francis (1580–1629); Fane, Mildmay (1602–66)

Burghley, Bn. *See* Cecil, Thomas (1542–1623); Cecil, William (1521–98)

Burghley, Lady. *See* Townshend, Letitia

Burghley House, Northants:

chapel at, unfurnished, **10.** 345

Chute may visit, **10.** 82

club at, **10.** 346

Cole's opinion of furnishing of, **10.** 344

Dolci picture at, **1.** 176

Exeter adds to, **10.** 344

—— refurnishes, **10.** 91

—— shows, to HW and Cole, **10.** 91, 344–6

—— to leave, temporarily, **10.** 344–5

HW calls, noble palace, **15.** 205

HW does not stop at, having seen it before, **35.** 266

Montagu may visit, **10.** 82

on road to Horton, **10.** 85

ornaments at, **10.** 91, 345–6

pictures at, **10.** 345–6, **15.** 204–5

regulations at, for practising fire engine, **10.** 347

tapestries after Raphael said to be at, **16.** 159

visitors to: Cole, **1.** 41, 46, 278n, **2.** 212, 213n, **10.** 91, 344–6; Dodd, **40.** 17; HW, **1.** 41, 46, 278n, **2.** 212, 213n, **10.** 82, 86, 91, 344–6, **40.** 288; Hamilton, **35.** 411; Whaley, **40.** 17

writing and vases at, **1.** 46, 175, 176

Burglar; burglars:

at Brentford, **42.** 109

at Freeman's house, **9.** 132–4

attempt of, to rob SH, foiled, **31.** 298

HW's town house ransacked by, **23.** 284–6

'impeached,' **35.** 367–8

tools of, found by HW, **9.** 133–4

Burglary:

prevalent, **25.** 316, **31.** 298, **39.** 391, 420

Burgoin. *See* Bourgoin

Burgomaster; burgomasters:

Ailesbury, Lady, frisks about with, **38.** 124

HW jokes about Lady Mary Coke subduing, **38.** 83

Burgoyne, Lady. *See* Johnston, Charlotte

Burgoyne, Miss:

SH visited by, **12.** 236

Burgoyne, Lady Charlotte. *See* Stanley, Lady Charlotte

Burgoyne, Lady Frances. *See* Montagu, Lady Frances

Burgoyne, John (1723–92); Gen.; M.P.; dramatist:

American campaigns and surrender of, **6.** 470, 486, 500n, **7.** 185, **24.** 98, 215n, 320, 323, 331, 335, 336, 339–41, 342, 345, 347, 349, 361–2, 408n, **28.** 328, 342–3, **29.** 167, 192n, **31.** 188, **32.** 286, 370, 374, 382, 392, 393, 394, 395, 400, 407, **33.** 12n, **35.** 363, 597, **39.** 321

Americans treat, with humanity, **32.** 400

appears in House of Commons, **33.** 12

Bath order offered to, for Ticonderoga, **32.** 380n

biographical information about, corrected, **43.** 94, 301

Boston thought to be destination of, **24.** 81n, 98n

—— visited by, on *Cerberus*, **32.** 286n

Burke parodies, **28.** 354–6

Chanteloup visited by, **5.** 269–70

Christianity of, doubtful, **28.** 332

Clinton's predicament like that of, **24.** 408n

dispatch of, parodied, **32.** 399

Du Deffand, Mme, sends parcel by, **5.** 272, 276

employed though asking for his recall, **41.** 314

epilogue by, to Murphy's *Way to Keep Him*, **33.** 563n

Gates's convention with, ratification sought for, **33.** 12n

HW calls: 'Hurlothrumbo,' **28.** 355, **32.** 393; 'Julius Cæsar Burgonius,' **32.** 376; 'Swagger, Gen.,' **32.** 399

HW gives history of, **28.** 336–7

HW indifferent to, **39.** 327

Harrington defends, in Parliamentary inquiry, **39.** 325

*Heiress, The*, by, **33.** 508–9, 514, 563–4, **43.** 357

Hertford will give HW parcel from, of Mme du Deffand's effilage, **39.** 165

House of Commons investigates, **24.** 383, **28.** 401, **33.** 12, **39.** 321, 325

*Letter* from, said to be answered by Payne and Dr Johnson, **33.** 136

Light Horse of, due in Boston, **24.** 197n

*London Gazette* to publish exploits of, **32.** 376

lucky but not dishonourable as a gambler, **28.** 336–7

*Maid of the Oaks* by, **32.** 217n, **39.** 211

Mason wants material on, for possible satire, **28.** 332

mistaken for Frenchman, **28.** 342–3

parentage of, doubtful, **28.** 336

Paris visited by, **5.** 269

Parliamentary committee chairman on India, **23.** 381n

Parliamentary questioning of, **24.** 474n (*see also under* House of Commons)

Parliamentary resolutions by, on East India Co., **5.** 355n, **23.** 483n

Parliamentary speech by, requesting trial, **24.** 387n

Petersham, Lord, recommended by, **32.** 336

pompous manifesto by, **24.** 320

proclamation by, **32.** 369

prohibited from appearing at Court until after court martial, **28.** 395

prologue or epilogue may be done by, **34.** 1n

quarrels of, with Germain and Gen. Howe, **24.** 424n

Quebec reached by, **24.** 215n

(?) Ragley visited by, taking letter to London to HW, **39.** 118

regiment of: band of music in, **32.** 115n; Harcourt, Hon. William, appointed to, **28.** 470

resignation saddens, **28.** 475

*Richard Cœur de Lion* by, **33.** 546

savage orders of, to army, **32.** 400

Spaniards checked by, at Valencia de Alcántara, **22.** 78n, **38.** 178

speeches and writings of, laboured, **28.** 337

unpopular, **24.** 383

wife of, **3.** 243n

Burgoyne, Sir John (1739–85), 7th Bt; army officer:

drinks claret and gambles at quinze at Adderbury, **10.** 297

genealogy of, **10.** 352

HW regrets reading by, of *Mysterious Mother*, **10.** 298

Montagu's youth restored by, **10.** 296–7

—— visited by, at Adderbury, **10.** 295–6

*Mysterious Mother* acted by, at Adderbury, **10.** 297, 300

(?) Ragley visited by, taking letter to London to HW, **39.** 118

wife of, **10.** 25n

Burgoyne, Sir Roger (ca 1710–80), 6th Bt; M.P.:

genealogy of, **10.** 352

Montagu dislikes, **10.** 169

——hears of Lady Barbara Montagu's death from, **10.** 169

——'s visit interrupted by return of, **10.** 169

wife of, **9.** 360n

Burgundians:

French formerly hated by, **7.** 360

Burgundy, Ds of. *See* Bourgogne, Duchesse de

Burgundy, D. of. *See* Bourgogne, Duc de

Burgundy, governor of. *See* Beauvillier, Paul-Hippolyte de

Burgundy (French province):

destruction of châteaux in, **11.** 67

English travellers in, **11.** 46n

Éon's accent of, **33.** 510

explosion in, **11.** 46

Frederick II may be made D. of, in Flanders, **19.** 223, 238

parliament of, *see* Dijon, parliament of

Burgundy (wine):

Fettiplace's marriage attributed to influence of, **9.** 140

Hertford drinks, only, **15.** 320

Muzell's shipment of, to Mann, paid through HW, **21.** 424, 427, 491

Rigby throws, at Oxford proctor, **30.** 330

served at Lincoln's Inn entertainment, **43.** 169

Skrine serves, in carafes, **20.** 145

Stanley serves, **32.** 115n

Taaffe smuggles, **20.** 289

Buri, Comtesse de. *See* Frotier-de-la-Méssalière, Marie-Élisabeth; Urre d'Aiguebonne, Anne-Marie d' (ca 1633–1724)

Burial; burials (*see also under* Funeral):

Christian, HW does not care to be killed far from, **37.** 66

Edgcumbe quarrels with 'Kitten' over paying for her, **30.** 90

Italian, éloges of the deceased put into tombs, **21.** 170

of Thomas Gray, **1.** 230–1, 232, 235

Scottish, vastly attended, even when most trivial, **37.** 267

Burial card:

HW expects, from Chute, **9.** 166

Burigny. *See* Lévesque de Burigny

Buriton, Hants:

Gibbon lives at, **14.** 176n

Burk, ——, Gen.:

Martin's message to, **18.** 43

Burke, ——, naval officer:

Russian naval command of, **25.** 6on

Burke, Mr:

Draper *or* Braber lives with, in Ireland, **30.** 224n

Burke, Mrs:

*Critical Review* criticizes novels of, **31.** 274n

Burke, Edmund (1729–97), M.P.; statesman:

agreeableness and vivacity of, diminished by business and politics, **31.** 242

*Appeal from the New to the Old Whigs* by, **11.** 300, **34.** 116, 118, 119

appointment of, as Paymaster, **25.** 392, 407

*Articles of Charge . . . against Warren Hastings*, **25.** 639

[Burke, Edmund, *continued*]

associations' effect on people gives opportunity to, **25.** 32

Barry includes, in allegorical painting, **29.** 296, 297

——'s patron, **2.** 189n

Beauclerk, Topham, visited by, **32.** 292

Beaconsfield the address of, **42.** 300

Bembridge and Powell restored by, to Pay Office, **25.** 407–8

bill of reformation or reduction proposed by, **25.** 20, 25, 26–7, 28

Bolingbroke imitated by, **43.** 125

Boswell sketches, **33.** 462n

Bribery Bill opposed by, **22.** 585n

Bristol election speech of, **33.** 230

—— elects, M.P., **39.** 207

—— seat given up by, **36.** 174

Burgh's *Scriptural Confutation* dedicated to, **28.** 200

Burgoyne parodied in speech by, **28.** 354–6

Burney calls on, **42.** 330n

Callington borough's possible vacancy may interest, **41.** 376n

Carlisle's choice ridiculed by, **28.** 365n

Chatham the object of protest by, **22.** 471n

—— would give secondary post to, **28.** 377

civil list regulations proposed by, **25.** 257n

clerkship of the Pells wanted by, for son, **29.** 264n, **33.** 345n, **42.** 23–8

Colman's portrait unworthy to be with that of, **41.** 400

Congress's petition not presented by, **39.** 231n

Cust does not restrain speeches by, **23.** 175n

dominating influence in administration, **29.** 261n

Du Deffand, Mme, desires opinion of, on Necker's *Éloge de M. Colbert*, **5.** 395, 405

——'s opinion of, **5.** 329, 331–2, 334

——'s opinion of speech of, **7.** 216

—— to send letter through, **5.** 335, 338, 339

Dundas warns, **29.** 271n

East India Co. inquiry opposed by, **41.** 65n

educated by Quaker, **29.** 63

eloquence of, in second printed speech better than in first, **28.** 203

entertaining, **31.** 214

*Essay Towards an Abridgement of English History* by, **43.** 126

'farcical grimace' of, **29.** 241

'feigned voice' of, **28.** 354

Fox, C. J. and, only efficient men in new Opposition, **25.** 295

Fox, C. J., denounced by, **11.** 263, 293

——'s apology to, **34.** 118

——'s India Bill probably planned by, **36.** 214n

French difficult for, **5.** 329, 331–2

French visit of, to put son in school, **32.** 103n

George III praised by, in speech, **29.** 241–2

Gordon rioters oppose, **2.** 224–5, **25.** 54, **29.** 62, **33.** 176

Gray mentions proposed history to, **14.** 122

Guibert's *Connétable* discussed by, **5.** 343

——'s *Tactique* admired by, **5.** 334, 335, 338

HW admires temper of, less than Fox's, **34.** 118

HW called on by: **41.** 375; after Yorke's death, **23.** 178n

HW has not seen, three times in three years, **34.** 100

HW indifferent to, **39.** 327

HW informed by, about Rockingham, **39.** 123

HW jokes about reform of sinecures as urged by, **31.** 241

HW prefers, to Mirabeau, **34.** 104

HW's correspondence with, **41.** 375, **42.** 23, 300

HW solicited by, for subscription to Dr Johnson's monument, **11.** 276

HW's opinion of, **9.** 380

HW talks with, **5.** 343

HW to be called on by, **42.** 23

HW to meet, at Lady Lucan's, **12.** 76

HW to receive book by, **5.** 334, 335, 338, 339

HW wishes history by, in Irish binding, **9.** 418

Hamilton entertains, **9.** 380, 405

Hastings accused by, of mistreating Begums of Oudh, **33.** 525n

——'s prosecution by, proved to be right, **25.** 653

history of England said to be written by, **9.** 408, (?) 418

history of Ireland said to be written by, **9.** 405, 407, (?) 418

House of Commons attacked by, **15.** 130, **23.** 170, 184

—— criticizes, for restoring dismissed men to Pay Office, **25.** 408

incorruptible save when buying land cheaply from naked Caribs, **39.** 239

Irish bills supported by, **28.** 395n

Junius papers not attributed to, **36.** 52

Kildare, Bp of, to entertain, **9.** 396

La Harpe's *Barmécides* heard by, **5.** 338, 339, 343

Léon, Bp of, friend of, **12.** 25n

*Letter* from, on American war, **28.** 309–10, 312, 330

*Letter from Mr Burke to a Member of the National Assembly*, **11.** 277, 299–300

*Letter from the Right Hon. Edmund Burke to a Noble Lord*, **34.** 214–15

list by, of sinecure offices to be abolished, **39.** 388

Llangollen ladies appeal to, against newspaper notoriety, **34.** 94n

Mann, Horace II, refers Maidstone freeholders to bill proposed by, **25.** 32n

'metaphoric vision' might be formed by, **39.** 356

Middleton notifies, about Congress, **24.** 85n

military suppression of Gordon Riots deplored by, in House of Commons, **25.** 77n

motion by, in East India Co. court of pro-

prietors, for inquiry into Benfield, **25**. 117n

*Mr Burke's Speech . . . on Mr Fox's East India Bill* will make England the horror of Europe, **36**. 221

North, Lord, accused by, of deceiving Parliament about impending Spanish war, **24**. 491n

—— ridiculed by, **32**. 404

——'s administration opposed by, **39**. 239

Opposition's coalition effected by, **15**. 128n

Paine called by, worst man in England but best in France, **34**. 180

pamphlets against, **11**. 169–70

Paris visited by, **5**. 329–38, **32**. 103

Parliamentary bill to regulate civil list establishments introduced by, **29**. 109, 116

Parliamentary motions by: for papers on India, **25**. 630n; on American conciliation, **32**. 274n; on St Eustatius, **25**. 218n, **36**. 199

Parliamentary speeches by: against Gage's conduct at Boston, **39**. 232; defending London's remonstrance, **39**. 126; denouncing sinecures, **31**. 241n; in debate on address to Q. Charlotte and George IV, **34**. 41n; on French Revolution, **34**. 104n; on Grenville's motion about Franco-American treaty, **28**. 373; on Parliamentary reform, **25**. 31, **33**. 169; on Saratoga, **32**. 400n; warm but not good, **23**. 248

Parr praises, **34**. 45n

paymaster of the Forces, **25**. 264n, 392, 407

Polish subscription not joined by, **15**. 224–5n

protest against Dividend Bill drawn up by, **22**. 534n

*Reflections on the Revolution in France* by, **11**. 125, 127n, 131–2, 135, 146, 151, 168–9, 209, 239, 277, **34**. 97–8, 100–4, 118, **42**. 300, 303, **43**. 144

remarks by: on Hunter's political lecture, **29**. 86; on Lady Mary Coke's quarrel with Miss Pelham, **28**. 402–3; on Lord Effingham, **29**. 235–6

resignation of, **35**. 519

rhetoric of, HW does not care for, **32**. 222

Richmond, D. of, prodded by, to attack North ministry, **41**. 310–11n

Rockingham's 'governor,' **23**. 209

Roman Catholics defended by, against Gordon, in Parliamentary inquiry, **39**. 325

Roman Catholics, petition against, opposed by, **29**. 52n

Roman Catholic sympathy of, **28**. 469, **29**. 63, 315, 318

Roscoe's pen more unadulterated than that of, **34**. 215

St Vincent's importance over-estimated by, **28**. 142

Shelburne attacked by, **29**. 266, 280–1

Sheridan opposes, in House of Commons on French Revolution, **31**. 343n

Shipley friend of, **28**. 269n

Smith's book given to, **15**. 52n

social relations of: in Paris, **5**. 329, 331, 331–2, 338, 339; with Mrs Vesey, **31**. 214, 242

son of, **31**. 206

Spanish war predicted by, in Commons, **24**. 483n

speeches said by, to be incorrectly reported in newspapers, **25**. 58n

*Speech of . . . on American Taxation*, **32**. 222

Strutt's bill said to be aimed at Fox and, **29**. 50

'stupid retreat' of, **28**. 283n

*Sublime and Beautiful*, quoted by Hannah More, **31**. 252

testimony by, at Powell's inquest, **25**. 407n

*Thoughts on the Cause of the Present Discontents*, **23**. 209

Thurlow called 'iron Pluto' by, **25**. 684

Townshend, Charles, surpasses, in metaphors, **10**. 242

*Two Letters Addressed to a Member*, **34**. 223

Vesey nominated by, for Club, **30**. 51n

*Vindication of Natural Society* by, imitates Bolingbroke, **9**. 380

Wedderburn's altercation with, in House of Commons, **32**. 401–2

——'s breach with, made up, **24**. 341

Wilberforce supported by, against slavery, **31**. 296n

wit, metaphors, etc. of, more attractive than his discretion, **34**. 116

wit of, **11**. 151

witty but in bad taste, **32**. 43n

Burke, Mrs Edmund. *See* Nugent, Jane

Burke, Richard (1733–94), brother of Edmund Burke:

Barnard's clash with Dr Johnson reported by, **32**. 288n

HW mistakes, for Boswell, **33**. 466

Reynolds bequeaths miniature to, **33**. 539n

speculates in land, **28**. 142n

testimony of, to Salisbury jury, **25**. 117n

Burke, Richard (1758–94), son of Edmund Burke:

Du Deffand, Mme, sends letter through, **6**. 41, 56

father places, at Auxerre, **32**. 103n

father puts, in school at Blois, **32**. 103n

father tries to make, clerk of the Pells, **33**. 345n, **42**. 24–8

HW called on by, in Paris, **7**. 299

HW's correspondence with, **42**. 24–8

King accompanies, **6**. 41, **43**. 96

leaves Paris, **6**. 41

social relations of, with Mrs Vesey, **31**. 214

SH visited by, **31**. 206

Burke, William (1729–98), M.P.:

Burke, Edmund, avoids England to escape St Vincent's involvement of, **32**. 103n

Junius papers attributed to, **36**. 52

*Remarks on the Letter Addressed to Two Great Men* attributed to, **16**. 39n

Burlace. *See* Borlace

Burleigh, —— (fl. 1777), carrier:
owns Cambridge wagons, **2**. 47
Burleigh. *See also* Burghley
Burleigh House. *See* Burghley House
*Burlesque*. See *Eviad, The*
Burletta; burlettas:
at Dublin, **9**. 394, 414–15, **10**. 20
at Florence: acted alternately with Rucellai's play, **20**. 151; almost ended, before D. of York arrives, **22**. 179; at 'little theatre,' **17**. 121, 128, 130, **19**. 356, 476; Botta to permit, on Francis I's day, **22** 171; Chute may attend Mme Grifoni at, **35**. 11; Cowper's, **22**. 393; dispute at, **17**. 162; Estevenon attends, **17**. 200; for Karl Friedrich, **20** 148; Leopold and Maria Louisa afraid to attend, **22**. 393; Mann to take Thomas Pitt to, **21**. 501; Mann, Lady Lucy, attends, **24**. 105; new, to be given, **22**. 28; Pepi substitutes, for *Don Pilogio*, **18**. 41; Pertici's, **18**. 198, 294; Pertici, Signora, considers play inferior to, **20**. 357; Ronchetti sings in, **18**. 462n; said to be good, **22**. 173; singers to perform, **22**. 245n
at Pisa, **22**. 424, **23**. 171
in London: at Covent Garden, **35**. 160; bad, **23**. 547; beginning, **20**. 4; Charlotte, Q., prefers, **38**. 143; make managers' fortunes, **22**. 473–4; prevalent, **35**. 192; rage for, **21**. 506; three a week, **20**. 410; unsuccessful, **20**. 41
Mann's procurement of copies of, for HW, **21**. 506, 512, 532, 533, 538, 561, **22**. 6
out of fashion in England, **10**. 4
Burley. *See* Burghley; Burleigh
Burlington, Cts of. *See* Compton, Lady Elizabeth (1760–1835); Noel, Juliana (1672–1750); Savile, Lady Dorothy (1699–1758)
Burlington, E. of. *See* Boyle, Charles (before 1674–1704); Boyle, Richard (1694–1753); Cavendish, Lord George Augustus Henry (1754–1834)
'Burlington air':
HW assumes, for SH, **20**. 361
Burlington Bay. *See* Bridlington Bay
Burlington Gardens, London:
Clifford St in, **43**. 262
fire reported to be at, **9**. 363
Frere lodges in, **30**. 76n
Queensberry's house in, **33**. 64n
Burlington House, Piccadilly, London:
Chatterton thinks that D. of Devonshire lives in, **16**. 347
Devonshire, D. of, brings HW to, to meet Ds of Bedford and see pictures from Hardwick, **38**. 119–20
—— said to have lent, to Ps Amelia, **9**. 316
Hartington, M. of, acquires, by marriage, **20**. 66n
Portland lives in, **29**. 265n
'Violette' (Mrs Garrick) a favourite at, **20**. 74nn

wedding at, **22**. 465n
Burlington Street, London:
Dickensons live in, **31**. 367n
Fox writes from, **30**. 133–4
Poyntz's house in, visited by Nivernais, **22**. 70n
Queensberry, Ds of, gives ball in cold gallery of her house in, **38**. 342–3
Wade's house in, **19**. 126n
*See also* Old Burlington St
Burlton, Philip (ca 1714–90), army surgeon; sportsman:
comes to HW three times a week, **32**. 131
HW asks Lord Ossory about, **32**. 133
HW's correspondence with, **32**. 134–5
'my friend,' **32**. 169
Rutland, Ds of, said to sponsor gaming-house of, **32**. 131n
Burn, Richard (1709–85), D.C.L.:
*Justice of the Peace and Parish Officer, The,* by, **29**. 115
Burn; burns:
deaths from, **33**. 460
Burnaby, Rev. Andrew, chaplain to English factory at Leghorn:
Leghorn consulate administered by, **22**. 526n
Burnaby, John (d. 1774), English minister to Switzerland 1743–50:
Berne will prefer Villettes to, **20**. 76
Fribourg's protection of Young Pretender opposed by, **19**. 509
Paoli's correspondence with, **23**. 27n
troops raised by, in Switzerland, **18**. *215*
Burnell, Elizabeth (ca 1704–68), m. 1 —— James; m. 2 (1741) George Whitefield:
Whitefield gives Lady Huntingdon's watch and trinkets to, **35**. 309
Burnells. *See* East Ruston Burnells
Burnestone, Anna Maria:
Burgoyne the son of, **28**. 336n
Burnet, Mrs:
print of, **40**. 237
Burnet, Elizabeth (1692–1748), m. (1714) Richard West:
death date of, **43**. 176
Gray searches for, **13**. *143*
—— suggests that HW ask, for West's MSS, **14**. 16–17
son of, **13**. 91, **17**. 468n
Williams said to be lover of, **13**. 210n
Burnet, Gilbert (1643–1715), Bp of Salisbury:
asseverations of, **31**. 22
Baker not supported by, **2**. 98, 343, 348–9, 350
——'s acquaintance, **2**. 348
changes his principles, **2**. 64–5, 66
Christina, Q., converses with, **2**. 60
Cole's poor opinion of, **2**. 359–60
Crew's treatment by, confirmed, **2**. 346
daughter of, **13**. 143n, **17**. 468n
death of, **2**. 349
Gunning, Bp, described by, **2**. 59–60, 64
HW quotes, **35**. 457

HW's portrait of, **15**. 192
*History of His Own Time* by, **1**. 59–60, **6**. 247, 253, **10**. 174n, **16**. 20–1, 52, **28**. 67, 451, **29**. 115, **31**. 294, **34**. 64n
*History of the Reformation* by, **1**. 79, 221, **2**. 348–9
Hurd's dialogues the 'offspring' of, **16**. 34
in Stratford's tragedy, **29**. 224
Johnson does not forgive, **2**. 359
letter of, cited, **2**. 356
Mackenzie receives account of Mary Q. of Scots from, **15**. 34–5
protestations by, of impartiality, **14**. 53–4
Robinson does not spare, **2**. 127
Roland, Mme, reads books by, **10**. 174
Suffolk, House of, described by, **2**. 357
*Vindication of the . . . Church and State of Scotland, A*, **2**. 64n, 65n, 66, 68n
West's grandfather, **13**. 91, **14**. 234
Wolsey's hat found by, **28**. 313n, **41**. 332

Burnet, Mrs John. *See* Jamesone, Mary
Burnet, Sir Thomas (1694–1753), son of Bp Burnet:
Wolsey's hat left to, **41**. 332
Burnet. *See also* Burnett
Burnet, great (pimprenelle):
Meinières,Mme de, asks about cultivation of, **4**. 124, 130
Burnett, James (1714–99), lord of session as Lord Monboddo, 1767; jurist and author:
*Ancient Metaphysics* by, **29**. 105n
Garrick, Mrs, wooed by, **29**. 271, **33**. 363
HW scoffs at, **29**. 105
*Of the Origin and Progress of Language*: **29**. 105n; alludes to men's tails, **33**. 363
social relations of, with Mrs Ord, **31**. 213
Burney, Charles (1726–1814), Mus.D.; historian of music:
Barry includes, in allegorical painting, **29**. 300
Bewley dies in house of, **16**. 351
—— friend of, **2**. 85n, **16**. 121n
——'s correspondence with, **43**. 64, 218, 351, 367
Boscawen, Mrs, visited by, **12**. 203
Chelsea College the address of, **42**. 331
daughter's resignation announced by, **42**. 329–30
Dryden praised by, **31**. 213, 221n
Duncan, Lady Mary, leaves bequest to, **11**. 153n
*General History of Music, A*, by, **28**. 248–9, 251
Grimaldi seen by, **13**. 64n
HW called on by, in Berkeley Sq., **42**. 428
HW congratulates, on daughter's Court post, **42**. 170–3
HW congratulates, on daughter's resignation, **42**. 331–2
(?) HW hears news from, **11**. 139–40
HW invites, to SH, **42**. 149–50, 331–2

HW's correspondence with, **42**. 149–50, 170–3, 202, 329–32, 425, 427–8
HW sees chariot of, **42**. 202
HW to be called on by, at SH, **42**. 299
HW too ill to see, but now recovering, **42**. 425
HW twice misses call from, **42**. 202
HW visited by, at SH, **12**. 203–4, **33**. 498
Hawkins's rivalry with, as historian of music, **43**. 64
Lock recommended by, **11**. 111n
*Memoirs . . . of the Abbé Metastasio*, HW thanks Burney for, **42**. 427, 428
Mt Edgcumbe, Cts of, friend of, **11**. 31n
Nivernais's *Jardins modernes* given to, **12**. 260
pianoforte heard by, **4**. 452n
social relations of, with: Garrick, Mrs, **31**. 213; More, Hannah, **31**. 213; Ord, Mrs, **31**. 213; Pepys, W. W., **31**. 243
Burney, Frances (1752–1840), m. (1793) Alexandre d'Arblay; novelist:
annuity granted to, **42**. 331n
Batt a favourite of, **11**. 17n
*Brief Reflections Relative to the Emigrant French Clergy* by, **12**. 73
Cambridge, Charlotte, friend of, **11**. 80n
—— hears HW praised by, **42**. 299
*Camilla* by, **12**. 204, **15**. 329–30, **31**. 403
*Cecilia* by, **15**. 165n, **16**. 256, **31**. 271, **33**. 356–7, 359, 518, **43**. 198
Charlotte, Q., sees, when with Mrs Delany, **42**. 171n
Court post accepted by, **31**. 247, 271, 360–1, **33**. 518
Delany, Mrs, probably recommends, **42**. 171, 172
*Evelina* by, **1**. 83n, **31**. 271, **33**. 356, 518
father announces to HW resignation of, from royal household, **42**. 329–31
Greville, Mrs, godmother of, **11**. 47n
HW calls: 'Cecilia,' **42**. 150; 'the prototype of Evelina and Cecilia,' **42**. 293
HW congratulates father on Court post for, **42**. 170–3
HW could inform, on etiquette, **33**. 518
HW gets apologies from, for silence, **42**. 290–1, 293
HW introduces Berrys to, **11**. 235n
HW invites to SH, **42**. 149–50, 331–2
(?) HW jokes about, as secretary of state, **25**. 599
HW points out to, a box to go (after his own death) to Lord Waldegrave, **43**. 369–70
HW's correspondence with, **42**. 290–1, 293–9
HW's good opinion of, **31**. 361, **33**. 498
HW's *Mysterious Mother* alienates, from HW, **31**. 247n
HW's regard for, **15**. 329
HW tells: to bring maid to SH, **42**. 150; to consult lawyer about Colomb, **42**. 293–4
HW told by, to have James Colomb call on her, **42**. 290, 293

[Burney, Frances, *continued*]
HW to send servant to, at St James's Palace, 42. 296
HW visited by, at SH, 12. 222, 33. 498, 42. 150n, 29, 331
health of, recovered, 31. 247
induction of, at Windsor Castle, 42. 172
keepership of the robes resigned by, 42. 330–1
Ord, Anne, travels with, 42. 330n
pension of, 42. 331n
'retired from the world into a closet at Court,' 42. 294
St James's Palace address of, 42. 293
servant's money to be divided by, 42. 298
social relations of, with: Garrick, Mrs, 31. 213; More, Hannah, 31. 213; Ord, Mrs, 31. 213; Pepys, W. W., 31. 243; Vesey, Mrs, 31. 247
SH visit described by, to Hester Maria Thrale, 42. 149n
Windsor Castle may not be left by, to visit SH, 42. 170, 173
Woodcock, lawyer of, tells her not to contest servant's will, 42. 297
Burney, Susanna, Mrs Phillips:
sister visits, at Mickleham, 42. 331n
sister writes to, about introduction at Court, 42. 172n
Burnham, Bucks:
Antrobus, vicar of, 13. 106n
Apthorpe leaves, 1. 328, 331n
—— lives at, 1. 35, 78
—— vicar of, 1. 35n
Britwell Place near, 13. 112n
Cole at, 1. 348, 370, 381, 2. 5, 371
—— intends not to live at, 1. 334, 337
——'s curate at, 2. 228
—— to go to, 1. 331, 339, 347, 360, 43. 59
—— vicar of, 1. 103n
Gray finds, dull, 13. 111
—— visits, 13. 105, 107, 110
living of, 1. 103, 106, 328, 330, 331–2, 334, 335–6, 337, 2. 57, 86, 228, 378, 379
wayward circumstances at, 2. 228, 229
Burning-glass:
Conway tries, on a bomb, 21. 155
French do not need, 32. 8
meat roasted by means of, in London, 21. 121
Burning on the hand. *See* Branding
Burns, Robert (1759–96):
Thomson's eulogy by, 11. 353n
'Burnus, Mr':
Old Pretender's name for D. of Argyll, 17. 479
Burrell, Lady. *See* Raymond, Sophia
Burrell, Mr, Lisbon merchant:
cash of, saved in Lisbon earthquake, 20. 520n
Burrell, Sir Charles Merrik (1774–1862), 3d Bt, 1796:
SH visited by, 12. 236
Burrell, Lady Elizabeth. *See* Bertie, Lady Priscilla Barbara Elizabeth

Burrell, Elizabeth (d. 1734), m. (1713) Thomas Trevor, 2d Bn Trevor:
genealogy of, 10. 352
Burrell, Elizabeth Amelia, m. (1766) Richard Henry Alexander Bennett:
marriage of, 24. 499
Burrell, Elizabeth Anne (1757–1837), m. 1 (1778) Douglas Hamilton, 8th D. of Hamilton (divorced 1794); m. 2 (1800) Henry Cecil, 10th E. of Exeter; cr. (1801) M. of Exeter:
marriage of, 24. 499, 33. 3
pretty member of Burrell family, 24. 499
Burrell, Frances Julia (1752–1820), m. (1779) Hugh Percy, styled E. Percy 1766–86, 2d D. of Northumberland, 1786:
marriage of, 24. 499
Burrell, Isabella Susanna (1750–1812), m. (1775) Lord Algernon Percy, 2d Bn Lovaine, 1786, cr. (1790) E. of Beverley:
Éon's rudeness to, after Dutens's introduction, 33. 548
HW does not know, 25. 422
Mann entertains, at Florence, 25. 402n
marriage of, 24. 499
Burrell, Peter (1692–1756), M.P.:
Bank director, 17. 411
broken merchant, 24. 499
family alliances of, 24. 499, 33. 206
Mann may remember, 24. 499
——'s correspondence with, 19. 77
money to be remitted to Jamaica by agreement by, 17. 411
Secret Committee may examine, 17. 410–11
Secret Committee reports on, 17. 475
sub-governor of South Sea Co., 19. 77n
Treasury agent, 17. 411n
Walpole, Sir Robert, has, as follower, 24. 499
Burrell, Peter II (1723–75), M.P.:
Townshend dismissed for asking place for, 10. 69n
West Looe election contests of, 21. 89n
Burrell, Peter III (1754–1820), Kt, 1781; 2d Bt, 1787, cr. (1796) Bn Gwydir:
Cholmondeley's wedding attended by, 11. 255
Irish peerage declined by, 33. 430n
lord great chamberlain, 39. 334
luck of, might make him a good naval commander, 39. 334
marriage of, 12. 193n, 24. 499, 33. 84, 206
possible owner of Glastonbury Abbey, 33. 206
to winter in France, 2. 235
Wales, Ps of, dines with, 12. 200n
Burrell, Mrs Peter. *See* Raymond, Amy
Burrell, Lady Priscilla Barbara Elizabeth. *See* Bertie, Lady Priscilla Barbara Elizabeth
Burrell, Sir William (1732–96), 2d Bt, 1788; L.L.D.; antiquary; M.P.:
drawings for Sussex collected by, 15. 203
gives franks to Cole, 1. 162
HW sends box through, 7. 404

HW sends letter through, **7**. 377
HW's social relations with, **7**. 267
possible owner of Glastonbury Abbey, **33**. 206
SH visited by, **12**. 236

Burrell. *See also* Burwell

Burrell family:
history of, **24**. 499, 505–6
luck of, **39**. 334

'Burrhus.' *See* Castellane, Jean-Baptiste de

Burrish, George, naval capt.:
investigation of, **19**. 25

Burrough, Sir James (1691–1764), vice-chancellor of Cambridge; antiquary; architect; master of Caius College:
acquainted with Vertue, **14**. 110
Clare Hall designed by, **1**. 161n
MSS of, about Bury St Edmunds, **2**. 36–8
note by, on King's College Chapel, **1**. 17

Burroughes, Rev. Jeremiah (1599–1646), nonconformist:
engraving of, **16**. 65

Burroughs, Capt.:
SH visited by, **12**. 246

Burroughs, Mrs Thomas Cooke. *See* Masters, Mary

Burroughs. *See also* Borough; Burrough; Burroughes

Burr St, Wapping:
Chandos, Ds of, 'bred up' in, **30**. 61n

Bursar:
at Cambridge, poor in arithmetic, **32**. 19

Burstonhaugh. *See* Burton Haugh

Burt, Rev. Robert (ca 1756–91), vicar of Twickenham:
denies Lord Camelford's authorship of pamphlet, **11**. 53
SH visited by, **12**. 233, 239

Burt, Mrs Robert. *See* Gascoyne, Sarah

Burton, Mrs, milliner:
HW asked by, for tickets to Coronation, **9**. 384

Burton, Mrs, of Richmond:
SH visited by, **12**. 247

Burton, Benjamin (d. ca 1756):
law suit over estate of, **21**. 65n

Burton, Francis (?1744–1832), M.P.:
(?) SH visited by, **12**. 222, 252

Burton, Harriet (ca 1751–1829), m. (1773) Hon. John Trevor, 3d Vct Hampden, 1824:
HW knows, and calls her 'gentle and pleasing,' **25**. 595
Mann enjoys company of, at Florence, **25**. 592

Burton, Henry (ca 1578–1648), Puritan divine:
engraving of, **16**. 65
minister of St Matthews, Friday St, **16**. 65

Burton, Rev. John (1696–1771):
takes living of Worplesdon, **1**. 106, 334

Burton, John (1710–71), physician; antiquary:
'Account of a Roman Sepulchre' by, **15**. 179n
*Monasticon Eboracense* by, **16**. 25, 26
rebels joined by, **19**. 180

Burton, Lora (1740–1812), m. (1763) **John** Dawnay, 4th Vct Downe, 1760:
SH visited by, **12**. 236

Burton, Ralph (d. 1768), army officer:
Craufurd's regiment assigned to, **38**. 468–9

Burton, Robert:
suit against, over Benjamin Burton's estate, **21**. 65n

Burton, Sarah (d. 1812), m. (1759) **Joshua** Rowley, cr. (1786) Bt:
(?) SH visited by, **12**. 239

Burton, Simon (ca 1690–1744), M.D.:
Thompson's disagreement with, satirized in *Discord*, **37**. 162, 165

Burton, Susan (d. 1764), m. Hon. James Brudenell; woman of the Bedchamber to Q. Caroline, 1731–7:
'Brunella' the wasp in HW's 'Patapan,' **30**. 295
son of, receives legacy, **9**. 184

Burton, William (1575–1645), topographer:
*Antiquities of Leicestershire* by, **16**. 64
Delaram's engraving of, **16**. 64

Burton, William, army officer:
England to be visited by, **10**. 13
HW to send *Anecdotes of Painting* through, to Montagu, **10**. 13
Montagu, Frederick, knows, **10**. 13

Burton, William Henry (d. 1818), army officer:
(?) Hertford appoints, aide-de-camp at Ponsonby's request, **30**. 200

Burton, Staffs:
Comings of, **2**. 39n

Burton Haugh, Suffolk:
manor of, **1**. 376

Burton Pynsent, Somerset:
Chatham at, **6**. 38n
—— sets out for, **39**. 89
parson of, made Pynsent's will, **22**. 276

Burton-upon-Trent, Staffs:
Whaley writes from, **40**. 42

Burwell, Lady. *See* Derehaugh, Elizabeth

Burwell, Edmund (*or* Edward) (d. 1652) **of** Woodbridge:
family of, **1**. 374n
HW's ancestor, **1**. 374n

Burwell, Mrs Edmund (*or* Edward). *See* Pitman, Mary

Burwell, Sir Jeffery (d. 1684), Kt:
HW's ancestor, **1**. 374, 376
Rougham sold by, **1**. 377

Burwell, Mary (d. 1711), m. Robert Walpole; HW's grandmother:
children's births recorded by, **22**. 26n
marriage of, **1**. 374

Burwell family:
arms of, **1**. 377
notes on, **1**. 374–5, 376–7

Bury, Comtesse de. *See* Frotier-de-la-Messalière, Marie-Élisabeth; Urre-d'Aiguebonne, Anne-Marie d' (ca 1633–1724)

Bury, Vct. *See* Keppel, George

Bury, Mr:
SH visited by, 12. 250 *bis*

Bury, Lady Charlotte Susan Maria. *See* Campbell, Lady Charlotte Susan Maria

Bury, John (1725–64):
uncle's estates go to, 34. 60n

Bury, Richard de (1730–94), historian:
*Histoire de la vie de Henri IV*, 4. 94, 158–9, 43. 88
social relations of, with Mme Geoffrin, 7. 349

Bury pear. *See under* Pear

Bury St Edmunds, Suffolk:
abbey at: 2. 31n; altar doors (or tablets) from, 2. 30–2, 35–6, 219–21, 16. 185, 42. 246, 43. 65; Babington abbot of, 2. 36, 38–9; Battely's history of, 2. 39, 222; patronized by House of Lancaster, 2. 32, 36–9, 40, 42, 222, 16. 184; Tate and, 2. 220, 221–2
agate-handled knives and forks at, 2. 12
Barnardiston of, 1. 189n
Bristol, E. of, nominates Felton Hervey as M.P. for, 30. 115
Burrough's MSS concerning, 2. 36–8
Conway elected M.P. for, 6. 177n
—— faces election contest at, 35. 612
election at, voided, 35. 196n
Elizabeth of York's portrait at, 2. 320
Fitzroy succeeds Conway as M.P. for, 39. 407n
former seat of abbots of, 2. 175
Gloucester, D. of, accompanied Henry VI to, 16. 184
Grafton gives borough of, not to Conway but to Davers and Hervey, with Conway later succeeding Hervey, 39. 194
Hardwick House near, 41. 103
Hervey's sale at, 2. 8n
La Rochefoucauld brothers lodge with Symonds at, 16. 225–6
mayor and corporation of, get letter from Thomas Hervey, 30. 115–16
MS account of Henry VI's visit to, 16. 183, 184, 187, 188
Norford, surgeon at, 16. 314n
revolutionary spirit at, 15. 243
St Mary's at, Mills preacher at, 16. 246n
Sudbury mob sends card to, about contested election, 35. 196

Bury St, St James's, London:
Clement, Anne, addressed at, 36. 279
fire in, 35. 210–11
La Cour lives in, 14. 93n

Busancy-Pavant, Jeanne-Pérette de, m. (1763) Charles-François-Ferdinand, Marquis de Champagne:
(?) social relations of, with Duchesse d'Anville, 7. 311

Busbecq, Augier-Ghislain de (1522–92), Flemish diplomatist; traveller:
*Omnia quæ extant . . . quibus accedunt epistolæ aliquot insignium quorundum vi-vorum lectu iucundissimæ Museum Minervæ*, grant in, 16. 151

Busbrig, John (d. 1541), gamekeeper:
Dacre hanged for killing, 35. 139–40

Busch, Mme de:
George IV said to have affair with, 25. 154n

Busch, Johann Clamor August von dem:
Hanoverian privy councillor, 20. 212n

Bush, Atkinson (ca 1735–1811), proctor:
(?) HW amused by letter from, 15. 267
(?) HW calls, 'Chanticleer,' 12. *141*
(?) 'intellectual,' 12. 141
(?) SH visited by, 12. 141, 239, 249

Bush; bushes:
lamps in, at ball, 35. 391

Bushe, Gervase:
Irish Parliamentary activity of, 39. 350n

Bushey, Herts:
Capper of, 14. 196n

Bushey House, Middlesex; E. of Guilford's seat:
Guilford's engagement acknowledged at, 12. 147–8
North, Lady Charlotte, and Mrs G. Cholmondeley come from, 11. 317
visitors to: Englefield, 11. 114; HW, 11. 114, 12. 120, 167, 29. 210; Storer, 11. 114

Bushey Park, Middlesex; royal park and home of Lords Halifax and North:
Brydone gains entrée to, 33. 232
Falkner, Anna Maria, has house at, 10. 335
HW convoys French ladies through, 11. 329
Halifax occupies seat at, 10. 207
—— ranger of, 10. 335
Hamilton entertains at, 9. 380, (?) 405
—— takes house near, 9. 329n, 358
Hampton Court near, 10. 335
landscape effects at Halifax's at, 9. 380
North, Lord and Lady, at, 32. 193
North, Lord, ranger of, 11. 82n
North, Hon. Frederick, returns to, 42. 385
road through, 11. 26n
solitary after Lord North's fall, 33. 347
storm damage at, 12. 175
visitors to: Boswell and Courtenay, 42. 143n; HW, 32. 156, 33. 235, 580–1; Hinchingbrooke, 10. 207; Malone and sisters, 42. 143n; Montagu, 9. 371; Montagu, John, 9. 371; Montagu Dunk, Lady Elizabeth, 10. 207; Osborn, Hon. Mrs, 10. 32, 207; Sandwich, 10. 207

Bushey Park Gate:
house at, mentioned for Berrys, 11. 26, 42, 50, 54, 55

Bushy Park. *See* Bushey Park

Bushy Run:
Indian battles near, 38. 213

Business:
English take no pleasure in, 25. 110
HW does not understand, 23. 122
HW fond of hurry of, 30. 72

Buskin; buskins:

Chandos wears, in Van der Myn's portrait, **30.** 61

Danish mender of, **35.** 327

HW prefers celebrities who do not wear, in their memoirs, **38.** 444

Busoni, ——, banker at Paris:

Orford, Cts of, invests money with, in French funds, **25.** 113

Bussy, Abbé de:

Benedict XIV sends, to Gages, **18.** 56

papal galleys commanded by, **18.** 56

Bussy, Comte de. *See* Rabutin, Roger de

Bussy, Mme de. *See* Messey, Marie-Charlotte-Justine

Bussy, François de (1699–1780), French chargé d'affaires at Vienna and London; minister plenipotentiary to England 1761–2; minister to Hanover:

Churchill tells puns to, **18.** 307

courier expected by, **38.** 112

departure from England deferred by, so wagoner can move his goods, **38.** 120

England left by, **9.** 389. **38.** 119, 128

France's possible negotiator with England, **21.** 355n

George II dislikes, **21.** 504n

HW dines with, **18.** 131

(?) Honywood's clash with, **35.** 33

London house in Suffolk St taken by, **21.** 514, **35.** 308, **38.** 97

peace negotiations of, **21.** 527n, 536n

peace overtures of, **18.** 245n

Pitt answers threat from, with witticism about French prisoners, **38.** 112

—— told by, that Belle-Île must be surrendered, **38.** 97n

politeness expected from, **18.** 283

Prague's resistance makes, pert towards England, **37.** 127

Stanley's exchange with, **21.** 504, 514, **38.** 89–90

stories by, **18.** *131*

Bussy-Rabutin, Comte de. *See* Rabutin, Roger de

Bust; busts:

ancient, show character, not passion, **35.** 445

at Stowe, **35.** 75–6

Bernini's, of Brutus, **35.** 268

Boyle, Charlotte, models, of brother, **35.** 385

coloured, of Sir Nicholas Bacon, **40.** 193

Damer, Mrs, does: of Ceres, **35.** 432; of infant Paris or Atys, **35.** 437; of Mary Berry, **43.** 155; well, **25.** 184

Delineator, the, may aid copying of, **41.** 366

export of, from Florence, forbidden, **20.** 465

HW buys, in Italy, **13.** 232, **15.** 12, **26.** 3, 4, 6, 7

Leigh, Miss, has nose broken by modelling, **34.** 258

Leopold II buys, of Gaddi family, **25.** 170

of Antinous, **35.** 217

of Brutus, received by National Assembly, **34.** 175

of Caligula, *see under* Caligula

of Caracalla, **13.** 232, **15.** 12, **26.** 7, 8n

of Cicero, **20.** 86

of Cts of Orford, **25.** 504

of Cromwell, **38.** 443

of E. and Cts of Pembroke, at Houghton Park House, **33.** 184, 351

of Faustina, **42.** 452

of Henry VII, owned by HW, **15.** 333

of Homer, **35.** 217

of James IV, **42.** 12n

of Jupiter Serapis, **39.** 442–3

of Newton, **37.** 270

of Venus and Apollo, in Nuneham garden, **35.** 484n

of Vespasian, *see under* Vespasian

on Shakespeare's monument, **35.** 151

Walpole, Sir Robert, has, at Houghton, **18.** 326

Wilton's, of Pitt, **20.** 397n

Bustle; bustles:

of cork, **33.** 379

'Busy,' Cole's dog:

never out of Cole's lap, its future provided for, **2.** 271

Butcher; butchers:

boy of, rings bell at SH gate, **35.** 331

English: bills of, unpaid, while noblemen pay fortunes to heralds, **22.** 226; newspaper squib warns, against England's conquest by Roman Catholics, **19.** 129

Flemish, English troops bicker with, over beef, **18.** 30

HW and Hardinge to share, **35.** 625

HW imagines Lord North joking with, **33.** 327–8

HW's, knows more politics than HW does, **39.** 197

in Piccadilly, rents lodging to Giustiniani, **23.** 287

Italian, compelled to kill meat at Leghorn, **17.** 304

Montagu corresponds with Cts of Guilford through, **10.** 197

Negro, might replace French cooks, **24.** 21

statesmen become, **39.** 176

weavers may be joined by, **38.** 562n

Bute, Cts of. *See* Windsor, Hon. Charlotte Jane (1746–1800); Wortley Montagu, Mary (1718–94)

Bute, E. of. *See* Stuart, John (1713–92); Stuart, John (1744–1814)

Bute, Marchioness of. *See* Windsor, Hon. Charlotte Jane (1746–1800)

Bute, M. of. *See* Stuart, John (1744–1814)

Butler, ——:

state coach built by, **22.** 104n

Butler, ——, Irish M.P.:
augmentation for Halifax proposed by, in Irish parliament, **10.** 18
Butler, ——, master of the studs to Louis XV:
Young Pretender said to be at house of, in Normandy, **20.** 508n
Butler, Mme:
Berwicks' social relations with, **7.** 272
Butler, Lady Amelia (ca 1660–1760):
brother of, dies, **21.** 261
Butler, Brinsley (1728–79) styled Lord Newtown (*or* Newtown Butler) 1756–68; 2d E. of Lanesborough, 1768:
children of, **25.** 601
Hamilton's affair with wife of, **38.** 250–1
Butler, Charles (1671–1758), cr. (1693) E. of Arran; *de jure* 3d D. of Ormond; chancellor of Oxford 1715–58:
carried to House of Lords to take oaths, **37.** 458
death of, **13.** 22n, **21.** 261
HW's *Royal and Noble Authors* discussed at table of, **9.** 219
King, Dr William, entertained by, **9.** 219
Pomfret, Cts of, thanked by, **20.** 470n
York, Cardinal, lodges with, at Avignon, **19.** 97n
Butler, Lady Eleanor, alleged paramour of Edward IV:
biographical information on, corrected, **43.** 188
'confession' of, a lie, **14.** 182
controversy over, **1.** 304, 318, 319
Edward IV's pre-contract with, **14.** 181, **35.** 609
——'s supposed marriage with, **15.** 170–1, 173–4, 175, 183–4
genealogy of, **1.** 218n
Masters's confusion about, **43.** 58
Butler, Lady Eleanor (ca 1546–1636), m. 1 (ca 1568) Gerald Fitzjames Fitzgerald, 14th E. of Desmond, 1558; m. 2 (ca 1597) Sir Donogh O'Connor Sligo:
Catherine, Cts of Desmond, confused with, **41.** 109–11
Butler, Lady Eleanor (ca 1739–1829), recluse of Llangollen; 'Miss Buttershaw':
HW does not know, **34.** 94–5
Butler, Henry (d. 1647):
monument for, **1.** 7
Butler, Henry Thomas (1746–1813), styled Vct Ikerrin; 2d E. of Carrick, 1774:
HW sends letter through, **7.** 389
Butler, J., Gray's correspondent:
'The Bard' criticized by, **14.** 101–2
Butler, Jacob (1681–1765), lawyer:
drawing of, by Tyson, **1.** 142
print of, **1.** 188
Butler, Sir James (1420–61), 5th E. of Ormond:
in Margaret of Anjou's escort, **14.** 73
Butler, James (1610–88), 12th E. of Ormond;

cr. (1661) D. of Ormonde; lord lieutenant of Ireland:
lord lieutenant of Ireland's ceremonies unaltered since time of, **39.** 37
print of, **9.** 118n
Butler, James (1665–1745), 2d D. of Ormonde, 1688; army officer:
Chesterfield's secret meeting with, to get Pretender to make Jacobites vote against Sir Robert Walpole, **17.** 133n, 232n, **19.** 69
death of, **19.** 78n
Dorset, E. of, replaced by, as governor of Dover Castle and warden of Cinque Ports, **20.** 63n
Hartington the first Irish viceroy since, to have Irish estates, **20.** 469n
head of, replaced by Vernon's, on signs, **37.** 266
Jacobite invasion of England planned by, **17.** 6n
Jacobitism of, **20.** 60
Old Pretender receives courier from, from Avignon, **19.** 85
——'s follower, in exile, **17.** 232n
print of, **1.** 179
Scots College has box of papers by, **7.** 359
social relations of, with Lady Browne, **7.** 311
Walpole, Sir Robert, opposed by, **17.** 232n
Butler, James (ca 1680–1741), M.P.:
death of, precipitates Sussex election, **30.** 20n
Butler, John (1707–66), M.P.:
death of, **30.** 242n
excise post lost by, **22.** 109n
Butler, John (d. 1780):
hanged for riot at Bath, **33.** 196n
Butler, John (1717–1802), Bp of Oxford, 1777; of Hereford, 1788:
*Address to the Cocoa-Tree, An*, by, **2.** 283n, **22.** 116n, **28.** 458n, **29.** 244n
Bell attacked by, **29.** 134
changes his politics, **2.** 283
chaplain to Ps of Wales, **20.** 344n
Clarendon's memorials bore, **29.** 149
*Concio ad clerum*, bad Latin of, **29.** 155
(?) Cresset's epithets resented by, **20.** 344
disappointed of St Paul's deanery, **29.** 188, 192
George III friend of, **35.** 535
Harcourt might cram, at election time, **35.** 507
—— often entertains, at Nuneham, **35.** 535
——'s brother's promotion should please, **28.** 470
Mason pillories, in *Archæological Epistle*, **29.** 244
Oxford college plate probably considered sacred by, **35.** 497
pamphlet by, attacks Warburton, **29.** 134
St Paul might out-flatter, in epistles, **29.** 309
Smithfield fires would be rekindled by, **35.** 497, 507

*Some Account of . . . Legge* by, **38**. 474, 481

turns from 'patriot opposition' to defence of the Court, **28**. 458

Waldegrave, Lady Maria, comments on, **32**. 411–12

Walpole, Sir Edward, hears from, that Harcourt should be tolerated, **35**. 497

—— visited by, **32**. 411–12

Butler, Joseph (1692–1752), Bp of Bristol, 1738; of Durham, 1750:

Caroline, Q., patronizes, **2**. 167

—— recommends book by, to Sir Robert Walpole, **20**. 167

Chandler succeeded by, **20**. 167

death of, vacates Durham bishopric, **20**. 323n

Hayter may succeed, **20**. 323

metaphysical writer, **20**. 167

Butler, Louis (ca 1700–75), Freiherr; Austrian army officer:

(?) daughter of, **25**. 101n

Butler, Louise-Charlotte (d. 1828), m. (1762) Pierre-Marie, Comte de Luppé:

(?) social relations of, with Comtesse d'Adhémar, **7**. 428

Butler, Robert, D. of Bedford's servant:

Tylney's legacy to, **25**. 534n

Butler, Robert Herbert (1759–1806), 3d E. of Lanesborough:

Leghorn merchants considerate of, **25**. 601

Butler, Samuel (1612–80), satiric poet:

*Genuine Remains* by, **9**. 242

*Hudibras* by: **2**. 52, 360, **9**. 242, **16**. 127, **28**. 259, **29**. 135n, 220, **31**. 333, **38**. 228, 500, 42. 241; Dr Johnson called, **11**. 272; Grey's edn of, **2**. 360; line from, in Chatterton, **2**. 52; Nash's edn of, **42**. 241, **43**. 389

paintings said to be by, **40**. 273

*Satyr upon Plagiaries* by, **9**. 242

style of, unsuitable to a description of a solemn funeral, **23**. 435

Butler, Thomas (ca 1424–1515), 7th E. of Ormond:

at Henry VII's court, **2**. 365

Butler (surname). *See also* Boteler; Buttler

Butler (servant). *See under* Servant

Butler Danvers, Hon. Augustus Richard (ca 1766–1820):

Leghorn merchants considerate of, **25**. 601

Butley Priory, Suffolk:

HW visits, **35**. 247

Butson, John Joseph (fl. 1744–61), King's messenger:

Gray, Sir James, receives Bath ensigns through, **21**. 507

Butt, Mary (1732–1819), m. (1755) Vere Poulett, 3d E. Poulett, 1764:

Twickenham house of, **12**. 74–5, **42**. 481

*Butta su*:

Pius VI's expression for *couvre salope*, **24**. 107

Butter:

at HW's breakfast, **35**. 342

Clement XIII permits, in Lent, **22**. 17n

England sends firkins of, to Portugal, **20**. 512n

——'s allies make, **35**. 61

English dare not use, **19**. 174

English scarcity of, **22**. 460

for breakfast, **30**. 132n

from Brittany, **7**. 436

good, at Abbeville, **7**. 334

HW almost famished for want of, **39**. 7

HW eats, at Adderbury, **10**. 312

HW scoffs at French for serving dishes of, **13**. 164

Ireland ships, to Portuguese earthquake victims, **37**. 423

Mann uses, at tea, **17**. 104

Mann, Galfridus, has, on bread, **20**. 554

melted, served in sauceboat, for hot rolls, **22**. 105, 113

monks serve, **13**. 182

Petersham, Lady Caroline, uses, in stewing chickens, **9**. 109

price of, **22**. 460n, **35**. 320

SH visitors eat, **33**. 530

veal counterbalanced by, to avoid gout, **35**. 21

'Buttered Peas' (tune):

popular in Italy, **13**. 201

Butterfield, Jane (b. ca 1747), mistress of William Scawen:

talked of, **32**. 262

Butterfly; butterflies:

Brooke, Lady, as a, **30**. 295

humans as evanescent as, **35**. 383

Butter plate:

HW procures, for Montagu, **9**. 155

'Buttershaw, Miss.' *See* Butler, Lady Eleanor

Butter-woman. *See* Owens, Mrs

Buttery:

at Hurstmonceaux, stained glass in, **35**. 138

Buttery-book:

at Almack's, **30**. 258

Buttler, Don ——, Ensign:

captured at Velletri, **18**. 492

Buttler *or* Butler, Mr:

Eliott sends packets to Mann by, from Gibraltar, **25**. 303

itinerary of, to England, **25**. 303

Buttler, Diego, Capt.:

captured at Velletri, **18**. 492

Buttler, Teobalde, Capt.:

captured at Velletri, **18**. 492

Buttler, Tobias, Capt.:

captured at Velletri, **18**. 492

Buttley Abbey. *See* Butley Abbey

Button; buttons:

Chartres, Duc de, displays horses' and dogs' copulations on, **25**. 409, 417

Chartres's, indecent, **43**. 311

diamond, given by Maria Theresa to Maria Louisa, **22**. 481

fur-edged, **32**. 182

gold, in regimental costume, **9**. 241

[Button; buttons, *continued*]
HW encloses, to show size of gun bore, 18. 232
HW has, of another hero, 37. 107
Montagu receives, from HW, 10. 41
——'s, consigned by HW to Brown, 10. 37, 38
on waistband of breeches, 37. 568
Buttonhole; buttonholes:
gold, 37. 289
St Andrew's Cross worn in, 23. 225
Buttress; buttresses:
HW criticizes, in plan for SH cloister, 35. 110
Buxton, Jedediah (1707–72), mathematician:
print of, 1. 216
Buxton, Robert John (1753–1839), cr. (1800) Bt; M.P.:
Hare's candidate in Norfolk election, 42. 437n
Buxton, Derbyshire:
Damer, Mrs, does sculpture for fountain at, 12. 272
HW not to visit, 31. 345
Pisa apartments as bad as those of, 11. 216
visitors to: Cholmondeley, 10. 96; Montagu, Henrietta, 9. 106; Roscoes, 15. 280
Buxton Wells, Derbyshire:
Bath and Tunbridge compared with, 40. 16
Dodd and Whaley visit, 40. 16
Buyot, ——, deputy lt of police at Paris:
HW called on by, 7. 267
Louis suspected by, of theft, 7. 267–8
Buzaglo, Abraham (ca 1716–88), quack doctor:
gout cured by, 32. 407–8
Buzançais, Comte (later Duc) de. *See* Beauvillier, Charles-Paul-François de
Bybrook, Kent:
Shorter of, 1. 52n, 28. 24n
Byde, Thomas Plumer (?1720–89), M.P.:
birth date of, 43. 60
stands for Cambridge, 1. 346
Byfleet, Surrey:
artillery encamps at, 9. 192n
Spence, Joseph, at, 20. 188n
—— given house at, by Lord Lincoln, 40. 62n
—— writes from, 40. 115
Bylandt, Lodewijk van (1718–93), Graaf van Bylandt; Dutch naval officer:
accompanies Dutch fleet as prisoner, 33. 155–6
Feilding intercepts, 25. 3
Bylaugh, Norfolk:
Lloyd of, 11. 184n
Byng, Mr:
Strafford's bequest to, 11. 305n
Byng, Hon. Cecilia (b. 1771), m. (1805) J. Robert Gregge Hopwood:
Berry, Agnes, friend of, 43. 156–7
(?) gone from SH, 43. 157
Byng, Hon. Edward (1706–56), Col.:
death of, soon after talking to brother, 20. 583, 21. 3
Byng, Frances (d. 1851), dau. of George Byng, M.P.:
(?) SH visited by, 12. 246

Byng, Sir George (1664–1733), cr. (1721) Vct Torrington:
George II forgets services of, 21. 63
HW attributes Port Mahon's capture to, 21. 52n
naval victory, not Port Mahon's capture, brought peerage to, 43. 274
prowess of, in Spanish war, 20. 569n
Byng, George (? 1735–89), M.P.:
testifies about Lord North's loan to Drummond, 29. 123n
North's partiality attacked by, in Commons, 36. 194n
Byng, George (1740–1812), 4th Vct Torrington, 1750:
brother ruined by, 33. 210
Brussels the refuge of, 33. 210n
Bunbury accompanies, at Florence, 21. 436
daughter of, 31. 238
feelings of, at brother's pension, 33. 225
leaves Florence, 21. 543
retirement preferred by, 21. 436
Byng, Mrs George. *See* Conolly, Anne
Byng, Georgiana Elizabeth (1768–1801), m. (1786) Lord John Russell, 6th D. of Bedford, 1802:
Russell, Lord John, to marry, 31. 238
Byng, Hon. Isabella Elizabeth (1773–1830), m. (1794) Thomas Thynne, styled Vct Weymouth; 2d M. of Bath, 1796:
Cardigan, Lady, succeeds, in Bedchamber, 11. 367n
wishes to be lady of Bedchamber to Ps of Wales, 12. 107–8
Byng, Rear-Adm. Hon. John (1704–57), M.P.:
Admiralty and ministry quarrel with, 21. 3
Admiralty orders Cleveland to send La Galissonnière's letter to, 20. 561n
—— receives minutes of Gibraltar council of war from, 20. 560n
—— signs execution warrant of, 21. 63
—— treats, leniently, 21. 55
Anson ill-treats, 21. 23
——'s party oppose reinvestigation of, 21. 66
—— to prepare trial and condemnation of, 20. 578n
*Antelope* boarded by, for England, 20. 573n
Brodrick joins, at Gilbraltar, 20. 573
brother talks to, 20. 583
Brough receives account from, 21. 66n
confined at Greenwich, 20. 586
consternation over, 35. 277
court martial of, 21. 3, 23, 39, 45, 50–2, 55–6, 61, 63, 68, 71, 81–2, 35. 95–6
death or success can alone retrieve, 20. 578
Edgcumbe and Bucareli talk to, at Gibraltar, 20. 566
English resentment against, 9. 191, 192, 20. 569, 578, 583, 22. 421, 35. 306
escape of, to Holland, rumoured, 21. 71
execution of, 10. 35n, 21. 66–7

fate of, condemned by French, **25.** 307

fleet of: at Gibraltar, **20.** 558, 571, 572–3, 577, 578; Minorca may not be reached by, in time, **20.** 545, 552–3, 558–9, 560, 573; ordered home, **19.** 489n; sails to Mediterranean, **20.** 538, 545, 552–3, 558–9; to defend Lérins islands, **19.** 376n; too weak to beat the French, **20.** 564, 566

Fox said to have planned sacrifice of, **21.** 55n

French landing on Lérins islands opposed by, **19.** 406

George II's possible pardon of, **21.** 51, 55, 63, 64, 73

—— thinks, guilty of cowardice, **21.** 55n

—— to consult Newcastle before confirming sentence on, **21.** 51n

Gibraltar denies reinforcements to, **20.** 560, 566, 576

—— not yet reached by, **37.** 471

—— reached by, **37.** 473

HW at first duped by clamour against, **21.** 143

HW hopes de Grasse will not be treated as inhumanly as, **25.** 307

HW's attempt to save, **9.** 332n, **13.** 27, **21.** 63–5

HW's verses on Anson's eagerness for death of, **21.** 66n

HW wants news of, **40.** 87

Hardwicke communicates evidence against, to Anson, **21.** 23n

Hawke and Saunders relieve West and, **20.** 573n

Hawke and Saunders sent to Gibraltar to punish, **20.** 561–2

infatuated, **35.** 92

Keppel's intervention does not save, **21.** 63–4, 68

letters of, suggest retirement to Gibraltar, **20.** 560

London enraged at, **9.** 191, 192

—— merchants press George II to execute, **21.** 55n

Minorca affair subject of 'lies' by, **37.** 468–9

—— may be captured before arrival of, **37.** 462

Newcastle blames, for Minorca's loss, **20.** 578n

Onslow demands expulsion of, from House of Commons, **21.** 63

Osborne's brother married to sister of, **21.** 191n

—— 's friend, **21.** 191

pamphlets on, sent by HW to Conway, **37.** 473

placards advocate execution of, **21.** 65–6

Sackville's plight compared to that of, **21.** 320–1, **30.** 158, **38.** 20

St Philip's Castle said to be reinforced by, **20.** 562

Saunders reassures George II about, **35.** 95

simpleton, **20.** 586, **21.** 3

superseded on basis of enemy information, **35.** 95

supporters and enemies of, **21.** 55n

tranquillity of, **20.** 560, 586, 590

Voltaire defends, before execution, **28.** 219

—— 's comment on, **35.** 555

—— sends Richelieu's letter to, **21.** 51, 61

witnesses for trial of, sail from Gibraltar to Spithead, **20.** 590n

Young summoned in behalf of, though his accuser, **20.** 586, 590–1

Byng, Hon. John (1742–1813), 5th Vct Torrington, 1812:

believes in Ireland's MSS, **15.** 321

(?) boxes sent to Craufurd by, **4.** 363

(?) boxes returned through, **4.** 365

brother causes ruin of, **33.** 210

Ossory, Lady, charitable to, **33.** 225

Byng, Hon. Mrs John. *See* Forrest, Bridget

Byng, Pattee (1699–1747), 2d Vct Torrington:

appointed capt. of Yeomen of the Guard, **19.** 221n

Yonge to succeed, as vice-treasurer of Ireland, **19.** 155

Byng, Hon. Sarah (1693–1775), m. (1710) John Osborn:

anecdote about, **12.** 262

Anson will not be lamented by, **10.** 35

appears older, **10.** 32

Boscawen's death not mourned by, **9.** *332*

Bushey Park visited by, **10.** 32, 207

HW receives Irish prints from, **10.** 34

HW sees, **10.** 32

HW to frank letter for, **10.** 251

HW unable to call on, **10.** 32

Halifax's appointment described by, **9.** 370

Hinchingbrooke wedding attended and reported by, **10.** 207

(?) Melvill, Margaret, discusses Vcts Hinchingbrooke with, **10.** 234

Montagu congratulated by, **10.** 251

—— 's correspondence with, **9.** 370, **10.** 251

—— sends Irish prints through, to HW, **10.** 30, 32

Osborne's brother married by, **21.** 191n

Byrd, William:

Percy, Lady, divorced for crim. con. with, **14.** 141n

Byres, Mr:

SH visited by, **12.** 237

Byres, James (1730–1817), dealer at Rome; architect and archaeologist:

Agincourt sends engravings to HW in care of, **42.** 63

—— 's letter to HW to have been delivered by, **42.** 101

HW mentions, **42.** 103n

Palestrina, Ps of, sells art to, resold to Hamilton, **33.** 485n

Portland vase bought by, resold to Hamilton, **35.** 444n, **42.** 63n, 267n

[Byres, James, *continued*]
retires to family estate at Tonley, Aberdeenshire, 42. 63n
Rutland's agent for Poussin's Sacraments, 33. 538n
Scottish antiquary at Rome and Florence, 42. 63n, 101
Byrne, William (1743–1805):
Hearne collaborates with, on topographical views, 42. 68n
Byrom, John (1692–1763), poet:
ballad by, on St George, 2. 162
HW quotes 'My time, O ye muses' from, 12. 35
HW quotes pastoral by, 32. 227
Byron, Bns. *See* Shaw, Elizabeth
'Byron, Miss.' *See under* Richardson, Samuel: *Sir Charles Grandison*
Byron, Lady Amelia. *See* Darcy, Lady Amelia
Byron, George Gordon (1788–1824), 6th Bn Byron, 1798:
Carlisle guardian of, 28. 34n
Jerningham's 'unpoetical day' preceded the rise of, 11. 67n
parents of, 28. 472n
Byron, Hon. Isabella (1721–95), m. 1 (1743) Henry Howard, 4th E. of Carlisle; m. 2 (1759) Sir William Musgrave, 6th Bt:
Avignon to be visited by, 7. 84
Beaufort, Ds of, hears from, 23. 508
Carlisle's correspondence with, 7. 63
Chaillot residence of, 7. 50, 61
Coke, Lady Mary, compared with, 37. 572
concert by, 2. 187, 9. 219
Conway calls, youngest, handsomest, and wittiest widow in England, 37. 561
Du Deffand, Mme, gives opinion of, 7. 50–1, 61
—— inquires about, 7. 50
Florence visited by, 23. 447
Gray described by, 9. 285–6, 286
HW criticizes, 23. 451
HW may see, in Paris, 35. 317
HW might wed, on her becoming widowed, 37. 561–2, 563, 564
HW's friend, 23. 447, 451
Hertford will pity, on brother's future trial, 38. 503
Magdalen House visited by, 9. 273–4
Musgrave's age falsified by, 9. 260
—— to marry, 9. 260
Naples visited by, 23. 449
Nicoll, Miss, subject of remark by, 9. 148n
(?) Petersham, Lady Caroline, rival of, 37. 359
Selwyn's correspondence with, 7. 61, 63
social relations of, with Mme du Deffand, 7. 50, 61
*Thoughts in the Form of Maxims* by, 34. 89
Tissot tells, to stay at Rome, 23. 447
Townshend's joke about, 9. 271
Warner to bring, from Aix, 36. 193

Byron, Hon. John (1723–86), naval officer:
bitterly declaimed against, 39. 323
Carlisle, Cts of, has no word of, 7. 61
Estaing avoids battle with, 24. 464n, 480–1
—— blockaded by, at Martinique, 24. 456
—— cannot be attacked by, in Fort Royal, 24. 466
—— defeats, 7. 175n, 24. 515, 39. 339
—— might be trapped by, 23. 408
—— undefeated and Martinique unconquered by, 24. 475
Falkland Islands skirted by, 23. 128n
fleet of: 33. 31–2, 34, 44, 116; damaged by storm, 24. 400; sails, 7. 47n
Grenada clash with d'Estaing reported by, 33. 122n
Howe may be reinforced by ships of, 24. 411
Martinique may be starved by, 24. 466
—— said to have been taken by, after d'Estaing's defeat, 24. 461
Montreal's reinforcements captured by, 21. 440
Patagonian 'giants' discovered by, 1. 126n, 3. 172n, 22. 420–1
sails to America, 24. 387
son of, 28. 472n
Toulon squadron may be encountered by, 24. 394
verses mention, 7. 179
victory of, in Chaleur Bay, 21. 433, 440; not certain, 7. 145, 39. 323
West Indies may be saved by, if unhurt by d'Estaing, 24. 447–8
Byron, John (1756–91), army officer; father of Lord Byron, the poet:
Mason lends parsonage to wife and, 28. 472, 484–5, 29. 20, 29n
raises recruits in Yorkshire, 28. 472, 485
Byron, William (1722–98), 5th Bn Byron, 1736:
Chaworth killed by; in duel in tavern, 10. 148n, 22. 284, 38. 501, 503
financial reverses of, 9. 299
forts built by, 9. 299
oaks sold and Scotch firs planted by, 9. 299
Shaw, Elizabeth, marries, 19. 19n
trial of, 10. 148, 149, 22. 293, 30. 177n, 38. 511, 527, 534–5
Byron family:
portraits of, at Newstead Abbey, 9. 299
Bysshe, Edward (fl. 1702–12), miscellaneous writer:
*Art of English Poetry* by, 32. 230
Byzantine emperors:
later popes as dull as, 24. 48
Byzantine Empire:
eighteenth-century England compared with, 23. 499
Grecian wits in time of, produce only folly and acrimony, 39. 120
Byzantine historians:
eighteenth-century history will be as unread as, 24. 55

# C

C, ——, 'concussionaire':
Conway writes to HW about, **39.** 211
C——, Lord:
stories of, divert HW, **33.** 73
C——, Mr:
family of, laugh at 'my vivacity at my age,'
**12.** 255
'C——,' Mr:
'Lord H.' to, **33.** 331
Caage, Thomas. *See* Carew, Thomas
Cabal; cabals:
clergy usually responsible for, **24.** 225
*Cabala sive scrinia sacra*:
Henry VIII's letter in, **16.** 10
*Cabales, Les. See under* Voltaire
Cabaret; cabarets:
Du Deffand, Mme, has, **4.** 305, 312, **6.** 97
girls of, **37.** 131
Cabarn, M. de, French naval officer:
commander-in-chief of Toulon squadron, **18.**
384n
Cabbage; cabbages;
Conway grows, for seed, **39.** 551
—— wants to forsake Ireland for, **37.** 450
garden of, at Passionist monastery, **42.** 406
laurels to be replaced by, at peace, **37.** 296
Cabin-boy; cabin-boys:
Quin's joke about, **20.** 210
Cabinet (administrative). *See* Cabinet Council
Cabinet; cabinets (furniture):
at Elizabeth Chudleigh's, **9.** 277
at Hardwick, **9.** 297
at Welbeck, **35.** 271
black, (?) for SH, **20.** 375
Boule, **7.** 286, 353
by HW's bedside at SH, **35.** 373
ebony: at Knole, **35.** 132; carved, at Boughton
House, **10.** 341; of Mme de Sévigné, **33.**
150-1
ebony and brass, at Hinchingbrooke, **40.** 283
ebony, decorated by Lady Diana Beauclerk,
at SH, **43.** 378
ebony, of Mme de Sévigné, left by Selwyn
with HW, **43.** 104
Electrice leaves, to Francis I, **18.** 207
Florence, **7.** 353
Frederick Augustus I gives, to Maria Aurora
von Königsmarck, **20.** 58
French royal, *see Recueil d'estampes*
HW's, in Arlington St house: for Roman and
Greek collections, **23.** 284-5; Montagu puts
flowers on, **10.** 204
HW's, to contain medals, **19.** 185, **20.** 128
India ('Walpolian'), Craon, Princesse de, has,
**18.** 78
mahogany, in Star Chamber at SH, **33.** 403n
Mann buys, for Cts of Pomfret, at Canonici's,
**17.** 129
memory resembles, **33.** 577
of glass, at Burghley House, **10.** 345
of ivory, at Ham House, **10.** 306
of japan, at Burghley House, **10.** 346
painted by Rubens, at Burghley House, **10.**
345
rosewood, HW buys, for enamels and miniatures, **18.** 277
white-and-gold, in every Paris hotel, **23.** 312
Cabinet; cabinets (room):
Conway as busy in, as Louis XV, **37.** 442, 448
HW may add, to SH, **21.** 238, 306
HW's, at SH. *See* Strawberry Hill: cabinet at
Townshend, Vcts, sends Frederick Campbell
to, **30.** 84
Cabinet Council:
appointments to, almost as many as to Privy
Council, **21.** 489
Bedford, D. of, avoids, **38.** 433
Bristol's recall deferred by, **38.** 120-1
bustle in, over appointing Irish archbishop,
**22.** 275
Bute and D. of York named to, **21.** 443
Byng's pardon to be decided by, **21.** 51
Canadian news discussed by, **32.** 284
Carteret reads his fiancée's letters to, **18.** 431
——'s defeat in, **18.** 349
Conway attends, **21.** 119n
——'s continuance in, demanded by George
III and Grafton, **22.** 571
—— to have seat in, **25.** 270
deliberations in, about return to Rochefort,
**30.** 142
East India Co. dispute divides, **39.** 82n
—— warned by, about coming Bengal in-
quiry, **30.** 238n
Egmont resigns Admiralty because Chatham
would differ from him in, **22.** 449n
Egremont summoned to, from Bath, **22.** 96n
Fox, Henry, joins, **20.** 461, **35.** 194
Frederick II supposed to have provoked meeting of, **20.** 364
French intelligence known only to, **40.** 106
French peace proposals considered by, **38.** 162
George II told by, to dismiss Carteret, **18.**
535-6
George III excludes members of, from Bedchamber, **38.** 118
—— lays French *mémoire* before, **21.** 515n
—— notifies, of regency plans, **22.** 295
——'s statement to, at Carlton House, of his
policy, **21.** 456n
Grenville attacks German war, and Prussian
and Portuguese subsidies in, **22.** 31n
—— to be in, **21.** 541n
HW's satirical reference to, **35.** 165
HW would reject peace proposals of, **32.** 404
Haddock's fleet ordered to defence of Italy
by, **17.** 267n
Halifax called to, **30.** 135n
—— prefers admission to, to Garter, **21.** 111n
Hertford glad he has no seat in, **39.** 304
Hillsborough's letter said not to express the
opinion of, **41.** 315n

[Cabinet Council, *continued*]

Holland's conditions for aiding England rejected by, **20.** 538n

investigation by, of alleged toasts to Old Pretender, **20.** 360, 364, 366

Leeds joins, **21.** 489

Martinique expedition considered by, **21.** 252n

meeting of: at Northington's, on princes' allowances, **22.** 425n; over Ravensworth's accusations, **43.** 271

members of, dance, **35.** 213

ministers 'pull caps' at, **35.** 559

misconduct of, **35.** 616

Münchhausen calls for, to examine D. of Cumberland's conduct, **21.** 145n

new, listed by HW, **25.** 262

Newcastle, D. of, may keep small post in, **22.** 79

—— recommended by, to George II for prime minister, **35.** 168

—— wants Fox omitted from, **21.** 92

—— will be opposed by, **21.** 93

North, Lord, empowered by, to order magistrates to keep peace in Gordon Riots, **25.** 53, **33.** 176

Northumberland, D. of, joins, **22.** 103

officers of, less permanent than church-wardens, **22.** 431

peace negotiations considered by, **21.** 526n, 536n

Pelham will have to remove, **18.** 537

Pitt and Pratt devise habeas corpus bill without consulting lawyers in, **21.** 205n

Pitt and Temple at odds with, **38.** 131n, 140

Pitt overruled by, on demanding Spanish war, **21.** 537n

—— proposes Spanish war to, **38.** 131

—— resigns in opposition to temporizing of, **21.** 537

—— to conquer, **21.** 290

places in, offered, **35.** 253

Regency formed from, **37.** 60

Richmond, D. of, will break, to pieces, **36.** 222

rumours of changes in, **12.** 19

Russian peace mediation with Holland accepted by, **25.** 188n

St-Malo, bad bread at, reported to, **12.** 77

Seilern's complaint considered by, **23.** 7

Shelburne vainly requests Rockingham to provide posts in, for Lords Gower and Weymouth, **25.** 261

Stanley's instructions, for mission to France drafted by, **21.** 504n

votes in House of Lords influenced by, **35.** 588

war in America fomented by, in sending troops there, **39.** 247

Weymouth may re-enter, **23.** 424

*Cabinet . . . d'architecture, peinture, etc. See under* Lecomte, Florent

Cabinet-makers:

association formed by, for labour strike, **22.** 49

shop of, at Englefield Green, **9.** 20

Cabinet ministers. *See under* Minister; ministers (cabinet)

Cable; cables:

of ships: Howe requests, **32.** 337; with springs, for Turkish fleet, **23.** 234

Raynal discusses, **39.** 168

Cabot (*or* Cabo, *or* Cabau), ——, HW's servant at Paris:

Du Deffand, Mme, sends letter through, **5.** 91, 93

(?) HW may be served by, **5.** 89

HW to be served by, **4.** 268

wages of, **7.** 408, 410, 411, 412

*Cabot*, American brig:

*Glasgow's* battle with, **24.** 216

*Cabot*, English sloop of war:

Conway embarks on, for Jersey, **24.** 472n, **33.** 102n

Cabre. *See* Sabatier de Cabre

Cabriolet; cabriolets (chairs for house):

Ailesbury, Cts of, to have, **7.** 411, **39.** 146

Du Deffand, Mme, receives, **7.** 430

Cabriolet; cabriolets (one-horse vehicles):

accident to, **6.** 499

Amelia, Ps, and others drive about Stowe gardens in, **10.** 313

Child introduces, **20.** 483

Louis XV rides in, **31.** 111

vogue for, in France, **20.** 483

Cacao:

Haddock captures, in Dutch ship, **17.** 53

Cacherano d'Osasco, Giuseppe Ottaviano (d. 1773), Conte della Rocca d'Arazzo:

Savona menaced by, **18.** 344–5, **19.** 313n, 429n

'Cacofogo,' character in Fletcher's *Rule a Wife*:

Cumberland, D. of, resembles, **20.** 49

Mountrath, Cts of, resembles, **9.** 135

Cade, 'Jack' (d. 1450), rebel against Henry VI:

James I alludes to, **15.** 341

Wilkes's success would astonish, **24.** 536

Cadell, Thomas (1742–1802), bookseller:

Conway's speech printed for, **29.** 96n

Dalrymple to receive *Historic Doubts* from, **15.** 118

Granger's *Supplement* published by, **16.** 235n

(?) HW asks, for Blair's 'head,' **42.** 56

(?) HW quoted by, for list of unengraved portraits, **16.** 234–5

HW receives Henry's *History* from, **15.** 183

HW's correspondence with, **41.** 439, **42.** 56

HW tells, to deliver Raspe's *Critical Essay* to Raspe, **41.** 439

Hamilton's *Campi Phlegræi* advertised by, **35.** 427n

——'s *Collection of Engravings* sold by, **35.** 442n

Piozzi, Mrs, writes to, attacking Boswell, **43.** 292

publications by: political pamphlets, **31.** 387; *Remarks on the Speech of M. Dupont,* **31.** 381, 386

Raspe's *Critical Essay* published by, **41.** 439n, **42.** 66

receipts of, diminished, **31.** 387

Roscoe asks HW to entrust medals to, **15.** 283

—— writes to, **15.** 286

Scots write for, **28.** 438

SH visited by, **12.** 225, (?) 248

Cadenberg, Joseph Slop von:

Minto visits, **15.** 167n

Cadesha. *See* Khadijah

Cadet, ——, Duchesse de Choiseul's lackey:

Orléans, Bp of, sought by, **3.** 360–1

Cadet; cadets, at Woolwich. *See under* Woolwich

Cadet de Chambine, ——, premier commis to Trudaine:

(?) slow in forwarding case, **6.** 181

Cadière, Catherine, (fl. 1710–31), Ursuline nun:

Hogarth's alleged print of, Father Girard and, **16.** 173

Cadiz ('Cades,' 'Cales,' 'Cadix'):

*Achilles* and *Buffon* captured near, **21.** 523

armaments prepared at, **24.** 98n

Artois to visit, to celebrate Gibraltar's expected capture, **25.** 334

Brest fleet said to be going to, **39.** 313

Bucareli governor at, **20.** 566n

Chartres, Duc de, at, **32.** 301

Córdoba's fleet retires to, **25.** 344

Darby arrives off, **29.** 138n

Don Gastón's fleet to join Córdoba's at, **25.** 25

Dutch ships bound for, seized, **17.** 53n

Dutch try to send naval stores to, **22.** 70

English fleet may attack, **25.** 17

English vessel escapes from, **24.** 307

Estaing to take ships to, from Brest, **25.** 345

fleet nearly a month on passage to Minorca from, **25.** 190

French and Spanish fleets sail from, **25.** 82, 173, 181

French fleet has not gone to, **33.** 140

French force will be collected at, **25.** 303

galleons said to arrive at, **17.** 84

Goldsworthy succeeds Hay as consul at, **20.** 433n

Haddock keeps Spanish fleet in, **17.** 219

——'s fleet to watch, **17.** 17n

Irish merchants at, **19.** 416, **21.** 269

Jesuit convoy from, **22.** 532n

Leigh, Irish merchant at, **19.** 416

Minorcan expedition from, would have little success, **25.** 59

news from, of Guichen's return to Europe, **25.** 94

Rowley follows Cartagena squadron to, **19.** 12n

—— supposedly near, **19.** 81

Russian consul at, reports capture of Russian ship, **25.** 39n

Saunders said to be planning attack on, **22.** 12

ship escapes to, **2.** 193n

ships at, said to be disarmed, **22.** 19

Spanish fleet at: **28.** 396n, **29.** 122n, **30.** 271, **39.** 368; braved by Darby, **25.** 147; not to join Brest fleet, **25.** 72; Philip, Don, to be accompanied by, **17.** 215; sails out, **17.** 23; sickly when it returns, **25.** 145; supposedly returns, exposing Gibraltar, **25.** 145

Spanish navy prepared at, **24.** 496

Spanish troops at, may threaten Gibraltar, **23.** 261

Strange and Molone merchants at, **21.** 269n

Torres said to have reached, with treasure, **17.** 83

Venetian ship from, **19.** 81

Cadmus:

teeth of, **31.** 335, **34.** 166, 183

Cadogan, Bns. *See* Churchill, Mary (b. 1750); Sloane, Elizabeth (after 1695–1768)

Cadogan, Charles (1685–1776), 2d Bn Cadogan:

death of, rumoured, **17.** 353, 356

guards alerted by, against riot, **23.** 7n

in cavalcade at Henley, **37.** 371n

regiment of, **17.** 353n

Cadogan, Charles Henry Sloane (1749–1832), 2d E. Cadogan, n.c., 1807:

death date of, corrected, **43.** 55

father must provide for, **36.** 137

in army, **33.** 52

insanity of, **33.** 51

suggested for Cambridgeshire seat, **1.** 198n, 199, 200, 202

Cadogan, Charles Sloane (1728–1807), 3d Bn Cadogan, 1776; cr. (1800) E. Cadogan, n.c.; Master of the Mint 1769–84; M.P.:

camping trip prevents father-in-law from bringing, to SH, **39.** 300

Caversham sold by, to Marsac, **36.** 152n

children of, **1.** 199n, **2.** 304, 306, **11.** 187n, **33.** 51, **36.** 137

Cole dines with, at Cambridge, **1.** 185

Du Deffand, Mme, asks if HW is to visit, **7.** 42

HW dines in party with, **30.** 252

HW does not mention, **6.** 480, **7.** 173

HW does not wish to be obliged to, **30.** 276

HW entertains, at SH, **33.** 565

HW informed by, of 3d E. of Orford's illness, **34.** 129

HW invited by, to meet Churchills at Caversham, **36.** 152–3

HW is glad of maturity of, **32.** 369

HW's correspondence with, **36.** 277, 336

HW's relationship to, **30.** 276

heir of Hans Stanley, **33.** 161

marriages of: first, **1.** 48n, 306; second, **1.** 185n, **2.** 306, **5.** 2n, **6.** 467n, **24.** 320, **32.** 368, **33.** 51, **36.** 127–8, 137

M.P. for Cambridge, **1.** 346

name of, corrected **43.** 326

[Cadogan, Charles Sloane, *continued*]
privy purse to Edward, D. of York, **37.** 479, **38.** 468
Santon Downham seat of, **34.** 129n
six sons of, leave small jointure for wife, **36.** 137
SH visited by, **12.** 223
surveyor of the Gardens, **38.** 377
Trevis liked by, **33.** 565
wife of, **1.** 48n, **5.** 2n, 403n, **9.** 104n
wife's marriage settlement from, **36.** 137n
wife's paramour arrested by order of, **36.** 329
Cadogan, Hon. Mrs Charles Sloane. *See* Bromley, Hon. Frances (d. 1768)
Cadogan, Charlotte (1781–1853), m. 1 Sir Henry Wellesley; m. 2 (1810) Henry William Paget:
husband of, **11.** 187n
Cadogan, Hon. Edward (1758–79):
father must provide for, **36.** 137
Cadogan, Hon. (from 1800, Lady) Emily Mary (1778–1839), m. (1802) Hon. and Rev. Gerald Valerian Wellesley:
age of, **2.** 306
birth of, **33.** 51
Cadogan, Frances (1747–1819), m. (1788) William Nicholl:
HW drinks tea with, at Mrs Garrick's, **11.** 33
Cadogan, Hon. George (1754–80):
father must provide for, **36.** 137
Cadogan, Hon. George (1783–1864), 3d E. Cadogan, 1832:
half-brothers all survived by, to inherit earldom, **36.** 137n
Cadogan, Hon. (from 1800, Lady) Louisa (b. 1787):
birth of, **33.** 579
Cadogan, Lady Sarah (1706–51), m. (1719) Charles Lennox, 2d D. of Richmond:
Arenberg not asked for dinner by, because he wants it at 11, **18.** 97
beauty of, **17.** 184, 338, **20.** 125, **30.** 42, 46
company seen in form by, after accouchement, **30.** 42
Conway afraid of offending, **37.** 54
costumed as Jane Seymour, **17.** 338
daughters' reconciliation mortifies, **19.** 371
death of, **17.** 338n
fondness of, for husband, **30.** 46
Foxes reconciled with, **30.** 112–13
Fox's wedding disapproved by, **37.** 157n
Goldsworthy, Mrs, companion to, **17.** 186, 334n
—— to urge, to plead for Goldsworthy, **18.** 13
Goldsworthy family asked by, for a visit, **18.** 158
HW jokes about husband's fondness for, **30.** 38, 42
HW presented by, to Mrs Goldsworthy, **18.** 158, 188
Hague, The, to be visited by, **18.** 209
husband leaves, wealthy, **20.** 182

husband's bequests to, **20.** 182n
husband's devotion to, **17.** 184, **20.** 125, **30.** 38, 42
husband shown by, letters to prove Ds of Norfolk's loyalty, **19.** 176
influence of, on foreign appointments, slight, **18.** 31
Macartney, Miss, companion to, **17.** 186
Marlborough friendly with, **18.** 451
masqueraders assemble at house of, **18.** 167
miscarriage of, **43.** 114
Mostyn and, **17.** 139
Newcastle urged by, to aid Goldsworthy, **18.** 246n
Pelhams friendly with, **18.** 451
pregnancy of, keeps her secluded, **9.** 57
pregnant for 28th time, **20.** 125
Queensberry, Ds of, rebukes, for being afraid to let her daughter attend ball, **19.** 28
sick servant follows, from Paris to Aubigny, **40.** 28
social relations of, with: Albemarle, Cts of, **18.** 166–7, **30.** 35; Amelia, Ps, **9.** 81; Banks, Margaret, **9.** 81; Bisshopp, Miss, **9.** 82; Burlington, Cts of, **9.** 81; Carteret, Bns, **18.** 442; Cumberland, D. of, **9.** 81; 'Fitzes,' **9.** 81; Frederick, P. of Wales, **18.** 442; Frederick, Charles, **9.** 80; Garrick, **9.** 81; George II, **9.** 81; Goldsworthy, Mrs, **18.** 158; HW, **18.** 158, 188, **30.** 35, **37.** 288, 291; Hartington, Marchioness of, **9.** 81; Holdernesse, **9.** 81; Jacobites, **9.** 81; Lincoln, Cts of, **9.** 81; Lincoln, E. of, **18.** 166–7, **30.** 35; Modena, D. of, **9.** 81; Moorish princes, **9.** 81; Norfolk, Ds of, **17.** 338, **19.** 176; Pitt, Mrs George, **9.** 81; Queensberrys, **9.** 82; Robinson, **17.** 184; Sabbatini, **9.** 81; Violette, Eva, **9.** 81
stays home, fearing miscarriage, **37.** 288
subscription masquerade attended by, in lady mayoress's costume, **20.** 49
supper given by, **30.** 35
Townshend, Vcts, makes witticism on childbearing of, in dropsy, **20.** 131
virtues of, **30.** 46
Cadogan, Hon. Thomas (1752–82), (?) naval capt.:
father must provide for, **36.** 137
(?) *Licorne* commanded by, **33.** 210n
Cadogan, William (?1671–1726), cr. (1716) Bn and (1718) E. Cadogan; army officer; M.P.:
birth date of, corrected, **43.** 352
daughter of, **20.** 125n
epitaph on, by Atterbury, **33.** 112
ingratitude of, to Marlborough, **33.** 112
Cadogan, William (1711–97), M.D.:
HW drinks tea with, at Mrs Garrick's, **11.** 33
Cadogan, Hon. William Bromley (1751–97):
father must provide for, **36.** 137
Cadoxton, Glamorganshire:
descent of manor of, **41.** 117, 127, 129, **43.** 352

Caducanus (probably Cadwgan) (d. 1241), Bp of Bangor 1215–36:
tomb of, **1.** 327, **10.** 43
Cadwaladr (d. 664), K. of Gwynedd (in N. Wales):
biographical information about, corrected, **43.** 114, 174, 356
HW descended from, **9.** 69, **13.** 81, **33.** 454–5
mother of, **13.** 225
Cadwallader; Cadwalladhor. *See* Cadwaladr
'Cadwallader, Dame.' *See* Raftor, Catherine
'Cadwallader, Mr.' *See under* Foote, Samuel: *Author, The*
Cadwgan. *See* Caducanus
Cædmon:
paraphrase attributed to, **40.** 248
Caen (France):
Churchill, Charles, at, **38.** 410
Churchills to visit, **5.** 60, 63, 65
English expedition feints at, **21.** 214n
William the Conqueror's portrait at, **15.** 123n
Caen Wood (Kenwood), near Highgate; Lord Mansfield's seat:
Mansfield said to flee to, **33.** 255
men marched to, **33.** 184
safe in Gordon Riots, **29.** 57n, **33.** 186
white roses in conservatory at, **33.** 334
Caerwis, Wales:
Lloyd rector of, **2.** 167n
'Cæsar.' *See* Joseph II
Cæsar, Augustus. *See* Augustus
Cæsar, Caius Julius (100–44 B.C.):
Attila and Haidar Alī as innocent as, **25.** 142
Baretti denounces assassination of, **29.** 139
Cicero's bons mots collected by, **28.** 280
Clodius born before death of, **23.** 400
collection of sayings made by, **16.** 309n
conquest of Gaul by, excuses his dictatorship, **39.** 121
Conway not fired by histories of, **37.** 37
correspondence of, compared to Brutus's, **41.** 305
Cumberland, D. of, does not imitate clemency of, **19.** 288
Curio and Clodius prepared the way for, **28.** 393
Du Deffand, Mme, likes, **6.** 337
—— mentions, **5.** 7
—— prefers, to Alexander, **3.** 321
Ellis a 'nurse' for future counterparts of, **32.** 250
fish and counters little regarded by counterparts of, **22.** 85
Fox, C. J., compared with, **23.** 498–9, 542, **32.** 198
George III called, **32.** 247
Guadagni played, **23.** 272
'guide' a term not used by, **38.** 140
HW as innocent of Chatterton's death as that of, **33.** 40
HW cites quotation about Marius and, **24.** 28
HW does not want, for sake of Brutus, **23.** 151
HW imagines himself advising Brutus in plot against, **12.** 56
HW jokes about hearing, scold in Temple of Concord, **38.** 187
HW's name for Joseph II, **23.** 107, 117, **25.** 224, 237
HW wants Wurmser to be, **29.** 84
Henri IV as brave as, **31.** 438
Mann's name for Joseph II, **25.** 238
medal of, bought by HW, **26.** 7
Montemar carries *Gallic Wars* of, in pocket, **18.** 146
North's losses greater than conquests of, **24.** 139
Pitt compared with, **23.** 82
political responsibility of, **32.** 274
Pomfret compares, to Bristol watchmen, **20.** 470
Pomfret, Cts of, makes absurd comparison with, **20.** 579
Portland frightened by reference to, **37.** 437
Rockingham was not a, **25.** 294
Roman enamellers might eclipse, **21.** 313–14
St Francis compared with, **20.** 478
value of, as member of society, **33.** 158
Whately compared with, **32.** 167
world is made for counterparts of, **22.** 348
yellow fever would cause, to look wretched, **21.** 290
Cæsar, Jane (d. 1802), m. 1 Sir Charles Cottrell Dormer; m. 2 (1782) Lt-Gen. Hon. George Lane Parker:
HW's opinion of, **9.** 290
Cæsar, Sir Julius (1558–1636), chancellor of the Exchequer:
HW buys MSS of, **15.** 73
memo about, frightens Portland, **37.** 437
Cæsar, Julius (d. 1762), army officer:
death of, **38.** 167
Sackville's court martial to include, **21.** 366n
Tyrawley's witticism on affair of, with Margaret Woffington, **21.** 157
Cæsar; Cæsars:
ancient, bestow crowns, **36.** 232
Tintoretto's and Van Dyck's paintings of, **16.** 155
twelve, Cottonian books arranged by names of, **40.** 305–6
*Cæsar*, Venetian ship:
capture of, **19.** 81
*Cæsar*. *See under* Bladen, Martin
Cæsarea, Bp of. *See* Crivelli, Ignazio Michele (1698–1768)
Cæsarean section:
Maria Anna has, **18.** 540n
Cafarelli. *See* Caffarelli
Cafaro, Pasquale (1706–87), composer:
birth date of, corrected, **43.** 274
*Disfatta di Dario, La*, by, **21.** 127

Caffarelli, Gaetano Majorono (1710–83), called; singer:
biographical information on, corrected, **43.** 176, 245
Charles III said to have ordered, to Naples, **19.** 439
Egizziello received by, when sitting on a close stool, **19.** 452
—— to be humiliated by, **19.** 438
Elisi nearly equals, in opera, **20.** 86
imprisoned for making Astrua sing out of time, **19.** 438
London is disappointed in, **13.** 142
Naples to be visited by, for cantata, **19.** 438, 439
sings well, **19.** 438
Walpole, Bns, has affair with, **17.** *448*
witticism of, to Zipoli, **19.** 438
Caffiéri, ——, customs director at Calais:
goods to be expedited by, **5.** 160, 301
(?) Guines's law suit involves, **6.** 129
Cage; cages:
cats sent in, to England, **17.** 474
iron, Pugachev sent in, to Moscow, **32.** 184n
Cagliari (Corsica):
Buttler is landed at, **25.** 303
neutral port, **25.** 303
Prussian privateer takes captured Tuscan vessel to, **21.** 330
Russian fleet may call at, **23.** 148
Russian ship takes refuge at, **23.** 202
Cagliostro. *See* Balsamo, Giuseppe
Caher, Bn. *See* Butler, James
Cahideuc, Emmanuel-Auguste de (1698–1764), Comte du Bois de la Motte:
convoy taken by, to America, **20.** 562n
Hawke and Boscawen fail to intercept fleet of, on way from Louisbourg, **21.** 145n
La Galissonnière might be superseded by, **20.** 562
squadron commanded by, **35.** 235n
(?) troops of, at Louisbourg, **21.** 130n
Cahusac, Louis de (d. 1759):
*Fêtes d'Hymen, Les,* by, **7.** 298
Caiaphas:
Henslow lists costume for, among stage properties, **11.** 292
Cailhava d'Estandoux, Jean-François (1731–1813), dramatist:
*Tuteur dupé, Le* ('La Fausse porte'), by, **7.** 265
Caillaud; Caillaut. *See* Caillot
'Caille, Abbé de la,' pseudonym of Voltaire. *See* Voltaire
Caillot, Joseph (1733–1816), singer and actor:
birth date of, corrected, **43.** 98, 300
Conway misses, **39.** 213
*Déserteur, Le,* played by, **6.** 127
Garrick jealous of, **28.** 285
Le Texier has talent of, **39.** 273
theatre abandoned by, **6.** 127
Caimo, Norberto:
*Voyage d' Espagne* by, **6.** 17n, **43.** 96

Cain:
Coke, Lady Mary, wanders like, **31.** 154
descendants of, possess empires, **32.** 83
HW jokes about Abel and, **35.** 335
Caïn *or* Kaïn, Henri-Louis (1729–78), called Lekain *or* Le Kain; actor:
*Alzire* acted by, **7.** 297
biographical information on, corrected, **43.** 94, 133–4, 300
*Britannicus* acted by, **7.** 277
death of, **7.** 17, 19
Du Deffand, Mme, praises reading of, **8.** 191
HW compares, to Garrick, **10.** 175
HW sees, in comedies, **7.** 263
HW sometimes pleased by, **39.** 212–13
imprisoned for refusing to act, **38.** 538n
*Lois de Minos* to be read by, to Mme du Deffand, **5.** 282–3, 287–8, 319
Piozzi, Mrs, comments on, **10.** 175n
verses on, and his successor, **7.** 23
Voltaire expects visit from, **28.** 278
Cairnes, Mary (d. 1790), m. 1 (1724) Cadwallader Blayney, 7th Bn Blayney, 1706; m. 2 (1734) Col. John Murray:
militia recruiting by, resisted, **39.** 323–4
Cairo (Egypt):
plague at, **11.** 302n
*See also* Grand Cairo
Cairo (Italy):
Charles Emmanuel III's army at, **19.** 304
Caius, John (1510–73), M.D.; co-founder of Gonville and Caius College:
monument to, **14.** 112
portraits of, **14.** 110
Caius College, Cambridge. *See* Gonville and Caius
Cake; cakes:
country ladies stock up with, after Session, **18.** 498
Florentine pastilles in, **21.** 565
hare, entremets of, **19.** 357n
plum, Mann to give, to Mme de Craon, **17.** 263
served with ale at Ranelagh, **17.** 401
veal, entremets of, **19.** 357n
Cake-house:
SH may become, **9.** 314, **39.** 381
Calabre, Duc de. *See* Jean II (1425–70)
Calabria, D. of. *See* Philip Anton
Calabria:
earthquakes in: **11.** 298, **25.** 374–6, 383, **33.** 396, 415; Hamilton's accounts of, **35.** 375
plague in, **18.** 270, 282, 283, 288
Calais:
ambassadors meet at, **4.** 481n
balloon descent at, **25.** 543n
bay of, English capture ships in, **20.** 500
Berrys' passage from, **11.** 373
Blanchard's *Trip to,* **33.** 458
boat from, **11.** 162n
book to be forwarded from, **40.** 29
Bussy to sail from, when exchanged for Stanley, **21.** 504

Caffiéri director of customs at, **5**. 160, **6**. 129n
chief magistrate of, **28**. 85n
Churchill said to have died at, **22**. 261
Churchill, Lady Mary, to post HW's letter at, **38**. 497, 498
Coke, Lady Mary, detained at, **31**. 25, 27
—— suspects plot to kill her on way to, **31**. 185
Comédie française rumoured to act at, **38**. 524
commandant at, wants Lady Fenouilhet's house, **5**. 366, 372, 373, 398
Craufurd may go by, **5**. 289
Croÿ governor of, **5**. 402, 405
Cumberland, D. and Ds of, insulted by actors at, **23**. 519–20, **32**. 150–1
currency exchange at, **1**. 98
custom house at, **3**. 92, **6**. 132, **37**. 39, 42
Dashwood brings the Barbarina in chaise to, **30**. 19–20
Dessein's inn at, occupied by Archduke Ferdinand and suite, **33**. 530n
Dover fifteen hours from, **32**. 270
—— mails to and from, stopped, **24**. 496n
drawbridge at, sketched by Hogarth, **20**. 13
Du Châtelet said to receive letters of recall at, **22**. 586n
Du Deffand, Mme, mentions HW's route through, **5**. 64, 92, 95, 97
embargo at, removed, **18**. 416
English ladies supposed to go to, to drink champagne, **38**. 524
English prisoners to be returned to, from France, **37**. 280
English quietly pass through, despite undeclared war, **24**. 412
English ships to be seized at, and crews imprisoned, **20**. 526n, **24**. 365n
English threaten, **21**. 221, 228
English visitors to, **34**. 78
Fenouilhet, Lady, lives at, **5**. 366, 373, 417n, **9**. 30n, **13**. 36n
—— writes from, of D. and Ds of Cumberland, **32**. 150–1
flag near, seen from Ramsgate, **12**. 122
Frenchman willing to endure hell to rescue, from English, **7**. 360
French prisoners to be returned to, from England, **37**. 280
French troops assemble at, **5**. 338, **19**. 193n
French visitors might see England from, through opera glass, **35**. 370
garrison of, given ball by D. of Cumberland, **5**. 143, **23**. 351
gates of: Hogarth's painting of, **41**. 449; locked at sunset, **31**. 117
*General Lally* captures *Dolphin* and takes her to, **21**. 75n
governor of: **20**. 13; *see also* Béthune, Armand-Joseph de; Croÿ, Emmanuel, Duc de
HW delayed at, by contrary winds, **10**. 297, **30**. 19
HW fails to land at, **7**. 258

HW mentions, **7**. 398
HW not to be expected at Paris till he reaches, **38**. 481
HW's expenses at, **7**. 409, 412, 413
HW's furniture to go by, **4**. 459, 461, 463
HW's trunks opened at, **17**. 142
HW surprised by, **13**. 199, 229
HW took 7 days to Paris from, on first trip, **38**. 380
HW writes from, **3**. 7, 8, 14, **4**. 273, 276, 277, **5**. 94, **7**. 381, 389, 390, 394, **10**. 283, **17**. 140, **22**. 413–16, **23**. 141–5, 153, **31**. 116, **39**. 253–4
Henry VIII's embarkation for, **16**. 181
Hertfords unable to land at, missing Croÿ's entertainment and lawyer's speech, **38**. 211
Hessians astonished to find the French no nearer than, **20**. 570
Kingston, Ds of, provides water-mill at, to grind for the poor, **31**. 289n
—— retires to, **28**. 268
—— sails from, for Leghorn, **24**. 398
—— to ship treasure to, **24**. 404
—— writes from, **32**. 299–300
Knight visits, annually, to see cliffs of England, **24**. 174, 180
Ligonier, Lady, and packet-boat captain spend week together at, **30**. 255
Lincoln, E. of, dies near, **24**. 420
Lion d'argent, inn at: **7**. 371; Cumberland, D. and Ds of, stay at, **23**. 344n; formerly Mme Grandsire's, **23**. 344n; HW to stay at, **37**. 38; imports British beef, **20**. 13
Lochiel's regiment at, **9**. 66
Mary, Q. and, **31**. 26
mayor of, compliments D. of Bedford, **28**. 85
Masserano may not live to reach, **24**. 328
Mozzi turns Cts of Orford back from, **23**. 158
Orford, Cts of, visits, twice, but returns to Paris, **23**. 141, 155, 158, 218, **25**. 641
packet boats to: delayed, **7**. 38; stopped, **18**. 401
post between Paris and, **3**. 5
post by Ostend compared to that by, **7**. 159, 162, 163, 172, 227
post from Dover to, stopped, **7**. 157, 161
postilions of, **7**. 342
Russian war ship ordered by Catherine II to take Ds of Kingston's treasure to, from Leghorn, **24**. 409–10
schedules for route from, to Paris, **37**. 40
siege of, **2**. 5
Somerset, D. of, lands in, with D. of Suffolk's expedition, **20**. 139n
Spanish privateer operates near, **17**. 153
storm at, **10**. 241, **11**. 148, 162, 166
Suffolk, D. of, captured between Dover and, **16**. 231n
transportation of goods through, **5**. 124, 160–1, 162, 163, 206, 212, 229, 301, **6**. 36, 39, 252
travellers delayed at, **11**. 355
vagabonds between Boulogne and, **11**. 88

[Calais, *continued*]

visitors to: Amorevoli, **17**. 141, **30**. 19; Ancram, Cts of, **37**. 131; Barbarina, **17**. 141,
**30**. 19; Bedford, D. of, **28**. 85; Belle-Isle,
**19**. 91n; Berrys, **11**. 373; Coke, Lady Mary,
**31**. 25, 27; Conway, **37**. 131, 295, **39**. 536;
Conways, **6**. 159, 162, 163, 165, 169; Coventrys, **20**. 324; Craufurd, **5**. 292, **6**. 228, 231,
489; Cumberland, D. (Henry) and Ds of,
**5**. 131–2, 143, **23**. 344, 351, 519–20, **32**.
150–1, **42**. 264; Damer, Mrs, **11**. 265; Dashwood, **30**. 19–20; Downe, **20**. 324; Du Barry,
Mme, **11**. 244n; Du Châtelet, **22**. 586n;
Gray, **13**. 162n, **28**. 95n, 114; Greville, Mrs,
**5**. 394; Guerchy, **38**. 211; HW, **3**. 18, 350,
352, 353, **4**. 279, 281, **5**. 94, **6**. 220, 221, **7**.
314, 315, 324, 333, 342, 353, **10**. 282–3,
297, **13**. 162n, 199, 229, **17**. 140–2, 161, **22**.
413–16, **23**. 141–5, 153, **28**. 95n, 114, **30**.
19–20, **31**. 116, **32**. 252, 253, **37**. 38–9, **39**.
90; Hogarth, **20**. 13; Kingston, Ds of, **24**.
202, 242, 398, **28**. 268, **31**. 289n, **32**. 299–
300; Knight, **24**. 174, 180; Lauzun, **3**. 311,
314, 316; Lennox, Lady Cecilia, **4**. 281;
Ligonier, Lady, **30**. 255; Mansfield, **28**.
189n; March, E. of, **38**. 527; Monticelli,
**17**. 141, **30**. 19; Mozzi, **23**. 158; Newcastle, Ds of, **9**. 66; Orford, Cts of, **23**. 141,
155, 158, 218, **25**. 641; Pars, **24**. 144; Pomfret, **30**. 23n; Saxe, **18**. 402n; Scott, David,
**39**. 536; Selwyn, **3**. 213, 221, **7**. 85, 86, 88,
89, 151, **38**. 527; Spencers, **6**. 231; Stormont,
**6**. 171; Tylney, **37**. 325; Vaneschi, **17**. 141;
Viscontina, **17**. 141, **30**. 19; Walpole, Edward, **5**. 57n, **23**. 300n; Wilkes, **22**. 137,
261; Wilkes, Mary, **23**. 143n; Young Pretender, **18**. 402

white bread not available at, **34**. 50

'Calais, Siege of.' *See* Buirette de Belloy, Pierre-
Laurent: *Siège de Calais, Le*

Calais, Sword of:

Anne Boleyn beheaded with, **17**. 233n

Calamy, Edmund (1671–1732), nonconformist
divine:

Cole dislikes biographies by, **2**. 72, 93

Calas, Jean (1698–1762), Huguenot merchant:

condemnation of, **3**. 251n

family of: defended by Élie de Beaumont, **28**.
7; HW associates, with Toulouse, **31**. 276n;
Voltaire's efforts for, **7**. 40

Calash; calashes (vehicles):

Esher toured by party in, **10**. 72

German princes furnish, to visitors, **39**. 390

Harlequin's, **9**. 96

Calcagnini, Carlo (1679–1746), cardinal, 1743:

Benedict XIV creates, cardinal, **18**. 302n

Calcidonio (chalcedony):

said to be in Lorraine, **18**. 207

*Calcio* (game):

English merchants give, at Leghorn, for Tuscan Court, **22**. 417–18, 423

Calcraft, John (1726–72), M.P.; politician:

Chatham's reconciliation with Temple and
Grenville contrived by, **10**. 272n

Fox called 'Twitcher' by, in dialogue in
*North Briton*, **38**. 200

Grafton's 'creature' but alienated by him,
**23**. 186n

Granby swayed by, **23**. 168n, 175n

*Heroic Epistle* might have included, **28**. 75

(?) letter to, **7**. 407, **43**. 108

peerage said to be granted to, **10**. 65

Pitt-Temple faction may dismiss, from regimental agencies, **9**. 233

Selwyn's witticism on, **32**. 38

(?) Shelburne and, keep up the Court's
spirits, **38**. 201

Shelburne's friend, turned out of deputy
commissary-generalship of musters for anti-
Court vote, **38**. 248

——'s resignation due to parley with Pitt and
Temple at house of, **22**. 168n

*Town and Country Magazine* satirizes, as
'Crafterio,' **32**. 38n

wealth of, **10**. 65

wishes to become E. of Ormond, **32**. 38

Calcutta:

'Black Hole' of, **32**. 110

Jones judge at, **29**. 35n

supreme court of, **29**. 396n

Caldara Polidoro. *See* Polidoro Caldara

Caldari, ——, Florentine embezzler:

arrested, **17**. 223

Caldecott, George:

Vernon, Borrodale, and, partners in Ludgate
St, **20**. 361n

Caldecott, Thomas (1744–1833), bibliophile:

believes in Ireland's MSS, **15**. 321

(?) SH visited by, **12**. 221

Calder, Sir Henry (ca 1740–92), 4th Bt, 1774;
army officer:

appointed Lt-Gov. of Gibraltar, **11**. 119

Calder, Dr John (1733–1815):

witticism by, on Dr Johnson and his biographers, **43**. 166

Calder, river, Yorkshire:

Zouch asks HW to aid navigation project for,
in Parliament, **16**. 28–9

Calderón de la Barca, Pedro (1600–81), Spanish
dramatic poet:

Shakespeare resembles, **41**. 153

*See also* Ceballos Cortes y Calderón

Caldwell, Lady. *See* Hort, Elizabeth

Caldwell, Capt. Benjamin (ca 1737–1820):

enemy's situation evaluated by, **25**. 183n

Caldwell, James:

Blair's portrait engraved by, **42**. 56n

'Caleb.' *See under* Pulteney, William

*Caledonian Mercury, The*:

rebels called 'Highlanders' by, **19**. 107

Calendar:

change in, **20**. 337n

French Revolutionary, **12**. 28, 170

HW jokes about reform of, **31.** 306
Parliament drops 11 days from, in 1752, **12.**
152–3
Calendar; Calendars, court:
new, every day, **32.** 7
*Calendrier des princes et de la noblesse. See
under* La Chesnaye-Desbois, Aubert de
Calendrini, Magdalen, of Geneva, m. Richard
Neville Aldworth Neville:
marriage of, **20.** 7n
Calends, Assyrian and Greek:
time-space between, **10.** 282
Calero, Pierre:
captured at Velletri, **18.** 493
Cales. *See* Cadiz
Caley, John (ca 1763–1834), F.S.A.; antiquary:
'On the Origin of the Jews in England' by,
in *Archæologia*, **12.** 262, **33.** 568–9
Calf; calves:
Bristol said to have, with 8 feet, **39.** 322
Essex the county for, **23.** 98
Hardinge begs, from HW's cows, **35.** 630–1,
633
—— rejects, as non-French, **35.** 633
York, D. of, receives, at Rome, **22.** 228
California:
Bošković to go to, with Royal Society's ap-
proval, **22.** 527
English victories extend to, **20.** 500, **21.** 352
HW compares, to England, **28.** 228
(?) Halifax would not choose secretary from,
**9.** 45
Seven Years War extends from Madras to,
**35.** 290
Caligula, Caius Julius Germanicus (A.D. 13–41);
Roman Emperor A.D. 37–41:
bust of, given by Mann to HW: **22.** 522–4,
528, **23.** 383, 425, **24.** 15, **25.** 56, 90, **26.**
56, **29.** 329, 333, 348
horse made consul by, **35.** 375
pharos at Boulogne supposedly built by, **16.**
211
played with cockle-shells at Boulogne, **16.** 211
Rome degenerates to, **28.** 175
'Caligulisms':
Frederick, P. of Wales's, **19.** 175
Calini, Maria, Florentine servant:
Mann's annuity to, **25.** 668n
Call, John (1732–1801), M.P.:
M.P. for Callington, **42.** 350n
Calladon, Anne (d. 1780), m. Charles Montagu:
biographical information on, corrected, **43.**
137, 138
Gower, Cts, visited by, at Bill Hill, **10.** 306
HW invites, to dinner at SH, **10.** 306
Callenberg af Huset Muskau, Ursula Margrethe
Constantia Louisa von (1752–1803), m.
(1772) William Christopher von Diede:
Du Deffand, Mme, gives opinion of, **6.** 347
neglected on her arrival in England, **23.** 402
social relations of, with M. and Mme Necker,
**6.** 347

Callendar House:
(?) Kilmarnock, Cts of, leaves papers at, **37.**
217
Callimachus:
Horace's name for Alcæus, **35.** 568
Callimanco, Prince. *See* Caramanico
Callington, Cornwall:
borough of: Boone may succeed Skrine as
M.P. for, **35.** 416–18; HW is M.P. for, **9.**
51, 113n, **13.** 11, 18, 238n, **17.** 73n; HW
prefers election from, because he need not
go there, **19.** 418–19; HW's election in, **19.**
413; HW's opponents for election in, **17.**
414n; Lucas looks after, for E. of Orford,
**25.** 462; Orford, Cts of, corresponds about,
with HW, **23.** 545–6, 548, 557; Orford, Cts
of, influences, **19.** 414n; Orford, Cts of,
loses, by not trusting HW, **24.** 308; Orford,
Cts of, promised, to Sir William Hamilton,
**23.** 548, 557, **24.** 52, **35.** 416–18; Orford,
E. of, controls, **28.** 121n, **39.** 192, **41.** 376;
Parliament's dissolution blamed by Cts of
Orford for neglect of, **24.** 57, 67; Shirley
M.P. for, **9.** 114n; Skrine sent to, by E.
of Orford, **24.** 46; Worsley M.P. for, **2.**
240n, **9.** 343n
HW jokingly proposes title of, for Patapan,
**17.** 76
HW receives unpleasant letter from, **42.** 350
Orford, E. of, heir to maternal estates in,
**30.** 169n
'Calliope':
HW uses name of, for: Miller, Mrs, **39.** 241;
More, Hannah, **33.** 533
Callis, Smith (ca 1709–61), naval officer:
birth date of, **43.** 245
George II to hear account from, of victory
at St Tropez, **17.** 471
Callot, Jacques (1592–1635), artist:
Chute recommends pictures by, to HW, **17.**
118
Du Deffand, Mme, would decorate SH with
grotesques in manner of, **3.** 195
Grisoni procures drawings by, for Mann, **17.**
58, 68
Callotti, Giuseppe, Florentine servant:
Mann's annuity to, **25.** 667n
Calmady, ——:
Callington election contested by, **19.** 414n
Calmet, Augustin (1672–1757), Benedictine
writer:
Calmette, Mme de la, may be related to,
**20.** 326n
*Dissertations qui peuvent servir de prolégo-
mènes de l'Écriture Sainte*, **41.** 157
*Dissertation upon the High Roads of the
Duchy of Lorraine* by, **35.** 163
Calmette. *See* La Calmette
Calmucks:
Pomeranian villages would have been burned
by, **22.** 14

Calne, Wilts:
  Shelburne buys borough of, **29.** 24n
  ——'s seat close to, **29.** 24n
Calomel:
  Orford, E. of, over-dosed with, **42.** 342n
Calonne, Charles-Alexandre (1734–1802), con-
    troller-general of finance:
  contrôleur général des finances, **11.** 44
  'convict,' **33.** 568
  *Correspondance* by, HW has glanced at, **36.**
    249
  *De l'État de la France* by, **11.** 127, 150–1
  England the refuge of, **11.** 44
  English rumour that Necker is to be replaced
    by, **6.** 473
  father eulogized by, **36.** 249
  French émigrés encouraged by lies by, **39.** 485
  HW doubts judgment and integrity of, **11.** 310
  HW knows nothing of, **34.** 37
  hissed out of theatre in Paris, **11.** 44
  La Chalotais's clash with, **11.** 43–4, **36.** 249
  Lamotte, Mme de, aided by, in *Mémoires*,
    **11.** 5n
  laughs at rage of populace in France, **34.** 73
  London reached by, **11.** 310
  *Mémoire présenté au roi* by, **3.** 151, 163, 170
  pamphlets written against, **11.** 44
  print satirizes, **11.** 54n
  *Réponse* by, to Necker, **36.** 249n
  rodomontades of, **11.** 359
  *Tant mieux pour elle* possibly by, **38.** 57n
  wife of, **11.** 36n
Calonne, Mme Charles-Alexandre. *See* Nettine,
    Anne-Rose-Josèphe de
Calonne, Jacques-Ladislas-Joseph (1743–1822),
    Abbé de:
  brother of, **11.** 310n
Calprenède. *See* Costes de la Calprenède
Calshot Castle:
  in Southampton view, **35.** 251
Calthorpe, Sir Henry (ca 1717–88), K.B., 1744;
    M.P.:
  Bath knighthood given to, **18.** 451
  mad behaviour of, **9.** 56
Calthorpe, James (1604–52):
  Cole gives print of, to HW, **1.** 32–3
Calthorpe, Sir William de:
  trustee of Henry de Walpole, **1.** 33n
Calthrop. *See* Calthorpe
Calumet:
  HW owns, presented to Sir William Johnson
    by Indians, **20.** 511n
Calvani, Giuseppe, secretary to Bp Dumesnil:
  Dumesnil accompanied by, **19.** 493
Calveley, Sir George:
  James I knighted at Leigh Hall, **41.** 446
Calveley, Sir Hugh (d. 1393):
  Aragon, Q. of, said to have married, **41.** 445
  John of Gaunt said to be accompanied by,
    to Castile, **41.** 445
  —— serves with, under Chandos, at Battle of
    Navarete, **41.** 445n

Calvert, Charles (1699–1751), 5th Bn Balti-
    more:
  Admiralty not joined by, because of prece-
    dence given to Lord Vere Beauclerk, **18.** 565
  Admiralty post given to, **17.** 366, **19.** 360n
  Boothby, Mrs, entertains, **17.** *173*
  death of, **19.** 360n, **30.** 304n
  Frederick II visited by, on way to St. Peters-
    burg with Algarotti, **37.** 64
  Frederick, P. of Wales, complimented by, **9.**
    18
  —— has, as head of ministry, **20.** 30
  ——'s lord of the Bedchamber, **18.** 8n
  —— transfers, from lord of the Bedchamber
    to Cofferer, **19.** 360
  Gideon said to have bought seat of, in Kent,
    **43.** 269
  good nature of, **30.** 304n
  HW calls, 'unhappy in his English,' **17.** 173n
  HW's opinion of, **20.** 30
  malapropisms of, **20.** 100, **30.** 304n
  offices held by, **30.** 304n
  Opposition led by, in Parliament, **19.** 360
  papers printed for, **18.** 565
  Parliamentary debate by, on privately-raised
    regiments, **26.** 14
  Parliament to have motion from, **9.** 31
  Townshend, Vcts, flirts with, **17.** 173
  Walpole, Sir Robert, told by, that Frederick,
    P. of Wales, does not refuse to see him,
    **18.** 8
Calvert Frederick (1731–71), 6th Bn Baltimore,
    1751:
  dejected-looking at Kingston, **16.** 347
  *Tour to the East, A*, sent by HW to England,
    **7.** 407
  wife of, **20.** 226n
Calvert, George, cr. (1625) Bn Baltimore:
  print of in Pennant's *Journey*, **42.** 16n
Calvert, Peter (1730–88), LL.D.; dean of the
    Arches Court of Canterbury:
  counsel for Ds of Kingston, **24.** 192, 196, **28.**
    261n
Calvert, Sir William (?1703–61), alderman;
    M.P.; Kt, 1744; lord mayor of London, 1749:
  election of, **19.** 425n
  Newcastle, D. of, attended by, at installation
    as chancellor, **9.** 241–2
  Parliamentary debate by, on privately-raised
    regiments, **26.** 23
Calvi, Filippo, Florentine servant:
  Mann's annuity to, **25.** 667n
Calvi, Corsica:
  Bastia garrison flees to, **19.** 162
  Corsican rebels to besiege, **19.** 163
  Corsicans blockade, **19.** 171
  France sends engineer to, to raise batteries,
    **20.** 573n
  Genoa reserves, **20.** 273n
  Jesuits escape from, **22.** 545–6
  —— land at, **22.** 526n, 535n, 545n

Paoli sends Corsican rebel troops and Jesuits
to occupy, **22.** 536
siege of, **2.** 303n
Calvin, John (1509–64), reformer:
alleged painting of, **22.** 179, 246, 291
burning of Servetus reveals, as monster worse
than popes, **34.** 111
French philosophes cannot be as effective as,
**5.** 356
HW's dislike of, **1.** 241, **2.** 61, 100
Luther envied by, **31.** 435
oceans of blood result from, **35.** 398
papal proclivities of, **31.** 385, 435
Priestley a frustrated, **31.** 385
Servetus burnt and St Francis pulled down by,
**20.** 555
Calvinism:
Voltaire's remark on, **17.** 429n
Calvinist; Calvinists:
HW inquires whether Louisa is, **31.** 207
Maclaine was, **20.** 168
Swiss, HW might become, **13.** 181
*Calypso. See under* Cumberland, Richard
Calypso:
hero should resist allurements of, **40.** 245
island of, **37.** 235
Cam, river:
Conservators of, **1.** 340n
HW alludes to, as 'Granta,' **13.** 108
Linton on, **1.** 223n
West alludes to, in verses, **14.** 15
'Camacho,' character in *Don Quixote*:
wedding feast of, excelled by game from
Houghton, **12.** 56
*Camaldule, La. See under* La Harpe, Jean-Fran-
çois de
Camaldules, Order of:
France suppresses, **39.** 147n
Camasse, Marianne (d. 1807), m. (1757) Chris-
tian IV of Bavaria, Duc de Deux-Ponts;
called Comtesse de Forbach:
Stormont's landlady, **7.** 34
Cambden. *See* Camden
Cambden-House. *See* Campden House
Camberwell, Surrey:
Seton of, **11.** 19n
Cambi, Signora. *See* Galli, Lucrezia
Cambiagi, Gaetano, Florentine printer:
Galluzzi's history printed by, **25.** 59n, 80n
Cambiaso, Luca (1527–85), painter:
'Venus Disarming Cupid' by, formerly as-
cribed to Correggio, **23.** 350, **32.** 70, **35.** 409
Cambis, Vicomtesse de. *See* Alsace-Hénin-Lié-
tard, Gabrielle-Françoise-Charlotte d'
Cambis, Henri-Marc-Amable de (d. 1794), Mar-
quis d'Orsan:
marriage of, **7.** 84
Cambis, Jacques-François-Xavier-Régis-Ignace
(b. 1727), Vicomte de, later Comte de Cambis-Orsan:
brother of, marries, **7.** 84
marriage of, **3.** 311n, **11.** 221n

(?) social relations of, with Mme du Deffand,
**6.** 310
Cambis, Marie de (b. 1746– living, 1793), nun
at St-Cyr:
HW admires beauty of, **7.** 329, **10.** *293*
HW hopes to dream about, **10.** 295
Cambis-Orsan, Comte de. *See* Cambis, Jacques-
François-Xavier-Régis-Ignace, Vicomte de
Cambis-Orsan, Comtesse de. *See* Alsace-Hénin-
Liétard, Gabrielle-Françoise-Charlotte d'
Cambo:
Erskine of, **15.** 186n
Cambon, Abbé de:
Du Deffand, Mme, allots suit to, **6.** 258
—— talks of Bp of Mirepoix with, **6.** 304
social relations of, in Paris, **6.** (?) 222, **7.** 344,
346, 348, 349
Cambon, François-Tristan de (d. 1790), Bp of
Mirepoix, 1768:
assembly of clergy attended by, **6.** 85, 168, 211
Barèges visited by, **6.** 187
Du Deffand, Mme, provides rooms for, **5.** 6,
13, 65n
—— receives copy of diocesan charge of, **7.**
435
——'s correspondence with, **5.** 90–1, **7.** 168,
426, 436, 438, 447, 450, 454, 458
——'s opinion of, **4.** 84, **5.** 6, 69, 85, **6.** 85, 316
——'s relations with, **6.** 200, 395, **7.** 100
—— whispers to, by mistake, **32.** 267
États de Languedoc to be attended by, **6.** 374
HW buys suits for, **6.** 235, 243, 246–7, 251–3,
255, 257, 258, **7.** 414
HW discusses America with **7.** 346
HW inquired after by, **7.** 102
HW liked by, **6.** 168, 310, **7.** 168
HW likes, **5.** 90, **6.** 174, 200
HW sends messages to, **5.** 304, **6.** 168, 316
HW sent messages by, **6.** 200, 310, **7.** 168
HW's *Gramont* given to, **5.** 304, 306
HW to see, **5.** 85, **6.** 209, 211, 214
Montpellier visited by, **6.** 255
Paris to be visited by, **6.** 174, 182, 183, 187,
198, 374
—— visited by, **5.** 304, **6.** 200, 204, 304, 316,
395, **7.** 100, 102
remark of, **28.** 222n
Roissy visited by, **7.** 346
St-Ouen visited by, **7.** 348
Sévigné letters transmitted by, **5.** 373
social relations of, in Paris, *see index entries
ante* **8.** 275
to leave Paris, **6.** 251, 252–3
Cambrai, Abp of. *See* Choiseul-Stainville, Léopold-Charles de (1724–74); Rosset de Ceilhes
de Fleury, Henri-Marie-Bernardin de (1718–
81); Salignac de la Mothe-Fénelon, François
de (1651–1715)
Cambrai ('Cambray'):
battle near, **11.** 97n
canal to St-Quentin from, **6.** 159n
French troops assembled at, **5.** 338

[Cambrai, *continued*]
league of, England menaced by repetition of,
   **20.** 571, 582, 585
More, Helen, becomes nun at, **1.** 289n
Mozzi perhaps to see Morice near, **25.** 303
Cambric:
contraband, Ailesbury, Cts of, tries to import,
   **38.** 124
Parliamentary bill prohibits foreign, **18.** 192n
Cambric Bill. *See under* Parliament: acts of
Cambridge, D. of. *See* Adolphus Frederick
   (1774–1850)
Cambridge, E. of. *See* Richard (Plantagenet)
   (ca 1375–1415)
Cambridge, Charles Owen (1754–1847):
   (?) HW visits, **12.** 61
Cambridge, Charlotte (1746–1823):
   Berry, Agnes, hears from, **12.** 20
   Berrys' house rented by, **11.** 149
   ——' return from Italy discussed by, **11.** 304
   —— to be aided by, in obtaining house, **11.**
      *80,* 94
   Burney, Frances, praises HW to, **42.** 299
   gossips, **11.** 305
   HW calls, 'Miss Au-près-du-pont,' **11.** 304
   HW does not see, **12.** 61
   HW hears news from, **12.** 15
Cambridge, Rev. George Owen (1756–1841):
   Archdeacon of Middlesex, **12.** 61n
   Berry, Mary, writes to, **11.** 236
   comment by, on his mother, **11.** 16n
   HW assured by, about Berrys' vessel, **11.** *116*
   HW calls, 'the Infallible,' **12.** 20
   HW's witticism on Duc de Bouillon repeated
      by, **33.** 425n
   HW to give potatoes to, for charity, **12.** 180
   HW visits, **12.** 61
   Hesketh, Lady, visited by, **11.** 236
   horse advice given by, to Agnes Berry, **12.** 15,
      20
   horse-selling by, for Robert Berry, **11.** 160, 162
   *Siege of Berwick, The,* attended by, **12.** 62
   Twickenham to be visited by, **12.** 20, 180
Cambridge, Richard Owen (1717–1802), poet:
   an 'old wit,' **11.** 181n
   Batt visits, **11.** 183
   benevolent and inoffensive, **29.** 71
   Berry, Mary, gets letter from, **28.** 49n
   Berrys' house rented by, **11.** 149
   ——' news given by, **11.** 149
   Camelford, subject of tales spread by, **11.** 53
   celebrated Twickenham resident, **35.** 234
   Charlton's blunder told by, to HW, **33.** 414,
      415
   Colman satirizes, as newsmonger, **29.** 70
   credibility of, **32.** 242
   dull people never bother, **11.** 29
   'echo in the neighbourhood,' **32.** 195
   *Elegy Written in an Empty Assembly-Room*
      by, **28.** *91,* **37.** 460
   *Fakeer, The,* by, **28.** 91n

family of, Whigs, **13.** 111
family prayers of, **12.** 177
field of, near Richmond, **39.** 418
finds authors vain and troublesome, **28.** 250–1
(?) gnats in Twickenham annoy, **11.** 29
gossip absorbs, **11.** 48, 53–4, 304, 305
Gray's *Odes* discussed by, **9.** 215
HW asks, about Lort, **16.** 282
HW called upon by: at SH, **42.** 297; to see
   HW's parody of Chesterfield, **32.** 203
HW calls, Berrys' 'morning gazetteer,' **11.** 60
HW contributes to charity drive of, **12.** 177
HW coolly treated by, because of passage in
   Mason's *Gray,* **28.** 213–14
HW declines dinner invitation from, **28.**
   330–1
HW gets no gossip from, **29.** 68, **35.** 245
HW identifies, **28.** 187n, 188n
HW jokes about stories of, **11.** 212, **12.** (?)
   266
HW praised by, **13.** 111
HW prepared by, for Fanny Burney's prob-
   lem, **42.** 297
HW rarely visited by, **11.** 60
HW receives Drayton quotation from, **11.** 71
HW's anecdotes of, **15.** 331–2
HW's news from, **11.** 31
(?) HW told by, of Batt's prospective inheri-
   tance, **11.** 322
HW to reassure, about Berrys, **11.** 117
HW visited by, **11.** 18, (?) 29, 48, 357
HW visits, **11.** 67, 160, 304, **12.** 15, 26, 49,
   61, 159, 177
has little gossip to relate, **29.** 68
*Heroic Epistle* supplemented by, **28.** 91, 95
highway robbery near house of, **34.** 143
house of, **11.** 31n, 63
'junto' of, **12.** 19
meadows of, **9.** 154n, **11.** 337
Montroses informed by, of Irish bill's withdrawal, **33.** 491
news and literature dispensed by, **32.** 192–3
newsmongering of, **33.** 171, 266
Nivernais's *Jardins modernes* given to, **12.** 259
'officious intelligencer,' **33.** 491
Parnassian vein of, **11.** 149
Pepys's social relations with, **31.** 243
poet of Twickenham, **32.** 31
'Progress of Liberty' by, in *Times,* **34.** 87
rumour concerning HW's MSS and, **29.** 202n
Seton, Barbara Cecilia, consults, **11.** 116
SH visitors sent by, **12.** 227, 247, 251
Suffolk, Cts of, probably learns news from,
   **31.** 123–4
Twickenham resident, **42.** 484
verses by, about Berrys, printed, **11.** 1n
wife of: feared to be declining, **12.** 32; still
   loved by him, **11.** 16
*World* contributions by, **20.** 395n
Cambridge, Richard Owen II (b. 1741):
baptism of, **28.** 187n
(?) HW visits, **12.** 61

Cambridge, Richard Owen III (d. 1775):
Cambridges resolve not to grieve for, **15.** 331–2

Cambridge, Mrs Richard Owen. *See* Trenchard, Mary

*Cambridge*, English ship:
HW's shipment to have been conveyed from Leghorn by, **18.** 196, 200, 215

Cambridge, Cambs (*see also* vols 1, 2, 13 and 14 *passim*):
Addenbrooke's Hospital (County Hospital) at, **1.** 267, 268, **2.** 94, 95, 331
almshouses at, **13.** 80
assizes at, attended by Gray, **13.** 155
Baker's proposed history of writers of, **2.** 98, 114–15, 342, 347–8, 350
Barrett Lennard initiated at, by Lyttelton, into College of Arms, **35.** 184
Baskerville prints Bible at, **40.** 275
Blanshard from, **38.** 442
Bryant fêted at, **2.** 172
Carter's *History* of, **2.** 354
Castle Hill and Castle Yard at, **2.** 219
clergyman at, rebukes daughter for praying by light of farthing candle, **17.** 85
clergy of, admire Burke's *Reflections*, **34.** 100n
coach to and from, **1.** 215n, 225, 361, **2.** 135; *see also* fly to and from
Cole a clergyman of, **33.** 575
—— dines in, **1.** 185, 210, 232n, 254, 272, 299, **2.** 35, 193, 232, 276, 281, 344
—— in, **1.** 30–1, 84, 121n, 155, 159, 331, **2.** 12, 97, 151n, 152, 180, 181, 218, 230, 234, 271, **28.** 59
—— justice of the peace for, **2.** 378
—— likes neighbourhood of, **1.** 24, 142, 146
—— seldom visits, **1.** 277, 326, **2.** 72, 148, 331
——'s inscription for Town Hall of, **2.** 311, 312, 313, **43.** 75
——takes supper in, **2.** 180
cross for Ampthill to be finished at, **1.** 296, 299
daily improvements at, **1.** 161
Dissenters at, **2.** 71
elections at, **1.** 346–7, **2.** 166–7, 219, **38.** 371, **43.** 60
Essex from, **32.** 294, **39.** 275
—— to leave, **2.** 81
festivities at, **1.** 168, 266n, 267, **2.** 95, 331 (*see also under* Cambridge University)
Fitzwilliam Museum at, **16.** 79n
flood in, **2.** 369
Florence fouler than, **30.** 3
fly to and from: parcels sent by, **1.** 260, 264, 295, 366, **2.** 41, 56, 57, 62, 95, 147, 148, 156, 157, 158, 202, 235, 295, 306, 319, 327; puts up at Gray's Inn Lane, **1.** 263, 264, 295, 359, 366, **2.** 41, 57, 62, 95, 157, 235, 295; schedule of, **1.** 263n, **2.** 202; *see also* coach to and from
Free School Lane at, **1.** 235, **14.** 103n

Glynn a physician and Chattertonian at, **16.** 225, **34.** 150
Gray compares, to a spider, **13.** 58
—— in, **1.** 124, 206, **14.** *passim*
——'s contempt for, **1.** 359
——'s delight in, when empty of inhabitants, **28.** 186–7
—— to return to, **35.** 66
Great St Mary's Church at, **2.** 94, 95, 97, 213, 331, **15.** 305, 315
HW alludes to Lyttelton's compliments on, **40.** 96
HW asks Lort to find clergyman at, to live with E. of Orford, **16.** 171
HW mentions, **10.** 86
HW's visitor from, **11.** 164
HW to dine at, with Cole, **36.** 125
HW visits Benthams at, **1.** 178, 185
hurricane at, **2.** 136
illuminates, in honour of Rodney's victory, **2.** 193
Legate, John, printer of, **40.** 297n
Lort at, **16.** 161, 165, 167, 169, 177, 193
——'s collection of prints at, **16.** 173
maps of, **2.** 356
market at, **2.** 15
Mason to see Gray at, **28.** 5
Merrill of, **16.** 194
Middleton of, **15.** 1, 7
——'s house at, **15.** 305, 313–14
music room planned at, **1.** 188
never produces anything, **1.** 379
Newham St at, **13.** 80n
opinion in: of Bryant, **1.** 370; of Burke's *Reflections*, **34.** 100n; of Gray's *Life*, **1.** 356, 358, 359
painted glass in, **1.** 30–1, 32
Perse Almshouses at, **13.** 80n
petitioning in, **2.** 207
post from, schedule of, **2.** 97, 106, 267
Pythagoras's school at, **1.** 263, **2.** 148
Rose and Crown inn at: **1.** 143; Cole dines at, **1.** 299, **2.** 88; County Club meets at, **1.** 299, **2.** 362; parcels to be directed to Cole at, **2.** 41, 57, 62n, 63, 202, 235, 295, 303
St Botolph's church at **2.** 23n
St Clement's church at: **1.** 321n; Cole gives steeple to, **2.** 379
St Edward's church at, **1.** 188n
St Mary's church at: Middleton's behaviour at, decent, **15.** 315; Middleton's house near, **15.** 305
St Michael's church at, **15.** 309, 313, 314, 315
Stone Yard Baptist Chapel at, **2.** 71n
Sun Inn, diligence sets out from, **1.** 225n
Three Tuns Tavern at, **14.** 91n
Town Hall of, **2.** 208
Town Hall of (new), **2.** 311, 312
Trinity St at, **15.** 303n
Trumpington St at, **13.** 60n, 80n
Tuers at, **1.** 51, 74, 81, 114
usury in, **2.** 35

[Cambridge, Cambs, *continued*]

visitors to: Christian VII, 23. 57n; Conway, 37. 20, 21; Gulston, 2. 27; HW, 1. 32n, 110, 124, 178, 185, 2. 46, 6. 145, 13. 89 *and passim*, 15. 21, 36. 125; Harding, 16. 324; Mason, 28. 5, 124, 129; Mount Stuart, 2. 27; Townshend, Charles, 38. 341; Wilkes, 43. 62

wagon (Burleigh's) sets out to, from Bull Inn, Bishopsgate St, 2. 47

wagon (Salmon's) to: parcels sent by, 1. 260, 2. 259, 260, 262, 263; puts up at Green Dragon, Bishopsgate St, 1. 263, 2. 259, 260, 262, 263; schedule of, 1. 263n, 2. 260; sets out from Black Bull Inn, Bishopsgate St, 2. 260n

Walpole, Lady, to send things to HW at, 37. 15

Cambridge, Mass.:

powder and ammunition seized at, 24. 45n

*Cambridge Chronicle, The*:

Cole disparages, 2. 127

—— quotes, on Houghton pictures, 2. 145–6

—— reads, 1. 93–4, 97, 2. 305

HW's letter to Rousseau published in, 1. 112n, 113

letter in, signed 'Scrutator,' 34. 149

Rousseau's letter from Wootton published in, 1. 112n, 113

verses in, against Cooke's sermon, 2. 213

Cambridgeshire:

Bromley from, 40. 13

Cole in, 1. 15, 48

——'s materials concerning, 1. 92, 159n

——'s offices in, 2. 378, 379

Cotton a Jacobite of, 19. 310n

County Club of, 1. 232n, 299, 2. 362

'dampest county,' 1. 164

draining of fens in, 1. 132

elections in, 1. 198–202, 198n, 2. 216, 219, 233, 234, 29. 47, 35. 612

Hinxton in, 35. 593

Jenyns injured by mob in, 29. 47

militia of, 1. 238n, 2. 88, 21. 312

Parliamentary reform rejected by, 29. 24, 26

riots in, over militia bill, 21. 137n, 35. 285n

Rutland, D. of, has debts in, 33. 219

Waldegrave sisters' real estate in, 42. 172n

Cambridge University, high steward of, *see* Pelham Holles, Thomas (1693–1768) D. of Newcastle; Yorke, Philip (1720–90), E. of Hardwicke

Cambridge University:

addiction of, to food, 20. 83

Anstey's *Patriot* aimed at, 14. 161

banquets at, 20. 71–2, 83

Baskerville's grant from, for printing prayer-books, 40. 275

Bentley, Dr, subject of legal action at, 15. 294

Bentley, Richard, at, 35. 643

bursar at, poor in arithmetic, 33. 19

Cambridge (town) engulfs, 10. 92

*caput* of, 1. 177

*Castle of Otranto* scene taken from college at, 6. 145

chancellor's post may be vacant at, 9. 71

chemistry chair at, contested, 32. 165n

Christian VII fortunate in not having tutor from, 23. 40

—— unable to go to, to hear Latin verses, 23. 48

clergy of, ungrateful to D. of Newcastle, 22. 38

Cole at, 10. 92

—— has not seen, since October, 2. 72

—— knew Exeter at, 10. 344, 345

—— knew Halifax at, 10. 334

—— knew Montagu at, 10. 333

—— knew Orwell at, 10. 334

——'s collections will revive, after colleges fall down, 2. 117

——'s love for, 1. 83

——'s MS 'Athenæ' of, 1. 370, 2. 134

collection of verses of, *see* Gratulatio

college head at, may be recommended by Newcastle for K.B., 22. 332

colleges of, described by Gray, 13. 58–60

commencement festivities at, 1. 168, 266n, 267, 2. 95, 331

contest after Hardwicke's death for high steward of, 38. 341, 355, 360, 362–3

Cornwallis at, 23. 43

dirges at, on P. of Wales's death, 20. 260–1

dress of students at, 13. 59–60

elections for, 2. 166–7

Essex chancellor of, 16. 367

examinations at, 13. 78–9

Fearne a fellow of, 21. 61

fellow-commoners of, described by Gray, 13. 58–60

fellows of, described by Gray, 13. 58

Ferne attends, 7. 373

Francis III receives degree at, 20. 57

Frederick, P. of Wales, persuaded to seek chancellorship of, 20. 10n

—— writes to, 9. 71

George II orders, to elect Newcastle chancellor, 9. 71, 20. 10n

George III's address from, presented by D. of Newcastle, 22. 78n

*Grace Book, A,* of, 1. 138

Grafton's installation as chancellor of, 1. 168, 10. 284n

Gray at, 10. 284, 13. *passim*

—— becomes Regius Professor at, 39. 106, 41. 163–4

—— is absent from, without regret, 13. 95

—— laments lack of variety in, 13. 73

—— reluctant to leave, though ugly, dirty and dull, 13. 154

HW at, 9. 8, 10. 92, 12. 208, 13. 6, 15. 19, 152, 16. 19, 37. 2n, 34

HW attends Batty's lectures at, 36. 123n

HW discouraged by Sanderson from studying mathematics at, 21. 353

HW has lost all connections with, 16. 217

HW learns astronomy at, **28.** 160

HW learns Italian at, **13.** 6

HW may write to Brown at, **28. 43**

HW quotes language of, **26.** 454

HW read Voiture's letters at, **30.** 75

HW returns to, **37.** 34, **40.** 21, 24

HW undertakes to carry election at, for E. of Sandwich, **32.** 165

HW visits, **6.** 145

HW would like to live at, **10.** 92

Hardwicke to succeed Newcastle as high steward of, **20.** 19

high stewardship of: **10.** 170, 309; contested by Hardwicke and Sandwich, **22.** 219; Sandwich wants to succeed Hardwicke in, **38.** 248, **43.** 186

Hume, Bp, tutor-companion at, to E. of Lincoln, **30.** 2n

Hurd's *Moral and Political Dialogues* much admired at, **16.** 34

improved appearance of colleges at, **10.** 92

Jones of Emmanuel College at, visits SH, **12.** 245

Keene acts as Newcastle's tool at, **20.** 346–7

—— turns, half Jacobite, **20.** 346–7

—— vice-chancellor of, **20.** 346n

King's College Chapel at, **10.** 284, **11.** 22

Latimer's story of foolish scholar at, **35.** 119n

Layard's *Charity* a prize poem at, **32.** 181n

libraries at, consulted by Gray, **28.** 28

Lind said to be tutor to Poniatowski at, **23.** 556n

loyal address presented by, **30.** 98

Lyttelton invited to visit at, by HW, **40.** 19

Mann cannot translate absurd address of, **19.** 144

Mann, Horace II, studies at, under Bp Keene, **21.** 409

manor of, at Landbeach, **2.** 11

manuscripts at, **15.** 145–6

manuscripts of Theophilus at, **29.** 6

Mason's *Gray* not admired at, **28.** 198

masters of colleges at, described by Gray, **13.** 58

Masters's *Some Remarks* distributed at, **1.** 290, 294n, 309n, 334, **2.** 162

Methodism should be resisted by, **1.** 135

Middleton chosen principal librarian to, **15.** 292

—— makes enemies at, by taking private pupils, **15.** 311–12

M.P.s for, **2.** 219

mummy given to, **15.** 17–18, 19

Newcastle, D. of, installed as chancellor of, **10.** 284, **20.** 71–2, 83

—— presents address of, to George III, **9.** 321, **22.** 78n

—— should found school of politics at, **38.** 30

—— succeeds Somerset as chancellor of, **20.** 9–10

—— wants to be chancellor of, **9.** 71

North, (?) Hon. Brownlow, at, **10.** 284

oath of matriculation at, **13.** 75

Oxford's rivalry with, **35.** 272

painted windows at, **1.** 21

Parker's *History* of, **1.** 148

pensioners of, described by Gray, **13.** 59

poems from, on P. of Wales's wedding, **9.** 1, 6, 6–7

price of board at, **13.** 59

Principal Librarian of, **2.** 94

proctors' election at, **43.** 175

professor of physic at, refuses to aid Gray, **23.** 329

proposal in, that Fellows might marry, **1.** 107

regius professor of divinity at, makes use of charm against the stone, **15.** 315

Richard III's relations with, **1.** 138, 144, 147, **43.** 50–2

Richardson returns to, **40.** 233

Senate House ('Theatre') at: **2.** 97, 145, 208, 330; Middleton's house near, **15.** 305, 310; students have mock election at, **38.** 363

sizars in, described by Gray, **13.** 59

sophs of, too low for anything but puns, **13.** 93

sophs' schools at, **13.** 78–9

Stourbridge Fair attended by students of, **10.** 11

Strype solicits subscriptions in, **2.** 145

student from, in coach, **37.** 21

tripos verses at, **13.** 119

tutor at: scolds pupils for leaving college often, **12.** 97; speaks English instead of Latin because of sore mouth, **18.** 148

undergraduates at, hiss at Sandwich's friends, **38.** 363

University Library at: **2.** 45, 354; Baker's MSS in, **2.** 346; Chaucer MS in, **14.** 108; Dugdale's *Baronage* not in, **14.** 80; Gray looks at book in, **14.** 186; HW's works wanted for, **2.** 246–7, 248; Northampton's letters in, **16.** 160; principal librarian at, **2.** 94

verses written at, mere juvenile exercises, **16.** 15

vice-chancellor of, chosen annually, **13.** 58; *see also* Richardson, William

Walpole, Sir Edward, attends, **7.** 373

Walpole, Sir Robert, tutored at, by Hare, **18.** 63–4

—— wrote verses at, **16.** 224, 226

West expects to visit, **13.** 109

Westmorland's installation at, as chancellor, **9.** 241–2

Whaley wants to know when HW returns to, **40.** 12

William, P., of Gloucester, entered at, **36.** 244n

York, Abp of, chancellor of, **43.** 51

*See also*: Christ's College; Clare Hall; Corpus Christi College; Cosin scholarship; Emmanuel College; Gonville and Caius College; King's College; Magdalene College; Pembroke College; Peterhouse; St Cath-

[Cambridge University, *continued*]
erine's Hall; St John's College; Sidney Sussex College; Trinity College; Trinity Hall
*See also under* Middleton, Conyers
Cambuskenneth, Clackmannanshire:
Erskine of, **28.** 242n
Camden, Bn. *See* Pratt, Charles (1714–94)
Camden, Cts. *See* Molesworth, Frances (before 1766–1829)
Camden, E. *See* Pratt, Charles (1714–94); Pratt, John Jeffreys (1759–1840)
Camden, Marchioness. *See* Molesworth, Hon. Frances
Camden, M. *See* Pratt, John Jeffreys
Camden, William (1551–1623), antiquary:
*Annales,* **1.** 262, **2.** 356, **37.** 306, **40.** 22, **42.** 242–3, 312
*Britannia,* **1.** 387, **2.** 277, **15.** 114n, 194, **35.** 146, **43.** 202
HW's anti-Gothic reflections may not be forgiven by, **40.** 311
*Remains Concerning Britain,* **2.** 202
Camden, South Carolina:
battle of, **25.** 92, **29.** 84n, 90n, **33.** 232, **36.** 183–4
Charleston's treasures stored at, **33.** 155n, **39.** 346n
settlers said to have seized, with Charleston's valuables, **39.** 346n
Camel; camels:
at Pisa, **11.** 181
Bruce's story of sending, to America, denied by Jenyns, **15.** 331
Campbell a pun upon, **39.** 174
caravan of, **24.** 510
HW imagines introduction of, into England, **33.** 212
HW's story about Campbells and, **32.** 242
London exhibition of, **21.** 199
Raynal discusses, **39.** 168
Russians capture, **23.** 160
Camel and the gnat:
HW cites proverb about, **21.** 86
Camelford, Bn. *See* Pitt, Thomas (1737–93); Pitt, Thomas (1775–1804)
Camelford, Bns. *See* Wilkinson, Anne (1738–1803)
Cameo; cameos:
Albani's, coveted by Mann for HW, **18.** 477
at Elizabeth Chudleigh's, **9.** 277
Ennery's collection includes, **7.** 325
HW buys, **26.** 5
HW wants ring of, **19.** 332
in Middleton's *Monumenta,* **15.** 17
Mann inherits, from Stosch, and sends it to HW in pill-box, through Mrs Damer, **25.** 650, 652–3, 657, **26.** 56
—— sends, to HW through Morice, **25.** 51, 56, 65, 88, 89–90, 94
Miller has fingers loaded with, **39.** 241
obscene, reproduced by d'Hancarville, **23.** 456n

of Alexander the Great, on snuff-box, **22.** 234n
of Augustus, in Barberini-Byres-Hamilton-Portland collections, **33.** 485n
Ottoboni presents, to Carlisle, **13.** 214
Pompadour, Mme de, makes, popular, **21.** 201
Portland vase is largest extant example of, **35.** 444
Stosch's: bequeathed to Mann, **21.** 149, **25.** 650; bought by France, **21.** 201; coveted by Caylus, **21.** 434; numerous, **21.** 151; to be sold separately, **21.** 186
Strozzi, Principessa, loses, **19.** 350
urn in, on mourning ring, **31.** 131n
Zanetti's, Mann will write about, to Venice, **22.** 6
Camera apostolica, at Rome. *See* Apostolical chamber
Camera obscura:
Delineator, The, a form of, **39.** 293
—— surpasses, **29.** 371
Farington's views painted in, **15.** 319
Storer's improvements of, **16.** 235
*See also* Delineator
*See also under* Storer, William
Camera, papal. *See* Apostolical chamber
Camerfort, ——, volunteer:
captured at Velletri, **18.** 493
Camerlengo; camerlingo. *See* Chamberlain
Cameron, Dr Archibald (1707–53):
execution of, **20.** 384, 387
Prussia supposedly commissions, for Jacobite invasion of England, **20.** 373, 384
physician and captain in Young Pretender's and French armies, **20.** 373n
(?) print of, **40.** 236
wife's parting from, **20.** 384, 387
Young Pretender's reception into Church of England confirmed by, **20.** 333n
Cameron, Donald (?1695–1748) of Lochiel:
Newcastle, Ds of, received by, at Calais, **9.** 66
Young Pretender accompanied by, in French landing, **19.** 319n
Cameron, Jean, m. Dr Archibald Cameron:
husband takes leave of, **20.** 384, 387
Cameron, Jean or Jeanie (ca 1699–1772), m. —— O'Neal; 'Miss Jenny':
birth date of, corrected, **43.** 281
capture of, **37.** 217
Rome visited by, to ask Young Pretender for a pension, **22.** 453
Cameron, John (d. 1748), cr. (1717) Lord Lochiel (Jacobite peerage):
(?) brother of, **37.** 252
Camœdris:
recommended for gout, **6.** 384
'Camilla.' *See under* Virgil: *Æneid*
Camilla. *See under* Burney, Frances
*Camilla, Regina de' Volsci,* burletta:
at Teatro S. Casciano, **18.** 294n
Camillus, Marcus Furius (d. ? 365 B.C.), Roman general:

England lacks, **35**. 62

Livy's lies about, **21**. 541

modern counterparts of, at balls instead of war, **24**. 86

Washington imitates, **24**. 287

Camillus de Lellis (1550–1614), saint:

canonization of, **19**. 171n

Camilly, Comte de. *See* Blouet, Pierre

Cammania:

La Condamine visits, **22**. 147n

Cammann, Schuyler V. R.:

'Serendipity' study by, **25**. 34

Camoens, Luiz Vaz de (ca 1524–ca 1579), Portuguese poet:

grandeur of, marred by faults, **29**. 256

Camomile:

Du Deffand, Mme, comments on, **5**. 80

Camomile tea:

Devonshire takes, **38**. 419n

HW takes, for vomiting, **12**. 194

Camp; camps, military:

English army: at Bradford Peverell, **37**. 490–2; Bolingbroke to wed at, **30**. 137; contagion of military vanity caught by living in, **37**. 139; continuance of, in London, is displeasing, **25**. 75; Conway going into, **37**. 121, 123, 483, 490–1; Conway inspects, **37**. 476; dull when inactive, **37**. 143, 283; England prepares, against invasion, **20**. 505; English march out of, at daybreak, **37**. 191; floods endanger, **35**. 365; George III and Howe visit, **24**. 414; HW hopes Conway will not be forced to gain reputation in, **37**. 448; idle stories infest, **37**. 153; in Isle of Wight, **21**. 190; in Kent and Sussex, **35**. 255; numerous in England, **24**. 377, 384, 387, 392; rainy season breaks up, **21**. 13

French army: break up in October, **24**. 413–14; formed at Compiègne, **38**. 410

Roman, **15**. 179, 202, **42**. 100

Roman, Saxon, and Danish, in Dorchester area, **37**. 491

Campagni. *See* Compagni

*Campaign, The. See under* Addison, Joseph

Campaign; campaigns, military:

may be popular in London, **30**. 35

Campanini, Barbarina (1721–99), called 'La Barbarina'; dancer; m. (1750) Karl Ludwig, Freiherr von Cocceji; cr. (1787) Gräfin von Campanini:

attack on, when she leaves opera house, **18**. 124

Auretti's rivalry with, **16**. 280n

becomes director of home for poor girls of noble birth, **17**. 141n

biographical information about, corrected, **43**. 237, 313

Calais visited by, **17**. 141, **30**. 19–20

Chiaretta will not do on same stage with, **18**. 31

Dashwood brings, to Calais in chaise, **30**. 19–20

debut of, in Berlin, **17**. 358n

Frederick II forces, to return to Berlin, **17**. 358n

Gräfin in own right, **17**. 141n

HW calls, 'vastly pretty,' **30**. 20

HW meets, at Calais, **17**. 141n, **30**. 19–20

London opera to retain, **17**. 358

looseness of, at Uzerches, **30**. 20

parties for, **18**. 131

Stuart Mackenzie elopes with, **17**. 358n, **30**. 59

Campbell, Lady. *See* Cheape, Marianne (ca 1773–1849); Ramsay, Amelia (d. 1813)

Campbell, Mr; Lyttelton's agent:

Mann will draw on, for expenses of Lyttelton's gesse, **20**. 577, 582

Campbell, Mr:

HW sends letters from Paris through, **7**. 380

Campbell, Mr:

Middleton sends proposals to, **15**. 7n

Campbell, Mrs:

social relations of, with Lady Mary Coke, **31**. 138

Campbell, Mrs, of Whitton:

SH visited by, **12**. 246

Campbell, Capt. Alexander (d. 1773):

wife of, **9**. 377n

Campbell, Sir Alexander (d. 1810), 4th Bt, of Ardkinglass:

wife of, **11**. 107n

Campbell, Mrs Alexander. *See* Meadows, Frances

Campbell, Anne (1594–1638), m. (1607) George Gordon, 2d M. of Huntly:

Jamesone's portrait of, **40**. 268

Campbell, Lady Anne (ca 1720–85), m. (1741) William Wentworth, 2d E. of Strafford, n.c.:

Abercorn complimented by, **38**. 292

angling and shooting avoided by, **35**. 335

at Twickenham, **32**. 192

birth date of, corrected, **43**. 123, 294, 325, 331

bullfinch of, whistles tune, **31**. 127

Coke, Lady Mary, corresponds with, **23**. 560n, **31**. 63, 150, 167

—— doubtless describes Stowe house-party to, **35**. 338

—— quotes, **4**. 16n

—— sends message to HW by, **31**. 178

——'s social relations with, **31**. 133

—— visits, at Wentworth Castle, **37**. 561

Conway and wife to be visited by, at Park Place, **37**. 483

Conway and wife visit, at Wentworth Castle, **37**. 559–62

(?) Conway may tear HW from, **37**. 301

Conway, Anne Seymour, visits, at Wentworth Castle, **37**. 560

death of, from falling into fire in a fit, **33**. 460, **36**. 232

Devonshire, D. of, accompanies to SH, **38**. 362

—— to be visited by, at Chatsworth, **38**. 72

Devonshires entertain, at Chatsworth, **9**. 295

[Campbell, Lady Anne (ca 1720–85), *continued*]
family of, **21.** 452n, **28.** 164n, **29.** 74n, **30.** 327n, **35.** 282n, 308n, 331n

Greenwich, Lady, sends news to, **35.** 349

HW abuses patience of husband of, **35.** 371

HW admires appearance of, at George III's coronation, **9.** 387

HW asks commands of, at Paris, **35.** 316–17, 341

HW buys paint-box for, **7.** 406

HW calls: 'Eve,' **35.** 335; 'huckaback,' **35.** 297n; 'lady of the menagerie,' **35.** 293

HW condoles with, on loss of animals, **35.** 378

HW, Conway and wife to visit, at Wentworth Castle, **37.** 472n

HW does not mention, **31.** 140

HW glad that poultry of, will be fed, due to grain embargo, **35.** 320

HW hopes Jones's *Muse Recalled* will charm, **35.** 362

HW hopes that chickens and ducks will not detain, **35.** 286

HW hopes to get news from, **35.** 332

HW hopes tranquillity for, in woods, **35.** 355

HW inquires after, **35.** 316, 340

HW known by, to have protested that his letters were unworthy, **35.** 385

HW mentions, **10.** 7, **20.** 292

HW's animals send regards to those of, **35.** 309

HW sends compliments to, and to her menagerie, **35.** 282, 289, 291, 293, 320, 324, 341

HW sends regards to pheasants of **35.** 324

HW shares opera box with, **31.** 14n, **35.** 350n

HW's influence with, **31.** 186

HW's 'The Beauties' compares, to Diana, **30.** 327

HW's social relations with, **31.** 133

HW takes leave of, **35.** 316

HW thanks, for hospitality at Wentworth Castle, **35.** 278

HW to be visited by husband and, **28.** 385

HW told by, to write to Lady Mary Coke, **31.** 163

HW to meet, in London, **35.** 353

HW to receive good wishes of, **28.** 232

HW to send letters to Lady Mary Coke through, **31.** 154

HW to visit, at Wentworth Castle, **35.** 318

HW urges, to come to London, **35.** 349

HW visited by: **32.** 345; at SH, for tea, **38.** 362

HW will be suspected by, of rambling like Northesk, **35.** 374

health of: alarming, **38.** 180; excellent, **31.** 144, 164; HW inquires about, **31.** 63, **35.** 340; HW rejoices in, **35.** 380

husband and, solitary but happy, **28.** 164

husband's insistence on HW's letters will be attested by, **35.** 385

impatient to leave London, **31.** 144

lambs of, to receive Tonton's greetings, **35.** 368

London's troubles will not concern, **35.** 335

Mason pays respects to, **28.** 230

—— visited by, **28.** 52

mother may be imitated by, **35.** 297, 299

Northumberland House dinner attended by, **38.** 529–30

Queensberry, Ds of, invites, to ball, **38.** 342

subscription masquerade attended by, in vast beauty, **20.** 49

Suffolk, Cts of, friend of, **35.** 320

Tonton's homage to, **35.** 368

tranquillity to be enjoyed by, in woods, **35.** 355

Twickenham house of, **38.** 362

Tylney to send pheasants to, **35.** 275, 277

Worksop visited by, **35.** 280n

Campbell, Anne (ca 1731–1812), m. (1752) Matthew Fortescue, 2d Bn Fortescue:
husband's suicide said to have been announced by outcry of, **10.** 166, **22.** 333

Campbell, Archibald (d. before 1440):
Jamesone's portrait of, **40.** 265

Campbell, Archibald (d. 1744), Bp of Aberdeen:
Deacon consecrated by, **13.** 32n

Campbell, Lord Archibald (1682–1761), cr. (1706) E. of Ilay; 3d D. of Argyll, 1743:
Bedford accuses, of favouring Jacobites, **20.** 310

(?) Bellenden visits, **9.** 60–1

bill of, attacked in House of Lords, **20.** 310

Bramston's epigram on garden of, on Hounslow Heath, **17.** 441–2, 462

brother sends to, communications from Old Pretender, **17.** 479

brother's retort from, about will, **26.** 11

brother succeeded by, **37.** 150

Bute to inherit Scottish patronage of, **9.** 358

Caroline, Q., hates, **15.** 153

cats wanted by, **17.** 164, 181, 394, 419–20, 462, 497, 506

censured for coming to London in 1745, **15.** 154

Coke's treatment of his wife condemned by, **9.** 60

cousin succeeds, **23.** 246n, **37.** 46on

dark and shrewd, **15.** 153

death of: **9.** 358; leaves Bute the chief power in Scotland, **21.** 527n; Stuart Mackenzie's Venetian appointment rescinded because of, **21.** 511n

Elcho appeals to, for protection, **19.** 272n

Elliot's retention in Admiralty offered to please, **21.** 73n

French burn house of, on Islay, **21.** 372

George II asks, to help restore unity in royal family with regard to Bute, **20.** 57on

—— commends, for showing Old Pretender's letters (to Argyll) to Sir Robert Walpole, **17.** 479

—— 'friend' of, **21.** 372

government places given to followers of, **9.** 55–6

(?) HW mentions, **17.** 124

ink made from privet discovered in household of, **35.** 204

London visited by, **19.** 102

Maule friend of, **19.** 107

Parliament act is excuse of, for not raising troops, **19.** 102n

plan by, for colonizing forfeited Scottish estates, **20.** 310

Pulteney attacked by, about Scottish taxes, **20.** 311

regent, **18.** 209n

Scottish bills softened in complaisance to, **19.** 389

Scottish elections managed by, for Sir Robert Walpole, **20.** 5n

Scottish patronage insisted on by, **20.** 5n

Stone's treatment of place-seekers praised by, **20.** 366

Stuart Mackenzie's affair with Barbarina checked by, **30.** 59n

——'s return to England requested by, **17.** 358n

suspected of temporizing in 1745 rebellion, **21.** 372n

toads, spiders, and projectors enthrall, **37.** 150

treachery of, **30.** 287

Turnpike Bill opposed by Scots peers led by, **20.** 124

Walpole, Sir Edward, to ask, about cobalt and zinc, **18.** 250

Walpole, Sir Robert, does not believe, to be treacherous, **17.** 347n

—— prevented by, from employing Hume Campbell and Marchmont, **20.** 5

——'s agent in Scotland, **15.** 152–3, **17.** 125n, **20.** 5n

white pines on estate of, **9.** 177

Whitton Place owned by, **17.** 441n, **41.** 437n

wife buried by, under stairs, **17.** 506

wife ill-treated by, **9.** 60

Campbell, Maj. Archibald (d. 1761):

death of, **9.** 379n

Campbell, Archibald (ca 1726–80), satirist:

*Lexiphanes* by, **28.** 152, 159, **29.** 290

*Sale of Authors, The*, by, satirizes Gray, **28.** 152

Campbell, Sir Archibald (1739–91), K.C.B., 1785; army officer:

death of, **11.** 247n

father-in-law dies on way to meet, **25.** 522–3

not yet beyond the Delaware valley, **39.** 321

returns from Jamaica, **25.** 522–3

Savannah captured by, **24.** 448n, **33.** 94n

Campbell, Mrs Archibald. *See* Ramsay, Amelia (d. 1813)

Campbell, Lady Augusta (1760–1831), m. (1788) Lt Henry Mordaunt Clavering:

Ailesbury, Cts of, entertains, at supper, **11.** 229

Argyll, D. and Ds of, accompanied by, to Italy, **11.** *48*

father of, **11.** 188n

Gunning match not suspected by, **11.** 229

in house attacked by mob, **23.** 7

marriage of, **34.** 17–18

mother of, **9.** 264

Campbell, Lady Caroline (1717–94), m. 1 (1742) Francis Scott, styled E. of Dalkeith; m. 2 (1755) Hon. Charles Townshend; cr. (1767) Bns Greenwich, s.j.:

acting of, at Queensberry House, **19.** 468n

(?) Anderson, Mrs, mimics, **11.** 237

(?) anecdote about, **11.** 303

assembly postponed by, **32.** 97

August and Sept. enlivened by, with speaking trumpet, **39.** 251

barony to be given to, **30.** 246

Blandford, Lady, entertains, **32.** 48n, 295n

——'s social relations with, **31.** 166, 181

'blatant beast' at Sudbrook, **11.** 63

Coke, Lady Mary, corresponds with, **23.** 560n, **31.** 144, 150

—— informed by, about Charles Townshend's death, **31.** 135

—— sends message to HW by, **31.** 178

—— smiles at, **38.** 567

death of, **34.** 197

Egremont affair explained by, **29.** 74

Euston, Lady, maligned by, **33.** 457–8, 485

father refuses to sign marriage articles of, **17.** 480n

finances of, **39.** 91

(?) Garrick, Mrs, entertains, at dinner, **11.** 310

'gazettes' from, unreliable, **32.** 295

George III excludes, from wife's Bedchamber, **38.** 142n

George IV's baptism attended by, **38.** 175

(?) Gloucester, D. and Ds of, disparaged by, **23.** 484n

HW calls: 'Green Which,' **33.** 144; (?) 'Lady Clack' or 'Lady Clackmannan,' **11.** 108, 237, 303, 310, 351; 'shrill *Morning Post*,' **39.** 197–8; 'Tisiphone,' **33.** 457–8

HW calls on, in Grosvenor Sq., **38.** 371

(?) HW entertains, at dinner, **11.** 351

HW jokes with, about Lady Mary Coke, **31.** 166

HW lives two miles from, but hears no news, **39.** 300

HW meets, little, after Lady Blandford's death, **33.** 171

HW mentions, **37.** 443

HW's ball attended by, in riding-dress, **28.** 447

HW's sympathy for, **31.** 135

HW thanks, for inquiries about his health, **31.** 148

Hobart, Mrs, entertains, **33.** 428n

house of, not safe from mobs, **33.** 93

husband's death blamed on, **39.** 90–1

[Campbell, Lady Caroline (1717–94), *continued*]
husband's death does not drive, to despair, 39. 94
husband's joking instructions to, 10. 33
husband's witticism to, at E. of Strafford's dinner, 37. 430
marriages of, 7. 360, 9. 171, 20. 138, 35. 236, 308n
news fully reported by, 31. 150
news-mongering of, at Twickenham, 30. 270
peerage of: given to gain husband's political support, 22. 549n; perhaps a bribe, 39. 94; perhaps premature, 39. 85
peevishness and political ignorance of, 39. 332, 333–4
physician stops, on way to husband's death-bed, 20. 137–8
pregnant, 20. 138
Queensberry, Ds of, omits, from ball, 38. 342
scandal-mongering of, 33. 171
Scott, Lady Jane, leaves miniature to, 33. 110n, 146n
—— nursed by, 33. 144–5
—— talked of, brutally, by, 33. 145
sister of, 11. 121n
sister rejoices that husband of, benefits politically, 38. 567
son of, baptized, 37. 550
Strafford, Cts of, gets news from, 35. 349
SH visited by, 31. 147, 297
Sudbrook residence of, 31. 147
—— still occupied by, 39. 90, 94
Suffolk, Cts of, visited by, 35. 321
theatre formed by, 19. 468–9
Tweeddale, Lady, talks with, about Saxons, 34. 17
'uglier than ever with rage,' 33. 93
verses may have been written by, 33. 299
Wedderburn entertained by, 10. 33
Wilkes blamed by, for lawlessness, 32. 213
Campbell, Caroline (1721–1803), m. 1 (1739) Charles Bruce, 3d E. of Ailesbury, 1741; m. 2 (1747) Hon. Henry Seymour Conway:
Albany, Cts of, given assembly by, 11. 280
—— great-niece of, 11. 258
Alexander, Mr, friend of, 38. 75
Amelia, Ps, discusses HW's *Historic Doubts* with, 31. 138
—— driven by, in small chaise, 31. 146
Arbuthnot says, is coming to Italy, 20. 285
army in Germany expects, 21. 485n
arrives in England, 22. 47
*Barbier de Seville* not heard by, 6. 162
Bath may be visited by, for health, 35. 408
Beauclerk Closet at SH not seen by, 39. 294
Berry, Mary, introduced to, 11. 5
—— visits, 12. 173
Berrys charm, 11. 79
Boufflers, Comtesse de, sends compliments to, 42. 33
brothers of, 7. 63, 9. 50, 10. 274n, 12. 273n, 21. 267, 450, 22. 549, 25. 263n, 33. 50–1, 37. 391, 527

Bruce praises, 20. 331
Bryant's *Observations* borrowed by, from HW, 33. 316
Calais visited by, 6. 159, 162
Campbell, Caroline, lives with, 25. 613
—— treated by, as her own daughter, 25. 618
Campbell, Lady William, writes to, 25. 208
carriage accident of, 39. 257
Chalfont visited by, 9. 284
characteristics of: coquette, loving crowds, 37. 407; cries several times during opera, 39. 218; good and happy, 38. 103; magnanimous, 38. 163; 'mean and mercenary,' 38. 124; not socially timid like HW, 39. 435; Spartan fortitude, 38. 163
Chatsworth and Worksop visited by, 37. 561, 564, 565
Chiswick to be visited by, before going to Southcote's, 37. 374
Choiseuls do not receive, 39. 236
Churchill, Lady Mary, cannot accompany, to Mt Edgcumbe, 39. 281
Cobhams visit, at Latimers, 37. 306
Coke, Lady Mary, corresponds with, 31. 200
—— invited to dine with, at SH, 31. 347
—— pities, on Jersey news, 33. 113n
Cole receives guinea eggs from, 2. 199, 202, 206, 216, 218
comedy attended by, in Paris, 6. 147
Compiègne visited by, 6. 156
concern of, for husband, 33. 24
contributions vainly solicited by, 38. 14
Conway and Lady Mary Coke accompany, to Germany, 38. 83n
Conway asks D. of Cumberland's leave to go through Flanders with, 37. 291
—— consoled by, for military inactivity, 35. 297
—— gives jerboa to, 9. 142
—— has not heard from, 37. 312
—— hears from, of Knyphausen and Lady Mary Coke, 38. 11
—— hurried by, 37. 389,
—— inspired to poetry by, 37. 260–1, 263
—— joined by, at Bevois Mount, 37. 516
—— joins, at Paris, 39. 539
—— lucky to have married, 37. 388
—— may be visited by: abroad, 37. 316; at camp at Bradford, 37. 490
—— may meet, at Combe Bank, 37. 345
—— mistakes screams for those of, 39. 497–8
——'s broken arm reported by, 33. 231
——'s correspondence with, 20. 299, 37. 316, 327, 392, 38. 3
——'s dismissal must afflict, 38. 382
——'s handwriting resembles that of, 20. 533
——'s promotion will cancel trip of, 20. 297
——'s safety relieves, 9. 50
——'s sow deemed pregnant by, 37. 349
——'s unsealed letter exposes, 37. 568–9
—— to be fetched by, from Paris, 35. 422

—— to be joined by: at Marseille, **20**. 285; at Turin, **20**. 293; in winter quarters at Osnabrück, **21**. 554

—— to be married by, before husband is buried, **22**. 132n

—— to be visited by, **35**. 283

—— to conduct, through Flanders to Dover, **37**. 291

—— to receive Bubb Dodington's *Diary* from, **39**. 411

—— to receive from, Guines's invitation to Metz, **39**. 178

—— to settle: at Rotterdam, **37**. 281; at Tunbridge to take waters, **37**. 345

—— will not prefer Florentine women to, **20**. 265

—— will regain weight when back with, **20**. 313

—— writes only to, **38**. 3

Craven, Lady, attended by, at Drury Lane, **29**. 43

cribbage played by, **12**. 58, 167, **39**. 540–1

Damer's death distresses, **6**. 351

Damer, Mrs, and Caroline Campbell send good accounts to, of Mann and nephew, **25**. 623

Damer, Mrs, daughter of, blooming but awkward, **22**. 155

Damer, Mrs, left with HW during absence of, in Ireland, **37**. 378n

—— less beautiful than, **9**. 237, **21**. 67

——'s bas-relief of, **12**. 271

——'s bust of, **12**. 272, 273, 274

——'s escape from storm makes, thankful, **39**. 481

——'s flight to France approved by, **24**. 234

——'s illness alarms, **38**. 334

——'s imprisonment alarms, **33**. 113

—— to live with, **39**. 282–3

—— urges, to read fairy tales, **37**. 435

—— will be consoled by, **6**. 351–2

daughters of, **25**. 576n

death of brother of, **9**. 50, **33**. 50–1

dog of, a barbette, **38**. 132

Dublin left by: for country, **37**. 455; for Sligo and Belturbet, **37**. 336

Du Deffand, Mme, asks HW what present would please, **6**. 329

—— asks if HW is to visit, **7**. 42

—— desires good opinion of, **6**. 135, 143, 156

—— given presents by, **6**. 133, 177, 181, 183, 328, 331, 339, **7**. 28, 29, 35, **39**. 269

—— hopes for news of, **6**. 215

—— inquires about summer plans of, **7**. 51

—— inquires after, **6**. 307, **7**. 8, 184

—— inquires from, about Stanhope-Stormont affair, **6**. 147

—— refers to, for confirmation, **6**. 103, 104

——'s correspondence with, **6**. 177

——'s efforts in behalf of, **6**. 138, 150

—— sends gifts to, **6**. 325

—— sends messages to, **6**. 158, 161, 164, 175,

177, 187, 201, 202, 223, 250, 263, 291, 339, 344, 352, 355, 358, 457, 484, **7**. 35, 70, 108

—— sent messages by, **6**. 452

——'s opinion of, **6**. 101, 104, 108, 126, 135, 142, 147, 156, 161, 187, 207, 344, 352, 358, **7**. 5, 111, **39**. 200–1

——'s relations with, **6**. 138, 141, 147, 156, 161, 165, 315–16, 457

—— suggests that HW might send package by, **6**. 85

—— wishes, would visit Paris, **6**. 250, 254, 282, 485–6, **7**. 108

—— wonders if incense-burner was sent by, **6**. 341

—— would like Choiseuls to know, **6**. 115, 118, 126, 133–4, 155, 156

Dutch greffiers and burgomasters frisk about with, **38**. 124

Ealing visited by, **11**. 48

Eccardt's painting of, **35**. 174

England to be revisited by, through Holland, when campaign in Germany re-opens, **38**. 154, 160

family of, **30**. 327n

father of: **36**. 81; a collector, **37**. 460; dies, **23**. 246

fire at house of, in Warwick St, **33**. 583–4

fire-screen worked by, for SH, **37**. 505

first husband's loss easily borne by, **22**. 132

Flanders visited by, **6**. 162

flitch of bacon appropriate for, **38**. 71

Fontainebleau visited by, **6**. 106, 112

Foote, Mrs, attends opera with, **22**. 304

Germany quitted by, **31**. 25

Gloucester, Ds of, resents alleged slight from, **36**. 80–1

goldfish observed by, **37**. 381

Goodwood might be visited by, **11**. 59, **39**. 332

Gower's witticism disliked by, **39**. 167

Gray described by, **9**. 286

—— visits in neighbourhood of, **9**. 285

HW accompanies, to theatre, **9**. 160

HW adapts parable of the sower to worstedwork of, **39**. 173

HW advises, not to visit Brunswick but to stay in Holland, **38**. 84–5

HW and, consider Conway only, **39**. 200

HW and E. of Orford thanked by, for (?) plovers' eggs, **37**. 484, 485, 489

HW and Mary Rich seen by, when falling off stile, **35**. 276

HW asked by: to get things at Pesters's sale, **37**. 465–6; to take daughter to SH, **37**. 330

HW assured by, of Conway's safety, **36**. 177

HW buys things for, **7**. 406, 409, 411, 413, **39**. 146, 151

HW calls: 'huckaback' from well-preserved beauty, **35**. 297n; 'mean and mercenary,' **38**. 124

HW calls to inquire about, **39**. 376

HW cannot call, a good soul, **37**. 431

HW cannot lure, to SH, **39**. 138

[Campbell, Caroline (1721–1803), *continued*]
HW does errands for, about muslins, china, and contraband goods, 38. 124
HW does not mention, 6. 111, 238, 250, 480, 7. 128, 130, 173
HW expects, at SH, 42. 111
HW gives commission of, to Ds of Richmond, 39. 36
HW gives small bull to, 38. 405
HW informed by: of Conway's illness, 33. 270; of visit of Guines family, 33. 402; that Mrs Damer abandons French trip, 30. 268
HW informs, about Conway, 37. 509, 510, 511
HW jokes with: about being rejected by her as daughter's suitor, 37. 333–4; about her Irish preoccupations, 37. 428–9
HW may have given treillage paper to, 35. 484
HW meets, in London, 33. 498, 37. 552
HW meets Foote family at concert given by, 22. 506
HW mentions, 4. 432, 5. 75, 37. 465, 490
HW might fetch, from Park Place, 31. 25
HW might meet Dutch people and Jews instead of Charles Townshend at house of, 38. 100
HW misses, 6. 132, 38. 128
HW mistakenly attributes knock to, 25. 343
HW not to accompany, to Paris, 32. 200
HW persuaded by, to go to Goodwood, 32. 375
HW prefers to write to, rather than to Conway, 37. 425
HW pities anxiety of, over husband's French expedition, 42. 104, 106
HW prompted by, to write to Conway, 38. 8
HW receives from: daughter's sketches, 38. 156; (?) German medal, 38. 154, 156; money, 7. 411; snuff, snuff-box, and bonbons, 38. 87
HW recommends tombs at Paris to, 39. 201
HW repeats Grenville's statement in presence of, 40. 331
HW reproaches, for failure to write, 38. 124
HW's *Beauties* compares, to Neptune's queen, 30. 327
HW's books to be procured through, from Paris, 39. 198
HW's commission to buy drawings executed by, in Amsterdam, 38. 129, 130, 142
HW's concern for Conway only surpassed by that of, 37. 513, 38. 94, 95
HW's correspondence with: 6. 105, 115, 116, 126, 127, 131, 133, 137, 7. 376–9, 381, 385, 389, 395, 396, 30. 160, 35. 310, 37.–39. *passim*; MSS of, 36. 313, 314, 315
HW sees, in husband's absence, 21. 155
HW sends letters through, 6. 100, 39. 188, 194, 195
HW sends things to, 6. 100, 116, 7. 377, 378, 39. 32, 35, 208, 219

HW's friendship with, 4. 332, 6. 125, 155, 158, 163, 187, 207, 316
HW shares opera box with, 31. 14n, 35. 350n
HW's legacy to, 15. 336, 30. 374
HW's letter read to, 6. 101
HW's *Royal and Noble Authors* read by, 37. 524
HW's 'two countesses' include, 12. 120
HW sympathizes with, on Conway's absence, 37. 498, 500
HW talks of Mme du Deffand with, 6. 163
HW thanked by, for aid to brother, 37. 401
HW thanks, for china, 38. 99–100
HW to accompany, to Wentworth Castle, 35. 333
HW to be thanked by, for goldfish, 37. 370, 371
HW to forward Weymouth's letter about Channel Islands to, 39. 319
HW to leave flower picture for, 37. 475
HW to welcome, on return from Sligo, 37. 364
HW urged by: to come to Paris, 6. 164, 215; to visit Mme du Deffand, 39. 255
HW will accept letter from, in lieu of husband's, 39. 11
HW writes regularly to, 38. 94
HW writes sheer politics to, 37. 433
Hague, The, visited by, 38. 128–9
Hamilton sends regards to, 35. 410
Hamilton, Mrs (Lady), corresponds with, 40. 383
——, told by, of HW's visit to France, 22. 354n
'handsomer than fame,' 38. 179
Harcourt to reconcile, with (?) D. of Gloucester, 35. 510
Hardinge, Mrs, emulates, 35. 627
Harrogate to be visited by, 37. 553
Haymarket Theatre attended by, 33. 189
health of: 6. 255; alum might improve, 39. 106; arm still swollen, 39. 262; Bath waters improve, 37. 360; better, 37. 350; disorder overcome, 39. 505; Duncan consulted about, 39. 106n; favourable news of, 37. 366; Hertford anxious about, 39. 422; illness, 21. 168; not quite well, 35. 408; physicians not needed for, 39. 423; recovered, 31. 144, 35. 333, 37. 348, 39. 413–14; seasickness, 37. 405; (?) stomach complaint, 39. 449; weak but recovering, 37. 520; wrist broken, 39. 257
Hertford, Cts of, plays cribbage with, 39. 540–1
—— visited by, in last illness, 33. 370–1
Hertfords to play loo with, 39. 274
Hervey's abuse of cousin reported to, 34. 86
Hillsborough urges, to have Mann made K.B., 22. 495, 502
Holland toured by, with Conway, 37. 286–7
Holles's *Memorials* enjoyed by, 37. 477
Houghton to be seen by, 32. 313

Hunloke plays commerce with, at Worksop, **37**. 565, 568
in mourning for Conway, **15**. 269
Ireland suits better than expected, **37**. 413
—— visited by, **20**. 316–17, **37**. 342–3, 403
Italian tour not to be made by, to Mann's regret, **20**. 304
Jerningham's correspondence with, **11**. 8n
Johnston, Lady Cecilia, asked by, to procure HW's writings, **38**. 142
—— leaves packages for, **39**. 24
Kildare, Cts of, admired by, **37**. 435
—— lends books to, **37**. 435
—— praises, **37**. 430
landscape in worsted-work by, for HW, **38**. 438
La Vallière, Mme de, does not meet, **6**. 155
Little Strawberry Hill visited by, in rain, **12**. 49
leaves Paris, **6**. 156
Legge wants to say more to, **38**. 382
London to be visited by, to hear Manzuoli and see Mrs Cornwallis, **38**. 470
—— visited by, **11**. 187, 244, **12**. 88
Lorn notifies, of Ds of Argyll's death, **39**. 480
Luxembourg, Mme de, likes, **6**. 101, 104, 115, 117
Lyttelton sympathizes with, **40**. 106
Lyttelton's verses on marriage of, **39**. 523–4
Lyttelton, Bns, friend of, and resembled her, **30**. 327n
—— intimate with, **38**. 14n
—— taken by, to feed pheasants, **39**. 158
magic lantern seen by, in London, **39**. 266
Malmesbury buys Park Place from, **15**. 334
Mann extols, for refusing to suspect her servants, **23**. 9
—— hopes that Conway will meet, in Florence, **20**. 296
——'s attentions to Lady William Campbell appreciated by, **25**. 286
Manzuoli to be heard by, **38**. 470
Marie-Antoinette favours, **6**. 127
marital felicity of, **6**. 108, **38**. 71
medallions suggested to HW by, as gifts for Mme du Deffand, **39**. 254
Mingotti gets letter by, in Italian, seeking opera box, **37**. 476
Mirepoix, Mme de, likes, **6**. 101, 104, 115, 117
mistakes pedestrians for mob, **11**. 249
Montmorency visited by, **6**. 116–19
Müntz's drawing of HW wanted by, for dressing-room at Park Place, **37**. 475
*Mysterious Mother* reading to be heard by, **10**. 260
Naples not to be visited by, **39**. 239
needlework pictures of: **35**. 395 (*see also* Worsted-work); suffers from her broken wrist, **39**. 257
niece of, to marry, **6**. 132
niece's death afflicts, **34**. 34

Norfolk trip given up by, **39**. 282
Nuneham visited by, **12**. 38
occupations of, at Park Place, **37**. 548
O'Hara notices changes in, **12**. 158
—— visits, **12**. 158n
opera box of Lady Mary Churchill coveted by, **37**. 480
Oxford and Elgin, Cts of, ancestress of, **39**. 139
Paris pleases, **6**. 129, 170, **35**. 351
—— visited by, **6**. 99, 115, **39**. 200–5, 206–9, 216–19, 229, 234, 237
Park Place occupied by, **11**. 145, **12**. 58
—— occupied by, in husband's absence, **38**. 33
—— purchased by, **20**. 316
party of, put off for Mingotti's benefit, **38**. 12
pheasantry of, **39**. 138
plans to return to Paris, **6**. 135, 177
pregnancy of, makes Conway anxious to return her to England, **37**. 290–1
protégé of, pardoned, **38**. 15
relatives of, may have influence with Stuart Mackenzie, **21**. 452n
return of, to England, **37**. 461
Richmond, Ds of, asked by, about Ds of Leinster, **32**. 204
Richmond, D. of, corresponds with, **6**. 452, 457
Rotterdam visited by, **37**. 283
St-Cyr visited by, **6**. 133, 144
St-Quentin visited by, **6**. 156, 159
Sally, Mrs, woman of, **38**. 129
servant of, **14**. 184n
servant sent by, to tell HW of Conway's arrival, **10**. 55
Sèvres porcelains bought by, **6**. 125
Seymour-Conway, Hon. Henry, to tell, of son-in-law's suicide, **39**. 281
shell bench at SH occupied by, **9**. 237
*Siege of Berwick* attended by, **12**. 88
social relations of, at Paris, *see index entries ante* 8. 276
social relations of, in England and Paris with: Albany, Cts of, **11**. 280, **42**. 326n; Albemarle, Cts of, **33**. 387; Amelia, Ps, **31**. 138, 146, **33**. 104, 463; Ansbach, Margrave and Margravine of, **39**. 500; Beauvau, Prince de, **6**. 118; Beauvau, Princesse de, **6**. 118, **39**. 218; Bedford, Ds of, **38**. 12; Bessborough, Cts of, **38**. 12; Boufflers, Chevalier de, **39**. 208, 218–19; Buller, Mrs, **11**. 229; Cambis, Mme de, **39**. 218; Campbell, Lady Frederick, **11**. 265, **39**. 419n; Campbell, Lord Frederick, **39**. 368, 419n; Choiseul, Duchesse de, **6**. 127, 155; Churchill, Charles and Lady Mary, **37**. 532–3, 537, 538, **38**. 165, **39**. 419n; Clive, Mrs, **35**. 275; Coke, Lady Mary, **31**. 133, 146, 156, 297; Cornwallis, Mrs Edward, **38**. 470; Damer, Mrs, **11**. 372, **12**. 96; Devonshire, D. of, **37**. 483, 486; Du Deffand, Mme, **6**. 100, 101, 106, 110, 134, 147, 152,

[Campbell, Caroline (1721–1803), *continued*]
152–3, **39.** 200, 203, 216, 218, 219; Footes,
**22.** 506; Fox, Henry and Lady Caroline,
**37.** 483, 486; George IV, **31.** 298; HW, **1.**
341n, **6.** 154, 158, 159, 207, 213, 353, **9.** 237,
**10.** 99, 100, 133, 260, **11.** 5, 48, 59, 126, 229,
244–5, 280, 339, **12.** 120, 167, **22.** 506, **29.**
242, **30.** 260n, **31.** 133, 146, 154, 156, **32.**
10–11, 124, 345, **33.** 104, 142, 281, **34.** 57,
107, 222, **35.** 98, 217, 275–6, 283, 489, **36.**
243, **37.** 346, 351, 366, 374, 395–6, 466, 468,
470, 483, 484–5, 487, 489, 491–2, 504–5, 525,
**38.** 34, 37, 39, 165, 179, 207, **39.** 119, 128,
295, 328, 368, 391–2, 419n, **42.** 111; Hamiltons, **37.** 527; Harrowbys, **39.** 419n; Hertford, Cts of, **32.** 375n; Hertford, E. and
Cts of, **37.** 538, **38.** 67, 70, **39.** 274; Hervey,
Miss, **39.** 419n; Hervey, Mrs William
Thomas, **39.** 500; Hobart, Mrs, **33.** 368;
Johnston, Lady Cecilia, **11.** 42, **12.** 169, **38.**
165, 180; Johnstons, **11.** 278–9; Ker, Lady
Louisa, **37.** 543n, 548; Kildare, **37.** 456;
Kildare, Cts of, **37.** 483, 486; Lennox,
Ladies Louisa and Sarah, **37.** 486; Luxembourg, Mme de, **6.** 129, 147, **39.** 218; Lyttelton, Bns, **37.** 396, **38.** 35, 165, **39.** 300;
Lytteltons, **37.** 349; Mirepoix, Mme de, **6.**
106, 152–3, **39.** 218; Ricciarelli, **37.** 396;
Rich, Mary, **37.** 351, 396; Richmond, Ds of,
**37.** 483, 528, 534, 537n, **39.** 283, 526; Richmond, D. and Ds of, **12.** 135, **37.** 483–4, **38.**
180, **39.** 419n, 469, 470; Stormont, **6.** 147,
156, **37.** 395; Strafford, E. and Cts. of, **37.**
472n, 483; Townshend, Hon. Mary, **37.** 317,
350; Viry, Contessa di, **6.** 106, 152–3; West
family, **37.** 396; Westmorland, **37.** 346
soldier's wife the only attendant of, **37.** 295
Stanhope, Lady Harriet, with, **39.** 219
Stormont talks with, of Mme du Deffand, **6.**
250
—— tells, of Conway's summons to Jersey,
**39.** 359
—— to offer lodging to, **6.** 291
story by, of old man who hatched chickens,
**22.** 586n
Stowe to be visited by, **9.** 152, **37.** 369
SH not visited by, **39.** 159
SH visits of, *see* SH: visitors to
success of, in Paris, **6.** 112, 115, 118, 119, 126,
132, 143
Surrey and Hampshire visited by, **37.** 304–5
syringa of, to be vaunted to HW, **37.** 527
'taken up', supposedly, with turnpike bills,
Popish recusants and Irish politics, **37.** 428
Taplow visited by, **37.** 538
to leave Paris, **6.** 143, 144, 151–5
'Tonton' spoken of to HW by, **6.** 174
Townshend, Hon. Mary, to get letter from,
asking her to see Eversley, **37.** 305
travels of, **6.** 64, 70, 98
triplets not suitable for, **37.** 294
tubs for, ordered from Hammersmith, **38.** 198

uncle of, dies, **38.** 84
Vauxhall and Court parties to be attended
by, **37.** 489
Versailles to be visited by, **6.** 148
—— visited by, **6.** 127
Viry, Contessa di, likes, **6.** 106
Waldegrave, Cts, should follow example of,
**22.** 132
wax figure addressed by, **32.** 98
weeps during Farmain de Rozoi's *Henri IV*,
**39.** 218
Welbeck Abbey visited by, **37.** 477
Welderen, Mme, will call, wicked, **38.** 99–100
well-received at Court, **38.** 236
winter quarters at Osnabrück occupied by,
**38.** 155n
witticism by, on Henrietta West's praise of
Col. Johnston, **35.** 305
*World* recognized by, as HW's, **37.** 440
worsted-work pictures of, **34.** 15, **38.** 438, **39.**
550 (*see also* Needlework)
Yorkshire visit may be made by, **37.** 547, 551
*See also* Park Place
Campbell, Caroline (1764–89):
Ailesbury, Cts of, gets good account from,
of Mann and nephew, **25.** 623
—— lives with, **25.** 613
'beggared orphan,' **33.** 50
Conway and Cts of Ailesbury treat, as their
own daughter, **25.** 618
Conway's elegy on death of, **39.** 553–4
Damer, Mrs, does bas-relief of, **12.** 271
—— does bust of, **12.** 272
—— takes, to continent, **25.** 613
death of, **11.** 3n, **34.** 34, **39.** 553–4
Du Deffand, Mme, sends messages to, **6.** 158
HW and Lady Mary Coke think, spoiled and
disagreeable, **31.** 156
HW's *Dice Box* written for, **31.** 156
HW to be visited by, at SH, **39.** 295
HW writes to Mme du Deffand about, **7.** 199
harp played by, at Richmond House, **34.** 34n
Mann will welcome, at Florence, **25.** 618
marriage of, rumoured, **33.** 580
Murphy's *Way to Keep Him* acted by, at
Richmond House, **33.** 563n, 580, **39.** 448n,
**43.** 388
play planned by, for Richmond House, **33.**
580n
(?) SH visited by, **12.** 232
Campbell, Lady Charlotte Susan Maria (1775–
1861), m. 1 (1796) Col. John Campbell; m.
2 (1818) Rev. Edward John Bury:
beauty and understanding of, **11.** *188*
Berry, Agnes, hears news of Brighton from,
**12.** 198
Gunning, Miss, scorned by, **11.** 199
Inverary visited by, **11.** 309
lack of discipline of, **11.** 188
Campbell, Colin (d. 1493), 1st E. of Argyll:
Jamesone's portrait of, **40.** 265

Campbell, Sir Colin (ca 1577–1640), of Glenorchy, 2d Bt, 1631; 8th Laird:
Jamesone's patron, **40**. 264–5
——'s portrait of, **40**. 265
Campbell, Colin (d. 1729), architect:
Mereworth by, **35**. 143
Wanstead designed by, **35**. 238n
Campbell, Coline (d. ca 1475), of Glenurchy, 1st Laird of Glenurchy, 1432:
Jamesone's portrait of, **40**. 265
Campbell, Sir Duncan (d. 1453), of Lochow, 1st Lord Campbell, 1445; Kt, 1448:
Jamesone's portrait of, **40**. 265
Campbell, Lady Elizabeth (ca 1722–99), m. (1749) Hon. James Stuart Mackenzie; 'Lady Betty Mackenzie':
acts in Queensberry House theatricals, **19**. 468n
Berry, Mary, identifies, **11**. 35n
Brighton visited by, **12**. 203
Coke, Lady Mary, compared in beauty to, **9**. 37
—— mourns for position lost by husband of, **38**. 567
——'s social relations with, **31**. 186
—— very different from, **24**. 381
—— writes to, **23**. 560n
Damer, Mrs, visits, **12**. 49
Douglas, Lady, visited by, **12**. 117
England reached by, **24**. 401
(?) Euston, Lady, maligned by, **33**. 457–8
Florence to be visited by, on way to Naples, **24**. 337
foreign travels of, **35**. 313
(?) Gloucester, D. and Ds of, disparaged by, **23**. 484n
HW called on by, at SH, **39**. 467
HW entertains, at dinner, **12**. 5
HW kept from, by gout, **12**. 174
HW mentions, **37**. 425
HW receives message from Lady Mary Coke through, **31**. 142
HW talks with, about Mann, **24**. 412
HW visited by, **11**. 35, **12**. 177
HW visits, **11**. 124, **12**. 12, 28, 37, 49, 138, 169
health of, perfect, **31**. 27
Mann to be visited by, at Florence on way to Venice, **24**. 381
marriage of, **28**. 164n
Merlin's easy chairs recommended by, to Mann, **24**. 346
Northumberland House dinner attended by, **38**. 529–30
only child of, dies, **38**. 24
Petersham residence of, **31**. 287–8
Queensberry, Ds of, omits, from ball, **38**. 342
Richmond stay of, **11**. 148
Richmond theatre attended by, **9**. 74
Strafford, Cts of, sister of, **21**. 452n
SH visited by, **31**. 127, 129, **39**. 467
Campbell, Lady Frederick. See Meredith, Mary

Campbell, Lord Frederick (1729–1816), lord register for Scotland; M.P.:
Batt to visit, **11**. 322
Bellenden's villa left to, **9**. 359n, **43**. 347
birth date of, corrected, **43**. 281
Bute made enemies by giving place to, **30**. 184
change planned for, **38**. 370
Combe Bank home of, **32**. 11n, **34**. 64n
Conway favours, ahead of HW, **39**. 531
Conways may be visited by, at Park Place, **37**. 350, 527
(?) Conways visited by, at Park Place, **39**. 419n
Damer, Mrs, entertains, at supper, **11**. 369
—— makes statue of George III at request of, **12**. 273
daughter (illegitimate) of, **12**. 64n
Dee's black stone given to HW by, **23**. 286–7, **33**. 324, **43**. 389
Fitzroy, Lady Caroline, selects, as 'confidente,' **30**. 87
Gunning affair interests, **11**. 229
HW and Cts of Ailesbury sup with, **39**. 368
HW asked by, to examine father's collection, **23**. 286
HW entertains, at breakfast, **11**. 280
HW jokes about Lady Townshend's 'training' of, **30**. *84*
HW's bequest to, **30**. 375
HW's executor and trustee, **15**. 336, **30**. 349, 374, 376, 377
HW's former house in Arlington St fitted up by, **34**. 46n
HW's petition to Pitt might be given legal terms by, **38**. 41
HW to dine at house of, **32**. *11*
health of, fevers, **37**. 391
House of Lords ejects, **23**. 256n
interestedness of, **32**. 11n
Irish may not enjoy, as a Scot, **22**. 549
'junto' includes, **11**. 197n
lord privy seal for Scotland, **38**. 568
marriage of, **10**. 274, **21**. 396n
Nivernais's *Jardins modernes* given to, **12**. 259
Park Place visited by, **35**. 386
Parliamentary speech by, **38**. 319
Porteus, Bp, entertains, at Fulham, **39**. 497
Queensberry House theatricals include, **19**. 468n
Ranelagh visited by, **30**. 87
sister visits, **34**. 46
SH to be visited by, **35**. 283
SH visited by, **12**. 238, **31**. 142
Stuart Mackenzie succeeded by, as lord privy seal of Scotland, **22**. 302n, **30**. 184
Townshend gives Irish post to, to make room for E. of March, **22**. 549n
—— takes, to Ireland as secretary, **22**. 549
Townshend, Vcts, pursues, **37**. 334
—— waited on by, **30**. 84
wife of, **9**. 283n, **11**. 265n

Campbell, George John (1763–4), styled E. of Campbell:
birth of, **22.** 121
Campbell, George William (1768–1839), styled M. of Lorn; 6th D. of Argyll, 1806:
ball for George IV not attended by, **11.** 329
Conway hears from, of mother's death, **39.** 480
father of, **11.** 188n
Gunning affair involves, **11.** 108, 197, 218, 252, 279, 331
Campbell, Lady Henrietta ('Harriot') (d. 1766):
death of, **7.** 397
Campbell, Capt. Henry (d. 1747):
killed at Laeffeld battle, **9.** 50, **37.** 275
Campbell, Hume. *See* Hume Campbell
Campbell, Lady Isabella Caroline. *See* Howard, Lady Isabella Caroline
Campbell, Hon. Sir James (ca 1667–1745), K.B., Lt-Gen.:
killed at Fontenoy, **19.** 42, **36.** 11, **37.** 192
knighted after Dettingen, **37.** 144
Campbell, (?) James (d. 1784), King's bookbinder, in Strand:
Mann, Horace II, tells, to bind Galluzzi's history for George III and HW, **25.** 192, 197, 205
Campbell (formerly Livingstone), James (?1719–88) of Ardkinglass; 3d Bt, 1771; M.P.:
Barré succeeded by, as governor of Stirling Castle, **38.** 255
Bute's friend, **21.** 465n
Campbell, Jane, m. (1788) Henry George Johnston:
HW invites, to meet Lady Guilford and family, **12.** 164
HW visited by, at SH, **12.** 51, 196
son of, **12.** 64n
Campbell, Lady Jemima (1722–97), Marchioness Grey, s.j., 1740; m. (1740) Philip Yorke, styled Vct Royston, 2d E. of Hardwicke, 1764:
ancestry of, **33.** 472
father of, **18.** 487
HW refuses SH ticket to, **33.** 502
heiress of D. of Kent, **30.** 304n
marriage of: **9.** 230, **37.** 70n; arranged by Secker, **30.** 304n
SH visited by, **12.** 226
succeeds, as Marchioness Grey, **9.** 5n
Wrest dining-room made by, **39.** 139n
Campbell, Sir John (1598–1662), cr. (1633) E. of Loudoun, chancellor of St Andrews:
HW's portrait of, **15.** 192
Campbell, John (1680–1743), 2d D. of Argyll, 1703; field marshal:
Admiralty board named by, **17.** 355–56, 363
army command of, would encourage Old Pretender, **17.** 388
Balmerinoch's loyalty affirmed by, **19.** 296
Barrymore delivers Old Pretender's letters to, **17.** 479

Blandford, Lady, entertains, **37.** 51
'Broad Bottom' ministry achieved by, **17.** 355
brother receives papers supposedly sent to, by Pretender, **17.** 478–9
brother's relations with, **15.** 153
brother's retort to, about will, **26.** 11
brother succeeds, in dukedom, **37.** 150
Bubb Dodington connected with, **30.** 292n
Carteret hates, **37.** 92
Chute speculates about resignations by, **35.** 26
Cockburn secretary to, **17.** 355n
Conway might get commission under, **37.** 24, 31
—— would be resented if forced into regiment of, **37.** 31
*Country Girl, The,* mentions, **18.** 24
daughters of, **11.** 35n, 121n, **12.** 11n, **19.** 295, 456n, 468n, **22.** 149n, **23.** 530n, **24.** 401n, 412n, **28.** 164n, **30.** 327n, **31.** 25, 155, 166, **35.** 277n, 282n
daughter's marriage articles delayed by reluctance of, to sign his name, **17.** 480n
death of, **17.** 164n, **18.** 321
disciplinarian, **37.** 31
Earle a protégé of, **17.** 243
—— deserts, **17.** 220n
English troops in Flanders to be commanded by, **17.** 353, 356, 370
Erskine brought into Parliament by, **20.** 229n
Flemish post declined by, **17.** 373
Frederick, P. of Wales, impelled by, against Sir Robert Walpole, **17.** 329
Garrick preferred by, to Betterton, **17.** 435
George II quarrels with, dismissing him, **37.** 61, 69
HW mentions plot revealed by, **17.** 475
Holland not to be visited by, **17.** 345
importance of, gone, **18.** 321
insists upon general command, but offered one camp instead, **37.** 61
letter to, HW comments on, **31.** 17–18
Lyttelton's *Dialogues of the Dead* mentions, **21.** 408
Mann thinks, to be advertising his conversion from Jacobitism, **17.** 498
Marlborough's quarrel with, over rank, **18.** 566
medal of, **17.** 229n, **21.** 202, 233
melancholy and eccentric after correspondence with Old Pretender, **17.** 480n
'Motion, The,' depicts, **18.** 21n
*New Ode, A,* mentions, **18.** 52
*Old Coachman, The,* mentions, **18.** 21
Old Pretender's correspondence with, **7.** 359, **17.** 479, 480n
ordnance command restored to, **17.** 345
Oxford's administration pays, but is deserted by him, **26.** 10–11
Parliament not attended by, **17.** 338, **18.** 159
Port Mahon officers' list discussed by, in House of Lords, **17.** 300

Pulteney and Sandys scolded by, **17**. 335
regiment of, **17**. 345, **19**. 283, **37**. 31
reputation of, established, **31**. 18
resignation of, **17**. 365, 388
Richelieu, Duc de, reminiscent of age of, **35**. 114
Smith, Adam, describes last years of, **7**. 360
son-in-law attacks memory of, **37**. 333
—— of, **17**. 320
Sudbrook built by, **35**. 282n
Tower of London dreaded by, **7**. 360
treachery of, **30**. 287
Walpole, Sir Robert, disliked by, **37**. 31
—— expects rudeness from, in House of Lords, **17**. 338
wife of, **9**. 37n, **35**. 297n
William III promotes, **26**. 14
wit of, **31**. 17
Campbell, John (ca 1693–1770), 4th D. of Argyll, 1761:
Bellenden, Mary, wife of, **31**. 419n
Conway favours, ahead of HW, **39**. 531
—— to be visited by, at Latimers, **37**. 302
—— told by, of invitation to HW, **37**. 346–7
cousin succeeded by, **23**. 246n, **37**. 150
daughter of, **2**. 199n, **11**. 59n, **21**. 67n, **23**. 246, **30**. 327n, **36**. 81
death of, **23**. 246
Dee's black stone given to, by Lady Betty Germain, **23**. 286, **33**. 324, **43**. 389
Fontenoy battle missed by, **36**. 12
George III omits, from Bedchamber, **21**. 460
(?) HW aids, in becoming aide-de-camp to George II, **37**. 401
HW at son's wish examines collection of, **23**. 286
HW bids against, for old tombstones, **37**. 460
HW informed by, about Conway's itinerary, **37**. 346
HW mentions, **37**. 425
interestedness of, **32**. 11n
old-fashioned politeness of, **30**. 45
Parliamentary membership of, corrected, **43**. 313
Selwyn's question to, about expedition, **37**. 531
son of, **9**. 50n, **11**. 229n, **23**. 7n
son's promotion may make, a 'dowager,' **35**. 295
Townshend, Vcts, admired by, **30**. 45, **38**. 346
Villiers, Mrs, may be abandoned by, **38**. 346
Young Pretender about to surrender to, **37**. 251
Campbell, John (1695–1777), M.P.; of Calder:
birth date of, corrected, **43**. 112
Treasury post given to, **9**. 33, **19**. 256
Walpole, Sir Robert, appoints, to Admiralty, **19**. 256
Campbell, John (1696–1782), styled Lord Glenorchy 1717–52; 3d E. of Breadalbane, 1752; M.P.:
ancestor of, **40**. 264

death of, rumoured, **39**. 220
George III orders Conway to send dismissal to, **22**. 439n
Lyttelton succeeds, as master of the Jewel Office, **21**. 25
Parliamentary membership of, corrected, **43**. 246
Sandys succeeded by, as justice in eyre, **21**. 25
son-in-law's father demands place for, in lieu of Admiralty post, **17**. 487
wife of, **9**. 5n
Campbell, John (1705–82), 4th E. of Loudoun; army officer:
commander-in-chief of forces in America, **19**. 102n
detachment from, captures *Hazard*'s passengers, **37**. 236
governor-general of Virginia, **19**. 102n
Halifax left by, for New York, **21**. 130n
Hay, Lord Charles, arrested for criticizing, in Nova Scotia, **21**. 367n
Inverness abandoned by, **19**. 221
Louisbourg expedition of, **21**. 130, **37**. 502
Mackenzie's men try to join, **37**. 236–7
Newcastle, D. of, informed by, of departure of House of Commons members from Ghent, **18**. 97n
Perth said to have defeated, **19**. 259
rebels beaten by, in north of Scotland, **19**. 153
rebels disperse troops of, **37**. 232–3
rebels may march after, **37**. 224
rebels to attack, at Inverness, **37**. 216
regiment of: arrives at Gibraltar with Brodrick's squadron, **20**. 576n; Mackintosh in, **37**. 244; to be augmented, coming from Ireland, **24**. 474n
Shirley, Gov. William, replaced by, in American command, **21**. 13n
Skye the objective of, **37**. 237
troops raised by, to oppose Young Pretender, **19**. 102–3
Walker, Kitty, mistress of, **30**. 316
Walpole, Sir Robert, writes to, **36**. 7
Campbell, John (1708–75), LL.D.; miscellaneous writer:
Bentley genealogy to be corrected by, in *Biographia Britannica*, **35**. 204
HW promised ink recipe by, **35**. 204
(?) HW's pamphlet answered by, **13**. 21
*Lives of the Admirals* by, **14**. 62n, **35**. 610
*Memoir of the Revolution in Bengal* by, **22**. (?) 36, (?) 49
*Political Survey of Britain* by, **28**. *140*, 144
Campbell, John (1723–1806), styled M. of Lorn 1761–70; 5th D. of Argyll, 1770; army officer; M.P.:
Ailesbury, Cts of, to take leave of, **39**. 469n
appearance of, **21**. 267
(?) Argyllshire militia commanded by, **37**. 229n
arrives in England, **11**. 107
Bellenden may leave villa to, **9**. 360

[Campbell, John (1723–1806), *continued*]
 Berrys to visit, **11.** 8
 brother-in-law would not please, **21.** 466
 brother of, **11.** 229n, **21.** 396n, **25.** 263n
 Cathcart friend of, **37.** 401
 Conway and wife may be visited by at Park Place, **37.** 350, 527
 Conway favours, ahead of HW, **39.** 531
 ——'s correspondence with, **37.** 473
 Ealing Grove bought by, **31.** 239
 family of, **11.** 188
 French revolutionists pelt chaise of, **11.** 107
 George III does not include, in Bedchamber, **9.** 324
 Gunning affair involves, **11.** 108, 197, 201, 204, 205–6, 217, 218, 225, 279
 (?) HW has print of, **10.** 7
 habits of, **11.** 187–8
 health of, bad, **11.** 309
 Hamilton, Ds of, weds, **15.** 48, **21.** 267, 278, **35.** 105, **38.** 7
 Highland regiment loses, as Lt-Col., **37.** 434
 interestedness of, **32.** 11n
 Inverary visited by, **11.** 48, 309
 Italian tour of, **11.** 48, 104
 'junto' includes, **11.** 197n
 later D. of Argyll, **21.** 267n, 458
 lord privy seal for Scotland declined by, **38.** 568
 made general, **35.** 295
 Parliamentary debates by: on privately-raised regiments, **26.** 18; on Scotch bill, **26.** 31
 Prado's grapes seen by, **32.** 208
 Queensberry, Ds of, routs, from warm room at her ball, **38.** 343
 Scotland visited by, **23.** 7
 Stuart Mackenzie to be succeeded by, as lord privy seal for Scotland, **38.** 565
 unmarried, **10.** 29
 wife of: **9.** 129n, **11.** 48n, 218n, **15.** 48n, **28.** 286n; death of, **39.** 480–1; quarrel of, with Queęn, moderated by him, **33.** 66; to accompany him to continent, **21.** 450–1, 466
Campbell, John (d. 1794), lt-col.:
 killed in action, **12.** 92n
Campbell, Col. John (d. 1809):
 wife of, **11.** 188n
Campbell, Mrs John. *See* Bellenden, Hon. Mary
Campbell, Lord John Douglas Edward Henry (1777–1847), 7th D. of Argyll, 1839:
 father of, **11.** 188n
Campbell, John Neil, of Milton Ernest:
 wife of, **1.** 367n **6.** 117n
Campbell, Mrs John Neil. *See* Mendez, Jael
Campbell, Louisa (1766–1852), m. (1799) Alexander Johnston, Kt, 1809:
 'beggared orphan,' **33.** 50
Campbell, Lt Malcolm:
 Thurot's plundering described in deposition by, **21.** 372n
Campbell, Lady Mary (1727–1811), m. (1747) Edward Coke, styled Vct Coke:

absent from Notting Hill, **33.** 185
age of, **10.** 315
Ailesbury, Cts of, should not imitate, **37.** 289
Albemarle, Cts of, criticized by, **31.** 172
Amelia Ps, chronicled by, **9.** 57n
American news brought by, **7.** 346
American news read by, **33.** 4
appearance of, **31.** 23, 162, **39.** 7–8
army in Germany expects, **21.** 485n
arrives: having missed Karl Wilhelm Ferdinand, **38.** 215; in England, **24.** 14, **32.** 196
Auteuil visited by, **7.** 347
Barrymore, Cts of, discusses servant's health with, **7.** 350
Bedford, Ds of, accuses, of inventing Gunning match, **11.** 121
Berry, Mary, identifies, **12.** 11n
Botta feared by, at Lerici, because she had seen him in Florentine theatre, **23.** 552
Boufflers, Comtesse de, displeases, **6.** 56
brother-in-law's death reported to, by HW, **7.** 319
brother-in-law's death returns, to England, **39.** 89, 94
brother-in-law's political prospects change, **38.** 567
Browne, Lady 'ordered' by, to send HW to England, **31.** 93
Brunswick, Ps of, to be seen by, **39.** 8
Brussels visit of, to see Archduchess, **33.** 292–3
Burke's comment on quarrel of, with Miss Pelham, **28.** 402–3
Cambis, Mme de, relations of, with, **6.** 56
Canadian news discussed by, at Ps Amelia's, **32.** 284–5
Caracciolo to bring gown to, from Paris, **38.** 252, 261
Carmarthen's engagement angers, **31.** 288
Catherine II's dethronement of husband may win sympathy of, **35.** 314
characteristics of: 'absolutely English,' **38.** 173; cosmetics not used, **31.** 23; debtors to, never reminded by her, **31.** 169; delusions, **31.** 175–8, 185; grief enjoyed, **39.** 94; kindness, **31.** 148; love of attention, **31.** 175; passion for royalty, **10.** 313, **25.** 647, **28.** 402–3, **31.** 149, 150, 153, 154, 155–6, 157, 160–3, 175, 177, **32.** 196, **33.** 439, 528; preference given to newest friend, **37.** 561; quarrelsomeness, **31.** 177; silent about own virtues, **31.** 18; sincerity, **31.** 70, 108, 175, 179
Chatsworth not visited by, from jealousy of Ds of Grafton, **37.** 561
clans would be led by, against French, **38.** 17
Cock Lane séance attended by, **10.** 6
comment by, on Lord Spencer Hamilton's match, **9.** 377n
Conway and wife accompanied by, to Germany, **38.** 83
Conway's unsealed letter exposes, **37.** 568
correspondence of, with: Ailesbury, Cts of, **31.** 200; Amelia, Ps, **23.** 534n, 553, 556; Greenwich, Bns, **31.** 144, 150; HW, *see*

*below under* HW's correspondence with; Rochford, Cts of, **31.** 134; Strafford, Cts of, **31.** 63, 150, 167
costume of, **39.** 7
Court attended by, **31.** 140, 171
courtly ceremony liked by, **12.** 11
court partisan, **25.** 564n
Coventry, Cts of, questioned by, **9.** 185
curio-dealer visited by, **7.** 318
dancing declined by, **31.** 146
diamond ring of, **31.** 159
Du Châtelet, Mme, disliked by, **32.** 40n
Du Châtelets rude to, **23.** 127n
Du Deffand, Mme, at loss to explain enthusiasm of, for her, **4.** 404
—— introduced to, by HW, **31.** 134
—— sends parcels by, **6.** 58–60, **31.** 179
——'s opinion of, **4.** 439, **6.** 39, 60
——'s relations with, **6.** 56
Du Muy family receives, at Grignan, **42.** 258
Euston, Cts of, discussed by, with Mrs Keppel, **31.** 239
(?) —— maligned by, **33.** 457–8
family of, accused of trying to murder her husband, **9.** 59–60
fleet visited by, at Portsmouth, **30.** 270n
Florence left by, for fear of Maria Theresa, **23.** 544
former dispatches of, to be disregarded, **23.** 560
Frederick II repulses, **23.** 539, **31.** 177, **35.** 346, 348
friends and acquaintances of: Amelia, Ps, **31.** 146–7, 153, 163, 178; Browne, Lady, **31.** 72; Eszterházy, Ps, **31.** 161; Harris, Mrs, **31.** 145; Hertford, Cts of, **31.** 27; Hesse, Ps of, **31.** 161; Ligonier, **31.** 8; Rochechouart, Marquise de, **31.** 161; Suffolk, Cts of, **31.** 63; Yarmouth, Cts of, **31.** 70
garden equipage of, **31.** 138
Genoa consul gets letter from, about her suspicions, **23.** 553
Genoa to be reached by, on boat from Lerici, **23.** 545
Gloucester, Ds of, arouses jealousy of, **23.** 530, 538, **24.** 179n, **31.** 168, 175, 177
—— blamed by, in Egremont affair, **29.** 74
(?) Gloucester, D. and Ds of, disparaged by, **23.** 484n
Granby to receive cabinet from, from Holland House, **32.** 280n
HW accompanies: to French localities, **31.** 134, 182, 183; to Louvre exposition, **7.** 346
HW and Mary Rich seen by, on fall from stile, **35.** 276
HW asks, to request Ligonier to advance Scots soldier, **31.** 8
HW believes Coke family's accusations against, **37.** 333
HW buys candlesticks and flower-pots for, **7.** 407
HW called a republican by, **33.** 2, 382
HW calls: (?) 'Hecate,' **31.** 239; 'Marie Alacaque,' **33.** 382; 'posthumous Duchess of York,' **23.** 556, **35.** 415, 418; 'Queen of Sheba,' **23.** 539; 'Scotch princess,' **23.** 542, 550; 'youngest, handsomest, and wittiest widow in England,' **37.** 563
HW calls himself *pastor fido* of, **31.** 72
HW compares: to Amazon, **31.** 160, 185; to Britannia, **31.** 25; to Cain, **31.** 154; to Cts of Carlisle, **37.** 572; to Maréchale de Guébriant, **38.** 83; to Mary Tudor, **31.** 26; to Pitt, **37.** 572; to Q. of Sheba, **31.** 156, 177; to Venus, **38.** 83; to Wandering Jew, **31.** 155
HW congratulates Hamilton on escaping, **35.** 418
HW criticized by, **31.** 133, 140, 141, 171, 178, 179, 186, 187, 188, 200
HW criticizes, **31.** 175, 177, 178, 186
HW discussed by, with 'sensible old man,' **31.** 200
HW does not listen to gossip about, **31.** 405
HW does not mention Paris trip of, to Mme du Deffand, **31.** 182
HW gives publications to, **31.** 141, 171, 182, 200, 297, 314
HW hears from, of Strafford's kindness, **35.** 319
HW in disfavour with, **32.** 196n
HW 'in love' with, **35.** 303, **37.** 563, 564
HW instructed by, to write to Hertford, **38.** 146
HW jokes about: balancing between, and Cts of Carlisle, **37.** 572; fame of, **31.** 20–2; Lady Ailesbury spurning husband, like, **37.** 289; marriage to, **31.** 14–15, **38.** 40; mysterious air of, **31.** 189; offering part of bed to, **37.** 563; passion of, for royalty, **10.** 313, **31.** 149, 150, 153, 154, 155–6, 157, 160–3; printing travels of, at SH Press, **31.** 154; subduing burgomasters, **38.** 83; taming ocean, **38.** 83; travels of, **31.** 149–50, 154, 155, 160–4
HW jokes about, with Lady Louisa Stuart, **31.** 186–7
HW may see, in Paris, **35.** 317
HW meets, near Amiens, **7.** 259, **39.** 7–8
HW mentions, **5.** 75, **9.** 260, **23.** 442
HW met by: at Hertford's, **32.** 365n; at Lady Blandford's, **32.** 365n, 366n, 368n, 375n
HW not mentioned by, to Mme du Deffand, **6.** 56, 58, **31.** 178
HW not surprised at behaviour of, at Florence, **23.** 538–9
HW not to argue with, **31.** 190
HW not to repeat scandal about Mme de Boufflers to, **38.** 222
HW offends: by considering Bp of Exeter a relative, **31.** 188; by forgetting gambling debt, **31.** 168–9; by leaving Bath two days before her arrival, **31.** 132; by not informing her of the Straffords' health, **31.** 140; by not returning from Paris, **31.** 156–7; by omitting condolence on her mother's death, **31.** 133; by trying to joke her out of her

[Campbell, Lady Mary, *continued*]
follies, **31.** 177; by verbal message, **31.** 165–7
HW plays cribbage with, **31.** 298
HW receives snuff-box brought by, from Paris, **22.** 94
HW recommends, to Mann, **23.** 530–1, 538–9, **31.** 175, 177
HW 'repeats' part of *Mysterious Mother* to, **31.** 139, 141
HW ridicules, **31.** 141, 156, 186
HW's *Castle of Otranto* dedicated to, **31.** 34, 429
HW's correspondence with, **7.** 377, 379, 380, 385, 393, **31.** 8, 14–15, 17–18, 20–4, 25–7, 61–3, 70–2, 92–4, 98, 104, 108–10, 128–9, 132, 133, 135–7, 142–6, 148–69, 171, 181, 182, 201, 299, 314, 347, 404–5
HW sends letters by, **7.** 385, **39.** 89, 90
HW sends vases for, **7.** 407
HW sent message by, **31.** 178
HW's friendship with, cooled by D. of Gloucester's marriage, **23.** 530, 538
HW's genius admired by, **31.** 141
HW's gifts from: haunch of venison, **31.** 179; snuff-box, **31.** 146; verses, **31.** 404–5
HW shares opera box with, **31.** 14n, 63, **36.** 39, **38.** 123, 128, 143
HW's mock sermon for, **13.** 36, **31.** 23, 423–6, 43. 329–30
HW's 'No rouge you wear' written for, **43.** 330
HW's opinion of, **10.** 313
HW's quarrel with, in Paris, **31.** 183–5
HW's relations with, **31.** 127, 133–5, 137–9, 140–2, 146–7, 168–9, 171–2, 175, 177–88, 200–1, 207–9, 314–15, **43.** 97
HW's remark to, **4.** 122n
HW's services to, at Paris, rudely requited, **24.** 179
HW's 'sovereign,' **38.** 172
HW's style and language admired by, **31.** 138
HW's 'The Advice' sent to, **43.** 330–1
HW's verses to, **9.** 413, **13.** 37
HW tells, of satisfaction with James Cholmondeley's will, **10.** 312n
HW to consult, as authority on European princes, **36.** 228
HW tries to embroil, with Lady Charlotte Edwin, **31.** 141
HW unable to see, when she calls, **31.** 149
HW unable to visit, **31.** 200
HW visits, at Notting Hill, **31.** 138–9, 141, 154
HW will execute commissions for, in Paris, **31.** 137
Harris, Mrs, commends, **31.** 145
Haszlang offends, **38.** 36
health of: cold, **31.** 8; erisypelas, **9.** 413, **13.** 37, **38.** 146; HW's concern for, **31.** 23, 108, 110
Herbert disputes with, over Berkeley Sq. property, **9.** 368
——'s verses to, **9.** 368

Hertford invites, to share Paris opera box, **38.** 298
—— sends compliments to, **38.** 239
Hertford, Cts of, informed by, of plan to visit Paris, **38.** 411
—— inspires 'passion' in, **37.** 561, 565
Holdernesses and Cts of Yarmouth might be met by, in Holland, **38.** 373
Holland, Bns, buys gown for, in Paris, **38.** 250
Holland or Paris may be visited by, **38.** 373
Horace read by, **31.** 61
Huntingdon, E. of, quarrels with, **23.** 543, 550n, 553, **31.** 177
—— to meet, in Italy, **35.** 348–9
husband of, **31.** 177
husband of, degenerates, **19.** 456–7
husband's lawsuit with, **9.** 59–60, **13.** 13n, **20.** 100, 114, **23.** 538n, **31.** 177, **37.** 288, 291
'importance of accent' of, **33.** 4
Italy to be visited by, **23.** 530–1, **35.** 415
itinerary of: **31.** 25, 27, 61, 132, 133–5, 142, 143, 148–9, 150–4, 161, 163–7, 175, 176–8, 182–5, **35.** 415n; arranged to escape Maria Theresa's emissaries, **23.** 542–3
Knyphausen and, **38.** 11
(?) 'lady politician,' **33.** 558
Lambert, Lady, to forward gown to, **38.** 261
Leopold of Tuscany regarded by, as her persecutor, **23.** 553
letter lent by, to HW, **31.** 17
loo played by, **31.** 138, 142, 179, 188
mad, **24.** 179, 361
Magdalen House visited by, **9.** 273–4
Mann forwards to HW a letter of, **23.** 545
——'s attentions to, **23.** 534–5, 543, 544–5, 550
——'s correspondence with, **23.** 553
——'s relations with, **31.** 176–8
March, E. of, not yet refused by, **37.** 557
—— 'refused' by, **37.** 564
Maria Amalia does not receive, at Parma, **23.** 535, 539, **31.** 176–7
Maria Carolina may antagonize, **23.** 547
Maria Louisa receives, coldly, **23.** 535
Maria Theresa adored by, **23.** 530, 539
—— gives present to, **31.** 168
——'s alleged persecution of, **23.** 535, 542–3, 544, 547, 552–3, 559, **31.** 176–8, 185, **32.** 251
Marie-Antoinette suspected by, **31.** 185
Marie-Josèphe's funeral oration attended by, **7.** 317, **31.** 134
marriage of, **9.** 36–7, **19.** 19n, 294–5
Mason contrasts, with Lady Strafford, **28.** 407
masquerade ticket returned by, **31.** 145–6
Masserano takes gown to, from Paris, **38.** 239, 250
Middleton, Catherine, driven by, in small chaise, **31.** 146
(?) Montagu comments on HW's verses to, **10.** 1
More, Hannah, generally admired by, for writings, **31.** 314
murder feared by, at Lerici, **23.** 552
nephews of, **31.** 132

Nivernais did not see, in Paris, 31. 62

old ladies countenance, 20. 100

Notting Hill reached by, 32. 196n

—— the villa of, 35. 341n

opera attended by, 10. 6, 38. 318

opera boxholders can be united only by HW's 'passion' for, 38. 128

opera-box subscription of, 38. 123

opera will be shunned by, if her box is inferior, 38. 128

Paris not yet visited by, 23. 568

Paris visited by, 5. 69, 6. 56, 216, 7. 317–51 passim, 30. 264, 31. 61, 133–5, 178, 182–5

Park Place visited by, 31. 146, 156

Parliament attended by, after opera, 38. 318

Pitt, Anne, suspected of disliking, 31. 139

Pitt, William, early admired by, 31. 21

plumes exchanged for mourning by, 38. 27

Prince William's birth may send, to Bedlam, 24. 179

punctilio of, 32. 246

pursuit of royalty brings mortifications to, 35. 348–9

quarrels of, with: Augusta, Ps of Wales, 31. 108; Barrymore, Cts of, 31. 183–5; Calais, governor of, 31. 25, 27; Coke, Vct, 31. 177; Du Châtelets, 31. 141–2; HW, 31. 183–5; Huntingdon, E. of, 23. 543, 550n, 553, 31. 177; Leicester, E. of, 31. 177

Queensberry, Ds of, omits, from ball, 38. 342

Ragley reached by, at night via Stratford, 37. 563, 564–5

recovers, at prospect of husband's death, 20. 114

residences of: Berkeley Sq., 9. 368, 31. 22; Green Park, 31. 22n; Notting Hill, 31. 138–9, 141, 154, 35. 341n; Sudbrook, 23. 538n

returns from travels with English preferences, 38. 173

Richmond's masquerade attended by, as Imoinda, 22. 149

royal signature of, 23. 550n, 553, 25. 564n, 28. 402–3

St-Denis burial vaults visited by, 24. 14

salon of paintings visited by, 7. 318

servant dismissed by, at Genoa, 23. 553

servant of, leaves, at Paris, 7. 350

Sévigné anecdotes learned by, 31. 143

Sion House ball to be described by, 35. 331

sisters of, see: Campbell, Lady Anne; Campbell, Lady Caroline (1717–94); Campbell, Lady Elizabeth

sister very different from, 24. 381

social relations of, with: Ailesbury, Cts of, 31. 133, 146, 156, 297; Amelia, Ps, 31. 138, 141, 32. 284–5, 307, 33. 104, 164, 185; Beaufort, Ds of, 33. 485n; Bedford, Ds of, 31. 171; Blandford, Lady, 31. 127, 156, 168, 172, 179–81, 187, 32. 48n, 295n, 365n, 366n, 368n, 375n, 33. 104n, 113n, 118n, 41. 319n; Boufflers, Comtesse de, 7. 347, 31. 183; Browne, Lady, 31. 142, 43. 102; Campbell, Mrs, 31. 138; Cavendish, Lord Fred-

erick, 35. 341; Christian VII, 23. 42n; Conway, H. S., 31. 146, 156, 168; Devonshires, 9. 295, 38. 72; Du Deffand, Mme, 5. 69, 6. 56, 216, 7. 318, 345, 347, 349, 31. 134, 182–3; Forbes, Lady Mary, 31. 138; Forcalquier, Comtesse de, 7. 318, 31. 134; Fronsac, 7. 319; Geoffrin, Mme, 7. 351, 31. 185; HW, 7. 317, 319, 343–6, 349–50, 10. 70–1, 31. 138–9, 141, 154, 179, 347, 32. 207, 33. 343, 353, 35. 225, 341, 38. 86, 39. 104, 256; Harris, John, 31. 133; Harris, Mrs John, 31. 142; Hertford, Cts of, 31. 133, 140, 168, 171, 178, 180, 181, 186, 188, 32. 82n, 37. 561, 563–5, 39. 165; Hertford, E. of, 23. 42n, 31. 133, 140, 171, 178, 179, 37. 561, 563–5, 39. 130, 165; Hobart, Mrs, 33. 370, 428n; Holdernesse, Cts of, 31. 139, 35. 341, 38. 36, 43. 304; Holdernesse, E. of, 38. 36, 39. 390n; Howe, Hon. Juliana, 31. 314, 347; Hume, David, 31. 139; Jeffreys, Mrs, 31. 315; Johnston, Lady Cecilia, 31. 297–8; Lloyd, Miss, 31. 171; Lowther, Lady Mary, 31. 168; Mackenzie, Lady Betty, 31. 186; Marchais, Mme de, 7. 348, 31. 183; Masserano, Principessa di, 31. 133; Onslow, Bns, 31. 347; Pelham, Frances, 10. 72–3; Pelhams, 35. 341; Powis, Cts of, 35. 341; Rochford, Cts of, 7. 318–19, 31. 134; Strafford, Cts of, 31. 133; Suffolk, Cts of, 31. 127; Temples, 4. 432, 10. 313–16; Townshend, Vcts, 31. 141; Viry, Contessa di, 7. 345, 31. 182–3; Waldegrave, Lady Elizabeth, 37. 556–7; York, D. of, 22. 521n, 38. 476n

Stowe house party doubtless described by, to Cts of Strafford, 35. 338

SH visited by, 31. 127, 129, 139, 142, 147, 168, 179–80, 197, 347, 33. 53

Sudbrook visited by, 31. 314, 35. 282

Sunning Hill visited by, with husband, 37. 288

Temple, Cts, writes verses on, 10. 57

terrible to be chambermaid of, 37. 572

Turgot's economy at royal wedding distresses, 39. 255

Turin visit of, 23. 543, 545, 553, 556, 559, 560

Vauxhall visited by, with Frances Pelham and Townshend, 37. 557

Versailles visited by, 7. 343

verses to HW from, 31. 15–16

victory might be celebrated by, 37. 567

Vienna no longer suspected by, 23. 560

—— to be visited by, 31. 148–9

—— visited by, 31. 150–4, 163–7, 175, 32. 251

virtues of, 31. 166, 175–7

Voltaire visited by, 31. 143

Waldegrave, Cts, boasts to, of Bedford's insolence to George III, 30. 185–6

Walpoles envied by, for royal marriage, 33. 528

Wentworth Castle to be visited by, 29. 164

Westminster Abbey burial vaults visited by, when Ps Louisa died, 24. 14

[Campbell, Lady Mary, *continued*]
—— to be attended by, for Ps Elizabeth's burial, 38. 27
windows of, broken by mob, 25. 564, 29. 356
would rejoice to add freckles for king and country, 33. 22
Wraxall's *Short Review* praised by, 33. 558n
York, Ds of, compared to, by HW, 12. 11
York, D. of, claimed by, to have married her, 12. 11, 23. 530, 550n, 24. 14, 179n, 25. 564n, 31. 175
—— discussed by, with Elector Palatine and HW, 31. 134
—— inquires about 'marriage' of, to HW, 9. 264
Young Pretender's wife might be visited by, 33. 439
Campbell, Mary, m. (1778) Donald Campbell of Barbreck, Cts of Ailesbury's niece:
(?) SH visited by, 12. 232
Campbell, Robert (d. 1758), merchant in Sweden:
son of, 37. 498
Campbell, Robert, army officer; English minister to Sweden:
England said to send, to Sweden, to seek alliance, 37. 497–8, 500
Campbell, Thomas:
Dalrymple's correspondence with, about Atterbury's letters, 15. 118n
Campbell, Lady William. *See* Izard, Sarah
Campbell, Lord William (ca 1732–78), M.P.; gov. of S. Carolina:
daughter of, 4. 158n
death of, 33. 50, 35. 489
HW to be visited by, at SH, 39. 295
health of, 7. 63, 39. 299
losses of, in American war, 33. 51
marriage of, 4. 63n
Park Place visited by, 38. 436
wife of, 25. 184, 263n
Campbell, William Conway (1773–1856), son of Lord William Campbell:
'beggared orphan,' 33. 50
Campbell clan:
Coke, Lady Mary, would like to lead, against French, 38. 17
HW may recruit, for regiment, 38. 40
troops of: attack rebel right at Culloden, 37. 240; with Gen. Bland pursue rebels, 37. 229–30
Campbell family:
camels confused with, 32. 242
Coke family quarrels with, 37. 333
HW's connection with, 21. 452
Hamilton, Lord Archibald, esteems, 21. 457
Hamilton family united with, through Elizabeth Gunning, 21. 267–8, 22. 121, 38. 7
Hardwicke marries son into, 37. 70
illegitimacy in, 26. 11
Jamesone's portrait of young lady of Argyll family of, 40. 267
members of, emigrate to America, 15. 331

of Glenurchy: genealogical book on, 40. 264–5; Jamesone's pedigree of, with miniature portraits, 40. 265
people who marry into, must expect their own relatives to object, 37. 333
Stuart Mackenzie's death would prevent pollution of noble blood of, 30. 59
Townshend family to be rivals of, 38. 36
Campden. *See* Camden
Campden House, Kensington:
Marlborough, Ds of, impertinent at, 9. 269
Pitt's Buildings near, 21. 183n
Campen:
battle of, 21. 444, 466
Campet de Saujon, Marie-Charlotte-Hippolyte de (1725–1800), m. (1746) Édouard, Comte (Marquis, 1751) de Boufflers-Rouverel; 'Comtesse de Boufflers'; 'l'idole du Temple':
afraid of highwaymen, 11. 329
anglomanie of, cured by English visit, 22. 270
anglophile, 22. 135, 435
appearance of, not handsome, 10. 71
Arles visited by, 6. 349, 355, 379, 430
arrival of, in England, 22. 135
Arty, Mme d', visited by, 38. 480
Auteuil house occupied by, 6. 67, 72, 75, 81, 185, 211, 345, 349, 459, 469, 472, 7. 153, 162, 165, 166, 168, 176, 218, 230, 347, 422–30, 31. 183
Barbantane much connected with, 22. 434
Beauclerk interests, 6. 367, 7. 218
——'s death does not move, 7. 218
Bedford, Holdernesse, and Hume accompany, 32. 14n
Boufflers, Comtesse Amélie de, loved by, 7. 219
Boufflers, Marquise de, not to be confused with, 22. 270n
Brunswick, P. of, admires, 3. 41
Bunbury, Lady Sarah, annexed by, 3. 205, 224, 311
Cambis, Mme de, attached to, 5. 226
Caraman, Comtesse de, admires, 3. 18
Caramans visited by, 6. 86
Chanteloup visited by, 6. 33, 41, 430–1, 441, 453, 8. 202
Chauvelin's campaign praised by, 4. 199, 200
Choiseul, Duc de, not on best terms with, 3. 16
—— reconciled with, 4. 177, 182, 188, 202n, 203
—— visited by, with Dutens at Chanteloup, 25. 627
Choiseul, Duchesse de, relations of, with, 3. 16, 6. 41
Coke, Lady Mary, displeased with, 6. 56
Conti, Prince de, does not marry, 4. 19n
—— forgotten by, 7. 218
—— loves, on public couch at l'Isle-Adam, 38. 221
—— may wed, 22. 135n, 270, 434, 38. 470, 477–8, 480
—— mourned by, 6. 345, 346, 347, 355

——'s provision for, **7.** 218

——'s relations with, **3.** 15n, 41n, **5.** 144n, 357, **6.** 473, **7.** 218, **14.** 153, **22.** 135n, 270n, 434, **31.** (?) 126

Conway and HW have met, **38.** 203

Craufurd corresponds with, **5.** 374n, 403

—— liked by, **5.** 280, 288

Cromwell's bust seen by, at D. of Grafton's, with HW, **38.** 443

discards the English for the Italians, **3.** 26

Du Deffand, Mme, compares, with Cts Waldegrave, **4.** 19

—— driven to and from Versailles by, **6.** 48

—— hears English news from, **4.** 132

—— mentions, **3.** 90, 175, 183, **4.** 139, 159, 394, **5.** 21

—— pays call of condolence on, **6.** 345, 346, 347

——'s correspondence with, **6.** 379, **7.** 459, 461

—— sends *Vie de M. Hume* to, **6.** 425

——'s opinion of, **3.** 26, 48, 76, 80, 109, 111, 172–3, 202, 209, 263, 281, 334, 338, 345, 396, **4.** 80, 109, 200, 203, **5.** 6, 107, **6.** 11, 41, 48, 219, 347, 473, **7.** 136, 168, 218–19

——'s 'portrait' of, **8.** 84–7

——'s relations with, **3.** 12, 109, 111, 117, 120, 132, 231, **4.** 16, 121, 130, 293, **5.** 417, **6.** 11, 304, 371, 431, 453, 473, **7.** 102, 136

—— talks of Hume's appointment with, **3.** 253

—— will not give *Cornélie* to, **4.** 100

eloquent but too eager for applause, **14.** 153

England visited by, **22.** 135, 434, **32.** *14*, **34.** 68, 76, 80, 109, **38.** 442

English celebrity of, **3.** 133

English garden of, **3.** 341, **7.** 316, 347, **28.** 222–3, **32.** 259

English predilections of, **8.** 87

'English solidity' remark of, shows her own lack of discernment, **22.** 280

English spoken by, **10.** 71

English struggle for diversion noticed by, to HW, **22.** 152

English visit of, will make Frenchmen believe her, **38.** 442

English ways known to, **6.** 11

finances of: **7.** 218; impaired by French Revolution, **34.** 68, 80

Fitzwilliam, Lord, lives next to, **11.** 285

Forcalquier, Mme de, ridicules, **3.** 50

Genlis, Mme de, comedy of, attended by, **7.** 212

Gloucester, D. of, may have been seen by, in Paris, **31.** 126

Gramont, Duchesse de, cultivated by, **6.** 33, 41

—— praises, **6.** 41

Greenwich visited by, to see ship-launching, **10.** 70

Guerchy discusses Hume and Rousseau with, **3.** 133

Gustav III's correspondence with, **5.** 135, 142, **7.** 427

—— sends son's portrait to, **7.** 427

——'s relations with, **7.** 230

—— to be joined by, at Spa, **7.** 230, 235, **239**

HW aids son of, **3.** 172

HW angers, by letter to Rousseau, **35.** 117

HW asks Hertford about books ascribed to, **38.** 442, 447, 477

HW describes, **22.** 434

HW escorts, through Bushey Park, **11.** 329

HW forsakes, to go to SH, **38.** 202

HW hears French news from, **11.** 76

HW inquired after by, **4.** 293

HW invited by, for Ash Wednesday supper, **41.** 2

HW jokes about Hume's correspondence with, **31.** 119

HW makes conquest of daughter-in-law of, **32.** 259

HW may take Thomas Walpole jr to, at Richmond, **36.** 276

HW mentions, **3.** (?) 342, **11.** 352

HW not disapproved of by, **3.** 283

HW praises remark of, **5.** 346

HW recommends son of, to Sir Horace Mann, **3. 172n**

HW scolded by, for letter to Rousseau, **14.** 156

HW's correspondence with, **7.** 381, 382, **41.** 2, 14–15, 32–3

HW secures kettle for, **5.** 417–18, 425, 433, 436, **6.** 2, 4, 7, 8–9

HW sees, in London, **34.** 80

HW sends compliments to, **38.** 214–15

HW's letters to Hume and Rousseau discussed by, **3.** 172, 174, **7.** 294

HW's lodging with Mme du Deffand might shock, **3.** 108

HW's present to, **3.** 83, 86, 89, 112, 120

HW's relations with, **4.** 293

HW's verses to, at SH party, **10.** 69, 71, 73, 74

HW to be received by, at Paris, **38.** 504

HW to see, at Paris, **10.** 172

HW visits, at Richmond, **11.** 248, **34.** 109

HW well treated by, in Paris, **22.** 434

HW will know much of, in Paris, **32.** 20

HW will miss, in Paris, **22.** 554

(?) Harcourt sends vase to, **36.** 168, 169

health of: **4.** 100, 106, **7.** 425; fever, **11.** 291

Hertford meets, at Mme d'Usson's, and talks of HW, **38.** 351

—— receives trees from, for Ps Amelia, **38.** 339, 366

—— sees, in Paris, **38.** 337

Hervey, Bns, often entertains, **22.** 135

—— told by, of French air helping HW's health, **41.** 14

—— to receive pomatums from, **31.** 103

*Historic Doubts* given to, **4.** 31–2, 34

Holdernesse attentive to, **3.** 24n, 25, 59, 77, 80, 172, **38.** 480

—— to visit, **6.** 185

Holdernesses visited by, in England, **38.** 480n

Holland, Bns, asks, about SH, **22.** 270

homage paid to, **4.** 106, 269

Hume always with, **38.** 480

[Campet de Saujon, M.-C.-H. de, *continued*]
—— hears from, a denial of books attributed to her, 38. 447
—— idolized by, 22. 434
——'s acquaintance with, 3. 15–16, 100, 119, 133n, 172, 250–1, 253, 4. 23, 161, 164, 269
——'s correspondence with, 3. 105–6, 109, 115, 117, 120, 6. 355
——'s letter to, on Conti's death, admired by Mme du Deffand, 6. 355
——'s life sent to, by Mme du Deffand, 6. 425
——'s pension spoken of by, 4. 87
husband's death puts, into retirement, 38. 480
Isle-Adam visited by, 3. 127, 172, 188, 303, 5. 51, 417, 6. 324, 22. 554, 31. 45
La Borde adores, 4. 188
La Fayette related to, 7. 113
La Tuilerie visited by, 7. 345
Lauzun, Duchesse de, visits, 6. 67, 72, 75, 81, 7. 162
Lauzuns cultivated by, 3. 241
Lespinasse, Mlle de, supported by, 6. 379
Luxembourg, Mme de, disparages, 5. 107
—— friend of, 3. 41, 47, 334, 4. 106
—— looked after by, 7. 153
—— shares expenses with, at Auteuil, 7. 218
—— visits, 6. 211, 7. 153, 162, 218
—— with, after Conti's death, 6. 345, 347, 348–9
Lyon visited by, 6. 371
Mann's attention to son appreciated by, 22. 463
Mirepoix, Mme de, hates, 3. 19
Montmorency descent attributed to, 10. 71
Montmorency visited by, 3. 191, 334, 338, 4. 243
Moranville brought by, from Richmond to SH, 39. 473
Normandy estate visited by, 6. 462
Orléans, Duc d', talks with, 3. 396
Palais-Royal visited by, 3. 396
Paris life of, easy, 10. 70
Plombières to be visited by, 7. 47–8, 53
Pont-de-Veyle receives English news from, 3. 321
Pougues visited by, 3. 59, 100, 303, 308–9, 311, 319, 334, 4. 106, 110
praised, 3. 76
Provence visited by, 6. 367, 441
Ranelagh visited by, 10. 70
returns to Paris, 3. 191, 330, 6. 467, 493
Richmond Green house taken by, 11. 221
Richmond parties include, 11. 148
Rochford attentive to, 3. 172
Rousseau does not want to see, 4. 434
—— may be abandoned by, 3. 91, 108–9
—— mentioned by, 3. 26, 281
—— not discussed by, with HW, 41. 32
—— protected by, 22. 434
——'s follies recounted by, 3. 301
——'s patroness, 3. 12n, 133, 172, 7. 294
—— thought by, to be crazy, 3. 172

—— writes to, 3. 15, 132, 188, 202
Rueil visited by, 4. 130
Saturday suppers of, 7. 135
Shakespeare not liked by, 6. 304
sightseeing tires, 10. 70
social life of, 7. 168
social relations of, at Paris, *see index entries ante* 8. 278
social relations of, in England and Paris, with: Coke, Lady Mary, 31. 183; Conti, 31. 45; Du Deffand, Mme, 31. 183; Garrick, Mrs, 11. 329; HW, 10. 69, 70, 71, 73, 74, 11. 104, 108, 248, 12. 236, 237, 31. 183, 34. 109; Hertford, Cts of, 38. 221–2; Hervey, Bns, 22. 135
son of, marries, 4. 58, 168
son of, recommended to HW, 41. 14, 32
son of, takes leave, 11. 88
son of, to visit Florence, 22. 434, 435, 445
Spa visited by, 7. 230, 235, 239
*Spectator* imitated by, in *L'Esclave généreux*, 22. 271
Stormont's misdeed told to, 6. 4, 7
SH visited by, 12. 236, 237
Tavistock's accident and death, send, into mourning, 3. 271, 278, 381
Temple residence of, 3. 41n, 6. 472
to return to Paris, 6. 430–1, 472
Trouillet's letter from, attacks Rousseau, 22. 475
Versailles visited by, 6. 48
Vierville, Marquise de, friend of, 5. 384, 422
Villeroy, Duchesse de, not an adorer of, 3. 213–14
visitors to, at Auteuil, *see* Auteuil: visitors to
Vorontsov lends Richmond House to, 34. 68
Waldegrave, Cts, object of curiosity to, 22. 136
Wiart's translation of Boswell admired by, 4. 113
witticism by, on Duc d'Orléans, 32. 264
Camp fever. *See under* Fever
Camp follower; camp followers:
clad in scoured regimentals, 35. 509
Conway may outlast, in army service, 38. 128
Camphor:
bruises treated with, 31. 305, 34. 50
Camphor, spirits of. *See* Spirits of camphor
Campigli, Andrea:
masked ball directed by, 25. 645n
Campigneulles. *See* Thoreau de Campigneules
Campillo. *See* Del Campillo
Campion, Maria Anna (ca 1685–1706), singer and actress:
Devonshire's epitaph for, 16. 368–9
*Campi Phlegræa. See under* Hamilton, Sir William
Campo, Del. *See* Del Campo
Campo di Fiore, Rome:
book burnt in, by hangman, 21. 477
Campofiorito ('Campoflorido'), Principe di. *See* Reggio e Branciforte, Don Luigi

Campofiorito, Principessa di. *See* Gravina, ——

Campo Morone:
Austrians advanced to, **19.** 359

Campo Santo, Marquis de. *See* La Torre, Don Ferdinand de

Campo Santo:
battle of, **18.** 153–5, 161, 163–5, 195–6, 312
McDonel commands Spanish Guards at, **18.** 336n
Spaniards cross the Panaro at, **18.** 151n

Campo Vaccino. *See* Rome: forum at

Campredon, Jacques de (1646–ca 1726), French envoy to Russia:
Magnan secretary to, **18.** 548n

Camps de Saujon. *See* Campet de Saujon

Camsillon, Baronne de. *See* Phélipot, Louise-Gabrielle

Camus, Graf von. *See* Brown, Ulysses Maximilien

Camus, ——, member of Royal Académie des Sciences at Paris:
Éon presents, to George III, **22.** 146n
Louis XV sends, to study discovery of longitude at sea, **22.** 146n

Camus, Armand-Gaston (1740–1804), lawyer and legislator:
named commissioner, **12.** 1n
(?) Necker accused by, **34.** 96n

Camus de Mézières. *See* Le Camus de Mézières

Can; cans:
antique, bought by HW at Mrs Kennon's sale, **37.** 439n

Canaan, K. of. *See* Jabin

Canada, governor of. *See* Du Quesne, Ange; Rigaud, Pierre-François de

Canada:
American colonies might cede, to France, **24.** 133
Americans driven from, by Carleton, **24.** 229
Americans may seize, **24.** 132–3, 138, 161, 336, 342
Amherst abandons embarkation for, **21.** 336n
—— prepares invasion of, **21.** 421n
*Anecdotes of Painting* does not discuss, **9.** 326
bills on, *see* Canada Bills
England demands, from France, **21.** 526
—— to keep, by peace terms, **22.** 76n
English army in, to be mostly of Russians, **24.** 127n
English bishops establish Roman Catholicism in, **35.** 587
France may regain fur trade with, **24.** 133
—— offers, in peace overtures, **21.** 498
French troops sail to, **20.** 541n
HW believes France will recover, **32.** 328
HW expects loss of, **28.** 237
HW thought as much of losing Aquitaine and Normandy as, **38.** 56
House of Commons considers bill about, **24.** 13
Indians are used against troops in, **28.** 333

—— in north of, subject of fabulous accounts, **35.** 187
—— of, said to have overwhelmed British western strongholds, **38.** 268
Jumonville's death supposedly in, **41.** 147
juries abolished in, **41.** 312
*London Gazette's* report about, incorrect, **32.** 284
loss of, feared, **32.** 395
Murray defeated in, **21.** 416
Pitt offered government of, **21.** 540n
—— the 'conqueror' of, **9.** 395, **21.** 541
—— to conquer, **21.** 290
requests union with the United States, **33.** 32
Richmond's dispatch on, **7.** 273
Roman Catholic Church permitted to collect tithes in, **24.** 161n
Roman Catholics favoured in, **41.** 312
savages of, the only fit allies of Lord George Gordon, **35.** 354
troops from, captured with Burgoyne, **24.** 345n
war will probably be decided by battle in, **21.** 327

*Canada*, English ship:
Conway, Capt., appointed to, **11.** 262n

Canada Bills:
Choiseul concedes payment of, **39.** 30
Dauberval to be exchanged for, **38.** 460
French arrêts concerning, **38.** 423, 432n
HW jokes about his concern for, **31.** 97
Hertford tired of hearing of, **38.** 447
Holland's speculations in, may explain his attentions to Hertford, **38.** 414
Richmond and HW settle affair of, **7.** 287, 290
Richmond obtains payment of, **30.** 213
subject of contention with France, **38.** 432

Canadian; Canadians:
Americans not to be fought by, **41.** 312n
Americans said to have been joined by, **24.** 161
England expects, to help conquer Bostonians, **28.** 216

Canal, Antonio (1697–1768), painter; called Canaletto:
(?) Montagu wants paintings by, **10.** 97
Smith employs, **35.** 185
——'s collection of, sold to George III, **35.** 186n

Canal; canals:
at Bruges, **37.** 153
at Hampton Court, **33.** 42
at Ranelagh, **20.** 47
behind Colisée at Paris, **39.** 145
bilander travels on, in Flanders, **37.** 118
Bridgwater's, Conway should be interested in, **39.** 438
Dudley's, near Thames, **35.** 389
French and English meanings of, **42.** 136
French lead prisoners through English outpost on, **37.** 207
Java's, praised by Byron, **22.** 421n
Oxford and Coventry, frozen, **32.** 186n

[Canal; canals, *continued*]
  project for, in Devonshire, 34. 184
  rioters throw people into, in Holland, 37. 286
  Rotterdam's, 37. 134
  Vilvorde, fortification of, 37. 204
Canal boat. *See* Bilander
Canale, Contessa di. *See* Pálffy, Maria Anna
Canaletto. *See* Canal, Antonio (1697–1768);
  Bellotto, Bernardo (1720–80)
Canary; canaries:
  Acciaioli resembles, 19. 497
  Du Deffand, Mme, has, 4. 77, 222, 224
  HW hopes Conway's, is with egg by bluebird, 39. 103
  HW's, 30. 93
  learned, HW as much sought after as, 14. 157
  Uguccioni couples, 18. 446
Canary Islands:
  Dutch fleet at, 12. 189
  fountain tree in, 10. 155
  Torres's arrival at, rumoured, 17. 83n
Canary seed:
  birds to feed on, 35. 154
Canbury, Surrey:
  Hardinge of, 12. 166n
Cancale Bay:
  Conway investigates, 39. 343
  English expedition to, 21. 205n, 210, 39. 526
  Wallace's raid on, 39. 321n
Cancelleria, Palazzo della, at Rome:
  York, Cardinal, lives at, 25. 150n
Cancer:
  occurrences of, 10. 36, 20. (?) 108n, 291, 22. 56, 345, 354, 24. 5, 353, 25. 78, 33. 211, 217, 38. 243n
  treatment of, 11. 60n
Cancin, Frans, Ensign:
  captured at Velletri, 18. 493
Candale, Comte ('Baron') de. *See* Foix-Candale, Bertrand-Léon de
Candelabra:
  of mahogany, 35. 119
'Candid':
  popular signature for letters to newspapers, 42. 500
Candida:
  Bèze's poem to, 40. 100
*Candid and Impartial State. See under* Marshall, Edmund
*Candide. See under* Voltaire
Candie. *See* Crete
Candish. *See* Cavendish
Candle; candles:
  at Kensington Palace, 20. 89
  at Mme Panciatichi's catafalque, 18. 405
  burn out, at Pantheon fête, 39. 331
  Byron takes, from waiter, 38. 503
  Craon, Casa, draws guests who merely want to use, 19. 477
  Craon, Princesse de, cannot bear light of, 18. 242
  —— has, covered with a fanale and green shade, 18. 228

Cumberland, D. of, holds, while surgeon opens his knee, 38. 456
draughts extinguish, 30. 211
Dumesnil's secretary moves, during mass, 19. 493
English should lay in, for long winters, 35. 474
farthing: clergyman rebukes daughter for praying by light of, 17. 85; in English opera, 19. 370; Montagu mentions, 9. 381; ploughman believes stars to be, 10. 184
fire set by, kills seven children, 25. 242
Forzoni uses, to kill gnats, 17. 179
glass protectors for, 17. 59, 73, 87
guides to Devil's Arse carry, 40. 16
HW carries: before Ps Amelia, 31. 133; to pursue burglars, 9. 133
HW forced to light, at 11 A.M., 32. 409
HW refers to burning inch of, 31. 129
HW's economy in, at Houghton, 32. 143
HW sees Northumberland's gallery by light of, 21. 88
HW's servants are not given time to light, before rabble breaks windows, 25. 343
HW's servants light, in his front windows for mob, 25. 563
Halifax and Sandwich call for, to retire, 10. 207
Harry awakes HW with, 35. 210
heat from, at Jewish wedding, 37. 312
Houghton gallery illuminated with, 18. 298
in gallery at SH, 10. 279
La Borde's expenses for, 31. 80
landlady unable to get, before Vcts Townshend rejects room, 30. 70
Minorcans light bonfire instead of, 37. 311
not lighted for Wilkes-Tooke quarrel, 31. 151
obelisk of, at Cts of Northumberland's festino, 10. 34
on supper table with lamps, 37. 454n
Parliamentary orators should speak by inch of, 25. 58
Riccardi spoils gallery by furnishing, with rock-crystal lustres, 22. 157–8
smoke of, spoils painting in Riccardi's gallery, 22. 157–8
SH visitors forced to see it by light of, 35. 370, 531
SH would be dirtied by, 38. 335
tallow: lights room for Cock Lane séance, 10. 6; Montagu, Lady Mary Wortley, uses, 22. 3; used for social occasions, 17. 85
'thief' in, misunderstood by Mme de Mirepoix, 20. 132
wax: at Bns Grey's, 10. 204; at Dublin entertainment, 9. 404; Cocchi to receive, for hospital services, 17. 57; Lucca gives, to D. of York, 22. 221; Montagu mentions, 10. 239; used by Mrs Damer for statuary, 38. 198n
Wookey Hole explored with, 40. 10
Candlelight:
  colours indistinguishable by, 33. 262

HW advises Conway not to read by, **39**. 408
HW reads by, **21**. 139, 147
HW reads only by, **16**. 20
HW unable to read faint ink by, **42**. 189
Montagu cannot long read by, **10**. 144
Pitt, Mrs George, threads needle by, **23**. 456
reading by, injurious to eyesight, **21**. 147, 163
Zouch writes by, **16**. 51
Candle-screen; candle-screens:
HW reads without, **21**. 139
Candle-snuffer; candle-snuffers (theatre menials):
actors send, with bouquets to Ds of Cumberland, **23**. 519
at Calais play, **32**. 150–1
audience pelts, at theatre, **23**. 348, **39**. 371
footman, who fails as actor, becomes, **37**. 141
modern French monks worthy only to be, **35**. 127
Candlestick; candlesticks:
at Elizabeth Chudleigh's, **9**. 277
Carmey's, from church in Kent, **40**. 259
Dresden, given by Sir John Bland to Lady Caroline Petersham, **9**. 106–7
HW buys, at Sheffield, **9**. 295
HW musters, for showing SH at night, **33**. 403
hand, of silver: HW's at Arlington St, **23**. 285; Mrs Delany's, **33**. 497n
of Chelsea china, **20**. 121–2
in Q. Elizabeth's collection, **33**. 324
silver, on church altars, **34**. 98–9
'Candour':
popular signature for letters to newspapers, **42**. 500
'Candour, Mrs.' *See under* Sheridan, Richard Brinsley: *School for Scandal*
Cane *or* Kane, Patrick:
conspiracy by, against Sir Edward Walpole, **43**. 365
Cane; canes:
Capponi receives, from Modenese princess, **17**. 70
gold-headed and diamond-studded, given to Serristori by Modenese princess, **17**. 64, 70
HW needs, more than a pastoral crook, **10**. 298
HW walks with, **24**. 440
heads for, may have been given by HW to Chute for Suares, **17**. 117, 456, **35**. 6
heads of, gold with 'spying glass,' **35**. 86
Portsmouth, Cts of, to carry, at Coronation, **9**. 387
*See also* Stick
Caneshop, the, Spring Garden Gate:
Irish giant at, **35**. 365n
Canevaro, Pietro, senator:
Genoese provided with arms by, **19**. 338n
Canfield, Benedict, Father:
memoir of, **16**. 203n
Cange, Du. *See* Du Cange
Canister; canisters:
of tea, **17**. 17

Canillac, Abbé de. *See* Montboissier-Beaufort, Claude-François de
Canillac, Comte de. *See* Montboissier-Beaufort, Ignace de
Canillac, Comtesse de. *See* Roncherolles, Anne-Michelle-Dorothée de
Canillac, Mlle de. *See* Montboissier-Beaufort-Canillac, Louise-Agnès-Élisabeth de
Canillac, Vicomte de. *See* Montboissier-Beaufort, Ignace de
Canillac, Vicomtesse de. *See* Roncherolles, Anne-Michelle-Dorothée de
Canisy, Marquis de. *See* Carbonnel, Charles-Éléonor-Hervé de
Canisy, Marquise de. *See* Marguerye de Vassy, Marie-Marguerite-Louise-Françoise de
Cannæ:
battle of, **14**. 2
Cannel coal:
snuff-boxes of, **31**. 105n
Cannenberg, Gen., Dutch officer:
Cumberland, D. of, and, attempt to rally the Dutch troops, **19**. 424n
Cannetti:
in Ponte Molle battle, **18**. 531
Cannibal; cannibals ('anthropophagi'; 'lestrygons'):
'cowardly,' mentioned by Lafayette, **43**. 165
do not eat in company with wild beasts, **33**. 197
French compared with, **31**. 360
world may become theatre of, **39**. 498
Cannich, Inverness-shire:
Young Pretender hides in a hut near, **19**. 295n
Canilliac. *See* Canillac
Canning, Ann (1748–1820), later Superior of English Augustinian nuns at Paris:
(?) social relations of, with Massereene, **7**. 294
Canning, Elizabeth (1734–73), impostor:
jury brings in, as guilty, **35**. 175
'modest impostor' compared to Cock Lane ghost, **10**. 6
Pitt may have met, at Enfield Wash, **38**. 131
Canning, George (1770–1827), statesman:
lines by Knight parodied by, **29**. 340–1
Canning; Canninge; Cannings. *See* Canynges
Cannon, Capt.:
packet-boat of, said to be lost, **25**. 210n
Cannon, Mr:
social relations of, with D. of Beaufort, **7**. 271
Cannon, Mrs (?) Sarah:
social relations of, with D. of Beaufort, **7**. 271
Cannon, Mrs Sidney. *See* Kennon, Sidney
Cannon:
accidental bursting of, in Paris, **11**. 96
at Breda, **19**. 255
at Culloden, **37**. 239
at Florence, fire salute for Francis I's birthday, **17**. 217n
at Leghorn, **21**. 16
at Marciana, **18**. 28
at Modena, **17**. 443

[Cannon, *continued*]

at Monaco, fire salute when D. of York's body leaves, **22.** 554

at Plymouth, **37.** 202

at Stade, **21.** 146

at Tortona, **19.** 100

audible from Bastille, at Paris uprising, **39.** 467–8

Austrians mount, on the Bisagno, **19.** 417

batteries of, surrounding St Philip's, **25.** 233

battering, Voyer and Paulin take, past Lyon, **20.** 536

big princes famous for, in Italy, **25.** 587, 589

brass: Leghorn armed with, **17.** 193; Norris captures, **18.** 455

Brunswick, D. of, takes, from French, **39.** 506

bullets for, **38.** 410

captured at San Lazaro, **19.** 267

captured at Piacenza, **19.** 270

Charles, P., captures, on the Rhine, **37.** 159

Charles Emmanuel III sends, from Savona to Brown, **19.** 353

Christianity not to be propagated by, **35.** 392

Del Monte family lacks, **20.** 423

English, in Germany, **37.** 136n

English captain throws, from captured Spanish ship, **18.** 406

English fire, at San Remo, **19.** 121, 124–5

English lose, at Korbitz, **38.** 32

English ships find, loaded when salutes are fired, **21.** 123

English the first to fire, in war with France, **20.** 488

English troops to go to Concord to spike, **24.** 110

English unable to bring, against St-Malo, **37.** 536

Eszterházys welcomed by, at Florence, **20.** 350

fired for George III's visit to House of Commons, **9.** 412

firing of, when ship burns up, **19.** 473

Florentine fortresses stripped of, **17.** 204

Frederick II nails up, **37.** 549

French: at Fontenoy, **36.** 11, **37.** 191; captured, **37.** 159; Charles, P., dislodged from island by, **37.** 146; eighty, at Hastenbeck, **37.** 497; numerous but ill-served, **37.** 497; superior to English, **19.** 318–19; use straw men for target practice, **38.** 410

French have difficulty drawing, from Ciudadela, **20.** 567

French land, at Ciudadela, **20.** 552

French lose, at Crefeld, **35.** 101n

from Cherbourg: **31.** 22; brought from Portsmouth to Hyde Park, **21.** 238; displayed in Hyde Park, **37.** 567, 569; paraded to Tower, **37.** 571

from Menin, can be heard at Ghent, **37.** 154

from Savona, retarded, **19.** 358

Gage's, captured, **39.** 221, 232

Genoese, may keep Medley's fleet away, **19.** 385

Genoese aim, at Palace, **19.** 359

Genoese mob sends, to the Bocchetta, **19.** 343

Genoese seize, in insurrection, **19.** 337

Genoese send, to Corsica, **18.** 455

HW could no more fire a pistol than carry a, **25.** 570

HW jokes about Pitt sending expedition after, **37.** 569

HW may mount, on SH battlements, **35.** 315

HW will fire, at Plymouth if Conway gains victory, **37.** 202

Howe opposed by, at New York, **24.** 229

in Anson's sea-piece, **20.** 38

in Holland, **33.** 562

Jesuits confronted by, at Civita Vecchia, **22.** 517–18

Joseph II's coronation celebrated by, at Florence, **22.** 225n

Kingston, Ds of, mentions, in will, **31.** 289n

lack of, prevents capture of Antibes, **19.** 352

large, Spaniards lack, **18.** 151

left by enemy in siege of Quebec, **15.** 71

Leghorn's, **21.** 334

Liechtenstein awaits, from Parma, **19.** 258

lost at Falkirk, **19.** 204

Murray will reply to Crillon by mouths of, **25.** 207–8

near Amoeneberg, **22.** 86

off-stage, in Farmain de Rozoi's *Henri IV*, **39.** 218

Paris visitors surprised not to see, in London streets, **34.** 157

Pitt does not make George III ride, to Tower, **37.** 571

—— sends, against St-Malo but not against Rochefort, **21.** 213

plaster busts cannot be melted to make, **34.** 184

Portuguese nail up, at Rio Grande, **24.** 224

privateer, Dunmore captures, from Americans, **24.** 157

Prussians spike, at Prague, **18.** 543

rebels fire, against walls of Blair, **37.** 237

rebels said to have left, behind, **19.** 178–9

rebels spike, **19.** 208

Ricardos captures ten, from the French, **12.** 40

Richelieu requests additional, **20.** 572

Russian, captured at Zorndorf, **37.** 562n

St-Malo siege impossible for lack of, **37.** 538

Schulenburg obtains, to subdue Genoa, **19.** 367

Spaniards capture, **19.** 119

—— demand, of Genoa, **18.** 455

—— land, in Genoa, **18.** 555

—— prepare, at Barcelona, for Minorca attack, **25.** 229

—— throw, into the sea, **18.** 412

—— to receive, from Naples by Adriatic, **19.** 30

—— withdraw, from Milan, **19.** 225

Spanish army advances with, **19.** 15

Wade demands, for Ostend, **19.** 69

Waldeck impregnable without, **22.** 55–6

woods might interfere with, **17.** 195

York, D. of, welcomed with, at Lucca, **22.** 222

Young Pretender lacks, **19.** 104–5

*See also* Artillery; Battery; Cannon-ball; Field piece

Cannon-ball; cannon-balls:

Grenville killed by, **19.** 403

Hamilton, James, deprived of leg by, **42.** 89

Montagu's head taken off by, **37.** 192

red hot, floating batteries sunk by, at Gibraltar, **39.** 394

Washington enjoys, **20.** 449–50

Cannonoci, Casa:

Uguccioni couples canary birds at, **18.** 446

Cannons Park, Middlesex, D. of Chandos's seat:

damage by visitors to, **2.** 275

demolished, **36.** 246

gardens at: destroyed, **30.** 60–1; discussed by Pope, **30.** 60–1

'great standard of bad taste,' **30.** 60

HW and Rigby visit, **30.** 60–2

Hallet buys, **10.** 77n

Lund laments destruction of hedges at, **30.** 61

'patchwork' room at, **30.** 61–2

Canoe; canoes:

lords of America cannot be afraid of, **21.** 338

Canonici, (?) Girolamo (1704–70), councillor:

sale of effects of, **17.** 129

*Canonici*:

Clement XIII regulates dress and conduct of, **21.** 224

*Canonisation de Saint Cucufin, La, see under* Voltaire

Canonizations:

Benedict XIV busy with, **19.** 171n

Canons Leigh, Devon:

Smith of, **11.** 37n, **12.** 152n, **29.** 104n

*Canons of Criticism, The. See under* Edwards, Thomas

Canons Park. *See* Cannons Park

'Canopus':

HW has no comment on verses of, **33.** 114–15

Canopy; canopies:

at Pitti Palace, **22.** 179

for Ds of Buckingham's funeral, **18.** 193

for George III's coronation, **38.** 121

in Anne of Denmark's furniture, **32.** 325

in SH Gallery, **10.** 53

purple velvet, at George II's funeral, **9.** 321

Canova, Antonio (1757–1822), sculptor:

Harwood's studio visited by, **25.** 93n

*Cantabrigia depicta*:

mistake in, **1.** 42

Cantata; cantatas:

Accademia dei nobili's celebration to be preceded by, **22.** 367

at Florence, for Karl Wilhelm Ferdinand, **22.** 458

Garrick's, **28.** 65–6

Naples to give, for D. of Calabria's birth, **19.** 437

Santa Croce gives, **17.** 20

Uguccioni's, sent to England, **18.** 545, 554

York, D. of, entertained by, in Siena theatre, **22.** 232

Canteen; canteens:

for army camp, **37.** 121

Canteloupe. *See* St-Vrain

Cantelupe, Vct. *See* West, George John (1791–1869); West, John (1729–77)

*Canterburies Doome. See under* Prynne, William

Canterbury, Abp of. *See* Abbot, George (1562–1633); Augustine, St, (d. 604); Bancroft, Richard (1544–1610); Becket, Thomas à (ca 1118–70); Bourchier, Thomas (ca 1404–86); Chichele, Henry (ca 1362–1443); Cornwallis, Frederick (1713–83); Courtenay, William (ca 1342–96); Cranmer, Thomas (1489–1556); Deane, Henry (d. 1503); Dunstan (924–88); Fitzalan, Thomas (1353–1414); Herring, Thomas (1693–1757); Hutton, Matthew (1693–1758); Kemp, John (ca 1380–1454); Laud, William (1573–1645); Moore, John (1730–1805); Morton, John (?1420–1500); Parker, Matthew (1504–75) Potter, John (?1674–1747); Robert de Winchilsea (d. 1313); Sancroft, William (1617–93); Secker, Thomas (1693–1768); Sheldon, Gilbert (1598–1677); Stafford, John (d. 1452); Tenison, Thomas (1636–1715); Tillotson, John (1630–94); Wake, William (1657–1737); Warham, William (?1450–1532); Whitgift, John (?1530–1604)

Canterbury, Dean of. *See* Bargrave, Isaac (1586–1643); North, Hon. Brownlow (1741–1820)

Canterbury, John (fl. 1450–70):

builder of King's College, Cambridge, **1.** 18

Canterbury, Kent:

American Revolution injures trade of, **7.** 342

archbishopric of: aspirants to, **39.** 104–5; Blackburne coveted, **15.** 143; Cambridge sizars aspire to, **13.** 59; Cornwallis appointed to, **10.** 265; HW and Hannah More would like to see Porteus in, **31.** 342–3; HW might plead to, about army chaplain, **40.** 91; Herring receives, **18.** 201n; Mann might bid Papal Conclave elect to, **21.** 214; refused by Gibson, **19.** 503; refused by Sherlock, **19.** 511; Secker no longer hopes to get, **20.** 187; Trevor may get, **21.** 185

army camp at, **37.** 476n

assembly and horse race at, **40.** 4

attacked, **7.** 368

Bourne near, **25.** 659

cathedral at, *see* Canterbury Cathedral

Dominican friar of, **2.** 161

Fountain inn at, **7.** 342

France to attack England from Cornwall to, **20.** 535n

HW pleased to have missed military review at, **30.** 20

HW prefers, to Italian cities, **17.** 142

Herne near, **42.** 60

King's Head inn at, **7.** 342, **40.** 3

[Canterbury, Kent, *continued*]

Lee Priory near, **12.** 111, **28.** 8on, **31.** 342

Methodists would not like domination by, **35.** 323–4

Parliamentary representatives instructed by, **23.** 98n

Paul, George, vicar-general of, **21.** 281n

Province of, regulates ecclesiastical costume, **41.** 222–4, 225

regiment quartered at, **40.** 4

singers from, to sing *Miserere*, **18.** 211

St Augustine's Abbey at, **7.** 258, **12.** 109

visitors to: **43.** 75; Bedford, Ds of, and son, **22.** 78n; Berrys, **11.** 374n; Dodd, John, **40.** 3–4; HW, **3.** 349, 353, 354, **7.** 229n, 258, 314, 315, 324, 333, 342, 386; Montagu, **10.** 321, 322; Mount Stuart, **33.** 134n; Whaley, John, **40.** 3–4

woman at, prayed for before marriage, **17.** 142, 162, **37.** 99

Canterbury Cathedral:

American tourists frequent, **7.** 342

Dodd and Whaley visit, **40.** 4

Essex repairs roof of, **2.** 26–7

Farmer to be prebendary of, **2.** 304, 308, **43.**

HW's fondness for, **12.** 105

St Augustine's Abbey affords view of, **12.** 109

SH chimney-pieces imitated from, **12.** 105

Tatton prebendary of, **2.** 304n

tombs at: of Black Prince, **12.** 105; of Henry IV, **7.** 258, **12.** 105; of Queen Joan, **2.** 257n, **7.** 258

whitewashing destroys effect of, **12.** 109

Canterbury Races:

Guilford attends, **10.** 164

*Canterbury Tales, The. See under* Chaucer, Geoffrey

Cantharides (aphrodisiac; 'Spanish fly'):

bawds provide, **30.** 309

Cumberland makes, ingredient of love potion, **2.** 150

Williams, Sir Charles Hanbury, takes, **21.** 183n

Canticles:

Methodists', **20.** 271

Cantillana, Conte di. *See* Baesa e Visentelo, Don Giuseppe

Cantillon, Henrietta (d. 1761), m. 1 (1743) William Matthias Stafford Howard, 3d E. of Stafford; m. 2 (1759) Robert Maxwell, 2d Bn Farnham, cr. (1760) Vct Farnham, (1763) E. of Farnham:

appearance, fortune, and religion of, **18.** 219

Eastbury visited by, **31.** 7n

family of, **18.** 429n

HW hopes, will aid in getting relics of Ninon de Lenclos, **31.** 7

HW mentions, **37.** 418

HW to be visited by, at SH, **37.** 537

husband leaves, in France, **18.** 430

husband to exile, to Shropshire, **9.** 95

London and Paris to be residences of, **18.** 277

marriage of, **18.** 219, 277, **38.** 42

peerage of second husband of, corrected, **43.** 328

pregnant, and changes religion, **38.** 42

Raoul, cat of, **31.** 7

second husband and, presented to Court after marriage, **38.** 42

Cantillon, Richard (1680–1734), Paris banker:

birth date of, **43.** 249

murder of, **18.** 219

Cantillon, Mrs Richard. *See* Mahony, Mary Anne

Canto de' Carnesecchi, Florence:

Giambologna's Hercules at junction of, **22.** 124n

Canton (China):

Anson arrives from, on *Centurion*, **18.** 436n

—— quenches fire at, **9.** 55

—— refuses to pay ships' duties at, **35.** 284n

Inquais Hong at, destroyed by fire, **40.** 45

merchants of, **17.** 277

Townshend, Hon. Augustus, goes to, to trade with Hong merchants, **40.** 45n

viceroy of, neglects Anson, **9.** 55

Cantonment:

English army going into, **37.** 286

preliminary stage of winter quarters, for French army, **37.** 207

Cant's Hall, Bucks:

Gray visits, **13.** 105

Canute, K.:

time of, **39.** 418

Canvas; canvasses:

cases covered with, **26.** 3

early painting on, **42.** 67

HW buys, in Paris for Lady Ossory, **32.** 53

Palais Royal's pictures transferred to new, **39.** 202

petticoat of, **37.** 78, 81

Canynges, William (ca 1399–1474), merchant; mayor of Bristol:

account of donation by, to St Mary Redcliff, **16.** 176

alleged MSS of, **42.** 2–3

appears in Rowley poems, **28.** 281

Chatterton may have changed dates of poems to agree with history of, **16.** 125

chests of: may contain Turgot's history, **16.** 337; six, of MSS, **2.** 289

death of, **16.** 240

Englefield's etching of, **16.** 345

HW alludes to times of, **31.** 219

house of, **16.** 104

Paston letter mentions, **16.** 241n

Rowley said to be advised by, to keep writing secret, **16.** 240

—— said to be employed by, **16.** 114

St Mary Redcliff founded by, **2.** 44, **16.** 102

sepulchre presented by, to St Mary Redcliff, **16.** 133n

William of Worcester mentions, **2.** 104

Cap; caps:

black, worn by jockeys, **31**. 108

brother snatches, from Lady Maria Waldegrave, **36**. 230

courier's, Young Pretender wears, **18**. 377

Cumberland, D. of, makes surgeon change,
during operation, **38**. 456

drunken lady loses, **35**. 306

English, of velvet, worn by Contessa Delci,
**18**. 85

Fox Strangways, Lady Susan, sends footman
back for, **38**. 367

French: round-eared, worn by St-Cyr pensioners, **10**. 293; worn at opera by Q. Caroline, **3**. 142

grenadiers of Young Pretender have inscription on, **19**. 106

high, worn by paraders, **32**. 331

Italian wears, in portrait at Drayton, **10**. 342

large, worn by Q. Caroline and Q. of France,
**35**. 113

Mann's of Bath order, **23**. 57, 59

Montagu, Lady Mary Wortley, does not wear,
**10**. 5

of estate, duke's, **2**. 31

of gold brocade, Bootle wears, at breakfast,
**20**. 184

price of, **31**. 400

queer, worn by Lady George Lennox, **31**. 124n

regulation of, for clergy, **41**. 223

Richard III wears, in portrait, **41**. 132

round-eared **31**. 21

soldiers', **35**. 94

Sophia, Ps, does not want to take off, before
gentlemen, **24**. 297

square: **2**. 351; bishop wears, in play, **9**. 336;
Gray swears he will wear, at Cambridge,
**13**. 59; Middleton wears, **15**. 315; Tesi
wears, **18**. 263

white, running footman wears, at races, **9**.
248

women wear, in shape of chaise-wheels, **20**.
483

*See also* Bavaro

'Capability Brown.' *See* Brown, Lancelot

Caparison:

of purple velvet for Charles I's horse, **32**.
325

Cape; capes:

blue, Bentley wears, in Mall, **9**. 373

ermine, Lichfield Hunt wears, **9**. 289

green, fashionable, **32**. 191n

half-a-dozen, of different colours, sign of
robustness, **30**. 86

high, forbidden at Madrid, **39**. 60

Cape Ann, Mass.:

destruction of, abandoned, **24**. 161n

Cape Breton Island, Nova Scotia:

Belle-Isle's comment on English capture of,
**21**. 123

English capture, **19**. 79, 190, 405, **20**. 23, **21**.
123, 232–3

Florentine ignorance about, **21**. 236

France to regain, by Aix Treaty, **19**. 481

France tries to retain, in peace negotiations,
**21**. 526n

French attempt to recover, thwarted, **19**. 403

French fleet reaches, **35**. 235

French have fleet off of, **21** 130n

*Gloucester* brings letters from, **21**. 230n

Guay ordered to go to rescue of, **20**. 498n

New Englanders may have captured, **20**. 474

Parliamentary debate mentions, **26**. 24

peace to decide fate of, **19**. 255

surrender of, rumoured, **20**. 498

*See also* Louisbourg

Cape Finisterre, France:

Anson and Boscawen quarrel at, **20**. 113

Anson's victory at, **19**. 402–3, 410, **37**. 273

battle of, **9**. 51n

Boscawen severely wounded off, **20**. 113n

Norris, Adm. Sir John, ordered to, **17**. 145n,
194n

Spanish fleet gobbles up English fleets near,
**25**. 78

Cape Henry, Va.:

battle of, **25**. 150n

Capel, Lady Anne (1730–1804):

chatters, **38**. 343

Capel, Lady Catherine. *See* Manners, Lady
Catherine

Capel, Lady Charlotte (1721–90), m. (1752)
Hon. Thomas Villiers, cr. (1756) Bn Hyde,
(1776) E. of Clarendon:

at Mrs Boyle Walsingham's ball, **42**. 222n

chatters, **38**. 343

Conway, Hon. Henrietta Seymour, might
have asked, for Clarendon's *Life*, **38**. 52

Guerchys entertain, at dinner, **38**. 510

uncle's bequest to, **37**. 358

Capel, Lady Diana (1728–1800):

chatters, **38**. 343

Capel, Lady Elizabeth (1755–1834), m. (1777)
John Monson, 3d Bn Monson, 1774:

acts in play at Cassiobury, **32**. 176

Cathcart rumoured to marry, **32**. 176n

rumoured to marry Lord Grimston, **32**. 176–7

Capel, Mary (1630–1715), m. (1657) Henry
Somerset, D. of Beaufort:

father's book given by, to Loutthorpe, **16**.
139

print of, **1**. 181

Capel *or* Capell, Lady Mary (1722–82), m.
(1758) Adm. Hon. John Forbes:

chatters, **38**. 343

HW asked by, to print her ancestor's letters,
**16**. 276

HW identifies, **30**. 326n

HW's *Historic Doubts* displeases, **31**. 138

HW's 'The Beauties' compares, with Ceres,
**30**. 326

social relations of, with: Coke, Lady Mary,
**31**. 138; Guerchys, **38**. 510

Capel, Thomas, jeweller; friend of Chatterton: opinion of, worthless, **16**. 355

Capel, William (1697–1743), 3d E. of Essex:
daughter of, **16**. 276n, **30**. 326n
death of, **18**. 143
denies that he exists, **18**. 137
Gentlemen Pensioners said to be commanded by, **17**. 457
mad from melancholia, **18**. 89
Villettes secretary to, at Turin, **17**. 13n
Walpole, Bns, tells about, **18**. 114

Capel, William Anne Holles (1732–99), 4th E. of Essex:
Bladen, Harriet, to wed, **30**. 241
George III does not retain, in Bedchamber, **9**. 324, **21**. 460
marriage of, **30**. 322
Mastership of Horse to Q. Charlotte coveted by, **23**. 176
pension for, **22**. 570n
Poulett applies for offices of, **43**. 272
(?) Saturday Club and, **43**. 185
to be lord of the Bedchamber, **20**. 470
wife of, **9**. 207n
Williams, Frances Hanbury, to wed, **35**. 177

Capel. *See also* Capell; Keppel

Capel Coningsby (before 1781, Capel), George (1757–1839), styled Vct Malden 1757–99; 5th E. of Essex, 1799:
Boyle, Miss, cousin of, **11**. 238n
—— to be accompanied by, to Italy, **11**. 238
Onslows visit, in Hertfordshire, **31**. 288
SH visited by, **12**. 233

Capel family:
Hardinge, Mrs, descended from, **35**. 610

Capell Arthur (1604–49). cr. (1641) Bn Capell of Hadham:
*Daily Observations* by, **16**. 139, **43**. 218
daughter of, **1**. 181n
*Excellent Contemplations* by, **16**. 139
execution of, **16**. 139
HWs article on, in *Royal and Noble Authors*, **14**. 167

Capell, Arthur (1632–83), 2d Bn Capell, cr. (1661) E. of Essex; conspirator:
father's advice to, **16**. 139
in Stratford's tragedy, **29**. 224
*Letters*, HW urged by Lady Mary Forbes to print, **16**. 276
(?) portrait of, by Mrs Beale, **30**. 370
Wilkes told to copy suicide of, **38**. 202

Capell, Edward (1713–81), Shakespearian scholar:
Dacre patronizes, **35**. 599
Hardinge advises subscription to publish Shakespeare notes of, since booksellers shun him, **35**. 599
Sacchini's *Tamerlane* sent by, for HW's perusal, **39**. 169

Capello, Signora. *See* Colalto, Eleonora (fl. 1742–51), Contessa di

Capello, Pietro Andrea (1702–63), Venetian ambassador to England 1744–8:
Constantinople post coveted by, **20**. 177
Florence to be visited by, **20**. 161–2
house of, in Thrift St, **19**. 134n
Leicester Fields visited by, with P. of Wales, **19**. 134
masquerade given by, **19**. 17–18
Pelham's letters from, **43**. 253
Querini, Cardinal, sent from Venice to Rome to aid, **20**. 190n
Rome left by, **20**. 173
translations of Cts of Pomfret's letters sent to, as instructions, **18**. 558, **19**. 4
Venice's recall of, from Rome, **20**. 161, 176, 177
Walpole, Sir Robert, talks Latin with, at Lady Brown's, **18**. 459
wife comments on age of, **18**. *431*
wife may be poisoned by relatives of, **37**. 289
wife of, **9**. 27n
wife persuades, to delay leaving Rome, **20**. 177n

Capello. *See also* Cappello

Cape Noli:
English ship stationed off, **19**. 236

Cape of Good Hope:
English capture, **12**. 179, **34**. 212
French lose almost all possessions beyond, **21**. 523
from St Petersburg to, French are defeated, **21**. 352
HW jokes about balloon arriving from, **39**. 425

Cape St Vincent:
combined fleet said to have approached, **25**. 173–4, 181
English fleet said to have left Gibraltar for, **25**. 9
Rodney's victory at, **7**. 205n, **25**. 16, 24

'Caperpillar, Mr.' *See* Capper, Francis

'Capet, Monsieur.' *See* Bourbon, Louis-Philippe-Joseph de, Duc d'Orléans

Capet, Hugh (ca 946–96), K. of France:
'guide' a term not used by, **38**. 140
HW considers, usurper, **11**. 76n

Capezzoli, Giovanni Battista (fl. 1755–77), sculptor:
Chute's servant hunts for, **23**. 568–9
HW cannot find, **23**. 562–3
lives with Wilton, **23**. 567
Mann sends letter to, **23**. 560

*Capias utlegatum*:
attorney-general does not take out, for Wilkes, **23**. 12

*Capi d'ordini* (administrative cardinals):
Delle Lanze's dispute with Cardinal York to be settled by, **21**. 207

*Capillaire*:
Hackman drank, **33**. 100

Capital punishment:
Du Deffand, Mme, gives opinion of, **3**. 53

*Capitana Ali Bey*, Turkish ship:
(?) Russians destroy, **23**. 227, 228, 234–5
'Capitano della Piazza de Spagna':
Acquaviva's guard headed by, **19**. 114
Capitation for actors:
*Armide* given as, **7**. 304
Capitol, at Rome:
backstairs compared to steps of, **32**. 371
medal of, **21**. 189, 201
statues in, **20**. 470
Capitolo. *See under* Pisa
Capoccio, John James *and* Vinia, sculptors:
shrine by, sent by Hamilton to HW, **1**. 244, 245, 256, **2**. 221, 370, **35**. 406, 429
Capo Corso, Corsica:
French conquest of, **17**. 46, 53
French frigates at, could capture English merchant ships, **24**. 352, 375, 397
Capoue, Béatrix de, m. (1734) Léopold-Marc, Comte de Ligniville:
Rucellai insulted by criticism by, of his work, **20**. 118
Cappa (ecclesiastical cloak):
York, Cardinal, to wear ermine on, **19**. 415
Cappelli. *See* Capello; Cappello
Cappello, Bianca (1548–87), m. 1 (1563) Pietro Bonaventuri; m. 2 (1578) Francesco I, Grand Duke of Tuscany:
Bronzino's fresco the only authentic portrait of, **20**. 398n
——'s medallion of, **43**. 128
brother-in-law said to have poisoned, **37**. 97n
career of, **20**. 414–15
dies at Poggio a Caiano, **23**. 296
Electress does not permit portrait of, among Medici grand duchesses, **20**. 399, 414–15, **21**. 561
Francesco I's mistress and wife, **21**. 561n
Galluzzi describes, **25**. 193, 214
Gray's Latin account of, **14**. 67–8
Montaigne describes dinner of, with Tuscan ducal family, **24**. 16
name of, corrected, **43**. 128
print of, among Medici heads, shows that Electress is dead, **21**. 561
'Vasari's' portrait of, sent to HW by Mann: **10**. 54, **20**. 398–9, 402–3, 404, 407, 414, **21**. 420, **23**. 315, 425, **24**. 16, **25**. 89, **26**. 56; (?) by Bronzino not Vasari, **43**. 128; HW exhibits, in Arlington St house, **20**. 407; HW places in Round Tower at SH, **21**. 420, **23**. 315; HW to frame, with Latin inscription and grand ducal coronet, **20**. 407; HW used to admire, in Casa Vitelli, **20**. 398, 402, 404; Mann hangs, in his bedchamber, **20**. 398; Montaigne's description agrees with, **24**. 16
Venice makes, daughter of the Republic, **20**. 399, 415
Cappello, Elena, m. Vittorio Cappello:
Montaigne sees, at dinner, **24**. 16
Cappello, Vittorio (b. 1547):
Montaigne sees, at dinner, **24**. 16

Cappello family:
arms of, to adorn Bianca's portrait, **20**. 407, 415
Cappello. *See also* Capello
Capper, Francis (1698–1764), barrister:
Chute and Miss Nicoll at house of, **14**. 56n, 204–5, 208–9, 212
continues as Miss Nicoll's guardian, out of regard for Walpoles, **14**. 216
family of: conduct of, defended by Miss Nicoll, **14**. 218–20; distressed by HW's and Chute's letters, **14**. 226; lampooned in ballad supposedly by HW and Chute, **14**. 227, 228; overhear Chute-Nicoll interview, **14**. 204–5, 208–9, 212
HW calls: booby, **14**. 213–14; 'caperpillar,' **41**. 418; fat-headed, mean, cringing, and dull, **14**. 197–8
HW requests Miss Nicoll to leave house of, **14**. 215
HW reveals to Miss Nicoll the supposed evildoings of, **14**. 210–12
HW's letter to, sent to Horace Walpole, sr, **14**. 221
Nicoll, Miss, kept at house of, **14**. 202–3
—— offered guardianship by, **14**. 199
—— receives permission to visit, **14**. 213
——unfavourably influenced by, **14**. 204, 206, 209
Nuthall comments on HW's letter to, **14**. 224–5
opinion of, in Nicoll affair, **14**. 196, 230–3
Orford, E. of, suggests that Miss Nicoll remain with, **14**. 214
treachery of, **20**. 273
Walpole, Horace (1678–1757), defends, **14**. 57, 224
——employs, as lawyer, **13**. 24
——'s correspondence with, **14**. 218, 221, 228–9
—— suggests that Miss Nicoll live with, **14**. 198
—— writes notes on HW's letter to, **14**. 221–4
Capper, Mrs Francis. *See* Bennet, Mary
Capper, Mary (1738–86), m. (1761) Rev. George Smallridge:
Chute tries to prejudice Miss Nicoll against, **14**. 219–20
Nicoll, Miss, unfavourably influenced by, **14**. 202–3, 208
Nuthall defends conduct of, **14**. 224–5
Capper, Richard (1730–1800) of Lincoln's Inn:
Walpole, Horace, sr, forgets that Miss Nicoll may be endangered by, **14**. 207–8
Capperonnier, Jean (1716–75), keeper of the Bibliothèque du Roi at Paris:
Dutens corresponds with. **41**. 58n
HW's correspondence with, **41**. 57–9, 64
negligent about HW's gift of SH Press imprints, **3**. 262, 263
social relations of, with Mme Geoffrin, **7**. 338
Cappock. *See* Coppock
Capponi, Signora. *See* Corsi, Maria Maddalena

Capponi, Camillo (1713–57):
Mann entertains, at dinner, 18. 17
Capponi, Elisabetta (1714–80), m. (1732) Cavaliere Pietro Grifoni:
Annunziata church attended by, 17. 433
ball at Casa Incontri attended by, 18. 65
beauty of, 17. 435n
Bonducci's dedication to, 17. 64n
brother of, 18. 202
burletta to be attended by, in Mann's box, 17. 121
Carducci attends, 17. 38
Chute hopes to attend, at burletta, 35. 11
—— meets, 35. 8
coach of, 17. 415
concert attended by, 17. 324
Conway has not seen, 37. 318
—— saw little of, and thought her not handsome, 37. 323
country life hated by, 18. 95
English visitors prefer Venuses of the Via del Giardino to, 35. 52
festino given by, 17. 150–1, 169
'Fottera' pronounced by, 18. 545
Galli, Mme, envies, 17. 239
HW asks Anne Pitt if beauty is preserved by, 24. 17
HW calls, 'most charming sight in Florence,' 30. 12
HW condoles with, on sister's loss, 20. 525
HW glad to escape presents from, 18. 366, 527
(?) HW hopes, will visit Reggio fair, 30. 14
HW imagines, in Mann's garden, 18. 497
HW mentions, 17. 42
HW might fall in love with, were she not already engaged, 30. 12
HW praises, at Reggio, 17. 44, 61
HW's 'belle,' 17. 33
HW's correspondence with, 17. 37, 47, 48, 51, 55, 61, 78, 84, 100, 181, 212, 255, 324, 415, 435, 488, 18. 42, 54, 63, 100, 148, 202, 254, 267, 286
HW sends compliments to, 18. 194, 529
HW sends presents to, 17. 152, 156, 181, 193–4, 200, 212, 229, 239, 325, 415, 416
HW's 'fair Geraldine,' 11. 153
HW's love for, 30. 294n
HW's 'Patapan' mentions, 13. 14n, 30. 294–6
HW's separation from, may be endless, 30. 16
HW thinks, is fully 60 years old, 24. 17
HW tired of his affair with, 18. 63, 146, 148
HW to receive compliments of, 17. 381, 18. 545
HW will find it hard to drop correspondence with, 18. 100
health of: fever, 18. 179, 182; miscarriage, 18. 65, 100
house of: Mann leaves letter at, 17. 37; too remote to be serenaded, 18. 485
in the country, 17. 193–4, 200, 202
Mann asked by, about HW, 18. 146, 182

—— borrows fanali from, 17. 499
—— delivers HW's letter to, 17. 37, 324, 415
—— discusses HW with, 17. 61, 121, 155–6, 324–5, 488
—— discusses his cocchiata with, 18. 1
—— escorts Oxenden to, 19. 232
—— exchanges calls with, 17. 121, 229, 239, 316, 415, 18. 65, 146
—— lends opera box to, 17. 69, 121, 151
—— persuaded by, to give conversazioni, 18. 281
—— receives enclosure from, 17. 442
——'s conversation with, after Rinuccini's visit to England, 19. 321–2
—— to ask Anne Pitt about beauty of, 24. 17
——walks in garden with, 17. 100
Mannelli's attentions to, 17. 202, 218, 18. 65, 19. 308, 308n, 322, 358
mask of, 17. 294
'memoirs of the Grifonis' sent to HW by Mary Berry, 11. 179
Modenese princess attended by, at uncle's Leghorn house, 17. 66, 70, 78
Modenese princess gives presents to, 17. 70, 78
Montemar supposed by HW to be pursuing, 18. 62–3
opera attended by, 17. 48, 51, 78, 18. 54
Panciatichi attends, 17. 37
'Patapan' given to HW by, 17. 41n, 30. 296n
Pisa visited by, 17. 33
Pistoia visited by, 17. 100
Pomfret, Cts of, and Cts Granville discuss, with HW, 18. 527
portrait of, by Richter, owned by HW at SH, 11. 154, 17. 33n, 24. 28, 30. 14
pregnant, 18. 95, 405, 19. 232
presents to be sent by, to HW, 18. 348, 366, 527
returns to Florence from villa, 17. 229
Riccardi consoles, 19. 358
San Miniato visited by, 18. 100
serenade attended by, 17. 97
sister of, 17. 33, 19. 308n, 20. 350, 520
sister's childbed left by, for Mann's party, 17. 499
social relations of, with: Craon, Mme de, 17. 416; Delci, 18. 459; Goldsworthy, Mrs, 17. 316; Grimaldi, Mme, 17. 151; HW, 18. 459; Mann, 17. 95, 121, 151, 169, 229, 239, 415, 483, 499, 18. 12, 65; Nigroni, Mme, 17. 151
Surrey's sonnets applied to, by HW, 18. 497
uncle's death would keep, from Mann's party, 18. 289
Vitelli, Mme, quarrels with, 17. 37–8
Capponi, Elisabetta (1729–1800), m. (1747) Cosimo Pasquali:
marriage of, planned, 19. 438
Capponi, Ferrante (1682–1752), Conte:
Mann and Veers entertained by, 19. 506
Capponi, Gino Pasquale (1716–81), Col.; 'Gigi':
cup-bearer at Grand Ducal dinner, 22. 379n

duel fought by, with Lorraine officer, **18.** 182, 202

Francis I to be informed by, **35.** 23

(?) HW's favourite, **17.** *112*

(?) piles feared by, **17.** 112

Pisa to be visited by, with troops, **18.** 85

regiment of, **17.** 156, 198, 214, 266, 288, **18.** 100n

Regency's protests against passage of troops renewed by, **17.** 341n

Riccardi discusses Leghorn earthquake with, **17.** 305

Riccardi, Mme, regains, after his marriage, **20.** 95

soldiers' riot not calmed by, **24.** 8n

Tuscany sends, to remonstrate with Montemar, **35.** 22–3

Capponi, Marchese Giuliano Gaspero (1667–1745), governor of Leghorn:

horses of, **17.** 260

Leghorn earthquake does not alarm, **17.** 305

Mann meets, at Braitwitz's **17.** 260

Modenese princess gives cane and snuff-box to, **17.** 70

Modenese princess visits, **17.** *66*, 70, 78

Capponi, Maria Laura (1726–77), m. (1744) Marchese Luigi Tempi:

father-in-law likes, more than husband does, **18.** 438–9

marriage of, **18.** 435, 438–9

Capponi, Maria Settimia (1728–82), m. (1748) Marchese Luca Torreggiani:

marriage of, **19.** 506

Capponi, Abate Ranieri Federigo (1705–43):

death of, **18.** 149

Pandolfini lives with, **18.** 149–50

(?) serenade managed by, **17.** *105*

Capponi, Teresa Maria (1715–55), m. (1734) Senator Vincenzo Antinori:

Braitwitz's courtship of Mme Vitelli described by, to Mann, **18.** 333

Conway prefers, to her sister, **37.** 323

daughter born to, **18.** 405–6

death of, **20.** 520–1, 525

English cocchiata serenades, **18.** 485

fat, **17.** 156

foreign lady visits, **20.** 191

HW sends thanks to, **17.** 45

HW to receive compliments of, **17.** 37, 381

Mann admires, **20.** 525n

—— called cicisbeo of, **19.** 308

—— calls on, **18.** 333

—— denies being cicisbeo to, **19.** 322

—— discusses HW with, **17.** 33

—— gives garden assembly for, **20.** 191

—— persuaded by, to give *conversazioni*, **18.** 281

——'s devotion to Mrs Barrett noticed by, **20.** 105

——'s relations with, **17.** 33n

——'s women guests to be secretly invited by, **20.** 369

—— takes, to Artimino to dine with Mme de Craon, **19.** 145

Montemar writes to, **18.** 46, 62–3

nephew's death grieves, **20.** 520–1

pregnancy of, **18.** 333

Serristori cicisbeo to, **17.** 381, **19.** 322

—— regained by, after his marriage, **20.** 95

social relations of, with: Eszterházys, **20.** 350; Feroni, Mme, **17.** *33*; Mann, **17.** 95, **18.** 333, **19.** 411, **20.** 191; Riccardi, **19.** 411

uncle's death would keep, from Mann's party, **18.** 289

Capponi family:

Carteret's wedding too simple for, **18.** 445

Capra, Villa del. *See* Vicenza: Villa Rotonda at

Capraiola. *See* Caprarola

Capraja, Corsica:

Corsican rebels capture, **22.** 527

Caprara, Conte; general. *See* Silvio, Enea (1631–1701)

Caprara, Marchese di. *See* Frescobaldi, Francesco

Caprara, Count, gonfaloniere at Bologna:

gallery of, described by HW, **13.** 194

HW and Gray see, **13.** 193

Caprara, Cornelio (1703–65), cardinal, 1761; governor of Rome, 1756:

as vice-chamberlain and gov. of Rome, signs book-burning edict, **21.** 477n

Clement XIII does not make, cardinal, because of gallantry with women, **21.** 333–4

Caprara, Corsica:

French may capture, from Paoli, **23.** 46

Caprarola, Italy:

Acquaviva's palace at, **17.** 389, **18.** 377

books of, see *Illustri fatti Farnesiani*

paintings in palace of, **25.** 403n

Young Pretender takes road to, **18.** 377, 388

*Capricious Lady, The. See under* Cooke, William

*Capricious Lovers, The. See under* Lloyd, Robert

Captain; captains:

Algiers visits described by, to Mann, **25.** 416

Austrian, allows French to lead prisoners through English outpost, **37.** 207

Clive's, at Florence, **21.** 279

English naval, in Italy: advise Mathews to buy Mann's coffee pot, **18.** 472; Albani and Thun dine with, **19.** 12; cannon thrown by, from Spanish ship, **18.** 406; Charles III addressed by, in English, **18.** 461; Charles III detests, **18.** 123; Civita Vecchia to be guarded by, **18.** 287–8, 296, 300; dances at 60, **18.** 78; Du Châtelet entertains, **18.** 77–8, 98, 100; Genoa said to have bribed, **19.** 120; Goldsworthy incites, **18.** 38; in India, **21.** 296, 303; Mann pleases Mathews by remonstrances for, **18.** 309; Mann's restraint of Martin irritates, **18.** 100; Mann wants to dismiss, from Leghorn, **18.** 38; prizes preferred by, to capture of artillery, **19.** 100; Susa gives ball and dinner for, **18.**

386 INDEX

[Captain; captains, *continued*]
360; tricolour cockades worn by, **18.** 336, 544; *see also under* Leghorn: English captains at

English naval, in England: letters concerning court martial printed by, **40.** 235; seek half-pay increase, **23.** 462; Vernon revered by, **18.** 151; vessels seized by, regardless of plague, **18.** 256

French, to blame for Quiberon Bay disaster, **21.** 356–7, 359

imprisoned at Algiers, **22.** 586

lodges with Bosvilles, **18.** 251

of Dutch smacks, **38.** 2

of *Great Duchess of Tuscany*, *see* Blackett, William

packet-boat, has affair with Lady Ligonier, **30.** 255

Swedish, at Leghorn, *see* Fleetrood

Tuscan, Tuscany disavows action of, to Genoa, **18.** 262–3

*Captain, The,* English ship:
Martinique ships captured by, **19.** 487n

Captain-general:
George III appoints D. of Cumberland as, **22.** 302, **38.** 562

Grenville ministry wants Granby to be, instead of D. of Cumberland, **22.** 302, **38.** 564–5

Captain of the horse:
Frederick II gives Giustiniani patent as, **22.** 465

Captain of the Pensioners. *See under* Yeomen of the Guard

Captain Pacha, at Constantinople. *See* Hasan Bey

Capua, Abbess of:
Maria Amalia dines with, weekly, **20.** 429

Capua, Italy:
English Opposition will not loiter in, **25.** 27

'Hannibal' not at, **22.** 211

Santa Maria and San Giovanni convents at, **20.** 429n

Capuccino (artist):
'Goliath' by, in Pierson's sale, **23.** 570n

'Capuche':
Craon, Princesse de, wears, **18.** 109

*Capuchin, The. See under* Williams, Sir Charles Hanbury

Capuchin; Capuchins:
abbés will stink like, if adhering to Pius VI's edicts, **24.** 107

Bussy's stories about, **18.** 131

church of, in Paris: HW visits, **7.** 281; Place Vendôme in vista from gate of, **7.** 282; Pompadour, Mme de, said to observe jubilee at, **20.** 236, 530n

convent of, at Girgenti, **35.** 409

Craon, Princesse de, resembles, **18.** 109

general of, *see* Barberini, Bonaventura

HW jokes about Delaval as joining, **35.** 288

HW to look for print of Joyeuse as, for Selwyn, **30.** 217

Jesuit churches taken over by, **23.** 507

Mann thinks, would be of more use in the world than nuns, **25.** 239

relics displayed by, at Radicofani, **37.** 67

submissive always, **8.** 177

Superior of, cuts his throat, **3.** 50

Wachtendonck's death-bed piety gratifies, **17.** 110, 117

Capuchin nuns:
Austrian convents of, suppressed, **25.** 236n

Capucines, Rue des, Paris:
Capucines' church in, **7.** 281n

chapel in church in, decorated in honour of Mme de Pompadour, **20.** 236n

Capusettin von Chapuset. *See* Chapuset

*Caput mortuum:*
Sluys can yield nothing but, **38.** 9

Carabinier; carabiniers:
French: HW glad, are cashiered, **23.** 323; regiment of, destroyed, **18.** 154; suppressed, **39.** 150

Caracalla (Marcus Aurelius Antoninus Bassianus, 188–217), Roman emperor 211–17:
bust of, **13.** 232, **15.** 12, **26.** 7

*Itinerarium* from reign of, **2.** 204n

Caracalla, Baths of, at Rome:
HW's marble eagle found near, **19.** 66n

Caracca:
ship of: captured, **17.** 276; HW would not let England take, **37.** 166

Caracci. *See* Carracci

Caraccioli, Louis-Antoine de (1719–1803), Marquis:
*Lettres intéressantes du Pape Clément XIV*, probably spurious, **31.** 278, **35.** 394

*Vie du Pape Clément XIV*, (?) owned by Mme du Deffand, **8.** 35n, **43.** 93

Caraccioli. *See also* Caracciolo

Caracciolo, Carlo Maria (1764–1823), Duca di San Teodoro:
(?) to be educated in Paris, **6.** 30

Caracciolo, Carmine Nicolò (1671–1726), Principe di Santo Buono, 1694:
Spanish governor in the West Indies, **17.** 7

Caracciolo, Domenico (1715–89), Marchese Caracciolo; Neapolitan ambassador to England 1764–71, to France 1771–81; viceroy of Sicily; secretary of state:
Aiguillon supported by, against the Church, **5.** 213–14

Alembert admired by, **5.** 211, **6.** 288

American news told by, **6.** 470

Beauvau wants to rent house to, **5.** 140

Beauvau, Princesse de, admired by, **5.** 232, 311, 381, 432, **6.** 218, 288

——'s relations with, **6.** 288

birth date of, corrected, **43.** 92, 283

Chanteloup visited by, **7.** 427

chapel of, **10.** 216

Coke, Lady Mary, to receive gown from Paris through, **38.** 252, 261

Conway and all Englishmen said by, to get drunk daily, **6.** 350

Du Barry, Mme, avoided by, **5.** 110, **23.** 338
Du Deffand, Mme, attends rehearsal of *Roland* with, **7.** 9
—— has at her chaise longue, **39.** 271
—— has not told, of HW's remark on Contessa di Viry, **5.** 424
—— prefers Stormont to, **6.** 68
——'s opinion of, **5.** 97, 108, 117, 138, 158, 184, 211, 231–2, 311, 381, 405, **6.** 30–1, 82, 200, 238, 288
——'s relations with, **5.** 432
—— suffers from aphasia while talking with, **5.** 208
Frederick II to be seen by, **6.** 30
French declaration opposed by, **23.** 399
health of, **5.** 311, 381, **6.** 350
Hume compared to, **6.** 22
Lespinasse, Mlle de, admired by, **6.** 288
Louis XV cordial to, **5.** 405
musicale given by, **6.** 445
Naples visited by, **6.** 22, 30, 68, 82
nephew to return with, **6.** 30
Piccinni aided by, **7.** 9, 19
popularity of, **6.** 22
returns to Paris, **6.** 200
Shelburne friend of, **5.** 145, 153
social relations of, in Paris, *see index entries ante* **8.** 279
thinks peace likely, **7.** 139
Thomas's *Essai sur les éloges* delights, **5.** 357–8
Tonton likes, **6.** 447
to return to Paris, **6.** 195
Turgot admired by, **6.** 314
viceroy of Sicily, **7.** 452
Voltaire's epistle admired by, **5.** 339–40
——'s work brought to party by, **5.** 323
Caracciolo, Gennaro Maria (1720–66), Duca di Girifalco (*or* Cirifalco):
dies in prison in Naples, **35.** 434
wife never accuses, **35.** 434
Caracciolo, Marino (1696–1745), Principe di Santo Buono, 1726:
Vernon's success not believed by, **17.** 7
Caracciolo, Martino Innico (d. 1754), titular Abp of Chalcedon, nuncio at Venice:
Venice to eject, **20.** 161, 173, 176
Caractacus (fl. A.D. 50), K. of the Britons:
Ossory, Lord, called, **33.** 49
*Caractacus. See under* Mason, William
Caradeuc de la Chalotais, Aimé-Jean-Raoul de (1733–94):
imprisoned in Château de Taureau, **11.** 44
omitted from Breton parliament, **4.** 259
(?) request for, **3.** 301n
reversion of procureur-général's place offered to, **23.** 207
Caradeuc de la Chalotais, Louis-René de (1701–85), procureur-général of the parliament of Rennes:
Aiguillon restores pension and arrears of, **39.** 144

——'s clash with, **3.** 65n, 109n, 118, **4.** 433n, **11.** 43, **23.** 206
arrest of, **7.** 285, **14.** 149n, **30.** 206n
Calonne's clash with, **3.** 151, 153, 163, **11.** 43–4, **36.** 249
Choiseul saves, from scaffold, **11.** 44
Duclos brings offers to, but they are rejected, **23.** 207
HW describes, **7.** 378, **11.** 43
imprisoned: in Bastille, **3.** 188, 190, **7.** 273; in Château du Taureau, **11.** 44
intended trial of, by commission, attacked by parliament of Paris, **30.** 206
Jesuits opposed by, **11.** 43
letter allegedly by, found, **7.** 273
Louis XV suppresses plea made by, **8.** 174
—— tries, at Versailles, **23.** 206
Mann hopes that persecution of, is over, **24.** 10
Marie-Antoinette and others ask Louis XVI for release of, **24.** 10n
mémoires of, **3.** *109*, 112, 128, 131, 151, 224, 301, 429
Ogier a friend of, **3.** 370n
omitted from Breton parliament, **4.** 259
Pitt's alleged correspondence with, gets him accused of treason, **30.** 216, **39.** 33
procureur-général of parliament of Rennes, **11.** 43
restored in 1774 to position, **11.** 44
Romans, Mlle de, said to have letter from, **7.** 371
trial of, **3.** 188, 200, 212
true patriot and martyr, **11.** 28
Voltaire's letter to, **11.** 28
Caradoc:
Gray's odes mention, **40.** 102, 105
Carafa, ——, m. (1758) Giovanni Battista Albertini, Principe di San Severino:
(?) letter to, **21.** 331
Carafa, Marzio Domenico (1758–1829), Duca di Matalona:
inscription on villa of, **35.** 427
Carafa, Pompeio (b. 1736), Duca di Noia:
(?) letter from, **21.** 331
Carafa. *See also* Caraffa
Carafe; carafes:
for liqueurs, bought by Mme du Deffand through HW, **4.** 146, 172, 177n
Mann measures wine by, **17.** 78
Skrine serves burgundy in, **20.** 145
Caraffa, Pier Luigi (1677–1755), cardinal, 1728:
Louis XV wants French candidate elected by, **17.** 20–1
Caraffa di Traietto, Francesco (1722–1818), cardinal:
congregation on Jesuits includes, **23.** 507n
Caraman, Abbé de. *See* Riquet de Caraman, Jean-Louis de
Caraman, Comte de. *See* Riquet, Victor-Maurice de (1727–1807); Riquet de Caraman, Maurice-Gabriel-Joseph de (1765–1835)

Caraman, Comtesse de. *See* Alsace-Hénin-Liétard, Marie-Anne-Gabrielle-Josèphe-Françoise-Xavière d'

Caraman, Duc de. *See* Riquet de Caraman, Victor-Louis-Charles de

'Caraman, Mme.' *See* Maupeou, Marie-Catherine-Charlotte de

'Caraman the elder.' *See* Riquet, Jean-Gabriel-Amable-Alexandre de

Caraman, Hôtel de, at Paris:
HW visits, **7.** 348

Caramanico, Principe di. *See* Aquino, Francesco d'

Caramel:
Jacob's, **29.** 353

Carausius (d. 293), Roman emperor:
Kennedy, Dr, has coins of, **18.** 347n

Caravaggio, Michelangelo Merisi (1573–1610), painter:
painting by, of Lot and his daughters, **10.** 334
paintings by, in Colebrook's sale, **23.** 569n

Caravan; caravans:
English, captured by Arabs, **24.** 510
Raynal discusses, **39.** 168

Caravol. *See* Carvalho

Carbery ('Carberry'), Bns. *See* Fitzwilliam, Hon. Frances

Carbine:
HW carries, to pursue burglars, **9.** 133

Carbon, ——, Ensign,
captured at Velletri, **18.** 492

Carbonali, Cosimo. Florentine servant:
Mann's annuity to, **25.** 667n

'Carbonari, island of':
Chute and Whithed's name for Newcastle and its mines, **19.** 143

Carbonelli, Alfonse, Capt.:
captured at Velletri, **18.** 493

Carbonnel, Charles-Éléonor-Hervé de (1729–1814), Marquis de Canisy:
marriage of, **4.** 242n
not made brigadier, **4.** 382

Carbonnel de Canisy, Marie-Françoise-Renée de (1725–ca 1796), m. 1 (1737) Antoine-François de Pardaillan de Gondrin, Marquis d'Antin; m. 2 (1742) Louis-Bufile de Brancas, Comte de Forcalquier; 'la belle Comtesse'; 'la Bellissima':
accident to Mme du Deffand and, **3.** 55–6, 61
account of Jacqueline and Jeanneton sent to, **3.** 351, 362, 364, 373
admitted to royal 'voyages,' **5.** 322, 330
Aiguillon, Duc d', friend of, **3.** 65n, **4.** 197
always tuning but never playing on her wit, **3.** 65
apologia of old age by, **3.** 10
Artois, Comtesse d', attended by, **5.** 337, 342, 347, 357, 359, 363–4, 412, **6.** 18–19, 54, 57, 60, 66
Boufflers, Mme de, ridiculed by, **3.** 50
—— will steal, from Mme du Deffand, **3.** 329

Boulogne house of, **3.** 155, **4.** 267, 270, **7.** 326, 331
Bourbon-Busset may be aided by, **5.** 349
——'s bride aided by, **5.** 347, 349
——'s bride close friend of, **4.** 242, 246, 305, **5.** 347
(?) Broglie, Comte de, hopes to make use of, **4.** 340
Canisy, Mme de, exchanges visits with, **4.** , 242, 245
*caput mortuum* of HW and Mme de Choiseul, **3.** 112
Choiseul, Duchesse de, pleases, **3.** 356
Cholmondeley, Mrs, coolly treated by, **4.** 238, 240–1, 284, 306
Comédie attended by, **3.** 237, **4.** 115–16
Comédie-Française box shared by Mme du Deffand and, **4.** 62, 73, 81n
Conti's friendship with, **3.** 229, 237
cousin of, **4.** 242n
Dampierre forced to translate English verses for, **7.** 296
Darget inspires, **4.** 307
Du Barry, Comtesse, friendly with, **4.** 191, **5.** 322
Du Deffand, Mme, mentions, **3.** 319, **4.** 139, 208, **5.** 363
—— receives paper cut-outs with verses from, **4.** 19–20
——'s correspondence with, **4.** 254
——'s opinion of, **3.** 9, 47–8, 65, 67, 112, 114, 124, 127, 139, 146, 155, 156, 182, 281, 356, 369, **4.** 16, 34, 72n, 83, 94, 124, 197, 242, 246, 247, 256, 299, 305, **5.** 330–1, 349
——'s quarrel and break with, **4.** 382–3, 388–9, 390–1, 393, 394, 395, 399, **5.** 368
——'s relations with, **3.** 55, 60, 67, 92, 112, 139, 319, 337, 356, **4.** 11, 16, 124, 203, 245, 251, 284, 287, 306, 310, 382–3, 388–9, 390–1, 394, 395, **5.** 349, **41.** 4, 162
—— suggests, as author of 'Sévigné' letter, **3.** 70
——'s verses on, **4.** 20, 302, 308, 310
—— to copy letter from HW for, **4.** 155
—— to tell, about HW and Voltaire, **4.** 97
Dupin, Mme, friend of, **3.** 10, 47, 65, 67, 369, **4.** 280–1
English understood by, **7.** 261, **31.** 97, **41.** 40
first husband of, **3.** 112n
Foire Ste-Ovide visited by, **7.** 319
Fontainebleau visited by, **3.** 351, 354, 356
Grave tells, that Mme du Deffand approves of her conduct, **5.** 349
HW called 'Robert' by, **4.** 77
HW gets condolences from, on Lady Suffolk's death, **41.** 93–4
HW gives vase to, **3.** 102
HW has sympathy of, at Bns Hervey's, **4.** 142
HW mentions, **3.** 342
HW's arrival awaited by, **3.** 339

HW's correspondence with, **3.** 47, 48, 50, 77, 86n, 114, 126–7, 135, 136, 151, 170, 171, 362, **4.** 77, 106, 115, 124, 132–3, 286, **7.** 381–3, 386, **41.** 33–5, 40–2, 93–4, 161–3

HW sees, at Mme du Deffand's, **39.** 13

HW sends compliments to, **4.** 68, 73, 77

HW's gifts of portrait arouse jealousy of, **3.** 402

HW shown Sévigné portrait by, **3.** 70, 73

HW's *'mie triste,'* **3.** 53

HW's opinion of, **5.** 348, 359

HW spoken of by, **3.** 391

HW's portrait desired by, **4.** 115

HW's relations with, **3.** 25, 36, 53, 67, 82, 148, 154–5, 233, 259, 315, 337

HW's verses about, **31.** 96

HW tells, to teach English to Mme du Deffand, **41.** 34

HW to give *Fugitive Pieces* to, **7.** 416

HW to regard, as old window-pane at SH, **41.** 94

HW to send *Anecdotes of Painting* to, **7.** 415

Hénault says that Choiseul would have treated, better than Praslin did, **8.** 122

——'s portrait painted by, and accompanied by verses, **3.** 66–7

*Historic Doubts* pleases, **4.** 34

Holland, Bns, acquaintance of, **4.** 292

illumination for Poix wedding seen by, **7.** 319

Irwin admired by, **4.** 94, 133

—— introduced to Mme du Deffand by, **4.** 93

—— likes, **4.** 232–3, 242

Jacqueline's and Jeanneton's installation attended by, **7.** 321

*Joueur, Le,* not attended by, **4.** 75

Lamballe wedding attended by, **3.** 229

Lesrocs attended by, **7.** 321

letter from HW to Mme du Deffand read to, **3.** 86

Luxembourg, Mme de, attentive to, **3.** 229

marriages of, **3.** 92n

Meinières, Mme de, influenced by, **4.** 11

mother-in-law tended by, **41.** 34–5

Normandy visited by, **4.** 242, 245

Palais-Royal attended by, **4.** 224

Penthièvre visited by, **4.** 68

Rambouillet visited by, **4.** 207

relatives of: ill, **3.** 112, 114, 118; in England, **41.** 94

resigns as Comtesse d'Artois's attendant, **6.** 60

Rochford's relations with, **3.** 303, 309, 311, 315, 337, 402, **4.** 94

Rochford, Cts of, corresponds with, **3.** 333

——'s relations with, **3.** 303, 309, 311, 315, 333, 337, 392, **4.** 207, 211, 231–2

Rueil visited by, **4.** 130

social relations of, in Paris, *see ante* **8.** 281

social success of, **3.** 229

Stormont attentive to, **4.** 348

to return to Paris, **4.** 256, 265

Toulouse, Comtesse de, cared for by, **3.** 114, 118, 124, 136, 146

—— visited by, **3.** 92, 99, 102

translates HW's inscription for Benedict XIV, **3.** 114–15

translates Mrs Elliot's letter to Mme du Deffand, **3.** 41

verses by, **3.** 66–7, 76, **4.** 19–20, 291, 305, 306–7, 310, **8.** 158

verses on tonneau attributed to, by Mme du Deffand, **4.** 289–91

very handsome, **14.** 144

Walpole, Edward, attentive to, **3.** 303

Walpole, Hon. Robert, corresponds with, **4.** 224, 231–2

——'s relations with, **4.** 182–3, 184, 221, 240–1, 245

writes obscurely, **4.** 207

Carbuncular state of blood:
occurrences of, **20.** 413

Carburi, Jean-Baptiste (d. 1789), Comte de:
Boucher's collection visited by, **7.** 304
social relations of, with HW, **7.** 303

*Carcass,* English ship:
involved in Mediterranean war, **19.** 352

Carcassone, Bp of. *See* Chastenet, Jean-Auguste de

Card; cards, burial. *See* Burial card

Card; cards, calling:
Bute's, labelled Mr Stuart,' **23.** 103
Clive, Mrs, enjoys, **36.** 54
Florentine ladies leave, on Charlotte Stuart, **25.** 535
Garrick, Mrs, and Mrs Montagu leave, for HW, **42.** 83
Hardinges leave, on Lady Diana Beauclerk, **35.** 631
Sulkowsky's, give his titles, **33.** 280

Card; cards, correspondence:
Lodomie tears and returns Lady Caroline Petersham's, **37.** 354
inquiries preferable to, when one is stricken, **36.** 153
Ireland's, to HW, requesting SH ticket, **42.** 175
Queensberry, Ds of, writes, to Ds of Newcastle, **37.** 436–7
*See also* Card; cards, message

Card; cards, drawing:
bistre will not take well on, **41.** 322

Card; cards, invitation:
Ailesbury, Cts of, sends, to HW, **37.** 525
—— wants copper plate for, **37.** 523, 525
HW misreads, **35.** 455
HW receives, from D. of York, **38.** 475
HW's servant to deliver, **31.** 406
Holman, Mrs, might send, for her assembly, **35.** 196
invitations to ball and excuses to those not invited, **39.** 450
Lincoln, Cts of, sends, for her assembly, **37.** 454
Petersham, Lady Caroline, sends, to exclude guests, **35.** 223

[Card; cards, invitation, *continued*]

Queensberry, Ds of, sends, for her ball, **38.** 342

sent only to women, **18.** 562

to assemblies, **9.** 238

whist invitations made by, **30.** 30

Card; cards, message:

George II's messages to Parliament answered by, **35.** 216

HW does not receive, to inquire about 'pain in his voice,' **30.** 86

Jewesses send, to Q. Charlotte, **22.** 72

mock, sent to Lady Susan Keck, to inquire for her palsy, **30.** 54

of Bubb Dodington, **9.** 344

of Diana Bertie, **9.** 29

Orford, Cts of, sends, to Margaret Banks, **19.** 234

Queensberry, Ds of, sends, to Lyttelton, about ball invitation, **20.** 226

Sudbury mob sends, to Bury mob, **35.** 196

*See also* Card; cards, correspondence

Card; cards, playing:

at Siena assembly, for D. of York, **22.** 224

Berrys not interested in, **11.** 267

Buccleuchs invite Montagu to play, **10.** 268

Burghley and friends play, **41.** 298n

Clive, Mrs, absorbed in, **35.** 456, 463, 464

—— dreads *vole* in, **35.** 456

'clubs and diamonds' played by HW and Montagu, **9.** 164

Coke, Lady Mary, plays, at Mann's in Florence, **23.** 543, **31.** 176

Conway and Frenchmen play, at Bruges, **38.** 4

Conway and officers play, at Sluys, **38.** 4

country ladies stock up with, after session, **18.** 498

Craon, Casa, draws guests who merely want to use, **19.** 477

Craons play, **17.** 178, 259, 463, **18.** 348, **24.** 23

Delorain, Cts of, plays, **18.** 71

Edgcumbe talks to, **30.** 37

English captains play, at Mann's, **18.** 98

English noblewoman resents inferiors playing ahead of her, **20.** 352

foretelling by, **4.** 201

Frederick, P. of Wales's outer room scene of, **20.** 232

French play, before and after supper, **38.** 238

George II watches game of, at time of son's death, **20.** 233

George III plays, with wife and daughters, **25.** 682–3

Grafton, Ds of, plays, **22.** 17

HW and Conway to play, **37.** 86

HW calls war a game at, **39.** 463

HW compares politics to, **20.** 503

HW defends playing of, on Sundays, **31.** 436–7

HW does not care a straw for, **34.** 25

HW fears he must exchange his occupations for, **21.** 139

HW has minchiate and tarocco, at SH, **17.** 193n

HW never asked to touch, at Paris, **39.** 12

HW plays, at Mrs Clive's, **35.** 96, 524

Hertford entertains Seilerns at party for, **32.** 19n

Hodges, Mrs, borrows pack of, **34.** 94

incessant, at The Hague, **37.** 150

Leghorn custom house impounds French, purchased by Mann, **20.** 146n

Lorenzi, Comtesse, always notices the king in, **20.** 276

Methodists do not play, on Sunday, **20.** 34

ministry could burn, at Smithfield, **37.** 445

Mirepoix, Mme de, addicted to, **39.** 212

Northumberland, Cts of, invites HW to play, **40.** 153, 237, 246

not played at Twickenham on Sundays, **34.** 25

old women will turn to art instead of, **35.** 390

played: **17.** 25, 194, 416–17, **18.** 82, 98; at Mann's *conversazione*, **20.** 427; at Massereene's ball, **30.** 211; at Twickenham, **10.** 259; in evenings, at the Vyne, **35.** 185; in Parlour, at SH, **31.** 406; in side rooms at Pisa ball, **25.** 581

royal proclamation forbids, on Sundays, **34.** 25n

Sarrazin, Mme, impatient to play, **19.** 161

satiric: sent by HW to Strafford, **35.** 280; *see also under* Print; prints, satiric

Skrine's losses at, **36.** 210n

Stair's party for, **37.** 149

tax on, **37.** 445

time annihilated by, **31.** 264

Tutet's, lack aces, **15.** 195

Wright murdered in game of, at Florence, **37.** 33n

*See also* Bambera; Basset; Berlan; Bilboquet; Biribis; Brag; Card-sharper; Card-table; Cavagnole; Cribbage; Comet; Faro; Hazard; Lansquenet; Loo; Loto; Macao; Minchiate; Momo; Ombre; Piquet; Quadrille; Quinze; Taroc; Trente et quarante; Tre-sept; Vingt-et-un; Whist

*See also under* Game; Gambling; Gaming

Cardano, Geronimo (1501–76), Italian physician, mathematician and astrologer:

HW uses name of, as pseudonym, **31.** 432

Card assembly. *See* Assembly

Cárdenas, Don Alonso, Spanish ambassador to England 1638–55:

pictures bought by, in England, **16.** 154–5

tapestries bought by, **16.** 147n

Carder, Mrs, Cts of Orford's 'woman':

Cowper's children to be accompanied by, to England, **25.** 151

informed of things Cts of Orford brought from England, **25.** 151, 169

letter from, tells of Orford's reproving Lucas, **25.** 181

Mozzi advised by, not to accept compromise, **25**. 419

—— sends papers to England by, **25**. 161, 163

——'s letter from, **25**. 168

—— to pay, **25**. 512

—— urged by, to come to England, **25**. 435

Orford's opinion of Mozzi improved by, **25**. 168

Orford, Cts of, brings, from England, **25**. 151, 169

—— makes wretched provision for, in will, **25**. *122*

Card games. *See under* Game, *and under their own names*

Cardiff, Bn. *See* Stuart, John (1744–1814)

Cardigan, Cts of. *See* Montagu, Lady Mary (ca 1711–75); Waldegrave, Lady Elizabeth (1758–1823)

Cardigan, E. of. *See* Brudenell, George (d. 1732); Brudenell, George (1712–90); Brudenell, Hon. James (1725–1811); Brudenell, Robert (1769–1837)

Cardigan, Wales:

Hardinge's address, **35**. 576

Cardigan House, Richmond Hill:

Cardigans owned, but did not live in it, **31**. 2n

Cardigan's Head, bagnio at Charing Cross, London:

bunters from, **38**. 206

Cardinal (costume). *See* Andrienne

Cardinal Dean. *See* Cavalchini, Carlo Alberto

Cardinal Legate of Bologna. *See* Doria, Giorgio

Cardinals, College of:

bandits' extermination by, **17**. 29n

Benedict XIV expected to fill vacancies in, **18**. 288

*capi d'ordini* in, **21**. 207n

Clement XIII may fill vacancies in, **21**. 304

Clement XIV reproached by, for want of confidence in them, **23**. 214–15

Conclave anxieties keep, from supporting Young Pretender, **22**. 387

Francis I should complain to, about Benedict XIV, **19**. 114

in Conclave: cross and obstinate, **37**. 66; HW could write about, **37**. 49, 53; *see also under* Conclave

Louis XV asks, to await his cardinals, **21**. 207

mass for destruction of Polish dissidents attended by, **22**. 577

Old Pretender nominates Luynes to, **20**. 464

Pius VI has D. and Ds of Gloucester courteously treated by, **24**. 174

summons to, **40**. 58

vacancies in: **18**. 150; will bring promotion to the *Corone*, **20**. 464

York, Cardinal, reveals Albani's letter to, **22**. 389

'Cardinal's Necklace':

discussion of affair of, spoils conversation, **31**. 242

*Cardinal Tencin's Plan*:

Cooper publishes, **18**. 379n

Cardini, Giuseppe, Worsley's servant; Mann's messenger:

dispatches carried by, to England, **25**. 180, 313, 323

HW assured by, in letter, of Mann's good health, **25**. 312

HW's correspondence with, **42**. 36–7

HW sends letter to Mann by, **25**. 185, 192, 309, 323

HW's past letters to Mann taken back to HW by, **22**. 477, 483, 490, **26**. 36

HW to reach, at Badiote's, **25**. 309n, **42**. 37

Kennicott may receive from, collation of MSS, **22**. 477n

Mann sends letters to HW by, **25**. 178, 179, 180, 188, 305, 306, 309, 315

may be frequent carrier of letters from Mann, **25**. 192

Cardon, Antoine (1739–1822), engraver:

Hamilton employs, **35**. 429n

Cardonnel. *See* De Cardonnel

Card-playing:

universal in Paris, **13**. 162

Cardross, Lord. *See* Erskine, David Steuart

Card sharpers:

Lincoln cheated by, **23**. 378

Card table; card tables:

Amelia's, HW hears news at, **25**. 368

at Cts of Berkeley's, **31**. 79

coat of arms symbolizes, **9**. 186

japan, at Burghley House, **10**. 346

Northesk sits by, **35**. 373

Carducci, Signora. *See* Suares de la Concha, Maria Vittoria

Carducci, Pierfrancesco (1715–60):

finances of, **18**. 526

marriage of, **19**. 145

St John cannot get payment from, **19**. 84

Suares de la Concha, Maria Vittoria, to wed, **18**. 439, 526, **19**. 136

Vitelli, Mme, abandoned by, **17**. *38*

—— may have, as cicisbeo, **17**. 136

wife to arouse jealousy of, **19**. 145, 311

Careggi, Grand Duke of Tuscany's villa:

Richecourt at, **19**. 97, 101, 402

—— rents, **20**. 116

Richmond, Mrs, visits, **19**. 97, 101

*Careless Husband, The. See under* Cibber, Colley

Carestini, Giovanni (ca 1705–ca 1760), singer:

Barlocci fatter than, **18**. 302

biographical information on, corrected, **43**. 245

Conway praises, **37**. *50*

Egizziello may be replaced by, **17**. 463

Carew, Lady. *See* Bryan, Elizabeth (fl. ca 1514); Courtenay, Joan (b. ca 1411)

Carew, Anne (d. after 1565), m. 1 (1549 *or* 1550) Sir Nicholas Throckmorton; m. 2 (1572) Adrian Stokes:

family of, **38**. 125

Carew, Coventry (? 1716–48), M.P.:
Parliamentary debate by, on amendment to the Address, 26. 23
Carew, Elizabeth:
son of, 28. 456n
Carew, Sir Francis (ca 1530–1611), Kt, 1576:
visit of Q. Elizabeth to, 33. 111
Carew, Sir George (1555–1629), cr. (1605) Bn Carew, (1626) E. of Totness:
HW wants Ware's passage about, 16. 9
Hibernica contains translation by, 10. 16, 16. 13
tomb of, 9. 120
translation by, mentioned by Ware, 16. 7
Carew, Sir Nicholas (d. 1539), K.G., 1536:
Beddington the seat of, 33. 111
family of, 38. 125
HW's ancestor, 33. 111
portrait of, 33. 111, 34. 131n
Carew, Sir Nicholas (1687–1727), cr. (1715) Bt; M.P.:
HW finds rare print of, 28. 456
Mason sends print of, to HW, 28. 459, 463
Carew, Sir Nicholas Hacket (ca 1716–62):
will of, 28. 456n
Carew, Thomas (ca 1595–ca 1639); 'Cary'; 'Carye'; courtier, poet, and wit:
Birch corrects reference to, in Lord Herbert's Life, 40. 357
Court positions of, under Charles I, 40. 357
Carew family:
Beddington owned by, 28. 455n
Howard family not as old as, 38. 125
Carew. See also Carey; Cary
Carey, ——:
Howard, Lady, said to have married, 38. 124
Carey, Sir Edmund (fl. 1580–1600):
second marriage of, 1. 6
Carey, Esquire (d. 1756), surgeon in Pall Mall:
Walpole, Sir Robert, angers, 17. 252
Whitehead accompanied by, 17. 252, 43. 241
Carey, Henry (1526–96), cr. (1559) Bn Hunsdon:
daughter of, 9. 101n
Q. Elizabeth gives peerage to, on death-bed, 25. 166, 33. 377
refuses earldom on death-bed, 33. 235
Robertson's Scots spelling of name of, 15. 45
son of, 1. 6
Carey, Henry (ca 1575–1633), cr. (1620) Vct of Falkland:
biographical information about, corrected, 43. 47
Van Somers's portrait of, owned by HW: 1. 88; inspires incident in Castle of Otranto, 42. 106
Carey, Henry (1596–1661), 2d Bn Leppington; 2d E. of Monmouth:
Romulus and Tarquin, translation by, 16. 7
Carey, Henry (d. 1743), dramatist and musician:
Learned Dissertation on Dumpling, A, by, 13. 62

Carey, Sir Lucius (1610–43), Kt; 2d Vct of Falkland, 1633; statesman:
biographical information about, corrected, 43. 215, 348
Chillingworth said to have been aided by, 16. 12
Clarendon partial to, 29. 179
Coke, Lady Mary, criticizes HW's depreciation of, 31. 200–1
HW buys miniature of, at Mead's sale, 20. 470n
HW disparages, in Royal and Noble Authors, 38. 39, 40. 137
head of, by Hoskins, copied by Lady Bingham, 32. 155
Lyttelton's Dialogues of the Dead mention, 21. 408
Carey, Margaret (d. 1605), m. Sir Edward Hoby:
monument of, in Bisham church, 9. 101
Carey, Robert (1560–1639), 1st E. of Monmouth:
HW's account of, 16. 32n
Carey, Walter (1685–1757), M.P.:
(?) HW mentions, 37. 337
Howe, Richard, replaces, as M.P., 21. 89n
name of, corrected, 43. 274
Carey. See also Carew; Cary
Carey family:
genealogist familiar with, 38. 133
HW's, the reverse of Lady Ailesbury's, 38. 125
Cargil, ——:
former schoolmaster, 21. 457
Hamilton, Lord Archibald, lives with, in Tuscan woods, 21. 457
Carhampton, E. of. See Luttrell, Henry Lawes (1743–1821); Luttrell, Simon (1713–87)
Carhampton, Vct. See Luttrell, Simon (1713–87)
Cariati, Principe di. See Spinelli, Scipione or Carlantonio
Cariati (Italy):
earthquake account mentions, 25. 376
Carib; Caribs:
English will hang, 23. 455
French aided by, at St Vincent, 24. 503
Parliament gives no representation to, 23. 462
'red,' on St Vincent, said to sell land cheaply, to Burke, 39. 239
Caricature; caricatures:
'Coalition Dissected,' 35. 381
Hamilton draws, 26. 46n
Hogarth does, of French, 20. 13
in the Turnstile, 21. 93–4
Laroon's, of Mat Ashton, 42. 282
of Newcastle and his cook, 17. 485n
out of fashion, 38. 489
Patch's, 23. 5, 27, 33, 37, 267, 275, 422, 427, 429, 26. 45
Townshend's: 21. 77–8, 90, 35. 280; 37. 444; in black lead, 37. 573; on cards, 9. 195;

Townshend forgets, when attacking libels, 38. 489
Carickfergus. *See* Carrickfergus
Carignan, D. of. *See* Luigi (1721–78)
Carignan, Prince de. *See* Luigi (1721–78); Vittorio Amadeo (1690–1741); Vittorio Amadeo (1743–80)
Carin Secchi. *See* Carnesecchi
Carisbrooke Castle:
Charles I imprisoned in, 23. 165
Carisdale. *See* Coradale
Caristini. *See* Carestini
Caritat, Marie-Jean-Antoine-Nicolas de (1743–94), Marquis de Condorcet:
Anckarström praised by, 15. 237, 34. 175
believed to be implicated in La Rochefoucauld's murder, 34. 174
compared with shepherd kings of Egypt, 34. 173
constitution by, 31. 384–5
HW calls: 'monster,' 12. 66, 34. 174; one of the worst men of 18th century, 34. 179
HW denounces, 31. 379, 384, 397
*Lettre d'un théologien à l'auteur des Trois siècles*, 6. 82, 88
Louis XVI's remark just before death printed by, 34. 179–80
marriage of, 34. 174
office to be given to, 6. 155
Priestley's correspondent, 34. 125
responsibility of, for French Revolution, 31. 385
rumoured to be in Switzerland, 12. 66
suicide of, 31. 397
Treasury position of, 34. 125, 39. 487
Voltaire edited by, 39. 385–6
worse than the partitioners of Poland, 39. 496
Caritat de Condorcet, Jacques-Marie de (1703–83), Bp of Lisieux 1761–83:
Ussé's sister gives ring to, 5. 287
Ussé's sister kept by, 5. 287
Carkett, Robert (d. 1780), naval officer:
*Monmouth's* action against *Foudroyant* continued by, 21. 193n
Carlby, Lincs:
Purkis rector of, 1. 361n
Carlepont (France):
Broglie, Charles de, dies at, 6. 479n
Carleton, Bn. *See* Boyle, Henry (d. 1725)
Carleton, Christopher (1749–87), army officer:
Fort Ann and Fort George captured by, 33. 266
Carleton, Sir Dudley (1574–1632), Kt; cr. (1626) Bn Carleton, (1628) Vct Dorchester; diplomatist:
birth date of, corrected, 43. 63
letters by, at Ragley, 9. 224
*Letters from and to*: 1. 379–80, 386, 43. 63; Hardwicke edits, 28. 246n, 29. 183; Hardwicke wants HW to reprint, 41. 283
peerage of, corrected, 43. 121

Carleton, Capt. George:
*True and Genuine History of the Two Last Wars* by, 43. 249
Carleton, Sir Guy (1724–1808), K.B., 1776; cr. (1786) Bn Dorchester; army officer:
aide-de-camp to D. of Cumberland, 21. 78n
Americans driven by, from Canada, 24. 229
—— reported to have captured, 31. 186
—— repulsed by, at Quebec, 24. 215
army of, at Quebec estimated, 24. 347n
Burgoyne's surrender announced by, 24. 339–41
Canadian-English army formed at Montreal by, for relief of St John's, 32. 284n
Conway predicts achievements by, 24. 215, 229, 238
Cumberland, D. of, takes, to Hanover, 21. 78
fights better than he writes, 24. 229
Germain opposed to appointment of, as commander-in-chief, 25. 241n
——'s incompatibility with, 29. 177n
later K.B. and commander at New York, 24. 215n
Montgomery said to have defeated, 24. 156, 161
not arrived in England, 32. 286
Quebec must be winter quarters for, 24. 263
reinforcements for, 24. 238n
set aside for Burgoyne, 32. 393
Carleton, Mrs John. *See* Moders, Mary
Carleton, Mrs Thomas. *See* Howard, Lady Anne (b. 1752)
Carleton House. *See* Carlton House
California. *See* California
Carlingford, Bn. *See* Fortescue, Chichester S. P.
Carlisle, Bp of. *See* Close, Nicholas (d. 1452); Douglas, John (1721–1807); Law, Edmund (1703–87); Lyttelton, Charles (1714–68); Merke, Thomas (d. 1409); Osbaldeston, Richard (1690–1764); Story, Edward (d. 1503)
Carlisle, Cts of. *See* Byron, Hon. Isabella (1721–95); Cavendish, Lady Georgiana Dorothy (1783–1858); Leveson Gower, Lady Margaret Caroline (1753–1824); Percy, Lady Lucy (ca 1600–60)
Carlisle, E. of. See Howard, Charles (ca 1629–85); Howard, Charles (1669–1738); Howard, Frederick (1748–1825); Howard, Henry (1694–1758)
Carlisle, governor of. *See* Durand, Col.
Carlisle, mayor of. *See* Patinson, ——
Carlisle, Cumberland:
Balmerinoch denies taking part in capture of, 19. 282
Carlisle, E. of, opposes Grafton ministry in, 39. 96
cathedral at, *see* Carlisle Cathedral
citadel of, reproduced in sugar, 19. 174–5
Cumberland, D. of, captures, 19. 193
Hertford writes from, 38. 91
Mann translates account of capture of, 19. 205
petition from, moderate, 25. 10

[Carlisle, Cumberland, *continued*]
  Portland's expenditure in election at, **30**. 250
  quartermaster captured on way to, **19**. 167
  rebels captured at, **19**. 296
  rebels leave garrison in castle of, **37**. 211
  rebels may besiege, **19**. 159
  rebels may halt at, **37**. 213–14
  rebels retreat to, **19**. 185n
  rebels take, **14**. 2n, **19**. 165–6, 190, 205
  Solway Moss battle near, **16**. 80
  Stanhope, Spencer, M.P. for, **28**. 492
  Wade to join troops at, **37**. 214
Carlisle Cathedral:
  Amphlett prebendary of, **13**. 173n
Carlisle House, Soho Sq.:
  assembly-rooms in, **29**. 31n
  Cornelys, Mrs, opens assembly in, **29**. 138n
  — takes, **23**. 271
  masquerade at, **39**. 322
  subscription ball for Karl Wilhelm Ferdinand at, **38**. 289, 291, 296
Carlo, St. *See* Borromeo, Carlo
Carlos, Don (1545–68) of Spain:
  HW thought of writing about, **41**. 290
  Howe, Lord, compared to, **12**. 24
  Monaco, P. of, has painting of, **7**. 335
  *Travels of Philip II King of Spain, The,* by, **12**. 24
  Williams does not write about, till mad, **41**. 290
'Carlos, Don.' *See* Charles III
Carlow, Vcts. *See* Stuart, Lady Caroline
Carlowitz, Treaty of:
  Austrian-Venetian borders defined by, **24**. 11n
Carlsbad, Bohemia:
  Chudleigh, Elizabeth, to visit, **38**. 473
Carlton, Sir Blundel. *See* Charlton, Sir Blunden
Carlton. *See also* Carleton
Carlton House, Pall Mall; P. of Wales's residence:
  artificial stone used in ornaments for, **42**. 311n
  ball at, **9**. 58, **25**. 476n
  Bubb Dodington first minister of, **20**. 96
  cold room at, opens off garden, **20**. 232
  colonnade of, supports nothing, **42**. 274
  'court' misnomer for, **17**. 210
  crowds at, **17**. 337
  Deerhurst in attendance at, **17**. 211
  Frederick, P. of Wales, changes clothes at, **20**. 232
  George II's levee resembles those at, **18**. 95
  George III and Q. Charlotte at, **23**. 375
  George III's statement at, to Cabinet Council, **21**. 456n
  George IV at, **11**. 227n
  —— gives dinner at, for Conway and Waldegrave families, **25**. 647
  ——'s ball at, **25**. 476n
  —— to give dinner at, for Hertford family, **31**. 298, **42**. 188
  HW mentions, **12**. 258n
  HW's stories of, not to be repeated, **12**. 150

Jersey, Lady, said to be forbidden to appear at, **12**. 193
Louisa, Ps, dies at, **23**. 22n
mob hisses at, in passing, **23**. 196
print of Porter formerly at, **42**. 126
Stanhope, Sir William, accosts strangers at, **17**. 279
Violette, Mlle, avoids, **9**. 29
visitors to: Christian VII, **10**. 264, **35**. 326; Durham, Bp of, **10**. 301; Friedrich III of Saxe-Gotha, **17**. 331n; HW, **10**. 301, **33**. 498–500
Walpole, Sir Robert, might not be received at, **18**. 8
Carlyle, Joseph Dacre (1759–1804), professor of Arabic at Cambridge:
  *Specimens of Arabian Poetry* by, **12**. 205
Carmarthen, Marchioness of. *See* Anguish, Catherine (1764–1837); Darcy, Lady Amelia (1754–84); Harley, Lady Elizabeth (d. 1713)
Carmarthen, M. of. *See* Osborne, Francis Godolphin (1751–99); Osborne, Thomas (1713–89)
Carmarthen, Wales:
  circuit of, **35**. 577
  Hardinge writes from, **35**. 575
Carmel, Mt:
  'odoriferous as,' **12**. 36
  order of, *see* Carmelite; Carmelites
*Carmelite, The. See under* Cumberland, Richard
Carmelite; Carmelites ('Carmes'):
  church of, at Paris: Guido Reni's paintings at, **32**. 261, **39**. 202; HW visits, **7**. 264, 336; Le Brun's 'Magdalen' at, **39**. 202
  convent of, at Paris: Louise, Ps, enters, **4**. 399–400, **23**. 207, 321n, 398; massacre at, **34**. 163n; prioress of, *see* Craig, Mme
  dowry of, **4**. 400
  friar; friars of: convent disciplines, for intercourse with heretic's daughter, **20**. 128; Mann asked by, at Siena, for leave to dedicate English-Italian grammar, **22**. 438; Mann recommends, as Maria Louisa's English teacher, **22**. 438
  Mann thinks, of more use than nuns, **25**. 239
  members of, **18**. 171n
  nuns of, Austrian convents of, suppressed, **25**. 236n
Carmen, ——, café-keeper in Saragossa:
  house of, threatened by mob, **8**. 120
Carmey, Angel, of Chelsea:
  HW may be shown curiosities owned by, **40**. 259
Carmi, Du. *See* Du Carmi
Carmi, Patrice, Don:
  captured at Velletri, **18**. 492
Carmichael, John (1701–67), 3d E. of Hyndford; envoy to Prussia 1741–4:
  Austrian-Prussian peace procured by, **17**. 483, 497
  becomes privy councillor, **20**. 135

Frederick II adds eagle to arms of, **18**. 107
—— gives audience to, **17**. 76n
—— gives plate to, **18**. 89, 107
George II's special envoy, **17**. 76n
George III does not retain, in Bedchamber, **9**. 324, **21**. 460
green ribbon awarded to, for procuring Prussian peace, **17**. 497
Maria Theresa's picture sent to, **18**. 107
——'s plenipotentiary, signs treaties, **17**. 456n
Stuart Mackenzie expelled from Berlin by, **17**. 358n, **30**. 58
wife ill-used by, **34**. 257

Carmichael, Hon. William (1702–65), Bp of Clonfert, 1753, of Leighlin and Ferns, 1758, of Meath, 1758; Abp of Dublin, 1765:
Bedford, D. of, urges appointment of, as Abp of Armagh, **22**. 276
(?) Conway's Irish friend, **37**. 434
death of, expected, **10**. 187
Hertford's clique to be relieved by death of, **10**. 187
'Scoto-Hibernian,' **22**. 276

Carmichael, William (d. 1795):
(?) La Fayette's agreement with, **6**. 427
(?) lives with Franklin, **6**. 427

Carmine, church of. *See* Santa Maria del Carmine

Carmona, Manuel Salvador (1734–1820), engraver:
Waddilove praises, **16**. 170

Carmontelle. *See* Carrogis, Louis

Carnac, John, official in India:
capitulation signed by, **24**. 510n
Puna expedition miscarries because of, **24**. 509n

Carnarvon, Cts of. *See* Wyndham, Lady Elizabeth Alicia Maria

Carnarvon, E. of. *See* Herbert, Henry (1741–1811)

Carnarvon, Marchioness of. *See* Nicoll, Margaret (ca 1735–68)

Carnatic, Nawab of. *See* Chanda Sahib

Carnation; carnations:
Clark cultivates, at Nuneham, **35**. 461
clove-carnations, HW sends, to Lady Ravensworth, **33**. 567
propagation of, by piping, **31**. 264

Carnavalet, Hôtel de, Paris home of Mme de Sévigné:
Androuet de Cerceau said to have designed, **41**. 258
HW recommends, to Cts of Ailesbury, **39**. 201
HW's *Ave Marias* before, **30**. 206, 250, **31**. 50
HW's devotion to, **3**. 309
HW sends 'blessings' from, to Selwyn, **30**. 206
HW's picture of, by Raguenet, **4**. 30, 31, **7**. 304n, 404, **28**. 196, **41**. 258
style of, un-French, **31**. 50–1

Carnegie, George (1716–92), 6th E. of Northesk:
daughter taken by, to see London sights, **35**. 373

HW's ramblings resemble those of, **35**. 374
Noel, Mrs, hears at Twickenham Park the tales by, of his voyages, **35**. 373

Carnegie, James, of Finhaven:
Strathmore's quarrel with, **21**. 364n

Carnegie, Lady Mary Anne (1764–98), m. (1797) Rev. John Kemp:
father shows London sights to, **35**. 373

Carnesecchi, Signora. *See* Barducci Cherichini, Vittoria

Carnevalino:
Barretts miss, at Florence, **20**. 92
Leopold amuses himself with masks at theatre during, **23**. 343

Carnival:
at Florence: **13**. 200–2, **17**. 394, **19**. 354–6, **35**. 52; bad, **20**. 216; bad weather impairs, **24**. 280; balls allowed in, despite Richecourt's prohibition, **19**. 14; beginning of, dull, but ending stormy, **20**. 115; begins with bad operas, **18**. 128, 454, 555, **20**. 115, 210–11; 'burial of,' the only day in Lent when amusements are permitted, **24**. 281; Conway may arrive for, **20**. 274; described by HW, **13**. 200–2; diversions of, exclude all other topics, **20**. 464; dull and cold, **20**. 357; Electress's death prevents, **18**. 159, 353; ending, **17**. 311, **19**. 364; excessive cold during, **25**. 248; Florentines mad with masking at, **19**. 207; Florentines to stimulate circulation by, **21**. 359; gayest ever, despite food shortage, **22**. 486; Karl Joseph's birth permits slight revival of, **19**. 8; last day of, **18**. 391; Leopold and Maria Louisa enjoy, to the fullest, **22**. 491; Leopold does not suppress, in compliment to Pius VI, **25**. 243; Leopold enjoys, **22**. 486; Lorraine, Duchess of, halts, by her death, **19**. 1, 8; Lorraine, Duchess of, might spoil, by dying, **18**. 352–3; Mann ill at, **17**. 78; Mann indifferent to, **20**. 404; Mann misses amusements of, because of his cold, **19**. 460–1; Mann's servants forbidden to attend, after his death, **25**. 670; Maria Louisa always pregnant during, **23**. 171; Maria Louisa enjoys, as spectator, **23**. 189; Maria Louisa miscarries because of over-indulgence at, **23**. 458; Maria Theresa's death prevents, **25**. 107; marked by poor theatricals, **22**. 477; morning opera to mark end of, **19**. 465; nearly ended, **17**. 291–2, **22**. 393; opening of, expected, **18**. 113; Pomfret, Cts of, considers, dull, **17**. 311n; popularity of, **18**. 372; Richecourt said to have countermanded Francis I's order for, **19**. 8; Sauveterre and Tesi engaged for, **18**. 322; spoiled by lack of masking, **20**. 219; Suares, Vittoria, may marry during, **18**. 138; Tempi family excluded from, by bereavement, **20**. 298; Tesi's opera to pay for one in, **18**. 302; Tuscan court may not return to Florence for, **23**. 262
at Leghorn, **18**. 526, **22**. 354

[Carnival, *continued*]

at Naples: Leopold, Maria Louisa, Ferdinand of Parma, and Maria Amalia to attend, **25.** 2; 'shows' lacking at, **22.** 492

at Paris: **3.** 236, **5.** 191, 197, **38.** 336; masked balls end with, **38.** 514; short in 1765, **38.** 477, 485

at Rome, replaced by Conclave, **37.** 46

at Venice: **17.** 134; Francis III may finish at, **18.** 161

cardinals would willingly have spent, in Conclave, **21.** 81

Du Châtelet does not want to spend, in country, **18.** 121

dull, all over Italy, **24.** 280–1

in England: **13.** 201; HW would probably go to London for, **20.** 216

Pius VI rejects proposal to close, **25.** 383

York, D. of, to spend, at Milan, **22.** 204

young people's health generally injured by, **38.** 485

Carnivalli (Carnavali *or* Carnevale), Pietro (d. ca 1791):

biographical information about, corrected, **43.** 146–7

(?) Fantoccini managed by, **11.** 216

(?) lottery prize won by, **11.** 216

Squibb's in Savile Row sold by, to Barrymore, **43.** 143

*Carolina*, English ship:

George II embarks on, **18.** 217n

Carolina, North *and* South:

alarm for safety of, **20.** 495

back settlers of, said to have risen in England's favour, **33.** 155, **39.** 345–6

Clinton said to have captured Lee in, **23.** 215

Cornwallis defeats Gates in, **25.** 92

English take frigate near, **6.** 452

estate in, confiscated, **33.** 50–1

exports to, **32.** 242

French and Spanish wars endanger England's reconquest of, **24.** 500

French menace the forts protecting, **20.** 448

HW's vision of future senate of, **23.** 210

North Carolina, Martin governor of, **24.** 157n

ship from, **38.** 169

South Carolina: Campbell, Lady William, born in, **25.** 263n; Campbell, Lord William, governor of, **25.** 263n

storm off coast of, **24.** 535

Tories in, promise aid if English troops invade, **24.** 157–8

Carolina Augusta Maria (1774–5) of Gloucester, Ps:

bathed in sea-water, **36.** 324

birth of, **6.** 69, **24.** 24

death of, after inoculation, **24.** 86

father may take, to southern France, **24.** 76

father to supplicate George III for aid to, **36.** 110–11

George III refuses burial to, in Westminster Abbey, **36.** 114n

HW solicitous about, **36.** 107–8, 111–12

legitimacy of, might be questioned if her father applied to Parliament, **36.** 108

to be inoculated, **24.** 82

Carolina cherry. *See under* Cherry

Caroline (1683–1737) of Ansbach, m. (1705) George II, K. of England, 1727:

Albemarle, Cts of, Bedchamber lady to, **20.** 111n

Baden-Durlach, Margrave of, related to, **20.** 148n

Bird gives ground to, at Richmond Park, **20.** 322–3

Blackburne and, **15.** 143, **31.** 421

Bolingbroke admits that Sir Robert Walpole had sole confidence of, **20.** 60n

burial of, **13.** 145

Butler patronized by, **20.** 167

——'s book recommended by, to Sir Robert Walpole, **20.** 167

Chesterfield's character of, unjust, **28.** 303

Churchill, Gen., questioned by, about Ward's Drop, **37.** 77n

Clarke, Alured, friend of, **17.** 279n

closet of, at Kensington Palace, **40.** 126n

Coronation petticoat of, **38.** 109–10

crystal hunting-bottle of, given by George II to Sir Robert Walpole, **25.** 464

daughter-in-law may equal, **19.** 62

death of: **13.** 144; premature reports of, **13.** 141–2

dines at Walpoles' Chelsea house, **15.** 333

divorce of, possible, **13.** 117n

Duck, Stephen, appointed ranger by, **31.** 220, **37.** 75n

Dunoyer's remark to, about D. of Cumberland, **30.** 28

France, Q. of, has cap like that of, **35.** 113

George II's relations with, **31.** 420–1

Grantham's tiptoe walk ascribed to fear of awaking, **18.** 104

Haymarket attended by, when other opera was fashionable, **38.** 123

health of, 'past recovery,' **37.** 37–8

Hermitage of: **29.** 34, 296; Green's lines on, **14.** 39–41

Hertford, Cts of, lady of Bedchamber to, **17.** 346

Hervey solicits preferment for Middleton from, **15.** 292

Hervey, Bns, maid of honour to, **31.** 415

Hervey, Hon. Felton, equerry to, **30.** 115n

Howe, Mary, former maid of honour to, **17.** 495n

Ilay hated by, **15.** 153

influence of, powerful, **31.** 420

inscription about, at Stowe, **35.** 76

Karl Friedrich, great-nephew of, **20.** 148

Kensington Palace mostly locked up after death of, **20.** 88

letter of, in *Utrecht Gazette*, **34.** 12

Louisa, Ps, resembles, **30.** 27

Magnan said to have been employed by, **18.** 548

malapropism of, in congratulating new bishop, 23. 313n

'Merlin's Cave' built for, 13. 118

Methuen twitted by, at Lady Walpole's at Chelsea, 33. 247–8

Modena, Ds of, as plump as, 18. 246

Montagu, Lady Mary Wortley, in time of, 14. 246, 248

Mordaunt, Anna Maria, maid of honour to, 20. 208n, 22. 163–4n

nephew of, becomes K.G., 20. 72

Onslow's boast provokes retort from, 30. 292n

opera attended by, 13. 142, 38. 123

Orléans, Duchesse d', corresponds with, 34. 12, 35. 394

Pembroke, Cts of, former 'maid of honour' to, 20. 281n

*Pietas Academiæ Cantabrigiensis* compiled for, 13. 145–6

Pomfret, Cts of, Bedchamber lady to, 17. 165n, 20. 389

Pomfret, E. of, Master of the Horse to, 17. 165n, 276

Pope avoids, 9. 305n

Portland, Lady, dismissed by, 34. 260

portrait of, at Navestock, 9. 244

Richmond displeases, by saying his children would precede D. of Cumberland's grandchildren, 19. 20

royal portraits assembled by, at Kensington Palace, 16. 322

Schutz, Augustus, friend of, 9. 112n

Selwyn, Mrs, subject of scandal reported by, 34. 12, 35. 394

Selwyn, Mrs, Bedchamber woman to, 20. 114n, 23. 94n, 31. 420

Selwyn, Col. John, treasurer to, 20. 114n, 23. 94n

Stair's remark to, 15. 153n

statue of, at Queen's College, Oxford, 13. 99

Suffolk, Cts of, does not prevail over, 34. 259

—— resigns Richmond to, 42. 188

——'s relations with, 31. 420–1

—— woman of the Bedchamber and Mistress of the Robes to, 22. 543n

summer house of, 10. 131n

Sundon, Bns, Bedchamber woman to, 14. 96n

—— has, in her power, 17. 276

Swift would have praised, if she would help him, 25. 8

Vertue catalogues collection of, 16. 143n

Walpole, Sir Robert, courts, to remain prime minister, 33. 422n

—— entertains, at Chelsea, 43. 213

—— favoured by, 2. 124

—— questioned by, about hernia, 17. 276n

——'s relations with, 31. 420–1

—— visits, 37. 37n

West's monody on death of, 14. 234, 17. 469n, 28. 115–16

Caroline (Amelia Elizabeth) (1768–1821) of Brunswick-Wolfenbüttel, m. (1795) George,

P. of Wales, K. of England as George IV 1820–30:

applauding reception of, 15. 325

Bedchamber ladies of, 11. 114n

Berry, Mary, would not want position of, 12. 127

betrothal of, rumoured, 34. 203n

bon mot on Lady Jersey and, 12. 142

Brighton not to be visited by, 12. 200

Cholmondeley, Henrietta Maria, killed by fall from carriage of, 4. 217n

England, escorts for journey of, to, 12. 107, 115, 123, 128–9, 136

Fitzroy, Mrs, Bedchamber woman to, 15. 325

George III's rumoured letter to, about Lady Jersey, 12. 193

Greenwich reception for, 12. 139

HW describes, 12. 139

household of, planned, 12. 129n, 131

Jersey, Cts of, reproached for lack of reverence for, 12. 149

Jersey, E. of, complains to George III about, 15. 328

letter of, intercepted, 15. 328n

marriage of, 12. 139

opera's acclaim for, 12. 185–6, 187

Pelham, Mrs, dismissed by, 12. 200–1

pregnancy of, at Brighton, 12. 142

reconciliation of, with husband, 12. 198

St James's Palace receives, 12. 138, 139

Sophia Matilda of Gloucester's life will be brightened by arrival of, 36. 330

Caroline Elizabeth (1713–57), Ps:

Adolf Fredrik might wed, 18. 203, 219, 278, 305

Bath to be visited by, for rheumatism, 19. 234

charity of, 21. 165

death date of, corrected, 43. 147, 249

death of, after long illness, 21. 165

Drawing-Rooms held by sisters and, in London, 30. 22

dresser to, 19. 427n

elopement of, would be astonishing, 18. 451

Finch, Lady Isabella, Bedchamber lady to, 19. 389n

George II greeted by, 18. 341

Hastings, Lady Elizabeth, rejected as Bedchamber lady to, for refusal to play cards on Sunday, 20. 34

Horner, Mrs, said to 'cuckold,' with Hervey, 30. 27

Mann wears weepers for, 21. 165, 174

Mary, Ps, to visit, 19. 295

Portland, Cts of, governess to, 34. 260

portrait of, 10. 338

summer spent by, at St James's Palace, 18. 218

Sussex, Cts of, Bedchamber lady to, 10. 338

vulgarism not understood by, 11. 265

witticism on Duchesse d'Orléans's tomb explained by, 35. 394

years spent by, shut up in chambers at St James's, 21. 165n

Caroline Matilda (1751–75) of England, m.
(1766) Christian VII, K. of Denmark:
arrested, 5. 183
biography of, 43. 91
birth of, expected, 20. 233
Bothmer steward to, 10. 35n
brothers will be distressed by disgrace of, 23.
384–5
Christian VII applauds anti-matrimonial
quips, 23. 57
—— husband of, 4. 104n
—— to thank mother of, for his bride, 35.
326–7
—— treats, too hastily, 23. 384
—— tries to see, 23. 409
Copenhagen may be revisited by, 23. 426
Danish revolution sacrifices husband as much
as, 23. 386
death of, 24. 104, 108
Denmark left by, 5. 230
Denmark ruled by, 23. 272–3
English fleet may rescue, 5. 203, 23. 401
enjoys herself in Hanover, 23. 426
Frederick II arranges deposition of, 23. 437
gallantries of, 28. 58
George III announces betrothal of, 38. 490
—— asks Parliament to vote dowry for, 22.
425
Göhrde to be visited by, 23. 409
HW jokes about weight and virtues of, 31.
162
health of: colic, 23. 402; (?) porphyria, 43. 285
imprisoned for amour with Struensee, 5. 178n,
23. 373, 31. 167
life of, spared, 5. 228, 23. 391–2
Mann's compassion for, 23. 396
marriage plans of, announced, 22. 275
may be sent to Norway, 23. 386
mother to visit, 4. 420
mourning for, 32. 237–8
obelisk to, in tableau, 38. 204
said to be going to Zell, 23. 409
sister visits, 23. 426
Sophia Matilda of Gloucester's godmother,
32. 129n, 130, 132
stepmother-in-law to protect, from open
scandal, 23. 380
Struensee rules, 23. 273
——'s relations with, 4. 420n
yacht flying Danish flag to take, to Hanover,
23. 409
Caroline of Orange, Ps. See Wilhelmina Carolina
Carolis, Palazzo, at Rome:
Bernis lives at, 25. 675n
Caron de Beaumarchais, Pierre-Augustin. See
Beaumarchais, Pierre-Augustin Caron de
Carow, Prussia:
Wartenlebens of, 12. 11n
Carp:
(?) Du Deffand, Mme, presented with, 7. 444

HW imagines brace of, presented to judges
on circuit, 41. 381
HW sees, at Chantilly, 7. 260
Strafford, Cts of, not to fish for, 35. 335
Carpenter, Hon. Alicia Maria (d. 1794), m. 1
(1751) Charles Wyndham, 2d E. of Egremont;
m. 2 (1767) Hans Moritz, Graf von Brühl:
Beauties, The, mentions, 25. 68n, 30. 327
Blandford, Lady, suspected by, of procuring
grapes, 32. 208
Charlotte, Q., has, as Bedchamber lady, 21.
517n, 25. 68n
—— to be attended by, at Lord Petre's, 33. 66
Coke, Lady Mary, visits, 25. 564n
(?) Court ball attended by, 9. 402, 403
dances much, at private Court ball, 38. 143
family of, 30. 327n
Garrick's reading attended by, 28. 286
HW mentions, 40. 284
HW's correspondence with, 7. 395
HW sees, at Gloucester House, 25. 68
HW's social relations with, 31. 409
HW's verses mention, 20. 141
HW to send paper to, 7. 416
husband taken ill at breakfast of, 22. 159
jointure of, 33. 205
Lyttelton's verses to, 9. 342
marriages of, 25. 68n
pictures rearranged by, at Petworth, 40. 319
Ranelagh visited by, 25. 68
Richmond, D. of, confers with, 41. 73
son's engagement pleases, 33. 205
Sussex revisited by, 40. 324
witticism by, 39. 167
Carpenter, Lady Almeria (1752–1809):
Campbell, Lady William, confused with, 30.
270
Gloucester, Ds of, has, as Bedchamber lady,
25. 638n
Gloucester, D. of, less attentive to, 36. 329
——'s mistress, 11. 50n, 25. 638n, 31. 298
La Coast, Louisa Maria, natural daughter of,
36. 245n
Mann, Horace II, cordially received by, at
Rome, 25. 674
—— did not respond to advances of, 25. 638
Carpenter, George (ca 1695–1749), 2d Bn Carpenter, 1732; M.P.:
daughter of, 25. 68n, 30. 327n
Moratt committed by, to Newgate, 37. 9n
Carpenter, George (1723–62), 3d Bn Carpenter, 1749; cr. (1761) E. of Tyrconnel; M.P.:
chimpanzee exhibited by, in HW's newspaper
parody, 9. 127
peerage granted to, 9. 344, 21. 490
Pitt, Anne, entertains, 32. 48n
Carpenter, Jenkin. See Carpenter, John
Carpenter, John (ca 1370–ca 1441), town clerk
of London:
painting of 'Dance of Death' in St Paul's
cloister commissioned by, 16. 144

Carpenter, John (d. 1476), Bp of Worcester 1444–76:
register of, to be searched for Rowley, 2. 104–5
Carpenter, Robert (d. 1745), Col.:
killed at Fontenoy, 19. 43, 36. 11
Carpenter; carpenters:
burglary attempted by, 9. 133
HW directs, at SH, 20. 371
HW to forestall, 42. 196
journeymen, form association to go on strike at SH for higher wages, 22. 49, 35. 315
Montagu's pictures to be boxed by, 10. 81
shop of, at Ampthill Park, 34. 5n
Townshend lives with, in Ireland, 23. 380
wooden legs manufactured by, joked about, 38. 509
yards of, covered by penthouses, 32. 237
See also Ship-carpenter
Carpentier, Antoine-Michel (1709–72), architect:
(?) Mme du Deffand's friend, 3. 373
Carpet; carpets:
embroidered, to cover cupboards, 32. 325
enchanted, in fairy tale, 35. 49–50
hung, from windows to be dusted, 35. 458
magic, 18. 303
Mann has, in house, 18. 109
Turkey, in Charlotte yacht, 21. 525n
velvet, Young Pretender wants, hung before his theatre boxes, 25. 536
Walpole, Sir Edward, promises, to Mrs Scott, 10. 329
Carpi, Ugo da (ca 1479–81–ca 1532), engraver:
wood engraving said to be invented by, 16. 96
Carpintero, Antoine:
captured at Velletri, 18. 493
Carpue, Joseph Constantine (1764–1846), surgeon and anatomist:
(?) SH visited by, 12. 246, 251, 252
Carr, Lady. See Little, Mary
Carr, Mr, of Whitton:
SH visited by, 12. 244
Carr, Mrs:
SH visited by, 12. 235
'Carr, old':
cousin's conversation with, about burial, 35. 107–8
Carr, Lady Anne (1615–84), m. (1637) William Russell, 5th E. of Bedford:
monument to, at Chenies church, 9. 102
Carr, Rev. Colston (1740–post 1797), schoolmaster at Twickenham:
SH visited by, 12. 225, 232, 242
SH visitors sent by, 12. 227, 237
Carr, Elizabeth (b. ca 1748):
Churchill the poet elopes with, 38. 234
Carr, Henry:
SH visited by, 12. 251
Carr, Isabella (1742–1808), m. (1762) James Hay, 15th E. of Erroll, 1758:
SH visited by, 12. 223

Carr, John (d.?1780), convict:
released by Gordon rioters, 29. 60n, 33. 194
three people robbed by, near Hayes, 29. 60n
(?) trial of, 25. 67
Carr, John (1723–1807) of York, architect:
Mason's rectory at Aston designed by, 43. 301
Carr, Joseph (fl. 1754–68), stone-mason:
daughter of, 38. 234
Carr or Ker, Robert (ca 1587–1645), cr. (1613), E. of Somerset:
HW's portrait of, 15. 191
Holles a friend of, 16. 163
marriage of, 9. 124
Northampton's letters to, 16. 160–1
spurious portrait of, 1. 208, 43. 55
trial of, 16. 161
wife of, 15. 192n
Carr, Sir Robert. See Ker, Sir Robert (1578–1654), E. of Ancram
Carr. See also Ker
Carracci, Agostino (1557–1602), engraver:
Correggio painting engraved by, 17. 167
Carracci, Annibale (1560–1609), painter:
compared with Shakespeare, 2. 221
Du Deffand, Mme, has portrait after, 8. 20
Mann to get painting by, for Royston, 21. 532
paintings by: in Colebrooke's sale, 23. 569n; sold by Francis III to K. of Poland, 19. 314n
self-portrait of, at Julienne's, 7. 287
'Triumph of Bacchus and Ariadne' by, copied through Mann for D. of Northumberland, 20. 328, 352, 490
Tuileries gallery copied after, 7. 308
'Virgin with St Francis and Infant Christ' by 43. 275
Carracci, Signora Annibale:
portrait of, at Julienne's, 7. 287
Carracci family:
Faenza ware said to be designed by, 25. 591n
school of the, 2. 221
Carrara, Ps of. See Novellara, Ricciarda di
Carrara or Carara, Agata (fl. 1776–7), opera singer:
beauty of, 32. 106, 111
HW hears, at opera, 32. 106
HW would sacrifice, for Lady Ossory, 32. 108
Carraway seed:
Conway grows, at Park Place, 39. 551
Carrbary. See Carbery
Carré, Jacques:
authorship of letter of, admitted by Voltaire, 21. 520
Carretto. See Del Carretto
Carriage; carriages:
Ailesbury, Cts of, overturned in, 39. 257
Austrians order, from Milan for artillery, 19. 406
Berry's: accident to, at Chailly, 11. 126, 126n; repaired at Fontainebleau, 11. 126n; surrounded by French at Bourgoin, 11. 138n

[Carriage; carriages, *continued*]

Coke, Lady Mary, has, break down, **31**. 142

Du Deffand, Mme, takes Bishop in, to Pont-de-Veyle's, **36**. 107

English, upset easily, **7**. 139

Englishwoman does not have footman for, **24**. 260

Fleury owes £500 for, **12**. 79

Gordon rioters tear Parliament members from, **25**. 53–4

HW does not have, for North, **10**. 320

HW too rheumatic for, **11**. 177

lozenges on, **11**. 23n

Melcombe's, in bad taste, **31**. 215

new travelling, to meet D. and Ds of Gloucester at Dover, **36**. 155n

number of, passing SH, diminished, **28**. 405

of ammunition, moving west, **28**. 460

Rutland, Ds of, in, followed by admirer at Ramsgate, **12**. 113

six-horse, hung with black, for Cts of Orford's funeral, **25**. 114

Vesey, Mrs, and Mrs Handcock can afford, **31**. 230n

York, Ds of, allows tradesmen two guineas apiece for, **39**. 493

*See also* Berlin; Cabriolet; Calash; Carrosse; Chair; Chaise; Chariot; Coach; Curricle; Gig; Hack; Landau Mail-coach; Phaeton; Post-chaise; Stage-coach; Voiture; Whisky

Carrick, E. of. *See* Butler, Henry Thomas

Carrick:

Campbell family of, **11**. 181

Carrickfergus, co. Antrim, Ireland:

Conway to attend election and assizes at, **37**. 74

French, under Thurot, capture, **9**. 254n, **21**. 371–4, 376, 381–2

mayor of, *see* Chapman, ——

Novillars killed in battle at, **10**. 12

Carrier, Jean-Baptiste (1756–94), member of National Convention:

refinements of, on barbarity, **12**. 162

Carrier; carriers. *See* Brackley carrier

Carriera, Rosalba (1675–1757), called Rosalba; pastel painter:

Chaloner's portrait by, **18**. 243n

copies never made by, **18**. 243n

Diana a favourite subject of, **35**. 6n

'Diana' sold by, to E. of Lincoln, **35**. 6

Ennery has poor examples of, **7**. 325

Fermor, Lady Sophia, painted by, **35**. 6

HW has portrait of John Law by, **15**. 167, 180, **42**. 386

HW has portrait of Mme Suares by, **17**. 39n

HW's portrait by, **18**. 243n, **43**. 250

Julienne has paintings by, **7**. 287

'Lord Boyne' by, **43**. 231

Nicoll, Margaret, drawn by, **43**. 189

sketches by, of Chute, Whithed, HW, E. of Lincoln, Spence, and Chaloner, **18**. 243n

Suares, Mme, visits studio of, with daughters, **18**. 243n

Carrillo de Albornoz, Don José (1663–1747), Duque de Montemar; Spanish army officer:

Acquaviva tells, to invade Tuscany, **17**. 266

Antibes said to be visited by, **17**. 198

Antinori, Mme, gets letter from, **18**. 46, 62

army of: attacked by hussars, **17**. 455; Neapolitans join, **17**. 265n; Neapolitans may withdraw from, **18**. 27; prepared at Madrid, **18**. 5; to reunite at Modena, **17**. 226; Tuscany may be surrounded by, **17**. 289

arrest of, rumoured, **18**. 29, 54

Austrians and Sardinians force to retire, **35**. 28

Barcelona visited by, **17**. *182*

Bitonto victory of, **17**. 427

Braitwitz's civilities refused by, **17**. 214

Cæsar's Gallic wars carried by, in pocket, **18**. 146

Capponi to remonstrate with, **35**. 23

Cento visited by, **17**. 455

Charles Emmanuel III opposes, **18**. 2, 455

courier from Spain awaited by, **18**. 42, 54

courier sent by, from Orbetello to Florence with invasion plans, **17**. 226

Craon and Regency asked by, for passports through Tuscany, **18**. 44

Craon receives demand from, for troops to pass, **17**. 226, 280–2

Deodati to compliment, at Antibes, **17**. 207

destruction of, **17**. 481

*Dialogue entre la Reine d'Espagne et le Duc de Montemar* satirizes, **18**. 5–7

dismissal of, **18**. 44, 46, 59

Duc de Bitonte the title of, **18**. 5, 46

Elizabeth Farnese said to be warned by, against Alberoni, **18**. 7

——'s general, **17**. 479

Empoli visited by, **18**. 54

English fleet not to be called to Tuscany without provocation by, **18**. 27

English fleet weakens, **17**. 408

Ferdinand VI said to include, in his new ministry, **19**. 278n

Ferrara may be refuge of, **17**. 455

Ferretti signs agreement with, at Orbetello, **17**. 214n

Finale may be approached by, after crossing Panaro to relieve Modena, **17**. 455

Florence formerly visited by, **17**. 239

Florentine correspondence of, **17**. 193

Foligno visited by, **18**. 27

Francis I refuses demand of, for passage of troops, **17**. 261–2, 280–2, 289–90

Francis III's correspondence with, **17**. 433

Galli attributes wife's pregnancy to Florentine visit of, **18**. 46, 62

Galli, Mme, has relations with, **17**. 193n, **18**. 46, 62

garrisons to be left by, **17**. 228–9, 289, 323, **18**. 27

Genoese visits of, **17**. 198, 207, **18**. 65

Grifoni, Mme, thought by HW to be pursued by, **18**. 62–3

HW enjoys Mann's accounts of, 18. 68

*histrioni* employed by, 17. 379

inscrutable, 17. 323

La Cattolica the station of, 18. 322

Las Minas may replace, 17. 449

Leghorn port visited by, in Genoese galley, 17. 214

Mann said to be asked by, for passport, 18. 46

Massa visited by, 18. 59

Mirandola threatened by, to relieve Modena, 17. 449n

Modena siege may be lifted by, 17. 443, 449n, 455, 501

Naples may be refuge of, 18. 2, 16

naval forces of, taken to the Giogo, 18. 296

officers swear at mismanagement of, 17. 262

Orbetello visited by, 17. 198, 204, 214, 226, 238, 239, 18. 7, 16

Orsi hope for Lombardy's conquest by, 17. 481

Panaro approached by, past Reno from Bologna, 17. 427

passage through Papal States and Tuscany demanded by, 17. 226, 228–9, 280–2

Pesaro visited by, 17. 323, 342, 350

Porto Spezia said to be reached by, 17. 195

Prati della Sala encampment of, 17. 427

Regency's correspondence with, 17. 261, 281

reinstatement expected by, 18. 59

Rimini abandoned by, 18. 16n

—— headquarters of, 17. 379

Rome visited by, 17. 281

route of, settled through Papal States to Foligno, 17. 261

Samoggia encampment of, 17. 427

Sardinian army feared by, 17. 341

Sardinian deserters paid by, 17. 500

Sicilies conquered by, 17. 427

Siena visited by, 18. 46

son-in-law of, 17. 349n

Spanish agent at Florence buys pistols for, 17. 207

Spanish agent at Florence sends news to, 17. 238

Spanish Court expected Modena to be relieved by, 17. 501

Spanish Court receives, after Campillo's death, 18. 54n

Spanish orders for return of, 18. 44n

Spanish or Neapolitan orders may require, to retire to Naples or aid Don Philip, 18, 27

speech by to Giovanni Gastone de' Medici, 17. 427

third convoy awaited by, 17. 323

titles given to, 17. 427n

Traun and Sardinian troops to attack, 17. 350

Traun feared by, 17. 341

Turin may be visited by, 17. 198

Tuscany may be invaded by, 18. 16

Velluti to receive orders from, at Pesaro, 17. 323

—— to see, at Bologna, 17. 314

Viareggio visited by, 18. 59

Viterbo meeting to be attended by, 17. 214

Viviani deserts upon arrival of, 20. 350

—— pimp to, 17. 239

Zambeccari to forward answer to, 17. 281

Carrington, Nathan (d. 1777), King's Messenger:

House of Commons examines, 38. 316, 317

Wilkes not arrested by, 38. 197n

Carrion, ——, Masserano's secretary:

(?) HW entertains, at SH, 10. 127

(?) Vauxhall visited by, 10. 127

Carro della Zecca (*or* di San Giovanni):

in Florentine procession, 35. 28

Carrogis, Louis (1717–1806), called Carmontelle; painter:

alleged portrait of Mme du Deffand by, 6. 479, 8. 216

Boufflers, Marquise de, and Thérèse painted by, 5. 298n

HW wants Mme du Deffand to have her portrait done by, 3. 392, 398, 399, 4. 10, 51

Gatti painted by, 4. 321

Gleichen painted by, 5. 360

group by, of Lauzun and Mmes de Gramont and de Stainville, 3. 217

Pont-de-Veyle painted by, 5. 28

portrait by, of Mmes du Deffand and de Choiseul: 3. 392n, 4. 3n, 6n, 13–14, 55, 66, 305, 6. 371, 8. 215–16, 12. 14, 28. 39n, 41. 136–7, 43. 86; Boisgelin sees, 4. 89; Carmontelle refuses copy of, 4. 19, 32; Choiseul, Duchesse de, wants to surprise HW with, 4. 13–14, 25; copies of, 4. 35, 6. 340, 371, 8. 215–16; Du Deffand, Mme, writes verses for, 4. 14; HW's opinion of, 4. 26–7, 29–30; HW to have, 3. 292n, 4. 6, 15; Necker sees, 8. 213; poor likeness of Duchesse, 3. 392n, 4. 13–14, 19, 25, 27, 29–30, 32, 41, 51, 8. 215; Selwyn to have copy of, 30. 252

proverbs of, 4. 278

Rondé, Mme, painted by, 5. 276n

social relations of, with Mme du Deffand, 4. 2, 13

Carron, Giuseppe Angelo Maria (d. 1796), Marchese di Aigueblanche:

no longer in Sardinian ministry, 6. 476, 477

Sardinia's exchange of Corsica with France not approved by, 24. 26n

Viry's disgrace attributed to, 6. 476, 477

*Carron Beaumarchais Memoirs*:

HW's copy of, 43. 96

Carron di San Tommaso, Giuseppe Gioacchino (d. 1709), Conte di Briançon; Savoyard envoy to England 1704–9:

coffin of, unburied, 25. 216, 230

Carrosse; carrosses:

and 3 horses, expense of, 4. 386

[Carrosse; carrosses, *continued*]
Choiseul, Duchesse de, travels in, **4**. 110
Cholmondeley's, **4**. 235
Du Deffand, Mme, has: **3**. 315, 342, 343, 349,
**4**. 368, 369, **5**. 229, **6**. 84; accident to, **3**.
55–6; *see also* Berlin
—— travels in, **4**. 253, 442
Mme Louise orders, **4**. 399
of Mme de Mirepoix, **7**. 66
'Carrousel, dames du.' *See* Compagnolt, Marie-
Anne-Louise-Charlotte de; Crussol, Anne-
Julie-Françoise de; La Baume le Blanc,
Adrienne-Émilie-Félicité de
'Carrousel, Duchesses du.' *See* Crussol, Anne-
Julie-Françoise de; La Baume le Blanc, Adri-
enne-Émilie-Félicité de
Carrousel, Place du, at Paris:
La Vallière, Mme de, lives in, **3**. 18, **5**. 125,
145–7, 155, 170, 191, 197, 210, 226, 233, 238,
256, 311, 312, 317, 361, 362, 376, **6**. 221,
224, 267, 329, 346, **36**. 204
Carrousel; carrousels:
Maria Theresa's ladies to give, for Francis
I, **18**. 99
Cars, Des. *See* Des Cars
Carshalton, Surrey:
HW dines at, with Hon. Thomas Walpole,
**39**. 331
Walpole, Hon. Thomas, lives at, **28**. 456, **33**.
110–11
Cart; carts:
creditors take C. J. Fox's books in, **39**. 376
Gothic, HW should carry SH on, **37**. 466
HW's, to take Montagu portraits to Acton,
**10**. 104
HW sends, twice to Hampton Court for pictures, **10**. 103
HW to send, to Hampton Court, for portraits,
**10**. 67, 81, 85
visible from SH, **25**. 532
Carta cerulea (paper):
HW wants his copy of Medici history printed
on, **25**. 88
Mann explains that his letter is written upon,
**25**. 93
Cartagena, Colombia:
Albemarle may now capture, **22**. 22
Caracciolo arrives at, **17**. 7n
Dutch ship captured on way to, **17**. 53
earthquake allegedly ruins, **22**. 22
English capture of, vainly expected, **13**. 243,
**17**. 71n, 83, 84, 92–3, 96, 126, **18**. 32, **30**.
29, 35, **37**. 101
forts at, disparaged by Ascanio, **17**. 86
Guise jokes about pelicans at, **17**. 485, **20**.
450
—— returns from, **17**. 485
Mann receives news of, **17**. 68
Torres abandons, on Vernon's approach, **17**.
71
Vernon bets on capture of, **17**. 126
—— bombards, **13**. 226, **37**. 83

Cartagena (Spain):
armaments prepared at, **24**. 98n
combined fleet seen near, **25**. 174
English ship's crew captured by Spaniards at,
**22**. 108
fleet prepared at, **23**. 474
Haddock's fleet to observe, **17**. 17n
Osborne fights French ships near, **21**. 188
Saunders near, **21**. 197
sea battle near, **21**. 192–3
Spanish defence preparations at, **23**. 252n
Spanish troops at, may threaten Gibraltar, **23**.
261
squadron of, followed by Rowley to Cadiz,
**19**. 12n
Squillace to embark from, for Naples, **39**.
63–4
Carte, Samuel (1653–1740), antiquary:
MS history of Leicester by, **2**. 243
Carte, Rev. Thomas (1686–1754), historian:
*General History of England, A*, by: cited, **1**.
223n; London employs Carte to write, **18**.
480; Richard III vindicated in, **14**. 165,
**35**. 607
MSS in hand of, from the Archives, Quai
d'Orsai, **43**. 253, 254–5
preferred by HW to Guthrie, **1**. 139
'projets' by, for Jacobite cause, **43**. 253
Whitaker's *Manchester* attacks, **1**. 361
Carteaux, Jean-François (1751–1813), painter;
army officer:
army of, estimated, **12**. *8*
Elliot cannot stop, **39**. 504
Elphinstone defeats, at Toulon, **12**. 8, **39**.
504n, 505n
Cartel; cartels:
for exchange of prisoners: **19**. 187, 202, 204,
**37**. 276; Conway to settle, with French, **21**.
261; English-French at Liège, violated, **37**.
279–80; English-French at Sluys, **37**. 584,
**38**. 1, 5, 7, 10, 11
(?) Montagu, Charles, affected by, **43**. 113–14
Cartel-ship:
Marlborough's teaspoons returned by, **21**. 221
Carter, Charles (fl. ca 1772– after 1788); Mason's 'painting servant':
acts as Mason's amanuensis, **28**. 76
engraving by, of Mason's and Wilson's portrait of Gray, **28**. 98, 100–1, (?) 140–1, **29**.
(?) 290, (?) 291, (?) 302
etching by, from Vaslet's painting of Mason,
**43**. 57
HW would be glad to recommend, **29**. 298–9
'half starving' in London, **29**. 291
Mason asks HW to send parcels through, **28**.
375
—— sketched by, **1**. 260n, **28**. 39n
Pegge painted by, **43**. 295
print by, of Pope's mother, **29**. 278
studies at Royal Academy, **28**. 369
Tyson praises, to Gough, **43**. 294–5

Carter, Edmund (fl. 1753), topographer; school-master:
  *History of Cambridge* cited, 2. 354
Carter, Elizabeth (1717–1806), poet; scholar:
  *Bishop Bonner's Ghost* sent to, by HW, 31. 318
  comments on Mrs Piozzi's style, 11. 21n
  Conyers, Sophia, esteemed by, 11. 57n
  HW admired by, for humanity rather than for wit, 31. 249
  HW asked by, to get act to put down faro, 34. 172, 210
  HW not soon to sit between Lady Louisa Macdonald and, 12. 38
  HW overhears conversation between Hannah More and, 31. 226
  HW's correspondence with, 42. 244–6, 250–2
  HW sends *Bishop Bonner's Ghost* to, 42. 250
  Hayley's *Old Maids* dedicated to, 33. 509n
  health of, headaches, 42. 245
  Hesketh, Lady, visited by, 11. 236
  Howe, Caroline, friend of, 11. 108n
  London to be visited by, 31. 336
  More, Hannah, corresponds with, 31. 252
  'Mrs Epictetus Carter,' 34. 210
  parties at Mrs Vesey's made by HW, Hannah More and, 31. 227–8
  social relations of, with: Garrick, Mrs, 31. 228; More, Hannah, 31. 228; Ord, Mrs, 31. 213; Vesey, Mrs, 31. 242–3
  SH visited by, 12. 229, 31. 262
  Vesey, Mrs, and Mrs Handcock receive attentions from, 31. 266
  Vesey, Mrs, distressing to, 31. 252
'Carter, John':
  HW's name for Carteret, 40. 88
Carter, John (1748–1817), draughtsman; architect:
  drawing by, of HW's oaken head of Henry III, 2. 275n, 16. *192*, 43. 73
  (?) HW goes to see Fenn's pictures at house of, 42. 191
  HW may apply to Palmer through, for purchase of Henry III's head, 16. 193
  HW mentions, 42. 103n
  health of, ague acquired at Croyland, 16. 193
  proposals by, for view of Croyland Abbey, 16. 193, 194–5
  *Specimens of the Ancient Sculpture and Painting* by: Henry III's head depicted in, 2. 275n; Saxon king's statue depicted in, 16. 198n
  statue of Saxon king drawn by, 16. 198
Carter, Mary (d. 1812), HW's friend and correspondent:
  HW's correspondence with, 42. 405–7
  HW sups with, at Lady Mary Churchill's, 11. 95
  HW to receive marble fragment and water incrustation from, 42. 406
  Hamilton, Sir William, deceives, 42. 406

Nivernais's *Jardins modernes* given to, 12. 260, 43. 143, 166
  Venice visited by, 42. 405n
Carter, Mary, m. Andrew Douglas, M.D.:
  sister of Elizabeth Carter, 42. 244n
Carter, Thomas (1690–1763), Master of the Rolls and secretary of state in Ireland:
  Boyle opposed by, on Money Bill, 20. 402n
  Hartington's agreement with, 37. 404
  member of Irish Speaker's party, 20. 402n
  removal of, ordered, 20. 426n
  Stone's removal wanted by, 20. 505n
Carter, Thomas (d. 1795), marble-mason:
  Adam's design for Roger Townshend's monument executed by, 40. 167n
  (?) Bentley schemes with, 35. 231
  Chute's monument by, at the Vyne, 35. 231n
Carter. *See also* Cartwright
Carteret, Bn. *See* Carteret, Hon. Henry Frederick (1735–1826); Carteret, John (1690–1763)
Carteret, Bns. *See* Fermor, Lady Sophia (1721–45); Granville, Lady Grace (1667–1744); Worsley, Frances (1694–1743)
Carteret, Hon. (later Lady) Frances (d. 1788), m. (1748) John Hay, 4th M. of Tweeddale:
  Argyll, Ds of, tries to rent house of, on Twickenham Common, 34. 17
  children starved by, 34. 28
  curiosity of, 31. 124
  father's gift of jewels displeases, 19. 294
  Greenwich, Lady, talks to, about Saxons, 34. 17
  half-sister resembles, 22. 275
  marriage of, 19. 195n
  Montagu, Lady Mary, calls 'ugly girl,' 17. 278n
  nephew's marriage may disconcert, 9. 301
  Nugents visited by, 9. 65
  sings, 9. 65
  Spanish spoken by, 17. *278*
  stepmother leans on, 18. 483
  Tabuerniga family live with, 17. 278
  Twickenham resident, 42. 486
  Williams, Sophia, lives with, 31. 333n
Carteret, Hon. (later Lady) Georgiana Caroline (d. 1780), m. 1 (1734) Hon. John Spencer; m. 2 (1750) William Cowper, 2d E. Cowper, 1723:
  death of, 25. 78, 84, 33. 211, 217, 35. 357
  Dick, Lady, to be proxy for, at step-grandson's baptism, 24. 233, 239
  Duncannons may have Richmond house of, 35. 357
  father's gift of jewels displeases, 19. 294
  forced to walk at Coronation with Cts of Macclesfield, 38. 122, 126
  HW visits, 35. 357
  half-sister resembles, 22. 275
  island of, in Thames, 32. 317n
  jewels and jointure of, go to stepson on her death, 25. 84–5

[Carteret, Hon. Georgiana, *continued*]
    jointures of, revert to son and stepson, **25.** 78
    nephew's marriage may disconcert, **9.** 301
    scenery near house of, at Richmond, **32.** 318
    son gives Queensberry House to, **33.** 541n
    Spencer's match displeases, **37.** 359
    stepmother leans on, **18.** 483
    stepson told by, not to return at once to England, **22.** 375
    (?) Williams, Sophia, lives with, **31.** 333n
Carteret, Lady Grace (1667–1744). *See* Granville, Lady Grace
Carteret, Hon. Grace (1713–55), m. (1729) Lionel Tollemache, 4th E. of Dysart:
    Cavendish, Mrs Richard, mourns, **9.** 171
    'daughter' of, **18.** 431
    death of, **9.** 171
    father's gift of jewels displeases, **19.** 294
    stepmother leans on, **18.** 483
Carteret (Thynne until 1776), Hon. Henry Frederick (1735–1826), cr. (1784) Bn Carteret:
    elder brother of, **33.** 140
    house of, in Curzon St, **33.** 548
    ill-informed on fleet movements, **33.** 140
    (?) print of, **10.** 7
Carteret, John (1690–1763), 2d Bn Carteret, 1695; 1st E. of Granville, 1744:
    address against use of Hanover troops discussed by, **18.** 158
    Admiralty appointments by, without Pelhams' knowledge, **18.** 349
    Admiralty selection may be influenced by, **20.** 17
    anti-Prussian policies of, hamper Villiers's negotiations, **19.** 223n
    Arenberg returns visit of, **18.** 79
    Argyll and Sir Robert Walpole both hated by, **37.** 92
    Arlington St house of, **18.** 96, 231, 349, **21.** 167n, **33.** 340
    army in Germany observes, **37.** 143
    attack on, to re-open, **18.** 366
    ball given by, **37.** 352
    Barnard defends, **26.** 10
    Berkeley a disciple of, **18.** 143
    Berlin diplomatic post predicted for, **9.** 53
    Board of Trade to be headed by, **20.** 249
    Bolton a friend of, **20.** 207
    Brown called 'Irishman' by, **19.** 220
    Cabinet Council tells George II to dismiss, **18.** 535–6
    Capello, Signora, comments on age of, **18.** 431, 446
    change in ministry must meet approval of, **18.** 147
    Charles, P., 'reprieves,' by crossing Rhine, **30.** 60
    Charles Albert's death may be regretted by, as coming too late, **19.** 3
    Chesterfield's witticism on marriage of, **18.** 424

Cholmondeley inclines towards faction of, **18.** 551
Clare resembles, **16.** 346
Clinton's new title supposedly due to, **9.** 36
Clutterbuck betrays, after being aided by him, **17.** 391
Colloredo's conversation with, about Austrian-French neutrality treaty, **20.** 578, 584
Colyear, Lady Juliana, may wed, **20.** 374, 383–4
conundrum on, **19.** 28
Court attended by, **9.** 89
Craon, Princesse de, thanks, for aiding her son, **18.** 286, 312
Cumberland, D. of, prevented by, from having command in Flanders, **19.** 287n
daughter of, **17.** 278n, **20.** 390n, **22.** 275, **23.** 263n, **25.** 78n
defeat of, in Cabinet Council, **18.** 349
Dettingen battle seen by, **18.** 259, 261, 265
—— victory will relieve, **35.** 40
*Discord* satirizes, as 'Craterus,' **30.** 49, **37.** 162
dismissal of, **30.** 291n
drinking habits of, heavy, **19.** 17, 213, **20.** 374, **30.** 40, 229
Drumgold translates HW's account of, **40.** 304n
Dutch reinforcements hurried away by, **18.** 457
Egmont criticizes Hanoverian loyalty of, **20.** 222n
England receives no word from, **18.** 283
estates of, **15.** 139n, **35.** 161n
faction of: **18.** 551; called 'Grand Villains,' **19.** 213
failure of ministry does not disconcert, **19.** 213
father-in-law entertains, **18.** 431
Fermor, Lady Charlotte, receives jewels from, **19.** 294
Fermor, Lady Sophia, to wed, **18.** 424
fiancée's letters read by, to Cabinet Council, **18.** 431
Flanders army debate pushed by, in Parliament, **18.** 382–3
followers of, court his wife, **18.** 442, 501
Fountain meeting not attended by, **17.** 335, 436
Fox persuaded by, to accept Newcastle's plea to lead House of Commons, **20.** 502
Frederick, P. of Wales, hates Pitt since fall of, **19.** 175
—— not joined by, for fear of antagonizing George II, **20.** 30
—— starts opposition after removal of, **20.** 30
—— supports, **18.** 551
—— told by, that Englishmen are grave, **20.** 231
—— whispers to, **9.** 89
friends not made by, **18.** 327
Garter award of, **9.** 89, **18.** 143, 245, **20.** 72, 84
Gashry's appointees may be removed by, **18.** 81

George II and Frederick, P. of Wales, support, **18.** 536, 551

George II and Wasner confer with, on Charles VI's death, **26.** 10

George II asked by, for provision for P. of Wales, **18.** 81

—— asks, to form new ministry, **19.** 211–12

—— awaits report by, from The Hague, **37.** 130

—— favours, **20.** 249, 259

—— induced by, to resist new ministry, **18.** 550

—— makes, K. G., **9.** 89n, **20.** 72, 84

—— persuaded by, that Young Pretender's invasion is unimportant, **19.** 105, 109, 117

—— said by ballad to be bullied by, **18.** 80–4

——'s back stairs descended by, **37.** 221

—— shows to, Fox's offensive letter, **21.** 6n

——'s nearest minister, **18.** 49

—— speaks to, at levee, **17.** 506

——'s reliance on, stressed by Lady Pomfret, **18.** 558

—— still partial to faction of, **18.** 564–5

—— talks with, about dismissal of Treasury people, **18.** 232

—— told by, that Sir Robert Walpole helped carry Hanover troops measure, **18.** 382

—— to remove Pelhams to make room for, **21.** 100n

grandson advised by, about marriage, **9.** 301

HW and Villiers entertained by, **20.** 17

HW buys picture at sale of effects of, **10.** 53

HW compares Bute to, **9.** 315

HW consults, about papers at Longleat, **15.** 77

HW discusses Winchilsea's retort to George II with, **18.** 565

HW disparages, **9.** 40

HW inclined to blame discomforts of inns upon, **18.** 315

HW jokes about glory of, **18.** 248

HW likes approach to house of, **20.** 17

HW mentions, **37.** 186

HW ridicules, **13.** 14n

HW's correspondence with, leads to interview granting apartment to Bentley, **35.** 161

HW's opinion of, **19.** 4, **30.** 229

HW's 'portrait' of: **13.** 37, **14.** 123–4; Gray revises, **14.** 124–5

HW's portrait of Mary Tudor formerly owned by, **40.** 365

HW's verses on, sent to Mann, **20.** 117, 119

HW's visit returned by, probably on Sir Robert Walpole's account, **18.** 527–8

HW to ask, about Lady Pomfret's Froissart, **15.** 60

HW to give Mann's compliments to, **18.** 463–4

HW told by, to ask wife to dance, **19.** 18

Hague, The, visited by, **18.** 61, 70

Ham House gates opened only for, **10.** 307

Hamilton, Lady Archibald, ousted from P. of Wales's court probably by, **19.** 62

Hanoverian policy of, may result in Whigs' defeat, **18.** 356n

Hanover news from, ridiculed, **18.** 264

Hanover to be visited by, with George II, **18.** 209

Harrington more civil than, to Mann, **18.** 363

—— refuses to coalesce with, **19.** 326n

health of: gout, **18.** 431; much broken, **22.** 33

Indemnity Bill opposed by, **17.** 436

Italy not notified by, of his becoming secretary of state, **19.** 213

Jersey estate of, **35.** 161n

Lee an Admiralty member under, **20.** 30

—— protégé of, **17.** 242n, **19.** 241

—— resigns Admiralty on disgrace of, **17.** 242n

levee of, **18.** 349

lord president of the Council, **9.** 115, **20.** 202n, 207, 216, 258–9, **22.** 569

Lovat's complaint investigated by, **19.** 347

Lyttelton secretary to, **18.** 551

Magnan writes to, **18.** 549

Mann glad that new ministry has been wrecked by association with, **19.** 225

—— need not expect letters from, **18.** 382

—— no favourite of, **18.** 363

—— pleased by conduct of, to Bns Walpole, **17.** 460

—— sends to, Theodore of Corsica's letter, **18.** 190

——'s inquiries about Theodore unanswered by, **18.** 205

—— writes to, **18.** 286, 312

Maria Theresa said to depend chiefly upon, for English support, **18.** 557

Mathews displeased with, **18.** 346, 395

matrimonial happiness of, **18.** 464

Mecklenburg, D. of, succeeds, in Garter, **22.** 227n

ministry of: **9.** 116n, **20.** 12; commands majority in House of Commons, **18.** 96; duty on tea proposed by, **18.** 141; Pension Bill shows power of, **17.** 392n; Theodore of Corsica said to have deceived, **18.** 221–2

ministry offered to, **35.** 253

mob hails, **35.** 39

mother-in-law of: mortified by his fall, **18.** 537; not encouraged by him, **18.** 430, 442; praises him in letters to Niccolini, **18.** 557–8; will expect to influence him, **18.** 424

mother of: (?) governs him, **30.** 55; offers to get people positions through him, **18.** 136; succeeded by him in title, **18.** 521n

motion of, at rebels' trial, **19.** 286–7

'Motion, The,' depicts, **18.** 21n

name of: forged to Young Pretender's passport, **18.** 378; used to lure Theodore from shelter, **20.** 164

Newcastle, D. of, and, **35.** 21

Newcastle, D. of, and Pelham jealous of, **18.** 537

[Carteret, John, *continued*]

Newcastle, D. of, and Pelham quarrel with, **30.** 49

Newcastle, D. of, and Pelham reconciled with, **18.** 349

Newcastle, D. of, approves of, for using victories to procure peace, **18.** 230n

—— believes all measures of, subservient to flattering George II, **18.** 327n

—— changes policy after ousting, **19.** 464

—— copies letter of, with Dettingen news, **18.** 258

—— enjoys discomfiture of, at rebels' progress, **19.** 109

—— entertains, at Claremont, **17.** 503, **18.** 20–2

—— induces George II to discard, as secretary of state, **40.** 88

—— informed by, of Fox's willingness to join ministry, **20.** 502n

—— jealous of assemblies of, **18.** 562

—— negotiates with, to strengthen himself against D. of Cumberland, Bedford, and Sandwich, **20.** 72n

—— never gets letters from, **18.** 382

—— said to be left in place by, but without power, **18.** 82

—— served under, **10.** 192n

——'s union with, **17.** 300–1

—— tells, about venison, **17.** 506

*New Ode, A,* satirizes, **18.** 49

*Old Coachman, The,* satirizes, **18.** 20–2

Onslow hails Parliamentary triumph over, **18.** 540

packet boat detained by, while he decides what to write to Holland, **19.** 213

parish subscription book not signed by, **19.** 167

Parliamentary motion by, against Sir Robert Walpole, **37.** 92

Parliamentary speech by, parodied in Williams's 'Pandæmonium,' **30.** 314

party betrayed by, **17.** 329n

Pelham betrayed by, into losing sugar tax, **22.** 489

—— opposed by, about privately-raised regiments, **19.** 158

—— strengthened by failure of, to form new ministry, **19.** 212

Pelhams might fear vengeance of, **19.** 17

physicians of, order him to Spa, **19.** 26

Pitt abuses, in Parliament, **18.** 383

—— attacks, **37.** 416

—— calls, 'Mazarin,' **26.** 10

——'s bequest from, **22.** 277n

——'s charges against, answered by Winnington, **18.** 351

——'s diction and views not esteemed by, **30.** 229

——'s Spanish war proposal opposed by, **38.** 131n

political situations of 1763 and 1765 like that in 1746 under, **22.** 158, 303

portrait formerly owned by, **15.** 139, 155, **40.** 365

Pucci predicts retirement of, **18.** 557

Pulteney captures Frederick, P. of Wales, from, **19.** 229

—— disowned by, **20.** 259

—— may break with, if French are not beaten, **18.** 328n

—— receives hint of Privy Seal offer from, **18.** 231

——'s followers desert to, **18.** 73, 74

——'s friend, **19.** 167

Ranelagh visited by, **18.** 464

Regency Bill defended by, **20.** 257

Regency Council not noticed by, **18.** 382

regent, **18.** 209n

resigns, **18.** 535, 549, 556

restoration of, unlikely, **19.** 105

return of, possible, **20.** 202

Richecourt through Francis I might persuade, to oust Mann, **18.** 363

rodomontade favourite figure of speech of, **30.** 229

rubs periwig off, scratches head, and bites nails, **37.** 92

Rushout may lead party of, in House of Commons, **19.** 212

sacrifices all, to please George II, **18.** 537

secretary of state, **17.** 333

secretaryship of state predicted for, by Gage, **17.** 296

son of, goes mad, **18.** 501

Spanish spoken by, **17.** 278

Spencer's match pleases, **37.** 359

Stair charges, with everything amiss, **18.** 311n

Stanislas I's candidacy for emperor supported by, **19.** 7n

Tabuerniga family live with, **17.** 278

Theodore of Corsica claims friendship of, **18.** 188, 194

—— claims that aid was promised him by, **18.** 188

—— claims to have heard from, of Bns Walpole's application, **18.** 194

—— formerly befriended by, **20.** 385

——'s connections with: amaze Sir Robert Walpole, **18.** 210, 225; shown by failure to mention him to Mann, **18.** 233

——'s deception discovered by, **18.** 216

—— wants, to send Mann a courier, **18.** 190

Thomas made bishop by, **18.** 537–8

Townshend, Vcts, entertains, **19.** 18

Treasury post coveted by, **18.** 265–6, 277

Tweeddale a follower of, **18.** 51

—— son-in-law and political ally of, **19.** 195n

Uguccioni has abbé do epithalamium for, **18.** 510

—— hopes for preferment through, **18.** 455, **35.** 53

——'s presents to, **18**. 553–4

unable to form government, **10**. 153n

Villiers's conversation with, **20**. 17

Walpole, Bns, deterred by, from English visit, **18**. 4

—— expects, to be eager to vex Sir Robert Walpole, **17**. 460–1

—— writes to, **17**. 441

Walpole, Sir Robert, drinks to health of, **18**. 259–60

—— kept ignorant of foreign affairs by, **18**. 30

—— not openly demanded by, for impeachment, **17**. 329

—— prevails upon George II to dismiss, **18**. 536n

—— receives from, Bns Walpole's letter, **17**. 441

—— said by, to attract all to his levees, **18**. 349

——'s coachman conveys, from New Park, **17**. 503, 506, **18**. 21–2

—— thanked by: for coachman, in Newcastle's presence, **17**. 506; for Hanover troops measure, **18**. 382

wedding of: **17**. 107n, **18**. 431; postponed, **18**. 430, 431: shocks Florentines by its simplicity, **18**. 445–6

wife of: **9**. 15n, **13**. 234n, **17**. 258n, **30**. 328n; continues assemblies after his resignation, **18**. 562; given dressing-plate and his mother's apartment, **18**. 562

wife's family may be shunned by, **18**. 430

wife's remark about, **17**. 258

wife's visit to Tunbridge may imply impotence of, **18**. 501

Williams bets with Fox over presidency of Council for, **20**. 216n

Winnington questions maxim of, about Crown support, **18**. 535

Worms treaty signed by, **18**. 311n

Wyndham promised title by, **20**. 81

Wyndham, George O'Brien, said to be godson of, **9**. 126

Yarmouth reached by, on return to England, **18**. 79–80

Carteret, Robert (1721–76), styled Bn Carteret 1744–63; 2d E. Granville, 1763; M.P.:

Bedfords visited by, **18**. 501

dances at Robinson's ball, **37**. 115

declines standing for re-election, **30**. 78

goes mad, and crops horses' ears, **18**. 501

Lincoln's superiority to, **30**. 41

Carteret, Lady Sophia (1745–71), m. (1765) William Petty, 2d E. of Shelburne, 1761; cr. (1784) M. of Lansdowne:

appearance and fortune of, **22**. 275

birth of, **19**. 105

death of, **23**. 263, **31**. 153

France visited by, **20**. 87

frightened, **9**. 193

grandfather's bequest to, **20**. 390

HW did not know, **33**. 115

less handsome and agreeable than her successor, **33**. 106, 115

marriage plans of, announced, **22**. 275

Pomfret, Cts of, accompanied by, at presentation of Pomfret marbles at the Sheldonian, **9**. 193

—— takes, to Italy, **20**. 97

separation of husband and, falsely rumoured, **14**. 141

Carteret family:

ancestral Manoir de St-Ouen of, in Jersey, **35**. 161n

Granville, Cts, gives ball for, **18**. 565

Carthage:

African civilization momentarily flowered in, **25**. 47

author from, would be proud to be translated by Scipio, **42**. 129

destruction of, **31**. 439, **33**. 49

England compared with ruins of, **29**. 295, **33**. 264

London mostly as unfamiliar as, **11**. 212

Spain formerly in subjection to, **29**. 232

Carthagena. *See* Cartagena

Cart-horse; cart-horses:

at Ghent, **37**. 125

Conway buys, for camp, **37**. 125

Carthusian; Carthusians:

Austrian, suppressed, **25**. 594n

diet of: Chute imitates, **35**. 23; Hardinge adopts, **35**. 578

George II lodges at convent of, near Mainz, **37**. 144

Louis XVI recompenses, for loss of Le Sueur's paintings, **35**. 430n

Carton, Ireland, Kildare's seat:

Conway visits, **37**. 428

Devonshire, Conway, and wife to meet at, **37**. 456

Carton Dancourt, Florent (1661–1725), dramatist:

*Curieux de Compiègne, Les,* by, **7**. 329

*Théâtre* of, owned by Mme du Deffand, **8**. 34

wife of, **18**. 334n

Cartoon; cartoons:

alleged Raphael painting resembles, **35**. 37

for tapestries, supposedly Raphael's, **16**. 157

for tapestry, **40**. 283

Raphael's: **35**. 37; at Hampton Court, **16**. 147; tapestry from, at Madrid, **16**. 169; tapestry from, at Rome, **16**. 169; tapestry from, supposedly at Burghley House, **16**. 159; Waddilove asks about, **16**. 168–9

Cartouche, Louis-Dominique (ca 1693–1721), thief:

HW imagines plea by, at Judgment Day, **28**. 427

National Assembly membership would not be thought an honour by, **31**. 386

Cartown. *See* Carton
Cartridge; cartridges:
    pandours carry, 37. 142
Cartwright, Mr:
    mistake for Carteret, 33. 140
Cartwright, Rev. Christopher (1602–58):
    Drake on, 2. 114–15
Cartwright, James *or* Nathaniel (fl. 1760–70),
    lace merchant:
    Cole sends parcels under care of, 1. *54*, 55, 58,
        58n, 59, 64, 67, 68, 101, 115, 126, 127
    lodges with John Rowley, 1. 68n
Cartwright, William (1611–43), dramatist:
    (?) HW confuses namesake with, 35. 134
    *Royal Slave, The*, to be acted, in HW's news-
        paper parody, 9. 129
Cartwright, William (d. 1687), actor:
    bequest of, at Dulwich College, 11. 289n
    portrait of, at Knole, 35. 134
Cartwright, Rt Rev. William (ca 1730–99), non-
    juring bishop; apothecary:
    HW's account of, 13. 31–2
    *Remarks on Mr Walpole's Catalogue* ascribed
        to, 13. 31–2, 14. 258, 16. 29–30
Carucates:
    surveys are full of, 35. 146
Carvajal y Lancáster ('Carvalho and Lancas-
    ter'), José de (ca 1701–54), Spanish states-
    man:
    Anglo-Spanish treaty of commerce signed by,
        20. 197n
    Huescar succeeds, temporarily, 20. 426n
    Wall to succeed, as Spanish secretary of state
        for foreign affairs, 20. 426
    Young Pretender urged by, to leave Spain,
        19. 390n
Carvalho e Melo, Sebastiaõ José de (1699–1782),
    Conde de Oeiras; cr. (1770) Marquês de
    Pombal; prime minister of Portugal:
    Benedict XIV's brief used by, to justify edicts
        against Jesuits, 21. 340n
    Brazilian seizure attributed to attempt by,
        to involve England, 36. 47n
    brother of, dies, 31. 144
    house of, 11. 160n
    in danger of assassination, 23. 359
    Jesuits accused by, of insults to Portuguese
        sovereignty in Brazil, Paraguay and Uruguay,
        21. 217n
    —— opposed by, 26. 49
    life of, can be preserved only by guards, bars,
        and bolts, 23. 100
    plot will be discovered by, 23. 166
    Portuguese bastards' elevation opposed by,
        21. 475n
    Portuguese conspiracy ascribed to, 21. 342
    Portuguese conspiracy well handled by, 21.
        276
    rooms of, closely guarded, 22. 94–5
    Saldanha related to, 21. 217n
    Souza receives account from, of attack on José
        I, 4. 328–9

Walpole, Hon. Robert, to ask, about Jesuit
    archives, 23. 533n
Carvel; carvels:
    Turkish, defeated by Russians, 23. 233
Carver; carvers:
    HW's, at SH, *see* Murray, George (d. 1761)
    working in Gallery, at SH. 10. 84
Carving:
    HW eschews at SH, 20. 382
    in ivory, 18. 277, 19. 420–1
    on picture frames, 31. 80
    profuse, at Lord Wilmington's at Eastbourne,
        40. 6
Carvoisin, Jacques-François de (b. 1727), Mar-
    quis d'Achy:
    wife of, 4. 406n
Cary, Elizabeth (ca 1740–1830), m. (1767) Jef-
    frey Amherst, cr. (1776) Bn Amherst:
    assemblies of, 33. 215
    Berry, Mary, identifies, 11. 230n
    social relations of, with: HW, 11. 230, 260,
        12. 88, 31. 351; More, Hannah, 11. 260,
        31. 351
Cary, Frances (d. 1768), m. (1721) John Vil-
    liers, 5th Vct Grandison, cr. (1721), E.
    Grandison:
    daughter and son-in-law to visit, at Dublin,
        10. 66
    death of, expected, 10. 194
    Montagu, Charles, to benefit from, 10. 194
    reversion of, 10. 234n
Cary, Lucius Charles (ca 1707–85) 7th Vct Falk-
    land, 1730:
    HW can get description from, of Burghley
        portrait, 41. 298
    HW's correspondence with, 41. 298
    HW to be called on by, 41. 298
    marriage of, 9. 139–40, 37. 339, 341
Cary, Thomas, friend of Chatterton:
    Chatterton considered by, a genius but in-
        capable of writing Rowley poems, 16. 333
Cary; Carye. *See also* Carew; Carey
Caryatides:
    on chimney-piece, 35. 214
Carysfort, Bn. *See* Proby, John (1720–72)
Carysfort, Bns and Cts of. *See* Grenville, Eliza-
    beth
*Carysfort*, English frigate:
    Joseph II to see, 23. 108
Carzon. *See* Curzon
Casale, Scipione Giuseppe (d. 1765), Genoese
    agent at Rome 1753–60; minister to Naples
    1760–5:
    Genoa notified by, of bishop's departure for
        Corsica, 21. 394
    Genoa will receive no letters from Rome but
        through, 21. 412
Casale:
    Austrians join Charles Emmanuel III at, 19.
        120
Casali, Cardinal:
    congregation on Jesuits includes, 23. 507n

Casalnuovo, Italy:
earthquake account mentions, **25.** 376
Casanova, François (1730–1805), painter:
Loutherbourg's paintings in the manner of, **7.** 317
Casanova de Seingalt, Giacomo Girolamo (1725–98), adventurer:
(?) daughter of, **31.** 333n
Desarmoises family mentioned by, **17.** 225n
mistress of, **29.** 31n
Rochford, Lady, subject of comment by, **9.** 42n
San Gillio, Contessa di, mentioned by, **20.** 309n
Casaquin:
Antinori calls, a *conc touché*, **18.** 486
Casas, Las. *See* Las Casas
Casati, Teresa, Contessa, m. (1783) Carlo Francesco Saverio Giuseppe Albani, Principe di Soriano:
SH visited by, **33.** 530
Casaubon, Meric:
Dee's *True and Faithful Relation* edited by, **43.** 389n
Cascade; cascades:
at Blenheim, **10.** 309
at Coldbrook, **30.** 48
at Hagley, **35.** 148
at Leeds Castle, **35.** 145
at SH: HW makes, **35.** 324–5; resemble cataracts, **39.** 133
at Warwick, **9.** 121
at Wroxton, **35.** 72, 73
Bentley's drawing of, **35.** 157
in Dublin ballroom, **37.** 412
Cascar, Don Gulielmo, Scottish sergeant-maj. in Spanish service:
campaign conditions on Spanish-Portuguese border described by, to Sandwich, **40.** 240
Cascine; Cascines, at Florence:
ballroom at, burns, **11.** 318
delightful but unfrequented, **25.** 585
Du Châtelet has entertainment at, for English captains, **18.** 98, 100
English verdure compared to, **11.** 267, 300
Ferdinand of Naples shoots in, **25.** 600
Mann escorts Karl Alexander to, **20.** 376
—— takes Ds of Kingston to, **24.** 6
—— visits, at sunset, **25.** 558, 585, 597
Richmond meadows compared to, **11.** 337
weather prevents Mann from visiting, **21.** 58
woods of, may be cut down, **17.** 195
Cascine Gate, Florence:
Corsini's house near, **17.** 101
Case, Miss, musician:
'Slingsby's Allemande' played by, **43.** 351
Case (surname). *See* Caus
Case; cases:
for HW's Italian purchases, charges for transportation of, **26.** 3, 4, 6
for scissors: best made in Paris, **31.** 85; common, would tarnish steel, **31.** 85

glass, at Elizabeth Chudleigh's, **9.** 277
tortoise-shell, belonging to Tromp, given to HW by Hamilton, **35.** 430–1
'Case Concerning the Late Disturbances.' *See under* Beard, John
Case-knife; case-knives:
Amsterdam expresses politics by, **25.** 496
*Case of Going to War, The. See under* Tucker, Josiah
*Case of John Hamilton, The. See under* Hervey, Hon. Thomas
*Case of Miss Gunning, The*:
published, **11.** 280n
'Case of the Entail, The,' by HW:
HW's controversy over Walpole estates detailed by, **36.** 295–304
letters concerning, **36.** 315
*Case of the Hanover Forces, The. See under* Stanhope, Philip Dormer, E. of Chesterfield; Waller, Edmund
*Case of the Hon. Alexander Murray, The*:
Owen's trial for publishing, **35.** 551n
Caserta (Italy):
Aquedotto Carolino brings water from Monte Taburno to, **21.** 379n
'building at,' *see under* Vanvitelli, Luigi: *Dichiarazione*
Charles III orders work on, to continue, **21.** 379
Chute and HW admire, **21.** 363
criticisms of, **21.** 379
Ferdinand gives balls and suppers at, **23.** 191
gardens at, **35.** 439
HW inquires about, **21.** 364
Hamilton writes about, **35.** 438
Herculaneum's treasures were to be deposited at, **21.** 364
Neapolitan Court at, **20.** 429
Cashel (Cashell), Abp of. *See* Agar, Charles
Cashiobury. *See* Cassiobury
Casimir, K. of Poland. *See* John II
'Casino, The,' Florentine coffee-house:
English visitors will not be as well received at, when refugees, **18.** 459
(?) Leopold's letter banning extravagant dress read at, **25.** 175
Mann entertains too many frequenters of, **18.** 286
Casino; casinos:
at Leghorn, **22.** 104
at Pisa, **22.** 221
at Pitti palace for Archduchess's women, **22.** 258, 290–1
Charlemont builds, at Marino, **9.** 391
Sixtus V's, at Villa Negroni, **24.** 7
Casino (game):
Gloucester, Ds of, has party of, **36.** 329
Casino de' nobili, at Florence:
ball at, for Archduke and Archduchess of Milan, **25.** 51
Leopold's letter to Nelli instructs, about ladies' dress, **25.** 175n

[Casino de' nobili, *continued*]
 masked ball at, **23**. 458n
 prince of, told to assert Mann's innocence, **19**. 498
 Young Pretender goes to, **23**. 226
Casino Rospigliosi, at Rome:
 Guido Reni's 'Aurora' at, **20**. 328n
Casket; caskets:
 enamel, at Burghley House, **10**. 345
 gold, at Burghley House, **10**. 345
 silver, Montagu to send, by HW, to Mme Roland, **10**. 246–8, 250, 251
Časlau:
 battle of, **17**. 429–30, 433, 464
Casley, David (ca 1682–*post* 1754), librarian:
 *Catalogue of the MSS of the King's Library*: Gray refers HW to, **14**. 109, 116, 173; Warbeck's proclamation not in, **14**. 176
Caslon, Guillaume (1692–1766), type-founder:
 death of, **7**. 397
Casotti:
 wood insufficient to build, **18**. 270
Casque; casques:
 Richelieu might wear, **32**. 246
 *See also* Helmet
Cassagnet, Aimery de (1696–1760), Marquis de Fimarcon, 1730; army officer:
 French invasion force said to be commanded by, **19**. 187
*Cassandre. See under* Costes de la Calprenède, Gautier de
Cassanea de Mondonville, Jean-Joseph (1715–73), composer:
 *Thésée* produced by, **3**. 208–9
Cassel (Germany):
 Conway and Scott visit, **39**. 536
 French may spend winter at, **21**. 254
 French said to capture, **38**. 69
 Isenburg stationed near, to defend Hesse, **37**. 554
 Lutterburg near, **40**. 144
 Mann hopes that Conway will help capture, **21**. 493
 siege of, raised, **9**. 353, **21**. 498, 502
 woods at, poor, **38**. 179
*Cassette verte de Monsieur de Sartine, La. See under* Tickell, Richard
Cassia:
 Du Deffand, Mme, takes, **3**. 378, 389, **4**. 275, 287, **5**. 80, 93, 94, 170, 196, 208–9, 283–4, **6**. 20, 99–100, 105, 229, 270, 448, **7**. 243, 245, 246, 425, 430, 436, 438, 439, 445, 449, 450, 454, 457, 459, 460, **41**. 195
 faintings caused by, **36**. 58
Cassiobury Park, near Watford, Herts; E. of Essex's seat:
 Bentley should be employed at, **35**. 177
 HW and Rigby visit, **30**. 62
 (?) Nugent to direct alterations at, with Cts of Essex, **37**. 447
 plays acted at, **32**. 176, 180
 Selwyn and Lord March visit, **32**. 77

 *See also* Little Cassiobury
Cassius Longinus, Caius (d. 42 B.C.), conspirator:
 HW cites, from *Julius Cæsar*, **22**. 567
 HW imagines letter from, to Brutus, **29**. 84
 HW refers to Norton as, **23**. 180
Cassock; cassocks:
 Baker wears, in old fashion, **2**. 351, 352
 girls should choose lovers clad in, as likely to be faithful, **25**. 424
 Hackman exchanges gorget for, **33**. 100
 Middleton wears, **15**. 315
Cassolette. *See* Cellini, Benvenuto: chest of
Cast; casts:
 Hamilton to send, to HW, of Mrs Damer's medallion, **35**. 432
 moulds for, **40**. 276
 of antique statues, collected by D. of Richmond, **21**. 173
 of Caligula's bust, **22**. 528
 of Cupid and Psyche, **35**. 484n
 of eagle, **19**. 197, 430, 438, 445, 457, **21**. 173
 of 'Livia' statue, *see under* Livia
 wax, of Sir Robert Walpole, **41**. 285
 *See also* Gesso
Cast, St. *See* St-Cast
Castalia:
 Mason not to be dipped in, **29**. 262
'Castalio and Polidore.' *See under* Otway, Thomas, *The Orphan*
Castaly, fountain of Parnassus:
 'Castalian state,' **32**. 223
 'Castalia's choicest lay,' **33**. 96
Castanets:
 women dance with, on Minorca, **37**. 311
*Castara. See under* Habington, William
Castejon. *See* González de Castejon
Castelbarco, Teresa di (d. 1765), m. 1 (1724) Conte Antonio Simonetta; m. 2 (1761) Francis III of Modena; cr. (1765) Principessa di Varese:
 death of, after becoming Ps of Varese, **22**. 331
 Ercole III imprisoned for disrespect to plans made by, at Vienna, for his daughter, **22**. 201
 Francis III arranges income for, **22**. 144
 —— marries, **22**. *126*, 135, 148
 HW saw, at Reggio fair, **22**. 134–5, 144, 148
 Maria Ricciarda Beatrice may be educated by, **22**. 171–2
 Maria Theresa caresses, at Vienna, **22**. 126
Castel Ceriolo e St Giuliano (Italy):
 Don Philip replaces Gages at, **19**. 84
Castelcicala, Principe di. *See* Ruffo, Fabrizio
Castelcicala, Principessa di (d. *post* 1816), m. (ca 1782) Fabrizio Ruffo, Principe di Castelcicala:
 dances at Queensberry House, **11**. 341
Castelcigala. *See* Castelcicala
Castel del Monte:
 Del Monte brothers escape from, **20**. 430
Castelferretti. *See* Ferretti di Castelferretti

Castelfranco, Princesse de. *See* Stolberg-Gedern, Karoline Auguste of (1755–1829)

Castel Gandolfo:
Albani, Palazzo, at, **24.** 214n, 248
Benedict XIV returns from, **20.** 442
Clement XIV returns from, **23.** 526
Gloucester, D. of, should have spent summer at, instead of Venice, **24.** 314
—— to occupy Albano villa at, **24.** 214
Gore family neighbours of D. of Gloucester at, **24.** 251
Laurenti goes to, on hearing of Benedict XIV's illness, **20.** 442n
Ruffo visits, to complain to the Pope, **19.** 416

Castellane, Comtesse de. *See* Rohan-Chabot, Alexandrine-Charlotte-Sophie de

Castellane, Marquise de. *See* Simiane, Julie de (1704–28)

Castellane, Angélique-Charlotte de (b. 1751), m. (1772) Claude-Camille-François, Comte d'Albon; Prince d'Yvetot:
marriage of, **5.** 225

Castellane, Jean-Baptiste de (d. 1790), Marquis d'Esparron et de la Garde; 'Burrhus':
Chanteloup visited by, **4.** 234, 238, 245, **6.** 75, 476, **41.** 198
Choiseul, Duchesse de, accompanied by, from and to Chanteloup, **7.** 26
—— confides in, **4.** 342, 359
—— friend of, **41.** 193, 258
—— governed by, **4.** 350
—— obtains Sévigné letters from, **41.** 109
Dauphiné visited by, **41.** 198
Du Deffand, Mme, presents HW's compliments to, **5.** 253
——'s offer of lodging to HW approved by, **4.** 391, 398
——'s opinion of, **3.** 255, 280, 303, 337, **4.** 302, 342, **7.** 35
——'s relations with, **4.** 359, 388, **5.** 44, 255, **6.** 22
Gennevilliers visited by, **7.** 328
HW knows not, if living, **34.** 85
HW liked by, **4.** 302, 304, **7.** 26
HW often sups with, **41.** 258
HW sent messages by, **5.** 243, **7.** 26
Paris to be visited by, **6.** 22
returns to Provence, **6.** 75
Sévigné letter obtained from, for HW, **4.** 72, **34.** 81, 85
(?) Sévigné letters supposedly discovered by, **35.** 393
Simiane, Mme de, mother-in-law of, **7.** 320
social relations of, in Paris, *see index entries ante* **8.** 283

Castellane-Adhémar de Monteil, François de (ca 1629–1714), Comte de Grignan:
HW finds print of, **9.** 21–2
wife of, **3.** 70n, **10.** 12n, **16.** 273n, **28.** 297n

Castellane-Adhémar de Monteil de Grignan, Françoise-Pauline de (1674–1737), m. (1695) Louis de Simiane du Claret, Marquis de Truchenu et d'Esparron:
Castellane not descended from, **34.** 85
daughter of, **3.** 255n, **7.** 320, **34.** 81
grandmother's portrait owned by, **31.** 7n, **35.** 198
grandmother venerated by, **41.** 257
HW admires letter to, from mother, **4.** *141*
house of, **34.** 85, **43.** 359
letters of: **5.** 380n; Du Deffand, Mme, disparages, **5.** 420; HW defends, **5.** 423; HW finds, uninteresting, **35.** 466, 601; Moulceau in, **32.** 172
mother's letters presumably destroyed by, **28.** 297n
name of, corrected, **43.** 89
picture of, not seen by HW, **34.** 85

Castellane de Monteil de Grignan, Louis-Provence de (1671–1704), Marquis de Grignan:
stabbed in bed by estranged friend, **41.** 257

Castellanos, Don Pedro Pascal, Spanish usurer:
house of, pillaged not burnt, **8.** 120
threatened by mob, **8.** 119

Castellar; Castellara; Castelar. *See* Patinho, Don Lucas Fernando

Castellars, Marquis de, commandant général of Saragossa:
mob demands lower food prices from, **8.** 119

Castellet, —— (d. 1790), Marquis de; director general of port of Toulon:
murder of, **34.** 95–6

Castelli, Signora, wife of Pierfrancesco:
oculist cures, **18.** 240

Castelli, Giuseppe Maria (1705–80), cardinal, 1759:
Bourbon Courts would exclude, from Papal councils, **23.** 16, 35

Castelli, Maria Medea, m. (1719) Agostino Dini:
daughter jealous of Corsi's attentions to, **19.** 452
fortune owned by, **17.** 203
Mann entertains, **17.** 95
Tempi cicisbeo to, for 30 years, **20.** 298

Castello, near Florence:
Corsini's villa at, **17.** 67
Craon to take Mann, Chute, and Whithed to, **17.** 443
*See also* Castello, villa

Castello, near Rome:
Del Monte besieged in palazzo in, **20.** 442
Del Monte family invades, **20.** 423, 428
Lobkowitz halts at, **18.** 531

Castello, villa, near Florence:
Craon takes Mann and others to, **18.** 1
furniture at, **20.** 116
Grafton, Ds of, declines to visit, **22.** 29
Leopold and Maria Louisa at, **25.** 644
Leopold moves from, with family, to Poggio Imperiale, **25.** 421
Mann sends news of Gibraltar to, **25.** 329
—— takes D. of York to, **22.** 224

[Castello, villa, *continued*]
 Maria Louisa visits, **25.** 203
 Tuscan Court prefers Lappeggi to, **22.** 412
Castello di Sangro:
 Charles III at, **18.** 438
Castello Gandolfo. *See* Castel Gandolfo
Castello San Giovambatista. *See* Fortezza da Basso
Castelmaine, Cts of. *See* Villiers, Barbara
Castelmaine, Vct. *See* Child, Richard (1680–1750)
Castelmoron, Marquis de. *See* Belsunce, Antonin-Louis de
Castelmoron, Marquise de. *See* Fontanieu, Cécile-Geneviève (d. 1761); Sublet d'Heudicourt, Charlotte-Alexandrine (b. 1722); Vergès, Marie-Madeleine de (1762–1837)
Castel St Angelo, at Rome:
 Jesuit agents sent to, **23.** 516, 517n, 526n
 Jesuits at, were to have been released by Pius VI when Charles III intervened, **24.** 115
 Leopold, Maria Carolina, and Maria Louisa saluted by, **23.** 23
 Sixtus V's treasure deposited in, **22.** 446, 448
Castera, —— (d. 1783), surgeon:
 (?) insane, **4.** 416
Casti, Giovanni Battista (1724–1803), poet:
 *Il Re Teodoro in Venezia,* HW buys book after seeing opera of, **33.** 586–7
Castiglione, Contessa. *See* Crivelli, Eleonora
Castiglione, Baldassare (1478–1529), Conte; author:
 Harcourt the perfect courtier of, **33.** 463
Castiglione, Giovanni Benedetto (1616–65), painter:
 painting by, at Burghley House, **10.** 346
 painting by, of (?) Tobit, sent by Mann to HW, **21.** 521–2, 524–5, 532, 538, **23.** 425, **24.** 15, **25.** 89, **26.** 56
Castile, Ps of. *See* Isabel (ca 1355–92)
Castile:
 Aranda president of Council of, **41.** 203
 arms of, **1.** 242
 Calveley said to have gone in John of Gaunt's expedition to, **41.** 445
Castilhon. *See* Castillon
Castilius, Don Francis Havers:
 *Constant of Teneriff* commanded by, **17.** 276n
Castille, Baron de. *See* Froment-Fromentès de Castille, Gabriel-Joseph de
Castillo, ——, painter:
 Cumberland speaks of, **29.** 232n
Castillon, —— de, avocat général of the parliament of Aix:
 extract of 'inflammatory speech' by, **1.** 99n
Castillon *or* Castilhon, Jean (1718–99), writer:
 Du Deffand, Mme, asks, to keep criticism of Hénault out of *Journal encyclopédique,* **4.** 158
Castle; castles:
 as garden ornaments at Wentworth Castle, **35.** 267

at Southampton, **35.** 251
at Stowe, **10.** 315
at Walpole St Peter, in stained glass, **40.** 224
Conway builds, in air, **37.** 122
'Druidic' temple resembles ruins of, **35.** 396
floating, England puts, at river-mouths, to prevent invasion, **20.** 505
HW calls, SH, **37.** 406, 411
HW prefers, to be shown by housekeeper rather than owner, **39.** 434–5
HW sees, ruined, **39.** 179
highwaymen bring back the dangers of, **35.** 525
King's *Observations* on, **33.** 353
Miller's, ruined, at Hagley, **35.** 148
Montagu sees, **10.** 229
More, Hannah, sees, in Wye valley, **31.** 320
mountains covered with, at Genoa, **37.** 319
on the Rhine, **37.** 150
Park Place lacks, **37.** 379
peers must eschew new façades to, for Coronation finery, **35.** 310
SH resembles Spenser's, **40.** 255
Sussex the 'holy land' of, **35.** 131
Castle Ashby, Northants:
 chapel and church at, **10.** 336
 Cole describes, **10.** 335–7
 HW and Cole visit, **10.** 88, 335–7
 HW criticizes, **10.** 88
 HW wants print of, **42.** 17
 itinerary to and from, **10.** 86, 335, 338
 Jones designs part of, **10.** 336
 Northampton's furniture at, returned to Comptons by wife, **10.** 337
 (?) ——'s lawn and chase at, converted to tillage, **10.** 287
 pictures at: **10.** 336–7; Pennant may want copies of, **41.** 251
 Shrewsbury portraits at, **41.** 220n
Castle Bear Hill:
 Fitzherbert, Mrs, buys villa at, **12.** 138n
Castlecomer, Vct. *See* Wandesford, Sir Christopher (1717–36); Wandesford John (1725–84)
Castlecomer, Vcts. *See* Montagu, Elizabeth (d. 1731); Pelham, Frances (d. 1756)
'Castlecomer, Lords':
 inconvenience to, **10.** 311, **35.** 91
Castlecomer, Ireland:
 Sherlock, vicar of, **29.** 104n
Castlecomer Park, Ireland:
 Wandesford gives vases from cave in, to Montagu, **10.** 12
Castle Coote, Bn. *See* Coote, Charles Henry
Castle Coote, Bns. *See* Tilson, Elizabeth Anne
'Castle Crambo':
 Pope builds, **18.** 35
Castle Ditch, Hereford:
 Cocks of, **12.** 18n
Castle-Durrow, Bn. *See* Flower, Henry
Castle-Durrow, Bns. *See* Tatton, Elizabeth
Castlehaven, E. of. *See* Tuchet, James

Castle Hill, Middlesex:
Burdett of, **12**. 54n
Castle Howard, Yorks:
Carlisle plans to retire to, **6**. 187n
——'s seat, **1**. 172
(?) Carlisle, Cts of, may retire to, **37**. 359
HW describes and praises, **30**. 256–8
HW visits, **28**. 37, 42, **30**. 256–8, **35**. 333
Holbein portrait of Henry VIII at, **40**. 226n
Hoyland of, **28**. 9n
landscape effects at, **30**. 256–8
royal family visits, **36**. 246n
Selwyn forgoes visit to, **39**. 262
Castle Inn, Richmond:
ball and supper at, for D. of Clarence, **43**. 150
boat race watched from great room at, **43**. 150
Castle Island, co. Kerry:
Herbert of, **14**. 126n
Castle Lyons, Bn of. *See* O'Brien, Daniel
Castle Lyons, Bns of. *See* O'Brien, Margaret Josepha
Castlemaine, Cts of. *See* Villiers, Barbara
Castlemaine, Vct. *See* Child, Richard
'Castle of Hercules':
in Hesse-Cassel, described by Conway, **38**. 141
*Castle of Otranto, The*, by HW:
ancient romances imitated in, **40**. 377
apparition from portrait in, **43**. 47
Barbauld, Mrs, imitates, **28**. 382
Barry's painting reminds HW of, **29**. 301
Bathoe publisher of, **15**. 92n
Beast of the Gevaudan might have been put into, **38**. 525
Bodoni prints, at Parma for Edwards, **35**. 436, **43**. 145
——'s edition of: arrives at Edwards's without vellum copies, **15**. 213; HW corresponds with Mary Berry about, **11**. 150, 150n, 170; HW gives, to Mary Hamilton, **31**. 369; received by Edwards, **15**. 212
Bute would have written from Otranto in memory of, **23**. 103, 107n
Chatterton calls HW 'Bn Otranto' because of, **2**. 107, 110, **16**. 347, 358
Cole receives, **1**. 85, 86, 88, 91, 92
composition of, hurried, **28**. 6
*Count of Narbonne* based on, *see* Jephson, Robert, *Count of Narbonne*
dedication of, to Lady Mary Coke, **31**. 34, 429
dramatization of, wanted by F. W., **41**. 170
drawing of castle may be frontispiece to Bodoni edn of, **35**. 436
dream provided inspiration for, **28**. 6, **30**. 177
Du Deffand, Mme, forwards, to Voltaire, **4**. 99
—— mentions, **4**. 6, 8
—— wants copy of, **4**. 102, 114, 115
—— wishes Florian to translate, **7**. 269
Duncombe, Mrs, sends sketch of scene of, to HW, **42**. 60
Eidous's translation of, **43**. 84

Falkland's picture at SH inspires scene of, **42**. 106
familiar dialogue in, too modern, **28**. 5, 6–7
Fenn's copy of, **43**. 222
Fenn, Mrs, to cite, in *Female Guardian*, **16**. 245
fictitious authorship of, **1**. 71n, **16**. 127n
Findlater to show, to Dalrymple, **15**. 105
French translation of, **3**. 256, 260, 270, **4**. 99, 100, 107, 116, **13**. 42, **35**. 436
girls' emotions depicted in, **36**. 154
Gothic shields will bring dreams like those in, **35**. 421
Gray encourages HW to print, **28**. 6
—— thanks HW for, **14**. 137
—— thought to be author of, **38**. 525
Greatheed's drawings of scenes in, **42**. 429–31
HW believes himself actually in, **33**. 406
HW calls Voltaire's attention to preface to, **41**. 149–50, 152
HW chooses title of, from map of Naples, **35**. 435–6, **42**. 178
HW comments on, **3**. 260–1, **5**. 316
HW compares himself with skeleton in, **10**. 147
HW complimented on, by F. W., **41**. 170
HW does not properly appreciate, **31**. 224
HW expects, to be his only book known outside England, **35**. 436
HW gives: to Bibliothèque du Roi, **41**. 58n; to Hertford, **38**. 502; to M. and Mme Élie de Beaumont, **40**. 378–80; to Montagu, **10**. 145; to Voltaire, **13**. 43, **41**. 149–50, 152; to Warton, **40**. 376–7
HW may write a second, **10**. 192
HW mentions, **5**. 398, **10**. 154
HW might send, to Lady Ossory, **32**. 41
HW scolds Hannah More for giving, to Mrs Yearsley, **31**. 221
HW sells, **28**. 23n
HW's opinion of, **31**. 221
HW's preface to 2d edn of, **1**. 92n, **3**. 256, 261, 270, **4**. 90, 95–9, 100, 102, 107, **6**. 268, **8**. 143–4
HW tranquil enough to write, **10**. 154
HW unwilling to have, translated, **7**. 269
HW will not write second part to, **33**. 364
'hand in armour' in, **32**. 66
Hardinge could have cried over, **35**. 575
—— mentions helmet and sighing picture in, **35**. 588
—— praises, **35**. 648
helmet of Otranto in, **32**. 216
Hertford receives, from HW, **38**. 502
*Hieroglyphic Tales* in style of, **2**. 141–2
Highmore's illustration for, **42**. 60–1
Italian translation of, **35**. 436, 438
Jephson skillful in adapting, to play, **41**. 409, 455
Mason at first duped by, **28**. 5–6
'Matilda' in, **40**. 380, **42**. 178
Mirepoix, Mme de, compares breaking into HW's house to, **5**. 54

[*Castle of Otranto,* continued]
Montagu asks for new edition of, **10.** 151
—— receives, from HW, **10.** 145, 146
——'s opinion of, **10.** 146
—— wants HW to write a second, **10.** 196
Montigny receives copy of, **4.** 100, 102, 114, 115
More, Hannah, discusses style of, **31.** 224
—— wants, for her library in Cowslip Green, **31.** 231
'much in vogue,' **38.** 502
novelty of, its greatest merit, **15.** 105
publication of, **10.** 145, **43.** 47
Reeve, Clara, imitates, **28.** 381–2
——'s *Old English Baron* criticizes, **2.** 107–8, 110
scene of, taken from Cambridge college, **6.** 145
second edn of: **43.** 133; Gray wants copy of, **14.** 139; needed, **40.** 377; to be issued with new preface, **38.** 526
SH the setting of much of, **1.** 91n
success of, less flattering to HW than Mason's praise, **28.** 6–7
success of, makes HW admit his authorship, **38.** 525
Voltaire receives, from HW. **13.** 43
Warburton says, is 'regularly a drama,' **41.** 409
Wiart's translation of preface to, **4.** 99, 100
Williams, G. J., ridicules, **30.** 177
writing of, **1.** 88
written and published, **13.** 41
Yearsley, Ann, writes poem to HW on reading, **31.** 221n
See also *Château d'Otrante, Le*
*Castle Rackrent. See under* Edgeworth, Maria
Castlereagh, Vct. *See* Stewart, Robert (1769–1822)
Castlereagh, Vcts. *See* Hobart, Lady Amelia Anne (1772–1829); Pratt, Frances (ca 1751–1833)
Castle Rising, Constable of. *See* Cromwell, Ralph de (1368–1417); Daniel, Sir Thomas (fl. 1448)
Castle Rising, Norfolk:
borough of: **43.** 111; Boone M.P. for, **10.** 7n, **30.** 167n, **36.** 34; Churchill M.P. for, **30.** 87, 330n, **36.** 16; HW M.P. for, **13.** 25, 27, 238n, **36.** 34, **41.** 78; HW quarrels over, with Sir Edward Walpole, **19.** 419; HW tries to get Rigby as M.P. for, **37.** 194n; Luxborough to be M.P. for, **19.** 419; Mackreth M.P. for, **1.** 347n, **24.** 53, 60, 62, **28.** 173; Orford, E. of controls, **19.** 419n, **28.** 121n, **30.** 87, 167n, 330n, **36.** 10, 33, 47; Rigby M.P. for, **30.** 87, 330n, **37.** 194n, **43.** 111; Walpole, Sir Edward, lists eligible candidates for, **36.** 14, 16; Walpole, Horatio (1723–1809), promised seat at, **36.** 10; Wedderburn M.P. for, **1.** 347n
Daniel and Cromwell, constables of, **40.** 224n
hospital at, **16.** 82n, 87

poor men at, eligible for Trinity Hospital, **16.** 90
Castle Street, Leicester Fields, London:
Matthews publisher in, **23.** 196n
Strange lives in, **24.** 24n
Castletown, Ireland; Conolly's seat:
Conolly of, **9.** 234n, 235n, **11.** 56n
Hartington goes to, **37.** 400
Castor; castors:
HW's, shaped like owls, **32.** 325
Castor and Pollux:
HW and Mann compared to, **25.** 615
'Castor et Pollux.' *See* Conzié, Joachim-François-Mamert de; Conzié, Louis-François-Marc-Hilaire de
*Castor et Pollux. See under* Bernard, Pierre-Joseph; Rameau, Jean-Philippe
Castration; castrations:
Clanwilliam performs, on rival, **24.** 544
HW informed about, by surgeons, **18.** 565
Castrato; castrati:
Englishman's singing contrasted to that of, **40.** 44
London chairman's encounter with, **17.** 248
Castre, —— de:
France's possible negotiator with England, **21.** 355n
Castres. *See* Sabatier de Castres
Castries, Duchesse de. *See* Bonnières de Guines, Marie-Louise-Philippine de
Castries, Marquis de. *See* La Croix, Charles-Eugène-Gabriel de (1727–1801); La Croix, Joseph-François de (d. 1728)
Castries, Marquise de. *See* Bonnières de Guines, Marie-Louise-Philippine de
Castries, Hôtel de, Paris:
mob sets fire to, **7.** 53n
Castris, Francesco de:
Ferdinando de' Medici associates with, **25.** 215n
Castro, Duca di. *See* Farnese, Orazio (d. 1554)
Castro, Duchessa di. *See* Diane (1538–1619)
Castro, Inès de (d. 1355):
named applied to Mrs Fitzherbert, **33.** 528
Castro, João:
garden of, **12.** 178n
Castro (Italy):
Clement XIII would sacrifice, to his brief, **23.** 10
Farnese family pawn, to Pope, **17.** 204, 205n
Neapolitans seize, **23.** 36
Parma to seize, **23.** 24
Rosa of, **17.** 8n
Spain may take, from Clement XIII, **23.** 45
—— to tell Clement XIV if he may keep, **23.** 413
Spaniards may take winter quarters in, **17.** 204
Castromonte, Marchese di. *See* Baesa e Visentelo, Don Giuseppe
Castropignano, ——, Neapolitan army officer:
Naples may recall, **18.** 16

Neapolitan troops to be led by, to Naples, 18. 3

Presidii troops commanded by, 17. 262n

Casualties:

newspapers fall back on, for news, 20. 321

Caswall, Timothy (ca 1733–1802), M.P.:

birth date of, 43. 64

duel at Mary-le-Bone stopped and reported by, to George III, 9. 319

franks letter for HW, 2. 1, 120

(?) HW sends letters by, 7. 385

(?) Marie-Josèphe's funeral oration attended by, 7. 317, 31. 134

(?) Rueil visited by, 7. 320

St James's Palace post of, as capt. of the guard, 9. 319

(?) social relations of, in Paris, 7. 317, 319–21

'Cat, the.' See 'Emely, Lady'

Cat; cats:

Agnes Berry's, 12. 101, 121

Angora: Du Deffand, Mme, offers, to HW, 4. 319–20; Walpole, Hon. Robert, takes one of, 4. 325

Chute's, 17. 182; see also 'Geoffrey' or 'Jeffery'; 'Luna'

Du Deffand, Mme, has: 5. 67, 8. 216; Cochin's engraving of, 6. 360

Dysart's fear of water compared to that of, 10. 307

Englishmen compared to, 6. 58–9, 61

Gray's letter on, 28. 124

——'s ode on, 33. 522

HW lacks, in London, 33. 81

HW might rescue, in ark, 35. 316

HW plays with, 41. 5

HW returns to his, 28. 225

HW's, 3. 12, 18. 136, 28. 101, 225, 39. 128, 370; see also 'Fanny'; 'Harold'; 'Mufti'; 'Ponto'; 'Selima'; 'Sophy'

HW's fondness for, 31. 68, 93

Hervey proposes, for his coat-of-arms, 35. 109

Johnston, Lady Cecilia, sits over fire with, 35. 474

'Lady Clackmannan' likes, 11. 303

Little Strawberry Hill's: amuses HW, 12. 213n; Seton, Miss, writes letter in name of, 12. 213n

Lunardi exhibits, after taking it in balloon, 25. 528, 543

Maltese, may be acquired by Chute, 35. 12

Maltese, sought by Ilay from Stosch through HW and Mann, 17. 164, 181–2, 212, 394, 413, 419, 433–4, 452, 462, 474, 482, 488, 497, 506

mandarin, Bentley draws, 9. 134

Mirepoix, Mme de, has, 31. 55, 41. 231

Montagu, D. of, jokes about, while making will, 9. 94

Montagu's, see 'Goldwin'; 'Reynolds'

motto on verses on, 12. 269

over a string, 35. 254

Pitt, Anne, hates, 31. 54

sail on bilander, 37. 118

Spectator character strokes, 41. 278

tiger at Horton the size of, 10. 334

Tonton compared to Spectator tradesman's, 33. 464

—— exiles HW's, 39. 370

Van Dyck's, 17. 495

Walpole, Sir Edward, promises, to Mrs Scott, 10. 329

Whittington's, 13. 47, 28. 40, 32. 84

See also 'Fanny'; 'Geoffrey'; 'Goldwyn'; 'Harold'; 'Jeffery'; Kitten; 'Luna'; 'Merlou'; 'Mufti'; 'Ponto'; 'Puss'; 'Raoul'; 'Reynolds'; 'Selima'; 'Sophy'

Catacombs. See under Rome

Catafalque; catafalques:

'builder' of, see Jadot

Doge's, at Venice, 17. 75

for Charles VI's obsequies at Florence, by Jadot, 17. 75, 30. 8–9

for Mme Panciatichi, at Florence, 18. 405

for Old Pretender, at Rome, 21. 392

Francis I's, at Florence, statues weep on, 22. 367

Louis XV's, 24. 26

'Catalan monsters' (Mediterranean pirates):

HW escapes, 17. 132

Catalans:

Greeks will be sacrificed like, 23. 212

revolutionary tendencies of, 12. 53

Catalan ships:

Jesuits sent in, from Barcelona, 22. 516n

Catalogue; catalogues:

HW makes, of collections at SH, 32. 216

HW reads, in London, 10. 267

of books and prints, HW amused by, 12. 58

of horses, for Orford's sale, 31. 174n

of Pitti Gaddi collection, 24. 80

of Sir Robert Walpole's collection, see Ædes Walpolianæ

of Stosch's collection, see under Stosch

of Strawberry Hill, by HW, see Description of Strawberry Hill

Catalogue and Description of King Charles the First's Capital Collection . . . , A:

cited, 1. 173

HW has copies of, 16. 289–90

HW writes preface to, 13. 27

Henry VIII's jewel may be listed in, 42. 289

Pinkerton finds copy of, 16. 289–90

Rembrandt's mother's portrait listed in, 42. 13

Titian painting listed in, 16. 168

See also under Van der Doort, Abraham

Catalogue of Books, A. See under Clavell, Robert

'Catalogue of English Heads.' See Granger, James: Biographical History of England

Catalogue of Engravers, A, by HW:

Anecdotes of Painting less faulty than, 42. 302

(?) Bathoe sends, to HW, 40. 290

Cole receives, from HW, 1. 53, 57–8, 61, 127

——'s corrections of, 1. 45, 47, 141, 155, 2. 352

[*Catalogue of Engravers*, continued]
   *Critical Review's* notice of, 1. 65
   Dalrymple's missing letter about, 15. 99
   Gray impatient for, 14. 130, 132
   —— receives, 14. 133
   HW asks Dalrymple's indulgence for, 15. 94
   HW begins and finishes, 13. 38
   HW busy writing, 10. 44
   HW must wait for aid on, 16. 53
   HW presents: to Bibliothèque du Roi, 41.
     58n; to Stanislas II, 42. 164
   HW sends, to Hillier, 16. 71–2, 73, 78, 93
   HW thanks Walker for additions and cor-
     rections to, 42. 301–2
   'list of very bad prints,' 28. 3
   Lort hopes, will soon appear, 16. 160
   Mason will not be amused by, 28. 2
   misnamed as 4th vol. of *Anecdotes of Paint-
     ing*, 41. 236
   number of copies printed of, 43. 72
   printing of, 1. 45n, 47, 43. 132
   publication of, 1. 53n, 15. 92
   second edn of, Cole's copy of, 43. 54
   Tyson's corrections for, 1. 172–6
   Zouch makes too generous a return for, 16.
     54
*Catalogue of Five Hundred Celebrated Authors
  of Great Britain Now Living, A*:
   HW applies witticism in, to Frances Burney,
     31. 271
*Catalogue of French Books, A*:
   HW transcribes, 18. 52–4
   Mann likes, 18. 78
*Catalogue of Honor. See under* Milles, Thomas
*Catalogue of Pictures and Drawings in the Hol-
  bein-Chamber at Strawberry Hill*:
   HW prints, 9. 248n
*Catalogue of the Antiquities, Houses . . . and
  Situations in England and Wales. See under*
  Gray, Thomas
*Catalogue of the Collection of Pictures, etc. Be-
  longing to King James II, A*:
   HW writes preface to, 13. 27–8
  *See also under* Chiffinch, W.
*Catalogue of the Curious Collection of Pictures
  of George Villiers, Duke of Buckingham, A*:
   HW writes preface to, 13. 27–8
*Catalogue of the Harleian Collection of Manu-
  scripts . . . in the British Museum*:
   Baker's MSS catalogued in, 2. 342
   cited, 1. 156, 174, 251, 252
   HW sends references from, to Fox and March-
     mont, 30. 153
*Catalogue of the Lords of Session. See under*
  Dalrymple, Sir David: *Catalogue of the Sena-
  tors of the College of Justice, A*
*Catalogue of the Manuscripts Preserved in the
  British Museum, A. See under* Ayscough,
  Samuel
*Catalogue of the Royal and Noble Authors of
  England, A*, by HW:
   Aldborough, Lady, wants her father inserted
     in, 33. 376, 421

Anglesey, E. of, criticized in, 31. 294
Atterbury and Wynne mentioned in, 15. 111
Barrington's eligibility for, 2. 122, 33. 469–70
Batheaston miscellany provides new names
  for, 32. 225
Belsham's 'Strictures' on, 31. 293–4
Birch may have found mistakes in, 40. 127
Bowle gives HW additions to, 40. 296–9,
  300–2
Bromfield suppresses letter giving HW addi-
  tions to, 40. 327
(?) Buchan, Cts of, alludes to, as 'the poets,'
  35. 119
Buckingham's *Rehearsal* praised in, 31. 294
Bull gives HW extra-illustrated copy of, 31.
  296–7, 33. 376–7
Cardigan, Cts of, does not resent grand-
  mother's treatment in, 9. 219
—— resents article on her grandfather in,
  10. 340
Charles I's defenders offended by passage in,
  15. 109
Chesterfield endorses opinions of, 9. 218–19
Cole comments on, 1. 38–9, 140–1, 2. 215
—— gives, to Glynn, 2. 197
—— needs, 2. 197
——'s copy of, 43. 45, 70, 71
Conway and wife read, 37. 524
Conway papers may form volumes the size
  of, 16. 17
Conway thanks HW for dedication of, but
  suggests changes, 39. 525–6
*Critical Review* attacks, 13. 30, 31, 14. 105
Cutts treated in, 9. 252
Dalrymple sends HW notes for, 15. 26, 28–30,
  37, 38
——'s notice attracted by publication of, 15.
  60
—— wishes, were in quarto, 15. 103
Dodsley and Graham buy copyright of, 21.
  262n
Dodsley wants new edition of, 28. 121
Ducarel's corrections to, 40. 129
Du Deffand, Mme, asks for, 4. 30
—— told by Stormont about, 6. 430
'ease' the only merit of, 15. 33
Edinburgh reprint of, 28. 121n
Edward VI's letter for, 40. 158
Effingham suggested as eligible for, 28. 208,
  29. 213
errata in, 21. 196
first printing of, 13. 29, 15. 37
future edition of, 2. 217
Grafton not to be enrolled in, 31. 323
Granby eligible for, 32. 181
Granger sends additions to 2d edn of, 41. 218
Gray censures style of, 15. 51
—— sends observations on, to HW, 14. 175,
  178
Greville, Lord Brooke, included in, 16. 367
Grimston mentioned in, 40. 193
HW adds works by Q. Elizabeth to, 40. 296n
HW alludes to, 12. 257, 14. 104, 25. 225

(?) HW answers inquirers about, in *Public Advertiser*, **41**. 220

HW apologizes for rapid and careless compilation of, **16**. 206

HW collects corrections to, for new edition, **40**. 175

HW compliments the Scots in, **1**. 139, **2**. 264, **13**. 37–8, **29**. 358

HW corresponds with Dalrymple about, **15**. 31

HW described by antiquary as 'the lively editor' of, **14**. 130

HW describes, as 'inaccurate and careless,' **15**. 26

HW discusses materials for, with Zouch, **16**. 3–16, 18, 20–1, 24–5, 27–8

HW displeased by Hill's defence of, **13**. 31

HW disregards Cole's comments when revising, **1**. 38, 39, 140n

HW does not mention Cts of Winchilsea's paraphrase in, **9**. 266–7

HW forgets, **16**. 32

HW gives: **28**. 23n; to Bibliothèque du Roi, **41**. 58n; to Brown, **28**. 27n; to Cole, **2**. 199, 201, 206–7, 209; to Cts of Northumberland, **40**. 162; to Hillier, **16**. 78, 93, 94; to Holland, **34**. 39, 92; to Lady Ailesbury, **38**. 142; to Lyttelton, **40**. 124; to Mann, **21**. 214, 253, 262, 458, 472; to Montagu, Lady Mary Wortley, **21**. 458, 472; to Mrs Anderson, **42**. 146; to Pinkerton, **17**. 259, 274; to (?) Royston, **40**. 125; to Selwyn, **30**. 278; to Zouch, **16**. 9, 22

HW gives, away, **28**. 23n

HW gives reasons for including Catherine Parr in, **16**. 207

HW involves D. of Devonshire in, **40**. 126

HW lists number of copies printed of, **43**. 79

HW may add Charles, Duc d'Orléans, to, **31**. 271

HW may add Cts of Northumberland in new edn of, **42**. 394

HW notes James I's first work in his copy of, **40**. 300

HW not to reprint, **42**. 254

HW offers copy of, to Scottish society of antiquaries, **15**. 157–8, 161

HW prefers visit from Lady Ossory to additions to, **34**. 6

HW quotes Wharton's verses in, **42**. 10

HW refuses to read books mentioned in, **15**. 241

HW seeks Hampden's poems for, **42**. 398

HW sends queries about, to Mann, **21**. 156–7

HW's Whiggism most apparent in, **33**. 276–7

HW thanks Dalrymple for notice of, **15**. 77

HW thanks Walker for notes on, **42**. 305

HW thinks, forgotten **9**. 256

HW to amend Crescimbeni reference in, **40**. 301

HW to complete, **16**. 292

HW uses best anecdotes on Bedford family in, **34**. 122

HW will not include Thomas, Lord Lyttelton in, **28**. 203

HW writes, **21**. 156

HW writes to Dalrymple about, **15**. 31

Harris's contributions to, **40**. 156–7

Henry VII's *Institution* to be mentioned in, **16**. 4

Hume's criticism of, **40**. 135

incorrect, because written with people in the room, **14**. 167, **15**. 51

Irish clergyman praises, **9**. 256

Jacobite pamphlet against, **13**. 31–2

King, Dr, praises HW's tribute in, to Sir Robert Walpole, **9**. 219

Kippis cites, **2**. 92

Lort's copy of, **43**. 218

——'s notes on, **16**. 137, 143, 364–71, **40**. 175–6

magazines abuse, **35**. 107

Mallet's contribution for, **40**. 129

Mann gives, to Firmian and wants another copy, **21**. 271–2, 278, 339, 446–7

——'s copy of, **43**. 276

Marchmont's queries about, **30**. 153

Marlborough, D. of, comments on, omitted from 2d edn of, **11**. 105

Mason mentions, **28**. 55, **29**. 120

Montagu, Ds of, offended by, **11**. 105

More, Hannah, wants HW to add to, **31**. 273

nearly completed, **16**. 24

Newcastle's comedies criticized in, **31**. 294

new edition of, **9**. 218

only dead authors eligible for, **34**. 6

Orrery praises, **28**. 465

Pembroke, Cts of, letter of, to Williamson printed in, **10**. 336

Percy's *Reliques* acknowledges, **40**. 372

Percy suggests including Cts of Northumberland in, **12**. 32

Pinkerton to supply list of Elibank's writings for, **42**. 197

popularity of, **9**. 218

postscript to, **33**. 552, 574, 575; see also *Postscript to the Royal and Noble Authors*

publication and copyright of, **43**. 120

readers resent treatment of their ancestors in, **42**. 122

Reed gives HW new material for, **41**. 280

revision of, **15**. 196

Richard I's Provençal poem in, **40**. 303

Robertson the first Scottish writer since publication of, **15**. 39

Rochford included in, **1**. 358

Rochford's alleged poem to be in a later edn of, **42**. 381–2

Ruthven article to be inserted in, **15**. 34

Sandby's notes for, **1**. 214

Scots complimented in, **1**. 139, **2**. 264, **13**. 37–8

second edition of: **11**. 105, **13**. 30, **15**. 34, 37, 38, 196, **16**. 3, 4, 9, 10, 22, 24, **21**. 262

Sharp contributes Edward VI's letter for, **40**. 158–60

smallness of edition of, **40**. 127

[*Catalogue of the Royal and Noble Authors*, continued]
Spence longs to see, **40**. 116
supplement to, to have Pinkerton's aid, **16**. 293–4
third edition of, not expected by HW, **15**. 38
unfavourably reviewed, **13**. 30, 31, **14**. 105, **15**. 54, **35**. 107
Walpole, Sir Robert, eulogized in, **40**. 171
Westmorland's poems mentioned in, **41**. 365
Wharton, D. of, included in, **29**. 247, 294
Wilkes accuses HW of flattering Scots in, **13**. 37–8
Williams, Sir, C. H., wants copy of, for friend, **30**. 147
Wilson's query about, **40**. 279–80
Zouch's letter on, **16**. 3
See also under Hill, John: *Observations*
*Catalogue of the Senators of the College of Justice, A.* See under Dalrymple, Sir David
*Catalogues of the Collections of Pictures of the Duke of Devonshire . . .* :
HW prints, **43**. 246
HW's copies of, exhausted, **9**. 398
HW sends, to Montagu, **9**. 396, 407, 415
HW to reprint, **9**. 398, **43**. 125
Ponsonby to receive, from Montagu, **9**. 396, 398
printed in *London and Its Environs Described*, **9**. 398
*Catalogus impressorum librorum bibliothecæ Bodleianæ*:
*Horæ subsecivæ* not attributed to Chandos in, **16**. 140
*Catalogus librorum manuscriptorum quod Collegio Corpus Christi*:
HW seeks, **43**. 66
*Catalogus universalis librorum. See under* Hartley, John
Catalonia:
Lestock's ships to patrol coast of, **17**. 408n
Catalonia. *See also* Catalans
Cataneo, Giovanni, Prussian agent at Venice:
peace rumour denied by, **17**. 483
Catanzaro ('Catanzaio'), Italy:
earthquake damages, **25**. 376
Cataract; cataracts (waterfalls):
HW's cascades resemble, **39**. 133
Cataract; cataracts (ocular):
'couching' of, **22**. 567
Ilmer famous for operations on, **18**. 240n
Sharp's operations on, **23**. 428n
Wentzel performs operation for, on D. of Bedford, **41**. 110n
*Catarro russo. See* Influenza
Catawba, S. Carolina:
battle of, **25**. 92
Catawba Indians:
Dinwiddie promises, to Braddock, **20**. 492n
Catcall; catcalls:
Parliament does not despise, **38**. 187
Catch; catches (musical):
Sandwich's fondness for, **33**. 30
yacht captain demands, **17**. 141

Catch Club:
collection of catches inscribed to, **33**. 424n
'Catchem, Mr' (dog):
Bedford, Charles, cannot find, **39**. 489–90
Lennox, Lord and Lady George, inquire about, **31**. 366
'Catchup' (dog):
died leaving puppies, **39**. 490n
Catcott, George Symes (1729–1802), pewterer:
Chatterton's career described by, **28**. 423n
——'s friend, **28**. 36n
——'s poems in hands of, **16**. 126
—— tells, that MSS were held by another person, **16**. 176
in Rowley controversy, **2**. 50n
Langhorne's review cites, on Chatterton, **16**. 122n
Warton opposed by, in *Gentleman's Magazine*, over Rowley poems, **16**. 178
Cateau-Cambrésis (France):
Mansell killed at, **12**. 97n
York, Duke of, wins victory at, **12**. 98
Catechism:
Gideon questions son about, **35**. 178–9
Grafton reported to have written, **31**. 322–3
*Catéchisme et décisions de cas de conscience. See under* Vaux de Giry de St-Cyr, Claude-Odet-Joseph de
Caterina (1593–1629), de' Medici, m. (1617) Ferdinando Gonzaga, D. of Mantua:
Henry, P., might have married, **25**. 224n
Caterpillar; caterpillars:
HW's elms stripped by, **33**. 462
on Cellini's bell, **23**. 383
plague of, **29**. 216, 242, 245, 248, **33**. 340
Cates, Mr, pawnbroker, at Five Balls, Chandos St, Covent Garden:
HW's watch and seals to be returned to, **40**. 65n
Catesby, Sir William:
keeps Tyrell down, **13**. 183n
Catharine. *See* Catherine; Katherine
Cathcart, Bns. *See* Elliot, Elizabeth (d. 1847); Malyn, Elizabeth (1691–1789)
Cathcart, Cts. *See* Elliot, Elizabeth (d. 1847)
Cathcart, Charles (1686–1740), 8th Bn Cathcart:
expeditionary forces of, paid by Treasury agents, **17**. 411n
Cathcart, Charles Schaw (1721–76), 9th Bn Cathcart:
(?) at Chesterfield's assembly, **37**. 327
black patch hides battle scar of, **36**. 12n
Campbell, John, may be aided by, **37**. 401
Capel, Lady Elizabeth, rumoured to wed, **32**. 176n
Cumberland, D. of, has accident caused by, **9**. 42–3
Diderot disparaged by, **33**. 37n
HW compares, to captive in Glover's *Boadicea*, **9**. 158
hostage after peace of Aix-la-Chapelle, **4**. 347

Ilchester told by, of daughter's affair, 38. 367

Macartney to be succeeded by, in Russian post, 22. 586

Ranelagh and Vauxhall visited by, 9. 42

Read, Catherine, informs, of Lady Susan Fox Strangways's affair, 38. 367

'simpleton,' 23. 208

Turkish ornament given by, to Lady Brown, 40. 89n

wounded at Fontenoy, 36. 12, 37. 191

Cathcart, Hon. Charlotte Catherine (1770–94): Paris visited by, 6. 401

Cathcart, Hon. Frederick. See McAdam, Hon. Frederick Cathcart

Cathcart, Hon. Louisa (1758–1843), Cts of Mansfield, s.j., 1793, m. (1776) David Murray, 7th Vct Stormont; 2d E. of Mansfield, 1793:
appearance of, 6. 337
brother and sister of, 6. 401n
Du Deffand, Mme, regrets departure of, 7. 28
Greville cousin of, 6. 379
Hamiltons not to visit, 31. 217
marriage of, 6. 305–8, 312
pregnant, 6. 344
sings for Mme du Deffand, 6. 357
social relations of, in Paris, 6. 335, 357
son born to, 6. 415

Cathcart, Hon. Mary (1757–92), m. (1774), Thomas Graham, cr. (1814) Bn Lynedoch: Paris visited by, 6. 401

Cathcart, William Schaw (1755–1843), 10th Bn Cathcart; cr. (1807) Vct, and (1814) E. Cathcart:
Du Deffand, Mme, asks, to send for Linguet's letter to Vergennes, 6. 416
Paris visited by, 6. 401
Twickenham house taken by, 11. 60, 42. 486

Cathedral; cathedrals:
chapters of, permit destruction of monuments when families are extinct, 42. 260
French: influenced by florid English design, 42. 305; prints of, 2. 177
Gothic, used for heathen temple in stage scenery, 31. 152
HW imparts gloomth of, to SH, 20. 372
Henry VIII plunders, 32. 323
Irish, absence of monuments in, 10. 11
Müntz to paint aisles of, 35. 186
Morvo in charge of masonry for, 42. 69

Cather, John:
conspiracy by, against Sir Edward Walpole, 43. 365

Catherine (de Ricci) (1522–90), St:
canonization of, 19. 171n

Catherine (of Russia), St:
order of, see Order of St Catherine

Catherine (of Siena) (?1347–80), St:
in Bagot's painting, 41. 430
in Correggio painting, 17. 167
in stained glass, at Hurstmonceaux, 35. 138
Sévigné, Mme de, may be eclipsed by, 35. 393

straw hat of, and her measure in ribbon, produce miracles, 20. 430

Catherine I (ca 1683–1727), m. (1711) Peter I of Russia; Empress of Russia 1725–7:
HW and Montagu contemporary with, 10. 39
HW calls, 'soldier's trull,' 31. 12n
Knyphausen promises anecdotes of, to HW, 31. 11–12

Catherine II (1729–96) the Great, m. (1745) Peter III of Russia; Empress of Russia 1762–96:
accusations by, against Peter III, 22. 75
acquisition or loss of acres by, inconsequential, 23. 420
acquisitive, 23. 562
agrees to peace terms, 11. 297
aims at universal monarchy, 11. 233
Albani calls, 'heroine of the north,' 22. 76
Alembert refuses request to educate son of, 31. 62, 41, 62n
——'s connections with, 4. 214
Alexander Paulovich, marriage of, attended by, 12. 53–4
Alexis and his sisters released by, 34. 3
allies of, insist on her ending the Turkish war, 24. 33
amours and murders of, disgust HW. 23. 452
armed neutrality of, 29. 29n, 76n
Asia and Europe would be bled by, 34. 146
assassination attempt against, by subalterns of her guards, 23. 440
Austria and Prussia ally with, against Poland, 34. 153
Azov the only conquest to be retained by, 23. 212
Bestuzhev recalled by, 22. 59
Biron restored by, to Courland duchy, 22. 118
Black Sea, should be confined in, 11. 230
blood spilled by, equals French massacres, 31. 373
box ornamented with portrait of, 5. 183, 23. 376
Buffon's correspondence with, 8. 64
Chernyshev's cession of precedence may not be allowed by, 23. 138
Chesterfield receives self-made box from, 23. 376
children of, perhaps not Peter III's, 35. 314
China the limit of territory of, 25. 545
Chinese emperor quarrels with, 24. 333, 32. 390–1
—— terms 'murderess,' 23. 116
Choiseul's diplomatic relations with, 23. 125, 127
——'s fall will please, 23. 259
Choiseul, Duchesse de, talks of, 3. 319
Choiseuls do not favour, 4. 483
Confederacy of Targowitz organized by, 34. 144n, 153n, 159n
Clement XIII considers congratulating, 22. 76
collection of, 34. 217
conspiracies against, 22. 205

[Catherine II, *continued*]

Constantinople menaced by, **11**. 186, 226, **23**. 146, 212, 240, **24**. 333, **25**. 545, 616n, **32**. 193

coronation of, **22**. 64n

Craven, Lady, might be sheltered by, **25**. 632, **42**. 183–4

Crozat collection bought by, thwarting HW, **39**. 146

Danish affairs displease, **23**. 273

Danish revolution attributed to, **5**. 183

Dashkov, Ps, former favourite of, **23**. 242

——'s bad relations with, **4**. 483, **22**. 65n, **31**. 162, **33**. 197

death of, **34**. 229

declaration of, on deposing Peter III, **22**. 56–7

Denis, Mme, corresponds with, **7**. 90, 91, **8**. 212

Dick receives Order of St Anne of Holstein from, **24**. 96

Dimsdale inoculates, **23**. 75

Dolgorukov's conduct in Montenegro disapproved by, **23**. 160

Du Deffand, Mme, mentioned by, to Shuvalov, **7**. 72

——'s opinion of, **5**. 198

—— to show to Comtesse de Genlis letters by, **8**. 64

Dutch to be aided by, **25**. 118n

Elizabeth, Czarina, probably poisoned by, **23**. 208

England may aid against Turks, **4**. 203

—— must seem despicable to, **29**. 65

—— offered Russian troops by, for American war, **24**. 127

——'s offer of Minorca thought by, to be lure for joining war, **25**. 187n

——'s relations with, **11**. 221, 236, 242, 288, 336

English in Paris treated like disciples of, **31**. 107

English intervention against France must please, **23**. 478

English revolutions pale beside that of, **22**. 91

English simpletons deceived by affability of, into thinking her innocent, **23**. 195

Europe's cause against France not supported by, **12**. 54

fearless, **11**. 232

fleet of: delayed, **23**. 157; destruction of, might make her more tractable, **23**. 479; sent to Ægean Sea, **23**. 212; to besiege Constantinople, **23**. 146, 240

forces of, irresistible by land, **23**. 148–9

foreign ministers congratulate, on accession, **22**. 75

Fox's bust ordered by, **11**. 323

France deserves, as its queen, **12**. 46, **34**. 153, 163

—— discusses recognition of, **3**. 286n

—— tries to turn Turkey and Poland against, **23**. 338

Frederick II and Joseph II may meet, in Poland, **25**. 44

Frederick II denounced by, as enemy, **22**. 62

—— deprived by, of her husband's friendship, **23**. 145

—— forbids, to aid England, **25**. 26, 39

——'s escape from, **22**. 119–20

—— told by, to return Russian troops from his army, **22**. 59

—— urges, to make Stanislas II resign crown to P. Henry, **25**. 44–5

French, Mrs, pictures of, offered to, **11**. 220–1

French philosophers extol, **22**. 333, 570, **23**. 195, 208, **25**. 39, 194, 206, **33**. 410

Geoffrin, Mme, receives furs from, **41**. 7

giants in menagerie of, **32**. 174

gigantic incendiary, **34**. 19

Goertz to alert, to Austrian designs on Poland, **25**. 45n

good princes survived by, **22**. 404

Gramont, Duchesse de, compared to, **3**. 358, 360

great figure in Europe, **25**. 389

Grimm subject of jokes by, **8**. 64

Gunning receives Bath order from, with diamond-studded sword, **23**. 508

Gustav III does not get approval of, **25**. 458

—— foils Joseph II and, **34**. 14

——'s reforms to be opposed by troops sent by, **23**. 439

——'s warfare with, **35**. 397

HW and Mann know more about, than about each other's friends, **23**. 260

HW calls: 'Alecto,' **22**. 253, **31**. 373; 'Amalasunta,' **25**. 613; 'Athaliah,' **22**. 64; 'Aurora Borealis,' **11**. 186; 'Brunehault,' **22**. 64; 'Catherine Slayczar,' **11**. 242, 288, 297, 323, **12**. 265, **31**. 391, **34**. 87, 153, 157, 217, 229; 'Crocodile,' **35**. 397; 'devil,' **22**. 570, **38**. 430; 'Fury of the North,' **34**. 153; 'Gallant Empress,' **33**. 336; 'Grand Usurperess,' **34**. 146; 'Great Turk at Petersburg,' **11**. 221; 'imperial freebooter,' **25**. 409; 'Legislatress,' **25**. 194, 545, **33**. 197; 'Mirabeau in petticoats,' **34**. 146; 'Minerva of the French literati,' **22**. 333; 'murderess,' **10**. 157, **35**. 334; 'Northern Empress,' **34**. 123; 'Northern Fury,' **31**. 149; 'Petruchia,' **11**. 236, 242, **12**. 54; 'philosophic tyrant,' **28**. 475; 'pillar of toleration,' **25**. 237; 'quintessence of friendship,' **31**. 162; 'Semiramis,' **11**. 186, 231, 233, **33**. 409, 561, **34**. 14, 32, 87; 'Thalestris,' **33**. 179; 'tigress,' **22**. 455; 'Tisiphone of the North,' **34**. 144, **39**. 180; 'Ursa Major of the North Pole,' **11**, 186; 'vulture,' **25**. 410, **33**. 452, **35**. 392

HW compares, with Beast of the Gévaudan, **31**. 56

HW 'declares war' on, **23**. 128

HW dislikes, **11**. 242

HW does not distinguish between Con Phillips and, **24**. 35

HW does not trust, to stay at peace, **25.** 422

HW doubts, would accept Minorca, **25.** 187

HW glad that Sweden is punishing, **35.** 397

HW has print of, with Ps Dashkov's verses, **23.** 242

HW hopes for fall of, **10.** 157

HW hopes that Frederick II, Joseph II, and, all vex one another, **25.** 567

HW impelled by, to sympathize with Turks, **23.** 116, **35.** 392

HW jokes about, **10.** 208

HW jokes about Lady Mary Coke's visiting, **31.** 149, 150, 162

HW mentions, **11.** 161, **12.** 93

HW might communicate with Mary Berry through, **11.** 161

HW prefers Turkish sultan to, **23.** 195

HW's abhorrence of, slightly cools, **22.** 80

HW's horror at praise of, **3.** 299–300, 319, **4.** 6, **5.** 396

HW sneers at legislation of, **23.** 437

HW suggests subject for Reynolds's picture for, **31.** 243

HW wishes: were Q. of France in place of Marie-Antoinette, **34.** 153, 163; would share fate of Hamlet's mother, **22.** 426

HW wonders how Ottoman world will be held by, **23.** 236

HW wonders what Galluzzi would say of, **25.** 193–4

HW would enjoy triumph of, if it meant French defeat, **23.** 236

Harris to tell, of Cabinet's acceptance of Russian mediation with Holland, **25.** 188n

'Hermitage' of, **8.** 205–6

Holland must be coveted by, **33.** 452

—— not to be aided by, **25.** 156n

Houghton pictures bought by, **2.** 146, 157n, 158, 170, **7.** 159, **9.** 56n, **11.** 81n, **15.** 228, **16.** 189n, **24.** 427–8, 434, 502, **33.** 86

House of Commons as imperialist as if composed of, **23.** 562

'husbands' of, her gentlemen of the bedchamber, **34.** 123

Ignatius may be replaced by, as tyrant, **23.** 514

inoculation of, **23.** 75

Italian art, good and bad, bought by, **25.** 93

Ivan VI perhaps murdered by, **22.** 253, 253n, **23.** 208

——'s murder increases HW's hatred of, **38.** 430

Jesuits protected by, **16.** 191, **25.** 389–90, 400

—— would not be blamed for attacking, **22.** 514

Joseph II and Maria Theresa tell, not to cross Danube, **23.** 310

Joseph II courts, **25.** 389

—— may join, to dismember Turkey like Poland, **25.** 399

(?) —— not expected to revisit, **25.** 156

——'s proposal from, of new state for her grandson, **25.** 399n

——'s rift with, over peace negotiation, **25.** 156n

—— the tool of, **34.** 87

—— to meet, in Poland, **25.** 61

Kingston, Ds of, acknowledged by, **32.** 390

—— favoured by, **24.** 332–3, **25.** 632

—— said to be learning Russian in order to visit, **23.** 559

—— said to have left jewels to, **35.** 397

Knowles president of the Admiralty to, **18.** 279n

laws of coursing prepared for, by E. of Orford, **33.** 312

legal code drawn up by, **23.** 376n

Louis XVI should dethrone, **24.** 35

lovers may prevent, from fully paying for Houghton pictures, **24.** 502

luck of, **22.** 257

manifestos of, **10.** 39–40, **22.** 64, 66, 71, 74–5, 209, 570n, **29.** 29n

Mann calls, 'slippery heroine,' **25.** 389

—— refuses to accept honours from, **24.** 96

—— said to have been promised diamond snuff-box by, **25.** 84

—— suggests sending Bp of Osnabrück to, **25.** 156

Maria Theresa called 'ma vilaine sœur' by, **25.** 128

Marie-Antoinette contrasted with, **12.** 54

mediation of, in Dutch war, rumoured, **25.** 139

megrim headaches for, would benefit Europe, **31.** 369

mother resembled by, **22.** 65

Muscovite librarian of, may thank HW for books given to Stanislas II, **36.** 281

naval victory celebrated by, **23.** 249

North's Pindaric ode to, on Peace of Galatz, **42.** 396n

Ogiński seeks support from, **33.** 511n

Order of St Anne conferred by, in son's name, **24.** 84

Orford, E. of, receives portrait of, **2.** 192

—— sells Houghton pictures to, **2.** 146, 158, 170, **7.** 159, **13.** 17n, **15.** 228, **24.** 427–8, 434, 502, **33.** 86, **43.** 68–9

Orlov, Alexei, the accomplice of, **23.** 207, **28.** 477

Orlov, Grigor, and Ps Dashkov aid, **22.** 64–5

Orlov, Grigor, expelled from bedchamber of, but not from his posts, **23.** 444

—— may be discarded by, as favourite, **23.** 441

—— responsible for putting, on the throne, **24.** 114

——'s place with, filled by two men, **24.** 143

—— the favourite lover of, **23.** 75n, **24.** 143n

—— wears portrait of, **24.** 143n

Orlov brothers the favourites of, **23.** 149, 444

[Catherine II, *continued*]

Ottoman Empire and eunuchs to be exterminated by, 42. 184

Ottoman Empire might be demolished by, 23. 169

Panin counteracts Harris's pleas to, 24. 520n

peace mediation in England's wars may be attempted by, 24. 487n, 519, 25. 139, 29. 118n, 30. 274, 33. 289, 36. 192

patron of the arts, 32. 71

pedantry of, 11. 323

Peter III betrayed by, 22. 53–4, 56–62, 65, 68, 81, 253

—— dethroned by, 10. 38–9, 35. 314–15, 38. 164

—— intended to imprison, 22. 68, 23. 215

—— 'murdered' by, 31. 162, 32. 390, 33. 36–7

—— never intended to execute, 23. 207

——'s accusations from, 22. 74–5

—— said to have intended to divorce, 22. 57

——'s death 'mourned' by, 22. 71, 75

pictures of Mrs French offered to, 11. 220–1

Pitt, Anne, jokes about coup d'état of, 10. 39

Pitt dismissed for opposing subsidy treaty with, 14. 88n

Pius VI asked by, through her minister, to re-establish Jesuits in Russia, 25. 389–90

—— persuaded by, to let Jesuits have novices, 16. 191

plague brought by, to Europe, 33. 409–10

Poland defeated by, 31. 369–70, 373, 391

Polish acquisitions to be visited by, 25. 44

Polish activities of, countenanced by Frederick II and Joseph II, 34. 144

Polish Constitution stifled by, 34. 157

Polish Dissidents aided by, 22. 574n

Polish partition by, 12. 73, 23. 419, 25. 399n, 32. 266, 33. 36, 39. 496, 497n

Portland vase might go to, 36. 237

portrait of Cardinal Pole bought by, 5. 178n, 7. 373n

Prussian uprising said to be fostered by, 12. 105n

Pugachev defeated by, 24. 3, 32. 184

Razumovskiĭ pensioned by, 22. 456

ready to be crowned in Hagia Sophia, 34. 14

religion lacked by, 25. 400

revolution smothered by, 33. 179

Reynolds's commission from, 36. 237

royal personages poisoned by, 32. 213

Rulhière's *Anecdotes* to be suppressed by, 4. 319n

Russia much improved by, 25. 389

Rutherfurd made baron by, and given a jewelled box with her portrait, 24. 453

Samoyeds decline code of laws from, 28. 475–6

self-preservation may be excuse for, 23. 202

Sheridan should worry, in Westminster Hall, 35. 392

ship of war ordered by, to convey Ds of Kingston's things from Leghorn to Calais, 24. 409–10

Shuvalov made grand chamberlain by, 7. 72

—— may hope for fall of, 10. 157

——'s reception by, 6. 492, 7. 72, 8. 205–6

—— wrongly said to be chief minister of, 22. 59

—— wrongly said to be cicisbeo of, 23. 149

son may be poisoned by, in imitation of Semiramis, 22. 253

son sent by, on travels, 33. 312

son's inoculation ordered by, 23. 76

Stanislas II's ultimatum from, 31. 371n

Stanley's embassy to, set aside, 3. 251n

still survives, 23. 329

stops at nothing, 23. 224

strong stomach of, 34. 163

Sweden and Poland drawn by, on her shoulders, 34. 32

Sweden's war with, 35. 397, 36. 251, 39. 462

Thiers's pictures sought by, 5. 141, 143, 148, 184

toleration preached by, 25. 400

travels of, 25. 44, 33. 561–2

triumphs of, 12. 46

Turkey might be given by, to son, 23. 236

—— said to have forestalled attack from, by satisfying her demands, 25. 409

Turkish peace with, rumoured, 39. 180

Turkish usurpations of, to be defended by her, 25. 436

Turkish war with, 23. 133–4, 143, 157, 25. 415, 35. 392, 39. 180

Turks dupe, 23. 438

upsetting the world, 34. 2

Voltaire and literati basely court, 7. 287

Voltaire apologist for, 3. 298, 299, 358, 8. 163, 22. 253, 570, 23. 195, 208, 25. 194, 206, 32. 31

——'s *Corneille* subsidized by, 8. 150

——'s correspondence with, 8. 150

——'s desire to see, objected to by Mme du Deffand, 4. 48, 49, 53

Vorontsov probably hates, 22. 195

Vorontsova, Countess, tries to surrender Order of St Catherine to, 22. 58–9, 65

war plans of, 23. 148–9

western nations lightly regarded by, 25. 359n

wisdom of, in educating son, 32. 59

wolves more easily tamed than progeny of, 31. 62

would allow no patriot orations, 32. 49–50

Young Pretender might sell pawned jewels to, 25. 526

Catherine (1401–37) of Valois, m. 1 Henry V of England; m. 2 Owen Tudor:

Chichele institutes masses for, 35. 387–8

love of, for Owen Tudor, 28. 318, 42. 19

portrait of, at Lambeth, 40. 215

Catherine (1485–1536) of Aragon, m. 1 (1501) Arthur, P. of Wales; m. 2 (1509) Henry VIII of England:

arms of, 1. 242, 342

Arthur's marriage to, 40. 198

Ashby asks if *Prayers or Medytacions* was written by, **16**. 203–4

attended only by servants, in scene in *Henry VIII*, **18**. 537

cross to memory of, at Ampthill Park, Beds, **1**. 225–6, 226n, 232, 235, 236, 240, 241, 242, 294n, 296, 299, 322, 338, 339, **2**. 1, 135, **32**. 53, 130, 146, **33**. 81, 256, **34**. 112

font of, **32**. 323–4

HW's reasons for not attributing prayers to, **16**. 207

Henry VIII's divorce from, **1**. 82, **2**. 259n, **13**. 117

——'s 'incest' with, **22**. 8

Kimbolton Castle, residence of, **10**. 77

lay at Ampthill, **33**. 256

Lort disagrees with Ashby on authorship by, of *Prayers or Medytacions*, **16**. 209

out of place in painting of Tudors, **40**. 319

painting of P. Arthur and, given by Myddelton to HW, **42**. 215

resentment of, at being considered Ps of Wales, **9**. 100

Shakespeare's *Henry VIII* portrays, **9**. 100

(?) stained-glass figure of, at Copt Hall, **9**. 92

virtues of, **1**. 270

Catherine (Howard) (d. 1542), m. (1540) Henry VIII of England:

Holbein portrait thought to be of, **40**. 365–6

Queensberry, Ds of, said to be, **32**. 363

Catherine (Parr) (1512–48), 6th wife of Henry VIII. *See* Parr, Catherine

Catherine (1638–1705) of Braganza, m. (1662) Charles II of England:

Hamilton, Miss, instigates, to invite Vcts Muskerry to appear in Babylonian dress, **20**. 50n

head of, on earthenware dish, **42**. 22n

milleleva won by, at faro, **19**. 494, 501

portraits of: at Cambridge, **16**. 324n; at Hinchingbrooke, **40**. 283; at SH, **33**. 472

print of, given by Bull to HW, **41**. 414

Somerset House apartment of, may be occupied by Portuguese royalty, **22**. 38

Twickenham Manor leased by, to Genew, **42**. 417

Wells, Winifred, maid of honour to, **41**. 242n

Catherine (1519–89) de Médicis, m. (1533) Henri II, K. of France, 1547:

as a subject for history, **15**. 53

can be trusted, now she is dead, **10**. 192

cipher of, on Henri II's tomb, **7**. 260n

England produces her own heroines instead of, **24**. 154

escaped murder, **34**. 73–4

Florence, the birth-place of, no longer noted for crime, **22**. 254

HW attributes poisonings to, **37**. 97

painting of, at Ste-Chapelle, **7**. 276

Yearsley, Mrs, worse than, **31**. 254

Catherine (1741–1807) of Brunswick-Wolfenbüttel:

Catherine II releases, **34**. 3

Catherine ——, HW's housekeeper at SH:

Bateman begs, not to discuss Ps Amelia's inquisitiveness, **35**. 227

Bentley's pictures might be exhibited by, **35**. 243

flood excites volubility of, **35**. 228

signs herself 'Noah,' **35**. 228

Catherine Court, Tower Hill, London:

Transport Office at corner of, **19**. 299n

Catherine-Henriette, m. (1619) Charles, Duc d'Elbeuf:

Henri IV's natural daughter, ancestress of Ps Craon, **19**. 262n

Catherine St, the Strand, London:

'Lamb, The,' opposite, **10**. 350

Millar, Andrew, opposite, **19**. 27n

Nourse, bookseller in, **10**. 349, 350

Walsh in, **13**. 103n

Catherlough, Bn. *See* Fane, John

Catherlough, Bns. *See* Cavendish, Mary

Catherlough, Cts of. *See* Knight, Mary

Catherlough, E. of. *See* Knight, Robert (1702–72)

Catholic; Catholics. *See* Roman Catholic

*Catholic Christian Instructed, The. See under* Challoner, Richard

Catholic Church. *See* Roman Catholic Church

Catholicism:

English churchmen not prone to, **23**. 40

HW's chapel to have air of, **21**. 306

Magdalen House suggests, **9**. 273

*See also* Popery; Roman Catholic Church

'Catholic Majesty, His.' *See* Charles III, Ferdinand VI, Philip V of Spain

*Catilina. See under* Crébillon, Prosper Jolyot de

Catiline (Lucius Sergius Catilina) (ca 108–62 B.C.):

Bubb Dodington imitates, **30**. 292n

Clive compared with, **23**. 491

conspiracy of, **3**. 97

counterparts of, spring from every street, **15**. 130

England unlikely to be saved by, **15**. 129

fierceness of, in Ps Dashkov's eyes, **23**. 248–9

Fox, C. J., compared with, **23**. 400, 491

Gordon rioters compared with, **25**. 67

maxim fit for, **35**. 566

Richelieu compared with, **21**. 172

Stosch's painting of conspiracy of, mistaken by English clergyman for Lord's Supper, **18**. 41

Wilkes compared with, **23**. 82

*Catiline. See under* Jonson, Ben; Sallust

Catinat, Nicolas (1637–1712), Maréchal de France:

Conway resembles, **39**. 260

éloges of, by La Harpe and Guibert, **39**. 260

*Catino di smeraldo orientale, Il. See under* Gaetano da Santa Teresa, Fra

Catley, Ann (1745–89), actress and singer:
pregnant 'virgin' in *Elfrida*, **28.** 109
  (?) principal 'virgin' in new version of *Elfrida*, **28.** 362
Catley, Cambs:
sale of Sclater Bacon's goods in, **1.** 19
Catlidge. *See* Kirtling Hall
Cato, Marcus Porcius (232–147 B.C.), the censor:
Akenside deserts, for Bute, **35.** 566
Clodiuses assume name of, **23.** 176
honoured only after death, **23.** 176
*Letters* of, **20.** 167
reproof of Beaumarchais befitting, **33.** 536
  (?) translated speech by, in Nichols's *Select Collection of Poems*, **42.** 18
Cato, Marcus Porcius (95–46 B.C.) the younger, 'Uticensis':
compared with justice of the peace, **33.** 158
counterparts of, do not now appear, **15.** 130
HW compared to, **11.** 241, **12.** 78, **35.** 19
lends wife to friend, **32.** 152, **33.** 257
not indifferent to his country's ruin, **28.** 462
Nugent's verses mention, **31.** 269
patriotism of, **32.** 81
'pent up in Utica,' **10.** 256
suicide of: **6.** 1, **32.** 274; achieves fame but does no good, **39.** 409
  (?) translated speech by, in Nichols's *Select Collection of Poems*, **42.** 18
'Cato':
popular signature to letters to newspapers, **42.** 500
*Cato. See under* Addison, Joseph; Trenchard, John
*Caton*, French ship:
capture of, **25.** 286n, 291n
Catone (Italy):
earthquake account mentions, **25.** 376
Catrani, Abbé:
imprisoned for anti-papal satire, **23.** 516n
Catsfield Place, Sussex:
Pelham of, **9.** 417n
Cattle:
Blakeney removes, from Minorca, **21.** 567
consuming winter stock, because of drought, **25.** 314
Corsican, seized, **24.** 26n
distemper in: aggravates burden of land tax, **42.** 497; kills, **42.** 504
Edinburgh Castle garrison captures, **19.** 133
foddered in vicinity of Greatworth, **10.** 120
French entrepreneurs scold general for saving, from enemy, **22.** 51n
Gage's, seized by Americans, **28.** 211
HW's, at SH, **4.** 267, 394
horned: disease among, **37.** 286; nonsense about, in answer to petitions, **23.** 197; Russians capture, **23.** 160
hurricane destroys, at Barbados, **25.** 109n
inoculation for, against distemper, **35.** 204
Jacob's nostrum for speckling, **30.** 72
loss of, in Irish troubles, **26.** 32

Loutherbourg paints, well, **24.** 93
meadow with, near Upton, **35.** 152
murrain strikes, in England, **19.** 174
surprise landing on Minorca prevented, from being driven into Castle, **25.** 190, 198
*See also* Bull; Calf; Cow
Cattolica, The ('La Cattolica') (Italy):
Austrians at, **18.** 335
Francis III may entrench himself at, **18.** 322
Gages may take refuge in, **18.** 324
Montemar's entrenchment at, **18.** 322
Spaniards abandon, **18.** 331
  —— at, **18.** 58, 322
  —— expected to settle at, **18.** 200
Catuelan, Comte de. *See* Merdy, Jacques de
Catullus, Caius Valerius (? 84–? 54 B.C.), poet:
Gray hears translations of, **13.** 143
  —— quotes, **13.** 228
sparrow of, **35.** 45
West paraphrases, **13.** 173
  ——'s imitations of, **14.** 16
Caudle:
at St James's, scene of gossip, **32.** 19, 29
Caudle-cup; caudle-cups. *See under* Cup
Caulfeild, ——:
Seymour, Lady, said to have married, **38.** 124
Caulfeild, Miss, dau. of Lord Charlemont:
Bath to be visited by, for health, **42.** 311n
Caulfeild, George, recorder of Oxford:
alleged daughter of, **38.** 125
Caulfeild, James (1728–99), 4th Vct Charlemont, 1734; cr. (1763) E. of Charlemont:
Bath to be visited by, for health, **42.** 311n
Beauchamp's pamphlet criticized by, **39.** 396n, 397n
Chatterton's poems strike, by their beauty, **16.** 350
confident of Lord Bellamont's recovery, **32.** 93
correspondence of, with Dr Haliday and Thomas Prentice, **42.** 311n
Dublin bookseller prevented by, from reprinting *Mysterious Mother*, **42.** 309
farm and casino constructed by, **9.** 391
folio volume of epigrams translated by, **42.** 234n
HW asked by: about costume of St-Esprit knights, **42.** 156, 157; for *Mysterious Mother*, **42.** 153, 155; to let his Hogarth prints be copied, **42.** 152–3, 154
HW asks, to let *Mysterious Mother* be reprinted, **42.** 309, 312
HW convinces, of Chatterton's fraud, **16.** 132–4
HW inquires about villa of, **9.** 417
HW lets Livesay make transcripts for, **42.** 154
HW outbid by, for Q. Elizabeth's bust, **9.** 417
HW's correspondence with, **41.** 190–2, 433–4, **42.** 152–7, 234, 308–10, 312
HW sends books to Malone for, **42.** 157
HW's 'lord chamberlain and licenser,' **42.** 310

HW thanks: for Preston's poems, **41.** 433–4; for 'specimen of poetic wit,' **42.** 234
health of: indisposition, **42.** 311
history of Q. Elizabeth's bust given by, **9.** 414
Hogarth engraving by, **20.** 13n
Ireland loses by departure of, for England, **39.** 48
King, Thomas, resembles, in *Clandestine Marriage*, **10.** 203
Livesay employed by, to copy Hogarth prints, **42.** 153
medals collected by, **9.** 414
Montagu sees collection of, **9.** 414
—— to show *Anecdotes of Painting* to, **10.** 17
—— visits villa of, **9.** 400
Nivernais's *Jardins modernes* given to, **12.** 260
Protestant landed interest endorses anti-Catholic bias of, in Ireland, **25.** 529n
Rome visited by, **37.** 324
'Caulfeild, Dr James':
alleged daughter of, **38.** 125
Caulfeild, Lettice (d. after 1627), m. 1 Francis Staunton; m. 2 William Peisley:
family of, **38.** 125
Caulfeild, St George (d. 1778), Chief Justice of King's Bench:
Cunninghame replaces, as M.P. for Tulsk, **20.** 316n
Dublin rioters compel, to administer oath to Chancellor, **9.** 266
lord chief justice, **20.** 316n
Caulfeild, Toby (1565–1627), Kt, 1603; cr. (1620) Bn Charlemont:
family of, **38.** 125
Caulfeild family:
Howards and Seymours not related to, **38.** 133
Caulfield. *See* Caulfeild
Cauline. *See* 'Sir Cauline'
Caumont, ——, Mme du Deffand's servant. *See* Common
Caumont, Baronne de. *See* Lustrac, Marguerite de
Caumont, Duchesse de. *See* Noailles, Marie-Louise de
Caumont, Antonin-Nompar de (1633–1723), Duc de Lauzun:
HW compares himself to, **10.** 310
Caumont, Marie-Françoise de, m. François de Hallencourt, Marquis de Boulainvilliers:
(?) daughter of, **6.** 323n
Caumont-La Force, Anne-Jacobé (1758–1842), m. (1776) François-Marie-Armand, Comte de Balbi:
Provence, Comtesse de, makes, 'dame d'atour,' **7.** 455
Caus, Mme de:
Chesterfield writes of, **6.** 37
Du Deffand, Mme, ignorant of, **6.** 41
*Causes célèbres. See under* Gayot de Pitaval, François
Causeway, Hyde Park, London:
Gunning, Miss, exhibited on, **11.** 202

Causeway; causeways:
ancient, near Dorchester, **37.** 491
'Causidicus':
poem to Conway by, in *Public Advertiser*, **43.** 290–1
Caussham. *See* Caversham
Cauterizing:
for hydrophobia, **20.** 509
Caux. *See* Caus
Cavagnole (game):
HW plays, at Mme du Deffand's, **30.** 220
played in Paris, **5.** 56, 101, 138, 206, 370, 372, **7.** 310, 327, 328, 334–40
played weekly at Mme de Jonsac's, **5.** 13
Talmond, Princesse de, cheats at, at French Court, **38.** 465, 469
Cavaillac, Marquise de:
assembly given by, **13.** 191n
Cavalcade:
at Henley, for Parliamentary candidates, **37.** 371
Cavalchini, Carlo Alberto (1683–1774), cardinal, 1743:
Bellarmino's canonization supported by, **21.** 216
Benedict XIV makes, cardinal, **18.** 302n
Clement XIII makes, *datario*, **21.** 224
—— persuaded by, to give audience to Almada, **21.** 423
—— summons, to advisory congregation, **21.** 308n
Conclave almost elects, **21.** 215–16
French cardinals protest against appointment of, **21.** 224
Louis XV thanked by, for preventing his becoming pope, **21.** 216
*Relatio Caroli Alberti Cardinalis Cavalchini* by, **21.** 216
Sardinian subject under Jesuit influence, **21.** 215n
Torreggiani to tell, to inform cardinals about Young Pretender's status, **22.** 392
York, Cardinal, and Cardinal Lanti uphold, despite French pressure, **21.** 219–20
Cavalier; cavaliers:
Herbert of Cherbury may have suffered from, **40.** 132
postpone shaving till the Restoration, **35.** 256
*See also* Royalist
*Cavaliere servente*:
post of dignity among Italian dames, **25.** 627
*Cavalieri*, Florentine:
ask Leopold to curb extravagance in ladies' dress, **25.** 175
Cocchi condescendingly treated by, **20.** 204–5
Florentine gates guarded by, **18.** 288
ignorant about American war, **21.** 236
Italy does not concede gentility to those below the rank of, **20.** 298
Madonna dell'Impruneta escorted by, **30.** 4
water carried by, to Uffizi fire, **22.** 68
Cavaliers' Fencing School, Florence:
Lenten concerts in, **19.** 374

Cavallini, Pietro (fl. 1250–1330), builder:
  Capoccio shrine at SH by, **1**. 244n, **2**. 370, **43**. 56
  Edward the Confessor's shrine ascribed to, **1**. 244n, **2**. 370, **35**. 406, **42**. 67
  HW's account of, in *Anecdotes of Painting* corrected by Agincourt, **42**. 66–7
  Vasari mentions work by, at St Paul's, **42**. 67
Cavalry:
  Croatian, **17**. 266n
  Dutch, run away at Fontenoy, **36**. 13
  English: at Minden, **38**. 20–3; Cumberland, D. of, has, **40**. 55; dragoons to be merged with, **19**. 340, **26**. 14, 17; English rebels pursued by, **19**. 185–6; Montagu raises troops of, **19**. 110; rebel right attacked by, at Culloden, **37**. 240; rebels pursued by, **37**. 213, 240
  French, rumoured reforms in, **6**. 379
  German, to cut off Spaniards, **18**. 197
  Lobkowitz pursues Spaniards with, **18**. 412
  —— to send, to Charles Emmanuel III, **18**. 509, 512–13
  Neapolitan, **19**. 297
  regiment of, to be formed from Tuscan militia, **17**. 123
  regiments of light, 'swarm,' **30**. 158
  Sackville fails to bring up, at Minden, **30**. 157
  Spanish: convoy of, **17**. 323; Havana the destination of, **38**. 169; inferior to Lobkowitz's, **18**. 312; 'ruined,' **35**. 51; to pass through Loreto, **18**. 45; to repass the Var, **19**. 51
  Turkish, **23**. 160
  Vernon disperses Cuban, **30**. 29
  *See also* Dragoon; Hussar
Cavan, E. of. *See* Lambart, Richard
Cavanac, Marquise de. *See* Couppier, Anne (1737–1808)
Cave, Mr, of Dublin:
  SH visited by, **12**. 245
Cave, Edward:
  Johnson offers to translate Italian for, **33**. 493n
Cave, Sir Thomas (1712–78), 5th Bt, 1734; M.P.:
  HW corrects misapprehension of, about *Anecdotes of Painting*, **41**. 236
  HW's correspondence with, **41**. 236
  HW thanks, for correcting error, **41**. 236
  HW to return visit of, **41**. 236
Cave; caves:
  at Esher, **10**. 73
  HW jokes about era when royalty lived in, **39**. 127
  Minorcan, compared to 'Devil's Arse' in Derbyshire, **37**. 315
  *See also* Grotto
Caveat:
  Martin's, over *Essay on Woman*, **38**. 231
  Orford's, against mother's will, **25**. 124, 126, 137, 143, 167, 492, 493, 504, 505, 509, 511

Torriano's, against James Mann's will, **22**. 240–2, 245, 247, **24**. 271
Cavendish, Lady. *See* Hardwick, Elizabeth
Cavendish, Anne (ca 1621–38), m. (1632) Robert Rich, styled Lord Rich 1619–41; 3d E. of Warwick, 1658:
  Van Dyck's portrait of, **39**. 139n
Cavendish, Lady Caroline (1719–60), m. (1739) William Ponsonby, styled Vct Duncannon, 2d E. of Bessborough, 1758:
  Ailesbury, Cts of, and friends invited by, **38**. 12
  at Chesterfield's assembly, **37**. 325
  birth date of husband of, corrected, **43**. 373
  brother and sister go with, to country on father's death, **37**. 423
  chambermaid of, loved by Edgcumbe, **30**. 90n
  death of, **9**. 272, **21**. 362, 429
  family of, suffers from epidemic, **9**. 271
  HW mentions, **20**. 326
  husband of, **37**. 422n
  marriage of, **20**. 66
Cavendish, Sir Charles (1553–1617), Kt, 1582:
  Stanhope assaults, **37**. 477
Cavendish, Lord Charles (ca 1693–1783), M.P.; F.R.S.; trustee of British Museum:
  Lowther's residuary legatee, **9**. 184
  Morton known to, **31**. 427
  portrait of, by Maratti, **10**. 345
Cavendish, Lady Dorothy (1750–94), m. (1766) William Henry Cavendish Bentinck, 3d D. of Portland, 1762:
  Amelia, Ps, entertains, **33**. 416n, **35**. 533n
  birthday of, celebrated at Chatsworth, **9**. 295
  brother's bequest to, **36**. 205
  Douglas, Lady Frances, told by, of mother-in-law's will, **33**. 489–90
  father's legacy to, **38**. 455
  HW entertains, at SH, **10**. 306
  marriage of, **22**. 465, **29**. 261n
  name of husband of, corrected, **43**. 368
Cavendish, Lady Elizabeth (1654–1734), m. 1 (1669) Christopher Monck, 2d D. of Albemarle; m. 2 (1692) Ralph Montagu, 1st D. of Montagu:
  Coke, Lady Mary, resembles, **25**. 564
  eccentricities of, **25**. 564n
  HW jokes about insane delusions of, **10**. 109
Cavendish, Elizabeth (d. 1779), m. (1732) Richard Chandler, later Cavendish:
  'above common size,' **31**. 53
  death of, expected, **30**. 270–1
  Dysart, Cts of, mourned by, **9**. *171*
  (?) HW mentions, **37**. 337
  HW speculates on half-nakedness of, in new Court dress, **38**. 155
  Isleworth house of, **33**. 524n
  Latimers owned by, **35**. 233
  Sandwich, Cts of, visited only by, **10**. 203
  statue reminds HW of, drunk in bath-tub, **39**. 139
  (?) *World* story about Maclaine's encounter with, **35**. 199

Cavendish, Lady Elizabeth (d. 1796), m. (1743) John Ponsonby:
brother and sister go to country with, on father's death, 37. 423
Cavendish, Lord John, visits, 28. *323*
husband of, 37. 422n
SH visited by, 12. 240
Cavendish, Frances (ca 1742–1808), m. (1769) Frederick Flood, cr. (1780) Bt:
at Pitt Place, 28. 480n
Lyttelton's party with, at Epsom, 24. 537
Cavendish, Lord Frederick (1729–1803), field marshal; M.P.:
army commission retained by, despite his political opposition, 40. 336n
Barillon's letters read by, 34. 113
brother's fits mentioned by, to Newcastle, 38. 419
brother's legacy to, 38. 455
Conway hears from about Hastenbeck, 37. 495, 497
—— led by, 38. 569
——'s friend, 37. 570
—— sorry for, 37. 575
—— to see, 38. 405
Cumberland, D. of, has, as lord of Bedchamber, 21. 78n
—— takes, to Hanover, 21. 78
Derbyshire seat sought for, by father, 9. 115
Devonshire, D. of, visited by, at Chatsworth, 38. 19
field-marshalship date of, corrected, 43. 363
Fitzwilliam's bequest to, 11. 49–50, 34. 59
Fox, Henry, confirms account by, 37. 497
French take, prisoner, 21. 244, 251
George III receives Devonshire's Garter from, 38. 455
HW does not want to meet, at Park Place, 39. 101
HW persuades, not to vote on Regency Bill, 38. 548
HW's correspondence with, 37. (?) 465
HW sees, at Lord Bessborough's, 32. 11
HW sups with: 29. 53n; after Gordon Riots, 33. 177
Hartington accompanied by, to Ireland, 37. 392n
Lambert's blunder cancelled by, 21. 255
Lowther leaves reversionary interests to, 9. 184
M.P., 28. 398n
Montagu, Frederick, friend of, 9. 303
Montrose, Ds of, succeeded by, at Twickenham Park, 36. 252
Mountrath, Cts of, leaves Twickenham Park to, 30. 223, 31. 123
'mute,' 39. 100
Newcastle informed by, of brother's health, 40. 362n, 364n
—— shows HW a letter from, on brother's illness, 38. 445

Parliamentary activity of, on Regency Bill, 38. 548–50
safe after St-Malo attempt, 37. 570
Shelburne's second, in duel, 25. 31n, 29. 14
social relations of, with: Coke, Lady Mary, 35. 341; HW, 29. 53n, 33. 177; Holdernesse, Cts of, 35. 341
thinks England has no enemies but Bute and Dyson, 39. 100
Thomond talks with, at White's, 41. 73
Twickenham Park House occupied by, 42. 484
Cavendish, Lord George Augustus (?1727–94), M.P.:
appointment of, as comptroller, 9. 406
biographical information on, corrected, 43. 119, 308
bon mot of, 29. 116–17
brother's legacy to, 38. 455
comptroller, 38. 142
Conway led by, 38. 569
Cornwall's dinner attended by, 33. 588n
Devonshire, D. of, visited by, at Chatsworth, 38. 19
HW persuades, not to vote on Regency Bill, 38. 548
HW receives book from, 2. 289n
HW's conversation with, 29. 263
HW sees, at Lord Bessborough's, 32. 11
Keith entertains, with Conway in Vienna, 39. 538
Lowther leaves reversion of annuity to, 9. *184*
M.P., 28. 398n
'mute,' 39. 100
nephew succeeded by, in Parliament, 36. 205
Parliamentary activity of, on Regency Bill, 38. 548–50
refuses to read Burke's *Reflections*, 34. 104
resignation of, as comptroller of the Household, 22. 97
thinks England has no enemies but Bute and Dyson, 39. 100
West's *Antiquities of Furness* given by, to HW, 39. 237
Cavendish, Lady George Augustus Henry. *See* Compton, Lady Elizabeth (1760–1835)
Cavendish, Lord George Augustus Henry (1754–1834), cr. (1831) E. of Burlington:
Compton, Lady Elizabeth, might be courted by, 33. 279
father's legacy to, 38. 455
French sends print to, 42. 268
French, Mrs, friend of, commemorated by Darwin as 'Milcena,' 42. 271
HW distinguishes between uncle and, 29. 117n
HW may get Darwin quotation from, 42. 271
marriage of, 29. 192
Cavendish, Lady Georgiana Dorothy (1783–1858), m. (1801) George Howard, styled Lord Morpeth to 1825; 6th E. of Carlisle, 1825:
birth of, impending, 33. 380

[Cavendish, Lady Georgiana Dorothy, *continued*]
father's apathy about, 33. 405
mother's supposed treatment of, 33. 408
Cavendish, Gilbert:
book ascribed to, 16. 140n
Cavendish, Lady Harriet Elizabeth (1785–1862), m. (1809) Lord Granville Leveson Gower, cr. (1815) Vct and (1833) E. Granville:
birth of, impending, 33. 481
Cavendish, Henrietta (1694–1755), m. (1713) Edward Harley, 2d E. of Oxford:
ancestral portraits collected by, 35. 271
death of, 35. 271
Cavendish, Henry (1630–91), 2d D. of Newcastle-on-Tyne:
daughter and co-heiress of, 25. 564n
Cavendish, Lord Henry (ca 1673–1700):
daughter of, 24. 401n
Cavendish, Sir Henry (1732–1804), 2d Bt, 1776:
English government defended by, 33. 141
house of, in Dublin, attacked, 24. 535n, 33. 141
Cavendish, Lord James (after 1698–1741), M.P.:
Charles, P., resembles, 37. 142
daughter of, 9. 171n, 33. 524n
death of, reported, 17. 197
Cavendish, Lord John (1732–96), M.P.; politician:
administration change affects, 33. 343–4
Barré's pension defended by, 29. 264
brother of, 29. 117n
brother's fits mentioned by, to Newcastle, 38. 419
brother's legacy to, 38. 455
Bryant's *Ancient Mythology* admired by, 28. 146
Buckinghamshire's entrenchments in Ireland described by, 28. 323
Burke defended by, 25. 408n
—— proposes to receive clerkship of the Pells from, 42. 23n, 25n
——'s *Reflections* admired by, 34. 99n
Cavendishes think, equal to Chatham, 39. 101
Cavendish family thought by, to have right to make Portland premier, 33. 342n
chancellor of the Exchequer, 25. 262, 293, 391, 29. 208, 213, 217, 328n
Chatham object of protest by, 22. 471n
—— praised by, insincerely, 28. 398
——'s high style resented by, 22. 444n
Coke, Lady Mary, dines with, 33. 343
Conway dominated by, 38. 549, 569
——'s illness does not alarm, 39. 281
——'s loyalty to, during Regency crisis, 22. 298n
—— to be visited by, 38. 405
declines to serve under Shelburne, 25. 293
Devonshire, D. of, visited by, at Chatsworth, 38. 19
dominating influence in Rockingham ministry, 29. 261n

elected M.P. for York after hard race, 28. 173
faction of, does not deserve Conway's struggles for them, 41. 65–6
Fox, C. J., will now dominate, 29. 267
Gibbon discussed by, 29. 126–7
Grafton on good terms with, 30. 232
——'s letter of resignation from, 30. 232
Fountayne gets political news from, 29. 221
HW accompanied by, to Hardwick, 9. 296
HW cannot persuade, to avoid voting on Regency Bill, 38. 548, 549
HW, Conway, and de Saussure received by, at Chatsworth, 41. 165
HW does not expect, to be moderate, 41. 86–7
HW does not want to meet, at Park Place, 39. 101
HW hears story from, about Bess of Hardwick, 9. 298
HW identifies, 29. 187n
HW meets, at Gloucester House, 29. 222, 226
HW notified by, of Devonshire's legacy to Conway, 38. 449
HW not taken for hero by, 38. 382
HW pities, on brother's death, 43. 380
HW's conference with, over Exchequer place, 42. 56n
HW sees, at Lord Bessborough's, 32. *11*
HW's opinion of, 9. 308
HW suspects traces of family madness in, 30. 232
HW tells, of satisfaction with Conway's retaining office, 33. 344n
Hardinge introduced by, to D. of Devonshire as counsel, 35. 618
Hardwick Hall exhibited by, to HW, 40. 182
Hertford meets, and discusses Conway's stroke, 39. 281
integrity of, 29. 54
Lowther leaves reversionary interests to, 9. 184
Mason decides, is not a true Whig, 29. 40
—— expects visit from, 1. 233, 28. 459
—— is as contradictory as, 28. 399
—— is curious about vote of, on Strutt's bill, 29. 50
—— perhaps considered impertinent by, 29. 189
—— probably alludes to, 29. 93n
——'s estrangement from, 29. 54
—— to visit, 29. 84n
may be secretary of state, 25. 295n
Montagu, Frederick, friend of, 9. 303
—— praises, 9. 303
Mountrath, Cts of, names, in her will, 30. 222, 31. 123
—— slightly acquainted with, 30. 222
'much broken,' 33. 253
Newcastle informed by, of Devonshire's health, 40. 362n
obstinate and conceited, 38. 548
Parliamentary activity of, on Regency Bill, 38. 548–50

Parliamentary bill by, for Exchequer reform, **33**. 406n

Parliamentary motions by: **29**. 197n; against preliminary peace articles, **25**. 371n; against Shelburne on preliminary peace articles, **33**. 388n; for amendment to the Address, **24**. 533n, **25**. 368n; for committee to consider George III's debts, **28**. 304; for George IV's allowance, **25**. 418n; on dismissal of officers, **38**. 502

Parliamentary resolutions by: against treaty, **25**. 367n; proposed, **25**. 253n, **29**. 197n

political allies of, few, **30**. 240

political 'mischief' of, **30**. 232

Portland, D. of, proposed by, as prime minister, **29**. 261

resignation of, **30**. 228, 232, **35**. 517–18

resignations urged by, **41**. 66n

Richmond influenced by, **30**. 232

Rockingham friend of, **25**. 293

—— governed by, **30**. 232n

——'s death leaves, with power (as chancellor of Exchequer) to appoint to vacant places, **42**. 25n

(?) Saturday Club and, **43**. 185

SH visited by, **12**. 246

sups at Richmond House, **33**. 344

Townshend proposed by, for Speaker, **23**. 180

Treasury quitted by, **22**. 444

war expenses stressed by, **25**. 255n

Weymouth wants, as chancellor of the Exchequer, **24**. 447n

Whigs led by, against Conway's support of East India Co.'s inquiry, **41**. 65n

Wyvill behaves 'infamously' to, **29**. 27n

York election of, opposed, **39**. 197

Yorkshire Association does not oppose reelection of, **29**. 79

—— opposed by, **29**. 20, 24, 329n

Cavendish, Mary (d. 1632), m. (1568) Gilbert Talbot, styled Lord Talbot, 7th E. of Shrewsbury, 1590:
chambermaid recommended for, **11**. 278

Cavendish, Mary (1698–1778), m. (ca 1720) John Fane, cr. (1733) Bn Catherlough; 7th E. of Westmorland, 1736:
Conway and wife to visit, **37**. 346
death of, **24**. 401
Foote, Mrs, friend of, **24**. 401
—— visited by, **22**. 72
HW admires appearance of, at George III's Coronation, **9**. 387, **21**. 535, **38**. 117, 122, 126

Cavendish, Philip (d. 1743), Adm.; M.P.:
Admiralty member, **17**. 366, **18**. 349n
Parliamentary memberships of, corrected, **43**. 244

Cavendish, Lady Rachel (1727–1805), m. (1748) Horatio Walpole, 2n Bn Walpole of Wolterton, 1757; cr. (1806), E. of Orford, n.c.:

Devonshire, Ds of, leaves money to, **6**. 442

father of, calls her 'Cat,' and exclaims to her over peace treaty, **9**. 58–9

HW proposes that son of, marry a Waldegrave, **25**. 132

HW writes to, about election instructions, **36**. 291

marriage of: HW attends, **9**. 54; impending, **19**. 469

miscarriage of, **20**. 42

son born to, **37**. 339, 341

son of, inherits Cavendish gait, **15**. 317

SH visited by, **12**. 240

Cavendish, Richard (d. ?1601), politician; author:
epitaph of, **1**. 38–9

Cavendish, Richard (d. 1769). *See* Chandler, Richard

Cavendish, Lord Richard (1752–81), M.P.:
birth of, **37**. 341
death of, **29**. 161, **33**. 294, 299
father's legacy to, **38**. 455
Reynolds's portrait of, **29**. 138, 285, **43**. 308
sister inherits money of, **36**. 205
uncle succeeds, in Parliament, **36**. 205
volunteer on Keppel's ship, **33**. 38
Walsingham's friend, **33**. 38n

Cavendish, Thomas (1560–92), circumnavigator:
American colonies planted by, **33**. 349

'Cavendish, Sir William.' *See* Cavendish, Sir Charles

Cavendish, Sir William (d. 1557):
wife inherits property of, **9**. 298, **40**. 182

Cavendish, William (1552–1626), cr. (1618) E. of Devonshire:
sister of, **11**. 278n

Cavendish, William (1593–1676), cr. (1628) E., (1643) M., and (1665) D. of Newcastle-upon-Tyne:
Belsham's defence of, inadequate, **31**. 296
——'s *Strictures on Walpole's Catalogue of Royal and Noble Authors* criticizes HW's treatment of, **31**. 294
*Country Captain* by, **15**. 198n
*General System of Horsemanship* by, **5**. 152n, **7**. 416
prints of, **1**. 182, **7**. 269, **14**. 145–6, 147
riding-stable of, **35**. 271
wife of, **16**. 367n

Cavendish, William (1641–1707), 4th E. of Devonshire, 1684; cr. (1694) D. of Devonshire:
(?) Dixon sells picture to, **41**. 97
epitaph by, on his mistress, **16**. 368–9
granddaughter of, **24**. 401n
Kennett prints writings of, **16**. 368
Macpherson casts suspicion of Jacobitism on, **28**. 192
son of, **9**. 171n

Cavendish, William (ca 1673–1729), 2d D. of Devonshire:

Pembroke, E. of, entertained by, with virtuosi at Devonshire House, 16. 208–9
—— sold medals to, 16. 208
son of, 9. 184n

Cavendish, William (?1698–1755), 3d D. of Devonshire:

Bessborough obtains English barony through, 20. 66
Brudenell received into White's by, in HW's newspaper parody, 9. 127
chess associations of, in HW's newspaper parody, 9. 127
Chesterfield succeeds, as lord lieutenant of Ireland, 18. 550
daughter-in-law of, 9. 81
daughters of, 19. 469, 20. 66, 21. 429
death of, from dropsy and drinking, 37. 423n
Domenichino painting admired by, 18. 292
Dorset succeeded by, as lord steward, 18. 550
drinking, gaming, and ugly wife loved by, 20. 66n
fare of, economical, 37. 341
Fox alienated by refusal of, to give post to Hamilton, 30. 130n
German treaties opposed by, 20. 501, 35. 88
King's College doctor's treatment of, 13. 174
Newcastle ministry appeases, by granting his son's wishes in Ireland, 37. 409
nicknames given by, to his children, 9. 58, 11. 265n
regent, 18. 209n
regiment raised by, 19. 110, 128, 26. 13, 30. 98
resigns as lord steward of the Household, 19. 211, 20. 66
retires to Chatsworth, with mad wife, 20. 66
Richmond rumoured to succeed, as lord lieutenant of Ireland, 17. 330n
Russian and Hessian treaties opposed by, 35. 88
Rutland's Derbyshire influence sought by, for son, 9. 115
signing of Aix-la-Chapelle treaty pleases, 9. 58–9
son of, 1. 233n, 9. 184n, 28. 146n
unpolished, 20. 270
Walpole, Horatio (1678–1757) hoped to ask, for peerage, 19. 469, 20. 66–7
Walpole, Sir Robert, liked by, 17. 176
wife made insane by, 20. 66
wife's promise from, not to wed their son to Burlington's daughter, 20. 66n
wife taken by, to London, 20. 66
wife tells, not to cut ham, 37. 341

Cavendish, William (ca 1720–64), styled M. of Hartington, 1729–55; 4th D. of Devonshire, 1755:

address of loyalty to George II moved by, in Parliament, 18. 399
Amelia, Ps, accompanied by, to Stowe, 22. 247n
—— said to have been lent Burlington House by, 9. 316
art collection of, 38. 455n
(?) at Chesterfield's assembly, 37. 325
ball for Karl Wilhelm Ferdinand chiefly by, 38. 289
Bath left by, after D. of Newcastle's fall, 22. 96
Bessborough visits, at Chatsworth, 38. 19
biographical information about, corrected, 43. 117, 233, 313
Bodens, Molly, and Mrs Garrick consult, about ministry, 35. 165
Boyle and Stone oppose, 37. 399
Boyle, Newport, and Stone confer with, 37. 393n
Boyle's negotiations with, 37. 448n
Bridgwater visits, at Chatsworth, 38. 19
brothers visit, at Chatsworth, 9. 295, 38. 19
Buondelmonti's retort from, at Rome, 37. 56–7
Burlington, Lady, leaves annuity to, 9. 226n
Bute opposed by, 38. 186
catalogue of collection of, see Catalogues of the Collections of Pictures of the Duke of Devonshire . . .
Cavendish, Lord John, sent by, with HW to Hardwick, 9. 296
chairman of committee to examine Secret Committee lists, 17. 383
chamberlain's staff and key taken by, 21. 91
characteristics of, candour, honesty, sense, and spirit, 37. 399
Chatsworth improved by, 9. 296
—— left by, for Kensington, 21. 11n
Coke, Lady Mary, to visit, at Chatsworth, 38. 72
Conolly lends Castletown to, 37. 400
Conway adheres to, 40. 334
Conway and wife to be visited by, at Park Place, 37. 483, 486
Conway anxious for George II to approve conduct of, 37. 404–5
—— in London settles Irish policy of, 37. 403n
—— must go into mourning for, 38. 452–3
—— obligated to, 38. 385, 386, 40. 334n, 41. 67
—— owes more to, than to Hertford and cannot desert him, 38. 425
—— praises, 37. 398n, 399
—— repairs honour of, in Ireland, 37. 406
—— secretary to, in Ireland, 20. 503, 505, 37. 392n
——'s legacy from, 10. 135–6, 22. 256, 38. 449, 450, 454
——'s release from Ireland depends on Dublin's need for, 37. 450
—— tells, of jerboa medal in his collection, 37. 467
—— thought by, to have favour with George II, 37. 575

—— to meet, at Carton, **37**. 456

(?) —— to visit, at Chiswick, **37**. 374

council on Rochefort expedition attended by, **37**. 494

Court attended by, **22**. 79n

Court would not get much quarter from, **22**. 102

Cumberland, D. of, visits, at Chatsworth, **38**. 19

dances at Robinson's ball, **37**. 115

daughter of, **29**. 261n

death and will of, **22**. 256

death of: **43**. 380; Grenville ministry not improved by, **38**. 458–9; leaves chasm, **38**. 470; sets Rockingham at head of Whigs, **25**. 288

Derbyshire visited by, **30**. 64

design for Wolfe's tomb selected by, **21**. 428

Dorset succeeded by, as lord lieutenant of Ireland, **20**. 469

Dublin acclaims, as only viceroy since Ormond with Irish estates, **20**. 469n

—— left by, for country, **37**. 455

Edgcumbe friend of, **22**. 471n, **41**. 67

father-in-law's will does not mention, **35**. 159

father won over by concessions to, in Ireland, **37**. 409

Foote's *Minor* defended by, from Secker's censorship, **9**. 326–7

Fox, Henry, disgusted with, for favouring Pitt, **21**. 31

—— notified by, of new ministerial plan, **35**. 168

—— offends, by not consulting him before attacking Hay, **21**. 23n

—— quarrels with, **22**. 134, **30**. 130

——'s letter carried by, **35**. 169

—— visits, after Pelham's death, **20**. 412n

Garrick, Mrs, gets interest from, on mortgage, **20**. 74n

garter of, returned by brother to George III, **38**. 455

George II orders: to induce Pitt to join Fox in ministry, **21**. 11; to visit Pitt, **21**. 22n

—— tells, to offer Garter to Temple, **21**. 345n

—— thought by, to favour Conway, **37**. 575

—— urged by, to give Pitt and Temple places, **21**. 86n

George III believed by, to force his resignation to make room for Bute, **22**. 97n

—— orders, to list pictures in royal palaces, **40**. 189

—— refuses to see, **10**. 45–6, **22**. 96

——'s treatment of, **22**. 106

Gideon's bequest to, **38**. 189

gold boxes received by, in Ireland, **37**. 400

Gower visits, at Chatsworth, **38**. 19

Grafton does not come to London to see, **38**. 435

—— succeeded by, as lord chamberlain, **21**. 91n

Graftons' visit to, put off for Derby races, **38**. 63

Granby's Derbyshire appointment accompanied by excuses to, **38**. 334

HW asked by, to write Mann for melon seeds, **18**. 384

HW and Straffords to visit, at Chatsworth, **38**. 72

HW disparages 'candour' of, **35**. 159

HW invited by, to Chatsworth, **35**. 303–4

HW jokes about pullet seen by, at Wentworth Castle, **38**. 72

HW mentions, **9**. 211, **20**. 326, **37**. 133

HW receives condolences of, **17**. 320

HW remarks upon, **17**. 7n

HW repeats to, Grenville's alleged statement about Conway, **40**. 331

HW's correspondence with, **40**. 126, 176–8, 181–3

HW's plans changed by visit of, to Spa, **10**. 133

HW summoned by, to Burlington House to see pictures from Hardwick, **38**. 119–20

HW tells Conway to wear mourning for, **38**. 452–3

HW to follow, to Chatsworth, **38**. 72

HW tries with, to preserve opera-box party, **38**. 123

HW urges, to let Churchill succeed Col. Pelham, **40**. 177–8

HW used to shock, **32**. 191

HW visited by, with Straffords at SH for tea, **38**. 362

HW visits, **21**. 427, 432–3, **22**. 247, **40**. 181–2

HW wants copies of portraits owned by, **40**. 182

heads of Q. Elizabeth owned by, supposedly by Vicentino, **16**. 157

health of: autopsy reveals growth on brain, **38**. 450; endangered, **40**. 361–3, 364; fits, **38**. 419; illness, **30**. 176; rash and miliary fever, **38**. 429, 444–5

Hertford does not think he should have joined, in breaking white stick of office, **38**. 424

—— never had the confidence of, **38**. 330

—— not treated with political friendship by, **38**. 424

—— visits, at Chatsworth, **38**. 18, 19

Hertfords visit, at Chatsworth, **38**. 91

hunting trip of, said to indicate Whig security, **9**. 144

incense pot might be given by, to SH chapel, **38**. 362

income of, £40,000 yearly, **38**. 445

Ireland not to be left by, for England, **37**. 398–9

—— receives, courteously but not enthusiastically, **37**. 392–3

—— to be station of, as lord-lieutenant, **35**. 220, **37**. 392n

—— to be visited by, **20**. 474

Irish elections shunned by, **37**. 422

Irish policy of: approved by George II and Boyle, **37**. 409–10; impartial, **37**. 394

[Cavendish, William (ca 1720–64), *continued*]
key and staff relinquished by, to Egremont, **22.** 96
Kildare's social relations with, **37.** 456
Knight of the Garter, **10.** 29, **21.** 27, **37.** 480
*Letter from the Cocoa Tree* abuses, **22.** 102n
legacies of, **38.** 455
lieutenancy lost by, **22.** 109n
London to be visited by, to go to Spa at physicians' wish, **38.** 422
London visited by, **10.** 45, **38.** 214
lord chamberlain, **15.** 160n, **22.** 96n
lord chamberlain's post resigned by, **10.** 46
lord lieutenant of Ireland, **37.** 392n
Mann sorry for, **22.** 106
—— thinks, fortunate to have Conway as secretary, **20.** 505
——trusts the calm, pacific disposition of, **21.** 28
Marlborough to vacate chamberlain's office for, **22.** 130–1
marriage of: **19.** 19; drives mother crazy, **20.** 66
Master of the Horse, **9.** 115, **20.** 258
Mattei civil to, **30.** 6
melon seeds for, from Florence, **18.** 384, 428, 496
ministry of: Minorcan investigation to be used against, **21.** 76–7; without influence in House of Commons, **21.** 67
Moore, Sir John, visits, at Chatsworth, **38.** 19
mother avoids, **20.** 66
mother-in-law of, **35.** 165n
Naples visited by, **17.** 16
Newcastle advised by, about retiring, **22.** 37n
—— replaced by, as prime minister, **21.** 17, 24
—— rumoured to succeed, in Treasury, **21.** 91n
——'s broken promises to Fox revealed by, **30.** 123n
Newmarket visited by, **37.** 511
officers assigned to Ireland summoned back there by, **35.** 220n
opera box-holders can be united only by tact of, **38.** 128
Orford writes to, about Castle Rising, **36.** 33
Pelham's death mourned by, **35.** 165–6
——'s favourite, **20.** 74n
pictures sent by, to cleaner, **40.** 182
Pitt opposed by, **20.** 223
——'s Spanish war proposal opposed by, **38.** 131n
—— tells, he will await George II's orders before resigning, **21.** 74n
—— urged by, to become minister, **21.** 11
portrait owned by, of Mary, Q. of Scots, **15.** 113n
resignation of, as lord chamberlain, **38.** 173, 190
return of, to England, **37.** 461
Richmond succeeded by, as Master of the Horse, **20.** 182n

Rockingham visits, at Chatsworth, **38.** 19
Rome governor talks to, about captured ship, **17.** 7–8
Sandwich opposed by, over Wilkes, in House of Lords, **38.** 293
—— rumoured to succeed, in Garter, **38.** 463
sister of, **21.** 362
sisters go to country with, on father's death, **37.** 423
sits 22 hours in Parliament, **17.** 383
social relations of, with: Bessborough, Bonfoy, and Coke, Lady Mary, **9.** 295; Grafton, Ds of, **21.** 427; HW, **40.** 181–2; HW, Ponsonby, Ladies Catherine, Charlotte, and Sarah, Straffords, and Thomond, **9.** 295
son born to, **20.** 19, **29.** 138n
Spa visited by, **10.** 132, **38.** 422, 429, 444–5, 447
steward of, **37.** 567
Stone's dismissal from Irish Regency, wanted by, **20.** 503n
Strafford put off by summons of, to London, **37.** 579
Straffords visited by, at Wentworth Castle, **38.** 72
Suffolk Cts of, advises Strafford to wear mourning for, on getting legacy, **38.** 452–3
Terrick obtains Peterborough see from, but deserts him, **30.** 209n
Thomond consulted by, about peerage, **21.** 24n
tickets desired from, for ball, **9.** 386
to be Bn Cavendish and Master of the Horse, **9.** 115
Treasury headed by, **9.** 202, **21.** 17, 24
—— retained by, temporarily, **21.** 74
uncle fetched by, **17.** 244
unmarried, **10.** 29
Venice the destination of, **17.** 23
Waldegrave visits, at Chatsworth, **38.** 19
Walpole, Horatio (1678–1757), favoured by, in Nicoll affair, **35.** 160n
Walpole, Lady Mary, may marry, **17.** 176–7
Walpole, Sir Robert, entertains, **17.** 176
Walpole party supported by, **17.** 247
wife brings houses and estates to, **20.** 66n
wife of, **9.** 81n
Wilmot attends, at Chatsworth, **38.** 419
Yarmouth, Cts of, approached by, on Conway's behalf, **37.** 542n, **38.** 84n
Cavendish, William (1748–1811), styled M. of Hartington 1755–64; 5th D. of Devonshire, 1764:
absentee tax opposed by, **23.** 524n
antiquities collected by, **32.** 139
apathy of, at daughter's birth, **33.** 405
arrival of, in London, **4.** 352
at camp, **15.** 162
birth of, **20.** 19
brother of, **29.** 161n
'buying the character of singularity very dear,' **32.** 139

Cavendish, Lord John, inherits mortgage on estates of, from Lady Mountrath, 30. 222, 31. 123
—— introduces Hardinge as counsel to, 35. 618
Chatterton thinks Burlington House is home of, 16. 347
coldness of, 33. 183
Court attended by, 38. 561
daughter of, by Charlotte Spencer, 25. 444, 455n, 459n
Devonshire House and art collection to be redeemed by, from father's estate, 38. 455
Du Deffand, Mme, sends letters and parcels by, 4. 327, 329, 330, 332, 333, 334n, 335–8, 348, 355
——'s social relations with, 4. 333
Farington mentions, 15. 317
Foster, Lady Elizabeth, paid by, to go to France with his daughter, 25. 459n
George IV envies, 33. 411
Gordon's scandal about, in Morning Post, 33. 117n
grandfather's bequest to, 35. 159
HW proposes to visit, 1. 66n
Hamilton, Lady Elizabeth, courted by, 32. 139n
hesitates to permit printing of wife's verses, 29. 183, 189, 192
illness of, 1. 66n
Isabella Clara Eugenia's portrait owned by, 7. 269
Knight of the Garter, 25. 273
Lort appointed by, to take care of his medals, 1. 313n
—— did not know that medals of, had been Pembroke's, 16. 209
Mann grateful for aid of, 23. 64
——'s declaration witnessed by, 23. 63n
—— to be accompanied by, at investiture, 23. 60
marriage of, 23. 562, 24. 14, 35. 422
medal of Ds of Portsmouth might be owned by, 16. 301
medals stolen from collection of, at Devonshire House, 15. 200, 16. 204
mob respects, 33. 175n
Mountrath, Cts of, bequeaths mortgage on estates of, 31. 123
no gamester, 16. 347
North's letter from, on absentee tax, 32. 164n
paintings owned by, 16. 323n, 42. 443
Paoli aided by, 23. 91n
Paris left by, 4. 327, 330, 338, 339, 344, 345, 347, 11. 27, 36
portrait belonging to, 15. 112, 139
portrait not owned by, 15. 163
Protestant mob cheers, 25. 54n
rumoured as Rockingham's successor, 25. 289
Stratford's comedy may be ridiculed by, 29. 234–5

SH visited by, 12. 251
treasures neglected by, 16. 208
uncle of, 29. 79n
Villiers handsomer than, 39. 152
Watts insults, 2. 274
wife of, 5. 280n, 28. 203n
York meeting attended by, 28. 488n
Cavendish, Mrs William. See Chandler, Barbara (d. 1786)
Cavendish, William George Spencer (1790–1858) 6th D. of Devonshire, 1811:
father's medals sold by, 16. 301n
Cavendish Bentinck. See Bentinck
Cavendish family:
arms of, 1. 39
Bessborough's connection with, 43. 380
Boyle and Clifford family estates descend to, through Lady Charlotte Boyle, 20. 545n
Bute and Dyson considered the sole enemies by, 39. 100
Cavendish, Lord John, thinks Grafton would not wish member of, on Treasury Board, 30. 232
Clavering's and Blackett's motion opposed by, 39. 126
Closet to be stormed by, 30. 238–9
Collins's account of, 42. 313
Conway cannot see, unless wearing mourning for Devonshire, 38. 453
—— urged by, to resign, 22. 471–2
credit lost by, in their own counties, 25. 488
George III dislikes, 25. 379
Grafton's rift not understood by, 38. 436
Grenville, George, deals with, 41. 73
HW abuses members of, for opposing Pitt-Grafton ministry, 30. 238
HW appears 'ashamed' of political intrigues of, 30. 176
HW dislikes, for intrigues at White's, 41. 73n
HW does not expect, to be moderate, 41. 86–7
HW does not want to see, at Park Place, since they think Rockingham and Lord John Cavendish equal to Chatham, 39. 101
HW ill-treated by, after breach with uncle, 10. 46
HW regarded, moderately, 39. 530
HW's great regard for, 43. 380
heir's birth encourages, 20. 19
hereditary gait of, 15. 316–17
madness hereditary in, 30. 232
Mann shocked by tragedy of, 21. 369
minority may be joined by, in East Indian dispute, 22. 473
Parliamentary reforms opposed by, 25. 29–30
Pelham proposes Hartington to George II as Master of the Horse to secure interest of, 20. 258n
political activities of, 10. 236
Portland wanted by, as prime minister, 33. 342n
portraits of, at Welbeck, 35. 270

[Cavendish family, *continued*]
portraits of kings and queens of England at Hardwick owned by, **42**. 443
resolution upholding Parliament's proceedings opposed by, **39**. 126
Rockingham faction ruled by, **25**. 379
Stanhope's rejection at Derby a blow to, **20**. 19
Walpole, Hon. Thomas, connected with, **38**. 546

Cavendish House, Cavendish Sq. *See* Cavendish Sq.: Amelia, Ps in

Cavendish Scott Bentinck, William Henry Cavendish (1768–1854), styled M. of Titchfield; 4th D. of Portland, 1809:
birth of, **35**. 408
Gunning, Miss, to angle for, **11**. 205
Léon, Bp of, friend of, **12**. 25n
marriage of, **12**. 68n

Cavendish Sq., London:
Amelia, Ps, lives in, **9**. 57n, **23**. 7n, **29**. 193n, **31**. 52, **33**. 393, 455, **38**. 343–4, **39**. 248, 262
———'s house in, to be sold, **33**. 535
Darby's house in, **29**. 145n
Fox, Lady Mary, lives in, **23**. 392
HW addresses Harcourt in, **35**. 494
Harcourt House in, **35**. 469n, 471n, **38**. 495n
Lovell near, **9**. 183n
Lyttelton's house in, **9**. 316
Salisbury, Bp of, lives in, **11**. 253n
Wilton's work-shops in Edward St in, **20**. 392n

Caverhill, Dr John (d. 1781), physician and author:
Mason threatens HW with, **28**. 57
*Treatise on the Cause and Cure of the Gout* by, **28**. 57n

Cavern. *See* Cave

Caversham, Berks:
Berrys with Lovedays at, **11**. 137
HW dines at, and describes it, **33**. 51
Hervey, Bns, at, **31**. 30
house of, visible from Park Place, **39**. 550
Loveday of, **41**. 218
Setons at, **43**. 144

Caversham Hill, Berks:
Seton, Barbara Cecilia, goes to, **11**. 129n

Caversham Park, Berks:
Cadogan, Lady, writes from, **36**. 152
Churchill writes from, **36**. 127

Cavillini, Contessa:
Modenese princess's first lady, **17**. 158n

Cavino, Giovanni (1500–71):
medal attributed to, **15**. 278n

Cavone. *See* Covone

Cawdor, Bns. *See* Howard, Lady Isabella Caroline

Cawode; Cawoode. *See* Cawood

Cawood Castle, Yorks:
Bowet, Abp, built hall at, **16**. 49

Cawood Palace, Yorks:
Henry VIII's ointment devised at, **2**. 332, 334

Cawston, Norfolk:
Addison holds living of, **14**. 90n

Caxton, William (ca 1422–91), printer:
*Æneid* a novelty to, **2**. 289
Benedictine connections of, **16**. 3–4
*Dictes and Sayings of the Philosophers* printed by, **40**. 119n
HW compares himself to, **28**. 40, **29**. 263
HW quotes epilogue by, **28**. 48
Le Fèvre's *Recueil* printed by, **40**. 255n
Middleton writes on, **15**. 295
miniature depicts presentation of, to Edward IV, **41**. 112n
print of, **1**. 140
SH reminiscent of age of, **40**. 255
Virgil cited by, as historical authority, **29**. 89

Caxton, Cambs:
Young Pretender is expected to pass through, **14**. 2

Cay, Henry Boult (d. 1795), lawyer:
(?) SH visited by, **12**. 228

Cayenne:
Chanvalon indicted for mismanagement at, **7**. 320n
Dumonts in, **4**. 492
Hertford sends, to London, account of French colony at, **38**. 521n
parrots from, not owned by Mme de la Vallière, **5**. 128

Cayley, Lady. *See* Seton, Isabella

Cayley, Sir George (1773–1857), 6th Bt, 1792; Berrys' cousin:
Brompton, Yorks, seat of, **12**. 13n
HW asks about brother of, **12**. 52
SH visited by, **12**. 244

Cayley, Mary Agnes, m. (1846) James Alexander:
named for Berrys, **12**. 52n

Cayley, Sir Thomas (1732–92), 5th Bt, 1791; Berrys' uncle:
Berrys' letters addressed in care of, **11**. 18, 24, 58, 62
seat of, **11**. 13n

Cayley, Mrs Thomas. *See* Seton, Isabella

Caylus, Comte de. *See* Tubières de Grimoard de Pestel de Levy, Anne-Claude-Philippe de (1692–1765)

Caylus, Marquis de. *See* Tubières de Pestel de Levy, Charles de (ca 1698–1750)

Caylus, Marquise de. *See* Villette de Murçay, Marthe-Marguerite de

Cazalet, ———:
(?) at Boulogne, sends report to brother in London, **39**. 306n

Cazalet, Peter (d. 1788), merchant in Austin Friars:
(?) brother of, at Boulogne, gets Sartine's notice about Brest fleet, **39**. 306n

Cazalet. *See also* Castellet

Cazeaux, ———, law student at University of Toulouse:
trial of, **7**. 134

*Cazzo*:
Benedict XIV's epithet, **19**. 492
Ceadda (d. 672), St:
cathedral to, **9**. 294
Ceballos Cortes y Calderón, Gen. Pedro, viceroy of Rio de la Plata:
expedition sails to Brazil under, **24**. 224n
'Cecca' or 'Cecchina,' la; Giuditta's 3d sister:
burletta acted by, **17**. 128
Romana's popularity surpasses that of, **17**. 162
Suares, Francesco, loves, **17**. 70, 121, 128, **35**. 29
'Cecchina.' *See* 'Cecca'
*Cecchina. See under* Piccinni, Niccolò
'Cecchino'; 'Cecco.' *See* Suares, Francesco
Cecconi, Giuseppe, of Florence:
Lady Orford's Declaration signed by, **43**. 288
Cecil, ——, in Old Bond St:
Lort lodges with, **16**. 165n
Cecil, Lady Anne (1746–1813), dau. of 6th E. of Salisbury:
SH visited by, **12**. 230
Cecil, Brownlow (1701–54), 8th E. of Exeter, 1722:
wife of, **9**. 388n
Cecil, Brownlow (1725–93), 9th E. of Exeter, 1754; M.P.:
arrival of, in Florence, **23**. 64
Burghley House enlarged by, **10**. 344
—— refurnished by, **10**. 91, 344
—— to be left by, temporarily, **10**. 344–5
Cole's opinion of, **10**. 344
France to be visited by, **10**. 344–5
HW mentions, **40**. 284
HW reveals cabinet to, **10**. 91
HW's correspondence with, **10**. 332
HW shown the Burghley House treasures by, **10**. 91, 344–5
Homer's bust bought by, at Mead sale, **35**. 217
——'s bust presented by, to British Museum, **16**. 153
hospitality of, limited, **10**. 344
Italy visited by, **10**. 344–5, **23**. 18, 64
Langton's writing shown by, to HW, **1**. 46
Livesay hopes to sketch Hogarths in collection of, **42**. 153n
Mann's letter from, announces future return to Italy, **23**. 18
marriage of, **10**. 344
Mastership of Horse said to be offered to, **39**. 311
nephew adopted by, as heir, **10**. 344
portrait discussed by, with Cole, **10**. 346
portrait of, at Burghley House, **10**. 345
wife leaves life use of money to, **9**. 184
Cecil, Lady Diana (d. 1654), m. 1 (1624) Henry de Vere, 18th E. of Oxford, m. 2 (1629) Thomas Bruce, 3d Lord Kinloss and Bn Bruce of Kinloss, cr. (1633) E. of Elgin:
Bruce, Lady, talks of, in letter, **34**. 189
portrait of, at Boughton House, **10**. 340
tomb of, **39**. 139

Cecil, Lady Dorothy (d. 1613), m. Sir Giles Allington, Kt:
marriage of, **1**. 374
tomb of, at Horseheath, **1**. 48, 49–50, 52
Walpoles descended from, **12**. 165n, **33**. 505
Cecil, Edward (1572–1638), cr. (1625) Vct Wimbledon:
Johnson's portrait of, said to be at Somerset House, **40**. 142
Cecil, Lady Elizabeth (1578–1646), m. 1 Sir William Hatton, m. 2 (1598) Sir Edward Coke:
portrait of, at Standon, **12**. 199
Cecil, Henry (1754–1804), 10th E. of Exeter, 1793; cr. (1801) M. of Exeter; M.P.:
uncle adopts, as heir, **10**. 344
Cecil, James (1713–80), 6th E. of Salisbury, 1728:
broad-wheeled wagons planned by, **10**. 348
Burghley would be horrified by, **9**. 349
coach invented by, **10**. 348
'cucumber of Burleigh,' **33**. 505
family of, **10**. 348
HW misses, at Hatfield, **40**. 199
Hatfield stage coach driven by, **9**. 349, **10**. 348
manners and disposition and low company of, **10**. 348
marriage of, **10**. 348
mistress of, **10**. 348
Piozzi, Mrs, comments on, **10**. 348
popular opinion of, **10**. 348
post-chaises invented by, **10**. 348
wife's family well treated by, **10**. 348
Cecil, James (1748–1823), styled Vct Cranborne; 7th E. of Salisbury, 1780; cr. (1789) M. of Salisbury; lord chamberlain:
HW invited by, to Hatfield, **33**. 402
lord chamberlain and a 'stately simpleton,' **39**. 494n
marriage of, **32**. 166, **35**. 467
Pantheon license given by, **11**. 95, 227–8
rumour concerning appointment of, **33**. 134
Taylor, William, attacks, **11**. 191, 227–8
wife of, **11**. 25n
Cecil (after 1821, Gascoyne-Cecil), James Brownlow William (1791–1868), styled Vct Cranborne; 2d M. of Salisbury, 1823:
birth of, **11**. 248
Cecil, John (ca 1648–1700), 5th E. of Exeter:
Giordano and Dolci employed by, **15**. 204–5
(?) Maratti paints, at Rome, **42**. 159n
(?) painting of, by Dolci, **10**. 346
Cecil, Margaret (ca 1696–1782), m. Sir Robert Brown, cr. (1732) Bt:
age of, **31**. 418
birth date of, corrected, **43**. 111, 184, 314
'Brina' the whale, in HW's 'Patapan,' **30**. 295
Capello and Sir Robert Walpole entertained by, **18**. 459
Cathcart gives Turkish ornament to, **40**. 89n
Chute can be nursed by, **35**. 118

[Cecil, Margaret, *continued*]
—— might be courted by, for her daughter, **35**. 86
daughter of, dies, **9**. 170
dies, leaving estate to Morice, **25**. 246
fat but comely, **30**. 295n
HW calls, a 'fat beauty,' **18**. 166n
HW hears Rowe's lines on Lady Hervey from, **33**. 37
HW mentions, **14**. 120
HW receives Sir Robert Walpole's head on white cornelian from, **16**. 69n
HW receives Turkish ornament from, **18**. 166n
HW's correspondence with, **40**. 89–90
HW sees, **9**. 317
HW's presents from, **40**. 89n
HW to avoid, **9**. 317
HW to introduce Cerretesi at Sunday night party of, **18**. *166*
husband and Maguire aided by, **37**. 132
husband leaves property to, **9**. 312, 317
husband of, needs preferment, **37**. 132
Knightsbridge visited by, **9**. 16
Maguire's 'reign' with, **30**. 84
Montagu expects Chute to court, **9**. 315
moves to Upper Brook St, **9**. 15
'old Lady Brown,' **33**. 37
returns to England from Venice with husband, **25**. 609n
Rosalba's portrait of, in Tribune at SH, **18**. 166n
Rowe's verses on Bns Hervey discussed by, with Bns Hervey, **31**. 418
soldiers admired by, **30**. 84
Sunday evening entertainments by, **9**. 15, **18**. 66, **30**. 84
Cecil, Robert (1563–1612), cr. (1605), E. of Salisbury:
Galluzzi mentions knavery of, **25**. 225
Gunpowder Plot detected by, **32**. 76
house of, **35**. 266
Cecil, Thomas (1542–1623), 2d Bn Burghley; cr. (1605) E. of Exeter:
daughter of, **1**. 50, 374
death date of, corrected, **43**. 45
portrait of, **10**. 346
wife of, **1**. 149n, **9**. 7n
Cecil, Hon. Thomas Chambers (ca 1728–78):
marriage of, **10**. 344
son of, **10**. 344
Cecil, Hon. Mrs Thomas Chambers. *See* Garnier, Charlotte
Cecil, William (1521–98), Bn Burghley; statesman; lord Treasurer; M.P.:
Burghley House built by, **10**. 91n
*Collection of State Papers*, includes, **17**. 30n
counselled when Shakespeare wrote, **33**. 86
degenerate descendant of, **9**. 349
Falkland's picture of, **41**. 298
HW praises, **18**. 357
HW's ancestor, **1**. 374, **33**. 505
house of, **35**. 266

Knole's associations with, **32**. 223
Newcastle, D. of, might equal, **35**. 240
portrait of, by Zuccari, **10**. 346, **41**. 298
print of, **1**. 180, **40**. 237
Salisbury, 6th E. of, the 'cucumber' of, **33**. 505
signs pages of Q. Elizabeth's gift book, **32**. 323
wife of, **2**. 34n
Cecil, William (1590–1618), 17th Bn Ros:
vindicated, **2**. 34
Cecil, William (d. 1745), Col.; equerry to George I; Jacobite:
Argyll believes papers were sent to him by, **17**. *478*
Florentines hear nothing more of, **18**. 433
imprisoned in Tower, **17**. 478n, **18**. 408
Mann hopes, will be punished, **18**. 426
Old Pretender's agent, **17**. 478–9
——'s secretary of state, **17**. 479n, **18**. 408
Walpole, Sir Robert, gets Jacobite information from, **17**. 479n
Cecil family:
'ashes' of, rekindling, **33**. 505
crest of, **1**. 49
HW praises, **18**. 357
painting of jewels of, **10**. 346
portraits of, **10**. 345
'Cécile, Milady.' *See* Lennox, Lady Cecilia Margaret
Cecilia, St:
celestinette appropriate to, **35**. 423
HW contrasts St-Cyr nun's violin-playing to music of, **10**. 294
Pope not successful in odes on, **16**. 257
*Cecilia. See under* Burney, Frances
Cecill, Thomas (fl. ca 1625–40), engraver:
Weever's portrait engraved by, **16**. 64
Cecily *or* Cecilia (Plantagenet) (1469–1507), m. 1 (1487) John Welles, cr. (1485) Bn and (1486) Vct Welles; m. 2 (ca 1503) Thomas Kymbe:
letters falsely attributed to, **1**. 221–2, 223–4, 227
marriage of, **1**. 227, **2**. 363, **16**. 233
Papal bull omits, **42**. 208n
preceded by Ds of Bedford, **2**. 363
Cecina (Italy):
Ginori retires to, **17**. 282
marquisate of, restored to Ginori, **20**. 463
Cedar; cedars:
Fitzpatrick doubtless entertaining on, **34**. 123
of Lebanon, *see* Cedar of Lebanon
Virginia, recommended to Montagu by HW, **9**. 177
Vyne, The, to have, **35**. 640
Cedar chest:
HW's, **36**. 312
Cedar of Lebanon; cedars of Lebanon:
Beauclerk, Lady Diana, draws, **32**. 289
exotic tree, **21**. 418
HW obtains, from nursery, **9**. 176
Ossory, Lady, must abandon, **32**. 236

Cedrati. *See* Citron; citrons

*Ceffalo e Procri. See under* Araia, Francesco

Ceiling; ceilings:
Le Brun designs, at Louvre gallery, **35**. 344
of Hinchingbrooke drawing-room, **40**. 283
*See also under* Architecture

Celadon:
Fox, C. J., called, **32**. 162
HW's pseudonym, **13**. 73, 76, 77, 91, 92
Strathmore too much a, **22**. 152

'Celadon, Mlle':
Conway's mistake for Mlle Sanadon, **39**. 214

Celbridge, co. Kildare (Ireland):
Marlay of, **9**. 379n

Celesia, Mme. *See* Mallet, Dorothea

Celesia, Pietro Paolo (d. 1806), Genoese minister to England 1756–9:
Byng's sailing reported by, **20**. 553
Mallet's daughter married by, **20**. 553n

Celestines. *See* Célestins

Celestinette (musical instrument invented by Mason):
HW jealous of, **28**. 178–80
HW mentions, **28**. 184, 320, 328, 342, **29**. 4, 137, 283, 312
HW suggests other combinations similar to, **28**. 195
harpsichord and violin combined in, **28**. 248, **35**. 423
Mason reproves HW for joking about, **28**. 183, 200
——'s essay on, approved by HW, **29**. 7
—— would give, for 'Delineator,' **28**. 334

Célestins, religious order:
church of, in Paris: column to François II in, **13**. 163; crowded with beautiful old tombs, **39**. 201; HW and Conway saw, in 1739, **39**. 201; HW recommends, to Cts of Ailesbury for its tombs, **39**. 201; HW visits, **7**. 271, 308, 337; Tresmes buried in, **13**. 163
France reduces, **39**. 147

'Celia':
name applied to Miss Phipps in affair with C. J. Fox, **32**. 163

*Célibataire, Le. See under* Dorat, Claude-Joseph

Cellamare, conspiracy of:
Du Deffand, Mme, ridicules, **7**. 278

Celle (Zell), Hanover:
Caroline Matilda confined in castle at, **5**. 178n, 230n, **23**. 409
Ferdinand, P., turned back from, **21**. 167n
message sent to, **32**. 130
Richelieu reassembles army at, after Rossbach, **21**. 158n, **43**. 274
visitors to: Conway, **39**. 537; Cressett, Mrs, **20**. 247n; Scott, David, **39**. 537

Celli, Antonio:
Mann's legacy to, **25**. 667n

Cellini, Benvenuto (1500–71), Florentine goldsmith and sculptor:
autobiography of, **23**. 383, **35**. 342
buckler attributed to, **23**. 407n

chest by, from Medici collection, sent to HW by Mann for SH: **23**. 404, 407, 415, 421, 425, 427, 429, 432, **24**. 15, **25**. 89, 165, **26**. 56; Chute says top of, is copied from Raphael print, **23**. 432
eagle of, inferior, **19**. 66
Florence now lacks, **24**. 478
gold lamina by, in gallery at Florence, **23**. 407
HW's silver bell supposedly by, **15**. 316, **16**. 254n, **23**. 383, **28**. 38n, **35**. 478
Mann's coffee-pot might be attributed to, **18**. 116, 137
medallions of Medici by, **25**. 215
Perseus by, in Florentine loggia, **11**. 154, **22**. 123
wax models by, **25**. 215n

Celsus:
controversies of, **41**. 386

Celt; Celts:
Lort's paper on, *see under* Lort, Michael
Pinkerton too much opposed to, **16**. 304

Celtic language:
Macpherson, James, pretends to be skilled in, **16**. 378
—— promotes study of, **16**. 377
Macpherson, John, professes skill in, **16**. 378

Cembali:
played by country girls in Boboli amphitheatre, **25**. 586

Cenci, Baldassare (1710–63), cardinal, 1761; Segretario della Consulta, 1753:
Clement XIII does not make, cardinal, because of spruce wig, **21**. 334

Cenci, Porcia (ca 1700–72), m. (1731) Nicola Soderini:
(?) Niccolini, Mme, serves, **18**. 251

Cenis, Mt:
HW and Gray cross, **13**. 188–9, 196
travel discouraged by, **13**. 230

Cenotaph. *See* Monument

Censer; censers:
Du Deffand, Mme, receives, **6**. 341
Montagu, Mrs, gives, to Mme du Deffand, **6**. 486, **7**. 24, **8**. 203–4

Censorship:
at Béarn, **10**. 192–3
of books, **3**. 109, 224, **5**. 308, **6**. 287
of plays, by Abp of Canterbury, **9**. 326–7
of post, **10**. 183, 197

Centaur; centaurs:
Bentley's satirical account of, **35**. 643
in Bentley's painting, **35**. 243
Mann advises Botta to put Giambologna's, in Loggia, **22**. 124
rump of, **35**. 46

*Centaur*, English ship:
Dutch contraband seized by, **25**. 3n
Keppel mentions, **28**. 415n
(?) sunk in storm, **25**. 326

Centlivre, Mrs Joseph. *See* Freeman, Susannah

Cento (Italy):
Montemar at, **17**. 455

Central America:
    Spanish fort in, captured, **24.** 543
'Centricality':
    word used by Sir Ralph Payne, **32.** 343
*Centurion*, English ship:
    Denis in command of, **19.** 402n
    Harrison instead of Hervey to command, **22.** 175n
    *Nuestra Señora del Cabadonga* captured by, off Manila, **18.** 463n
    Walter chaplain of, **33.** 424n
    York, D. of, sails on, **22.** 166, 175, 251n
    —— to sail to Italy on, with Capt. Hervey, **22.** 155n
*Century of the Names . . . of Such Inventions, A. See under* Somerset, Edward, M. of Worcester
Cephalonia:
    possible revolt by, against Turks, **23.** 146n
*Ce qui plaît aux dames. See* Favart, Charles-Simon: *Fée Urgèle, La*
Cerati, Gaspare (1690–1769), Monsignore; Conte:
    eye troubles of, cured by bathing eyes in Hungary water, **21.** 147
    Guasco and Niccolini indulge with, in mutual praise, **22.** 531
    Prior of San Stefano order, and *provveditore generale* of University of Pisa, **21.** 147n
    satiric print or drawing of, **22.** 531
*Cerberus*, English ship:
    Bunker Hill news brought by, **32.** 247n
    Burgoyne, Clinton, and Gen. Howe sail on, to Boston, **32.** 286n
    *Mercury* parts from, **24.** 229n
    officers sail to Boston on, **24.** 97n
Cerberus:
    Howard family unlike story of, **32.** 384
    Lempster's debts compared to heads of, **20.** 209, 470, **32.** 384
Cerceau, Du. *See* Androuet
Cerchi, Mme. *See* Degli Alessandri, Maria Cristina
Cerchi, Alessandro dei (1704–67):
    Suares, Mme, related to, **17.** 123
Cerda, Cardinal de la. *See* Cordova Spinola de la Cerda
Cerdic (fl. ca 495), leader of West Saxons:
    Chatterton mentions, **16.** 102
    reign of, **16.** 110
Cere-cloth:
    Edward I's corpse supposed to have a new, yearly, **24.** 4
Ceres:
    Capel, Lady Mary, compared with, **30.** 326
    Damer, Mrs, does bust of, from medal, **35.** 432
    French reformation compared to vengeance of, **34.** 101
    HW might send, to reproach Noah, **35.** 384
    HW's bronze of, in SH gallery: drawn by d'Hancarville, **15.** 13, **33.** 479; illustrated in Knight's *Account*, **42.** 193

Homeric hymn to, **16.** 179
    Homer would ascribe English success to favour from, **33.** 444–5
    lack of flowers must mortify, **35.** 372
    symbols of, **30.** 326
Céreste, Comte de. *See* Brancas de Forcalquier, Bufile-Hyacinthe-Toussaint de
Céreste, Duc de. *See* Brancas, Louis-Paul, Marquis de
Ceretesi. *See* Cerretesi
Cerigati family:
    house of, at Vicenza, **35.** 4
Cerigo (Cythère):
    Du Deffand, Mme, mentions, **4.** 186
Cerjat, ——, of Lausanne:
    Pembroke addressed in care of, **25.** 493n
Cernikoff. *See* Chernyshev
Cerretesi, Giuseppe (b. 1702), freemason and poet:
    (?) Dashwood lends money to, **18.** 225
    (?) English and Latin not spoken by, **17.** 503
    (?) Flanders visited by, **18.** 225
    (?) Florence the destination of, **18.** 225
    (?) freemason lodge attended by, **19.** 364n
    (?) grotto and other points of interest described by, in pocket book, **17.** 503
    (?) HW meets, in park, **17.** *459*
    (?) HW to introduce, at Lady Brown's Sunday night party, **18.** 166
    (?) HW told by, that Mme Galli is dead, **18.** 166, 186
    (?) lodges in bagnio in London, **17.** 459
    (?) Mann pleased by Sir Robert Walpole's entertainment of, **18.** 14
    (?) Richecourt's affair with Wachtendonck told by, to HW, **17.** 467–8
    (?) Venetians take, to Oxford and Blenheim, **18.** 166
    (?) Walpole, Sir Robert, entertains, at Chelsea, **17.** 503
Certosi. *See* Carthusians
Cervantes, Miguel de (1547–1616):
    *Don Quixote*: aeronauts resemble hero of, **33.** 447; Coke, Lady Mary, compared with hero of, **33.** 292; Conway wears costume of Duke in, **20.** 49; Coypell's prints for, **33.** 547; Du Deffand, Mme, hates, **5.** 16, **7.** 72; Dulcinea in, **30.** 39, **31.** 209, **35.** 557; galley slaves in, compared with new Irish peers, **33.** 260; HW compares Herbert of Chirbury to hero of, **30.** 176, **35.** 585; HW compares himself to hero of, **32.** 220; HW compares Lund to Trifaldin in, **30.** 62; HW criticizes character of Duchess in, **31.** 209; HW mentions, **4.** 211, **11.** 356, **12.** 56; HW's opinion of, **7.** 72; HW's signature, 'governor of Barataria,' **32.** 211; Kingston, Ds of, resembles Countess Trifaldine in, **23.** 557; Maritornes in, **31.** 235; print of Lord Herbert of Chirbury illustrates period of, **42.** 43; 'Sancho Panza' and the Doctor in, **31.** 67; 'Sancho Panza' in, **21.** 312, **35.** 525;

'Sancho Panza' in, resembles Raftor, **35.** 525; 'Sancho Panza' in, would have talked chapters about game from Houghton, **12.** 56; stories of Barataria in, divert HW, **33.** 73; Warburton describes *Tristram Shandy* as in vein of, **15.** 66; *see also* Quixote, Don
HW regrets that chivalry was laughed out of fashion by, **24.** 22

*César*, French ship:
captured, **25.** 278
Cesena, Bp of. *See* Agoselli, Francesco
Cesena (Italy):
Charles Emmanuel III and Traun at, **18.** 13
Lobkowitz returns to, **18.** 331
Cestrum:
HW discusses Pliny's use of, **9.** 252
Cethegus, Gaius Cornelius (d. 63 B.C.):
maxim fit for, **35.** 566
Cette (France):
English invasion might land at, **21.** 223
Ceunot, John:
Conway gets dragon design from, **37.** 345
(?) drawing of Conway's chimney-piece to be shown by, to HW, **37.** 331
(?) in Warwick St, Golden Sq., or Marylebone, **37.** 331
Ceuta (N. Africa):
prisoners from, to be used in storming St Philip's, **25.** 180
Cevallos, Capt.-Gen. Don Pedro de, Spanish officer:
Santa Catarina captured by, **24.** 310n
Ceylon, K. of. *See* Rajadhi Rajasingha
Ceylon:
called 'Isle of Serendip' in *Arabian Nights*, **25.** 277
Conway's letters in, **36.** 314, **37.** xxii
HW's acquaintance with, in 'fairy days,' **34.** 212–13
Holland to bewail loss of monopoly in, **25.** 283
sumach from Ampthill as precious as if from, **34.** 44
Trincomalee in, captured by British, **25.** 277, **34.** 212–13
Ch., Mr:
verses by, **12.** 255
Chabannes, Mme de:
refused permission to visit Chanteloup, **5.** 76n
Chabannes, Claude-François (1721–86), Marquis de:
social relations of, with Mme Rondé, **7.** 345
Chabannes, François-Antoine (1686–1754), Comte de:
wife of, **3.** 351n
Chabannes, Rochon de. *See* Rochon de Chabannes, Marc-Antoine-Jacques
Chabanon, Michel-Paul-Gui de (1730–92):
Académie française elects, **7.** 438
*Épitre sur la manie des jardins anglais*: Du Deffand, Mme, to get for HW, **6.** 196; Mason receives, from HW, **28.** 200, 205, 207

Chabenat de Bonneuil, André-Louis-Charles:
(?) attends session of parliament of Paris, **8.** 173
Chabillard de Montillet de Grenaud, Jean-François de (ca 1702–76), Abp of Auch, 1742:
HW's former lodging in Paris taken by, **6.** 209
Chablais, Duc de. *See* Benoît-Maurice-Marie (1741–1808)
Chabot, Comte de. *See* Chabot, Louis-Charles de (d. 1780); Rohan-Chabot, Guy-Auguste de (1683–1760); Rohan-Chabot, Louis-Antoine-Auguste de (1733–1807)
Chabot, Comtesse de. *See* La Rochefoucauld, Élisabeth-Louise de (1740–86); Stafford Howard, Lady Mary Apolonia Scolastica (1721–69)
Chabot, Duc de. *See* Rohan-Chabot, Louis-Antoine-Auguste de
Chabot, Duchesse de. *See* La Rochefoucauld, Élisabeth-Louise de (1740–86)
Chabot, Vicomte de. *See* Rohan-Chabot, Marie-Charles-Rosalie de
Chabot, Vicomtesse de. *See* Smyth, Elizabeth (d. 1843)
Chabot, Louis-Charles (d. 1780), Comte de:
death of, **7.** 446
Chabot, Lady Mary. *See* Stafford Howard, Lady Mary Apolonia Scolastica
Chabrillan, Bailli de. *See* Moreton, Antoine-Apollinaire Guigues de
Chabrillan, Comte de. *See* Moreton, Jacques-Aimar-Henri de
Chabrillan, Marquis de. *See* Moreton, Joseph-Dominique Guigues de (b. 1744); Moreton de Chabrillan, Hippolyte-César de Guigues de (1767–1835)
Chabrillan, Marquise de. *See* Vignerot du Plessis-Richelieu d'Aiguillon, Innocente-Aglaé
Chace. *See* Chase
Chadd, St. *See* Ceadda
Chadeau de la Clocheterie, Jean-Isaac-Timothée (d. 1782), French naval officer:
*Arethusa's* combat with, **24.** 394
biographical information on, corrected, **43.** 104
frigate of, attacked by British, **7.** 52
Chadwick, Mr, of Ditton:
SH visited by, **12.** 227, 230
Chadwick, Sir Andrew:
will of, forged, **32.** 73n
Chadwick, Thomas (d. 1746):
execution of, **19.** 287n
Chafer; chafers:
elms stripped by, **33.** 462
Chafey. *See* Chafy
Chaffault; Chaffaut. *See* Du Chaffault
Chaffont. *See* Chalfont
Chafing-dishes:
French antechambers full of, **31.** 54
Chafy, Rev. John (1720–82):
death of, **2.** 304n

Chagford, Devon:
Hayter, rector of, **15.** 143n
Chagres, Colombia:
Vernon captures, **13.** 226
Chaigneau, William (1709–81), novelist; regimental agent:
Conway to be addressed in care of, in Lower Castleyard, Dublin, **37.** 330–1
Chaillot (France):
Carlisle, Cts of, settles at, **7.** 50, 61
convent of Visitation de Ste-Marie at, **4.** 486
Du Deffand, Mme, mentions, **3.** 285, **4.** 268
Meinières, M. and Mme de, live at, **6.** 469
Montagu, Mrs, has house at, **6.** 357
soap factory near, **6.** 449n
visitors to: Boisgelin, Mme de, **6.** 357; Cambis, Mme de, **6.** 357; Du Deffand, Mme, **6.** 357, 469; Eglintoun, **6.** 357; Gibbon, **6.** 469; Gregory, Dorothea, **6.** 357; Marchais, Mme de, **6.** 357; Mirepoix, Mme de, **6.** 357; Richmond, **6.** 357
Chaillou, Marquis de. *See* Amelot, Antoine-Jean
Chailly (France):
Berrys' carriage breaks down at, **11.** 126n
Chain; chains:
all people links of one, **33.** 450
coaches barred by, from serenade, **17.** 105
for watch: George II gives, **20.** 111; price of, **21.** 295–6
HW 'hanging' in, **35.** 27
HW sends, to Duchesse de Choiseul, **4.** 365, 370, 385, 404, 407, 443, 450, 454
lord mayor's, **17.** 295
of brilliants, **17.** 70
of gold or pearls, **42.** 12
prisoners', **9.** 192
slaves', **40.** 11
smuggler's body hangs in, **35.** 141
streets barred with, near D. of Gloucester's sick-room in Leghorn, **23.** 335
Chair; chairs:
Ailesbury, Cts of, wants frames for, **37.** 466
armchairs: **30.** 204, 281; at Norfolk House, for royal family, **9.** 337–8; for Methodist clergy, **35.** 119; HW buys, in Paris, **5.** 141 *and passim*; HW lives in, **38.** 69; Louis XIII's valet expects him to have, in heaven, **42.** 152; peeresses sleep in, to preserve hairdos for Coronation, **38.** 122
at Hurstmonceaux, scanty, **35.** 138
at Mamhead, broken, **30.** 67
at Osterley, **28.** 414, **34.** 238
at Stoke and Esher, discussed by Gray, **14.** 60
Bateman's, **1.** 90, 93, 325n, **9.** 384
Bentley designs, for HW, **35.** 181–2
blue cloth, at St-Cyr, **10.** 293
blue velvet and gold, at Boughton House, **10.** 341
Bonner's, **34.** 54
Chinese, in garret, **35.** 301

chintz, in SH Blue Bedchamber, **35.** 173
Craon supplies, to rented villas, **20.** 116
curule, **10.** 112, **33.** 327–8, **35.** 286
Delorain, Cts of, pulls, from under George II, **18.** 71
easy: idle man uses, **21.** 295; Mann sends to Merlin's for, **24.** 346; now prevalent, **24.** 342
ebony: at Wanstead, **35.** 238; wanted by Conway for cottage, **38.** 206
elbow: HW's, **31.** 328; Plymouth prefers, to other amusements, **23.** 378
English ladies made to sit on, by French duchesses, **20.** 144
flock, at Blenheim, **9.** 289
for George III and Q. Charlotte in Westminster Hall, **38.** 121
French tapestry, in HW's Exchequer chest, **23.** 285
from Glastonbury Abbey, acquired by HW, **33.** 208–9, **35.** 106
fruit on, at Chudleigh ball, **35.** 301
great: HW's, **31.** 340; Walpole, Sir Robert, has, at Houghton, **18.** 68
HW's: HW's embroidered suit hung on, **35.** 210; in Round Tower at SH, **21.** 420
in Bletchley parish, **1.** 93
Leghorn residents sleep in, after earthquake, **17.** 303
Lyttelton misses, **15.** 330–1
mahogany, Rowley gives, to Mann, **19.** 9
mahogany gilt, covered with blue damask, might be copied in 20th century for farmhouse use, **38.** 206–7
Mann sends, to opera, **17.** 69
—— to be put in, to receive Ds of Gloucester, **24.** 291
Merlin's: Mann confined to, by gout, **24.** 404; Mann sends for, **24.** 346; Mann supplied with locomotion by, at home, **24.** 462
model of, Botta imports, from France, **21.** 556–7
monk's, from Glastonbury, owned by HW, **33.** 208–9, **35.** 106
Newcastle, D. of, takes, to Germany, **19.** 485
oak, in Mme de Maintenon's apartment at St-Cyr, **10.** 293
of painted wood, at Osterley, **28.** 414
opera spectators sit back-stage on, **38.** 289
pattern for, Mann receives, from Galfridus Mann, **19.** 20
plump, in SH Breakfast Room, **20.** 382
price of, **1.** 90n
purple velvet, occupied by Mme de Maintenon in portrait by Ferdinand, **10.** 294
rustic: Bateman collects, **9.** 384; HW wants Wettenhalls to seek, **9.** 385
sold out of Palazzo Pitti, **25.** 230–1
stiff, at Knole, **35.** 132
two rows of, in every Paris hotel, **23.** 312
Waldegrave moved to, from couch, **36.** 259

Windsor: in Mann's garden, 18. 479; Mann wants a double one, 18. 332; pattern of, 19. 20; single ones made by Mann, 18. 332

Wren's, sold, 40. 348

Yorke, Sir Joseph, leaps over back of, 30. 280

*See also* Crane-chair; Fauteuil

Chair; chairs (for transportation; sedan chair):

Andreoni too fat for, 17. 248

Benedict XIV takes air in, 21. 124

Bute said to use Miss Vansittart's, in visits to Ps of Wales, 38. 462n

carriers of, *see* Chairmen

Chute goes to opera in, 18. 386

Conway, Hon. Henrietta takes, from election ball, 39. 80

costumes worn by carriers of, 10. 204

Fox taken to Pitti Palace in, 22. 528

Godfrey, Mrs, goes in, to St James's Park, 25. 571

Gray carried home in, after seizure by fit, 23. 455n

hackney: 22. 102n; Bedford, Ds of, points out, when HW cannot find one, 9. 232; Carteret, Bns, goes home in, 18. 431; Chesterfield takes, in Dublin, 19. 190; Fox Strangways, Lady Susan, elopes in, 38. 367; HW sees Wilkes pass his window in, 23. 5; HW takes, 30. 45; Pelham, Frances, loses earrings in, 20. 114

maker of, *see* Vaughan, George

mob breaks glass of Cts of Boyle's, 38. 560

mobs watch Gunning sisters enter, 20. 311

Montagu expects tasselled, for Mrs Bentley, 9. 309

obsolescent in London, 11. 249

Oldfield, Mrs, uses, 17. 435

one-horse (cabriolet): 11. 283, 35. 247; used by D. of Newcastle in garden, 38. 419; *see also* Cabriolet

Onslow, Bns, goes home in, 39. 454

open, Cole rides in, 10. 343

Pelham, Miss, awaits, 31. 36

Pitt (Chatham) brought in, to House of Lords, 24. 308n

——'s, has boot for his gout, 22. 159n

—— takes, to Buckingham House, preceded by two servants, 22. 159

Richecourt and Stampa dispute over, 20. 320

Scarbrough's servant fetches, 37. 47

Temple not visited by, 30. 222

Vernaccia, Mme del, carried in to *le mal maritate*, 18. 112

Walpole, Bns, takes ptisan in, to Richecourt, 18. 67

Westminster Hall affords passage for, to Exchequer House assembly, 37. 454

*See also* Crane-chair; Sedan chair

Chairman; chairmen (carriers of sedan chairs):

Andreoni's quarrel with, over fare, 17. 248

burglars pursued by, 9. 133

costume of, 10. 204

crowds pursue, when they fight, 18. 8

Delaval uses, to help punish mistress and her lover, 20. 41

drunken, accuse occupant of being drunk, 33. 568

earrings sunk by, 20. 114

flap their arms in hard frost, 7. 333

Fox, C. J., supported by, in Westminster election, 25. 489

from hotel, bring Cellini's chest, 23. 425

hackney: call 'Oddman' when they want helpers, 19. 213, 33. 394; in London are mostly Irish, 25. 489n

Irish, in Gordon Riots, 33. 193

La Condamine's landlady dresses, as bailiffs, 22. 151

of Brentford, Clarke represented as being killed by, 23. 98

pigs taken by, to waterside, 37. 347

strong legs of, 33. 196

Theodore of Corsica unable to pay, 21. 45

Chaise; chaises:

Almada travels in, 21. 436

Amelia, Ps, travels in, 12. 11

and pair: barber's boy may want to drive HW to Epsom in, 30. 86; Joseph II and Leopold II drive in, to Florentine theatre, 23. 112

at Twickenham boat race, 11. 86

Argyll's, pelted in France, 11. 107

Bentley cannot afford to hire, 35. 69

Berrys': aired by HW's coachman, 11. 153; HW uses, 11. 134, 153

Boufflers killed by overturn of, 20. 236

Cardigans travel with, 10. 89

Charlotte's arrival proclaimed by, 35. 314

Chute's and Whithed's, inadequate for painting, 35. 5

Cole's: Cole gets into, 1. 264; Cole's accident in, 2. 180–1; Cole takes airings in, 1. 339, 2. 20

Conway loses, near Chester, 37. 355–6

——'s at door to go to London, 37. 391

—— tells HW to have, well-greased and free from contraband goods, 37. 39

Corso thronged with, 17. 3

couples go to White Hart in, 19. 298

courier tied to, 18. 516

Cowley's portrait to lie flat in, 42. 203

Dashwood brings the Barbarina to Calais in, 30. 19–20

Delany, Mrs, arrives at Windsor in, 33. 498

double, four horses needed for, on bad roads, 37. 41

Douglas, Ds of, ties servant's body to front of, 39. 9

drunken lady refuses to ride in, 35. 306

English visitors', enrich Picardy, 39. 8

Esher toured by party in, 10. 72

Fitzpatrick in, almost runs over Ds of Queensberry, 12. 57

[Chaise; chaises, *continued*]

Fitzroy, Lady Caroline, invites G. W. Hervey to accompany her in, **30.** 86

four-wheeled, HW wants to borrow Selwyn's, **30.** 133

French mail carried in, **25.** 619

George III takes airings in, **22.** 288

Gloucester, D. of, travels in, **26.** 50

Grafton runs over man when in, **31.** 134, **39.** 87

green, of Lady Mary Coke, **37.** 557

Grifoni, Mme, tries to pass Mme Vitelli in, **17.** 37–8

Gunning, Mrs, invites M. of Blandford into, **11.** 204

HW about to enter, at SH, **25.** 579

HW again reads in, **21.** 139

HW and Lady Browne attend fireworks in, **33.** 183

HW and Spence ride in, to Genoa, **17.** 91, **30.** 17

HW crosses Alps in, **17.** 257n

HW does not ride in, at Bath, **10.** 232

HW enters, at 5 A.M. to escape from inn, **35.** 124

HW gallops about in, during flirtation, **37.** 126

HW goes in: to Carshalton, **39.** 331; to see Galfridus Mann, **21.** 32

HW has Louis with him in, **39.** 8

HW in, when robbed, **33.** 295

HW offers, to Lady Townshend at Houghton, **41.** 261

HW rides in, **32.** 122, 123, 326, 360, **33.** 21, 26

HW's: **28.** 139; accidents to, **9.** 195, **35.** 278; at his door at SH, **31.** 217; Cholmondeley's, passes, **25.** 331; fractured, **35.** 278; HW goes to Park Place in, **10.** 103, 105; HW goes to Stowe in, **10.** 312; has no springs, **37.** 66; Louis opens door of, **10.** 59; motion of, moves gout from knee to foot, **35.** 489; set up at Twickenham Park, **31.** 236; to be lent to Lady Browne, **31.** 201; to bring Hardinge to Lady Diana Beauclerk's, **35.** 636

HW writes 'The Dice Box' in, **31.** 156

HW writes verses when riding in, **40.** 182

hackney: **35.** 325; Christian VII takes, **35.** 326; HW afraid of, **11.** 134

Hertford's, broken, **39.** 18, 25

Hervey, Bns, to travel in, **31.** 84

hired, HW afraid of, **11.** 134

Holbein Chamber at SH has view of, **10.** 168

load suitable for, **37.** 40

London exodus of, in Gordon riots, **33.** 192

Mann gets into, to go to Leghorn, **21.** 117

——  may go to Leghorn in, **23.** 333

——'s: ready for D. of York, **22.** 180; to take him to Leghorn, **18.** 503

Mann, Horace II, prevented by bad roads from travelling in, **25.** 204

Maria Louisa lends, to Gatti, **24.** 330

messenger travels slowly in, **20.** 581

Midleton takes Mordaunt in, **30.** 144

Montagu goes 'fox-hunting' in, **10.** 230

——'s: Montagu comes from Lady Anne Jekyll's in, **10.** 160; Montagu rides in, **10.** 256

Montemar to travel in, **17.** 207

Neapolitan Court may flee in, to Rome, **18.** 3

on *cigne*, Old Pretender has, at Albano house, **19.** 135

open, of French hatless in, in rain, **35.** 112

Ossory, Lady, returns to England in, **32.** 5

Palgrave's, **29.** 365

plentiful on road, **39.** 498

Pomfret, Cts of, carried picture behind, **25.** 227

Pulteney's, bequeathed to Colman but must be sold for debt, **22.** 146

rattle of, disturbs HW, **11.** 306

renting of, in France, **37.** 40

Richecourt's secretary said to transport stolen goods in, **17.** 224

seat of, may be searched by Customs, **37.** 40

small, used at Park Place, **31.** 146

Temple killed when thrown from, **28.** 463

Trigge never leaves, between Florence and Ostend, **24.** 377n

Twickenham boat-race attended by, **11.** 86

two-wheeled: two-horse, accoucheur travels in, **23.** 220; Young Pretender goes to Florence in, **23.** 318

visible from SH, **37.** 269

Walpole, Robert, in, **35.** 123

Werpup killed by overturn of, through postilion's obstinacy, **22.** 306

wheels of, imitated by women's hats, **20.** 483

Young Pretender said to have taken, from Rome, **17.** 113

*See also* Carriage; Phaeton; Post-chaise

Chaise longue; chaises longues:

Choiseul, Duchesse de, has, **4.** 200

Du Deffand, Mme, in, **39.** 271

HW uses, for gout, **41.** 343

Chaise merchant; chaise merchants:

French, seldom provided with chaises proper for purchase, **37.** 40

Chaise-percée:

mahogany seat for, **35.** 55

Chait Singh, Rajah:

Indian districts dependent on, **25.** 14n

Chalais, Comte de. *See* Talleyrand, Henri de

Chalais, Prince de. *See* Talleyrand, Élie-Charles de

Chalcedon, Abp of. *See* Caracciolo, Martino Innico (d. 1754); Doria, Giorgio (1708–59)

Chaldæa:

Montagu might have died in, **10.** 282

Chaleur Bay (France):

Byron's victory at, **21.** 433

Chalfont Park, Bucks, Lady Mary Churchill's house:

Bentley designs Gothic stable for, **9.** 285

Churchill inexactly executes Bentley's designs for, **35**. 644

Churchill of, **2**. 280n, **5**. 2n, **13**. 183n

Churchill, Lady Mary, at, **9**. 71n

Churchills' purchase of, **43**. 114

Chute's plans for altering, too expensive, **35**. 233

landscaping at, unfinished, **9**. 285

visitors to: Ailesbury, Cts of, **9**. 284; Bentley, **9**. 249; Chute, **35**. 233; Conway, **9**. 284, **38**. 59, **39**. 173; HW, **9**. 71, 249, 284, **10**. 104, **35**. 233, **38**. 34, 59, **39**. 173, 199; Lyttelton, Bns, **9**. 284; Shirley, Mrs, **9**. 284

Chalice; chalices:
at Trinity Hospital, Greenwich, **16**. 91
saved from Gordon Rioters, **33**. 178
Selwyn drinks out of 'popish,' at tavern, **30**. 89

Chalk:
drawing in, **42**. 71n
French landscape built of, **10**. 298, **31**. 55, **35**. 336
HW dislikes, in France, **10**. 298
liquid, HW's fingers exude, **25**. 622
trees in Paris planted on pedestals of, **31**. 45
wall of, in Paris garden, **35**. 126

Chalk-egg:
HW compares parliament of Paris with cuckoo on, **31**. 111

Chalkstone; chalkstones:
Chute has, in hands, **24**. 211
HW's fingers discharge, **2**. 286, 337, **12**. 12, 72, 76, **15**. 241, **16**. 199, 318, **25**. 149, 242, 618, 622, 629, 635, **28**. 241, **29**. 7, 152, 165, 176, 281, 337, 358, **31**. 237, 242, 298
Mann's physician and surgeon tell him, are painful, **25**. 626
treatment of, **2**. 290
*See also under* Gout

Challenge; challenges:
Mann almost receives, for not inviting insignificant Englishmen to dinner, **25**. 341

Challerange. *See* Rolland de Challerange

Challis, Martin (ca 1711–92):
(?) HW reimburses, for Customs salary shared with E. L. Mann. **4**. 359n, **24**. 276–7, 284–5

Challoner, Richard (1691–1781), D.D., Bp of Debra, 1738; Roman Catholic apostolic vicar in England:
*Catholic Christian Instructed, The,* answered by Middleton, **15**. 8n, 295

Chalmers, George (1742–1825), antiquary:
believes in Ireland's MSS, **15**. 321

Chalmers, Margaret (ca 1709–65), m. Arthur Elphinstone, 6th Bn Balmerinoch, 1746:
faints, at husband's death warrant, **9**. 46
husband enjoys, **19**. 296
husband joined by, in Tower, **19**. 281

Chalon, Mme de. *See* Andlau, Jeanne-Françoise-Aglaé d'

Chaloner, ——:
Rosalba's portrait of, **18**. 243n

Chaloner, Sir Thomas (1561–1615):
HW adds note on, **13**. 17n
Henry, P. of Wales, under care of, **25**. 224n

Châlons, Bp of. *See* Andigné de la Chaise, Joseph-François

Châlons:
visitors to: Gloucester, D. of, **6**. 485; Stainville, **6**. 485

Chalotais. *See* Caradeuc de la Chalotais

Chalybeate springs:
at Buxton Wells, **40**. 16

Chambars, Thomas (ca 1724–89), engraver:
Bacon's portrait at Gorhambury copied by, **40**. 196–7
Grimston advises, to stay at St Albans, not Gorhambury, **40**. 193
Perrot's picture copied by, in chalk, for HW, **40**. 272n, **43**. 384n
prints made by, for HW, **15**. 96n, 97n, (?) **31**. 78n

Chambars. *See also* Chambers

Chambellan; chambellans, Tuscan:
ante-chamber of, **22**. 346
give festival for Maria Louisa, **22**. 491
Richecourt escorted by, to Corsi christening, **20**. 432
wrongly introduces Guasco as 'Count,' **22**. 531

Chambellan, Grand. *See* Grand Chambellan

Chamber, Apostolical. *See* Apostolical Chamber

Chamber, Lady. *See* Boyer, Anna

Chamber, Lady Mary. *See* Berkeley, Lady Mary

Chamber, Sir Thomas (d. 1692), Kt, 1666:
Fort St George, scene of wedding of, **9**. 62
Hanworth House belonged to, **33**. 294n
wife of, 'black,' **9**. 62

Chamber, Thomas (d. 1738), of Hanworth:
daughters of, **10**. 342
leg of, 'black,' **9**. 62
wife of, **10**. 342

Chamber, Mrs Thomas. *See* Boyer, Anna

Chamber. *See also* Chambars; Chambers

Chamberlain (surname). *See* Chamberlaine; Chamberlayne

Chamberlain; chamberlains:
French lord of the Bedchamber in waiting is equivalent to, **38**. 451
HW thought Q. Charlotte would be attended by, **39**. 511
Manchester, D. of, to be, **38**. 96
of London, Wilkes to be, **24**. 535
Papal ('Camerlengo'): Albani, Annibale, is, **13**. 220n, 227, **17**. 16; Colonna may become, **20**. 589
to Q. Charlotte, aspirants to post of, **10**. 29
*See also* Chambellan; Lord Chamberlain; Vice-Chamberlain

Chamberlaine, Mrs, of Twickenham:
SH visited by, **12**. 237

Chamberlaine, Frances (1724–66), m. (1747) Thomas Sheridan:
*Dupe, The,* by, **38**. 265

Chamberlaine, John (1745–1812), antiquary;
  keeper of the King's drawings and medals,
  1791:
  Farington expects to meet, at SH, **15**. *319*
  HW leaves money to, for engravings, **42**. 375n
  *Imitations of Original Drawings, by Hans
    Holbein* edited by: **30**. 371; HW aids Lodge
    in biographies for, **43**. 326; HW thanks
    Nicol for, **42**. 375
  SH visited by, **12**. 241, 243
Chamberlaine. *See also* Chamberlayne
Chamberlayne, Cassandra Agnes (d. 1821), m.
  (1763) John Hamilton, cr. (1776) Bt:
  (?) SH visited by, **12**. 228 *bis*
Chamberlayne, Edward (1616–1703), author:
  *Angliæ notitiæ*, frontispiece to, **1**. 180
Chamberlayne, Rev. Edward (?1699–1773):
  son of, **2**. 310n
  tutor to Bn Walpole's elder son, **2**. 314
Chamberlayne, Edward (1741–82), joint-secre-
  tary to the Treasury:
  suicide of, **2**. 310, 314, 316
Chamberlayne, Elizabeth. *See* Denton, Elizabeth
Chamberlayne (later Denton), George (?1703–
  57), M.P.:
  birth date of, **43**. 120
  Chamberlayne, Thomas, to inherit from, **9**.
    208–9
  daughter compelled by, to wed, **9**. 209
  daughter's elopement plans revealed to, by
    Sir James Chamberlayne, **9**. 209
  death of, **9**. 209
  name changed by, **9**. 209
Chamberlayne, Rev. George (1739–1815), fel-
  low of King's College, Cambridge:
  Lincoln travels with, **23**. 224
  Mann to welcome, **23**. 228
  Newcastle wants HW to recommend, to
    Mann, **23**. 224
Chamberlayne, Sir James (d. 1767), 4th Bt:
  Chamberlayne, George, warned by, that
    daughter may elope, **9**. 209
  son tells, of elopement plot, **9**. 208–9
Chamberlayne, Thomas (d. ?1764), army officer:
  Chamberlayne, George, leaves estate to, **9**.
    208–9
  Denton, Elizabeth, to elope with, **9**. 209
  father told by, about elopement plan, **9**. 208–9
Chamberlayne, Rev. Thomas (1743–1801):
  brother and fiancée of, die, **2**. 15–16
  (?) SH visited by, **12**. 221
Chamberlayne, William (fl. 1768–82):
  HW aided by, in seeing wardrobe account,
    **41**. 123n
  under-clerk of the Great Wardrobe, **28**. 238n
Chamberlayne, William, solicitor to the Trea-
  sury:
  House of Lords informed by, of message from
    Fielding, **33**. 176n
Chambermaid. *See under* Servant
Chamberpot; chamberpots:
  emptied on Lord Chatham, **33**. 20
  Louis XV throws, at nymph, **23**. 87

silver, bought by Mrs Ward, **13**. 156
some planet empties, for impertinence, **33**.
  367
woman unable to stop using, **18**. 307
Chamberri. *See* Chambéry
Chambers, Capt.:
  *London* commanded by, **24**. 13n
Chambers, Anne (ca 1709–77), m. (1737) Richard Grenville (Grenville Temple after 1752),
  styled Vct Cobham, 1749; 1st (2d) E. Temple,
  1752:
  Amelia, Ps, entertained by, in house-party at
    Stowe, **4**. 431–3, **10**. 313–16, **22**. 247, **31**. 146,
    **39**. 127–8
  assembly given by, **20**. *123*, 145, **26**. 29
  (?) at Chesterfield's assembly, **37**. 327
  birth date of, corrected, **43**. 91
  Conway and wife visited by, at Latimers, **37**.
    306
  Conway visited by, at Park Place, **37**. 380
  family of, **9**. 62, **10**. 342
  forty years old when she discovered 'a turn
    for genteel versification,' **40**. 294n
  (?) Germain, Lady Elizabeth, gives dinner to,
    **38**. 358
  HW calls, pagan landlady, **39**. 127
  HW consoled by, **41**. 343–4
  HW entertained by, at Stowe, **4**. 431–3, **10**.
    313–16, **22**. 247, **31**. 146, **39**. 127–8
  HW entertains, at SH, **10**. (?) 126, **35**. 454n
  HW's correspondence with, **40**. 294, 295,
    366–7, **41**. 268–9
  HW shown by, verses by Lady Harcourt, **35**.
    465
  HW's opinion of, **10**. 313
  HW thanked by, for *Magpie and her Brood*,
    **40**. 366
  HW thanks, for verses, **40**. 294, 295
  HW to call on, **41**. 269
  HW told by, about Pitt's inheritance, **22**. 277
  HW writes 'warrants' and 'patent' for, **10**.
    115–17
  Harcourt, Cts, writes verses to, approved by
    HW, **35**. 646
  health of: gout, **22**. 247; lame, **10**. 315; not
    well, **35**. 467
  Hotham, Henrietta, brings amusing trifles
    to, in child's wagon, **10**. 116
  —— visits, **10**. 115–17
  Macclesfield's body seen by, **38**. 358–9
  Nugent visited by, in Essex, **35**. 467
  Nugent, Hon. Mary Elizabeth, gets diamonds
    from, **39**. 238
  *Poems by Anna Chamber Countess Temple*,
    printed at SH: **10**. 130, 131, 133, **35**. 459;
    HW lists number of copies printed of, **43**.
    79; HW praises, **40**. 294; HW's preface to,
    **43**. 131; HW's slight alterations to, **40**. 295
  sister of, **28**. 62n
  Stapleton, Miss, conveys offer of miniatures
    to HW through, **41**. 269
  Stowe occupied by, **10**. 313–16

Suffolk, Cts of, asks HW to write verses to, **10.** 115
—— entertains, **10.** 113–14
verses by: (?) for Lady Mary Coke in reply to HW's verses to Pitt, **31.** 15–16; (?) in Seeley's *Stowe*, **35.** 75n; on Lady Mary Coke, **10.** 57; to accompany Henrietta Hotham's ring, **10.** 114, (?) 114–15
'Verses Sent to Lady Charles Spencer' by, **35.** 459
Chambers, Ephraim (ca 1680–1740), lexicographer:
*Cyclopædia, or an Universal Dictionary* by, **35.** 31
Chambers, Hannah Sophia (ca 1702–65), m. (1724) Brownlow Cecil, 8th E. of Exeter:
George III complimented by, at Coronation, **9.** 388
HW disparages appearance of, at Coronation, **9.** 388
house of, burnt near Derby, **19.** 178
wig 'scratched' off by, at Coronation, **38.** 127
Chambers, (?) Isabella, actress and singer:
biographical information on, corrected, **43.** 175
in *King Arthur*, **13.** 97, 98, **43.** 175
Chambers, Mary (d. 1783), m. (1736) Lord Vere Beauclerk, cr. (1750) Bn Vere of Hanworth:
Albemarle, Lady, mourns for, **33.** 386–7
aunt of, **17.** 356
family of, **9.** 62, **10.** 342
Gothic lantern at SH coveted by, **9.** 151
grandmother of, 'black,' 'Portuguese,' **9.** 62, 67, 151
HW and Cts of Albemarle frequent home of, after Lady Blandford's death, **33.** 386n
HW rebuked by, for foolish anxiety over Conway, **38.** 102–3
HW visits, **9.** 62
husband's bequest to, **33.** 294n
SH visited by, **9.** 151
Chambers, Sir Robert (1737–1803), Kt, 1778; Indian judge:
Percy shows Chatterton's specimens to, **16.** 350n, **43.** 231
——'s letter from, sent to HW by Lort, **16.** 228
resigns as Vinerian Professor, **2.** 228n
Chambers, Sir William (1726–96), architect:
Ampthill improved by, **1.** 226n
Banks's acquaintance with, **11.** 6n
casino designed by, **9.** 391n
commission for Wolfe's monument may have been given by, to Breton, **21.** 422
criticism of panegyric of, over Somerset House, **16.** 188
'Description of the New Buildings at Somerset House' attributed to, **16.** 187
design submitted by, for Wolfe's tomb, **21.** 428
*Designs of Chinese Buildings* by, **28.** 29n
disappearance of, causes rumours, **29.** 37–9, 42, 47

*Dissertation on Oriental Gardening, A*, by, **1.** 212n, **28.** 28–9, 34, 35–6, 40, 77, 113n, 222, **29.** 275
Essex might be helped by, with George III, **1.** 212
frightful and surprising prospects relished by, **28.** 106
garden pavilions at Kew built by, **20.** 187n
Gostling sells Whitton Place to, **41.** 437n
HW's bill from Mrs Coade examined by, **41.** 227–8
HW's correspondence with, **41.** 227–8
house of, at Whitton, **15.** 287
Knights of Polar Star ask, to 'Sir Williamize' himself, **28.** 28–9
(?) Mann employs, to get sepulchral *ara*, **20.** 353
(?) —— gives commissions to, **20.** 368–9
(?) —— helped by, at Rome, in finding art objects, **20.** 391–2
Mason leaves gardens to, **28.** 33
——'s attack on, actually directed at throne, **28.** 77–8
—— sends HW notes on, **28.** 450–1
——'s *Heroic Epistle* to, *see under* Mason, William
Roehampton house designed by, for Bessborough, **36.** 42n
satirized, **16.** 186n
state coach designed by, **22.** 104n
Stephens pupil of, **23.** 423n
Strada Felice, Roman location of, **20.** 392n
taste of, for the Asiatic, **33.** 97
*Treatise on . . . Civil Architecture* by, **1.** 212n, **9.** 391, 392, 400, 417, **28.** 29n
Wilton lived with, in Rome, **20.** 368n
—— returns to England with, **20.** 392n
'Chambers':
distribution of, in toasts by Leghorn merchants, **19.** 151–2
Chambers. *See also* Chambars; Chamber
*Chambers' Dictionary. See under* Chambers, Ephraim
Chambers, Treasurer of the. *See* Treasurer of the Chamber
Chambéry ('Chamberri'; 'Chamberry'):
Berrys at, **11.** 113n, 137, 141, 142, 146
Charles Emmanuel III evacuates, **18.** 142
Grande Chartreuse near, **37.** 150
HW's impression of, **11.** 138, 140
'little nasty old hole,' **13.** 190
Philip, Don, may retire to, **17.** 513
theatre at, **11.** 140
Chamblain de Marivaux. *See* Marivaux
Chambly ('Chamblee,' Canada):
Americans capture, **32.** 284n
English forces in, **24.** 347n
Chambon, Mme de. *See* Sarre, Marguerite
Chambon, Jacques de (1687–1753), Comte de Marcillat:
wife of, **8.** 193n
Chambonas, Marquis de. *See* La Garde, Scipion-Louis-Joseph de

Chambonas, Marquise de. *See* Lespinasse-Langeac, Aglaé-Josephine-Amélie-Louise-Édmée de

Chamboneau. *See* Chambonas

Chambors, Comte de. *See* La Boissière, Joseph-Jean-Baptiste de

Chambre des Comptes:
Louis XVI receives deputation from, 6. 60
Richmond's title to be registered in, 6. 455

Chameleon:
HW resembles, in looking backward, 33. 383

Chamfelt, Countess:
Bubb Dodington's joke about, 9. 167
languages learnt by, 9. 167
Petersham, Lady Caroline, protects, 9. 167

Chamfort, Sébastien-Roch-Nicolas (1741–94):
Condé gives position to, 6. 374
*Éloge de La Fontaine* by, 6. *114*, 115, 39. 220
(?) *Éloge de Molière* by, 7. 326
HW dislikes 'fables' by, 39. 243–4
Marie-Antoinette gives pension to, 6. 374
*Mustapha et Zéangir* by, 6. 374, 7. 10
verses attributed to, 4. 168n

Chamier, Anthony (1725–80):
Arras, Bp of, to have letter to, 4. 451
Cholmondeley, Mrs, may borrow from, 4. 369
contraband belonging to, 4. 439, 453, 461
courier of, 4. 383
Du Deffand, Mme, hears from, of Grafton's resignation, 4. 355
—— instructed in English politics by, 4. 374
—— mentions, 4. 448
—— regrets recall of, 5. 8
—— sends books, letters, and objects by, 4. 294, 295, 296, 303, 377, 379, 383, 422, 425, 427, 428, 429
——'s sends message to, 4. 300
——'s opinion of, 4. 294, 347, 453, 5. 8
——'s relations with, 4. 427, 435, 453, 5. 8
Dulac, Mme, sends china to, for HW, 4. 302, 305
East India Co. recalls, 4. 294
Fontainebleau visited by, 4. 301
gardens visited by, 7. 329
HW accompanies, to theatre, 7. 332
impatient for English mail, 4. 360
leaves Paris, 4. 427
mother visited weekly in London by, 4. 439
Paris to be visited by, 4. 347
Presle's correspondence with, 5. 352
social relations of, with: Choiseul, 4. 301; Cholmondeley, Mrs, 7. 332; Du Deffand, Mme, 4. *228*, 241, 352, 7. 332; HW, 4. 453, 7. 327, 329, 332; Irwin, 7. 332; Sanadon, Mlle, 7. 332; Walpole, Hon. Robert, 7. 332
to leave Paris, 4. 424
Walpole, Hon. Robert, says nothing of Choiseul's invitation to, 4. 301

Chamier, Mrs Daniel. *See* La Mejanelle, Suzanne de

Chamillard, Guy (1624–75):
Nanteuil's print of, 15. 100

Chamillart-la-Suze, Anne-Madeleine de (1753–1820), m. (1767) Louis-Henri de Villeneuve, Marquis de Trans:
Artois, Comtesse d', attended by, 5. 420
dances at ball in honour of Dauphin's marriage, 4. 410

Chamisso, Marguerite de, m. (1699) Albert, Baron de Pouilly:
officers' arrival at Reims expected by, 13. 179n

Chammilly. *See* Camilly

Chamnys, ——, actor; singer:
*Fairies, The*, sung by, 35. 209n

Chamois:
shoes of, 39. 44

Chamouni (France):
Chetwynd, Pocock, and Wyndham visit, 30. 2n

Champagne, Marquise de. *See* Busancy-Pavant, Jeanne-Pérette de

Champagne, Gaspard de, Comte de la Suze:
wife of, 3. 44n

Champagne, Philippe de (1602–74), painter:
paintings by, at Carmelites', 7. 264
Richelieu's portrait by, 16. 323n

Champagne (France):
Churchills go to, 38. 428
Marmier, Comte de, in, 42. 90
Montagu familiar with province of, 10. 196
Reims in, 13. 9

Champagne (wine):
Albemarle, Lady, drinks two glasses of, 33. 387
Bedford faction requires, 39. 101
Cheltenham water stronger than, 34. 47
Du Deffand, Mme, has stock of, 8. 11
English ladies supposed to visit Calais to drink, 38. 524
George, P. of Wales, drinks, at Epsom Races, 39. 446n
Granby drunk on, 9. 108
——'s heart expanded by, 40. 242
HW drinks, at Reggio, 17. 44
lady addicted to, 9. 140
no longer served at La Borde's suppers, 6. 404
served at extravagant dinner at White's, 20. 260
served at Lincoln's Inn entertainment, 43. 169
Stanley serves, 32. 115n

Champagne-La Suze, Anne-Marie de (1713–84), m. (1732) César-Gabriel de Choiseul, Duc de Praslin:
(?) Gaillard's verses to, 7. 363
HW describes, 35. 114
(?) HW mentions, 3. 341
Hertford, Cts of, asks about, 39. 37
—— glad that HW is seeing, 39. 264
social relations of, with: Choiseul, Vicomte and Vicomtesse de, 7. 349; Craon, 7. 263; Du Deffand, Mme, 7. 346, 349, (?) 427, (?) 429, 431–2, (?) 448; Estrées, Maréchal and Maréchale d', 7. 263; HW, 7. 262–3, 291,

349, **39**. 264; Hertford, **38**. 236, 253, 517; Hertford, Cts of, **7**. 262–3, **38**. 236, 517; Lorges, **7**. 349; Mirepoix, Mme de, **7**. 349; Montrevel, Comtesse de, **7**. 263; Pérusse, Marquise de, **7**. 349; Praslin, Marquise de, **7**. 349; Rians, Marquise de, **7**. 349; Richards, **7**. 263; Rochefort, Comtesse de, **7**. 342; Rondé, Mme, **7**. 349; Sanadon, Mlle, **7**. 349; Selwyn, **3**. 369

Champagne-Mouton, Comte de. *See* La Rochefoucauld, Frédéric-Guillaume de Roye de

Champcenetz, Marquise de. *See* Nieukirchen de Nyvenheim

*Champ de drap d'or, Le*:
'Embarkation of Henry VIII' to be companion to print of, **16**. 181
print of, **1**. 299, **2**. 277n

*Champ de la Confédération, Le. See* Champ de Mars

Champ de Mars, Paris:
balloon launching at, **25**. 450n
Berrys visit, **11**. 128
ceremony at, **11**. 100n
Condé's duel at, **7**. 438
Fête de la Fédération held in, **31**. 340

Champ du drap d'or. *See Champ de drap d'or*; Field of the Cloth of Gold

Champignelles, Marquise de. *See* Y, Charlotte-Louise-Thérèse d'

Champigny, Jean (1717–87), historian:
(?) Augusta, Ps of Wales, and, **36**. 8

Champion, Col. Alexander (d. 1793):
Teshu Lama's letters may have been mentioned by, in testimony about India, **25**. 14n

Champion, Anthony (1725–1801), M.P.; lawyer:
believes in Ireland's MSS, **15**. 321

Champion, The. *See* Dymoke, John (d. 1784)

*Champion*, frigate:
Conway arrives on, **33**. 140, 142–3

*Champion, The* (periodical):
Fielding writes, **18**. 32n
Walpole, Lady Mary, mentioned by, **18**. 32

Champion de Cicé, Jean-Baptiste-Marie (d. 1805), Bp of Auxerre:
social relations of, with Maurepas, **7**. 309

Champion de Cicé, Jérôme-Marie (1735–1810), Bp of Rodez, 1770:
Berry, Mary, submits Mme du Deffand's MSS to criticism by, **3**. xli
Du Deffand, Mme, gives opinion of, **4**. 469, **5**. 13
Gennevilliers visited by, **4**. 469
MS copies by, **5**. 402n
social relations of, with: Choiseul, Duchesse de, **4**. *469*; Du Deffand, Mme, **6**. 115, 250, **7**. 351–2, **41**. 194

Champlain, Lake:,
American army assembling at, **24**. 133n

Champlâtreux, Comte de, *See* Molé, Édouard-François-Mathieu

Champlâtreux, Comtesse de. *See* Lamoignon, Marie-Louise de

Champneys, Lady. *See* Minchin, Henrietta

Champrond, Abbé de. *See* Vichy, Nicolas-Marie de

Champrond, Comte de. *See* Vichy, Abel-Claude-Marie-Gœric-Cécile de (1765–1832); Vichy, Abel-Claude-Marthe-Marie-Cécile de (1740–93); Vichy, Gaspard de (d. 1736); Vichy, Gaspard-Nicolas de (1699–1781)

Champrond, Comtesse de. *See* Albon de St-Marcel, Marie-Camille-Diane d' (1714–73); Brulart, Anne (fl. 1690); St-Georges, Claude-Josèphe-Marie de (1742–75)

Champrond (France):
Du Deffand, Mme, receives letter from, **7**. 455

Champs, Des. *See* Des Champs

Champs de Marcilly. *See* Des Champs de Marcilly

Champs de Mars. *See* Champ de Mars

Champs-Élysées:
Sévigné, Mme de, inhabits, **41**. 109

Champs-Élysées, Rue des, Paris:
La Reynières live near, **5**. 370n

Chançay. *See* La Martillière de Chançay

'Chance.' *See* Nugent, Lady Louisa

Chance:
HW's reflections on, **24**. 387–8, **32**. 344–5, 378

'Chancelier, le.' *See* Maupeou, René-Nicolas-Charles-Augustin de

Chancellor; chancellors:
English, *see* Lord chancellor
French, hanged, arouses Maupeou's interest, **39**. 151
*See also under* Maupeou, René-Nicolas-Charles-Augustin de

'Chancellor, the Dancing.' *See* Hatton, Sir Christopher

Chancellor of Cambridge; Chancellor of Oxford. *See* Cambridge University: chancellor of; Oxford University: chancellor of

Chancellor of the Duchy of Lancaster:
Hyde may succeed Strange as, **23**. 313

Chancellor of the Exchequer. *See under* Exchequer

Chancellor of university:
Montagu not soliciting votes for, **10**. 142

Chancery, Court of:
accountant-general of, *see* Waple, John
Bolton, Ds of, gets unscrupulous lawyer from, **21**. 365
Camden advises HW against seeking decree from, on Shorter estate, **40**. 79
cannot stand still, **23**. 79
Daye, Catherine, involved in suit in, **36**. 59
Dunstable prose of bill in, **33**. 287
Gloucester, Ds of, has bill in, **36**. 72n
HW has saved Mozzi from suit in, **25**. 448
HW might become solicitor in, **32**. 121
HW might sue himself in, for distribution of Shorter estate, **40**. 79

[Chancery, Court of, *continued*]

HW must have request by Cts of Orford as his guarantee before, **23**. 496

HW's suit in, over his house in Berkeley Sq., **28**. 453, **33**. 108, **34**. 250–2

HW to get Walpole heirs' consents, as justification to, **36**. 93

Jenyns, Soame, checked by, **28**. 86

Kingston, Ds of, wins case in, over husband's will, **24**. 118

Lucchi money to be deposited at, **22**. 267

Mason's lawsuit in, with Murray, **28**. 310–11, 322, 326, 452

Nicoll, Miss, is allowed maintenance by, **14**. 194

Orford's affairs and, **32**. 118, 135

Orford, Cts of, could not be made her son's keeper by, unless she lived in England, **23**. 481, 510

Pomfret, Cts of, quibbles about, **17**. 210

register of, *see* Beauclerk, George, 3d D. of St Albans

suits in: **11**. 236; reduce the contestants, **21**. 261; Turkish war resembles, **23**. 432; would be no more involved than Mozzi's affair, **25**. 397

testimony in, **11**. 227

trust money in, used to keep stocks up, **41**. 315

Walpole, Sir Edward, would be declared by, younger than HW, **24**. 529

wills set aside by, **22**. 578

would not sell horses with engagements, **32**. 135

Chancery, Court of, Irish:

clerk of the Crown and Hanaper in, to revert to Conway on Domvile's death, **38**. 145, 146

Chancery, Master in:

animals could act part of, **35**. 375

*See also* Pepys, Sir William Weller

Chancery Lane, London:

Dixons lived in, **41**. 96

god of, counts sheets of paper, **32**. 173

Gapper, attorney in, **42**. 418

HW's remark about families in, **14**. 208–9

Shorter, Erasmus, dies in, **13**. 25n, **20**. 403n

Society of Antiquaries in, **28**. 40, **38**. 371

sonnet 'writ' in, **35**. 557

Tonson's publishing house in, **15**. 57n

Chanclos de Rets Brisuila, Charles-Urbain (1686–1761), Comte de; army officer; governor of Ostend:

Ostend defended by, **37**. 204

Chanda Sahib, Nawab of the Carnatic, 1749:

Dupleix makes, nawab, **22**. 212n

Chandelier; chandeliers:

at Covent Garden theatre, **22**. 120n

crystal, HW breaks, at Norfolk House, **9**. 331

silver, at George II's funeral, **9**. 321

Chandler, Mrs. *See* Vertue, ——

Chandler, Mrs, of Twickenham:

(?) HW mentions, **20**. 292

SH visited by, **12**. 224, 226, 230, 234

SH visitor sent by, **12**. 243

'treads,' **9**. 53

Chandler, Barbara (d. 1786), m. 1 (1731) William Cavendish; m. 2 (1751) Hon. John Fitzwilliam:

husband and servants of, **34**. 59

servant of, inherits fortune from General Fitzwilliam, **11**. 49

Chandler, Edward (ca 1668–1750), Bp of Lichfield, 1717; of Durham, 1730:

Collins, Anthony, opposed by, **20**. 167n

controversial writer, **20**. 167

daughter of, **11**. 49n

death of: **20**. 167n; falsely rumoured, **18**. 246

rich, **20**. 167

son of, **9**. 171n, **14**. 245

Chandler, Richard (d. 1744):

publishes *History of House of Commons*, **29**. 295n

Chandler (later Cavendish), Richard (d. 1769), son of Bp Edward Chandler:

Montagu, Lady Mary Wortley, writes verses to, **14**. 245

wife of, **9**. 171n

Chandler, Richard (1738–1810), D.D.; antiquary and traveller:

*Travels in Greece* by, **28**. 257

Chandler, Mrs Richard. *See* Cavendish, Elizabeth

Chandler's shop:

at Englefield Green, **9**. 20

chambermaid gets credit at, **33**. 201

plums cannot be bought at, without danger from highwaymen, **35**. 521

Chandos, Bn. *See* Brydges, Giles (ca 1547 *or* 1548–94); Brydges, Grey (ca 1579–1621)

Chandos, Ds of. *See* Gamon, Anne Eliza (d. 1813); Hatten, Lydia Catherine van (ca 1693–1750); Willoughby, Cassandra (1670–1735)

Chandos, D. of. *See* Brydges, Henry (1708–71); Brydges, James (1674–1744); Brydges, James (1731–89)

Chandos, Sir John:

Calveley and John of Gaunt serve under, at Battle of Navarete, **41**. 445n

Chandos St, Covent Garden:

Cates, pawnbroker in, **40**. 65n

'Three Tuns' in, **19**. 389n

Chandos St, Marylebone:

Foley House in, **33**. 261n

Change:

Latin motto about, **38**. 567

Change Alley, Cornhill:

Devonshire, Ds of, and Lady Duncannon in, **12**. 213

Greek and Roman defeats were not reflected in, **21**. 558

HW's observations on, **25**. 287

HW will not deal in 'garbage' of, **35**. 125

in Stratford's tragedy, **29**. 224

path to House of Commons from, **22.** 498

rumours benefit, **10.** 36

stock prices changed by rumours in, **39.** 512

Changuion, —— (fl. 1765–6), secretary of embassy at Paris:

Richmond's secretary at Paris, **22.** 405n

social relations of, in Paris, **7.** 291, 293, 296, 304

Changuion, Philip (fl. 1755–71), secretary of embassy at Naples:

Gray leaves, at Naples, **22.** 112

Halifax's orders to, about D. of York, **22.** 173n

Channel, The. *See* English Channel

Channel Islands:

Arbuthnot leaves naval force to protect, **39.** 320

*See also* Alderney; Guernsey; Jersey; Sark

Channell, Capt. William:

(?) ship of, from Newfoundland, brings news to Leghorn, **24.** 246

Channel Row House, London:

Clifford, Anne, conceived at, **2.** 323n–4n

'Chanson; chansons':

ballad to tune of, **33.** 45

*Chanson de Roland*:

Abp Turpin in, **28.** 313

*Chanson on Lady Caroline Petersham and Col. Conway*:

in HW's hand, **10.** 325–7, **43.** 138

*Chant de l'enfer. See under* Gudin de la Brenellerie, Paul-Philippe

Chanteloup (France):

Arras, Bp of, unable to escort Mme du Deffand to, **5.** 108

Balbastre composes airs for, **6.** 115

Boufflers, Marquis de, dies at, **6.** 92

Choiseul, Duc de, banished to, **11.** 341n, **23.** 257, **39.** 134, **41.** 196–8

—— manages, **5.** 253–4

—— occupies, **3.** 302, **4.** 9, 85, 86, 88, 102n, 103, 436, 469, **5.** 1, 7, 243, 246, 253, 331, **6.** 62, 190, 204, 244, 439, **7.** 44, 365, 447, **8.** 207

—— should prefer, to power, **23.** 315

—— to occupy, **3.** 338, **4.** 134, 243, 266, 463, 464, **5.** 42, **6.** 163, 174, 196, 198, 272, 281, 319, 441, 445, 468, 476, 478, **7.** 36, 68–9, 124

Choiseul, Duchesse de, likes life at, **4.** 437

—— occupies, **3.** 57, 59, 284, 286, 289, 319, **4.** 61, 68, 70, 79, 110, 234–5, 237, 240, 243, 248, 254, 261, 263, 404, 406, 411, 425, 427, **5.** 1, 6, 7, 15–16, 322, 331, 426, **6.** 196, 198, 212, 240, 244, 441, **7.** 44, 447

—— recuperates at, **4.** 223

—— rides at, **5.** 96n

—— to occupy, **6.** 163, 272, 281, **7.** 36, 124

Choiseul's acquisition of, **43.** 94

Coigny, Comte and Comtesse de, might settle at, **6.** 22

comedies acted at, **5.** 382, 385, 388

Du Châtelet sends courier to, **5.** 166

Du Deffand, Mme, considers difficulties of going to, **5.** 42–4, 370, 386

—— has news from, **5.** 327, 381, 395, 411–12, 426, **6.** 8, 110

—— invited to, **4.** 121, 126, **5.** 363, 395, 396, **6.** 40, 44, 46, 324

—— lacks news from, **4.** 85, 85–6, 88, 93, **5.** 15, 80, 84, 185–6

—— mentions, **4.** 120, 266, 296, 298, 453, 470–1, **5.** 38, 60, 61, 235, **6.** 248, 375, 378, 380, 499, **7.** 81 192

——'s correspondence with, **4.** 238, 244, 263, **5.** 11, 23, 81, 109, 129, 144, 153, 224, 270, 281, 300, 305, 336, 337, 351, 373, 377, 385, 388, 416, **6.** 33, 69, 93, 187, 221, 324, 361, **7.** 48, 155, 435, 457, 461

——'s deliberations about visiting, **5.** 15, 16, 23, 30, 37, 42, 52, 63, 73, 76, 78, 79, 93, 96–7, 102, 108, 109, 117, 118, 122, 127, 150, 152, 153–4, 156, 158, 168, 170, 195–6, 215, 216, 221, 224, 228, 231, 234, **6.** 270

——'s journey from, **5.** 251, 257, 259

——'s journey to, **5.** 237–40

—— thinks Choiseul regrets, **6.** 127

fashionable, **39.** 143

flocks at, **4.** 437

gardens of, **8.** 208

Gramont, Duchesse de, important to life at, **5.** 395, 396, 399–400

HW invited to, **5.** 41, **6.** 167, 376, **7.** 88

HW sees model of, **7.** 331

HW sends messages to, **6.** 98

health of company at, **5.** 322

Joseph II's proposed visit to, **6.** 445, 447, 453, 455

life at, **4.** 240, **5.** 243, 255–6

Monaco, Prince de, postpones visit to, **31.** 136

occupants of, visit Richelieu, **6.** 463

pagoda ('obélisque') at: **7.** 88, 124, **8.** 208; in parfilage, **7.** 197

peace reigns at, **5.** 253

pencils forwarded to, **7.** 154

postal service to, **5.** 242, 243, 244, 246

poultry yard at, **4.** 437

runaway horses from, **6.** 430

St-Simon's *Mémoires* at, **5.** 6, 57, 78

schedule of hours at, **5.** 243

'Strawberry Hill' of Mme de Choiseul, **4.** 261

theatricals at, **5.** 382, 385, 388

time of journey between Paris and, **4.** 110, 406, 436, **5.** 43, **7.** 126

tonneau for Mme du Deffand to be brought from, **6.** 268, 275

Véret 2 leagues from, **6.** 196

visitors to: **7.** 72, 153, 34. 54, 79; Achy, Mme d', **4.** 406; Amblimont, Mme d', **4.** 469; Anville, Duchesse d', **5.** 95, 231; Arras, Bp of, **5.** 234, 253, 254, **6.** 373, **7.** 456; Artois, **6.** 445, 450–1; Barthélemy, Abbé, **3.** 297, 312, **4.** 234, 240, 245, 253, 254, 260n, 261, 263, 406, **5.** 1, 6, 7, 16, 63, 96, 130n, 168, 173, 240, 243, 245, 404, 426, **6.** 184, 212, 291, 332, 348, 349,

[Chanteloup, *continued*]
353, 441, **7.** 424, **8.** 201–2, 207–8, **41.** 197;
Barthélemy, Marquis de, **6.** 184; Bauffremont (Listenois), **4.** 71, 411, **5.** (?) 268, **7.**
448, **41.** 197–8; (?) Beauteville, **7.** 423, 448,
456; Beauvau, **5.** 34, 37, 45, 48, 169, 225, 256,
345, 380, 391, **6.** 3, 82, 212, 214, 417; Beauvau, Princesse de, **4.** 464, 469, **5.** 1, 37, 48,
169, 225, 256, 264, 380, 432, **6.** 3, 212, 214,
**41.** 197; Besenval, **5.** 243; Boufflers, Chevalier de, **5.** 245; Boufflers, Comtesse Amélie
de, **6.** 441, 453; Boufflers, Comtesse de, **6.**
33, 41, 431, 441, 453, **25.** 627; Brienne, **5.**
331, **6.** 232; Brionne, Mme de, **5.** 59, 231,
243, 245, 363, **7.** 150, **8.** 207; Burgoyne, **3.**
243n, **5.** 269–70; Cambrai, Abp of, **41.** 197;
Caracciolo, **7.** 427; Castellane, **4.** 234, **5.**
238, 243, 245, 253, **41.** 198; Chabot, **5.** 95;
Chabot, Comtesse de, **5.** 95, 231; Chartres,
**5.** 331; Chauvelin, Mme de, **7.** 150, **8.** 207;
Choiseul, Comte de, **7.** 69, 72, 73; Choiseul-
Beaupré, Comtesse de, **4.** 234, 425, **5.** 7, 183,
350, 352, 363, 403, 426, **6.** 330; Choiseul-
Beaupré, Marquis de, **5.** 7, **7.** 69; Choiseul-
Beaupré, Marquise de, **5.** 7; Choiseul-
Stainville, Marie-Stéphanie de, **7.** 69, 72,
73; Corbie, Mme, **4.** 416; Cotte, **8.** 207;
Du Buc, **7.** 448; Du Châtelet, **5.** 84, 86, 165,
241, 243, 245, 246; Du Châtelet, Comtesse
(Duchesse), **5.** 84, 86, 165, 241, 243, 245,
246, **6.** 450; Du Cluzel, Mlle, **8.** 207; Du
Deffand, Mme, **5.** 236, 240–58, 259, 261, 270,
284, 331, 396, **6.** 312, **8.** 191; Du Hamel,
Mlle, **4.** 469; Duras, Duchesse de, **8.** 207;
during exile numbered 210, **6.** 121; Dutens,
**25.** 627; Gatti, **4.** 234, 261, 263, 406, **5.** 7;
Gleichen, **4.** 250, 252; Gontaut, **5.** 7; Gramont, Duchesse de, **3.** 338, **4.** 126, 134, 463,
464, 469, **5.** 7, 30, 42, 245, 363, 370, 373; **6.**
33, 41, 163, 174, 184, 347, 353, 441, 468,
476, **7.** 68–9, **41.** 197; Imécourt, **8.** 207;
Imécourt, Mme d', **7.** 150–1, **8.** 207; La
Fayette, Marquise de, **8.** 207; La Rochefoucauld, **5.** 231; Lauzun, **5.** 7, 426; Lauzun,
Duchesse de, **5.** 7, 231, 243, 426, **6.** 441;
Ligne, Princesse de, **5.** 243, 245; Lorraine,
Princesse Anne-Charlotte de, **5.** 245, **8.**
207; Luxembourg, Mme de, **5.** 122, 125,
127, 129, 135, 136, 169, 180n, 228, 231, 234,
238, 241, 243, 350, 353, 358, 404, 412, 418,
426, 431, **6.** 33, 48–9, 54, 103, 104, 110, 441,
450, 452, 453; Montesson, Mme de, **7.** 124,
150, 153; Montpipeau, M. and Mme de, **8.**
207; Mouchy, Maréchale de, **8.** 207; Noailles, Vicomtesse de, **8.** 207; Orléans, **7.**
124, 150, 153; Poissonnier, **8.** 207; Poix,
Princesse de, **5.** 317; Schomberg, **5.** 245;
Selwyn, **7.** 124; servants of, given party by
Choiseul, **6.** 162–3; Stainville, **5.** 7, 15, 30,
**41.** 197; Stanley, **5.** 270; Tessé, Mme de, **4.**
469, **5.** 59; Thianges, **8.** 207; Thiers, **4.**
234, 240; Tingry, Princesse de, **5.** 256; Toulouse, Abp of, **5.** 331, **7.** 150, 153; Tours,

Abp of, **7.** 450; Valentinois, Duchesse de,
**5.** 363; Vaudémont, Princesse de, **7.** 150
water route to, **5.** 350, 352–3
wing of, collapses, **5.** 122, 128
Chanteloupe. *See* St-Vrain
Chanterac, Charles de la Cropte de. *See* La
Cropte de Chanterac
Chanteur, Le. *See* Le Chanteur
'Chanticleer.' *See* Bush, (?) Addison
Chantilly (France), Condé's seat:
balloon flight to, **25.** 527n
Bourbon exiled to, by Louis XVI, **7.** 31
——'s house and gardens at, **37.** 41
brass from, **37.** 71
china from, **7.** 401, 402, 403, 405, 406, 407,
410, **8.** 24
Condé at, **5.** 15, **6.** 163
—— entertains Karl Wilhelm Ferdinand at,
**41.** 19
*corbeilles* at, **31.** 54
crowded, **39.** 143
Du Deffand, Mme, mentions, **3.** 230, 340
—— sends letter to Mlle de Prûlé at, **7.** 459
five hours from Paris, **3.** 1
gallery at, inspired HW's at SH, **31.** 46
HW calls Goodwood Richmond's, **30.** 92
HW loses portmanteau at, **1.** 98, **38.** 17
HW meets Cts of W. at, **35.** 124
HW's expenses at, **7.** 399
HW writes from, **3.** 1, 32, 126, 128, 169, 310,
**4.** 273, 292, **7.** 381, 386
Herbert's mistaken spelling of, **14.** 127, 129
Le Nôtre designs gardens at, **28.** 30n
mob damages Condé's property at, **11.** 207
Montmorency's statue at, **31.** 46
Paris robbed of company by, **5.** 82
spring not arrived at, **31.** 117
suitable for over-night stay, **37.** 40
trees scarce budded at, **7.** 314
unchanged in twenty years, **31.** 46
visitors to: Brunswick, **3.** 42; Choiseul, Duchesse de, **4.** 130, 134; Christan VII, **4.** 154,
166; Du Barry, Comtesse, **4.** 447; HW, **3.**
1, 344, 346, **7.** 260, 314, 324, 334, 353, **31.**
46, **35.** 123, **39.** 9; Karl Wilhelm Ferdinand,
**41.** 19; Louis XV, **3.** 122, 333, **4.** 257, 447,
458; Luxembourg, Mme de, **3.** 338; Marie-
Antoinette, **4.** 447; Mesdames de France,
**4.** 257, 447; Mirepoix, Mme de, **3.** 127, **4.**
257; Nivernais, **41.** 19; Pars, **6.** 236; Pembroke, Cts of, **4.** 159; Selwyn, **7.** 151, 152
Chanvalon. *See* Thibaut de Chanvalon
Chapeau, Mrs Edward Robert Nassau. *See*
Strange, Sarah
Chapel; chapels:
Amelia, Ps, attends, in riding-clothes with
dog, **37.** 341
at Bulstrode, **35.** 233
at Burford, **35.** 155
at Casa Craon, **21.** 468
at Fulham Palace, **31.** 313
at Glamis Castle, **42.** 346–7

at Hartlebury Castle, **35**. 149

at Hurstmonceaux, **35**. 138

at Standon, Roman Catholic, **40**. 198

Chute's, at the Vyne, **9**. 164, **20**. 485, 489, 529, 539, **35**. 639–40, 641, 642

Cordon's, demolished by Gordon rioters, **25**. 55

HW's 'Cabinet' to resemble, **21**. 238, 306

Haszlang's, plundered by Gordon rioters, **25**. 54

Hertford's, at embassy in Paris: attended by Wilkes, **38**. 343; crowded to hear Sterne, **38**. 353; Scottish Presbyterian said to conduct, **38**. 347, 352

Huntingdon, Cts of, has, **35**. 118–19

in bishop's house at Gloucester, **35**. 153

Chapel Royal. *See* St James's Palace: Chapel Royal at

Chapelain, Jean (1595–1674):

Du Deffand, Mme, writes verses in the manner of, **7**. 213

*Pucelle, La,* mentioned by Mme du Deffand, **7**. 214

Chapelle, Claude-Emmanuel Lhuillier (1626–86), poet:

Broussin's friend, **4**. 284

Du Deffand, Mme, repeats verses from, **4**. 284

Chaplain; chaplains:

at All Souls, **35**. 388

Augusta, Ps of Wales's, **20**. 344

Charlotte's, in Zoffany's painting, **24**. 539

Dodd removed as, **32**. 185

French invasion of England to include, **21**. 311

Louis XVI told to have two, **34**. 142

Murray's, *see* Lind, John

Newcastle's, *see* Hurdis, Rev. Thomas

Northumberland, Cts of, may have had her *Meditations* compiled by, **42**. 394

Northumberland's, attend assembly in gowns and scarves *à l'irlandaise*, **22**. 239, **38**. 401

Onslow's, injured in carriage accident with HW at Richmond, **39**. 454

portrait of, at Burghley House, **10**. 346

Strafford's, **37**. 559, 560

to regiment: Charles Montagu gives post of, to brother's parson, **35**. 265; desires leave, **40**. 91

to Hon. Robert Walpole, **34**. 132–3

Zouch is, to Lady Rockingham, **35**. 323n

Chaplet, cut paper:

on warrant, **10**. 116

Chaplin, ——, mayor of Carrickfergus:

Thurot captures, **21**. 376, 386

Chapman, Lady. *See* Edmondson, Rachel

Chapman, Edward, senior, builder and bricklayer of Twickenham:

Davenport sues, for brickmaking on common field, **43**. 155

(?) misunderstands orders for new road at Little Strawberry Hill, **12**. 162

Chapman, Mrs (?) Edward, of Twickenham:

SH visited by, **12**. 236

Chapman, Rev. John (1704–84):

bookseller's conversation with, over sale of his works, **33**. 247

*Eusebius* by, **33**. 247

*Jesuit Cabal Farther Opened* by, **15**. 297

Middleton's controversy with, **15**. 297, **33**. 247

*Popery the Bane of True Letters* by, **15**. 297n

*View of the Expediency and Credibility of Miraculous Powers among the Primitive Christians, A,* by, **15**. 304, **43**. 212

Chapman, Sir John (ca 1710–81), 2d Bt; M.P.:

impotence of, and wife's lewdness made public, **37**. 232

Chapman, Thomas (1717–60), D.D.; Master of Magdalene College, Cambridge:

dies of eating fish, **28**. 154, 259

HW identifies, **28**. 188n

Chaponay, Jacques-Hugues de:

trial of, **3**. 35

Chapone, Mrs John. *See* Mulso, Hester

Chappe d'Auteroche, Jean (1722–69):

*Voyage en Sibérie* by, **5**. 190

Chappelow, Rev. Leonard:

Piozzi, Mrs, gets comments from, on her style, **42**. 245n

Chappuzeau, Samuel (ca 1625–1701):

*Europe vivante, L',* by, **8**. 26

Chapt de Rastignac, Pierre-Louis (b. 1713), Comte de Puyguilhem:

(?) social relations of, with Duchesse d'Anville, **7**. 311

Chapter Coffee-house, Paul's Alley, Paternoster Row:

Reed, Isaac, adressed at, **41**. 280n

Chapuset, Anna Maria Apolonia Capusettin von (1747–1837), m. 1 (ca 1765–8) Baron Christof Adam Karl von Imhoff; m. 2 (1777) Warren Hastings:

bribes of diamonds allegedly received by, **11**. 207n

brilliance of, **12**. 55

first marriage date of, corrected, **43**. 146

gold muslins presented by, to Q. Charlotte, **31**. 272n

influence of, at Court, **11**. 207

ivory and gold bed presented to Q. Charlotte by, **11**. 295

presentation of, at Court, **11**. 340

rumour about sale of, to Hastings, **11**. 295

Chapuy, René-Bernard (1746–1809), French army officer:

captured at Cateau-Cambrésis, **2**. 98

'Jacobin commander,' **12**. 98

Character:

can only be hurt by itself, **38**. 366

*Character and Conduct of Cicero Considered, The. See under* Cibber, Colley

*Characteristics. See under* Cooper, Anthony Ashley

*Character of . . . Lucy, Countess of Carlisle. See under* Matthews, Sir Tobias

'Character of Sir Robert Walpole.' *See* **Hume,** David: *Essays, Moral and Political*

Character of the Life and Administration of the Late . . . Earl of Orford, A. See under Ashton, Thomas

Characters of Eminent Personages. See under Stanhope, Philip Dormer, E. of Chesterfield

'Characters of the Christ-Cross Row, The':
Gray sends, to HW, 14. 27–30

Charade; charades:
(?) 'alteration,' 37. 242
'blockhead,' 33. 508, 509, 510
(?) 'character,' 33. 446
'cimitière,' 39. 39
'courage,' 7. 374
Fitzpatrick's, sent to HW by Lady Ossory, 33. 533, 39. 445, 545
HW cannot guess, 34. 41
HW sends, to Harcourt, 35. 525, 526
HW thanks Lady Ossory for, 33. 533
HW thinks, making and solving of, as wise as anything we do, 39. 446
'Italien,' 6. 340, 344, 32. 309–10
'lutestring,' 33. 533, 39. 445, 545
(?) 'plainsong,' 33. 533, 39. 445, 545
Powys's, 33. 446
'Tartar,' 12. 268
'Tonton,' 35. 525, 526
'trout,' 7. 360
'vapeur,' 33. 508

Charborough, Dorset:
Drax of, 9. 252n

Charcoal:
Henri IV sketches with, 35. 244
princesses' dishes heated over, at Versailles, 10. 292
pubic hair depicted by, on statue at Wilton, 25. 178

Chardin, Jean (1643–1713):
Journal du voyage du Chevalier Chardin en Perse et aux Indes, quoted by Mme du Deffand, 3. 9, 337

Chardon, Mme:
Lauzun takes, into confidence, 4. 136n

Charente, river:
forts at mouth of, may be attacked, 37. 507n

Charenton-St-Maurice, hospital for insane at:
patients at, 4. 416

Charette de Montebert, Marie-Madeleine-Élisabeth (1706–78), m. 1 (1733) Louis de Sérent, Marquis de Kerfilis; m. 2 (1745) Henri-François de Bretagne, Comte de Vertus; m. 3 (1752) Anne-Léon, Baron de Montmorency:
death of, 7. 6
social relations of, with Mme Geoffrin, 7. 327

Chargé d'affaires; chargés d'affaires:
English, at Florence, see Mann, Horatio (1706–86)
English, at Naples, see Changuion, Philip (fl. 1755–71); Preston, Rev. William (fl. 1771)
English, at Paris, see Hume, David (1711–76); Thompson, Anthony (d. 1756)
French, at Florence, see Billerey, —— (fl. 1777–81); Roland, Luigi (d. 1766), Conte Lorenzi

French, at Rome, see Guérin de Tencin, Pierre (1680–1758); Montboissier-Beaufort, Claude-François de (ca 1693–1761); Polignac, Melchior de (1661–1742)
French, in London, see Barthélemy, François (1747–1830); Bussy, François de (1699–1780)
French, in Russia, see Sabatier de Cabre
Genoese, at Paris, see Sorba, Giambattista (d. 1738)
Genoese, in London, see Gastaldi, Giambattista
Hessian, in London, see Alt, Justus Heinrich
Mann's losses as, 18. 516, 21. 370, 483
Modenese, in France, see Cioia (or Cioja) des Forges
Neapolitan, at Florence, Viviani ceases to be, 22. 349
Prussian, at The Hague, see Hellen, Bruno von der
Prussian, in London, see Michell, Abraham (or Andreas Ludwig) (ca 1712–82)
Spanish, in London, see Abreu y Bertodano, Felix de (fl. 1754–60); Escarano, Caballero d'
Tuscan, at Naples, see Bonechi, Giuseppe
Tuscan, at Paris, see Favi, Francesco (fl. 1780–92); Niccoli, Abbé Raimondo (d. 1780)
Tuscan, in London, see Pucci, Domenico (1718–83); Pucci, Vincenzo (ca 1675–1757)

Charibdis. See Charybdis

'Charing Cross, Ds of.' See Seymour, Lady Elizabeth, Ds of Northumberland

Charing Cross, London:
Atterbury wants to proclaim Old Pretender at, 20. 60
ballad about Q. Eleanor at, 9. 251, 256, 14. 156, 32. 348
Balmerinoch buys gooseberries at, 9. 38
Biddulph, banker in, 42. 453
Cardigan's Head a bagnio at, 38. 206
Charles I's statue at, 13. 86
Craig's Court in, 42. 455
crowds all the way from, to House of Lords, 21. 389
Drummond, HW's banker in, 11. 134n, 21. 457; see also Drummond & Co.
estates at, owned by Trinity Hospital, Greenwich, 16. 91
fire does not reach, 29. 56
French invasion to be observed in, 9. 23
HW jokes about battle in, 18. 179
Hedge Lane in, Wilton plaster-worker in, 20. 392n
houses in, left to Trinity Hospital, 16. 90
illuminated during Gordon Riots, 33. 188
mob riots in, 23. 200
Northampton lived at, 16. 91
Northumberland House in, 20. 328n
sign of the Golden Cross at, 35. 643

trunk shop at: **32.** 322n; given as D. of Somerset's address, **32.** 322
Vertue's drawing of, **15.** 203
Chariot; chariots:
absent from White's Club, **38.** 459
Ashburnham torn from, **33.** 175
Barberini's, **19.** 428
Burney's, at HW's door, **42.** 202
Castle-Durrow's, **20.** 21
Cole and Middleton drive in, **15.** 313
Cutts', **9.** 252
filled, during London storm, **10.** 14
Fox, C. J., stoned by mob when riding in, **23.** 291
Fox brothers dragged from, by mob, **23.** 290
French servants may wear hats in, in Paris, **35.** 112
Glover's, **9.** 398
gold, antiquated dukes in, **33.** 259
Gray's verses mention, **28.** 169
HW goes through Pall Mall in, **38.** 199
HW's: Conway, Anne Seymour, may ride in, **37.** 334; HW and Cole travel in, **10.** 332; HW stopped in, to be told about Cape Breton, **20.** 474; HW to carry Bentley to SH in, **35.** 69; HW to let down glass window of, to inspect lodgings, **10.** 270; held up at Whitehall by crowd at fire, **17.** 496; held up by highwayman, **40.** 65; hissed and pelted by weavers' mob, **38.** 560; in Paris, decorated with Cupids, **10.** 176
Harley's, broken by mob, **22.** 187n
Hertford's, **38.** 77
Hillsborough goes in, to Court, **22.** 445
Hulse carries clergyman in, to avoid suspicion of unorthodoxy, **30.** 30
Lorenzi's, lined with yellow and green, **21.** 501
Lyttelton's, at theatre, **32.** 286
Malton family's, has Japanese decoration, **30.** 50
Mann's, **25.** 667n
Margaret of Anjou's, **14.** 74
merchants presenting address to George III ride in, **10.** 273
Merril's, **43.** 185
modern, varnished, **42.** 2
Montagu may buy, from Castlecomer estate, **9.** 196, 197
North's, torn to pieces by London mob, **23.** 290
Richecourt orders, to be made for Bns Walpole, **17.** 54
Saville's and Turner's, demolished by mob, **25.** 54
Spencer rides in, **31.** 204
Stanhope's, **20.** 108
Temple's, **9.** 233
tides of, in London, **11.** 249
Walpole, Sir Robert, forbidden to drive in, **18.** 538
Winnington's, **30.** 70, **34.** 89

*See also* Carriage; Chaise; Phaeton
Chariot-and-pair:
Pitt and Temple drive in, to Lord Mayor's dinner, **21.** 547
Chariot-and-six:
sheriff rides in, **21.** 399
Chariot race:
at Florence, **22.** 237n
French merchants at Leghorn give, for Tuscan Court, **22.** 418, 423
in Piazza di Santa Maria Novella at Florence, **17.** 79n
Charitable Corporation, London:
Belloni threatens to expose scandal of, **43.** 258
*Charité, La*, French ship:
involved in war, **19.** 222
Charité, La. *See* Hôpital de la charité des hommes
*Charity. See under* Layard, Charles Peter; Manners, Charles, 4th D. of Rutland
Charity; charities:
apt to cool before second call, **34.** 167
beds bestowed, in Florence, **19.** 461
Bligh's, Howe's, and P. Edward's, to Cherbourg's poor, **21.** 238
bread given to Florentine poor: by Cowper, **24.** 232; by Lorenzi, **19.** 14; by Rinuccini, **19.** 461; on P. Charles's wedding day, **18.** 364
Florentine debtors released, **19.** 461
for French emigrants, **31.** 397
for poor, **31.** 397
Gloucester, Ds of, aids poor, **31.** 396
'grandmother of,' HW speculates on identity of, **33.** 299
HW answers appeals for needy persons, **40.** 270, 345
HW's, for Hannah More's protégés, **31.** 338
HW supports real objects of compassion with, **37.** 172
Jamesone's bequests to the poor, **40.** 285
mountains should be moved by, **37.** 108
old women misinterpret, **25.** 584
to the sick, in Fleet Prison, **40.** 345
weddings of poor Florentine girls, **22.** 491
*See also* Benevolent activity
*Charity: a Poetical Essay*:
Granby said to have written, **32.** 181
Charity children:
sing in Twickenham church choir, **34.** 115
Charity girls:
Dysart treats Waldegrave sisters as, **36.** 327
Charity house:
Durazzo, Marquis, keeps, at Genoa for decayed nobility, **37.** 319
Charity school:
HW pretends to be hackney writer educated at, **42.** 502
Rose the founder of, at Amesbury, **42.** 45
Charlbury, Oxon.:
Dodd and Whaley visit, **40.** 12, 13

Charlemagne (742–814), Holy Roman Emperor:
descent from: 23. 435; Gunning, Gen., claims,
11. 185, 196n, 197n, 229; HW jokes about
his, 31. 155
George III may be successor to, 21. 515
'Charlemagne, Cour de.' See under Colbert,
Élisabeth-Pauline-Gabrielle, Marquise de
Jonzac
Charlemont, Bn. See Caulfeild, James (1728–
99); Caulfeild, Toby (1565–1627)
Charlemont, Cts of. See Hickman, Mary (d.
1807)
Charlemont, E. of. See Caulfeild, James
Charlemont, Vct. See Caulfeild, James
Charleroi (France):
Conway and Scott visit, 39. 536
Charles, St. See Borromeo, Carlo
Charles V (1500–58), K. of Spain 1516–56; Holy
Roman Emperor 1519–58:
abdication of: 2. 46; should never have been
repented by him, 23. 554–5; shows his
ambition, 20. 449
anecdotes of reign of, 34. 65
François I's meeting with, 35. 423n
HW detests, 3. 318
HW tries to dissuade Robertson from writing
on, 15. 50, 125
health of, gout, 23. 555
helmet of, not bought by HW, 15. 19
Henry VIII and, in picture, 1. 305
——'s ambassador to, 14. 116n
Hume's friends magnify Rousseau quarrel to
level of, 41. 51
Japhet, Don, incompatible with, 41. 154
López de Gómara's account of, 15. 67–8
Malta's grant from, 20. 406
retort of, 33. 503
Robertson consults HW about writing on, 15.
45–6, 50, 125
——'s History of reign of, 13. 44, 28. 243
—— writing on, 15. 59
Voltaire's passage about age of, 23. 523
Wolsey's treating with, 2. 259
Wyatt ambassador to, 42. 370n
See also Robertson, William
Charles VI (1685–1740), Holy Roman Emperor 1711–40:
catafalque of, 17. 75
Corradini's candidacy opposed by, 17. 5n
councillors hold title in lifetime of, 17. 40
Craon made a prince by, 18. 298
daughter of, treated as Maria is now treated
on father's death, 24. 309–10
death of: 13. 236, 237, 17. 231, 21. 141, 24.
310, 26. 10; Florentine mourning for, may
be repeated for Maria Theresa, 25. 102n;
Lucca first told of, 17. 134; Pomfret, Cts
of, does not recognize, 19. 53; Tuscan
neutrality maintained after, 21. 112
Flanders said to have been left by, to younger
daughter, 18. 331
Francis I commands armies of, 37. 97n

Frederick II assumes Silesian loan or mortgage of, 17. 483, 20. 348n
history of, 42. 494
Maguire enters service of, 17. 420
obsequies planned for, at Florence, 30. 8–9
peace of 1736 with, 17. 446
Rinaldo of Modena's opposition from, 40. 18n
Whigs offer bribes to ministers of, 7. 354
Charles VII, Holy Roman Emperor. See Charles
Albert
Charles I (1600–49), K. of England 1625–49:
Aberdeen magistrates put low price on Jamesone's full-length of, 40. 267
added to Gloucester Cross, 15. 204n
adornments for horse of, made into bed, 32.
325
adulation demanded by, from Presbyterians
as well as bishops, 23. 100
Ancram, E. of, gives 'Rembrandt's Mother' to,
40. 108n, 43. 59
Anecdotes of Painting the best defence of,
16. 152
artistic taste of, better than his literary taste,
as shown in patronage of Bernini and
Quarles, 41. 191
attempt to remove, from roll of martyrs, 6.
146
Barker bitter against, 1. 362n
Barry includes, in allegorical painting, 29.
300
Bate, physician to, 36. 140n
biographers of, usually fall in love with him,
32. 340
Capel objects to measures against, 16. 139
cards played on Sunday by, at Mildmay's, 31.
437
Carew's positions at Court of, 40. 357
catalogue of pictures of, see Catalogue and
Description . . .
chalice used at last sacrament of, in Portland
collection, 9. 114
Church of England regards George III as,
36. 221
Clarendon praises conjugal affection of, 16.
32
collection of: catalogue of, see Catalogue and
Description of King Charles the First's
Capital Collection, A; James IV's portrait
formerly in, 16. 382; Leonardo da Vinci
drawings supposedly in, 12. 263; pictures
from, bought by Cárdenas, 16. 154–5; pictures from, in Spain, 16. 179; Raphael
cartoons in, 16. 147n; Titian's painting at
Escurial formerly in, 16. 168
committee headed by, 16. 151n
Court established by, at York, 28. 466
Critical Review's defence of, 13. 30n
Cromwell's descendants intermarry with those
of, 33. 443, 37. 186n
daughter of, 1. 30n, 7. 335, 15. 191
Desmond, Cts of, dies in reign of, 40. 109
educational progress a credit to, 16. 152
Eglisham's petition to, 43. 186

Elizabeth's tyranny merely continued by, **35.** 214

execution of: **1.** 8, 8n, **28.** 175n; Quin's witticism on, **29.** 34; verses allude to, **13.** 94, **30.** 126; warrant for, hung by HW at his bedside, **9.** 197

Faithorne's print of, **35.** 346

Falkland's attitude towards, defended by HW, **40.** 137

family of, in Hollar's view of Richmond Palace, **16.** 74

Fox's ancestor, **6.** 24

French parliamentary magistrate writes paper which would not be permitted by, **39.** 23

George III advised to imitate, **28.** 378n

——'s ministers address him as if he were, **22.** 302

Glamorgan empowered by, to enlist Irish and foreign Roman Catholics, **40.** 138

Gloucester besieged by, **1.** 341n

Goodwin defends proceedings against, **16.** 65n

Grey a judge of, **1.** 8n

Gustav III, an usurper, must sympathize with descendant of, **25.** 455–6

HW dates letters by martyrdom of, **33.** 383

HW declines offer of heel piece of boot of, **28.** 338, 339

HW does not consider, a good king because a good collector, **16.** 158

HW impartial towards, **15.** 94, 109

HW jokes about descendants of, **19.** 71

HW jokes with Selwyn about, **30.** 121

HW owns portrait of, **15.** 190

HW ridicules alleged virtues of reign of, **25.** 605

HW's attitude to, criticized, **34.** 243

HW's letter might have been written in time of, **25.** 15

HW's palliation of, **34.** 103

HW's severity towards, **2.** 189

Henry VIII's jewel depicting Bosworth Field perhaps owned by, **42.** 289

Herbert attends, at York, **16.** 5

Herbert of Chepstow would not have been called by, to Parliament, **40.** 130

Herbert of Chirbury forsakes, **40.** 132, **41.** 270

High Church party reveres, **15.** 27–8

Hume's life of, praised, **15.** 328

inventory of jewels given by, to Infanta Maria, **1.** 58

James I calls, 'baby,' **15.** 340

——'s letters to, **15.** 339–42

——'s psalms printed by order of, **16.** 366

Jamesone leaves portrait of, to E. of Rothes, **40.** 285

—— paints, while wearing hat, **40.** 264, 267

Junius papers could not have been written before imprisonment of, at Carisbrooke, **23.** 165

knives and forks belonging to, **2.** 12, 13, 14

(?) Knole's associations with, **33.** 223

Lilly's observations on, **16.** 152

lived on site of Queensberry House, **11.** 152

lords join, at Oxford, **40.** 131

Louis XVI's exile might be like that of, **39.** 468

Macaulay, Mrs, abuses, **2.** 210n

martyrdom of: **13.** 94n; and Cromwell's descendant, **7.** 18; **33.** 444; observed, **31.** 437; verses on, **13.** 94

Matson visited by, **1.** 341, **34.** 7, **35.** 152

Mayerne introduces Petitot to, **40.** 238

—— physician to, **16.** 67n

medals of, **16.** 49, 50, 54, 150, 157n, **40.** 238n

memorials to, at Matson, **1.** 341

might have kept his head, had he not 'sultanized,' **23.** 386

More, Hannah, compared with, **31.** 342

Morton, Lady, governess to children of, **30.** 370

Murray, tutor and secretary to, **40.** 285n

niece of, **1.** 182n

Norwich the wit of Court of, **23.** 308

Olivier's verses on birth of 5th child of, **42.** 44

pearl from ear of, in Portland collection, **9.** 114

picture given to, **1.** 329n

pictures of reign of, at Queensberry's at Richmond, **33.** 541

plaster cast of face of, **1.** 344

poems printed in reign of, **15.** 265n

Poor Knights of Windsor loyal to, **28.** 135

portraits of: **1.** 180n; HW owns, **15.** 190; in armour, **30.** 370; in Bodleian Library, **9.** 114; Jamesone's, **40.** 264, 285; Van Dyck's, **2.** 169n, **16.** 166; verses on, **16.** 48

portrait of Mrs Wright modelling head of, **29.** 33

portrait resembling, in red, **40.** 283

portraits of two children of, attributed to Van Dyck, **30.** 149

prerogative enforced by, more than by Louis XVI, **11.** 28

present era resembles that of, **23.** 142, 170–1

priest reprieved by, provoking Parliament to refuse to pay army, **42.** 235

print of chimney sweeper of, **28.** 47

prints of, **16.** 166, **40.** 236

prints of descendants of, **40.** 236

prints of sufferings of, **17.** 358

proclamation of, **9.** 224

Quin's witticism on, **29.** 34

rebellion against: **17.** 346; started 100 years before attempted impeachment of Sir Robert Walpole, **20.** 315n

reign of, mentioned, **15.** 77

Richmond, D. of, approves of execution of, **7.** 18

Richmond Palace favoured by, **11.** 152n

Richmond Park enlarged by, **11.** 98n

Roubiliac's bust of, placed by Selwyn at Matson, **30.** 121n

Scotland visited by, **40.** 264

Shuckburgh and, **2.** 75–6n

Simon engraves medals for, **40.** 238n

[Charles I, *continued*]

sons of, at Matson, **1**. 341, **34**. 7, **35**. 152

spaniels of breed of, *see under* Spaniel

Spanish marriage proposed for, **15**. 339–42

Spanish visit of, **32**. 325

statue of, **1**. 342n, **13**. 86

Steenwyk worked for, **16**. 155n

Strafford and, **6**. 430

taste of, deficient, **34**. 84

third son of, born at Oatlands, **34**. 7

trial of, **29**. 171

true English retired to America under, **32**. 404

Van Dyck granted annuity by, **16**. 35n

——'s portraits of, **2**. 169n, **16**. 166

——'s portraits of followers of, convert Dodd and Whaley to his cause, **40**. 12

victory would have rendered, despotic, **23**. 106

warrant for execution of, **9**. 197

wife of, **1**. 180n, **19**. 397

Wynn holds office under, **41**. 160n

York Minister organ removed by, **16**. 47

*See also under* Dalrymple, Sir David: *Memorials and Letters . . . Reign of Charles I*

Charles II (1630–85), K. of England 1660–85:

Abercorn had Bedchamber position with, **42**. 89

*Account of the Preservation of King Charles II after the Battle of Worcester, An*, **1**. 214, 223n

agent of, in France, **15**. 103

anecdotes of, from Sandwich's memoirs, mislaid, **15**. 132

Arlington, adviser of, **28**. 72n

atheist and bigot, **28**. 72

Barker bitter against, **1**. 362n

Bate, physician to, **36**. 140n

Brisbane employed by, **15**. 103n

Buckingham minister to, **28**. 72n

builds palace, **16**. 71n

Burford House conveyed by, to Nell Gwyn, **1**. 350n

*Character* of, by M. of Normanby, **1**. 223n

character of, shown in Dalrymple's *Memoirs*, **28**. 67

Clarendon omits conversion of, **16**. 33

——'s partiality to, **16**. 34

Clifford wears armour because he accompanied, at Battle of Worcester, **35**. 148

Cole mentions, **10**. 336

conversion of, in papers left in strong-box, **31**. 323

Conway papers end in reign of, **9**. 223

coronation of, **1**. 52n

costumes of reign of, for quadrilles, **32**. 102

Court of, **32**. 8

daughter of, **35**. 138

descendants of, **1**. 375, **9**. 307, **18**. 450, **21**. 67, 285, **25**. 508, **28**. 110n, **33**. 387

Dixon said to have been keeper of pictures in Closet of, **41**. 97

Dover visited by, **9**. 267n

England might have suffered from, **23**. 106

—— 'sold' by, **35**. 364

escape of: **1**. 197n; in Fuller's paintings, **42**. 380

father of his people because he begot so many, **24**. 393

Fauconberg, privy councillor of, **1**. 182n

Fitzroy, Hon. and Mrs George, descended from, **25**. 508

French domination of, **18**. 247, **28**. 174n

gardener of, **2**. 200, 239, **12**. 258, **14**. 120n, **29**. 45n

good humour of, **32**. 212

Grafton, descendant of, **31**. 323, **32**. 264

granddaughter of, **9**. 307n

great-granddaughter of: **10**. 129n; weds footman's son, **18**. 450; worthy of him, **25**. 508

Gwyn, Nell, mentions, **1**. 350

HW jokes about, **9**. 407

HW quotes motto from medal of, **18**. 424

HW ridicules alleged virtues of reign of, **25**. 605

HW's lines on, praised by Gray, **14**. 36

HW's portrait of, **15**. 190, **29**. 45

HW would decorate Ragley salon with portraits of, **9**. 223

Hamilton, James, to have been given peerage by, **42**. 89

head of, on earthenware dish, **42**. 22n

Heath's *Brief Chronicle* printed soon after restoration of, **31**. 437

Highlanders refuse to attend, to Worcester, **19**. 107

Hollar drawing-teacher to, **14**. 96n

——'s view of Richmond Palace depicts, **16**. 74

illegitimate son of, **1**. 350n, **4**. 114n, **11**. 347n, **16**. 11n

*imprimatur* needed in later years of, **16**. 68

James I's book reprinted by command of, **16**. 365

James II's journal illuminates reign of, **38**. 479

Keppels descended from, **9**. 307n, **21**. 285

King's Plate race founded by, **13**. 89n

knavery of, revealed by Dalrymple, **32**. 105

Knight, John, serjeant-surgeon to, **14**. 82

Lauderdale intimate with, **28**. 72n

Lely's portraits of beauties of reign of, at Windsor, **15**. 96n, **30**. 326n

letter of, transcribed by Dalrymple, **15**. 103–4

letters between Louis XIV and, **28**. 68

Louis XIV 'buys' British isles from, **18**. 247

Macaulay, Mrs, abuses, **2**. 210n

Matson visited by, **1**. 341, **33**. 7

medals struck under, **40**. 239

mistresses of, **1**. 350, **3**. 39n, **9**. 16n, **10**. 106n, **15**. 158n, **16**. 301n, 323n

Montrose's attempt to restore, **16**. 7n

name of, corrected, **43**. 362

Nonsuch Palace placed in trust by, **2**. 150n

Norwich's wit not appreciated by Court of, **25**. 308

Oglethorpe, Mrs, laundress and seamstress to, **37**. 353n

old woman describes farting at dance in time of, **37**. 55

Penderels shelter, **10**. 105n

portraits of: **15**. 190, 191n; at Hinchingbrooke, **40**. 284; at Navestock, **9**. 244; with Rose the gardener, **2**. 200, 239, **29**. 45

Powell's estates restored by, **16**. 159n

print of, **1**. 180, **16**. 74n, **40**. 237

queen dowager of, **19**. 494–5

Raphael cartoons owned by, **16**. 168n

restoration of: **16**. 61n; Walpole, Sir Robert, first commoner a K.G. since, **22**. 27

Scots force, to sign covenant at Scone, **33**. 163

Scottish Kirk lectured, before battle of Worcester, **23**. 386

Shaftesbury characterized by, **16**. 368

Simon a medallist in time of, **1**. 319n

statues of: at Gloucester, **40**. 44; at Lichfield, **9**. 294

Stratford's tragedy includes, **29**. 224

thought too little to be a Protestant, too much to be a true Catholic, **16**. 34

Tiberius said to resemble, **16**. 48, 52

Twickenham Manor lease granted by, to E. of Rochester, **42**. 417n

'tyrant,' compared with Louis XIV, **32**. 105

unconditional restoration of, endangered British constitution, **31**. 324

Van der Borcht employed by, **1**. 24n

Waller's answer to, **3**. 81

warrant of, for barons' coronets, **30**. 153

Westbrook built in reign of, **16**. 196n

Whitehead's lines on, praised by HW, **29**. 281

Winchester Palace designed for, by Wren, **35**. 249

witticism by, on Wolley's nonsense suiting his parishioners, **22**. 57, **24**. 52, **34**. 426, **35**. 496

witty but unfeeling, **33**. 223n

Wren's gifts from, **40**. 349

Charles III (879–929) 'le Simple,' K. of France 893–923;
title of, **34**. 76

Charles V (1337–80), K. of France 1364–80:
astrologer to, **2**. 195n

Christine de Pisan's life of, **31**. 245

Doumenil has portrait of, **7**. 313

Joseph II may be like, **6**. 447

name of, **2**. 104

*Paris sauvé* deals with minority of, **5**. 379

Charles VI (1368–1422), K. of France 1380–1422:
Buchan created Constable of France by, **15**. 182n

carried hawk on fist, **14**. 77

Charles the Bad defeated by, **4**. 385n

HW finds sketch of, in Vertue's MSS, **42**. 217

Harcourt serves spice-plate to, **35**. 486

horrors in reign of, **33**. 196, **34**. 57

(?) Mary Stuart's prayer book illuminated in reign of, **7**. 359

René I lived in reign of, **16**. 156

Charles VII (1403–61), K. of France 1422–61:
age of, in 1444, **14**. 76

chancellor of, said to have been hanged, **39**. 151

Choiseul as gay as, **4**. 327

Doumenil has portrait of, **7**. 313

entry of, into Paris, **14**. 78

*Histoire* of, owned by Mme du Deffand, **8**. 34

horrors in reign of, **33**. 196

John, D. of Burgundy, murdered by, **12**. 267

Margaret of Anjou entertained by, **14**. 71

(?) Mary Stuart's prayer book illuminated in reign of, **7**. 359

René I lived in reign of, **16**. 156

Charles VIII (1470–98), K. of France 1483–98:
fleur-de-lis said to have been granted to, by Medici family, **20**. 415

Gudin's poem on, **4**. 243

Henry VII aided by, **4**. 4

Charles IX (1550–74), K. of France 1560–74:
believed himself warranted to slaughter, **34**. 161

Doumenil has drawing of, **7**. 313

effigy of, at St-Denis, **39**. 203

monument erected by, **13**. 163n

Charles (-Philippe) X (1757–1836), Comte d'Artois, K. of France 1824–30:
American service wanted by, **33**. 399n

anecdote about eldest son of, **33**. 310

appearance and dancing of, **32**. 255, 264

Bastard, chancellor to, **7**. 442

Besenval allowed to visit, in exile, **7**. 32

Bourbon, Duc and Duchesse de, reconciled with, **7**. 30

Bourbon, Duc de, fights with, over insult to Duchesse, **7**. 29–31, 32

Bourbon family continued by, **32**. 264

Breton expedition made by, **12**. 156

bull-fight attended by, **25**. 337n

Calonne's mission from, **11**. 310n

capitainerie obtained by, **6**. 397

Choiseul to be visited by, at Chanteloup, **6**. 445, 450–1

Choisy visited by, after Louis XV's death, **6**. 50

Coigny, Duc de, may serve, **5**. 220

copy of letter supposedly written by, to Duc de Bourbon, sent to HW, **25**. 329

Cossé ball attended by, **6**. 162

Crillon to be advised by, at Gibraltar, **25**. 300

Crussol, capt. of the Guard to, **7**. 30

—— second to, in duel, **7**. 30

dances at ball in honour of Dauphin's marriage, **4**. 410

Du Barry, Mme, might be restored by, **32**. 266

Eszterházy allowed to visit, in exile, **7**. 32

500,000 livres set on head of, **11**. 39

Flanders visited by, **12**. 118

[Charles (-Philippe) X, *continued*]

floating batteries reported by, to have been demolished, 25. 325

foolish jaunt made by, to see projected bombardment of Gibraltar, 25. 320.

'genius' of, 10. 291

Gibraltar siege begins with arrival of, 25. 313n

HW describes, 10. 291, 35. 113

HW hopes Mann will be able to feast on arm of, 25. 327

HW presented to, 7. 266

HW sees, dine, 7. 330

health of: 6. 418; inoculation, 6. 58, 62, 64, 66, 69, 35. 422

Hénin to serve, 5. 220

Holyrood House the lodging of, 34. 213

horse race of, 39. 270

horse-racing losses of, 6. 418

household of, 5. 296, 347

Italians expect, to return to Paris *colle trombe in sacco*, 25. 334

La Marck, Comtesse de, aided by, in finding another house, 6. 398

La Vauguyon, governor of, 5. 179

—— first gentleman of Bedchamber to, 3. 258n

'Le roi Pepin' owned by, 24. 266n

Louis XV could give crown to, instead of to Louis XVI, 23. 304

Louis XVI accompanied by, to National Assembly, 11. 40

—— exiles, to Choisy, 7. 31, 32

—— has letter from, in Bourbon affair, 7. 32

—— treated familiarly by, 32. 226

Louis XVIII's proclamation to be conveyed by, 12. 151n

Marie-Josèphe's funeral oration attended by, 7. 318

Marly visited by, 6. 62

marriage of: 5. 337, 342, 412; celebrations for, 5. 418, 421, 425, 427; planned, 23. 465

mob embraces, 11. 215n

Montyon chancellor to, 7. 442

Nassau allowed to visit, in exile, 7. 32

Paulmy's library sold to, 4. 264n

Piedmont, Princess of, dances with, 7. 343n

Polignac may serve, 5. 220

preparations at Cadiz to receive, to celebrate conquest of Gibraltar, 25. 334

Quaker, with hat on, dines with, 24. 53, 32. 212

'ridiculous flippancy' of, 25. 337

St-Germain château (new) acquired by, 6. 397

St Petersburg allegedly visited by, 11. 355

son of, 11. 298n, 12. 156n

Swiss Guards given to, 5. 155n, 161, 167, 209

Vauban accompanies, to St Petersburg, 7. 139n

Vaudreuil friend of, 4. 410n

Versailles to be visited by, 6. 450

Voltaire's *Irène* attended by, 7. 30

wife attributes her amour to ill-usage by, 36. 220, 223

wife of, 11. 96n

William, P., writes about, 12. 118

wishes to visit England, 33. 399

'Charles X,' of France:

Bourbon, Cardinal de, styled as, by the League, 25. 482, 520

Charles II (1332–87) the Bad, K. of Navarre:

daughter of, 2. 257n

defeated by Charles VI, 4. 385n

Sedaine's play about, 4. 384–5

Charles II (1661–1700), K. of Spain:

portrait of, as 'ridiculous boy,' 40. 283

will of, 28. 296n

Charles III (1716–88), K. of Naples (as Charles IV *or* VII) 1735–59, K. of Spain 1759–88:

abdication of, rumoured, 39. 237

accession of, to Spanish throne, 21. 321

Admiralty court accused by, of confirming unjust Minorcan sentence, 25. 189

Aix treaty set aside by paper of, 21. 323

Aix treaty's Neapolitan arrangements opposed by, 21. 264n

alarmed, 18. 3, 19. 237

Albertini told by, to thank George II for Gray's promotion, 21. 160

Algiers demolished by, 24. 118, 122, 39. 420

Allens might be seized by, as hostages, 19. 57–8

Almódovar tells England of intention of, to join France, 24. 495

American independence not to be acknowledged by, 28. 448, 33. 60

American mercantile agents may have been received by, 24. 476

Aranjuez the retirement-place of, 7. 312, 39. 64

army of: defeated, 18. 486–91; may be led by him against Austrians, 18. 419–20; *see also* Naples: army of; Spain: army of

Austrian army may aim at, 18. 336

Baiardi dismissed by, 21. 142n

——'s *prodromo* distributed by, 21. 142

Balchen's fleet might intimidate, 24. 506

barks and galleys sent by, to intercept German troops in Adriatic, 19. 220

Bayeu and Maella, painters to, 16. 170

behaved better at Naples than in Spain, 21. 560

Benedict XIV meets, at Monte Cavallo, 23. 389n

—— obeyed by, in restoring commerce with Malta, 20. 406n

—— receives, 18. 533

——'s relations with, may be investigated by Leghorn squadron, 18. 67

Botta told by minister of, to observe strict neutrality, 21. 270–1

Bourbons exemplified by, 21. 442

brother's marriage regulated by, 36. 307–8

brother to meet, at Lerici, **21.** 280

Caffarelli said to have been ordered by, to sing at Naples, **19.** 439

Caserta volume required by, to be completed, **21.** 379

Castello di Sangro occupied by, **18.** 438

cavalry of, to return through Tuscany, **19.** 297

(?) Clement XII acknowledged, as Great Prince of Tuscany, **22.** 406

Clement XIII implores, not to expel Jesuits, **22.** 517

——'s answer to, offends Madrid, **22.** 532

——'s letter from, about shipping Jesuits, **22.** 509n

—— to compliment, when he passes through papal states on way to Spain, **21.** 280

Clement XIV receives harsh letter from, about Jesuits, **23.** 214

—— sets example to, in lack of bigotry, **23.** 436

—— soothes, **23.** 190

——'s promise to suppress Jesuits might be produced by, **23.** 527

—— to influence Louis XV against, **23.** 372–3, 431

confessor of, a 'bad man,' **25.** 33n

Conway as secretary of state might bully, **39.** 11

Córdoba does not satisfy, **25.** 344

—— ordered by, to destroy Geary's fleet and take Gibraltar, **25.** 82

courier sent by, to Llano with instructions, **23.** 446

courtiers told to divert, on wife's death, **21.** 442

Crillon ordered by, to assault Gibraltar, **25.** 300

daughter of: alarmed by prophecies of his death, **24.** 50; apprehensive about his sanity, **22.** 438; intended by him to be Joseph II's wife, **21.** 323; loved by him, **25.** 43

daughter's letters from: about destruction of floating batteries, **25.** 329; about pacific intentions, **24.** 476, 480; about Spain's opposition to French policy, **24.** 375; contradicted by son, **25.** 32–3; deceptive, **24.** 498; freely discuss international affairs, **24.** 467; must be delivered by Spanish minister, **25.** 334; unintentionally untruthful, **25.** 334

death of, **34.** 33

declaration of war by: against Pitt, **21.** 559; brought by courier to Naples, **22.** 5

delays over Jesuits unendurable to, **23.** 414

Doria to seek aid from, **19.** 345

Du Tillot removed by, from Parma, **23.** 324

edict of, against Clement XIII's brief, **23.** 10–11

engineers blamed by, for loss of floating batteries, **25.** 329

England and France get ultimatum from, **24.** 458n, 463n

England assured by, of neutrality, **21.** 347

—— favourably regarded by, **21.** 551, 551–2

—— has opportunity to be in good graces of, **21.** 323–4

—— hated by: **33.** 103; ever since he was at Naples, **23.** 349–50

—— may expect war declaration from, **23.** 245, **24.** 489

—— receives rescript from, **24.** 482–3

—— should be told by, to dismiss the French clergy, **23.** 420

—— will humbly sue to, after railing at him, **39.** 333

English attack on Spanish ship will offend, **24.** 306

English bombers to influence, **18.** 32

English captain addresses, in English, **18.** 461

English capture of barks offends, **19.** 56–7

English disliked by, **19.** 77

English fleet demands withdrawal of troops by, **18.** 15

English fleet may threaten son of, at Naples, **38.** 186

English fleet suspected by, of South American objectives, **25.** 339n

English harmony with, predicted by Sir James Gray, **21.** 275

English merchants fear retaliation from, for Marciana outrage, **18.** 28

English newspaper letter on, nearly chokes Masserano, **23.** 230

English peace ratified by, **23.** 277

English peace with, rumoured, **25.** 145

English Royal Marriage Act imitated by, **36.** 307

English sea-captains detested by, **18.** 123

English war reluctantly declared by, **24.** 483

English war sought by, **5.** 355

escapes from Velletri in slippers, **35.** 52

Europe's comfort depends on mood of, about war, **24.** 480

Falkland Islands restored by, to George III, **23.** 506

—— still claimed by, **23.** 282

family compact forces, to join France, **24.** 495

Farnese palace at Caprarola owned by, **17.** 389n

Ferdinand VI may dethrone, **19.** 307

—— succeeded by, **21.** 363

Ferdinand of Naples allegedly told by Louis XVI and, to exclude Russian fleet, **25.** 616n

——'s letter from, about war intentions, **24.** 489

Ferdinand of Parma's rift with, to be mediated by Clement XIV, **23.** 473n

—— submits to, **23.** 518

fleet of, said to be preventing Russian fleet from going to Greek islands, **25.** 415

Florida Blanca, prime minister to, **11.** 54n

Fogliani accompanies, **20.** 458

[Charles III, *continued*]

—— minister of, to Holland, **18.** 183

France advises, to use elsewhere the troops held at Gibraltar, **25.** 345

—— and Austria give up Naples and Sicily to, **21.** 280n

France deceives, into thinking he can get Portugal, **22.** 99

—— has no leisure to join, **23.** 283

—— offends, by American treaty, **24.** 375n

French alliance will not be abandoned by, despite bribes, **25.** 46

French ambassador to Naples quiets fears of, **21.** 275

French conduct may be resented by, **25.** 147

French policy condemned by, **33.** 10–11

French pressure on, to spare Jesuits, **23.** 372n

French victory will not comfort, **25.** 152

Gages to receive troops from, **19.** 15

Genoa's possible aid from, **19.** 65, 345

George III said to be favourably regarded by, **21.** 539n

——'s negotiations with, **21.** 544, **39.** 479

Gibraltar defeat may not stop persistence of, in the impossible, **33.** 358

——'s capture by: said to be possible, **25.** 416; still to be pursued, **25.** 345; to wipe off affront of naval defeat. **25.** 149

——'s fate will regulate conduct of, **25;** 300

——'s relief upsets, **25.** 152, 337, 339

—— straits might be closed by, to Turkey's foes, **25.** 415n

Girifalco's punishment wished by, **35.** 434

Gray, Sir James, complimented by, on supposed transfer to Spain, **21.** 159–60

—— given audience by, at Caserta, **20.** 370n

—— liked by, **21.** 556–560n

—— makes Anglo-Neapolitan commercial treaty with, **20.** 458

HW and Mann know more about, than about each other's friends, **23.** 260

HW calls 'mule,' **25.** 337, 358, 366

HW expects, to make separate peace, **29.** 138

HW forgives, for hatred to Jesuits, **23.** 452

HW jokes about: destroying English thieves, **39.** 420–1; drinking glass of wine and talking botany with Squillace, **39.** 61

HW not harmed by, at Naples, **35.** 11

HW's gout does not concern, **35.** 331

HW's name put by, on list for future Herculaneum and Caserta volumes, **22.** 547

HW will give SH imprints to, in return for Herculaneum book, **21.** 131

hackney to be presented by, **18.** 462

Halifax defends, against accusations of being pro-French, **38.** 233

Hamilton's assurances about, vain, **24.** 498

Havana's capture may affect, **22.** 77n, 83

health of: sick, **22.** 414–15; smallpox, **23.** 238

Herculaneum publication of: books reserved by, for English, **22.** 422n; distribution of,

restricted by him, **21.** 142, **22.** 35, 457; required by him to be completed, **21.** 131n, 379; research on, patronized by him, **14.** 123n; unlikely to be completed after his departure for Spain, **21.** 363

——'s site bought by, **13.** 222n

*Hermione's* capture silences, for two days, **22.** 51, 89

hunting preferred by, to commercial negotiations, **20.** 458

inoculation opposed by, on religious grounds, **24.** 330

insanity threatens, **21.** 442, **22.** 89, 438

'instrument to chastise the pride of England,' **21.** 564

Jesuits not permitted by, to live in any community, **24.** 118

——' landing in Corsica arranged by, with Genoa and France, **22.** 535n

——' only great enemy, from fear for his life, **24.** 106

—— pensioned by, **22.** 516

——' suppression by: entirely due to his efforts, **23.** 518; 'foolish,' **23.** 514; may relieve him, **23.** 473; must be total, to satisfy him, **23.** 446

—— would have seized or imprisoned, **22.** 518–19

Johnstone said to offer Florida and Gibraltar to, **25.** 46n

Joseph II and Maria Theresa receive message from, about Parma, **23.** 446

Leopold convinces, that English war is a mistake, **25.** 58

—— esteemed by, **25.** 43

——'s announcement not awaited by, in giving credentials to Viviani, **22.** 350

less likely to be bullied, than when he was at Naples, **22.** 70

Llano sent by, to Parma, **23.** 445

Lobkowitz's failure to defeat, may not be repeated, **19.** 237

—— tries to seize, at Velletri, **18.** 487, 489–90, 504

Louis XV reluctant to aid, **23.** 277

—— said to be about to meet, **21.** 283, 289

—— said to influence, about Papal election, **17.** 20–1

——'s relations with, **23.** 277, 414

Louis XVI does not please, **25.** 21

—— would not be allowed by, to restore Jesuits, **24.** 9

Madrid insurrection frightens, **22.** 509

—— not to be visited by, **22.** 414–15

—— will be treated by, with great condescension, **22.** 441

Malta's dispute with, **20.** 405

Maltese claims of, based on Urban I's bull to Roger, Count of Sicily, **20.** 406n

manifesto of, sent by Mann to Newcastle, **18.** 420

Mann bullies, with English fleet, 19. 71
—— persuades Leopold and Maria Louisa to urge, to cease supporting France against England, 25. 43–4
—— refused permission by, to copy paintings by 'veiling,' 20. 328n
—— thanked by, 19. 383–4
Maria Amalia of Parma's quarrel with, over dismissal of Llano and Du Tillot from Parma, 23. 412n, 444–6
Maria Theresa asked by, for another bribe for Ferdinand, 22. 564
Martin's ultimatum to, 18. 37–9, 42–3, 22. 564
Masserano's declaration might not be ratified by, 23. 269
Mathews sends message to, 18. 461
——'s treatment of, unjustifiable, 18. 195
may become P. of Asturias, 19. 307
Mengs favoured by, 16. 170
Messina's plague elicits isolation orders from, 18. 252
Mexican revolts would be as good as guarantee by, of peace, 24. 384
Minorca called by, a nest of Jews and rabble, 25. 189
Moñino threatens papacy with vengeance of, if Jesuits are not suppressed, 23. 428, 430–1, 24. 115
Monte Cassino may be visited by, 18. 447
Montemar's preference of, to Don Philip, said to irritate their mother, 18. 5
Montmorin's recall wanted by, 24. 375n
named Carlo VII of Naples in papal bull, 17. 20n
Naples not to be left by, 19. 15
—— to be reserved by, for his second son, 21. 270
—— unlikely to be left by, to mercy of France and Vienna, 21. 280
—— will not be relinquished by, to brother, 21. 264, 270
naval victory mentioned by, 13. 211
Neapolitans' demand secret conference with, 21. 330
—— not trusted by, 18. 446
nephew of, 5. 214n
neutrality to be observed by, even when on Spanish throne, 21. 271, 22. 5–6
new regiments raised by, 18. 542
Norris, Sir John, may be disliked by, 17. 145
obstinacy of: English peace may be prevented by, 22. 99; forces France to aid Spain against Gibraltar, 25. 292; humbled, 23. 253; in wanting Gibraltar, defeated, 25. 358, 366; Jesuits suppressed by, 23. 472, 506, 518; will not admit that English war is a mistake, 25. 58
Palafox's canonization advocated by, 23. 123n
Parma gets orders from, 23. 324, 444–6, 518–19
Philip, Don, to be met by, at Lerici, 21. 264n

Pitt almost tossed in blanket by, 22. 276
Pitt and Madrid might force, to have a pro-British ministry, 22. 441n
Pius VI may persuade, to admit Jesuits, 24. 106
—— would have released Jesuits but for, 24. 115
Porto Longone owned by, 18. 28
Portuguese attack may provoke, 24. 224
Portuguese royal family related to, 21. 560, 22. 49
pragmatic sanction issued by, 3. 294n
proclaimed king at Madrid, 21. 323n
Revilla recalled by, from Parma, 23. 446
rioters' demands met by, 39. 61, 63
Rodney's victory must vex, 25. 21
rôle of, La Passion des Jésuits, 5. 315
Roman pilgrimage expected from, after deliverance from Austrians, 18. 519
Rome visited by, 18. 525, 532, 20. 43
San Roque encampment helps England more than, 25. 72
Sardinian successes in Lombardy alarm, 19. 237
Sicily may become refuge of, 18. 453
Silva sent by, to Mann, 19. 57
sister and nieces fought by, with no compassion for Lisbon earthquake, 22. 49, 38. 186
soldiers deserting from, form banditti, 13. 221
son may be put in place of, 22. 519
son receives Naples from, 21. 270, 322, 333, 335
son's incapacity judged by, 21. 322–3, 329–30, 333, 347
son will not be compelled by, to sign family pact, 22. 6
Spain displeased with, 25. 32
——'s failure to bribe Sardinia disappoints, 17. 145
—— will be approached by, by sea to avoid meeting Louis XV, 21. 318
Spanish fleet ordered home by, 24. 530
Spanish fleet to escort, from Naples, 21. 333
Spanish throne to be ascended by, 21. 264, 270, 275, 335
Spanish troops to be sent by, to Naples, 21. 335
Squillace dismissed by, 7. 312
—— prime minister to, 22. 414n
successor of, might reinstate Jesuits, 23. 472
Tanucci a professor at Pisa when first met by, 21. 495n
—— in confidence of, 21. 330
—— reluctant to inform, that Maria Josepha's engagement to Archduke Joseph is broken, 21. 323n
—— says that neutrality is aim of, 22. 5–6
——'s dissertation on Italian kingship done on arrival of, as Tuscany's heir, 21. 494–5

[Charles III, *continued*]

tapestries at Pitti palace shot at by, **23**. 238, 241, 242, 254

tapestry horse may be mounted by, to declare war, **23**. 245

tapestry horse said to have been flogged by, **23**. 230–1, 254

tenacious of his word, **24**. 118

Testa sent to Malta by, as ecclesiastical visitor, **20**. 405n

thousands of lives sacrificed by, **22**. 81

troops held at Gibraltar are called a 'blockade' to please, **25**. 345

troops of: may join Gages's army, **18**. 405; withdraw from Spanish army, **17**. 291n; withdrawn by him from confines of Naples, **21**. 275

Tuscan claims abandoned by, on his daughter's betrothal to its heir, **22**. 87n

Tuscan throne was to have been inherited by, **21**. 495

Tuscany exposed to, **18**. 509

—— may receive war declaration from, **19**. 65

United States recognized by, **24**. 459n

Velletri visited by, **18**. 447, 454, 487–91, 533

viceroy appointed during absence of, **18**. 420

villa of, at Portici, **13**. 222

Viviani made envoy by, **22**. 349

Wall has confidence of, **21**. 347

—— not to support England if France is preferred by, **21**. 333n

—— urges English confidence in, **21**. 347n

wife rewarded by, for son's birth, **19**. 423

Young Pretender may be set up by, in Ireland, **23**. 328

Charles IV (1748–1819), P. of the Asturias; K. of Spain 1788–1808:

claim of, to French throne, debated, **34**. 66, 76

father's throne may be given to, **22**. 519

father to be succeeded by, **21**. 322

Florida Blanca consulted by, about sending troops to aid Louis XVI, **11**. 54

forces of, make no progress in France, **12**. 53

Inquisition probably not to be relaxed by, **31**. 324

(?) Maria Louisa's letters from, contradict her father's, **25**. 33

Spanish revolution feared by, **12**. 53

Charles X (1622–60), K. of Sweden 1654–60:

reign of, interesting, **15**. 56–7

Charles XI (1655–97), K. of Sweden 1660–97:

last descendant of, **10**. 39n

reign of, interesting, **15**. 56–7

Charles XII (1682–1718), K. of Sweden 1697–1718:

Alexander the Great compared to, **20**. 477

general of, **9**. 107n

*Histoire* of, owned by Mme du Deffand, **8**. 34

Poland wanted by, to choose Stanislas I, **22**. 403n

Porquet alludes to, **4**. 325

reign of, interesting, **15**. 56–7

sister of, **17**. 255n

Stanislas profited by wars of, **22**. 404

Charles XIII (1748–1818), K. of Sweden 1809–18. *See* Karl XIII

Charles (1433–77) the Bold, D. of Burgundy:

Comines saw Edward IV and Richard III at Court of, **41**. 112–13

daughter of, **14**. 77n

Exeter and Somerset trudge after army of, **35**. 256

La Marche's account of, **42**. 192

wife of, **1**. 320n, **6**. 76n, **14**. 163n

Charles IV (1604–75), D. of Lorraine:

Elector Palatine ambushed by, **2**. 1–2

Charles (Joseph) (1745–61), archduke:

birth of, **18**. *8*, 14

Botta probably to arrange brother's succession to, **22**. 87

brother to succeed, in Tuscany, **21**. 556

death of, **21**. 556

Charles (1686–1714) de Bourbon, Duc de Berry:

wife of, **4**. 23n

Charles (1785–95), P. of France. *See* Louis XVII

Charles (1744–1836), P. of Hesse-Cassel:

Amelia, Ps, leaves legacy to, **33**. 534

——'s portrait of her grandmother perhaps left to, **42**. 180

Charles (Joseph Ignaz) (1680–1715), P.; of Lorraine:

Lunati-Visconti, Marquise de, mistress of, **20**. 351n

Charles (Alexander) (1712–80), P.; of Lorraine; army officer; gov.-gen. of the Austrian Netherlands ('Prince Charles'):

advances of, **18**. 241, **19**. 62n

Alsace may be invaded by, through Basel, **18**. 290

—— or Lorraine may be objective of, **37**. 160

Amelia, Ps, rumoured to wed, **18**. 278n

appearance of, when Conway sees him, **37**. 142

army command may be taken by, **21**. 470

army of: crosses Rhine, **18**. 466, **30**. 53n, 60; on the Neckar, **18**. 267

Austrian army under, **9**. 206n

birthday of, celebrated in Florence despite his military blunders, **19**. 451

Bohemia entered by, **18**. 528

Botta administers Brussels in absence of, **22**. 44n

Broglie defeated by, **17**. 464–5

—— pursued by, **37**. 140

brother not to permit Prague to be taken by, **18**. 58

Brown replaced by, as commander-in-chief, **21**. 95n

Brussels to be visited by, **18**. 331

Charles Albert opposed by, **18**. 234

Coigny defeats, at Weissenbert, **30**. 60n

Conti defeated by, **18**. 249

——'s baggage returned by, **37.** 137
Conway sees, at review, **37.** 141–2
courier expected from, **37.** 160
couriers proclaim victories of, **21.** 112
Cumberland, D. of, may replace, in Flanders, **19.** 324
Daun compared with, **21.** 470
defeat of: **17.** 430, 433, 454, **19.** 61, 127; falsely rumoured, **30.** 60
drunk and unintelligent, **19.** 61
Elbe crossed by, **18.** 543
Electress leaves jewels to, **18.** 171
English await arrival of, at Hanau, **18.** 276n
festival of, at Florence, **20.** 451
Flemish command given to, **19.** 288
Florentine celebrations for wedding of, **18.** 364
France might be invaded by, **18.** 285
Frederick II defeats: at Hohenfriedburg, **19.** 61–2, **35.** 58; at Sohr, **19.** 127
—— driven back by, **18.** 540
—— forces, to recross Rhine, **37.** 175–6; to retreat to Bohemia, **18.** 505
—— may be given good opportunities by, **21.** 470
—— may confer with, **17.** 465, 472
—— proposes to march against, **18.** 512n
—— said to be defeated by, **18.** 521
—— traps, at Prague, **21.** 95n
French defeated by, **17.** 457
French invasion by, would result in Spanish invasion of Tuscany, **18.** 285, 295
French moving against, from Flanders, **18.** 481
French preparing to fight, **18.** 276
French progress to be halted by, **18.** 478
French to keep, from crossing Rhine, **37.** 144
Garter should be awarded to, **18.** 245
George II chooses, to command allied army, **18.** 457n
governor-general of Austrian Netherlands, **17.** 205n
HW does not repeat news about, **18.** 494
HW laughs at campaigns of, **18.** 68
HW thinks Braunau victory of, important, **18.** 249
Hungarian troops commanded by, at Časlau, **17.** 430n
James invited by, to Vienna for Joseph II's wedding, **21.** 462
Keith defeated by, near Rusyn, **21.** 109n
Königseck visited by, **17.** 205
Laschi, Filippo, in service of, **20.** 41n
Liechtenstein may be replaced by, **19.** 324
Lobkowitz joined by, to defeat the French, **17.** 451n
Lorraine threatened by, from the Rhine, **18.** 457
—— unlikely to be threatened by, **18.** 297
Louis XV to have driven, across Rhine, **18.** 505

Maria Anna and, make ceremonial entry into Brussels, **18.** 2n
—— to marry, **18.** 330
Maria Theresa appoints, to command army in Low Countries, **18.** 331n
—— induces Francis I to give command to, despite incompetence, **21.** 96n
military success of, makes brother's interference unpopular, **18.** 2
Naples may be reward of, for conquering it, **18.** 336
Neckar reached by, **18.** 267
Pernklö commands army of, **37.** 159
Prague may be taken by, **17.** 465, 472
—— townspeople conciliated by, **18.** 512
print or book of, to be sent by Lort to HW, **16.** 195–6
Prussian retreat intercepted by, **21.** 109
Puebla ordered by Serbelloni and Daun to join, near Prague, **21.** 96n
retreats to Reichenau, **19.** 62n
Rhine crossed by, **18.** 466, **30.** 53, 60, **37.** 158–9, 175
Rhine crossing of: encourages Florentines, **18.** 478; fruitless, **18.** 481, **30.** 60
Rhine not yet crossed by, **18.** 276n, 297, 311
Rhine recrossed by, **18.** 505
sale of collections of, **16.** 195–6n
Saxe prevented from preventing, from driving Frederick II from Bohemia, **18.** 526
Simbach and other victories by, **37.** 137
Theodore of Corsica's marriage to Maria Anna said to be opposed by, **18.** 208
Tuscany may be given to, **18.** 2, 30, 331, 336
—— would prefer, as ruler, to Francis I, **18.** 2
Valkenswaard reached by, to take command of allied army, **19.** 288n
victories of: in vain if England withdraws from continent, **37.** 165; near Braunau, **18.** 234, 249; persuade Frederick Augustus II to make peace, **17.** 499
wife of, dies, **18.** 540
wounded and returning to Vienna, **17.** 430
Charles, P., of Mecklenburg-Strelitz. *See* Karl Ludwig Friedrich
Charles (1775–8), P., of Naples:
inoculated, **24.** 330
Charles (1391–1465), and Charles (d. 1545), Ducs d'Orléans. *See* Orléans, Charles d'
Charles (Christian name):
English use of, **2.** 104
Charles, George:
Cumberland, D. of, not taught by, to spell, **23.** 230n
Charles, J.-A.-C., physicist:
balloon ascent by, **25.** 450n, **39.** 419n
Charles Albert (1697–1745), Elector of Bavaria 1726–45; Holy Roman (German) Emperor 1742–5 as Charles VII:
Bavaria defended only by, **18.** 241

[Charles Albert, *continued*]

Bavarians proud of, when he is emperor, **29.** 69

Benedict XIV gets letter from, thanking him for influence on imperial election, **17.** 351–2, 372

brother of, **9.** 50

*Catalogue of French Books, A,* satirizes, **18.** 52

Charles, P., marches against, **18.** 234

coronation of, as emperor, **17.** 144n, 151n

death of, **19.** 2–3, 5, 8, 10, 19, **26.** 10

election of, as emperor: **17.** 144n, 290, 351–2; costs him Bavaria, **29.** 69

England's alleged support of, satirized in ballad, **17.** 188

France may ally with, **17.** 119, 133

—— may have ulterior views in not letting, take Hanover, **17.** 203

French sympathies of, **19.** 24

French unable to aid, **18.** 241

Giacomazzi, Margherita, 'virtuosa' of, **23.** 570n

health of, gout and stone, **18.** 139

history of, **42.** 494

letters of, show that his representative confers with Young Pretender, **18.** 397

Linz entered by, **17.** 143n

—— threatened by, **17.** 151

medal with head of, **17.** 380, 401

Milan may be given by, to Don Philip, **17.** 290

peace terms to appease, **17.** 380

Roman representative of, calls on Young Pretender, **17.** 445

Salzburg and Passau said to be entered by, **17.** 108

son does not succeed, as emperor, **42.** 494

Suares, Mme, may seek, **17.** 161

titles to be assumed by, **17.** 151

Valenti Gonzaga's sympathy for, enrages Maria Theresa, **18.** 55n

Vienna to be besieged by, **17.** 144, 151, 155

Young Pretender and Prussia allied with, at France's instigation to attack Hanover, **18.** 396

Charles Edward (Stuart) (1720–88), Count of Albany, the Young Pretender:

Acquaviva and young Tencin aid, in escaping, **18.** 376

advisers of, prevent his serving in French army, **18.** 394n

Affry denies participation of, in French invasion, **21.** 298n

Aiguillon, Mme d', tells anecdotes of, **7.** 274

Albani asked by, to urge Clement XIII to let him return to Rome, **22.** 368

——'s letter gives false hope to, **22.** 389

Albano may be visited by, **17.** 10, 14, **18.** 377–8, 387–9

'Albany, Count' the pseudonym of, **23.** 225, **25.** 427n

Amelot thinks, will aid Don Philip, **18.** 415

American ship from Boston in service of, **37.** 237

Anglican church joined by, **20.** 333n, **21.** 392n, **22.** 325, 336, **23.** 402

Antibes reached by, **18.** 385

Argenson and Tencin meet, **17.** 393n

Argenson remonstrates with Louis XV over, **18.** 415

—— urges clemency for, **19.** 264n

army of: advance guard of, **37.** 229; arrest of, **19.** 509n; cannon lacked by, **19.** 104–5; deserters from, **19.** 159; Edinburgh taken by, **30.** 96, 97, 98; Elcho and Perth join, **19.** 118; George II indifferent to progress of, **30.** 94; grenadiers of, **19.** 106; HW describes, as '3000 banditti,' **30.** 96; London may be reached by, in fortnight, **30.** 94; may wait in Scotland for French aid, **19.** 117; size of, **30.** 97

arrest of, at Paris, **19.** 509n, **20.** 8, 15, 22

Ashburnham fears seizure as hostage for, **19.** 454

Atholl's house occupied by, **19.** 106

Aubeterre's support of, unauthorized, **22.** 384, 399, **25.** 526

Avignon may be visited by, **19.** 140, 368, 376, 378, **20.** 22–3, 35, 44, 84n, 508

Balmerinoch praises, **19.** 301

Bar, Confederacy of, may be headed by, **5.** 111

Barbantane told by, that Mann spoiled his project, **25.** 526

—— wants English public house at Florence to be used by, **24.** 137

Bavarian representative at Rome calls on father of, to ask about son's health, **17.** 445

Beauvau family claim relationship to, **19.** 262, **43.** 260

Beavor rejects offers by, **19.** 168

Bedchamber attendants often struck by, **26.** 47

behaves well when sober, **24.** 201

Belle-île visited by, for escort, **19.** 87

Benedict XIV and cardinals hope to bring, to Rome, **20.** 22–3

Benedict XIV and father ignorant of whereabouts of, **20.** 508

Benedict XIV might make, a martyr, **19.** 131

—— refuses money to, **20.** 27

—— said to have furnished, with money and briefs, **18.** 427

——'s blessing asked by, **19.** 85, 90

—— urges, to leave Avignon: lest English bomb Civita Vecchia, **20.** 35n; to go to Rome, Bologna or Ferrara, **20.** 22n

Berlin may be visited by, **20.** 35, 44

Berne said to be visited by, as 'Chevalier Browne,' **22.** 90n

Berry, Mary, identifies, **11.** 258n

birthday of father of, **11.** 296n

birthday of, **19.** 191, 196

Bologna gazettes call, P. of Wales, **19.** 205

Bologna may be visited by, **20**. 15, 44

—— passed by, with handkerchief over face, **23**. 319

Bolognetti, Contessa, entertains, **17**. 10, 16

Bouillon, Duc de, and Campo Florido promise aid to, **19**. 105n

Bouillon, Duc de, harbours, at Bouillon, under name of Bn Douglas, **21**. 298n, **22**. 389, 393, **43**. 280

breeches lost by, **19**. 320

Brescia said to be visited by, **17**. 113

Brest fleet may convey, **18**. 375, 378, 393, 404

Breteuil attends, in France, **22**. 385

brother abused by, for rebuff to daughter, **25**. 548–9

brother administers viaticum to, **25**. 627

brother asks, to await instructions, **22**. 385, 387

brother avoided by, **20**. 15

brother convinced by, of Cts of Albany's intrigue with Alfieri, **25**. 396–7

brother does not trust, with gems, **25**. 525

brother enrages, by becoming priest, **19**. 501, **20**. 333

brother has Jews fix apartment for, at Rome, **22**. 379

brother injures, **7**. 275

brother may join, **18**. 436, **19**. 99

brother might have to 'raise up issue to ,' **25**. 115

brother said to have met, at Avignon, **19**. 140

brother's correspondence with, **22**. 388n, 389, **35**. 61

brother's folly leaves, worse off than ever, **22**. 402

brother's quarrel with, **19**. 415n, **25**. 468

brother's remark about journey of, **23**. 403

brother's witticism about, **22**. 325

brother takes, on his right hand through Rome in coach, as sign of royalty, **22**. 392

brother urges, not to insist on royal honours for wife, **23**. 406

brother would condemn, at congregation for change of religion, **22**. 336

bust of, owned by Redmond, **7**. 279

Butler's house in Normandy allegedly visited by, **20**. 508n

Calais said to be visited by, **18**. 402

calls himself: 'Bn Douglas,' **22**. 389, 399, **23**. 225; 'Count of Albany,' **23**. 225, **25**. 427n; 'Count Renfrew,' **23**. 225; 'Mr Smith,' **21**. 59n, **23**. 218; 'Regent,' **19**. 103

Cameron, Archibald, confirms reception of, into Church of England, **20**. 333n

—— physician and capt. in army of, **20**. 373n

Cameron, Jeanie, unkindly received by, **22**. 453

can exist decently in Rome only, **22**. 394

capture of: necessary to discourage rebels and France, **19**. 131; rumoured, **19**. 254, 279

captures announced to, **19**. 106

cardinals to decide about, **22**. 384–5, 387, 388–9, 392–3

Carteret persuades George II that invasion by, is unimportant, **19**. 105, 109, 117

Caxton, Cambs, may expect, **14**. 2

Charles III may set up, in Ireland, **23**. 328

Charles Albert said to be allied with, **18**. 396

——'s representative consults with, **18**. 397

Charles Emmanuel III to stop, **17**. 14

Château de St-Antoine the Paris home of, **19**. 509n

Choiseul not to use, against England, **21**. 298n

Chute and HW confer about, **19**. 378

Chute and Whithed dislike, **19**. 318

Chute rebukes Rivera for calling, 'Altesse,' **19**. 142–3

—— says, is not in Scotland, **19**. 198

Civita Vecchia said to be approached by, **17**. 14

clans awaited by, at Inverness, **37**. 238–9

clans threaten to desert, unless others join him, **19**. 167

Clement XIII decides about royal pretensions of, **22**. 368–9, 374, 384–5, 387, 392–3, 394, 406, 408, **23**. 402, **25**. 526

—— does not recognize for fear of Pitt, **30**. 216

—— receives, with Cardinal York, **22**. 516

—— tells Aubeterre he will acknowledge, when Louis XV does, **25**. 526

coach of: given by D. of Cumberland to Mordaunt, **9**. 35; has 8 horses, **22**. 389

Coke, Lady Mary, should visit court of, at Rome, **23**. 550

companions of: brought from France to Rome, **23**. 351; on return journey to France, **19**. 270n

confessors tell Roman Catholics in Florence to pray for success of, **19**. 112

confessor to, *see* Macdonald, Allan

conversion of, to Church of England could not be understood by father, **22**. 336

Conway hunts for, in Scotland, **37**. 250–3

——'s letter threatens with George III's resentment any who countenance, **22**. 408

Cope defeated by, at Prestonpans, **19**. 116–17, 125, 198

—— out-marched by, **19**. 101–2

correspondence with, declared treasonable, **18**. 440

costume of: at departure from Loch Nuagh, **19**. 320n; courier's said to be, **18**. 375; Garter, **23**. 225; girl's, **19**. 320n, **30**. 103, **37**. 252; St Andrew's Cross, **23**. 225

council of, meets daily at Holyrood, **19**. 118n

Cowper's quarrel with, over Florentine house, **24**. 201, 245, 255

Craon, Princesse de, fond of, **20**. 132

Craons may assist, across Tuscany, **17**. 15

Culloden escape of, **19**. 248

[Charles Edward, *continued*]

Cumberland defended by, 7. 274–5

daughter of: acknowledged as his sole heiress, 25. 512–13, 516n, 520, 522, 535, 459, 33. 438, 442; registered by him at Paris and Florence as Ds of Albany, 25. 513, 516n, 521–2; resembles him, 25. 535; summoned to Bouillon but not found, 26. 46–7; summoned to Florence and called Ds of Albany, 25. 513, 538n; the only child, 25. 516n; to be married to Florentine cavaliere, 25. 513, 522; wears father's jewels, 25. 536

Daullé's print of, 23. 422n

Dauphin would aid, 21. 59

Dauphiné route taken by, 20. 35

death of, rumoured, 19. 268, 274, 279, 20. 168, 333, 25. 482, 33. 438, 442

declaration of, threatens those who attend British Parliament, 19. 138

Del Monti describes departure of, from Rome, 18. 418, 421–2

Derby reached by, 19. 178, 398, 23. 32, 164, 329

descendants of martyrs of, restored to forfeited Scottish estates, 25. 520

destinations of, rumoured, 20. 35n

dinner guests of, arrive at 2 P.M., 25. 467

disappearance of, 19. 367–8, 23. 324

drinks and quarrels at Rome, 23. 351

drunk, 23. 427, 26. 47

'drunk half the day and mad the other,' 23. 406

Dublin offers reward for apprehension of, 18. 393n

'Duncombe,' HW's name for, 17. 18

Dunkirk said to have been visited by, 19. 153, 269n

Dutch letters imply that an impersonator may represent, in Scotland, 19. 227

dying but wants an heir, 24. 144

earthquake prophecy might have helped, to conquer England, 20. 147

Edinburgh's capture by, 19. 89, 96, 102, 125–6, 142, 198, 30. 96, 35. 61

Elizabeth Farnese of Spain denies interview to, 19. 390n

embarks at St-Nazaire with volunteers collected in Paris, 19. 86–7

England may be invaded by, 17. 15, 18. 419

—— secretly visited by, 20. 333n, 43. 270–1

——'s privately-raised regiments show, that populace is not for him, 26. 16

——'s use of Paoli will resemble France's of, 23. 139n

English arms taken down from door of, 22. 408

English cause defended by, to Frenchman, 24. 531

English invasion to be headed by, 21. 298

English Jacobite visitors call on, because forbidden to see his father, 19. 112, 136

English *Mémoire justificatif* approved by, 24. 531

English military strength might be diverted by, 18. 379

English ministers must be doubtful about presence of, in Scotland, 19. 199

English people asserted by, to love him, 30. 92

English Roman Catholics say, is not in Scotland, 19. 172, 198

English Roman Catholics send contributions to, 19. 176

English troops might be diverted from Flanders by invasion of, 19. 90

English visitors at Rome believe in success of, 19. 191

extreme unction administered to, 25. 468, 482n

fate of, uncertain, 19. 271, 279, 295, 298

father denies rumoured marriage proposal of, 20. 44n

father informed by, of departure from Avignon, 20. 35n

father may go to France to guide course of, 19. 94

father not in touch with, 21. 59, 255–6

father recommends, to Clement XIII, 21. 391

father required by, as condition for return to Italy, to dismiss O'Brien, 20. 45n

father said to have resigned pretensions to, 17. 19

father's bequests to, 22. 387

father's correspondence with, 18. 385, 19. 85, 87, 89, 259, 451n

father's furniture brought by, from Rome to Florentine house, 25. 525

father should not be told of apostasy of, 22. 325

father's illness probably drives, to drink, 22. 90

father's pension wanted by, 22. 368

father's quarrel with, 20. 341, 345

father's rebellious subjects to be punished by, 19. 311

father told by, to dismiss O'Brien, 20. 45

Ferdinand VI grants sum to, 19. 390n

—— interviews, 19. 390n

Ferrara may be visited by, 20. 44

finances of, 5. 218–19, 19, 105, 109, 319n, 22. 368, 387, 406, 24. 244, 25. 107, 442, 475, 536–7

first minister of, see Spada, Conte

Fitzjames escorts, 5. 111

Fitzjames family do not want to support daughter of, after his death, 25. 516, 522

Flanders and the Rhine may be visited by, 18. 434

flees before his army, 40. 56

flight of, from Scotland, expected, 19. 213–14

Florence traversed by, 22. 389

—— visited by, at public inn, 23. 225

Florentine casino and theatre attended by, 23. 226

Florentine house of, 24. 201, 245, 255

Florentine house sought by, 24. 136–7

Florentine theatre box of, **23.** 226, **24.** 244–5, **25.** 536

Foligno said to be visited by, **17.** 113

Forbes, Master of the Horse to, **21.** 364n

foreign aid expected by, **19.** 137

foreign reinforcements needed by, **19.** 130

Fortrose, Loudoun, and Panmure raise troops to oppose, **19.** 102

Fossombrone said to be visited by, **17.** 113

France and Spain disregard, **22.** 399

France and Spain do not encourage, greatly, **19.** 105

France and Spain will probably be urged by, to make Clement XIII give him royal honours, **22.** 369

France augments forces of, **19.** 221–2

—— may be destination of, **17.** 14, 113, 114, 116, **18.** 101, 389, 433–4, **19.** 269n, 317n, 319–20, 393n, **22.** 393, **23.** 324

—— may hesitate to antagonize Benedict XIV over, **20.** 23

—— may induce English-Spanish friction through, **19.** 378, 393

—— may support, **17.** 14–15, **19.** 109

—— may use, to embarrass England, **19.** 399

—— must dictate operations of, **19.** 393

—— regards Paoli's position as equivalent to that of, **23.** 139–40

——'s aid to, **17.** 202–3, 306, **18.** 273, **19.** 87, 130, 508–9

——'s answer to Thompson about, **18.** 409

——, Sweden, and Prussia to rescue, **19.** 311

—— tells Holland not to oppose, **19.** 134

—— threatens to force, from Avignon to Marseille for Civita Vecchia, **20.** 23n

—— turns back, from Paris, **23.** 398

—— will not deny presence of, **20.** 508

Francis I may pretend French alliance with, to embroil England with France, **18.** 373–4

——'s estates may become refuge of, **20.** 93

Frederick II may aid, **19.** 311

French acknowledge, as P. of Wales, **18.** 552

French and Spanish Courts tell their Roman ministers to disavow, **22.** 399, **25.** 526

French army may be entered by, at Paris, **18.** 378

French Court seems to approve of sojourn of, **20.** 6

French expedition at Dunkirk may aid, **19.** 103

French financial support sought by, **25.** 442

French hotel allegedly taken by, **19.** 509

French invasion of England mentioned by, **19.** 451n

French possessions of, allowed by Louis XVI to go to his daughter, **25.** 536–7

French reinforcements do not reach, **19.** 137–8

French schemes for, still alarm Mann, **19.** 376

French ships hover to rescue, **19.** 254

Fribourg canton asked by France to receive, **19.** 509

frigate of, said to be forced back to Brest, **19.** 91

Garter and Cross of St Andrew worn by, **23.** 225

George II awaits England's reaction to invasion by, **19.** 95

—— might recall D. of Cumberland if impersonator led armies of, **19.** 174, 199

—— tells Parliament of French move of, **18.** 399

George III's coronation allegedly attended by, **11.** 296

Germany may be refuge of, **20.** 93

Gloucester, D. of, meets, on Genoa street, **23.** 343, 345

Gordon, Lord Lewis, joins, **19.** 102n

Goring, Henry, his equerry, accompanies, on journey from Avignon, **20.** 35n

governor, to *see* Murray, Hon. James, E. of Dunbar

Gravelines visited by, **18.** 402n

Grisons said to be visited by, **17.** 113

Gustav III discouraged by Bernis and Cts of Albany from aiding, **25.** 475

—— may well pity, **25.** 455–6

—— to aid and visit, in Florence, **25.** 442–3, **33.** 449–50

HW asks about, **23.** 236

HW calls, 'Tooanohowy,' **30.** 94

HW congratulates, on not becoming king, **24.** 104

HW despises Rome for disavowing, when he lost all for her sake, **24.** 255

HW does not disapprove of Mann for halting Roman recognition of, **24.** 255

HW doubts that an impersonator represents, **19.** 172–3, 174, 210

HW expects to see, **13.** 217

HW jokes about probable reception of, by Regency, **30.** 91

HW owns portrait of, **9.** 304n

HW refuses to worry about, **19.** 398

HW remembers, at Derby, **23.** 32, 164

HW wants recent print of, **23.** 422

Hanover may be attacked by, with French army, **17.** 306, 315, **18.** 434

Hawley's defeat by, **19.** 227–8

health of: bloody flux, **19.** 295n; body swollen, **25.** 394; decays fast, **25.** 513–14, 549; discharge from legs necessary to, **24.** 118, 137, 244; disorder in legs, **25.** 549; distempers, **19.** 295; dropsy of breast feared, **25.** 394; eating and drinking injure, **24.** 244; epileptic fits, **24.** 245, **25.** 627; fever, **25.** 627; fistula, **24.** 479–80; insanity rumoured, **20.** 508; legs swollen, **24.** 137, 244, **25.** 442; miserable, **19.** 311; mortification in legs, **25.** 394; rallies somewhat, **25.** 470, 475; shortness of breath, **25.** 394; sick at his stomach in theatre corridor, **24.** 244; slight illness, **17.** 113n; slow fever, **24.** 118; sores in legs, **24.** 118, 480; speechless and insensible, **25.** 467, 470; stroke, perhaps apoplectic, **25.** 467; walks almost double, **25.** 442

[Charles Edward, *continued*]

Herbert, Lady Mary, rescued by, **7.** 288

Hervey, Bp, should not be trusted by, **25.** 455

hidden in a corner of France, **22.** 106

Highlanders may not follow, to England, **19.** 107, 137

Hillsborough regards Mann as responsible for Clement XIII's refusal to recognize, **22.** 429–30

Holdsworth carries pictures of, to England, **19.** 172

Holyrood House said to be vacated by, **19.** 126

homosexuality rumoured by, **37.** 244

hunts near Cisterna, **18.** 377, 387–9

impotence of, blamed by him on potion administered by wife on Mann's instigation, **25.** 102

incognito of: as 'Baron Douglas,' **22.** 389, 399; as 'Mr Smith,' **21.** 59n

income of, **23.** 402

insupportable in stench and temper, **24.** 480

invited to Pitti Palace gala, **25.** 50n

Irish Catholics said to withhold money from, because he renounced faith at Liège, **23.** 402

Irish might proclaim, **35.** 221

Irish tumults may arouse hopes of, **25.** 443, 455

Jablonowsky, Ps, said to have offered Polish crown to, at Rome, **23.** 318–19

Jacobites lose politically after attempt of, **19.** 425

Jesuits unconcerned about Clement XIII's failure to recognize, **22.** 406

jewels redeemed by, **22.** 387n

Johnson, Bp, should give absolution to, **22.** 324

Kelly mistaken for, **19.** 153n

—— to ask for French aid for, **19.** 153

Kilmarnock said to have betrayed, **19.** 262

Le Moine's bust of, **7.** 279

Leopold denies theatre box decorations to, at Florence, **25.** 536

—— receives complaints from, **25.** 102

——'s son said to be heir to kingdoms of, **25.** 394–5

lethargic from wine, **23.** 319

Liège said to be visited by, **21.** 59n, **23.** 402

linen not to be changed by, until he lies at St James's, **30.** 94

Lockhart aide-de-camp to, **20.** 27n

—— sent by, to Rome, **20.** 25

London said to be threatened by, **35.** 61

—— unlikely to be conquered by, **19.** 398

Louis XV embarrassed by departure of, **18.** 378n

—— hates, **21.** 44, 59

—— orders arrest of, **20.** 8n, 35n

—— said to have sent Fitzjames to, **23.** 338

—— said to proclaim pretensions of, **17.** 114

Lovat supports, **14.** 10n

Lucchese envoy invites, to concert, **23.** 229

Lyon reached by, **19.** 368n

Macdonald, Flora, protects, **37.** 252

Macdonald's house the refuge of, **18.** 394n

Mackintosh, Bns, said to be favourite of, **37.** 244

Madrid visited by, **19.** 390n, 392–3

Maltese vessel takes, to Genoa, **18.** 376n

manifesto of, **19.** 103

Mann avoids, **23.** 229

—— calls heir of the Palazzo di Santi Apostoli, **22.** 383–4; 'nauseous tyrant,' **25.** 150

—— combats influence of those wanting Clement XIII to recognize, **22.** 388–9

—— disappointed by false alarm about escape of, **17.** 114n, 118–19, 144–5

—— disappointed that HW thinks so little of Rome's attitude towards, **22.** 405, **24.** 244

—— does not believe conversion of, **22.** 336

—— doubts if Scotland is really invaded by, in person, **19.** 140–1, 149, 172, 174, 197–9, 205, 227

—— hears nothing of, **17.** 159

—— hopes, will be hanged, **18.** 421

—— prevents Roman recognition of, **22.** 394n, 422, 441, **23.** 244, 255n, 329

—— sees, at theatre, **25.** 467

—— sends accounts of family of, which now do not interest England, **25.** 625

—— tells D. of Richmond of plan of, to return to Rome, **22.** 369, 374

—— to confer with Gustav III about, **25.** 442–3

—— to tell, of HW's *Historic Doubts*, **24.** 104

—— urged to transmit information about, **17.** 159, 160, 203

marriage of, **5.** 218, **23.** 398, 402–3, 405–6; rumoured, **18.** 378, 385, **19.** 335, 417, **20.** 35, 44, **22.** 393

Massa, Ds of, rejects, as son-in-law, **22.** 393

medals of: coined, **21.** 45; die for, **17.** 18–19; Mann sends, to D. of Newcastle through HW, **17.** 218; Parker mentions, **26.** 3

mind of, as weak as his body, **25.** 549

mistress of, *see* Jablonowska, Marie-Louise, Princesse de Talmond; Walkinshaw, Clementina

Modena visited by, **23.** 318

money dispensed by, **19.** 105

mother's jewels acquired by, **25.** 525

Murray (Dunbar) admits absence of, from Scotland, **19.** 140

—— fears that Mann may tell Mathews to intercept, **18.** 419

—— may follow, **19.** 378

—— tells lies about, **19.** 311

Murray, William, would probably entertain, **30.** 91

Murray of Broughton secretary to, **9.** 40n

Murrays join, **19.** 104

must be kept the other side of Derby, **35.** 235

Newcastle, D. of, asks Mann about, **17.** 159, 160, 203

—— has declaration of, burnt at Royal Exchange, **19.** 161

—— misunderstands message as denoting approach of, **37.** 436–7

Newdigate would formerly be glad to be chief mourner at funeral of, **24.** 144

no more a king at Rome than at London, **22.** 399

Norfolk, Ds of, does not expect, **37.** 454

Ogilvie, Bns, expects throne for, **37.** 245

Orford, Cts of, said to be friend of, **19.** 310

—— used to fuss over, **19.** 70

Orsini and Guglielmi do homage to, **22.** 392

Ostend said to be landing-place of, **19.** 311

Oxford no longer drinks health of, **23.** 329

page sent by, to France for songs, **30.** 92

Papal election may delay departure of, **17.** 10

Paris letters tell of new schemes for, **19.** 451

Paris may be visited by, **18.** 378, **20.** 44, **24.** 102

—— visited by, **18.** 394, **21.** 59n, **23.** 398

Parliament in Scotland called by, **19.** 118

Parliament makes correspondence with, treasonable, **18.** 440

——'s disapproval of peace treaty may be caused by, **20.** 27

Philipps said to be friend of, **19.** 310

physician of, tells Mann he is in great danger, **25.** 467

physicians implored by, to keep him alive, **25.** 395

pineapples first tasted by, at Blair Atholl, **19.** 106

Pisa baths to be visited by, **23.** 226

Pisa quitted by, for Siena, **23.** 318

pistols always carried by, **25.** 101n

Pius VI continues allowance of, **24.** 244

—— does not acknowledge, as king, **24.** 244, **25.** 526, 552–3

—— permits creation of duchess by, **25.** 552–3

—— to give half of pension of, to wife, **25.** 107

plate received by, **25.** 525

Polish aspirations of, rumoured, **23.** 318–19, 324, 337–8, 352

Pont Beauvoisin said to be destination of, **20.** 9

portrait of: HW owns, **9.** 304; not engraved because he is too unimportant, **23.** 429, 436; on Mme d'Aiguillon's bracelet inspires witticism, **8.** 58, **22.** 325

Prestonpans victory of, **14.** 87n

print of, sought by Mann for HW, **23.** 422, 427, 429, 436

proclamation for arrest of, **19.** 91

Puisieux warns, to leave French dominions, **20.** 8n

quail shooting pretence of, for escape from Rome, **17.** 13

Regency offers reward for capture of, **30.** 91

religion of: said to be changed, **20.** 333, **22.** 324–5, 336, 368, **23.** 402; unchanged, **22.** 379–80

reward offered by, for George II's head, **19.** 105

Rivera boasts to Chute of successes of, **19.** 142

Roman Catholic Church rejoined by, **21.** 392n

Roman Catholic gentlemen send remittances to, **19.** 176n

Roman Catholics hope for success of, **19.** 130

Roman churches have prayers for, **19.** 171n

Roman discussions about Spanish connections of, **19.** 97

Roman nobility said to be jealous of, **22.** 394

Roman return of, expected, **17.** 15, 21

Romans doubt virtue of, in curing King's Evil, **21.** 392

Rome calls, P. of Wales, **22.** 389

—— certainly left by, **18.** 374, 376–8, 384, 386–9, **19.** 98

—— disliked by, **20.** 15

—— hoots at, on his return, **23.** 343

—— insists, is still in Scotland, **19.** 311

—— left by, **5.** 111

—— may be left by, **17.** 1–15, 113–16, 118–19, 159, 202–3, 315n, **18.** 101, 373, **20.** 393

—— may be visited by, **20.** 333

—— proclaims success of, **19.** 257, 259

—— said to finance French trip of, **18.** 101

—— to become family home of, **25.** 627

sails for Scotland, **19.** 85n

St Andrew's day always celebrated by, in drunkenness, **25.** 100

St-Joseph, convent of, hiding-place of, in Paris for three years, **20.** 44n

Savona visited by, **18.** 385

Saxe's projected invasion in favour of, **15.** 133n

says he will never marry, **22.** 325

'scandalous rebellion' of, **37.** 223

Scotland provides few recruits for, **19.** 104

—— said not really to be visited by, **19.** 140–1, 149, 172, 174, 197–9, 205, 227

—— said to be destination of, **18.** 373, 375, 378, 404

—— said to be left by, **19.** 270, 310, 317

—— unlikely again to be invaded by, **20.** 35

Scottish coast approached by, for embarkation, **37.** 218

Scottish invasion by, **9.** 23n, 33–4, **19.** 85–319, *et passim*, **35.** 61

Scottish localities visited by, **19.** 102n, 152n, 248n, 254n, 269n, 270n, 279n, 295n

Scottish projects of, not laid aside, **17.** 202

Scottish wanderings of, after Culloden, **37.** 250–3

Scottish west coast hiding-place of, **37.** 245–6

servants of: leave France for Rome with his effects, **18.** 433–4; support him as he walks, **25.** 442; support him when sick in theatre, **24.** 244

Seymour probably follows, to Paris, **24.** 102

Sheridan arrested with, **20.** 9n

—— in charge of effects of, at Avignon, **20.** 9n

—— tutor to, **19.** 312n

[Charles Edward, *continued*]

Siena quitted by, for Florence, **23**. 318

Silesian claims relinquished by, **22**. 387n

Sinigaglia visited by, **23**. 225

Skye escape of, in women's clothes, **30**. 103

*Sortes Virgilianæ* drawn for, **37**. 79

Spada accompanies, at Floernce, **23**. 229

Spain briefly visited by, **19**. 390, 392–3

—— may aid, **17**. 14, **19**. 97, 130, 330, 335

—— may be visited by, **17**. 6n, 14, **19**. 140–1, 198, 377–8, **23**. 328

Spanish courier's costume worn by, **18**. 377

Spanish reinforcements do not reach, **19**. 139

Spanish ship brings arms to, **19**. 137–8

speeches of, to Highlanders repeated at Rome, **19**. 170

Stafford with, at Avignon, **20**. 9n

still called P. of Wales after father's death, **22**. 389

Stormont leaves Paris to avoid meeting, **6**. 160n

Stosch writes weekly letters about, **20**. 333

Stuart sent by, to Paris to fetch daughter, **25**. 513

subscriptions collected in Scotland for, **20**. 373n

Sweden may be visited by, **20**. 44

Switzerland often visited by, **21**. 59n

Talmond, Princesse de, mistress of, **4**. 258n, **8**. 57–8, **20**. 44n

—— probably visited by, in Paris, **20**. 44

tapestry horse might be borrowed by, **23**. 242

Tencin gives set of plate to, **17**. 114

——'s valet attended, **19**. 98–9

—— to ship, to England, **18**. 32

theatre boxes of, at Florence, **23**. 226, **24**. 244–5, **25**. 536

Theodore of Corsica's rights might be bought by, **21**. 45, 59

title of successor to, in doubt, **24**. 480, **25**. 482, 520

Traquair discussed affairs of, **19**. 381

travelling bed made for, **17**. 13

travels with French passport, **22**. 389

Tullibardine joins, **19**. 106

Turin does not recognize, **19**. 143

Tuscany crossed by, **18**. 378

—— may be destination of, **17**. 13–15, **20**. 93

valet of, reaches Rome, **19**. 311–12

Van Hoey transmits peace overtures about, **19**. 264

Venice reported to be visited by, incognito, **20**. 84n

—— said not to have received, royally, **17**. 98

Verona said to be visited by, **17**. 113

victory attributed to, **19**. 197, 253

Vienna express to England announces escape of, **18**. 404

Villa Patrizi entertainment attended by, **17**. 25

Vincennes the prison of, **20**. 8, 22, 44

Wade opposes, **19**. 127, 128

whereabouts of, unknown, **20**. 44, 84, **21**. 59, 255–6

wife attached to Seymour with consent of, **24**. 94

wife can seldom leave convent in lifetime of, **25**. 107

wife flees from, to convent, **25**. 101–2, 108n, 150, **26**. 47

wife ill-treated by, **33**. 260

wife jealously watched by, to avoid illegitimate heir, **24**. 94, 137, 245

wife met by, at Loreto, and conducted to Macerata and Rome, **23**. 406

wife not spared the stench and temper of, **24**. 480

wife of: **11**. 258n, 270, **39**. 180; may marry Alfieri, **33**. 438–9

wife pitied when Alfieri's affair with her is disclosed, **25**. 397

wife separated from, through Alfieri, **25**. 396

wife's income after separation from, **25**. 535–6

wife subjected by, to indecencies, **25**. 100–1, 108n

wife treats tenderly, **24**. 137

wife will be disappointed by recovery of, **25**. 395

will made by, **25**. 394

(?) wounded at Culloden, **43**. 260

York, D. of, does not mention, **7**. 364

Charles Emmanuel II (1634–75), D. of Savoy:

HW copies inscription referring to, **13**. 190

Charles Emmanuel III (1701–73), D. of Savoy; K. of Sardinia, 1730:

Admiralty scolded by, for court-martialling Townshend, **19**. 332

Aix treaty wins reluctant consent of, **19**. 508

Albenga the headquarters of, **19**. 312

Alessandria near camp of, **19**. 82

——'s preservation preferred by, to peace treaty, **19**. 231

Alps and Riviera di Ponente to be defended by, **19**. 478

Amalia (d'Este) not permitted to marry, **17**. 55n

armistice rejected by, **19**. 279

army of, estimated, **17**. 291

Austria gives troops to, for reduction of Genoa, **19**. 401

—— may be attacked by, **22**. 55

Austrian army wanted by, at Bologna, **18**. 461

Austrian conquest of Naples not wished by, **18**. 441, 461

Austrian generals to negotiate with, through Wentworth, **19**. 401

Austrian ignorance of geography to be corrected by, **19**. 401

Austrian pride irritates, into peace overtures with France, **19**. 223

Austrians join: at Casale, **19**. 120; at the Trebbia, **19**. 269

Austrians urged by, to drive French across the Var, **19**. 436

Austrian troops outfitted by, **19.** 431

Austria reluctant to accept demands of, **18.** 228

Bavarian elector may conciliate, by giving Milan to Don Philip, **17.** 290

Benedict XIV's permission asked by, to invade Bologna, **17.** 482

birth date of, corrected, **43.** 95

Blonay sent by, to protest against Genoese aid to Spanish army, **19.** 64

Bologna place of assembly for troops of, **18.** 55

—— threatened by army of, **17.** 500

Bormida River the theatre of, **19.** 262, 297

Botta may get troops from, to chastise Genoese, **19.** 353

——'s peace terms condemned by, **19.** 312

Bourbons encircle, **17.** 290

Braitwitz calls, 'potence,' **18.** 524n

Brown fails to execute requests of, **19.** 436

—— receives cannon from, **19.** 353

Cairo the station of army of, **19.** 304

camp of: as remote as Scottish rebels, **19.** 190; at Popolo, **19.** 137n

Carlisle invested by, with Order of the Thistle, **22.** 554, **23.** 59

Cavalchini a subject of, **21.** 216

Cesena visited by, **18.** 13

Chambéry evacuated by, **18.** 142

Civita Vecchia saved by intervention of, **18.** 314

complaints of, sent by courier to Vienna, **19.** 312

Corsican undertakings of, **19.** 146, 157, 171, 183, 232, 258, 260, 275–6, **20.** 274

Cuneo may be defended by, **18.** 513

Dauphiné to be invaded by, from Stura, **19.** 432

death of, **5.** 337

defeat of, **18.** 521

Dunbar persuades Rivera that Young Pretender should be aided by, **19.** 142

England and Hungary sign treaty with, **18.** 311

English failure to attack Corsica shocks, **19.** 258

English fleet cannot be expected to do much without troops from, **19.** 120–1

English fleet wished by, to attack Genoese coast, **19.** 100

English ministers alarmed by retreat of, **18.** 142

English naval officer's disloyalty known to, **19.** 147–50

English subsidy to, **18.** 342–3

English throne might be claimed by, after Pretender's family, **19.** 142

Faenza visited by, **18.** 7

Ferdinand VI empowers Las Minas to conclude suspension of arms with, **19.** 279n

Finale and Savona attacked by, **19.** 313

France and Spain may be joined by, **17.** 85, 312

France may order, to restore territory to Austria, **20.** 576

Francis I negotiates with, for mutual guarantee, **19.** 6

Francis III covets furniture of, **18.** 323

—— said to have agreement with, **17.** 442–3

——'s revenues seized by, **17.** 464

Frederick II compared with, **19.** 239

French and Spanish escape from Placentia with connivance of, **19.** 275

French attacks upon, **19.** 36

French couriers avoid territory of, **18.** 64, 75

French may divert, from move against Genoa, **19.** 417

French moving against territory of, **19.** 417

French negotiations with, **19.** 223, 230, 239

French treaty and armistice repudiated by, **19.** 219n

Gages escapes from, **19.** 291

galleys of: convey Mann to meet Rowley, **18.** 506; cruise on Genoese coast and in Piombino channel, **19.** 236n

general of, captured, **18.** 153

Genoa and Spain may be left to mercy of, by peace treaty, **19.** 219

Genoa approached by, **19.** 297, 304

—— disgusted by cession of Finale to, **18.** 360

—— hates, **18.** 554–5

—— may declare war on, **19.** 58

—— said to have been captured by, **19.** 309

Genoese blockade and Corsican conquest expected by, of English fleet, **19.** 232

Genoese peace terms do not mention, **19.** 312

Genoese to be punished by, **19.** 263

George II said to have hired army to aid, **18.** 461–2

Gorsegno meets Villettes at quarters of, **19.** 150

—— ordered by, to have Mann confer with Townshend and raise funds for Corsican conquest, **19.** 183

—— secretary of state to, **19.** 87, 150

—— to ask, to tell Osorio to inform George II or Newcastle about disloyal English officer, **19.** 147–50

HW compliments Osorio upon, **18.** 342

HW enjoys Mann's accounts of, **18.** 68

HW regrets absence of, from Flanders, **19.** 318

health of: drunk to, at Leghorn, **19.** 151, 152; recovered, **19.** 334n, 353; recovering, **19.** 336, 344; smallpox, **19.** 334

heroism of, grows rusty, **21.** 277

Imola visited by, **18.** 7

Kaunitz summoned by, **18.** 142

La Chavanne gets instructions from, for Aix congress, **19.** 446n

Lobkowitz cannot aid, and save Tuscany too, **18.** 513

——'s army to join, at Pavia, **19.** 55

[Charles Emmanuel III, *continued*]
—'s son to report victory to, 19. 487, 491
—'s weakness ignored by, 18. 515
— to imitate, 18. 324
— to send troops to, 18. 502, 509, 512, 513, 515
Maillebois may abandon Genoese to, 19, 237
— pursued by, 19. 262–3, 264–5
— to be approached by troops of, 19. 237
— to be opposed by, 19. 258
Mann expects letters from camp of, 19. 82
— might join, in attack on Leghorn or Parma, 21. 266
— ordered by, to plan Corsican rebellion, 20. 274, 386
— praised by, through Gorsegno, 19. 170
— regrets recommending Townshend to, 19. 169–70
—'s message from, through Gorsegno, 19. 260
— tells, that he is unable to raise money for him, 19. 183
— urged by, to save Corsican rebels, 19. 258, 275–6
— wants galleys of, put to sea, 19. 236
Maria Theresa blamed by, for wanting to capture Naples, 18. 461
— said to have signed treaty with, 17. 342
—'s alliance with, 17. 350, 18. 311
—'s negotiations with, awaited by Traun, 18. 263
—'s treaty with, gives him towns, 17. 379
— suspected of instigating retreat of, 18. 142
— to grant cessions to, by Aix treaty, 19. 481
— well regarded by, 17. 291
Marsan, Mme de, well treated by, 32. 268n
Mathews blames Maria Theresa for not aiding, 18. 346
— inquires about plans of, 18. 271
— wants, to coop up Spaniards in Tuscany, 18. 108
Milan coveted by, 17. 323n, 22. 55
Modena administered by, 17. 489
— citadel's surrender demanded by, 17. 464
— entered by troops of, 17. 442
Modenese duchess gets small allowance from, 18. 39
Modenese junction with Spaniards prevented by, 18. 322
Modenese princesses said to be pensioned by, 18. 223
Montemar fears, 17. 341
— forestalled by, 17. 455
— pursued by, towards Rimini, 18. 2–3
—'s defeat by, satirized, 18. 5
mourning for, 5. 339, 32. 101–2
Naples hopes that Spain may bribe, 17. 145, 291
— invasion to be shared by, 18. 3
Newcastle, D. of, refuses to supply troops for, 18. 462n

Nice to be attacked by, 19. 313
Oneglia victory will bind, to allied cause, 37. 160
on other side of Po, 19. 156
Osorio's communications from, 19. 306n, 431n
palace of, at Turin, 13. 190–1
Panaro may be crossed by, 17. 449, 472
Philip, Don, annoys, by invading Savoy, 18. 58–9
— may persuade, to permit Spanish invasion, 17. 323
— prevented by, from joining Francis III, 18. 322
—'s promotion from Parma to Naples wished by, 21. 264
— threatens, with retaliation in Piedmont for English bombardment of Genoese coast, 19. 121
— to be expelled from Savoy by, 18. 59, 322–3
physicians sent by, to Hercules III, 17. 489
Piacenza bombardment angers, 19. 276
— ceded by, in exchange for Savoy and Nice, 19. 508n
—'s evacuation demanded by, 19. 279
— visited by, 17. 392
Pitt calls, 'impregnable,' 26. 10
Po crossed by, near Pavia moving towards Rivalta, 19. 292n
Ponte del Reno visited by, 17. 500
Provençal invasion of, to be co-ordinated with Lorient's capture, 19. 323n
Richelieu to persuade, to exclude English ships, 20. 576
rôle of, in *La Passion des Jésuites*, 5. 315
Rowley asked by, to pacify Genoa, 18. 509
— blamed by, for Corsican rebellion, 19. 276
rumoured to be on man of war at Leghorn, 18. 145
Savona captured by, 19. 313, 352
Schulenburg's requests granted by, 19. 367
son succeeds, 5. 402n
Spain breaks peace negotiations of, with France, 19. 223
Spaniards attacked by, at River Lambro, 19. 278–9
— deterred by troops of, from invading Tuscany, 18. 58
— dislodge, from Mont Castello and the Tanaro, 19. 120
— intercept news from, 19. 190
— said to be defeated by, on the Var, 18. 466
— to be pursued by, 19. 292
Spanish armies do not alarm, by proposed junction, 19. 47
Spanish army may be resisted by, in Lombardy, 17. 266
Spanish invasion through Nice to be resisted by, 18. 395
Spanish stores at Ventimiglia destroyed by troops of, 19. 58

station of, behind the Tanaro near Pavon e Moncastello, 19. 84

Theodore of Corsica cheats, 20. 386

Tortona's evacuation demanded by, 19. 279

—— siege expected by, to decimate the besiegers, 19. 100

—— to be besieged by, 19. 262n

Townshend's conduct pleases, 19. 325

——'s ship boarded by, 19. 314

—— to cooperate with, 19. 292, 297

Traun joins, at Piacenza, 17. 312n

—— might be saved by intercession of, 18. 285

——'s ardour checked by, 18. 13

—— to be joined by troops of, 17. 350

Trebbia approached by, 19. 276n

Trino occupied by, 19. 156

troops of, at Bomporto, 18. 151; at the Panaro, 17. 424; Austrians joined by, 17. 312n; await his leave to cross the Panaro, 18. 197; inactive, 19. 258; in Riviera di Ponente, 19. 344; recalled by him, 19. 422

Turin left by, 18. 59, 19. 432

—— to be visited by, 19. 353

uncle of, 19. 226, 21. 207

Valenza to be besieged by, 19. 237

victories of: 18. 330; please England, 19. 228–9, 239

Vienna's answers awaited by, before army operations, 19. 393

Viennese Court cannot expect too much loyalty from, 19. 156

Villafranca to be attacked by, 19. 313

Villettes and Kaunitz summoned by, to approve his evacuation of Chambéry, 18. 142

Villettes doubtful about, 17. 312

—— persuades, about Corsican rebels, 19. 260

—— receives picture of, 20. 76

—— reports favourable attitude of, 17. 264

—— to forward reports of, about battle, to England, 18. 155

Vintimille siege may be directed by, 19. 441

wife of, dies, 17. 84–5, 87

Young Pretender to be stopped by, 17. 14

Charles Emmanuel IV (1751–1819), P. of Piedmont; D. of Savoy; K. of Sardinia, 1796:
Macartney visits, 12. 191
marriage of, 5. 337, 7. 343n, 41. 343

Charles George Augustus. See Karl Georg August

Charles Louis (1617–80), Elector Palatine:
rescue of, 2. 1–2

Charles Sq., Hoxton:
Roman Catholic school in, 25. 56n

Charles St, London:
Chute in, 10. 204, 205

Charles St, Berkeley Sq., London:
Lucans live in, 12. 152n, 33. 138n
(?) Nash lodges in, 43. 385
Pocock's house in, 33. 347n

Charles St, Covent Garden, London:
brothel in, 30. 40n

Charles St, St James's Sq., London:
Burke's house in, 2. 225n

Charles St, Westminster:
Taylor, Henry, of, 37. 254n

'Charles's Wain':
'Georgian' planet named in imitation of, 33. 367

Charleston, S.C., U.S.A.:
attack on, 6. 354n
English capture of, 7. 233, 25. 62, 73–4, 88, 500, 33. 198–9
English expedition to, fails, 24. 236–7, 241, 32. 318–19
HW imagines earls of, 33. 421
Leslie is ordered to, 29. 90n
Mason expects accounts of Clinton at, 29. 51
no news from, 25. 48
siege of, said to be lifted, 25. 69
valuables from, stored at Camden, 33. 155n, 39. 346n

Charlestown, Mass., U.S.A.:
powder and ammunition seized at, 24. 45n

Charles Town. See also Charleston

Charles William Ferdinand. See Karl Wilhelm Ferdinand

Charleton, Walter (1619–1707), M.D.; F.R.S.; President of Royal College of Physicians:
Chorea gigantum by, describes Stonehenge, 39. 460

Charleton. See also Charlton

Charleville, Cts of. See Coghill, Hester (d. 1789)

Charleville, E. of. See Moore, Charles (1712–64)

Charlevoix, Pierre-François-Xavier de (1682–1761):
Histoire . . . de la Nouvelle France by, 35. 186–7

Charlotte, Ps, of Lorraine. See Anne-Charlotte (1714–73)

Charlotte (1716–1801) of Prussia, m. (1733) Karl, D. of Brunswick-Wolfenbüttel:
death of, reported, 22. 509

Charlotte (1751–1827) of Saxe-Meiningen, m. (1769) Ernst, D. of Saxe-Gotha, 1772:
godmother to P. William of Gloucester, 24. 181, 36. 115–16

Charlotte, English ship:
(?) American news brought by, 24. 335n, 32. 394n, 396

Charlotte, Q. Charlotte's yacht:
painting of, should turn Q. Charlotte's stomach—or head, 21. 525

Charlotte-Aglaé (1700–61) de Bourbon d'Orléans, m. (1720) Francis III, D. of Modena:
Ancona visited by, 18. 222
Charles Emmanuel III gives little to, 18. 39
father too familiar with, 33. 531n
fatter and more fatigued, 18. 273
Florence visited by, 18. 227, 246, 273
France may be visited by, 18. 237, 246
Gages requests Tuscan passports for, 18. 223
gambling of, 17. 46
Genoa to be visited by, 18. 222
George II admires, 18. 246n

[Charlotte-Aglaé, *continued*]
  HW asked by, about Sade, **17**. 46
  HW contrasts Princesse de Craon with, **18**. 246
  HW describes, **18**. 246
  HW entertained by, **13**. 242, **17**. *43*–6, **33**. 531, 531n
  husband's restoration to Modena will take, from pleasant exile, **20**. 76
  Lorenzi meets, **18**. 228
  Luxembourg Palace to be Paris home of, **18**. 222
  Mann meets, **18**. 227, 246, 273
  Modena to be home of, **20**. *45*, 76
  mother dislikes, **18**. 385–6, **33**. 531
  Old Pretender's legitimacy not believed by, **17**. 43–4
  Orbetello not to be visited by, **18**. 222, 223
  Paris visited by, **18**. 222n
  Pucci, Mme, does not accompany, **18**. 246, 273
  —— lady of the Bedchamber to, **18**. 25n
  —— quarrels with, **17**. 158
  Regency Council and Mme de Craon entertain, at Tempi's villa, **18**. 228
  relatives to support, **18**. 222
  Rimini visited by, **18**. 222
  Sade supplied by, **18**. 39
  St Crispino and Venice on route of, from Modena, **17**. 442
  sister's apartment to be taken by, **18**. 222
  sisters-in-law must bore, **18**. 237
  Venice left by, **18**. 222
  would not have been scrupulous about a second marriage, **22**. 134
Charlotte Augusta (1796–1817) of England, m. (1816) P. Leopold of Saxe-Coburg:
  birth of, **12**. 142n, **34**. 213
  miniature of, **11**. 145n
  subgoverness to, **11**. 104n
Charlotte Augusta Matilda (1766–1828) of England, Ps Royal, m. (1797) Friedrich Wilhelm Karl, K. of Württemberg:
  approaching birth of, **31**. 126
  approaching marriage of, **12**. 196, 210
  at Garrick's reading, **28**. 285
  birthday of, **36**. 247
  Cheltenham visited by, **34**. 12n
  Cosens, tutor to, addresses Windsor ode to her, **33**. 476n
  father requests provision for, **24**. 371–2
  (?) HW visited by, at SH, **39**. 510–12
  proposed marriage of, with Joseph II, **33**. 275, 291
  Sherwin includes, in drawings of beauties, **29**. 185
  sponsor to Ds of Chandos's daughter, **33**. 59n
Charlotte-Élisabeth. *See* Élisabeth-Charlotte
Charlotte Sophia (1744–1818) of Mecklenburg-Strelitz, m. (1761) George III of England:
  Abercorn visited by, at Witham, **21**. 528
  accouchements of, **10**. 167, **22**. 562, **30**. 166, 250, **31**. 126, **38**. 166

Adhémar departs without taking leave of, **39**. 449–50
Akenside physician to, **35**. 566n
Albany, Cts of, presented to, **11**. 270, 271
Allen, Gentleman Usher to, **23**. 327
'Amphitrite,' **32**. 130
Ancaster, Master of the Horse to, **30**. 186
Anson transports, to England, **21**. 528
appearance of, **21**. 529, **38**. 116
applause for, at theatres, slight, **38**. 276
Argyll, Ds of, affronted by, **33**. 65, 66
arrival of, in England: **9**. 384, **21**. 528, **35**. 311–12, **38**. 116–19; expected, **21**. 517, 525
aspirants to Mastership of Horse to, **23**. 174
Baker, Sir George, scolded by, **25**. 680n
ball and dinner given by, for Ps Augusta and Karl Wilhelm Ferdinand, **22**. 197
ball given by, for P. of Wales, **29**. 108
Barnard, Anna, offers bull to, in place of cow requested, **33**. 568
Beaufort resigns as Master of Horse to, **23**. 174
Bedchamber of: appointments to, **11**. 367n, **21**. 518; Berry, Mary, does not want to join, **12**. 126–8; Brudenell, Mrs Robert, woman of, **11**. 242n; candidates for, **38**. 96–7; Dalkeith, Cts of, excluded from, **38**. 142n; Egremont, Cts of, lady of, **25**. 68n; Hertford, Cts of, lady of, **25**. 338n; ladies of, at St James's, **32**. 19; ladies of, cannot attend her at Kew for fear of highwaymen, **24**. 47; members of, **21**. 518; vacancy in, **11**. 367n; Weymouth, Vcts, lady of, **41**. 342
bed of, in Great Drawing Room for son's baptism, **38**. 174
Bedford, Ds of, sends watch to, **22**. 104–5
Bedford faction could be driven away by anger of, **30**. 190
Bentley's *Wishes* compliments, **9**. 383
—— uses, as character in *Philodamus*, **9**. 414
birthday of, **6**. 139, **10**. 1, 204, **11**. 179, 272, **22**. 196, 197, 199, **25**. 236, **28**. 131n, **32**. 182, 226, 343, 345, 346, **33**. 335, 554n, **34**. 1, 3, **38**. 204–5, 286, **39**. 273–4, **43**. 145
Blenheim, Nuneham, and Castle Howard to be visited by, **36**. 246n
bridesmaids of, **35**. 312
brother receives Chelsea china from, **22**. 121–2
brothers of, **10**. 3, 10, 34, **22**. 3n, 8, 227n, 437
Brunswick, Ps of, snubbed by, **23**. 379n
Buckingham House ball attended only by husband's servants and those of, **38**. 290
—— furnished by, **10**. 33
—— to be chief residence of, **10**. 33, **15**. 160n
burlettas preferred by, **38**. 143
Burney, Frances, introduced to, by Mrs Delany, **42**. 171n
—— is second keeper of robes to, **42**. 170–3
—— resigns from service of, **42**. 330, 331
—— set by, to folding muslins, **31**. 271n

Bute's and Gloucester's Garter installations attended by, at Windsor, **22**. 79

Carlton House occupied by, **23**. 375n

caudle of, **32**. 19

chamberlain of: Harcourt may be succeeded by Lord Charles Spencer as, **23**. 66; Northumberland becomes, **22**. 103, **43**. 127

chamberlain's post in household of: **10**. 29; much sought for, **32**. 7

chaplain of, erased by Zoffany from painting of Tribune, **24**. 539–40

characteristics of, **38**. 101, 116–17, 127

Cheltenham visited by, **34**. 12n

Chetwynd, Deborah, sempstress and laundress to, **35**. 325n

Christian VII entertained by, **10**. 264

Chudleigh, Elizabeth, celebrates real birthday of, **38**. 204–5

—— has tableau representing, **38**. 204

Churchill, Lady Mary, well received by, for not championing Ds of Gloucester, **36**. 77

codicil added by, to George III's will, **25**. 680

comes from Mecklenburg-Strelitz, **29**. 35n

concerts may be substituted by, for opera at Haymarket, **38**. 101

Conway should escort, through France, **38**. 106

coronation date set for, **21**. 513

coronation medal of, **40**. 214

coronation of, **21**. 534–6

costume of, **21**. 529, **32**. 325, **34**. 110, **38**. 116

Covent Garden theatre attended by, with no applause, **38**. 288

Cowslade, gentleman usher to, **9**. 251n, **41**. 276n

'crimson-coloured shop glasses of,' **28**. 182

Cumberland, D. of, waits on, at Buckingham House, **22**. 288n

Dalton draws picture of, **21**. 525

Dashwood, Catherine, duenna to, **21**. 531

daughters of, **11**. 145

Delany, Mrs, noticed by, **15**. 334

De la Warr succeeds Ancaster as Master of Horse to, **22**. 473

Del Campo gives ball at Ranelagh for, **39**. 465n

diamond necklace would not have been relinquished by, **33**. 495

Drawing-Room of, postponed, **12**. 42

Elgin, Lady, reports on breakfast of, **12**. 160

English triumphs will make, feel as if marrying Alexander the Great, **21**. 517

Eton visited by, from Windsor, **22**. 83

farce to be seen by, joked about by HW, **33**. 135

feathers forbidden by, at Court, **25**. 183, **28**. 285

fourth son born to, **22**. 562

Fox, C. J., opposed by, in Westminster election, for 'debauching her son,' **25**. 489n

French spoken by, **21**. 529

friseur of, waits on table, **38**. 434

Garter might be worn by, **22**. 80n

gentleman usher to, *see* Smith, John

George III alienated by, from sons, **25**. 680, 682

—— and daughters play cards with, **25**. 682–3

—— dances with, at private ball, **38**. 143

—— intends to marry, **9**. 376

—— meets, in garden, **21**. 529

——'s portrait shown to, **22**. 501

—— taken by, to Ranelagh, **38**. 128

George IV vainly asks, to stop brother's duel, **39**. 464

Gloucester, D. of, attends Drawing-Room of, **31**. 299

Gloucester, D. and Ds of, may have been proscribed by, **36**. 77

government to be assumed by, **25**. 680

Graeme resigns places about, **32**. 183

Gray asks HW for description of, **14**. 119

Grenville, James, resigns as vice-treasurer to, **23**. 180

Guilford made treasurer to, **32**. 176

HW advises Selwyn how to remove probable bad impression of Kennedy received by, **30**. 254

HW contrasts, to Lady Ossory, **32**. 2

HW describes, **21**. 529, 542, **32**. 2, 3

HW does not want to show, to Fleury, **22**. 135

HW jokes about, **9**. 378, 379, **33**. 135

HW jokingly suggests plot against, **33**. 21

HW mentions, **9**. 402, 403

HW presented to, at Drawing-Room, **38**. 115

HW's 'character' of, **42**. 224

HW's correspondence with, **35**. 545

HW sends prospectus of *Cheap Repository Tracts* to Harcourt for, **31**. 396

HW's feelings if summoned to house of, **33**. 393

HW's new room at SH: might be visited by, **32**. 195n; to have been visited by, till hearing of his niece's match, **36**. 323

HW's servants repulse, from SH, **33**. 503

HW's visits from, arranged by Harcourt, **35**. 544–5

HW visited by, at SH, **35**. 544–5, **39**. 510–12

HW wishes, to see Great Bed at SH, **31**. 169

Halifax, and possibly Sandwich, call on George III at house of, **22**. 297n

Hamilton, Ds of, reassures, on reaching St James's, **21**. 528

Handel's *Samson* attended by, **32**. 110

Hanoverian dialect disparaged by, **21**. 530

Hanover may be visited by, **38**. 355

Harcourt should go to Court if summoned by, **35**. 481

Harcourt to fetch, **9**. 376, 379

Harcourt, Cts, shows anonymous verse letter to, **29**. 364

Harcourts neglected by, on death of first earl, **29**. 332, 348

Hardinge, solicitor-general to, **35**. 621

[Charlotte Sophia, *continued*]

harpsichord played by, to royal family, **21.** 530, **35.** 312, **38.** 101n

Harris becomes secretary to, **28.** 131n, **32.** 183

Hastings, Mrs, gives ivory bed to, **11.** 295n

Hellevoetsluis to be visited by, **9.** 377

Hertford to come to London for accouchement of, **38.** 166

Hertford, Cts of, to transmit correspondence of, with brother, **38.** 473–4

—— wants to be in household of, **38.** 104, 113

household of, **9.** 376–7, **21.** 517–18

Hussey resigns as attorney-general to, **23.** 180, **39.** 122

Jersey, Lady, favoured by, **12.** 186

Karl Ludwig Friedrich resembles, **10.** 10

Karl Wilhelm Ferdinand turns back towards, **38.** 289

Keppel's ship serves dinner to, **24.** 377n

Kingston, Ds of, presented to, **23.** 106n

Knight, Cornelia, dedicates book to, **34.** 168

La Luzerne gives ball for, **11.** 38n, **39.** 465

livery of, worn by Waldegrave's servants, **33.** 541

London's lord mayor and aldermen to present address to, **21.** 531

Lysons's drawings of Roman pavements requested by, **12.** 198, **34.** 222–3

maids of honour to receive, **9.** 377

manner of, gracious, **32.** 6

Mann presents box of essences to, **22.** 241, 243

Maria Louisa's rival in fertility, **25.** 425

Marie-Antoinette's death mourned by, **12.** 42

Markham's speech to, **29.** 281

Marlborough, Ds of, called proudest woman in England by, **11.** 81n

marriage of: **21.** 529, **32.** 3, 4, **28.** 131n, **38.** 116–19; considered by Privy Council, **21.** 513; delayed by mother's death, **21.** 517, **38.** 95–6, 100; plans for, **35.** 310

Mason's *Heroic Epistle* mentions, **28.** 45

——'s resignation of chaplaincy involves, **29.** 349

medallion of, **11.** 363

ministers have name of, inserted in Regency Bill, **22.** 296

Mogul, through Clive, gives diamonds to, **22.** 540, 547

Montagu, Mrs, visited by, **11.** 290

mother-in-law of: breakfasts with her, **39.** 116n; might be offended by her being regent, **22.** 294; receives her, **21.** 529; talks with her on death-bed, **23.** 379

Mount Edgcumbe visited by, **11.** 32

Newcastle, D. of, in retiring-room of, at Coronation, **21.** 535, **38.** 122

Northumberland, Ds of, has more footmen than, **34.** 23

——'s pomp exceeds that of, **38.** 469

numerous children of, **25.** 425, **28.** 341, **29.** 19

Oatlands and Wanstead visited by, from Richmond, **38.** 418

Octavius a favourite child of, **25.** 403

—— born to, **33.** 95

opera attendance by, **11.** 203n, **38.** 123, 126

opera crowded when attended by, **38.** 123

Opposition press attacks, **22.** 53, 76

palace of, *see* Buckingham House

Paoli presented to, **23.** 142n, 150

Petre, Lord, visited by, **33.** 66

Piccinni's *Buona figliuola* enjoyed by, **22.** 474

Pitt and Temple eclipse, at lord mayor's dinner, **21.** 547

Pitt, William II, protégé of, **25.** 680

plays attended by, **38.** 127

Polignacs go away without taking leave of, **39.** 449

Port presented to, for entrance to Charterhouse, **33.** 498n

pregnant, **22.** 8

prints of, **1.** 188, **21.** 554, **39.** 550

Regency Bill's inclusion of, debated, **22.** 294, **38.** 541–4, 549

resentment toward, for few invitations to balls, **33.** 325

Reynolds, Sir Joshua, advises, to buy Zoffany's 'Tribuna,' **24.** 540n

Richmond House play watched by, **33.** 563n

Richmond regatta watched by, **32.** 318

Salvadore, Mrs, and Mrs Mendes send card to, on George IV's birth, **22.** 72–3

Sandwich said to have kept fleet at Portsmouth for diversion of, **24.** 377

servants of, not new-dressed for sister-in-law's wedding but for her own birthday, **38.** 286

Shelburne summoned to house of, **25.** 261

Shirley comptroller to, **9.** 113–14n

sings, **21.** 530, **35.** 312, **38.** 101n

sons born to, **10.** 167, **22.** 64, 66, 562, **23.** 312, 557, **24.** 454, **33.** 95

sons' disagreements with, **39.** 464–5

sons of, **11.** 145, **32.** 171

sons unlikely to be ruled by, **25.** 683

stoned in Pall Mall, **34.** 212n

Stone treasurer to, **17.** 6n

SH visited by, **12.** 144, 248, **22.** 426, **33.** 503, **35.** 544–5, **38.** 418, **39.** 510–12

Titian's Venus would not please, **24.** 540

Vernon, Caroline, maid of honour to, **11.** 184n

—— not dismissed by, till after oratorio, **32.** 110

vice-chamberlain to, Charles Fitzroy becomes, **23.** 66

visits camp, **28.** 446n, 448–9nn

voyage of, to England, **21.** 528

Waldegrave becomes Master of Horse to, **23.** 180, **33.** 448, **38.** 568

—— shown concern by, **34.** 84

—— supposed to become chamberlain to, **38.** 568

Waldegrave, Cts, summoned by, to Windsor for Ps Charlotte's birthday, **36.** 247

Wales, P. of (George IV), reconciled with, **11.** 227

—— vainly asks, to stop brother's duel, 39. 464

Wales, Ps of (Caroline), to have fewer attendants than, 12. 131

Werpup attended, to England, 22. 306

Weymouth visited by, 11. 32n

William IV cautioned by, not to mention dukedom to George III, 25. 684n

Winchester visited by, 33. 59n

Windsor charms, 22. 79

—— mercer told by George III of gown wanted by, 33. 226n

wit of, 32. 3

yacht painting should turn head or stomach of, 21. 525

Yertzin, Mme de, speaks to, at Birthday, 38. 401

York, D. of, meets, at garden gate, 21. 529

—— might be temporary king if George III dies before delivery of, 22. 42

zebra belonging to, stuffed, 28. 90–1

Zoffany allegedly sent to Florence to paint Tribune scene for closet of, 24. 540

——'s 'Tribuna' bought by, 33. 138n

Charlotte St, Portland Place, London:
Lorimer of, 16. 311n

Charlotte St, Rathbone Place, London:
Farington lives in, 12. 187

Charlton, Sir Blunden (ca 1682–1742), 3d Bt, 1729; 'Sir Blundel Carlton':
nurse repulsed by, 33. 414, 415

Charlton, Elizabeth (d. 1817), m. (1785) Matthew Montagu (formerly Robinson), 4th Bn Rokeby, 1829:
fortune of, 31. 321
More, Hannah, praises, 31. 321

Charlton, Emma (d. 1748), m. 1 Thomas Cornwallis; m. 2 John Robinson, Bp of London:
Chandos, Ds of, does portrait of, 30. 61n

Charlton, John (fl. 1709), Master of Jewel Office:
Treasury warrant to, 13. 89n

Charlton, John (fl. 1768–?1806), 'page-surgeon' to D. of Gloucester:
Gloucester, D. of, treated by, at Leghorn, 23. 334, 336, 342, 393

Charlton. See also Charleton

Charlton, Kent:
Cholmondeley's villa at, 12. 200n

Charlton House, Kent:
Ancram, Cts of, may fetch daughter to, on husband's return, 37. 543

Charlton Place, Kent:
Foote of, 11. 81n
Foote, Mrs F. H., dies at, 24. 205n

Charlus, Comte de. See La Croix de Castries, Armand-Charles-Augustin de

Charlus, Comtesse de. See Bonnières de Guines, Marie-Louise-Philippine de

Charm; charms:
Whalley uses, for stone, 15. 315

Charmante, La, French schooner:
Pigot captures, 25. 318

'Charming ('charming man'), The.' See Jerningham, Edward

Charming Kitty, English brigantine:
Conelly, master of, 22. 174n
Moroccan emperor releases, 22. 174n

Charming Molly, English merchant ship:
French war ships encountered by, 18. 463n

Charming Nancy, English ship:
arrival of, 22. 174

Charmoisy, Mme Claude de. See Duchâtel, Louise

'Charms of the Athenians.' See under Pope, Alexander

Charolais, Comte de. See Bourbon, Charles de (1700–60)

Charolais, Mlle de. See Bourbon-Condé, Louise-Anne de

Charon, English ship:
Luttrell, capt. of, 24. 543n, 33. 150n
Omoa's capture reported by, 33. 150n

Charon:
boat of, 11. 285
HW jokes about, 32. 74
Stowe guests worthy of, 35. 339

Charost, Duc de. See Béthune, Armand-Joseph de (1738–1800); Béthune, Paul-François de (1682–1759)

Charost, Duchesse de. See Martel, Louise-Suzanne-Edmée

Charost, Marquis de. See Béthune, Louis-Joseph de (1681–1709)

Charost, Marquise de. See Brulart, Marie (ca 1685–1763)

Charpentier, François (1620–1702):
Louis XIV flattered by, 7. 356

Charpentier, Victor-Thérèse (1732–76), Marquis d'Ennery; governor of French Leeward Islands:
at Martinique, 41. 11
biographical information on, corrected, 43. 101
death of, ascribed to thunderbolt, 6. 403
Janssen buys country house of, at Ennery, 41. 11
ladies mourn, 6. 403

Charpentier d'Ennery, Marie-Cécile-Pauline (b. ca 1734), m. (1749) Gilbert de Chauvigny, Baron de Blot:
admired, 3. 76, 6. 41
Chartres, Duchesse de, attended by, 6. 293
Chesterfield praises, 6. 37, 41
Du Deffand, Mme, gives opinion of, 6. 41
HW knows, 39. 214
Necker, Mme, recommends, to HW, 39. 292
social relations of, with Mme de Luxembourg, 7. 304

Charrier. See Carrier

Charron, ——, Leghorn merchant:
Dick gets complaint from, about confiscated cargoes, 21. 273n

Charter; charters:
Middleton sends, to HW, 15. 1, 3

[Charter; charters, *continued*]
of Scottish kings, 15. 159, 182
Scottish, 42. 280

Charter Act. *See under* Parliament: acts of

Charterhouse (London), master of. *See* Bearcroft, Philip (1696–1761); Garrard, George (b. 1580); Mann, Nicholas (d. 1753); Salter, Samuel (1713–78)

Charterhouse, London:
Bryant declines mastership of, 2. 172
Law one of first governors of, 16. 48n
Middleton seeks mastership of, 15. 292–3, 306
Morton seeks mastership of, 31. 427
Port enters, on Q. Charlotte's presentation, 33. 498n
Sutton of, 16. 65,

Charterhouse Yard, London:
Wyat lives in, 41. 231

Charteris, Col. Francis (ca 1660–1732):
grandson inherits estate from, 19. 148–9
HW does not remember, clearly, 15. 142
immorality of, celebrated, 19. 148n
(?) West alludes to, 13. 138

Charteris, Francis (1723–1808). *See* Wemyss, Francis

Charters; Chartres. *See* Charteris

Chartier, Jean:
*Histoire de Charles VII* by, 8. 34

Chartres, Bp of. *See* Rosset de Rocozel de Fleury, Pierre-Augustin-Bernardin de

Chartres, Duc de. *See* Bourbon, Louis-Philippe de (1725–85); Bourbon, Louis-Philippe-Joseph de (1747–93); Louis-Philippe (1773–1850)

Chartres, Duchesse de. *See* Bourbon, Louise-Marie-Adélaïde de (1753–1821); Bourbon-Conti, Louise de (1726–59)

Chartres, Mlle de. *See* Bourbon d'Orléans, Louise-Marie-Adélaïde-Eugénie de

Chartres (France):
Louis XV hunts near, 3. 291
St-Hubert in diocese of, 3. 292n

Chartreuse (Lombardy):
suppression of, releases wealth, 25. 594

Chartreuse (Rue de l'Enfer, Paris):
cloister of, repainted, 32. 261
HW at, 7. 270, 308, 319, 337
HW buys pastilles at, 7. 410
HW pleased by gloom of, 13. 168
paintings at: 35. 425, 429–30; Angiviller saves, to be taken to Versailles and replaced with copies, 35. 425, 429–30; HW praises, 14. 145, 35. 126–7

Chartreuse, Grande, (in Savoy):
album of, 2. 302, 307
(?) Cambridge compared with, 20. 83

Chartreux. *See* Chartreuse

Charwood, Surrey:
Sanders of, 2. 220n

Charybdis:
Anderson, Mrs, compared to, 12. 145

Chase, Thomas (1729–88):
(?) Mann leaves ring to, 25. 667n
Tylney's legacy to, 25. 534

*Chase, The. See under* Somerville, William

Chase; chases:
Baskerville prepares, 40. 276

*Chasse de Henri IV, La. See under* Collé, Charles: *Partie de chasse*

Châsse de Ste-Geneviève, Paris:
uncovered, 7. 286

Chasseloup. *See* Chanteloup; Chasselup

Chasselup, ——:
HW seeks position for, from Edgcumbe, 40. 54

Chasseur; chasseurs:
Gévaudan beast shown by, 35. 113, 39. 14

Chastelet. *See* Hay du Chastelet

Chastellier du Mesnil, Charles-Louis-Joachim de (ca 1700–64), Marquis du Mesnil:
Ligonier's letter from, about prisoners' exchange, 37. 279n
parliament of Grenoble orders arrest of, 38. 301
recalled, 38. 301

Chastellux, François-Jean (1734–88), Chevalier (Marquis, 1784) de:
Académie française elects, 6. 116
HW entertains, at SH, 23. 468
lady talking with, 7. 121
Mann entertains, at Florence, 23. 468
social relations of, with: Helvétius, 7. 299; Holbach, 7. 267, 272
Wilkes knew, in Paris, 23. 28
—— talks with, in King's Bench Prison, 23. 28

Chastenet, Barthélemi-Athanase-Hercule de (b. 1729), Vicomte de Puységur:
(?) Du Deffand, Mme, expresses opinion of, 4. 350
(?) social relations of, with Duchesse de Choiseul, 4. 350

Chastenet, Jacques-François-Maxime de (1716–82), Marquis de Puységur:
(?) Du Deffand, Mme, expresses opinion of, 4. 350
(?) made maréchal de camp, 7. 147n
(?) social relations of, with Duchesse de Choiseul, 4. 350

Chastenet, Jean-Auguste de (1740–1815), Abbé de Puységur; Bp of St-Omer 1775–8, of Carcassone 1778–88; Abp of Bourges 1788–1802:
St-Omer bishopric given to, 6. 98
social relations of, with Mme du Deffand, 7. 428, 429
SH visited by, 12. 248

Chastenet, Louis-Pierre de (1726–1807), Comte de Puységur:
(?) Du Deffand, Mme, expresses opinion of, 4. 350
(?) social relations of, with: Choiseul, Duchesse de, 4. 350; Luxembourg, Mme de, 7. 301

Chastity:
  HW's reflections on vows of, **31**. 434
  St-Germain professes, **26**. 20
Chastleton, Oxon.:
  Greenwood of, **14**. 109
Chastre, La. See La Chastre
Chastres, Marquis de. See Du Deffand de la
  Lande, Jean-Baptiste-Jacques-Charles
Chastres, château of:
  Du Deffand, Mme, has legal rights to, **8**. 30
*Château d'Otrante, Le* (French translation of
  HW's *Castle of Otranto*):
  Choiseul wishes to read, **3**. 280
  Du Deffand, Mme, discusses reception of, **3**.
    256, 260, 270, 271, 283
  —— lends, to Mme de la Vallière, **5**. 123
  —— mentions, **5**. 115
  —— sends, to HW, **3**. 270, 271, 275, 280
  HW mentions, **3**. 260
  imperfect translation, **35**. 436
  See also *Castle of Otranto, The*
Château du Taureau, French prison:
  La Chalotais and son committed to, **11**. 44
Château-Giron. See Le Prestre de Château-
  Giron
Châteaurenaud, Marquise de. See Montmorency,
  Anne-Julie de
Châteauroux, Duchesse de. See Mailly-Nesle,
  Marie-Anne de
Châtel. See Du Châtel
Châtelain, Nicolas:
  *Atlas historique* by, **35**. 435n
Châtelet (surname). See Du Châtelet
Châtelet, Le, at Paris:
  arrêté of, **8**. 200
  Cazeaux imprisoned in, **7**. 134
  Mme du Deffand's will delivered at, **8**. 11
  papers of, searched to incriminate Marie-
    Antoinette, **34**. 176
  prisoners transferred to, **6**. 256
  Wortley Montagu and Taaffe imprisoned in,
    **20**. 287, **43**. 263
Châtelet, Place du, at Paris:
  Petits-Pères in, **13**. 164n
'Chatereux.' See Charterhouse
Chatfield, Mr (d. 1765):
  death of, **7**. 396
Chatham, Bns and Cts of. See Grenville, Lady
  Hester (1720–1803)
Chatham, E. of. See Pitt, John (1756–1835);
  Pitt, William (1708–78)
*Chatham*, English ship:
  in danger, **21**. 350
  Mann sends, to cruise, **18**. 460
Chatham, Kent:
  Amherst begins works at, **28**. 455
  army camp at, **37**. 476n
  barracks at, **11**. 57n
  Conway quits, for Park Place, **38**. 37n
  —— writes from the Lines at, **38**. 30–3
  Hanoverian troops embark at, **21**. 13n
  Hanoverian troops land at, **20**. 526n

(?) incendiary attempt upon, **23**. 470
Lines, The, at, **38**. 17, 30–3
naval title, that might have gone to Con-
  way, **38**. 135
SH as barren of events as, **38**. 34
visitors to: Conway, **38**. 17; Stephens, **38**. 33
Chatham Annuity Bill. See *under* Parliament:
  acts of
Chatham barony:
  Pitt, Lady Hester, receives, **9**. 395
Chatham earldom:
  annuity settled on, by Parliament, **24**. 382
'Châtillon, Dame de':
  in *La Réduction de Paris*, **32**. 269
Châtillon, Duchesse de. See La Baume le Blanc,
  Adrienne-Émilie-Félicité de (1740–1812); Le
  Veneur de Tillières, Anne-Gabrielle (1699–
  1781)
Châtillon, Amable-Émilie de (1761–1840), m.
  (1777) Marie-François-Emmanuel, Duc de
  Crussol:
  marriage of, **6**. 431, 436, 439
  SH visited by, **12**. 248
Châtillon, Louis de (1639–1734), painter:
  Ennery has medallion of, **7**. 325
  Petitot's pupil, **7**. 325
Châtillon, Louis-Gaucher, Duc de:
  wife of, **4**. 83n, **12**. 31n
Châtillon, Louise-Emmanuelle de (1763–1814),
  m. (1781) Charles-Bretagne-Marie-Joseph,
  Prince de Tarente, and (1792) Duc de la
  Trémoïlle:
  HW visits, **12**. 3, 44
  Marie-Antoinette's relations with, **12**. 31
  mother and grandmother of, arrested in Paris,
    **12**. 31
Châtillon. See also Du Plessis-Châtillon
Châtillon, near Paris:
  visitors to: Chabot, **7**. 331; Choiseul, Duc and
    Duchesse de, **7**. 331; Du Deffand, Mme, **4**.
    245; HW, **7**. 331; Invault, M. and Mme d',
    **7**. 331; Lavaur, Bp of, **7**. 331; Mercy-Ar-
    genteau, **7**. 331; Orléans, Bp of, **7**. 331; St-
    Brieuc, Bp of, **7**. 331; Trudaine de Mon-
    tigny, M. and Mme, **7**. 331
Chat qui dort (game):
  played, **7**. 335, 336
Châtre. See La Châtre
Chatres. See Chartres
Chatsworth, Derbyshire, seat of D. of Devonshire:
  Bess of Hardwick builds, **40**. 182–3
  bridge designed for, **9**. 296
  chapel at, **9**. 296
  Coke, Lady Mary, thinks of visiting, **37**. 561
  'condemned,' **9**. 296, **43**. 123
  Devonshire, Ds of, tired of, **32**. 392
  Devonshire, D. of, invites HW to, **35**. 303–4
  ——leaves, for Kensington, **21**. 11n
  Devonshires occupy, **9**. 295
  —— retire to, **20**. 66
  fountain at, **9**. 296

[Chatsworth, *continued*]
  Gaubert's plans at, 33. 499
  Graftons' visit to, put off, 38. 63
  HW and Conway to visit, 38. 415, 422
  HW describes, 9. 295–6
  HW pleased with, 35. 305
  HW sees Bonfoy at, 13. 166n
  HW to accompany Ds of Grafton to, 21. 427
  HW to visit, 1. 66n
  HW writes from, while visiting D. of Devonshire, 21. 432
  Hardwick Hall compared with, 40. 182
  Lort to visit, 16. 171
  public dinner at, 38. 72
  stables of, 9. 296
  Talman designer of, 9. 292
  visitors to: Bessborough, 9. 295, 38. 19; Bonfoy, 9. 295, 13. 166n; Bridgwater, 38. 19; Cavendish, Lords George Augustus, Frederick, and John, 38. 19; Coke, Lady Mary, 9. 295, 38. 72; Conway, 41. 165n; Conway and wife, 37. 561, 563, 564; Cumberland, D. of, 38. 19; Gower, 38. 19; Grafton, Ds of, 37. 561; HW, 9. 295, 13. 166n, 21. 432, 35. 305, 38. 72, 40. 181, 41. 165; Hertford, 38. 18, 19, 91; Hertford, Cts of, 38. 91; Montagu, Frederick, 9. 303; Moore, Sir John, 38. 19; Ponsonby, Ladies Catherine, Charlotte, and Sarah, 9. 295; Rockingham, 38. 19; Saussure, 41. 165; Straffords, 9. 295, 38. 72; Thomond, 9. 295; Waldegrave, 38. 19
  Wilmot treats D. of Devonshire at, 38. 419
Chatteauleux. *See* Chastellux
'Chatte blanche, la.' *See under* Le Jumel de Barneville, Marie-Catherine, Mme d'Aulnoy
Chatterpost, Mrs:
  husband to have been brought by, to dine with HW, 12. 179n
Chatterton, Alanus (d. 1415):
  epitaph of, 16. 179n
Chatterton, Mary (1749–1804), m. Thomas Newton:
  Chatterton's sister, 29. 183n
Chatterton, Thomas (1713–52), father of the poet:
  poetry in old parchments would be noticed by, since he was musical, 16. 332
  wife of, 16. 125n
Chatterton, Thomas (1752–70), poet:
  ancient deeds imitated by, in forging MSS, 16. 241
  ancient diary might have been found by, in MSS of St Mary Redcliff, 16. 355–6
  Barrett and Catcott told by, that MSS were in another's possession, 16. 176
  Barrett received no poetical MSS from, 16. 362
  ——'s argument in favour of, 16. 220–1
  ——'s documents should disillusion proselytes of, 16. 222, 227
  Beckford's death mentioned by, 2. 288
  *Biographia Britannica* includes: Gregory's

  life of, 16. 212, 360, 31. 326; Lort's account of HW's relations with, 16. 212–13, 217
  'Bristowe Tragedie,' Fenn hoped Bryant would explain, 16. 239
  Broughton publishes *Miscellanies* of, 28. 422–3
  Bryant and Milles consider, no genius, 16. 332
  Bryant and Milles on controversies over, 33. 316–17
  Bryant ascribes poems of, to a third person, 16. 354
  —— too severe upon, 16. 236–7
  Cary considers, a genius but incapable of writing Rowley poems, 16. 333
  Catcott rejects Tyrwhitt's theory of debt of, to Skinner's glossary, 16. 178–9
  character of, inverted by Milles and Bryant, 29. 171–2
  Charlemont buys MSS of, 16. 132
  concert in memory of, at Bristol, 16. 351, 363
  'Consuliad' HW calls, unintelligible, 16. 346
  controversies over, 42. 13–14
  Courtenay refers to HW's relations with, 12. 94
  death of, 2. 50, 52, 77–8, 205, 318, 319
  deed may have been seen by, 16. 342
  easily believed, in Bristol, 16. 223
  *European Magazine* prints H.I.'s attack on HW concerning, 2. 335
  'Execution of Sir Charles Bawdin, The' ('Bristowe Tragedie') by, dismal and dull, 28. 36
  false Latin syntax used by, in forged epitaph, 16. 358–9
  Fielding and Walker want more MSS by, for future edition, 16. 177
  forgeries of, 34. 214, 35. 584
  genius of: 2. 52, 81, 305–6, 16. 361, 28. 281–2, 424; 'gigantic,' 33. 475
  *Gentleman's Magazine* prints controversy over, 16. 243
  HW accused of having driven, to despair, 16. 122–3, 214–15
  HW asked by, to return Rowley papers, 16. 115, 116
  HW asks Percy's advice about affair of, 41. 395–6
  HW called 'Baron Otranto' by, 2. 107, 110, 288, 291
  HW denies receiving letters supposedly sent by, 31. 326
  HW determined to avoid controversy over, 16. 221–2, 226, 236
  HW indifferent to controversy over, 33. 319
  HW probably could not have saved, 16. 132
  HW receives anonymous letter accusing him of contributing to death of, 43. 230
  HW said to have been told by, that MSS were Barrett's property, 16. 358
  HW's alleged denial of letters written to, 34. 149–51

HW's answer to Broughton's attack over, *see Letter to the Editor of the Miscellanies of Thomas Chatterton*

HW's collection of pieces concerning, **16.** 331–63

HW's correspondence with: **31.** 222, 326, 331, **34.** 149–51; HW's side of, stifled, **16.** 227; in Barrett's history, **16.** 219–20, 222, **34.** 150; Lort sees, at Barrett's in Bristol, **16.** 174–5; mentioned, **16.** 123, 125–6, 127–9; text of, **16.** 101–18

HW's letter to Bewley about, **2.** 85, 87, 90, 92, 102, 104, 107, 109, 114, 132, 133

HW's reasons for not publishing his *Letter* on, **33.** 319

HW's relations with, recounted by Lort for *Biographia Britannica*, **16.** 212–13, 217

HW's remarks on poems of, are cursory, **16.** 236

HW's repulse to, described by Broughton, **16.** 345

HW's respect for talents of, **33.** 41

HW's scepticism about, confirmed by Gray and Mason, **28.** 441

HW's treatment of, gentle, **28.** 422–3

HW's writings on, requested by Bowle, **42.** 42, 45

HW unlikely to publish anything about, **16.** 122

honesty rather than forgery would have been better policy for, **16.** 176–7

ignorance of, concerning D. of Devonshire's house, **16.** 347

illustrations of Bristol Castle in Barrett's *History* probably forged by, **16.** 221

Lamington monument may have inspired, **16.** 341

Latin said to be unknown to, **16.** 178

Lort tells Steevens of HW's letter about, **16.** 225

'lost to the Muses,' **29.** 338n

*Love and Madness* gives account of, **2.** 205–6, 208

Malone sends essay on affair of, to HW, **42.** 1–4

Mason's garbled account of 'confession' of, **29.** 182

——'s verses on exposure of, **28.** 430–2, 435–8, **29.** 373–4

—— thinks poems of, were antiquitized after being written in modern English, **28.** 428

mausoleum of, described in *Lady's Magazine*, **16.** 350–1, 360

*Miscellanies in Prose and Verse* by: **2.** 102, 107, **43.** 67; HW quotes from, **33.** 475; HW's notes on, **16.** 345–8; Lort receives, from publishers, **16.** 177; published, **33.** 40–1

*Monthly Review*'s account of, **2.** 50

original of 'Battle of Hastings' not brought to Barrett by, **16.** 361

Ossian imitated by, **2.** 288

paper used in 15th century unknown to, **16.** 243

poems of: believed because they seemed old, **41.** 357; Bryant and Milles mistaken about, **42.** 1–3; no genuine antiquity in, **16.** 237–8; quoted, **16.** 104, 108–9, 111

*Poems Supposed to have been Written at Bristol . . . by Thomas Rowley*: **28.** 309n, **29.** 196n, **43.** 74; accepted by Milles and Bryant, **29.** 129, 169; *Archæological Epistle* concerning, **2.** 311–12, 314, 314–15; believers in authenticity of, **2.** 277–8; Bryant's *Observations* on, **2.** 284, 287–9, 290, 291, 296; Cole on, **2.** 104–5; footnote to, **16.** 175; Glynn seeks proof of authenticity of, **2.** 50, 92, 104, 107, 288; HW on authenticity of, **2.** 52, 205, 288–9, 305–6; HW's name introduced into account of, **16.** 122; HW's notes on, **16.** 331–45; Malone on, **2.** 291, 295, 296, 298, 305, 307; Milles's edition of, **2.** 284, 287, 288, 290, 296; Milles seeks proof of authenticity of, **2.** 92, 277–8; not mentioned by Bale or Pits, **2.** 105, 106; not mentioned by William of Worcester, **2.** 104, 105; pronounced gospel though HW doubts, **33.** 317; rejected by Warton, **28.** 381; reported proof of forgery of, **2.** 205; submitted to HW, **2.** 50, 52, 78, 80–1, 112, 113, 128, **28.** 36; Tyrwhitt convinced of forgery of, **2.** 82–3, 85, 90, 287–8, **15.** 165n; Tyrwhitt publishes, **28.** 281, 292, **29.** 374

poetic models of, **16.** 127

prints by, reveal ignorance, **31.** 326

*Rambler, The*, copied by, **16.** 333–4

Rowleian controversy over, settled by Tyrwhitt's book, **15.** 165

Scrutator's letter on HW and, **34.** 148–51

Smith calls genius of, 'universal,' **16.** 361

suicide attempted by, when he was not in want, **16.** 223–4

suicide of, told by HW to Goldsmith, **16.** 130

*Supplement to the Miscellanies of Thomas Chatterton, A*, **16.** 177n, 362–3, **43.** 357

*Town and Country Magazine* said to be source of story of, about HW and Mrs Clive, **16.** 346

——'s contribution by, **16.** 175

Turgot may have been read by, **16.** 336–7, 341, 343

Tyrwhitt's exposure of, **15.** 165n

versatility of, **16.** 131

Warton on, **2.** 77–8, 81, 287–8, **16.** 171, 223

will of, contains Latin, **16.** 179

words of, more antiquated than phraseology, **16.** 338

wrote little after leaving Bristol, **16.** 224

See also *Letter to the Editor of the Miscellanies of Thomas Chatterton, A*, by HW

Chatterton, Mrs Thomas. *See* Young, Sarah

Chaucer, Alice (ca 1404–75), m. 1 Sir John Philip, K.B.; m. 2 Thomas de Montagu, 4th

[Chaucer, Alice, *continued*]
E. of Salisbury; m. 3 William de la Pole, 1st
D. of Suffolk:
HW hopes he is descended from, 9. 68
in Margaret of Anjou's escort, 14. *70*, 73, 74
second husband of, corrected, 43. 114
Chaucer, Geoffrey (? 1340–1400), poet:
black-letter edition of, offered to HW, 29.
163–5
*Canterbury Tales, The*, by: HW finds couplet
applicable to Ds of Kingston in, 28. 191;
HW quotes, 11. 62; Parson's Tale in, men-
tioned by Mason, 28. 321
Chatterton's imitations unconvincing to
readers of, 35. 584
dissertations on language of, 35. 523
'Flower and the Leaf' attributed to, 11. 10n,
29. 331n
French enthusiasm for, 40. 304
HW hopes he is descended from, 9. 68
HW prefers, in Dryden's versions, 28. 191, 29.
165
Hoccleve's portrait of, 14. 108–9, 116
Mason wants to antiquitize Chatterton in
manner of, 28. 428–9
Montagu's wit as unintelligible as, to yokels,
10. 259
Pinkerton's scheme would make all English
poetry as obsolete as, 16. 264
Pope and Dryden did not improve, according
to Warton, 28. 143–4
print of, by John Speed, 14. 108–9
*Troilus and Criseyde*: Kynaston's translation
of, 16. 151; MS of, at St John's College,
Cambridge, 14. 108
Tyrwhitt's edition of, 2. 82, 83n, 28. 281n
Vertue sought MSS and portraits of, 16. 134
Chaucer, Thomas (ca 1367–1434), M.P.:
daughter of, 9. 68n, 14. 70n
tomb of, shown in print of Geoffrey Chaucer,
14. 108
Chaucer family:
arms and alliances of, 14. 108–9
'Chaucerides':
HW's nom-de-plume, 9. 73
*Chaud d'eau*:
Craon, Princesse de, gives, to Mann, 19. 385
Chaudière River:
expedition against, 20. 495n
Chauffepié, Jacques-Georges de (1702–86):
*Nouveau dictionnaire*, HW may have used,
21. 253n
Chaulieu, —— de, Broglie's aide-major-gen.:
Versailles notified by, of victory over P.
Ferdinand, 21. 287n
Chaulieu. *See also* Amfrye de Chaulieu
Chaulnes, Duc de. *See* Albert d'Ailly, Charles d'
(1625–98); Albert d'Ailly, Marie-Joseph-
Louis d' (1741–93); Albert d'Ailly, Michel-
Ferdinand d' (1714–69)
Chaulnes, Duchesse de. *See* Bonnier de la Mos-
son, Anne-Josèphe

Chaume, Rue du, Paris:
Hôtel de Soubise near, 7. 283n
Chaumont, Antoine-Martin de (1697–1783),
Marquis de la Galaisière; Stanislas I's chancellor; conseiller d'État:
Boufflers, Marquise de, has intrigue with,
22. *244*
social relations of, with Mme de Mirepoix,
7. 341
speech of, at suppression of Court des aides,
5. 58–9
Stanislas I's chancellor, 7. 341, 22. 244
Chaumont de Quitry, Marie-Anne de (1736–
1812), m. (1754) Claude-Marguerite-Fran-
çois Renart de Fuchsamberg, Comte d' Am-
blimont:
Choiseul and Duchesse de Gramont entertain,
at Chanteloup, 4. 469
Chauncy, Charles (1706–77), M.D.:
Cuyp view bought by, 23. 569n
HW's correspondence with, 41. 145
Sunderland's etchings bought by, at Pond's
sale, and sent to HW by Bathoe, 41. 145
Chaussée, Nivelle de la. *See* Nivelle de la
Chaussée
Chauveau-Lagarde, Claude-François (1756–
1841), counsel for Marie-Antoinette:
Marie-Antoinette's 'defamatory spy,' 12. 48
Chauvelin, Marquise de. *See* Mazade d'Arge-
ville, Agnès-Thérèse
Chauvelin, Anne-Sabine-Rosalie (b. 1732), m.
(1752) Jean-François de la Rochefoucauld,
Vicomte de la Rochefoucauld; Comte de
Surgères:
(?) social relations of, with Duchesse d'Anville, 7. 311
Chauvelin, Charlotte-Ferdinande de, m. (1778)
Marie-Louis-Charles de Vassinhac, Vicomte
d'Imécourt:
Chanteloup to be visited by, 7. 150–1
—— visited by, 8. 207
pension of, 5. 431, 435
Chauvelin, François-Bernard (1766–1832), Marquis de:
master of the wardrobe at 7, 5. 431, 435
Chauvelin, François-Claude *alias* Bernard-Louis
(1716–73), Marquis de; army officer; diplomatist:
acts at Chanteloup, 5. 382n
ambassadorships of, 5. 433
Argental, friend of, 6. 120
Conti's friendship with, 5. 431
Corsican campaign of, 4. *64*, 66, 199, 200, 202,
23. 62n
Curzay arrested by orders of, 20. 353
——'s transfer to Antibes ordered by, 20.
353n
death of, 5. 427, 428
Du Deffand, Mme, cites song of, 6. 274
——'s opinion of, 5. 428
——'s relations with, 5. 433
Du Tillot installed by, at Parma, 23. 445

(?) England threatened by, **20.** 497

France blames, for Corsican reverses, **23.** 68

French troops under, to garrison Corsican ports, **23.** 27

Genoa has pledge from, **20.** 353n

grandes entrées granted to, **4.** 339

house of, in Rue de Bourbon, **5.** 431, 435, 436

Lauzun leaves for Corsica ahead of, **4.** 135

—— ordered to join, **4.** 135n

Lorenzi told by, of Curzay's arrest, **20.** 353

Louis XV's benefactions to family of, **5.** 431, 435

Noailles temporarily replaces, at Turin, **20.** 497n

social relations of, with Mme du Barry, **4.** 288

song by: for Ds of Parma: **4.** 89–90, 97; attributed to Mme du Deffand, **6.** 26

verses by, on seven deadly sins, admired by HW, **33.** 580

wife of, **3.** 210n

York, D. of, does not return visit of, at Turin, **22.** 230n

Chauvelin, Henri-Philippe de (1714–70), theologian; abbé:

address of, on Pragmatic Sanction, **3.** 293–4

death of, **4.** 342

*Discours* by, **3.** 293–4, 43. 86

Du Deffand, Mme, compares, to Wilkes, **4.** 342

HW discusses Jesuits with, in Paris, **23.** 524

'Henri V,' **4.** 342

Jesuits demolished by, in France, **23.** 524n

—— denounced by, to French parliament, **22.** 513–14

name of, corrected, **43.** 85

Chauvelin, Jacques-Bernard (1701–67), seigneur de Beauséjour; intendant des finances:

death of, from gout, **3.** 265

Chauvelin, Louise-Philippe de, m. (1781) Charles-Esprit-Clair de la Bourdonnaye, Comte de Blassac; Marquis du Timeur:

pension of, **5.** 431, 435

Chauvigny, Gilbert de (1720–85), Baron de Blot:

marriage of, **3.** 76n

social relations of, with Mme de Monconseil, **7.** 297, 332

Chavanne. *See* Borré de la Chavanne

Chavannes. *See* Le Rat de Chavannes

Chavaudon, ——:

attends session of parliament of Paris, **8.** 173

Chavignard, Anne-Théodore de (ca 1688–1772), Chevalier de Chavigny; Comte de Toulongeon; French diplomatist:

Denbigh, Cts of, quotes observation by, on English parliaments, **22.** 294

Lorenzi assured by, that Louisbourg would be saved, **21.** 235

Chavigny, Chevalier de. *See* Chavignard, Anne-Théodore

Chavigny, Théodore de (d. 1771), diplomatist:

France's possible negotiator with England, **21.** 355n

(?) social relations of, in Paris, with HW, Sir James Gray, Nicol, and Hon. Robert Walpole, **7.** 317

Chaville (France), Comtesse de Tessé's seat:

Gramont, Duchesse de, to visit. **5.** 363

—— visits, **7.** 449

Chaworth, William (d. 1765):

Byron kills, in duel, **9.** 299n, **10.** 148n, **22.** 284, 293, **38.** 501, 503

——'s trial for killing, **30.** 177n

house of, in Berkeley Sq., **38.** 503

Chayla, ——, French army officer:

Eger relieved by, **18.** 217n

Cheam, Surrey:

Evans, rector of, **14.** 36n

Henry VIII's palace at, **28.** 167n

Cheam School, Surrey:

Gilpin, master of, **29.** 80n

Cheap, Mrs:

SH visited by, **12.** 233

Cheap, Thomas, of Ealing:

(?) SH visited by, **12.** 231

Cheape, Marianne (ca 1773–1849), m. 1 (1792) Sir Alexander Campbell, 4th Bt; m. 2 (1817) Thomas Lyon-Bowes (later Bowes-Lyon), 11th E. of Strathmore, 1820:

(?) HW meets, at Mrs Udny's, **11.** 107

(?) tells HW Mrs Udny's age, **11.** 109

*Cheap Repository Tracts. See under* More, Hannah

Cheapside, London:

Andrews in, **2.** 371n

Booth a 'tradesman' in, **33.** 99

Boydell lives in, **16.** 194

Briscoe of, **9.** 74n

Cutler lives near, **31.** 84

French invasion to be observed in, **9.** 23

Hayley's annotation as long as, **29.** 257

looking-glass sought in shops of, **20.** 141

Mereworth church suitable for, **35.** 143

*North Briton* to be burnt at, **22.** 187

riot at, on burning *North Briton*, **38.** 256–7

windows broken in, on Bastille Day, **11.** 314

Cheddar, Somerset:

More, Hannah, attempts reforms at, **31.** 328, 334

More sisters plan for Sunday School at, **31.** 321n

Chedworth, Bn. *See* Howe, John (d. 1742); Howe, John Thynne (1714–62)

Chedworth, Margaret (d. 1494), Ds of Norfolk:

not at Henry VII's Court, **2.** 364

Cheek; cheeks:

convulsion of, **23.** 280

Cheeke, Anne (d. 1728), m. (ca 1699) Sir Thomas Tipping, Bt:

daughter of, **17.** 333n

Cheeke, Joanna (1721–1819), m. (1763) William Melliar, of Castle Cary, Somerset:
HW sends love to, 40. 252
Holland, Lady, makes no bequest to, 32. 198
Cheere, Sir Henry (d. 1781):
statue by, 13. 100n
Cheese; cheeses:
between pear and, 35. 230n
Brescia trades in, 17. 324n
Choiseul, Duchesse de, sends, to Mme du Deffand, 5. 240
Clement XIII permits, in Lent, 22. 17n
Cotenham, 1. 199, 216, 2. 277
ditchers' diet, 37. 172
Dodd and Whaley have, at Deane House, 40. 5
English scarcity of, 22. 460
HW could send, from Windsor, 19. 331
HW does not receive, from Montagu, 10. 266
HW's, made at SH, sent to Montagu, 9. 168, 170
Marzolini: English cream cheese less delicate than, 18. 195; Grifoni, Mme, to send, to HW, 18. 348; Mann gives, to Mathews, 18. 195
monks serve, 13. 182
Montagu sends, to HW, 10. 265, 266
rebels send, to Carlisle, 37. 211
recipe for: 4. 60; offered to HW, 3. 394
See also Viri cheese
Cheesecake house:
Greek architecture inappropriate for, 20. 127
Mann fears his villa would become, 20. 160
Cheese-milk:
peasants' food, Shakespeare's plays considered as, 35. 629
Cheese-mongers:
peerages enjoyed by, 41. 361
Cheesman, Capt. (d. 1776):
killed at Quebec, 24. 185n
Cheetham. See Chetham
Cheevers, Sarah, Quakeress:
Cole has book on imprisonment of, on Malta, 1. 251–2
Cheke, Lady Dorothy. See Sidney, Lady Dorothy
Cheke, Sir John (ca 1514–57):
Ridley's letter to, 1. 273n
Cheke: See also Cheeke
Chekin, ——:
Ivan VI's possible murderer, 22. 253n
Chelles, Abbess of (d. ca 1743):
Ds of Modena's sister, 18. 222n
Chelmsford, Essex:
Griffin leads voters to election in, 38. 263
Karl Wilhelm Ferdinand complimented at, by Quaker, 22. 197
Mildmay's monument at, 9. 183n
Rigby going to, 30. 222
Chelotti, Bargello of Florence:
grenadiers want to kill, 24. 8n
Chelsea, Vct. See Cadogan, Charles Sloane

Chelsea, Middlesex:
Anstey dies at, 14. 5n
Blanchard's balloon launched at, 39. 423
Bolingbroke's house in, 33. 78n
Botanical ('Physic') Garden at: tea seed said to be found at, 18. 183, 216, 250, 284; Sloane's house near, 20. 358n
Carmey lives near Ranelagh House at, 40. 259
Caroline, Q., dines with Walpoles at, 15. 333, 33. 248
China of, see under China (ware)
church at, HW and Anne Pitt to visit, 31. 139
Cole's aunt confined at, 1. 321n
grotto at, 17. 503
HW at, 40. 21
HW plays with Chudleigh children at, 24. 198
HW revisits, 9. 40
HW writes from, 18. 7, 26
HW writes to his mother at, 36. 3, 4
'heathen temples' in, 30. 56n
'Jenny's Whim,' tavern at, 9. 108
King's Road from Battersea to, 31. 273n
Kyrwood, Mrs, at, 9. 15
Lens, Bernard, of, 2. 222
Maclaine lodges at, 20. 168
Mann knew Ds of Kingston at, 23. 559, 24. 203
Mann, Edward, dies at, 21. 555
Middleton visits Walpoles at, 15. 4
Newcastles at, 9. 40–1
Newton (Farren), Mary, of, 30. 360
operas eclipsed by, 17. 421
Orford House at: 2. 223n, 13. 7n, 15. 252n, 24. 198n, 43. 170, 175; HW at, 40. 1, 2, 21; Houghton paintings formerly at, 9. 348; parlour and summer house at, 37. 126; unbearable to HW after mother's death, 40. 24; Walpole, Lady, dies at, 13. 140n; Walpole, Sir Robert, entertains at, 17. 502–3, 18. 14; Walpole, Sir Robert, fetched to, by brother, 17. 386; Walpole, Sir Robert, occupies, 9. 40n, 13. 118, 161n, 24. 198, 33. 248, 36. 5; Walpole, Sir Robert, stores paintings at, 18. 249, 24. 441n; Walpoles lived at, 24. 198
Paradise Row at, 13. 4n
porcelain from, see under China
Ranelagh at, see under Ranelagh
Senauki swims from, to Fulham, 42. 236
Sloane's collection to be kept at his house in, 20. 358n
Stanley's estate at, left to Lord Cadogan, 33. 161
visitors to: Cerretesi, 17. 503; Conway, 37. 102; Fitzwilliam, 17. 502; HW, 17. 502–3; Paxton, 17. 502
Walpole, Sir Edward, at, 18. 250, 284
Walpole, Sir Robert, employed Van Huysum at, 36. 238n
—— moves to, 17. 334n
Watts's address, 16. 194

Whitefield, George, preaches at, **9**. 74

Winchester House at, **9**. 222

Zinzendorf buys Lindsey House at, for Moravians, **20**. 359n

Chelsea china factory:

Morgan buys stock of, **10**. 270n

Chelsea College. *See* Chelsea Hospital

Chelsea Company:

reservoirs of, have water for fire-fighting, **17**. 496n

Chelsea Hospital ('Chelsea College'):

Adair surgeon to, **36**. 130n

balloon ascent at, cancelled, **25**. 528n

Bland, chaplain to, **18**. 245n, **40**. 24n

Burney, Dr, addressed at, **42**. 331

——'s apartment at, **42**. 330n

Chudleigh deputy governor to, **24**. 198

Chudleigh, Mrs, carries footpad's body to, **24**. 203

Chute's proposed arms more appropriate to, **35**. 108–9

Estwick resigns as secretary and register of, **33**. 400n

government of, **15**. 88

Mann, Robert, deputy treasurer of, **17**. 27n, **24**. 198n

Monsey physician to, **1**. 364

Orford House in stableyard of, **13**. 118n

Pelham succeeded by Winnington as paymaster of, **18**. 313n

pensioners of: escort Mrs Chudleigh, **24**. 198; to mount guard, **19**. 69

secretary to commissioners of, *see* Eyre, Kingsmill

Walpole, Horatio (1752–1822), kisses hands for place at, **33**. 400

Chelsea Reach:

boat anchored in, raided by pirates, **11**. 31

Chelsum, Rev. James (1738–1801), D.D.:

Gibbon replies to, **33**. 84

*History of the Art of Engraving in Mezzotinto, A*, by, presented to HW who offers to aid him in new edition, **42**. 209

Cheltenham, Glos:

ancient painting at, **2**. 191

Carlisles to go to, perhaps with Selwyn, **34**. 13

Fox, Lady Caroline, not to visit, **30**. 48

George III's attack of insanity attributed to waters at, **12**. 147, **34**. 47

Keppels to visit, **36**. 246

Sudeley Castle near, **11**. 165n

visitors to: Berry, Agnes, **12**. 99, 103, 134; Berrys, **12**. 139, 143–7, 151, 154, 158–9, 161, 162, 163, 165, 167, **15**. 266, 269, 271; Carlisle, **31**. 287; Charlotte, Q., and daughters, **34**. 12n; Darells, **12**. 203; Fox, C. J., **33**. 536; George III, **12**. 147, **31**. 268, **34**. 6, 12n, 47, **36**. 251; Keppel, Mrs, **31**. 287; Lockhart, Mrs, **12**. 99, 103n; Orford, **20**. 273; Selwyn, **31**. 287; Williams, Sir C. H., **30**. 48, 58, 62, 67n

Waldegrave may go to, **36**. 257, 258, 260

Chemesov, E. P. (1737–65), engraver:

Catherine II's print by, **23**. 242

Chemist; chemists:

Branchi one of the best, in Italy, **18**. 177

Ginori employs Wandelin as, **18**. 184n

Rock, Richard, quack, on Ludgate Hill, **21**. 132n

Chemistry:

Conway's experiments in, **39**. 551

of paints, Beale interested in, **40**. 367n

Patch studied, **23**. 275

progressed through search for fanciful discoveries, **31**. 325

Chenevix, Paul Daniel (d. ?1743), toy-shop-keeper:

Craon, Princesse de, hopes to get things from, **20**. 24

HW mentions, **37**. 133

library of, at SH, **37**. 270

wife of, **9**. 32n, **13**. 103n

Chenevix, Mrs (?) Paul Daniel. *See* Deard, Elizabeth

Chenevix, Richard (1698–1779), Bp of Killaloe, 1745; of Waterford and Lismore, 1746:

brother of, **13**, 103n

Synge succeeds, **14**. 10n

Cheneys. *See* Chenies

Chenies, Bucks:

HW sees Russell family tombs in church at, **9**. 102, **37**. 298n

Sissinghurst resembles, **35**. 145

Chenille:

Roland, Mme, uses, in La Malle plan, **10**. 196

Chennevières. *See* Nouveau de Chennevières

Chenonceaux (France):

Dupin, Mme, at, **4**. 281

Chepstow, Monmouthshire:

Setons move to, **43**. 144

Cher, river:

Aiguillon's country seat on, **4**. 253n

Cherbourg (France):

cannon from, brought to England, **21**. 238, **31**. 22

Cocks wounded at, **21**. 245

Coke, Lady Mary, talks about, **37**. 561

cones at, damaged, **34**. 3

English capture of, **9**. 222, **21**. 225–6, 232, 234, 243, **30**. 146, **35**. 102–3, **37**. 557–9

English charity to poor of, **21**. 238

English expedition 'peeps at,' **39**. 526

English feint at, **37**. 541

English have not drunk tea under cannon of, **39**. 526

HW jokes about restoration of, to protect Hanover, **30**. 146

Howe demolishes works at, **30**. 148

quatrain on English attack on, **21**. 244

Walpole, Edward, behaves gallantly at, **21**. 246

Cherbury, Lord Herbert of. *See* Herbert, Edward (1583–1648)

Cherichini. *See* Barducci Cherichini

Chernyshev, ——:
Mann presents, at Tuscan Court, **25.** 84

Chernyshev, Daria Petrovna, m. Count Ivan Petrovich Saltykov:
born in England, **33.** 352
breakfasts at SH, **33.** 362
highwaymen feared by, **33.** 352
La Vallière, Duchesse de, recommends, to HW, **33.** 352
Ossory, Lady, hears about, from Vernon, **33.** 353

Chernyshev, Count Ivan Grigor'evich (1726–97), Russian ambassador to England 1768–9:
ambassadorship of, corrected, **43.** 108
Azov's capture reported to, **23.** 116n
Catherine II told by, of England's aversion to American war, **24.** 138n
Chinese emperor repulses, as murderess's ambassador, **23.** 116, **24.** 333
Du Châtelet's quarrel with, **23.** 125–8, 137–8, **31.** 141–2, **35.** 334
HW told by, of Catherine II's inoculation, **23.** 75
Mecklenburg princes entertained by, **23.** 116n
recalled, **7.** 368
(?) Russian officer and son recommended by, to Mann, **25.** 84

Chernyshev, Petr Grigor'evich (1712–67), Russian ambassador to England 1746–55:
daughter of, **33.** 352
(?) Frederick II notified by, of Catherine II's recall of her troops, **22.** 59n, 62n
George II lends Somerset House for masquerade by, **35.** *199*
HW asked by, for goldfish, **35.** 226, **40.** 85
Lincoln refuses to lend house to, **35.** 199

Chernyshev, Count Zachar Grigor'evich (1705–81), Russian general and diplomatist:
Berlin menaced by, **21.** 441n
captured at Zorndorf, **37.** 562n
Catherine II orders army of, to return, **22.** 59n
Frederick II gives gold sword to, at parting, **22.** 62n
—— hears of Russian revolution before, **22.** 62
Peter III orders, to warn Loudon that he would no longer cooperate against Prussia, **22.** 11n

Cheroffini, Contessa. *See* Gherardi, Francesca

Cherokee; Cherokees:
chiefs of: Clive, Mrs, sings for, **10.** 36; Macclesfield entertains, at Twickenham, **10.** 36
Dinwiddie promises, to Braddock, **20.** 492n
French compared with, **31.** 357
HW compares the English to, **35.** 306
Oglethorpe brings, to England, **30.** 94n

Cherrington, Glos:
Lysons, rector of, **15.** 269n

Cherry, cherries:
Carolina, to be sent by HW to Montagu, **9.** 177
Chudleigh, Elizabeth, serves, at ball, **35.** 301
Conway's, may be ripe, **39.** 407
cooked, **7.** 88
Du Deffand, Mme, presented with, **7.** 458
fed to horse, **32.** 329
from Alps, mentioned by HW, **21.** 113
HW might 'smell to,' **11.** 29
honeysuckle bearing, **21.** 113
James I gives, to Ds of Buckingham, **15.** 341
more exuberant than their leaves, **34.** 8
Morello, HW tries, for gout, **22.** 322
Petersham, Lady Caroline, and guests eat, **9.** 109
price of, cheapest ever at halfpenny a pound, **34.** 7
Queensberry, Ds of, dies of surfeit of, **32.** 366
troughs of, at Elizabeth Chudleigh's ball, **35.** 301

Cherry brandy:
black, drunk by Ds of Kingston, **28.** 225
coach passenger imbibes, **37.** 22
HW asks for, at Stowe, **10.** 314n, **31.** 146

Cherry Hinton:
Serocold, Mrs, of, **2.** 303n

Cherry orchards:
HW admires, **11.** 98

Cherry seat:
HW mentions, **38.** 157

Cherry trees:
two 'bird-cherries' cut down because of caterpillars, **33.** 340

Chersonesus:
Diana's altar in, **22.** 196

Chertsey, Surrey:
Woburn Farm at, **1.** 44n

Cherubim:
HW interested in sex of, **21.** 70n
never out of order because they have no legs, **39.** 157

Cherufini, Vittoria (living, 1789), m. Marchese Giuseppe Lepri:
beautiful, **25.** 385
England visited by, **25.** 384
Rota at Rome decides in favour of, **25.** 587–8

Cherwell River:
Lyttelton boys drowned in, **13.** 100n, **40.** 20

Chery. *See* Nery

Chesapeake Bay:
English fleet turns back before reaching, **25.** 209
French fleet off, **29.** 137n
Graves and Hood attack French fleet at mouth of, **25.** 194

Chéseaux, Jean-Philippe-Loys de (1718–51):
comet discovered by, **18.** 406n

Cheselden, William (1688–1752), surgeon:
Monro's epigram on, **17.** 168, **30.** 30, **35.** 11
Pope friend of, **30.** 30
Chesham, Bucks:
Latimers in parish of, **37.** 299
Cheshire:
Allen, John, lives in, **1.** 129
Cholmondeley dislikes, **10.** 312
Cole's MSS from, **1.** 59, 87, 90, 92
—— to look for chairs for HW in, **1.** 90, 93
deputies of, to convention in London, **43.** 305
George II addressed by, **21.** 13n
Grosvenor family of, **42.** 191
HW not to visit, **10.** 312
HW wants Wettenhalls to seek chairs in, **9.** 384
militia of, under 4th E. of Cholmondeley, **24.** 481n
Montagu dreads journey to, **10.** 286
—— to take rose window to, **10.** 11
Nixon's prophecies from, **34.** 43
Parliamentary reform rejected by, **29.** 30, 32
Roman Catholics in, estimated, **25.** 66n
Schroeder affair elicits instructions from, **35.** 291n
Talbot has estate in, **19.** 176
Vernon's estate in, **20.** 361n
visitors to: Blencowe, **9.** 194; Cole, **1.** 4, 34, 87, 90, 94; Crewe, Mrs, and daughter, **31.** 287; Ferns, Bp of, **10.** 24; Montagu, **9.** 175, 190, 194, 201, 286, 290, 300, **10.** 11, 133, 225, 229, 286, 299, **35.** 261; Montagu, John, **10.** 225
Wettenhall to leave, for Greatworth, **10.** 246
Wettenhall, Mrs, leaves, **10.** 173, 246, 248
Whigs of, do not sign petition, **33.** 166
Cheshunt, Herts:
Cranmer's picture at, **16.** 47
Denny of, **14.** 148n
Chesma; Chesme. See Tchesmé
Chesnay; Chesnaye, La. See La Chesnay; La Chesnaye
Chesneau, Nicolas (b. 1601), French physician:
rheumatism defined by, **22.** 451n
Chess:
American war compared with, **33.** 119–20
Conway plays, with abbé, **13.** 181
——'s correspondence with HW not to proceed like game of, **37.** 86
Craufurd fond of, **6.** 56
Devonshire, D. of, associated with, in HW's newspaper parody, **9.** 127
figures from, **33.** 119–20
Howe's movement compared to that of king in, **12.** 18
Lucas slow enough to be inventor of, **25.** 509
Malézieu and Mme de Staal play, **7.** 322
Mirepoix plays, with John Black, **38.** 104n
Montagu's correspondence with HW compared to game of, **9.** 2
players of, at White's Club, invited by Mirepoix, **20.** 289

St-Cyr pensioners play, **10.** 294
Chess-board:
French terminations compared to, **42.** 231
life resembles, **25.** 510
Chest; chests:
at Elizabeth Chudleigh's, **9.** 277
attributed to Cellini, sent by Mann to HW, **23.** 407, 415, 421, 425, 427, 429, 432, **24.** 15, **25.** 165, **26.** 56
exchequer see Exchequer chest
military, Russians capture, from Turks, **23.** 479
physic, HW to take, to France, **10.** 248
Chester, Bp of. See Dawes, Sir William (1671–1724); Ferne, Henry (1602–62); Keene, Edmund (1714–81); Markham, William (1719–1807); Morton, Thomas (1564–1659), Porteus, Beilby (1731–1809); Wilkins, John (1614–72)
'Chester, Comte de.' See Edward Augustus, D. of York
Chester, E. of:
arms of, **2.** 29
See also George IV
Chester, Mrs, of Hampton Court:
SH visited by, **12.** 251
Chester, English man of war:
Dutch intercepted by, **22.** 71
Chester:
assembly at, Irish girls fit to appear at, **37.** 336
Cholmondeley's house at, **11.** 255n
Conway's chaise broken 3 miles from, **37.** 355–6
distances on road to, **1.** 38
Dodd's birthplace, **40.** 15
election at, **12.** 193
Falconer of, **2.** 266n
Flintshire rebels may seize, **19.** 167
Gower's regiment's mutiny reported from, **19.** 209
Hertford's reception at, **39.** 18
—— writes from, **38.** 118
Hertford, Cts of, writes from, **39.** 74
Latin translation of 'The Bard' printed at, **1.** 386, 388
Lee, Mrs Sydney, of, **42.** 199n
mayor of, see Ollerhead, Richard
militia-bill inquiry requested by, **21.** 12n
Rainsford governor of, **25.** 271n
rebels unlikely to go to, **37.** 211
recorder of, see Townshend, Robert (ca 1708–91)
Roman Catholics in, estimated, **29.** 125n
Talbot justice for, **9.** 181n
Thurlow chief justice of, **39.** 136n
visitors to: Ashton, Mat, **42.** 282n; Cholmondeley, 3d E. of, **37.** 221n; Cole, **1.** 6; Dodd, **40.** 15; Ferns, Bp of, **10.** 25; Montagu, **10.** 25; Whaley, **40.** 15–16
writ regulating coinage dated at, **40.** 221n
Chester Castle:
Gloucester, Ds of, committed to, **14.** 75n

Chester family:
Hardinge, Mrs, descended from, **35**. 610
Chesterfield, Cts of. *See* Schulenberg, Petronille
Melusine de (1693–1778); Thynne, Lady
Henrietta (1762–1813)
Chesterfield, E. of. *See* Stanhope, Philip (ca
1634–1714); Stanhope, Philip (1755–1815);
Stanhope, Philip Dormer (1694–1773)
Chesterfield:
corporation members of, fight, and fall asleep
when naked, **37**. 567
postmaster at, informs Conway about Zorn-
dorf, **37**. 566
Chesterfield House:
Chesterfield gives assembly to display, **20**. 302,
**37**. 325–7
Chesterfield St, Mayfair, London:
Milton's house near, **38**. 295n
Selwyn addressed in, **30**. 216, 261
—— moves from, **33**. 236n
Vachel in, **35**. 595
Walpole, Catherine, dies in, **11**. 28n
Chesterford, Great, Essex:
fly from Cambridge to London passes through,
**1**. 263n
Orford, 3d E. of, ill at, **1**. 298
urn found at, **1**. 210
Chesterton, Cambs:
Chettoe of, **2**. 119n
Chestnut; chestnuts:
*bouilli* of, invented at Paris, **14**. 157
roasted, not one in twenty is sound, **33**. 213
Chestnut tree; chestnut trees:
hailstorm injures, at Geneva, **37**. 104
Chesupiades, the (venereal disease):
Suares and Pecori share, **18**. 345
Chétardie, La. *See* La Chétardie
Chetham, Humphrey (1580–1653):
Chetham Hospital and Library founded by,
at Manchester, **40**. 16
Chettoe, John (fl. 1778) and Mrs John (d.
1798):
Hardwicke defended by, **2**. 119n
Chetwood, William:
*Travels and Adventures of Three Princes of
Serendip*, a translation by, **26**. 34
Chetwynd, Vcts. *See* Berkeley, Mary
Chetwynd, Hon. Deborah (d. 1788), royal
laundress and sempstress:
HW's naiads inferior to, in water production,
**35**. 324–5
Chetwynd, John (ca 1680–1767), 2d Vct:
brother of, **18**. 191n
Gower sends, to vote for Hessians, **26**. 24
Chetwynd Hon. Susannah (d. 1818), m. (1782)
Munbee Goulburn:
separation of, from husband, **12**. 80
Chetwynd, Walter (1710–86), fellow of King's
College, Cambridge:
(?) HW sends compliments to, in dumb
show, **30**. 2
(?) Turin visited by, **43**. 178

Chetwynd, Mrs Walter. *See* Berkeley, Mary
Chetwynd, Hon. William Richard (?1683–1770),
3d Vct Chetwynd, 1767; M.P.:
Admiralty appointment of, **17**. 356
Arundel replaced by, as Master of the Mint,
**18**. 551
biographical information on, corrected, **43**.
243
Bolingbroke's agent, **17**. 356
——'s friend, **10**. 117, **18**. 191, **22**. 544n
Gower sends, to vote for Hessians, **26**. 24
HW seeks reversion of Mint mastership of,
**40**. 146
HW sends regards to, **31**. 81
Hotham, Henrietta, accompanied by, **35**. 322
—— 'courted' by, **31**. 40
House of Commons never left by, in long
session, **38**. 317
Master of the Mint, **10**. 117, **18**. 191n, 551
plans for fairy-tale dénouement laid by, **10**.
117
Suffolk, Cts of, sups with, **22**. 544
—— visited by, **35**. 321
Walpole, Horatio (1678–1757) duels with,
**18**. 191–2, 207
youthfulness of, **31**. 40, 66
'Chevalier, le.' *See* Beauvau, Ferdinand-Jérôme
de; Boufflers, Stanislas-Jean de
Chevalier, John *or* Abraham, sea-capt.:
law suit detains, so goldfish await transport,
**35**. 222
Chevalier, John, London merchant:
(?) Walpole, Hon. T., sends parcel to HW
by, **7**. 205, 209
Chevallier, John (1730–1809), master of St
John's College, Cambridge:
goes out of office as vice-chancellor, **2**. 69
lends Baker's history to Cole, **2**. 53
wife of, **2**. 235n
Chevance, ——, wood merchant in Paris:
Du Deffand, Mme, has receipt from, **8**. 41
Chevau-légers:
cost of, to d'Aiguillon, **4**. 340
reduced in number, **6**. 251
Cheveley, Cambs:
tapestry from, **1**. 169
Chevening Park, Kent, E. Stanhope's seat:
*poissardes* might call on Stanhope at, **11**. 97
Chevert, François de (1695–1769), army officer:
Düsseldorf to be besieged by, **21**. 228n
HW considers, best French officer, **21**. 233
Hastenbeck battle distinguishes, **21**. 233n
Imhoff defeats, **21**. 228n, 233–4
impoverished origins of, **21**. 233n
Soubise awaits, **21**. 227n
verses on, **9**. 254
Chevilly. *See* Perrin de Cypierre de Chevilly
Chevis, Robert, of Murtown:
witness at Lovat's trial, **19**. 381n
'Chevreuil.' *See* Chevreuse
Chevreuse, Duc de. *See* Albert de Luynes, Marie-
Charles-Louis d'

Chevreuse, Duchesse de. *See* Rohan, Marie de (1600–79)

Chevreuse, Mlle de. *See* Lorraine, Charlotte de

Chevrier, François-Antoine:
*Acadiade, L'*, by, Jumonville lauded in, **41.** 147

'Chevy Chace,' ballad:
Conway alludes to, **37.** 521
Dacre hunts in style of, **35.** 139
HW knows no duel later than that of, **32.** 103
HW paraphrases, **23.** 264, **28.** 309, **29.** 85, **32.** 229, 241, **33.** 527
Widdrington's 'stumps' in, **23.** 264, **33.** 326, 375, **34.** 106

Chewton, Vct. *See* Waldegrave, George (1751–89); Waldegrave, George (1784–94)

Chewton, Vcts. *See* Waldegrave, Lady Elizabeth Laura (1760–1816)

Chewton Mendip:
HW's MSS at, **36.** 316

Chewton Priory:
HW's MSS at, **36.** 316

Cheylus, Joseph-Dominique de (1719–97) Bp of Tréguier:
Du Deffand, Mme, plans to rent apartment to, **3.** 12, 19
social relations of, in Paris, **7.** 281, 283, 291, 294, 298, 300, 301, 306, 309, 311, 312

Cheyne, Bns. *See* Pierrepont, Gertrude

Cheyne Walk, Chelsea:
Lindsey House at Beaufort St and, **20.** 359n

Cheyneys. *See* Chenies

Cheyneys Court. *See* Chiras Court

Chiaretta, dancer:
Amorevoli abandons, when he is ill, **17.** 197
—— and Blighe to welcome, in London, **18.** 32
Barbarina's presence makes London opera unsuitable for, **18.** 31
England to be visited by, **18.** 14–15
HW to receive Gerini's views of Florence through, **18.** 14
Mann refuses letter of introduction to, **18.** 15

Chiari, Giuseppe Bartolommeo (1654–1727), painter:
Maratti painting probably mistaken for one by, **21.** 172
paintings by, at Burghley House, **10.** 345, 346

Chiaroscuro:
ceiling design may be executed in, **31.** 106

Chiavacci, Clementina (fl. 1772–82), opera singer:
(?) Pembroke goes with, to Florence, **25.** 497n

Chiaveri, Caterina, actress:
girl mispronounces last name of, **18.** 42, 62

Chichele, Henry (? 1362–1443), Abp of Canterbury, 1414:
All Souls founded by, because he prefers prayers for the dead to hospitals, **35.** 387–8
Henry VI prompted by, to invade France to keep him from fleecing the clergy, **35.** 387
portraits of: at Lambeth, **40.** 215; at New College, Oxford, **38.** 43–4

Chichester, Bp of. *See* Ashburnham, Sir William (1710–97); Buckner, John (1734–1824); Hare, Francis (1671–1740); Mawson, Matthias (1683–1770); Montagu, Richard (1577–1641); Patrick, Simon (1621–1707); Story, Edward (d. 1503); Waddington, Edward (ca 1670–1731)

Chichester, Cts of. *See* Cobbe, Catherine (ca 1762–1839); Frankland, Anne (ca 1734–1813)

Chichester, E. of. *See* Pelham, Thomas (1728–1805)

Chichester, Vct. *See* Chichester, George Augustus (1769–1844)

Chichester, Mrs, of Richmond:
SH visited by, **12.** 238

Chichester, Arthur (1563–1625), cr. (1613) Bn Chichester of Belfast; diplomatist:
letters by, at Ragley, **9.** 224
print of, **1.** 181

Chichester, Arthur (1739–99), 5th E. of Donegall; cr. (1791) M. of Donegall; M.P.:
Irish tenants of, rebel against fines for renewal of leases, **23.** 391

Chichester George Augustus (1769–1844), styled Vct Chichester 1769–91 and E. of Belfast 1791–9; 2d M. of Donegall, 1799:
engagement of, broken, **11.** 326
'rich Irish heir-apparent,' **11.** 326

*Chichester*, English ship:
Dilke, captain of, **19.** 33n
involved in Mediterranean war, **18.** 396

Chichester, Sussex:
Baker of, **11.** 52n
Bull, Mr, of, **7.** 398
Conway, Hon. Henrietta Seymour, from, **37.** 483–4
—— writes from, **38.** 46–7, 51–2, 159–60, 383, **39.** 69, 80–1
Conway, William, at, **31.** 353
Daye, Mrs, of, **2.** 371–2, **30.** 358, 359, **32.** 245
—— to come from, **11.** 306
Dodd and Whaley to visit, **40.** 6
Goodwood near, **11.** 39n
HW dreads meeting people from, at Goodwood, **39.** 295
Miller of, **10.** 304n
Petworth near, **12.** 206n
Stanstead Park near, **12.** 200n
Stoke near, **31.** 353–6, 366
surgeons at, **11.** 262n

Chichester Cathedral:
pictures of the kings in, **1.** 23
Richmond, D. of, orders father's body removed to, **20.** 182n
Richmond, Ds of, buried in, **34.** 222n
Trevigar canon of, **2.** 371n

Chichester Cross:
HW has Bentley copy, in Gothic temple, **9.** 295, **11.** 66–7
HW's altar-piece for Westminster Abbey modelled after, **2.** 185, **28.** 214, 216

Chicken; chickens:
  boiled: HW aspires no higher than, **13.** 172;
    HW has, at dinner at SH, **41.** 366
  Conway eats, **39.** 365
  feathers of, worn by Florentine ladies, **25.** 175
  HW hopes that Lady Strafford's, will not detain her, **35.** 286
  HW likes, cold, **31.** 67
  HW may send, to mother, **36.** 2
  HW's, **3.** 80, 105, 107
  legs and wings of, left over from supper,
    **39.** 330
  Mann lives on, **17.** 61
  Mann scandalizes Italians by eating, in Holy
    Week, **20.** 308
  marinades and cocks' combs from, for hors
    d'œuvres, **19.** 356n
  Orford eats, **36.** 122
  Petersham, Lady Caroline, and guests, mince
    and stew, **9.** 109
  pie of, **18.** 162
  sea captain keeps, at Algiers, **22.** 586
  Selwyn, John, eats, **37.** 94
  sent from Le Mans, **7.** 436
  Shrove-tide cock, **35.** 534
  sick fox in Gay's *Fables* covets, **39.** 234
  West dines on, **13.** 174
  *See also* Bantam; Guinea-fowl; Peafowl;
    Poultry
Chicken-pox:
  occurrences of, **38.** 106
Chicksands Priory, Beds, Sir George Osborn's
  seat:
  columbarium at, **10.** 170
  Montagu thinks, needs improvement, **10.** 169
  —— visits, **10.** 169
  Montagu, Lady Mary, married at, **10.** 169
  Osborn of, **9.** 149n, 248n
Chicoyneau, Jean-Joseph-François de (d. 1783),
  Baron de la Valette:
  (?) Du Deffand, Mme, has notes signed by,
    **7.** 39–40
  (?) ——'s 'rescription' money received by, **7.**
    434
Chictaws. *See* Choctaws
Chidley Court, Pall Mall:
  Adair, army agent in, **42.** 47n
Chief justice:
  changing of name by permit from, **10.** 119
  *See also under* Court of Common Pleas; Court
    of King's Bench
Chief justice in eyre:
  changes in post of, **9.** 33, 181, 341
  Leeds, D. of, succeeds Sandys as, **21.** 489
  Monson resigns as, **22.** 471
  Pelham becomes, **23.** 562
  Sandwich to become, **35.** 263
  Sandys succeeds D. of Leeds as, **20.** 518
Chief justiciar:
  functions of, **20.** 65n
Ch'ien-lung (Hung Li) (1711–99), Emperor
  of China 1736–96:

Anson at Canton refuses to pay ship's duties
  ordered by, **35.** 284n
Catherine II of Russia negotiates border
  with, **32.** 390
Russian embassy rejected by, **23.** 116, **24.**
  137–8
Voltaire's *Épître* to, **4.** 489
'Chifang, Mr':
  Conway picks, as Chinese name, **37.** 377
Chiffinch, William (ca 1602–88), closet-keeper
  to Charles II:
  catalogue by, of James I's collection, **16.** 142–
    3n, **40.** 187, 189
  HW buys portrait of, by (?) Riley, **35.** 227–8
Chigi, Signora. *See* Galli, Teresa
Chigi, Fabio. *See* Alexander VII
Chigi, Flavio Maria (1711–71), cardinal, 1753:
  Jesuits might have sought election of, as pope,
    **23.** 89
Chigi, Principe Sigismondo (1736–93), Marshal
  of the Conclave:
  *Il Conclave* attributed to, **24.** 69n, 73
Chigi Zondadari, Cecilia (b. 1744), m. (1762)
  Angelo Ugurgieri Malavolti:
  York, D. of, entertained by, **22.** 224
Chigi Zondadari, Marchese Flavio (b. 1714):
  daughters of, **22.** 224
Chigi Zondadari, Vittoria (1742–1818), m.
  (1762) Alceo Bulgarini, cavaliere di Malta:
  (?) relative of, was Oxenden's cicisbea, **43.**
    279
  York, D. of, entertained by, **22.** 224
Chignall St James, Essex:
  Gower, rector of, **1.** 210n
Chigwell, Essex:
  Harvey of, **9.** 314n, **11.** 61n, **25.** 12
  Tyson temporarily at, **2.** 101, 114
  —— to get living near, **2.** 77
Child, Lady Dorothy (d. 1786):
  Monro attends, at Lake House, where she retires with Child, **37.** 309n
  Tylney leaves, inconsolable, **37.** 309
Child, Sir Francis (1642–1713), Kt, 1689:
  Rubens portrait bought by, in Holland, **34.**
    239
Child, Francis (ca 1735–63), banker; M.P.:
  Adam rebuilds Osterley for, **32.** 125n
  birth date of, corrected, **43.** 317
  death of, from quinsy at Hampden House,
    **10.** 103, 104
  fiancée's legacy from, **10.** 104, **30.** 172
Child, Hon. Josiah (d. 1759), E. Tylney's
  brother:
  cabriolets introduced by, **20.** 483
  may live abroad after scandal, **20.** 356–7
  sister retires with, to Lake House, **37.** 309n
  Tylney's brother, **20.** 483n
  woman ruins, **20.** 357
Child, Josiah jr (d. 1774), E. Tylney's nephew:
  death of, from deep consumption, **24.** 22
  Tylney to destroy rich codicils in favour of,
    **24.** 23

Child, Mrs Josiah. *See* Knight, Hon. Henrietta

Child, Rebecca (d. 1712), m. 1 (1683) Charles Somerset, styled M. of Worcester; m. 2 (1703) John Granville, Bn, of Potheridge:
HW's pedigree for Cts of Hertford includes, **38**. 482

Child (after 1734, Tylney), Richard (1680–1750), cr. (1718) Vct Castlemaine, (1731) E. Tylney; M.P.:
name-change of, redated, **43**. 285
nose-bleed precedes fatal dropsy of, **24**. 145
portraits at Wanstead as ugly as children of, **35**. 238

Child, Robert (1739–82), banker; M.P.:
Adam rebuilds Osterley for, **32**. 125n
brother's legacy to fiancée confirmed by, **10**. 104
daughter of, **12**. 63n
death of, **33**. 347
diamonds given by, to brother's fiancée, **10**. 104
disposal of property of, **12**. 72
Fairfax's library bought by, **42**. 354n
forgery on, expected, **32**. 361
house of, in Leicester Sq., **32**. 126n
income of, **34**. 238
seal and ring mysteriously sent to, **32**. 361, 363
wife of, **11**. 176n
will of, **33**. 347

Child, Mrs Robert. *See* Jodrell, Sarah (1741–93)

Child, Samuel (ca 1694–1752), M.P.:
(?) Rubens portrait brought by, from London to Osterley, **34**. 239

Child, Sarah Anne (ca 1764–93), m. (1782) John Fane, 10th E. of Westmorland, 1774:
beauty and good humour of, **12**. 63, 64
daughter inherits fortune of, **12**. 68
death of, **12**. 63–4
(?) delicacy of, in toasts, **33**. 356
moves to Ireland, **12**. 64
SH visited by, **12**. 225
Waldegrave, Cts, friend of, **12**. 64

Child & Co., bank in London:
Child, Mrs, receives income from, **11**. 176
Fane, Lady Sarah Sophia, to receive income from, **12**. 72

Childebert:
Karl Theodor should call himself, **36**. 233

*Childers*, English sloop:
Tobago's capture reported by, **25**. 172n

Childhood:
HW's reflections on second, as similar to first, **25**. 133

Child Okeford:
Hall rector of, **2**. 213n

Children:
Beauclerk, Lady Diana, paints, **42**. 490
HW lies on grass with, at Ragley, **9**. 225
HW prefers, to 'Christians,' **32**. 204

HW to cultivate friendships with, to replace dying friends, **40**. 181
Montagu dances with, at Dallington, **10**. 195, 196
—— dislikes, **10**. 81
nurses train, by hand, **30**. 84
parson and clerk played by, **30**. 60
travelling, Mann's visitors limited to, **20**. 454
*See also* Natural children

*Children in the Wood. See under* Morton, Thomas

'Children in the Wood,' ballad:
HW shed tears over, at age of 6, **12**. 78
HW tells stories of, **32**. 229

Chile:
Gray's *Odes* mention, **40**. 105

Chile, viceroy of. *See* Amat y Junient Planella Aimeric y Saint Pau, Manuel de

Chillingworth, William (1602–44), theologian:
Falkland may have aided, **16**. 12
HW quotes letter of, **9**. 77–8
*Religion of Protestants a Safe Way of Salvation, The*, by, **16**. 12n

Chilly, Seigneur de. *See* Du Chilleau, Jean-Baptiste

Chilly, ——, (d. 1779), commandant at Cassimbazar:
Arabs waylay, **24**. 510n

Chiltern Hundreds:
Palliser resigns by accepting, **24**. 444n

Chimay, Prince de. *See* Alsace-Hénin-Liétard, Philippe-Gabriel-Maurice-Joseph d' (1736–1804); Riquet de Caraman, François-Joseph-Philippe de (1771–1842)

Chimay, Princesse de. *See* Beauvau, Gabrielle-Françoise de (1708–58); Fitzjames, Laure (1744–1814)

Chimay:
Maria Theresa cedes, to France, **21**. 117n

Chimenti, Margarita:
opera performance of, **18**. 361

*Chimère*, French frigate:
Toulon squadron includes, **21**. 431n

Chimney; chimneys:
bacon flitch carved over, at Wichnor, **38**. 71
earthquake demolishes, in London, **20**. 130
Florentine, shut up in April, **25**. 397
French, low and straddling, **31**. 88
hurricane blows over, **24**. 431n
in SH Gallery, fire in, **38**. 175
Mann fears that wind will injure, **20**. 25
—— stops up, in warm weather, **19**. 391
Mereworth spoiled by, **35**. 143
niches in, **35**. 70–1
Pitti palace fitted with, **22**. 291
smoky, at Massereene's, **30**. 211
stack of, falls at Mrs Angerstein's, **39**. 481
storm blows down, in London, **12**. 176
storm injures, on New Year's Day, **24**. 431
whitewash for, better than Lady Mary Wortley Montagu's paint, **37**. 79

Chimney-back; chimney-backs:
Henry VII's: 9. 161, 20. 391, 395; bought by
Bentley for SH, 35. 174; HW's servant
mistakes, for armour, 20. 396
*See also* Grate
Chimney-board; chimney-boards:
by Barlow, at Burghley House, 10. 345
information about, 43. 360
Müntz paints, 35. 100
Chimney-piece; chimney-pieces:
at: Belhus, 35. 184; Boyle Farm, 42. 197, 204;
SH, 35. 644; The Vyne, 35. 639, 640; Welbeck, 35. 270–1; Wentworth Woodhouse,
35. 267
Bentley designs: for Strafford, 35. 214; for
SH Blue Bedchamber, 35. 174
Boyle, Charlotte, designs and carves, in
marble, 31. 251, 42. 197, 204
bust to adorn, 20. 86
Ceunot's drawing of, for Conway, to be
shown to HW, 37. 331
English sculptor makes, in Florence for Pitti
palace and for Russia, 25. 93
in Yellow Bedchamber at SH, 33. 273
marble tablets for, at Boyle Farm, 35. 390
polished like looking-glass, 20. 398
sculpture seldom rises above, 20. 398
unopened in boxes, at Wentworth Wood-
house, 35. 267
Volterra vases to adorn, 17. 395
Chimney-sweep; chimney-sweeps:
dance with garlands on May 1, 25. 275, 39.
407
HW mentions, 25. 272
Parliament aids, 16. 217
Porter's efforts in behalf of, 16. 217, (?) 25.
353, 39. 428
Chimpanzee:
Carpenter exhibits, in HW's newspaper
parody, 9. 127
Harcourt's portrait resembles, 35. 481
Yertzin, Mme, is, 38. 402
China, Emperor of. See Ch'ien-lung (Hung-Li)
China:
Anson claims to have punished, with one
man of war, 35. 284
*Augusta* bound for, 19. 277n
balloon might fly to, 39. 425
baskets from, 37. 439
Bolton, Ds of, to take refuge in, 9. 22, 37.
206n
bow, quiver and arrows from, at SH, 31. 26
chairs from, 35. 301
Chambers, Sir William, visits, 28. 450
Coke, Lady Mary, might visit, 31. 166
English strangers become friends if they meet
in, 33. 348
existence of, doubted, 42. 183
Fiesole villas resemble fan or screen from,
20. 191, 193, 21. 462

Florence as remote as, from English news,
19. 214
from California to, French are defeated, 21.
352
goldfish from, 35. 222, 37. 376
HW admires unsymmetrical landscaping of,
20. 127
HW and Hervey interested in, 40. 18
HW could walk across room as easily as to,
38. 65
HW's *Letter from Xo Ho* supposedly from,
21. 92
HW's presents leave no desire for anything
in, 40. 38
history of, *see* Du Halde, Jean-Baptiste:
*Description géographique de la Chine*
(?) Irby, Lady, may flee to, 37. 206
Jesuit conversions in, 18. 305
(?) Kwangtung, HW may imagine himself
in, 40. 17
Macartney's embassy to, 12. 191, 34. 202
Mandeville does not name, correctly, 42. 183
Mason's *Heroic Postscript* mentions monarch
of, 28. 113
Montagu, D. of, pretends to be emperor of,
when marrying Ds of Albemarle, 25. 564
Morice says that Petraia palm-tree is largest
outside of, 22. 29
obscene drawings and prints from, 21. 202
oranges from, 17. 352
pocket spying-glasses might see to, 37. 293
Russian lands near, uninhabited and uncivil-
ized, 25. 545
ships from, at St Helena, 25. 110
tapestry from, at The Vyne, 35. 640
Townshend, Augustus, loses imports from,
40. 45
vastness of, to pismires, 33. 569–70
Walpole, Lady, gets India ink from, 17. 436
China (ware):
Ailesbury, Cts of, gives, to HW, 38. 99–100
—— has errands about, 38. 124
at: Burghley House, 10. 91, 345; Drayton,
10. 90; Ham House, 10. 306; Osterley Park,
32. 126
auction of, at Twickenham, 21. 122
Brunswick, not yet come, 39. 177
Buckingham, D. of, manufactures, 10. 345
Burlington, E. of, tries to give, to Mrs Brace-
girdle, 25. 74
Cardigans', 38. 357
Chantilly, *see under* Chantilly
Chelsea: Grafton, Ds of, gave, to Mann, 22.
180–1, 191; Sprimont's, given by George
III and Q. Charlotte to D. of Mecklenburg,
22. 121–2, 43. 278
Chelsea porcelain, 6. 429n
Cole's, bought by HW, 1. 109, 111, 115, 116,
117, 119, 120
——'s St-Cloud or Sèvres, 1. 107–8
Colquhoun collects, 42. 322n

Craon, Princesses de, packs, 17. 193, 199
cup of, HW's gift to Lady Ossory, 32. 275, 278
Cutler and Margas charge high prices for, 37. 348
Delft, *see under* Delft
Dresden: Ailesbury, Cts of, can now afford, 38. 145; at Elizabeth Chudleigh's, 9. 277; candlesticks of, 9. 106–7; cows of, 19. 414; Ranelagh shops sell, 20. 47; snuff-box of, 42. 464; *see also under* Saxony
Du Deffand, Mme, has, 8. 12–13, 24–6
Dutch, seen by Conway and wife in Holland, 37. 286
duty on importation of, 41. 437, 43. 349–50
earthquake damages, in London, 20. 130, 155, 158
Electress wills, 18. 169
French: affected by Palladian architecture, 31. 99; HW brings, from Paris, 1. 112, 10. 171, 297–8, 299, 32. 270; heavy duty on, 32. 270; skilled design of, 25. 635
from Ginori's factory, *see* China factory, Ginori's
Fürstenberg and Frankenthal, sent by Beauchamp to HW, 39. 177
George III provides, for Mrs Delany, 34. 497
HW asks about Leopold II's, at Florence, 25. 215, 231
HW buys, at Dulac's for Craufurd, 41. 5
HW compares varieties of, 25. 635
HW gives, to Mrs Gostling, 41. 437
HW must ruin himself buying, in Rue St-Honoré, 39. 47
HW's, from Paris, 1. 112, 41. 7
HW's brown boar reminiscent of, 37. 348
HW's collection of, in China Closet at SH, 25. 591, 31. 216
HW's fondness for, mentioned by Whaley, 40. 49
HW stops buying, to plant trees, 20. 53–4
Hertford, Cts of, asks HW not to buy for her in Paris, 39. 47
idol of, 20. 226
Indian, Frederick II gives, to Frederick Augustus II, in exchange for dragoons, 38. 103n
jars of, among scagliola table ornaments, 18. 292
Mann's coat of arms painted on, 18. 184
—— sends, to HW, 25. 619, 620, 635
manufactured at Sèvres, 31. 125
medals of, 7. 262
Michelangelo's 'Bacchus' in, of Comte de Lauraguais, 39. 32n
Mirepoix, Mme de, has 'little closet' full of, 31. 99
paste of, at Derby, Bristol, and Worcester superior to all but that of Saxony, 25. 635
Petersham, Lady Caroline, stews chickens in dish of, 9. 109
Pitti, Palazzo, sells, blue and white, 25. 231

plates attributed to Rubens, 2. 152–3, 155–8
porcelain, Leopold's factory for, *see* China factory: Leopold II's
price of French coffee set, 32. 270
prices of, low at Mrs Dunch's auction, 9. 412
raffle of, 17. 159
Raphael's vases of, at Burghley House, 10. 345
Raynal discusses, 39. 168
rearranged in Uffizi gallery, 25. 170
Sally, Mrs, gets teapots from The Hague, 38. 129
Saxon (?Dresden): Craon, Mme de, has, 18. 78; Du Deffand, Mme, has, 8. 13, 24; Mann's cups of, 18. 162
Sèvres, 25. 645, 31. 125, 38. 278, 39. 40, *and see under* Sèvres
teapot of, 35. 477n
Townshend, Augustus, loses, from fire, 40. 45
Turkish, HW's, 42. 52
Walpole, Sir Edward, promises, to Mrs Scott, 10. 329
workmen from Saxony brought by Ginori to Florence to make, 18. 184
*See also* Porcelain
China factory:
Ginori's: 18. 184, 21. 369; earthenware the chief product of, 25. 598; Ginori seeks colours for, 18. 184, 202, 216, 250, 283–4, 323; HW assumes that vases are from, 25. 635; HW has not yet received china from, 25. 629; Mann orders two pieces from, for HW, 25. 598, 604, 26. 56; only one in Tuscany, 25. 598, 645; vases from, took 4 months and were exhibited afterwards, 25. 645
Leopold II's: HW asks about, 25. 590–1; HW assumes that vases are not from, 25. 635; never made more than earthenware for stoves, 25. 645
China shop; china shops:
monkey in, 36. 222
Morgan's, 10. 270
Chine (meat):
HW does not eat, at Christmas, 20. 16
*Chine, Epître au Roi de la. See under* Voltaire
Chinese, the:
Conway as lonely as, at Marseille, 37. 312
early promise of, in the arts unfulfilled, 15. 211
East India Co. called 'Mr Company,' by, 30. 216
prudence of, in refusing European ties, 34. 202
Temple, Sir William, first to attribute 'Shariwaggi' to, 20. 127n
Voltaire on, 33. 206–7, 34. 22
Xo Ho is, 33. 107
Chinese architecture. *See under* Architecture
Chinese fence:
at Park Place, 39. 534

Chinese gardens:
English gardens modelled on, **28**. 222, **29**. 275
Chinese language:
ambiguities in, **33**. 262
difficulty of learning characters of, **31**. 248
'Chinese machine' (artificial penis):
Campbell, Frederick, brings to Lady Townshend instead of bottle of salts, **30**. 84
Chinese pheasant. *See under* Pheasant
Chinese pigs. *See under* Pig
Chinese present:
Craon, Princesse de, thanks HW for, **24**. 6
Chinese wall-paper:
Chambers's *Dissertation* more extravagant than, **28**. 34
Chingford, Essex:
Otterbourne rector of, **14**. 78n
Chintz; chintzes:
bed and chairs of, in SH Blue Bedchamber, **35**. 173
bed of, at SH, **39**. 285
idle topic, during world crisis, **38**. 130
nightgown of, **37**. 124
Ossory, Lady, needs, **33**. 63
Chios (Scio), Ægean island:
Russian-Turkish naval hostilities near, **23**. 226, 232–5
wine of, **30**. 217
Chippenham, Wilts:
Earle M.P. for, **15**. 326n
election at, **13**. 11n, **17**. 318, **19**. 302
Lackham near, **10**. 229n
Chiras ('Cheyneys') Court, near Frome Hill:
Withinbury, Mrs, of, **42**. 123n
Chirbury, Lord Herbert of. *See* Herbert, Edward (1583–1648)
Chirk Castle, Denbighshire, Myddelton's seat:
Myddelton of, **42**. 215n
Ossory, Lady, enchanted with beauty of, **34**. 92–3, 94
Chiron:
mentioned in verses, **12**. 96
Chisel; chisels:
burglars', found by HW, **9**. 133–4
lava rocks might be modelled by, **35**. 433
Chishull, Edmund (1671–1733), chaplain at Smyrna 1698–1702:
*Travels in Turkey*, quoted, **1**. 20
Chislehurst, Kent:
Jordan, Thomas, of, **11**. 104n
Townshends buried at, **13**. 4n
Chiswick, Middlesex:
Conway to visit, **37**. 374
Grove, The, at, *see under* Grove, The
HW meets D. of Norfolk at, **35**. 280
Pope visits Lady Burlington at, **18**. 449, **43**. 253
Towneley's house at, **33**. 407n
Chiswick House, Chiswick, Middlesex; E. of Burlington's villa:
Hartington acquires, by marriage, **20**. 66n

Mary, Q. of Scots's alleged portrait at, **42**. 321
model of Grecian architecture, **20**. 362
(?) Montagu compares, with Lying-In Hospital at Dublin, **9**. 391
print of, **2**. 274
Pulteney's epigram mentions, **30**. 24
shown only by ticket, **2**. 274
SH compared with, **9**. 169, **35**. 237
Violette, Mlle, invited to, **9**. 28
Chitry:
Lillebonne, Baron of, **5**. 83n
Chivalry:
Edgcumbe's 'sagacity' in, **30**. 55
pageantry of, HW regrets loss of, **11**. 22
print of Lord Herbert of Chirbury exemplifies, **42**. 43
Chivers, Gen.:
captured at Zorndorf, **37**. 562n
'Chloe':
HW's term for Mary Rich, **35**. 276
Chloé (*or* Cloiié, Cloué, *or* Clouet), D. of Newcastle's cook:
Albemarle's maître d'hôtel at Paris, **20**. 450n
caricature of, **17**. 485n
dinners by, **30**. 91
Grafton dismisses, for playing bowls instead of dressing dinner for Belle-Isle, **30**. 91n
Guise says, could make pelican pie, **17**. 485, **20**. 450
HW jokes about distress of, on destruction of mushroom bed, **31**. 11
Newcastle said to be governed by, **17**. 485n
spelling of name of, **43**. 246
Chloe:
Prior's, **32**. 32
Strephon's match with, restricted by Parliament, **37**. 361
'Chloe,' Lady George Lennox's dog:
(?) death of, **31**. 125–6
Chloe. *See also* Cloe
Choart, Gabriel (d. 1787):
(?) attends session of parliament of Paris, **8**. 173
Chocolate:
Clement XIV poisoned by dish of, served by his innocent butler, **24**. 49
Corsini forces Cenci to drink, **37**. 70
Danvers spurns, **35**. 70
dish of, spilled on Lady Sophia Fermor, **30**. 7
Elizabeth, Empress, gives, to Berrue and Princesse de Craon, **17**. 205
French customs will confiscate, **37**. 40
George II drinks, in morning, **9**. 311, **21**. 443
HW prepares, for Archduke and Archduchess of Austria, **33**. 529
HW serves, to Ds of York at SH, **12**. 11
Hervey, John, Bn, resembles cold cup of, **40**. 28
Mann serves, **17**. 259, 413, 424
Pitt, Anne, takes, with milk for breakfast, **23**. 567
Riccardi family give, at party, **20**. 192

tray for, **18.** 553
York, D. of, receives: at Lucca, **22.** 221; at Rome, **22.** 228
Chocolate cup; chocolate cups:
HW sends, to Mann, **17.** 42, 45, 52
Chocolate house:
White's Club first met at, **25.** 483n
Choctaw; Choctaws:
French compared with, **31.** 357
Choczim:
Russian defeat at, **35.** 334
Choeb:
imposture of, **19.** 123
*Choice of Harlequin*, pantomime:
at Covent Garden, **33.** 321n
Choin. *See* Joly de Choin
Choir-stall; choir-stalls:
Chute's, at The Vyne: **35.** 641, 642; Roma paints, **35.** 642
in Westminster Abbey, **9.** 323
Choiseul, Baron de. *See* Choiseul, Louis-Marie-Gabriel-César de
Choiseul, Baronne de. *See* Girard de Vannes, Marie-Françoise de
Choiseul, Cardinal de. *See* Choiseul, Antoine-Clériadus de
Choiseul, Chevalier de. *See* Choiseul-Beaupré, Michel-Félix-Victor de (1754–96)
Choiseul, Comte de. *See* Choiseul, Antoine-César de (1756–1808); Choiseul-Beaupré, Claude-Antoine-Clériadus-Gabriel de (1760–1838); Choiseul-Beaupré, Marie-Gabriel-Florent-Auguste de (1752–1817)
Choiseul, Comtesse de. *See* Choiseul-Stainville, Marie-Stéphanie de (1763–1833); Lallemant de Betz, Marie-Françoise (d. 1793); O'Brien de Thomond, Charlotte-Antoinette-Marie-Septimanie (1759–1808)
Choiseul, Duc de. *See* Choiseul, César-Auguste de (d. 1705); Choiseul-Beaupré, Claude-Antoine-Clériadus-Gabriel de (1760–1838); Choiseul-Stainville, Étienne-François de (1719–85)
Choiseul, Duchesse de. *See* Bouthillier de Chavigny, Marie (1646–1728); Choiseul-Stainville, Marie-Stéphanie de (1763–1833); Crozat du Châtel, Louise-Honorine (1735–1801)
Choiseul, Marquis de. *See* Choiseul, Charles-Antoine-Étienne de
Choiseul, Marquise de. *See* Raby, Louise (ca 1755–72); Walsh de Serrant, Françoise-Élisabeth-Charlotte de (d. 1793)
Choiseul, Vicomte de. *See* Choiseul, Renaud-César-Louis de (1735–91)
Choiseul, Vicomtesse de. *See* Durfort de Lorges, Guyonne-Marguerite-Philippine de
Choiseul, Mme —— de:
SH visited by, **12.** 244
Choiseul, Antoine-César de (1756–1808), Comte de Choiseul; Comte de Praslin; Duc de Praslin:
honours given to, **7.** 448

Choiseul, Antoine-Clériadus (1707–74), Cardinal de:
Conclave expects, at Rome, **23.** 95n
social relations of, with HW and Cts of Hertford, at Paris, **7.** 262–3
Choiseul, César-Auguste de (d. 1705), Duc de:
wife of, **5.** 188n
will of widow of, 8, 36
Choiseul, César-Gabriel de (1712–85), Duc de Praslin; secretary of state:
advises on choice of controller, **4.** 326
Aiguillon investigation favoured by, **4.** 197
alternates with Choiseul as minister of foreign affairs, **3.** 1n
Beaumarchais subject of letter by, **7.** 439
Bouillon said to have sold office to, **3.** 68–9
Choiseul becomes successor to, **8.** 122
—— grants marine and colonies to, and makes him chief of finance council, **39.** 65
Clugny served under, **6.** 311
daughter-in-law of, **6.** 66
daughter of, **3.** 53n
Du Buc serves under, **5.** 332n
Du Deffand, Mme, has accident in front of house of, **3.** 55–6, 61, 63, 8. 122
—— scolded by Choiseul for telling of discourtesy of, **8.** 122
—— sends to, for news, **5.** 161
——'s opinion of, **5.** 196
——'s relations with, **5.** 173
Du Barry, Mme, tosses orange called after, **23.** 85
Du Châtelet to succeed, in marine department, **23.** 258
Éon's book offensive to, **38.** 356, 372
Éon's controversy with, involving Guerchy and Nivernais, **22.** 217–18
exiled, **5.** 5, **23.** 257–8, **39.** 134, **41.** 198
footmen of, **35.** 112
French to be made universal language by, by publishing monthly reviews, **22.** 218
(?) Gaillard's verses to wife of, **7.** 363
gout prevents, from interceding with Louis XV, **41.** 195
HW at dinner of, for diplomatists, **35.** 113–14, **39.** 14
(?) HW mentions, **3.** 341
Hénault calls, 'un faquin,' **3.** 56
Hertford calls on, at Fontainebleau, **38.** 218, 465
—— gets complaint from, about d'Éon, **38.** 373n
—— hears from, Guerchy's news of Grenville, **38.** 570–1
—— mentions Dauberval's commission to, **38.** 477
——'s parley with, over Turk's Island, **38.** 428n
(?) letter of, may explain Guerchy's neglect of HW, **31.** 115
letters by, in d'Éon's book, characteristic, **39.** 14

[Choiseul, César-Gabriel de, *continued*]
Lorenzi told by, that he is dismissed with pension, **22.** 356
Louis XV attended by, **4.** 196
'man of sense,' **38.** 218–19
marriage of, **3.** 369n
ministry of cousin and, said to totter, **38.** 380
Opéra attended by, **5.** 325, 333
parliament of Paris attended by, **8.** 172
retirement of, rumoured, **39.** 34
Richmond, D. of, assured by, that Aubeterre acted without permission, **22.** 369
—— converses with, **7.** 273
Sanadon, Mlle, a favourite of, **5.** 250n, 325, 333, **6.** 66
'satrape,' **3.** 63, 69
social relations of, in Paris, **5.** 173, 183, 196, 363, **6.** 156–7, **7.** 266, 298, 348, 429, 430–2
son of, to visit England, **38.** 531
Vergennes's correspondence with, **7.** 439
wife of, **3.** 369n
Young Pretender's recognition not authorized by, **22.** 384n
Choiseul, César-Hippolyte de (1757–93), Comte de Choiseul-Praslin:
marriage of, **7.** 450
social relations of, with Mme du Deffand, **7.** 450
Choiseul, Charles-Antoine-Étienne (b. 1739), Marquis de:
(?) Choiseul, Duc de, enemy of, **5.** 110
grandes entrées obtained by, **6.** 52
(?) joke by, on English weather, **9.** *413*
wife of, **5.** 110
Choiseul, Claude-Antoine-Clériadus de (1733–94), Marquis de Choiseul-Beaupré; 'Marquis de Choiseul-la Baume':
Chanteloup to be visited by, **7.** 69
Choiseul, Duc and Duchesse de, accompanied by at Chanteloup after their disgrace, **5.** 7
social relations of, with: Choiseul-Beaupré, Comtesse de, **7.** 439; Du Deffand, Mme, **7.** 445
son of, marries, **7.** *69*, 72, 73
Choiseul, Élisabeth-Céleste-Adélaïde de (1737–68), m. (1752) Florent-Alexandre-Melchior de la Baume, Comte de Montrevel:
death of, **4.** 150, 151
(?) HW's letter to Rousseau disliked by, **7.** 294
Sanadon, Mlle, close friend of, **4.** 151
social relations of, in Paris, **3.** *53 and see index entries ante* 8. 292
Choiseul, François-Joseph de (ca 1695–1769), Marquis de Stainville; French diplomatist:
birth date of, corrected, **43.** 90, 242
Choiseul, Duchesse de, in mourning for, **4.** 406
Craon may be succeeded by, at Florence, **20.** 29, 45, 84, 162, 192n, 197, 210
death of, **4.** *313*, 320

Fleury warns, **17.** 205n, *290n*
Francis I's *grand maître* and envoy at Paris, **20.** 29
governor of Florence but never came there, **20.** 29n
mistress of, generously treated by Duc de Choiseul, **4.** 320
Richecourt disapproves of appointment of, **20.** 45
—— seems to dread approach of, **20.** 84, 162, 192
supposed letter to, from Lubeck, about Young Pretender, **20.** 93n
Choiseul, Jacques-Philippe de (d. 1789), Comte de Stainville; army officer:
Châlons visited by, **6.** 485
Chanteloup to be visited by, **7.** 69, **41.** 197
Choiseul, Duc and Duchesse de, accompanied by, at Chanteloup after their disgrace, **5.** 7, 15, 30
Conway to be taken by, to see fortifications, **39.** 224n
daughter of: **4.** 280n; marries, **7.** 69, 72, 73
death of, at Wilhelmsthal, rumoured, **38.** 161
Du Deffand, Mme, entertains, at supper, **41.** 194
—— pays, **7.** 431
—— receives dress purchased through **7.** 432
——'s commissions executed by, **7.** 430
—— sends parcel by friend of, **7.** 108
——'s informant on Barthélemy's pension, **5.** 168
——'s letters from Chanteloup delayed by, **4.** 15, 15–16
Ferdinand, P., defeats, **22.** 46–7, 60
Gloucester, D. of, seen by, at Châlons, **6.** 485
grenadiers of; suppressed, **39.** 150n
Hobart friend of, **7.** 108
Karl Wilhelm Ferdinand defeated by, **21.** 498n
Lorraine visited by, **6.** 222, 485, **7.** 431
marriage of, **3.** 217n
Saxon army to be aided by, **22.** 60n
sensible, but harsh and brutal to wife, **39.** 224
social relations of, in Paris, **41.** 195; *see also index entries ante* 8. 292
troops for Roussillon commanded by, **7.** 151
Valentinois, Comtesse de, bequeaths house at Passy to, **6.** 71
wife confined by, in convent at Nancy, **3.** *217*–18, 218–19, 225, 226–7, 239
Choiseul, Louis-Marie-Gabriel-César, Baron de:
France may send, as ambassador to England, **25.** 363n
Choiseul, Rénaud-César-Louis (1735–91), Vicomte de; later Duc de Praslin; ambassador to Naples 1766–72:
arrives in Paris, **5.** 141
Conway saw, in England, **39.** 65
England to be visited by, **38.** 531, 535
'good-natured polite man,' **38.** 531
Guerchy to be visited by, **38.** 531

Neapolitan embassy for, **39.** 65

recent ambassador to Vienna, **6.** 157n

social relations of, in Paris, **7.** 349, 433, 444, 457

wife of, **5.** 5n

Choiseul, Hôtel de, in Paris:

changes hands, **7.** 144

Du Deffand, Mme, can always go to, **6.** 432

—— sends letters to, **5.** 93

HW sees Choiseul at, **23.** 143

news of Richelieu-St-Vincent trial awaited at, **6.** 293

Choiseul-Aillecourt, Comte de. *See* Choiseul-Aillecourt, Gaspard-Marie-Victor de (1779–1854); Choiseul-Beaupré, Michel-Félix-Victor de (1754–96)

Choiseul-Aillecourt, Gaspard-Marie-Victor (1779–1854), Comte de:

birth of, **7.** 438

Choiseul-Beaupré, Chevalier de. *See* Choiseul-Beaupré, Michel-Félix-Victor de

Choiseul-Beaupré, Comte de. *See* Choiseul-Beaupré, Marie-Gabriel-Florent-Auguste de

Choiseul-Beaupré, Comtesse de. *See* Gouffier d'Heilly, Marie de (1752–1816); Lallement de Betz, Marie-Françoise (d. 1793)

Choiseul-Beaupré, Marquis de. *See* Choiseul, Claude-Antoine-Clériadus de

Choiseul-Beaupré, Marquise de. *See* La Baume-Montrevel, Diane-Gabrielle de

Choiseul-Beaupré, Claude-Antoine-Clériadus-Gabriel de (1760–1838), Comte (Duc, 1785) de Choiseul:

Chanteloup to be visited by, **7.** 69, 72, 73

La Trémoïlle, Duchesse de, visited by, **12.** 3

Louis XVI aided by, in attempted escape, **11.** 301

marriage of, **7.** 69, 72, 73

returns to Paris, **11.** 301

wife of, **3.** 226n, **4.** 280n

Choiseul-Beaupré, Marie-Gabriel-Florent-Auguste (1752–1817), Comte de; 'Comte de Choiseul'; 'Comte de Choiseul-Gouffier':

Brittany visited by, **7.** 429

Chartres, Duc de, might accompany, to the Levant, **25.** 243n

Du Deffand, Mme, gives opinion of, **7.** 76

HW's approbation pleases, **7.** 232

(?) Lauzun's taking of Senegal joked about by, **7.** 125

marriage of, **5.** 113

returns to Paris, **7.** 190

secretary of, ill, **7.** 141

social relations of, with Duchesse de la Vallière, **5.** *113*

*Voyage pittoresque de la Grèce* by: **7.** 75–6, 82, 86, 94, 96, 102, 106, 108, 114–15, 118, 121, 123, 125, 126, 128, 133, 138, 141, 143, 145, 151, 171, 190, 196, 200, 203, 213, 225, 227–30, 232, 250, 253, 451; HW procures, through Hon. Thomas Walpole, **36.** 179, 195, 196, 206–7, 223, 241–2

with regiment, **7.** 190

Choiseul-Beaupré, Michel-Félix-Victor de (1754–96), Chevalier de Choiseul, Comte d'Aillecourt:

(?) Ducis's Académie election commented on by, **7.** 100

Flanders visited by, **7.** 429

Choiseul-Betz, Comtesse de. *See* Lallement de Betz, Marie-Françoise

Choiseul d'Esguilly, Louise-Joséphine de (b. 1765), m. (1780) César-Hippolyte de Choiseul, Comte de Choiseul-Praslin:

social relations of, with Mme du Deffand, **7.** 450

Choiseul family:

Broglies may succeed, in ministry, **22.** 227

dispersed, **28.** 51

fall of, may not revoke their plots, **23.** 260

Choiseul-Gouffier, Comte de. *See* Choiseul-Beaupré, Marie-Gabriel-Florent-Auguste de

Choiseul-Gouffier, Comtesse de. *See* Gouffier d'Heilly, Marie de

Choiseul-Gouffier, Louis-Félix-Octave de (d. 1848):

(?) birth of, **7.** 429

Choiseul-la-Baume, Marquis de. *See* Choiseul, Claude-Antoine-Clériadus de

Choiseul-la-Baume, Marquise de. *See* La Baume-Montrevel, Diane-Gabrielle de

Choiseul-Meuse, Mlle —— de (d. after 1821), m. Pierre-Marie, Marquis de Suffren de St-Tropez:

(?) SH visited by, **12.** 237

Choiseul-Meuse, François-Joseph (1736–1816), Comte de:

Condé makes, capt. of the guard, **7.** 441

Choiseul-Praslin, Comte de. *See* Choiseul, César-Hippolyte de

Choiseul-Praslin, Comtesse de. *See* Choiseul d'Esguilly, Louise-Joséphine de

Choiseul-Praslin, Alphonse-Charles-Guy de, (1780–1802):

birth of, **7.** 457

Choiseul-Stainville, Comte de. *See* Choiseul-Beaupré, Claude-Antoine-Clériadus-Gabriel de

Choiseul-Stainville, Comtesse de. *See* Choiseul-Stainville, Marie-Stéphanie de

Choiseul-Stainville, Duc de. *See* Choiseul-Beaupré, Claude-Antoine-Clériadus-Gabriel de (1760–1838); Choiseul-Stainville, Étienne-François de (1719–85)

Choiseul-Stainville, Béatrix de (1730–94), m. (1759) Antoine-Antonin, Duc de Gramont:

absorbs attentions, **5.** 169

Aiguillon, Duchesse d', shocks, by countenancing Mme du Barry, **5.** 116

Amazonian, generally detested, **14.** 155

arrested in Paris, **12.** 28

Barèges visited by, **4.** 407, 421, 444–5, 450, **6.** 64

[Choiseul-Stainville, Béatrix de, *continued*]

Beauvau, Princesse de, at Chanteloup with, **4**. 464

—— dominates, **6**. 308

—— friend of, **41**. 192

—— hostess in absence of, **4**. 195

Boufflers, Comtesse de, attentive to, **6**. 33, 41

—— praised by, **6**. 41

(?) Bourbon-Busset loses support of, **5**. 349

Bourbonne to be visited by, **6**. 184, 198

Brienne to be visited by, **6**. 174, 319

Broglie, Comte de, avoided by, **5**. 363, 374

'Catherine' after Catherine II, **3**. 358

Chanteloup to be visited by, **3**. 338, **4**. 126, 134, 463, **5**. 42, 245, 363, 370, 373, **6**. 41, 93, 163, 174, 184, 347, 441, 468, 476, **7**. 68–9, **41**. 197

—— visited by, **4**. 464, 469, **5**. 7, 30, **6**. 33, 353

—— would lose life without, **5**. 395, 396, 399–400, 401

Chartres's acquaintance with, **5**. 340, 341

Chaville visited by, **5**. 363, **7**. 449

Choiseul, Duc de, advised by, not to lend MS copy of St-Simon's *Mémoires*, **34**. 30, 54

—— corresponds with, **5**. 241, 246

—— 's friendship with Comtesse de Boufflers accepted by, **4**. 188, 202n, 203

—— 's intrigue with, **3**. 30n

—— 's relations with, **4**. 196, 372, **5**. 399–400, 401, **10**. 198

—— 's sister, **5**. 89n

—— 's violence against Mme du Barry incited by, **23**. 144, 264

—— visits, in her illness, **6**. 161

Choiseul, Duchesse de, corresponds with, **5**. 241

—— laughs with Mme du Deffand over, **3**. 358, 360

—— overshadowed by, **5**. 169

—— praised by, **4**. 196

—— 's opinion of, **6**. 149

—— 's relations with, **4**. 450, **5**. 338

Choiseul-Stainville, Mlle de, marriage contract of, drawn up by, **7**. 68–9

Cirey to be visited by, **6**. 174

Comédie attended by, **5**. 363

death of, would benefit Duchesse de Choiseul, **4**. 445

deserts own party to sup with Louis XV, **4**. 195

Du Barry, Comtesse, hated by, **5**. 63, **28**. 290

—— subject of wager by, **4**. 196, 203–4

Du Deffand, Mme, fears HW's letter to Duchesse de Choiseul might displease, **5**. 41

—— has, at her chaise longue, **39**. 271

—— mentions, **5**. 284n, **6**. 197

—— receives cup from, **7**. 440

—— 's correspondence with, **6**. 71, 324, 453

—— sends letter by, **7**. 454

—— 's opinion of: **3**. 358, 360, **5**. 63, **6**. 161; improves, **5**. 255, 401, **6**. 18, 33, 149

—— 's relations with, **4**. 196, **5**. 43, 44, 240, 241, 245, 368, 373, 401, **6**. 15, 18, 21, 33, 71, 142, 179, 270, 426–7

—— 's visit to Chanteloup disclosed by, **5**. 240–1

—— 's visit to Chanteloup disclosed to, **5**. 240

—— unwilling to visit Chanteloup because of, **5**. 42, 158

—— urged by, to accept Barthélemy's escort, **5**. 108

—— wagers with, on Mme du Barry, **4**. 196, 203–4

Du Hamel, Mlle, to remain near, **4**. 469

foreigners not received by, **6**. 155

Gramont, Comtesse de, relationship of, to, **4**. 441

Guerchy, former lover of, now hated for opposing marriage, **22**. 551n

HW calls 'Hermione,' **10**. 198

HW plays loo with, **32**. 24

HW sees, at theatre, **32**. 22

HW's lessons on, **3**. 371

HW will flirt with, **32**. *13*

health of, **5**. 395, 399, **6**. 33, 149, 161, 187, 189–90

kingdom upset by, **5**. 63

La Borde's presents from, **31**. 80

La Borde to be visited by, **5**. 231, 234, 238, 363

La Ferté to be visited by, **5**. 363

leaves Paris, **6**. 180

letter of, on Duchesse de Choiseul's health, **4**. 291

Le Val visited by, **7**. 454, 458

L'Isle's verses about, **6**. 411

Louis XV conducts, out, **4**. 193, 195

—— 's summer-time parties with, **38**. 389

Luxembourg, Mme de, relations of, with, **6**. 21, 26, 29, 33 42

Mirepoix, Mme de, avoids and is avoided by, **5**. 363, **6**. 18, 26–7

Orléans, Bp of, to be visited by, **5**. 231, 234, 238, 239, 241

Paris visited by **5**. 363, **6**. 11, 15, 21, 33, 175, 347, 348, 500, **7**. 68–9, 192

Plombières visited by, **6**. 295, 319, 324, 347, 348

Poix, Princesse de, confinement of, brings, to Paris, **6**. 468, 472

Pompadour, Mme de, might be succeeded by, **38**. 372

Pompom sent to call on, in monk's garb, **7**. 2

popularity of, **5**. 245, **6**. 21, 30, 33

Raincy visited by, **6**. 29

said to have gone to Choiseul's bedside, **4**. 86

Ste-Assise visited by, **7**. 452

social relations of, in Paris, *see index entries ante* 8. 294

Stanley attached to, **38**. 427

stays up late, **5**. 246, 255, **6**. 250

summer plans of, in 1776, **6**. 295, 319

sups at the Temple, **4**. 188

Tessé, Comtesse de, to be visited by, **5**. 363

*(see also under* Chaville visited by)

to leave Paris, 6. 29, 30, 270, 426

Valentinois, Comtesse de, avoided by, 5. 363

Versailles visited by, 4. 195, 5. 363

York's misunderstanding about, 3. 333

Choiseul-Stainville, Caroline-Eugénie de (1723–1816), Abbess of Metz:

lawsuit lost by, 7. 456

social relations of, in Paris, 7. (?) 439, (?) 442, 450, 451, 452

Choiseul-Stainville, Étienne-François de (1719–85), Comte de Stainville; Duc de Choiseul, 1758; minister of foreign affairs; 'petit-fils'; 'grand-papa':

administration of: 5. 332n; Fitzjames and Du Menil recalled by, to appease provincial parliaments, 38. 301; Paris parliament asked by, for financial advice and care of sinking fund, 38. 301; Paris parliament's union with provincial ones dreaded by, 38. 301; parliaments oppose, 38. 271, 280; said to totter, 38. 380

advises on choice of controller, 4. 326

affairs of the heart occupy, 11. 36

Aiguillon may succeed, 23. 79, 85

——'s enemy, 3. 349n, 4. 196–7

Alembert's preface to Exposé succinct enrages, 3. 171

anecdote of, and Monclar's pension, 4. 285

anecdotes by: of king's message to Bp of Orléans, 3. 360–1; (?) of Senegal's capture, 7. 123

appointees of, removed, 23. 321–2, 480

Arras, Bp of, appointment of, to Tours, pleases, 6. 98

—— wants to see, 5. 251

'Arsame' in Barthélemy's Anacharsis, 34. 78

Artois, Comte d' (Charles X) to visit, 6. 445, 450–1

Aubeterre chosen by, to treat Rome with high hand, 22. 384

Austria and Spain (but not Russia, Turkey, and Corsica) may dislike fall of, 23. 259

author of Bourbon family compact, 23. 259

Avignon may not be relinquished by Aiguillon because it was obtained by, 23. 527

Ayen to visit, in exile, 5. 45

bankers saved by, 4. 373, 376, 404

Barbantane shocked by disgrace of, 23. 261

Barèges to be visited by, 6. 64

Barthélemy aided by, with emoluments, 34. 79

—— to visit, 5. 6

Beaumarchais's pamphlet's suppression demanded by, 7. 195n

—— subject of letter by, 7. 439

Beauvau, Prince de, promoted by, 4. 340

—— to speak to La Borde about, 8. 187

—— upholds, 41. 192

—— visits, 5. 30, 32

Beauvau, Princesse de, influences, 4. 372, 421

—— upholds, 41. 192

—— visits, 4. 469, 5. 30, 32

Bedford, D. of, negotiates peace with, 22. 81n

Benedict XIV resents deferred entry of, 20. 589

Berkenroode warns, of Dutch intervention if Pretender is involved, 21. 298n

Bernis's recall arranged by, 38. 298

Besenval consults, on troops, 5. 32

—— visits, 5. 32

biographical information about, corrected, 43. 272

Boswell's Account of Corsica translated for, and lent to Mme du Deffand by him, 4. 113, 124, 126

Boufflers, Chevalier de, corresponds with, 4. 60, 8. 137–8

Boufflers, Comtesse de, not pleasing to, 3. 16

—— reconciled with, 4. 177, 182, 188, 202n, 203

Boufflers, Marquis de, death of, afflicts, 6. 92

—— visits, 5. 30, 6. 92

boundary disputes with Austria and Sardinia settled by, 23. 143

Bourbon's fall would surprise, 34. 55

(?) Bourbon-Busset loses support of, 5. 349

Bourbonne to be visited by, 6. 198

breaks bone in hand, 5. 381, 385

Brienne, Comte and Comtesse de, to be visited by, 6. 195

Brienne to be visited by, 6. 174

Brionne, Comtesse de, friend of, 4. 341, 372, 5. 169

—— may be accompanied to Limours by, 6. 473

—— to visit, in exile, 5. 45

—— visited by, 6. 439

Broglie conceals affairs from, 4. 214n

——'s pension secured by, 3. 57

brother of, 3. 217n, 4. 280n, 441n

Burgoyne's intimacy with, 3. 243n

Canada Bills settled by, 39. 30

Caramans defended by Mme du Deffand to, 3. 369

Carmontelle's portrait of Duchesse and Mme du Deffand expedited by, 4. 14

Castries expected to succeed, 7. 326

——'s appointment arranged by, 4. 330, 340–1

——'s relations with, 4. 340–1, 372

Catherine II may rebuke, 23. 125

—— not favoured by, 4. 483

—— receives agent from, and may receive a minister, 23. 127

——'s Turkish war instigated by, 23. 133–4, 143, 154

Chanteloup country seat of, 3. 57n

—— managed by, 5. 253–4

—— occupied by, 3. 302, 4. 9, 85, 86, 88, 103, 435, 436, 469, 5. 1, 7, 243, 244, 246, 253, 331, 6. 62, 190, 204, 439, 7. 44, 365, 447, 8. 207, 39. 134

[Choiseul-Stainville, Étienne-F. de, *continued*]
—— should be preferred by, to power, **23.** 315
—— to be occupied by, **3.** 338, **4.** 134, 243, 266, 431, 463, 464, **5.** 42, **6.** 163, 174, 196, 198, 272, 281, 319, 441, 445, 468, 476, 478, **7.** 36, 68–9, 124, **39.** 134
Chartres's acquaintance with, **5.** 340
——'s letter from, **5.** 336, 340–1
——'s letter to, **5.** 336, 338, 340
——'s visit declined by, **4.** 333, 340–1
—— to visit, **5.** 331, 340
Châtillon visited by, **7.** 331
Chauvelin sent to Corsica by, **4.** 200, 202
Choiseul, Duchesse de, brought to Paris by, **4.** 294, 445
—— can be sincerely treated by son of another prime minister, **41.** 16
—— desired by, to return to Paris, **4.** 289
—— entertains friends of, **4.** 318
—— greeted by, **4.** 110
—— included by, in reply to Chartres, **5.** 340, 341
—— reads HW's letter to, **41.** 110
——'s date of return set by, **4.** 103
——'s intercession with, asked by HW, **41.** 43
——'s relations with, **3.** 23, 59, **4.** 10, 188, 298, 299–300, 418, 445, 450, **5.** 319, 338, **6.** 155, 293, **7.** 197, **10.** 198, **14.** 155
——'s suppers seldom attended by, **3.** 337–8
——, wife of, **3.** 1, **10.** 198n, **14.** 154n, **16.** 199n
Choiseul, Hôtel de, returns to ownership of, **7.** 144
Choiseul, Marquis de, enemy of, **5.** 110
Choiseul-Beaupré, Comtesse de, visits, **5.** 7
Choiseul-Beaupré, Marquis and Marquise de, visit, **5.** 7
Choiseul-Stainville, Mlle de, marriage contract of, drawn up by, **7.** 68–9
Choisy visited by, **4.** 257
Cholmondeley, Mrs, lent lodging by, for Dauphin's marriage, **4.** 402, 407
—— talks with, **4.** 272
Cirey to be visited by, **6.** 174
Clairon, Mlle, appeals to, **38.** 518, 524
Clement XIV contributed greatly to fall of, **23.** 372
—— 'made' by, **23.** 133
colonists sent to French Guiana by, **4.** 492n
Compiègne visited by, **4.** 445
Condé covets Swiss Guards command of, **23.** 265n
—— opposed to, **5.** 45
Conti reconciled with, **4.** 177, 182, 202n, 203
Conway and wife being foreigners are not received by, **39.** 236, 242
Conway and wife may see, **6.** 115, 118, 126
Corbie offers millions to, **4.** 416
Corsica conquered and oppressed by administration of, **4.** 202, **23.** 38, 62, 67, 69, 75, 81, 87, 90, 121, 124, 130, 133, 153–4, 157, 258, 263, **39.** 112, 135

courier of, **3.** 215, 219, 220, **4.** 42, 66, 73, 74, 91, 94
Court attended by, at end of exile, **6.** 62
Court's visit to Fontainebleau may overturn, **39.** 119
cousin of, **4.** 351
criticism of, **4.** 158n
Dalrymple, Sir John, gets from, copies of letters, **28.** 67n
Dalrymple's letter of introduction to, **28.** 368n
Dauphin said by, to resemble James II, **7.** 297
departure from Paris postponed by, **39.** 270
diplomatic successes of, **23.** 133–4
disgrace confers immortality upon, **41.** 201
Du Barry, Comtesse, bans friends of, **5.** 48
—— braved by, to please Mmes de Beauvau and de Gramont, **23.** 144, 264
—— called on by, without yielding, **23.** 144
—— contrasted with Mme de Maintenon by, **7.** 369
—— does not favour, **4.** 169n, 185–6, (?) 188, 297–8, 300–1, 304n, 381, **23.** 75, 85, 115, 117, 125, 130, 134, **28.** 290–1
—— makes faces at, at whist, with Louis XV, **23.** 157
—— must quickly aid Paoli by overturning, **23.** 75, 81, 87, 90
—— unwisely treated by, **4.** 372, **23.** 85, 134, 144
Du Châtelet not permitted to visit, **23.** 258, **39.** 134
——'s friendship with, **41.** 193
Du Châtelet, Comte and Comtesse, to be visited by, **6.** 174, 195–6
Du Deffand, Mme, accused of servility to, **4.** 382
—— allots suit to, **6.** 258
—— asks, about date of wife's return, **4.** 97
—— asks for mémoire by, **4.** 69
—— believes, is disturbed, **4.** 285
—— concerned over affairs of, **4.** 185–6, 193, 196, 202–3, 210, 234, 297–8, 300, 304, 311, 318, 327, 329, 341, 347, 371–3, 376–7, 380–1, 441, 444, 447, 449–50, 456, 458, 464, 491, 495, 496, **5.** 48, 49, 55–6, 74
—— entertains, at supper, on eve of his fall, **41.** 194
—— fears that HW's letter may displease, **5.** 41
—— given seat at Comédie by, **4.** 272, 275
—— gives supper for, **39.** 269
—— has, at her chaise longue, **39.** 271
—— invited to Chanteloup by, **6.** 204
—— lent letters of Mme de Maintenon by, **4.** 44, 62, 68–9, 74, 88, 108
—— lent St-Simon's *Mémoires* by, **4.** 478
—— may never see, again, **5.** 322
—— mentions, **3.** 29, **4.** 157, **6.** 90, 197, 450
—— not seen by, on first return from exile, **6.** 62, 64, 66, 71, 97, 115, 123
—— not to mention HW to, **4.** 60
—— occupies opera box of, **7.** 331

—— offers to confess to, **7.** 252n
—— receives New Year's gift from, **3.** 205, 405, 406, **4.** 7, 7–8, 38
—— receives porcelain from, **41.** 197
——'s Christmas Eve party for, **6.** 115, 118, 123, 125, 131, 133
—— scolds, over Praslin's reaction to her street accident, **3.** 61, **8.** 122
——'s correspondence with, **3.** 406, **4.** 69, 86, 88, 383, 406, 414, **6.** 97
—— secures book from, for HW, **4.** 378
—— sends letter and book through, **3.** 268, 269, 271
——'s finances a concern to, **4.** 91, 103, 315, 354, 355, 358, 361, 362, 364, 365, 375, 379, 383, 385, 406
——'s letter to HW will not be opened by, **3.** 269
——'s messages from and to, **4.** 428, **8.** 208
——'s opinion of, **3.** 205, 218, 256, 359–60, 371n, **4.** 202, 206–7, 298, 315, 342, 360, 365, 379, 407, 437, **5.** 14, 49, 253–4, 255, 257, **6.** 85, 299
——'s presence at supper with Christian VII desired by, **4.** 163
——'s quarrel with Mme de Forcalquier known to, **4.** 391
——'s relations with, **3.** 210, 256, 265, 324, 358–60, 406, **4.** 2, 6, 121, 137, 174, 177, 183, 191, 375, **5.** 43, 44, 61, 107–8, 241–3, **6.** 74, 97, 115, 142, 161, 166, 270, 273, 426, **7.** 36
——'s verses for, **4.** 178, 183
——'s verses on, **6.** 122–3
——'s visit disclosed to, **5.** 241
——'s visit to surprise, **5.** 238, 240
—— talks with, about: Chamier, **4.** 301; Guines, **4.** 492; Richmond, D. of, **4.** 297
—— thinks Chanteloup regretted by, **6.** 127
—— to ask, about Ossory, **4.** 114
—— to give Boufflers's verses to, **39.** 236
—— to receive game from, **4.** 445
—— unwilling to settle at Chanteloup because of, **4.** 42, 60
—— wagers with, on Mme du Barry, **4.** 203–4
—— wants to show HW's letter under name of Émile to, **3.** 11
—— would like Conways to know, **6.** 115, 118, 126, 133–4, 156
Du Hamel, Mlle, interests, **4.** 469, 470–1
Dupuits to address books to, **4.** 21
Dutens and Comtesse de Boufflers visit, at Chanteloup, **25.** 627
Egremont's peace negotiations with, **22.** 38n
employees of, ill, **6.** 97
enemies of, **4.** 464n
England may get agent from, offered by La Borde, **21.** 488n
——'s invasion planned by, **15.** 134
——'s peace with France considered by, as made, **22.** 65n, 66n
——'s possible plot with, suspected, **5.** 53n
English enjoy fall of, because he endangered them, **41.** 201

English, especially Chatham, disliked by, **39.** 236
English threatened by, **20.** 497, **23.** 142
exile of: **23.** 257; ended by Louis XVI, **6.** 50, 52, 53, 56, 57, 59, 60, 62, 64n
fall of: **4.** 191n, 491n, 497, **5.** 4, 7, 14, 249n, **7.** 341n, **28.** 51, 153, 290, **31.** 152, **34.** 30, **39.** 134–6, **41.** 193–9; expected, **23.** 70, 79, 155; rumoured, **39.** 112, 135
finances of, **5.** 155, 159, 162, 165–7, **7.** 144
fluttering and unsettled, **14.** 149
Fontainebleau visited by, **4.** 294–5, 469
Forcalquier, Mme de, opposed to, **4.** 382
foreign and military departments taken by, leaving others to Praslin, **39.** 65
foreigners not received by, **6.** 126, 133–4, 155, 156
Francès's condition alarms, **4.** 344
France tells, to foment Italian quarrels, **20.** 589
Franklin and Deane meet, at Mme du Deffand's, **24.** 273n
French credit supported by, **4.** 376, 378
French foreign-office archives opened by, for *Historic Doubts*, **4.** 4
French gazette says, is to be made a Maréchal, **23.** 154
French pecuniary distress largely due to, **34.** 78
Fréron arouses anger of, over attack on HW, **3.** 206n, 228
garden of, adjoins house built by Marquise de la Ferrière, **6.** 11
Gatti visits, **5.** 7
gay in the face of trouble, **4.** 327, 456, 458, 491, **5.** 167
gazette article by, stresses Turkish defeat of Russians, **23.** 143, 154
generous to his father's mistress, **4.** 320
Gennevilliers visited by, **4.** 458
Gibbon meets, **6.** 445
——'s acquaintance desired by, **6.** 442, 445
——'s *Decline and Fall* may be translated at expense of, **6.** 301
——'s *Decline and Fall* pleases, **6.** 442, 445
gives party for servants of former guests at Chanteloup, **6.** 162–3
Gleichen tells, that Mme du Deffand now prefers Gleichen to HW, **4.** 212
Gluck's *Armide* to be attended by, **6.** 478
Gontaut visits, **5.** 7
governed by self-seekers, **4.** 298
Gramont, Comtesse de, banished during absence of, **4.** 436–7, 441
—— not close friend of, **4.** 441
Gramont, Duchesse de, corresponds with, **5.** 241, 246
—— intrigues with, **3.** 30n
——'s relations with, **4.** 196, 372, **5.** 399–400, 401, **10.** 198
—— visited by, in her illness, **6.** 161
—— visits, **3.** 338, **4.** 134, 463, 464, 469, **5.** 7, 30 (*see also under* Chanteloup: visitors to)

[Choiseul-Stainville, Étienne-F. de, *continued*]
'grand-papa' the nickname of, **41**. 192
Grimaldi might plot with, **23**. 260
guests delight, **5**. 331
Guines approved by, **4**. 492
——'s suit reported by, to Mme du Deffand, **6**. 168
Gustav III ostensibly regrets absence of, **5**. 48
HW and Mme du Barry talk about, **11**. 341
HW and others await, **7**. 329
HW because of Corsica does not regret fall of, **39**. 135
HW calls, 'Oberon,' **10**. 198
HW complimented by, **4**. 417
HW concerned over illness of, **4**. 101, 102, 103, 133
HW congratulates wife of, on his retirement, **41**. 200–1
HW could predict consequences of return of, **24**. 13
HW describes, **35**. 114
HW desired by, to visit Chanteloup, **5**. 252–3, 255, **7**. 88
HW esteems, **5**. 255
HW hears gazette article read by, at his own house, **23**. 143
HW hints to friends of, that Wilkes might bring Pitt back to power, **23**. 143
HW hopes for restoration of, to power, **39**. 189
HW indignant over failure of, to help Mme du Deffand, **4**. 358
HW inquired after by, **4**. 294, **7**. 88
HW introduced to, **7**. 266
HW liked by, **3**. 373, **4**. 272, 344
HW not in disfavour with, **3**. 71
HW not to have medallion of, **4**. 349–50
HW occupies opera box of, **7**. 331
HW praised by, **3**. 359, 404
HW presented to, by Guerchy, **39**. 14
HW's acquaintance desired by and for, **3**. 171, 175, 206, 223, 233n, 239, 241–2, 256, 263–4, 267, 280, 324, **28**. 291, **41**. 75
HW's affairs inquired after by, **3**. 266, 290, 319, 359, **4**. 183
HW sees Flemish pictures of, **7**. 331
HW sends book on medicine to, **4**. 114, 119, 133
HW's letter on *Testament politique* discussed by, **3**. 220, 223
HW's letters charm, **3**. 171, 175, **4**. 38
HW's letter to Rousseau discussed by, **3**. 22, **4**. 183
HW spoken ill of, to, **3**. 59
HW's proposed epic of war in Mme Geoffrin's salon delights, **4**. 217
HW suggested by, as ambassador to France, **4**. 344, **23**. 183, 190
HW suspected of secret correspondence with, **5**. 55
HW thinks, agreeable but with taste not exquisite, **39**. 236
HW to have medallion of, **4**. 25, 333, 338

HW to talk to, **41**. 7
happy in retirement, **5**. 253–4
Harcourt, E., unsatisfactory to, **4**. 343
Havrincourt's correspondence with, about Anglo-French negotiations, **21**. 360n
health of: **3**. 236, **4**. 4–6, 85, 86, 88, 91, 102n, 133, 136, 257, 311, 360, 400, 437, **5**. 1, 7, 15, 37, 297, 381, 385, **6**. 92–5, 110, **7**. 440
Hénault ridicules, **3**. 56
Hertford gets complaint from, about d'Éon, **38**. 373n
—— should not receive letters through, **38**. 566
Holland might have been forced by, to give ships for invasion of England, **23**. 269
Hôtel des Halles à blé assigned to, in joke, **8**. 181
Hume not highly thought of by, **3**. 266
hunts, **4**. 179, 458, **5**. 241
in good humour, **4**. 335
Invault a favourite of, **23**. 164, 169
Irwin likes, **4**. 154
—— occupies opera box of, **7**. 331
Jesuits expelled by, **23**. 87, **26**. 49
jokes with Mmes du Deffand and de la Vallière, **4**. 68, 70–1
Joseph II cordial to, **6**. 445
——'s proposed visit to, **6**. 445, 447, 453, 455
La Balue's closing remedied by, **4**. 373, 376
—— said to be influenced by, **4**. 373
La Borde said to be influenced by, **4**. 373
—— visited by, at La Ferté, **4**. 458, 459
La Chalotais's life saved by, **11**. 44, **23**. 206n
La Harpe translates Suetonius by order of, **4**. 482
La Touche proves to, impossibility of defending Martinique, **22**. 21n
Lauzun, Duc de, displeases, **3**. 242
—— visits, **5**. 7
Lauzun, Duchesse de, visits, **5**. 7
leaves Paris, **6**. 426
letter of, on wife's health, **4**. 291
Limours visited by, **6**. 439, 473
L'Isle attached to, **41**. 193
——'s verses about, **6**. 411
lively, **38**. 218–19
Lorenzi notified by, that he must surrender post to a Frenchman, **22**. 346, 351, 371
Louis XV aided England by dismissing, **23**. 314
—— attended by, **4**. 196, 257
—— does not forbid visits to, but remembers the visitors, **23**. 321
—— gracefully replied to by, **4**. 153–4
—— has devotion of, **4**. 441
—— reproaches, for fomenting war, **23**. 258
——'s correspondence with about exile, delivered by La Vrillière, **41**. 196–7
—— sends note to, **4**. 195
——'s treatment of Du Châtelet told of by, **3**. 361
—— tells: of approaching visit to parliament of Paris, **4**. 459; of wish for peace, **39**. 135

Louis XVI cool to, **6**. 127

—— said to have conference with, **25**. 291

——'s consecration to be attended by, **6**. 163, 167, 195, 198

Luxembourg, Mme de, cool to, **5**. 122

—— given gold torches by, **6**. 174

—— jokes about, **4**. 12

—— reconciled with, **5**. 169

Luynes informed by, through Rochechouart, excluding Cavalchini, **21**. 215n

'Mlle de Montpensier,' **3**. 270

Maillebois cabals against, **23**. 283

Mann anxious to hear that Mme du Barry has expelled, **23**. 90

—— can believe anything of, **23**. 277

Marie-Antoinette favours, **6**. 397, **25**. 291, **32**. 266, **39**. 270

—— said to be influenced by, **25**. 291n

Marly visited by, **4**. 241

marriage and career of, **3**. 1n

Maupeou contrasted with, **8**. 179

—— told by, to name new controller, **23**. 164

medallions of, **4**. 25, 322–3, 333, 338, 349–50, **8**. 27

Meinières, Mme de, praises, **3**. 364

*Mémoire historique sur la négociation* by, **21**. 546n

memoirs of, published without authority, **5**. 96n

Mirepoix, Mme de, at odds with, **3**. 152, 214, 283, **4**. 298, 300, 339, **6**. 261

Monaco, Prince de, postpones visit to, **31**. 136

Monteynard speaks courteously of, **5**. 15

—— subject of remark by, **5**. 5n

Morfontaine impersonated by, **3**. 211, 218, 223, 233, 270

niece given watch by, **4**. 295, 299

Nivernais rumoured to succeed, **23**. 62

nothing heard of, **24**. 18

Old Pretender complains to, of Benedict XIV's neglect, **20**. 590

Orléans, Bp of, friend of, **23**. 321

—— may be visited by, **6**. 92

Panthémont, abbess of, asked by, to keep Miss Cholmondeley, **4**. 400

Paoli might be saved by fall of, **23**. 75, 81, 87, 90

——'s letters from, show perfidy, **23**. 154

Paris house of, open, **6**. 127

—— to be visited by, **4**. 435, 469, **6**. 95, 118, 120, 121, 240, 242, 299, 314, 315, 439, 468, 495, 499, 500, **7**. 68–9, 73, 230

—— visited by: **4**. 9, 134, 360, 459, **6**. 125, 195, 204, 244, 380, 473, 478, **7**. 88, 94, 192, 438, 451, 452, 461; on return from exile, **6**. 62, 64, 66, 71, 97, 115, 123, **24**. 19, **32**. 268

parliament of Brittany restored by, **23**. 134

Parliament's Corsican decision will please, **23**. 69

parliaments said to receive clandestine aid from, **23**. 259

party of, desires war, **5**. 111

peace considered by, as made with England, **22**. 65n, 66n

peace desired by, **4**. 315, **22**. 60

peace negotiated by: with Bedford, **22**. 81n; with Egremont, **22**. 38n; with Pitt, **21**. 515n, 526n

peace not earnestly wanted by, **23**. 269

peace would be obstructed by, **25**. 291

pension for, **5**. 155, 159, 162, 166, **23**. 322, 363

permission necessary to visit, in exile, **5**. 1, 6, 30, 32, 43–4, 45, 48, 76

Pitt (Chatham) probably dreaded by, more than Mme du Barry, **23**. 134

—— proclaims, as greatest French premier since Richelieu, **41**. 201

——'s peace negotiation with, **21**. 515n, 526n

political changes not to involve, **6**. 85

political possibilities for, **6**. 299, 311n, 314, 322, 323, 397, **7**. 58

Pompadour, Mme de, aided, **4**. 301

—— persuaded by, not to publish minutes condemning Broglie, **21**. 519n

—— promotes, to become Duc, **21**. 242

popularity blinds, to his faults, **23**. 321

popularity of, **4**. 377, 381, 389, **23**. 303

portrait of, often on snuff-boxes, **23**. 303

Praslin's successor, **3**. 56, **8**. 122

print of, **41**. 284

recalled to Paris, **24**. 19

reports on departments of war and foreign affairs, **4**. 371–2

resignation threatened by, to avoid being expelled by Mme du Barry, **23**. 85

restoration of, rumoured, **32**. 266, 299

retirement of, rumoured, **22**. 30

return of: to power, would mean war with England, **24**. 1, 10–11; would gratify Mme du Deffand, **39**. 223

Richelieu and Mmes du Barry and de Mirepoix leagued against, **41**. 192

Richelieu ridiculed by, for reconciliation with Mme de Mirepoix, **7**. 369

Richelieu-St-Vincent trial attended by, **6**. 293

Richelieu (place) visited by, **6**. 461, 463

Richmond, D. of, desires favour of, **4**. 287, 297, 413, 414

(?) ——'s speech scandalizes, **7**. 19

——'s status regarding Aubigny explained by, to Mme du Deffand, **4**. 417–18, 424, 427–8

Roman entry delayed by, **20**. 589

Rome opposed by, **22**. 384, **23**. 117

Rousseau's pension astonishes, **3**. 320, 322

runaway horses of, **6**. 430

Russian successes a blow to, **23**. 151, 154

Ste-Assise visited by, **7**. 452

St-Esprit, Ordre du, ceremonies of, attended by, **6**. 127, 314, 441

St-Florentin, enemy of, **3**. 262n

St-Hubert to be visited by, **8**. 122

St-Simon's *Mémoires* copied by order of, **34**. 29–30, 54–5

——'s *Mémoires* guarded by, **5**. 78

[Choiseul-Stainville, Étienne-F. de, *continued*]
——'s *Mémoires* lent by, to Mme du Deffand, **4.** 478
——'s *Mémoires* said not to be owned by, **5.** 88
——'s papers seized by order of, **34.** 29n
sale of pictures of, **5.** 221
Salis consults, on troops, **5.** 32
—— visits, **5.** 32
Sanadon, Mlle, occupies opera box of, **7.** 331
says, at Vienna, that it is tiresome to be French, **21.** 307
sedition the chief weapon of, in conquering Corsica, **23.** 153–4
Sévigné letters lent by, to Mme du Deffand, **4.** 81n
Sigorgne aided by, **4.** 453
'sick of the war,' **22.** 30n
sister-in-law of, **3.** 217n, 218n
sister of, **3.** 30n, **4.** 188n, **12.** 28n, **28.** 290n, **38.** 372
slight to, **4.** 288n
social life of, **6.** 161, 378
social relations of, in Paris, with: HW, **39.** 89, 292; Schomberg, **39.** 292; Wood, **39.** 89; *see also index entries ante* **8.** 298
Solar told by, of France's proposal to compensate Sardinia for Placentia's revenue, **21.** 275n
Sorba instigated by, to invade Corsica, **23.** 363
Spanish negotiations of, **41.** 195
spirits of, low, **5.** 297, 385
Stainville visits, **5.** 7, 30
Stanley much with, **38.** 427
—— no longer cared about by, **4.** 461
—— presented by, to Louis XV, **21.** 514n
Starhemberg tries to persuade, not to negotiate with England, **21.** 360n
stays up late, **5.** 255
successor to, not yet named, **23.** 261
Suetonius translated by order of, **4.** 482
suppers given for, on return from exile, **6.** 118, 120–3
Sweden 'bought' by, **23.** 133
Swedish aid for invasion of England mentioned by, **21.** 296n
Swiss Guards taken from, **5.** 155, 165–7, **23.** 322, 363, **41.** 200
Swiss oppressed by, **23.** 130
Terray convinced by, that war funds cannot be raised, **39.** 135
—— enemy of, **4.** 334n
—— restores Mme du Deffand's pension at request of, **4.** 375–6
——'s fiscal support of war 'confuted' by, **23.** 258
——'s reforms opposed by, **4.** 365
——'s relations with, **4.** 358, 372–3, 373
Tessé, Comtesse de, to visit, **5.** 45
Tingry, Prince and Princesse de, visit, **5.** 32, 45
*Toison d'or* conferred on, **21.** 560

to leave Paris, **6.** 174, 175, 177, 179, 272, 273, 275, 281, 288, 295, 299, 419, **7.** 214
Treaty of Paris signed by, **22.** 118n
triumphs over England and Mme du Barry, **23.** 125
Turgot may be succeeded by, **24.** 208
Turkish and Polish causes might be espoused by, **24.** 11
Turks attack Catherine II at instigation of, **23.** 133–4, 143, 154
—— must be abandoned or joined by, **23.** 202
Vergennes's correspondence with, **7.** 439
Versailles visited by, **4.** 86, 88, 253, 360, 383, **6.** 127, **35.** 422, **41.** 194
verses for, at Mme de Luxembourg's supper, **6.** 405
verses on, **4.** 300–1, **5.** 7, **6.** 122–3, 194
Versoix favoured by, **4.** 396, **23.** 130n
victory of financial policy of, **4.** 376–7
Vienna post disparaged by, in letter, **21.** 242
visitors to, at Chanteloup, *see* Chanteloup: visitors to
vivacity of, uncommon, **24.** 498
Voltaire enlists aid of, for Genevese emigrants, **4.** 411
—— praises, **32.** 50
——'s letters to, on: La Bletterie, **4.** 171, 181; MM. de Pompignan, **3.** 202, 203
——'s return not to be sought by, **7.** 329
——'s treatment of La Bletterie scandalizes, **4.** 105, 113, 171
—— suspects, of being HW's intermediary, **8.** 144
Walpole, Hon. Robert, relations of, with, **4.** 306, 311, 344, 378, 461, 480
Walpole Hon. Thomas, relations of, with, **4.** 378, 461
—— suspects, is not very firm, **39.** 34
Walpole of Wolterton's *Case* translated by order of, **4.** 119n
war will not disturb power of, **23.** 253
Weymouth preferred by, to Rochford, **23.** 62n
Wilkes has probably been approached by, **23.** 143
witticism by, to Clairon when she threatens to quit stage, **38.** 518, 524, 526
Wood preferred by, to other English, **39.** 236
Young Pretender not to be used by, in operations against England, **21.** 298n
Choiseul-Stainville, Léopold-Charles de (1724–74), Abp of Cambrai:
Choiseuls to be visited by, at Chanteloup, **41.** 197
death of, **6.** 94–5
Du Deffand, Mme, wagers with, on Mme du Barry, **4.** 203–4
Gramont, Comtesse de, close friend of, **4.** 441
house of, at Arsenal, **6.** 218
social relations of, in Paris, **3.** 240, **4.** 164, **41.** 194
Choiseul-Stainville, Marie-Stéphanie de (1763–1833), m. (1778) Claude-Antoine-Clériadus-

Gabriel de Choiseul-Beaupré, Comte (Duc, 1785) de Choiseul:
Chanteloup to be visited by, **7.** 69, 72, 73
(?) Choiseul gives watch to, **4.** 295, 299
(?) Du Deffand, Mme, prepares doll for, **4.** 280, 295, 299-300
financial provision for, **3.** 226
health of, **4.** 381
marriage of, **7.** 69, 72, 73
(?) rival suitors of, **33.** 515-16
social relations of, with Comtesse de Choiseul-Beaupré, **7.** 442
Choiseul-Stainville, Thérèse-Félicité de (1767-94), m. (1782) Joseph-Marie-Jérôme-Honoré Goyon-de-Matignon de Grimaldi, 'Prince Joseph of Monaco':
financial provision for, **3.** 226
Choisi. *See* Choisy
Choisy, Abbé de:
journey of, **7.** 461
Choisy, Marquise de. *See* Ourches, Marguerite-Jeanne d'
Choisy, Louis, Marquis de:
(?) social relations of, in Paris, **7.** 274, 282, 285, 289, 312, 321, 325, 327
(?) Voltaire's pieces read by, **7.** 274
Choisy (France):
account of, **3.** 122n
*Alix et Alexis* given at, **4.** 257, 258, 259
Artois, Comte d', exiled to, **7.** 31, 32
Bauffremont's home at, **7.** 339
Court at, **5.** 71, 322, **6.** 476
——'s visit to, postponed, **41.** 193
—— to visit, **6.** 460, **7.** 178
Du Deffand, Mme, mentions, **3.** 337
Louis XV returns from, **23.** 115
Louis XVI countermands Court visit to, **20.** 500n
Port à l'Anglois near, **5.** 69n, 79n
royal family at, after Louis XV's death, **6.** 50
visitors to: Artois, Comtesse d', **5.** 421; Avaray, Marquise d', **4.** 258-9; Beauvau, Chevalier de, **7.** 339; Boufflers, Marquise de, **7.** 339; Choiseul, **4.** 257; Choiseul, Duchesse de, **4.** 48, 137, 8. 136; Conti, Princesse de, **6.** 51; Du Barry, Comtesse, **4.** 258-9, 472; Du Bois de la Motte, Mme, **7.** 339; Duras, Duchesse de, **4.** 258; Flavacourt, Marquise de, **4.** 258; Forcalquier, Mme de, **5.** 330; Joseph II, **6.** 441, 443, 450; La Tournelle, Mme, **18.** 103n; L'Hôpital, Comtesse de, **4.** 259, 472; Louis XV, **3.** 35, 122, 291-2, **4.** 243, 256-8, 472, **5.** 97, **18.** 103n, **38.** 268, 338; Louis XVI, **6.** 50-4, **7.** 431, **24.** 5n; Maurepas **6.** 53; Mazarin, Duchesse de, **4.** 472; Mesdames, **6.** 50, 55; ministers, **6.** 54; Mirepoix, Mme de, **4.** 15, 258, 472, **5.** 421; Montmorency, Princesse de, **4.** 472; Pons, Vicomtesse de, **4.** 259; (?) Porquet, **7.** 339; St-Maigrin, Marquise de, **4.** 259; Talmond, Princesse de, **4.** 258; Valentinois, Comtesse de, **4.** 258, 472

*Choix de coquillages. See under* Regenfuss, Franz Michael
*Choleric Fathers, The. See under* Holcroft, Thomas
Cholmeley, Francis (1750-1808) of Brandsby Hall, Yorks:
SH visited by, **12.** 247
wife of, **2.** 304n, **11.** 29n
Cholmeley, Mrs Francis. *See* Englefield, Teresa Ann
Cholmeley. *See also* Cholmley; Cholmondeley
Cholmley, ——, lawyer:
law chambers of, burnt, **20.** 321n
Cholmley, Alice (d. 1756), m. Samuel Forth:
Mann, Galfridus, inherits little from, despite promise, **20.** 556, 564
Cholmley, Anne, m. —— Taylour; Lady Anne Clifford's governess:
portrait of, at Appleby Castle, **10.** 185
Cholmley, Nathaniel (1721-91), M.P.; sheriff of Yorkshire, 1754:
opposes Yorkshire petition, **28.** 491
Cholmley, Mrs Nathaniel. *See* Smelt, Anne Jessie
Cholmley. *See also* Cholmeley; Cholmondeley
Cholmondeley, Cts and Marchioness of. *See* Bertie, Lady Georgiana Charlotte (1764-1838)
Cholmondeley, Charles (1685-1756), M.P.:
Place Bill to be prepared by, **17.** 295n
Cholmondeley, Charlotte Georgiana (d. 1828), m. (1818) Hugh Henry Seymour:
marriage of, **12.** 158n
Cholmondeley, George (1703-70), 3d E. of Cholmondeley, 1733; M.P.; HW's brother-in-law:
absence of, from London keeps HW from executing Mrs Hayes's commands to him, **30.** 28
Arlington St house of, sold for debt, **19.** 340n
Bisham Abbey altered by, **9.** 101, 101-2
(?) Boone, Daniel, abused by, **30.** 31
brother of, **17.** 296n, **19.** 203
Buxton visited by, **10.** 96
Cabinet Council's move to oust Carteret not aided by, **18.** 536
Carteret faction almost includes, **18.** 551
Chester the station of, **37.** 221
Chesterfield answered by, **17.** 230
Cholmondeley Castle dismantled by, **10.** 96
Courten resembles, **7.** 270n, **30.** 214
Craon's epitaph already familiar to, **17.** 169
death of, **10.** 309n, 310, **23.** 217, **36.** 60-1
drinking destroys the constitution of, **23.** 217
Du Deffand, Mme, finds, strange, **4.** 211-12
—— mentions, **4.** 237
——'s social relations with, in Paris, **4.** 210, 218, 228, **36.** 49
financial difficulties of: **38.** 346, **43.** 238; over Bisham Abbey, **9.** 101-2; over new room, **9.** 35
George II relinquishes, with regret, **18.** 551
——'s representative, in dealing with Frederick, P. of Wales, **17.** 296

[Cholmondeley, George (1703–70), *continued*]
Gower replaces, as lord privy seal, **18.** 551
granddaughters' board paid by, **4.** 235
grandson of, **11.** 88n
HW asked by, to get house for daughter-in-law, **36.** 42
HW does not ask about, **36.** 56
HW in mourning for, **10.** 310, 311
HW rebukes, for abuse of (?) Boone, **30.** 31
HW's brother-in-law, **5.** 203n, **13.** 50n
HW's correspondence with, **36.** 42
house of, in Piccadilly, **23.** 217n
House of Lords asked by, to search for precedents of riots, **38.** 257
houses of, at Arlington St and Richmond, **43.** 238
improvident, survives impoverished son, **38.** 346
Irish lord lieutenancy sought by, **19.** 327n
Irish preferment promised to, **18.** 536, 551
London said to be vainly visited by, at ministerial crisis, **37.** 221
money borrowed by, on pretence of buying Genoa damask, **20.** 325n
opera attended by, **38.** 470
Orford buys lantern at sale of, **20.** 163
Paris visited by, **4.** 210, 218, 228, 233, 235
pictures of, to be sold for debts, **19.** 405
portrait by Highmore, **43.** 366
Potter succeeds, as joint vice-treasurer of Ireland, **21.** 109
privy seal granted to, **18.** 159, 356
property of, seized for debt, **19.** 340
Queensberry House built by, **33.** 541n
Ragman's Castle, Twickenham, occupied by, **42.** 483
regiment raised by, **19.** 128
resigns as Master of the Horse to P. of Wales, **20.** 245n
Richmond home of, **9.** 35
Schaub, Lady, said to be pursued by, **17.** 185
solitaire worn by, **38.** 470
son of, **13.** 26n, **19.** 177n, **20.** 554n, **22.** 210n, **24.** 524n, **25.** 418n
speeches of, composed by others, **30.** 31
Vane succeeded by, as vice-treasurer of Ireland, **18.** 551, **19.** 221n
Walpole, Lady, entertained by sisters of, at his Windsor Castle apartment, **43.** 169
Walpole, Sir Robert, gets letter from, **18.** 260
Walpoles neglected by, **30.** 63
will of, **4.** 423, **36.** 60–1
Yonge succeeded by, as vice-treasurer of Ireland, **20.** 518
Cholmondeley, George (1724–64), styled Vct Malpas; M.P.; army officer:
administration seeks Parliamentary vote of, **38.** 345n
Anstey sends news and compliments of, to HW, **40.** 25
army service of, **19.** 177

Cholmondeley Castle to be fitted up by, **10.** 96
creditor administers shrunken estate of, resulting in auction, **38.** 346n
Crewe Hall visited by, **10.** 96
death of, **22.** 210, 225, **36.** 38, **38.** 345–6, 358
entail, as proposed, prejudicial to, **36.** 26, 27–8, 296–304
Fontenoy leaves, unscathed, **36.** 12
HW defends rights of, **13.** 26–7
HW's affection for, **38.** 346
health of: inflammation of bowels, **38.** 345
Hertford wears mourning for, **38.** 353
Mann, Galfridus, seen by, **20.** 554
marriage of, expected, **19.** 340
Montagu praises, **9.** 78
Northumberland recalls, from Ireland, at Grenville's request, **43.** 279
Orford has not been offended by, **36.** 302
regiment accompanied by, to Ireland, **22.** 210
returns from Ireland, **38.** 345–6
son of, **23.** 316n
Walpole, Horatio (1678–1757), gets protest from, over entail of Walpole estates, **36.** 300–4
wife of, **16.** 126n
Cholmondeley, Mrs George. *See* Walpole, Mary (ca 1705–32)
Cholmondeley, George Horatio (1792–1870), styled Vct Malpas, and (1815) E. of Rocksavage; 2d M. of Cholmondeley, 1827:
Berry, Mary, identifies, **12.** 122–3
entail of HW's Norfolk estates mentions, **30.** 345–6
Kent visited by, **12.** 122
Cholmondeley, George James (1749–1827), Vct Malpas; 4th E. of Cholmondeley, 1770; cr. (1815) M. of Cholmondeley; HW's grand-nephew:
account by, of HW's health, 'shot flying,' **25.** 331
appearance of, **4.** 213, 218–19; grown large but looks well, **36.** 137
Batoni's portrait of, **43.** 284
Bedford, Ds of, proposes to, **7.** 347n, **33.** 279
Berlin appointment resigned by, **25.** 314, 319–20, 324, 333, **33.** 336
Berry sisters have 'civil parley' with, **12.** 128
Cheshire disliked by, **10.** 312
—— militia under, **24.** 481n
—— politics reported by, to HW, **33.** 166
—— residents approve of, **10.** 309
Cholmondeley Castle to be pulled down by, **10.** 312
Cholmondeley, Mrs, loves, **4.** 235
—— mentions, to Mme du Deffand, **39.** 219
Compton, Lady Betty, courted by, **33.** 279
—— to be yielded to, by HW, **33.** 186
cousin of, **24.** 524
daughter of, **12.** 158n
does not speak in Mme du Deffand's presence, **4.** 218–19

Du Deffand, Mme, hears nothing of, **7.** 103
—— may return HW's letters by, **4.** 229, 230, 231
—— never sees, though he brings HW's letter, **39.** 219
——'s acquaintance not desired by, **4.** 235
—— sends letters by, **4.** 233, 237n, (?) **6.** 114
——'s social relations with, **4.** 211–12, 218–19, 228, **36.** 49–50
England returned to by, **12.** 44
entail prejudicial to, **36.** 26
family of, **30.** 345, 357
faro banker with Aston at Brooks's, **39.** 368–9
father of, **20.** 554n
father protests exclusion of, from Walpole estates, **36.** 300, 301
finances of, **10.** 312
Florence, Bologna, and Venice visited by, during D. of Gloucester's illness, **23.** 348–9
Florence enjoyed by, more than Leghorn, **23.** 342–3
—— visited by, **23.** 337, 342–3, 348–9, **25.** 314, 319, 323, 346, 348
fortune of, small but may be repaired by great-uncle, **23.** 217
Fox, C. J., by resigning, deters, from Berlin post, **25.** 314, 319–20
France to be visited by, **11.** 255n
gallantry of, **33.** 336
Gloucester, Ds of, acknowledges, as cousin, **36.** 323–4
—— suspects, of misinforming HW, **36.** 159
Gloucester, D. of, accompanied by: from Genoa, **23.** 335; in Paris, **5.** 430, 435; throughout Italian tour, **23.** 343, 349, 370; to Florence, **23.** 353
—— does not see, **23.** 335
—— informed by, **36.** 208
—— insists, should see Florence, **23.** 394
——'s attendants joined by, in slighting Mann, **23.** 377
—— takes leave of, **23.** 336
—— thought by, not to know of brother's marriage, **23.** 355
—— to play quinze with, **23.** 356
—— totally attaches, **23.** 357
Gloucester family visited by, at Trent, **36.** 132, 134, 135, 137
Grasse accompanied by, **25.** 314n
great-uncle disapproves of HW's marriage plans for, **23.** 408–9
great-uncle fond of, **23.** 409
great-uncle to leave property to, **4.** 423n, **10.** 312, **23.** 217, 362
(?) HW approves of, **4.** 240
HW believes, in Italy, **25.** 228
HW called on by, **23.** 408
HW does not refer to, **24.** 53
HW doubts influence of, at Court, **12.** 126, 131–2
HW has bride in mind for, **23.** 362
HW has not lately seen, **36.** 159

HW informed by, of Rockingham's death, **35.** 517
HW leaves paintings to, **16.** 324n
HW might make, his heir, **23.** 361–2
(?) HW notifies, of Orford's recovery, **24.** 368
HW not 'of privy council' of, **25.** 320
HW recommends, to Mann, **23.** 316
HW sends letter to Conway to Paris by, **39.** 204, 208
HW sent regards of, **23.** 336, **36.** 61
HW's correspondence with, **36.** 107, 158
HW's good opinion of, **22.** 210, **23.** 316
HW's great-nephew and Ds of Gloucester's cousin, **24.** 319n
HW's MSS inherited by, **12.** 202n, **36.** 311
HW's memorandum on, **29.** 220
HW's missing letter to Mme du Deffand probably brought by, **43.** 97
HW's Norfolk estates entailed upon, **15.** 336–7, **30.** 345–6
HW's reluctance to ask favour of, **12.** 131
HW thinks, should cultivate him more, **23.** 361–2
HW to receive compliments of, **23.** 356
HW to 'scheme' for, **10.** 309
HW to sign marriage articles of, **11.** 251
HW visited by, **11.** 241, **12.** 115
HW wants portrait done of, at Rome by Batoni, **23.** 349
HW would rather not have Mann write to, about marriage proposal, **23.** 379, 382
Houghton visited by, **15.** 326
house of, in Piccadilly, **23.** 316n
Kent revisited by, **12.** 122, 128
law suits of, over Houghton, **15.** 322–4, 327, 332, 335, **16.** 313, **25.** 148n, **30.** 370, 372, **36.** 297n
Lee (? or Leigh) accompanies, **23.** 353, 357, 364
Leigh, James Henry, visits, in Kent, **12.** 128
Mann and Duc de Chartres dine with, **25.** 348
Mann assured by, of HW's good health and spirits, **25.** 323, 331
—— has no reason to write panegyric on, **23.** 367
—— procures passport for, for France, **25.** 348
—— questions, about resigning Berlin embassy, **25.** 333
—— receives, kindly, on second visit to Florence, **23.** 392–3
——'s banker receives credit for, **25.** 314
——'s correspondence with, about HW's marriage hints, **23.** 371, 379, 382, 388
—— tells, of HW's wish for his portrait, **23.** 357
—— told by, to tell Leopold of D. of Gloucester's plan to revisit Florence, **23.** 397
—— tries to excuse rudeness of, **23.** 395
marquessate of, **43.** 89

[Cholmondeley, George James (1749–1827) *cont.*]
marriage of, **11**. 241, 251, 255–6, **12**. 12, **34**. 108, 110
meritorious son, **34**. 204
mistresses of, **33**. 181
Montagu congratulates HW on behaviour of, **10**. 299
mother taken leave of by, at Hampton Court, **25**. 331
Naples left by, after receiving letter from England, **25**. 346
natural daughters of, **11**. 245n, 255n
nieces of, **12**. 102n
Nivernais receives *Mysterious Mother* from, **42**. 352
Orford has not been offended by, **36**. 302
Paris visited by, **4**. 210, **5**. 430, 435, **42**. 352
Prospect House in connection with, **12**. 116, 122, 128, 133
Rockingham recommends, for Bedchamber, **25**. 266n
Rome and Naples to be visited by, not for health, **25**. 324
Russian embassy refused by, **33**. 336
St Albans, Mme, mistress of, **11**. 87–8, 109–10, 245
Shelburne did not give preferment to, **25**. 319
Spa and Italy to be visited by, before Parliament opens, **23**. 316
Strasbourg to be visited by, **36**. 132
SH entail mentions, **30**. 351
theatre to be built by, **11**. 191n
Trent to be visited by, to aid D. and Ds of Gloucester, **24**. 319
Venice to be visited by, **36**. 137
Vestris teaches dancing to, **33**. 268n, 282n
Vienna should be visited by, **36**. 134
Wales, P. of (George IV) makes chamberlain, **12**. 107n, 115, 123, 128, 129, 133
Wales, Ps of (Caroline) visits, **12**. 200n
Walpole, Horatio (1752–1822) doubts HW's right to permit, at Houghton, **15**. 324
Walpole family papers to be delivered to, **30**. 372
wife of, **2**. 235n
Worsley, Lady, involved with, **25**. 228
Cholmondeley, George James (1752–1830), HW's grand-nephew:
Agincourt to be recalled by, to HW's remembrance, **42**. 104
Beauvau asks for passport for, **8**. 211
Buller, Mrs, visited by, **11**. 250
Cholmondeley's marriage may affect, **11**. 241
dines with HW, **32**. 388
entail of HW's Norfolk estates mentions, **30**. 346
entail prejudicial to, **36**. 26
Florence to be visited by, **25**. 418–19
HW appoints, trustee under his will, **30**. 356
HW recommends, to Mann, **25**. 419
HW's bequest to, **30**. 357
HW visited by, **11**. 82–3

health of: headache, **11**. 250; toothache, **11**. 83
humorous, vocal, musical, but in low health and spirits, **25**. 419
Mann entertains, in Florence, **25**. 435–6
Marchesi may be heard by, in Florence, **25**. 425–6
marriage settlements of, **11**. 83, 109
Nivernais's *Jardins modernes* given to, **12**. 259
Orford has not been offended by, **36**. 302
(?) Strafford kind to, **35**. 368
SH visitors sent by, **12**. 229
Vienna should be visited by, **36**. 134
wife of, has dead child, **11**. 275
Windham a friend of, **24**. *524*
Cholmondeley, Lady Henrietta (b. 1701):
Walpole, Lady, entertained by, at Windsor Castle, **43**. 169
Cholmondeley, Henrietta (d. 1815), m. (1812) John George Lambton, cr. (1828) Bn Durham, and (1833) E. of Durham:
father settles money on, **11**. 245n
St Albans, Mme, mother of, by Lord Cholmondeley, **11**. 87n, 245
Cholmondeley, Henrietta Maria (*or* Mary Harriet) (1754–1806); HW's grandniece:
balls attended by, **4**. 445
Comédie attended by, **4**. 222
Du Deffand, Mme, has not asked to see, **4**. 218
—— pities, for mother's folly, **5**. 69
——'s correspondence with, **4**. 488, **5**. 143, 147
——'s opinion of, **4**. (?) 415, 445
entail prejudicial to, **36**. 26
grandfather pays board of, **4**. 235
HW's bequest to, **30**. (?) 357
HW sends kisses to Panthémont for, **36**. 55
HW to send Mme du Deffand's letter to, **5**. 143, 147
may be sent to convent of the Presentation, **4**. 226
Montrouge visited by, **4**. 442
Panthémont school of, **4**. 230, 233, **7**. 328
—— will not allow, to return, **4**. 400
Rueil visited by, **4**. 443
St-Joseph convent school of, **4**. 217, 220, 223, 225, 226, 230, 233
St-Joseph convent shocked by, **4**. 226
St-Joseph convent to be left by, **4**. 228, 230
Sceaux visited by, **4**. 442
(?) social relations of, with Mme du Deffand, **4**. 415
to be with her mother, **4**. 400
Walpole, Hon. Robert, to give New Year's gift to, **4**. 328
with her mother, **4**. 369, 381, 404
Cholmondeley, Lady Hester (1755–1828), m. (1773) William Clapcott Lisle, HW's grandniece:
brother's kindness to, **34**. 204–5

daughters of, **12.** 102n, **34.** 205
entail prejudicial to, **36.** 26
father leaves small portion to, **22.** 210
father protests exclusion of, from Walpole estates, **36.** 300
HW's bequest to, **30.** 357
marriage of, **43.** 157
villa for Ps of Wales sought by, **12.** *200*

Cholmondeley, Hester Frances (1763–1844), m. (1783) Sir William Bellingham, cr. (1796) Bt; HW's grandniece:
Choiseul-Stainville child's doll not to be prettier than that of, **4.** 280
Du Deffand, Mme, has not asked to see, **4.** 218
—— pities, for mother's folly, **5.** 69
entail prejudicial to, **36.** 26
grandfather pays board of, **4.** 235
HW's bequest to, **30.** 357
HW sends kisses to Panthémont for, **36.** 55
health of, **4.** 368, 369, 374, 378, 381
Panthémont school of, **4.** 230, 233, 400, 404, **7.** 328, **36.** 55
St-Joseph convent school of, **4.** 217, 220, 223, 225, 226, 228, 230, 233, 400
SH visited by, **12.** 223
Walpole, Hon. Robert, to give New Year's gift to, **4.** 328
with her mother, **4.** 369

Cholmondeley, Hon. James (1708–75), army officer; M.P.:
appointed to staff for South Britain, **20.** 73n
brother names, as trustee and executor in will, **4.** 423n, **36.** 60–1
Cholmondeley, Mrs R., writes of, to Mme du Deffand, **5.** 203, 210, 212
date of general's rank for, corrected, **43.** 242
death of, **7.** 398
Du Deffand, Mme, wishes, had left annuity to Mrs Cholmondeley, **6.** 225
—— writes to Mrs Cholmondeley on death of, **6.** 248
fights well at Falkirk, **19.** 203
finances of, **23.** 362n
great-nephew liked by, **23.** 409
great-nephew may be enriched by, **4.** 423n, **10.** 312, **23.** 217, 362
HW named executor by, in will, **6.** 225, **13.** 50, **32.** 271
HW's hints about great-nephew disapproved by, **23.** 408–9
Parliamentary speech by, **17.** *296*
regiment of: Hervey an officer in, **17.** 34n; not allowed to pay at public-houses, **18.** 408
temperate, **23.** 217
Weymouth election to favour, **17.** 421n
wife to be received by, **37.** 2
will of, **10.** 312n, **23.** 362n

Cholmondeley, Margaret (b. 1761, d. in infancy):
birth date of, corrected, **43.** 326

HW's will mistakenly mentions, **30.** 357

Cholmondeley, Lady Mary (1714–83):
Cony arranges payment to, **26.** 55
Walpole, Lady, entertained by, at Windsor Castle, **43.** 169

Cholmondeley, Lady Penelope. *See* Barry, Lady Penelope

Cholmondeley, Rev. Hon. Robert (1727–1804), HW's nephew:
Anstey sends news and compliments of, to HW, **40.** 25
army breaks, for cowardice at Laeffeld, **37.** 277, **43.** 113
army quitted by, after disgrace at Fontenoy, for holy orders, **19.** 340n
children of: **30.** 346, 357; house to be sold to aid, **4.** 423n
earldom's possible heir, **11.** 110n
entail as proposed prejudicial to, **36.** 26, 27–8, 296–304
entail of HW's Norfolk estates mentions, **30.** 346
finances of, **5.** 184, **6.** 225
HW defends rights of, **13.** 26–7
HW lacks picture of, **36.** 160
(?) HW mentions, **37.** 186
HW's bequest to, **30.** 356
HW's correspondence with, **7.** 376, 378, **36.** 44, 60–1
marriage of, **19.** 339–40
not in London, **36.** 56
not invited to nephew's wedding, **11.** 256
Orford has not been offended by, **36.** 302
social relations of, with Mrs Clive, **3.** 298–9
son of, **11.** 83n, **24.** 524n, **25.** 418n
SH visited by, **12.** 230
wife of, **9.** 269n

Cholmondeley, Mrs Robert. *See* Woffington, Mary

Cholmondeley, Robert Francis (1756–77):
death of, **6.** 440
entail prejudicial to, **36.** 26
goes to Indies, **5.** 184
shipwrecked, **5.** 364
social relations of, with Mme du Deffand, **7.** 343

Cholmondeley. *See also* Cholmeley; Cholmley

Cholmondeley Castle, Cheshire, E. of Cholmondeley's seat:
Cholmondeley, 3d E. of, dismantles, **10.** 96
Cholmondeley, 4th E. of, to have, pulled down, **10.** 312
HW may visit, **10.** 309
HW not to visit, **10.** 312
lack of furniture in, **10.** 312
Malpas fixes up, **10.** 96
Montagu hopes Cholmondeley will live at, **10.** 309
Wettenhall, Mrs, lives near, **10.** 309

Cholmondeley family:
Cholmondeley House built by, **11.** 152n, **33.** 541n

[Cholmondeley family, *continued*]
HW dresses younger members of, in masquerade clothes, **23.** 194
Montagu hopes Cholmondeley will revive, **10.** 309
Walpole estates should go to, after HW's and Sir Edward's deaths, **25.** 132
Cholmondeley Hall:
Malpas's furniture at, to be sold, **22.** 210n
Cholmondeley House, Richmond:
Cholmondeleys build, **11.** 152n
Cowper, Cts, receives, from her son, **32.** 318n
Duncannons may live at, after Cts Cowper's death, **35.** 357
Queensberry buys, **11.** 152n, **33.** 541n, **35.** 357n
*See also* Queensberry House
Cholmondeley Terrace:
Barrett and Gray meet Mrs Nicholls at, **28.** 80n
Cholwick, John (d. 1765), Samuel (d. 1775), *or* William (d. 1764):
Florence visited by, as Sainthill's 'ass,' **35.** 30
Mann to take, to Pratolino, **17.** 484
Newcastle recommends, to Mann, **17.** 483
Chomley. *See* Cholmeley; Cholmley; Cholmondeley
'Choosing King and Queen' (game):
Christmas revel, **34.** 1
Daun and Frederick II play, **21.** 362
*Chorea gigantum. See under* Charleton, Walter
Chorier, Nicolas (1612–92), advocate; pornographic writer; 'Meursius':
*Aloisiæ Sigeæ Toletanæ satyra sotadica* by, **17.** 273n
*Elegantiæ latini sermonis*, Lady Ossory would not read if she could, **33.** 428–9
HW compares *Le Portier des Chartreux* with, **17.** 273
Chorister; choristers:
at Birthday Serenata, **38.** 87
Chotek, Johann Karl (1705–87), Graf; *and* Rudolf (1707–71), Graf:
Hofkriegsrat members, **21.** 96n
Chotzim. *See* Khotim
Chouin. *See* Joly de Choin
Chrestien, Dom Jacques-Nicolas, Grand Prior of St-Denis 1763–6:
Foncemagne's letter to, recommending HW, **40.** 389
*Chrétien mourant, Le. See under* Hélyot, Pierre
Christ. *See* Jesus Christ
'Christ, Charles':
portrait of, in Bodleian, **10.** 149, **34.** 179
'Christ and Apostles':
Poelenburg's paintings of, **7.** 287
'Christ and St John':
painting by Tubi, at Sceaux, **7.** 322
'Christ and the Angels':
Faithorne's print of, **40.** 236
Christ Church, London:
bust of Lady Digby in, **1.** 27, 28

Christ Church, Oxford:
Aldrich's services to, **1.** 172
Avergavenny matriculates at, **19.** 387n
Batt attends, **11.** 17n
Beauchamp attends, **9.** 287, **13.** 35
—— writes from, **38.** 43–6, 50–1, 52–3, 62, 150–1, 157–9
behaviour good at, though study is lax, **38.** 46
buttery at, **9.** 289
cathedral at, *see* Christ Church Cathedral
Fox, C. J., at, **34.** 253
Guise to leave his pictures to, **21.** 429
HW and Conway to eat college commons at, **38.** 62
HW visits, **9.** 287, 289
Harcourt and Stone flattered by people of, **20.** 261
(?) Holbein portraits at, discovered by HW, **9.** 289
Montagu, Lord Charles Greville, attends, **9.** 303
Peckwater Quadrangle in, **1.** 172
Scott, Lord Charles, matriculates at, **19.** 387n
Wolsey feasted by members of, **38.** 62
—— satirized in stained-glass window at, **16.** 47
——'s foundations at, **1.** 269
Wren's Tom Tower at, **35.** 154
Wyatt's Canterbury Gate at, **33.** 54
Christ Church Cathedral, Oxford:
dean of, *see* Gregory, David (1696–1767)
Gregory embellishes, **10.** 41–2
Montagu, Bns, buried in, **10.** 42
Christ College, Cambridge. *See* Christ's College
'Christ Disputing with the Doctors':
water-colour of, at Deane House, **40.** 4
*See also under* Ghezzi, Giuseppe; Guido Reni
Christendom:
wisest heads in, grow in Scotland, **32.** 296–7
Christening; christenings. *See* Baptism
Christian I (1425–81), cr. (1448) K. of Denmark:
Orkneys and Shetlands pledged by, **37.** 298n
Christian VI (1699–1746), K. of Denmark 1730–46:
death of, **19.** 295
George II demands aid from, **17.** 38n
Christian VII (1749–1808), K. of Denmark 1766–1808; 'le polisson'; 'le petit poinçon'; 'la petite pagode':
Alembert's eulogy of, before Gustav III, **5.** 39
——'s speech before, **4.** 168–9
Amelia, Ps, entertains, at ball and fireworks at Gunnersbury, **23.** 48
amorous, **35.** 323
anti-matrimonial quips applauded by, **23.** 57
appearance of, white and pert, **39.** 109
behaviour of, puerile, **23.** 374, 384, 385
Benthagen, Anna Catherina, has affair with, **35.** 327
Bernstorff and Ds of Northumberland to accompany, to York races, **35.** 329

Bernstorff's servility to, **23**. 43

*Buona figluola* seen by, at opera, **23**. 42–3

Cambridge and York not to be visited by, **23**. 48

Carlton House visited by, **10**. 264

Charlotte, Q., entertains, **10**. 264

confined at St James's, **23**. 48

Danish revolution sacrifices, as much as his wife, **23**. 386

Denmark left by, to administrators and Providence, **39**. 108

Du Deffand, Mme, gives opinion of, **4**. 159, 163, 165–6, **5**. 34, 198

Duras, MM. de, escort, **4**. 153, 168

England visited by, **4**. 104, 108, 115, 127, 128, 130, 134, **10**. 264–5, **23**. 40–58, **35**. 323, 325–9

English mob enjoys travels of, **23**. 57

favourites of, **39**. 106

France and Italy to be visited by, **23**. 41

Frederick II inspires Danish nobility to enslave, **23**. 437

Frederick, P. of Wales, resembled by, **10**. 264

George II resembled by, **10**. 264, 265, **23**. 41

George III announces sister's betrothal to, **38**. 490

—— gives ball for, **23**. 57

—— receives, at Buckingham House, **35**. 326

—— refuses nothing to, **23**. 58

HW awaits, at time when Mann expects D. of Cumberland, **23**. 50

HW calls: 'Scipio,' **35**. 327; 'Telemachus,' **35**. 329

HW jokes about showing perfect specimens of last age to, **39**. 106

HW's account of, **4**. 128, 132, 139, **10**. 264–5, **35**. 327, **41**. 161–2

HW to see, **39**. 105

Harley to give ball for, **23**. 57

Harrington, Cts of, ambushes, at Shooter's Hill, **35**. 327

—— gets plea from, for daughter to marry Holck, **39**. 108

—— receives letter from, **35**. 407–8

health of: bellyache, **23**. 48; gripes, **39**. 108

Hertford first to receive, at St James's, **23**. 42

Hertfords entertain, **10**. 264, **23**. 42

Holck a favourite of, **4**. 128n, **35**. 407–8

incognito of, **23**. 43

itinerary of, **23**. 41, 57

La Fontaine's fable applied to, **4**. 146

levees held by, at St James's, **23**. 41

Mann calls, 'young despotic,' **23**. 396

marriage plans of, announced, **22**. 275

masquerade given by, at Ranelagh, **23**. 58, **35**. 330, 407

money flung by, to mob, **35**. 328

Montesquieu praised by, **4**. 165–6

More, Hannah, hates, **31**. 274

near-sighted, **23**. 43n

nose picked by, **23**. 43n

opera and Ranelagh attended by, **10**. 265

Paris and French Court give fêtes for, **4**. 153–4, 155, 159, 161, 163, 165–6, 167–8

Paris no longer mentions, **4**. 169

—— to be visited by, **4**. 108, 134, 138

*Provok'd Wife* attended by, **23**. 57

Ranelagh and Vauxhall visited by, **23**. 41

Rantzau guards, closely, **23**. 386

St James's Palace apartment at first spurned by, **39**. 105

St James's Palace visited by, **10**. 264, **23**. 41–2, 48

Soho ball more magnificent than that of, **23**. 193

Stanhope, Lady Isabella, dances with, **35**. **327n**

Stanislas II's treaty with, over Polish Dissidents, **22**. 574n

stepmother may put her son in place of, **24**. 108

Stowe visit brings memories of, to HW, **10**. 314

Struensee accused of drugging, **23**. 380

—— rules, **23**. 273

Swedish princes favourably compared with, **5**. 34

tutor does not accompany, **23**. 40

verses on, **3**. 268, **4**. 166, 167–8, **8**. 131

Voltaire praised by, **4**. 165

——'s verses to, **3**. 268, **8**. 131

'votre beau-frère,' **4**. 132, 153

wife kept from, **23**. 409

wife of, **28**. 58n

wife too hastily treated by, **23**. 384

Christian IV (1722–75), Prince de Deux-Ponts 1735–75:

camp of, at Plauen, captured, **21**. 428n

(?) claims of, prevail, **7**. 24n

escape of, from Prague, reported in English newspapers, **18**. 68–9

morganatic wife of, **7**. 34n

resignation of, expected, **21**. 304

Christian, Mrs Thomas. *See* Hughes, Anne

Christian; Christians:

and lovers, allowed to brag of pains, **32**. 42

Burke makes, in Paris, **32**. 103

expect rewards for merit, **32**. 35

Fitzgerald, Lady Anne, to curtsy like, **33**. 268

HW does not imitate, **23**. 365

HW prefers children and dogs to, **32**. 204

nymphs and satyrs at Covent Garden behave like, **32**. 66

should pray for riches for the Crown, **32**. 325

Turks persecute, at Smyrna, **23**. 232, 233, 235

Wilkes should be murdered by, **32**. 213

Christianborg (Denmark):

masked ball in palace of, **23**. 373n

Christian Friedrich Karl Alexander (1736–1806), Margrave of Brandenburg-Ansbach, 1757; abdicated, 1791:

Ailesbury, Cts of, expects visit from, **39**. 500

Bath visited by, with D. of Gloucester, **33**. 136

Chudleigh, Elizabeth, opens ball with, **38**. 205

Craven, Bns, with, at Ansbach, **34**. 27n

death of, rumoured, **11**. 100

first wife of, dies, **11**. 219

[Christian Friedrich, *continued*]

Frederick William II fails to pay annuity to, **12**. 151

Gloucester, D. and Ds of, supported by, **35**. 533n

godfather to P. William of Gloucester, **36**. 115–16

HW visited by, **29**. 365

HW visits, **33**. 159

marriage of: **34**. 132–3, **11**. 361n; left-handed, **11**. 342

name of, corrected, **43**. 143, 147, 266, 271, 279, 285, 312, 367, 374

'nincompoophood' of, **11**. 274

nominated K. G., **9**. 89n

second marriage date of, corrected, **43**. 150, 151

wife of, **5**. 358n, **11**. 219n, **28**. 247n, **29**. 360n

*Christianisme dévoilé, Le. See under* Damilaville, Étienne-Noël

Christianity:

despotism makes converts faster than, **35**. 126

HW's, repelled by wars of forcible conversion, **35**. 392

*Christian Plan, The. See under* Hodges, Walter

Christie, Maj.-Gen. Gabriel:

West Indian news from, **25**. 235n, 236n

Christie, James (1730–1803), auctioneer:

Ansell's collection sold by, **23**. 299n

auction by, of (?) Mrs Pritchard's effects, **32**. 124n

Bateman's auction by, **1**. 325n

Claude's 'Departure of Jacob' sold by, **32**. 102n

Colebrooke's pictures to be sold by, **23**. 569n

Cony plans with, for sale of Houghton pictures, **26**. 55, **43**. 286

Cooper's paintings sold by, **12**. 70

Dalton's print warehouse acquired by, **32**. 289n

'Description of SH' compared with auction catalogues of, **32**. 386

exhibition by, in Pall Mall, **23**. 210n

Frankland sale by, **42**. 125n

French, Mrs, leaves pictures sold by, **11**. 221n

'Great Room' of in Pall Mall, **25**. 543n

Greville's effects auctioned by, **33**. 249n

HW 'playthings' may be sold by, **34**. 184

Hindley's Twickenham house sold by, **33**. 180n

Holland House contents sold by, **32**. 279n, 280n

Houghton sale handled by, **2**. 168n, **26**. 55

Lort hears from, of Sheldon sale, **16**. 195

Montfort's pictures sold by, **2**. 57, **28**. 252n

Musin Pushkin's interview with, about sale of Houghton pictures, **43**. 286

Ossory's house auctioned by, **32**. 215n

Pierson's paintings sold by, **23**. 570n, **35**. 428

Savoir Vivre clubhouse sold by, **32**. 205n

Strafford's goods to be sold by, **11**. 283n

Strange's pictures sold by, **23**. 466n

valuation by, of house at Hampton, **11**. 284

Van Dyck painting to be sold by, **32**. 289

*See also* Christie and Ansell

Christie and Ansell, auctioneers:

Hillier's sale at, **16**. 59n

Sheldon's collection sold by, at Weston, **16**. 195n, **33**. 292n

'Christie and Mansell,' auctioneers:

Villiers's house in Grafton St sold by, **32**. 371n

Christie's:

Waller sale by, **36**. 315

Christina (1626–89), Q. of Sweden 1644–54:

Arckenholtz's *Mémoires* of: **9**. 117; Alembert abridges, **15**. 56, **29**. 119–20; Dalrymple wants HW to condense, **15**. 30

Ferrers compared with, **9**. 272

Fontainebleau's associations with, **39**. 208

HW declines writing on, **15**. 32

HW disapproves of Cole's defence of, **2**. 60, 61

HW has S. de la Bella's drawing of, **24**. 15n

Kingston, Ds of, imitates, by buying Roman villa, **24**. 14

More, Hannah, calls, 'unprincely vagabond,' **31**. 223

reign of, interesting, **15**. 56–7

remark by, on Vossius, **31**. 223

retains title but no power, **35**. 352

Stosch steals MSS of, from Vatican, **21**. 284n

Christina, Archduchess. *See* Maria Christina (1724–98)

Christina; Christine, Ps. *See* Marie-Christine

Christine de Pisan. *See* Pisan, Christine de

Christinich, Capt.; Russian officer:

Florence visited by, with Orlov, **23**. 191n

'Christ in the Garden':

Vyne chapel to have painting of, **35**. 639

Christmas, Gerard (d. 1634), sculptor:

monument to Elizabeth Drury by, in Hawstead church, **41**. 106n

Northumberland House gateway ascribed to, by Vertue, **41**. 106

Christmas:

annuity payments to be made on, **30**. 348, 361, 362, 372

Boyle Walsingham, Mrs, spends, with Garrick and Hannah More, **42**. 205

Clive, Mrs, to have venison for, **10**. 240

country visits fashionable during, despite weather, **35**. 370

diversions scanty until, **38**. 142

entertainments suitable to, **34**. 1

Florentines will return to town for, **20**. 290, **22**, 191

Glastonbury Thorn blooms at, **24**. 148, **32**. 195

HW cannot spend, at SH because of workmen, **20**. 348, **35**. 68

HW describes typical English activities during, **38**. 273

HW dislikes, **18**. 367

HW hopes dull season will mend after, **32**. 279

HW mentions, **32**. 44

HW not fit for gambols of, **33**. 72

HW's friends leave town on, **39**. 167

HW's house-party on, **38**. 276

HW spends: at SH, **9**. 267, 332, 417, **10**. 298, **20**. 16, 212, **21**. 558, **24**. 55, **32**. 64, 216, **35**. 200–1, **38**. 276, **39**. 208, **42**. 202; in London, **10**. 241, **33**. 251

HW wants society without a mob on, **33**. 429

HW wants to confer happiness on Lady Ossory's, **32**. 340

Henry VIII often kept, at Greenwich Palace, **16**. 80

holly and ivy nosegays at, **25**. 639

laurel-covered boar's head at, **38**. 462

laurel in windows at, **38**. 1

London deserted at, **10**. 299, **22**. 191, **24**. 149, **39**. 167

—— letters welcome in country at, **31**. 195

Lorenzi sends citrons to Fleury on, each year, **17**. 317

Madonna dell'Impruneta brought to Florence on, **30**. 4

Mann surprised that HW spends, in country, **20**. 25

—— the only Florentine to entertain during novena of, **18**. 353

mince pies at, **18**. 367

Montagu to spend: at Adderbury, **10**. 299; at Wroxton, **10**. 185

morris dancers move around to open houses at, **32**. 408

Ossory, Lady, sends wishes on, to HW, **34**. 88

Parliamentary session deferred till after, **22**. 169, 256, **25**. 103, 519–20, 608

Parliament not to flee London during season of, **24**. 543

pastry-cooks display Twelfth-cakes at, **34**. 231

vacancies not to be filled until, **20**. 512

Christmas ale:

Allen, Lady, gives, at Dublin, **9**. 415

Christmas-box:

HW ridicules English charity at Cherbourg as, **21**. 238

Christmas Eve:

fire engines to be played on, at Burghley House, **10**. 347

HW attends Midnight Mass on, in Paris, **7**. 289, **39**. 233

*Christmas Tale. See under* Garrick, David

Christoforo 'Armeno';

*Peregrinaggio* by, **26**. 34

'Christopher,' inn. *See under* Eton

'Christ Praying in the Garden':

by Filippo Lauri, bought by HW, **3**. 306, **7**. 406

Christ's College, Cambridge:

HW holds leasehold estates of Master and fellows of, **30**. 344–5, 347, **42**. 438n

painted glass in chapel of, **1**. 31, 32

Rooke afterwards Master of, **35**. 643

treasures in, **15**. 19

'Christ's Kirk of the Green.' *See under* James V

Christ Walking on the Sea:

Vyne chapel to have painting of, **35**. 639

*Chronicle. See* London Chronicle; St James's Chronicle

*Chronicle of the Kings of England. See under* Baker, Sir Richard

*Chronicus canon Ægyptiacus . . . . See under* Marsham, Sir John

*Chronique de Paris*:

(?) Condorcet prints Louis XVI's alleged remark in, **34**. 179–80

*Chronique scandaleuse, La. See* Roye, Jean de: Journal

*Chronologica series simulacrorum regiæ familiæ Mediceæ. See under* Allegrini, Francesco; Zocchi, Giuseppe

Chrysostom, St:

Orford, Cts of, and Lady Pomfret should have studied, instead of Newton, **20**. 555

'Chrysostome, la'; 'Chrysostome, Mlle St-.' *See* Sanadon, Mlle

Chudleigh, Elizabeth (ca 1720–88), m. (privately, 1744) Augustus John Hervey, 3d E. of Bristol, 1775; m. 2 (bigamously, 1769) Evelyn Pierrepont, 2d D. of Kingston-upon-Hull:

age of: falsified, **24**. 198; not more than 55, **24**. 203

almost forgotten, **24**. 121

antiquities to be dug up by, at Villa Negroni, **23**. 567n

appearance and costume of, **10**. 245, **20**. 49, **23**. 556, **24**. 6, 242

army camp at Newport visited by, **37**. 503

auction of Mrs Dunch's effects attended by, **9**. 412

Augusta, Ps of Wales's former protection of, cited at trial, **24**. 196

——'s maid of honour, **30**. 328n

——'s retort from, in satiric print, **21**. 487

ball given by, with fireworks, **10**. 73, 75, 76, **35**. 299–301, **38**. 204–5

band of music said to accompany, **23**. 556, 564, 567

Bath, E. of, befriends, **35**. 81n

Bathurst attacks, **24**. 150

——'s decree may protect, **24**. 123

believed to have died in debt, **31**. 289

bigamy charge faced by, **2**. 10, **5**. 406, **6**. 292, 305, 307, **24**. 24, 25, 31, 123, 196, **28**. 219, 488–9, **32**. 169

branding on the hand may be the punishment of, **24**. 25, 31, 123, 196

Bristol, Cts of, may be title of, **24**. 87

Calais visited by, **24**. 202–3, **28**. 268, **32**. 297, 299–300, **43**. 350

Carlsbad to be visited by, for alleged pleurisy, **38**. 473

Cascines remind, of her English parks, **24**. 6

Catherine II acknowledges, **32**. 390

—— lends courier to, **24**. 333

—— makes her Admiralty care for yacht of, **24**. 333, **32**. 390

[Chudleigh, Elizabeth, *continued*]

—— orders Russian war ship to take treasure of, from Leghorn to Calais, **24**. 409–10

—— shelters, **25**. 632

Chancery decree favours, regarding husband's will, **24**. 118

Chaucer's couplet applicable to, **28**. 191

children of, **32**. 145

Clement XIV friend of, **24**. 175

—— might have given dispensation to, **24**. 21

—— to get letter of thanks from, for attentions, **24**. 6–7

—— to negotiate for Villa Negroni for, **24**. 6–7

Coke, Lady Mary, expects, to be well received at Florence, **31**. 180

collation given by, **9**. 276–7

concert given by, for Edward Augustus's birthday, **9**. 276

conduct of: at husband's death, **32**. 145–7, 149–51; at trial, **28**. 261, 265

contributes to relief of distressed clergy in America, **28**. 254–6, 270

Cooper's miniature of Cromwell said to be bought by, **41**. 263, **42**. 125

counsel for, *see* Calvert, Peter; Mansfield, James; Wallace, James; Wynne, William

Court presentation of, **11**. 340, **23**. 106n

Craven, Lady, compared to, **11**. 219

debts of, **39**. 105

diamonds the pride of, **24**. 143

Du Deffand, Mme, gives opinion of, **6**. 197, 250, 305

Ecclesiastical Court admits oath of, **23**. 93

—— denounces, **24**. 226–7

—— said to declare Kingston marriage of, invalid, **39**. 221

——'s decision upon, **24**. 31, 62, 220

—— summons, to meet its agents in Paris, **24**. 83

Field (lawyer) writes to, **24**. 24

finances of, **6**. 311

flees England to avoid prosecution for bigamy, **24**. 24

Florence to be revisited by, **24**. 404–5

Florence visited by, **24**. 6–7, 83–4

Foote ridicules, in *Evening Post*, **24**. 126

——'s farce about, suppressed, **24**. 121, 126, **33**. 459n, **39**. 252

——'s quarrel and correspondence with, **5**. 192n, **28**. 218, 222, 225, 236–7, 256, **32**. 297, **41**. 309–10

forgotten, **35**. 464

Forster, chaplain to, makes affidavit for her, **41**. 310n

Frankland, Lady, may have sold Cromwell miniature to, **42**. 125

Frederick II will not protect, **32**. 145

Frederick, P. of Wales, makes, write letter asking for warrant as secretary of war, **19**. 175

French find history of, as strange as English politics, **28**. 222

furniture may be brought by, from England, **24**. 7

George II gives jubilee masquerade for, **20**. 57, 122

—— gives watch fairing to, **20**. 57

—— makes mother of, Windsor housekeeper, **20**. 213

—— might give title to, **20**. 213

George III and Q. Charlotte receive, **23**. 106n

George III asked by, for *nolle prosequi*, **24**. 151, 162

Gloucester, D. of, might deter, from Rome, **24**. 220

guard kept by, at her door at Calais, **24**. 242

HW and Mason exchange anecdotes about, **28**. 224–5, 227, 228

HW asks Mann to write about escapades of, **23**. 556–7

HW calls: 'Ælia Lælia,' **9**. 276, **24**. 196n; 'Andromache,' **32**. 149; 'dashing virgin,' **38**. 203; 'Duchess of Bristol,' **39**. 252; 'Duchess of Rudd and Butterfield,' **32**. 262; 'Duchess Robin Hood,' **32**. 375; 'heroine of Doctors Commons,' **24**. 125; 'Messalina,' 333; 'paltry mountebank,' **24**. 411; 'Porcia,' **32**. 152

HW entertained by, **9**. 276–7, **10**. 73

HW informs Mme du Deffand about, **6**. 311

HW jokes about, **10**. 274

HW no longer interested in, **34**. 20

HW played with, at Chelsea, **24**. 198

HW's long acquaintance with, **28**. 260

(?) HW's mock sermon alludes to, as 'St Lubrica,' **31**. 423–4

HW speculates about appearance of, at Westminster Hall, **24**. 87, 187

HW's 'The Beauties' mentions, **30**. 328

HW tells Mann not to bother with, **23**. 560–1

HW to avoid, **9**. 306

Hamilton may be entertained by, **35**. 418

Harcourt, Cts, writes verses on censure of, **35**. 491

health of: asthma, **24**. 31; bad, **24**. 404; bled, **24**. 193; gout, **20**. 122; palsy, may be intoxication, **28**. 234–5, 236–7

Hervey (her first husband) did not divorce, **31**. 289

—— husband of, **31**. 416

—— might be visited by, at Nice, **24**. 203

—— might inherit peerage, **24**. 55–6

—— said to have been bribed by, **24**. 151, 196

—— said to have connived with, to deceive Ecclesiastical Court, **24**. 150–1, 195, 227

—— said to have given bond to, not to molest her, **24**. 196

—— said to seek divorce from, **23**. 88, 93, 196, **39**. 105

—— says that nothing can be done against, **24**. 63

——'s calf must have doubled feet because of, **39**. 322

——'s letter not answered by, 39. 105n

—— to prove marriage to, 31. 139

—— visits, after D. of Kingston's death, 32. 151–2

house and furniture of, 9. 277, 32. 145n

house of, in London: has pistol-mark in wainscot, 24. 198; in Hill St, 35. 300n; in Knightsbridge, 24. 87n

House of Lords petitioned by, for her trial, 24. 143

hysterical at opera, when guard has fit, 35. 80–1

Joan of Arc compared with, 28. 204

Joseph II showed honours to, 24. 7

Keith refuses to present, at Viennese Court, 24. 398n

King's Bench treats, with respect, 28. 204

Kingston, D. of, keeps, 9. 412

—— said to be threatened by, with pistol, 24. 198

——'s bequest to, 23. 520, 32. 149, 151, 35. 346–7, 39. 221

—— should have been permitted by, to leave more to his family, 24. 31

——'s 'marriage' to, uncertain, 39. 105–6

——'s nephews to fight his bequest to, 24. 21, 227

—— to marry, 23. 93

laudanum used by, 24. 152

Leghorn reached by, from Calais, 24. 398, 404

letter of, from Calais, 32. 297, 299–300

lives abroad, 32. 375

London visited by, 32. 306

Los Balbases, Marquise de, gets letter from, explaining her position, 24. 220

Lyttelton does not pity, 24. 151

—— might keep, 32. 286

madness feigned by, 24. 151

Mann asks about, 24. 95, 190, 410

—— astonished by law suit against, 24. 30

—— calls, 'Hermione,' 20. 218

—— enraged by follies of, 23. 102

—— entertains, at dinner and takes her to Cascines, 24. 6

—— knew, at Chelsea, 23. 559, 24. 198, 203

—— might have to demand treasures of, from Pius VI, 24. 191

—— pities, 24. 233

——'s French letter from, signed with her Bavarian title, 24. 404

Mansfield protects, 28. 237

—— wants, to have private Parliamentary hearing, 24. 150

Maria Louisa, at Electress of Saxony's request, to entertain, at Florence, 24. 40–1, 31. 180

Maria Theresa would treat, worse than Lady Mary Coke, 23. 559

marriage register of: lost, 28. 168; said to be fabricated, 24. 195; said to be torn out, 24. 151

marriages of, 20. 213n, 24. 88–9, 32. 169

Mason's letter to, intended for newspapers, 28. 254–6, 257

Maximilian Joseph I said to have made, Comtesse de la Warth, 24. 404

may have to stand in a white sheet, 24. 162

Medows, Evelyn, adopted by, as heir, 33. 572

Medows, Lady Frances, sues, 6. 185

Medows family mourn, 31. 289

Medows family sue first husband of, for second husband's estate, 24. 227

memory of, fails, 28. 234, 236

might become Maid of Honour again if she returned, 24. 464

Molyneux threatened by, with sight of pistol-mark, 24. 198

Montagu jokes about Irish pension for, 10. 76

mourning worn by, 28. 225, 261

'naked as Andromeda,' 20. 49

name of, corrected, 43. 363

Naples to be visited by, 24. 220

Naylor, Mrs, struck by, from list for concert, 9. 329

notoriety of, will alienate Italians, especially great ladies of Rome, 24. 95

opera attended by, 35. 80

opera box of, 38. 123

Paris visited by, 6. 311, 24. 83, 88, 95, 242

peerage trial assured to, if Hervey becomes earl, 35. 351

Pitt, Anne, blames, for mentioning Ps of Wales, 24. 203

—— does not see, but exchanges messages, 24. 7

—— makes witticism about, 24. 6

Pius VI cannot cleanse, with all holy water in Tiber, 24. 126

—— promises to keep jewels and furniture for, at Rome, 24. 123, 162, 167, 191, 234

print of, shows her retorting to Ps of Wales's reproaches, 9. 338, 21. 487

Pulteney repeats Vcts Townshend's stories to, 9. 148

rank of, will save her from being burnt in the hand, 24. 121

Rena, Contessa, may profit by example of, 23. 106

resumes her senses, 24. 162

returns to avoid outlawry, 24. 226

Rome visited by, 23. 559, 564, 566–7, 24. 79, 123, 398, 404, 409–10

roses and sweet peas worn by, in hair, 10. 245

Russian said to be studied by, to converse with Catherine II, 23. 559

St-Port purchased by, 5. 386n

salary mostly spent by, on ball, 35. 299

Saxony, Electress of, said to excuse bigamy of, 24. 25, 31

screams in St James's chapel, 24. 150, 39. 272

Selwyn's epigram on, weeping for her mother, 37. 447

Sixtus V's villa could hardly be occupied by, after conviction for bigamy, 24. 24–5

[Chudleigh, Elizabeth, *continued*]

Strafford and Lady Mary Coke will not occupy opera box over that of, **38**. 128

subscription masquerade attended by, as Iphigenia, **20**. 49

*Tom Thumb* passage applicable to, **28**. 489

Townshend jokes about grief of, at George II's death, **9**. 318

Townshend, Vcts, tells stories about, **9**. 148

tradespeople of, on scaffolds in courtyard for fireworks, **38**. 204

train of black crêpe worn by, **23**. 556

treasure of: deposited with Clement XIV, **24**. 398; shipload of, may be stolen by captain, **24**. 59–60; to be brought back to Rome from Leghorn, **24**. 409–10; to be brought to Civita Vecchia, **24**. 118; transported to Albani's villa, **24**. 70; wagons and vessels take, from Monte di Pietà to Leghorn, to go to Calais, **24**. 404

trial of, in House of Lords: **2**. 10, **5**. 406, **6**. 292, 305, 307, **11**. 5n, **28**. 260–6; approaching, **32**. 285; confidently awaited, **24**. 84; could not be endured by her, **24**. 167; described by HW, **24**. 192–3, 195–6, **28**. 260–6; evidence of physicians at, **28**. 234–5; future course of, doubtful, **28**. 245; HW too unwell to attend, **28**. 260–1; Mann's and Anne Pitt's comments on, **24**. 198–9, 202–3; ostensibly desired but really opposed by her, **24**. 150; plea of insanity abandoned, **28**. 237; put off, **24**. 175; Thurlow summarizes her career for, **28**. 263, 264; tickets for, in great demand, **24**. 187; verdict in, **28**. 266; will probably be escaped by her, **24**. 126

tried to introduce polygamy, **33**. 555

Tuscan Court receives respectful message from, **24**. 7

Vernon, Lady Harriet, sees, at Colisée in Paris, in feathered hat, **24**. 242

Vienna rebuff may cause, to shun Tuscan Court, **24**. 398

Villa Negroni sought by, **23**. 567, **24**. 6–7, 14, 31

virginity of, long past, **38**. 144

virtue preserved by, from two husbands, **10**. 274

will of, **31**. 288, **35**. 397

witticism by, on Louis XV's new mistress, **37**. 364

Chudleigh, Harriet (d. 1756), m. Col. Thomas Chudleigh:

Beauclerk, Lady Henry, succeeds, as Housekeeper, **20**. 527n

footpad's body tied to coach of, and carried to Chelsea Hospital, **24**. 203

footpads routed by, in coach, **24**. 198

George II makes, Windsor housekeeper, **20**. 213

Selwyn's epigram on daughter's weeping for, **37**. 447

Chudleigh, Thomas (ca 1689–1726), Col.: deputy governor of Chelsea Hospital, **23**. 559n, **24**. 198

Chudleigh, Sir Thomas (d. 1741), 5th Bt, 1738; army officer: HW played with, at Chelsea, **24**. 198

Chudleigh family: Mann remembers, at Chelsea, **24**. 198

Chudleigh (*or* Chudley's) House. *See* Kingston House

Church, Thomas (1707–56), D.D., controversialist:

*Appeal to the Serious and Unprejudiced, An*, **15**. 301

Lowth's reply to, **15**. 302

Middleton's reply to, **15**. 301

Oxford makes, D.D., for attacking Middleton, **15**. 298

Toll's remarks on, **15**. 301

*Vindication of the Miraculous Powers, A*, **15**. 298

Church; churches:

and gout, 'screw one to the uttermost,' **33**. 69

at Berlin, Querini sends ornaments for, **20**. 329

at Chelsea, **31**. 139

at Rome, furbished up by Benedict XIV, **20**. 98

chancel of, at Houghton, unroofed, **32**. 141

Clement, Anne, to attend, **36**. 279

collegiate, at Manchester, **40**. 16

Coventry, Cts of, at, **37**. 351

Crown aids the looting of, and then quarrels over it, **25**. 596

cup stolen from, at Venice, **17**. 85

dampness of, conducive to colds, **20**. 228

Florentine: archbishop tells women to uncover breasts in, **21**. 292; bankrupts take refuge in, **17**. 61–2, 65; coachmen take refuge in, **17**. 488; deserters take refuge in, **20**. 424; Gavi takes refuge in, **17**. 217, 223, 239; gens d'armes take refuge in, when mobbed, **17**. 79; proposal for plundering, **17**. 193; to be added to Pitti palace, **22**. 258

Gothic, in *King Arthur*, with painted glass windows, **39**. 133

HW attends, **30**. 25, **34**. 115, **39**. 173–4

HW has 'always gone now and then,' **34**. 115

HW no longer enjoys, since religion ebbs away, **35**. 127

HW prefers, to monarchs, **33**. 488

HW proposes an 'after-room' in, to attract nobility, **11**. 15

HW's views on attending, **34**. 115

Hertford attends, before going to Kew, **39**. 194

Huntingdonshire has, in place of milestones, **35**. 266

in Paris: gout prevents HW's visits to, **31**. 60; HW to begin visits to, **31**. 73; visits to, unfashionable, **31**. 73

Italian: called 'resorts of gallantry,' **21.** 292;
cleaned for *anno santo,* **20.** 43; pastilles
burnt in, **21.** 554

Jesuit, Capuchins take over, **23.** 507

Lysons, Samuel, draws, in Gloucestershire,
**12.** 59

mountains crowned with, at Genoa, **37.** 319

revolutionary doctrines preached from, **34.**
80, 98–9

silver candlesticks stolen from altar of, **34.**
98–9

Townshend posts papers on doors of, against
Militia Bill, **21.** 138

Winchelsea's, all destroyed, **40.** 5

*See also* Cathedral; Chapel; Quaker meeting;
Religion, *and under* Church of England;
Church of Scotland; Presbyterian Church;
Roman Catholic Church, *and under* names
*of individual parishes*

Church-going:

hags use, as excuse for scandal, **25.** 584

*Church History of Britain. See under* Fuller,
Thomas

Churchill, Bns. *See* Jennings, Sarah

Churchill, Miss (b. 1744), dau. of Charles
Churchill and the Frasi:

Winnington calls, 'opéra comique,' **18.** 481

Churchill, Lady Anne (1683–1716), m. (1700)
Charles Spencer, 3d E. of Sunderland, 1702:

army prefers, **34.** 262

Bubb Dodington's ballad calls, 'the little
Whig,' **33.** 557, **34.** 262

Lonsdale courts, **14.** 244

Marlborough's daughter, **9.** 34n

Churchill, Arabella (1648–1730), m. Col. Charles
Godfrey; James II's mistress:

Berwick never heard of marriage of, **38.** 406

daughter of, **9.** 104n

HW jokes about James II's affair with, **9.** 412

HW meets, at her daughter's, **25.** 571

HW remembers, **22.** *485*, **25.** 559, 571

HW saw, in St James's Park in her chair,
**25.** 571

James II gives miniature to, **9.** 412

——'s mistress, **22.** 485, **25.** 559, 571

*Mémoires* of Gramont describe, **25.** 571n

portrait of, at Navestock, **9.** 244

son of, **9.** 244n, **10.** 129n

superannuated, **22.** 485, **25.** 571

Churchill, Charles (ca 1679–1745), Lt-Gen.;
M.P.:

army career of, corrected, **43.** 313

birth date of, **43.** 237

Boothby, Mrs, entertains, often, **17.** 174

(?) —— mistress of, **10.** 181

—— produces children resembling, **30.** 298n

Caroline, Q., questions, about Ward's Drop,
**37.** 77n

Castle Rising represented by, **36.** 14n, 16

Cobham gets regiment of, **19.** 62

Cope promoted by, **19.** 117

daughter of, **17.** 184

death of, **19.** 62n, **30.** 85

Duck Island under, as deputy ranger of St
James's and Hyde Parks, **37.** 75–6

Dunmore gets Plymouth post of, **19.** 62

dying, **36.** 10

George II's groom of the Bedchamber, **17.**
221n

HW compares Richelieu with, **10.** 181

HW in disguise accosts, at masquerade, **17.**
359

Houghton's regiment reviewed by, at Canterbury, **30.** 20

illiteracy of, **30.** 42, 289, 289n

impotence of, implied, **17.** 174n

Manchester, Ds of, loved by, **30.** 317

Montagu, Lady Mary Wortley, enemy of, **14.**
246

Oldfield, Mrs, mistress of, **13.** 66n

Parliamentary debate attended by, on
crutches, **30.** 29–30

practised dancing, in gouty shoe, before mirror, **33.** 283

Pulteney claims promise of, about Hedon
election, **17.** 221

——'s reply to, **17.** 331

pun by, **17.** 171–2

puns translated by, out of old jest books, **18.**
131, 307

Richelieu reminiscent of age of, **35.** 114

Rigby succeeds, as M. P. for Castle Rising,
**30.** 330n

son of, **2.** 292n, **11.** 42n, 97n, **13.** 183n, **19.**
104n, **28.** 389n

teeth lost by **17.** 271

Townshend, Vcts, makes witticism about, **17.**
174, 207

trustees of, buy Chalfont Park for son, **35.**
233n

Vane told by, that he was never married nor
beaten, **17.** 139

Walpole, Sir Robert, always called, 'Charles,'
**30.** 289n

—— could never have been approached by,
about son's marrying a Walpole, **19.** 132

—— could not read letters of, **30.** 289n

—— tells, to choose between Pulteney and
himself, **17.** 221

—— wrote letter to, **2.** 291, **30.** 42, **43.** 74

Williams, C. H., satirizes, **30.** 313, 317

wit of, **17.** 271

witticism by, to Frederick, P. of Wales, **30.**
29–30

Churchill, Rev. Charles (ca 1712–58), father of
the poet:

Churchill the poet, curate to, **7.** 374

Crosse, Sir John, his patron, preached against
by, **7.** 374

Churchill, Charles (? 1720–1812), M.P.; HW's
brother-in-law:

Bentley's designs for Chalfont inaccurately
followed by, **35.** 644

birth date of, corrected, **43.** 74, 90

[Churchill, Charles (? 1720–1812), *continued*]
Boutin's garden visited by, **7.** 336
Briennes, friends of, **6.** 207
Cadogans invite HW to meet, at Caversham, **36.** 152–3
Chalfont bought by, **43.** 114
Champagne visited by, **38.** 428
Chute and HW visit, at Chalfont, **35.** 233
Conway and wife visited by, at Park Place, **37.** 532–3, 537, 538, **39.** 419n
(?) Conway reconnoitres with, **37.** 153
(?) Conway's trip to Bath learned by, from Stanley, **39.** 317
Coventry, Cts of, asked by, to give order of Biblical books, **20.** 367
Cumberland, D. of, accepts resignation of, **30.** 85
(?) Dampiers friends of, **6.** 207
daughter of, **1.** 185n, 312n, **2.** 280n, 306n, **25.** 418n, **36.** 8
daughter tended by, in pregnancy, **42.** 201
Du Deffand, Mme, commiserates with, on death of sister, **6.** 409
—— expects, with letter from HW, **5.** 32, 34, 37
—— has no news of, **5.** 86, 87
—— inquires after, **5.** 145, 364, 386, **7.** 8
—— sends messages to, **5.** 163, 198
—— sends word of Fawkener to **5.** 435
——'s offer of lodging accepted by, **5.** 65, 83, 86
——'s opinion of, **5.** 51–2, 56
—— thinks HW may send parcels by, **5.** 23, 27, 28
—— would like to have, visit Paris, **6.** 462
Eccardt's painting of, with family, **35.** 174
expected marriage reported by, **32.** 358
family of, **30.** 358, 372, 374–5
Farington finds, at HW's, **15.** 319
father of: dies, **30.** 85; would not dare to approach Sir Robert Walpole about marriage, **19.** 132
Fawkener nephew of, **5.** 429n
——'s correspondence with, **30.** 85
Foley banker to, **38.** 464
France may be visited by, **6.** 80, **20.** 324, **22.** 362
Frasi has daughter by, **18.** 481, **36.** 8
Frenchman asks, about relationship to poet, **22.** 262
French travels of, **5.** 60, 63, 65, 79, 80, 83, 89, **20.** 324, **22.** 262
Geneva visited by, **13.** 183
HW accompanies: **6.** 76; to theatre, **7.** 336
HW and Conway to visit, at Chalfont, **39.** 173
HW appoints, trustee under his will, **30.** 358–9
HW asks about, **38.** 423
HW consults, as joint trustee for Daye daughters, **11.** 307
HW does not mention, **6.** 480, **7.** 173
HW given 'Norman titles' by, **1.** 65n

HW influenced by, in favour of Parry for Eton fellowship, **40.** 65
HW may have heard from, of Conway's country house, **37.** 296
HW mentions, **12.** 153
HW pays Wiart for, **7.** 411
HW procures ruffles for, **7.** 411
HW's correspondence with, **22.** 324, **36.** 37–41, 43, 127–8, **37.** 340, **40.** 290, **43.** 366
HW sends letter by, **5.** 32, 38, **7.** 392, **39.** 144
HW sent titles by, **1.** 65n
HW should bring, to Park Place, **37.** 485
HW's house-breaking astounds, **5.** 53
HW's reversionary bequest to, **30.** 358, 359
HW tells, to have Liotard portray Crébillon and Marivaux, **20.** 324–5
HW to be repaid through, for purchase, **5.** 21
HW to be visited by, at SH, **38.** 27, 165
HW told by, of distress in France, **37.** 339, 340
HW to visit, at Chalfont, **39.** 199
HW visited by, at SH, **15.** 251, 319, **16.** 302, **32.** 124, 357, **33.** 355, 565, **34.** 57, **37.** 289, **39.** 276
HW wants Col. Pelham's place for, **40.** 177–8
HW will find in Paris, **5.** 66, 82
Harcourt to aid, **5.** 65, 86
Hedges's epigram on, **13.** 183
Hertford sees, in Paris, **38.** 409
—— to send newspapers to, **38.** 495
house of, **11.** 95n
law suit over wife's fortune leaves, impoverished, **40.** 177
leaves Paris, **7.** 336
Lewisham visited by, **12.** 38, 69, 138
London visited by, **4.** 293, **5.** 2
Lorraine, probably Nancy, visited by, **38.** 464
Lyttelton, Bns, to be brought with Cadogans to SH by, **39.** 300
marriage of, **1.** 165n, **13.** 15n, **19.** 104, 221n, 239, **21.** 353n, **22.** 27, **25.** 609n, **36.** 296, **37.** 218, **43.** 254, 260, 373
Mazarin, Hôtel de, visited by, **7.** 336
Nancy visited by, **22.** 244, 324, **33.** 419
nephew of, **5.** 429n, **11.** 95n
Nicolet attended by, **7.** 336
Nivernais's *Jardins modernes* given to, **12.** 259
not in London, **12.** 153
Nubécourt, Château de, near Clermont in Argonne occupied by, **38.** 495
Paris may be visited by, **6.** 213
—— not to be visited by, **6.** 217
—— visited by, **5.** 2, 38, 46, **35.** 123
—— would bore, **6.** 84
Parliamentary service of, to administration, **40.** 177
Parliamentary vote by, on privately-raised regiments, **26.** 19
plans of, for settling in France, **38.** 410
Raynal rebuked by, at SH dinner, **32.** 357
reports marriage expected, **32.** 358
Roissy visited by, **7.** 334
Rueil visited by, **7.** 335

social relations of, in Paris, **5.** 62, 63, 79, 83, **7.** 318, 334–6

social relations of, with: HW, **11.** 42, 95, 179, 350, **12.** 18, 29, 38, 46, 69, 104, 196, **15.** 251, **16.** 302, **32.** 124, 357, **33.** 355, 565, **34.** 57, 107, **35.** 217, 225; Lillebonne, **5.** 83, **36.** 39; Pitt, George, **20.** 367; Robinson, **17.** 222, **37.** 115

son of, **11.** 264n, **12.** 212n; believed safe, **34.** 219; letter of, from Jamaica, **12.** 213; prowess of, pleasing to him, **34.** 218; to receive fortune, **19.** 104n

Spa to be visited by, **6.** 206–7, **36.** 113

(?) Stanley tells, of Conway's flight to Bath, **39.** 317

SH visited by, **12.** 105, 106, **15.** 251, **16.** 302, **35.** 225, **37.** 289, **38.** 27, 165, **39.** 276

SH visitor sent by, **12.** 233, 235

Sunning Hill visited by, **37.** 289

to leave Paris, **5.** 60, 63

to serve as army volunteer despite ill-usage, **30.** 85

Townshend, George, to be befriended by, **36.** 7

Versailles visited by, **7.** 334

Wales, Ps of, seen by, at Greenwich, **12.** 138–9

Whiteknights preferred by, to Woburn Farm, **35.** 71

wife of: **1.** 165n, **2.** 292n, **4.** 173n, **9.** 71n, **11.** 97n, **15.** 251n, **22.** 262n, **28.** 389n, **37.** 202n; under charge of Isabella Leneve until married, **21.** 353n, **25.** 609n

Churchill, Rev. Charles (1731–64), poet:

alleged to be in France after confessing to writing, *Essay on Woman*, **38.** 270

(?) Bentley's *Patriotism* satirizes, **43.** 131

books by, autographed, **28.** 150

Brussels visited by, **38.** 270n

career of, **7.** 374, **22.** 260–2

Combe imitates, **28.** 470

death of: **7.** 258–9, **22.** 260–2, **38.** 469; French ministerial gazette mentions, **22.** 272; silences Temple, **22.** 290; will deprive Wilkes of material for his history, **22.** 281

debaucheries of, **7.** 374

Dryden compared with, **40.** 379

*Duellist, The*, by: **22.** 198n; satirizes Holland, Warburton, Sandwich and Norton, **38.** 290

Flamen compared with, **38.** 188

France visited by, perhaps to seek chaplaincy, **38.** 234

Hogarth's portrait of, **15.** 142n

literary dissections by, **32.** 90

'lost to the Muses,' **29.** 338n

love affair of, diverts him from aiding Wilkes, **38.** 233–4

Mann's low opinion of, **22.** 272

*North Briton* by, **22.** 53

Pitt and Townshend to have been attacked by, **22.** 261, 304

pugilism of, **38.** 188

*Rosciad, The*, most famous work by, **22.** 261

sermons of, dedicated to Warburton, **22.** 261–2

*Times, The*: autographed, **28.** 150n; mentions Pope's admiration for Lady Hervey, **31.** 417

Wilkes prepares edition of works of, **10.** 180, **22.** 261, 304

—— visited by, at Calais, **22.** 261

Churchill, Charles (b. 1747, d. 1783 *or* 5):

birth of, **19.** 371, **43.** 262

death date of, corrected, **43.** 365, 375

Eccardt's painting of, **35.** 174

entail prejudicial to, **36.** 26

father's plans for, uncertain, **38.** 410

Churchill, Charles:

Churchill the poet's son, **7.** 374

Churchill, Mrs Charles, wife of the poet. *See* Scott, Martha

Churchill, Chatham Horace (1791–1843), army officer:

Astley's visited by, **12.** 197

birth of, **11.** *245*, 256

Chatham, E. of, HW, and Ps Sophia godparents to, **11.** 264

HW jokes about name of, **11.** 264–5

Churchill, Lady Elizabeth (1688–1714), m. (1703) Scroop Egerton, 5th E.; cr. (1720) D. of Bridgwater:

painting of, at Althorp, **9.** 6

Churchill, George (1654–1710), Adm.:

HW's enamel of, **9.** 412n

Churchill, George (d. 1808), army officer:

believed safe, **34.** 219

entail prejudicial to, **36.** 26

false report of death of, **12.** *212*, 213, **34.** 218

father's plans for, uncertain, **38.** 410

HW appoints, trustee under his will, **30.** 358

HW's bequest to, **30.** 375

HW to be aided by, in entertaining royalty, **39.** 510

parents get letter from, from Jamaica, **12.** 213

Churchill, Harriet (1726–77), m. 1 (1747) Sir Everard Fawkener, Kt; m. 2 (1765) Hon. Thomas Pownall:

dances at Robinson's ball, **37.** 115

daughter of, **38.** 394

death of, **6.** 409

Lovat's remark about, at trial, **19.** 382

marriage of, **19.** 371

Robinson entertains, **17.** *184*

Churchill, Harriett (d. after 1864), dau. of Horace Churchill:

Astley's visited by, **12.** 197

Churchill, Henrietta (1671–1733), m. (1698) Francis Godolphin, 2d E. of Godolphin; Ds of Marlborough, s.j., 1722:

army prefers, **34.** 262

daughter of, **2.** 26n, **24.** 228n

Howe, Sophia, table companion to, **34.** 256

urinates in front of footmen, **34.** 257

Churchill, Henry:

entail prejudicial to, **36.** 26

father's plans for, uncertain, **38.** 410

HW's bequest to, **30.** 375

Churchill, Horatio (Horace) (1759–1817), Maj.-Gen.:
Astley's visited by, with family, **12**. 196–7
birth of, **21**. 279, **43**. 147
entail prejudicial to, **36**. 26
father's plans for, uncertain, **38**. 410
HW appoints, trustee under his will, **30**. 375
HW entertains, at SH, **12**. 105
HW's bequest to, **30**. 375
HW to be aided by, in entertaining royalty, **39**. 510
HW visited by, in Berkeley Sq., **12**. 196
illness of, feared by HW, **12**. 177, 179
in the country, **12**. 179
son of, christened, **11**. *264*
(?) Spa visited by, **36**. 113
SH visited by, **12**. 243
wife of, **11**. 245n
William I's pavement might be torn up by, **36**. 41
Churchill, Mrs Horatio (Horace). *See* Modigliani, Harriot Ann
Churchill, John (1650–1722), cr. (1702), D. of Marlborough:
Argyll's quarrel with, over rank, **19**. 566
army prefers daughters of, **34**. 262
Atterbury's ingratitude to, **33**. 112
avarice of, **21**. 480–1, **24**. 309
Blenheim Palace's inscriptions honouring, **9**. 6, 289
cabal of Oxford and Bolingbroke overbears, **25**. 605
(?) Cardigan, Cts of, resents HW's treatment of, in *Royal and Noble Authors*, **10**. 340
Carmarthen a descendant of, **2**. 26
Comyns respected by, **7**. 362
Craggs private secretary to, **20**. 181n
Cutts called 'salamander' by, **9**. 252
daughter of, **9**. 34n, 94n, **33**. 557, **37**. 297n
design on Brest revealed by, to wife, **28**. 387–8
dotage of, **7**. 362, **28**. 361
forgotten, **19**. 460
Francavilla statues desired by, **21**. 480–1
France in awe of, **2**. 84
Gage and Parker will not succeed to renown of, **28**. 280–1
general of, replies to stupid alderman at Lord Mayor's feast, **21**. 198, **24**. 29, 414, **25**. 340
glory of, not worth one soldier's life, **18**. 423
grandson of, **19**. 272
HW hoped his nephew would be a second **34**. 218
HW jokes about title of, possibly scaring French by being in Flanders, **30**. 35
HW's account of, in *Royal and Noble Authors*, **10**. 89n, 340, **11**. 105
HW saw burial of, **25**. 559
HW signs himself as, **30**. 39, **35**. 39
Holywell House occasionally occupied by, **28**. 390n
ironic song mentions, **33**. 215
Jacobite entanglements of, **7**. 362, **20**. 322

James II would not have been restored by, **28**. 388
Joseph I grants imperial principality to, **11**. 197n, **21**. 221n
Macpherson deprecates, **24**. 309, **28**. 281, 387
Mallet's life of: delayed, **15**. 54; in return for legacy from Ds of Marlborough, **18**. 528, **20**. 62
marriage of, **1**. 349n
Mindelheim principality never preferred by, to English duchy, **24**. 360
nephew fought in wars of, **11**. 97n
Old Pretender's correspondence with, **7**. 362
——'s pardon for, **20**. 332
Oxford's impeachment sought by, **7**. 362
'purified from obloquy,' **42**. 502–3
Ramillies victory of, **29**. 147n
Raphael painting offered by, to Victor Amadeus II, **18**. 235
Scots traduce, **29**. 105, 135
Selwyn, John, served under, **13**. 14n
sister of, **10**. 129n, **22**. 485n, **25**. 571n
Swift portrays, as coward, **21**. 185
sword of, **18**. 248
Tallart carried off by, **22**. 381
Tower of London the prison of, **35**. 153
triumphal car of, in military procession, **9**. 192
Tunbridge visited by, **7**. 362
veterans of, made to guard palaces, **19**. 69
victories of, ignored by boastful Villars, **34**. 173
Wade may rival, **18**. 456
widow of, has Glover and Mallet write his life, **18**. 528
wife of, **9**. 6n, **13**. 248n
Windsor guide displays tapestry of, **9**. 18n
winter weather not braved by, **9**. 268, **21**. 361–2
Churchill, John:
Churchill the poet's son, **7**. 374
Churchill, Mrs John. *See* Jennings, Sarah (1660–1744)
Churchill, Lady Louisa. *See* Greville, Lady Louisa
Churchill, Lady Maria (*or* Mary). *See* Walpole, Lady Maria
Churchill, Lady Mary (1689–1751), m. (1705) John Montagu, 2d D. of Montagu:
Fairfax trustee for, **9**. 95
genealogy of, **10**. 351
husband's bequest to, **9**. 94, **20**. 80
illness of, makes HW anxious about her daughter, **37**. 297
Manchester, Ds of, dislikes, **9**. 94, 95
'Marlborough humour' of, **9**. 95
'old Duchess Montagu,' **33**. 299
portrait of, at Boughton House, **10**. 341
South Sea bonds reclaimed by, **9**. 95
Turkish costume worn by, at masquerade, **10**. 341

Churchill, Mary (b. 1750), m. (1777) Charles Sloane Cadogan, 3d Bn Cadogan, cr. (1800) E. Cadogan; divorced, 1796:
birth date of, **21.** 279, **43.** 75, 116
birth of child of, **33.** 579
Briennes friends of, **6.** 206–7
Conway invites, to Park Place, **37.** 379
Cooper's elopement with, at Monmouth, **36.** 329
(?) Dampiers, friends of, **6.** 207
daughter of, **2.** 306, **11.** 105n, 187n, **33.** 51
delighted with husband, **33.** 51
divorced for misconduct with Rev. Mr Cooper, **36.** 113n
Du Deffand, Mme, asks if HW is to visit, **7.** 42
—— desires marriage for, **5.** 403
—— has no news of, **5.** 86, 87
—— inquires after, **5.** 145, 364, 386, **6.** 34
—— sends presents and messages to, **5.** 163, 198, 235, **6.** 160, 325, 467, **7.** 51
——'s friendship with, **5.** 120, **7.** 111
——'s lodging to be occupied by, **5.** 65, 83, 86
——'s netted purse from, **6.** 325
——'s opinion of, **5.** 52, 56, **6.** 27
—— suggests, as wife for E. of Orford, **6.** 27, 41
—— would like to have, visit Paris, **6.** 462
entail prejudicial to, **36.** 26
father's plans for, uncertain, **38.** 410
father to bring, to SH, **39.** 300
France may be visited by, **6.** 80
French travels of, **5.** 60, 63, 65, 79, 80, 83, 89
goes camping, **39.** 300
HW at house of, **25.** 246
HW buys 'head and ruffles' for, **7.** 411
HW does not mention, **6.** 480, **7.** 6, 130, 173
HW entertains, at SH, **33.** 565
HW invited by, to meet her parents at Caversham, **36.** 152–3
HW lacks picture of, **36.** 160, 161
HW's bequest to: **30.** 354; converted into a trust, **30.** 375
HW's correspondence with, **7.** 396, **36.** 112–13, 132–3
(?) HW to be godfather to, **9.** 104
HW to be visited by, at SH, **37.** 378
HW to receive snuff-box from, **36.** 112–13
HW will find, in Paris, **5.** 66, 82
HW with, **6.** 76
happy, **7.** 73
Harcourt to aid, **5.** 86
health of: sick, **37.** 378
husband of, **1.** 185n
jointure of, small, **36.** 137
leaves Paris, **7.** 336
Marie-Antoinette resembled by, **5.** 27
marriage of, **1.** 185n; **6.** 467, **24.** 320, **32.** 368, **36.** 127–8, 137
Mirepoix, Mme de, fond of, **5.** 56
—— to give ball for, **5.** 26–7
Monaco, P. of, sends respects to, **41.** 213

mother brings, to SH for health, **37.** 378
name of husband of, corrected, **43.** 326
news of father's arrival affects, **5.** 38
Nivernais's *Jardins modernes* given to, **12.** 259
Paris may be visited by, **6.** 213
—— not to be visited by, **6.** 217
—— visited by, **5.** 2, 46
pretty, **5.** 27
relatives of, **7.** 177
social relations of, in Paris, **5.** 19, 26–7, 38, 62, 63, 83, **7.** 334–6
Spa to be visited by, **6.** 206–7, **36.** 113
Stavely's portrait of, at SH, **24.** 320n
to leave Paris, **5.** 60
Versailles visited by, **7.** 334
Churchill, Robert (1748– ? ):
arrival of, **36.** 38
birth of, **19.** 465, **43.** 264
deserves care and attention, **36.** 40
entail prejudicial to, **36.** 26
father's plans for, uncertain, **38.** 410
Churchill, Sophia (d. 1797), m. (1781) Hon. Horatio Walpole, 2d E. of Orford, n.c., 1809:
(?) birth of, expected, **9.** 285
born before 1759, **21.** 279
Churchill, Lady Mary, visited by, **11.** 101, **12.** 46, 107
Conway praises, **6.** 189
*doubles entendres* of, **12.** 155
Du Deffand, Mme, inquires about, **7.** 177
entail prejudicial to, **36.** 26
father's plans for, uncertain, **38.** 410
HW mentions, **12.** 270n
HW's bequest to, **30.** 354
HW speaks of, with kindness, **15.** 324
HW strolls with, at Hampton Court, **33.** 42
HW sups with, **12.** 69
HW takes, home, **11.** 101
HW told by, about portrait at Piddletown, **42.** 389–90
HW visited by, **11.** 42, **12.** 81, **16.** 302, **34.** 57
harp played by, **12.** 268, **33.** 41
husband of, **1.** 312n
marriage of, **2.** 280, 282, **25.** 132, 172–3, **31.** (?) 202, **36.** 202
Nivernais's *Jardins modernes* given to, **12.** 259
Orford, E. of, invites, to Houghton, **25.** 418
parents tend, in pregnancy, **42.** 201
peerage of husband of, corrected, **43.** 275
pregnant, **36.** 205
rumours of offers refused by, **33.** 91
sings, **33.** 41
son of, **25.** 418n
SH visitors sent by, **12.** 247 *bis*
(?) Vesey's social relations with, **12.** 270n
Churchill, Sophia Marianna (ca 1785–1865), m. (1814) John Craufurd:
Astley's visited by, **12.** 197
Churchill family:
coat of arms of, at Boughton House, **10.** 340

Churching:
  Maria Louisa has, **22.** 486–7
Church lands:
  HW always abominated, **34.** 145
  HW must renew fine for, **34.** 145
Churchman; churchmen:
  HW prefers the artful conquests of, to the forcible ones of princes, **25.** 596
  HW's dislike of, **1.** 186n, **2.** 100, 155, 372, 373, 374
  Hume's hatred of, **16.** 266
  lawyers and, compared, **33.** 486
Church of England:
  archbishops of: oppose Pearce's resignation from Rochester see, **38.** 364; subject of bishops' inquiries when ill, **39.** 414
  Articles of Faith of (Thirty-Nine Articles): clergy's subscription to, to be debated, **23.** 366, 376; Socinians cannot subscribe to, **31.** 328
  Bible often read by, in services, with no regard for punctuation, **20.** 186
  *Biographia Britannica* defames, **2.** 190n
  bishops of: adultery opposed by, **24.** 455; American war approved by, **29.** 159–60, 186; Bath visited by, **31.** 131; Bolingbroke not to be answered by, **35.** 167; Catholic relief approved by, **29.** 66; Charles I not content with adulation of, **23.** 100; Cock Lane Ghost avoided by, **22.** 9; Cole's veneration for, **1.** 136; convocation of, ridiculed by HW, **29.** 99; Conway's stricture on, **29.** 113, 116; Dacre acquires, **35.** 572; favour toleration of Roman Catholics, **25.** 66; figure of, on gateway at Peterborough, **10.** 347; Grafton upheld by, on Paddington Road Bill, **37.** 464; Grenville administration does not nominate, **38.** 392; HW considers, 'household troops' in House of Lords, **25.** 368; HW hates, **35.** 602, 603; HW's opinion of, **2.** 89; HW's reflections on, **23.** 313; HW's second assembly to be attended by, **10.** 107; HW would defend religion against bench of, **31.** 261; Hardinge ridicules, **35.** 587; James II imprisons, **38.** 202; Markham's speech before, **29.** 254–5; Mason accuses, of nepotism, **28.** 255; Mason advises, in writing prayer after Bunker Hill, **28.** 215; medal of, **1.** 319; might court Nancy Parsons for promotion, **39.** 105; need earthquakes as excuse to stop masquerades, **35.** 408; Newcastle, D. of, avoided by, after fall, though he made most of them, **22.** 36–7, 324n; Newcastle's appointees among, flee Opposition, **38.** 248; Nugent accuses, in Parliament, **17.** 431; oppose ball at Soho but 4 of their wives attend, **23.** 193; oppose masquerades, **23.** 58; oppose Pearce's resignation from Rochester see, **38.** 364; painting of Saxon, **1.** 160, 164; Pelham's house thronged with, **18.** 231; postpone masquerades till after fast for earthquake,

**37.** 428, 430; thumbs of, worn flat from page-turning in Bibles, **37.** 35; Tucker's treatise approved by, **29.** 132; want church to be supreme, **35.** 587; wealth of, **28.** 255; Wilkes calls himself the 'eighth,' **38.** 202; Zouch dissuaded by HW from attacking, **16.** 30; *see also under* Clergyman; Priest
  Book of Common Prayer dominates Sydenham's mind, **30.** 292n
  bowing at Jesus' name practised in, **17.** 3n
  clergy of: anti-Popish zeal resented by, **15.** 9; as absurd as Roman ones, **20.** 186; Barbauld, Mrs, 'curses,' **31.** 361; Bolingbroke's enmity with, **16.** 20; categorizing by, in sermons, **30.** 183; Charles III of Spain should insist on dismissal of, **23.** 420; costume of, **10.** 7on; Court aided by, to infatuate England, **24.** 491; Fielding's, gross, **16.** 270; from Manchester, join rebels, **19.** 179; HW mistrusts sincerity of, **11.** 288; Henry V diverted from squeezing, **35.** 387; interpret earthquake as a judgment, **20.** 133–4, 150, 155, 158, 548; misuse English language, **30.** 25; Montagu's opinion of faith of, **10.** 112; Montagu's partiality for, **10.** 140, 142, 258; Montfort brings, to Richmond Green for cricket matches, **20.** 74; Newcastle patronizes, **22.** 323–4; Newcastle ungratefully treated by, **22.** 38; not inclined towards Catholicism, **23.** 40; Opposition's triumph must surmount attack from, **35.** 617; Pinkerton obnoxious to, **16.** 327; subscribe to relieve distressed brethren in America, **28.** 254–6; suspected of designs on Middleton's papers, **20.** 215–16; worst Tories, **24.** 491; *see also* Clergy; Clergyman; Priest
  clerical petition against, **2.** 11, 71
  Cole's zeal for Establishment in, **2.** 359
  Daniel's prophecy may be applied by, to modern times, **23.** 236
  doctrines of, **2.** 152
  fasts of, observed by Methodists, **22.** 17n
  funds of, for church-building, **18.** 20n
  George III supported by, as another Charles I, **36.** 221
  Gibbon attacked by, **41.** 386
  Gordon, Lord George, organizes demonstrations by, against Roman Catholics, **33.** 173
  Gordon rioters called 'conservators' of, **25.** 53
  gossips bestow Sunday morning on, **33.** 457
  HW a good member of, **34.** 51
  HW's verses to Lady Ossory disparage, **33.** 204
  Henry VIII's motives in founding, **33.** 390
  'heresiarchs' help to preserve, **34.** 51
  High Church party of: opposes Middleton's advancement, **15.** 292; Oxfordshire supports, **9.** 320; revere Mary, Q. of Scots and Charles I, **15.** 27–8; would be pleased if prime ministers were abolished, **33.** 292
  idolatry avoided by, **2.** 186n

Jacobite parson of, would hate the Revolution, 34. 20
James I advises Charles to have confidence in, 15. 341
lands of, fines for, 39. 494
livings in, HW gets letters about pretensions to, 31. 363
Middleton does not deprecate, 15. 315
Northumberland's assembly attended by robed chaplains, 38. 401
Oxford, 2d E. of, 'attached' to, 30. 87
Oxford University's devotion to, 33. 483
Parliament less fashionable than, 20. 357–8
Patapan to adhere to, 35. 9
penalties for dissent from, upheld by bishops, 35. 587
Presbyterians and Roman Catholics allied against, 2. 82
rôle of, in English constitution, 42. 403
Roman Catholic reconciliation with, 2. 83–4
Roman Catholic told that head of, is accoucheur, 38. 264
St John wants to unite, with Roman Catholic Church, 19. 358
Secker a popular preacher in, 30. 304n
services of, Edwards to call on HW after, 15. 259
solemnity of, fails to entertain aging women, 20. 378
Table of Consanguinity, incest with male ancestors condoned by, 31. 360
Townshend, Vcts, may desert, 10. 216
Trail, allegedly Presbyterian, reads liturgy of, 38. 347
Winnington tells Nugent to respect, 17. 431
Young Pretender joins, 20. 333n, 21. 392n
Church of Ireland (Anglican):
bishop of, pleads for Roman Catholics while Joseph II suppresses convents, 25. 439
bishops and clergy of, bibulous but learned, 37. 35–6
Church of Scotland (Episcopal):
clergyman of, watches Cameron's disemboweling, 20. 384
Church of Scotland (Presbyterian):
Burke or Jesuits' general might be head of, so far as HW cares, 39. 327
Dalhousie's speech to general assembly of, denounces Roman Catholics, 39. 325n
Church Stretton, Salop:
Mainwaring rector of, 28. 429n
Churchwarden; churchwardens:
Cabinet officers less permanent than, 22. 431
HW wants to inscribe Langley and Hallet as, over doors of their constructions, 35. 233
names of, improperly displayed in English churches which they have repaired and whitewashed, 18. 480, 25. 527
Churchyard. See Gray, Thomas: Elegy
Chute, Ann (d. 1748):
brother loved by, 20. 26
death and will of, 20. 19n, 26, 43. 189

Chute, Ann (d.?1754), wife of Francis Chute:
Chute, John, corresponds with, 19. 92
—— names, in bill, 14. 229
—— to leave, in charge of the Vyne, 35. 83
—— tries to force Miss Nicoll into accepting, as guardian, 14. 198, 219–20, 231, 232
forbidden by Lord Chancellor to see Miss Nicoll alone, 14. 229
HW tries to inform, of Anthony Chute's death, 35. 83
jail threatens, 35. 29
Nicoll, Miss, lodged with, 14. 195
Chute, Anthony (1691–1754), of the Vyne; M.P.:
'capricious monster,' 20. 19
Chute, Ann, leaves legacy to, 20. 19n
Chute, John, corresponds with, about Miss Nicoll, 14. 200–1
—— inherits estate of, 20. 433
—— in 'purgatory' of, 20. 199
—— quarrels with, over Nicoll affair, 14. 201, 20. 257
—— reconciled with, by HW, 20. 273, 278
—— unkindly treated by, 20. 102
—— visits, on Mrs Mildmay's death, 20. 96
—— would be neglected by, at any excuse, 19. 458
—— would have left estate of, to Whithed, 20. 238
death of, 9. 161, 14. 82, 17. 458n, 20. 433, 35. 83–6
fat and comely, 35. 23
grief of, for Mrs Mildmay, 20. 102
HW contributes obituary of, to newspaper, 35. 84, 85
HW discusses Chute and Whithed with, 17. 301
HW mentions, 17. 124
Harrison holds living from, 14. 195
—— wants Miss Nicoll to go to, but changes mind, 14. 196
health of: (?) gout, 35. 21, 85; gout in stomach, 20. 102
Mann hopes that brother's worth will be recognized by, 20. 263
sister's will may affect, 20. 19
Tracy, Robert, does not mention his negotiations with, 14. 199
—— prejudices, against John Chute, 14. 211
vinegary temper of, 20. 433
Vyne, the, owned by, 17. 234n, 19. 458n
Vyne alterations by, 35. 642
Walpole, Sir Robert, entertains, 17. 301
—— supported by, in politics, 17. 124n
Chute, Chaloner (d. 1659), Speaker:
Carter's monument to, at the Vyne, 35. 231n, 642
Vyne, the, bought and altered by, 35. 641
Chute, Chaloner (d. 1666), M.P.:
descendants of, 35. 642
Chute, Edward (1658–1722):
son of, 1. 36n
son's political opinions formed by, 24. 211

[Chute, Edward, *continued*]
son would have been knocked down by, for telling lie, **35.** 35

Chute, Mrs Edward. *See* Keck, Katherine

Chute, Francis (ca 1696–1745), M.P.; F.R.S.:
attachment of, to Sir Robert Walpole, caused hardships, **14.** 195
birth date of, **43.** 189, 237
brother surprised by newspaper reference to, **35.** 29
death of, **17.** 234n. **19.** 39, 47, 48
eminent lawyer, **17.** 234n, **19.** 39n
HW concerned about election of, **35.** 20
HW mentions, **17.** *124*
HW sends regrets to Mann for death of, **35.** 58
health of: (?) gout, **35.** 21
Hedon seat lost by, **17.** 234n, 355, **19.** 342, 371
Mann to discuss, with brother, **17.** 263
Parliamentary speeches by, **17.** 234, 297
petitioner at Hedon election, **17.** 220
Robinson allied with, at Hedon, **17.** 234n, **19.** 371
Walpole, Sir Robert, praises, **17.** 234
—— supported by, in politics, **17.** 124n

Chute, Mrs Francis. *See* Chute, Ann (d. ? 1754)

Chute, John (1701–76) of The Vyne:
abilities of, unrecognized, **19.** 448
'able geometrician,' **35.** 641
Accademia to be visited by, **18.** 187
Acquaviva and Valenti subjects of stories by, **19.** 330
Acquaviva hated by, **19.** 318, 339
Albani, Cardinal, and Mann to get gesse of eagle from, **19.** 149
Albani, Cardinal Alessandro, asked by, about eagle, **19.** 121–2
—— introduced to, by Mann, **19.** 59
——'s protection alone keeps, at Rome, **19.** 196
—— to receive letter of thanks from, **19.** 197
'all vehemence,' **35.** 244
anecdote by, on woman who turned Roman Catholic in old age, **20.** 378, 416
architectural taste of, **21.** 363
Argyle Buildings, the address of, **35.** 84n
Ashburnham's character well known to, **19.** 453
Ashe, Miss, satirized in epigram by, **20.** 140
asks why Taylor calls himself chevalier, **21.** 252
Austrian brutality disgusts, **19.** 279
authorship of literary piece suspected by, **18.** 411
Aylesford talks with, **10.** 7
Badminton not to be visited by, **10.** 228
ballad supposedly written by HW and, sent to Cappers, **14.** 227, 232
Barrett Lennard not well known by, **20.** 100
—— related to, **20.** 100n
——'s correspondence with, **20.** 87

——'s improved health to be reported to, **20.** 94
——'s social relations with, **10.** 4, 150
—— to take Mann's pedigree from, **20.** 78
—— visited by, with HW, at Belhus, **35.** 183–4
Barrett Lennards received by Mann merely because of, **20.** 173
Bath visited by, **10.** 228, **24.** 210
*Bawdy Guardian, The,* by, **43.** 189
Beaufort feared by, **10.** 228
bedchamber of, at SH, **20.** 381
behaviour of: causes Fowle to resign guardianship of Miss Nicoll, **14.** 223–4; deplored by Horace Walpole, sr, **14.** 217–18; in Nicoll affair, **14.** 193–233 *passim*
Benedict XIV's ignorance about England shows unworldliness, according to, **21.** 138
Bentley's correspondence with, **35.** 177, 256
——'s design for urn for Galfridus Mann admired by, **21.** 250
——'s drawing copied for, **35.** 232
——'s landscape criticized by, **35.** 207
——'s plan for Vyne ante-chapel disregarded by, **9.** 216
——'s taste equalled by that of, **21.** 250
Bocchineri, Mme, known by, **20.** 447
Bologna trip proposed by, to see Domenichino painting, **17.** 312–13, 340
Bologna visited by, **17.** 227–8, 235, 240, 241, 257, 267, **19.** 257, **30.** 16, **35.** 513
Bolognese school understood by, **18.** 284
bootikins worn by, every night, **23.** 76
Bosville, Mrs, described by, **19.** 286
—— dislikes, **35.** 41
Bracegirdle, Anne, friend of, **17.** 435
Bristol to be visited by, **10.** 228
'broken,' **19.** 317
Brown, Lady, can nurse, **35.** 118
Brownlow loved by, **19.** 472
Burghley may be visited by, **10.** 82
cane heads disquiet, **17.** 117
Capper will not permit, to see Miss Nicoll, **14.** 221, 232
Capper family insulted by, **14.** 228
(?) Carey genealogy known to, **38.** 133
carriage accident of, **9.** 96
Caserta admired by, **21.** 363
Castello may be visited by, **17.** 443, **18.** 1
cat of, to be replaced, **17.** 181–2
Cellini chest admired by, **23.** 432
Chalfont Park's alterations planned by, **35.** 233
chapel of, at the Vyne: absorbs him, **9.** 166; Mann to get 'Last Supper' for, **20.** 485, 489, 529, 539
Churchill, Lady Mary, might visit, in Hampshire, **35.** 68
Churchills visited by, at Chalfont, **35.** 233
Chute, Anthony, by dying intestate enriches, **9.** 161, **14.** 82n, **20.** 433, 436, **35.** 83–6

——'s poor relations with, 14. 200–1, 17. 263, 20. 96, 102, 199, 257, 263, 273, 278

'Chutehed,' 9. 54, 14. 18, 19. 420, 435, 442, 462, 467, 485

Clinton pretensions of Rolle family remembered by, 18. 126

coachman of, killed, 7. 398

coat-of-arms proposed by, 35. 108–9

Cocchi gives book to, 20. 438

——'s *parere* to be sent to, 19. 329

—— to receive thanks of, 20. 199

Cole to be visited by: at Bletchley, 10. 84; with HW, 1. 36

'college of arms' of, at SH, 20. 382, 387

Correggio painting recommended by, to Sir Robert Walpole, 17. 167n

Correggio painting thought by, to cost more than HW expects, 18. 370

Cowdray visited by, 9. 98–9

Craon and Guadagni play ombre with, 17. 416–17

Craon's correspondence with, 35. 59–60

——'s social relations with, 17. 416–17, 443, 498, 18. 1, 101, 132, 372, 381, 35. 28

—— tells, his painter makes him look too young, 18. 263

Craon, Princesse de, has social relations with, 17. 443, 498, 18. 1, 372, 35. 28

—— thought by, to be 90, 22. 324

Creti's copy criticized by, 18. 303

critical nature of, 10. 259

Cutts, Bns, identified by, in portrait, 9. 259

Dacre, Lady, ancestress of, 35. 73

Dagge pressed by to conclude Lucchi affair, 21. 418

—— recommended to, 22. 268

Dal Borgo entertains, 18. 84

Dashwood's perfidy astonishes, 17. 369

Davis's copy not detected by, 19. 348

death of: 6. 320, 24. 209–13, 222; HW's letters returned to him after, 32. 306

Del Sarto painting criticized by, 18. 214

diet of: 'Carthusian,' 35. 23; milk, 18. 132; milk and water, 35. 41, 42; ravioli, spinach tarts, stewed apples, currants, 17. 218; turnips and water, 18. 100; veal with bread and butter, 35. 21

Domenichino painting known to, 17. 167

domino worn by, to hide legs, 18. 386

Drayton may be visited by, 10. 82

Du Deffand, Mme, asks why HW never mentioned, 6. 320

Dugdale's *Baronage* wanted by, 14. 80, 81

Dunbar tells Romans that Whithed is pupil of, 19. 136

eagle bought by, for HW, 19. 65–6, 79, 97, 100, 121–2, 135, 149, 176–7, 197, 20. 489

eclogues of Lady Mary Wortley Montagu praised by, 19. 450

Edgcumbe dubbed chief herald painter by, 9. 186

effeminate and witty, 35, 648

Electress's will discussed by, 18. 171

Ely may be visited by, 10. 82

England disappoints, 19. 329, 371

English captains' gratitude to Mann witnessed by, 18. 115

epigrams by, on Lady Caroline Petersham, 20. 140, 150

essence of roses bought by, 18. 214

fan of, disliked by English visitors, 17. 116–17, 121

father establishes political opinions of, 24. 211

finances of, 24. 210

floods immure, at the Vyne, 35. 265

Florence may be life residence of, 35. 52

—— reached by, 17. 112, 30. 16

—— to be left by, 19. 47, 252, 254, 257, 40. 57

Florentine domicile of, *see* Ambrogi, Casa

Florentine sojourn of, 17–19. *passim*, 30. 16, 35. 1–64

fortune of, makes him independent of the world, 35. 107

Fotheringhay may be visited by, 10. 82

Franciabigio painting will be remembered by, 19. 392

Frogmore visited by, 10. 296

genealogical and heraldic knowledge of, 20. 93, 169

generosity of, 20. 254

'genius that presided over SH,' 24. 209

Ginori, Mme, to entertain, 17. 161

Giogo, the, crossed by, 17. 241, 257

Goldsworthy, Mrs, irritates, 17. 351, 372, 35. 25

—— with, 17. 313

'Gothland' disgusts, 19. 311

Gramont enjoyed by, 35. 146

Grandison, Vcts, sends compliments to, 10. 136

grandmother of, 19. 372

Gray at Reggio with, 17. 50n

—— at Venice with, 13. 10

——'s relations with, 14. 3, 6, 18, 21, 25, 27, 30, 41, 58, 80, 83, 86, 92, 17. (?) 50

——'s verses identified by, 28. 97n

grief buried by, in seclusion, 20. 251

Grifoni, Mme, may be attended by, at burletta, 35. 11

Guercino and Holbein drawings rejected by, 18. 116

Guido painting admired by, 17. 138, 162

HW accompanied by: 20. 338; at Reggio, 17. 50n; to Bath, 10. 227; to Greatworth, 9. 152; to Penshurst, 20. 389; to Winchester and Netley Abbey, 11. 8on, 35. 249–51; *see also* HW travels with

HW agrees with, not to tell Mann about new political changes, 19. 326

HW aided by, in pedigree, 2. 47n

HW and Anthony Chute discuss, 17. 301

[Chute, John, *continued*]

HW and Gray accompanied by, from Florence to Reggio, **43**. 235

HW and Sir Robert Walpole thank, for procuring Domenichino painting, **17**. 256–7

HW apologizes to, for recommending Maynard, **18**. 451

HW asked by: to point out his room at Houghton, **18**. 17, 36, 60; to recommend Musgrave to Mann, **23**. 375

HW asks: to await his return to Florence, **18**. 482; to go to SH with him in a post-chaise, **35**. 69

HW asks about cicisbea of, **18**. 497

HW asks Cowslade about, **41**. 276

HW asks Montagu to share letter with, **10**. 212

HW blames, for anti-Jacobite behaviour at Rome, **19**. 139

HW buys blue and copper vases for, in Paris, **43**. 108

HW cannot visit, but wants him to come to SH, **35**. 98–9

HW condoles with, on Whithed's death, **35**. 66–7

HW condoles with Mann on loss of, **19**. 61, 224

HW congratulates, on Dettingen victory, **35**. 39

HW consults, on Gray's and West's Italian letters, **28**. 99, 103, 107–8

HW discusses Venetian prospect with, **19**. 448, 457–8

HW dislikes advice to Mann by, to seclude himself, **17**. 419

HW entertains: at Arlington St, **20**. 234; at dinner at SH, **23**. 310, **24**. 103

HW exchanges calls with, **9**. 310, **10**. 263, **20**. 474, **22**. 316, **24**. 210

HW exchanges messages with, **10** 161, **18**. 459

HW expects letter from, if Mann is ill, **18**. 71

HW finds, in London, **19**. 316

HW forwards Bentley's letter to **35**. 256

HW gets eye cure from, **21**. 139, 156, 163

HW gets false notions from, about Mann's health **19**. 382

HW gets genealogical theories from, **9**. 69

HW gives Montagu's messages to, **9**. 239

HW glad that Mann has regained, **19**. 209–10

HW has, at Bedford's house for Coronation, **38**. 123n

HW hears of Lady Bingley from, **20**. 141

HW hopes for return of, to England, **18**. 410

HW hopes that brother's death will prolong life of, **35**. 85

HW imagines, at masquerade, **18**. 149

HW impatient to see, **19**. 272

HW inquires about health of, **10**. 202

HW jokingly offers his sister to, **17**. 257

HW knows no architecture but from Bentley and, **35**. 103

HW liked by, **17**. 112

HW longs to chat with Montagu and, at SH, **10**. 202

HW may have given cane heads to, for Suares, **35**. 6

HW mentions, **5**. 75, **14**. 120, **20**. 326, **37**. 175

HW plays cribbage with, **10**. 228

HW praises, **19**. 329, 442

HW pretends his gout is that of, **35**. 259

HW provides additional news for, **19**. 182

HW quotes, **18**. 465

HW receives game from, **41**. 276

HW receives news of Montagu from, **10**. 128, 258

HW regrets condition of, **18**. 179

HW relieved by indolence of, in letter-writing, **19**. 442

HW requests, to sketch Steane chimney-piece, **9**. 156

HW reproached by, for being so English, **19**. 343

HW's advice to: about the Vyne, **9**. 216; to Mann about Dashwood, **17**. 412

HW's and Mann's jokes communicated to, **17**. 146

HW says, is only person to whom he can confess that his loves are life-long, **35**. 127–8

HW's Bologna picture said by, to be finished, **17**. 118

(?) HW's cipher known by, **17**. 124

HW's close connection with, surprises Mann, **24**. 222

HW scolds, for not writing of Mann's illness, **18**. 60

HW's correspondence with, **7**. 376–7, 385, 389, 393, 396, **9**. 214, **10**. 38, **17**. 112, 114, 115, 117, 147, 153, 164, 169, 181, 211–12, 241, 257, 262, 267, 280, 325, 343, 355, 365–6, 389, 432, 435, 441, 450, 456, 460, 476, 498, **18**. 25, 236, 244, 256, 258, 271, 274, 275, 278, 286, 291, 308, 314, 326, 339, 384, 410, 451, 465, 482, 506, 560, **19**. 6, 20, 70, 90, 97, 107, 135, 256, 268, **20**. 234n, 427, **31**. 97, 32. 306, **35**. 1–128, **36**. 313, 315, **38**. (?) 555

HW sees, in London, **10**. 101

HW sends pamphlets to, **35**. 48

HW's entertainment for Italians could be described by, **19**. 331

HW's health described by, **10**. 319

HW shows new cottage at SH to, **10**. 168

HW shows to, Mann's account of Papal-Portuguese quarrel, **21**. 428

HW's letters returned to him on death of, **32**. 306

HW's letter to Mann relieves depression of, **19**. 197

HW's library searched by, **20**. 64

HW's *Mysterious Mother* liked by, **10**. 259

HW's obligation to, **17**. 365

HW's Parliamentary speech liked by, **17**. 407

HW's purchases for, in Paris, **7**. 401, 409, 414

HW's suggestions for Vyne alterations not followed by, **35**. 232, 252

HW's version of *bon mot* questioned by, **17.** 135

HW's *World* contributions show influence of, **20.** 385

HW tells: to buy eagle, **19.** 79; to look after Mann, **17.** 124

HW tells Mann to congratulate, **20.** 433

HW to accompany: to Bath, **10.** 227; to Great-worth, **9.** 152

HW to be told by, of Montagu's anxiety, **10.** 213

HW to be urged by, to go to Bath, **10.** 48

HW to consult: about cabinet at SH, **9.** 385; about Young Pretender's movements, **19.** 378

HW to encourage, to build and plant, **20.** 449

HW to exchange visits with, **9.** 243, **19.** 435, **20.** 449, **21.** 1, **35.** 65–6, 66–7, 85, 91, 177

HW to forward Montagu's letter to, **9.** 261

HW to furnish, with news to confute Riviera, **19.** 176

HW told by: about eagle, **19.** 65–6, 197; about sale of D. of Modena's pictures, **19.** 321; of Halifax's death, **23.** 310

HW to send pictures to, **7.** 416

HW to tell: about affair in Mann's garden, **19.** 499; about Albani's dismissal, **19.** 475; about Bubb Dodington, **20.** 254; about Montagu's cheerful prospects, **9.** 347; how much Angiola Lucchi depends on him, **20.** 306; that Lucchi family must be reassured, **20.** 254

HW travels with: in Hampshire, **9.** 172, **11.** 80n; in Kent, **9.** 141, **35.** 131–46; in Sussex, **9.** 96, **35.** 131–46

HW urges, to leave Vyne because of damp-ness, **35.** 109

HW visited by: at SH, **10.** 168, 226, **19.** 442, 497, **20.** 361, 456, **22.** 257, 265, **23.** 284, **24.** 103, **38.** 453; in Arlington St, **35.** 164

HW visits, at the Vyne, **9.** (?) 88, 162–4, 222, **37.** 388, **38.** 27

HW will laugh with, over Ashburnham's failure, **19.** 420

HW writes to, about Gray, **20.** 234n

habits of: abstinence, **10.** 277; patience, **10.** 304

Hampshire visited by, **19.** 420

health of: better every year, **10.** 277; bilious attack at Marseille, **35.** 25; 'broke,' **10.** 199, 204; chalkstones in hands, **24.** 211; cold, **19.** 484; eyesight and hearing fail, **24.** 211; fasts, **17.** 365; fever, **35.** 96; fever, common, **18.** 138; good, **10.** 179; gout, **1.** 41, **9.** 54, 57, 196, 208, 209, 212, 213, 302, 312, **10.** 86 87, 98–9, 100, 101, 136, 149, 151, 154, 161, 263, 277, 296, 304, **14.** 93–6, **18.** 100, 123, 132, 149, 175, 179, 197, 381, 386, 391, 394, 560, **19.** 216, 221, 227, 229, 232, 239, 243, 246, 247, 252, **21.** 1, 10, **22.** 257, 265, 266, 288, **23.** 252, **24.** 210–11, **31.** 97, **35.** 84,

(?) 95, (?) 96, 105, 106–7, 115, 117, **232,** **38.** 453; gout, free from, **10.** 206; gout assuaged by bootikins, **23.** 76, 252, 310; gout avoided, **17.** 218; gout feared, **41.** 276; grows gouty and old, **35.** 34; 'half blind,' **35.** 8; heart palpitations, **24.** 210; ill, **14.** 102; improved, **9.** 374, **10.** 151, 154, 304; low lingering fever, **24.** 210; pain in breast, **24.** 210; polypus, **24.** 210–11; rheumatism, **10.** 263; teeth nearly all gone, **10.** 204; uri-nary complaint, **19.** 329; walks better than he did seven years previously, **23.** 76; well, **17.** 365, **19.** 200

heraldic interests of, **9.** 97, 103

Heralds Office visited by, to search for Mann's pedigrees, **20.** 13, 31

Hertford's Taplow house may be taken by, **38.** 26

Hervey's conversation with, **19.** 372

Hobart does not resemble, **19.** 63

—— liked by, **19.** 275, 507

—— replaces, **19.** 261

Holdernesse snubs, at Lady Betty Germain's, **19.** 371–2

horse race attended by, **17.** 456

Horton may be visited by, **10.** 82

Houghton object of curiosity to, **18.** 17, **35.** 44, 46

—— plans enjoyed by, **17.** 428

house in Berkeley Sq. taken by, **9.** 330, 358

house in Charles St taken by, **10.** 202, 204, 206

house in Hampshire inherited by, *see under* Vyne, The

house in Tilney St sold by, to Henrietta Speed, **9.** 330

Hurstmonceaux's armorial carvings please, **35.** 138

ink of, inferior, **9.** 57

Italian sojourn of, for seven years, **20.** 114, **28.** 99

itinerary of: from Florence to England, **19.** 257; from Florence to Rome, **19.** 48–9; from Vienna to Berlin, **19.** 279

Jacobite lies contradicted by, **19.** 135–6

La Cour treats, **35.** 108, 109

landlady tells, to share bed with smuggler, **35.** 137

Langlois employed by, for furniture, **10.** 207

last of the male line, **24.** 209n

Leghorn gossip about Walpoles reported by, to Mann, **17.** 146

—— may be visited by, **18.** 27

letter-writing shirked by, **18.** 203, **20.** 199, 312, 440

London to be visited by, **9.** 249

Lorenzi disputes with, about colours in char-iot, **21.** 501

—— mistakes Schutz for, **20.** 89–90

——'s statement to, about landing at Bristol to make acquaintances, **20.** 114

Lovat's execution attended by, **19.** 387

[Chute, John, *continued*]

Lucchi, Sophia, rescued by, from foundling hospital, **22.** 265

Lucchi family's annuity facilitated by, at Mann's instigation, **20.** 246, 254, 306, 312, 330, **21.** 412–13, **22.** 265–7, 268, 278–9

Maison Carrée recommended by, to HW, **17.** 121

Mann accompanied by, **17.** 116

—— asks about, **17.** 101

—— attended by, after operation, **35.** 22

——brags to, of conversation with Richecourt, **18.** 12

——communicates HW's letters to, **35.** 7

—— consults: about buying Gabburri's drawings, **18.** 313; about Domenichino price, **17.** 227, 241; about model of 'Livia' statue, **18.** 179; about selling HW's coffee pot, **18.** 115, 472

—— discusses, with Morice, **21.** 442

—— distressed by family troubles of, **20.** 26, 102, 263

—— does not complain of correspondence dropped by, **22.** 278

—— encouraged by, to expect HW and Sir Robert Walpole at Florence, **18.** 254

—— excludes, during Theodore's visit, **18.** 187

—— expects, at Florence, **17.** 97, 106, 235, 241

—— fears that Jacobites may harm, at Rome, **18.** 113

—— hopes to prolong Florentine visit of, **17.** 146

—— knew merit of, in middle age, **24.** 221

—— left by, with great regret, **35.** 57

—— likes Barrett Lennards for sake of, **20.** 84

—— lodges, in his house, **19.** 197

—— may confide in, **17.** 124

—— not expected by, to be shifted to Genoa, **20.** 272

—— often discusses HW with, **19.** 35

—— persuaded by, to stay in seclusion, **17.** 393

—— preferred by, to visiting Rome, **35.** 46–7

—— reassured by, after false alarm over Young Pretender, **17.** 119

—— recommended to, by HW, **17.** 365

—— remembered by, but not in pen and ink, **20.** 312

——'s answer to Pucci's remonstrance approved by, **18.** 325

——'s apprehensions to be allayed by, **18.** 384

——'s baronetcy will please, **20.** 467

——'s correspondence should not have been dropped by, **22.** 268

——'s correspondence with, **17.** 262–3, **19.** 59, 65–6, 121–2, 257, 279, 346, 348, 354, 382, 387–8, 414, 429, 436, 441, 453, 462, 463, **20.** 243, 439–40, 441, **21.** 107n, **22.** 268

——'s disposal of coffee pot advised by, **18.** 115, 472

——'s excuses to be conveyed by, to HW, **19.** 329

——'s guests entertained by, at Casa Ambrogi, **18.** 386

——'s hospitality to be attested by, **19.** 349

——'s inability to amass money known to, **21.** 55

——'s 'little apartment' to be occupied by, **17.** 146, 154

——'s 'little friend' sent by, to Albano to spy on Old Pretender, **19.** 141

——'s motto sought by, **20.** 475, 480, 482, 487

——'s 'other apartment' occupied by, **19.** 216

——'s pedigree searched by, **20.** 13, 24, 31, 77–8, 88, 96, 129, 138, 150, **35.** 65

——'s portrait criticized by, **20.** 309, 313

——'s quotations from Bubb Dodington not to be revealed by, **20.** 254

——'s relations with, **17.** 112, 209, 283–4, 343, 349, 360, 365, **19.** 48, 90, 261, 265, 339, 443, 448, **20.** 433, 436, 439–40, 441, **22.** 278

——'s social relations with, **17.** 112, 116–17, 146–7, 161, 218, 328, **18.** 7, 140

—— summons to read HW's letter **18.** 132

—— to be accompanied by, if exiled, **35.** 10–11

—— to congratulate, on Henry Benedict (Stuart)'s probable capture, **19.** 177

—— to hear from, about SH's beauties, **19.** 497

—— to send reports to, of English zeal, **19.** 128

—— wants, to become minister to Venice, **19.** 444

—— will not trouble, with compliments to Theodore, **20.** 29

Mann, Edward Louisa, confers with, about letter to Thistlethwayte, **22.** 316

Mann, Galfridus, called on by, **21.** 523, 529

—— grateful to, **21.** 540

—— tells, that Linton estate is entailed, **23.** 101

—— to be reduced by, to abstinence and health, **20.** 63

—— writes about, **20.** 251

Martelli, Francesco, servant of, **20.** 119, **24.** 569

Martinelli writes to, on Whithed's death, **25.** 554n

Mason's *Gray* praised by, **28.** 193, 194

Mathews and Villettes laughed at by, **18.** 279

Maynard disliked by, **18.** 439

Mildmay visits, **10.** 149–50

Mildmay, Miss, friend of, **10.** 81

Modenese princesses entertain, **19.** 257

money might be withdrawn from stocks by, and put into annuity, **24.** 210

Montagu asks about, **10.** 126, 261

—— exchanges calls and visits with, **9.** 152, 155, 162, 163, 165, 370, 371, 374, **10.** 34, 37, 38, 75, 81, 82, 97, 199, 204, **37.** 388, **38.** 27

—— expects, to court Lady Brown, **9.** 315

—— invites: to Adderbury, **10.** 264; to Greatworth, **9.** 291, **10.** 62
—— may visit, **9.** 243
—— offered London lodging by, **9.** 356, 358
—— pities, **9.** 303
——'s banker cannot find, **10.** 126
——'s correspondence at the Vyne discussed by, with HW, **10.** 38
——'s correspondence with, **9.** 154, 261, **10.** 264
—— sees, in London, **10.** 319
——'s health and spirits favourably described by, **10.** 34
——'s Irish bill not paid by, **10.** 126
——'s opinion of, **10.** 230
—— taken by, to Langlois's shop, **10.** 207
—— to be visited by, at Greatworth, **9.** 152, 155, **10.** 81, 82
—— to inform, of HW's delay in seeing him, **35.** 97
—— told by, about available house, **10.** 258
—— visited by, at Greatworth, **10.** 34
—— visits, at the Vyne, **10.** 37, 38
—— wishes information from, about Cutts portraits, **9.** 252, 256
Montagu, Bns, may be well known to, **10.** 43
Montagu, Charles, and Vcts Grandison to arrange Vyne visit with, **10.** 97
Montagu, Charles, receives game from, **10.** 179
——'s social relations with, **10.** 199, 206, 264, **37.** 388, **38.** 27
'more agreeable than Christmas,' **18.** 367
Morice a friend of, **21.** 389
—— must have enjoyed discussing, **22.** 39
—— to intercede with, for Sophia Lucchi, **22.** 266
—— visited by, **10.** 164
Müntz might be employed by, at the Vyne, **35.** 185–6
—— pleases, **35.** 232
—— to be sent by, to SH, **35.** 89
—— with, at the Vyne, **35.** 256
'Musæ pueriles' of, **35.** 21
*Mysterious Mother's* subject found by, in Q. of Navarre's *Heptaméron*, **39.** 103
Naples visited by, **19.** 171
nephew of, preferred by Camden at HW's request, **41.** 182
*New Lesson for Pope* already seen by, **18.** 60
Nicoll, Miss, forbidden by Lord Chancellor to see, alone, **14.** 229
—— gets bill from, **14.** 229–30
—— gets letter from, **14.** 225–6
——'s escape facilitated by, **14.** 194–5, 197
——'s involvement with, in affair, **13.** 23, **14.** 56n, 57–8, 195, 197, 204 214–15, 216–17, 218–20, 227–8, 231, 232
——'s marriage to E. of Orford first proposed by, **14.** 194, **20.** 256–7, 262–3
Old Pretender said to be offended at, **19.** 136
opera attended by, **18.** (?) 322, 386, **19.** 372

opera avoided by, **17.** 269
parental discipline for, **35.** 35
Parker's collection missed by, **18.** 240
Patapan subject of poem by, **18.** 314n, **35.** 45–6, 48
Penny pleases, **17.** 241, 267
——tells, of Domenichino sibyl at Bologna, **17.** 268
—— to be rewarded by, **17.** 228
Pergolesi's *Olimpiade* to be bought by, at Naples, **19.** 149
Persius quotation pleases, **10.** 233
Peterborough may be visited by, **10.** 82
Petworth visited by, **9.** 97
physician at Marseille visits, at inn, **35.** 25
physicians disliked by, **24.** 210
Pisa visited by, **18.** 455
portraits of: half-length, at the Vyne, **35.** 639; in pastels, painted for Mann, **18.** 243, 263, **24.** 222, **35.** 38; Rosalba's, **18.** 243n, **35.** 6n
prints collected by, **18.** 284
Pucci, Mme, civil to, **17.** 42
Ragley would be improved by designs of, **9.** 223
reflections by, *see* Laughter
Reggio visited by, **30.** 16
'religiously inclined,' **35.** 29
returns from Vyne: **35.** 177; after Whithed's death, **20.** 238
Rivera rebuked by, at Albani's, **19.** 142–3
——'s accusations against English fleet heard by, **19.** 120
Roman letter to Goldsworthy amuses, **19.** 226
Romans to hear from, about English zeal, **19.** 128–9
Romans told by that Young Pretender is not really in Scotland, **19.** 198
Rome left by, **19.** 196–7, 210
—— soon to be revisited by, **19.** 171
—— to be left by, for Naples, **19.** 149
—— visited by, **19.** 59, 65–6, 84–5, 97, 113, 128, 135–6, 139, 161, 171, 196
Sade's verses on Frederick II criticized by, **17.** 46n
Sarrazin, Mme, discusses smallpox with, **17.** 498
—— forces, to play quadrille, **18.** 132
Scamozzi's *Cinq ordres d'architecture* owned by, **43.** 292
servant of, employed by Glass, **10.** 261; *see also* Martelli, Francesco
sets out for the Vyne, **35.** 200
Sherlock, Bp, not believed by, **20.** 137
sister-in-law's correspondence with, **19.** 92
sister of: beloved by him, **20.** 26; dies, **20.** 19
sketches by, for SH bookcases, **43.** 292
(?) sketch of Gothic arch by, **43.** 278
smells enjoyed by, **18.** 230
Smith informs, of Mann's operation, **35.** 4
——'s ignorance amuses, **18.** 465
Somerset family scandal discovered by, in Herald's Office, **20.** 138–9

[Chute, John, *continued*]

*sortes Walpolianæ* commented on by, **20**. 407

spirits of: good, **10**. 199, 204; improve, **20**. 273

Stanhope's house admired by, **19**. 485

Stosch procures for, rare print by 'Marc Antonio' after Raphael, **23**. 432

SH cloister designed by, **35**. 110–11

SH garden chapel façade designed by, **2**. 370n

SH garden cottage designed by, **4**. 147n

SH library bookcases designed by, **35**. 157

SH not visited by, in autumn, for fear of gout, **35**. 115

SH to be visited by, to see armour of Francis I, **23**. 350

'Strawberry King-at-Arms,' **9**. 97, 186, **20**. 93, 138

Strozzi family troubles known to, **19**. 350

Suares invites, to opera at villa, **35**. 5

Suares, Mme, entertains, with play, **17**. 120

—— greets, with HW's present, **35**. 29

—— persuades, to back Tesi's opera, **18**. 280–1

subscriber to concert at Florence, **18**. 13

swans to be procured for, **35**. 89–90

tea taken by, **17**. 438

Tesi quarrels with, **18**. 322

Thames voyage of, from SH to London, **19**. 497

Thistlethwaytes prefer Galfridus Mann to, as trustee, **20**. 312

—— urged by, to pay Sophia Lucchi's annuity, **22**. 268, 316

Thomas, Dr, consulted by, **24**. 210

Torri painting liked by, **17**. 268

trustee for Sophia Lucchi, **20**. 246

Tunbridge visited by, **19**. 436

Ubaldini's apartment occupied by, **17**. 146

Uguccioni to introduce, at Baronessa Ricasoli's, **17**. 129

*uomo nero* unknown term to, **20**. 291

vehemence of, prevents his flattering HW, **35**. 244

Venice visited by, **17**. 74, 101, **18**. 63, 465, **19**. 257, 268, **35**. 4, 21, 27

Vienna to be visited by, on way to England, **19**. 207, 257

Violette's dancing disliked by, **19**. 342

Vyne alterations by, **35**. 641–2

Vyne, the, residence of, **9**. (?) 88, 161–4, 166, 167, 172, 216, 222, 243, 249, 370, 378, **10**. 37, 38, 40, 75, 97, 98, 100, 264

Vyne visited by, at brother's death, **20**. 433

walks in Mann's garden, **19**. 252

Walpole, Bns, wanted by, to die, **17**. 432

Walpole, Horace sr, disagrees with, over Miss Nicoll, **14**. 214–15

Walpole, Sir Robert, congratulated by, on peerage, **35**. 25–6

—— revered by, **17**. 408

West mentions, **13**. 240

Whithed brought up by, **20**. 238, **22**. 268

—— persuaded by, to provide for Lucchi family, **22**. 265

——'s affair may keep, from going to Rome, **35**. 52

——'s bequest to, **14**. 49, **20**. 238

——'s fit alarms, **18**. 109

——'s marriage arranged by, **20**. 238, 256

——'s relationship to, **43**. 181

——'s will partly administered by, **20**. 246

——'s will seen by, **20**. 251

—— tended by, in last illness, **20**. 237–8

—— the 'other half' of, **35**. 52

—— to have been heir to, **20**. 238

wine-drinking of, brings on gout, **18**. 100

wine shunned by, **18**. 149

wit of: **17**. 124, **19**. 317; praised by Bentley and HW, **24**. 212

witticisms by: about knowing what he ought to like, **17**. 74; on Battle Abbey and Mrs Chenevix, **35**. 140; on lady who died of drams, **20**. 4; on Lee's remark about consistent servants, **20**. 246; on Mrs Goldsworthy, **17**. 351, 373, **20**. 93, 298; on mourning ring presented by covetous cousin, **21**. 52; on Niccolini's banishment, **20**. 3–4; on poetry, **14**. 36; on Primate of Lorraine's smallpox, **17**. 480, 498, **35**. 28, 32; on Ps Eleonora, **17**. 74; on Royal Marriage Bill at time of Young Pretender's marriage, **23**. 398

Young Pretender said by, not to be in Scotland, **19**. 198

——'s invasion called by, a hoax, **19**. 97

Chute, Mary Lobb (d. 1822), m. Wither Bramstone:

(?) SH visited by, **12**. 229

Chute, Thomas Lobb. *See* Lobb, Thomas

Chute, William John (1757–1824) of the Vyne:

SH visited by, **12**. 227, 228

Vyne, the, seat of, **35**. 641

Chute family:

Bentley designs 'Gothic columbarium' for, **9**. 216

Chute, John, last of male line of, **24**. 209n

Mildmay, Mrs, distant cousin of, **20**. 96n

'Chuteheds.' *See* Chute, John; Whithed, Francis

Chute pedigree:

Vyne window to display, **35**. 639

Ciampi, ——, composer:

burlettas composed and conducted by, **20**. 4n

Ciarlii, Giuseppe:

Mann's annuity to, **25**. 667n

Cibber, Caius Gabriel (1630–1700) sculptor:

figures by, **9**. 128n

Cibber, Colley (1671–1757), actor and dramatist:

*Apology for the Life of Colley Cibber*: HW quotes, **38**. 60; HW's opinion of, **10**. 298; quoted, **19**. 92, **33**. 402

as Bayes superior to Garrick, **33**. 88, **38**. 525

birthday odes by: discussed with Fox, **30**. 111; HW's contempt for, **10**. 298, **29**. 307

Bland's bet with Montfort over Nash's being survived by, **35**. 258

*Cæsar in Egypt* by, acted by Mrs Oldfield, **13**. 183n

*Careless Husband, The*: HW alludes to, **29**. 45; HW and Pinkerton admire, **33**. 492; HW's opinion of, **10**. 298; 'Mrs Edging' in, **38**. 208; praised, **41**. 374; successful on the stage, **18**. 34

*Character and Conduct of Cicero Considered* by, **14**. 13–14, 21, **15**. 296, **43**. 181, 212

death of, **20**. 214n

dying, **20**. 214

Garrick surpassed by, in acting men of fashion, **38**. 524

genteel comedy of, **33**. 563

*Gentleman's Magazine* compares Stephens and, with Quin, **13**. 64n

Gray not inclined to see, **13**. 96

HW attributes *Sir Courtly Nice* to, **25**. 564n

HW compares Garrick to, **10**. 298, **33**. 88, **38**. 524, 525

HW congratulates, on hearty appearance, **35**. 258

HW parodies Birthday odes of, **29**. 307

HW quotes, **36**. 221

Jones recommended by, to D. of Grafton, **20**. 214, 218

——'s *Earl of Essex* revised by, **20**. 214n

*King Lear* acted by, **19**. 342n

*Letter from Mr Cibber to Mr Pope, A*, **18**. 8, 34–5, **30**. 310n, **37**. 125

*Love's Last Shift* by, **9**. 129, **13**. 57, **42**. 158

*New Lesson for Pope* satirizes, **18**. 34–5

*Nonjuror, The*, by, **33**. 87, 492

odes by, **10**. 298

Pilkington, Lætitia, friend of, **14**. 13n

*Provok'd Husband, The*, by: **2**. 250; approached by *School for Scandal*, **41**. 363; acted at Cassiobury Park, **32**. 180n; came out when HW was at Eton and has never been surpassed, **35**. 350; characters in, **31**. 332; Garrick as Lord Townly in, **33**. 87, **38**. 525; HW compares *School for Scandal* to, **28**. 309, **41**. 363; HW likes, **33**. 514, **35**. 350; preface to, quoted by HW, **22**. 46, **23**. 132n, **31**. 157

*Provok'd Wife* to be acted by, **17**. 222n

'retirement' of, **17**. 222n

Robinson's ball atttended by, though not of 'first fashion,' **37**. 114

snuff-box used by in 'fop' parts, given to HW by Raftor, **42**. 158

to act, **17**. 222

Whitehead succeeds, as laureate, **28**. 243n

witticism by, on Beaufort's potency, **18**. 185

writings of, pert and dull, **14**. 14

Cibber, Theophilus (1703–58), actor and playwright:

*Devil to Pay* adapted by, from Jevon's *Devil of a Wife*, **35**. 51n

wife of, **13**. 96n, **28**. 183n

Cibber, Mrs Theophilus. *See* Arne, Susannah Maria

Cibizen, F. K.:

print of, **40**. 236

Cibo. *See* Cybo

Cicciaporci, F., art dealer:

collection of, **18**. 313

name of, corrected, **43**. 251

Cicé. *See* Champion de Cicé

Ciceri, Conte Giuseppe di (d. 1753), Austrian field marshal:

Spaniards capture, **18**. 153

wounded at Campo Santo, **18**. 164

Cicero, Marcus Tullius (106–43 B.C.):

Atticus friend of, **9**. 394n

*bons mots* of, collected by Cæsar, **28**. 280

Bull's partiality would have given joy to, **42**. 107–8

bust of, in Uffizi, copied by Hoare, **20**. 86

Catilines no longer confronted by, **15**. 130

Chute quotes, **35**. 19

Cibber attacks Middleton's life of, **15**. 296

—— sometimes right about, **14**. 14

Conway in Jersey compared to, in Sicily, **24**. 526

correspondence of, disillusioning, **35**. 561–2

Cumberland's play about, **10**. 243

*De amicitia*, **11**. 181

*De finibus bonorum et malorum*, **28**. 467

*De officiis*, **15**. 257n, **33**. 407

Du Deffand, Mme, mentions, **4**. 203

—— reads, **6**. 324

——'s opinion of, **6**. 337

'enchanting pen' of, weakened by flattery, **35**. 569

*Epistolæ ad Atticum*, **28**. 406

*Epistolæ ad familiares*, quotes Euripides, **13**. 198

*Epistulæ*, quoted by HW, **42**. 108

Ferdinando II buys bust of, from Ludovisi family, **20**. 86n

Fox, C. J., ranked with, by Catherine II, **11**. 323

Gray paraphrases, **14**. 12

HW compares Mason to, **29**. 86

HW lacks vanity of, **42**. 108

HW's name for: George Grenville, **23**. 163; William Pitt II, **25**. 278

HW's opinion of, **9**. 105, 394

Hardinge quotes, **35**. 556

humble birth boasted of by, **30**. 334–5

lamentations of, in banishment, **16**. 272

letters of: **11**. 295n; admired by Mme du Deffand, **6**. 332; disillusioning, **35**. 561–2; Melmoth's translation of, **15**. 304

Livy makes rough generals talk like, **4**. 490

loved glory, **28**. 440

medal of Sir Robert Walpole has figure of, copied from statue of Lucius Antonius, **16**. 300

Middleton's *Epistles of*, **15**. 10, 296, 304

——'s *History of the Life of*, **6**. 332, **15**. 6–8, 20, 293, 296, 302, 304, **37**. 94–5, 98

[Cicero, Marcus Tullius, *continued*]
   modern use of 'major' would not be under-
     stood by **2.** 313
   Nugent's verses mention, **31.** 269
   orations of: **17.** 83, **20.** 74, **23.** 490–1; Fox,
     C. J., equals, **23.** 400, 491; puerile, **33.** 543
   *Orator*, quoted by West, **13.** 124
   Pitt (Chatham) surpasses, **35.** 260, 262
   prejudice confutes eloquence of, **35.** 624
   son of, **9.** 105, **15.** 257, **21.** 57
   Stanley's dialogue in imitation of, **28.** 8
   statue of, at Easton Neston, **9.** 5, 122, **20.** 390
   style of, conveyed by Middleton, **15.** 10–11
   tomb of, **37.** 59
   *Tusculan Questions* re-edited by Davies, **2.**
     354
   vain, **6.** 356
   Warburton writes on, **15.** 302
   West fears influence of, on SH, **40.** 311
Cicero, Marcus Tullius (the younger) (b. ca 65
   B.C.):
   father despises, **9.** 105
   HW compares himself to, **15.** 257
   *L'Histoire des quatres Cicérons* celebrates,
     **21.** 57
*Cicero. See under* Greville, Sir Fulke
Cicisbea; cicisbeas:
   lovers' marriages permitted by, on promises
     of instant return, **20.** 95
   Mann finds, too much trouble, **20.** 94
   ——'s, **22.** (?) 180, **23.** 295, 306
Cicisbeatura ('Cicisbeship'):
   at Florence, **37.** 323
   double chairs without a division required
     for, **18.** 332
Cicisbeo; cicisbeos:
   conversation about, the chief Florentine topic,
     **20.** 284
   Conway diverted by, **37.** 320
   dark gardens favoured by, **17.** 498–9
   duties of, **13.** 204–5
   English travellers derange system of, **20.** 284
   Florentine customs of, **13.** 199–200
   Genoese abbé reported to be Lady Mary Wort-
     ley Montagu's, **30.** 11
   HW compares, to parakeets, **37.** 77
   HW is Lady Ossory's, **32.** 148
   HW tires of seeing, **13.** 238
   ladies to be regaled by, with macaroni pie,
     **20.** 219
   Mann becomes, for theatre attendance only,
     **22.** 180
   —— unlikely to become, **19.** 48
   Palazzo Ridolfi's gardens suitable for, **37.** 68–
     9
Cicognani, College of:
   Leopold names Jesuits to direct, **23.** 512n
*Cid, Il* (opera). *See under* Sacchini, Antonio
   Maria Gaspare
*Cid, Le. See under* Corneille, Pierre
Cider:
   counties producing, join Opposition, **38.** 459

Montagu sends hamper of, to HW for Bent-
   ley, **9.** 277, 281
Parliament threatens to tax, **10.** 58
tax on, **22.** 129, 132–3, 277n, **30.** 188
Verdea wine like, **23.** 204
Williams, Sir C. H., sends, to HW, **16.** 85
Cider Tax. *See under* Parliament: acts of
Cigala:
   HW compares Grenville to, **10.** 254
   Piozzi, Mrs, comments on, **10.** 254n
Cignani, Carlo (1628–1719), painter:
   painting by: bought for E. of Lichfield, **21.**
     231; from Arnaldi collection, probably
     bought by E. of Leicester, **21.** 478; Hamil-
     ton buys, supposedly for Lichfield, **21.** 208;
     Hoare asks Mann to buy, from Arnaldi col-
     lection, **21.** 208; sold cheaply because it
     decays fast, **21.** 208; sold by Arnaldi to
     Court of Dresden, **21.** 208n
Cigoli (Italy):
   Theodore stays in, at house of Baldanzi. **18.**
     217n
Cimabue, Giovanni (? 1240–? 1302), painter:
   Agincourt begins with, in study of church
     paintings, **42.** 104
   egg-white probably used by, **40.** 215
Cimaroli. *See* Brentano-Cimaroli
Cimino, Lt Nicholas:
   captured at Velletri, **18.** 493
'Cimitière':
   charade on, **39.** 39
Cimitile, Principe di. *See* San Severino Albertini
Cimon (d. 449 B.C.), Athenian statesman:
   George III compared with, **32.** 132
   Pope's *Dunciad* mentions, **17.** 451, **37.** 89,
     **39.** 150
Cincinnati, Society of the (U.S.A.):
   instituted in 1783, **29.** 323n
   Washington sends order of, to La Fayette, **29.**
     323, **33.** 431
Cincinnatus, Lucius Quinctius (ca 519–ca 439
   B.C.), senator:
   counterparts of, now to be found at hazard
     table, **24.** 86
   HW imitates, **23.** 285
   statues of, in Pomfret collection, **20.** 390
Cinders:
   'large glassy,' in Hagley grotto, **40.** 82n
Cineas (d. before 276 B.C.), ambassador from
   Epirus to ancient Rome:
   HW paraphrases conversation of, with Pyr-
     rhus, from Plutarch, **31.** 160–1
   Roman senate compared by, to assembly of
     kings, **23.** 562
Cingles:
   chaise on, **19.** 135
'Cinna.' *See under* Shakespeare, William: *Julius
   Caesar*
*Cinna. See under* Corneille, Pierre
Cinnamon:
   England will get, from Ceylon conquest, **25.**
     277

Holland to bewail loss of Ceylon monopoly of, **25.** 283

in quack medicine, **7.** 208

oil of, in Hoffman's medicine, **36.** 140

*Cinquantaine, La. See under* Fouques, François-Georges

Cinque, Don Cesare:
Neapolitan physician, **21.** 325

Cinque Fronde (Italy):
earthquake account mentions, **25.** 376

Cinque Ports:
barons of the: Coronation dinner for, **38.** 133; George III's coronation attended by, **9.** 389; Talbot's treatment at banquet resented by, **9.** 389

Dodd and Whaley tour, **40.** 5–6

Dorset to have life custody of, **21.** 109

—— lord warden of, **21.** 104n

Holdernesse gets reversion of wardenship of, **9.** 344, **21.** 489

—— lord warden of, **28.** 145

North appointed to, **7.** 49

Ormond replaces Dorset as warden of, **20.** 63n

Cintra:
De Castro's garden at, **12.** 178n

Ciofani, Matthäus, abbé; Prussian agent at Rome:
Clement XIV informed by, of Frederick II's wish to protect Jesuits, **23.** 157n

Frederick II's supposed letter to, **5.** 427

Cioia de Forges, Bernardo, Conte di Monzone;
Modenese representative at Paris 1739–58:
Francis III's letter to, **18.** 280

Ciotat (France):
Sicard from, **20.** 319n

Cipher; ciphers:
dispatches in, deciphered at Turin, **19.** 12

HW and Mann use, in their correspondence, **17.** 98, 111, 124, **25.** 42–3

Jesuits', unsolved, **23.** 517

Murray told that Mann can forward Murray's communications in, **24.** 469, **25.** 42

Old Pretender's letters in, **18.** 280

Palombo not entrusted with, **17.** 156

Sandys would take Conway's handwriting for, **37.** 181

Villettes does not write in, **18.** 385

—— to write in, **18.** 97

—— writes in, **18.** 59

Cippenham, Bucks:
seat of Jacob Bryant, **1.** 349n, **2.** 5n

Cipriani, Giovanni Battista (1727–85), painter:
artists at D. of Richmond's gallery to be corrected by, **21.** 174n

drawings by, auctioned, **43.** 369

frontispiece should be drawn by, for Cts Harcourt's poems, **35.** 459

HW calls, 'clumsy scene-painter,' **25.** 316

Hollis's memoirs decorated with cuts by, **29.** 19

Houghton pictures to be appraised by, **24.** 441

Orford, 3d E. of, buys drawings by, **36.** 237

—— refurnishes Houghton with pictures by, **25.** 247, 316, 418

satirical account of, **16.** 186n

state coach painted by, **22.** 104n

story of Theodore and Honoria to be painted by, for E. of Orford, **25.** 247

Cipriani, Pierre, Col.:
captured at Velletri, **18.** 493

Cipriani, Pietro (fl. ca 1735), sculptor:
Bacchus figure not copied by, **19.** 48

death of, lowers price of gesse figures, **19.** 47

'Circæa.' *See under* Darwin, Erasmus: *Botanic Garden*

Circassia:
maidens of: **30.** 36; Raynal discusses, **39.** 168

seraglios of, **31.** 279

slaves of, *see under* Slave

*Circassiennes*:
Florentine ladies dress in, **25.** 175

Circe:
Éremans, Mlle, acts, in *Ballet de la Paix*, **18.** 496

Rochefort, Mme de, compared to, **31.** 54

Circle:
Pomfret, Cts of, squares, **17.** 240

*Circumstantial and Authentic Account of a Late Unhappy Affair*:
HW's copy of, **22.** 284n

Cirencester, Glos:
Bathurst's park at, **40.** 11

Dodd and Whaley visit, **40.** 11

Lysons, Samuel, digs up Roman antiquities near, **12.** 59

Cirey (France):
visitors to: Choiseul, **6.** 174, 198; Gramont, Duchesse de, **6.** 174, 198; Tessé, Comtesse de, **6.** 198

Ciries. *See* Siries

Cirifalco. *See* Girifalco

*Ciro reconosciuto, Il. See under* Cocchi, Gioacchino

Cistercians. *See* Bernardins

Cistern; cisterns:
at Burghley House, **10.** 346

at Newstead Abbey, **9.** 299

black marble, for Cts of Elgin's statue in mausoleum, **39.** 139

HW mentions, **38.** 157

Cisterna (Italy):
Young Pretender's escape aided by brother at, **18.** 377, 387

Citeaux, Abbé de. *See* Trouvé, Dom François

*Cité des Dames. See under* Pisan, Christine de

*Cithère* [Cythère] *assiégée. See under* Favart, Charles-Simon; Gluck, Christophe Willibald

'Citizen of the World':
as world is constituted, a useless animal, **33.** 158

Citron; citrons:
Clement XIII gives, to D. of York, **22.** 228, 229

HW will grow, if mild weather persists, **20.** 131

[Citron; citrons, *continued*]
  jar of, in liqueur, sent by Mann to HW, 17.
    317, 322, 398, 413, 439
  Lorenzi sends, to Fleury, 17. 317
  Mann gives: to Mathews, 18. 195; to Trevor,
    17. 413
  —— receives, from Mme Feroni, 17. 317
  ——'s, may be killed by cold weatther, 19. 3
Citron water:
  country ladies stock up with, after Session,
    18. 498
Cittadella (Minorca). *See* Ciudadela
*Cittadini*, society of:
  plays acted by, at Florence, 22. 393
City; cities:
  French planning of, inferior, 25. 635
  Rousseau's alleged pronouncement about, 23.
    400, 24. 62
  unnatural attitude of, HW's reflections on,
    24. 385
*City Latin. See under* Thornton, Bonnell
Ciudadela (Minorca):
  Conway visits Lockhart at, 37. 314
  French capture, 20. 552
  French may have difficulty in drawing cannon
    from, 20. 567
  Minorca's capital under the Spaniards, 37.
    314
Civilian:
  legal meaning of, 21. 104n
Civilization:
  progress in, makes ancient crimes seem in-
    credible, 22. 65
*Civil Liberty. See under* Cooke, Rev. William
  (1749–1824)
Civil list:
  Frederick, P. of Wales, can fill, 20. 80
  George II does not charge watch to, 20. 57
  ——'s, 20. 500
  George III's, 22. 264n
  Stosch's allowance paid out of, 17. 10n
Civil rights:
  Hardinge thinks moral values should not be
    applied to, 35. 613
Civil War, English:
  Bedford, 1st D. of, in, 34. 128
  destruction by Presbyterians in, 32. 75
  few private letters of time of, 34. 148
  sabbatarianism during, 31, 435–6
Civita Castellana (Italy):
  Austrians send baggage towards, 18. 534
  Gages may retreat to, 18. 325
  Neapolitan reinforcements for Gages reach,
    19. 10
  Young Pretender pretends to be from, 18. 388
Civita Vecchia (Italy):
  Austrian invalids sent to, by land, 18. 519
  commissary sent to, to adjudge capture of ship,
    17. 8
  Cumberland, D. and Ds of, at, 23. 565n
  Cumberland, D. of, wants Genoese galley to
    take him from, 23. 553, 564

  eagle shipped from, 19. 200
  English captain to guard, 18. 287–8, 296,
    300–1
  English fleet might threaten, 20. 35n, 21. 214,
    22. 386
  feast at, 17. 14
  France threatens to send Young Pretender to,
    20. 23n
  governor of, told to exclude Jesuits, 22. 516n,
    518; *see also* Gonzaga, Carlo
  HW's purchases sent to, 26. 4
  Jesuits' attempts to land at, 21. 340, 348, 22.
    515–16, 517–18, 532
  Kingston, Ds of, to sail to, with rich cargo,
    24. 118
  Leghorn squadron may visit, 18. 67
  Louis XV orders Young Pretender arrested
    and conducted to, 20. 35n
  Mann saves, from fury of Adm. Mathews,
    18. 314, 22. 386
  painting shipped from, 2. 170n
  Pretender's sons said to approach, under
    pretence of quail-shooting, 17. 14
  *Seahorse* captured under cannon of, 37. 57
  ships arrive at, after Rodney's victory, 25. 24
  ships lacking at, 18. 161, 175
  Spanish xebecs at, 18. 287, 296, 300–1
Civitella (Italy):
  Austrians hope to capture, 18. 460
Civrac, Duc de. *See* Durfort-Civrac, Émeric-
  Joseph de
Civrac, Duchesse de. *See* La Faurie de Mon-
  badon, Marie-Anne de
Civrac, Marquis de. *See* Durfort, François-Aim-
  ery de
'Clackmannan, Lady.' *See* Campbell, Caroline
  (1717–94)
Clairfait. *See* Clerfayt
Clairien, Françoise (1753–1815), called Mlle
  Raucourt; actress:
  acts at Choisy, 5. 322
  anecdote of Villette and, 6. 157
  Du Deffand, Mme, discusses, 5. 312, 6. 213
  no longer at Comédie, 6. 213
  *Rhadamiste et Zénobie* acted by, 7. 349
Clairon, Mlle. *See* Leris, Claire-Joseph
Clairval. *See* Guignard, Jean-Baptiste
Clam shell. *See under* Shell
Clan; clans, Scottish. *See under* Scotland
Clanbrassill, E. of. *See* Hamilton, Hon. James
  (1730–98)
Clancarty, E. of. *See* Maccarty, Robert
Clandestine Marriages Act. *See under* Parlia-
  ment: acts of
*Clandestine Marriage, The. See under* Colman,
  George; Garrick, David
Clane (Co. Kildare), monastery of:
  (?) Franciscans of, 14. 174n
Clanricarde, Cts of. *See* Walsingham, Frances
Clanricarde, E. of. *See* Bourke, John Smith
  (1720–82); Bourke, Richard (ca 1572–1635)
Clanrickarde. *See* Clanricarde

Clanville Lodge. *See* Blissmore Hall

Clanwilliam, Cts of, and Vcts. *See* Hawkins Magill, Theodosia (1743–1817)

Clanwilliam, E. of, and Vct. *See* Meade, Sir John (1744–1800)

Clap, the:
occurrences of, **17.** 444, **18.** 196–7

Clapcott, William, governor of Portland Castle:
turned out of office, **17.** 420

Clapham, Surrey:
Thornton of, **12.** 113n

Claramont, Waltham Cross:
Waldegrave, Hon. William, writes from, **36.** 271, 272

Claramount. *See* Claremont

Clarck, Mr:
illness of, **37.** 402
son may succeed, at Orford, **37.** 402–3

Clarck, Mr, jr:
father may be succeeded by, at Orford, **37.** 402–3

Clarck. *See also* Clark

Clare, E. of. *See* Fitzgibbon, John (1763–1802); Holles, Sir John (1564–1637); Pelham Holles, Thomas (1693–1768)

Clare, Vct. *See* Nugent, Robert (1709–88); O'Brien, Charles (1699–1761)

Clare, Vcts. *See* Bulkeley, Charlotte

Clare, ——:
(?) Brudenell succeeds, as deputy, **20.** 517

Clare, Robert Ippeswell (d. 1495):
Alcock, Bp, makes, justice of peace, **2.** 256

Clare (county in Ireland):
Killaloe in, **14.** 9n

Clare Hall (now Clare College), Cambridge:
Cole educated at, **2.** 371, 378, 379
hall of, **1.** 161
living in gift of, **1.** 126
Mann and Folkes enrolled at, **24.** 290n
Montagu meets fellow of, **10.** 170
Tories at, **13.** 58

Clarelli, (?) Girolamo (d. 1764), Bp of Rieti, 1761:
(?) Benedict XIV appoints, to meet Montemar at Viterbo, **17.** 214–15
Montemar awaits answer from, **17.** 226
(?) Rosa's claim investigated by, **17.** 8n

Clare Market, Lincoln's Inn, London:
Newcastle called 'king' of **9.** 333

Claremont, Surrey, D. of Newcastle's seat:
a show place, **1.** 44
Clinton, Lady Lucy, visits, **30.** 22
Clive buys, and alters it, **32.** 71n
gardens of, **9.** 71
George II to dine at, in cook's absence, **20.** 72
HW dines with Newcastle at, **38.** 418–20
HW to call on D. of Newcastle at, **40.** 343, 344, 362
mushroom beds at, destroyed, **31.** 10–11
Newcastle, D. of, entertains at, **3.** 84n, **17.** 503, **18.** 20, **20.** 72, **22.** 78n
—— forces people to dine at, **30.** 194

——'s party for Fuentes family at, cancelled, **21.** 417n
—— to entertain Conway at, **22.** 332
—— to retire to, for a few days, **21.** 92
—— would probably give dinner to Young Pretender at, **30.** 91
—— writes from, **40.** 343, 361, **41.** 35, 36
Newcastles invite HW and Conway to, **41.** 35, 36, 38
Newcastles write from, to HW, **35.** 331
Shaw, Dr, called to, **31.** 10
sold in parcels, **36.** 246
SH compared with, **9.** 169, **35.** 237, 421
Tyrconnel occupies, **34.** 8n, **42.** 472n
visible from Esher, **10.** 73
visitors to: HW, **9.** 71, **38.** 418–20; Hertfords, **39.** 284; Hume, Bp, **38.** 419–20; Mecklenburg, P. of, **22** 78n; Nivernais, **10.** 72; Onslow, **38.** 419; Powis, Cts of, and children, **39.** 284; Stanley, **31.** 11
York, Frederick, D. of, takes Oatlands to be near mistress at, **34.** 8n

Claremont, Waltham Cross:
Waldegrave, Hon. William, addressed at, **43.** 387

Claremont. *See also* Claramont

Clarence, Ds of. *See* Nevill, Lady Isabel (1451–76)

Clarence, D. of. *See* George (Plantagenet) (1449–78); Lionel (Plantagenet) (1338–68); William IV (1765–1837)

Clarence, title of:
supposedly restored to E. of Warwick by Richard III, **15.** 221–2

Clarence House, London:
Conway and wife said to visit Gloucester House on way to, **36.** 80–1

Clarendon, Cts of. *See* Aylesbury, Frances (1617–67); Capel, Lady Charlotte (1721–90)

Clarendon, E. of:
Hardwicke rumoured to become, **35.** 170
*See also* Hyde, Edward (1609–74); Hyde, Henry (1638–1709); Hyde, Henry (1672–1753); Villiers, Thomas (1709–86)

Clarendon House, London:
style of, **18.** 316

Clarendon Printing House. *See under* Oxford University

Clare Priory, Suffolk:
Barker of, **11.** 57n

Claret:
Bedford faction requires, **39.** 101
Granby may take to, if lord lieutenant of Ireland, **22.** 131n
HW compares effect of sea on, to that of distance on news, **10.** 113
HW considers Montagu fortunate in getting only gout from, **10.** 101
in Ireland, **10.** 2, 27, 29, 61, 97
Mason advises HW to drink, **28.** 418
Montagu promises to avoid, **9.** 383
——'s complexion coloured by, **10.** 97
——'s guests drink, at Adderbury, **10.** 297

[Claret, *continued*]

Mountrath, Cts of, addicted to, **9.** 135

Norfolk, D. of, drinks 'sea of,' **12.** 206, **39.** 310

Rockingham dies from excess of, **20.** 208

sea of: Cholmondeley drinks, **23.** 217; Wilkes's ghost laid in, **23.** 5

served at Dublin entertainment, **9.** 404

served at Lincoln's Inn entertainment, **43.** 169

Stanley serves, **32.** 115n

Claret-bottle ticket:

coat of arms encircled by, **9.** 186

Clarges, Lady. *See* Skrine, Louisa

Clarges, Anne (d. 1782), m. Hon. Laurence Shirley:

daughter-in-law's letter from, **21.** 399

George II petitioned by, to pardon her son, **21.** 388, 397

Clarges, Sir Thomas (1688–1759), 2d Bt; M.P.:

HW leaves burglars' tools with, **9.** 134

Clarges, Sir Thomas (1751–81), Bt:

Conway sends letters to England by, **39.** 242

—— sends papers by, **6.** 138n

Du Deffand, Mme, sends book to HW, by, **6.** 129, 137

Keith entertains, with Conway at Vienna, **39.** 538

Clarges St, Piccadilly:

Clarke, Misses, live in, **31.** 214n, 232, **42.** 99n, 186n

Clopton dies in, **12.** 201n

Hamilton, Mary, addressed in, **31.** 214, 232, 234, **42.** 186n

highwaymen rob between Hounslow and, **20.** 188n

Veseys in, **31.** 214n, 222, 233, 247, 255, 336, **32.** 229n, **42.** 99n

'Clarice.' *See* Bulkeley, Charlotte

Clarinet; clarinets:

at Bedford House, **9.** 369

at Comte and Comtesse d'Egmont's, **7.** 301

at Cts of Northumberland's *festino*, **10.** 35

at Dr Graham's, **33.** 217

at Lord Stanley's ball, **32.** 115

dinner for Mendips to be accompanied by, **12.** 141

HW has, for party at SH, **10.** 69, 71, 127, 279

Claris de Florian, Philippe-Antoine (b. 1707), Marquis de Florian:

social relations of, with: Du Deffand, Mme, **7.** 269; Élie de Beaumont, **7.** 304

Voltaire's nephew, **7.** 269

*Clarissa. See under* Richardson, Samuel

Clark, ——, footman to Old Pretender:

Ashburnham twitted by, on jealousy, **19.** 454

Rome avoided by, because of brother, **19.** 454

Clark, ——:

Jewish passenger on *Great Duchess of Tuscany*, **25.** 480n

Clark, Mrs, of Pitt's Buildings, Kensington:

Brown's profanity described by, to Sir C. H. Williams, **9.** 219

Williams, Sir Charles Hanbury, confined at house of, **21.** 183n

Clark, Daniel, coal-heaver:

trial of, **23.** 39n

Clark, Elizabeth (ca 1655–93), m. 1 (1671) William Morley; m. 2 (1679) John Trevor; m. 3 (1690) John Cutts, 1st Bn Cutts:

Cutts abducts and ill-treats, **9.** 252

genealogy of, **9.** 252, **10.** 352

HW cannot find, in Montagu's pedigree, **9.** 218

health of: pox, **9.** 252, 261

Montagu's grandmother, **9.** 187n

—— writes to Chute about, **9.** 261

portrait of, **9.** 251, 252, 256, 258, 259

print of, **9.** 191

Clark, Lady Mary. *See* Mackenzie, Lady Mary

Clark, Walter (d. 1784), Harcourt's gardener:

flowers of, immortalized by Cts Harcourt, **35.** 461

HW calls, 'Linnæus,' **35.** 473

HW wants disciple of, to be his gardener, **35.** 473

Clarke, Mr:

defrauded by Dignam, **28.** 288n

Clarke, Mr:

SH ticket not used by, **12.** 248

Clarke, Mr:

social relations of, in Paris, with HW and Massereene, **7.** 268, 293, 294

Clarke, Mrs:

social relations of, in Paris, with Massereene, **7.** 294

Clarke, Alured (1696–1742), Dean of Exeter, 1741:

Caroline, Q., friend of, **17.** 279n

Exeter bishopric desired by, **17.** 279

Clarke, Sir Alured (ca 1745–1832), K.B., **1797**, army officer:

Hunter, Elizabeth, weds, **22.** 9n

wife of, **10.** 14n

Clarke, Mrs Alured. *See* Hunter, Elizabeth Catherine

Clarke, Anna Maria (living 1806):

Clarges St address of, **31.** 214n, 232, **42.** 99n

Dickensons left by, **31.** 277

HW calls on, in Conduit St, **31.** 336

HW gets Dickensons' address from, **31.** 336

HW invites, to SH, **31.** 215, 232, 262, **42.** 99

HW jokes about John Dickenson and, **31.** 275

HW's correspondence with, **42.** 186

HW thanks, for news of Mrs Dickenson's delivery, **42.** 186

Hamilton, Mary, corresponds with, **31.** 257

—— lives with, **42.** 99

Norfolk St former residence of, **31.** 336

self-sacrifice of, **31.** 277

Sunninghill may be visited by, **31.** 336

(?) woodcocks from the Dickensons sent to HW by, **31.** 335

Clarke, Anne Melicent:

scenes by, from *Castle of Otranto*, **42.** 430n

Clarke, Charles:
  letter from, on Patagonians, **22**. 421n
Clarke, Dr George:
  Jones's designs bequeathed by, to Worcester College, Oxford, **21**. 364n
Clarke, George (d. 1768):
  Brentford chairmen represented as killing, **23**. 98
Clarke, Hester (1723–52), m. (1748) John St John, 2d Vct St John:
  Florence visited by, in seclusion save for Schutz and Smith, **20**. 23
  Rome visited by, **20**. 23
  Schutz to take, to England after husband's death, **20**. 15, 23
Clarke, Isabella:
  Clarges St address of, **31**. 214n, 232n, **42**. 99n
  HW invites, to SH, **31**. 215, 232, **42**. 99
  Hamilton, Mary, lives with, **42**. 99
  mad, **31**. 277
  sister sent for by, **31**. 277
Clarke, Jeremiah (ca 1669–1707), composer:
  Dryden's *Alexander's Feast* set to music by, **28**. 345n
Clarke, John (1682–1757), D.D.; Dean of Salisbury:
  daughter of, **2**. 137n
Clarke, Mary, m. John Henry Jacob:
  husband of, **2**. 137n
Clarke, Matthew (d. 1786), actor:
  broad Irish accent of, in *Elfrida*, **28**. 109
  'Caractacus' acted by, **28**. 277n
Clarke, Richard (b. ? ca 1723):
  *Belisarius* by, submitted to HW, **42**. 448
  HW's correspondence with, **42**. 448–9
Clarke, Col. Robert. See Clerk, Robert
Clarke, Rev. Samuel (1599–1683):
  engraving of, **16**. 67
Clarke, Rev. Samuel (1675–1729), D.D.; metaphysician:
  bust of, in Hermitage, **14**. 39n, **29**. 34n, 296
  parental tenderness lacked by, **35**. 577
Clarke, Sir Thomas (1703–64), Kt, 1754; Master of the Rolls 1754–64; M.P.:
  biographical information on, corrected, **43**. 279
  death of, **22**. 263, **38**. 468
  Macclesfield, not Yorke, inherits from, being his alleged half-brother, **38**. 468
Clarke, William, London bookseller:
  SH visited by, **12**. 247
Clarke. See also Clark; Clerk
Clarkson, Thomas (1760–1846), abolitionist:
  *Essay on the Impolicy of the African Slave Trade, An*, by, **31**. 328n
  (?) mechanical sugar-cultivation thought practical by, **31**. 328
Classen. See Clossen
Classical art:
  HW's reflections on insipidity of, **35**. 443–5
Classics, Greek and Roman:
  Hardwicke meditates, at Blenheim, **10**. 309

Heinel, Mlle, copies attitudes from, **35**. 343
  library of unpublished, at Naples, **31**. 278–9
  quoted by retired lawyers and schoolboys, **34**. 104
  renaissance of, **2**. 289
Clate (Scotland):
  rebels try to surprise, **37**. 229–30
Claud; Claude (artist). See Lorrain, Claude
Claude (1499–1524), m. (1514) François I, K. of France:
  portraits of: at Ste-Chapelle, **7**. 276, **39**. 203; said to be in Vyne chapel window, **20**. 485n, **35**. 641
Claude Lorrain. See Lorrain, Claude
Claudian (Claudius Claudianus) (d. ca 408), poet:
  Cole cites, **2**. 100n
  HW quotes lines in Virgil similar to, **13**. 194
  ranting style of, **29**. 223, 256
  soldiers would despise war poetry of, **16**. 269
  West alludes to, **13**. 118
Claudius (Tiberius Claudius Drusus Nero Germanicus, 10 B.C.–A.D. 54), Roman emperor:
  (?) arch of, **33**. 54
  mother of, **15**. 12
  Pætus ordered by, to end his life, **5**. 424n
  wife remarries in lifetime of, **24**. 333
Clausen, Baron de, French Lt-Gen.:
  Karl Wilhelm Ferdinand defeated by, **21**. 498n
Clausonet, Marquis de, French minister to Württemberg:
  (?) social relations of, with Mme de Forcalquier, **7**. 340
Claussonette, —— de:
  HW entertains, at SH, **10**. 156
Claustre, André de (18th c.) abbé:
  *Dictionnaire de mythologie* by, **8**. 25
Clavecin:
  Balbastre, famous player of, **6**. 115
  Du Deffand, Mme, prefers harp to, **4**. 446
  ordered from London by Duchesse de Choiseul, **4**. 189
Clavell, Robert (d. 1711):
  *Catalogue of Books . . . since the dreadful fire, A*, by, **40**. 298
Clavering, Lady. See Yorke, Catherine
Clavering, Alice (1705–76), m. (1735 or 7) Herbert Windsor, 2d Vct Windsor:
  Coleraine, Bns, lives with, **24**. 235
  daughter of, **10**. 237n
  HW's epitaph on daughter of, **39**. 156
  house of, in Hill St, **24**. 236n
  unlucky days avoided by, **22**. 465n
Clavering, Lady Augusta. See Campbell, Lady Augusta
Clavering, Lady Diana. See West, Lady Diana
Clavering, Henry Mordaunt (1766–1850), army officer:
  Argyll, D. and Ds of, accompanied by, to Italy, **11**. 48
  marriage of, **34**. 17n
  wife of, **9**. 264n

Clavering, Sir James John (d. ? 1778), Lt-Gen.: wife of, **12.** 69n

Clavering, John (1698–1762), M.P.:
George III dismisses, for not sitting up with George II's body, **9.** 323
—— omits, from Bedchamber, **9.** 324, **21.** 460
Piozzi, Mrs, comments on, **9.** 323n

Clavering, Sir John (1722–77), K.B., 1776; army officer; councillor of India:
daughter of, expected to marry Sir John Dick, **25.** 153
French military difficulties reported by, **21.** 511
Hastings deposes, **28.** 396
hero of Guadeloupe action, **21.** 301
Mann's correspondence with, **20.** *294*, **21.** 301n
——'s friend, **21.** 301
son of, **11.** 48n

Clavering, Maria Margaret (ca 1757–1812), m. (1784) Francis Napier, 8th Bn Napier, 1775:
impotence of Sir John Dick would soon have been discovered by, **25.** 182
India's climate makes, a giantess, **25.** 153
marriage of, to Dick falsely rumoured, **25.** 153, 173

Clavering, Sir Thomas (1719–94), 7th Bt, 1748; M.P.:
death date of, corrected, **43.** 283
Parliamentary motions by: against denial of Parliament's validity, **39.** 125–6; to address George III to lay remonstrance before House of Commons, **23.** 198
resolution proposed by, for address opposing London's remonstrance, **39.** 126n

Clavering Cowper, Hon. Edward Spencer (1779–1823), M.P.:
Carder, Mrs, to accompany, **25.** 151
father sends, to England to be educated, **22.** 363n, **25.** 391n

Clavering Cowper, George Augustus (1776–99), styled Vct Fordwich 1776–89; 4th E. Cowper, 1789:
baptism of, **24.** 199, 206, 219, 232, 238–9
birth of, **24.** 232
Carder, Mrs, to accompany, **25.** 151
father sends, to England to be educated, **22.** 363n, **25.** 391n
father should send, to England and have him refuse to return, **24.** 242

Clavering Cowper, George Nassau (1738–89), styled Vct Fordwich 1738–64; 3d E. Cowper, 1764; M.P.:
burletta of, **22.** 393
children of, sent to England, **22.** 363n, **25.** 151, 391n
Conway asked by, for favour, **22.** 438
Corsi, Marchesa, kept, in Florence, **21.** 415, **22.** 361, 363n
courier of, brings HW's letter to Mann, **22.** 363

Cunningham tells, that Mann is to be K.B., **22.** 317
Dick, Sir John, expected to marry into family of, **25.** 161
—— writes to, **25.** 182
Dorset, D. of, may be succeeded by, as lieutenant of Kent, **22.** 361
England avoided by, for 20 years, **25.** 191
—— should not be visited by, just for profit, **22.** 363
English bride may be sought by, **23.** 449
false report of arrival of, in England, **25.** 191
father-in-law leaves Emily Gore with, **25.** 390
father's entreaties to return to England unheeded by, **21.** 543, **22.** 363, 375, **24.** 242n
Florence soon to be revisited by, **25.** 660
Florentine amours and marriage of, **22.** 363n
Florentine sojourn of, unduly prolonged, **21.** 543, **22.** 88, 363, 375, **24.** 242n, 529, **25.** 191, 390
Francis II promised by, to attend wedding, **25.** 661
generosity of, makes him popular, **24.** 232
Genoese doge resembled by, **25.** 646
George III permits, through Carmarthen, to accept Order of St Hubert, **25.** 470
—— to be godfather to child of, with Mann as proxy, **24.** 199, 206n
Grafton's correspondence with, about making Mann a K.B., **22.** 339, 469, 546
grandfather's provision for, **35.** 195n
green ribbon of Thistle order expected by, **23.** 502, 508, 511, 513
Gustav III often entertained by, **25.** 457
HW considers, mad, **24.** 187
HW introduced to, by Dutens at Mrs Cosway's concert, **25.** 646
HW ridicules: for accepting foreign titles, **12.** 201, **24.** 529, **25.** 572, 606, 646; for generosity to Florentine populace, **24.** 242
Hamilton to exhibit collection at house of, **42.** 460
Handel's *Alexander's Feast* performed at villa of, followed by ball, **23.** 64
heralds deny Nassau arms to, **24.** 370
Hesketh, Lady, related to, **23.** 202–3
house taken by, in Florence, **23.** 429
imperial diploma of: held up for lack of pedigree, **24.** 353; received, **24.** 382
indolence of, keeps him away from England, **22.** 375
installation of Knights of St Hubert to be attended by, **25.** 568
invited to Pitti Palace gala, **25.** 50n
Jermy leaves legacy to, as a prince, **25.** 206
Joseph II gives principality to, **12.** 201, **24.** 298, 302n, 369–70
—— tells, of rift with Catherine II, **25.** 156n
Kent lieutenancy may go to D. of Dorset instead of, **22.** 374–5
Leghorn to be visited by, to greet D. of York, **22.** 171

Leopold asks D. of Gloucester to get honours for, 23. 502
—— favours, in quarrel with Young Pretender, 24. 245
—— receives, 22. 345n
——'s comptroller has beer and punch served to, 22. 379
—— tells: of Charles III's misunderstanding, 25. 32n; of Polish disturbances, 25. 44
—— visited by, in country, 23. 335
letter from, enclosed by Mann, 22. 165n
letter received by, about Ds of Kingston at Calais, 24. 202
letters to be sent to, at Frankfurt, before he reaches Vienna, 25. 661
*London Gazette* mentions confirmation of principality of, 25. 606
London house of, 42. 460
Mann complimented by, on Bath ribbon, 23. 9
—— dissuades, from appealing case with Young Pretender to higher court, 24. 245
—— fears he may be supplanted by, 25. 660–1
—— remonstrates with, on possible marriage to Florentine lady, 23. 457
——'s call from D. of Gloucester witnessed by, 24. 297
——'s correspondence with, 23, 335, 25. 646
——'s declaration witnessed by, 23. 63n
——'s dispatch communicated by, to Leopold, 25. 43–4
——'s parting with D. of Gloucester witnessed by, 23. 395
—— tells, that HW caused his promotion, 22. 376
—— tells Zoffany to put, in painting of Tribune, 24. 539
—— to be accompanied by, at investiture, 23. 60
—— to represent George III at baptism of child of, 24. 206n
—— urges, to return to England, 22. 438
—— would have given tips to servants of, at christening, 24. 219
Maria Louisa often accompanied by, 23. 429
marriage intentions announced by, 24. 38, 40, 46, 48
marriage of: happy, despite rumours, 24. 181–2, 190; may take him away from Mann, 24. 48; rumoured to end in separation, 24. 181–2, 187; to take place in France, 24. 94
Milan visited by, on way to England, 25. 641
Morelli formerly running footman to, 33. 587n
mother of: Grantham's daughter and coheiress, 24. 360n; pedigree of, awaited, 24. 353
musical farces of, at Poggio a Caiano before Tuscan Court, 23. 325–6
Nassau and Auverquerque cousins object to assumption of their names and arms by, 24. 369–70

Padua visited by, 43. 277
(?) Palazzo Peruzzi taken by, 23. 449n
palazzo rented by, at Florence, 23. 449
Pall Mall house taken by, 33. 522n
Parliamentary seat lost by, 21. 543
pension given by, to aunt's old friend, 23. 416
Pius VI might sell cardinal's hat to, 25. 572
—— should be asked by, for bishopric for son, 25. 606
plate and jewels to be fetched for, from England, 23. 449
plate kept in bank during minority of, 25. 661
price paid by, for princedom, 24. 370
principality of: does not give him ducal rank, 36. 132; must wait till Joseph II returns to Vienna, 24. 312
relative's letter to, shown to Mann, 23. 139
return of, to England, promised but unlikely, 22. 438
Rome visited by, 24. 94, 251
servant of, takes Mann's letter to Conway, 22. 345n
Seymour's attachment to Cts of Albany does not amuse, 24. 94–5
Seymour, Lady Caroline, afflicted by absence of, 23. 449
son's treatment of, should resemble treatment by Cowper of his own father, 24. 242
Spencer, stepbrother of, 43. 280
star ordered by, from London, 25. 568
stepbrother will be entertained by, 22. 173
stepmother of: dies, 25. 78, 84–5; jointure of, 25. 78, 84; releases family jewels to, by her death, 25. 84–5
Strange's drawings may be bought by, 22. 108n
Thistle order coveted by, 22. 554–5, 23. 502, 508, 513
title of, as Prince: dropped because it gives him no precedence, 24. 302n; 'Highness' not used by him, 24. 382; Orange dynasty opposes 'Nassau' for, 25. 78n; 'Overkirk' may be form of, 24. 353; ridiculous, 24. 302; to be P. Cowper, 24. 370
Tuscan Court to entertain, at Poggio a Caiano, 23. 296
Tuscan lady's family rejects marriage proposals of, on religious grounds, 23. 449, 457
valet-de-chambre of: hurries back to Florence, 22. 374; returns with Conway's letter to Mann, 22. 374; takes Mann's letter to HW in Paris, 22. 361, 366; took Conway's letter through Paris without stopping for HW's, 22. 380
Villa Palmieri acquired by, 20. 191n
wife of: 11. 136n; given money and diamond necklace by, on son's birth, 24. 232; return to England will probably be urged by family of, 25. 353; rumoured to be separating from him, 24. 181–2, 187
York, D. of, entertained by, 22. 173, 213, 223

[Clavering Cowper, George Nassau, *continued*]
—— told by, to help Mann become K.B., **22.**
318
Young Pretender's quarrel with, over Floren-
tine house, **24.** 201, 245, 255
Zoffany's painting of Tribune correctly in-
cludes, **24.** 529
Clavering Cowper, Hon. Peter Leopold Louis
Francis Nassau (1778–1837), 5th E. Cowper:
Carder, Mrs, to accompany, **25.** 151
father sends, to England to be educated, **22.**
363n, **25.** 391n
Claverly, ——:
Mitchell sends, with news of Palzig, **21.** 316n
Claveyson, Marquise de. *See* Tournon, Rose-
Marie-Hélène de
Clavières, Comte de. *See* Guasco, Octavien de
Claxby, Lincs:
Markham of, **1.** 6n
Clay, Sir John (d. before 1465):
(?) in Margaret of Anjou's escort, **14.** 73
Clay Hall, near Windsor:
Herschels move from, to Slough, **33.** 569n
Claymore; claymores:
English killed by Scottish rebels with, **19.**
116n
verses mention, **30.** 126
Claypole, John (d. 1688), Cromwell's son-in-
law:
house built by, **1.** 129n
Claypole, Mrs John. *See* Cromwell, Elizabeth
Clayton, Jasper (d. 1743), Lt-Gen.:
killed at Dettingen, **18.** 258
mob hails, **35.** 39
Clayton, Lady Louisa. *See* Fermor, Lady Louisa
Clayton, Sir Richard (d. 1828), Bt:
Ten Hove's *Mémoires* translated by, **15.** 275n
Clayton, Samuel, auctioneer:
HW buys Berkeley Sq. house through, **33.**
67n, **34.** 250
Clayton, Thomas (fl. 1692–1711):
Dryden's *Alexander's Feast* set to music by,
**28.** 345n
Clayton, William (1671–1752), cr. (1735) Bn
Sundon; M.P.:
election of, invalidated by presence of sol-
diers, **17.** 220n, 252
government post lost by, **17.** 332
Parliamentary membership of, corrected, **43.**
241
salary of, as commissioner of the Treasury,
**17.** 333n
testimony against, about Westminster election, **17.** 246
wife of, **9.** 193n, **14.** 96n, **17.** 276
'Clearcake':
HW's term for Hobart, **19.** 263
Clearwell, Glos:
Wyndham of, **28.** 302n
Cleaver; cleavers:
in Arlington St, **18.** 96
London streets full of, **17.** 196
used by mob, **33.** 340

whetting of, **30.** 141
*See also* Marrow-bones and cleavers
Cleeve, Anne (d. 1833), m. (1765) Sir George
Yonge, 5th Bt, 1755:
Hotham, Miss, entertains, **12.** 154
Cleeve, Bourchier (1715–60), pewterer:
Dutch pictures bought by, **21.** 173
house at Foot's Cray built by, **21.** 173n
Cleitus (ca 380–328 *or* 327 B.C.), Macedonian
general:
Selwyn compared with, **30.** 216–17
Cleland, John (1709–89), writer:
*Fanny Hill* by, **20.** 134n, 149
Cleland, William (ca 1674–1741):
widow of, hates Walpoles for dismissing him,
**35.** 94
Cleland, Mrs William. *See* Du Pass, ——
*Clélie. See under* Scudéry, Madeleine de
Clement VII (Giuliano de' Medici) (d. 1534),
pope:
Cellini said to have made silver bell for, **28.**
38n, **35.** 477n
——'s medal of, **25.** 215n
Florence tries to escape usurpation by, **21.**
233n
HW's verses on, **37.** 97
statue commissioned by, **28.** 472n
Wolsey's treating with, **2.** 259
Clement VIII (1536–1605), pope, 1592:
Cardinal San Marcello's intimacy with, **15.**
80n
James I not excommunicated by, **15.** 80
——'s correspondence with, **15.** 80
Clement X (Emilio Altieri) (1590–1676), pope:
medal of, **1.** 319, 321
nephew of, **13.** 216n
Clement XI (Gianfrancesco Albani) (1649–
1721), pope, 1700:
Albani, Cardinal, nephew of, **13.** 208n, **18.**
467n
cardinals created by, **13.** 212n, 220
Colonna family not permitted by, to sell antique fragments, **13.** 213
(?) Maintenon, Mme de, receives gift from,
**10.** 294
Old Pretender given use of Palazzo Muti by,
**19.** 85n
—— officially recognized by, **17.** 9n
——'s marriage conducted by, **25.** 448n
——'s pension settled by, **21.** 391n
Unigenitus, bull of, condemns Jansenism, **5.**
12n, **20.** 337n
Clement XII (Lorenzo Corsini) (1652–1740),
pope, 1730:
bull of, against freemasons, renewed, **19.** 364n
cardinals created by, **13.** 220, 227n
(?) Charles III acknowledged by, as Great
Prince of Tuscany, **22.** 406
death of, **13.** 9, 203n, 236, **17.** 4n, **37.** 46
German baron tells, that the Roman sight
which he'd like to see is a pope's death,
**20.** 546
HW not presented to, **14.** 240

Hamerani medallist to, **17**. 18n

inability of soul of, to find rest, blamed for cold weather, **13**. 217

Old Pretender officially recognized by, **17**. 9n

St-Aignan granted private audiences with, **17**. 12n

Tencin presents credentials to, **17**. 12n

Clement XIII (Carlo Rezzonico) (1693–1769), pope, 1758:

abbés' appearance and dress regulated by, **21**. 224, 230

Acciaioli's valet-de-chambre returns letter to, **21**. 340–1

Albani, Alessandro, ordered by, to tell Mann that D. of York will be welcomed at Rome, **22**. 171

Albani, Giovanni, communicates with, about Young Pretender's return, **22**. 368, 369n, 389

Almada has audience with, at Cavalchini's and Corsini's insistence, **21**. 423

—— joins Bourbon ministers against Parma brief of, **23**. 26

——'s secretary's book burnt by order of, **21**. 476–7

Aubeterre, Azpuru, and Orsini bring pressure upon, **23**. 10, 15–16, 35

Aubeterre, Azpuru, Breteuil, and Cardinal York persecute, to make him acknowledge Young Pretender, **22**. 386

Aubeterre told by, that he will acknowledge Young Pretender if Louis XV does, **25**. 526

Avignon and Benevento unlikely to be regained by, **23**. 38

Avignon, Benevento, Castro, and Ronciglione would be sacrificed by, to his brief, **23**. 10, 24

Benedict XIV's Jesuit policy not to be changed by, **21**. 340n

——'s pension to Cardinal York confirmed by, **21**. 391, 392

bishop sent by, in armed ship to Corsica, **21**. 393

Bourbon family compact terrifies, **23**. 38

Bourbon family support D. of Parma against, **23**. 10

Bourbons and Francis III may unite to plunder, **23**. 35

—— menace temporal possessions of, **23**. 24

cardinals advise, not to negotiate in Almada's presence, **21**. 425

cardinals' costume regulated by, **23**. 18

cardinals created by, **21**. 304, 333–4

cardinals may be created by, **21**. 304

Catherine II to have been congratulated by, **22**. 76

Cavalchini made *datario* by, **21**. 224

Cenci and Caprara excluded by, from cardinals, **21**. 333–4

Charles III corresponds with, about expelling Jesuits to Italy, **22**. 509n, 517–18, 532

——'s edict and parliament of Paris's *arrêt* against brief of, **23**. 10

—— to be complimented by, as K. of Spain, **21**. 280

Clement XIV made cardinal by, **23**. 117

Corsica might have been given by, to Old Pretender, **21**. 418

Corsican situation eclipses, **23**. 45

Corsini advises, **21**. 424, 425, 426

—— manages election of, **21**. 219n

courier from Lisbon expected by, **21**. 430

crucifix addressed by, **23**. 46

dancing forbidden by, except at balls for D. of York, **22**. 229, 234

death of: **4**. 29n; blow to Jesuits, **22**. 331, **23**. 92; expected, **21**. 291–2; opportune, **23**. 88

despised, **21**. 304

election of, **21**. 219–20

England not to be offended by, because she treats Roman Catholics leniently, **22**. 386

English squadron might chastise, if he acknowledges Young Pretender, **22**. 386

experience of, in maintaining dignity in difficult circumstances, **22**. 236

family of, honoured by Venice, **21**. 230

Ferdinand of Naples accused by, of dumping Jesuits on him, **22**. 573

Ferdinand of Parma's edict rebukes, **23**. 10

——'s rift with, **4**. 36

Fiore falsified briefs of, **22**. 327–8

fish shortage might compel, to allow meat in Lent, **22**. 101

France and Spain applauded by, for disregarding Young Pretender, **22**. 399

France and Spain may urge, to acknowledge Young Pretender, **22**. 369

French cardinals not supported by Austria in opposing, **21**. 219n

Genoese quarrels with, **21**. 392–3, 394n, 405, 410, 411–12, 422

George III treated with deference by, in rejecting Young Pretender, **22**. 393

HW asks if Wilkes prompts, to annihilate Jesuits, **22**. 290

HW calls, 'old dervish,' **22**. 394

HW glad to see France and Spain carting, **23**. 32

HW hopes, will not be exiled to England with Jesuits, **22**. 34

HW tells Mann not to bother about, **21**. 238

HW wants pasquinades about, **21**. 491

health of: asthma and blindness, **21**. 291–2; fever, **22**. 331; fit, **22**. 331, 380; ill, **21**. 236

Hillsborough credits Mann with refusal of, to recognize Young Pretender, **22**. 429

Jesuits and nephews will alone regret, **22**. 331

Jesuits befriended by, **21**. 308, 424, 426, **22**. 515, 517, 527, 574

—— complain to, of persecution, **21**. 230

—— recommended by, in letter to Portuguese king, **21**. 340–1

—— suffer from rejection by, **22**. 527, 535–6, 545

—— unconcerned with refusal of, to recognize Young Pretender, **22**. 406

[Clement XIII, *continued*]

——unwillingly accepted by, because of financial burden, **22.** 515–16, 517–18, 573–4

José Manoel may be appeased by, through Torreggiani, **21.** 348–9

—— mortifies, by making him yield about Jesuits, **21.** 383

——refers Jesuits' conspiracy to, **21.** 308

——'s correspondence with, **21.** 340–1, 383, 423–4

—— sends Jesuits to, **21.** 340

—— unable to reach possessions of, **23.** 26

Joseph II may dethrone, **23.** 117

—— not likely to hold stirrup of, **22.** 555

lacks character, **21.** 230

lacks money to buy corn abroad, for people, **22.** 446

Leopold quarrels with, over disposal of church plate, **22.** 475–6

Loredan, Doge Francesco, sends Venetian Senate's decision to, **21.** 230n

Mabillon's *Annales* dedicated to, by Venturini, **18.** 392n

major-domo of, gives presents to D. of York, **22.** 229

Mann combats pressure upon, for recognition of Young Pretender, **22.** 388–9, 396–7, **24.** 244, 255n

—— notified of Young Pretender's reception by, **22.** 516–17

——'s account of Portuguese quarrel of, diverts Chute and Bentley, **21.** 428

——'s letters to Albani shown to, **22.** 388–9, 408

—— to thank, for attentions to D. of York, **22.** 179

Maria Carolina, Leopold, and Maria Louisa not to visit, at Rome, despite preparations, **23.** 2

mass and procession ordered by, for destruction of Polish dissidents, **22.** 577

medal of, **21.** 272, 278

ministers of, attacked in book by Almada's secretary, **21.** 476

mob surrounds coach of, and throws bad bread into it, **22.** 446

Modena may take Ferrara from, **23.** 45

nephews of: compliment Leopold, Maria Carolina, and Maria Louisa, **23.** 23; put him on diet to prolong his life and their revenues, **22.** 380; Trasteverini may stone, **22.** 229; will mourn his death, **22.** 331

nudities in paintings to be covered by order of, **21.** 292

Old Pretender asks, to omit funeral oration, **21.** 391

—— blessed by, **21.** 390, 392

—— recommends sons to, **21.** 391

——'s sons make over unto, their Silesian claims, **22.** 387n

Parma brief of, **23.** 26, 38, 399n

—— threatened by, with excommunication, **4.** 36, **22.** 582

party of, at Conclave of 1774, **24.** 59n

Polish dissidents opposed by, **22.** 574, 577

Portugal quarrels with, **21.** 422–4, 425–6, 428, 436–7

——'s abject devotion to, **21.** 430

printing of Portuguese *Sentença* at Rome forbidden by, **21.** 275n

Romagna's epidemic must concern, **21.** 359

sacraments administered to, **22.** 331

St Odile not summoned by, because he will not wait in Torreggiani's ante-chamber, **22.** 573

sayings of, **21.** 230

Schwartzenberg thanks, for civilities to Leopold, Maria Carolina, and Maria Louisa, **23.** 23

Sixtus V's treasure must be used by, **22.** 446, 448

Spain may take Castro and Ronciglione from, **23.** 45

Spaniards permitted by, to eat meat 4 days a week in Lent, **22.** 5

Spanish Court carts, **23.** 32

sturgeon the favourite food of, **22.** 327, 331, 380, **23.** 4

sturgeon will console, for parliament of Paris's support of Parma, **23.** 4

successor honours, by choosing his name, **23.** 117

tears of, consoled only by dish of sturgeon, **22.** 327

Torreggiani, Cardinal York, and Jesuits aid, against anti-Jesuit champions, **21.** 476

Torreggiani complains to, about Corsini, **21.** 425

Tron's dismissal from Vienna depends on Benedict XIV's parley with, **20.** 190n

Tuscany bullies, about ecclesiastical immunities, **22.** 449

Vatican visited by, when D. of York is at Monte Cavallo, **22.** 228

Venetian ambassador rebuked by, **21.** 230

Venice's correspondence from, ridiculous, **21.** 236–7

Walkinshaw, Mrs, banished by, **26.** 47

weeps, **21.** 477, **22.** 233, 327

women ordered by, to cover their faces in church, **21.** 292

York, Cardinal, corresponds with, about Young Pretender's recognition, **22.** 384, 386, 388

York, D. of, refuses to make concessions in order to see, **22.** 233

——'s welcome from, **22.** 171, 176–7, 179, 227, 228, 236

Young Pretender and Cardinal York received by, **22.** 516–17

Young Pretender assured by, of pension but not of royal honours, **22.** 368–9

—— not recognized by, from fear of Pitt, **30.** 216

——'s attempts to get royal honours from, **22.**

374, 384–7, 392–3, 394–5, 405–6, 408, 429, 23. 402, 24. 244, 25. 526
—— tells Albani to ask, for permission to return to Rome 22. 368
Clement XIV (Giovanni Vincenzo Antonio Ganganelli) (1705–74), pope, 1769:
abasement of, would counterbalance Catherine II's triumph, 23. 169
alleged letters of (Lettres intéressantes; Nouvelles lettres intéressantes), 31. 278, 35. 393–4
assassination and poison feared by, 23. 136
Avignon's and Benevento's restitution the prerequisite of, for Jesuits' suppression, 23. 477n
Bernis's negotiations with, over Jesuits, 23. 414
bishops and cardinals await mitres and hats from, 24. 39
body of, too putrefied to be dissected, 24. 42
Bontempi the sole confidant of, 24. 50
Bourbon Courts placated by, 23. 147
Bourbon ministers at Rome press, to dissolve Jesuits, 23. 214, 306
bowels of, break earthen pan with their fermentation, 24. 43
cardinals' hats to be conferred by, 24. 39
cardinals' poor relations with, 23. 147, 190, 214, 431, 24. 49–50
Charles III and Louis XV soothed by, 23. 190–1
Charles III's quarrel with, over Jesuits' suppression, 23. 214, 221, 527
Choiseul makes, pope, 23. 133
——'s fall accelerated by, 23. 372
——'s fall not due to, 5. 191
Christian VII's marriage could not be dissolved by, 23. 409
Clement XIII makes, cardinal, 23. 117
——'s name chosen by, 23. 117
Cumberland, D. and Ds of, to have been entertained by, 24. 559
Cumberland, D. of, accepts ship of, to take him to Toulon, 23. 566
—— received by, with royal honours, 23. 564
death of: attributed to poison, 24. 42–3, 49, 51, 75, 154, 25. 237, 32. 209, 212; deemed heaven's judgment for suppressing Jesuits, 24. 49; inconsequential, 24. 48; prevents his going insane, 24. 41; the only recent murder in Rome, 24. 154; will alarm Bourbons and cardinals, 24. 51
does not pretend to be a bigot, 23. 436
election and description of, 23. 117–18
England thinks no more of, 23. 128
—— will be glad of diverting news of, 23. 121
family of, more favourably described now he is pope, 23. 123, 125
Ferdinand of Parma blessed by, 23. 518
——'s rift with Charles III to be mediated by, 23. 473n
foreign ministers' relations with, 23. 123, 428, 430

France and Spain may be disappointed in, but HW is not, 23. 157
France may offer Avignon to, 23. 306
—— restrains authority of, 23. 399
Franciscan, from duchy of Urbino, 23. 117
French and German letters ask about health of, 23. 43–4
French Jesuit said to have written against election of, 23. 526–7
Gloucester, D. of, welcomed by, at Rome, 23. 343, 348, 388, 389
guards no longer outdistanced by, when riding horseback, 23. 526
HW asks about, 23. 212
HW rallies Cole about, 2. 47, 48
HW thanks Mann for description of, 23. 125
hated, 24. 49
health of: bled for loss of rest and appetite, 23. 215; impaired, 24. 29; scurvy and suppression of urine, 24. 39; takes waters, 23. 428, 430
Jenkins, Thomas, has free access to, 20. 174n
Jesuits allegedly murder, 24. 51, 75
—— cannot be saved by, 23. 420
——' crimes may be published by, 23. 533
——' papers enrage, 23. 517
——' relations with, before suppression, 23. 118, 135, 157, 214, 372, 511
——' revenues in Bologna legation granted by, to city under Malvezzi, 23. 494
——' suppression by, 5. 302, 401, 23. 506–8, 511, 523, 527
——' suppression delayed by, 23. 147, 472, 477, 487, 493, 494
——' wealth sought by, 23. 516–17
Kingston, Ds of, favoured by, 24. 6–7, 21, 398
lack of bigotry of, 22. 436
Leopold's dispute with, over Arezzo bishopric, 23. 504
Louis XV may be influenced by, through Mme du Barry and Ps Louise, 23. 372, 430–1
—— will send courier to, to ask absolution, 24. 8
Louise, Princesse, alleged 'agent' of, 23. 321, 372, 413n, 430–1
Mann might consult, about England's affairs in India, 23. 392
medal struck by, on reconciliation with Portugal, 23. 221–2
Moñino threatens, for not expelling Jesuits, 23. 413, 428, 430, 446
nephews of, in humble posts, 23. 117
Norfolk, Ds of, partisan of, 5. 361, 23. 485
old Roman princesses offended by, 23. 431
old women, instigated by Jesuits, said to have killed, 24. 41–2
Palafox canonization may be resumed by, 23. 123
Pallavicini chosen by, as secretary of state, 23. 118
Parma pretensions relinquished by, 23. 518

[Clement XIV, *continued*]

Petroni chamberlain and master of the horse to, **17.** 9n

physicians do not permit, to go on his *villeggiatura*, **24.** 39

Pius VI not so politely educated as, **24.** 275

poison allegedly administered to, in chocolate at Vatican on Holy Thursday, **24.** 49

poison feared by, because of Jesuits, **23.** 136, 480

Portugal detached by, from Spanish and French negotiations, **23.** 221

prophecies of death frighten, **24.** 29, 39–40, 41–2

Ricci coldly received by, **23.** 135

rides horseback, **23.** 526

rôle of, in *La Passion des Jésuites*, **5.** 315

Rome receives, well, on his return, **23.** 526

secretary of briefs to foreign ministers removed by, as Jesuit supporter, **23.** 123

Sixtus V imitated by, **23.** 157

Spanish minister assured by, of Palafox's canonization, **23.** 123

verses on, **5.** 401

*Vie de*, owned by Mme du Deffand, **8.** 35n

wax mask over face of, **24.** 43

Clement, Anne (d. 1813), m. Gen. William Edmestone:

Bury St, St James's, the address of, **36.** 279

church attended by, **36.** 279

Dysart visited by, at Ham House, **36.** 328

Gloucester, Ds of, corresponds with, **36.** 263, 285, 327–30

HW's correspondence with, **36.** 156–7, 268–9, 279

HW tells: to accompany the bereaved E. of Dysart, **36.** 268–9; to call on him, **36.** 279

(?) love affair of, **32.** 186–7

Waldegrave's improvement to be reported to, **36.** 262

Waldegrave, Lady Anna Horatia, to sleep with, at Sir Edward Walpole's, **36.** 325

Clement, Dorothy (ca 1715–ca 1739), Sir Edward Walpole's mistress:

children of: **9.** 13n, 302n, **11.** 24n, 56n, **16.** 310n, **17.** 209n; Montagu predicts brilliant future for, **9.** 302

name of, corrected, **43.** 140

Secker, Mrs, rescues, from dustcart, **43.** 111

Walpole, Sir Edward, tired of, **17.** 240

Clément, Jacques (1567–89), assassin:

forgotten, **12.** 117

modern counterparts of, **20.** 287, 294, 388, **21.** 48

Clement, Jane (ca 1722–98), sister of Dorothy Clement:

Baddeley wants to see, **36.** 63

Customs clerkship deemed by, unsuitable for Vilett, **36.** 89–90

Dysart visited by, at Ham, **36.** 63

Gloucester, Ds of, corresponds with, **36.** 323–7, 330

HW's correspondence with, **36.** 277–8

HW wants, to call on him, **36.** 156

Hertford tries to get Windsor lodging for, **36.** 323

Keppel, Bp, writes advice to, **36.** 321–2

'often knocking at the gate of death,' **34.** 230n

Reed and Bp of Exeter intercede for, **36.** 320

Waldegrave, Lady Maria, makes comment to, **32.** 412

Waldegrave daughters to be supervised by, **24.** 76n

Walpole, Sir Edward, corresponds and quarrels with, **36.** 317–21

Clément, Jean-Marie-Bernard (1742–1812), writer:

*De Despréaux à Voltaire* by, **5.** 195

*Médée* by, **7.** 115

*Mon dernier mot* by, **6.** 181

Clement, Margaret, wife of Hammond Clement:

Walpole, Sir Edward, leaves annuity and house to, **36.** 156n, 317n

Clément de Ris, Louis:

(?) attends session of parliament of Paris, **8.** 173

Clemente de Arostegui, Alfonso, Spanish minister to Rome 1747–8, to Naples 1753–70:

in council at Naples, **21.** 325

Clementina (1777–1801), archduchess, m. (1797) Francis I, later K. of the Two Sicilies:

birth of, **24.** 291

living, **25.** 549

*Clementina. See under* Kelly, Hugh

Clements, Mr:

at Primate's Hill, Dublin, **37.** 333

Clements, Rt Hon. Nathaniel (d. 1777), Irish deputy vice-treasurer:

son of, **10.** 107

Clements, Robert (1732–1804), cr. (1783) Bn, (1793) Vct, (1795) E. of Leitrim; M.P.:

Montagu deplores rumoured engagement of, to Lady Anne Seymour-Conway, **10.** 107

peerage of, **25.** 433

Clementson, John (d. 1805), deputy serjeant-at-arms to House of Commons:

Crosby accompanied by, **23.** 291

Clent, Staffs:

Amphlett of, **13.** 173n, **28.** 480n

Cleopatra (69–30 B.C.), Q. of Egypt:

Antony slung into monument of, **32.** 147

—— toasts, in bumper of mother of pearl, **11.** 295

bed at SH would become, **28.** 42

bust of, in Cottonian collection, **40.** 306n

Grafton, Ds of, dresses as, at masquerade, **22.** 148

loves of, **5.** 187

medals of, **15.** 14

portrait supposedly of, **9.** 6

Cleopatra Thea (d. ca 121 B.C.), Q. of Syria, 126 B.C.:

Catherine II comparable to, **22.** 54

'Cleopatra':

character in *Ballet de la paix*, **18.** 496

*Cleopatra. See Cléopâtre*

*Cléopâtre. See under* Costes de la Calprenède, Gautier de

Cleosa. *See* Fregosa, Rosa

Clephane, Dr John (d. 1758), physician:
Bouverie pays travelling expenses of, **17.** 70
Chute's fan disliked by, **17.** 116–17
Florence visited by, **17.** *63*, 67, 70, 97, 100, 116–17, 132, **18.** 479
HW's statue investigated by, **17.** 317
languages not known by, **17.** 70
Mann entertains, **17.** 70, 116–17
—— not courted by, **17.** 97
(?) —— ridicules behaviour and costume of, **17.** 132
——'s guest house occupied by, **17.** 67, 146, 154
Mansell accompanied by, **17.** *63*, 70, **43.** 235
physician, **17.** 100
Pisa visited by, **17.** 67
Rome visited by, **17.** 154, 317
silent, **17.** 67, 70, 116
Turkey merchant's correspondence with, about Cartagena, **17.** 71

Clerc, Le. *See* Le Clerc

Clere, Lady. *See* Boleyn, Alice

Clere, Sir Edward (d. 1606), Kt:
Blickling sold by, **2.** 32n, 163, 176

Clere, Sir John (d. 1557):
Blickling comes to, **2.** 32n

Clere, Sir Robert (d. 1529), Kt:
heir of, **2.** 32n
marriage of, **2.** 163, 176

Clérembault, Mme de, the younger:
death of, **6.** 214

Clérembault, Mlles de:
(?) Du Deffand, Mme, quoted by, to L'Isle, **8.** 177
——'s opinion of, **4.** 243
(?) —— taken from Gennevilliers to Paris by, **8.** 177
—— to depend on, for company, **3.** 385
Gennevilliers visited by, **8.** 177
social relations of, in Paris, **3.** *350–1*, **4.** 243, **7.** 327

Clerfayt, Comte de. *See* Croix de Drumez, François-Sébastien-Charles-Joseph de

Clergy:
cabals usually instigated by, **24.** 225
English, *see under* Church of England
French: admire Burke's *Reflections*, **34.** 99n; assembly of, **5.** 214, **6.** 85, 168, 183, 190, 211, **7.** 230; at odds with Louis XV, **20.** 199, 287, 294; benefit of, **11.** 164; Burke's pamphlet overlooks violation of consciences of, **11.** 277; controversy between French parliaments and, **31.** 69; forced to choose between starving and perjury, **31.** 361; HW bored by affairs of, **10.** 177; Loménie de Brienne considered first man of, **31.** 114; may be crushed by Revolution, **42.** 251; prefer a royal to a popular yoke, **11.** 28; Rousseau imagines, are among his persecu-
tors, **29.** 48; satires on, **31.** 69; useless, **11.** 175
French émigré: HW puts his name to second subscription for, **31.** 383; More, Hannah, attacked for supporting, **31.** 388–9; More, Hannah, publishes *Remarks on the Speech of M. Dupont* for relief of, **31.** 381
HW calls, pious rogues, **24.** 516
HW mistrusts sincerity of, **11.** 288
HW satirizes, in verse, **20.** 134
HW's low opinion of, **25.** 441
kings' infallibility upheld by, **23.** 292
preach against propagation and not against lust for destruction, **24.** 516
*See also* Clergyman; Priest
*See also under* Church of England; Church of Scotland; Roman Catholic Church

Clergyman; clergymen:
at Cambridge, rebukes daughter for praying by light of farthing candle, **17.** 85
at Drayton, exhibits house to HW and Cole, **10.** 90
at Stowe, directs Berwicks to inn, **10.** 131
Balmerinoch attended by, **19.** 301
costume of, **10.** 70n
dissenting, Sandwich's affair with coffee-girl observed by, **22.** 284
English, in Italy: advises Mann to drink wine to bring on gout, **22.** 335; Mann offends, by not asking him to say grace, **18.** 162; opera not attended by, on Sunday, **18.** 162; picture of Catiline's conspiracy mistaken by, for Lord's Supper, **18.** 41, 62
fears scandal for son's execution, **40.** 194
HW's reflections on advantages of marrying, **25.** 424
Hulse carries, in chariot to avoid suspicion of unorthodoxy, **30.** 30
mad Leviathan compared by, to Sir Robert Walpole, **17.** 197
Osborns', disapproves of *Mysterious Mother*, **10.** 297
Rigby fights with, on Sunday, **30.** 93, 330
Shaftesbury's letters to, **16.** 369
tallies at Townshend family's faro-playing, **30.** 69
Townshend, Vct, accompanied by, **21.** 138
*See also* Preacher; Priest
*See also under* Church of England; Roman Catholic Church

*Clergyman's Vademecum, The. See under* Johnson, John

Clerici, Marchesa. *See* Visconti, Fulvia (d. 1777)

Clerici, Antonio Giorgio (1715–68), Marchese:
ambassador to Conclave of 1758, **18.** 252n
child wanted by, **18.** 252
regiment of, reinforces Lobkowitz, **19.** 30

Clerk, Sir Alexander of Balbirnie, co. Fife:
daughter of, **34.** 189

Clerk, John (1728–1812) of Eldin; draughtsman and writer:
HW declines Buchan's offer of etchings by, **15.** 192

Clerk, Magdalen (fl. ca 1631), m. 1 Edward Bruce, 1st Lord Kinloss and Bn Bruce of Kinlosse; m. 2 (1616) Sir James Fullerton: letter of, to grandson, 34. 189

Clerk (or Clerke, Clark, or Clarke), Robert (d. 1797), army officer:
Bute favours, despite court martial, 37. 582n
Dury gets faulty intelligence from, in expedition against France, 37. 574–5
Rochefort fortifications spied on by, 7. 357
Wales, Ps of, favours, 37. 582
wife of, 9. 121n

Clerk. See also Clarck; Clark; Clarke; Clerke

Clerk; clerks:
at All Souls, 35. 388
customs, embezzles, 35. 493
House of Commons's, forces, to sit in empty halls, 25. 572
merchant's, Furnese bred as, 30. 305n
Newcastle, D. of, restores, to offices, 22. 323
parish, lectern for, in chapel, 35. 119
postal, see under Post Office

Clerke, Lady:
SH visited by, 12. 233

Clerke, Capt. Charles (d 1779):
King succeeds, as capt. of the Discovery, 33. 436n

Clerke, Clementina (b. 1776), m. (1791) Richard Vining Perry:
elopement of, from school in Bristol, 11. 253
More, Hannah, interested in, 11. 253
wealth of, 11. 253

Clerke. See also Clarck; Clark; Clarke; Clerk

Clerkenwell:
Albemarle, Ds of, lives in, 25. 564n

Clerk of the Buck-Warrant:
Lyttelton gives place of, to Bower, 35. 176

Clerk of the Closet:
Hales becomes, to Augusta, Ps of Wales, 29. 347

Clerk of the Estreats:
HW fêted on being called to the bar as, 43. 169
HW offers to sell place of, to Bn Holland, 41. 209

Clerk of the Green Cloth. See Fanshawe, Simon (1716–77); Morice, Humphrey (1723–85)

Clerk of the Hanaper. See under Hanaper

Clerk of the Pells:
Burke wants his son to be, 33. 345n, 42. 24–8
Irish: Bubb Dodington is, 21. 75; Fox, Henry, becomes, after Bubb Dodington's death, 21. 75; value of, 21. 75n
Walpole, Sir Edward, was, 17. 209n, 25. 462n

Clerk of the Pipe:
Shelley to have reversion of, after Arundel, 21. 26

Clermont. Bn. See Fortescue, Chichester S. P. (1823–98); Fortescue, William Henry (1722–1806)

Clermont, Bns and Vcts. See Murray, Frances Cairnes (ca 1733–1820)

Clermont, Comte de. See Bourbon-Condé, Louis de (1709–71)

Clermont, Cts of. See Murray, Frances Cairnes (ca 1733–1820)

Clermont, E. of. See Fortescue, William Henry (1722–1806)

Clermont, Marquise de. See Lameth, Marie-Angélique de; Rohan-Chabot, Marie-Sylvie de (1729–1807)

Clermont, Vct. See Fortescue, William Henry (1722–1806)

Clermont, Vcts. See Murray, Frances Cairnes (ca 1733–1820)

Clermont, Jean-Baptiste-Charles-François (1728–92), Chevalier de, later Marquis de Clermont d'Amboise and de Renel; diplomatist:
ambassador to Naples, 6. 87n, 89–90
(?) estate of, seized after his death, 34. 174
formerly ambassador to Portugal, 6. 89–90
HW describes, 7. 281
Naples diverted by, 24. 280
sings, 7. 281, 297, 298
social relations of, in Paris, 7. 281, 297, 298

Clermont, Jean-François (1717–1807), called Ganif; French painter:
(?) cabinet at Sceaux painted by, 7. 322, 8. 57, 114
HW's library ceiling at SH painted by, 35. 79–80, 171, 173

Clermont (in Picardy, France):
Au Cigne (or Cygne) inn at, 7. 353, 370
court to be held at, 5. 30n
Fitz-James near, 6. 464n
HW at, 4. 273, 315, 7. 260, 333, 353, 399, 39. 8–9
HW buys knife at, 7. 399
HW writes from, 4. 272, 273, 6. 218, 218–19, 7. 390, 39. 8–9
Louis XVI and Marie-Antoinette said to be taken at, 11. 298
suitable for overnight stay, 37. 40

Clermont d'Amboise, Marquis de. See Clermont, Jean-Baptiste-Charles-François de

Clermont d'Amboise, Diane-Jacqueline-Louise-Josèphe de (1733–1804), m. 1 (1753) Marie-François-Auguste de Goyon-de-Matignon, Comte de Gacé; m. 2 (1766) Pierre-Charles-Étienne Maignard, Marquis de la Vaupalière:
affection of, for husband, cools, 5. 210
Durfort, Chevalier de, embarrassed by visit of, 6. 2
HW entertains, at SH, 4. 236n, 10. 278
marriage of, to La Vaupolière, 3. 84
Monaco, Ps of, accompanied by, to Belle-chasse, 4. 438
Naples to be visited by, 5. 210
sings, 7. 298
social relations of, in Paris, 7. 280, 297, 298, 302, 306, 310
son of, marries, 5. 210, 225
son's death to be broken to, 6. 2

Clermont d'Amboise, Thomassine-Thérèse de (b. 1746), m. (1761) Jacques-Philippe de Choiseul, Comte de Stainville:
arrested and taken to convent at Nancy, **3.** *217*–18, 218–19, 225, 226–7, **39.** 224n
daughter of, **4.** 299n
Lauzun's conduct with, **3.** 242
social relations of, with Comtesse de Valentinois, **3.** 217
to have danced at Mirepoix ball, **3.** 217, 218
Clermont-Dampierre, Claude-Catherine de (1543–1603), m. Albert de Gondi, Duc de Retz:
tomb of, **7.** 285
Clermont-en-Argonne (France):
Nubecourt near, **38.** 495
Clermont-Gallerande, Comtesse de. *See* Bragelongne, Marie-Charlotte de
Clermont-Gallerande, Armand-Henri (1688–1776), Comte de:
(?) wife of, dies, **32.** 258
Clermont-Montoison, Marquise de. *See* Cléron, Charlotte-Louise de
Clermont-Tonnerre, Vicomtesse de. *See* Bernard de Boulainvilliers, Anne-Marie-Louise
Clermont-Tonnerre, Charles-Henri-Jules (1720–94), Comte (later Duc) de:
dances at ball in honour of Dauphin's marriage, **4.** 410
Clermont-Tonnerre, Gaspard de (1688–1781), Maréchal de Tonnerre, Marquis de Vauvillars:
Bourbon-Busset's marriage attended by, **5.** *349*
grandson of, marries, **7.** 109
Maillebois receives Louis XV's judgment from, **23.** 284n
——'s appointment protested by, **6.** 322–3
social relations of, in Paris, with: Forcalquier, Mme de, **5.** 349; Maximilian, **6.** 156
Clermont-Tonnerre, Gaspard-Paulin (1753–1806), Vicomte de:
marriage of, **7.** 109
Clermont-Tonnerre, Jean-Louis-Aynard de (1724–1800), abbé:
Bourbon-Busset's marriage attended by, **5.** 349
social relations of, with Mme de Forcalquier, **5.** 349
Clermont-Tonnerre, Stanislas (1747–92), Comte de:
(?) estates of, seized after his death, **34.** 174
Cléron, Charles-Louis-Bernard de (1770–1846), Comte d'Haussonville:
mother loves, **7.** 107
Cléron, Charlotte-Louise de (1773–1853), m. (1801) Anne-Charles, Marquis de Clermont-Montoison:
mother loves, **7.** 107
Cléron, Joseph-Louis-Bernard de (d. 1806), Comte d'Haussonville:

Choiseul's social relations with, **6.** 441
Du Deffand, Mme, has good opinion of, **4.** 63, 68
Haussonville, Comtesse de, loves, **7.** 107
made grand louvetier, **7.** 443
marriage of, **4.** 63, 68, 72
sister of, **4.** 338
Cléron, Marie-Anne-Victoire de (d. 1826), m. (1803) Gabriel-Elzéar-Joseph de Rosières, Comte de Sorans:
mother loves, **7.** 107
Cléron, Marie-Jeanne-Thérèse de, m. (1749) Charles-François-Antoine, Marquis de Lénoncourt:
Du Deffand, Mme, gives opinion of, **4.** 338
relatives of, **4.** 338
social relations of, with Mme de Meinières, **4.** 338
Clerval. *See* Clairval
Cletzlaw. *See* Czaslau
Cleve (*or* Kleve *or* Cleves) (Germany):
army of observation to contain troops retiring out of, **21.** 73n
Conway's letter postmarked at, **37.** 133
Ferdinand crosses Rhine from, to Gelderland, **21.** 222n
Ferdinand reaches, **21.** 223n
Karl Wilhelm Ferdinand captures, **38.** 77
Voltaire asks for asylum in, **3.** 110n
Cleveland, Ds of. *See* Finch, Lady Henrietta (ca 1705–42); Pulteney, Anne (1663–1746); Villiers, Barbara (1641–1709)
Cleveland, D. of:
Grafton, D. of, may inherit title of, **24.** 5
*See also* Fitzroy, Charles (1662–1730); Fitzroy, William (1698–1774)
Cleveland. *See also* Cleland; Clevland
'Cleveland.' *See under* Prévost d'Exiles, Antoine-François
Cleveland, Yorks:
Blackburne, archdeacon of, **29.** 19n
Cleveland Court *or* Row, St James's, London:
Bridgwater's house in, **33.** 351n
Gisborne lives in, **14.** 158n
Grantham's office in, **42.** 36
Musgrave writes from, **40.** 312
Russell, Lady Rachael, marries at her house in, **19.** 189n
Selwyn addressed in, **30.** 277
—— dies in, **11.** 182n, **30.** 283
—— ill at his house in, **34.** 6
—— reclaims house in, from nephew, **33.** 236n
——'s 'paternal mansion' in, **33.** 236
Sundon, Bns, dies at house in, **17.** 276n, 277n
Clever, Mr:
social relations of, with HW, **7.** 268
Cleverness:
pretence of, **37.** 526
Cleves, Anne of. *See* Anne (1515–57)

Clèves, Marie de (1553–74), m. (1572) Henri de Bourbon, Prince de Condé:
affairs of, **5**. 187
Clèves; Cleves. *See also* Cleve
Clevland, John (ca 1706–63), M.P.: secretary to the Admiralty:
Admiralty orders, to send, to Byng, an extract of La Galissonnière's letter, **20**. 561n
Boscawen describes Battle of Lagos to, **21**. 326n
——'s letter to, **21**. 332n
Byng sends letters to, **20**. 560n
Rodney's letter to, in *London Gazette*, **21**. 309
Saunders notifies, of Cadiz attack, **22**. 12n
Clewer, Berks:
St Leonard's Hill at, **10**. 42n
Clichy (France):
Walpole, Hon. Thomas, has house at, **11**. 28n
Cliefden. *See* Cliveden
Clies, Henrietta (ca 1739–1829), m. (1764) George Brydges Rodney, cr. (1764) Bt, (1782) Bn Rodney:
husband's letter from, **25**. 79n
Clifden, Bn. *See* Agar, James
Clifden, Bns. *See* Martin, Lucia
Clifden, Vct. *See* Agar, Henry Welbore (1761–1836); Agar, James (1734–89)
Clifden, Vcts. *See* Martin, Lucia (ca 1732–1802); Spencer, Lady Caroline (1763–1813)
Clifden. *See also* Cliveden
Cliff; cliffs:
at Dover, *see under* Dover
Clifford, Bn. *See* Southwell, Edward
Clifford, Bns. *See* Berkeley, Isabel de (d. 1362); Langdale, Apollonia (ca 1755–1815)
Clifford, Mr (Dutchman):
SH visited by, **12**. 226, 227
Clifford, Lady Anne (d. 1592), m. (1577), Philip Wharton, 3d Bn Wharton:
portrait of, at Appleby Castle, **10**. 185
Clifford, Lady Anne (1590–1676), m. 1 (1609) Richard Sackville, 3d E. of Dorset; m. 2 (1630) Philip Herbert, 4th E. of Pembroke; Bns Clifford, s.j.:
Cole's opinion of, **10**. 336
Cromwell 'bullies,' **9**. 125
Dalrymple mistakenly attributes letters to, **15**. 82–3
HW's account of, **16**. 28n
Knole's associations with, **33**. 223
mother of, **1**. 38, **2**. 323n, **9**. 125
portraits of, at Appleby Castle, **10**. 185; at Castle Ashby, **10**. 336; at Knole, **35**. 133
portraits of family and household of, at Appleby Castle, **10**. 185
second marriage of, **9**. 125
Williamson's alleged letter from, **9**. 125, **10**. 336, **35**. 133
writings of, **9**. 125
Clifford, Lady Anne (1715–93), m. 1 (1739) James Joseph Mahony, Comte Mahony; m. 2 (1773) Don Carlo Severino:

Albano visited by, **17**. 28
Shrewsbury to accompany, **17**. 28
Clifford, George (1558–1605), 3d E. of Cumberland:
arms of, **1**. 149
Ferne's patron, **1**. 149
portrait of, at Appleby Castle, **10**. 185
print of, **1**. 355, 357, 360
wife of, **1**. 38n, **2**. 323n, **9**. 124n
Clifford, Isabelle, Lady. *See* Berkeley, Isabel de
Clifford, Lady Margaret (d. 1596), m. (1555) Henry Stanley, 4th E. of Derby:
portrait of, at Appleby Castle, **10**. 185
Clifford, Margaret, E. Ferrers's mistress:
Cornwallis excludes, from Ferrers's prison, **21**. 398
Ferrers's execution attended by, in hackney coach, **21**. 401
——'s gifts to, **21**. 397, 402
——'s mistress, ill-used by him, **21**. 396
Clifford, Martin (d. 1677), master of the Charterhouse:
HW alters first name of, **16**. 5
*Treatise of Human Reason, A*, by, **16**. 6n
Clifford, Hon. Mary (1731–97), m. (1766) Sir Edward Smythe, 4th Bt:
(?) at Chesterfield's assembly, **37**. 326
Norfolk, D. of, lives with, for 20 years, but leaves her a 'dirty legacy,' **32**. 384, **36**. 151
Clifford, Robert de (1305–44), Bn Clifford:
wife of, **1**. 148n
Clifford, Rosamond (d. ?1176), Henry II's mistress:
bower of: **1**. 91; HW alludes to bower at Nuneham as that of, **35**. 484
Clifford, Thomas de (1414–55), 8th Bn Clifford:
in Margaret of Anjou's escort, **14**. 73
Clifford, Thomas (1630–73), cr. (1672) Bn Clifford; treasurer of the Household:
portrait of, at Hagley, **35**. 148
Clifford:
descent of title of, **18**. 144
Clifford family:
Burlington leaves estates of, to Lady Charlotte Boyle, **20**. 545n
of Frampton, quarter Ayliffe arms with theirs, **30**. 136n
Clifford's Inn, London:
Clifford, Bns, owned, **1**. 148
Clifford St, Burlington Gardens, London:
Granville, Mrs, settles in, **35**. 108
Langlois of, **43**. 262
Clifton, Catherine (ca 1592–1637), m. 1 (1609) Esmé Stuart, 3d D. of Lennox; m. 2 (ca 1632) James Hamilton, 2d E. of Abercorn:
biographical information on, corrected, **43**. 195
HW corrects Dalrymple's spelling of name of, **15**. 74
Clifton, Lady Margaret. *See* Howard, Lady Margaret (d. 1433)

Clifton, Sir Robert (1690–1762), 5th Bt, 1731; K.B., 1725; M.P.:
Clifton Hall, seat of, **35.** 279n
Clifton, Devon:
Howe, M.P. for, **21.** 89
Clifton, Notts:
St Mary's church at, **35.** 279
Clifton, Somerset:
Agar, Diana, dies at, **12.** 158n
Warton visits, **31.** 281
Clifton, Westmorland:
Cumberland, D. of, attacks Murray's rearguard at, **19.** 186n
Clifton Hall, Notts:
HW visits, and describes it, **35.** 279
Clifton St, London:
Lyttelton dies at house in, **41.** 119n
Clignet, Jeanne-Pauline-Antoinette (d. 1775), m. (1760) Vincent-Joseph de la Fontaine-Solar, Comte de Solar:
accused of plot with Cazeaux against son, **7.** 134
Climate:
subject to Aquarius and Pisces, **1.** 164
Clinton, Bn. *See* Clinton, Edward (1624–57); Clinton, George (1745–52); Fortescue, Hugh (1696–1751); Pelham Clinton, Henry Fiennes (1750–78); Trefusis, Robert Cotton St John (1787–1832); Trefusis, Robert George William (1764–97)
Clinton, Bns. *See* Fitzgerald, Lady Elizabeth (ca 1528–90); Rolle, Margaret (1709–81)
Clinton, E. *See* Fortescue, Hugh
Clinton, Lady Arabella, m. Robert Rolle:
descendants of, may inherit Clinton barony, **18.** 143n
Orford, Cts of, descended from, **25.** 501n
Clinton, Edward (1624–57), styled Bn Clinton:
Van Dyck's alleged portrait of, supposedly sent to 3d E. of Orford, **25.** 151, 227, 240, 292, 298, 298n, 304, 501, 504
Clinton, George (1745–52), styled Bn Clinton:
birth of, **9.** 16n
Pelham secures Custom House reversion for, **20.** 18
Clinton, Henry (1684–1728), 7th E. of Lincoln:
portrait of, **10.** 338
wife never recovers from death of, **21.** 93
Clinton, Sir Henry (1730–95), K.B., 1777; Gen.; M.P.:
account by, in *London Gazette*, **24.** 408
alarmed for safety of New York, **29.** 151n
American attacks said to have been repulsed by, **24.** 331
American troops will not surrender to, **25.** 135
Arbuthnot's correspondence with, about attack on Rhode Island, **25.** 99n
army of: dares not leave New York despite alleged superiority, **39.** 333; in New York, estimated, **24.** 347n
Arnold and Putnam now rank with, **41.** 401

Arnold betrays others to, **33.** 239
——'s correspondence with, **29.** 124n
beaten back, **28.** 434n
Boston thought to be destination of, **24.** 81n, 98n
—— visited by, on *Cerberus*, **32.** 287n
Charleston captured by, **7.** 233n, **25.** 62, 70, **33.** 198n
Charleston expedition of, fails, **24.** 236
commander-in-chief, **29.** 90n
Conway brings bad news from, **29.** 161
Cornwallis's controversy with, printed, **25.** 370
——'s departure from, **39.** 383
Dalrymple sent by, to England with bad news, **25.** 88
death of, rumoured, **25.** 69–70
dispatches from, **32.** 318n
fort captured by, near New York, **24.** 500
groom to D. of Gloucester, **38.** 468
HW sails with, **7.** 314
Hillsborough sends news of victory of, **25.** 70
Howe succeeded by, as peace commissioner, **24.** 358n, 420n
humanity of, to captives, **32.** 400
Lee said to be captured by, in Carolina, **24.** 215
manifesto to Congress signed by, **24.** 426n
messengers of, delivered to Congress, **25.** 135
New England forces may join Washington to besiege, **24.** 342
news from, lacking, **25.** 52
New York may have been abandoned by, **24.** 416
—— reached by army of, after battle, **24.** 405, 408
not yet beyond the Delaware valley, **39.** 321
Pelham Clinton, Lord Thomas, to be aide-de-camp to, **24.** 263n
Philadelphia evacuated by, **28.** 409, **33.** 25n
proclamation by, causes alarm, **24.** 426–7
regiment of, now at Gibraltar, **24.** 377n
reinforcements for, **24.** 238n
returns to New York on news from Yorktown, **25.** 209n
Rhode Island's capture announced by, **32.** 348n
sails to America, **24.** 98
sheep and oxen captured by, **24.** 419
troops said to be embarked and disembarked by, for West Indies, **24.** 424
two forts taken by, in attempt to relieve Burgoyne, **24.** 339
Washington's mutinous troops will not join, **29.** 112
Clinton, Lord John. *See* Pelham Clinton, Lord John
Clinton, Lady Katherine (d. 1643), m. (1639) George Booth, cr. (1661) Bn Delamer:
HW thinks, died childless, **18.** 143n
Clinton, Lady Lucy (1721–63):
Claremont visited by, **30.** 22

[Clinton, Lady Lucy, *continued*]
dances at Robinson's ball, **37.** 114
HW anxious to be well thought of by, **30.** 76
HW does not find, at Henry Pelham's in Spring Garden, **30.** 22
HW pleased at recovery of, **30.** 76
HW's discussion of Lincoln would please, **30.** 22
HW well thought of by, **30.** 76
Clinton, Lady Margaret (d. 1688), m. Hugh Boscawen:
Clinton barony goes to descendants of, **18.** 143n
Clinton, Theophilus (ca 1600–67), 4th E. of Lincoln:
Clinton barony in family of, **18.** 143n
son of, **25.** 501n
Clinton, Lord Thomas. *See* Pelham Clinton, Lord Thomas
Clinton. *See also* Fiennes Clinton
Clinton, barony of:
HW explains descent of, **18.** 143n, **25.** 165
Orford, Cts of (Bns Walpole), heiress to, **17.** 360, 367, 389–90, 406, **18.** 126, **21.** 385, **25.** 151, 195, 226, 501n
Orford, 3d E. of, cannot transmit, **25.** 165
—— is expected to claim, **25.** 151, 157, 240, 304
Clinton, Fort. *See* Fort Clinton
Clinton family:
arms of, to be on Cts of Orford's monument, **25.** 226, 240
Orford, Cts of, brought out of England a bad portrait of member of, **25.** 240
pedigree of, **18.** 126n, 143n
Clio:
Harcourts to rejoin, in Wales, **35.** 465
writes ode from Lady Ossory, **32.** 220
'Cliquetée'; 'Cliquetis.' *See* Bentley, Richard (1708–82)
'Cliquetis, Hannah.' *See* Bentley, Mrs Richard
Clitherow, James, deputy lt of Middlesex:
SH visited by, **12.** 224
Clivden. *See* Cliveden
Clive, Bns. *See* Herbert, Lady Barbara (1758–1830); Maskelyne, Margaret (ca 1734–1817)
Clive, Sir Edward (1704–71), judge of Court of Common Pleas:
Wilkes freed by, **38.** 200–1
Clive, Hon. Edward (1754–1839), 2d Bn Clive, 1774; cr. (1804) E. of Powis, n.c.; M.P.:
English peerage declined by, **33.** 430n
Clive, Mrs George. *See* Raftor, Catherine
Clive, Lady Henrietta Antonia. *See* Herbert, Lady Henrietta Antonia (1758–1830)
Clive, 'Kitty.' *See* Raftor, Catherine
Clive, Richard (ca 1693–1771), M.P.:
birth date of, corrected, **43.** 276
George III at levee asks, about son. **38.** 275
house of, in Swithin's Lane, Lombard St, **21.** 429n

Pitt said to receive offer from, of India's wealth in return for aid to son, **21.** 404
Clive, Robert (1725–74), cr. (1762) Bn Clive; M.P.; governor of Bengal:
Arcot taken by, **29.** 35n
arrives in England full of wealth and diamonds, **21.** 429
Asia subdued by, **38.** 188
associate of, writes to Mogul, **23.** 381
Attila and Haidar 'Alī as innocent as, **25.** 142
Barré replaced by, at Bengal, **38.** 378
Bath knighthood of, **22.** 243, 318, 323, 540, 581
Bath visited by, **24.** 60n, **32.** 218n
Bengal, Nawab of, defeated by, **21.** 181n
—— presents, with Shah Goest, **21.** 378n
Bengal cleared of French by, **21.** 181n
Bengal fortified by, **22.** 540
Bengal governor's salary reduced by, **22.** 540
Bengal secured by, from Great Mogul, **22.** 416
brave, but not tall and handsome enough for a hero, **40.** 241
candour of, brings threats of punishment, **28.** 87
captains of, return to England through Florence, **21.** 279
Carlisle's Thistle order delayed by, in transit, **23.** 14
charged with usurpation, **29.** 123
Claremont bought and altered by, **9.** 71n, **32.** 71n
death of: **6.** 115, **32.** 218–19; expected, **30.** 250; said to be suicide by taking laudanum for pains, **24.** 60–1, 68
diamond house of, to be pointed out in school-boys' lessons, **23.** 400
diamonds imported by, to make him popular in England, **38.** 128
diamonds may have to be sent by, to help England pay for food, **22.** 455
diamonds of, **39.** 199
diamonds taken by, **21.** 541
East India Co. 'begot,' and macaronies were 'begot' by him, **23.** 400
East India Co. elects, gov.-gen. of Bengal, **22.** 211, **38.** 344
East India Co. rejects *jagir* claim by, as substitute for annuity, **38.** 275
East India Co. voter bribed by, away from Sulivan, **38.** 378
East Indian affairs debated by, **28.** 86n
England can spare, **35.** 418
father said to offer Pitt a share of India's spoils, in return for aid to, **21.** 404
Florence visited by, **43.**
Fox and Bedford support, **13.** 26n
George III and Charlotte get presents from Mogul through, **22.** 540, 547
Grenville ministry buys off, by promising to restore *jagir* in return for Parliamentary vote, **38.** 248–9

HW hears about, from Grenville, **38.** 347–8
HW jokes about conquests of, **31.** 80
HW mentions, **22.** 239
HW tired of, **38.** 368
health of: convulsions and pains, **24.** 60;
  laudanum for, **24.** 61, 68; pain in stomach,
  **24.** 68; precarious, **22.** 561
house of: in Berkeley Sq., **23.** 530n, **35.** 418n;
  in Berkeley St, **24.** 60n
House of Commons exonerates, **5.** 360, **23.**
  484–5, 562
India's groans will accuse, in heaven, **23.** 387
Italy to be visited by, **23.** 530
*jagir* of, to be decided by law, **38.** 348
Jews and usurers commit as much rapine as,
  **23.** 231
made K.B. on departure for India, **22.** 318
Mann ought to get diamonds from, for foiling
  Francis I's schemes on India, **22.** 547
Masulipatam said to be captured by, **21.** 378
Meredith and C. J. Fox drive, out of House
  of Commons, **23.** 490–1
Mīr Ja'far friend of, **38.** 310
Montpellier visited by, **23.** 14n
Parliamentary speech by, on India, **23.** 399n
Parliament attacks, **23.** 483
——'s acquittal of, authorizes English depredations in India, **23.** 562
'patron' of the arts, **32.** 71
Pitt calls, 'heaven-born,' **21.** 181n, **22.** 176,
  243, 391n, **23.** 387, **35.** 418
——'s eulogy of, mimicked by HW, **31.** 21
riches engrossed by, like Plutus, **23.** 381
rising prices may leave, the only man rich
  enough to keep a cow, **22.** 49
Rumbold nearly as rich as, **39.** 369–70
Sandwich and Fox fail to win Mitchell election contest in behalf of, **35.** 215n
Shah Goest presented to Pitt by, **21.** 378n
share of, in victory over £200,000, **21.** 182n
spoils brought by, from India, **22.** 540, 547
Sulivan opposed to, **22.** 497n
survival of, lessens Mann's hope for Bath
  knighthood, **22.** 540
ten members of Parliament named by, **24.** 61
verses mention, **31.** 16
victories of, in India, **21.** 181
wealth of, **10.** 247, **30.** 250, **31.** 21, 159
Clive, Mrs Robert. *See* Maskelyne, Margaret
Cliveden, Bucks:
Frederick, P. of Wales, injured by fall at, **20.**
  240n
visitors to: Bootle, **20.** 184; Frederick, P. of
  Wales, **19.** 436; French players, **18.** 305;
  Niccolini, **19.** 436
'Cliveden,' Twickenham. *See* Little Strawberry
  Hill
Clivedon, Katharine (d. 1385), m. 1 Sir Peers
  le Veel; m. 2 (1347) Thomas de Berkeley,
  3d Bn Berkeley:
HW's drawing of, **15.** 204

headdress of, **1.** 344
Cloak; cloaks:
black: funeral procession wears, **33.** 20; Louis
  XV's daughters wear, **35.** 113
Cumberland, D. of, wears, at George II's funeral, **9.** 322
drunken lady loses, **35.** 306
French, **30.** 45, **32.** 205
Goldsmith wears, in play, **32.** 171
Italian wears, in portrait at Drayton, **10.** 342
ladies don, to go to see Macclesfield's body,
  **38.** 358
Mann wears: at open-air dinner, **18.** 98; to
  meet Theodore of Corsica, **18.** 187
red, Martin wears, **13.** 202
scarlet and yellow, worn by Naunton, **35.** 248
Scott, Lady Caroline, wears, **32.** 338
short: Craon, Princesse de, wears, **18.** 109;
  Niccoli wears, **19.** 49
Spaniards resent ordinance for shortening of,
  **7.** 311, **39.** 60–1
sphinxes wear, on gateposts near Livry, **7.**
  357, **10.** 212
Stowe guests wear, to avoid catching cold, **10.**
  314, **35.** 339
worn at night, in April at Florence, **25.** 397
*See also* Bavaro; Joseph
Cloak bag. *See under* Bag
Clobery. *See* Glynn
Clocheterie. *See* Chadeau de la Clocheterie
Clock; clocks:
at Shrewsbury: **40.** 14; inaudible at West-
  minster, **37.** 444
Florentine, put on French time, **20.** 26
French regulate lives by, **31.** 72
HW shops for, in Paris for Lord Ossory, **32.**
  54
Henry VIII gives, to Anne Boleyn, **2.** 334
in Q. Elizabeth's collection, **32.** 324
musical: in Colebrooke's sale, **23.** 569n; of
  Frederick, P. of Wales, **19.** 447
Clodia, vestal virgin:
urn of, **26.** 8
Clodius, Publius (ca 98–52 B.C.), 'Pulcher';
  demagogue:
born before Julius Cæsar's death, **23.** 400
Cato's name assumed by, **23.** 176
HW's letter might have been written in time
  of, **25.** 15
London riots reminiscent of, **23.** 19
one must talk of, for lack of a Scipio, **23.** 499
'paved the way to the throne of Cæsar,' **28.**
  393
Wilkes compared to, **4.** 203
Cloe:
Conway's, *see* Fitzroy, Lady Caroline
evening prayer relinquished by, **9.** 49
Clog; clogs:
actresses wear, **17.** 435
Kilmarnock, Cts of, requests, **37.** 218
Clogher, Bp of. *See* Garnett, John (1709–82)
Cloiié. *See* Chloé

Cloister; cloisters:
  at Battle Abbey, **35.** 140
  at Gloucester, **35.** 154
  at Hurstmonceaux, **35.** 138, 139
  at Newstead Abbey, **9.** 299
  at SH, *see under* Strawberry Hill
  at Westminster Hall, lighted with lamps and
    Volterra vases, **37.** 454
  in convent of the Chartreuse, **13.** 169
Clonfert, Bp of. *See* Carmichael, Hon. William
  (1702–65); Cumberland, Dr Denison (ca
  1708–74); Marlay, Richard (d. 1802); Oswald, Dr John (d. 1780); Smyth, Arthur
  (1706–71); Wolley, Edward (ca 1604–84)
Clonmell, E. of. *See* Scott, John
Clonmell, Vct. *See* Scott, John
Clonmell, co. Tipperary:
  (?) Franciscans of, **14.** 174n
  turnpike bill for, **37.** 426n
Clontarf (Ireland):
  Charlemont's seat near, **9.** 391n
Cloos. *See* Close
Clopton, Anne (ca 1699–1776), m. (1721)
  Thomas Boothby Skrymsher:
  (?) Baltimore and Vcts Townshend enter-
    tained by, **17.** 173
  (?) Churchill always with, **17.** 174, **43.** 134
  (?) —— has children by, **30.** 298
  (?) HW entertained by, at ball, **17.** 278
  (?) 'Madame Bona' in HW's *Patapan*, **30.** 298
  'old Boothby,' **32.** 49
  plays loo with Lady Harrington, **32.** 49
  (?) remarks on George II's going to and
    leaving Court, **17.** 365–6
  Walpole, Lady, cousin to, **21.** 497
Clopton, Catherine (d. 1754), m. (1725) Henry
  Talbot; 'Tigress':
  ancestral tombs of, at Stratford, **9.** 120
  death of, **9.** 161
  HW may visit, **9.** 61, 71, 73, 76–7
  (?) HW mentions, **14.** 52
  HW related to, **9.** 20n
  Jekyll, Lady Anne, visits, **9.** 20
  (?) Maclaine robs, **20.** 168
  Montagu may visit, **9.** 71, 73, 76–7
  —— not to visit, **9.** 61
  —— sends invitation to HW from house of,
    **9.** 51
  —— visits, **9.** 20
  Walker, Sir Edward, ancestor of, **9.** 120
Clopton, Charles Boothby Skrymsher (ca 1740–
  1800), called 'Prince Boothby':
  admires Mrs Siddons's acting, **33.** 359
  Cowper, E., and, **12.** 201
Clorinda:
  (?) HW's) poem about, **17.** 93–4
Close, —— (fl. 1425):
  supposed architect of King's College Chapel,
    **1.** 18
Close, Nicholas (d. 1452), Bp of Carlisle, 1450,
  of Lichfield, 1452:
  Master of the King's Works at Cambridge,
    **1.** 18

Close stool; close stools:
  'anointed velvet,' for Q. Charlotte in West-
    minster Abbey, **21.** 535n
  Caffarelli receives visitor when seated upon,
    **19.** 452
  Mann makes indelicate reference to, **17.** 284
Closet; closets:
  HW comments on use of word, **12.** 254
  HW's, at SH, *see under* SH
  HW's green, at Downing St, **37.** 112
  Mann, Galfridus, sleeps in, after dinner, **20.**
    525
  royal, *see under* George II; George III
Clossen, Maria (1739–89), m. Gamaliel Night-
  ingale:
  mother-in-law objects to, **1.** 239n
Clostercamp:
  battle of, **21.** 444
Closterman, Johann Baptist:
  Lyttelton's portrait by, **35.** 147n
Closterseven; Clostersoeven. *See* Kloster-Zeven
Clotaire:
  Karl Theodor should call himself, **36.** 233
Cloth; cloths:
  black, with raised pile, for mourning, **20.**
    211n
  blue, chairs covered with, at St-Cyr, **10.** 293
  English: contraband in Tuscany, **20.** 205;
    France considers admitting, **7.** 375
  export restrictions on, removed, **24.** 542n
  forehead, worn by St-Cyr nuns, **10.** 293
  HW sends, to Bentley, **35.** 264
  Müntz orders, for Bentley, **35.** 263
  Rowe's transactions about, in Treasury, **41.**
    206
  scarlet, for receiving Kilmarnock's severed
    head, **19.** 300
  unobtainable in Tuscany, save from England,
    **20.** 205
  wax, HW's Roman purchases wrapped in, **26.**
    4
  *See also* Cloth of gold
Clothes:
  Colomb's, valued, **42.** 298
  Du Deffand, Mme, has, at death, inventory
    of, **8.** 21–3
  extravagant suit of, described, **30.** 18–19
  Florentines resume March dress, in June, **21.**
    510
  for George III's wedding, much discussed,
    **38.** 118
  Franceschi's, sold, **17.** 122
  French and Spanish snatch, from Genoese,
    **19.** 306
  (?) given away on marriage, **30.** 56
  HW jokes about letting out, **37.** 347
  HW's: bequeathed to Philip Colomb, **30.** 360;
    for Birthday, **37.** 116; HW sends away,
    from Italy, **37.** 93; stolen at Paris, **39.**
    190; unpacked, **30.** 22
  Keyt assembles in room, before suicide, **30.**
    23

laced: for Tylney's servants, **23.** 60, 64; Gore gives, to King's Arms waiters, **20.** 209

man cuts, into strips to hang himself, **31.** 339

Marie-Antoinette carries, in bundle on way to prison, **31.** 388

suits of, owned by Francis I, **19.** 58–9

Watson Wentworth, Lady Henrietta, gives away, on marrying footman, **38.** 456–7

winter, Italians leave off, in warm March, **20.** 143

*See also* Costume

Clothing, regimental:

Conway's, promised to Galfridus Mann, **37.** 254

Montagu, Charles, gives contract for, to Galfridus Mann, **35.** 265

Cloth of gold:

hangings of, **42.** 314n

Richard III wears, **41.** 132

Clotilde, Mme. *See* Marie-Adélaïde-Clotilde-Xavière

Cloud:

bloody, earthquake foretold by, **20.** 119, 143

Cloud, St. *See* St-Cloud

Cloué; Clouet. *See* Chloé

Clouet, François, painter:

Mary, Q. of Scots, painted by, **30.** 122n

Clough, Miss, actress:

Garrick to produce, **9.** 74

HW praises acting of, at Richmond, **9.** 74

Clough, Mrs John. *See* Palliser, Alice

Clouwet, Peeter (1629–70), engraver:

prints by, **1.** 182, **14.** 147

Clove-carnations. *See under* Carnation

Clovelly Court, Devon:

Hamlyn of, **11.** 88n

Clover:

Conway confined in, in Ireland, **37.** 419

Clovio, Don Julio (1498–1578), miniature painter:

Giulio Romano's pupil, **42.** 165n

missal illuminated by, bought by HW at Portland sale, **12.** 255n, **39.** 442, **43.** 357

Cloyne, Bp of. *See* Berkeley, George (1685–1753); Hervey, Hon. Frederick Augustus (1730–1803)

Club; clubs:

Albemarle St, *see under* Ladies Club

at Burghley House, **10.** 346

atheists', **39.** 104–5

at Stapleton's, **32.** 361

English, riotous in their generosity, **23.** 137

Hood's, in Westminster, **34.** 31

in London, drink Sir Robert Walpole's health, **18.** 142

new, opened in St James's St, **22.** 186

political, in Paris, the excrement of legislators, **34.** 158

stories of, **32.** 103

Virtue, **32.** 6

*See also* Almack's; Arthur's; Beefsteak Club; Board, The; Brooks's; Dilettanti; Hell-Fire Club; Jockey Club; Kit-Cat Club; Ladies' Club; Macaroni Club; Rockingham Club; Savoir Vivre Club; Weltjie's; White's; Wildman's Club

*See also under* Drury Lane Theatre

Clubbe, John (ca 1703–73), satirist:

*Physiognomy*, sent by Lort to HW, **16.** 173

Clue, La. *See* La Clue

Clugny, Jean-Étienne-Bernard de (1729–76), Baron de Nuits-sur-Armançon; intendant of Bordeaux; controller-general:

controller's office given to, **6.** 311, 314

death of, **6.** 369

Du Deffand, Mme, hears nothing about, **6.** 326

health of, **6.** 365, 367

ministry of marine to go to, **6.** 300, 311

to work with Maurepas, **6.** 315

Clumber Park, Notts, seat of D. of Newcastle:

HW is not tempted to stop at, **28.** 42

Hertford to visit, **39.** 268

Worksop compared with, **32.** 375

Clun, Shropshire:

hospital at, **16.** 82n, 87

Cluny, clan of:

Young Pretender not joined by, **37.** 239n

Clutterbuck ('Clutturbuck'), Thomas (1697–1742), M.P.:

birth date of, corrected, **43.** 240

Carteret betrayed by, after being his benefactor, **17.** 391n

death of, **17.** 391n

government post lost by, **17.** 332, 391

Navy post to go to, **17.** 391

Onslow persuaded by, to resign Navy treasurership who then took it himself, **30.** 293n

——'s election as speaker seconded by, **17.** 219

—— to be succeeded by, **17.** 391

Pelham made scrupulous by, **17.** 391n

salary of, **17.** 333n

Walpole, Sir Robert, employs, but distrusts, **17.** 291n

—— had low opinion of, **30.** 293n

Cluzel. *See* Du Cluzel

Clymore. *See* Claymore

'Clytemnestra to Sappho.' *See under* Williams, Sir Charles Hanbury

Clytus. *See* Cleitus

Coach; coaches:

Amelia, Ps, and Lady Mary Coke travel in, **31.** 146

articles sent by, **1.** 101

at Richmond, diminished in number, **28.** 406

at Shelburne's, **33.** 174

attacked during Gordon Riots, **33.** 177

at Twickenham boat-race, **11.** 86

at Wanstead, for Tylney's ball, **21.** 417

Augusta, Ps of Wales, rides in, to shake numb legs, **23.** 364

Austrian visitors send, to George Inn, **33.** 532

bantams to come in basket by, from London, **37.** 345

Bedford's: at George III's birthday, **11.** 284; glasses of, broken by mob, **23.** 139

[Coach; coaches, *continued*]

beggars thrust mutilated limbs into, to excite charity, **10.** 201

Berrys', repaired at Bologna, **11.** 363, 364, 365n

body: HW jokes about Onslow's, **37.** 378; Wachtendonck leaves, to Mrs Goldsworthy, **17.** 110

books delivered to Mason by, **28.** 148, 310, **29.** 175

Botta provides, for Leopold, **22.** 123, 157

Braitwitz's, **18.** 66

—— sleeps in, in earthquake, **17.** 284

—— to give, to Mme Vitelli, **18.** 334

—— to sell, **17.** 195

Brentford allows, to pass without No. 45 on doors, **23.** 360

Cameron sees wife depart in, **20.** 384

Carteret watches battle from, **18.** 261

chained off, from serenade on Lung'arno, **17.** 105

Charlotte, Q., jumps out of, **38.** 117

——'s, **38.** 418

——'s arrival proclaimed by, **35.** 313

Chatham's, full of Grenville-looking children, **39.** 76

Chernyshev's, **23.** 126

Christian Friedrich Karl Alexander's, **20.** 376

Chudleigh, Mrs, held up by footpads when asleep in, **24.** 198

—— ties footpad's body to, **24.** 203

Clement XIII's, mobbed in Rome, **20.** 446

conservatori take, to call on Cardinal York, **19.** 428

Conway's trip in, from Cambridge, **37.** 20–1

—— to send leaf-silver to HW by, **37.** 15

correspondence delivered by, **34.** 49

Corso thronged with, **17.** 3

Craggs and Moore enter, **20.** 181

Craon's, **17.** 199

Cumberland, D. of, appears in, after operation, **38.** 456

draped for Dauphin's death, **31.** 89

Du Barry, Mme, uses Barrymore arms on, **32.** 55n

Dunstable, **32.** 174

early leathern wagons known as, **42.** 2

earthquake refugees sleep in, **17.** 303

Edgcumbe about to go in, to Moyle's, **41.** 54

Edgcumbe family spends four days in, en route to Mamhead, **30.** 66

Electress's, has long traces, **19.** 370

English compared with Dutch, **33.** 269

etiquette of seating arrangements in, **22.** 378

fast, for mail, **31.** 234n

filled, during London storm, **10.** 14

flitch of bacon might be sent by, **38.** 71

Florentines do not dare venture out in, in snow, **22.** 478, 574, 575

footman opens door of, for Duchesse d'Aiguillon, **22.** 163

Forbici, near Fiesole, accessible in, **20.** 191

former footman forgetfully climbs into back of, **20.** 181, 195

French servants wear hats when handing ladies into, **35.** 112

from Calais to Paris, baggage unsuitable for chaise may be sent by, **37.** 42

from King's Lynn, **40.** 48

from London to Southampton, carries seeds and nursery stock, **35.** 161

from Ranelagh, **32.** 53

Garrick, Mrs, afraid to send deed by, **42.** 211

—— hurts hip in jumping from, **22.** 203

George II's, **17.** 437

George III's, **35.** 325; new, draws crowds, **22.** 102n

glass windows of, **17.** 399, **23.** 15, 49, 139, 201–2, **33.** 174–5, **38.** 256, 560

Gloucester, D. of, to go out in, **36.** 142

Grafton, Ds of, easily tired by, **22.** 29

Grifoni, Mme, drives in, **17.** 415

Grosvenor, Cts, has glass in, broken by mob, **38.** 560

guests', come at 7 P.M. after 4 o'clock dinner, **38.** 530

HW and Conway ride in, to Vauxhall, **10.** 279

HW and others take, to visit Bois Prévu, **35.** 115

HW barely able to go out in, **42.** 394

HW converses through window of, **39.** 376

HW lifted into, to take air, **30.** 195

HW rides in, alone with Lady Mary Wortley Montagu, **30.** 10

HW's: **31.** 154, 171, 215; Mann terrified by mob's breaking the glass of, **23.** 15, 49; stopped in Piccadilly by mob, **23.** 6

HW sends Bentley a parcel by, **35.** 168, 197

HW sends letters by, **10.** 155, **33.** 167, **35.** 168, **39.** 102, 288, 319

HW's humours unsuited for travel in, **18.** 498

HW's letter to be sent by wagon or, **29.** 66

HW takes Dangeul in, **23.** 6

HW to send, for D. Lysons, **15.** 252

hackney: **35.** 505; anti-Catholic sign on, at Hammersmith, **33.** 193; at Shelburne's, **33.** 174; Blakeney takes, to Court, **21.** 24; Caswall rides in, **9.** 319; Conway takes, on way to Ireland, **37.** 356; Craufurd robbed in, **33.** 413; Ferrers's mistress attends his execution in, **21.** 401; George III may have to take, **32.** 129; mob pulls Wilkes in, **23.** 19; Sandys said to hire, to wait at his door, **18.** 232; Selwyn in, **37.** 13; visitors to Cock Lane séance take, **10.** 6; Wales, P. of, and Breton, leave Ps of Wales and Cts of Middlesex in, **30.** 95; Williams rides to pillory in, **38.** 512

Hare Naylor family visit Houghton in, **18.** 63

Harley's, has glass broken by mob, **38.** 256

Hertford goes hunting in, **38.** 218

——'s, rained on, at Grantham, **38.** 91

Hertford, Cts of, will take care of, **39.** 274

Hodges, Mrs, robbed in, **37.** 422

Hyde Corner passed by, in flight from earthquake, **20.** 137

Incontri, Abp, and attendants whisper Te Deum in, **21.** 151–2

Italian, difficulty in getting into, **20.** 579

Johnston, Lady Cecilia, has, **12.** 55

La Tour injured in, **21.** 442

Leghorn people sleep in, for fear of earthquake, **23.** 261

Leopold and Maria Louisa use only their own, for travelling, **23.** 220

Leopold's, moves with difficulty through Florentine mob, **22.** 337

London-Bristol: **31.** 313; HW to send books to Williams by, **30.** 147

London crowded with, at peace celebration, **20.** 47

London exodus of, **20.** 137, **33.** 191–2

London mob demands that glasses of, be pulled down, **23.** 201–2

London-Salisbury, **40.** 65n

lord mayor's, **11.** 210

Louis XVI's, mob intends to draw, to *lit de justice*, **24.** 61–2

lozenge, **19.** 298

Luxembourg, Duc de, summons, for Cts of Coventry, **20.** 338

mail coaches: Cowslip Green not on route of, **31.** 264–5; HW wants frequent visits of, from Bristol, **31.** 267; introduction of, by Palmer, **33.** 480n; More, Hannah, jokes about her book going by, **31.** 315–16; service by, on London-Bristol road, **31.** 265n; space annihilated by, **31.** 264–5

Mann afraid of squeezing Princesse de Craon in, **19.** 358

—— and D. of York talk while riding in, **22.** 558

——escorts a lady home from theatre in, **22.** 180

—— has not been out in, since gout, **24.** 307

—— might drive in, to Cascine gardens or Fiesole, **25.** 558

—— need not ride backward in, when representing George III, **24.** 206, 209

—— offers, to D. of Gloucester, **24.** 291

—— orders, from England through Pembroke, **25.** 667n

——'s: **35.** 30; Cumberland, D. and Ds of, use, **25.** 644; fur bag in, **25.** 248; Oxenden to use, **19.** 232; seldom used by D. of Gloucester, **23.** 395; used by D. of Gloucester, **24.** 291; used by Magnan, **19.** 13; waits at his door, **20.** 354; yellow, left to Mme Minerbetti, **25.** 667n

Mansfield's, Gordon rioters break glasses of, **32.** 174, 175

Maria Louisa follows husband to Florence in, **22.** 427

Marie-Antoinette's, Tessé has, in Florence, **24.** 353

Mason sends a print by, to HW, **28.** 463

may be put into mourning, on Electress's death, **18.** 175

merchants presenting address to George III ride in, **10.** 273

ministers drive home from Claremont in, **17.** 503, 506

mob holds flambeaux to windows of, **23.** 194

Modenese princess met by, at Florence, **17.** 68

Monnerat, David, falls from box of, **39.** 209

Mt Edgcumbe, Cts of, lends, to Mme de Cambis, **12.** 41

mourning: **17.** 122, **21.** 399; in Lady Buckingham's funeral procession, **18.** 207n

New Burlington St blocked by, **11.** 101

Northumberland, Cts of, has footmen attend her own, with her women in another, **42.** 380

Nugent, Mrs, says she jumps out of, **37.** 347

open, Electress's body carried in, **18.** 173

Orford, Cts of, makes Villa Medici accessible by, at Fiesole, **24.** 190

—— orders, to be made, **19.** 59

Orford, E. of, illness of, notified by message sent in, **36.** 119

Orlov and Mann ride in, **24.** 96

overturns in Thames, **35.** 279

papal legate rides in, **12.** 77

Pitti palace to be made more accessible to, **22.** 124

Proctor's and Cooke's, torn to pieces by mob, **23.** 6

ranks of, at Florentine *corsi*, **21.** 179

rape attempted in, by Richards, **38.** 507

'rattling,' **40.** 49

Ray, Martha, gets into, at Covent Garden, **33.** 98

Regency sends, to Modenese princess, **17.** 60

rich citizens descend backwards from, **35.** 86

Richecourt's, waits at Mrs Richmond's door, **19.** 97, 101

Richecourt's secretary said to transport stolen goods in, **17.** 224

robbery of, **34.** 143

royal, representatives of royalty ride backwards in, in England, **24.** 206

Salisbury, invented by E. of Salisbury, **10.** 348

Seilern's, stopped by mob, **23.** 7

Selwyn, George, brings Lord George Gordon to White's in, **33.** 169

(?) Selwyn, John, would like place in C. H. Williams's, to Houghton, **30.** 64

Siena does not have, for hire, **19.** 232

Spanish, stopped by mob, **39.** 63

stage, *see* Stage-coach

state: 'a gold glass-case,' **34.** 210; dolphins should have been attached to, **22.** 113; newly made in England, with tritons, **22.** 104; slow, **33.** 156

Strafford sends, for Conway and D. of Cumberland, **37.** 212

streets littered with straw to deaden noise of, **23.** 323

[Coach; coaches, *continued*]

strings of, obstruct departure from Vauxhall party, **10**. 279

'swagging,' Chute to drive in, with fat mares, **35**. 86

tax on, **41**. 432

Temple not visited by, **30**. 222

tides of, in London, **11**. 249

Townshend, Vcts, goes to chapel in, **10**. 216

——'s, **30**. 70

Twickenham's, said to outnumber France's, **35**. 234

vast and unwieldy, used by Roman princesses, **13**. 209

visible from SH, **20**. 380, **25**. 532, **37**. 269

visiting, dowagers order, before sunset, **9**. 53

Wachtendonck's, **17**. 110, 260

Walpole, Sir Edward, maintains, for Mrs Keppel, **24**. 349

—— promises, to Mrs Scott, **10**. 329

wedding, Kingston's, **23**. 99

Wilkes's rivals', attacked by mob, **23**. 461n

Wilton, Joseph, makes, for Coronation, **20**. 391n

York, Cardinal, takes brother through Rome in, **22**. 392

—— to lend, to Cts of Albany, **25**. 107

York, D. of, makes Tuscan tour in, **22**. 220

Young Pretender exchanges, for chaise, **23**. 318

——'s, has 8 horses, **22**. 389

*See also* Bath coach; Cambridge coach; Cambridge fly; Mail-coach; Speaker's coach

Coach-and-four:

Dodd and Whaley take, at Canterbury, **40**. 4

HW meets Lady Mary Coke in, near Amiens, **39**. 7–8

housebreakers travel in, **31**. 298

Coach-and-pair:

at Corso, **17**. 3

Mann drives in, to christening with only 2 horses, **24**. 239

Coach-and-six:

at Corso, **17**. 3

at weddings of poor Florentine girls, **22**. 491

Cardigans travel in, **10**. 89

Child, Lady Dorothy, regrets loss of, **37**. 309n

Hardwicke's, at Blenheim, **10**. 309

Mann disappoints Florentines by not driving in, **24**. 239

—— rides in, to escort Almada, **21**. 436

mourning, at Ferrers's execution, **21**. 399

Pitt will not keep, **38**. 136

Richecourt attended by, at Corsi christening, **20**. 432

SH passed by, **35**. 275–6

Young Pretender followed by, **22**. 389

Coach-driving:

popularity of, **10**. 348

Coach-horse. *See under* Horse

Coach-house:

at Battle Abbey, **35**. 140

HW refuses to accommodate Goodere with, **42**. 317

Coachmaker:

apprentice of, sent by HW's maid to tell Conway and HW of housebreaking, **23**. 286

Fleury, Duc de, owes £500 to, **12**. 79

Poggelini recommends, at Bologna, **11**. 364–5n

Coachmaker's Hall, London:

Protestant Association meets at, **25**. 52n

Coachman. *See under* Servant

'Coach-surgeon':

HW's carriage needs, after accident, **39**. 454

Coade, Mrs Eleanor (ca 1732–1821):

HW's transactions with, for artificial stone pier, **41**. 227–9

Coal; coals:

cannel, snuff-boxes of, **30**. 214, **31**. 105

Conway makes coke from, **39**. 551

Cornelys, Theresa, professes to give, to the poor, **23**. 271

Dee's black stone made of, **23**. 287

from Newcastle, **9**. 210, **10**. 262

HW buys, in London, **9**. 53

HW has to buy, in June and July, **10**. 218, **34**. 50, **39**. 128

HW makes sunshine with peck of, **10**. 215

HW's economy in, at Houghton, **21**. 353–4, **32**. 143

Hampden receives, **10**. 257

Hardinge, Mrs, makes witticism about George III's use of, **21**. 460

high price of, in London, **25**. 274

June ruinous from consumption of, **34**. 50

Leneve, Isabella, tells HW not to waste, **21**. 353–4

machine for picking, from hearth, **20**. 203

pit, Hannah More puns about, **31**. 213

sea: fire of, unsuitable for dog-days, **10**. 315; London's sunshine consists of, **10**. 239; Montagu must economize in, **10**. 281

small, Gavi, Mme, hides money in, **17**. 223

Warwickshire colliers bring, to George III, **32**. 186

Coal-heaver; coal-heavers:

all Irish Whiteboys, **23**. 33

London and Wapping terrorized by, **23**. 33–4

mob of, rises in London, **24**. 21

ringleaders of, hanged, **23**. 39

riots of: at Hexham, **30**. 163n; suppressed, **35**. 324

sailor aids Green against, **23**. 39

sailors' feud with, in London, **23**. 30, 33

Coal-heaving:

handkerchief-hemming considered equal to, as work, **31**. 365

Coal hole:

at SH, **40**. 150

'Coalition':

mistaken for 'collation,' **39**. 472–3

Coalition, English:

patronesses of, **35**. 62

'Coalition Dissected, The' (satiric print):

Abingdon lays, before House of Lords, **35**. 381

Coal mine; coal mines ('coal pits'):
at Louisbourg, **23**. 49n
at Quebec wanted by Amherst, **23**. 48–9
England's compensation for cold summers, **32**. 64, **34**. 143, **36**. 282
Lowther, 'prince of,' **21**. 527
Stuart, Lady Mary, 'infanta' of, **21**. 527

Coal miners (*see also* Collier):
riot of, at Hexham, **30**. 163n

Coan, John, dwarf:
(?) brag to be played by, at Mrs Holman's, **9**. 126

Coardi di Carpanetto, Caterina Maria Teresa (d. 1800), m. Vittorio Francesco Vignati, Conte di San Gillio ('Mme St-Gilles'):
Boswell, Casanova, and Gibbon mention, **20**. 309n
Hamilton's affair with, **20**. 309

Coast, La. See La Coast

Coat; coats:
Balmerinoch doffs, at execution, **19**. 302
beaver, worn by Pamfili, **19**. 445
black: considered a sign of mourning, **20**. 175; for mourning Joseph II, **34**. 97
black freeze, **19**. 320n
blue, worn by Balmerinoch, **19**. 299
brown, unfamiliar to soldiers, **37**. 129
canonici and abbés forbidden to have pockets in, **21**. 224
claret-coloured, HW orders, for Montagu, **9**. 358
cloth, worn by Mann in winter apartment, **20**. 69
Conti's, old, **38**. 221
crimson, lined with scarlet and turned up with cherry colour, **30**. 18
Fitzwilliam's: probably given away on his wedding, **30**. 55; worn by Polonius in *Hamlet* performance, **30**. 55
'French,' fashion in, **32**. 182–3
frock: HW's only summer costume, **9**. 305; Huntingdon wears, at ball at Norfolk House, **9**. 338
gala: **38**. 571; Mann feared he might need, for Cowper christening, **24**. 219
great: Mann's, **23**. 72; Stowe guests wear, to avoid catching cold, **10**. 314
green: deputy ranger's costume, **10**. 191, 196, 198, 200; Montagu hopes to wear, as ranger, **10**. 200; Montagu jokes about, **10**. 230
HW unable to put on, because of rheumatism, **31**. 204, **39**. 341
horseman's: Montagu, Lady Mary Wortley, wears fur of, **10**. 5; rug, worn by Craon indoors in winter, **18**. 109
in *A Tale of a Tub*, **28**. 158
laced, Horatio Walpole (1723–1809) wears, **20**. 342
lace for, **37**. 106
lappet of, **18**. 501
Mann gets, **17**. 433

milk-white, Bentley wears, in Mall, **9**. 373
morning grey, Conway wears, **13**. 179
new, for Q. Charlotte's birthday, **28**. 131, **29**. 354
numerous red and blue, in London, please George III, **29**. 65
of diamonds, **19**. 71
oilskin, made in Ireland, **37**. 420
Palliser's, pulled by mob, **24**. 442
red, Bosville makes, **18**. 309
regulation of, in ecclesiastical costume, **41**. 223
riding, Montagu, Lady Mary Wortley, wears, **22**. 3
scarlet, mankind can still be oppressed by, **23**. 514
silk, George II wears, **21**. 410
tail, not suitable at supper, **7**. 131
tawdry, worn at Reggio by Piedmont officers, **17**. 46
*See also* Petticoat; Watch-coat

Coates. *See* Cotes

Coat-of-arms; coats-of-arms:
at Hurstmonceaux, **35**. 138, 139
at Mereworth, **35**. 144
at the Vyne, **35**. 641
at Welbeck Abbey, **35**. 270
Boynets', unknown to HW, **35**. 256
Chute proposes change in, **35**. 108–9
Damer, Mrs, consults HW about, **35**. 494–5
foreign ministers in Italy affix, over doorways, **19**. 317n
gamblers: Edgcumbe paints, for White's Clubs, **9**. 186; HW sends, to Montagu, **9**. 188
HW's quarterings in, do not exceed Thomas Walpole jr's, **36**. 227
Hervey proposes cat for, **35**. 109
Hyndford's, granted an eagle by Frederick II, **18**. 107
lady's, containing tree and five of hearts, **33**. 427
Mann's, **18**. 184, **20**. 482, 487
Maule's maid reveals, to Edinburgh magistrates, **19**. 107
of Anne Boleyn, **32**. 323
of Fox family, in Harleian MSS, **30**. 153
of John Dudley, **32**. 323
of Sidney family, **33**. 350
of Sir Philip Sidney, **33**. 350
on tiles at Malvern Priory, **35**. 151
on Ximenes's Bible, **42**. 240
Wolsey's, on frankincense ship, **32**. 324
*See also* Crest

Coats-of-mail:
goldfish said to be dressed in, **35**. 221

'Coaxer, Mrs':
'Vixen, Mrs,' not to be confused with, **35**. 526
*See also* Walpole, Laura (Mrs Keppel)

Cob; cobs (Spanish dollars):
English vessel escapes with, from Cadiz, **24**. 307
value of, **24**. 307n

Cobalt:
  Ginori wants, from England for painting china, **18.** 184, 202, 216
  HW fails to find, **18.** 283–4
  Mann, Galfridus, mistakes, for mineral water, **18.** 216
  pewter by-product, **18.** 323
  Walpole, Sir Edward, hears, is in Lancashire, **18.** 284
  —— to ask Islay for, **18.** 250
Cobb, Anne (d. 1789), m. 1 (after 1741) John Besey; m. 2 (1745) John Blagrave; Montagu's landlady:
  steward of, willing to make alterations for Montagu at Adderbury, **10.** 266
Cobb, Christian (d. 1779), m. (1749) Paul Methuen; Montagu's landlady:
  steward of, willing to alter house for Montagu, **10.** 266
Cobb, Sir George (ca 1670–1762), 3d Bt:
  Montagu occupies house of, **10.** 257–8n
Cobb. *See also* Cobbe
Cobbe, Catherine (ca 1762–1839), m. (1788) Hon. Henry Pelham, cr. (1801) E. of Chichester:
  coarse remark by, **15.** 328
  Wales, Caroline, Ps of, dismisses, as Bedchamber woman, **12.** 200–1
Cobbe. *See also* Cobb; Orde
Cobbett, William (1762–1835):
  *Porcupine's Gazette*, story inserted in, **29.** 135n
Cobbler; cobblers:
  Cromwell made peers of, **31.** 267
  France's new national assembly full of, **34.** 124, **39.** 487
  wives of, acted by Mrs Clive, **40.** 61
Cobden, Rev. Edward (1684–1764):
  Spence's correspondence with, **2.** 214
Cobenzl (Cobentzl), Johann Karl Philipp (1712–70), Graf; Imperial statesman:
  Botta replaced by, as first minister of Austrian Netherlands at Brussels, **20.** 320n
  (?) Francis I's chief governor, **17.** 327n
Cobenzl, Johann Philipp (1741–1810), Graf von:
  Joseph II accompanied by, at Necker's, **6.** 443
  —— dines with, **6.** 440
  ——sends, to negotiate at Brussels, **34.** 87n
Cobh, Ireland:
  troops embark from, **24.** 74n
Cobham, Bn. *See* Oldcastle, Sir John (ca 1370–1417); Temple, Sir Richard (1675–1749)
Cobham, Bns. *See* Cobham, Margaret (d. 1470); Halsey, Anne (d. 1760); Pole, Joan de la (d. 1434)
Cobham, Vct. *See* Grenville Temple, Richard (1711–79); Temple, Sir Richard (1675–1749)
Cobham, Vcts. *See* Chambers, Anne (ca. 1709–77); Halsey, Anne (d. 1760); Temple, Hester (ca 1690–1752)
Cobham, Eleanor (d. 1454), m. (1428) Humphrey, D. of Gloucester:
  imprisoned, **14.** 75
Cobham, Margaret (d. ca 1470), Bns Cobham; Cts of Westmorland:
  tomb of, **1.** 140
Cobham, Surrey:
  drum to go to, **9.** 152
  Painshill near, **9.** 71
'Cobham cousins'; 'Cobhamites':
  dismissal of, likely, **19.** 188
  Hammond belongs to, **17.** 451
  Walpole, Sir Robert, calls 'nepotism,' **17.** 451
  *See also* Grenville family; Lyttelton family; Pitt family
Cobham Hall, Kent:
  Darnley dies at, **16.** 197n
Coblentz (Germany):
  visitors to: Artois, Comte d' (Charles X), **11.** 355n; Coigny, **11.** 345n
Cobourg. *See* Saxe-Coburg
Cobourg; Coburg, Prince. *See* Friedrich Josias (1737–1815)
*Cobwebs to Catch Flies. See under* Frere, Eleanor (Mrs Fenn)
Cocceji, Freiherre von. *See* Campanini, Barbara
Cocceji, (?) Karl Ludwig, Freiherr von:
  Frederick II's aide-de-camp, sent to London with news, **21.** 456n
Cocceji, Samuel (1679–1755), Freiherr von; jurisconsult:
  *Exposition des motifs* attributed to, **21.** 281
  works by, **21.** 281n
Cocchi, Signora. *See* Piombanti, Teresa
Cocchi, Antonio (1695–1758), Florentine physician:
  anatomy lecture delivered by son in place of, **20.** 152
  antiquarian, **21.** 194
  autopsy on, **43.** 275
  Barrett Lennard advised by, to leave off all drugs and medicines, **20.** 94–5
  bed called by, in winter, 'the only good climate,' **20.** 216
  Benevoli recommended by, **17.** 77
  Betange discusses Craons with, **35.** 16
  book by, on Greek surgeons, *see below under Græcorum chirurgici libri*
  books for England sent by, to Leghorn, **20.** 437
  cavaliere condescends to sit with, **20.** 204–5
  children of, carefully educated but will inherit no money, **21.** 164
  churches criticized by, as conducive to colds, **20.** 228
  Chute has not asked, about Mann's health, **35.** 4
  —— to receive *parere* of, **19.** 329
  —— treated by, for gout, **14.** 93
  Conway instructed by, about medals, **20.** 297
  —— sends Pringle's book to, **20.** 544
  copyist of Santo di Tito painting heeds suggestion of, **20.** 529
  Craon entertains, to discuss Pisa baths, **17.** 342

Crescimbeni's book on Provençal poets known to, 21. 157

death of, HW hears, from Huntingdon, 21. 178

*Dei Bagni di Pisa*: HW receives, 20. 151, 158, 165, 196–7, 204; officially requested, 19. 487, 20. 151, 158; pension awarded for, 20. 204; Richecourt interferes with, 20. 158

*Del matrimonio ragionamento* by, disapproved by Rome, 22. 204

*Del vitto pittagorico*: 18. 477, 19. 20, 20. 519; translation of, 18. 567, 19. 14–15, 29

diet of, 21. 164

disciples of: do not believe in excessive use of drugs, 22. 460; Mann to recommend, to Lady William Campbell, 25. 263; Maria Louisa may choose physician from, 22. 460; occasionally employed by Mann, 25. 270

*Discorsi Toscani*: Fossi's *Elogio* printed in, 21. 170n; Scacciata's medal engraved in, 21. 202n

distilled orange flower water not advised by, 22. 469

éloge of, 21. 170, 178

English decadence bemoaned by, 21. 20

English visit of, 43. 234

English well understood by, 20. 204, 544

*Esprit des lois* not read by, 20. 117

Fitzwalter's diet will astound, 20. 519

Florentine faults admitted by, 20. 401

Florentine hospital may be under regulation of, 17. 57

Florentine malice against, 17. 95

Florentine neglect of, 17. 57

Francis I grants pension to, 20. 204

Frederick, P. of Wales's death diagnosed by, 20. 244

freemason lodge in Florence attended by, 19. 364n

friend of, writes him about Correggio picture, 17. 199

Gabburri's drawings priced by, 18. 338

Gatti a disciple of, 22. 342

Giberne attended by, 19. 83

good rather than great, 13. 231

*Græcorum chirurgici libri*: Cocchi may print part of, with own funds, 20. 179n; Cocchi stops printing of, and refunds subscribers' money, 20. 179n; HW to aid, 20. 34; Mann mentioned in, 20. 438; Mead, Dr, to aid, 20. 179; to be sent to HW and other Englishmen, 20. 437–8

HW asks about, 18. 321, 19. 244

HW asks Mann about successor of, 23. 451

HW asks opinion of, on book, 20. 107

HW attended by, 13. 1on, 17. 51, 54, 57, 66, 30. 17

HW cannot compose letter of thanks to, 20. 196–7

HW embarrassed by enthusiasm of, for *Ædes Walpolianæ*, 20. 79

HW laughs at Mann's advice from, about snuff, 20. 389

HW mentions, 21. 160

HW's correspondence with, 17. 90, 91, 94, 99

HW's gifts to: *Ædes Walpolianæ*, 19. 497, 504, 505, 20. 64, 79; Gray's *Odes*, 21. 120, 163; Hentzner's *Journey*, 21. 156; prints of eagle, 20. 485, 489

HW sorry not to be able to send book to, 21. 214

HW's version of *bon mot* questioned by, 17. 135

HW tells, that Anglican divines are as absurd as Roman ones, 20. 186

HW thanked by, 17. 31

HW thanks, for book, 18. 496, 19. 20

HW wants certificate from, of Mann's health, 17. 249

HW well acquainted with, 13. 231

HW wishes, were at Mann's side to assuage bereavement, 22. 237

health of: asthma, 20. 152; dropsy in breast, 21. 162, 163; heart trouble, 20. 152

hospital services of, paid in wax candles, 17. 57

Huntingdon, 9th E. of, takes, to England, 21. 170n

Huntingdon, 10th E. of, sees medals of, 20. 457

Inquisition suspects free-thinking of, 20. 389n

*Lettera critica sopra un manoscritto in cera*, 20. 107n

Mann accompanied by, to Palazzo Pitti, 20. 489

—— advised by: to avoid strong liquors, 22. 469; to take a little snuff, 20. 377; to visit Pisa baths, 19. 477

—— attended by, 17. 48, 66, 77, 89, 90, 91, 100, 104, 340, 369, 372, 19. 461, 20. 216

—— consults: about Gabburri's drawings, 18. 313; about Galfridus Mann's illness, 20. 527–8, 529–30, 536, 540, 543, 544, 549, 21. 35–6; about HW's eye trouble, 21. 147, 163; about miliary fever, 19. 477; about motto, 20. 480, 487

—— gives Gray's poems to, 21. 163

—— gives money to, 17. 57

—— kept in bed by, 18. 322

—— no longer has, to watch him, 24. 432

—— revived by return of, 17. 66

——'s correspondence with, 17. 51

——'s headaches thought by, to be periodical, 21. 370

—— shows HW's verses to, 18. 372

——'s only confidant about grief for brother, 21. 43, 58

——'s opinion of, 17. 90

——'s stomach pains not diagnosed by, 22. 468–9

——'s visits to deathbed of, 21. 164

—— tells, to urge HW to return to Florence, 17. 54

—— to reward, for professional services, 17. 106

[Cocchi, Antonio, *continued*]
—— will be aided by, in seeking Richard I's poems, **21.** 157, 162
Marsili friend of, **20.** 549n
Mead, Dr, helps finance book by, **20.** 179
——'s bankruptcy might involve, **20.** 165, 179, 185, 189
——'s correspondence with, **20.** 179
medal design suggested by, **18.** 471–2
medal of, **21.** 202
medals not discussed by, with Craon, **17.** 342
Medici history contemplated but never executed by, **21.** 284
Middleton's book desired by, **20.** 179
milk diet recommended by, **20.** 543
Panciatichi attended by, **20.** 36
Philipps may consult, **17.** 67
Pringle's medical description of Galfridus Mann wanted by, **20.** 544, 554, **21.** 35–6
professor of anatomy, **21.** 194
quicksilver not approved by, as medicine, **20.** 543
Richecourt abandoned by, **18.** 133
—— called on by, with Mann's apologies, **17.** 394
—— hints at ennoblement for, **20.** 204
—— may dislike HW's defence by, **17.** 448
—— offended by attachment of, to Mann, **18.** 133
—— orders, to insert his praises in book on Pisa baths, **20.** 158
Rucellai warns, against defending Sir Robert Walpole, **18.** 133
son of, **21.** 152, 164, **22.** 73n
son secures posts of, **21.** 194
Sturgis not attended by, **18.** 198
Tanucci schoolmate and friend of, **21.** 495n
Tozzetti performs autopsy on, **21.** 162n
Trumbull attended by, **19.** 184–5
villa of, adjoining church, borrowed by Mann, **20.** 308
Walpole, Bns, contradicted by, about HW, **17.** 448
—— rebukes, for not congratulating her on Sir Robert Walpole's retirement, **17.** 371
Walpole family respected by, **17.** 387
Whithed attended by, **18.** 109
——'s death diagnosed by, **20.** 244
Cocchi, Beatrice, m. (1763) Angelo Tavanti:
education is father's only provision for, **21.** 164
'letter to a spouse' written by, **22.** 204n
Cocchi, Gioacchino (ca 1715–1804), composer:
*Ciro reconosciuto, Il,* by, **21.** 278
*Gli amanti gelosi* by, **20.** 410, **35.** 160, **43.** 272
*Tempio della gloria, Il,* by, **35.** 106, **38.** 1
Cocchi, Dr Raimondo (1735–65):
antiquarian in Uffizi gallery, **20.** 152
*Canneto* by, sent to HW, **22.** 50, 73
education is father's only provision for, **21.** 164
father may be succeeded by, **20.** 152

father's posts secured by, **21.** 194
Florentine galleries directed by, **21.** 152n
Lyttelton disliked by, **22.** 251n
Mann will be aided by, in seeking Richard I's poems, **21.** 162
Medici history might be attempted by, if circumstances permitted, **21.** 284
Paoli intimate with, **23.** 68
——'s correspondence with, **23.** 27n, 51n, 68n
public anatomy lecture read by, in father's place, **20.** 152
Richard I's poems copied by, **21.** 186
*Spectator* by, imitated from Addison, **22.** 73n
writing may more safely be practised by, in England, **22.** 74
Cocchiata:
English have, at Florence, **18.** 485
Mann promises, to HW if he revisits Florence, **18.** 56
——'s, **18.** 1, 30
—— to give, in his garden, **17.** 498–9
on Lung'arno, **17.** 105
Spaniard gives, in Florence to sweetheart, **22.** 158
Cocchi family:
financial success of, **21.** 201
Cochin, Charles-Nicolas (1715–90), designer; engraver:
engraving by, of Mme du Deffand's cats, **6.** 360
Hénault's *Abrégé* illustrated by, **4.** 4–5, **5.** 283
(?) print of Bns Hervey after painting by, **31.** 415
social relations of, with Mme Geoffrin, **7.** 283, 291, 304, 345
Cochineal:
*Postilion* has cargo of, **19.** 82n
Cochran, printer. *See* Sands, Donaldson, Murray, and Cochran
Cochrane, Susan (d. 1754), m. 1 (1725) Charles Lyon, 4th E. of Strathmore; m. 2 (1745) George Forbes:
crazed after intervening in husband's quarrel, **21.** 364n
Mann remembers, at Florence, **21.** 364
Cock, ——, auctioneer, of Covent Garden:
Oxford's collection sold by, **42.** 266n
Cock, Jeronimus (ca 1510–70):
Hondius's prints after, **16.** 59n
Cock, Rev. John (1715–96):
preferment of, **1.** 107
town house of, **2.** 172n
Tuer's picture owned by, **1.** 83, 85, 87
Cock, William, King's Messenger:
Mann mentions, **23.** 377
(?) Masaccio's designs brought by, to HW, **23.** 266
Cock; cocks:
black, pie made of, **36.** 324
dunghill warfare of, **37.** 291
St Peter's, **37.** 67
Cockade; cockades:

blue: Gordon rioters wear, **33.** 174, 186n, 191n, 192, 193, 193n; mob compels Middlesex voters to wear, **23.** 6

'bucks' wear, **10.** 296–7

Conway wears, **37.** 37

Cumberland, D. of, orders making of, **19.** 464n

English captains wear, for Triple Alliance, **18.** 336, 544

green, Acquaviva's guard tears, from Romans, **19.** 114

green and orange for 'New Interest,' **37.** 371n

of embroidered French ribbons, given to Tuscan Grand D. and Ds, **22.** 423

orange, **39.** 457

red and white, carried by French fleet, **24.** 483, **39.** 329

tricolour, **18.** 336, 522, 544

white, Wesket wears, at execution, as sign of innocence, **38.** 490

Cockain, (?) Francis:
print of, **40.** 237

Cock and bull:
story of, **42.** 504

'Cock and the Fox, The.' *See under* Dryden, John: *Fables*

Cockatoo; cockatoos:
at Bois Prévu, **7.** 293, **35.** 116
new hair style like crest of, **39.** 271
Paris shops sell, **33.** 515

Cockayne, Thomas (d. 1749), army officer:
HW may have seen, **37.** 244
Mackintosh, Bns, loved by, **37.** 244

Cockbert. *See* Coquebert

Cockboat; cockboats:
English capture, from Calais to California, **20.** 500
news not brought by, **12.** 75

Cockburn, Lt-Col.:
expedition to Puna under, **24.** 509n

Cockburn, James (1723–1809), army officer; alleged 6th Bt, 1782:
French 'purchase' St Eustatius from, **25.** 235

Cockburn, Sir James (1729–1804), 8th Bt; M.P.:
hothouses of, not envied by HW, **35.** 473

Cockburn, Jane:
at Boughton Park, **37.** 212
Coke, Lady Mary, sends, on errand, **31.** 127

Cockburn, John (ca 1679–1758), M.P.:
Admiralty appointment of, **17.** 355, 363, 366, **18.** 550
Argyll's secretary, **17.** 355n
Parliamentary membership of, corrected, **43.** 243

Cockburn, W.:
print of, **40.** 236

Cocker, Edward (1631–76), engraver:
Cole calls attention to, **1.** 45

Cockermouth, Bn. *See* Wyndham, George O'Brien (1751–1837)

Cockermouth, Cumberland:

Somerset leaves borough of, to Wyndham, **20.** 11

Stanhope, M.P. for, **28.** 492n

Cocket, Mary, m. John Foote:
(?) HW gives breakfast to, at SH, **39.** 475
SH visited by, **11.** 81n

Cock-horse:
child puts boots on, when preparing to ride, **10.** 321

Cock Lane:
Arlington St near, **10.** 282
ghost of: crowds see, **10.** 6; exposure of, **22.** 8–9; Gévaudan beast compared with, **22.** 289; HW gives history of, **10.** 5–7; HW jokes about, **10.** 282; HW mentions, **10.** 10, 15, **11.** 46; HW to see, **22.** 3; HW visits, because fashionable, **22.** 17; Mann thinks story of, 'horrid,' **22.** 13; might be believed in Italy, **25.** 1–2; would-be auditors of, **10.** 6

Cockleshell; cockleshells:
Battle Abbey cloister adorned with, **35.** 140
Caligula played with, at Boulogne, **16.** 211

'Cockney, Castle of':
HW refers to English Court as, **37.** 406, 411

'Cockney, King of':
Norfolk does not care about, **37.** 406

Cockpit, Whitehall, London:
Bute's levee at, **13.** 38n
council at, **20.** 360n
Fox, Henry, to preside at, **20.** 503
HW calls on his uncle Horace at, **14.** 222
HW to attend meeting at, **18.** 103
meeting at **18.** 103, **37.** 413
Orford and Miss Nicoll brought together at, **14.** 223
Privy Council examines Cameron at, **20.** 373n
prize ships adjudged at, **21.** 287n
Selwyn's witticism to Wilkes at, **38.** 223
Walpole, Horatio (1678–1757) lives at, **14.** 203n, 222, **15.** 326n
—— writes from, **36.** 29, 302

Cocks, Charles (1725–1806), cr. (1784) Bn Somers:
brothers of, **12.** 18n

Cocks, James (d. 1758), ensign:
death of, at St-Cast, after being wounded at Cherbourg, **21.** 245, **37.** 571
fortune of, **21.** 245

Cocks, James (1734–1804), banker:
banking firm of, **42.** 453n
(?) HW meets, at Mrs Buller's, **12.** 18

Cocks, Margaret (d. 1761), m. 1 John Lygon; m. 2 (1719) Philip Yorke, cr. (1733) Bn Hardwicke and (1754) E. of Hardwicke:
ale forbidden by, **21.** 4
daughter of, married, **9.** 54–5
death of, **38.** 122
husband's wand not to be refused by, **9.** 39
nephew of, **21.** 245, **37.** 571
(?) picture of, falls down, **33.** 426

Cocks, Thomas Somers (1737–96), banker:
banking firm of, **42**. 453n
brothers of, **12**. 18n
Cock-sparrow. *See under* Sparrow
Cockspur St, Haymarket, London:
British Coffee-House in, **20**. 124n
Pinchbeck's shop in, **2**. 222n, **33**. 128n
Wright, Patience, exhibits wax figures at
house in, **32**. 98n
Cocoa Tree, The, coffee-house:
Board, The, moves from St Alban's Tavern
to, **20**. 5on, **43**. 249
hazard played at, **25**. 12
Jacobite rendezvous, **18**. 186, **25**. 12n
laundry-maid finds letter dropped near, **35**.
230
Pretender's coach to stop of its own accord at,
**9**. 35
See also *Letter from The Cocoa-Tree*
Cocomero, Via del, at Florence:
theatre in, *see* Teatro del Cocomero
Cocuffsoff, Capt.:
Russian ship commanded by, **33**. 214
Cod:
Farinelli said to seek, in Newfoundland, **18**.
119
Coddrington. *See* Codrington
Codille (term in ombre):
HW quotes Pope on, **32**. 123
Codlin tart:
HW eats, **28**. 162
Codoré *or* Coldoré, Olivier (fl. ca 1575–ca
1600), artist:
Mariette attributes works to, confusing him
with Fontenoy, **16**. 149n
sardonyx of Q. Elizabeth probably by, **16**.
148–9
Codpiece; codpieces:
Brandon's, **35**. 359
Capponi's, pierced in duel, **18**. 182
Henry VIII's, **17**. 233, **23**. 87
looking-glasses possibly related to, **9**. 79
Montagu jokes about Cromwell's, **10**. 158
Codrington, Miss:
SH visited by, **12**. 244
Codrington, Christopher (1668–1710):
HW describes will of, from (?) *Biographia
Britannica*, **35**. 178
Codrington, Sir William (1719–92), 2d Bt,
1738; M.P.:
Mann receives, **17**. 408
Cod smack:
Pembroke abducts Miss Hunter in, **22**. 16n
Coelson, Lancelot:
print of, **40**. 236
Coëtlogon, Comtesse de. *See* Johanne de la Carre
de Saumery, Marie-Madeleine
Coëtlogon, Marquise de. *See* Du Roy de Vac-
quières, Françoise-Bernarde-Thérèse-Margue-
rite-Eugénie
Coëtlosquet, Jean-Gilles de (1700–84), Bp of
Limoges:
made member of order of St-Esprit, **6**. 199

Coëtnempren de Kersaint, Guy-François de:
(?) Brest sailed from by, **21**. 101n
Coëtquen, Louise-Françoise-Maclovie-Céleste de
(d. 1802), m. (1736) Emmanuel-Félicité de
Durfort, Duc de Duras:
Chanteloup visited by, **8**. 207
Du Barry, Mme, at Choisy with, **4**. 258
social relations of, with: Guerchy, Comtesse
de, **7**. 317; Hertford, Cts of, **38**. 482
Coffee:
after dinner, while hearing music, **33**. 541n
Beauclerks serve, at Drayton, **10**. 343
Cole drinks: at Bentham's, **1**. 299n; at Em-
manuel College, **2**. 44
—— invited for, by Masters, **2**. 11
—— serves, to Glynn, **2**. 107
expense of, for Mesdames de France, **20**. 500
French Customs will confiscate, **37**. 40
HW attributes double meaning to Swift's use
of, **10**. 219
HW drinks, **10**. 312, **31**. 93
HW may have taken, with Lady Diana Beau-
clerk, **35**. 624
HW prepares, for Archduke and Archduchess
of Austria, **33**. 529
HW serves, at SH party, **10**. 69, 127, 168, 170,
279, **31**. 216
Hertford serves, on George III's birthday, **38**.
398
Johnson, Dr Samuel, apologetic for putting
milk into, **33**. 494
Karl Wilhelm Ferdinand takes, with D. of
Cumberland, **38**. 288
Mann and P. of Mecklenburg drink, with
Leopold and Maria Louisa, **22**. 438
—— serves: after dinner, **17**. 117; in HW's
Saxon cups, **18**. 162; with milk, **17**. 33
Mason had wished HW to drink, **28**. 273
Old Pretender serves, to Craons, **17**. 9
Oxford Loungers peruse politics over, **38**. 46
Pecquigny takes, as snuff, **38**. 215
Pelham, Frances, serves, at Esher party, **10**. 73
Raynal discusses, **39**. 168
Schaub, Lady, entertains HW and K. Theo-
dore with, **20**. 40
served at Robinson's ball, **17**. 185
served in Wroxton library, **35**. 72
Temples and guests drink, at Stowe, **10**. 313,
**31**. 146
York, D. of, receives: at Lucca, **22**. 221; at
Rome, **22**. 228
Coffee-girl:
Sandwich takes, into room, **22**. 284
Coffee-house; coffee-houses:
American agitation descends from Parliament
to, **24**. 87
at Minorca, provides lemons and greens for
ship, **37**. 314
at Oxford, **38**. 45–6
at Quirinal in Rome, **18**. 533
Blandford, Lady, keeps equivalent of, **35**. 349
Cholmondeley's begging letters compared at,
**20**. 325n

Dunn declares in, that he will kill Wilkes, **22.** 189, **38.** 265

English: Frederick II left to, **21.** 101; sources of political gossip, **21.** 13

English at Florence discuss politics as they would in, at home, **25.** 393

Florentine: **11.** 287, **17.** 406; false rumours in, **18.** 206; Mann mortified by talk in, about English fleet, **19.** 151; *see also* Casino, The; Pannoni's

French, not kept separate from clubs, **38.** 336

Gage declaimed in, **30.** 291n

HW calls politicians of, real patriots, **39.** 108

HW does not want to be game for, **34.** 100

HW gleans verses from, **9.** 7

HW might go to, **12.** 70

HW's house in Berkeley Sq. resembles, **12.** 84, **25.** 371, **33.** 396, 460, **34.** 37, 107, 180

hackney writer haunts, to see his letters in newspapers, **42.** 503

House of Commons compared with, **21.** 52

Howard, Edward, believed in, to have been poisoned, **22.** 484

invalid's room a, **32.** 343

Joseph II's aggressions reported in, **36.** 228

Mahon addresses mob from balcony of, **33.** 177

near Parliament St, **22.** 189n

Newcastle's friends gather in, to speculate on political shifts, **38.** 156

newspapers collect news from, **34.** 231

Nourse's conversation in, **17.** 248

of Pella, **32.** 388

on Parnassus, **33.** 527

Pannoni's, *see under* Pannoni

Parisian, have English newspapers, **28.** 356–7

politicians of: easily diverted to home topics from continental events, **25.** 562; gather material for bewailing their country, **39.** 108

Sturgis frequents, **17.** 462

Swiss, near Duomo in Florence, **17.** 406

two houses of Parliament are, **34.** 138

White's Club not separated from, **38.** 336

Winstanley's remark in, on recent crime, **20.** 317

*See also* British Coffee-house; Chapter Coffee-house; Coca-Tree, The; Holyland Coffee House; Lloyd's Coffee-house; Lucas's Coffee-house; Nando's Coffee-house; St-James's Coffee-house; Smyrna Coffee-house; Somerset House Coffee-house; Tom's Coffee-house; Union Coffee-house; Wardour St Coffee-house

Coffee-pot:
given by HW to Mann: **25.** 56; Mann may give, to D. of Newcastle, **18.** 115–16, 137, 151–2, 201, 518; sold by Mann to Mathews, **18.** 472

Coffee-room:
at White's Club, **35.** 313

Coffee service:
of Chelsea china, **22.** 122

Coffer; coffers:
at Welbeck, still sealed, **35.** 271
Cellini's, *see* Chest
Jamesone's, of medals, **40.** 285
red velvet, for dram-bottles, **37.** 439n

Cofferer of the Household:
Baltimore replaces Lord Archibald Hamilton as, **19.** 360–1
candidates considered for, by D. of Newcastle, **20.** 518n
Grenville, James, resigns as, **21.** 540n, **38.** 137
—— succeeds D. of Leeds as, **9.** 341, 343, **21.** 488, 489
Hill, Wills, is, **17.** 436n
Leeds, D. of, resigns as, **21.** 98
—— succeeds Lyttelton as, **9.** 181, **20.** 517, **35.** 263
Lyttelton does not resign as, **35.** 194
Richmond, D. of, declines to be, **30.** 194n
Sandys becomes, **17.** 249n, **18.** 365
—— to become, **18.** 350, 357
Stanley succeeds Scarbrough as, **22.** 473
Thomond becomes, **9.** 406, **38.** 142
—— succeeded by Scarbrough as, **22.** 311
Waller succeeds Winnington as, **30.** 291n
—— succeeded by Lincoln as, **19.** 347
Winnington is, **17.** 172n

Coffey, Charles (d. 1745), dramatist:
*Devil to Pay, The*, by: **12.** 33n, **18.** 51n; French have pieces like, **13.** 167; 'Lady Loverule' in, **12.** 150; *New Ode* refers to, **18.** 51

Coffin, Capt.:
tea ship at Boston commanded by, **23.** 550n

Coffin, Richard, of Exeter; engraver:
(?) plate by, of Exeter Cathedral window, **41.** 102n

Coffin; coffins:
Bright, Edward, measured for, **20.** 208n
Byng measured for, **21.** 66
Coventry, Cts of, seen in, by mob, **21.** 451
Edward (1453–71), P. of Wales's, supposedly discovered, **30.** 274
HW a Methusaleh who belongs in, **32.** 130
HW will order his, and pair, **33.** 461
Harrington dragged from, into House of Lords, **37.** 458
in monument at Trinity Hospital, Greenwich, **16.** 87
lead, Del Monte melts, to make musket balls, **20.** 428
leather, red, covers, **22.** 216n
made at Monaco for D. of York, **22.** 554
Mann takes, on voyage to Naples, **24.** 180
Moore's, chained to his whore's, **20.** 181
Scott, Lord Charles, disintegrates when put into, **20.** 138
Selwyn's joke when Lovat's body is put into, **37.** 268
stone, period of, **2.** 243
velvet, in Westminster Abbey, for Spanish ambassador, **22.** 216

Cogan, Francis:

[Cogan, Francis, *continued*]
  Newcastle's pension reported to, at Smyrna coffee-house, 21. 26n

'Cogge, Tom.' *See* Carew, Thomas

Coghill, Lady. *See* Hoyt, Mary

Coghill, Hester (d. 1789), m. 1 Charles Moore, 2d Bn Moore, 1725; cr. (1758) E. of Charleville; m. 2 (ca 1764) John Mayne (Coghill from 1779), cr. (1781) Bt:
  gout of, 33. 525
  HW jokes about being third husband of, 33. 525, 526
  HW told by, of her visitors' ideas about him, 34. 23–4
  house at Isleworth taken by, 33. 524
  second marriage of, 33. 524–5
  SH visited by, 12. 229
  SH visitors sent by, 12. 230, 231
  will of, 34. 60

Coghill (Mayne until 1779), Sir John (d. 1785), cr. (1781) Bt; M.P.; army officer:
  marriage and death of, 33. 524–5

Coghill (formerly Cramer), Sir John (1732–90), cr. (1778), Bt:
  cousin's heir-at-law, 34. 60

Coghlan, Miss, m. (?) —— Goodwin:
  (?) Florence visited by, 20. 103

Coghlan, Anne (d. 1786), m. (1745) Hon. Thomas Hervey:
  biographical information about, corrected, 43. 267, 314, 349
  Hervey, Elizabeth, friend of, 34. 86
  husband acknowledges, on death-bed, 39. 248
  husband re-acknowledges, 32. 231
  husband's description of, in letter to Mayor and Corporation of Bury St Edmund's, 30. 116
  husband's insulting remark to, about her costume, 30. 116
  poverty of, before marriage, 30. 116
  (?) sister of, 20. 103
  son of, 34. 86

*Coglione*:
  Benedict XIV's exclamation, 19. 492

*Coglionerie*:
  HW's use of, might have offended delicate ears, 21. 253

Coif:
  HW jokes about fight between wig and, 37. 365
  in portrait, 35. 72
  Montagu might as well be wearing, so far as Buccleuchs are concerned, 10. 259

Coiffure; coiffures:
  Barrymore, Cts of, gets, from Paris, 35. 477
  of St-Cyr pensioners, 10. 293
  Tesi's, 18. 263
  *See also* Hair-dressing; Headdress; Tête naissante; Wig

Coign; coigns ('coins'):
  at the Vyne, in parlour, 35. 639

Coignet de la Thuilerie de Courson, Mlle de (b. ca 1724):

(?) apartment of: 8. 3; (?) Aulan, Marquis and Marquise, to have apartment over, 7. 94; Du Deffand, Mme, borrows, to entertain, 4. 38
(?) social relations of, with Mme du Deffand, 7. 310, 431

Coigneux, Le. *See* Le Coigneux

Coigni. *See* Coigny

Coigny, Chevalier de. *See* Franquetot, Jean-Philippe de

Coigny, Comte de. *See* Franquetot, Ange-Augustin-Gabriel de (1740–1817); Franquetot, François de (1670–1759)

Coigny, Comtesse de. *See* Névet, Marie-Thérèse-Corentine de (d. 1778); Roissy, Anne-Josèphe-Michelle de (ca 1754–75)

Coigny, Duc de. *See* Franquetot, Augustin-Louis-Joseph-Casimir-Gustave de (b. 1788); Franquetot, François de (1670–1759); Franquetot, Marie-François-Henri de (1737–1821)

Coigny, Duchesse de. *See* Andlau, Jeanne-Françoise-Aglaé d'

Coigny, Marquis de. *See* Franquetot, François-Marie-Casimir de

Coigny, Marquise de. *See* Conflans, Louise-Marthe de (1759–1825); Névet, Marie-Thérèse-Corentine de (d. 1778)

Coigny, Vicomte de. *See* Franquetot, Pierre-Auguste de (b. 1757)

Coigny, Aimée de. *See* Franquetot de Coigny, Anne-Françoise-Aimée de (1769–1820)

Coigny, Légion de:
  Chauvelin may command, in Corsica, 4. 64n

Coin; coins:
  Achesoun's, of Mary, Q. of Scots, 42. 321n
  Arundel's, 16. 152, 42. 447
  at Devonshire House, 16. 209, 210
  brass, Roman, of two-horned rhinoceros, 20. 128n
  clipping of, in Yorkshire, 23. 498
  Colquhoun collects ancient, 42. 322n
  counterfeiting of, at Birmingham, 31. 277
  Florentine: HW's, 15. 278, 280, 283, 284, 285–6; in Stosch's collection, 21. 189, 201–2
  Folkes's, to be sold, 37. 425
  Frederick II adulterates, 23. 515n
  George III's, lacking in Q. of Sweden's cabinet, 40. 214
  Greek, not influenced by barbarous types, 15. 211–12
  Greek and Roman, in Kennedy's collection, 35. 347n
  HW's case of, 42. 262
  HW's collection of, 1. 67, 17. 4n; Roman, 35. 477n; silver, Florentine, drawn by S. Lysons for Roscoe, 42. 439; untouched by housebreakers, 14. 189, 23. 285
  HW sends, to Ashton, 13. 225–6
  Henry III's, gold, 40. 214
  high price of, in England, 23. 466
  Mestrell's, of Q. Elizabeth, 16. 150
  Middleton's, 15. 16–17

old, may be dug up at Dorchester, **37**. 491
of Q. Elizabeth, **42**. 278
Oxford's: English coins among, **17**. 358; sell
for high prices, **17**. 374, 378
portrait of Mary, Q. of Scots, on, **15**. 113, 139,
166, **42**. 321n
Rawlinson leaves, to Oxford, **42**. 239n
Roman: exhibited by Felton, **34**. 10n; Mid-
dleton's, **15**. 16–17
Saxon and Norman, **16**. 108
silver: in William III's time, **16**. 77; scarce,
**30**. 276n
Theodore of Corsica's, **21**. 140
Wheler's *Journey into Greece* mentions, **16**.
158
White's collection of, **1**. 67–9
Wren's, sold, **40**. 348n
writ regulating, dated at Chester, **40**. 221n
*See also* Coign; Currency; Medal
Coire (*also called* Chur):
Salis minister at, **18**. 215
Coirmheadhain, Scotland:
Young Pretender at, **19**. 279n
Coislin, Marquise de. *See* Mailly-Rubempré,
Marie - Anne - Louise - Adélaïde - Mélanie - Fran-
çoise de
Cokayne, Francis (d. 1767), sheriff of London
and Middlesex 1745–6:
Balmerinoch's speech to, **19**. 301
Cokayne, Lt-Col. Thomas (d. 1749):
prisoners' exchange arranged by, **37**. 279n
Coke, Lady. *See* Cecil, Lady Elizabeth (1578–
1646)
Coke, Lady Anne. *See* Osborne, Lady Anne
Coke, Sir Edward (1552–1634), Kt; lord chief
justice of Common Pleas and King's Bench:
Hardinge reveres Chesterfield in place of, **35**.
586
insinuations by, against Northampton at Somerset's trial, **16**. 162
Northampton's letters read by, at Somerset's
trial, **16**. 161
parody by, at Holles's trial, **16**. 163
portrait showing wife weeping over coffin of,
**40**. 199
Stoke manor bought by, **14**. 59n
Coke, Edward (1719–53), styled Vct Coke;
M.P.:
Address moved by, **18**. 351
advised at White's to shoot himself, **37**. 288
appearance of, short, **30**. 39
Bellenden's duel with, **9**. 59–61
'bound to the peace,' **9**. 153
Campbells' feud with, over his marriage
troubles, **9**. 59–61
Conway does not have, to write about, **37**. 291
death of, **17**. 247n, **19**. 456n, **30**. 120–1
degeneration of, **19**. 456–7
Deskford claims, as friend, **17**. 371
dying, **20**. 114
Edgcumbe, Hervey, and Ellis to visit, at
Holkham, **18**. 25

father absorbed in lawsuit of, **20**. 105
Florence visited by, **37**. 79
Grafton visited by, at Euston, **18**. 254
HW brought by, to and from Euston, **18**. 254
HW crosses Giogo with, **17**. 257
HW has not imitated the vices of, **37**. 333
HW jokes about, as matrimonial lawyer, **37**.
333
HW quotes, **35**. 624
HW receives condolences from, **17**. 320
HW says that Anne Seymour Conway is being
snatched from HW, just as the wife of, was
snatched by her family, **37**. 333–4
HW's *Lesson for the Day* dispersed by, **18**. 33
HW's pamphlet copied by, **13**. 13
HW used to shock, **32**. 191
HW visits, at Holkham, **30**. 39
half mad, **23**. 558n
insolvent and spreads grievances at White's
Club, **37**. 288
marriage of: **19**. 19n, 294–5; arranged, **9**.
36–7; rumoured, **19**. 19, 27
Norfolk visited by, **30**. 64
Onslow hears witticism by, about Taaffe and
Wortley Montagu, **20**. 289
Parliamentary committee headed by, **19**. 387n
Parliamentary speeches by, **17**. 297–8, **26**. 23,
32
Parliamentary vote by, on privately-raised
regiments, **26**. 18, 19
Selwyn indebted to, **30**. 120n
Shelvocke tutor to, **20**. 436n
sits 22 hours in Parliament, **17**. 383
*Sortes Virgilianæ* drawn by, **37**. 79
Sunninghill visited by, **9**. 60, **37**. 288
Walpole, Sir Robert, visited by, at Houghton,
**18**. 254
Walpole party supported by, **17**. 247
widow of, **4**. 404n, **11**. 121n, **12**. 11n, **13**. 36n,
**22**. 149n, **23**. 538n, **28**. 164n
wife defeats, **31**. 177
wife shut up by, **23**. 538n
wife's lawsuit against, **20**. 100, 114
wife's parents disparaged by, **37**. 333
wife's rift with, **37**. 288, 291
Coke, Lady Jane. *See* Wharton, Lady Jane
Coke, Lady Margaret. *See* Tufton, Lady Margaret
Coke, Lady Mary. *See* Campbell, Lady Mary
Coke, Robert (d. 1750), of Longford:
wife of, **9**. 332n, **34**. 256
Coke, Thomas (d. 1727), vice-chamberlain of
the Household:
copies list of Charles I's collection, **16**. 290n,
**42**. 354n
wife of, **14**. 243n
Coke, Thomas (1697–1759), cr. (1728) Bn
Lovel; (1744) E. of Leicester; M.P.:
Albani procures release of statues for, **20**.
104n
Bedford called 'Muley' by, **17**. 497
Brettingham agent of, **20**. 104n

[Coke, Thomas (1697–1759), *continued*]
brother of, **34.** 256
Chesterfield discusses Westminster election with, **17.** 272
—— to visit, **30.** 70
(?) Cignani painting bought by, **21.** 208n, 478
Coke, Lady Mary, defeats, **31.** 177
——'s denunciations from, believed by HW, **37.** 333
—— shut up by, **23.** 538n
comment by, on Dettingen victory, **35.** 39
conversation of, lost on younger generation, **34.** 39
earldom given to, through Sir Robert Walpole's aid, **18.** 441
Grafton visited by, at Euston, **18.** 254
HW brought by, to and from Euston, **18.** 254
Manchester, Dowager Ds of, admired by, **17.** 247n, **30.** 42
Mann prefers HW's witticism to, to Lady Townshend's on Whitefield, **20.** 70
——'s correspondence with, about statues to be sent from Rome, **20.** 104
—— sends compliments to, **18.** 455–6
Montemar's arrest reported by, **18.** 29, 54
mother of, **18.** 144
nephew of, marries, **9.** 209
Pulteney's *Epistle* in name of, **37.** 82
rebus sent to, about Ds of Manchester, **30.** 42
saying by, about John, **18.** 316
servants of, receive paltry gratuity from Pulteney family at Holkham, **19.** 443
Shirley, Lady Frances, admired by, **17.** 247n
son of: **12.** 11n, **13.** 13, **17.** 247n, 257n, **19.** 456n, **22.** 149n, **23.** 538n; affair of, absorbs father, **20.** 105; not to imitate Walpole and Townshend marriages, **19.** 27
statue owned by, **16.** 300
Walpole, Sir Robert, patron of, **34.** 38n
—— supported politically by, **17.** 247n
—— visited by, at Houghton, **18.** 254
White's Club frequented by, **34.** 38
wife of, **9.** 37n
Williams, Sir C. H., describes love of, for Ds of Manchester, in 'Isabella, or the Morning,' **25.** 308n, **30.** 317
wit of, not admired when he returned after retirement, **25.** 308
witticisms by: at rebel's trial, **19.** 286; to HW, on his trees, **20.** 53–4
Coke, Mrs Thomas:
Berkeley's amour with, **14.** 243n
Coke, Thomas William (1754–1842), cr. (1837) E. of Leicester; M.P.:
Albany, Cts of, loved by, **24.** 102n, **39.** 180
father of, **9.** 209n
(?) HW's correspondence with, **42.** 436–7
mother of, **33.** 105
opposition to, in Norfolk, **12.** 185, **42.** 436–7
Parliamentary motions by: against Pitt administration, **25.** 471n; for partial disavowal of peace commissioners' manifesto, **24.** 426n, 429n

signs Norfolk petition, **33.** 166
Coke, Mrs Thomas William. *See* Dutton, Jane (1753–1800)
Coke, Wenman Roberts. *See* Roberts, Wenman
Coke, Mrs Wenman Roberts. *See* Denton, Elizabeth
Coke. *See also* Cook; Cooke
Coke (fuel):
Conway makes, at Park Place, **39.** 551
Coke family:
Coke, Lady Mary, denounced by, **37.** 333
Coke ovens:
Conway might convert, to balloon-making, **39.** 419
Conway's, experimental, **35.** 437n, **39.** 392, 408, 419, 456, 551–2
Coker (Cokes *or* Coques ?), —— (fl. 1684), silversmith:
Nell Gwyn employs, **1.** 350
Cokesey, Sir Hugh (fl. 1413–45), Kt:
in Margaret of Anjou's escort, **14.** 73
Colalto, Eleonora (fl. 1742–58), Contessa di, m. (1742) Cavaliere Pietro Andrea Capello, Venetian ambassador:
biographical information about, corrected, **43.** 112, 253
Carteret's marital eligibility doubted by, **18.** *431*, 446
Conway entertained by, at Rome, **37.** 324
English society ridiculed by, **20.** 175
exile of, may be ended, **21.** 219
Florence to be visited by, **20.** 162
Granville, Cts, entertained by, **19.** 18
HW's old acquaintance, **20.** 162, 481, **21.** 219
HW's opinion of, **20.** 169, 179
harlequin dance to be performed by, in tragedy given by Romans at Frascati, **20.** 481
Hesse, Landgrave of, notices, **9.** 27
husband persuaded by, to delay leaving Rome, **20.** 177n
husband's relatives may poison, **37.** 289
Lobkowitz escorts, to P. of Wales's barge, **37.** 289
Mann gives garden assembly for, **20.** 174, 191
masquerade by, for Frederick, P. of Wales, excludes Pelham faction, **19.** 18
miscarries, as result of country dances, **37.** 324
negotiations of, would be entertaining, **20.** 176
Niccolini entertains, at dinner, **20.** 174
Rinuccini, former lover of, **20.** 174–5
smallpox ruins beauty of, **20.** 175
Stevens's witticism to, **20.** 175
wit of, less evident in Florence than in England, **20.** 175
Colardeau, Charles-Pierre (1732–76), poet:
Académie française elects, **6.** 274, 284
Académie française elects La Harpe to succeed, **6.** 333
dying, **6.** 284
'Colas,' Lady Ailesbury's pet:

HW condoles with Cts of Ailesbury on death of, **39.** 166–7

Colberg (Germany):
Peter III may be induced by conquest of, to stay in Pomerania, **22.** 10–11
—— 's generosity to inhabitants of, **22.** 22

Colbert, Élisabeth-Pauline-Gabrielle (d. 1786), m. (1736) François-Pierre-Charles Bouchard d'Esparbez de Lussan, Marquis de Jonzac; 'la nièce':
absent from Paris during HW's visit, **5.** 206
account by, of scene between Orléans and Chartres, **3.** 159, **8.** 127–8
addresses of, sent to HW, **3.** 50
Aguesseau subject of anecdote by, **7.** 276
Aubeterre's return pleases, **4.** 244
bled 7 times in 6 days, **7.** 101
Boudot friend of, **8.** 178
Bouillon, Chevalier de, mourned by, **3.** 357
Broglie, Comtesse de, visited by, at Ruffec, **6.** 211
Chabot, Comtesse de, correspondent of, **3.** 37, 314, 324
Chaillot refuge of, **4.** 486
Cholmondeley, Mrs, conveys messages to HW from, **4.** 480
—— cordially treated by, **4.** 240, 477, 480
Churchill, Lady Mary, meets, **5.** 23
'court of Charlemagne' of, **3.** 11, 14, 130, 182
Czernieski, Mme, writes to, **4.** 49
Du Deffand, Mme, asks for HW's picture for, **3.** 360
—— asks HW what to tell, **5.** 367, 375
—— engages, for numerous parties, with HW, **39.** 257–8
—— entertains Hénault to free, **4.** 119, 125, 416
—— has message from, **4.** 181
—— lends medal owned by, to Barthélemy, **7.** 445
—— mentions unhappy situation of, **6.** 164, 169
—— misses, **3.** 259, 261–2
—— 's correspondence with, **5.** 238
—— 's opinion of, **3.** 47, 182, 225, 244, 247, 309, 314, 319, 356, **4.** 16, 72n, 236, 300, 407–8, 486, 492, **5.** 56, **6.** 130, 164, 436, **7.** 50
—— 's relations with, **3.** 262, 324, **4.** 16, 137, **5.** 8, 431, **6.** 7–8, 130, 211
—— talks about HW to, **3.** 3
—— to consult, **4.** 95
—— to tell, about HW and Voltaire, **4.** 97
—— wishes HW to call on, **3.** 343
—— wishes HW to send message for, **3.** 190, 202, 215, 225
finances of, **4.** 486, **5.** 61
Forcalquier, Mme de, sends Hénault's portrait to, **3.** 66–7
forgets she has asked Mme du Deffand to supper, **7.** 435
guests of, **5.** 61
HW esteemed by, **3.** 38, 73, 148, 256, 314, 324, 343, 354, 356, **5.** 206

HW inquired after by, **6.** 130, **7.** 14
HW omits, from list of presents, **3.** 83, 85
HW receives bas-relief from, **3.** 129, 136
HW's correspondence with, **3.** 78, 86n, 87, 277, 362, **5.** 377, **7.** 382, 386, 388
HW sends compliments to, **41.** 29
HW sends messages to, **3.** 25, 155, 324, **5.** 206, **6.** 137, **36.** 55, 242
HW sent messages by, **3.** 36, **4.** 49, 287, 480
HW's friendship for, **4.** 293, **6.** 137
HW's *Gramont* given to, by Mme du Deffand, **5.** 436
HW's letter to Rousseau read by, **3.** 4
HW solicitous for, **4.** 272, **7.** 105, 107
HW's portrait sent to, **3.** 399, 402
HW's present to, **3.** 85, 92, 99
HW's return desired by, **4.** 259
HW to have vest embroidered by, **4.** 24, 73–4, 82, 85, 143, 154
HW to send mahogany table to, **7.** 415
HW writes about, **3.** 247
health of, **4.** 275, **5.** 61, 436, **6.** 34, 35, **7.** 101, 105, 107
Hénault attended by, for 6 years, **4.** 486
—— reassured by, **4.** 92
—— 's bequest to, **4.** 486
Jonzac, Marquis de, relations of, with, **4.** 486, **5.** 56
—— takes out, **4.** 131
Jonzac to be visited by, **5.** 56, 61, 225, 231
letter by, **41.** 199
letter from HW to Mme du Deffand read by, **3.** 86
L'Isle to convey parcel for, **4.** 24
Man in the Iron Mask discussed by, **7.** 270
Necker answers Mme du Deffand about protégé of, **7.** 430
reports on Hénault's health, **4.** 36
returns to Paris, **5.** 421, **6.** 380
Rochford, Cts of, talks with, **3.** 315
'Rosette' inquired after by, **4.** 233
Rousseau article in *St James's Chronicle* read to Mme du Deffand by, **3.** 37
Sévigné, Mme de, letter under name of, in hand of, **3.** 51, 73
—— snuff-box with portrait of, prepared by, **3.** 73
Shuvalov given commission by, **3.** 129
sister-in-law of, dies, **3.** 259
social relations of, in Paris, *see index entries ante* **8.** 305
tea table of, **3.** 23, 50, 85, 92, 112, 113
Thursday suppers of, **5.** 13
Tillières to be visited by, **6.** 211
Torcy educates, **7.** 270
*Triomphe de l'amitié, Le*, read to, **3.** 363–4

Colbert, Jean-Baptiste (1619–83), Marquis de Seignelay, minister under Louis XIV:
Doumenil has portraits from collection of, **7.** 313
Du Deffand, Mme, compares Terray to, **4.** 372–3
—— mentions, **6.** 95

[Colbert, Jean-Baptiste, *continued*]
HW compares Pitt with, **9**. 228
HW contrasts Sully and, **5**. 407
HW on, **5**. 407
Necker's *Éloge* of, **5**. 395, 396, 400, 405, 406–7, 408, 409
Sceaux built by, **7**. 322
Séguier cites, **41**. 346
tomb of, **7**. 279
Colbert, Jean-Baptiste (1665–1746), Marquis de Torcy:
family of, **3**. 155n, **7**. 215–16
Jonzac, Mme de, 'bred up' by, **7**. 270
Man in Iron Mask discussed by, **7**. 270
monument to, **7**. 279
Strafford prefers San Felipe's *Commentarios* to *Mémoires* of, **35**. 283
Colbert, Louis-Jean-Baptiste-Antonin (1731–living, 1780), Marquis de Seignelay:
wife of, **3**. 259, **5**. 147n
Colbert, Marguerite-Louise (1738–86), m. (1757) Joseph-Marie, Comte de Lordat:
social relations of, with Hénault, **7**. 323
Colbert, Marguerite-Thérèse (1682–1769), m. 1 (1701) Louis de Clermont d'Amboise, Marquis de Renel; m. 2 (1704) François-Marie Spinola, Duc de St-Pierre:
death of, **4**. 193, 195
Hénault's 'portrait' of, **8**. 97
social relations of, in Paris, **3**. 107, **7**. 298, 300–1, 303, 306, 308
Colbert, René-Édouard (1706–71), Marquis de Maulévrier:
apartment of, over Mme du Deffand's, **4**. 351, 376, 384, 391, *398*, 403, **8**. 3
country seat of, **4**. 351
Colbert de Seignelay, François (1736–1815), Bp of Rodez 1781–90:
Berry, Mary, informed by, **3**. xxiv, xli, 30n, **14**. 155nn
(?) Du Deffand, Mme, corresponds with, **7**. 443
(?) Paris visited by, **7**. 450
(?) social relations of, in Paris, **7**. 295, 298, 300, 302, 309, 450, 459, 460
SH visited by, **12**. 250
Colbert de Torcy, Catherine-Pauline (1699–1773), m. (1718) Louis du Plessis, Marquis du Plessis-Châtillon:
daughter of, **3**. 351
death of, **5**. 404
health of, **5**. 232
relatives of, **7**. 215–16
retort by, to husband's regret for his first wife, **7**. 370
social relations of, in Paris, **3**. *155*, **5**. 404, **7**. 316, 323, 338
Colbert de Torcy, Constance (1710–34), m. (1732) Augustin-Joseph, Comte de Mailly, Marquis d'Haucourt:
relatives of, **7**. 215, 216
Colbert de Torcy, Françoise-Félicité (ca 1699–1749), m. (1715) André-Joseph d'Ancezune

de Caderousse, Marquis d'Ancezune:
relatives of, **7**. 215
Colbert de Torcy, Jean-Baptiste-Joachim (1703–77), Marquis de Croissy:
Coigny sends, to Louis XV with battle news, **30**. 6on
married bliss of, **5**. 183
promotion of, in Ordre du St-Esprit, expected, **5**. 179
social relations of, in Paris, **4**. 288, **7**. 288, 300, 352
wife of, dies, **5**. 183
Colbert de Villacerf, Marguerite (1696–1772), m. (1714) François-Emmanuel, Marquis de Crussol:
Aiguillon, Duchesse d', trusted, **5**. 175
death of, **5**. *175*, 177
Du Deffand, Mme, mentions, **3**. 319
——'s friendship with, **5**. 175
——'s opinion of, **5**. 175
social relations of, in Paris, *see index entries ante* **8**. 305
Colbroke. *See* Colebrooke
Colbrook. *See* Coldbrook
Colchester, Walter de, painter and sculptor:
Paris, Matthew, praises, **42**. 42
sacrist of St Albans, **42**. 42
*Colchester*, English ship:
Admiralty orders Capt. Young to sail in, for Byng's trial, **20**. 590n
Colchester, Essex:
Clara Reeve's *Champion of Virtue* published at, **41**. 410n
Colton about to move to, **2**. 281
elections at, discussed by House of Commons, **20**. 469n, **35**. 208
Lort's accident at, **16**. 228n
Morant of, **40**. 247
Nassau M.P. for, **9**. 324n
Colcorton Hall, Leics:
Beaumont's seat, **42**. 240n
Cold; colds:
bed recommended for sufferers from, **20**. 216
churches conducive to, **20**. 228
epidemics of, **9**. 271, **18**. 145, 200, 213, **38**. 512; *see also* Influenza
HW infrequently has, **10**. 201, **11**. 279, 311, **12**. 51, 184, **30**. 250, **33**. 311
HW mentions, **12**. 9
Holman, Mrs, makes, an excuse for an invitation, **20**. 142
Mann afraid of catching, **18**. 85
occurrences of: **1**. 85, 89, 128, 169, 177, 269, 295, 301, 311n, 317, 332, 335, 339, 381, 385, **2**. 5, 198n, 207, 317, 318, **9**. 271, **10**. 26, 30, 147, **11**. 281, **12**. 19, 170, 212–13, **16**. 193, 201, 202, **17**. 122, 170, 197, 218, 369, **18**. 94, 98, 117, 119, 145, 147, 159, 174, 200, 213, 321, 365, 372, 449, 527, 546, **19**. 460–1, 484, **20**. 79, 155, 216, 228, 231n, 520, 569, **21**. 30, 58, 139, 256, **22**. 42, 173, 285, 348, 413, 506, **23**. 450, 512, **24**. 145, 188, 190, 230, **25**. 115, 280, 343, **30**. 28, **31**. 8, 29–30, 86,

112, 149, 193, 237, 239, 290, 295, **32.** 26, 27, 57–8, 64, **33.** 104, 275, 458, **34.** 5, 33, 34, 209, **35.** 210, 630, **36.** 239–40, 332, **37.** 505, **38.** 155, 342, 494, 508, 522, **39.** 452, **40.** 1, 27, 120, 371, 388, **41.** 377, 468, **42.** 191
Quin afraid of catching, in buttocks, **20.** 209
treatment for: ass's milk, **20.** 520; bleeding, **18.** 200, 213; blisters, **22.** 42; Confectio Raleana, **23.** 450; James's Powders, **1.** 337, 338, **22.** 42
'Cold and raw' (tune):
popular in Italy, **13.** 201
Coldbrook Park, near Abergavenny, Monmouth; C. H. Williams's seat:
air at, helps restore Williams's health, **30.** 147
cascade at, Williams writes by, **30.** 48
Essex, Lady, at, **30.** 147, 321
HW hopes to visit, **30.** 95
HW to write to C. H. Williams at, **30.** 48, 83
name of, corrected, **43.** 313
Williams, C. H., at, **30.** 58, 147, 321, 322
—— to fit up library at, on model of that at SH, **30.** 147
Colden, Cadwallader:
*History of the Five Indian Nations*, **35.** 186
Coldham Hall, Suffolk:
Gage of, **1.** 171n
Coldoré. *See* Codoré
Cold Pike Hill:
name of, corrected, **43.** 357
Coldstream Guards:
colonelcy of, not settled, **35.** 203
Cole, —— (d. ca 1770), of Ely:
left fortune to nephews, **1.** 284n
Cole, Abdiah:
print of, **40.** 237
Cole, Anne (d. before 1742), m. Ralph Pole; William Cole's half-sister:
sells portrait of Dalton, **1.** 362–3
Cole, Catherine (fl. 1718–82), Cole's sister:
HW sends card for, **1.** 308n
lives at Hackney, **1.** 42n, 317
ticket of admission to SH for, **1.** 307, 311, 315, 316, 317
Cole, Rev. Charles (b. ca 1757), rector of (?) Stutton, Suffolk:
(?) SH visited by, **12.** 230, 233
Cole, Charles Nalson (1723–1804), lawyer:
Cole's account of, **1.** 284n
Dugdale edited by, **1.** 283–4
Cole, Lady Elizabeth Henrietta. *See* Stanley, Lady Elizabeth Henrietta
Cole, Harriet, dau. of Thomas Rea Cole; m. Capt. William Tudor:
(?) SH visited by, **12.** 239
Cole, James (fl. 1726), engraver:
prints by, **1.** 141–2
Cole, Jane (? 1719–ca 1790), William Cole's sister:
Apthorpe visited by, **1.** 78
Cole's sister, **1.** 30n
—— visited by, **1.** 235
HW opens letter of, by mistake, **1.** 115–16

HW requested to frank letter to, **1.** 93, 114
Cole, Mary, m. Hector Mawdesley:
William Cole's sister, **1.** 15n
Cole, Stephen (ca 1707–90), of Twickenham; brewer; J.P.:
(?) HW refuses election invitation from, **24.** 48
robbed, **33.** 445
Cole, Stephen Thomas (1765–1835), army officer:
SH visited by, **12.** 161, 249
Twickenham resident, **42.** 485
wife of, **12.** 159n
Cole, Thomas Rea (d. 1807), army officer:
SH visited by, **12.** 225
Cole, William (d. 1734), father of Rev. William Cole:
family of, **2.** 378
Cole, Rev. William (1714–82), antiquary; HW's correspondent:
*See* vols 1–2 *passim*
antiquarian of Cambridge, **10.** 84
'Athenæ Cantabrigiensis' by, **43.** 63, 72
bachelor's degrees taken by, **13.** 115
birthplace of, **1.** 2n
Brown gives print to, **28.** 37
Cambridge attended by, **10.** 333, 334
Cambridgeshire estate of: **1.** 121, 167, 168, 177; sale of, **1.** 213, **2.** 35
Cambridge town hall inscription by, **43.** 75
Chute to visit, **10.** 84
Conway thanks, through HW, **37.** 24
death of, **2.** 379, **16.** 201, **33.** 575–6
*Des. of SH* presented to, and sold after his death, **33.** 575–6
design for cross at Ampthill to be selected by, **32.** 53
Edward VI's letters copied by, **32.** 45, 53
Ely may be visited by, **10.** 91, 92
epitaphs of, **2.** 378–9
Eton attended by, **10.** 333
Exeter discusses portrait with, **10.** 346
financial situation of, **1.** 106, 121, 167n, 243, 245, 303
garden of, **1.** 54, 257n, 310, 311n, 332, 369, 372, **2.** 166, 198, 210
Gooch's drawing of, **43.** 62, 63
Gough's correspondence with, **43.** 73
Granger cites HW on authority of, **41.** 220
——'s correspondence with, **43.** 55
Gray calls, 'Tozhy,' **13.** 143
—— entertains, at Cambridge, **10.** 92
—— has not seen, **14.** 187
—— informed by, of HW's illness, **14.** 158
—— sends service to, **14.** 107
—— to deliver books to, **13.** 185
HW accompanies: on English tour in 1763, **10.** 332–47; to St-Denis, **7.** 274, **31.** 73n; to St Roch, **31.** 73n
HW called on by, in Paris, **43.** 106
HW dines with, in Paris, **7.** 273
HW discusses Chatterton affair with, **42.** 2
HW expects parcel from, **29.** 183

[Cole, Rev. William (1714–82), *continued*]
HW gives 'Des. of SH' to, at his request, **42**. 39
HW goes to Cambridge to dine with, **36**. 125
HW hurries, **10**. 344
HW lived familiarly with, from boyhood, **42**. 169
HW patron of, **1**. 277
HW reads notes to, **10**. 346
HW's correspondence with: 1–2, **7**. 379, 380, 393, **28**. 19, 37, 39, 40, 57–8, 59; MSS of, **36**. 310, 315, **43**. 31–2
HW sends box by, **7**. 404
HW sends knotting-bags to England by, **31**. 76–7
HW sends letters by, **7**. 377
HW's letter to, inserted in Gough's *Sepulchral Monuments*, **42**. 168–9
HW's notes copied but not always understood by, **10**. 346
(?) HW's remark about letter from, **39**. 337
HW to visit, **10**. 84
HW visited by, at SH, **43**.
habits of: drinking, **2**. 4, 13, 234–5, 271n, 291; eating, **2**. 234n, 271n; hours, **1**. 311n
health of: **1**. 54, 59, 310, **2**. 20, 53, 71, 101, 118–19, 128, 157–9, 163, 165, 176, 179, 180, 197–8, 198n, 228, 234, 241–2, 247, 252, 261, 267, 282, 284, 310, 316, 325, 329, 334–5, 336–8; affected by heat, **1**. 185; ague, **1**. 35; colds, **1**. 128, 169, 177, 269, 295, 311n, 332, 335, 339, 381, 385, **2**. 5, 207, 317; eyesight, **1**. 278, **2**. 34n; fear of colds, **1**. 76, 337, 339; fever, **1**. 35, 83–4, 128, 159, 164, 335, 339, 360, 371, 376, **2**. 57, 140, 265, 276; gout, **1**. 241, 326, 330, 358, 360, 369, 371, 372n, 373, 376, 381, 385, **2**. 4, 7, 13–14, 14, 16–18, 23, 42, 53, 67–8, 70, 71, 73, 113, 133, 136, 140, 141, 143, 151, 155, 241–2, 254–5, 260, 264, 271, 276, 277, 279, 284, 290–1, 293–4, 362; gravel, **1**. 54, **2**. 276; headaches, **2**. 247, 250; HW recommends James's powder for colds, **1**. 337, 338; injures leg at Dover, **1**. 100, 106; insomnia, **1**. 369, 371, **2**. 14, 27, 118, 316, 338; lameness, **1**. 34, 348, **2**. 7, 10, 20, 23, 27, 29, 41n, 42; precautions necessary to, **2**. 210; rheumatism, **1**. 241–2, 243; St Anthony's Fire, **2**. 157, 158, 165; sore throat, **1**. 76, 78, 169, 177, 269, 273, 295n, 311n, 339, 376, **2**. 74, 137, 198n, 210, 232; stomach complaints, **1**. 102, 326; swimming in head, **1**. 274; tumour, **2**. 335; weakness in knee, **1**. 237–8, 241; weight, **1**. 126
hermitage of, **2**. 166n
horses run away with, **2**. 180–1, 183–4
Johnston, Lady Cecilia, sends parcel by, **7**. 404
Lort's correspondence with, **43**. 58
—— sends papers to, **16**. 172
lozenge commemorating, on St Clement's Church, **43**. 79
MSS of: **12**. 270; 'Commonplace Book,' **1**. 56n, 58, 60–5; contain his undisguised opinions, **2**. 42, 63; HW begs Cole not to take, to

France, **1**. 89; HW offers to print, **1**. 255, 260–1, 294, 296, 298; HW's interest in, **1**. 62, 72, 75, 80, 89, 92, 227–8, **2**. 40, 61, 67, 117, 258; index to, **2**. 10–11; 'Initials,' **2**. 156n; 'my wife and children,' **1**. 92
Middleton, Conyers, described by, **15**. 305–15
—— 's third wife may be procured by efforts of, **15**. 309
Montagu may see, at SH, **10**. 135, 136
Montagu, Christopher, friend of, **10**. 333
painted-glass portraits of, **2**. 172n, 182–3, 184, 192, 198, 200–1
parsonage of, at Bletchley, **10**. 84
Pennant a friend of, **11**. 93n
pocket-book of, used by HW, **10**. 346
portrait of, by Gooch, **1**. 354, 365, **2**. 182n, 184
Roman Catholicism and, **43**. 48
royalist sympathies of, **10**. 91
servant of, **10**. 347
Steevens's correspondence with, **43**. 75
SH to be visited by, **10**. 135, 136
SH visited by, **1**. 28n, 30n, 48, 145n, 151n, 176–7, 178n, 185, 263, 306n, 307n, 348, **2**. 370–5
Tyson a friend of, **16**. 181n
visits by, to: Boughton House, **10**. 89, 340–1; Burghley, **10**. 91, 344–6; Cambridge, **10**. 92; Drayton, **10**. 89–90, 341–3; Fotheringhay, **10**. 91–2, 343–4; Gothurst, **10**. 332–3; Horton, **10**. 333–5; Huntingdon, **10**. 92; Lowick Church, **10**. 343; Paris, **1**. 94–8, 99, 104–5, 111n, **7**. 268, 273; Peterborough, **10**. 92, 346–7; Wellingborough, **10**. 88
Western family portrait includes, **43**. 62
will of, **1**. 30n
Cole, Rev. William (1722–93), of Ely:
Cole's account of, **1**. 284n
—— talks with, **1**. 283
Cole, Mrs William. *See* Tuer, Catharine
'Cole, Old King':
paraphrase of, **32**. 186
Colebroke, Josiah (d. 1775), treasurer of Society of Antiquaries:
death of, **7**. 398
Colebrooke, Mrs. *See* Hudson, Mary
Colebrooke, Sir George (1729–1809), 2d Bt, 1761; M.P.:
Address debated by, **37**. 414
auction sale of pictures of, **23**. 569
(?) HW mentions, **37**. 428
Parliamentary motion by, on Sulivan's proposals, **22**. 497n
Colebrooke ('Colebrook'), James (1680–1752), money-scrivener:
HW's transactions with, **37**. 243
son's conversation with, **30**. 114–15
son's debts to be paid by, in return for extempore exile to Richelieu, **30**. 114–15
will of, **30**. 114
Colebrooke, Robert (1718–84), M.P.; minister to the Swiss Cantons 1762–4:
dances at Robinson's ball, **37**. 115

father's allowance to, to be stopped for payment of debts, **30.** 114–15

father to pay debts of, in return for extempore exile to Richelieu, **30.** 114–15

gambles and goes to White's despite promise to father, **30.** 114

Italy visited by, **17.** 185

mother will give to, part of her husband's legacy, **30.** 114

Colebrooke, Mrs Robert. *See* Powlett, Henrietta

'Cole-Hole,' theatre:

in Red Lion St, Holborn, **14.** 15n

Coleman, Mr:

Daye, Catherine, to order deeds sent by, **36.** 59

Coleman, John (d. before 1773), farmer at Dunmow, Essex:

daughter of, **22.** 240n

Coleman, Sarah ('Mrs Wright'), Edward Louisa Mann's mistress:

daughter's income during life of, **24.** 160

Mann, Edward Louisa, may wed, to legitimate her children, **22.** 242

—— to provide for, **22.** 240–1

Coleman. *See also* Colman

Coleman Street, London:

King's Arms Yard in, **14.** 97

Colepeper, Elizabeth (ca 1637–1709), m. (1661) James Hamilton:

genealogy of, **42.** 89

Colepeper, John (ca 1600–60), cr. (1644) Bn Colepeper:

daughter of, **42.** 89

Coleraine, Bn. *See* Hanger, Gabriel (1697–1773); Hanger, Hon. George (1751–1824); Hanger, John (1743–94); Hanger, Hon. William (1744–1814); Hare, Henry (1636–1708); Hare, Hugh (ca 1606–67)

Coleraine, Bns. *See* Bond, Elizabeth (1715–80)

Colesso, Gaetano, of Venice:

Lady Orford's Declaration signed by, **43.** 288

Colet, Dame Christiana. *See* Knyvet, Christian

Colet, John (ca 1467–1519), dean of St Paul's:

Mercers' Co. remembers, for benefactions, **16.** 84

St Paul's School founded by, **16.** 84

Colic:

bullet as treatment for, **33.** 147

hemorrhoidal, **33.** 36

occurrences of, **3.** 224, **4.** 85, 86, **17.** 37, 223, 275n, 481, **18.** 318, **19.** 369, **23.** 332, 402, **37.** 286

possible deterrent, **31.** 348

West, James, blames, on women, **20.** 379n

*Colifichets:*

Conway can despise, **37.** 140

Coligni brothers (Odetus, Gaspar, Franciscus):

Pass's print of, **1.** 173

Coligny, Marquise de. *See* Rabutin de Bussy, Louise-Françoise de

Coligny, Gaspard de (1519–72), Adm.:

Doumenil has portrait of, **7.** 313

Coligny, Henriette de (1618–73), m. 1 (1643)

Thomas Hamilton, 3d E. of Haddington; m. 2 Gaspard de Champagne, Comte de la Suze:

Du Deffand, Mme, disparages, **3.** 55, 87, 143

HW compares Mme du Deffand to, **3.** 44, 54

'Colin's Complaint.' *See under* Rowe, Nicholas

'Colin's Complaint' (tune):

HW's poem to be sung to, **33.** 423

Colisée, at Paris:

Barrymore, Lady, visits, with Duncannon and his tutor, **7.** 350n

Churchills and HW visit, **7.** 335

proprietors of, face ruin, **39.** 145

Ranelagh imitated by, **39.** 144–5

Vernon, Lady Harriet, sees Ds of Kingston at, **24.** 242

Coliseum, at Rome:

HW calls, 'fine ruin,' **30.** 5

HW would like to buy, **37.** 57

in parfilage, **7.** 197

medal of, **26.** 7

Paris's Colisée will not outlive, **39.** 145

Collar; collars:

clergyman wears, in painting, **10.** 346

gold, worn by Richard III, **41.** 132

of diamonds, **25.** 603

of fur, **40.** 225

Collar-day:

Selwyn's witticism on, **25.** 275

Collation, cold:

Chudleigh, Elizabeth, serves, **9.** 276–7

Collé, Charles (1709–83), dramatist:

*Anthologie françoise* edited by, **10.** 186

*Île sonnante, L',* **4.** 43n

*Partie de Chasse de Henri IV, La,* by: **3.** 285, 286, 289, **4.** 154, **6.** 116, **39.** 216–17; Dodsley's *King and the Miller* translated in, **39.** 217

Colle, Pietro, Capt. of Corsican recruits at Minorca:

Mann commissions, **25.** 249

(?) sails to Minorca, **25.** 199

Collecting of books. *See* Book-collecting

*Collection d'anciens Évangiles. See under* Voltaire

*Collection des meilleurs ouvrages françois composés par des femmes. See under* Guinement de Keralio, Louise-Félicité

*Collection of all the Ecclesiastical Laws. See under* Johnson, Rev. John

*Collection of all the Wills . . . of the Kings and Queens of England, A:*

HW acquires, **43.** 72–3

HW makes corrections to, **42.** 21n

*Collection of Curious Discourses, A. See under* Hearne, Thomas

*Collection of English Proverbs, A. See under* Ray, John

*Collection of Engravings from Ancient Vases. See under* Hamilton, Sir William

*Collection of Etruscan, Greek and Roman Antiquities, The. See under* Hamilton, Sir William

*Collection of Poems by Several Hands, A. See under* Dodsley, Robert
*Collection of Prints*, HW's:
Haistwell's prints to be inserted in, **42**. 53
*Collection of Prints in Imitation of Drawings, A. See under* Rogers, Charles
*Collection of State Papers. See under* Cecil, William, Bn Burghley
Collections:
HW thinks that simpletons', are as foolish as philosophers' systems, **25**. 604
'Collections for a History of the Manners, Customs . . . of England,' by HW:
transcripts from the Ashmolean presumably concerned with, **38**. 157
*Collection universelle des mémoires particuliers relatifs à l'histoire de France*:
HW acquires 23 volumes of, **31**. 245, **43**. 150
HW lends volumes of, to Hannah More, **31**. 245, 412
HW reads in, about E. of Warwick, **42**. 192
Collectors:
'mighty apt to steal,' **2**. 250
SH Press books prized by, **31**. 244, 313
College, ——:
money reserved for, **42**. 438
College; colleges:
authors left to, by British public, **41**. 55–6
fellows of: HW's worldly ignorance like that of, **23**. 122; Mann thinks, tiresome from pedantry, **17**. 107, **30**. 17–18
hall ceilings of, resemble Hinchingbrooke's, **40**. 283
Collège de Louis le Grand, Paris:
Jesuit taught at, **38**. 349
Collège des Quatre Nations, Paris:
fire at, **7**. 444
HW visits, **7**. 276
Mazarin's tomb in, **13**. 165
Collège du Plessis, Paris:
Sigorgne professor at, **4**. 421n
College for Old Maids:
Walker wants to have, in Ireland, **41**. 55
College Hill, London:
Godschall dies at his house at, **17**. 478n
College of Arms (Heralds' Office):
Ancasters' decline a blow to, **24**. 499–500
Burrell family's rise must perplex, **24**. 499–500, 505–6
Chute's, at SH, **20**. 382, 387
Chute works in, on Mann's pedigree, **20**. 13, 31, 138, **35**. 65
Coke, Lady Mary, better informed than, **36**. 228
Derby House given to, **1**. 148
French turn galleys into, **34**. 144
George III complains of negligence of, **21**. 535–6
HW and Chute told at, about Egmont's book, **20**. 31
HW jokes about, **31**. 360

HW's account of George III's wedding worthy of, **21**. 532
HW to see roll at, **42**. 285
Hertford has low opinion of, **38**. 555
hours and operation of, **20**. 13n
House of Lords as antiquated and idle as, **25**. 153
land-jobbers conduct, **38**. 555
Latin ('Lancastrian') version of Rous Roll owned by, **41**. 134n
Lyttelton initiates Barrett Lennard into, at Cambridge, **35**. 184
Maclaine might have got certificate from, **20**. 169
MSS of Howard and Talbot families found in, **15**. 209
Norfolk, D. of, gives Talbot papers to, **11**. 277
Selwyn searches, for precedents of K. T. elections of under-age men, **30**. 246
Somerset family scandal in, **20**. 138–9
tickets to Chatham's funeral to be obtained from, **33**. 19n
Tudor descent must be recorded at, **42**. 19
Welsh royal descents would puzzle, **33**. 454
Collemant. *See* Colmant
Collet, John (fl. ca 1777–ca 1786), English consul at Genoa:
Foote noticed by, at Genoa, **25**. 108n
Murray informed by, of enemy's approach, **25**. 349
Collet, Matthew (d. 1777):
(?) memorandum on, **15**. 14
Collevaux (*or* Collevause), picture cleaner:
Devonshire, D. of, to have pictures cleaned by, **40**. 182
Colley, Richard, merchant and broker:
bankruptcy of, **23**. 426
Collier, ——, servant to Sir Edward Walpole:
Walpole, Sir Edward, scolds Jane Clement about, **36**. 321, 322
Collier, Sir George (1738–95), Kt; naval commander:
American fleet attacked by, in Penobscot Bay, **33**. 123n
American ships destroyed by, **28**. 467
Collier, Jeremy (1650–1726), theologian:
*Ecclesiastical History of Great Britain*, 'Dance of Death' mentioned in, **16**. 47
Collier, Lady Juliana. *See* Colyear, Lady Juliana
Collier, Mary (fl. 1739–62), poetical washerwoman:
'turned poet and starved,' **31**. 220n
Collier, Mirabella (ca 1670–ca 1755), m. Rev. Joseph Spence:
HW talks to, about Pope, **20**. 189
son 'fondles' in imitation of Pope, **20**. 188–9
Collier, Susan, Sir Edward Walpole's housekeeper:
son of, **36**. 317n
Collier; colliers (coal-miners; *see also* Coal miners):
Ferrers attacked by, **9**. 272

from Warwickshire, pay tribute to George III, **32**. 185–6

in Northumberland, fight militia, **21**. 491

of Newcastle, said to feed their children with fire-shovels, **20**. 450

Parliament members resemble, **38**. 324

Collier; colliers (ships):

Anson pays, to resist French invasion, **21**. 306n

English capture, from Calais to California, **20**. 500

fleet of, prevented by bad weather from reaching port, **25**. 274

Collier's Hill, near Ware, Herts:

balloon descent at, **25**. 543n

Colliery:

all west Yorkshire is, **35**. 270

Colligara (Italy):

Spaniards at, **18**. 151

Collignon, Charles (1725–85), physician:

Lort's friend, **2**. 277

Collingbourne Ducis, Wilts:

Scudder, minister at, **16**. 66n

Collins, Anthony (1676–1729), deist:

Ashton attacks, **14**. 43n

Chandler writes against, **20**. 167n

*Discourse of the Grounds and Reasons of the Christian Religion, A*, by, **15**. 298

*Letter from the Late Anthony Collins, A*, **15**. 300

Collins, Arthur (ca 1690–1760), herald; genealogist:

Allington pedigree given by, to HW, **1**. 52

*English Baronage, The*, by, **40**. 131

HW jokes about obscure baronets known only to, **10**. 40

*Historical Collections of the Noble Families*: **2**. 324, 327; Vertue's print in, of Bess of Hardwick, **42**. 313–14

*Life . . . of Edward . . . the Black Prince*, **20**. 381n, **33**. 417n

Newcastle told that Sir Robert Walpole ordered £200 for, **22**. 24n

*Peerage of England*: **2**. 325; Bruce and Mann study, **20**. 331; cited, **2**. 1, 5; HW gets father's dates from, **22**. 24; Percy, Bp, contributes Percy genealogy to new edn of, **34**. 227n; Sackville pedigree in, **15**. 83

Wotton's *Baronetage* attributed to, **9**. 118–19

Collins, Charlotte (d. 1803), m. (1783) George Richard St John, 3d Vct Bolingbroke, 1787:

father of, **34**. 34

husband of, elopes, **34**. 56

jointure of, **34**. 56

Collins, Elizabeth (ca 1763–80):

hanged for rioting, **33**. 214n

Collins, George (d. 1758), King's Messenger 1738–58:

(?) news brought by, **20**. 498

Collins, John (fl. 1680), engraver:

print by, **1**. 149

Collins, John, Florentine inn-keeper:

inn of: (?) Karl Friedrich lodges at, **20**. 149; mud in front of, **30**. 3; St-Aignan lodges at, **17**. 78

Collins, Rev. Thomas:

daughter of, returns to him, **34**. 56

Collops:

'remove' of, **19**. 357n

*Colloquia mensalia. See under* Luther, Martin

Colloredo, Karl Octav (1723–86), Graf von; Imperial ambassador to England 1753–7:

Aix treaty negotiated by, **20**. 400n

(?) Cowper hears from, about his principality, **24**. 382n

Firmian fails to get English post of, **21**. 282

George II gives audience to, **21**. 18

Granville's conversations with, on Austrian-French neutrality treaty, **20**. 578, 584

Pucci's name joined to recall of, in newspapers, **21**. 108, 113–14

Colloredo-Melz und Wallsee, Joseph Maria (1735–1818), Graf von:

(?) Conway sees, at Vienna, **39**. 537

(?) Cowper hears from, about his principality, **24**. 382n

Francis II to be attended by, **25**. 474n

Joseph II accompanied by, at Necker's in Paris, **6**. 443

—— dines with, **6**. 440

—— not to be attended by, at Poggio Imperiale, **24**. 108n

Collot d'Herbois, Jean-Marie (1750–96):

comedian who became legislator, **12**. 23n

Collyer, Joseph (1748–1827), engraver:

heads for Johnson's *Poets* engraved by, **28**. 413n

print by, of Bp Trevor, **2**. 27, 28, 29, **41**. 350n

Colman, Francis (d. 1733), English Resident at Tuscany 1724–33:

Bubb Dodingtons and Mme Venturini lodge with, **18**. 392

reprimanded for expense at George II's coronation, **21**. 534

Colman, Mrs Francis. *See* Gumley, Mary

Colman, George (1732–94), the elder; dramatist; manager of Covent Garden Theatre:

Arne and, adapt Mason's *Elfrida*, **28**. 54–6, 58

Bath, E. of, recommends, to brother, for Bradford estate, **22**. 560

*Beggar's Opera* continued by, at Covent Garden, **23**. 524n

*Clandestine Marriage, The*: **3**. 208; acted by King, **33**. 87; by Garrick and Colman, **10**. 203n; Montagu's opinion of, **10**. 203

Cornelys, Mrs, alarms, with rival shows, **23**. 271

dramas by, **22**. 146n

*Dramatic Works*, presented to HW, **41**. 351, 383–4

*English Merchant, The*, seen by HW, **33**. 341

Garrick collaborates with, **3**. 208n, **10**. 203n

[Colman, George (1732–94), *continued*]

*Genius of Nonsense*, satirizes Graham, **33.** 217n

HW allows, to alter *Nature Will Prevail*, **41.** 244

HW calls on, at Richmond, in thanks for gifts of books, **41.** 383

HW cannot influence, to take Jephson's *Vitellia*, **41.** 362

HW concerned at meeting, so seldom, though his neighbour, **42.** 56

HW gives French version of *Modern Gardening* to, **42.** 150–1

HW gives Pinkerton's play to, **16.** 254, 259, 265

HW not surprised by bad play of, **10.** 205

HW's correspondence with, **41.** 242–4, 351, 383–4, **42.** 50–1, 56, 150–1

HW sends *Letters of Literature* to, **16.** 265, 267

HW's *Nature Will Prevail* pleases, **13.** 48

HW submits *Nature Will Prevail* to, **41.** 242–4, 383–4

HW thanks, for translation of Horace, **42.** 50, 150

*Jealous Wife, The*: indifferent but well acted, **16.** 43; to be acted at Richmond House, **34.** 1

lives near Marble Hill, **32.** 31

London officials quarrel with, at Richmond, **33.** 207

*Manager in Distress*: at Haymarket, **33.** 189n; Cambridge, R.O., satirized in, **29.** 70

manager of little theatre in Haymarket, **22.** 146n

*Man of Business, The*, **32.** (?)189, 191

Mason advises HW to present *Mysterious Mother* to, **28.** 55

—— exchanges 'pert' letters with, **28.** 60

Nivernais's *Jardins modernes* given to, **12.** 259

O'Keeffe's *Agreeable Surprise* a daring choice for, **16.** 256

Penneck attacks, **32.** 97–8

Pinkerton's *Letters of Literature* praises, **16.** 265

*Polly Honeycombe* by, **41.** 401n

probable criticism by, of Pinkerton's play, **16.** 253

prologue by, altered by Powys, to *Provok'd Husband*, **32.** 343n

Pulteney, Gen., angry with, for theatrical activities, **22.** 560

Pulteney, Vct, mentions, in will, **22.** 146

quarrels with City of London over embankment at Richmond, **29.** 69–70, **33.** 207

satiric verses on Reynolds's portrait of, **41.** 400

theatre of, will not open till 1785, **16.** 254

*Two Odes* by Lloyd and, satirize Gray and Mason, **28.** 193, 198, **29.** 338

witticism by, on Ayscough's *Semiramis*, **32.** 342–3

Colman, Seymour (d. 1850), maid of honour 1795–1818 to Q. Charlotte:

rumoured as Bedchamber woman to Ps of Wales, **12.** 201

Colman, William (1728–94), Master of Corpus Christi College, Cambridge:

apostle spoon to be conveyed by, **1.** 313, 317

Cole receives cast of Henrietta Maria's seal from, **2.** 128–9

—— sends HW's *Letter to the Editor . . .* to, **2.** 149

——'s informant, **1.** 386, **2.** 72n, 196n

——'s life of, **2.** 226n

finds error in *Biographia Britannica*, **2.** 198, 202–3

has print of J. Cowper, **2.** 307

letter about Cooke lent by, to Cole, **2.** 213–14

ticket and flower roots to be conveyed by, **1.** 317

Colmant, Catherine, (?) wife of Jean-Godefroy Colmant; kitchen girl:

Du Deffand, Mme, leaves legacy to, **8.** 6

furniture in bedroom of, **8.** 15

(?) wages of, **8.** 46

Colmant, Jean-Godefroy (d. 1778), Mme du Deffand's footman:

comes on duty at 7 A.M., **4.** 94

death of, **7.** 45, 81n

drinks, **5.** 384, **6.** 415n, 418

Du Deffand, Mme, arranges Mme and Mlle de Loménie's annuity to, **8.** 43

—— awaits 6 A.M. to awaken, **6.** 386

—— sends, on errand, **6.** 473

——'s morning secretary, **6.** 267

——'s verses on, **4.** 19–20

forwards letters, **5.** 240, 249, 252

(?) HW pays, **7.** 412

health of, **5.** 376, **6.** 408, 409, 415n, **7.** 45

papers copied by, **4.** 99n, 118n, 223n, **8.** 145n

Sanadon, Mlle, quarrels with, **5.** 252

writes letters for Mme du Deffand, *see index entries ante* **8.** 306; *see also* **5.** 368n

Colnbrook (Bucks):

ground floors at, uninhabitable from floods, **35.** 265

Colne Lodge, Twickenham:

Whitehead, Paul, occupies, **42.** 486

Colne Priory, Essex:

King's drawings of tombs of Earls of Oxford at, **42.** 59n

Colneri, ——, officer in Austrian army:

revolt led by, **18.** 446n

Colney Hatch, Middlesex:

Nicoll of, **4.** 193n

Cologne, Abp and Elector of. *See* Klemens August (1700–61); Maximilian Friedrich (1708–84)

Cologne:

Birckmann's 'Dance of Death' published at, **42.** 431n

Contades at, **37.** 555

England loses, as ally, **42.** 496
French subsidy to, **42.** 496
gazette of, see *Gazette de Cologne*
Hessian minister may go to, **42.** 494
*Imagines mortis* printed at, **16.** 146
kings of, **37.** 67
Monteil minister at, **5.** 209n
Roman disputes as uninteresting as those of canons of, **21.** 491
Serbelloni nuncio to, **20.** 428n
visitors to, Conway and Scott, **37.** 150
Colomb, Mlles, sisters of Jacob Colomb:
brother's debts to be incurred by, if they contest his will, **42.** 297
brother's money needed by, **42.** 294
in Switzerland, **42.** 297, 298
Colomb, Elizabeth, HW's cook:
HW's bequest to, **30.** 362
Colomb, Jacob (d. 1790), Fanny Burney's servant:
alleged will of: **11.** 139n; may be forgery, **42.** 294
assets and debts of, **42.** 297
Burney, Frances, asks what to do with money left by, **42.** 290
dying wish of, to provide for mistress and child, **42.** 298
setting aside will of, would be too expensive, **42.** 297
Colomb, James, HW's footman:
advice of, not to contest cousin's will, **42.** 298
Bayond's name tied with, as Jacob Colomb's executor, **42.** 298, 299
—— suspected by, of forging will, **42.** 294
Burney, Fanny, to arrange with, for payment, **42.** 298
—— wants to see, about his cousin's effects, **42.** 290, 293
footman, **11.** 368n
HW mistakenly given emetic by, **11.** 316
HW's bequests to, **15.** 338n, **30.** 362, 375
(?) HW sends, to Fermor at Richmond, **42.** 277
HW to send letter to Fanny Burney by, **42.** 294
HW tossed in bed by, **34.** 211
(?) illiterate, **25.** 118
(?) letter mistakenly posted by, **25.** 118
(?) messages sent by, **31.** 205
(?) Perkins abuses, **12.** 222n
Colomb, Maria, HW's servant:
HW's annuity to, **30.** 362-3
Colomb, Philip (d. 1799), HW's valet:
advice of, not to contest cousin's will, **42.** 298
Bayond suspected by, of forging will, **42.** 294
Berrys aided by, in search for house, **11.** 19-20, 80, 94
children of, **30.** 362
Chute's death reported by, **24.** 211
collects news of explosion on Hounslow Heath, **32.** 75
dinner at SH hard to organize by, **39.** 404
Du Deffand, Mme, dislikes naïvetés of, **5.** 189

—— intended garment for, **5.** 285
footman's death told by, **11.** 369-70
(?) HW awakened by, **31.** 184
HW cannot do without, on visit to Park Place, **42.** 299
(?) HW may be served by, **5.** 89
HW pays bills through, **7.** 405, 406, 410
HW pays wages of, **7.** 405, 408, 410, 411, 413
HW's annuity to, corrected, **43.** 326
HW's awakening greeted by, with Lady Ossory's vest, **32.** 219
HW's bell answered by, **35.** 373
HW's bequests to, **15.** 336, 338n, **30.** 345, 348-9, 360, 366, 373
HW's chaise ordered by, in Paris, **39.** 272
HW's companion, **5.** 294
HW's letter to be delivered by, to Fanny Burney, **42.** 299
HW's recovery judged by, from his resuming a book, **35.** 529
HW tossed in bed by, **34.** 211
mentioned, **11.** 156, 347
(?) Montagu's letter to Mme Roland to be posted by, **10.** 261
Nivernais's *Jardins modernes* given to, **12.** 259
Ossory, Lady, corresponds with, **33.** 74-5
——'s letter shown to HW by, **33.** 70
'Philip Pança,' **32.** 220
philosopher, **32.** 75
SH shown by, **12.** 242, 244, **28.** 258
SH visitor sent by, **12.** 241
'sulky Swiss,' **15.** 336
tax for, to be paid to excise, **41.** 433
to put off seller of land, **32.** 122
wages of, **43.** 108
Wiart asks, to buy white flannel, **6.** 246
——'s correspondence with, **6.** 123-4
Colombier, Rue du, Paris:
Doumenil lives near, **7.** 313, **39.** 204
HW lodges in, **1.** 99, **7.** 266
Hôtel de Saxe in, **38.** 280n
Hôtel du Parc-Royal in, **3.** 342n, **43.** 47
Law's wife moves to, **15.** 180n
'Colombini, Abbé':
Frederick II's supposed letter to, **5.** 427
Colomiès, Paul (1638-92), *or* Colomesius:
*Keimélia literaria*, mentions Vigenère's cipher book, **40.** 250
Colonel; colonels:
departure of, changed, **7.** 446
pot-bellied, lead militia, **35.** 291
Read's regiment coveted by, **37.** 356
rebellions made by, **42.** 252
*Colonel Draper's Answer. See under* Draper, William
Colonia, ——, fermier général:
social relations of, with Mme du Deffand, **7.** 236
Walpole, Hon. Thomas, consults, **7.** 236
Colonies, British, in America. *See* America, English colonies in
Colonna, Principessa. *See* Barberini, Cornelia (ca 1711-97); Salviati, Caterina Zephyrina

Colonna, Conte:
Mann presents, at Tuscan Court, **24**. 251n
Colonna, Agnese (1702–80), m. (1723) Principe
Camillo Borghese:
benevolence and penetration of, **30**. 6
Conway and Signora Capello entertained by,
at Rome, **37**. 324
English visitors abandoned by, **35**. 63
Greville known to, **20**. 58
HW calls, fine ruin, **30**. 5
HW thanks, for remembering him, **30**. 13
husband's presence may have curtailed atten-
tions of, to Lincoln, **30**. 6
Lincoln impressed by, **30**. 6
Lorraine primate's gambling discussed by,
**17**. *12*
Nivernais's hostess, **20**. 286
Colonna, Fabrizio (1700–55), constable of Na-
ples; Principe di Palliano:
Florence visited by, **18**. 545
'hackney' presented by, **18**. 462n
silent, **18**. 545
Colonna, Fabrizio (ca 1760–1813):
(?) appearance and manner of, **7**. 102, 119,
125
(?) Du Deffand, Mme, may send parcel by,
**7**. 118, 123, 126, 128, 133, 134, 141
(?) ——'s account of, **7**. 99
(?) ——'s opinion of, **7**. 119, 125
(?) England to be visited by, **7**. 118, 125
(?) Gloucester, D. of, has devotion of, **7**. 102
(?) Gloucesters ask HW to recommend, to
Mme du Deffand, **7**. 80
(?) HW hears from, about Mme du Deffand,
**7**. 149
(?) HW scarcely known to, **7**. 102
(?) health of, **7**. 99
(?) social relations of, in Paris, **7**. 99, 102,
118, 119, 125
Colonna, Federigo (1728–65), son of the Con-
stable:
(?) Florence visited by, **18**. 545
Colonna, Filippo (1663–1714):
Clement XI will not permit, to sell antique
fragments, **13**. 213
Colonna, Giovanni Battista (1729–46), son of
the Constable:
(?) Florence visited by, **18**. 545
Colonna, Girolamo (1708–63), cardinal, 1743:
Benedict XIV asked by, about giving vice-
chancellorship to Cardinal York, **20**. 590
—— makes, cardinal, **18**. 302n
Old Pretender asks intercession of, for son,
**20**. 589–90
Colonna, Giulio Cesare (1702–87), Principe di
Palestrina e di Carbognano. *See* Barberini
Colonna
Colonna, Lorenzo (1723–79), Grand Constable
of Naples 1755–79:
(?) Florence visited by, **18**. *545*
Kingston, Ds of, sends regards to, **32**. 300
Leopold to be entertained by, at Rome, **23**. 95
Rosenberg keeps, waiting, **23**. 104n

York, D. of, invited by, to Naples, **22**. 224,
229
Colonna, Marcantonio (1724–93), cardinal,
1759:
Conclave left by, **24**. 73
(?) Florence visited by, **18**. 545
Kingston, Ds of, sends regards to, **32**. 300
Colonna, Marcantonio (1724–96), Principe Co-
lonna; Principe di Stigliano e d'Aliano:
horses to be furnished by, **43**. 263
Colonna, Maria Felicità Barberini. *See* Bar-
berini Colonna, Maria Felicità
Colonna, Maria Vittoria (1721–77), m. (1738)
Joaquín Spinola, Marqués de los Balbases:
Kingston, Ds of, writes to, **24**. 220, **32**. 299–
300
Colonna, Olimpia Maria Maddalena (1731–
1800), m. (1748) Gennaro Maria Caracciolo,
Duca di Girifalco (*or* Cirifalco):
Genlis, Mme de, ill-informed about, **35**. 433
Hamilton sees, with her mother at Rome,
**35**. 434
husband never accused by, for his crimes,
**35**. 434
Colonna, Pietro Maria Giuseppe (1725–80),
cardinal, 1766:
(?) Benedict XIV holds public dispute with,
though Colonna is only 19, **19**. 114
(?) Florence visited by, **18**. 545
Kingston, Ds of, sends regards to, **32**. 300
Colonna, Prospero (1672–1743), cardinal, 1739:
death of, **18**. 183
Colonna, Via della, at Florence:
Craon, Casa, in, **17**. 36n
Colonna Barberini, Carlo (1735–1819), Principe
di Palestrina:
(?) Leopold II to be entertained by, **23**. 95
mother sells art during minority of, **33**. 485n
Rosenberg keeps, waiting, **23**. 104n
Colonnade; colonnades:
Carlton House's, supports nothing, **42**. 274
Colonna di Sciarra, Prospero (1707–65), car-
dinal, 1743:
Benedict XIV makes, cardinal, **18**. 302n
Colonna palazzo, Rome:
Houghton gallery better than, **35**. 44
Wentworth Castle gallery modelled on that
of, **35**. 267
Colonna Rossi, Bianca (fl. 1739–49), Corsican
leader:
Corsican rebels led by, **17**. 147, 163
Coloredo. *See* Colloredo
Colossus:
statues of, at Easton Neston, **9**. 5
Colour; colours:
alphabet of: HW's, **39**. 296–7; in Peruvian
quipu, **33**. 261–3, 266–7
grey no colour, **32**. 70
perception of, varies, **41**. 394–5
Petitot indebted to Mayerne for vitrifying, **40**.
238
pigments for, **40**. 215, 219
white said by Newton to be offensive, **18**. 228

See also Colours (flags); Paint
Colour-blindness:
HW's comments on, **12**. 253
Colours (ensign's commission):
Baldwyn gets pair of, **39**. 431, 441
Colours, regimental (flags):
Conway's regiment captures, at Laeffeld, **37**. 274
English and French lose eleven pairs of, at Laeffeld, **39**. 274
HW jokes about Pitt sending expedition after, **37**. 570–1
Louisbourg's, parade through London, **37**. 567
weavers display, in London, **22**. 301
Colpoys, John (ca 1742–1821), naval officer:
French ships nearly captured by, **34**. 228
Colquhoun, Sir James (1741–1805), 2d Bt, 1786:
HW receives from: books of Scottish engravings and engraved portraits, **42**. 431–2, 436; goat's horn, **42**. 322–3
HW's correspondence with, **42**. 322–3, 431–2, 436, 437–8
Colson, Jean-Claude-Gilles (1725–78), called Bellecour; actor:
biographical information about, corrected, **43**. 103
Collé's *Partie de chasse* acted by, **39**. 217
social relations of, with Voltaire, **7**. 18
Colston Hall, Suffolk:
ring inscribed with name of, **2**. 24
seat of Derehaughs and Burwells, **1**. 374n, 376, 377
Colt; colts:
at Wentworth Woodhouse, **35**. 280
HW 'vends,' **23**. 495
'tooth' of: Grenville may cut, **20**. 374; HW's, **32**. 117; sometimes cut a second time, **32**. 217; the discreetest never sheds, **32**. 284
Coltellini, Agostino (1612–93), lawyer:
account of, **1**. 130
Ménage's letter from, **1**. 131–2
Colton. *See* Colston; Coughton
Columb. *See* Colomb
Columbarium; columbaria:
at Chicksands Priory, **10**. 170
Bentley adapts design of, to urn for Galfridus Mann's monument, **21**. 157, 250
——— designs, for Chute, **9**. 216
Gothic, HW expects to build, at SH, **21**. 157, **36**. 39
Sion House's gallery resembles, according to HW's suggestion, **38**. 429
'Columbine,' character in Italian comedy:
Fermor, Lady Sophia, resembles, **18**. 103
Columbus, Christopher (ca 1451–1506), explorer:
America as forgotten as if never 'routed out' by, **24**. 194
dogs employed by, **28**. 332n
Giustiniani's verses on, **22**. 465n
HW's name for: Cornwallis, **25**. 210; Herschel, **25**. 614
invasion of, to be set aside, **24**. 367

*Columbus*, American warship:
*Glasgow's* battle with, **24**. 216
Column; columns:
at Florence: buried underground, **21**. 343, 356; HW's 'inscription' on, **21**. 355–6, **37**. 96–7
at Stowe, **35**. 77, **39**. 127
at Wentworth Castle, **35**. 267
drawing of, at Welbeck, by Marchioness of Carmarthen, celebrated by Prior, **35**. 271
Ionic, fluted, at Wrest, **39**. 139
pierced, in SH library bookcases, **35**. 200
ridiculous in small buildings, **20**. 127
taper, HW uses, in SH hall, **20**. 372
Coluthus (5th century):
Beloe translates, **15**. 217n
Colville, Alexander (1717–70), 7th Bn Colville; naval officer:
eagle taken by, to Port Mahon, **19**. 268
Genoese fleet attacked by, **19**. 245
*Leopard* commanded by, **19**. 232n
Colville, Camilla (d. 1775), m. (ca 1715) Charles Bennet, 2d E. of Tankerville:
daughter of, **17**. 399
death of, **7**. 398
Colyear, Lady Caroline (1727–1812), m. (1750) Sir Nathaniel Curzon, 5th Bt; cr. (1761) Bn Scarsdale:
lives alone, **10**. 230
Colyear, Charles (1700–85), 2d E. of Portmore; M.P.:
daughter of, **20**. 374
Colyear, Elizabeth (d. 1768), m. (1709) Lionel Cranfield Sackville, 1st D. of Dorset:
Amelia, Ps, plays with, at time of P. of Wales's death, **20**. 233
Athenry, Bns, used to frequent 'court' of, **37**. 442
daughter influenced by, **20**. 179
familiarity with, difficult, **37**. 302
HW mentions, **37**. 418
Knole's associations with, **33**. 224
son's disgrace attributed to malice by, **30**. 158
Colyear, Lady Juliana (1735–1821), m. (1759) Henry Dawkins:
Granville may wed, **20**. 374
Colyear, Walter Philip, army officer:
Germain, Sir John, associated with, in Dutch service, **17**. 221n
Colyton and Escott, Devon:
Yonge of, **10**. 122n
*Comandante*, Genoese bark:
Corsican bishop to be intercepted by, **21**. 393
founders at Pineto near Bastia, **21**. 393n
Comb; combs:
HW buys, at Mrs Kennon's sale, **37**. 439
in Swift's *Gulliver's Travels*, **18**. 495
Combaud, Mrs, of Richmond:
SH visited by, **12**. 243
Combe, Charles (1743–1807):
Pinkerton obliged to, **16**. 325n
Combe, Harvey Christian (d. 1818), alderman:

[Combe, Harvey, *continued*]
owner of MS copy of *Rolliad*, **11.** 34n
(?) Sheridan gives *Probationary Odes* to, **33.** 465n
Combe, John (d. 1614):
tomb of, **9.** 120
Combe, Richard (? 1728–80), M.P.:
biographical information about, corrected, **43.** 353
death of, mentioned by Burke, **33.** 230
Combe, William (1742–1823), satirist and editor:
birth date of, corrected, **43.** 204
*Diabo-Lady, The,* satire by, **28.** 304n
*Diaboliad, The,* satire by, **28.** 303, 304n, 470
Farington talks to, at Shakespeare Gallery, **15.** 321
*First of April, The,* attacks Hertfords, **28.** 303
HW declines to see, **15.** 217
*History of the Principal Rivers . . . The Thames,* **15.** 217, 218n, 319, 321, 322, **35.** 542, **43.** 156
*Justification, The,* satire by, **28.** 304n
satires by, on Ds of Devonshire, **28.** 313
*Tours of Doctor Syntax* by, **28.** *303n*
*World as It Goes, The,* imitates Churchill, **28.** 470
Combe, Kent:
Saunderson of, **9.** 38n
Combe, Surrey:
Grafton, Ds of, takes Grosvenor's former house at, **32.** 30n
HW calls on Ds of Grafton at, **39.** 102
Combe Abbey, Warwickshire, Bn Craven's seat:
Elizabeth of Bohemia's things brought to, from Hampstead Lodge, **10.** 286
HW visits, **10.** 264n
Montagu visits, **10.** 286
Combe (or Coomb) Bank, near Sundridge, Kent:
Ailesbury, Cts of, invites HW to, **37.** 346
Campbell, Lord Frederick, lives at, **11.** 322n, **32.** 11n
Damer, Mrs, born at, **37.** 290–1n
HW may meet Conway and wife at, **37.** 345, 346
HW prefers SH to, **39.** 460
HW said to have gone to, **34.** 64
spelling of, corrected, **43.** 150, 359
SH a rival to, for antiquities, **37.** 460
Comber, Rev. Thomas (d. 1778), LL.D.; writer:
*Examination of the Introductory Discourse,* **15.** 297
Combe Wood, Surrey:
Light Horse disperse freed prisoners from, **35.** 355
Comedians:
amateur, might walk at a coronation, **24.** 86
'Comédie du magistrat':
Cambis, Mme de, reads, **7.** 441
Comédie-française, Paris:
*Barbier de Séville* acted at, **6.** 21n

Boufflers mentions, **5.** 354
box at: Choiseul gives seat in, to Mme du Deffand, **4.** 272, 275, 277; Du Deffand, Mme, and Mme de Forcalquier rent, **4.** 62, 73, 81; Du Deffand, Mme, occupies Conti's, **3.** 236–7; Du Deffand, Mme, retains, **4.** 73n, 218, 222; HW to have, **6.** 217; Necker, Mme, will lend, to Mme du Deffand, **6.** 213; poor, **6.** 440; small, **6.** 469
Collé's *Partie de chasse* acted at, **6.** 116, **39.** 217
Comédie-italienne better than, **14.** 145
*Cornélie* acted at, **41.** 106
direction of, **6.** 28
Du Deffand, Mme, attends, **3.** 234, 236–7, **4.** 115–16, 138, 140, 208, **6.** 440, 469
—— mentions, **3.** 201, **4.** 276, 445
excellent, but unpopular except on fashionable nights, **13.** 162
Gibbon attends, **6.** 469
Gramont, Duchesse de, attends, **5.** 363
Joseph II attends, **6.** 443–4
Lauzun, Duchesse de, attends, **6.** 469
Louis XVI and Marie-Antoinette attend, **5.** 376
Luxembourg, Mme de, attends, **6.** 440, 469
members of, want citizenship, **39.** 62n
Mirepoix, Mme de, suggests going to, **4.** 362
Necker, Mme, attends, **6.** 440
plan to close, twice a week for sake of Colisée, **39.** 145
Pont-de-Veyle frequents, **5.** 314
Raucourt, Mlle, no longer acting at, **6.** 213
rumoured to act at Calais, **38.** 524
Sanadon, Mlle, attends, **6.** 75
Voltaire called on by actors of, **7.** 18–19
Comédie-italienne, Paris. *See* Opéra-comique
Comedy; comedies:
delay makes, obsolete, **41.** 362
excess not acceptable in, **33.** 265
farce need not be as chaste and sober as, **16.** 257
French: (?) arrives at Ghent, **37.** 124; at The Hague, **37.** 150
genteel: can be written and acted by those only, who live in good society, **33.** 563–4; Mary Berry's face fitted for, **34.** 25
HW more inclined towards, though unsuccessful in it, **41.** 289
HW's high opinion of, **32.** 334, **34.** 25
Hawkins, Sir John, on, **32.** 334
ill-acted at Compiègne, **38.** 408
in *She Stoops to Conquer,* **32.** 108
Italian, given once a week at Fontainebleau, **38.** 448, 451
modern, has no novelty, **24.** 62
Molière's, sometimes serious, **41.** 153–4
of Court life, unintelligible save to those who know it, **33.** 253
passion play mistakenly called, by theatre manager, **23.** 459
Pertici acts, at Florence, **20.** 357

'singular characters' not a subject for, **28.** 16
'this world a, to those that think, a tragedy
  to those that feel,' **23.** 387, 397, **32.** 315, 344,
  **33.** 444
*See also under* Drama
Comet; comets:
  'ambiguous lines' about, **32.** 309
  De Chéseaux's, discovered at Haarlem, **18.**
    406n
  Du Deffand, Mme, arranges party to see, **10.**
    290
  Grifoni, Mme, frightened by, **18.** 405
  HW asks about, **9.** 49
  HW mentions, **9.** 100
  HW's speculations about, **33.** 475
  Halley's: **38.** 13; hot weather attributed to,
    **9.** 249; Newton foretold, **21.** 294
  Montagu mentions, **10.** 297
  Norfolk House's reopening resembles, **37.** 438
  seen in England, **17.** 399
  Voltaire mentions, **35.** 413
Comet (comète), game:
  Conway family plays, at Sandywell, **37.** 105
  HW, Lady Mary Walpole, and Miss Leneve
    play, **18.** 36
  Louis XV popularized, **17.** 173n
  played at Paris, **6.** 378
*Comète*:
  headdress *à la*, **20.** 148
Comfit; comfits:
  at Florentine wedding, **13.** 230
  Twelfth-cake decked with, **33.** 429
Comines, Philippe de (1447–1511), chronicler:
  dates of, corrected, **43.** 188, 362, 364
  Edward IV and Richard III seen by, at D. of
    Burgundy's court, **41.** 112–13
  Exeter and Somerset seen by, trudging after
    Burgundy's army, **35.** 256
  Froissart MS executed for, **42.** 37n
  Gray mentions passage in, **14.** 175, 180–1
  HW inquires about, **14.** 178
  *Memoirs* of: mention Edward IV's beauty,
    **41.** 112–13; to be found in *Collection uni-
    verselle des mémoires*, **31.** 412
  Richard III mentioned by, **35.** 608–9
Comings, Fowler (1728–82), prebendary:
  dines with Cole, **2.** 39
  'Scoto-Hibernic,' **43.** 65
  wants to see SH, **2.** 39, 40–1, 42
Comings, Mrs Fowler. *See* Hartstonge, ——
Comings, Richard (d. 1799), merchant:
  attends Gray to grave, **1.** 231
  brother of, **2.** 39
  husband of Gray's cousin, **1.** 231
Comings, Mrs Richard. *See* Antrobus, Dorothy
Commandant:
  at Sluys, **38.** 4
Commander-in-chief, English:
  Conway becomes, **25.** 264n
  —— busy as, **39.** 390, 392, 408
  —— is, **25.** 262, 270, 354
  —— succeeds Amherst as, **25.** 276
  Granby becomes, **22.** 449

Stair becomes, **18.** 400
*Commèdia in commèdia, La*, burletta:
  Haymarket opens with, **20.** 4n
  Latilla, Resta, and Ciampi composed, **20.** 4n
*Commentaire historique sur les Œuvres de
  l'auteur de la Henriade. See under* Voltaire
*Commentaries. See under* Blackstone, Sir Wil-
  liam
*Commentarios de la guerra de España. See
  under* Bocallar y Saña, Vicente, Marqués de
  San Felipe
Commentary:
  whatever wants, is sure to be admired, **32.** 54
Commentators:
  HW's reflections on, **5.** 348, **28.** 118
Commerce:
  Francis I fond of, **20.** 277–8
  French dissertations on, **30.** 203
  French esteem, but do not understand, **31.** 43
  Goldsmith's argument that villages are de-
    stroyed by, ridiculous, **15.** 329
  HW does not understand, **30.** 203, **31.** 331
  HW's verses on destruction of the French navy
    fail to mention the advantages of, **38.** 51
  North's peace terms propose, with America,
    **24.** 354
  Raynal discusses, **39.** 168
  used as an excuse for war, **22.** 39
  with the Indies, **15.** 136
  *See also* Trade
Commerce (game):
  Amelia, Ps, and guests play, **32.** 308, (?) 518,
    **33.** 416n, **35.** 533n, **39.** 441, **42.** 166n
  Chewton, Vcts, does not suckle child while
    playing, **35.** 532
  Hunloke and Cts of Ailesbury play, at Work-
    sop, **37.** 565, 568
  played at SH, **33.** 355
  York, D. of, introduces, at Northumberland
    House, **9.** 334
Commercy, château in Lorraine:
  Lorraine, Dowager Ds of, lives at, **18.** 352n
Comminges, Bp of. *See* Médaby d'Osmond,
  Charles-Antoine-Gabriel
Commissary; commissaries:
  at Fivizano, **19.** 35
  Conway appoints, to treat with France about
    cartel, **37.** 584
  English, to live at Dunkirk, **22.** 118
  Florentine, Montemar to give directions to,
    **17.** 228
  HW examined by, in Paris, **7.** 268
  of Cortona, threatened by Del Monte broth-
    ers, **20.** 423
  Papal, *see* Ricci, Francesco
  rapacity of, in Seven Years War, **31.** 53
  Sienese, welcomes D. of York, **22.** 224
  Viennese Court might appoint, to suppress
    Jesuits, **23.** 135
Commissary *dei fossi. See* Federighi, Giovanni
Commissary-general:
  in Italy: Botta succeeds Stampa as, **20.** 320;
    Stampa is, for Francis I, **20.** 295

[Commissary-general, *continued*]
See also Boone, Daniel; Huxley, George
Commissary-general of musters:
Calcraft succeeded by Agar as, **38.** 248n
Commissioner; commissioners:
American, in France, hasten to get news of treaty to Congress, **24.** 369
England sends, to Americans, **41.** 316
English, in America, see Eden, William; Johnstone, George; Howard, Frederick, E. of Carlisle
Commissioner for hurt and sick seamen:
Gashry is, **18.** 81n
Commissioner for taxes. See Rigby, Christopher
Commissioner for the tariff:
Bladen is, at Antwerp, **17.** 336
Commissioner of Customs:
Hooper becomes, **20.** 17
Mann's absence excused to, by HW, **24.** 177
Commissioner of Public Accounts:
Bedford appears before, **42.** 32
HW's income from Exchequer place miscalculated by, **42.** 328n
Commissioner of salt:
Onslow, Denzil, replaces Thomas Sutton as, **20.** 518n
Commissioner of the Great Seal. See under Seal
Commissioner of the lottery:
Bentley becomes, **35.** 645
Commissioner of Trade and Plantations:
Dick promised position as, **23.** 222
Oswald one of, **17.** 299n
See also Gilmour, Sir Charles; Keene, Benjamin; Philipps, Sir John; Pitt, John
Commissioner to examine public accounts:
voting for, **17.** 437–8
Commission of accounts:
Philipps proposes, in House of Commons, **38.** 192
Commission of lunacy:
Orford, E. of, would lose his positions if subjected to, **23.** 482
*Committé*, French ship:
Georgia news brought by, from Philadelphia to Nantes, **24.** 545n
Committee; committees (county, in England):
Mann distrusts, **25.** 23–4
Opposition did not start, **25.** 30
petitions from, **25.** 18–19
reforms proposed by, **25.** 29–30
Yorkshire, Saville tries to humour, **25.** 18
See also under Associations
Committee; committees (Parliamentary):
petitions to be examined by, **25.** 35–6
Committee of elections:
chairman chosen for, **17.** 220, 242–3, 250
Committee of Secrecy. See Secret Committee
Commode; commodes:
Ailesbury, Cts of, to acquire from Selwyn through HW, **30.** 160, 161
at Elizabeth Chudleigh's, **9.** 277
at Navestock, **9.** 244

Cardigan, Cts of, wants HW to buy, in Paris, **31.** 98, 106, 110
HW orders, from Langlois, **10.** 207
of granite, **31.** 110
ornamented with ormolu, **31.** 98
Vyne parlour to have, **35.** 639
*Commodore*, English ship:
Dutch contraband seized by, **25.** 3n
Commodore; commodores:
English, Mann may have to govern, in coming war, **20.** 486
Commodus (Lucius Ælius Aurelius Commodus) (161–192), Roman emperor:
Marcus Aurelius's virtues not inherited by, **15.** 51
Common, ——, Mme du Deffand's servant:
Du Deffand, Mme, read to by, **7.** 223, 238
(?) —— shares lottery ticket with, **7.** 422, 455
——'s bequest to, **8.** 6
furniture in bedroom of, **8.** 15
wages of, **8.** 46
writes letters for Mme du Deffand, **7.** 81, (?) 127, (?) 209
Common Council. See under London: city of
Common field:
at Twickenham, brick-making on, **43.** 155
Common law. See under Law
Common Pleas. See Court of Common Pleas
Commons, House of. See under Parliament
*Common Sense, or The Englishman's Journal*:
Bouverie receives, weekly, **17.** 83
Chesterfield's contributions to, **28.** 294
Glover extravagantly praised in, **13.** 133
'Receipt to Make a Lord' in, **17.** 470
Common sense:
becoming to old people, **25.** 307
Du Deffand, Mme, on, **5.** 134–5
first quality in a prime minister, **25.** 275
HW has 'taken into keeping that old abandoned harridan,' **32.** 191
HW on, **5.** 132–3
HW praises, **24.** 213
HW says that fools and knaves hoodwink, **24.** 81
HW's philosophy consists in, **24.** 327
laws of, better than those of criticism, **42.** 51
seems to have taken flight, **34.** 169
theatre is pulpit of, **7.** 361
Commonwealth, The (English):
HW does not remember mention of, in conversation about Conway, **40.** 334–5
uncomfortable period to have lived in, **24.** 117
Communion:
Egizziello takes, **17.** 463
in Italy, carried everywhere during epidemic, **22.** 512
Louis XV to take, at Easter, **20.** 530
Communion plate:
Kingston, Ds of, sends, to Russia, **31.** 288n
Communion table:
at Trinity Hospital, Greenwich, **16.** 86
Compagni, Braccio (1691–1762), senator, 1736:

annuity to be paid to, as Electress's executor, **18.** 168

Compagni, Giovanni (1686–1755) and Girolamo Francesco Libri (b. 1699, living 1744), bankers:

courier paid by, **17.** 114n

Domenichino painting's purchase financed by, **18.** 57, 79

HW draws money from, **17.** *11*

HW's statue to be paid for by, **18.** 59

Mann discourages, from lending credit to Bns Walpole, **17.** 422

Mazzuoli fails to receive orders from, **17.** 11

Parker draws money from, **17.** 81

Venetian correspondent of, **17.** 422

Walpole, Bns, applies to, for credit to England, **17.** 422, 461

Compagnie des Indes (French East India Company):

ceases, **4.** 294

Lally acts against, **3.** 38

mémoires of Morellet and Necker on, **5.** 400

Paris exchange closed because of damage to, **19.** 330n

ships of, captured off Finisterre, **19.** 410–11

stock value of, **21.** 344

stores and fleet of, destroyed at Lorient, **19.** 330n

Compagnolt, Marie-Anne-Louise-Charlotte de (1728–1804), m. (1759) Étienne-Louis-Alexandre Berthelot de Baye, 'la complaisante':

(?) Du Deffand, Mme, makes acquaintance of, **4.** *284*

(?) HW admired by, **5.** 96, 210

(?) HW sent messages by, **5.** 139, 181

(?) social relations of, in Paris, *see index entries ante* **8.** 307

*Comparison of the Old and New Ministry. See under* Bubb Dodington, George

Comparse (theatre 'supers'):

humps of, **19.** 439

Compassion:

animals do not feel, **7.** 360

self-love hopes never to need, **7.** 361

Compiègne (France):

amusements at, **38.** 408–9, 410

army camp at, **38.** 410

camp at, omitted in 1770, **4.** 443

Court, French, at, **3.** 338, 340, **4.** 440, 441, 453, **5.** 82, 386, 391, **6.** 84, 85, **39.** 5

—— goes to, **38.** 573

—— returns from, **3.** 136, **4.** 265, **5.** 395

—— to abandon, **39.** 143

—— to go to, **3.** 303, 308, 319, **4.** 79, 80–1, 198, 231, 235, 243, 253, **5.** 76, 83, 86, 225, 256, 378, 380, **6.** 60, 73, 80, 81, 281, **7.** 11

—— to leave, **4.** 447, **5.** 394

—— to omit visit to, **4.** 93, **5.** 350, **6.** 319, 460, **7.** 136

forest of, **4.** 404n

George III forbids D. of York to visit, **7.** 365

HW alludes to, **13.** 178

Hertford invites HW to, **38.** 399

—— to follow Court to, **38.** 399, 404, **39.** 5

—— writes from, **38.** 408–14

Laval, Duc and Vicomte de, governors of, **4.** 441–2

Louis XV at, **3.** 122, 289, 333, **4.** 406, 449n

—— to go to, **4.** 73, 404

Louis XVI to go to, **6.** 54, 55, 60, 62, 194–5, 460

manœuvres at, watched by Louis XV and royal family, **38.** 410

Marie-Antoinette at, **4.** 406

visitors to: Barrymore, Cts of, **32.** 55, **35.** 344; Barrymore, E. of, **35.** 344; Beauchamp, **5.** 388, **38.** 408; Beauvau, **3.** 114, 118, 319; Choiseul, **4.** 445; Choiseul, Duchesse de, **3.** 132, 302–3, 319, **4.** 117, 130, 137, 250, 256, 259, 267, 269, 407, 427, 437, 439, 443; Conways, **6.** 156; Du Barry, Vicomte and Vicomtesse, **5.** 381; Egmont, Comte d', **20.** 572n; Elliot, **38.** 413; Fronsac, **20.** 572n, 574n; Guerchy, **3.** 114, 332; Harcourt, Earl, **5.** 86; Hertford, **38.** 408–14, **39.** 5; Hertford, Cts of, **38.** 408; March, **38.** 413; Mirepoix, Mme de, **5.** 264; Rochfords, **3.** 319, 333; Selwyn, **38.** 413; Seymour-Conway, Hon. H., **5.** 388; Stormont, **6.** 156; York, D. of, **22.** 550n, 552, 553

York, D. of, prevented from supping at, **7.** 364

Compiègne, Treaty of:

Pujol's negotiations lead to first, **20.** 573n

*Complaisant, Le. See under* Ferriol, Antoine

'Complaisante, La.' *See* Compagnolt, Marie-Anne-Louise-Charlotte de

*Compleat Angler. See under* Walton, Isaak

*Compleat Country Dancing Master:*

'Hempdresser' instructions in, **33.** 284n

*Compleat Embassador. See under* Digges, Sir Dudley

*Compleat Gentleman, The. See under* Peacham, Henry

*Complete Body of Heraldry, A. See under* Edmondson, Joseph

*Complete Collection of Genteel and Ingenious Conversation. See under* Swift, Jonathan

*Complete Collection of State Trials, A:*

Essex's trial in, **1.** 87, 89

Holles's trial in, **16.** 163, **40.** 187

*Complete History of the Most Remarkable Transactions at Sea. See under* Burchett, Josiah (? 1666–1746)

Compliment; compliments:

HW in old age more receptive to, **34.** 117–18

*Complot découvert, Le:*

Du Deffand, Mme, copies, for HW, **6.** 194

Composer (opera):

Middlesex cheats, **19.** 294

Compton, Bn. *See* Compton, Henry (1538–89); Townshend, George (1753–1811)

Compton, Bns. *See* Shirley, Elizabeth (1694–

[Compton, Bns., *continued*]
1741); Spencer, Anne (d. 1618); Spencer, Elizabeth (d. 1632)
Compton, Lady. *See* Beaumont, Mary (ca 1570–1632)
Compton, Mr:
HW's letters stayed with, till Hon. Henrietta Seymour Conway ordered things from him, 38. 159
HW to return franks to, and receive payment, 38. 47
Compton, Mr, of Derby:
draft on Bracey & Co. by, 38. 259n
Compton, Mrs. *See* Hoby, (?) —— Anne
Compton, Lady Anne (d. 1747):
(?) family piece of, 10. 336
Compton, Hon. Charles (1698–1755), M.P.; British representative in Portugal:
birth date of, corrected, 43. 252
Correggio painting might be known to, 18. 373
death of, 20. 517
English consul at Lisbon, 22. 151n
son of, 10. 337
Compton, Charles (1737–63), 7th E. of Northampton, 1758; ambassador to Venice 1761–3:
appearance of, 10. 337
appointed ambassador to Venice, 21. 505
at private Court ball, 38. 144
brother of, 9. 324
cold and dignified, 21. 294, 313
Court ball attended by, 9. 406
daughter of, 23. 372, 397
drinks, 10. 337
dying, 10. 337, 22. 142–3, 150
entrance ceremony of, at Venice, 22. 132, 142, 150, 154
family of, 10. 337
Florence visited by, 22. 132
Florentine mistress ungallantly treated by, 21. 303, 313
Geneva visited by, 22. 154
Grosvenor Sq. house of, 21. 272n
HW mentions, 9. 402, 403
HW often asked by, about Mann, 21. 374
Harwood copying Venus for, 25. 93n
health of, consumption, 22. 132, 142–3, 145, 150–1, 154, 155
heiress of, 29. 192
Lisbon, his birthplace, may be visited by, 22. 151
Mann's friend, 21. 294, 313, 505, 23. 372, 397
marriage of: 35. 295; almost broken for lack of dowry, 21. 313
messenger brings news of uncle's death to, 21. 272
Naples to be visited by, 22. 132
Northampton races attended by, 9. 247–8
running footman of, 9. 247–8, 249
Somerset, Lady Anne, to wed, 21. 294, 303, 313
steward of, 21. 272

Tronchin may be consulted by, at Geneva, 22. 150–1, 152, 154
Venice accepts, instead of Stuart Mackenzie, 23. 325
wife of, 9. 387n
Compton, Lady Charlotte (d. 1770), m. (1751) Hon. George Townshend, 4th Vct Townshend, 1764; Bns Ferrers, s.j., 1749; Bns Compton, s.j., 1754:
(?) at Chesterfield's assembly, 37. 326
death of, 31. 148
(?) family piece of, 10. 336
husband's letter to, 40. 168n
Compton, Lady Elizabeth (1760–1835), m. (1782) Lord George Augustus Henry Cavendish, cr. (1831) E. of Burlington; 'Lady Betty Compton':
Florence to be visited by, 23. 397
grandmother accompanied by, at Pisa, 23. 372, 397
HW entertains, at breakfast at SH, 33. 278–9
HW guards, during Gordon riots, 33. 186, 189
Maria Teresa, archduchess, plays with, 23. 372
marriage of, 29. 192
suitors of, 33. 278–9
Tuscan Court favours, at Florence, 23. 406
Vestris teaches dancing to, 33. 268n
Compton, George (1692–1758), 6th E. of Northampton, 1754; M.P.:
death of, 21. 272
'dish-clout,' 18. 350
marriage of, 10. 337
Montagu's colleague, 9. 137
named in Secret Committee lists, 17. 385
Northampton election sought by, 9. 141
Parliamentary silence of, 30. 304
prophetic abilities of, 9. 137
Sandys, Rushout and Gybbon outvote, 18. 50n
Treasury post of, 17. 337, 18. 350, 551
wife of, 9. 401n
Compton, Henry (1538–89), cr. (1572) Bn Compton; M.P.:
portrait of, at Castle Ashby, 10. 336
Compton, Hon. Henry (1632–1713), Bp of Oxford, 1674, of London, 1675:
portraits of, 10. 336, 337
Compton, James (1687–1754), 5th E. of Northampton; M.P.:
Bedford and Fox oppose, on turnpike bill, 20. 112n
dukedom declined by, 21. 26
familiarity with, difficult, 37. 302
(?) family piece of, 10. 336
Compton, James (1723–39), styled Bn Compton, 1727:
(?) family piece of, 10. 336
Compton, Lady Margaret (ca 1703–86), dau. of 4th E. of Northampton:
Amelia, Ps, entertains, 32. 307, 33. 104
—— tells, about Morice, 33. 357

Crewe, Mrs, has former house of, **35**. 390
Fitzwilliam, Vcts, visited by, **31**. 236
'General Compton,' **33**. 286
HW receives news from, **33**. 300
HW to invite, to SH, **31**. 406
Hampton Court society pleases, **31**. *199*
Hertford, Cts of, to be visited by, **31**. 409–10
Hobart, Mrs, entertains, at fête, **33**. 285
Holdernesse entertains, at Syon Hill, **39**. 390n
Holdernesse, Cts of, entertains, **43**. 304
poverty of, **29**. 193
servant of, sent in search of highwayman, **33**. 296–7
SH visited by, **31**. 297
Twickenham Park to be visited by, **31**. 203
weeps over loss of lurch, and wig almost lost, **39**. 420
wig and gambling of, **31**. 199n
wig of, well powdered, and lucky at loo, **32**. 308n
Compton, Spencer (1601–43), 2d E. of Northampton:
death of, at Hopton Heath, **10**. 336
portrait of, **10**. 336
Compton, Sir Spencer (? 1674–1743), cr. (1730) E. of Wilmington, Speaker of House of Commons 1715–27; first lord of Treasury:
Bath to be visited by, **18**. 135
Carteret said to express opinion of, **18**. 83
death of: **18**. 265, **30**. 315; expected, **18**. 135, 255
Downing St house offered by, to Sandys, **17**. 478, 494–5
fortune accumulated by, as Speaker, **30**. 292n
George II gives no orders to, for Hill's dismissal, **18**. 25
HW identifies, **30**. 302n
HW pities, **17**. 320
HW ridicules, **13**. 14n
house of, at Eastbourne, **40**. 6
incompetence of, **2**. 124
issues warrant against Prior, **13**. 187n
Kilmarnock's pension stopped by, **19**. 283–4
merchants referred by, to the Admiralty, **17**. 211
*New Ode, A*, satirizes, **18**. 50
Pelham succeeds, **43**. 178
prime ministry previously missed by, **18**. 50n
protuberant nose of, **30**. 302
Pulteney's followers desert to, **18**. 74
regent, **18**. 209n
relative of, gets Treasury post, **17**. 337
Sandys, Rushout and Gybbon outvote, **18**. 50n
Treasury headed by, **17**. 319, 320, 332
Walpole, Sir Robert, outwits, **33**. 422
—— supplants, **18**. 50n
Williams, C. H., abuses, in 'A Letter to Mr Dodsley,' **30**. 315
Young's *Night Thoughts* alludes to, **30**. 315
Compton, Spencer (1738–96), 8th E. of Northampton, 1763; M.P.:
appearance and family of, **10**. 337
Castle Ashby, seat of, **41**. 251

election expenses beggar, **10**. 256n
George III makes, groom of the Bedchamber, **9**. 324, **21**. 460
(?) lawn and chase of, at Castle Ashby, turned to tillage, **10**. 287
Northampton seat controlled by, **10**. 194n
portrait of, **10**. 336
retirement of, to Compton, **10**. 288
second marriage of, **10**. 287–8
Compton, William (ca 1560–1630), cr. (1618) E. of Northampton:
portrait of, at Castle Ashby, **10**. 336
Compton, Rev. William (1733–1824):
chancellor of Ely, **2**. 51
Masters deputy to, **2**. 181
Compton family:
coats of arms of, **10**. 336
cold and dignified, **21**. 294
De Ferrers, Lord, of, **2**. 136
Elizabeth, Q., gives bed to, **10**. 337
formality of, exemplified in their house, **10**. 88
Northampton, Cts of, returns Castle Ashby's furniture to, **10**. 337
portraits of, at Castle Ashby, **10**. 336
pride of, **10**. 337
Compton House, Compton Verney, Warwickshire; Bn Willoughby de Broke's seat:
Montagu to call at, **10**. 286
Compton Wyniates, Warwickshire, E. of Northampton's seat; 'Compton in the Hole':
Northamptons retire to, **10**. 288
Comptroller of finances, French. *See* Controller-general
Comptroller of the Household:
Cavendish, Lord George, becomes, **9**. 406, **38**. 142
—— resigns as, **22**. 97
Edgcumbe is, to George II, **25**. 518n, **37**. 481
—— succeeds Buckinghamshire as, **21**. 25
Hobart succeeds Hillsborough as, **9**. 181, **20**. 517
Morice becomes, **22**. 103, 113
Comptroller of the Pipe:
HW fêted on being called to the bar as, **43**. 169
HW offers to sell place of, to Bn Holland, **41**. 209
Comptroller of the Table, Tuscan. *See* Salviati, Averardo
Comptroller of the Victualling Accounts:
Gashry is, **18**. 81n
Comptroller to the Prince of Wales. *See* St Leger, Arthur
*Comte d'Artois*, French frigate:
Arras, Bp of, pledged province to pay for, **7**. 241
captured, **7**. 241
*Comte d'Essex, Le. See under* Corneille, Thomas
*Comte de Warwik, Le. See under* La Harpe, Jean-François de

'Comtesse, la belle.' *See* Carbonnel de Canisy, Marie-Françoise Renée de, Comtesse de Forcalquier

'Comtesse, la divine.' *See* Campet de Saujon, Marie-Charlotte-Hippolyte, Comtesse de Boufflers

*Comtesse de Bentheim*, privateer:
Hanover captured by, and taken to Brest, **21.** 75n

*Comtesse d'Escarbagnas, La. See under* Molière

*Comus. See under* Milton, John

Comyn, Valens (d. 1751), M.P.:
HW to ask about Eversley, Hants, owned by, **37.** 304–5

Comynes, John, Scottish Jacobite:
Argyll, D. of, favours, **20.** 310n

Comyns, Mrs:
disorderly house said to have been kept by, **9.** 19
Fitzroy, Lady Caroline, said to have incited attack upon, **9.** 19
Montagu urged by HW to visit, **9.** 19

Comyns, Sir John (d. 1740), chief Baron of the Exchequer:
Marlborough shows respect to, at Tunbridge, **7.** 362
Oxford's counsel, **7.** 362
——'s mission to Marlborough declined by, **7.** 362

Comyns. *See also* Comings; Cummings

'Con.' *See* Phillips, Teresia Constantia; Seymour-Conway, Francis (1743–1822), Vct Beauchamp; 2d E. of Hertford

Conant, Mr:
SH visited by, **12.** 235

Conca, della. *See* Suares de la Concha

Concale (*or* Concalle) Bay. *See* Cancale

Concert; concerts:
after Richecourt's dinner, **20.** 478
Ailesbury, Cts of, gives, **22.** 506
Albani, to give, for D. of York, **22.** 229
at Bristol, in Chatterton's memory, **16.** 351, 363
at Florence: **37.** 78; by subscription, **18.** 12–13; horn, at Epiphany, **18.** 134; Lenten, **17.** 316, **19.** 374
at Lucca, by Genoese musicians, for D. of York, **22.** 222
at Richmond's fireworks, **20.** 56
at St James's Palace, **38.** 287–8
at Venice, for doge's election, **17.** 77
Bracciano gives, for D. of Gloucester, **23.** 388–9
Charlotte, Q., may have, instead of opera, **38.** 101
Cornelys, Theresa, gives, **23.** 271
Cosway, Mrs, gives, **11.** 285, **25.** 646
fireworks to open with, **37.** 297
for Mingotti's benefit, **38.** 12
Franks gives, **35.** 350
Gloucester, D. of, attends, with Leopold and Maria Louisa, **23.** 405
Grafton, Ds of, invited to, at Rome, **22.** 17

Grifoni, Mme, attends, **17.** 324
HW gives, **37.** 4
Lucchese envoy gives, for Roman lady, **23.** 229
Mann attends, **17.** 324
—— gives: for Karl Wilhelm Ferdinand, **22.** 458; for Turinese lady, **19.** 499; in garden, **19.** 421; on eve of villeggiatura, **18.** 64
—— invites Hollands to, **22.** 467
morning, Montagu frequents, at Dublin, **10.** 20
Piozzi, Mrs, gives, **11.** 106
Queensberry, D. of, gives, **11.** 152, 153
Richecourt gives, **20.** 148
subscription, Chudleigh, Elizabeth, strikes Mrs Naylor's name from list for, **9.** 329
Udnys give, **11.** 107, **12.** 198
Young gives, weekly, in Florence, **20.** 327
*See also* Cocchiata

Concerto; concerti:
Corelli's and Geminiani's, **18.** 68

*Concetti*:
HW might imitate Italians in, **21.** 361

Concha, la. *See* Suares de la Concha

Concièrge. *See under* Servant

Conciergerie du Palais, Paris:
Billard at, **5.** 190
fire may have started in, **6.** 256
Lally's property to be confiscated for use of poor people of, **3.** 30n
Marie-Antoinette confined in, **31.** 388n, **34.** 185n

*Concilia. See under* Spelman, Sir Henry

Conciliation, Bill of. *See under* Parliament, acts of

Concini, Concino (d. 1617), Maréchal d'Ancre; Bn de Lussigny:
heart of, torn by enemies' teeth, **34.** 57
Louis XIII applauds assassination of, **25.** 225n

*Concise Statement of Transactions and Circumstances respecting the King's Theatre in the Haymarket. See under* Taylor, William

Conclave, papal:
*1740*, after Clement XII's death: **13.** 9, 203, 212–13, 215–17, 220, 226–7, 240, **17.** 9, 16–29, **21.** 22, 206, **35.** 37, **37.** 46, 57, 66, 69, 70, 77, **40.** 30; Chute would sacrifice wives to, for Raphael painting, **35.** 37; opening date of, corrected, **43.** 179, 233
*1758*, after Benedict XIV's death: **21.** 197, 204, 206–7, 214, 215–17, 219–20; preparations for, continue despite Benedict XIV's recovery, **21.** 81
*1769*, after Clement XIII's death: **23.** 88, 95–6, 104, 107, 113, 117–18, 533; cardinals fear Bourbon intimidation at, **22.** 387; Jesuits' suppression promised by, **23.** 533
*1774–5*, after Clement XIV's death: **24.** 50, 58–9, 64–5, 68–70, 73, 75, 79, 82, 86; Chigi the marshal and Colonna the vicar of, **24.** 73; Joseph II sees mock election at, **24.** 104, 107; satire on, *see* Sertor, Gaetano, *Con-*

*clave, Il;* winter weather will probably stop, **24.** 59

cardinals dislike, in hot weather, **21.** 81, 197, **23.** 113, **24.** 161–2

English shifts in administration compared to operation of, **25.** 377–8

*Conclave dell'anno 1774, Il. See under* Sertor, Gaetano

Concord, Massachusetts:
 Gage sends troops to: to seize magazine, **28.** 206n; to spike cannon, **24.** 110

Concorde, Place de la, Paris:
 Place Louis XV becomes, **11.** 99n

*Conc touché. See* Contouche

Concubines, French, royal:
 HW's 'chapter of,' **10.** 295

*Condamine. See* La Condamine

Condé, 'great.' *See* Bourbon, Louis de (1621–86)

Condé, Mlle de. *See* Bourbon-Condé, Louise-Adélaïde de

Condé, Prince de. *See* Bourbon, Henri de (1552–88); Bourbon, Louis de (1621–86); Bourbon, Louis-Henri de (1692–1740); Bourbon, Louis-Henri-Joseph de (1756–1830); Bourbon, Louis-Joseph de (1736–1818)

Condé, Princesse de. *See* Bourbon-Condé, Louise-Adélaïde de (1757–1824); Bourbon d'Orléans, Louise-Marie-Thérèse-Bathilde de (1750–1822); Brignole, Marie-Catherine de (1739–1813); Clèves, Marie de (1553–74); La Trémoïlle, Charlotte-Catherine de (1568–1629)

Condé (France):
 occurrences at, a good sign, **34.** 185

Condé, Hôtel de, Paris:
 compared with Carlton House, **33.** 499
 Holland's architecture influenced by, **33.** 499

Condé, Rue de, Faubourg St-Germain, Paris:
 Petit Hôtel d'Entragues opposite Hôtel de Provence in, **37.** 41

Condell, Henry (d. 1627), actor:
 dedication by, **35.** 629

Condé-sur-l'Escaut (France):
 Allies' difficulty in capturing, **12.** 67

*Condi. See* Conti

Condillac, ——:
 Ferdinand of Parma's preceptor, **23.** 17n

Condillac, Étienne Bonnot de. *See* Bonnot de Condillac

Condorcet, Marquis de. *See* Caritat, Marie-Jean Antoine-Nicolas de

Condorcet, Marquise de. *See* Grouchy, Sophie

*Conduct of the Last and Present Ministry Compared, The:*
 attributed to Bubb Dodington, **18.** 8–9

Conduit St, London:
 Clarke, Anna Maria, lives in, **31.** 336
 Eustons live in, **36.** 287
 house in, destroyed, **12.** 176n
 Jerningham in, **41.** 381

Conduitt, Catherine (ca 1722–50), m. (1740) John Wallop, styled Vct Lymington:

(?) child of, attributed to Nugent, **9.** 104

Conecte, Thomas (d. 1434), preacher; reformer:
 burnt at Rome for censuring clergy, **9.** 78
 'piked horns' preached against by, **9.** 78, **25.** 183n

Cone; cones:
 Bentley sends, to HW, **35.** 207–8

Conelly, William:
 *Charming Kitty* commanded by, **22.** 174n

*Coney. See* Cony

Coney Court, London:
 Baynes lives in, **29.** 247
 *See also under* Gray's Inn

Confectioner; confectioners:
 Clement XIV's, said to have been poisoned, **24.** 43, 49
 HW must borrow someone's, **37.** 404
 La Cour's prescriptions worthy of, **35.** 108

Confectionery:
 Carlisle citadel in sugar, **19.** 174–5
 cupids in sugar, **20.** 125–6
 dessert depicting *chasse* at Herrenhausen, **21.** 191
 Wilton Bridge in sugar, **9.** 363

Confectio Raleana:
 HW's cold and cough cured by, **23.** 450
 Montagu recommends, to HW, **10.** 119

Confederate Hawks of Great Britain. *See* Falconers' Society

Confederation of Bar:
 Ogiński joins, to oppose Stanislas II, **33.** 511n

Confederation of Targowitz:
 Catherine II organizes, to keep old Polish constitution, **34.** 144n, 153n, 159n
 Stanislas II adheres to, **34.** 159n

Confession; confessions:
 Bussy's stories about, **18.** 131
 Crawford's French servant makes, before going to save his master, **20.** 110
 Jesuits again permitted to hear, **24.** 106
 —— prohibited from hearing, **23.** 507
 Louis XV's, at Easter, **20.** 542
 Richecourt retires to country to make, **19.** 31

Confessional; confessionals:
 niches for, **35.** 138

*Confessions. See under* Rousseau, Jean-Jacques

Confessor, Edward the. *See* Edward (d. 1066)

Confessor; confessors:
 Charles III's, **25.** 33n
 Damiens's, talks with La Condamine, **22.** 147
 Electress's, *see* Giacomini, Ignazio
 Florentines told by: to hate the English, **19.** 196–7; to pray for Young Pretender's success, **19.** 112
 Leopold's and Maria Louisa's, is a Jesuit, **22.** 519
 Louis XV's, *see* Desmarets, Abbé (ca 1701–80); Pérusseau *or* Perrusault, Sylvain (ca 1678–1753)
 Maria Josefa's, removed by Maria Theresa because he is a Jesuit, **22.** 519
 Marie Leszczyńska's, *see* Bieganski, ——

[Confessor; confessors, *continued*]
St John's, receives Latin letters from him, **18**. 205
Confirmation:
of nuns, attended by Mann, **18**. 45
*Confirmation of the Introductory Discourse*:
pamphlet in miracles controversy, **15**. 297
Conflagration; conflagrations:
Gordon rioters use, for reform, **35**. 354
philosophers ascribe phenomena to, **35**. 383
Conflans, Comte and Maréchal de. *See* Conflans, Hubert de
Conflans, Marquis de. *See* Conflans d'Armentières, Louis-Gabriel de
Conflans, Hubert de (ca 1690–1777), Chevalier de Brienne de Conflans; Comte de Conflans; Maréchal de France; naval officer:
Aiguillon's transports to be convoyed from Vannes by, **21**. 350n
death of, **6**. 403
defeat attributed by, to captains' confusion, **21**. 356–7, 359
English defeat, at Quiberon Bay, **9**. 268n, **21**. 350–1, 356–7, 358–9, 377
French invasion fleet commanded by, **13**. 35n
French invasion troops to be embarked by, at Dunkirk, **21**. 296n
Hawke to be fought by, **21**. 346n
Ireland saved by defeat of, **21**. 377
Louis XV offered the head of, for Quiberon Bay disaster, **21**. 359
—— reconsiders orders to, too late, **21**. 358n
Maximilian's social relations with, **6**. 156
plan of, to sail from Brest and conduct French convoys from West Indies, **20**. 579n
St-Florentin's alleged letter from, called spurious, **21**. 356n
ships at Ouessant and Belle-Île may be attacked (*or* Morbihan fleet escorted) by, **21**. 358n
Thurot's diversion to allow, out of Brest in Hawke's absence, **21**. 336n
Vannes in Quiberon Bay approached by, to embark Aiguillon's troops for Scotland, **21**. 350n
vice-admiral, **6**. 403
Conflans, Louis de (1711–74), Marquis and Maréchal d'Armentières:
cook of, marries, **4**. 345–6
death of, **6**. 7
in command at Metz, **6**. 110
social relations of, in Paris, **5**. 233, **7**. 298, 306
Conflans, Louise-Aglaé de (1763–1819), m. (1781) Charles-Alain-Gabriel de Rohan-Guéménée, Prince de Guéménée:
Agenois to marry, **7**. 453
Conflans, Louise-Marthe de (1759–1825), m. (1775) François-Marie-Casimir de Franquetot, Marquis de Coigny:
England visited by, **25**. 408, **34**. 155
marriage of, **6**. 159
smallpox inoculation of, **6**. 336

witticism by, on French burning Esprémesnil's bust, **34**. 155
Conflans d'Armentières, Louis-Gabriel de (1735–89), Marquis de Conflans:
Choiseuls greeted by, at Longjumeau, **41**. 197
Du Deffand, Mme, gives opinion of, **3**. 278
England visited by, **3**. 237, 274n, 278, **25**. 409, **41**. 193, **43**. 85
French ambassador to Poland, **31**. 102n
HW entertains, at SH, **43**. 85
horse race of, **39**. 270
second in command at Metz, **6**. 110
'Congratulatory Letter to a Certain Right Hon. Person upon his Late Disappointment.' *See under* Williams, Sir Charles Hanbury
*Congratulatory Letter to Selim. See under* Mallet, David
Congregation of cardinals: Benedict XIV to summon, **19**. 416; cardinals at, order prelates to pay no royal honours to Young Pretender, **22**. 392; England said to have bribed, **22**. 395; France and Spain applauded by, for disregarding Young Pretender, **22**. 399; quarantine lifted by, **18**. 287n; to decide about Young Pretender, **22**. 388–9; Young Pretender would be damned to, if he changed religion, **22**. 336
Congress:
for peace would interest Horatio Walpole (1678–1757) more than Norwich assizes, **30**. 72
Congress, American (Continental Congress):
acts with harmony and spirit, **24**. 194
aggressive, **39**. 204, 207–8
American-French treaty to be brought to, by 4 ships, **24**. 369
army may be increased by, at will, **24**. 339
Articles of Confederation adopted by, **24**. 354n
Boston's aid from other colonies voted by, **39**. 226
Chatham praises, **39**. 228n
clergy would be willingly sent to England by, **28**. 255
Clinton's messengers bound and delivered to, **25**. 135
delegates of, to go to France, **39**. 344–5
Dunmore said to have captured member of, **24**. 157
England humbly sues to, with peace proposals, **39**. 333
English peace commissioners spurned by, **24**. 362, 400, 426n, **28**. 421
four colonies falsely reported to have revolted against, **25**. 321
France wants to get ahead of England's peace efforts with, **24**. 369
Franklin may be losing credit in, **39**. 345n
——'s mission from, **24**. 269n
HW dreams Lord Guilford was sent to, **32**. 304
HW not waiting for news from, **32**. 239

independence declared by, **24**. 230
'John the Painter' not directed by, **28**. 284
Lafayette's alleged quarrel with, **24**. 456
Laurens president of, **25**. 91, **36**. 179
no news of, **24**. 61
non-importation, non-exportation, and non-consumption voted by, **39**. 226
non-importation pact expected from, **39**. 210–11
North administration and, concerning peace terms, **32**. 406
North's conciliatory approaches to, **24**. 354, 358, **32**. 406
Parliamentary acts' repeal demanded by, **39**. 227
peace negotiations may have been intended by, as feint to conceal reliance on France and Spain, **24**. 271
petitions by, to George III, House of Commons, and English people, **39**. 227, 231
resolves to pursue war, **28**. 210, 217
session of, to begin in May, **24**. 85
terms of accommodation from, rumoured, **39**. 252, 253
treaty with France ratified by, **28**. 409
Washington appointed by, **24**. 120
—— named *generalissimo* by, **32**. 248
——'s troops demand pay from, **29**. 112
wisest course known to, **24**. 348
Congress, provincial, of Massachusetts:
Derby sent by, to Franklin, **24**. 109n
resolution by, **24**. 97n
Congreve, William (1670–1729), dramatist:
Berry, Mary, considers, her favourite author, **12**. 161
*Doris*, quoted by HW, **18**. 424, **30**. 47
*Double Dealer, The*: Gray quotes, **13**. 56–7; HW alludes to, **29**. 256; HW alludes to characters in, **31**. 332; Henderson's benefit performance of, **42**. 4n; Kemble superior to Quin in, **11**. 64; Lady Froth's star-gazing in, **32**. 16; Sir Paul Pliant in, **38**. 65
genteel comedy of, **33**. 563
HW read, in his 11th year, **18**. 424n
interest in, survives to next age, **28**. 280
*Judgment of Paris*, Frederick, P. of Wales, to act in, **19**. 45
(?) Keally's correspondence with, **10**. 28
letters by, in Dublin, **10**. 28
*Love for Love*, HW sees, **11**. 8
Montagu to send works of, to Mme Roland, **10**. 174, 182
*Mourning Bride* by: acted at Hall Place, **33**. 369n; Alphonso in, **20**. 291; (?) epilogue to, **43**. 133; Mrs Siddons appears in, **11**. 237n
*Old Batchelour, The*, by: Capt. Bluffe and Sir Joseph Wittol in, **38**. 137; HW alludes to, **9**. 60, **11**. 19n
prices of works of, in France, **10**. 180
songs and 'piece' by: HW jokes about indecency of, **10**. 33; Montagu finds, in Dublin, **10**. 28; Montagu sends, to HW, **10**. 28

Stowe visit brings memories of, to HW, **10**. 314
Stratford unfamiliar with, **29**. 234
translations of Horace by, too free, **13**. 101
Voltaire ridicules, for preferring rank of gentleman to that of author, **21**. 486
*Way of the World, The*, by: Gray alludes to, **13**. 77; Gray sees, **13**. 113; HW alludes to, **13**. 206, **29**. 45, 85–6, 256; HW paraphrases, **9**. 200, **31**. 292–3; HW quotes, **10**. 16, **19**. 71, **33**. 217; HW refers to 'Petulant' and 'Millamant' in, **22**. 431; 'Lady Wishfort' in, **39**. 213; Mason alludes to, **28**. 60; 'Millamant' in, **1**. 370n; 'Mincing' in, **35**. 246; West mentions, **13**. 131
witty but not natural, **33**. 492
Coni (Italy):
loss of, reported, **18**. 521
Maillebois and Don Philip may approach, **19**. 58
siege of, raised, **18**. 528
Stura valley near, **19**. 432
Coniers. *See* Conyers
Coningsburgh, Richard de. *See* Richard (ca 1375–1415), E. of Cambridge
Coningsby, Lady Frances (1709–81), m. (1732) Sir Charles Hanbury Williams:
daughter's letter from, about Sévigné snuff-box, **43**. 82
husband 'poxed,' **30**. 312
husband's ill-treatment of, **39**. 244
ill in private lodgings in London, **18**. 104
*Conjectures. See under* Young, Edward
'Conjectures on the System of the Universe.' *See under* Walpole, George, 3d E. of Orford
Conjurer; conjurers:
failure of, to appear at Little Haymarket Theatre causes riot, **20**. 29n
fashionable in London, **38**. 406–7
HW is not, **39**. 150
'Conjuring room':
D. of Norfolk's, at Worksop, **37**. 566, 572
*Connétable de Bourbon. See under* Guibert, Jacques-Antoine-Hippolyte, Comte de
Connolly, John (d. 1813):
arranges treaty with Indians, **28**. 355n
Connolly. *See also* Conelly; Conolly
Conolly, Lady Anne. *See* Wentworth, Lady Anne
Conolly, Anne (d. 1805), m. (1761) George Byng:
dines with HW at SH, **38**. 73
(?) HW confuses invitation to visit, **31**. 236
(?) HW's correspondence with, **31**. 236
Conolly, Caroline (ca 1755–1817), m. (1770) John Hobart, 2d E. of Buckinghamshire, 1756:
Conolly, Lady Anne, to meet, in Staffordshire, **31**. 199
dines with HW at SH, **38**. 73
HW calls, 'Queen,' **31**. 199
HW praises, **23**. 316
husband's bequest to, **12**. 5
marriage of, **35**. 340n

Conolly, Catharine (d. 1771), m. (1754) Ralph Gore, 6th Bt, 1746; cr. (1764) Bn Gore, (1768) Vct Belleisle, (1772) E. of Ross: (?) dines with HW at SH, 38. 73

Conolly, Frances (ca 1742–1817), m. (1765) Hon. Sir William Howe, K.B., 1766, 5th Vct Howe, 1799:
dines with HW at SH, 38. 73
husband of, 35. 352n

Conolly, Jane, m. George Robert Fitzgerald:
dines with HW at SH, 38. 73

Conolly, Lady Louisa. See Lennox, Lady Louisa Augusta

Conolly, Thomas (?1737–1803), M.P.:
guests of, at ball: Edward Augustus; HW; Irish; Richmond, Ds of; Tavistock, 9. 234
Hartington may occupy Castletown house of, 37. 400
(?) Ireland discussed by, in House of Commons, 28. 378n
Irish independence advocated by, in Parliament, 33. 332
Irish Parliamentary motion by, 25. 453n
sister of, 23. 316n
wife of, 7. 19n, 9. 235n

Conolly, William (d. 1754), of Castletown, Co. Kildare; M.P.:
wife of, 9. 235n, 11. 56n, 283n

Conqueror, English ship:
French frigates pursued by, 21. 303
Howe to be joined by, 24. 411

Conqueror; conquerors:
HW abominates, 31. 44
HW thinks, never excusable even though successful, 25. 141–2

Conquest, Mary Christina (ca 1743–1813), m. (1763) Henry Arundell, 8th Bn Arundell:
tapestry pictures left to, 1. 6n

Conquest, Norman:
manorial families dating back to, 15. 267

Conquest of Granada. See under Dryden, John

Conquête de Naples par Charles VIII, La. See under Gudin de la Brenellerie, Paul-Philippe

Conquête des Pays-Bas, La. See under Zambault, ——

Conscious Lovers. See under Steele, Richard

Conseil, grand. See Council, grand

'Conseiller de commerce.' See under Magnan, ——

Conseils raisonnables à M. Bergier. See under Voltaire

Conseils, supérieurs. See Councils, superior

Conserva, Genoese bark:
Corsican bishop to be intercepted by, 21. 393
founders near Bastia, 21. 393n

Conservatori:
Roman senate represented by, 19. 428

Conservatorio delle Quiete. See Quiete

Conserves:
monks serve, 13. 182

Considerations on Criminal Law. See under Dagge, Henry

Considerations on the Means of Preventing

Fraudulent Practices on the Gold Coin. See under Stanhope, Charles (1753–1816)

Considerations on the Present Dangerous Crisis. See under Ruffhead, Owen

Considerations on the Present German War. See under Mauduit, Israel

Considerations on the Present State of the Peerage of Scotland. See under Murray, Patrick

Considérations sur la nature de la révolution de France. See under Mallet du Pan, Jacques-François

Considérations sur les mœurs, Les. See under Toussaint, François-Vincent

Considérations sur les mœurs de ce siècle. See under Pinot Duclos, Charles

Considerazioni sopra le rime del Petrarca. See under Tassoni, Alessandro

Consistory, at Rome:
Benedict XIV to call, 19. 157
Pius VI's plan to visit Joseph II submitted to, 25. 239
Rohan should be tried by, 25. 658

Consistory Court:
Chudleigh, Elizabeth, brings jactitation suit in, 39. 106n

Consols:
HW buys, from Gomes through Harris, 42. 435

Conspiracy, The. See Jephson, Robert: Vitellia

Constable, William (ca 1721–91):
Brussels visited by, 23. 244
Florence visited by, with Dr Johnson, 23. 244
Granby's friend, 23. 244
Mann talks with, about Le Fevre's gout remedy, 23. 243–4

Constable; constables:
elections invalid if supervised by army instead of, 17. 252
Furness's constable says the times are hard on, 39. 237
London: Bedford House defended by, 38. 560; Covent Garden bagnio raided by, 17. 505; Ferrers attended by, 21. 399; mob beats, at burning of North Briton, 22. 188; Northumberland House festivities guarded by, 35. 107; Palliser's house guarded by, 24. 442; stationed about, for fear of riots, 23. 205; Westminster election testimony of, 17. 246; Westminster Hall garrisoned by, 23. 12; women rounded up by, in St Martin's roundhouse, 17. 503–4
of Dublin Castle, 39. 77

Constance of Brittany, m. (1186) P. Geoffrey (Plantagenet):
in Shakespeare's King John, 41. 294, 373

'Constant, Lady.' See Campbell, Caroline (d. 1789); see also under Murphy, Arthur: Way to Keep Him

Constant Couple. See under Farquhar, George

Constante, Spanish ship:
in Battle of Toulon, 18. 414n

Constant Husband. See under Steele, Sir Richard